Halliday
WINE COMPANION

ESTABLISHED 1986 – WINECOMPANION.COM.AU –
2022

This edition is dedicated to Paula Grey, earth mother of the *Companion* from January 1991 until her untimely death in June 2021.

Hardie Grant

BOOKS

Published in 2021 by Hardie Grant Books,
an imprint of Hardie Grant Publishing

Hardie Grant Books (Melbourne)
Wurundjeri Country
Building 1, 658 Church Street
Richmond, Victoria 3121

Hardie Grant Books (London)
5th & 6th Floors
52–54 Southwark Street
London SE1 1UN

hardiegrantbooks.com

Halliday Wine Companion 2022
ISBN 978 1 74379 733 4

Cover design by Pidgeon Ward
Illustration by Yoshiko Hada
Photography by Andrew Poole
Typeset by Megan Ellis
Printed in Australia by McPherson's Printing Group, Maryborough, Victoria

Hardie Grant acknowledges the Traditional Owners of the country on which we
work, the Wurundjeri people of the Kulin nation and the Gadigal people of the
Eora nation, and recognises their continuing connection to the land, waters and
culture. We pay our respects to their Elders past, present and emerging.

Contents

The tasting team

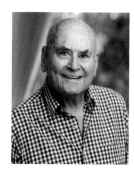

James Halliday

Respected wine critic and vigneron James Halliday is the
founder of the *Wine Companion*. With a wine career spanning
more than 50 years, he was one of the founders of Brokenwood
in the Hunter Valley, and later, Coldstream Hills in the Yarra
Valley. James is an unmatched authority on all aspects of the
wine industry, and for more than 30 years, was among the most
senior and active wine judges in Australia. He has won a clutch
of awards for his contributions, including the Australian wine
industry's ultimate accolade, the Maurice O'Shea Award. In 2010
he was made of Member of the Order of Australia for his
services to the wine industry. James has written or contributed
to more than 80 books on wine since 1970 and has written a
weekly wine column for Australian newspapers since 1978.

Tyson Stelzer

Tyson Stelzer fell in love with wine more than 20 years ago between the pages of James Halliday's *Australia & New Zealand Wine Companion 2000*. He is now a multi-award-winning wine writer, TV host and producer, and international speaker. He was named The International Wine & Spirit Competition Communicator of the Year in 2015, The Australian Wine Communicator of the Year in 2015 and 2013, and The International Champagne Writer of the Year in 2011. Tyson is the author of 17 wine books, including six editions of *The Champagne Guide*, and a contributor to Jancis Robinson's *The Oxford Companion to Wine* (3rd edition), and regularly writes for many wine magazines. As an international speaker, Tyson has presented at wine events in 12 countries, and is also a regular judge and chair of wine shows throughout Australia. Tyson also hosts intimate Champagne tours.

Tyson is the chief editor for the *Halliday Wine Companion 2022*.

Regional focus: Barossa Valley, Tasmania, Queensland

Twitter: @TysonStelzer | **Facebook:** TysonStelzer
Instagram: @tyson_stelzer | **YouTube:** Tyson Stelzer
Website: tysonstelzer.com

Erin Larkin

Erin Larkin is an independent wine writer, judge and presenter in Perth, Western Australia. Erin has a unique, grassroots approach to her work and a focus, and curiosity for, Western Australian wines. Multi-skilled when it comes to the business of wine, she is a regular contributor to *Halliday* magazine, a prolific presenter and educator across multiple platforms, and an Australian wine show judge. Erin is also an active consultant for retail and private clients, with a keen eye for quality and creativity in wine, marrying classic and contemporary perspectives. She has a weekly column in *The Post* and a YouTube channel where she opens and discusses a vast array of wines, releasing up to two videos a week.

Regional focus: Western Australia

Instagram: @erinllarkin | **YouTube:** Erin Larkin
Website: erinlarkin.com.au

Jane Faulkner

Jane Faulkner is a journalist by training and wine writer by vocation. A long-time contributor and columnist for the *Halliday* magazine, Jane has been reviewing for the *Wine Companion* since 2016. She started her career in newspapers, later writing for *The Age/The Sydney Morning Herald*, and has also worked in TV and radio. Respected for her honesty and fairness yet rigour and independence in her writing and tasting, Jane is a sought-after wine judge, locally and internationally, and chairs numerous shows. On a personal level, Jane is an Italophile, spending considerable time each year visiting its wine regions, and dreams of living in Piemonte. Yet she never tires of travelling throughout the wine world in search of stories and bottles from inspirational, thoughtful producers.

Regional focus: Southern New South Wales including Canberra; Coonawarra and the Limestone Coast, Clare Valley, Riverland, Southern Flinders Ranges, Southern Eyre Peninsula; Mornington Peninsula, Macedon Ranges, Sunbury, Gippsland, Yarra Valley and North West Victoria

Twitter: @winematters | **Facebook:** Jane Faulkner
Instagram: @winematters

Jeni Port

Jeni Port is a trained journalist, who caught the wine bug when she was a cadet in Melbourne's *The Sun News-Pictorial* newspaper (now *Herald Sun*). She was working in the paper's Women's Section (yes, really) and her first story was on a woman winemaker – a subject that would become a recurring theme over her career. During her time there, she wrote a weekly food market review, which quickly incorporated wine stories, and was the start of the paper's first wine column. She later worked at *The Age*, writing about wine for 30 years. Jeni is also the author of *Crushed by Women: Women and Wine*, and is a wine judge here and overseas, including in Europe for Mundus Vini and for Concours Mondial de Bruxelles. Jeni has served on various wine bodies, is a founding board member of the Australian Women in Wine awards and has won numerous awards for wine writing over her career.

Regional focus: Geelong, Central Victoria, North East Victoria, Western Victoria

Twitter: @jeniport

Ned Goodwin MW

Born in London, raised in Australia and educated in Tokyo and Paris, Ned Goodwin usually splits his time between Tokyo and his beloved Sydney. Ned is a dux of the Len Evans Tutorial and Japan's first Master of Wine as well as an educator, consultant, judge, critic, presenter and motivational speaker. He has served as wine director for one of Asia's largest restaurant groups, has had his own TV wine show in Japan, and was also the 'wine face' for All Nippon Airways. He is also an Asian-focused ambassador for a Champagne house, the host of Langton's TV, is on the Wine Committee at Italy's illustrious Biondi-Santi, and has his own import company, Wine Diamonds. Previously, Ned was a sommelier, including at Michelin-starred Veritas in New York, which had arguably the finest wine list in the world.

Regional focus: McLaren Vale; Hunter Valley and regional New South Wales

Instagram: @NedGoodwinMW | **Twitter:** @rednedwine

Tony Love

Tony Love is a South Australia–based freelance wine writer. As a career journalist and editor, Tony has worked across the newspaper, magazine and book industries Australia-wide, covering lifestyle content – from outdoor adventures to arts and culture. For the past 15 years, Tony has turned his focus onto food and wine, and has been published in major industry and consumer magazines. He was at Adelaide's *Advertiser* until 2018; his roles included features editor, senior restaurant reviewer, food and wine section editor, and, finally, national wine industry editor and writer for all NewsCorp's Australian daily mastheads. In 2018, Tony was named South Australia's Legend of the Vine by the Wine Communicators of Australia. Tony's work now includes a regular *InDaily* column on South Australian wines, freelance writing for magazines, copy writing and consulting to small wine businesses, corporate entities, and regional and national authorities. He also occasionally writes travel features for *The Australian* and *Escape*.

Regional focus: Adelaide Hills, Langhorne Creek, Kangaroo Island, Currency Creek, Southern Fleurieu

Twitter: @TonyLoveTaste | **Facebook:** @Anthony H Love
Instagram: @tloveeeeee | **Website:** tonylove.com.au

Australia's geographical indications

Regions and subregions marked with an asterisk are not registered but are in common usage.

NEW SOUTH WALES

WINE ZONE		WINE REGION		SUBREGION
Big Rivers	(A)	Murray Darling	1	
		Perricoota	2	
		Riverina	3	
		Swan Hill	4	
Central Ranges	(B)	Cowra	5	
		Mudgee	6	
		Orange	7	
Hunter Valley	(C)	Hunter	8	Broke Fordwich Pokolbin Upper Hunter
Northern Rivers	(D)	Hastings River	9	
Northern Slopes	(E)	New England Australia	10	
South Coast	(F)	Shoalhaven Coast	11	
		Southern Highlands	12	
Southern New South Wales	(G)	Canberra District	13	
		Gundagai	14	
		Hilltops	15	
		Tumbaramba	16	
Western Plains	(H)			

SOUTH AUSTRALIA

WINE ZONE		WINE REGION		SUBREGION
Adelaide Super Zone includes Mount Lofty Ranges, Fleurieu and Barossa wine regions				
Barossa		Barossa Valley	17	
		Eden Valley	18	High Eden
Fleurieu	(J)	Currency Creek	19	
		Kangaroo Island	20	
		Langhorne Creek	21	
		McLaren Vale	22	
		Southern Fleurieu	23	
Mount Lofty Ranges		Adelaide Hills	24	Lenswood Piccadilly Valley
		Adelaide Plains	25	
		Clare Valley	26	Polish River* Watervale*
Far North	(K)	Southern Flinders Ranges	27	
Limestone Coast	(L)	Coonawarra	28	
		Mount Benson	29	
		Mount Gambier	30	
		Padthaway	31	
		Robe	32	
		Wrattonbully	33	
Lower Murray	(M)	Riverland	34	
The Peninsulas	(N)	Southern Eyre Peninsula*	35	

AUSTRALIAN CAPITAL TERRITORY

WINE ZONE	WINE REGION	SUBREGION

NORTHERN TERRITORY

WINE ZONE	WINE REGION	SUBREGION

VICTORIA

WINE ZONE		WINE REGION		SUBREGION
Central Victoria	(P)	Bendigo	36	
		Goulburn Valley	37	Nagambie Lakes
		Heathcote	38	
		Strathbogie Ranges	39	
		Upper Goulburn	40	
Gippsland	(Q)			
North East Victoria	(R)	Alpine Valleys	41	
		Beechworth	42	
		Glenrowan	43	
		King Valley	44	
		Rutherglen	45	
North West Victoria	(S)	Murray Darling	46	
		Swan Hill	47	
Port Phillip	(T)	Geelong	48	
		Macedon Ranges	49	
		Mornington Peninsula	50	
		Sunbury	51	
		Yarra Valley	52	
Western Victoria	(U)	Ballarat*	53	
		Grampians	54	Great Western
		Henty	55	
		Pyrenees	56	

WESTERN AUSTRALIA

WINE ZONE		WINE REGION		SUBREGION
Central Western Australia	(V)			
Eastern Plains, Inland and North of Western Australia	(W)			
Greater Perth	(X)	Peel	57	
		Perth Hills	58	
		Swan District	59	Swan Valley
South West Australia	(Y)	Blackwood Valley	60	
		Geographe	61	
		Great Southern	62	Albany Denmark Frankland River Mount Barker Porongurup
		Manjimup	63	
		Margaret River	64	
		Pemberton	65	
West Australian South East Coastal	(Z)			

QUEENSLAND

WINE ZONE	WINE REGION		SUBREGION
Queensland	Granite Belt	66	
	South Burnett	67	

TASMANIA

WINE ZONE	WINE REGION		SUBREGION
Tasmania	Northern Tasmania*	68	
	Southern Tasmania*	69	
	East Coast Tasmania*	70	

New in the *Halliday Wine Companion* this year

TASTING TEAM OF REGIONAL SPECIALISTS

Represented in five states, our expanded tasting team of seven regional experts provide connection with every region, continuity and specialist knowledge (page 11).

AWARDS JUDGING BY THE TASTING TEAM

For the first time, the *Halliday Wine Companion* Awards were judged collaboratively by the full tasting panel (page 11).

RIGOROUS SCORING

We tackled bracket creep head-on with rigorous scoring consistent with international benchmarks (page 12).

STAR RATINGS RECEIVE A REFRESH

A three-year rolling average replaces discretionary winery star ratings (page 14).

MORE THAN 9100 WINES TASTED

Presenting the largest number of wines tasted in five years and the third largest in the 36-year history of the *Companion*.

RECORD NEW WINERIES REVIEWED FOR THIS EDITION

Our expanded tasting team has been more active than ever in seeking out 60% more new wineries than last year.

WINERY OF THE YEAR AND WINEMAKER OF THE YEAR RUNNERS-UP

We announce our runners-up for Winery of the Year (page 21) and Winemaker of the Year (page 24) for the first time.

VITICULTURIST OF THE YEAR

Introducing our inaugural Viticulturist of the Year and runners-up (page 26).

WHITE WINE OF THE YEAR, RED WINE OF THE YEAR AND SPARKLING WINE OF THE YEAR

Anointing just one Wine of the Year was a monumental undertaking. Our top sparkling, red and white wines emerged organically from our Awards judging (see the full story on page 35).

NEW VARIETAL CATEGORIES

Australian wine is evolving rapidly in new and exciting directions, and we are pleased to announce Sparkling Rosé (page 38) and Cabernet Shiraz (page 47) as two new varietal categories.

DETAILED VITICULTURAL AND VINIFICATION BACKGROUND

More in-depth background on all the wines tasted for this year's *Companion* can be found on www.winecompanion.com.au.

Introduction

The world of Australian wine is a dynamic and rapidly changing place, and there has perhaps never been a period that more dramatically exemplified its far-flung extremes in all directions than 2020–21. From the opening days of the growing season all the way through to the sales dynamics in domestic and export markets, this has been one roller-coaster year of white-knuckle turns and loops like nobody could ever have anticipated.

In mid-May 2021, as I pen the final words in this edition, the collective industry is heaving a sigh of relief at the conclusion of this late and tumultuous season. Off the back of relentless years of drought and its dire repercussions in bushfires and smoke taint in 2020, the rains of La Niña came as a welcome relief in spring 2020, only to later unleash a deluge on the east and west coasts that would mercilessly coincide with the 2021 vintage. Spared the extremes of the coasts, most of Victoria and all of South Australia and Tasmania flourished under mild conditions harking back to those wonderfully cool, classic seasons of decades past.

Labour-intensive viticultural and picking attempts to mitigate rain impact were doubly challenged by labour shortages in the wake of pandemic-induced border closures. Winery staff were redeployed in vineyards, and unexpected helpers heeded cries for assistance, with even grey nomads joining picking teams. The full, blow-by-blow account of this unusual harvest across the country is recounted on pages 59–63.

The pandemic played out dramatically in the market too. With international borders shut tight for the foreseeable future, a surplus of discretionary spending fuelled unprecedented domestic demand for premium wine both on- and off-premises. The balance of supply and demand was thrown into turmoil as domestic sales experienced an acute shift, while cellar doors and venues continued to struggle with the ongoing uncertainty of lockdowns and travel bans.

The diplomatic tussle with China, which saw Australia's biggest wine export partner and more than 40% of exports all but erased in 2020, has shown no signs of abating, and the industry continues to scramble to get its eggs out of this crumbling basket. Yet for all that this wild year has thrown at them, the optimism, adaptability and resilience for which Australian winemakers are respected for the world over has again flourished in the face of adversity on every side.

In such a period of profound change across our vast industry, it is timely to introduce a brand new era for the *Halliday Wine Companion*. Stepping up as chief editor for the first time, the responsibility of vigorously seeking out and championing the finest wines of the year has been a tremendous joy and privilege. Fundamental to this has been elevating an expanded tasting team to new region-specific roles and a stronger voice in every detail of the process, right up to judging of the *Companion* Awards. Together we are proud to introduce a record number of new wineries this year, more winery award categories (including runners-up for each), new wine categories, refreshed star ratings and nigh on the largest number of wines tasted in the history of the *Companion*.

The finest wines to be unleashed this year rank among the greatest this country has ever witnessed – testimony that, against all odds, Australian wine has never been in a stronger place. It is to the celebration of these wines and their resilient and tireless growers and makers that this edition is devoted.

The tasting team of regional specialists

James' decision to step back from tasting the majority of wines in the *Companion* this year has opened up the opportunity for the tasting team to step into new roles. The wine world in 2021 is a very different place to when James created his very first edition in 1986. It's no longer possible for one person to taste every wine, to know every winery and maintain connections with every region.

In place of the rolling system of the past, in which wineries were allocated variously to tasters every year, the *Halliday Wine Companion* tasting team now comprises a panel of regional specialists in a model tried and proven by other key global wine communication platforms, including JancisRobinson.com, *Wine Advocate*, *Decanter* and JamesSuckling.com. This change provides stronger links with the regions and wineries, offering continuity, connection and specialist expertise. See pages 5–7 for each taster's focus regions.

James stays on the team as, in his words, the 'taster at large', and as an example, mentor and ever-present inspiration. He and I are joined by his existing tasting panel of Ned Goodwin MW, Jane Faulkner and Jeni Port. We welcome for the first time Tony Love (based in Adelaide) as an experienced taster and writer, and Erin Larkin (based in Perth), the most energetic and talented new blood in Australian wine communication. All are respected tasters and writers in their own right; we are a team with a fantastic diversity of age, experience and gender, and, importantly, for the first time, there is representation in every one of Australia's key wine states (with a slight stretch for this Tasmanian residing in Queensland!).

In our regional roles, we are best placed to communicate, celebrate and scrutinise the ever-increasing diversity of the wonderful kaleidoscope that is Australian wine today. The panel has been on the ground this year, more active than ever, in seeking out all the best wines to introduce in the *Companion*. Particularly pertinent in a year in which interstate travel has been all but shut down by the global pandemic. Each taster brings their own unique approach, tastes and network of relationships, which has proven to be a tremendous blessing in expanding the scope of the *Companion* by the number and the diversity of wineries stepping forward this year. One of the spin-offs is a record 102 new wineries in this year's line-up, 60% more than last year. All the who's who are here as always, and this year we are proud to introduce our favourite little estates off the beaten track, brand new players, and even the odd 'skinsy dude' or two along the way! The Australian wine landscape has never been more dynamic or more thrilling, and it's our greatest pleasure to keep you right up to speed.

Awards judging by the tasting team

For the first time this year, judging of the *Halliday Wine Companion* Awards was conducted by the full tasting panel. This not only facilitated a rigorously collaborative and ecumenical result but also offered the ultimate context for the team to calibrate and benchmark at the top end. It also proved to be a blessing to have the chance to connect in person for the first time for the judging, which took place on the Mornington Peninsula in late March 2021, after a year defined by Covid-induced isolation.

Each of the seven tasters was invited to nominate their top wine in each of the 17 categories to progress to the trophy judging. In order to ensure that those tasters with multiple key regions had proper opportunity to champion each region, each taster was offered the option of nominating a second top wine from a different region in the six big categories of riesling, chardonnay, pinot noir, shiraz, cabernet sauvignon, and cabernet and family. This permitted those with two key regions to choose one from each (e.g. Hunter and McLaren Vale shiraz for Ned Goodwin). Each judge was also offered a maximum of three 'wild card' nominations of second (or third) nominations, again from different regions.

There were no points thresholds defined for nomination of top wines, so as not to encourage overscoring in order to qualify. The wines put forward obviously had to be the highest or equal-highest scoring for that variety in that region for that judge. (Nominated wines are marked with ♥ at the end of their tasting notes.) See pages 37–50 for winners of each category. Because each taster was only permitted to submit their single best wine from each region, the judges' nominations did not encompass all the top-scoring wines listed.

True to the history and spirit of the *Companion*, wines were not judged blind but considered with their full identity, context, region, variety, vintage, history and pedigree in mind, with full viticultural and vinification background provided. James has always upheld tasting for the *Companion* with the labels revealed. Blind tasting is obviously important in the context of judging, and we are privileged in Australia to have one of the best show systems in the world for wines to be assessed blind. The *Companion* offers something different that complements our show system, and this is the reason for upholding James' legacy of tasting wines with their labels revealed.

Members of the tasting panel were given time to taste each flight individually and to write their own notes. At the conclusion of each class, we had an open panel discussion before each member cast their vote using the Borda count method (as per wine show best practice). In instances where the results were close, there was a revote on the top two, three or four wines.

In determining our winners for each category, we made the decision to uphold individual tasters' scores and reviews for every wine, resisting the temptation to meddle with scores in hindsight to inflate points based on group consensus. Thus, every review can rightly be considered in the context of every other rating from that taster. The winner of each category was the favourite of the whole team, which is why it does not always appear as the highest-scoring entry in its category.

The opportunity to make the Awards judging truly collaborative and ecumenical certainly complicated the process vastly, but represented a very important transition in our evolving story and future of the *Companion*. I am immensely proud of the team and of our tireless Tasting Manager, Emily Lightfoot. James later congratulated us all on 'that most difficult challenge to steer the ship that might have ended up sideways in the Suez Canal'. The results speak for themselves, and we are united in our pride to present the longest list of winners ever featured in the *Halliday Wine Companion*.

Rigorous scoring

Wine scores are, by their nature, subjective. Each of us as members of the tasting team have our own voice in how we describe wine, and we all score slightly differently. This diversity is something that we celebrate, and this is why we encourage each taster to adopt their own style in their reviews (which, of course, always reveals so much more about the wine than the score).

Get to know a taster and you'll come to understand what their scores and descriptions mean. This is one of many reasons why we have appointed the tasting team as regional specialists this year, for continuity within each region and from one vintage to the next. This is also why we publish their initials next to each review.

There has been much discussion of late around 'bracket creep' – the concept that wine scores are progressively drifting upwards in time. This has been a hot and controversial topic among wine reviewers, winemakers, the wine trade and our readers for at least the past seven years, and it dominated much of the response around our transition announcement last year.

There's good reason that scores should be on the rise, especially in a winemaking nation that is developing as rapidly as Australia. The wines we're reviewing today are a world away from what they were when James created his first edition in 1986.

In the late 1990s, the average score awarded by the *Companion* was around 87 points. Last year, this average increased to close to 92 points. Over the past decade, the proportion of 98–100 point scores increased almost seventy-fold. Is this improvement of the breed or of grade inflation? Both are difficult to deny.

With a larger and more geographically diverse team, we are purposely more rigorous in ensuring that our ratings remain consistent, first and foremost, with the points as we define them here and, secondly, with international benchmarks.

This is why scores this year are a little more conservative than in recent editions. This year, the average score awarded is just over 90 points, which is similar to our average a decade ago. There is also greater spread in the scores this year, with two-thirds of the scores falling between 85 and 95 points. The proportion of 95-point scores this year is just under 11%, down from 12–16% over the past seven years. And the proportion of 98–100 point scores is just under 0.6%, down from 0.7–1.1% over the past three years.

This puts our average ratings at roughly where they were between 2010 and 2012, with sufficient spread to properly celebrate high scores, while remaining consistent with international benchmarks and other key tasters and publications globally.

These trends are a natural reflection, too, of challenging vintages in south-eastern Australia. The severe, ongoing drought has taken its toll in recent years, not to mention the dramatic impact of bushfires and smoke taint in 2020.

It's important to emphasise that it doesn't take 95 points to distinguish a great wine. There are cracking wines out there at 88 or 91 points. OK, so they're not Domaine de la Romanée-Conti La Tâche. They're also not $3000!

Ultimately, our responsibility comes down to nothing more than assessing the wine in the glass on its merits. As independent reviewers, it is our responsibility to you to rigorously scrutinise every wine. As you turn these pages, you will see that we are always generous when praise is due, vigorously seeking out and championing the finest wines in the country. As always, top wines deserve top scores.

Tyson Stelzer
Chief Editor, *Halliday Wine Companion*
May 2021

How to use this book

Wineries

Yarra Yering

Briarty Road, Coldstream, Vic 3770 **Region** Yarra Valley
T (03) 5964 9267 **www.**yarrayering.com **Open** 7 days 10–5
Winemaker Sarah Crowe **Est.** 1969 **Dozens** 5000 **Vyds** 112ha
In September 2008, founder Bailey Carrodus died and in April '09 Yarra Yering was on the market. It was Bailey Carrodus' clear wish and expectation that any purchaser would continue to manage the vineyard and winery, and hence the wine style, in much the same way as he had done for the previous 40 years. Its acquisition in June '09 by a small group of investment bankers has fulfilled that wish. The low-yielding, unirrigated vineyards have always produced wines of extraordinary depth and intensity. Dry Red No. 1 is a cabernet blend; Dry Red No. 2 is a shiraz blend; Dry Red No. 3 is a blend of touriga nacional, tinta cão, tinta roriz, tinta amarela, alvarelhão and sousão; Pinot Noir and Chardonnay are not hidden behind delphic numbers; Underhill Shiraz (planted in 1973) is from an adjacent vineyard purchased by Yarra Yering in '87. Sarah Crowe was appointed winemaker after the 2013 vintage. She has made red wines of the highest imaginable quality right from her first vintage in '14 and, to the delight of many, myself (James) included, has offered all the wines with screw caps. For good measure, she introduced the '14 Light Dry Red Pinot Shiraz as a foretaste of that vintage and an affirmation of the exceptional talent recognised by her being named Winemaker of the Year in the *Wine Companion 2017*. Exports to the UK, the US, Singapore, Hong Kong, China and NZ.

Yarra Yering

The producer name appearing on the front label is used throughout the book.

★★★★★

Star ratings provide a highly coveted and oft-quoted snapshot of the calibre of a winery based on the ratings of its wines in recent years. In the past, James has applied a modicum of discretion in determining promotions, demotions and rolling over of past years' ratings. Under our new structure, in which tastings are shared across a wider team, a more transparent, objective and consistent system of applying ratings is appropriate.

James' age-old criteria for calculating star ratings from wine scores have been upheld for consistency and continuity, with the same cut-offs maintained, as set out below. For the first time this year, I have introduced a three-year rolling average, in which ratings are calculated for each year and the average of the star ratings for the three most recent years is then rounded to the nearest 0.5. This removes subjectivity, providing a sufficiently up-to-date snapshot, while smoothing out the fluctuations of erratic harvests.

The three-year rolling average replaces James' judgement calls, based on the most recent three years' ratings, and his mercy rule, in which a demotion had previously been no more than half a star. Further, this also supersedes his decision that nobody's rating would be reduced for the 2021 edition, due to drought, poor flowering, bushfires and Covid in 2020. Admittedly, none of these effects influenced the wines tasted for the 2021 edition, though have, of course, significantly impacted our tastings for this edition.

To be fair, equitable and transparent, I have gone back to all 18000+ wine reviews in the 2020 and 2021 *Companions* and recalculated their star ratings based on the cut-offs (I knew I'd use that degree in computational mathematics one day!). These are the star ratings I've averaged together with the 2022 ratings as calculated from the 9129 wines tasted for this edition to determine the star ratings that you see throughout this book.

As in the past, five red stars are awarded to wineries who have upheld 5-star ratings this year and in the previous three years (hence four years in total). Here I have used the star ratings that James published in 2019, 2020 and 2021 along with my 2022 rating. Winery names printed in red again denote the best of the best with a long track record of excellence, and to formalise this criterion I have introduced the rule that they must have upheld a 5-star rating this year and in the previous nine years (10 years in total).

The result of these changes has naturally been a slight shuffling in the ranks of our top-rated wineries to single out those who have set the very highest standards in the most recent seasons. The inherent challenges in the 2020 harvest (dubbed by James as 'freakishly terrible') across many regions of south-eastern Australia, and, to a lesser extent, the ongoing impact of drought in 2018 and 2019, has resulted in an expected lowering of the averages. This is particularly stark in the context of the mercy rule and absence of demotions applied in the 2021 edition. Nonetheless, this year we have singled out a record 207 5-star wineries with names printed in red, more than twice as many as last year. In total, more than one-quarter of wineries awarded a star rating have achieved the coveted 5-star status.

Of a total of 2926 wineries on www.winecompanion.com.au, 1618 submitted wines for review in the past three years and hence were awarded a star rating this year. Space constraints dictate that not every review and score can be printed in this book, which means that star ratings are best understood in the context of the website, where all the scores appear.

The number at the end of each rating below notes the number of wineries in that category in this year's edition, and the percentage is that of the total number of wineries awarded a star rating this year (in contrast to previous editions, where the percentages were based on the total number of wineries in the *Wine Companion* database).

     Outstanding winery regularly producing wines of exemplary quality and typicity. Will have at least two wines rated at 95 points or above, and has held a 5-star rating for the previous three years (i.e. 4 years in total at 5 stars). 91 wineries, 5.6%

Where the winery name itself is printed in red, it is a winery with a long track record of excellence, having held a 5-star rating continuously for 10 years – truly the best of the best. (Formerly a winery generally acknowledged to have had a long track record of excellence in the context of its region.) 207 wineries, 12.8%

★★★★★   Outstanding winery capable of producing wines of very high quality, and did so this year. Will have at least two wines rated at 95 points or above. 115 wineries, 7.1%

★★★★☆   Excellent winery able to produce wines of high to very high quality, knocking on the door of a 5-star rating. Will have one wine rated at 95 points or above, and two (or more) at 90 or above. 384 wineries, 23.7%

★★★★   Very good producer of wines with class and character. Will have either one wine rated at 95 points or above, or two (or more) at 90 or above. 457 wineries, 28.2%

★★★☆   A solid, usually reliable maker of good, sometimes very good wines. Will have one wine at 90 points or above. 211 wineries, 13.0%

★★★   A typically good winery, but often has a few lesser wines. Will have at least one wine at 86–89 points. 102 wineries, 6.3%

NR   The NR rating is given when there have been no wines scoring more than 86 points, or where the tastings have, for one reason or another, proved not to fairly reflect the reputation of a winery with a track record of success. The NR rating mainly appears on winecompanion.com.au. 51 wineries, 3.2%

The vine leaf symbol indicates the 77 wineries that are new entries in this year's *Wine Companion*. (There were 102 wineries in total, with the remaining 25 on the website.)

Briarty Road, Coldstream, Vic 3770 **T** (03) 5964 9267

Contact details are usually those of the winery and cellar door, but in a few instances may simply be a postal address; this occurs when the wine is made at another winery or wineries, and is sold only through the website and/or retail.

Region Yarra Valley

A full list of zones, regions and subregions appears on page 8. Occasionally you will see 'various', meaning the winery sources grapes from a number of regions, often without a vineyard of its own.

www.yarrayering.com

An important reference point, normally containing material not found (for space reasons) in this book.

Open 7 days 10–5

Although a winery might be listed as not open or only open on weekends, many may in fact be prepared to open by appointment. A telephone call will establish whether this is possible or not. For space reasons we have simplified the open hours listed; where the hours vary each day or for holidays, we simply refer the reader to the website.

Winemaker Sarah Crowe

In all but the smallest producers, the winemaker is simply the head of a team; there may be many executive winemakers actually responsible for specific wines in the medium to large companies (80000 dozens and upwards). Once again, space constraints mean usually only one or two winemakers are named, even if they are part of a larger team.

Est. 1969

Keep in mind that some makers consider the year in which they purchased the land to be the year of establishment, others the year in which they first planted grapes, others the year they first made wine, and so on. There may also be minor complications where there has been a change of ownership or break in production.

Dozens 5000

This figure (representing the number of 9-litre/12-bottle cases produced each year) is merely an indication of the size of the operation. Some winery entries do not feature a production figure: this is typically because the winery (principally, but not exclusively, the large companies) regards this information as confidential.

Vyds 112ha

The hectares of vineyard/s owned by the winery.

In September 2008, founder Bailey Carrodus died and in April '09 Yarra Yering was on the market. It was Bailey Carrodus's clear wish and expectation that any purchaser would continue to manage the vineyard and winery, and hence the wine style, in much the same way as he had done for the previous 40 years. Its acquisition in June '09 by a small group of investment bankers has fulfilled that wish. The low-yielding, unirrigated vineyards have always produced wines of extraordinary depth and intensity …

Winery summaries have been written by James, except in instances where initials denote another member of the tasting panel.

Tasting notes

ΨΨΨΨΨ   **Dry Red No. 1 2019** This is mesmerising. Do take time to bask in its fragrance – all floral and spicy with some aniseed and fresh herbs. Enjoy the poised fruit flavours of blackberries, mulberries and a hint of blueberries coated in spicy oak and tethered to the body of the wine. Pulsing acidity and beautiful tannin structure shape this and offer a promise of more to come in time. Wow – what a wine. Screw cap. 13.5% alc. **Rating** 98 **To** 2039 $120 JF ❂

ΨΨΨΨΨ

The inadequacies of reducing the complexities of a wine to a number are patently apparent, but nonetheless we persist with the international 100-point system because it is universally understood. Space constraints dictate that only 3280 notes are printed in full in this book, with points, drink-to dates and prices included for a further 5352 wines. Tasting notes for wines that are 95 points and over are printed in red. Tasting notes for all wines receiving 84 points or above appear on www.winecompanion.com.au.

97–99	**G O L D**	🍷🍷🍷🍷🍷	**Exceptional** Wines of major trophy standard in important wine shows.
95–96		🍷🍷🍷🍷🍷	**Outstanding** Wines of gold medal standard, usually with a great pedigree.
94	**S I L V E R**	🍷🍷🍷🍷🍷	Wines on the cusp of gold medal status.
90–93		🍷🍷🍷🍷🍷	**Highly recommended** Wines of silver medal standard, demonstrating great quality, style and character, and worthy of a place in any cellar.
89	**B R O N Z E**	🍷🍷🍷🍷	**Recommended** Wines on the cusp of silver medal standard.
86–88		🍷🍷🍷🍷	Wines of bronze medal standard; well-produced, flavoursome wines, usually not requiring cellaring.
84–85		🍷🍷🍷🍷	**Acceptable** Wines of good commercial quality, free from significant fault.
80–83		🍷🍷🍷	**Over to you** Everyday wines, without much character, and/or somewhat faulty.
75–79		🍷🍷🍷	**Not recommended** Wines with one or more significant winemaking faults.

✪   **Special value** Wines considered to offer special value for money within the context of their glass symbol status. This can apply at any price point, and for consistency a basic algorithm is applied to take into account the price of a wine and the points it is awarded. A value rosette is given, for instance, to $11 wines scoring 85 or more points, $21 wines scoring 90 or more, $35 wines of 95 or more and $200 wines with 98 or more.

♥   **Shortlisted for 2022 Awards** Nominated by the tasting panel as the best example of this variety/style in its region.

Dry Red No. 1 2019 This is mesmerising. Do take time to bask in its fragrance … Screw cap. 13.5% alc. **Rating** 98 **To** 2039 $120 JF ✪

This year, we have compiled the full details available on the viticultural and winemaking background of each wine. In most cases, space constraints do not permit these to be included in book, but you can find the full details at the start of the note at www.winecompanion.com.au.

This tasting note will usually have been made within the 12 months prior to publication. Even that is a long time, and during the life of this book the wine will almost certainly change. More than this, remember that tasting is a highly subjective and imperfect art.

The initials EL, JF, JH, JP, NG, SC, TL and TS appearing at the end of the note signify that Erin Larkin, Jane Faulkner, James H-alliday, Jeni Port, Ned Goodwin, Steven Creber, Tony Love or Tyson Stelzer tasted the wine and provided the tasting note and rating. Biographies for each member of the tasting team and their regional focuses can be found on pages 4–7.

Screw cap

The closures in use for the wines tasted are (in descending order): screw cap 86.8% (last year 86.2%), one-piece natural cork 6.0% (last year 6.8%), Diam 5.6% (last year 4.4%) and crown seal 0.8%. The remaining 0.8% (in order of importance) are Vino-Lok, agglomerate, Twin Top, synthetic cork, ProCork, Zork and Zork SPK. It seems the market dominance of screw caps has almost plateaued, with the biggest shift a continuing move from natural cork to Diam.

13.5 % alc.

This piece of information is in one sense self-explanatory. What is less obvious is the increasing concern of many Australian winemakers about the rise in levels of alcohol, and much research and practical experimentation (for example picking earlier, or higher fermentation temperatures in open fermenters) is occurring. Reverse osmosis and yeast selection are two of the options available to decrease higher-than-desirable alcohol levels. Recent changes to domestic and export labelling mean the stated alcohol will be within a maximum of 0.5% difference to that obtained by analysis.

To 2039

The optimal time to drink a wine is of course subjective; some of us love young wines and others old. This is as personal to the taster as their review and their score. We have proposed dates according to when we would most love to drink this wine, and we commend these to you as a reference for managing your cellar and when to drink each bottle.

$120

Prices are provided by the winery, and should be regarded as a guide, particularly if purchased retail.

Winery of the Year

Yarra Yering Yarra Valley

In 1973 Dr Bailey Carrodus released the first commercial vintage in the Yarra Valley in 50 years. Almost another 50 years on, the wines crafted from the fabled site that he chose so meticulously at the foot of the Warramate Hills have stepped forward as the very finest in the country.

Winemaker Sarah Crowe embraced the vision and legacy so clearly set by Dr Carrodus from the outset, winning her the accolade of *Halliday Wine Companion* Winemaker of the Year in 2017 for the wines of 2014, her very first vintage at Yarra Yering.

Sarah is an intuitive winemaker with a profound insight into the contribution of each component in a blend. Her acute attention to the finer details has elevated the beautiful fruit from this site, through less reliance on new oak, and the resulting wine is immaculately preserved under screw caps.

Her wines in this edition hail from the 2019 harvest, marking the 50th anniversary of the planting of the vines. Even in this warm season in the Yarra, her wines carry a beguiling grace and breathtaking refinement. Every wine she has put forward this year is exceptional, and none more so than cabernet sauvignon and its blends – the true hero variety of the Yarra.

In the panel taste-off for Red Wine of the Year, the winner of Cabernet and Family (Yarra Yering Dry Red No. 1 2019) went head-to-head with the winner of Cabernet Sauvignon (Yarra Yering Carrodus Cabernet Sauvignon 2019) and it effectively became a two-horse race. The blend took the honours and went all the way to Wine of the Year. (JF & TS)

Runners-up

Bindi Wines Macedon Ranges

While exemplary standards across this year's releases are fundamental to all our awards, our criteria for Winery of the Year, Winemaker of the Year and Viticulturist of the Year are quite distinct, making it highly improbable that one estate could be a strong contender for all three. Whether you look at Bindi from the perspective of its vineyards (see page 26), its winemaking (page 24) or its wines, it qualifies on every level, which is why the tiny and beloved estate of the Dhillon family, high in the Macedon ranges, is the only winery to pull off the unlikely hat-trick of nominations this year. (TS)

Cullen Margaret River

Cullen, under the tutelage and direction of the irrepressible Vanya Cullen, is responsible for a swathe of wines that feature among the very best in Australia. Biodynamics and Cullen's fortunes have become entwined, shaping the direction and expression of this celebrated vineyard in Margaret River. The nomination for Winery of the Year is based on a remarkable catalogue of wines that express Margaret River in a way that has captured the minds, hearts and palates of drinkers (and writers) around the country. (EL)

Duke's Vineyard **Porongurup**

Duke's Vineyard is nestled into the northern face of the Porongurup range in the Great Southern. It was planted with the determination and charm of one man: Ian 'Duke' Ranson. He was one-eyed in his vision to produce great wine in the tiny region and has led the way, hand in hand with his winemaker Rob Diletti. Riesling, shiraz and cabernet are planted, and despite a move to Albany, Duke (who is in his 80s) can still be found tending the vines with a twinkle in his eye. Duke's Vineyard is a truly remarkable realisation of a dream, and one of which Western Australia is very proud. (EL)

Helen's Hill Estate **Yarra Valley**

Helen's Hill is not only a fully-fledged winery (and restaurant) but is also an important contract grape grower. The vineyard is meticulously managed using state-of-the-art equipment, and (unusually) devotes the same care with grapes for its own use as for those sold to other wineries in the region. (JH)

McHenry Hohnen Vintners **Margaret River**

Winemaker Japo Dalli Cani is as considered and detailed in his winemaking as he is in the words that he chooses to describe wines. This year we witnessed an impressive array of wines from McHenry Hohnen that spoke precisely of their vineyard sites and their varietals, carrying us off in each instance with imagination, gentle flair and utter focus. While the style of the house emphasises Margaret River regionality, the hand that shapes them exhibits a balance, finesse and distinct preference for minerality, line and form. Beautiful wines. (EL)

Moss Wood **Margaret River**

Moss Wood has long been responsible for some of the finest cabernet wines, not only in Margaret River and Western Australia, but in Australia at large. The nomination for Winery of the Year recognises not just the superb achievements of the Wilyabrup Cabernet (the current 2018 release is one of the greatest to date), but also the stunning attributes of the Chardonnay, Pinot Noir, Semillon and others. Keith and Clare Mugford and their team at Moss Wood have, through their work over the years, cemented themselves in the hall of fame of Margaret River and of Australia. (EL)

Oakridge **Yarra Valley**

There's no question that Dave Bicknell is a cracking winemaker. His prowess with chardonnay is well celebrated, reinforced by no fewer than six gold-medal scoring chardonnays in this edition. That he can back this with similarly rating pinot noir, syrah and even gris and rosé is what puts Oakridge in the running for Winery of the Year. Clever fruit sourcing, even in the competitive environment of the Yarra, matched with intuitive and attentive winemaking makes for a stunning line-up of no fewer than 20 reviews above 93 points this year. (JF & TS)

Shaw + Smith **Adelaide Hills**

Such is the evolution of refinement, precision and beauty in the wines of Shaw + Smith that I (Tony) had to resist the temptation to nominate every wine they make for our Awards judging. This is a brand that epitomises the best of what the Hills can do, taking it to new heights with new plantings in Piccadilly and single-vineyard releases from Lenswood. Chardonnay, shiraz, pinot noir and, of course, sauvignon blanc share the limelight, with a cracking riesling ascending through the ranks. Its future is in capable hands with the talented David LeMire and Winemaker of the Year nominee Adam Wadewitz (see page 25) stepping into managerial roles. This company is the number-one ambassador for the Adelaide Hills and was an unsung hero behind the scenes in supporting the community following the bushfires last year. (TL & TS)

Yeringberg Yarra Valley

From what is perhaps the most historic site in the Yarra Valley, Yeringberg crafts a wonderful suite of wines of subtlety and gentleness, amassing gold-medal scores this year for chardonnay, pinot noir, shiraz, viognier and, of course most of all, its iconic cabernet blend. Following the landscape of their precious patch in the Yarra, and staying true to the varieties that work best instead of chasing fashions, they are future-proofing their vineyard by planting on rootstocks. (JF & TS)

Previous Winery of the Year recipients were Paringa Estate (2007), Balnaves of Coonawarra (2008), Brookland Valley (2009), Tyrrell's (2010), Larry Cherubino Wines (2011), Port Phillip Estate/Kooyong (2012), Kilikanoon (2013), Penfolds (2014), Hentley Farm Wines (2015), Tahbilk (2016), Mount Pleasant (2017), Mount Mary (2018), Seville Estate (2019), Jim Barry Wines (2020) and Henschke (2021).

Winemaker of the Year

Winemaker of the Year is awarded to the individual whose wines in the *Companion* this year most exemplify best winemaking practice. It is acknowledged that, even in the smallest winery, credit is never due only to one individual but to a team. In listing each nomination we also recognise and applaud the teams around them.

For the first time we are proud to announce the runners-up for Winemaker of the Year. Each taster put forward one nomination. The shortlist was discussed rigorously while tasting at least one of each nominee's wines together during our Awards judging, a conversation that continued over the weeks to follow. Our final decision was multifaceted, taking into account all of the wines submitted for this edition, the full history of wines submitted in the past, and our personal knowledge of each of the individuals and their winemaking talents. To say that narrowing down to one winner was a difficult process is an understatement of the highest order. All are every bit worthy. And one, as it turns out, especially so.

Michael Dhillon, Bindi Wines Macedon

Conjuring a pinot noir that elicited an almost unanimous vote from the tasting team for best of the year, not to mention another three in the top 12, would be sufficient reason to be named Winemaker of the Year, but there is much more to Bindi winemaker and viticulturist Michael Dhillon. A reflective and insightful thinker, Michael embodies a deep and intimate connection with his land, his history and his community. From vineyards planted by his family high in the Macedon Ranges in 1988, he tends to pinot noir and chardonnay, with shiraz sourced from Heathcote.

Michael credits his sympathetic treatment of pinot noir to his predecessor and mentor, Stuart Anderson. A focus on drawing out elegant fruit from distinguished sites calls for gentle and minimal winemaking, which he is constantly fine-tuning and is inspired by regular sojourns to Burgundy. Ferments occur naturally without nutrients or enzymes, and red wines are worked gently, delicately pressed and aged long with minimal racking, no fining and restricted filtration. His wines speak of Macedon and of Bindi, never overworked but with effortless purity and distinctive refinement – a joy to taste and to drink.

Each of his releases arguably owe as much to Michael's fastidious approach in the vineyards than in the cellar, hence his nomination also for Viticulturist of the Year. See page 26 for detail on his initiatives in the vines. (TS & JF)

Runners-up

Duane Coates, Coates Wines Adelaide Hills

Across a four-month tsunami of tasting, not once did I come across a range of wines as unequivocally delicious as that from Duane Coates. I am speaking of each cuvée, meticulously crafted by a modest man with ample foreign experience up his sleeve, along with the academic moxie demanded by his Master of Wine studies and his recent inauguration to the Institute. From Nebbiolo and Chardonnay, to the most exciting sparkling wine yet tasted from these shores, these are wines that push boundaries as much as they sit in the mouth with an uncanny effortlessness ... before the bottle is gone. (NG)

Scott Ireland, Provenance Wines Geelong

Scott Ireland has gone from winemaker at Austin's in the Geelong region to a fully-fledged Western Victorian wine specialist focusing on cooler-climate wines from Geelong, Ballarat and Henty. He offers a wonderful celebration of regions and individual sites, crafting wines with a clean purity and a real sense of adventure. Scott has approached winemaking with a sense of bravery, professionalism and humility, and hasn't let limited resources hold him back from embracing opportunity. (JP)

Adam Wadewitz, Shaw + Smith Adelaide Hills

Everything Adam Wadewitz touches turns to gold. First at Best's Great Western, then subsequently at Shaw + Smith and its Tolpuddle Vineyard, and more recently The Other Wine Co and his own Elderslie wines. It is of course Shaw + Smith that leads his nomination, with a suite of gold-medal scoring wines embracing chardonnay, shiraz, sauvignon blanc and even riesling. His chardonnay ranks high among the best in the Hills, but it is perhaps his focus on elevating his famous sauvignon blanc, tighter and more modern than ever, that is his most laudable achievement. Adam Wadewitz is a go-to of elite Adelaide Hills winemaking and is to be credited for some of the finest wines in the region. (TL & TS)

Ian Hongell, Torbreck Vintners Barossa Valley

In the space of less than five years, Ian Hongell has transformed one of the leading estates of the Barossa, elevating its vines and its wines to hitherto unseen heights. A grower and winemaker with tremendous depth of experience, he embodies a restless fanaticism to always strive harder, tweaking the finer details to bring out the best in his team, his vines and his wines. Ian is a deep thinker who has fundamentally challenged my own preconceptions about red winemaking in a warm climate. He contrasts his insightful and considered approach with a down-to-earth common sense that builds firm bonds with his winemaking and viticultural team. After almost two decades at Peter Lehmann Wines, 'Honky' clearly has inherited Peter Lehmann's tremendous loyalty and devotion to the Barossa and its people. (TS)

Glenn Goodall, Xanadu Wines Margaret River

Glenn Goodall may come across as an unassuming, laid-back, comical Kiwi with a penchant for surfing, but his wines are a different story altogether. They are made with assiduous attention to detail, deliciousness and quality at the very forefront. At the value end of the spectrum, his wines routinely smoke peer-group competitors, and at the very top end (Steven's Road and Reserve ranges), they occupy a venerated place in the top echelon of wines produced each year in Margaret River. It is not hyperbole to state that Glenn has changed the fortunes of Xanadu, forging its reputation for show-winning, delicious wines. Its success is built upon his vision and execution. Long may it continue. (EL)

Previous Winemaker of the Year recipients were Robert Diletti (2015), Peter Fraser (2016), Sarah Crowe (2017), Paul Hotker (2018), Julian Langworthy (2019), Vanya Cullen (2020) and Brett Grocke (2021).

Viticulturist of the Year

We are proud to announce our inaugural Viticulturist of the Year, awarded to the individual whose wines in this year's *Companion* most fully exemplify best practice in the vineyard. As for Winemaker of the Year, we recognise that credit is never due only to one individual and in naming each nomination we recognise and applaud also the teams who support them.

Along with our winner, we are pleased to announce five runners-up. Each taster put forward one nomination from across their regions. We discussed each nomination rigorously while tasting at least one of their wines together during our Awards judging, a discussion that carried on for many weeks to follow. Our final decision was multifaceted, taking into account all of the wines submitted for this edition, the full history of wines submitted in the past, and our personal knowledge of each of the individuals and their viticultural initiatives. It was again an extremely difficult task to name a winner from such an exemplary line-up, but the wines, actions and spirit of one remarkable woman confirmed our winner.

Vanya Cullen, Cullen Wines Margaret River

Vanya Cullen possesses a deeply emotional connection with her vines and her land like nobody else. This symbiosis has nurtured a set of benchmark wines that stand proud among the greatest in Australia's modern era, proving that by placing the health and vitality of the vines and soil first, greatness can only follow.

It was feeling and intuition more than science that led Vanya to pursue biodynamics 18 years ago; the determination with which she has since embraced this regime makes it impossible to overstate the impact she has had on the reputation of biodynamic viticulture in Australia. The influence that biodynamics (and by extension organic viticultural and land management) has had, not only on Margaret River and Western Australia but on the whole Australian wine industry in totalis, can be measured by the sum of the great wines now made under this banner. The story of 'the land' is ultimately at the heart of the industry within which we all live and breathe, and, as Australia's most vocal proponent of biodynamics, Vanya Cullen has led a charge of producers who now proudly grow grapes and make wine biodynamically.

She sums it up eloquently: 'From the soil to the vine to the grapes to the people, "biodynamics" is the same word for me as "terroir": the life of the wine and the land; this is the essence of Australian wine.' As surely as Cullen is interwoven into the history of Margaret River, biodynamics is now inextricably a part of the story of Cullen Wines. We raise a glass with Vanya this year to celebrate the 50th anniversary of this remarkable story. (EL & TS)

Runners-up

Michael Dhillon, Bindi Wines Macedon Ranges

Michael Dhillon is the epitome of what the French call a vigneron. His fastidious, intensive, hands-on, organic techniques in vineyards, planted by his family high in the Macedon Ranges since 1988, are the embodiment of his thoughtful and methodical ways. Michael's crowning glory is arguably his inaugural pinot noirs from his Darshan and Block 8 vineyards, planted in 2014 and 2016 at a phenomenal 11300 vines/ha. But for these we shall all have to wait until next year. (JF & TS)

Mark Walpole, Fighting Gully Road **Beechworth**

Well-known on the Australian viticultural scene – for many years he was chief viticulturist at Brown Brothers with a deep understanding of alternative grape varieties (at one point he had some 80 varieties under his custodianship) – Mark Walpole knows the soils of North East Victoria like few others. Respected, influential and generous, he marries a deep historical knowledge with a brave and exploratory sense of daring. At Fighting Gully Road Wines in Beechworth, decades of knowledge are coming into exciting fruition. (JP)

Neil Jericho, Jericho Wines **McLaren Vale/Adelaide Hills**

Neil Jericho is an understated man, much like his range of wines that speak strongly of place while providing unrivalled value. Yet, Jericho is largely a négociant. He purchases leased fruit and crafts delicious wines. His recent purchase of an octogenarian vineyard of Blewitt Springs bush-vine grenache, however, has changed this dynamic. He intends on respecting the vineyard as a holistic proposition, untempered by commercial pressures to provide quantity and shift the viticultural framework. His ambition is to convert the site to organics while applying his trademark courage to crafting transparent wines, not only from grenache but other varieties of the future. (NG)

Mark and Peter Saturno, Longview Vineyard **Adelaide Hills**

The Saturno family vineyard at Macclesfield is more than an engine room of the Adelaide Hills, it is a highly revered, go-to source vineyard for many of the top wines of the region. The family's commitment to the community is integral to the Hills, and when the bushfires of December 2019 destroyed one-third of the region's vineyards, they took the lead in donating many tonnes of fruit to hard-hit growers. This included the New Era Grüner Veltliner 2020, which went on to win the trophy for best Grüner Veltliner at the Adelaide Hills Wine Show in 2020. (TL & TS)

Ronald Brown, Maverick Wines **Barossa Valley**

When I first tasted the wines of Ronald Brown, I exclaimed that they very clearly communicate that his vines are relishing the attention that he is evidently bestowing upon them. Even in extreme drought seasons in the Barossa, he has demonstrated that fragrant lift, bright natural acidity, medium-bodied elegance and impeccably ripe tannins can be achieved even at low alcohols. His pursuit of purity at the expense of yields has reportedly raised eyebrows in the region. With a focus on sustainable farming and minimalist practices, he sees himself first and foremost as a vigneron. 'Perhaps because of my European wine upbringing,' he says, 'I have always believed that the main actors in producing great wines are not so much the winemakers as the vines themselves and the terroirs which give them birth, of which we are the temporary custodians.' (TS)

Best Value Winery

Best Value Winery of the Year is closely tied to the awarding of rosettes for wines offering special value for money at their price point (see page 18). With more than 1400 rosettes awarded this year, the number of value wineries featured throughout these pages is considerable indeed. In narrowing down a top ten, I prioritised not only the highest number of rosettes and the highest strike rate but also inclusion of at least one value wine at $20 or below. While great value can occur at any price point, the wine holds a special place for us all at an everyday quaffing price.

I put my shortlist of contenders to the tasting team, and a couple of weeks of rigorous discussion ensued. As in every winery awards category, I was quietly pleased to see that my suggested winner was not always a foregone conclusion. When it comes to value, Western Australia leads the country, with eight of our ten top contenders, but it was ultimately Langhorne Creek for the win!

Lake Breeze Wines Langhorne Creek

Line 'em up, wine for wine and dollar for dollar and the value for money represented by Lake Breeze is nothing short of extraordinary: four wines under $20 scoring 90–95 points and four wines under $30 scoring 92–97 this year. Case closed.

The Follett family is privileged to a deep history; the family has been tending its vines on the shores of Lake Alexandrina since the 1880s and picking up hundreds of trophies and gold medals in major wine shows across the country for decades. The calibre of Lake Breeze Wines in the wider Australian wine landscape was reaffirmed by nominations for our final taste-off for both Cabernet Sauvignon of the Year and Cabernet and Family of the Year, pitted against wines of more than 17 times their price.

The Follett family are fabulous ambassadors for an oft-neglected region and embody the heart and soul that we all love about Australian winemaking. It's a bonus that their wines also happen to represent the best value in the country. (TL & TS)

Runners-up

Castelli Estate Great Southern

Castelli Estate sources fruit from all over Western Australia's south west and specifically the Great Southern region, meaning their diverse offering spans a number of styles and price points. All are united by Castelli's ability to extract eloquent regional expressions from the vineyards and present them in a manner that is worthy of both immediate drinking and cellaring potential, too. With five $18 wines clocking in between 90 and 94 points, the value for money is outstanding. (EL)

Castle Rock Estate Porongurup

Rob Diletti has spent years building an enduring reputation for the cool-climate and exceedingly elegant wines of Porongurup. His wines – particularly, but not exclusively his rieslings – are consistently brilliant and all priced under $40. This year, nine wines that were priced from a tantalising $20 to just $35 won ratings from 90 to 97 points, making Castle Rock a shoo-in nomination for this award. (EL)

Deep Woods Estate **Margaret River**

Fogarty group chief winemaker and *Halliday Wine Companion* Winemaker of the Year 2019 Julian Langworthy has built a reputation nationwide for his jocular and irreverent approach to almost everything, except the outstanding wines that he creates. He and his team of winemakers (Andrew Bretherton and Emma Gillespie) make seriously styled, seriously structured wines from great vineyards within Margaret River. Never underestimate their ability to wow and please. They consistently clean up at wine shows with wins, including the 2019 Jimmy Watson trophy. (EL)

Duke's Vineyard **Porongurup**

If you're a fan of riesling, you must try Duke's Magpie Hill Reserve Riesling. At $45, it is one of Australia's greatest examples of the variety, making it a ridiculous bang-for-buck proposition. The wines are made by Rob Diletti (Castle Rock) and are famed for their cool-climate elegance, light touch and finesse. The vineyard is planted to just shiraz, cabernet and riesling, ranking among the very best in the region and the finest in the state. Marvellous wines. (EL)

Harewood Estate **Denmark**

Harewood is lodged among the Karri trees in Denmark, arguably one of the prettiest wine regions in Western Australia. The wine offering spans a host of varieties and styles, most of which are sourced from vineyards within the Great Southern. Refreshingly priced between $20 and $30, a line-up of no less than nine labels clocked in with scores between 90 and 95 points this year. (EL)

Mike Press Wines **Adelaide Hills**

The story of Mike Press is well told: he retired from an illustrious winemaking career with the big icon companies to plant a vineyard at a cool 500m of elevation in Lobethal in 1998. Returning to winemaking was never the plan, but he soon found himself personally delivering tantalisingly priced bottles to an increasing list of loyal fans. Two decades on, his wines continue to improve, as Mike settles into his groove and his vines attain maturity. For single-vineyard, cool-climate wines priced almost entirely between $12 and $15, Mike Press is in a league all of his own. (TL & TS)

Stella Bella Wines **Margaret River**

Recent vintages have seen a decided increase in quality and definition of house style, making Stella Bella great wines to purchase at any price point. Two-thirds of its wines this year won value rosettes, including all three of its $19 Skuttlebutt range and even its $90 Luminosa flagship. Nestled in the heart of 'cabernet and chardonnay country', Stella Bella, under the guide of Luke Jolliffe, is well positioned to continue its inexorable rise. (EL & TS)

West Cape Howe Wines **Mount Barker**

This estate in Mount Barker epitomises value for money, consistently producing superb and satisfying wines that offer joy and pleasure beyond their price. Of West Cape Howe's 10 submissions priced between $17 and $30 and scoring between 88 and 95 points this year, nine were awarded value rosettes (and the tenth was only $1 off qualifying). Impressive. (EL & TS)

Xanadu Wines **Margaret River**

No estate in Australia offers more comprehensive value for money than Xanadu Wines this year, amassing an unmatched 16 value rosettes, the majority for its $20 Exmoor and $26 DJL series but extending all the way up the tree to its $110 flagships. It's not possible to overstate the exceptional value for money that this offering represents, with every wine scoring in the 90s and as high as 98. All credit to Glenn Goodall and Brendan Carr's desire to let the fruit do the talking. Their sensitive winemaking has yielded astoundingly impressive wines, the very best of which (Stevens Road and Reserve) belong alongside the most elite in Margaret River in any given year. (EL & TS)

Previous Best Value Winery recipients were Hoddles Creek Estate (2015), West Cape Howe (2016), Larry Cherubino Wines (2017), Grosset (2018), Provenance (2019), Domaine Naturaliste (2020) and Best's (2021).

Best New Winery

The Best New Winery of the Year is the finest winery submitting to the *Companion* for the first time. This year we are proud to introduce nine wineries swinging into our line-up for the first time with 5-star ratings. The competition was stronger than ever this year, with our expanded tasting team seeking out a record 102 new wineries. Our winner was confirmed by two 96-point scores, two 95, a 93 and a 92 – a tiny inaugural release that you must seek out, from an estate destined for great things indeed.

Place of Changing Winds Macedon

It would be difficult to imagine a vineyard concept more rigorously or more courageously conceived than Place of Changing Winds. The obsessive and fanatical Robert Walters is Australia's leading importer of the growers of Europe through his Bibendum Wine Co, having spent more than a quarter of a century scrutinising their methods, inspired by 'wines of great intensity, finesse and perfume, wines that spoke loudly of place'. The list of growers and scientists to whom he pays tribute who 'inspired, chastised and encouraged' his own vineyard ambitions reads like a who's who of the wine world.

His organic pinot noir and chardonnay vines on a rocky site high in the Macedon Ranges are nothing short of revolutionary, close planted at an extraordinary and unprecedented 12 000 to 33 000 vines/ha, ten times the Australian norm. In the ground between just three and nine years at the time of writing, already the miniscule quantities of his inaugural release make a profound statement of greatness, and instil a dramatic and thrilling sense of expectation for the possibilities that the future holds when these vines really hit their straps. (TS)

Runners-up

Battles Wine Western Australia

Lance Parkin and Kris Ambro have been around the Perth wine industry for many years, but their joint project in Battles Wine really does define the 'new winery' category. With only three vintages under their belts in 2021, already the wines (the reds, particularly) show attention to detail, smart sourcing and winemaking, and an energy and vitality that is at once refreshing and satisfying. Only great things lie in store for these two. (EL)

Bellebonne Tasmania

The accumulated investment of both knowledge and tirage age that is mandatory in crafting truly great sparkling wine makes it impossible for an upstart, dedicated sparkling house to ever be shortlisted for Best New Winery. Unless, that is, it is the passion project of a remarkable woman who has spent 20 years building an intimate knowledge of the vines and the wines of northern Tasmania. Natalie Fryar has a hand in defining the greatness of many of the finest sparkling brands on the island, none more graceful nor more characterful than her own beloved Bellebonne – the most important and the most sublime new sparkling label Australia has seen this century. And it must be the smallest, too. (TS)

Corryton Burge **Barossa Valley**

The finest new brands never come out of nowhere, and the new enterprise of siblings Trent and Amelia Burge takes full advantage not only of the Burge family's 300ha of vines and Illaparra Winery but also of Trent's almost 20 years of experience working in both. The brand has hit the ground running this year, with a smart set of inaugural releases appropriately led by an impressively polished Barossa shiraz and a cabernet hailing from the Corryton Park Vineyard, long the unsung hero of the family holdings. (TS)

Kerri Greens **Mornington Peninsula**

Winemaker Tom McCarthy (Quealy Wines) and viticulturist Lucas Blanck (Domaine Paul Blanck, Alsace) are a formidable duo working tirelessly to bring back to life the vineyards they manage on the Mornington Peninsula. With mandates of organics, sustainability and 'treading gently', their approach is respectful of their region and its history, yet with the youthful willingness to push boundaries. Their cracking wines are delicious, fresh and well priced. (JF & TS)

Lowboi **Great Southern**

Lowboi is the product of winemaker Guy Lyons and his wife Nicky. They bought the Springviews Vineyard on the south face of the Porongurup range in 2017 and make tiny quantities of wine from chardonnay and riesling vines (supplemented with grüner from the Forest Hill vineyard in Denmark). These wines are made with excruciating attention to detail and sensitive winemaking, acutely expressing the ground from which the vines spring. Lyons will be moving into the fifth vintage from this vineyard in 2021, but given the infinitesimal yields in 2019 and 2020, it may be the first time we see them on the market again since the glorious 2018s. Take your eyes off this label if you dare. (EL)

LS Merchants **Margaret River**

Dylan Arvidson has only been making wines at his own LS Merchants since 2017, and already we have been treated to a bevy of classy, well-constructed, minimal-intervention releases. Those in the know in Western Australia have been onto him since the brand's inception, resulting in increasingly short 'available' times in which to buy the limited wines. The new cellar door (opened in January 2021) has only amplified interest in his offering. Don't miss this little producer. (EL)

Pipan Steel **Alpine Valleys**

Paula Pipan and Radley Steel are turning a single-minded obsession with the nebbiolo grape into a successful reality. Their search for a suitable site took them to the Hunter Valley, Margaret River and Italy before ending in the foothills of the Australian Alps on a hillside of decomposed granite soil in Mudgegonga in North East Victoria. Using just three individual clones, they produce a stunning array of styles by clone, which culminate in a blend of all three. (JP)

Protero **Adelaide Hills**

Protero is a standalone brand of legendary McLaren Vale winemaker Steve Pannell that is devoted to nebbiolo, which has been sourced from the Protero vineyard at Gumeracha since 2005. Steve purchased the site in December 2019, just weeks before it was surrounded by bushfire, not for the first time. Mercifully, it survived on both occasions. Other Italian varieties and some gewürztraminer and riesling have been planted, but his real passion for this site is nebbiolo. Later this year he will release his most iconic offering from the top of the hill – and it's freaking awesome! (TL & TS)

Vino Volta **Swan Valley**

Vino Volta is owned by winemaker Garth Cliff and his wife Kristen. Born of a desire to support and showcase lesser-known regions in Western Australia, specifically the Swan Valley and its surrounds, Vino Volta has burst onto the scene with a wealth of edgy restaurants and bars opting to list his wines almost immediately. Highlights include a grenache and a red blend, but the chenins are also not to be missed. In such a short time, Cliff has dragged this brand and story out into the light, much to the delight of the drinking public. (EL)

Previous Best New Winery recipients were Rob Dolan Wines (2014), Flowstone (2015), Bicknell fc (2016), Bondar Wines (2017), Dappled (2018), Mewstone (2019), Shy Susan (2020) and Varney Wines (2021).

Dark Horses

Dark Horses are wineries that are not new to the *Companion* but who have received a 5-star rating for the first time this year. In the past, a history of at least four lesser ratings has been mandated. However, our new system of awarding star ratings based on a three-year rolling average makes it inherently difficult for wineries to qualify for a Dark Horse listing. Consequently, the requirement of a four-year track record has been dropped.

Renzaglia Wines Central Ranges

Minimal imprint in the vineyard and winery, judicious use of high-quality oak and courageous extraction gift us with a suite of detailed, precise and prodigiously digestible wines. These are the sort of savoury mid-weighters across price points that this country should make more of. With growing traction on the best lists of Sydney, I suggest you grab some of these wines while the going is still good. (NG)

Runners-up

Galafrey Mount Barker

This year, Galafrey ascended on the wings of a number of wines that showcased the strength and vitality of this dry-grown vineyard in Mount Barker. While the winery has been around for some time, the vines (planted in the late 1970s) are reaching a maturity that is starting to show in the wines. Winemaker/owner Kim Tyrer's continuation and evolution of style has yielded wines of poise and line. (EL)

South by South West Margaret River

Liv and Mij (Livia Maiorana and Mihan Patterson) have been making South by South West wines since 2016 and this year sees a swag of wines that really hit at the heart of modern drinkers' desires. There are field blends and alternative varieties sourced from all over the state, offering skin-contact and classically constructed wines, and a bevy of flavours and styles within. A very smart offering from a lovely duo. (EL)

Valhalla Wines Rutherglen

A vintage stint at Campbells, Rutherglen, in the late 1990s turned into a life-changing epiphany for Anton Therkildsen, who has gone on to establish his winery and his own take on regional specialities shiraz, durif, grenache, viognier and a stunning marsanne – not to mention a delightful riesling sourced from the King Valley. (JP)

Whistling Eagle Vineyard Heathcote

As can often be the case, Heathcote grapegrower Ian Rathjen got into winemaking unexpectedly when he decided to try his hand at creating wines with an oversupply of fruit. The rest is history. While he is best known for shiraz, watch out for his grenache. (JP)

Wine of the Year

Anointing just one Wine of the Year from the 9129 wines tasted for this edition was no trivial task. This year, the complexity of the challenge was compounded to an all new level by bringing the full tasting panel in on the final decision. Every standout wine of every style from every taster was on the table to be tasted, rigorously discussed and voted upon. The winner of each category was then in the running for Wine of the Year. Lining up 17 winners (19, in fact, with three winners of Chardonnay of the Year inseparable even on a second vote) in one taste-off to single out one winner would have proven insurmountable. The collaborative decision was thus made on the fly to first vote on our top sparkling, our top white and our top red wine. And so were born the inaugural *Halliday Wine Companion* Sparkling Wine of the Year, White Wine of the Year and Red Wine of the Year (there's something special when new awards evolve organically rather than being fabricated or contrived). The three were then lined up for the panel to cast its votes for Wine of the Year. It was decided that the Fortified Wine of the Year would not be judged for Wine of the Year. The age and rarity of Seppeltsfield 100 Year Old Para Vintage Tawny 1921 put it in a class of its own.

Yarra Yering Dry Red No. 1 2019

This is mesmerising. Do take time to bask in its fragrance – all floral and spicy with some aniseed and fresh herbs. Enjoy the poised fruit flavours of blackberries, mulberries and a hint of blueberries coated in spicy oak and tethered to the body of the wine. Pulsing acidity and beautiful tannin structure shape this and offer a promise of more to come in time. Wow – what a wine. JF

Previous Wine of the Year recipients were Bass Phillip Reserve Pinot Noir 2010 (2014), Xanadu Stevens Road Cabernet Sauvignon 2011 (2015), Serrat Shiraz Viognier 2014 (2016), Best's Thomson Family Shiraz 2014 (2017), Henschke Hill of Grace 2012 (2018), Duke's Vineyard Magpie Hill Reserve Riesling 2017 (2019), Yangarra Estate Vineyard High Sands McLaren Vale Grenache 2016 (2020) and Brokenwood Graveyard Vineyard Hunter Valley Shiraz 2018 (2021).

Sparkling Wine of the Year

Deviation Road Beltana Blanc de Blancs 2014

Opens with aromas of apple and lemon cream streusel bun. With a fine pithy mousse, the palate is compelling, with all the citrus/lemon chardonnay excitement it can muster. This is added to by a subtle aldehydic complexity that expresses itself in a light quinine character. Totally engaging. Always among the finest – this is next level. TS

Runners-up
Bellebonne Natalie Fryar Vintage Rosé 2017
Ashton Hills Sparkling Shiraz 2015

White Wine of the Year

Penfolds Yattarna Bin 144 Chardonnay 2018

An ultra-cool climate blend of Tasmania, Tumbarumba and Adelaide Hills fruit wastes no time in setting the terms of engagement with a wine of infinite class. The flinty/smoky aromas introducing an almost painful intensity on the mercurial palate, a celebration of white-fleshed stone fruits. It has made light work of 8 months in 100% new French oak. Struts its stuff without a care in the world. JH

Runners-up

Pooley Wines Margaret Pooley Tribute Single Vineyard Riesling 2020
Meerea Park Alexander Munro Individual Vineyard Aged Release Semillon 2011
Terre à Terre Crayeres Vineyard Sauvignon Blanc 2019
Oakridge 864 Single Block Release Drive Block Funder & Diamond Vineyard
    Chardonnay 2019
Leeuwin Estate Art Series Chardonnay 2018
Coriole Rubato Reserve Fiano 2020
La Prova Nebbiolo Rosato 2020

Red Wine of the Year

Yarra Yering Dry Red No. 1 2019

Runners-up

Bindi Block 5 Pinot Noir 2019
Thistledown Sands of Time Old Vine Single Vineyard Blewitt Springs Grenache 2019
SC Pannell Aglianico 2019
Tyrrell's 4 Acres Shiraz 2019
Yarra Yering Carrodus Cabernet Sauvignon 2019
Yalumba The Caley Cabernet Shiraz 2016

Top Rated by Variety

The evolution of Australian wine in new and exciting directions has been something to behold, and we have freshened up our varietal categories accordingly. Sparkling rosé has ascended to assume its own listing, as has cabernet shiraz, in recognition of Australia's definitive blend. Shiraz enjoys the company of an increasing diversity of blending partners, prompting a discontinuation of our shiraz viognier class, instead rolling it into shiraz. With insufficient highlights this year, semillon sauvignon blends have been subsumed into other whites and blends, and we mothballed the sweet wines category when our top-scoring wine was withdrawn from the market, and no worthy contenders stepped up in its place.

The winner of each category was determined collaboratively by the full tasting panel for the first time. Page 12 explains the tasting team's judging process to determine the wine of the year in each category. The winner of each category is the favourite of the whole team, which is why it does not always appear as the highest scoring entry in its category. Wines nominated by the tasting panel for judging are marked with ♥ at the end of their tasting notes. A full list of nominated wines can be found at www.winecompanion.com.au.

The lists below represent the 335 top-scoring wines in this edition. As always, the number of wines in each category is limited by a rating cut-off that reflects the strength of its class. Wine names have been shortened, but still enable the exact wine to be identified. Full tasting notes for each of these wines can, of course, be found in the body of the book.

Sparkling White

Australian sparkling is coming of age, and increasingly receiving global recognition. The sparkling epicentre of Tasmania again takes the lead in our list of superstars, with a line-up of splendour spanning three decades that dominates almost 40% of our shortlist. The cool mainland zones of Adelaide Hills and King Valley each mount a noble challenge, and one of the finest sparkling wines ever to emerge from the Adelaide Hills pipped Tasmania at the post for the top gong. Champagne, look out! The diversity of the balance of our list is exciting and promising in equal measure, with Victoria, New South Wales and Western Australia putting forward 10 contenders from seven regions. Even prosecco has fought its way to the top this year – not once, but thrice!

Sparkling White of the Year: Deviation Road Beltana Blanc de Blancs 2014

Rating	Wine	Region
97	Apogee Deluxe Brut 2016	Tasmania
97	Deviation Road Beltana Blanc de Blancs 2014	Adelaide Hills
97	House of Arras Grand Vintage 2009	Tasmania
96	Brown Brothers Patricia Brut Pinot Noir Chardonnay 2014	King Valley
96	Coates The Blanc de Blancs 2016	Adelaide Hills
96	Jansz Late Disgorged 2012	Tasmania
96	Jansz Single Vineyard Vintage Chardonnay 2013	Tasmania

95	Bellebonne Natalie Fryar Vintage Cuvée 2016	Tasmania
95	Centennial Vineyards Limited Blanc de Blancs NV	Southern Highlands
95	Colmar Estate Vintage Brut 2017	Orange
95	Dal Zotto Pucino Col Fondo Prosecco 2019	King Valley
95	Dal Zotto Tabelo Col Fondo Prosecco 2018	King Valley
95	Henschke Johanne Ida Selma Blanc de Noir MD NV	Adelaide Hills
95	Home Hill Ms Daisy Cuvée 2017	Tasmania
95	Josef Chromy ZDAR Sparkling 2008	Tasmania
95	Kerri Greens Terrestrial Flowers Blanc de Blancs 2017	Mornington Peninsula
95	Mitchell Harris Sabre 2017	Victoria
95	Mt Lofty Ranges Vineyard Late Disgorged 2013	Lenswood
95	Paul Conti Lorenza Sparkling Chenin Blanc NV	Western Australia
95	Petaluma Croser Pinot Noir Chardonnay 2015	Piccadilly Valley
95	Pipers Brook Vineyard Kreglinger Brut de Blancs 2016	Tasmania
95	Risky Business Prosecco NV	King Valley
95	Stefano Lubiana Prestige Pinot Noir Chardonnay 1999	Tasmania
95	Vinea Marson Prosecco 2019	Alpine Valleys

Sparkling Rosé

Elevated to its own listing for the first time, sparkling rosé is now firmly established as a very serious contender in the Australian wine landscape. Tasmania rightly leads the way, representing almost half of the list, with the Adelaide Hills hot in pursuit, and Victoria, New South Wales and Western Australia all claim a listing. Having established her credentials as Australia's Sparkling Rosé Queen during her long tenure at Jansz, Natalie Fryar is responsible for three of our finalists (consulting to Piper's Brook, while making her own brand of Bellebonne). In an almost unanimous clean-sweep vote by the tasting panel, Bellebonne is a fitting winner of our inaugural Sparkling Rosé of the Year.

Sparkling Rosé of the Year: **Bellebonne Natalie Fryar Vintage Rosé 2017**

Rating	Wine	Region
96	Bellebonne Natalie Fryar Vintage Rosé 2017	Tasmania
96	House of Arras Rosé 2008	Tasmania
95	Deviation Road Altair Brut Rosé NV	Adelaide Hills
95	Mitchell Harris Sabre Rosé 2017	Victoria
95	Pipers Brook Vineyard Kreglinger Brut Rosé 2016	Tasmania
95	Sittella Cuvee Rosé Brut NV	Swan Valley
94	Greenhill Pinot Noir Brut Rosé 2013	Adelaide Hills
94	Pipers Brook Vineyard Ninth Island Sparkling Rosé NV	Tasmania

Sparkling Red

Shiraz again accounts for the lion's share of Australia's best sparkling reds, with South Australia and Victoria fighting it out. In the final taste-off between Ashton Hills and Best's, it was a clean sweep to the Clare Valley's sole contender and the oldest inclusion in our shortlist – testimony to the value of age in this category (in this case, interestingly and unusually, not so much bottle age but four years in large-format oak).

Sparkling Red of the Year: Ashton Hills Sparkling Shiraz 2015

Rating	Wine	Region
95	Ashton Hills Vineyard Sparkling Shiraz 2015	Clare Valley
95	Charles Melton Sparkling Red NV	Barossa Valley
94	Turkey Flat Sparkling Shiraz NV	Barossa Valley
93	Bush Track Sparkling Shiraz 2017	Alpine Valleys
93	Kimbolton Bella Monte Sparkling Montepulciano 2019	Langhorne Creek
93	Kyneton Ridge Estate The John Boucher Sparkling Shiraz NV	Heathcote
93	Morris Sparkling Shiraz Durif NV	Rutherglen
93	Rutherglen Estate Sparkling Shiraz Durif NV	Rutherglen
92	Best's Sparkling Shiraz 2017	Great Western

Riesling

On sheer numbers, riesling again ranks behind only shiraz, chardonnay and cabernet as the strongest category in the country – proof again that we all ought to be drinking more of this sublime variety. The dominance of Great Southern and the Clare and Eden valleys in Australia's top riesling stakes is complete, together putting forward more than five in every six wines in our short list. Adelaide Hills, Great Western, Henty and Tasmania share the balance. With just two inclusions in our top 40 (both from Pooley), Tasmania was the surprise dark horse that swept in from the sidelines with a convincing win for Riesling of the Year!

Riesling of the Year: Pooley Margaret Pooley Tribute Single Vineyard Riesling 2020

Rating	Wine	Region
98	Duke's Vineyard Magpie Hill Reserve Riesling 2020	Porongurup
98	Forest Hill Vineyard Block 1 Riesling 2020	Mount Barker
98	Jim Barry Loosen Barry Wolta Wolta Dry Riesling 2017	Clare Valley
98	Pikes The Merle Riesling 2020	Clare Valley
97	Castle Rock Estate A&W Riesling 2020	Porongurup
97	Grosset G110 Riesling 2019	Clare Valley
97	Henschke Julius Riesling 2020	Eden Valley
97	Howard Park Howard Park Riesling 2020	Mount Barker
97	Jim Barry Loosen Barry Wolta Wolta Dry Riesling 2018	Clare Valley
97	Leo Buring Leonay Riesling 2020	Eden Valley
97	Peter Lehmann Wigan Riesling 2016	Eden Valley
97	Pooley Margaret Pooley Tribute Single Vineyard Riesling 2020	Tasmania
97	Rieslingfreak No. 2 Riesling 2020	Eden Valley
97	Silverstream Limited Release Riesling 2018	Denmark
96	ATR Hard Hill Road Writer's Block Riesling 2019	Great Western
96	Best's Riesling 2020	Great Western
96	Bleasdale Vineyards Riesling 2020	Adelaide Hills
96	Capel Vale Whispering Hill Riesling 2020	Mount Barker
96	Castle Rock Estate Riesling 2020	Porongurup
96	Coates The Riesling 2020	Adelaide Hills

96	Crawford River Riesling 2020	Henty
96	Duke's Vineyard Single Vineyard Riesling 2020	Porongurup
96	Gaelic Cemetery Vineyard Premium Riesling 2019	Clare Valley
96	Galafrey Dry Grown Reserve Riesling 2020	Mount Barker
96	Grosset Polish Hill Riesling 2020	Clare Valley
96	Henschke Peggy's Hill Riesling 2020	Eden Valley
96	Larry Cherubino Cherubino Riesling 2020	Great Southern
96	Lowboi Riesling 2020	Porongurup
96	Max & Me Mirooloo Road Riesling 2020	Eden Valley
96	Mount Horrocks Watervale Riesling 2020	Clare Valley
96	Naked Run Place in Time Sevenhill Riesling 2016	Clare Valley
96	Naked Run The First Riesling 2020	Clare Valley
96	Penfolds Bin 51 Riesling 2020	Eden Valley
96	Pikes Traditionale Riesling 2020	Clare Valley
96	Pooley Coal River Valley Riesling 2020	Tasmania
96	Rieslingfreak No. 6 Aged Release Riesling 2015	Clare Valley
96	Singlefile Single Vineyard Riesling 2020	Mount Barker
96	Vickery The Reserve Zander Kosi Block Riesling 2018	Eden Valley

Chardonnay

Chardonnay tussles with shiraz for the strongest category in Australian wine today. Western Australia does the heavy lifting, putting forth half of our highlights, the vast majority, of course, from Margaret River. The Yarra Valley, Adelaide Hills and Tasmania are next in line, though a long way behind the dominance of the west in sheer numbers. Reflecting the strength and diversity of the category, three winners emerged from the 11 nominations in our Awards judging, each receiving first-place votes and total scores too close to separate. Put to a second vote, the scores were again too close to single out a winner, so we have done the unprecedented and put forward three very different wines from three of the top producers in three very distinct regions. Seek them out. We love them all.

Joint Chardonnays of the Year:
**Oakridge 864 Drive Block Funder & Diamond Vineyard Chardonnay 2019,
Leeuwin Estate Art Series Chardonnay 2018,
Penfolds Yattarna Bin 144 Chardonnay 2018**

Rating	Wine	Region
99	Giaconda Estate Vineyard Chardonnay 2018	Beechworth
99	Penfolds Yattarna Bin 144 Chardonnay 2018	Various
98	Cullen Kevin John 2019	Margaret River
98	Cullen Kevin John Legacy Series Fruit Day Chardonnay 2020	Margaret River
98	Hoddles Creek Estate Road Block Chardonnay 2018	Yarra Valley
98	Leeuwin Estate Art Series Chardonnay 2018	Margaret River
98	Mewstone Hughes & Hughes Lees Aged Chardonnay 2019	Tasmania
98	Penfolds Reserve Bin A Chardonnay 2019	Adelaide Hills
98	Shaw + Smith M3 Chardonnay 2020	Adelaide Hills
98	Tolpuddle Vineyard Chardonnay 2019	Tasmania

98	Voyager Estate MJW Chardonnay 2018	Margaret River
97	Ashton Hills Vineyard Chardonnay 2020	Piccadilly Valley
97	Bindi Quartz Chardonnay 2019	Macedon Ranges
97	Dappled Les Verges Single Vineyard Chardonnay 2019	Yarra Valley
97	De Bortoli (Victoria) Lusatia Chardonnay 2018	Yarra Valley
97	Dexter Chardonnay 2019	Mornington Peninsula
97	Domaine Naturaliste Artus Chardonnay 2019	Margaret River
97	Fighting Gully Road Black Label Smith's Vineyard Chardonnay 2018	Beechworth
97	Flametree S.R.S. Wallcliffe Chardonnay 2019	Margaret River
97	Garagiste Terre Maritime Chardonnay 2019	Mornington Peninsula
97	Helen's Hill Estate Winemakers Reserve Chardonnay 2017	Yarra Valley
97	Larry Cherubino Cherubino Chardonnay 2019	Margaret River
97	Larry Cherubino Dijon Wychwood Vineyard Chardonnay 2019	Margaret River
97	Mount Mary Chardonnay 2019	Yarra Valley
97	Oakridge 864 Drive Block Funder & Diamond Vineyard Chardonnay 2019	Yarra Valley
97	Paul Nelson Karriview Vineyard Chardonnay 2018	Denmark
97	Pierro Chardonnay VR 2017	Margaret River
97	Singlefile The Vivienne DChardonnay 2018	Denmark
97	Stella Bella Luminosa Chardonnay 2019	Margaret River
97	Vasse Felix Heytesbury Chardonnay 2019	Margaret River
97	Windows Estate La Fenetre Chardonnay 2017	Margaret River
97	Xanadu Reserve Chardonnay 2019	Margaret River
97	Xanadu Stevens Road Chardonnay 2019	Margaret River

Semillon

The Hunter again corners the globally unique category of dry semillon, topping the charts with an aged release that received an almost unanimous vote for Semillon of the Year.

Semillon of the Year: Meerea Park Alexander Munro Individual Vineyard Aged Release Semillon 2011

Rating	Wine	Region
96	Audrey Wilkinson The Ridge Semillon 2011	Hunter Valley
96	Hungerford Hill Blackberry Vineyard Semillon 2013	Hunter Valley
96	Keith Tulloch Field of Mars Block 2A Semillon 2018	Hunter Valley
96	Leogate Estate Creek Bed Reserve Semillon 2013	Hunter Valley
96	Leogate Estate Creek Bed Reserve Semillon 2014	Hunter Valley
96	Meerea Park Alexander Munro Individual Vineyard Semillon 2011	Hunter Valley
96	Moss Wood Wilyabrup Semillon 2020	Margaret River
96	Peter Lehmann Margaret Semillon 2015	Barossa
96	RidgeView Generations Reserve Semillon 2007	Hunter Valley
96	RidgeView Generations Reserve Semillon 2013	Hunter Valley
95	Briar Ridge Vineyard Stockhausen Semillon 2013	Hunter Valley
95	Carillion Aged Release Tallavera Grove Semillon 2013	Hunter Valley
95	De Iuliis Aged Release Semillon 2014	Hunter Valley

95	Drayton's Family Susanne Semillon 2015	Hunter Valley
95	Eagles Rest Maluna Semillon 2019	Hunter Valley
95	Eagles Rest The Wild Place Semillon 2019	Hunter Valley
95	Fermoy Estate Reserve Semillon 2019	Margaret River
95	First Creek Single Vineyard Black Cluster Semillon 2014	Hunter Valley
95	Glenguin Estate Glenguin Vineyard Semillon 2017	Hunter Valley
95	McLeish Estate Semillon 2009	Hunter Valley
95	McLeish Estate Semillon 2011	Hunter Valley
95	Meerea Park Alexander Munro Individual Vineyard Semillon 2015	Hunter Valley
95	Mistletoe Reserve Semillon 2019	Hunter Valley
95	Pokolbin Estate Phil Swannell Semillon 2013	Hunter Valley
95	Silkman Reserve Semillon 2014	Hunter Valley
95	Thomas Synergy Vineyard Selection Semillon 2020	Hunter Valley
95	Tinklers Vineyard Reserve Semillon 2017	Hunter Valley
95	Two Rivers Museum Release Stone's Throw Semillon 2015	Hunter Valley
95	Tyrrell's Single Vineyard Belford Semillon 2016	Hunter Valley
95	Tyrrell's Vat 1 Hunter Semillon 2009	Hunter Valley
95	Tyrrell's Vat 1 Hunter Semillon 2016	Hunter Valley
95	Vinden Single Vineyard Reserve Semillon 2015	Hunter Valley

Sauvignon Blanc

Off the back of a line-up of strong vintages in the west, Margaret River dominates the Adelaide Hills in the sauvignon stakes this year, both in top scores and sheer numbers. Age comes into play here, with more than three in five of our top contenders hailing from the 2018 or 2019 vintages. Oak is another increasingly important element of Australia's top sauvignons, with five out of seven nominations for Sauvignon Blanc of the Year relying on barrels for fermentation and/or maturation. The final taste-off was hotly contested by the Margaret River big guns of Moss Wood and Cullen, but the great work of Xavier Bizot in Wrattonbully proved to secure the win (just!).

Sauvignon Blanc of the Year: Terre à Terre Crayeres Vineyard Sauvignon Blanc 2019

Rating	Wine	Region
97	Cullen Legacy Sauvignon Blanc 2019	Margaret River
97	Flowstone Queen of the Earth Sauvignon Blanc 2019	Margaret River
96	Cullen Amber 2019	Margaret River
96	Flowstone Sauvignon Blanc 2019	Margaret River
96	Jericho Kuitpo Lockett Vineyard Fumé Blanc 2019	Adelaide Hills
96	Moss Wood Ribbon Vale Elsa 2019	Margaret River
96	Shaw + Smith Sauvignon Blanc 2020	Adelaide Hills
96	Terre à Terre Crayeres Vineyard Sauvignon Blanc 2019	Wrattonbully
95	Bay of Fires Sauvignon Blanc 2020	Tasmania
95	Clairault Streicker Bridgeland Block Fumé Blanc 2019	Margaret River
95	Domaine Naturaliste Sauvage Sauvignon Blanc 2018	Margaret River
95	First Foot Forward Amphora Ferment Sauvignon Blanc 2020	Yarra Valley

95	Gembrook Hill Sauvignon Blanc 2019	Yarra Valley
95	Geoff Weaver Single Vineyard Sauvignon Blanc 2019	Adelaide Hills
95	Geoff Weaver Single Vineyard Sauvignon Blanc 2020	Adelaide Hills
95	Hesketh Wine Company Jimi's Ferment Sauvignon Blanc 2019	Limestone Coast
95	Mandala Fumé Blanc 2020	Yarra Valley
95	Murdoch Hill Sauvignon Blanc 2020	Adelaide Hills
95	Redgate Ullinger Reserve Sauvignon Blanc 2020	Margaret River
95	Ross Hill Pinnacle Series Griffin Road Vineyard Sauvignon Blanc 2019	Orange
95	Sidewood Estate Sauvignon Blanc 2020	Adelaide Hills
95	Vasse Felix Blanc X 2020	Margaret River
95	Windows Estate Petit Lot Fumé Blanc 2019	Margaret River

Other Whites and Blends

With insufficient numbers to warrant their own category this year, sauvignon blanc semillon blends join this category. Method and madness define the vast expanse of diversity in Australia's other whites and blends as much as a broad spectrum of varietal and regional distinctiveness. With seven different varieties and a dozen approaches on the table, this represented the most diverse and hotly debated category in our Awards judging. With a plethora of new names and techniques at play, it's fitting that a longstanding champion of the great varieties of Italy should take out the mantle of Other White of the Year.

Other White of the Year: **Coriole Rubato Reserve Fiano 2020**

Rating	Wine	Region
97	John Kosovich Bottle Aged Reserve Chenin Blanc 2015	Swan Valley
97	Stoney Rise Grüner Veltliner 2020	Tasmania
96	Coriole Rubato Reserve Fiano 2020	McLaren Vale
96	L.A.S. Vino CBDB Chenin Blanc Dynamic Blend 2019	Margaret River
96	Meerea Park Indie Individual Vineyard Marsanne Roussanne 2019	Hunter Valley
96	Pierro L.T.C. Semillon Sauvignon Blanc 2020	Margaret River
96	Rouleur Pinot Gris et al 2020	Yarra Valley
96	Tahbilk Museum Release Marsanne 2015	Nagambie Lakes
96	Turkey Flat White 2019	Barossa Valley
96	Windows Estate Petit Lot Chenin Blanc 2019	Margaret River

Rosé

Food-friendly, refreshing and increasingly sophisticated, Australian rosé is deserving of the attention of us all. And, it must be said, far more so than cheap imports. The diversity has never been more compelling. Our eight shortlisted finalists for Rosé of the Year hail from eight different regions and at least six varieties, testimony to the grand spectrum of styles that make this category so exciting. The winner is a masterfully executed and thrilling take on nebbiolo from an iconic site in the Adelaide Hills!

Rosé of the Year: **La Prova Nebbiolo Rosato 2020**

Rating	Wine	Region
96	Deep Woods Estate Rosé 2020	Margaret River
96	Dominique Portet Single Vineyard Rosé 2020	Yarra Valley
95	Cobaw Ridge Il Pinko Rosé 2019	Macedon Ranges
95	Devil's Corner Pinot Noir Rosé 2020	Tasmania
95	Emilian Single Vineyard Nebbiolo Rosé 2020	Strathbogie Ranges
95	Hahndorf Hill Rosé 2020	Adelaide Hills
95	Jericho Selected Vineyards Rosé 2020	Adelaide Hills
95	L.A.S. Vino Albino PNO 2019	Margaret River
95	La Prova Nebbiolo Rosato 2020	Adelaide Hills
95	Lake Breeze Rosato 2020	Langhorne Creek
95	Larry Cherubino Willows Vineyard Rosé 2020	Margaret River
95	mazi Limited Release Rosé 2020	McLaren Vale
95	Medhurst Estate Vineyard Rosé 2020	Yarra Valley
95	Nocturne Sangiovese Nebbiolo Rosé 2020	Margaret River
95	Oakridge Rosé 2020	Yarra Valley
95	Tahbilk Grenache Mourvèdre Rosé 2020	Nagambie Lakes
95	Willow Bridge Estate Rosa de Solana 2020	Geographe

Pinot Noir

It could be argued that discretion pays more dividends in the selection of pinot noir than any other category, which would make this list the most important in this book. Victoria leads the way, first in Macedon (thanks almost exclusively to Bindi, Curly Flat and Best New Winery of the Year, Place of Changing Winds), very closely followed by the who's who of the Yarra, Mornington and Tasmania. The work of Michael Dhillon in the vineyard and winery sets the standard, making Bindi an almost unanimous favourite of every member of the tasting team in the final judgement.

Pinot Noir of the Year: **Bindi Block 5 Pinot Noir 2019**

Rating	Wine	Region
98	Ashton Hills Vineyard Reserve Pinot Noir 2020	Adelaide Hills
98	Stargazer Palisander Vineyard Coal River Valley Pinot Noir 2019	Tasmania
97	Ashton Hills Vineyard Reserve Pinot Noir 2019	Adelaide Hills
97	Bindi Block 5 Pinot Noir 2019	Macedon Ranges
97	Bindi Dixon Pinot Noir 2019	Macedon Ranges
97	Bindi Original Vineyard Pinot Noir 2019	Macedon Ranges
97	Helen's Hill Estate Winemakers Reserve Pinot Noir 2017	Yarra Valley
97	Sidewood Estate Oberlin Pinot Noir 2019	Adelaide Hills
97	Yarra Yering Carrodus Pinot Noir 2019	Yarra Valley
96	Bannockburn Vineyards Serré 2018	Geelong
96	Bass Phillip Premium Pinot Noir 2019	Gippsland
96	Bindi Kaye Pinot Noir 2017	Macedon Ranges
96	Curly Flat Central Macedon Ranges Pinot Noir 2019	Macedon Ranges
96	Curly Flat Western Macedon Ranges Pinot Noir 2019	Macedon Ranges
96	Dappled Appellation Upper Pinot Noir 2019	Yarra Valley

96	Dappled Champs de Cerises Single Vineyard Pinot Noir 2019	Yarra Valley
96	Dexter Black Label Pinot Noir 2018	Mornington Peninsula
96	Garagiste Merricks Pinot Noir Cuve Beton 2019	Mornington Peninsula
96	Garagiste Terre de Feu Pinot Noir 2019	Mornington Peninsula
96	Handpicked Auburn Road Vineyard Tinot Noir 2019	Tasmania
96	Handpicked Capella Vineyard Pinot Noir 2019	Mornington Peninsula
96	Handpicked Collection T Pinot Noir 2019	Tasmania
96	Helen's Hill Estate First Light Single Clone Pinot Noir 2017	Yarra Valley
96	Hurley Vineyard Garamond Balnarring Pinot Noir 2019	Mornington Peninsula
96	Mewstone Hughes & Hughes 25% Whole Bunch Pinot Noir 2019	Tasmania
96	Moss Wood Wilyabrup Pinot Noir 2018	Margaret River
96	Mount Mary Pinot Noir 2019	Yarra Valley
96	Oakridge 864 Aqueduct Block Henk Vineyard Pinot Noir 2019	Yarra Valley
96	Paul Nelson Karriview Vineyard Pinot Noir 2018	Denmark
96	Place of Changing Winds Clos de la Connerie Pinot Noir 2019	Macedon Ranges
96	Place of Changing Winds High Density Pinot Noir 2019	Macedon Ranges
96	Seville Estate Pinot Noir 2020	Yarra Valley
96	Shadowfax Little Hampton Pinot Noir 2019	Macedon Ranges
96	Tamar Ridge	Pirie Tamar Ridge Reserve Pinot Noir 2019	Tasmania
96	Tapanappa Foggy Hill Vineyard Pinot Noir 2019	Fleurieu
96	Victory Point Pinot Noir 2019	Margaret River
96	Yarra Yering Pinot Noir 2019	Yarra Valley

Grenache and Grenache Blends

Grenache was the stuff of history a decade ago. My, how things have changed! Attentive detail in the vines and elegance in the wines have ushered in a brand new day. A short list of only five wines in our final judging for Grenache of the Year should not be construed to reflect any lack of strength in the category, but rather the dominance of two regions (McLaren Vale and Barossa) with one stunning outlier – the Swinney family has proven that Frankland River can play at this game, too. At the end of the day, it's McLaren Vale for the win, putting forward more top-scoring wines than every other region put together. Thistledown's 80-year-old Blewitt Springs bush vines proved to be convincing and worthy in the final showdown.

Grenache of the Year: Thistledown Sands of Time Old Vine Single Vineyard Blewitt Springs Grenache 2019

Rating	Wine	Region
98	Chalk Hill Alpha Crucis Old Vine Grenache 2019	McLaren Vale
98	Chapel Hill 1897 Vines Grenache 2018	McLaren Vale
98	Swinney Farvie Grenache 2019	Frankland River
97	Bekkers Grenache 2019	McLaren Vale
97	McHenry Hohnen Hazel's Vineyard GSM 2019	Margaret River
97	Thistledown Sands of Time Old Vine Grenache 2019	McLaren Vale
97	Turkey Flat Grenache 2019	Barossa Valley

97	Yalumba Carriage Block Dry Grown Grenache 2017	Barossa Valley
96	Aphelion Wine Rapture Grenache 2020	McLaren Vale
96	Dandelion Vineyards Faraway Tree Grenache 2019	McLaren Vale
96	Paralian Marmont Vineyard Grenache 2020	McLaren Vale
96	Purple Hands Old Vine Grenache 2019	Barossa Valley
96	Samson Tall Grenache 2019	McLaren Vale
96	SC Pannell Smart Clarendon Grenache 2019	McLaren Vale
96	Serafino GSM 2019	McLaren Vale
96	Serrat Grenache Noir 2020	Yarra Valley
96	Sittella A-G Rare Series Golden Mile Grenache 2020	Swan Valley
96	Swinney Grenache 2019	Frankland River
96	Teusner Avatar 2019	Barossa Valley
96	Thistledown This Charming Man Grenache 2019	McLaren Vale
96	Torbreck Vintners Les Amis Barossa Valley 2018	Barossa Valley
96	Varney GSM 2018	McLaren Vale
96	Yalumba Vine Vale Grenache 2019	Barossa Valley
96	Yangarra Estate Vineyard Hickinbotham Grenache 2019	McLaren Vale
96	Yangarra Estate Vineyard High Sands Grenache 2018	McLaren Vale
96	Yangarra Estate Vineyard Old Vine Grenache 2019	McLaren Vale

Shiraz

In an age in which everything new is cool (varieties, regions, producers, techniques), it remains that Australia's top-performing variety is good ol' shiraz and its only close contender is chardonnay. The diversity of Australian shiraz has never been more profound, and our best-of list spans five states and 13 regions. From the cool reaches of Porongurup and Canberra to the might of the Barossa and McLaren Vale, we never cease to be in awe of the remarkable dexterity of this chameleon variety across this vast continent. It was three of the more elegant styles that separated themselves from the pack of 15 hopefuls in our final Awards judging: Mount Pleasant, Tyrrell's and Yarra Yering, with Tyrrell's claiming a worthy first place for the Hunter Valley in the final vote.

Shiraz of the Year: Tyrrell's 4 Acres Shiraz 2019

Rating	Wine	Region
99	Henschke Hill of Grace 2016	Eden Valley
99	Mount Pleasant Maurice O'Shea Shiraz 2018	Hunter Valley
99	Penfolds Grange Bin 95 2016	Various
98	Angove Family Winemakers The Medhyk Shiraz 2017	McLaren Vale
98	Karrawatta Tutelina Shiraz 2018	Various
98	Koomilya Shiraz 2017	McLaren Vale
98	Poonawatta The 1880 Shiraz 2015	Eden Valley
98	Scotchmans Hill Bellarine Peninsula Shiraz 2018	Geelong
98	Swinney Farvie Syrah 2019	Frankland River
98	Torbreck Vintners The Laird 2016	Barossa Valley
98	Yarra Yering Carrodus Shiraz 2019	Yarra Valley
98	Yarra Yering Dry Red No. 2 2019	Yarra Valley
97	Chalk Hill Clarendon Syrah 2018	McLaren Vale

97	Clonakilla Murrumbateman Syrah 2019	Canberra District
97	Duke's Vineyard Magpie Hill Reserve Shiraz 2019	Porongurup
97	Dutschke Single Barrel St Jakobi Vineyard 75 Block #2 2008	Barossa Valley
97	Hewitson Monopole Mother Vine Shiraz 2018	Barossa Valley
97	Maverick Trial Hill Shiraz 2018	Eden Valley
97	Mount Pleasant 1880 Vines Old Hill Vineyard Shiraz 2018	Hunter Valley
97	O'Leary Walker Polish Hill River Armagh Shiraz 2018	Clare Valley
97	Orlando Centenary Hill Shiraz 2016	Barossa
97	Paul Nelson Loam Syrah 2019	Frankland River
97	Penfolds RWT Bin 798 Shiraz 2018	Barossa Valley
97	Peter Lehmann Stonewell Shiraz 2017	Barossa
97	Peter Lehmann VSV Valley View Road Shiraz 2018	Barossa Valley
97	Plantagenet Tony Smith Shiraz 2018	Mount Barker
97	Poonawatta The 1880 Shiraz 2018	Eden Valley
97	Saltram No. 1 B Shiraz 2017	Barossa
97	Serrat Shiraz Viognier 2020	Yarra Valley
97	Shingleback The Gate Shiraz 2018	McLaren Vale
97	St Hallett Planted 1919 Shiraz 2015	Eden Valley
97	Tyrrell's 4 Acres Shiraz 2019	Hunter Valley

Cabernet Shiraz Blends

Cabernet shiraz blends played a defining role in the history of Australian red winemaking and deserve to be judged outside the context of other cabernet blends, prompting us to introduce this category for the first time. South Australia's deep history with the blend makes it the dominant force. One of the long-standing champions of this historic blend, Yalumba The Caley reincarnates the great Coonawarra/Barossa blends of the past in a sublime and truly classic flagship – a near unanimous winner in our final taste-off.

Cabernet Shiraz of the Year: Yalumba The Caley Cabernet Shiraz 2016

Rating	Wine	Region
99	Yalumba The Caley Cabernet Shiraz 2016	Coonawarra/Barossa
98	John Duval Integro Cabernet Sauvignon Shiraz 2017	Barossa
97	Castelli Estate Il Liris Rouge Cabernet Shiraz 2018	Frankland River
97	Jacob's Creek 1819 The Birth of Johann Shiraz Cabernet 2018	Coonawarra/Barossa
97	The Maverick Shiraz Cabernet Shiraz 2018	Barossa

Cabernet Sauvignon

Only shiraz and chardonnay surpass the noble cabernet sauvignon as Australia's top-performing variety this year, and if all of its blends are accounted for, there's compelling argument that cabernet is king. By contrast to the dexterity of other varieties, cabernet's fastidious preferences confine its rule largely to Coonawarra, Great Southern and, most of all, Margaret River, with the Yarra Valley asserting its pedigree at the very top end. Western Australia claims pride of place, dominating the list with almost two-thirds of the highlights – thanks in no small part to the sublime

2018 season. In our hotly contested taste-off of east versus west, one wine soared ahead of the flock with an elegance and beauty that made it the favourite of almost every judge. It seems the Yarra is still far from relinquishing its mantle to the west!

Cabernet Sauvignon of the Year: **Yarra Yering Carrodus Cabernet Sauvignon 2019**

Rating	Wine	Region
99	Cullen Vanya Wilyabrup Cabernet Sauvignon 2018	Margaret River
98	Duke's Vineyard The First Cab 2019	Porongurup
98	Larry Cherubino Budworth Cabernet Sauvignon 2018	Frankland River
98	Moss Wood Wilyabrup Cabernet Sauvignon 2018	Margaret River
98	Penfolds Bin 707 Cabernet Sauvignon 2018	Various
98	Xanadu Reserve Cabernet Sauvignon 2018	Margaret River
98	Yarra Yering Carrodus Cabernet Sauvignon 2019	Yarra Valley
97	Amelia Park Reserve Cabernet Sauvignon 2018	Margaret River
97	Corymbia Cabernet Sauvignon 2019	Margaret River
97	De Bortoli Melba Vineyard Cabernet Sauvignon 2018	Yarra Valley
97	Deep Woods Estate Reserve Cabernet Sauvignon 2018	Margaret River
97	Deep Woods Estate G5 Cabernet Sauvignon 2019	Margaret River
97	Duke's Vineyard Magpie Hill Reserve Cabernet Sauvignon 2019	Porongurup
97	Hickinbotham Clarendon Vineyard Trueman Cabernet Sauvignon 2019	McLaren Vale
97	Lake Breeze Cabernet Sauvignon 2019	Langhorne Creek
97	Larry Cherubino Cherubino Cabernet Sauvignon 2018	Frankland River
97	Leeuwin Estate Art Series Cabernet Sauvignon 2017	Margaret River
97	Moss Wood Ribbon Vale Cabernet Sauvignon 2018	Margaret River
97	Nocturne Sheoak Vineyard Cabernet Sauvignon 2019	Margaret River
97	Penfolds Bin 169 Cabernet Sauvignon 2018	Coonawarra
97	Penley Estate Helios Cabernet Sauvignon 2019	Coonawarra
97	Plantagenet Lionel Samson Cabernet Sauvignon 2018	Mount Barker
97	Stella Bella Luminosa Cabernet Sauvignon 2018	Margaret River
97	Voyager Estate MJW Cabernet Sauvignon 2016	Margaret River
97	Wynns Black Label Cabernet Sauvignon 2019	Coonawarra
97	Wynns Harold Cabernet Sauvignon 2018	Coonawarra
97	Wynns John Riddoch Cabernet Sauvignon 2018	Coonawarra
97	Wynns Johnsons Cabernet Sauvignon 2019	Coonawarra
97	Xanadu Stevens Road Cabernet Sauvignon 2018	Margaret River
97	Yeringberg Cabernet Sauvignon 2019	Yarra Valley

Cabernet and Family

Cabernet and family embraces cabernet-dominant blends as well as other Bordeaux varieties and their blends. Margaret River again reigns supreme, putting forward as many highlights as every other region put together, with the Yarra Valley responsible for half of the balance. Malbec, merlot and cabernet franc all come out to play in force here, but ultimately prove to be no match for blends led by the distinguished cabernet sauvignon itself. It was a Yarra Valley taste-off for the winner, with Mount Mary and

Yarra Yering neck and neck. Yarra Yering does it again! And goes all the way to Red Wine of the Year and the Wine of the Year. Game over.

Cabernet and Family of the Year: **Yarra Yering Dry Red No. 1 2019**

Rating	Wine	Region
98	Cullen Diana Madeline 2018	Margaret River
98	Cullen Diana Madeline 2019	Margaret River
98	Mount Mary Quintet 2019	Yarra Valley
98	Peccavi Estate Merlot 2018	Margaret River
98	Yarra Yering Dry Red No. 1 2019	Yarra Valley
97	Cullen Legacy Series Fruit Day Malbec 2019	Margaret River
97	Deep Woods Estate Single Vineyard Cabernet Malbec 2019	Margaret River
97	Dominique Portet Single Vineyard Cabernet Sauvignon Malbec 2019	Yarra Valley
97	Lake's Folly Cabernets 2019	Hunter Valley
97	McHenry Hohnen Vintners Rolling Stone 2017	Margaret River
97	Vasse Felix Tom Cullity Cabernet Sauvignon Malbec 2017	Margaret River
97	Wills Domain Paladin Hill Matrix 2019	Margaret River
97	Yeringberg 2019	Yarra Valley
96	Domaine Naturaliste Le Naturaliste Cabernet Franc 2018	Margaret River
96	Flametree Jeremy John Cabernet Malbec 2018	Margaret River
96	Hickinbotham The Nest Cabernet Franc 2019	McLaren Vale
96	Hickinbotham The Revivalist Merlot 2019	McLaren Vale
96	Jim Barry The James Cabernet Malbec 2018	Clare Valley
96	Juniper Estate Aquitaine Rouge 2018	Margaret River
96	Moss Wood Ribbon Vale Merlot 2018	Margaret River
96	Patina Museum Release Cabernet Merlot 2006	Orange
96	Penley Estate Chertsey 2018	Coonawarra
96	Wendouree Cabernet Malbec 2019	Clare Valley
96	Woodlands Emily 2019	Margaret River
96	Yarra Yering Agincourt Cabernet Malbec 2019	Yarra Valley
96	Yeringberg 2018	Yarra Valley

Other Reds and Blends

Diversifying tastes and evolving climate are driving extensive experimentation with different varieties and blends, making this category an exciting and dynamic space – but also one riddled with lowlights to dodge. Stick with our highlights and you're in more than safe territory! Our eleven nominees for the top gong represent eleven different varieties and blends, with a worthy winner that prompted its nominator Ned Goodwin MW to ask the question, 'Why were we not planting this 100 years ago?'

Other Red of the Year: **SC Pannell Aglianico 2019**

Rating	Wine	Region
96	Best's Old Vine Pinot Meunier 2020	Great Western
96	Cobaw Ridge Lagrein 2018	Macedon Ranges
96	Denton Nebbiolo 2017	Yarra Valley
96	La Prova Colpevole Nebbiolo 2018	Adelaide Hills

96	Mazza Touriga Nacional 2018	Geographe
96	Mount Majura Vineyard Little Dam Tempranillo 2019	Canberra District
96	Protero Gumeracha Capo Nebbiolo 2018	Adelaide Hills
96	Protero Gumeracha Nebbiolo 2018	Adelaide Hills
96	Teusner Righteous Mataro 2018	Barossa Valley
96	Virago Nebbiolo 2017	Beechworth
96	Wendouree Shiraz Mataro 2019	Clare Valley

Fortified

Extraordinary age and distinctive varietal composition make Australia's top fortifieds unique in the world. Tawny, muscat and topaque/muscadelle are all fully deserving of top rankings in our short list of heroes again this year. They hold their status among the greatest wines of all, and for everything they represent, they are arguably the best value too. The showdown for Fortified of the Year was between the Barossa and Rutherglen. While Rutherglen muscat and topaque/muscadelle rightly dominate our best-of line-up, there is no contender anywhere on the planet for Seppeltsfield's mighty 100 Year Old!

Fortified of the Year: **Seppeltsfield 100 Year Old Para Vintage Tawny 1921**

Rating	Wine	Region
99	All Saints Estate Museum Muscadelle NV	Rutherglen
99	Seppeltsfield 100 Year Old Para Vintage Tawny 1921	Barossa Valley
98	All Saints Estate Museum Muscat NV	Rutherglen
98	Bleasdale Vineyards 18 Year Old Rare Tawny NV	Langhorne Creek
98	Chambers Rosewood Rare Muscat NV	Rutherglen
98	Morris Old Premium Rare Topaque NV	Rutherglen

Best wineries by regions

This is the full roll call of 5-star wineries of the year arranged by region. This encompasses a three-tier classification (fully explained on pages 14–16). The winery names printed in red denote the best of the best with a long track record of excellence in upholding a 5-star rating for the past ten years. Five red stars are awarded to wineries who have upheld 5-star ratings for the past four years. Five black stars denote a 5-star rating based on the rolling average of the three most recent years. With 413 wineries qualifying this year, this heroic list is your quick reference guide to the finest estates in the country.

ADELAIDE HILLS

Ashton Hills Vineyard ★★★★★
Bird in Hand ★★★★★
BK Wines ★★★★★
Catlin Wines ★★★★★
Charlotte Dalton Wines ★★★★★
Coates Wines ★★★★★
Deviation Road ★★★★★
Geoff Weaver ★★★★★
Hahndorf Hill Winery ★★★★★
Karrawatta ★★★★★
La Prova ★★★★★
Longview Vineyard ★★★★★
Mt Lofty Ranges Vineyard ★★★★★
Murdoch Hill ★★★★★
Ochota Barrels ★★★★★
Petaluma ★★★★★
Pike & Joyce ★★★★★
Protero ★★★★★
Riposte ★★★★★
Shaw + Smith ★★★★★
Sidewood Estate ★★★★★
Tapanappa ★★★★★
The Lane Vineyard ★★★★★
View Road Wines ★★★★★

ADELAIDE

Heirloom Vineyards ★★★★★

ALPINE VALLEYS

Billy Button Wines ★★★★★
Clay Pot Wines ★★★★★
Mayford Wines ★★★★★
Pipan Steel ★★★★★

BALLARAT

Eastern Peake ★★★★★
Tomboy Hill ★★★★★

BAROSSA VALLEY

Bethany Wines ★★★★★
Charles Melton ★★★★★
Corryton Burge ★★★★★
David Franz ★★★★★
Elderton ★★★★★
Glaetzer Wines ★★★★★
Grant Burge ★★★★★
Hart of the Barossa ★★★★★
Hayes Family Wines ★★★★★
Head Wines ★★★★★
Hentley Farm Wines ★★★★★
JJ Hahn ★★★★★
Laughing Jack ★★★★★
Penfolds ★★★★★
Peter Lehmann ★★★★★
Purple Hands Wines ★★★★★
Rockford ★★★★★
Rolf Binder ★★★★★
Ruggabellus ★★★★★
St Hallett ★★★★★
Schwarz Wine Company ★★★★★
Seppeltsfield ★★★★★
Sons of Eden ★★★★★
Soul Growers ★★★★★
Spinifex ★★★★★
St Hugo ★★★★★
Teusner ★★★★★
Torbreck Vintners ★★★★★
Turkey Flat ★★★★★
Two Hands Wines ★★★★★
Utopos ★★★★★

Vindana Wines ★★★★★
Wolf Blass ★★★★★
Z Wine ★★★★★

BEECHWORTH

Fighting Gully Road ★★★★★
Giaconda ★★★★★
Indigo Vineyard ★★★★★
Savaterre ★★★★★
Traviarti ★★★★★

BENDIGO

Balgownie Estate ★★★★★
Sutton Grange Winery ★★★★★

CANBERRA DISTRICT

Clonakilla ★★★★★
Collector Wines ★★★★★
Helm ★★★★★
Mount Majura Vineyard ★★★★★
Nick O'Leary Wines ★★★★★
Ravensworth ★★★★★

CENTRAL RANGES

Renzaglia Wines ★★★★★

CENTRAL VICTORIA

Tar & Roses ★★★★★

CLARE VALLEY

Gaelic Cemetery Vineyard ★★★★★
Greg Cooley Wines ★★★★★
Grosset ★★★★★
Jaeschke's Hill River Clare Estate
   ★★★★★
Jeanneret Wines ★★★★★
Jim Barry Wines ★★★★★
Kilikanoon Wines ★★★★★
Mount Horrocks ★★★★★
Naked Run Wines ★★★★★
O'Leary Walker Wines ★★★★★
Pikes ★★★★★
Rieslingfreak ★★★★★
Wendouree ★★★★★

COONAWARRA

Balnaves of Coonawarra ★★★★★
Hollick Estates ★★★★★
Leconfield ★★★★★
Lindeman's (Coonawarra) ★★★★★
Majella ★★★★★
Parker Coonawarra Estate ★★★★★

Penley Estate ★★★★★
Wynns Coonawarra Estate ★★★★★

DENMARK

Harewood Estate ★★★★★
Silverstream Wines ★★★★★

EDEN VALLEY

Flaxman Wines ★★★★★
Heathvale ★★★★★
Henschke ★★★★★
Poonawatta ★★★★★
Yalumba ★★★★★

FRANKLAND RIVER

Alkoomi ★★★★★
Ferngrove ★★★★★
Frankland Estate ★★★★★

GEELONG

Banks Road ★★★★★
Bannockburn Vineyards ★★★★★
Ceres Bridge Estate ★★★★★
Clyde Park Vineyard ★★★★★
Farr | Farr Rising ★★★★★
Lethbridge Wines ★★★★★
Mulline ★★★★★
Oakdene ★★★★★
Paradise IV ★★★★★
Provenance Wines ★★★★★
Robin Brockett Wines ★★★★★
Scotchmans Hill ★★★★★
Shadowfax ★★★★★
Spence ★★★★★

GEOGRAPHE

Capel Vale ★★★★★
Iron Cloud Wines ★★★★★
Willow Bridge Estate ★★★★★

GIPPSLAND

Bass Phillip ★★★★★
Dirty Three Wines ★★★★★
Lightfoot & Sons ★★★★★
Narkoojee ★★★★★
Philippa Farr ★★★★★

GLENROWAN

Baileys of Glenrowan ★★★★★

GRAMPIANS

ATR Wines ★★★★★

Fallen Giants ★★★★★
Montara ★★★★★
Mount Langi Ghiran Vineyards
  ★★★★★
Seppelt ★★★★★
The Story Wines ★★★★★

GRANITE BELT

Boireann ★★★★★
Ballandean Estate ★★★★★

GREAT SOUTHERN

Byron & Harold ★★★★★
Castelli Estate ★★★★★
Forest Hill Vineyard ★★★★★
Lowboi ★★★★★
Marchand & Burch ★★★★★
Paul Nelson Wines ★★★★★
Singlefile Wines ★★★★★
Staniford Wine Co ★★★★★

GREAT WESTERN

Best's Wines ★★★★★
Black & Ginger ★★★★★

GUNDAGAI

Nick Spencer Wines ★★★★★

HEATHCOTE

Jasper Hill ★★★★★
Kennedy ★★★★★
Munari Wines ★★★★★
Paul Osicka ★★★★★
Sanguine Estate ★★★★★
Syrahmi ★★★★★
Whistling Eagle Vineyard ★★★★★
Wren Estate ★★★★★

HENTY

Crawford River Wines ★★★★★
Henty Estate ★★★★★

HILLTOPS

Moppity Vineyards ★★★★★

HUNTER VALLEY

Andevine Wines ★★★★★
Audrey Wilkinson ★★★★★
Bimbadgen ★★★★★
Briar Ridge Vineyard ★★★★★
Brokenwood ★★★★★
Carillion Wines ★★★★★

De Iuliis ★★★★★
First Creek Wines ★★★★★
Glenguin Estate ★★★★★
Gundog Estate ★★★★★
Hart & Hunter ★★★★★
Keith Tulloch Wine ★★★★★
Lake's Folly ★★★★★
Leogate Estate Wines ★★★★★
McLeish Estate ★★★★★
Meerea Park ★★★★★
Millbrook Estate ★★★★★
Mistletoe Wines ★★★★★
Mount Pleasant ★★★★★
RidgeView Wines ★★★★★
Silkman Wines ★★★★★
Thomas Wines ★★★★★
Tinklers Vineyard ★★★★★
Tyrrell's Wines ★★★★★
Vinden Wines ★★★★★
Whispering Brook ★★★★★

KING VALLEY

Brown Brothers ★★★★★
Dal Zotto Wines ★★★★★
Pizzini ★★★★★

LANGHORNE CREEK

Bleasdale Vineyards ★★★★★
Bremerton Wines ★★★★★

MACEDON RANGES

Bindi Wines ★★★★★
Cobaw Ridge ★★★★★
Curly Flat ★★★★★
Granite Hills ★★★★★
Place of Changing Winds ★★★★★

MARGARET RIVER

Amato Vino ★★★★★
Amelia Park Wines ★★★★★
Ashbrook Estate ★★★★★
Brookland Valley ★★★★★
Brown Hill Estate ★★★★★
Cape Mentelle ★★★★★
Churchview Estate ★★★★★
Clairault Streicker Wines ★★★★★
Credaro Family Estate ★★★★★
Cullen Wines ★★★★★
Deep Woods Estate ★★★★★
Devil's Lair ★★★★★
Domaine Naturaliste ★★★★★

Evans & Tate ★★★★★
Evoi Wines ★★★★★
Fermoy Estate ★★★★★
Flametree ★★★★★
Flowstone Wines ★★★★★
Flying Fish Cove ★★★★★
Fraser Gallop Estate ★★★★★
Ground to Cloud ★★★★★
Hay Shed Hill Wines ★★★★★
Heydon Estate ★★★★★
Higher Plane ★★★★★
House of Cards ★★★★★
Howard Park ★★★★★
Jilyara ★★★★★
Juniper ★★★★★
LS Merchants ★★★★★
Marq Wines ★★★★★
McHenry Hohnen Vintners ★★★★★
Moss Wood ★★★★★
Mr Barval Fine Wines ★★★★★
Oates Ends ★★★★★
Pierro ★★★★★
Redgate ★★★★★
Robert Oatley Margaret River
    ★★★★★
Sandalford ★★★★★
South by South West ★★★★★
Stella Bella Wines ★★★★★
Thompson Estate ★★★★★
tripe.Iscariot ★★★★★
Vasse Felix ★★★★★
Victory Point Wines ★★★★★
Voyager Estate ★★★★★
Walsh & Sons ★★★★★
Watershed Premium Wines ★★★★★
Wills Domain ★★★★★
Windance Wines ★★★★★
Windows Estate ★★★★★
Wise Wine ★★★★★
Woodlands ★★★★★
Xanadu Wines ★★★★★

MCLAREN VALE

Angove Family Winemakers ★★★★★
Aphelion Wine ★★★★★
Bec Hardy Wines ★★★★★
Bekkers ★★★★★
Bondar Wines ★★★★★
Chalk Hill ★★★★★
Chapel Hill ★★★★★
Clarendon Hills ★★★★★

Coriole ★★★★★
Dabblebrook Wines ★★★★★
Dodgy Brothers ★★★★★
Dune Wine ★★★★★
Fox Creek Wines ★★★★★
Gemtree Wines ★★★★★
Hardys ★★★★★
Haselgrove Wines ★★★★★
Hickinbotham Clarendon Vineyard
    ★★★★★
Hugh Hamilton Wines ★★★★★
Jarressa Estate Wines ★★★★★
Kay Brothers ★★★★★
Longline Wines ★★★★★
Ministry of Clouds ★★★★★
Mr Riggs Wine Company ★★★★★
Oliver's Taranga Vineyards ★★★★★
Primo Estate ★★★★★
SC Pannell ★★★★★
Serafino Wines ★★★★★
Smidge Wines ★★★★★
Thomas St Vincent ★★★★★
Ulithorne ★★★★★
Varney Wines ★★★★★
Wirra Wirra ★★★★★
Yangarra Estate Vineyard ★★★★★

MORNINGTON PENINSULA

Crittenden Estate ★★★★★
Eldridge Estate of Red Hill ★★★★★
Foxeys Hangout ★★★★★
Garagiste ★★★★★
Hurley Vineyard ★★★★★
Kerri Greens ★★★★★
Main Ridge Estate ★★★★★
Montalto ★★★★★
Moorooduc Estate ★★★★★
Paringa Estate ★★★★★
Port Phillip Estate ★★★★★
Principia ★★★★★
Quealy Winemakers ★★★★★
Scorpo Wines ★★★★★
Stonier Wines ★★★★★
Ten Minutes by Tractor ★★★★★
Willow Creek Vineyard ★★★★★
Yabby Lake Vineyard ★★★★★

MOUNT BARKER

Galafrey ★★★★★
Plantagenet ★★★★★
Poacher's Ridge Vineyard ★★★★★

Towerhill Estate ★★★★★
West Cape Howe Wines ★★★★★

MOUNT LOFTY RANGES

Michael Hall Wines ★★★★★

MUDGEE

Craigmoor | Montrose ★★★★★
Robert Stein Vineyard ★★★★★

NAGAMBIE LAKES

Mitchelton ★★★★★
Tahbilk ★★★★★

NORTH EAST VICTORIA

Eldorado Road ★★★★★

ORANGE

Canobolas-Smith ★★★★★
HOOSEGG ★★★★★
Patina ★★★★★
Printhie Wines ★★★★★
Ross Hill Wines ★★★★★
Swinging Bridge ★★★★★

PERTH HILLS

Millbrook Winery ★★★★★

PORONGURUP

Castle Rock Estate ★★★★★
Duke's Vineyard ★★★★★
Zarephath Wines ★★★★★

PYRENEES

Blue Pyrenees Estate ★★★★★
Dalwhinnie ★★★★★
Mitchell Harris Wines ★★★★★
Summerfield ★★★★★
Taltarni ★★★★★

RIVERINA

Michel Marie ★★★★★
R. Paulazzo ★★★★★

RUTHERGLEN

All Saints Estate ★★★★★
Campbells ★★★★★
Chambers Rosewood ★★★★★
Morris ★★★★★
Pfeiffer Wines ★★★★★
Stanton & Killeen Wines ★★★★★
Valhalla Wines ★★★★★

SOUTH AUSTRALIA

Dandelion Vineyards ★★★★★
Thistledown Wines ★★★★★

SOUTHERN HIGHLANDS

Centennial Vineyards ★★★★★

SUNBURY

Craiglee ★★★★★

SWAN VALLEY

Houghton ★★★★★
John Kosovich Wines ★★★★★
RiverBank Estate ★★★★★
Sittella Wines ★★★★★
Vino Volta ★★★★★

TASMANIA

Bay of Fires ★★★★★
Bellebonne ★★★★★
Bream Creek ★★★★★
Freycinet ★★★★★
Goaty Hill ★★★★★
House of Arras ★★★★★
Jansz Tasmania ★★★★★
Mewstone Wines ★★★★★
Pipers Brook Vineyard ★★★★★
Pooley Wines ★★★★★
Riversdale Estate ★★★★★
Sailor Seeks Horse ★★★★★
Shy Susan Wines ★★★★★
Stargazer Wine ★★★★★
Stefano Lubiana ★★★★★
Tasmanian Vintners ★★★★★
Tolpuddle Vineyard ★★★★★

VARIOUS

EPIC Negociants ★★★★★
Handpicked Wines ★★★★★
Sentio Wines ★★★★★
Stonefish ★★★★★
Woods Crampton ★★★★★
Wine Unplugged ★★★★★

WESTERN AUSTRALIA

Larry Cherubino Wines ★★★★★

WRATTONBULLY

Terre à Terre ★★★★★

YARRA VALLEY

Ben Haines Wine ★★★★★
Bicknell fc ★★★★★
Bird on a Wire Wines ★★★★★
Buttermans Track ★★★★★
Chandon Australia ★★★★★
Coldstream Hills ★★★★★
Dappled Wines ★★★★★
De Bortoli (Victoria) ★★★★★
Denton ★★★★★
Dominique Portet ★★★★★
Fetherston Vintners ★★★★★
Gembrook Hill ★★★★★
Giant Steps ★★★★★
Goodman Wines ★★★★★
Helen's Hill Estate ★★★★★
Hoddles Creek Estate ★★★★★
Journey Wines ★★★★★
Kellybrook ★★★★★
Mandala ★★★★★
Mayer ★★★★★
Medhurst ★★★★★
Mount Mary ★★★★★
Oakridge Wines ★★★★★
Out of Step ★★★★★
Pimpernel Vineyards ★★★★★
Punch ★★★★★
Punt Road ★★★★★
Rochford Wines ★★★★★
Serrat ★★★★★
Seville Estate ★★★★★
TarraWarra Estate ★★★★★
The Wanderer ★★★★★
Thick as Thieves Wines ★★★★★
Thousand Candles ★★★★★
Tokar Estate ★★★★★
Toolangi ★★★★★
Wantirna Estate ★★★★★
Yarra Yering ★★★★★
Yering Station ★★★★★
Yeringberg ★★★★★
Mac Forbes ★★★★★

Australian vintage charts

Each number represents a mark out of 10 for the quality of vintages in each region. As always, these ratings are volunteered by key winemakers in each region. Of course, every variety and vineyard is unique, so these numbers should thus be regarded as indicative rather than prescriptive, and bear relative reference only to that region (and not to cross-regional comparisons).

 Red wine   White wine   Fortified

	2016	2017	2018	2019	2020
NSW					
Hunter Valley					
	6	8	9	8	–
	7	9	8	9	–
Mudgee					
	8	7	9	7	–
	9	6	8	7	–
Orange					
	8	7	9	8	–
	7	8	8	9	–
Canberra District					
	9	9	9	9	–
	9	8	8	9	–
Hilltops					
	9	9	9	9	–
	8	7	8	8	–
Southern Highlands					
	8	6	8	7	–
	8	6	8	8	–
Tumbarumba					
	8	9	9	8	–
	9	8	9	8	–
Riverina/Griffith					
	7	8	8	8	7
	7	8	8	8	7
Shoalhaven					
	8	7	8	7	–
	8	8	8	8	–

	2016	2017	2018	2019	2020
SA					
Barossa Valley					
	8	7	9	9	8
	7	8	7	7	7
Eden Valley					
	8	7	9	9	7
	9	10	9	9	8
Clare Valley					
	8	8	7	8	6
	9	9	7	9	8
Adelaide Hills					
	8	8	8	9	8
	7	9	7	8	9
McLaren Vale					
	8	9	8	8	8
	7	8	7	7	9
Southern Fleurieu					
	8	9	10	8	9
	8	8	8	7	9
Langhorne Creek					
	9	8	9	9	8
	7	7	7	7	7
Kangaroo Island					
	9	8	9	8	–
	9	9	9	9	–
Adelaide Plains					
	9	8	–	–	9
	8	8	–	–	9

	2016	2017	2018	2019	2020
Coonawarra					
	9	7	9	10	8
	8	9	8	8	8
Wrattonbully					
	10	9	9	10	10
	10	9	9	10	10
Padthaway					
	–	8	–	10	10
	–	8	–	9	9
Mount Benson & Robe					
	8	7	9	8	8
	9	9	9	9	9
Riverland					
	8	7	8	8	7
	7	8	8	8	8
VIC					
Yarra Valley					
	7	8	7	9	8
	7	8	7	8	8
Mornington Peninsula					
	8	8	9	8	7
	7	9	8	9	8
Geelong					
	7	8	8	10	5
	8	7	7	8	7
Macedon Ranges					
	8	7	9	8	8
	9	8	7	7	10

	2016	2017	2018	2019	2020
Sunbury					
	7	–	–	7	7
	7	–	–	8	8
Gippsland					
	8	9	9	9	9
	8	9	9	9	10
Bendigo					
	8	8	8	9	9
	8	7	8	8	8
Heathcote					
	9	7	8	9	9
	8	7	7	6	7
Grampians					
	6	9	8	9	8
	7	8	8	9	7
Pyrenees					
	7	8	10	8	8
	8	8	8	8	7
Henty					
	10	5	10	9	6
	10	8	10	8	8
Beechworth					
	8	7	8	8	–
	8	7	8	9	–
Nagambie Lakes					
	8	8	9	9	8
	9	7	7	7	7
Upper Goulburn					
	8	7	9	8	8
	9	9	8	9	8
Strathbogie Ranges					
	7	7	9	8	8
	7	7	9	8	7
King Valley					
	7	8	9	9	–
	8	10	9	7	–
Alpine Valleys					
	6	9	9	7	–
	6	10	10	9	–

	2016	2017	2018	2019	2020
Glenrowan					
	8	7	8	9	–
	9	7	7	7	–
Rutherglen					
	7	6	9	8	–
	9	6	9	8	–
Murray Darling					
	7	7	7	8	8
	8	8	8	8	8

WA

	2016	2017	2018	2019	2020
Margaret River					
	9	8	9	8	9
	9	8	9	9	9
Great Southern					
	8	7	10	8	8
	9	9	9	8	8
Manjimup					
	6	7	8	7	8
	7	8	9	8	8
Pemberton					
	8	7	9	10	9
	9	9	9	9	8
Geographe					
	8	8	8	8	9
	8	8	8	8	8
Perth Hills					
	9	9	8	8	9
	8	9	9	7	7
Swan Valley					
	6	6	9	8	9
	7	7	8	10	8

QLD

	2016	2017	2018	2019	2020
Granite Belt					
	8	6	10	8	–
	7	9	9	8	–
South Burnett					
	–	8	9	9	7
	–	8	9	8	9

	2016	2017	2018	2019	2020

TAS

	2016	2017	2018	2019	2020
Northern Tasmania					
	8	8	8	9	7
	8	7	8	9	6
Southern Tasmania					
	8	9	8	9	8
	8	9	9	8	9

Australian vintage 2021: a snapshot

As if reincarnating Dorothea Mackellar's land 'of droughts and flooding rains', if the theme of vintages 2019 and 2020 across the nation came down to the management of drought, that of 2021 was the precise opposite: mitigating the effects of rain. The heavens opened with the onset of La Niña through spring and, sporadically and nail-bitingly, continued pouring all the way through to the conclusion of the harvest. Flooding ensued down the east coast in late March, while vineyards in the west hoped desperately to dodge the spin-offs of cyclones. From one region to the next, the difference between a dismal and a stunning season simply came down to the timing of rain events and harvest. This was a grower's vintage in which there was more at stake than ever in careful management of the vines and stringent selection in picking. This proved a challenge in some regions suffering labour shortages in the wake of pandemic-induced border closures. Between the drenching of Queensland, New South Wales, eastern Victoria and Western Australia, other states enjoyed a stunning harvest. Most of Victoria and all of South Australia and Tasmania flourished under mild conditions, timely rainfall, good yields and elongated ripening in a vintage that harks back to those wonderfully cool, classic seasons of the late 1980s and 1990s. As always, publishing timelines dictated that this vintage snapshot had to be written just days after the last fruit of the harvest had been picked (and in a season as late as this, for some the last fruit is still being picked!). No 2021 wines have yet been completed, so these accumulated opinions of the vintage are the initial impressions of key winemakers in each region.

New South Wales

The **Hunter Valley** was blessed with an optimistic start to the season, when the debilitating four-year drought broke in February 2020. It proved to be a vintage unimpeded by heat spikes, and while February rainfall was less than 80% of average, a 60mm downpour in January imposed disease stress. Attentiveness in the vineyards paid stronger dividends than usual, even by Hunter standards. Heavy crops in some places made optimal ripeness a challenge in red varieties, and most semillon showed green characters. Chardonnay emerged the unlikely hero of the season. **Mudgee** experienced a wet growing season and inherent disease pressure, but moderate temperatures and a slightly later start to picking yielded medium-bodied wines of vibrant acidity. The hangover effects of years of drought impacted bud numbers, making for a small harvest. This was particularly pronounced in **Orange**, and especially for red grapes, where one key grower reported just 25% of normal yields. A cool season dictated that grapes lingered into the deluge of mid-March, especially at higher elevations on Mt Canobolas. Fruit harvested before the rains was reported to be exceptional. Rain was frequent and plentiful in the **Canberra District**, making attentiveness to spray regimes paramount. A cool season saw picking dates close to those of 20 years ago, and a strong white harvest was largely safely put to bed before the rains hit in late March, inflicting splitting and botrytis on almost-ripe reds, with shiraz hardest hit. Those who made stringent selection are quietly confident of the outcome, particularly for the later ripening cabernet sauvignon. **Hilltops** was inflicted with the same challenges, with one top grower reporting 50% loss of shiraz to botrytis. Cabernet was again the saving grace, blessed by a long, slow maturation in warm, sunny days and cool nights, potentially the best since 2014. The cooler growing season nurtured elegant wines of high acidity in the **Southern Highlands**, where leaf plucking, shoot thinning and stringent selection in hand picking proved essential to dodge Downey mildew and botrytis. Aromatic whites, chardonnay and pinot noir were regarded as the strongest performers. After a string of hot vintages, a cool season proved a welcome relief in **Tumbarumba**. Near-perfect ripening conditions were punctuated by significant rain events in January and February, necessitating diligent canopy management and disease control to save the crop. After complete losses to 2020 bushfires, one top grower reported potentially the best pinot noir to date, exclaiming, 'It's official – Tumbarumba is back!' After experiencing budburst a week ahead of normal, those who succeeded in mitigating disease in the **Shoalhaven Coast** reported excellent fruit. Timing of ripeness in the **Riverina** dictated that disease pressure was more intense for whites than reds, calling for judicious harvesting. Pinot grigio and chardonnay were listed as the highlights, with shiraz and other reds showing good colour and flavour. The **Murray Darling** escaped the worst of the rain, reporting an 'absolute cracker' season of mild, dry days and cool nights producing very good quality and slightly higher yields than 2020.

South Australia

The **Barossa Valley** experienced mild conditions of generally below-average temperatures for the entire growing season, making for an elegant and classic vintage boasting the best acidities in many years. Good rainfall made for close-to-average crops, a welcome relief after two tiny drought harvests. Extended and unhurried picking proved to be a blessing, without the labour shortages feared in the wake of border closures. Quality was said to be exceptional across every variety, with reds showing great density of colour and flavour and whites pristine aromatics, finesse and high natural acidity. One top maker declared it the best odd-year vintage since 1991. **Eden Valley** likewise experienced an outstanding season, in spite of significant frost damage in October and November knocking the yields of later-budding varieties. The **Clare Valley**, too, produced wines with excellent quality and high acidities across every variety, the only caveat low yields in riesling, down 30–40% as vines continue to recover in the aftermath of drought. **McLaren Vale** enjoyed healthy yields, bolstered by early February rainfall, and the equal earliest start of vintage on record, triggered by some February heat. A mild autumn kept sugar levels at bay and furnished excellent quality in whites and reds, with strong varietal definition, concentrated aromatics and deep colours and tannins in red varieties. The **Adelaide Hills** heaved a sigh of relief to harvest a large crop of outstanding quality, a welcome reprieve after the challenges of the previous vintages. Fears of ripening a big crop in a cool season were alleviated by an Indian summer, making for remarkable flavour development, producing elegant, aromatic wines of high levels of natural acidity. As an earlier ripening region, the **Adelaide Plains** loves cooler seasons, and 2021 was touted by one grower as his best in 16 years across all varieties. **Coonawarra** and

Wrattonbully experienced warm conditions during flowering, locking in big yields, and thereafter much colder conditions than usual. A long, cool, dry ripening season made way for a late harvest, lingering right until the end of April, reminiscent of the late 1980s and 1990s. Exceptional, long-enduring reds promise cool-season characters of red fruits and black pepper, backed with fine tannins and intense colours. Similar conditions in **Padthaway** made for standout sauvignon blanc, chardonnay, shiraz and cabernet sauvignon. Apart from one day of extremes in the high forties, it was the same story in **Mount Benson** and **Robe**, with amazing flavours in sauvignon blanc and pinot gris and great colour, density and structure in shiraz, in spite of high yields. **Langhorne Creek** enjoyed a 'cracker' vintage that is already being compared with the best (2016 and 2012), with firm tannins reminiscent of 2015. Yields were decimated in the **Southern Fleurieu**, first by a late September hail storm, then cold and windy flowering, and finally very dry conditions from December through to harvest, with one estate reporting 60% losses. Cool conditions made for a late harvest of exceptional wines of delicacy and high natural acidities. **Kangaroo Island** deserved a kind season after the devastation of 2020, and 2021 certainly delivered, described by one prominent grower as 'nearly perfect'. Yields were up and quality was above average, on par with 2018 and 2013. Dry conditions in the **Riverland** necessitated careful irrigation, while a mild season made for a late harvest of fresh, vibrant whites and bountiful volumes of promising reds.

Victoria

With healthy yields in the **Yarra Valley,** ideally timed rainfall and ripening season temperatures tracking long-term averages, 2021 was an idyllic season for cool-climate varieties. Chardonnay was a highlight, gris the best in several years, and pinot noir perfumed, ethereal and outstanding. Higher yields and cooler conditions favoured growers who moderated yields in shiraz and cabernet, producing generous wines of immediate appeal. The **Mornington Peninsula** delivered a textbook year described as 'quite possibly the perfect growing and ripening season': wet winter and spring, the mildest of mild summers and a classic autumn Indian summer that never seemed to end. Bountiful yields of chardonnay, pinot gris of vibrant natural acidity, and pinot noir and shiraz of extraordinary colour and flavour confirm a very special vintage. In **Geelong**, this cool, long growing season favoured warmer sites. Wetter conditions made vigilance in fighting Downey mildew prudent, while conditions across the region during flowering produced significant variation in yields of pinot noir. In **Gippsland**, cool conditions and well-timed rainfall made for a vintage plentiful in both quality and quantity. Chardonnay and viognier were standouts, thanks to unusually high acid levels. Similar conditions in the **King Valley** made for the best vintage in several years, albeit with some yields moderated by lower-than-average bunch numbers. At the time of writing, harvest was still underway in the **Alpine Valleys**, with one top grower leaving his post at the fermenters to sum it up for me as 'very protracted but frickin' awesome for those folk with low crop levels!' Likewise in **Beechworth**, a late harvest yielded good to exceptional quality. Picking was more condensed in **Upper Goulburn**, with most varieties ripening together, and showing strong promise. **Henty** experienced moderated yields in some varieties after a cool flowering period, though chardonnay and pinot noir were more generous, making for later ripening. Quality was reported as excellent across the region, particularly across earlier ripening varieties. The **Macedon Ranges** enjoyed a 'quite incredible' season, cool and wet, made – rather than saved – by a sunny and warm autumn of golden days and cool nights. Average yields of ripe but very bright pinots, and chardonnays of excellent concentration and cool acidity, prompted great enthusiasm from the region's top growers. **Sunbury** suffered in volume due to weak shoot growth following 2020 frost. Quality was strong, thanks to even ripening producing whites of clean fruit and good acid balance, and spicy reds of strong colour. **Nagambie Lakes** reported excellent sparkling and whites, with reds still coming in at the time of writing. **Strathbogie Ranges** experienced a season not overly wet, but with well-timed rain events ensuring 'happy vines'. Slightly heavier crops in this cool season saw red harvests carrying all the way into May, while sparkling, whites and pinot noir showed considerable energy and drive. In **Bendigo**, a mild growing season and extended harvest produced bright fruit flavours at lower baumes, very good natural acid levels and reds of intense and vibrant colours – an excellent year for both whites and reds. The year 2021 in **Heathcote** delivered what one high-profile winemaker described as quite possibly the perfect growing and ripening season: 'The wines will be of the highest quality and winemakers will sleep well through a long winter of content!' In the **Grampians**, a very cool to mild summer was summed up as 'almost like we went straight from spring to autumn, skipping summer … a winemaker's dream!' Slow ripening led to challenges with managing acid levels, but careful management produced quality of above-average levels. The **Pyrenees** reiterated Victoria's idyllic theme of timely rainfall, good yields, long ripening and protracted picking, producing whites of great natural acidity and reds of impressive concentration. In **Rutherglen** and **Glenrowan**, moderate temperatures and regular rain events up to bunch closure made for high-quality whites of pretty aromatics and bright natural acidity, elegant and well-structured reds and fortifieds infused with the concentration of elongated ripening.

Western Australia

Margaret River experienced an unusually challenging and wet season (41% above the 10-year rainfall average), most notably the wettest February in 20 years inflicting botrytis pressure. Canopy management, timing of harvest and careful fruit selection through stringent hand picking proved vital, a tricky balancing act in a season of labour shortages, with winery teams brought in to assist in the vineyards. Those who remained vigilant brought in a promising harvest, with bright chardonnay of higher-than-average acidity the standout of the whites. Cooler and drier conditions in March and April infused perfume, lift, vibrancy and fine tannins in cabernet sauvignon, the star of the reds. In **Great Southern**, virtually no indigenous tree flowered, placing huge bird pressure on fruit and necessitating early netting, which then all had to be removed for spraying when a rain event in early February brought the threat of splitting and disease. A cooler season produced a later start to harvest in the north (Frankland River) but right on average in the south (Albany and Denmark). Dry and slightly warmer conditions through March sealed a rapid harvest of good to exceptional quality and solid yields, provided canopy management was effective. In **Manjimup**, whites ripened two weeks earlier than usual, with good flavour and acid retention. A cool change slowed the reds, building depth of flavour while retaining acidity and elegance. **Pemberton** was hit by 70mm of rainfall in mid-February, followed by successive rain events and cool conditions. Vigilant vineyard management and selective hand picking proved essential. With a shortage of backpackers, Picardy rallied a posse of grey nomads from Dunsborough to help out. In the end, the most difficult season in a generation yielded good wines of low alcohols, albeit not of the standard of the previous three (exceptional) harvests. Similarly wet, cool and challenging conditions prevailed in **Geographe**, where low yields became a blessing in disguise in rallying fruit to ripeness. Chardonnay quality was dependent on the timing of harvest before or after the rain. It was a vintage of halves in the **Swan Valley**, with fruit picked after a hot December and cool January, or after heavy rains in February and March. Later ripening vineyards west of the river were particularly impacted by rot. A major bushfire nearby in early February added to the region's woes, with smoke taint sampling still inconclusive at the time of writing. Early picked whites were the standout, with delicate aromatics. **Perth Hills** fared much better, with earlier ripening whites escaping the rain events of autumn, thanks to a warm summer. Reds ripened evenly, with cool nights upholding acidity.

Tasmania

East Coast Tasmania experienced lower-than-average yields, and was hit by 100mm of rain mid-harvest, yet still put forward some of the finest chardonnay grown in years. **Southern Tasmania** enjoyed a classic growing season of moderate temperatures and intermittent rainfall. Harvest dates were in line with long-term averages (late by recent standards), yielding high-quality sparkling base, pinot noir and chardonnay of great natural acidity and concentration. **Northern Tasmania** saw cooler-than-average temperatures and plenty of rain right up until just a few weeks before harvest. Calm, sunny weather ensued, topping off a harvest of pristine flavours and high natural acidity in spectacular chardonnay, and amazing concentration and structure in pinot noir. One of the great seasons in Tasmania in the making.

Queensland

A cracking start to harvest with cool conditions and moderate rainfall in the **Granite Belt** produced beautiful whites and early ripening reds of intensity. Rain toward the end of the season had growers racing to pick later-ripening reds a little early. The rains came in early January in **South Burnett**, making verdelho and other early whites the stars of the season. Clear weather and vigilance in the vineyards saw reds through to ripeness, with tempranillo the standout.

Cover illustration

In commissioning the artwork for this year's cover, our brief was simple: we asked for a response to the broad theme, 'the joy of wine'. The shape of the bottle is a nod to last year's Wine of the Year – Brokenwood's Graveyard Vineyard Shiraz. Its tasting notes of blackberry and aniseed aromas, savoury oak characters and floral and herb garden notes inspired the illustration. The same theme will form our brief for the *Companion* going forward.

About the illustrator

Yoshiko Hada is a freelance illustrator based in Tokyo. She studied graphic design in Musashino Art University and has created art for posters, magazines, TV and music albums. Yoshiko's illustrations have been shown in exhibitions around the globe and have garnered accolades, most recently at the 2021 Bologna Children's Book Fair. Fascinated by the creativity that manifests on the canvas, she loves playing with colour using oil pastels and creating black–and–white art in acrylics.

For more information about her and her work, visit www.yoshikohada.com.

Australian wineries and wines

A. Rodda Wines

PO Box 589, Beechworth, Vic 3747 **Region** Beechworth
T 0400 350 135 **www.**aroddawines.com.au
Winemaker Adrian Rodda **Est.** 2010 **Dozens** 800 **Vyds** 2ha
Adrian Rodda has been winemaking since 1998. Originally working with David Bicknell at
Oakridge, he was involved in the development of the superb Oakridge 864 Chardonnay, his
final contribution to 864 coming in 2009. At the start of '10 he and wife Christie, a doctor,
moved to Beechworth and co-lease Smiths Vineyard with Mark Walpole of Fighting Gully
Road. Smiths Vineyard, planted to chardonnay in 1978, is a veritable jewel.

Triangle Block Smiths Vineyard Beechworth Chardonnay 2018 A stylish,
well-polished 3yo laying the groundwork for some time to come. Delicate aromas
of spring blossom, white peach, grapefruit and lemon drop. Not quite as upfront
as some Beechworth chardonnays, but rather quietly building complexity and
texture against a solid patchwork of spiced, nutty, vanillan oak, fine-edged acidity
and sustained fruit flavour. Watch it grow. Screw cap. 13% alc. **Rating** 94 **To** 2030
$85 JP
Tête de Cuvée Beechworth Cabernets 2018 Tête de Cuvée refers to a
wine of the highest quality. Celebrating a top vintage with a new reserve wine, it is
unusual (and quietly exciting) to see a quality cabernet blend out of Beechworth.
Offers a tight-knit wine, a mere youngster still, firm in dry, grainy tannins, smart
oak and serious, dark fruit flavours. It's varietally on point, well balanced and
assured of a big future. Screw cap. 14% alc. **Rating** 94 **To** 2034 $75 JP

Abbey Creek Vineyard

2388 Porongurup Road, Porongurup, WA 6324 **Region** Porongurup
T (08) 9853 1044 **www.**abbeycreek.com.au **Open** By appt
Winemaker Castle Rock Estate (Robert Diletti) **Est.** 1990 **Dozens** 1000 **Vyds** 1.6ha
This is the family business of Mike and Mary Dilworth. The name comes from a winter creek
that runs alongside the vineyard and a view of The Abbey in the Stirling Range. The vineyard
is split between pinot noir, riesling and sauvignon blanc. The rieslings have had significant
show success for a number of years.

Porongurup Sauvignon Blanc 2019 This delicate and fresh little sauvignon
blanc is one of only 3 varieties planted here and the 2019 vintage was sadly the
last for owners Mary and Mike. This is their curtain call. Screw cap. 12% alc.
Rating 92 **To** 2025 $22.50 EL ◆

Abbey Vale

1071 Wildwood Road, Yallingup Hills, WA 6282 **Region** Margaret River
T (08) 9755 2121 **www.**abbeyvalewines.com.au **Open** Wed–Sun 10–5
Winemaker Ben Roodhouse, Julian Langworthy **Est.** 2016 **Dozens** 2000 **Vyds** 17ha
Situated in the north of the Margaret River region, the Abbey Vale vineyards were established
in 1985 by the McKay family. The highest quality fruit comes from the original plantings of
chardonnay, shiraz and cabernet sauvignon. The picturesque cellar door offers a range of local
produce and artisan cheeses to accompany the wines, and overlooks a large dam that provides
visitors with one of the most sublime views in the region.

Premium RSV Margaret River Chenin Blanc 2020 Flinty, funky and
delicious, this has concentrated flavour for days, and (like all the Abbey Vale wines)
it offers extreme value for money. Unthinkable that you should buy anything
else for the same amount. Saline acid courses and weaves through the lanolin,
apricot and beeswax characters. Ultimately the oak cradles and supports the finish,
rather than coercing it. What a wine. Screw cap. 12.5% alc. **Rating** 95 **To** 2031
$25 EL ◆
Premium RSV Margaret River Shiraz 2020 Ridiculous value for money here.
Balanced, savoury/sweet, rich/fine, dense/layered – all the good things we want to

see in shiraz. At \$25 – run, don't walk. Screw cap. 14.5% alc. **Rating** 95 **To** 2031 \$25 EL

Premium RSV Margaret River Cabernet Sauvignon 2019 Now we're talking – this is serious cabernet at a ridiculous price. The tannins form a streamlined shape that cup the fruit and urge it along the palate. Cassis and raspberry fall over themselves to beat licorice and star anise to the fore. The acidity keeps everything fresh and relevant. Lovely wine, great price. Screw cap. 14% alc. **Rating** 95 **To** 2030 \$25 EL ❂

♟♟♟♟♟ **Choosy Beggars Rosé 2020 Rating** 92 **To** 2022 \$11 EL ❂
Choosy Beggars Sauvignon Blanc Semillon 2019 Rating 90 **To** 2022 \$13 EL ❂

AER   ★★★★

The Prince Hotel, 2 Acland Street, St Kilda, Vic 3182 (postal) **Region** Mornington Peninsula
T 0417 014 367 **www**.aer.wine
Winemaker Andrew Santarossa **Est.** 2019 **Dozens** 665
Andrew Ryan, former director of Mitchelon wines cum managing director of Melbourne's Prince Hotel, leapt at the opportunity to source a small stash of premium pinot noir from asunder, on the Mornington Peninsula. All Dijon 114 and 115, the fruit offered opportunity to explore clonal nuances. Given the strong points of differentiation between the clones, Ryan opted to craft 2 separate wines, each an arbiter of one of the clones respectively. Grown in a warmer northern subzone of The Peninsula, the inaugural cuvées are thus named The 114 and The 115. (NG)

♟♟♟♟♟ **114 Clone Tuerong Single Vineyard Mornington Peninsula Pinot Noir 2019** From a warmer site at the end of the Peninsula dominated by clay loams. Subsequently, a darker fruit profile mitigated by a hand that is just firm enough, extracting with confidence while placating the sub-zone's proclivity for teeming fruit with fine-boned tannins and pithy dark cherry flavours that result. This expands beautifully in the glass. A real long-limbed cadence to the tannins. Impressive. Cork. 12.9% alc. **Rating** 93 **To** 2028 \$45 NG
115 Clone Tuerong Single Vineyard Mornington Peninsula Pinot Noir 2019 Sweet dark cherry, bergamot and clove, sublimated nicely by the structural reins as the flavour intensity forces itself across them, expanding with sweetness and sap in the glass. Cork. 13.3% alc. **Rating** 93 **To** 2030 \$75 NG

Alex Russell Wines   ★★★★☆

1866 Pipers River Road, Lower Turners Marsh, Tas 7267 **Region** Northern Tasmania
T 0400 684 614 **www**.alexrussellwines.com.au
Winemaker Alex Russell **Est.** 2014 **Dozens** 1200 **Vyds** 21ha
Alex Russell's story brings back memories of Steve and Monique Lubiana's 1990 move from the family winery in the Riverland to Tasmania's Derwent River to make high-quality sparkling wine. Alex studied viticulture at La Trobe Bundoora. After finishing that degree he moved to Mildura to take on a technical role. He then enrolled in wine science at Charles Sturt University, made wine at Zilzie (2008) and then at Angove Family Winemakers, where he was introduced to the Riverland Vine Improvement Committee (RVIC). He volunteered as experimental winemaker for RVIC and was exposed to everything from albariño to zinfandel, while still working for Angove. After establishing RVIC's Cirami Estate brand he moved on in '14 to establish his own winery in a leased shed in Renmark, making 17 different varietal wines. That business continues notwithstanding his move to Tasmania, simply because the Riverland vintage is largely finished before that of Tasmania starts. Exports to the EU, the US, the UK and NZ.

♟♟♟♟♟ **Alejandro Riverland Fiano 2020** A neat combo of honeysuckle, creamed honey and lemon zest topping stone fruit, plus some apricot kernel, all of which fleshes out the palate. It's juicy, refreshing yet textural and ready for summer. Or perhaps right now. Screw cap. 12.5% alc. **Rating** 92 **To** 2022 \$24 JF ❂

Alejandro Riverland Graciano 2019 Heady aromas of mulberries, dried herbs and damp earth plus a waft of the distinctive hot-metal character of the variety. Tight and sinewy across the palate with hazelnut-skin-like tannins and blood-orange acidity. Screw cap. 14.5% alc. **Rating** 91 **To** 2025 $24 JF

Alkimi Wines ★★★★

PO Box 661, Healesville, Vic 3777 **Region** Yarra Valley
T 0410 234 688 **www**.alkimiwines.com
Winemaker Stuart Dudine **Est.** 2014 **Dozens** 700 **Vyds** 0.5ha
The name is taken from the phonetic spelling of alchemy, the medieval concept of transmuting base metals into gold and similar works of magic. It's somehow appropriate for owner/winemaker Stuart Dudine, because there are unexplained gaps in his wine journey. We do know that he worked in Europe with Emmerich Knoll (a particularly gifted winemaker) in Austria, and with Stéphane Ogier at Château Mont-Redon in France. His love of the Rhône Valley sprang from his time at Henschke, working with syrah, grenache and mourvèdre. Since 2012 he has been based in the Yarra Valley, working (inter alia) for Yarra Yering, Oakridge and Mac Forbes. His overall raison d'être is to find vineyard parcels that perform exceptionally well in their patch of soil, year in and year out, no matter the season. Exports to Singapore.

♀♀♀♀♀ **Mistral Series Yarra Valley Syrah Rosé 2020** Wild fermentation in old barriques. An appealing pale pastel pink hue shot with copper. Mouth-watering freshness, with crisp, perky acidity mingling with the apple and watermelon rind and citrus flavours. It's savoury and most importantly, it's a delicious drink. Screw cap. 12.5% alc. **Rating** 92 **To** 2023 $30 JF
Yarra Valley Chardonnay 2019 There's a gentle persuasion to this. It offers a touch of citrus, hints of nougatine and florals. It's savoury with a smidge of leesy texture. An easy to like wine. Screw cap. 12.9% alc. **Rating** 91 **To** 2027 $40 JF
Yarra Valley Pinot Noir 2019 A lighter shade of garnet belying the fruit intensity within. Lovely aromatics, florals and fruit, warm spices and earth. Sweet strawberries and red cherries strewn across the medium-bodied palate. Led by acidity rather than the tannins, which are fine and light. Screw cap. 13.5% alc. **Rating** 91 **To** 2026 $40 JF

Alkoomi ★★★★★

1411 Wingebellup Road, Frankland River, WA 6396 **Region** Frankland River
T (08) 9855 2229 **www**.alkoomiwines.com.au **Open** 7 days 10–4.30 Frankland River Mon–Sat 11–5 Albany
Winemaker Andrew Cherry **Est.** 1971 **Dozens** 80 000 **Vyds** 164ha
Established in 1971 by Merv and Judy Lange, Alkoomi has grown from a single ha to one of WA's largest family-owned and operated wineries. Now owned by daughter Sandy Hallett and her husband Rod, Alkoomi is continuing the tradition of producing high-quality wines which showcase the Frankland River region. Alkoomi is actively reducing its environmental footprint; future plans will see the introduction of new varietals. Alkoomi has a second cellar door at Albany. Exports to all major markets.

♀♀♀♀♀ **Black Label Frankland River Shiraz 2019** Viognier is well enveloped by powerful shiraz, but it still manages to contribute a slinkiness to the tannins – a slip on the tongue. This is both concentrated and floral, with tannins that create form and structure on the palate and provide framework from which the fruit hangs. A very smart wine indeed, especially at this price. Screw cap. 14.5% alc. **Rating** 95 **To** 2031 $35 EL
Jarrah Frankland River Shiraz 2014 At 7 years old this year, everything has started to soften and evolve, exposing a core of still-sweet black fruits, cloistered by finely textured and supporting tannins. The density is a standout; the texture is completely satisfying and full, finished by exotic spice, star anise, clove, quince, fig, satsuma plum and salted licorice. Complex and spicy. Screw cap. 14.5% alc. **Rating** 95 **To** 2031 $52 EL

Black Label Frankland River Riesling 2020 Fine, talcy phenolics and layers of citrus fruit almost obscure the tight coil of acid that springs from the centre. This has delicacy, poise and grace – but it's also powerful, making it an intriguing, beautiful and well-crafted wine. A lot to love right now, or cellar it – it'll go for years and years. Screw cap. 12% alc. **Rating** 94 **To** 2038 $33 EL

White Label Frankland River Riesling 2020 If ever there was a segment of wines that represented great value it would have to be riesling. The wines have potential in the cellar, they offer deliciousness early and with change from $20, what more could you possibly ask for? This vintage holds true to the success of all of the others that came before. It is taut, powerful, pretty and plump. Cracking value, and a cracking wine. Screw cap. 12% alc. **Rating** 94 **To** 2035 $18 EL ✪

Black Label Frankland River Sauvignon Blanc 2020 This is very classy. Restrained Granny Smith, lychee, guava and lemongrass mingle with cape gooseberry and juniper berry. On the palate the acidity is austere/rigid yet refreshing; the entire package being one of textural complexity and restraint. Bravo. Screw cap. 12.8% alc. **Rating** 94 **To** 2026 $35 EL

Black Label Frankland River Chardonnay 2020 Grilled yellow peach, crushed pistachios, briny acid and layers of exotic spice through the finish (think star anise, cracked pink peppercorn and fennel flower). The acidity, which has the potential to be fierce in Frankland, is entrenched and soft, in concert with all other elements of the wine. Screw cap. 13% alc. **Rating** 94 **To** 2031 $33 EL

Black Label Frankland River Cabernet Sauvignon 2019 This is frequently one of the 'if you know, you know' cabernets in the sub-$30 bracket. It's got it all: supple, succulent and spicy fruit, fine yet firm, structuring tannins and great length of flavour. The characteristic ferrous, gravel, petrichor flavours endemic to Frankland cabernet are all there. Through the lens of the 2019 vintage, this is elegant and long, packing punch within the confines of its restraint. Screw cap. 14% alc. **Rating** 94 **To** 2030 $28 EL ✪

♟♟♟♟♟ **White Label Frankland River Late Harvest 2020** Rating 93 To 2031 $21 EL ✪
Black Label Frankland River Chardonnay 2019 Rating 92 To 2028 $28 EL
White Label Frankland River Sauvignon Blanc 2020 Rating 91 To 2022 $18 EL ✪
White Label Frankland River Semillon Sauvignon Blanc 2020 Rating 90 To 2023 $18 EL ✪

All Saints Estate   ★★★★★

205 All Saints Road, Wahgunyah, Vic 3687 **Region** Rutherglen
T 1800 021 621 **www.**allsaintswine.com.au **Open** Sun–Fri 10–5, Sat 10–5.30
Winemaker Nick Brown **Est.** 1864 **Dozens** 22 000 **Vyds** 47.9ha
The winery rating reflects the fortified wines, including the unique releases of Museum Muscat and Muscadelle, each with an average age of more than 100 years (and table wines). The 1-hat Terrace Restaurant makes this a must-stop for any visitor to North East Victoria, as does the National Trust–listed property with its towering castle centrepiece. All Saints and St Leonards are owned and managed by fourth-generation Brown family members Eliza, Angela and Nick. Eliza is an energetic and highly intelligent leader, wise beyond her years, and highly regarded by the wine industry. Exports to the US, the Philippines, Hong Kong and China.

♟♟♟♟♟ **Museum Rutherglen Muscadelle NV** Very, very few fortified makers in Australia have the depth and breadth of cellaring material to enter into Museum territory. Wines need to have been put aside for generations, as they have here to produce this special wine. It reaches across time to present this glorious, concentrated wine that glides across the palate unwaveringly and long. It's surprisingly not all about sugar intensity and richness but fineness and a deep intrigue of flavours. Stunning. 375ml. Vino-Lok. 18% alc. **Rating** 99 $1000 JP ♥

Museum Rutherglen Muscat NV One of those rare occasions where you could literally inhale the scent of this ancient wine all day long, without considering the next logical step. It is intensely concentrated, while leaving a diaphanous trail that lingers in the senses, filled with rose oil, treacle, honey, fig, nougat and roasted hazelnut. Remarkably, it reaches an even higher beauty when tasted. 500ml. Vino-Lok. 18% alc. **Rating** 98 $1000 JP

Rare Rutherglen Muscat NV Utter deliciousness and just a touch decadent. That olive glimmer gives away the old age: the average age of the wines in the blend is 35 years old. An aromatic treat of raisins, prunes, cracked walnut, roasted coffee beans and salted toffees. Hugely complex but also with a real touch of elegance and clean driving power. 375ml. Vino-Lok. 18% alc. **Rating** 97 $120 JP ✪

Grand Rutherglen Muscat NV Average age in oak is 25 years. The house certainly has a marvellous legacy of old wines to call upon for its fortified program. The scent is heavenly, like inhaling the dessert counter at Alain Ducasse Le Chocolat in Paris. Intense dark chocolate, caramel, coffee bean, toasted hazelnut and dried fruits. So harmonious, so decadent and so, so lasting in the mouth. 375ml. Vino-Lok. 18% alc. **Rating** 97 $75 JP ✪

🍷🍷🍷🍷🍷 **Pierre 2018** Named in honour of the owners' father, Peter Brown, who loved a good bordeaux blend. A more prominent merlot presence than in the '17, Pierre needs a good decant for the wine's aromatics to soar. Violet, musk, red/black berries, licorice and earth with dried herb. Tannins run deep and fine. Well composed and quite the beauty. Screw cap. 14% alc. **Rating** 95 **To** 2030 $40 JP

Durif 2018 All Saints Estate sees the beauty and elegance in the durif grape – yes, it most definitely exists – and produces a style that can overcome any varietal prejudice. With forest-floor notes, wild berries, violets, top spice nuances and vanilla, it's an arresting introduction. Smooth palate, yet retains the grape's robust nature and power. Sensitive handling and winemaking on show. Screw cap. 14% alc. **Rating** 95 **To** 2028 $32 JP ✪

Grand Rutherglen Tawny NV Keeping the traditions of Australian tawny fortified wine production alive, All Saints shows us the beauty of this most under-valued art form. Deep tawny brown, with age apparent immediately in complex raisin, peel, Saunders' Malt and walnut. Not heavy or syrupy in the least, but with a light freshness, a true indication of quality, together with excellent depth, richness and length. 375ml. Vino-Lok. 18% alc. **Rating** 95 $75 JP

Classic Rutherglen Muscat NV Blending is an art form, achieving both youthful freshness and a degree of complexity with an average age of 15+ years. Nose and palate suggest that this has older material, such is the complexity, flavour depth and sustained finish. Aims higher than most classic muscats. Dark amber/olive green. Chocolate-covered licorice, dried fruit, orange rind, soused raisins. Mixes the sweet with a touch of savoury. Outstanding value. 375ml. Vino-Lok. 18% alc. **Rating** 95 $40 JP

Grand Rutherglen Muscadelle NV All Saints avoids the use of the name Topaque in favour of Muscadelle. The deep, burnished walnut colour prepares you for a fortified of some age, something special. So concentrated and mellow, with an immediate immersion in the deep, toffee/nutty complexities of time in barrel. And that's just the bouquet. What follows is an opulent feast for the senses: malt, honey and raisined fruitcake, finishing fresh and clean. 375ml. Vino-Lok. 18% alc. **Rating** 95 $75 JP

Rare Rutherglen Muscadelle NV In the Rutherglen Classification, Rare is the 2nd-top level attainable. This wine is an average age of 30+ years. The blender's art is allowing age to speak but also keeping it fresh and relevant. This is over the top on the intensity scale. The mood darkens, the colour too, as the flavours evolve into an almost treacly unctuousness, molasses-rich and warm with dark malt biscuit, nutty caramel and, importantly, a lifted freshness. 375ml. Vino-Lok. 18% alc. **Rating** 95 $120 JP

ￇￇￇￇￇ Rutherglen Muscat NV Rating 92 $26 JP
Classic Rutherglen Muscadelle NV Rating 92 $40 JP
Family Cellar Marsanne 2019 Rating 91 To 2026 $38 JP
1920 Old Vine Shiraz 2018 Rating 91 To 2034 $75 JP
Rosa 2020 Rating 90 To 2024 $32 JP

Allegiance Wines   ★★★★

3446 Jingellic Road, Tumbarumba, NSW 2653 **Region** Various
T 0434 561 718 **www**.allegiancewines.com.au **Open** By appt
Winemaker Contract **Est.** 2009 **Dozens** 40 000 **Vyds** 8ha
When Tim Cox established Allegiance Wines in 2009 he had the decided advantage of
having worked in the Australian wine industry across many facets for almost 30 years. He
worked on both the sales and marketing side, and also on the supplier side with Southcorp.
He started Cox Wine Merchants to act as distributor for Moppity Vineyards, with whom he
successfully partnered for over 5 years. Having started out as a virtual wine business, Allegiance
has recently purchased its own vineyards and now has 8ha under vine in Tumbarumba, planted
to 5.5ha pinot gris, 2ha chardonnay and 0.5ha shiraz. It also purchases fruit from the Barossa,
Coonawarra, Margaret River, Hilltops and Tumbarumba. Exports to NZ and China.

ￇￇￇￇￇ Unity Coonawarra Cabernet Sauvignon 2018 This is jangly from youth,
with the oak not quite meshing into the wine's body, although that should happen
in time. Cassis and currants infused with gum leaves are working with plentiful
tannins, ripe yet raspy, although the finish does smooth out. Screw cap. 14.5% alc.
Rating 92 To 2033 $100 JF
Alumni Eden Valley Riesling 2020 Pale to medium straw hue. A ripe, plump
and complex riesling of baked apple, mixed spice, fig and wild honey. Bright
acidity and well-handled fine phenolic grip unite on a finish of rich fruit sweetness
and lingering persistence. Drink now. Screw cap. 12% alc. **Rating** 90 To 2022
$25 TS
Single Vineyard Hilltops Shiraz 2019 An excellent dark purple/garnet. Bold
flavours abound including charry oak, but there is good fruit in the mix. Quite
savoury with cedar, cardamom and cured meats working across a fuller-bodied
palate with raspy yet ripe tannins. There's a vibrancy and appeal to this cool-
climate shiraz. Screw cap. 14% alc. **Rating** 90 To 2029 $30 JF
Unity Margaret River Cabernet Sauvignon 2020 Sweet, juicy, ripe. Verging
on simple, and very, very young. The fruit has a syrupy, sarsaparilla character to it
and it will most certainly benefit from another year in bottle. Screw cap. 14% alc.
Rating 90 To 2036 $100 EL
Single Vineyard Hilltops Cabernet Sauvignon 2019 A delightfully fragrant
offering with florals, cassis and a hint of mulberries wrapped up in leafy freshness.
Medium bodied at best, with oak in the background, supple tannins and a bright
line of acidity making this ready now. Screw cap. 13.5% alc. **Rating** 90 To 2027
$30 JF
Sweet Betty Botrytis Semillon 2018 Mid weighted and stuffed with riffs of
dried mango, orange zest, honey blossom and canned pineapple, there is plenty
going on. The ample sweetness is mopped up by oodles of acidity. The finish:
dutifully long with a soft cloy and plenty of tang. Screw cap. 12.5% alc. **Rating** 90
To 2026 $25 NG

ￇￇￇￇ Unity Margaret River Chardonnay 2020 Rating 89 To 2025 $60 EL
The Artisan McLaren Vale Shiraz 2018 Rating 89 To 2026 $40 NG

Allies Wines   ★★★★☆

200 Fullers Road, Foster, Vic 3960 **Region** Mornington Peninsula
T 0412 111 587 **www**.allies.com.au **Open** By appt
Winemaker David Chapman **Est.** 2003 **Dozens** 1200 **Vyds** 3.1ha

A former chef and sommelier, David Chapman began Allies in 2003 while working at Moorooduc Estate. He makes pinot noir, emphasising the diversity of the Mornington Peninsula by making a number of wines sourced from different districts. David spends much of his time in the vineyard, working to ensure well-exposed and -positioned bunches achieve ripe, pure flavours and supple tannins. His winemaking focuses on simple techniques that retain concentration and character: no added yeasts, fining or filtration. Production of Allies Wines is small and will probably remain that way, given that any expansion will limit the number of vines David can personally tend. Exports to Japan, Hong Kong and China.

ŸŸŸŸŸ Merricks Mornington Peninsula Pinot Noir 2019 Really perfumed with flavours working off a savoury theme aside from the injection of blood orange, morello and black cherries. There are plenty of woodsy spices, autumn leaves, sarsaparilla and a fleck of dried herbs. There's an appealing freshness throughout, a juiciness with acidity working in unison with the tannins. Diam. 13.8% alc. **Rating** 92 **To** 2025 $47 JF

Altus Rise

10 North Street, Mount Lawley, WA 6050 (postal) **Region** Margaret River
T 0400 532 805
Winemaker Laura Bowler **Est.** 2019
Altus Rise was founded by Chris Credaro, Kim O'Hara and Jan Skrapac, friends for many years, all with experience of the wine industry. Chris is a highly experienced viticulturist and member of the Credaro family and its extensive vineyard holdings. Kim O'Hara has 20 years of wine sales and marketing experience, while Jan Skrapac has a wealth of financial and management expertise.

ŸŸŸŸŸ Ascension Margaret River Cabernet Sauvignon 2019 Great flavour intensity that deep dives on the palate: raspberry, blackberry, mulberry and blood plum are laced together by a spicy line of tannin that whips around, creating line and length. This wine gives great satisfaction. It may not be the most complex wine, but it is desperately delicious. Screw cap. 14% alc. **Rating** 94 **To** 2030 $35 EL

ŸŸŸŸŸ Ascension Margaret River Shiraz 2019 Rating 93 **To** 2030 $35 EL
Wildlight Margaret River Sauvignon Blanc Semillon 2020 Rating 91 **To** 2024 $24 EL
Wildlight Margaret River Chardonnay 2020 Rating 91 **To** 2027 $24 EL
Wildlight Margaret River Cabernet Sauvignon 2019 Rating 91 **To** 2028 $24 EL

Amadio Wines

461 Payneham Road, Felixstow, SA 5070 **Region** Adelaide Hills/Kangaroo Island
T (08) 8365 5988 **www**.amadiowines.com **Open** Wed–Sun 10–5.30
Winemaker Danniel Amadio **Est.** 2004 **Dozens** 50000 **Vyds** 220ha
Danniel Amadio says he has followed in the footsteps of his Italian grandfather, selling wine from his cellar (cantina) direct to the consumer. Amadio Wines has substantial vineyards, primarily in the Adelaide Hills and Barossa Valley. They also source contract-grown grapes from Clare Valley, McLaren Vale and Langhorne Creek, with a strong suite of Italian varieties. The Kangaroo Island Trading Company wines are produced with fifth-generation islanders Michael and Rosie Florance from their Cygnet River vineyard; there is a second cellar door in the main street of Kingscote. Exports to Asia, the US, Canada and Sweden

Amato Vino

182 Stevens Road, Margaret River, WA 6285 **Region** Margaret River
T 0409 572 957 **www**.amatovino.com.au **Open** By appt
Winemaker Brad Wehr **Est.** 2003 **Dozens** 5000

Established in 2003 by Brad Wehr, Amato Vino makes small-batch 'lo-fi' wines (wild ferments, minimal adjustments, unfined and unfiltered) using grapes from a core group of independent growers who employ organic and sustainable farming practices. The 'Wilds' feature Mediterranean varieties, Fusa are blends of emerging varieties, and the Mantra wines are made from classic Margaret River varieties. Exports to Singapore.

🍷🍷🍷🍷🍷 **Space Girls Margaret River Savagnin 2020** Bitter citrus zest, salted preserved lemon and straw on the nose. The palate follows suit in the salty way that savagnin does. If you're a salt/acid/texture freak then this one is for you. Made in a juicy, modern and slinky way rather than an oxidative, textured, Jura way. A salivating curl of brine winds its way through this wine … in and out of the citrus fruit. Yes, yes and yes. Screw cap. 13.4% alc. **Rating** 95 **To** 2027 $40 EL ❤
Mantra Margaret River Cabernet Sauvignon 2018 Dense and succulent, this is a picture of Margaret River cabernet: power without heft, and concentration without girth. The fruit is ripe and plush and the tannins have a chewiness to them. Overall, extremely satisfying, almost decadent. Screw cap. 14% alc. **Rating** 95 **To** 2027 $40 EL
Mantra Margaret River Sauvignon Blanc 2020 Texturally complex and layered, this is an intensely flavoured, long, restrained sauvignon blanc with a cascade of interesting flavours within it. Bitter orange, cinnamon and rhubarb are followed by licorice, aniseed, walnut and ginger. Likely a fascinating food match. Screw cap. 13.9% alc. **Rating** 94 **To** 2026 $40 EL
The Pig Cabernet Sauvignon Nebbiolo 2018 Two extremely unlikely bedfellows that have physicality and chemistry in this glass. Both varieties require little tannic assistance, so why they are blended is a mystery, yet it works here. Plush, juicy, tannic and quite delicious. Definitely worth crossing the road for, even if just to satisfy some curiosity. Satisfaction awaits. Screw cap. 13.7% alc. **Rating** 94 **To** 2031 $40 EL
The Stars Baby, The Stars Trousseau 2020 Wild ferment in amphorae. Extraordinarily pale, as trousseau can be. The nose reveals strawberry, graphite, brine, pink peppercorn and apple skin. On the palate this is very fine and delicate, with layers of deliciousness that cascade from the front of the mouth and tumble their way through into the finish. The acid backbone is a highlight. This is a beautiful wine. Lyrical, in a way. Screw cap. 12.5% alc. **Rating** 94 **To** 2028 $50 EL

🍷🍷🍷🍷 **Rosso Margaret River 2020 Rating** 93 **To** 2025 $28 EL
Fiume Terra Sangiovese 2020 Rating 93 **To** 2027 $40 EL
The Bear Margaret River Teroldego 2018 Rating 93 **To** 2028 $50 EL
Margaret River Bianco 2020 Rating 92 **To** 2028 $28 EL
Mantra Margaret River Chardonnay 2020 Rating 91 **To** 2027 $40 EL
Lava Sunset Margaret River Verdelho 2020 Rating 91 **To** 2026 $35 EL
Chenski Margaret River Chenin Blanc 2020 Rating 90 **To** 2028 $35 EL
Pink Moon Rosato 2020 Rating 90 **To** 2025 $35 EL

Amelia Park Wines   ★★★★★

3857 Caves Road, Wilyabrup, WA 6280 **Region** Margaret River
T (08) 9755 6747 **www**.ameliaparkwines.com.au **Open** 7 days 10–5
Winemaker Jeremy Gordon **Est.** 2009 **Dozens** 25 000 **Vyds** 9.6ha
Jeremy Gordon's winemaking career started with Evans & Tate, and Houghton thereafter, before he moved to the eastern states to broaden his experience. He returned to Margaret River, and after several years he and wife Daniela founded Amelia Park Wines with business partner Peter Walsh. Amelia Park initially relied on contract-grown grapes, but in 2013 purchased the Moss Brothers site in Wilyabrup, allowing the construction of a new winery and cellar door. Exports to Singapore, China, Indonesia, Taiwan, South Korea, Myanmar, Philippines, Thailand, India, Russia and Vietnam.

🍷🍷🍷🍷🍷 **Reserve Margaret River Cabernet Sauvignon 2018** Cabernet can be so exciting when it walks the tightrope between ripe/succulent/supple and herbaceous (fresh garden herbs, with sprinklings of Margaret River salt bush). This is everything we expect from the perfect 2018 vintage: concentrated ripe cassis, raspberry, pomegranate and red licorice. The acidity is bright and salty and punched deep into the fruit. The oak, wherever that is, is completely, seamlessly integrated. A triumphant wine. Bravo. Screw cap. 14.5% alc. **Rating** 97 **To** 2041 $65 EL ✪

🍷🍷🍷🍷🍷 **Reserve Frankland River Shiraz 2018** From the exceptional 2018 vintage springs this aromatic, brooding, concentrated and complex shiraz from one of WA's great shiraz regions. Salted mulberry, raspberry, blackberry and licorice, layered with red licorice, bitter cocoa, star anise and that regional stamp of ferrous/ red dirt/earth. Ripe acidity weaves in and out of the long finish. This will bring pleasure now, and well into the future. Screw cap. 14.5% alc. **Rating** 96 **To** 2036 $65 EL ✪

Reserve Margaret River Chardonnay 2019 Matured in French oak for 10 months. Potently powerful fruit cascades over the palate in a rush of yellow peach, nectarine, crushed nuts; and some intriguing wisps of sweet paprika, jasmine tea, saffron and star anise. It is tightly bound up in the cool vintage that was 2019, but it has a lot to give. Needs decanting. Screw cap. 13% alc. **Rating** 95 **To** 2036 $65 EL

Amour Wines   ★★★★

69 Bruce Road, Orange, NSW 2800 **Region** Orange
T 0423 240 720 **www**.amourwines.com.au **Open** By appt
Winemaker Matt Eades **Est.** 2014 **Dozens** 300 **Vyds** 2.4ha
Like others before him, Matt Eades embarked on a career in insurance and law, but the lure of wine was too strong to be held at bay. It all began in 1997 with his first visit to a nearby wine region. In 2009 he enrolled in the Charles Sturt oenology degree, graduating in '13. His first vintage was in the Yarra Valley in '10, making his first wines from Beechworth shiraz in '12 and '13. Together with wife Katie, he has adopted Orange as their principal home base.

🍷🍷🍷🍷🍷 **Orange Chardonnay 2019** A resinous mid yellow, seldom seen on young chardonnay these days. Truffled earthen scents mingle with stone fruits, orange verbena and a tinge of oak-derived vanilla pod and cedar smokiness. A richly flavoured wine, belying the lowish alcohol. Sits confidently in the mouth. The finish is long and saturates the palate. Despite the 980m elevation of the site, there is nothing anaemic or edgy about this. Just a sheath of forceful flavour, delivered with admirable poise and a juicy plume of freshness. Screw cap. 12.5% alc. **Rating** 95 **To** 2026 $50 NG

🍷🍷🍷🍷 **Orange Pinot Noir 2019 Rating** 89 **To** 2025 $60 NG

Anderson   ★★★★☆

1619 Chiltern Road, Rutherglen, Vic 3685 **Region** Rutherglen
T (02) 6032 8111 **www**.andersonwinery.com.au **Open** Mon–Sat 10–4
Winemaker Howard and Christobelle Anderson **Est.** 1992 **Dozens** 2000 **Vyds** 8.8ha
Having notched up a winemaking career spanning over 55 years, including a stint at Seppelt (Great Western), Howard Anderson and family started their own winery, initially with a particular focus on sparkling wine but now extending across all table wine styles. Daughter Christobelle graduated from the University of Adelaide in 2003 with first-class honours, and has worked in Alsace, Champagne and Burgundy either side of joining her father full-time in '05. The original estate plantings of shiraz, durif and petit verdot (6ha) have been expanded with tempranillo, saperavi, brown muscat, chenin blanc and viognier.

🍷🍷🍷🍷♀ **Verrier Sparkling Lizzie 2017** Early-picked muscat grapes, made sparkling in the traditional method, aged on yeast lees in the bottle for 3 years. Essentially a moscato in style, with bottle age and upfront sweet, grapey appeal. Apple pie, lemon, nougat aromas. Bottle age has imparted a delightful biscuity, honeysuckle character. Punchy acidity matched with a light grapey sweetness completes this excellent summer sparkling. Cork. 12% alc. **Rating** 90 $27 JP

🍷🍷🍷🍷 **Verrier Basket Press Saperavi 2017 Rating** 88 To 2034 $35 JP

Anderson & Marsh ★★★★

6815 Great Alpine Road, Porepunkah, Vic 3740 **Region** Alpine Valleys
T 0419 984 982 **Open** By appt
Winemaker Eleana Anderson, Jo Marsh **Est.** 2014 **Dozens** 60
A joint project between Alpine Valleys winemakers Eleana Anderson (of Mayford Wines) and Jo Marsh (of Billy Button). The first vintage of Catani Blanc de Blanc was made in 2014 and was joined by Parell Albarino in '18 and Parell Tempranillo in '19 (Parell is Spanish for pair). Close friends and neighbours, they set out to produce the style of sparkling wines they love to drink – crisp and tight – from the town where they both live, Porepunkah. A local parcel of albariño became available in '18 which they were both very interested in, so they decided to make it together under their new label. Tempranillo was an obvious choice to partner with the Albarino.

🍷🍷🍷🍷🍷 **Parell Alpine Valleys Tempranillo 2019** The '19 fulfils many of the things drinkers love about tempranillo: it's medium bodied, with dark cherries, licorice and a touch of savouriness. Do we expect anything less than a masterclass on the grape from these 2 winemakers? Plush, even and balanced, there is plenty of generous fruit flavour, a pinch of toasty oak, ripe tannins and a whole lot of tempranillo character to embrace. Screw cap. 14.3% alc. **Rating** 94 **To** 2026 $45 JP

🍷🍷🍷🍷♀ **Catani Alpine Valleys Blanc de Blancs 2015 Rating** 91 $65 JP
Parell Alpine Valleys Albariño 2018 Rating 90 To 2024 $35 JP

 # Anderson Fort ★★★★

PO Box 712, Heathcote, Vic 3523 **Region** Heathcote
T 0438 133 311 **www.**afwines.com.au
Winemaker Liam Anderson, Bryan Fort **Est.** 2016 **Dozens** 400 **Vyds** 5ha
Anderson Fort is a collaboration between great mates Liam Anderson and Bryan Fort. Liam Anderson is a trained winemaker who has been involved in his family's wine business, Wild Duck Creek Estate in Heathcote, after studying viticulture at The University of Melbourne's Dookie College and wine science at Charles Sturt University. Bryan Fort is a trained sommelier who has worked in Melbourne restaurants, with stints in wine retail and distribution. They met in the early noughties, struck up a great friendship and dreamt of making wine one day under their own label. Anderson Fort specialises in Heathcote shiraz-based wines that highlight the variation and quality of the region's most significant grape. (JP)

🍷🍷🍷🍷🍷 **Mia Mia Heathcote Shiraz 2017** A powerful essay on Heathcote shiraz, but not without its share of elegance. Deep, dense purple. An almost unassuming bouquet, rich in cassis, smoky/spice oak aromas and dark chocolate. Opens up on the palate with a whoosh. Ripe, sweet, intense fruit but still tightly coiled, with good structure and a firm, tannic backbone. Balance is the key here. Will live long. Cork. 14.6% alc. **Rating** 94 **To** 2032 $85 JP

🍷🍷🍷🍷♀ **Toolleen Heathcote Shiraz 2017 Rating** 92 To 2032 $55 JP

Anderson Hill ★★★★☆

407 Croft Road, Lenswood, SA 5240 **Region** Adelaide Hills
T 0407 070 295 **www.**andersonhill.com.au **Open** Wed–Sun 11–5
Winemaker Ben Anderson **Est.** 1994 **Dozens** 4000 **Vyds** 9ha
Ben and Clare Anderson planted their vineyard in 1994. A substantial part of the grape production is sold (Hardys and Penfolds have been top-end purchasers of the chardonnay),

but enough is retained to produce their wines. The cellar door has panoramic views, making the venue popular for functions. Exports to Norway and China.

🍷🍷🍷🍷🍷 **Art Series Found in a Forest Adelaide Hills Pinot Noir 2020** Lenswood fruit, made straight and easy with 8 months' rest in French oak. Bright cherry red in the glass, pure cherry and woody spice flavour notes with a really well-toned and balanced finish that weaves an earthy, rocket/peppery savoury edge to the exit. Screw cap. 13.7% alc. **Rating** 92 **To** 2026 $30 TL

Art Series Sarah Jane Lenswood Chardonnay 2020 Ripe white peachy fruit notes, a delicate suggestion of ginger – possibly from 8 months in seasoned French oak with lees stirred. Creamy palate feels, without too much further complexity, some sticky and fulfilling texture and spice on the finish. Quite tidy. Screw cap. 13.5% alc. **Rating** 91 **To** 2025 $30 TL

Andevine Wines ★★★★★

119 McDonalds Road, Pokolbin, NSW 2320 **Region** Hunter Valley
T 0427 948 880 **www**.andevinewines.com.au
Winemaker Andrew Leembruggen **Est.** 2012 **Dozens** 15 000

Andrew Leembruggen has been a Hunter Valley boy since his cadetship at Mount Pleasant in 1998, becoming senior winemaker in 2002; he led winemaking operations for Drayton's Family Wines from '10 to '12 before his departure to create Andevine Wines. Andrew has also made wine in the Rhône Valley, Bordeaux, Napa Valley and Coonawarra. There are 3 ranges of wines: Reserve (available exclusively from the cellar door); varietals (available exclusively through Naked Wines); and wines sourced from regions across NSW.

Andrew Peace Wines ★★★★

Murray Valley Highway, Piangil, Vic 3597 **Region** Swan Hill
T (03) 5030 5291 **www**.apwines.com **Open** Mon–Fri 8–5, Sat 12–4
Winemaker Andrew Peace, David King **Est.** 1995 **Dozens** 180 000 **Vyds** 270ha

The Peace family has been a major Swan Hill grapegrower since 1980, moving into winemaking with the opening of a $3 million winery in '96. Varieties planted include chardonnay, colombard, grenache, malbec, mataro, merlot, pinot gris, riesling, sangiovese, sauvignon blanc, semillon, tempranillo and viognier. The planting of sagrantino is the largest of only a few such plantings in Australia. Exports to all major markets.

🍷🍷🍷🍷🍷 **Colour of Raven Limestone Coast Cabernet Sauvignon 2019** A black/red colour. While sitting smack in the middle of the riper spectrum, this hits the mark well, offering a combination of juicy, plump blackberries spiced with licorice and cedary/coconuty oak. The full-bodied palate is marked by a suppleness until the gritty tannins come into play. Screw cap. 14.5% alc. **Rating** 91 **To** 2029 $25 JF

Full Moon Victoria Shiraz Sagrantino 2019 Just 13% sagrantino, yet its amaro tang and richness come to the fore, so too the 30% new French and American oak barriques, aged 1 year. And yet, there's a suppleness across the full-bodied palate. Ripe fruit, baking spices galore and it all seems to work. Screw cap. 14.5% alc. **Rating** 90 **To** 2028 $20 JF ✪

Australia Felix Premium Barrel Reserve Wrattonbully Cabernet Shiraz 2018 A whorl of blackcurrants, blackberries, baking spices and mint leaves stake its regional claim. It's as rich as molasses, full bodied yet a juiciness abounds and the tannins are spot-on, oak too. Screw cap. 14.5% alc. **Rating** 90 **To** 2028 $28 JF

Australia Felix Swan Hill Sagrantino 2018 Oak tannins meet sagrantino tannins. Wham! A touch brutish at first, and more time in bottle could help, yet the ripe, sweet fruit starts to come out. Aniseed, coffee grounds, dark plums and eucalyptus. The acidity is somewhat jarring on the finish. Those who dig full-bodied reds with a difference, come and get it. Screw cap. 14.5% alc. **Rating** 90 **To** 2028 $45 JF

🍷🍷🍷🍷 **25th Anniversary Swan Hill Shiraz 2019** **Rating** 88 **To** 2028 $25 JF

Angove Family Winemakers   ★★★★★

Bookmark Avenue, Renmark, SA 5341 **Region** McLaren Vale
T (08) 8580 3100 **www**.angove.com.au **Open** Mon–Fri 10–5, Sat 10–4, Sun &
public hols 10–3
Winemaker Tony Ingle, Paul Kernich, Ben Horley, Amelia Anspach **Est.** 1886
Dozens 1 million **Vyds** 300ha

Founded in 1886, Angove Family Winemakers is one of Australia's most successful wine
businesses – a 5th-generation family company with a tradition of excellence and an eye for the
future. Angove wines includes The Medhyk, Warboys Vineyard, Family Crest, Organics, and
Long Row brands. The McLaren Vale cellar door is nestled in the family's certified organic
and biodynamic Warboys Vineyard on Chalk Hill Road, the Renmark cellar door (home of
the St Agnes Distillery) in Bookmark Avenue. In early 2019 Angove acquired the celebrated
12.7ha Angel Gully Vineyard in Clarendon from Primo Estate, and renamed the vineyard
Angels Rise. Angove is committed to remaining privately owned and believes remaining
in family hands enables the company to be master of its own destiny. Exports to all
major markets.

🍷🍷🍷🍷🍷 **The Medhyk McLaren Vale Shiraz 2017** Disciplined attention to detail
has produced a perfectly balanced medium- to full-bodied palate with supple,
juicy and smooth plum and blackberry fruit; a hint of dark chocolate; integrated
cedary oak and built-in tannins. It sings from start to finish. Screw cap. 14.5% alc.
Rating 98 **To** 2042 $65 JH ✪ ♥

🍷🍷🍷🍷🍷 **Single Vineyard Sellicks Foothills McLaren Vale Shiraz 2018** Most
impressive here is the licorella tannic detail and pungent – almost volcanic –
whack of anise, wood smoke and dried-cherry skin. Lilac and iodine, too.
Powerful, mineral/pumice precision and impressively vinous. Superlative extraction
techniques. Screw cap. 13.5% alc. **Rating** 95 **To** 2028 $44 NG
Single Vineyard Blewitt Springs McLaren Vale Shiraz 2018 Whole berries
imbue the wine with a jubey, energetic pulpiness. The oak, smart. Less reductive
and tense than the other 2 bottlings. Dark cherry, root spice, bitter chocolate
and cedar. Straightforward now, with an underlying arsenal of quivering, forceful
tannins, suggesting this will be a shapeshifter. Time, the essence. Screw cap.
14.5% alc. **Rating** 95 **To** 2032 $44 NG
Warboys Vineyard McLaren Vale Shiraz 2018 Classic regional interpretation,
eschewing the reductive approach of whole bunch and/or berry in favour of
basket pressing and regular plunging. The result is a sumptuous billow of floral
scents segueing to blue- and dark-fruit accents, licorice, clove and smoked
meats. A powerful wine that is nevertheless light on its feet. Screw cap. 14% alc.
Rating 94 **To** 2032 $46 NG

🍷🍷🍷🍷🍸 **Single Vineyard Willunga McLaren Vale Shiraz 2018** Rating 93 To 2032
$44 NG
Warboys Vineyard McLaren Vale Grenache 2018 Rating 93 To 2032
$46 NG
McLaren Vale Shiraz 2018 Rating 91 To 2025 $22 NG ✪
McLaren Vale GSM 2018 Rating 91 To 2024 $22 NG ✪
McLaren Vale Tempranillo 2019 Rating 91 To 2026 $22 NG ✪
Wild Olive Organic McLaren Vale Shiraz 2019 Rating 90 To 2025 $22 NG
Organic Cuvée Brut NV Rating 90 $18 NG ✪
Grand Tawny Average Age 10 Years NV Rating 90 $29 NG

Angullong Wines   ★★★★

37 Victoria Street, Millthorpe, NSW 2798 **Region** Orange
T (02) 6366 4300 **www**.angullong.com.au **Open** 7 days 11–5
Winemaker Jon Reynolds, Drew Tuckwell, Ravri Donkin **Est.** 1998 **Dozens** 20 000
Vyds 216.7ha

The Crossing family (Bill and Hatty, and 3rd generation James and Ben) has owned a 2000ha sheep and cattle station for over half a century. Located 40km south of Orange, overlooking the Belubula Valley, more than 200ha of vines have been planted. In all there are 15 varieties, with shiraz, cabernet sauvignon and merlot leading the way. Most of the production is sold. Exports to Germany and China.

Fossil Hill Montepulciano 2019 Montepulciano can be ferruginous and powerful, with considerable tannic mettle. And yet this is made with a lighter touch, presumably given the young vineyard and its first crop. Maturation, wisely for this sort of structural kit, in older oak. This allows for a suppleness and notes of bitter cherry amaro and blood stone to flow across the palate, rather than stifling it. A nice drink, best enjoyed on the cooler side. Screw cap. 13.2% alc. **Rating** 92 **To** 2022 $28 NG

Fossil Hill Chardonnay 2019 A luminescent yellow in the glass transpiring as nectarine, white peach and honeydew melon aromas. The palate, flinty and light of feel, with a delicate infection of cashew and praline. Well-nestled oak and a lively finish. Screw cap. 12.5% alc. **Rating** 91 **To** 2023 $26 NG

Crossing Reserve Shiraz 2017 A cooler year iterated as a sheath of peppery tannins and violet, anise, verdant herb, tapenade, clove and boysenberry aromas. Maturation in French oak (30% new) has imparted a savoury underbelly of cedar and smoky charcuterie notes. The finish, a bit shins and elbows; the reduction, still palpable. A little more time may bring greater poise, but my bet is on drinking this young. Screw cap. 14.5% alc. **Rating** 91 **To** 2025 $48 NG

Crossing Reserve Harriet Sagrantino Montepulciano Sangiovese 2019 **Rating** 88 **To** 2025 $48 NG

Angus the Bull ★★★☆

2/14 Sydney Road, Manly, NSW 2095 (postal) **Region** Central Victoria
T (02) 8966 9020 **www**.angusthebull.com
Winemaker Hamish MacGowan **Est.** 2002 **Dozens** 20 000

Hamish MacGowan took the virtual winery idea to its ultimate conclusion, with a single wine (Angus the Bull Cabernet Sauvignon) designed to be drunk with a perfectly cooked steak. Each year parcels of grapes are selected from a number of sites across Central Victoria, the flexibility of this multiregional blending approach designed to minimise vintage variation. Recently the range has been extended to include the Wee Angus Merlot and a limited Single Vineyard Heathcote wine called Black Angus. Exports to NZ, the UK, Ireland, Sweden, Denmark, Canada, Japan, South Korea, China, Hong Kong, Singapore, Thailand, Vietnam, Philippines, Indonesia, Fiji, Papua New Guinea amd Vanuatu.

Black Angus Heathcote Cabernet Sauvignon 2017 A single-vineyard expression that combines all the things we expect from Heathcote – deep colour, intensity, concentration, bush mint/eucalypt/bay leaf spice, warm oak – with a bit of a surprise. The medium-bodied cabernet bursts with just-picked red berries, blackberry/plum freshness and fragrant aromatics. It's a fine cabernet with earthy, leafy overtones and savoury tannins. What's more, it's sourced from the warmer north of the region. Quite a standout wine from a standout year. Cork. 14% alc. **Rating** 94 **To** 2030 $60 JP

Wee Angus Central Victoria Merlot 2019 **Rating** 89 **To** 2026 $19 JP **○**
Central Victoria Cabernet Sauvignon 2018 **Rating** 89 **To** 2026 $23 JP

Anim Wine ★★★★

PO Box 65, Tas 7052 **Region** Southern Tasmania
T 0400 203 865 **www**.animwine.com **Open** By appt
Winemaker Max Marriott **Est.** 2018 **Dozens** 500

The production may be small, but the story of owners Max and Siobhan Marriot is anything but. Max started his 15 years in wine in NZ studying at Lincoln University, emerging with a bachelor of viticulture and oenology. He then managed vineyards in Central Otago, and worked vintages in the Mosel, Oregon (Cristom) and Burgundy (Domaine du Comte Liger-Belair). After a few years in Oregon, 'my wife Siobhan and I discovered we were expecting twins, so we made the decision to repatriate ourselves and settle in Tasmania.' Max is involved with Clarence House and also leases/manages the Tinderbox Vineyard. Anim is a very small label, named after their children (Audrey, Niamh and Imogen), but also has other musical and Latin meanings. Grapes are sourced from the Clarence House and Tinderbox vineyards, Tinderbox the source of pinot, chardonnay and riesling, the 'fun grapes' coming from Clarence House.

ŸŸŸŸŸ **Tinderbox Blanc 2020** The spicy, white peach body and flesh of chardonnay takes the lead here, heightened by the texture of wild ferment and the creaminess of partial mlf. Riesling speaks more confidently on the finish, drawing out a long tail of lemon and lime, energised by the crystalline acidity of Tasmania's far south. A compelling blend from the outset, and I dare say it will age confidently, too. Screw cap. 13% alc. **Rating** 92 **To** 2030 $35 TS

Anvers   ★★★★☆
633 Razorback Road, Kangarilla, SA 5157 **Region** Adelaide Hills
T (08) 7079 8691 **www**.anvers.com.au **Open** Sun 11–5
Winemaker Kym Milne MW **Est.** 1998 **Dozens** 10 000 **Vyds** 24.5ha
Myriam and Wayne Keoghan's principal vineyard is in the Adelaide Hills at Kangarilla (17ha of sauvignon blanc, chardonnay, shiraz, barbera and gamay). Winemaker Kym Milne has experience gained across many of the wine-producing countries in both northern and southern hemispheres. Exports to the UK and other major markets.

ŸŸŸŸŸ **Limited Release Adelaide Hills Cabernet Sauvignon 2018** A combo of cooler-climate location and a warmer vintage has worked together to deliver classic cabernet dark berries, with atypical leafy and herbal notes. There are mint aromas, but not dominant. The success of this wine is thanks to its medium weight yet saturation of cabernet flavour, supported by superfine tannins and the very faintest of suggestions of gastronomic bitterness on the finish. Great value. Screw cap. 14.5% alc. **Rating** 95 **To** 2028 $24 TL ✪ ♥
The Warrior Adelaide Hills Langhorne Creek Shiraz 2018 A best-parcel selection, in this vintage 64% from Anvers' Adelaide Hills estate and 36% from Langhorne Creek. Each district was vinified and matured separately for a year in new and 1yo French oak, before best barrels were chosen, blended and settled together for a further 6 months. The result is a delicious, sophisticated shiraz. It's dark-fruited, smooth and lengthy, with the faintest hint of moreish bitters on the exit. Screw cap. 14.5% alc. **Rating** 94 **To** 2030 $65 TL

ŸŸŸŸŸ **Langhorne Creek Cabernet Sauvignon 2018 Rating** 91 **To** 2030 $32 TL
Kingsway Adelaide Hills Chardonnay 2020 Rating 90 **To** 2025 $32 TL

Aphelion Wine   ★★★★★
18 St Andrews Terrace, Willunga, SA 5172 **Region** McLaren Vale
T 0404 390 840 **www**.aphelionwine.com.au **Open** By appt
Winemaker Rob Mack **Est.** 2014 **Dozens** 2500
Aphelion Wine is akin to a miniature painting done with single-hair paintbrushes. When you consider the credentials of winemaker Rob Mack, supported by co-founder wife Louise Rhodes Mack, great oaks come to mind. Rob has accumulated 2 degrees (first Accounting and Management in 2007, then the bachelor of wine science from CSU in '16). He scaled the heights of direct marketing as wine buyer and planner (June '10–Jan '13) for Laithwaites Wine People, and spent the next 18 months as production manager for Direct Wines in McLaren Vale. Woven through this has been significant employment with 5 wineries, 4 in McLaren Vale, which he obviously knows well. Rob was voted Young Gun of Wine '18 and Aphelion won Best Small Producer at the McLaren Vale Wine Show in '19. Exports to the UK, the US, Canada and Hong Kong.

ŸŸŸŸŸ **Rapture McLaren Vale Grenache 2020** A wine that is now firmly entrenched in the pantheon of the country's finest. A limpid light ruby. Transparent. Firecracker aromas of sour cherry, cranberry, white pepper, raspberry, clove and tamarind. The tannins, a scaly carapace that directs, tones and services a savoury, chiselled frisk to the work at hand. Brilliant. Cork. 13.7% alc. **Rating** 96 **To** 2029 $100 NG

Pir Blewitt Springs Chenin Blanc 2020 50% was barrel fermented and left on lees for several months, conferring textural detail as much as imparting a chord of authoritative match-struck tension. Brilliant aromas of lemon drop crystals, cheese rind, quince, dried hay and lanolin. The acidity, pungent, juicy and electrifying, towing this very long like an elastic band pulling the saliva from the back of the mouth, unlike most Australian wines that roll across the front. Exceptional. Screw cap. 13.4% alc. **Rating** 95 **To** 2027 $35 NG ✪

Project 5255 Welkin Langhorne Creek Malbec 2020 Part of a creative project out of Langhorne Creek, for which 3 winemakers were offered access to the region's fruit for the first time. From the Wenzel vineyard, 2 separate blocks were co-fermented, then steered via a range of vinification techniques and maturation vessels. The deep purple colour is astounding, aromas of masses of violets, flint, and dark plum cake with baking spices. The palate then turns to pure dark plum and garden herb freshness. High intensity flavours, yet with an ease of flow and fine tannin grip. An exciting malbec expression. Screw cap. 13.5% alc. **Rating** 95 **To** 2030 $28 TL ✪

The Emergent McLaren Vale Mataro 2020 Fine aromas of black molten rock, tobacco leaf, kirsch and hung meat. Billowing South Oz sweetness marks the mid palate, but a burr of ferruginous tannins, Indian spice and juicy acidity resets a mien of savouriness. Very good. Screw cap. 14.2% alc. **Rating** 94 **To** 2029 $35 NG

ŸŸŸŸŸ **The Confluence McLaren Vale Grenache 2020** **Rating** 93 **To** 2026 $35 NG
The Ardent McLaren Vale Sagrantino 2019 **Rating** 93 **To** 2026 $35 NG
The Tendance McLaren Vale Shiraz 2019 **Rating** 92 **To** 2028 $35 NG
The Affinity McLaren Vale G, S & M 2020 **Rating** 92 **To** 2025 $35 NG
Welkin McLaren Vale Sagrantino Mataro 2020 **Rating** 92 **To** 2025 $28 NG
Welkin McLaren Vale Grenache 2020 **Rating** 91 **To** 2024 $28 NG
Welkin McLaren Vale Nero d'Avola 2020 **Rating** 91 **To** 2023 $28 NG
Project 5255 Welkin Langhorne Creek Malbec 2020 **Rating** 91 **To** 2026 $28 NG

Apogee ★★★★☆

1083 Golconda Road, Lebrina, Tas 7254 **Region** Northern Tasmania
T (02) 6395 6358 **www**.apogeetasmania.com **Open** By appt
Winemaker Dr Andrew Pirie **Est.** 2007 **Dozens** 1000 **Vyds** 2ha
Andrew Pirie (or Dr Andrew Pirie AM) has stood tall among those viticulturists and winemakers who have sought to understand and exploit Tasmania's terroir and climate over the past 40 years. He is as far removed from soap-box oratory as it is possible to be, quietly spoken and humble. His vision almost 50 years ago – longer still on some measures – saw the establishment of Pipers Brook Vineyard in 1974, using the detailed studies of Tasmania's regional climates in '72. In '77 he became the first (and last) person to complete study for his doctorate in viticulture from The University of Sydney. While making some of the best table wines to come from Tasmania in the last quarter of the 20th century, his focus shifted to sparkling wine in '99. In 2007 he acquired a 2ha site near Lebrina in the Pipers River district, planting pinot noir (62%), chardonnay (16%) and a little pinot meunier (2%) for sparkling wine, as well as pinot gris (20%) for table wine. Apogee's historic farm cottage is now an intimate cellar door where (by appointment) visitors can observe a hand disgorging demonstration. Pinot gris and pinot noir are also made under the Alto label. Exports to Germany and the US.

🍷🍷🍷🍷 **Deluxe Brut 2016** 53.3/39/7.7% chardonnay/pinot noir/meunier, traditional method, with 45 months on lees, disgorged Jan '20. Pale salmon hue; the bouquet is very complex, the palate even more so, with spiced strawberry fruits, brioche and soft acidity on the long finish. Diam. 12.6% alc. **Rating** 97 $63 JH ✪

🍷🍷🍷🍷 **Alto Pinot Noir 2019 Rating** 92 **To** 2029 $65 TS

Apricus Hill ★★★★☆

550 McLeod Road, Denmark, WA 6333 **Region** Denmark
T 0427 409 078 **www**.apricushill.com.au
Winemaker James Kellie **Est.** 1995 **Dozens** 800 **Vyds** 8ha
When the then owners of Somerset Hill Vineyard, Graham and Lee Upson, placed the vineyard on the market, James and Careena Kellie (of Harewood Estate) purchased it with 2 purposes: first, to secure a critical fruit source for Harewood, and second, to make and market a small range of single-vineyard, single-varietal wines for sale exclusively through the spectacular cellar door, with its sweeping vista. Thus Somerset Hill is now Apricus Hill. Exports to Japan.

🍷🍷🍷🍷 **Single Vineyard Denmark Pinot Noir 2019** Wildly aromatic – black cherry, chinotto, strawberry and olive tapenade. The palate follows suit; layered and distinctly Western Australian in its savoury, tannin-led approach to the palate. The phenolic structure carries the succulent fruit over the tongue and leads it through into a long finish. Really impressive. Screw cap. 14% alc. **Rating** 95 **To** 2028 $35 EL ✪

Arakoon ★★★☆

7/229 Main Road, McLaren Vale, SA 5171 **Region** McLaren Vale
T 0434 338 180 **www**.arakoonwines.com.au **Open** By appt
Winemaker Raymond Jones **Est.** 1999 **Dozens** 3000 **Vyds** 3.5ha
Ray and Patrik Jones' first venture into wine came to nothing: a 1990 proposal for a film about the Australian wine industry with myself (James) as anchorman. In 1999 they took the plunge into making their own wine and exporting it, along with the wines of others. As the quality of the wines has improved, so has the originally zany labelling been replaced with simple but elegant labels. Exports to Sweden, Denmark, Germany, Singapore, Malaysia and China.

🍷🍷🍷🍷 **Sellicks Beach McLaren Vale Shiraz 2019** A strongly regional wine which, while assertive and full bodied, is not as overpowering as the alcohol on the label suggests. Clove, black cherry, damson plum, Dutch licorice and violet. A meld of French and American oak imparts cedar, vanilla and some mocha notes. The finish is an open throttle, the flavours running smooth, long and a bit hot and sweet. Screw cap. 15% alc. **Rating** 90 **To** 2025 $22 NG
Sellicks Beach McLaren Vale Shiraz 2018 There is little integration between the oak and the rest of the wine's components here; instead, bourbon/vanilla flavours and cedary tannins are planted in the middle of the palate, directing blackcurrant, varnish, cherry and chinotto scents. Fairly long finish. Sweet across the end. Uncomplicated, but for those seeking a mouthful of flavour at a generous price, it is not a bad drink. Screw cap. 15% alc. **Rating** 90 **To** 2024 $22 NG

Aramis Vineyards ★★★★☆

411 Henley Beach Road, Brooklyn Park, SA 5032 **Region** McLaren Vale
T (08) 8352 2900 **www**.aramisvineyards.com
Winemaker Renae Hirsch (red), Peter Leske (white) **Est.** 1998 **Dozens** 12 000 **Vyds** 26ha
Aramis Vineyards was founded in 1998 by Lee Flourentzou. Located barely 2km from the Gulf of St Vincent, it is one of the coolest sites in McLaren Vale, planted to shiraz (18ha) and cabernet sauvignon (8ha), the 2 varieties best suited to the site. This philosophy leads Aramis to source grapes from other regions that best represent each variety, including sauvignon blanc and chardonnay from Adelaide Hills and riesling from Eden Valley. The city-based cellar door also features wines from other boutique producers. Exports to the US, Japan, Hong Kong, Singapore and NZ.

Aravina Estate

61 Thornton Road, Yallingup, WA 6282 **Region** Margaret River
T (08) 9750 1111 **www**.aravinaestate.com **Open** 7 days 10–5
Winemaker Ryan Aggiss **Est.** 2010 **Dozens** 10000 **Vyds** 28ha
In 2010 Steve Tobin and family acquired the winery and vineyard of Amberley Estate from Accolade, but not the Amberley brand. Steve has turned the property into a multifaceted business with a host of attractions including a sports car collection, restaurant and wedding venue.

Wildwood Ridge Reserve Margaret River Chardonnay 2019 Whole-bunch pressed direct to barrel (38% new), wild ferment, matured for 11 months, 60% mlf. Stone fruit and saline acidity are the first cabs off the rank, quickly followed by high-impact, toasty oak. The wood makes a splash, but it's good quality and well matched to the fruit, so we don't mind. 2019 was cool and produced aromatic wines of finesse and grace, of which this is one. Screw cap. 12.3% alc. **Rating** 95 **To** 2031 $45 EL

Limited Release Classic Muscat NV Brown muscat from 2019, with 7% 1960 frontenac from Swan Valley blended in. RS 258g/L. Quince, fig and date on the nose. The palate is rich and layered, with folds of christmas pudding, brandy sauce, salted caramel and dark chocolate. The aged component shines here, giving the wine depth and stature. There is a lot of sugar, perhaps a touch too much, but only by a whisker. This is very smart. Screw cap. 17.5% alc. **Rating** 95 $45 EL

The 'A' Collection Margaret River Cabernet Merlot Malbec 2020
Every year it seems there are more wineries in Margaret River producing cabernet malbec blends – and thank goodness. This blend is a match made in southwest heaven. Vibrant, juicy fruit bounces out of the glass: pomegranate, pink peppercorn, raspberry and licorice. This is brilliantly delicious, and the value for money is superb. Drink it while you wait for other such blends to come of age. It's a beauty. Screw cap. 13.5% alc. **Rating** 94 **To** 2031 $23 EL ✪

Single Vineyard Block 4 Margaret River Chenin Blanc 2019 **Rating** 93 **To** 2031 $35 EL
Single Vineyard Margaret River Shiraz 2020 **Rating** 93 **To** 2031 $35 EL
Wildwood Ridge Reserve Margaret River Cabernet Sauvignon 2018 **Rating** 93 **To** 2036 $50 EL
The 'A' Collection Margaret River Chenin Blanc 2020 **Rating** 92 **To** 2031 $23 EL ✪
Limited Release Margaret River Tempranillo 2020 **Rating** 92 **To** 2027 $35 EL
Wildwood Ridge Reserve Margaret River Malbec 2019 **Rating** 91 **To** 2031 $40 EL
The 'A' Collection Margaret River Shiraz Tempranillo 2020 **Rating** 90 **To** 2027 $23 EL

Arlewood Estate

679 Calgardup Road West, Forest Grove, WA 6286 **Region** Margaret River
T (08) 9757 6676 **www**.arlewood.com.au **Open** Fri–Sun 11–5 or by appt
Winemaker Cath Oates **Est.** 1988 **Dozens** 3000 **Vyds** 6.08ha
The antecedents of today's Arlewood shifted several times; they might interest a PhD researcher, but – with 1 exception – have no relevance to today's business. That exception was the 1999 planting of the vineyard by the (then) Xanadu winemaker Jurg Muggli. Garry Gossatti purchased the run-down, close-planted vineyard in 2008, and lived in the onsite house from '08–12, driving to Perth 1 day per week for his extensive hospitality/hotel business (which paid Arlewood's bills). His involvement in the resurrection of the vineyard was hands-on, and the cool site in the south of Margaret River was, and remains, his obsession. Garry's sons Jordan and Adrian now work in the vineyard and Garry drives down every weekend from Perth, clearly believing that the owner's footsteps make the best fertiliser. Exports to the UK, Hong Kong and China.

🍷🍷🍷🍷♀ **La Bratta Bianco Margaret River 2018** Very oak-driven at this stage, the characters associated with a year in French oak permeate the aromatics and the palate. Seriously structured, very long and concentrated. Green pineapple, citrus pith, guava and white currant. Flecks of cassis riddled throughout. The texture has an attractive waxiness to it. Suggest decanting to bring all the components together – that, or a vigorous swirl session. Screw cap. 13.5% alc. **Rating** 93 **To** 2028 $50 EL
Villaggio The Fumé Blanc Margaret River 2020 Intense passionfruit, gooseberry and kiwifruit on the nose and palate. The oak is surprisingly well integrated at this stage, perhaps owing to the very concentrated fruit. A well-executed partnership. Screw cap. 12% alc. **Rating** 92 **To** 2027 $22 EL ❂
Margaret River Cabernet Sauvignon 2018 While cabernet has a proclivity towards oak, in this case, the oak just wins out over the ripe fruit. The combination of the two will see it through a long life, but the oak is a bit assertive for short-term pleasure. Otherwise all things in place, and from a near-perfect vintage. Screw cap. 14% alc. **Rating** 92 **To** 2036 $40 EL
Villaggio Margaret River Nebbiolo 2019 Black cherry on the nose, a hint of tinned beetroot through the periphery, but this has some sarsaparilla charm. The fine tannins add structure and shape, but they're not seductively prohibitive, like nebbiolo tannins can be. Good length of flavour and a salivating coffee trace to the acid on the palate. Screw cap. 14% alc. **Rating** 90 **To** 2027 $40 EL

🍷🍷🍷🍷 **Margaret River White Blend #3 2020 Rating** 89 **To** 2024 $22 EL
Villaggio Margaret River Red Blend #3 2019 Rating 89 **To** 2031 $22 EL

Arlo Vintners ★★★★

8 Jones Road, Rutherglen, Vic 3685 **Region** Rutherglen
T 0431 037 752 **www.**arlovintners.com
Winemaker Dan Bettio, Lennie Lister **Est.** 2016 **Dozens** 400 **Vyds** 2.5ha
If you are thinking about starting a small winery from scratch, you must have a business plan. Dan Bettio and Lennie Lister are the owners of Arlo Vintners, each with over 20 years experience working in wine, chiefly in North East Victoria. Their plan is close to a template for others to adopt. Its credo is to select vineyards with something special about the region and adopt small-batch winemaking to produce 100 dozen bottles of each of their wines. They intend to open a cellar door in Rutherglen, the beating heart of North East Victoria.

🍷🍷🍷🍷🍷 **Old Vine Glenrowan Shiraz 2018** Glenrowan shiraz in all of its medium-bodied, velvety-tannined, fruit-forward beauty. Lifted aromatics, briar, mulberry, native pepper. Fine display of red/blue fruits with well-managed oak (a feature with this producer) falling away to a soft, quiet conclusion. Screw cap. 13.6% alc. **Rating** 94 **To** 2026 $29 JP ❂

🍷🍷🍷🍷♀ **King Valley Tannat 2018 Rating** 92 **To** 2031 $29 JP
Old Clone Glenrowan Durif 2018 Rating 92 **To** 2030 $29 JP
Gamay King Valley 2019 Rating 90 **To** 2024 $25 JP

Armstead Estate ★★★★

366 Moorabbee Road, Knowsley, Vic 3523 **Region** Heathcote
T (03) 5439 1363 **www.**armsteadestate.com.au **Open** 1st w'end of month 11–5 or by appt
Winemaker Rob Ellis **Est.** 2003 **Dozens** 1100 **Vyds** 0.6ha
The Armstead Estate vineyard is centrally located within the Heathcote region on the banks of Lake Eppalock. Founder Peter Armstead planted the first shiraz vines in 2003 on an east-facing slope just metres from the lake. Tom and Emily Kinsman purchased the estate in July '17, and intend to continue the business, growing and sourcing fruit from a number of well-known vineyards across the Heathcote region, making quality wines with the assistance of Rob Ellis.

♟♟♟♟♀ **Lakeside Heathcote Marsanne 2019** A full-bodied expression of the grape almost to the point of richness. Walks a fine line, but is saved by seamless acidity. Pronounced jasmine, honeysuckle with white peach, cut pear, preserved ginger, fig. It's complex with long length and persistence. Screw cap. 13% alc. **Rating** 92 **To** 2025 $28 JP

Moorabbee Road Heathcote Shiraz 2018 Looks the goods – deep, dark purple – and manages to typify what we love about Heathcote shiraz with its generosity and plushness. A rich vein of blackberries, plums lifted by high spice, pepper and blackstrap licorice. A gentle palate of savoury tannin and balanced oak tannins. Screw cap. 14.1% alc. **Rating** 92 **To** 2028 $30 JP

Roxy's Paddock Heathcote Shiraz 2018 Made with further ageing in mind, such is the tightness and structure of this wine. A fragrant young wine with complex aromas and flavours of plums, berries, spice and oak seamlessly folded in. Intense with length and a degree of elegance. Give it the time it deserves. Screw cap. 14.6% alc. **Rating** 92 **To** 2028 $35 JP

Coliban Block Heathcote Cabernet Sauvignon 2018 Presented as a lighter style of cabernet. It's certainly chock-full of lively fruit. Ripe, composed fruit on show with cassis, black cherry, Asian spice and pepper. The latter makes its presence known on the palate, together with an attractive leafiness and fine-grained tannins. Screw cap. 13.9% alc. **Rating** 90 **To** 2025 $35 JP

♟♟♟♟ **Little Vineyard Heathcote Sparkling Shiraz 2018** Rating 89 $45 JP
The Matilda Reserve Heathcote Shiraz 2018 Rating 88 To 2033 $55 JP

Artisans of Barossa ★★★★☆

16 Vine Vale Road, Tanunda, SA 5352 **Region** Barossa Valley
T (08) 8563 3935 www.artisansofbarossa.com **Open** 7 days 9–5
Winemaker Corey Ryan **Est.** 2005 **Dozens** 4000
Artisans of Barossa is a group of winemakers that share a like-minded approach to winemaking and enjoyment of wine. They are Hobbs of Barossa Ranges, Schwarz Wine Company, John Duval Wines, Sons of Eden and Spinifex. Each is highly successful in its own business, but relishes the opportunity of coming together to build on their collective winemaking skills and experience, knowledge of the vineyard landscape and their connections through the local wine community. The Artisans wines are made from grapes grown in the Barossa Valley, the Eden Valley, or both. Exports to Malaysia, Singapore, the UK and China.

♟♟♟♟♟ **Project 20 Duval Barossa Valley Grenache 2020** I love the detail and accuracy that John and Tim Duval have extracted from this vineyard. This is pure, unadulterated Barossa grenache in all of its flamboyant and fragrant exuberance. Rose petals, raspberries and strawberries, perfectly propelled by bright acidity and powder-fine, well-scaffolded tannins. Oak, whole bunches, method and madness are mere anecdotes. Delicious! Screw cap. 14.7% alc. **Rating** 95 **To** 2025 $42 TS

Project 20 Schell Barossa Valley Grenache 2020 Made by Spinifex. Gently fragrant and softly succulent, a testimony to Pete Schell's sensitivity with drawing out the supple, graceful side of grenache. Carbonic maceration heightens poached strawberry character and juicy texture, contrasting the exotic spice lift, herbal complexity and fine tannin grip of whole bunches. Excellent line, length and effortless glide. Delicious. Now. Screw cap. 14.7% alc. **Rating** 94 **To** 2024 $42 TS

♟♟♟♟♀ **Lot 8 Barossa Valley Grenache 2020** Rating 93 To 2023 $45 TS
Project 20 Schwarz Barossa Valley Grenache 2020 Rating 93 To 2025 $42 TS
Project 20 Ryan/Cowham Barossa Valley Grenache 2020 Rating 91 To 2025 $42 TS
Small Batch Barossa Valley Graciano 2018 Rating 91 To 2024 $38 TS

Artwine   ★★★★

72 Bird in Hand Road, Woodside, SA 5244 **Region** Adelaide Hills/Clare Valley
T 0411 422 450 **www**.artwine.com.au **Open** 7 days 11–5
Winemaker Contract **Est.** 1997 **Dozens** 10 000 **Vyds** 21ha
Owned by Judy and Glen Kelly, Artwine has 3 vineyards. Two are in Clare Valley: one on Springfarm Road, Clare; the other on Sawmill Road, Sevenhill. The 3rd vineyard is in the Adelaide Hills at Woodside, which houses their cellar door. Artwine currently has 15 varieties planted. The Clare Valley vineyards have tempranillo, shiraz, riesling, pinot gris, cabernet sauvignon, fiano, graciano, grenache, montepulciano, viognier and cabernet franc. The Adelaide Hills vineyard has prosecco, pinot noir, merlot and albariño.

♀♀♀♀♀ **Wicked Stepmother Clare Valley Fiano 2020** Trademark saline, field grass and faintly tonic-like aromas here with a touch of grapefruit on the palate, both flavour and pith. There's a pleasing weight and texture to the wine. Screw cap. 12.5% alc. **Rating** 92 **To** 2023 $35 TL

Ashbrook Estate   ★★★★★

379 Tom Cullity Drive, Wilyabrup, WA 6280 **Region** Margaret River
T (08) 9755 6262 **www**.ashbrookwines.com.au **Open** 7 days 10–5
Winemaker Catherine Edwards, Brian Devitt **Est.** 1975 **Dozens** 12 500 **Vyds** 17.4ha
This fastidious producer of consistently excellent estate-grown table wines shuns publicity and is less known than is deserved, selling much of its wine through the cellar door and to a loyal mailing list clientele. It is very much a family affair: Brian Devitt is at the helm, winemaking is by his daughter Catherine, and viticulture by son Richard (also a qualified winemaker). Exports to Singapore, Indonesia, Japan, China, Denmark, Germany, the UK and the US.

♀♀♀♀♀ **Reserve Wilyabrup Cabernet Sauvignon 2018** The nose here is reticent to open at this early stage in its life, although it does sing a song of pure cassis and blackberry, the oak resting in there as well. The palate has mellifluous density and very good length of flavour. This is medium-bodied elegance, and a perfect example of how 2018 produced wines of ripeness and clarity. Screw cap. 13.5% alc. **Rating** 95 **To** 2035 $65 EL

Margaret River Verdelho 2020 Crunchy acidity and a salivating plump mid palate which is crammed to bursting with nashi pear, green apple, soft talcy florals and gentle suggestions of citrus pith. Incredibly pretty, almost dusty, very satisfying and has great length of flavour. Screw cap. 13.5% alc. **Rating** 94 **To** 2027 $27 EL ✪

♀♀♀♀♀ **Gold Label Margaret River Riesling 2020** Rating 93 To 2031 $27 EL ✪
Margaret River Semillon 2020 Rating 93 To 2030 $27 EL ✪
Reserve Margaret River Chardonnay 2017 Rating 93 To 2036 $65 EL
Margaret River Cabernet Sauvignon 2018 Rating 93 To 2031 $35 EL
Margaret River Cabernet Franc 2018 Rating 92 To 2030 $45 EL
Margaret River Shiraz 2018 Rating 91 To 2028 $32 EL

Ashton Hills Vineyard   ★★★★★

126 Tregarthen Road, Ashton, SA 5137 **Region** Adelaide Hills
T (08) 8390 1243 **www**.ashtonhills.com.au **Open** Fri–Mon 11–5
Winemaker Stephen George, Liam Van Pelt **Est.** 1982 **Dozens** 3000 **Vyds** 3ha
Stephen George made Ashton Hills one of the great producers of Pinot Noir in Australia, and by some distance the best in the Adelaide Hills. With no family succession in place, he sold the business to Wirra Wirra in April 2015. (It had been rumoured for some time that he was considering such a move, so when it was announced, there was a sigh of relief that it should pass to a business such as Wirra Wirra, with undoubted commitment to retaining the extraordinary quality of the wines.) Stephen continues to live in the house on the property and provide ongoing consulting advice. Exports to the US, Hong Kong, Denmark, the Netherlands and China.

∇∇∇∇∇ **Reserve Pinot Noir 2020** As with the Reserve releases we've witnessed over many years, this has a latent power, deep down in the aromatic wells. Say it again – deep down. The fruit has a darker cherry expression, the fragrance in the nose rising gently, savoury forest-like elements on the palate well entwined. The weight is ethereal and exhibits a class, medium-bodied line and length, all of it lingering around the top and sides of your mouth for eons. So special, even tasted in its early stages of a long life. Screw cap. 13.5% alc. **Rating** 98 **To** 2030 $85 TL ✪ ♥

Piccadilly Valley Chardonnay 2020 This is straight-out-of-the-blocks pure and delicious chardonnay, with just the right amount of all the elements fitting exactly together: exact ripeness in the white stone-fruit flavours, citrus acidity, oak-encouraged creaminess and finishing pithy texture. Purity, refreshment, A-list. Screw cap. 12.5% alc. **Rating** 97 **To** 2028 $40 TL ✪

Reserve Pinot Noir 2019 A darker, more earthy and foresty feel here than the Estate version, and a different proportional mix of clones. The cherry sense is blacker fruit, while the acidity and mouthfeel are ramped up, evenly, to be more powerful once you engage. Likewise the aromatics, nose and palate, are poised, waiting to find their lift in time. Experience says this wine will be on another level in 5 years. Screw cap. 13.5% alc. **Rating** 97 **To** 2030 $80 TL ✪

∇∇∇∇∇ **Estate Pinot Noir 2020** There's a purity and gentility to this iteration, aromas teased with cherry fruits and woody forest notes. There's a sense of lightness. The faintest of Aperol-like bitters, deliciously balanced, gently savoury. Just right on all counts. Screw cap. 13.5% alc. **Rating** 95 **To** 2030 $60 TL

Estate Pinot Noir 2019 Aromatics and flavour profile run the full pinot fruit gamut of cherry and red plum. That's offset with a subtle bitters note on a palate that hums with an energetic acidity and even tannin length. Delicious. Screw cap. 13.5% alc. **Rating** 95 **To** 2028 $55 TL

Clare Valley Sparkling Shiraz 2015 Savoury, layered aromas to start. The palate shows off juicy crimson-berried flavours, a delicate mint jube note in there too, not too sweet at all. It's lifted by a fine mousse. Tannins coat the mouth to finish. A sophisticated iteration of sparkling shiraz that really should be heritage listed. Diam. 14% alc. **Rating** 95 $55 TL ♥

Piccadilly Valley Pinot Noir 2020 Created from estate fruit trickled down from higher-end wines, as well as from a few Valley neighbours. Woody forest notes weave their aromatic feel through the black cherry fruits, a decent portion (40%) of whole bunches showing its stemmy impact. Bright and breezy, with the house style's even tannins. Screw cap. 13.5% alc. **Rating** 94 **To** 2027 $40 TL

Single Vineyard Cemetery Block Adelaide Hills Pinot Noir 2020 This grower's block sits lower in the Piccadilly Valley, and has a warmer aspect than the estate vineyard, and yes the wine has more richness, more plushness of fruits, the herb and spice elements are more kitchen than forest – think anise-like flavours. Beautifully rounded and sculpted, a familiar house-crafted, gently tannin-coated exit completes the deal. Screw cap. 13.5% alc. **Rating** 94 **To** 2026 $55 TL

∇∇∇∇∇ **Piccadilly Valley Pinot Noir Rosé 2017 Rating** 91 **To** 2025 $40 TL

Atlas Wines   ★★★★☆

PO Box 458, Clare, SA 5453 **Region** Clare Valley
T 0419 847 491 **www**.atlaswines.com
Winemaker Adam Barton **Est.** 2008 **Dozens** 8000 **Vyds** 24ha
Before establishing Atlas Wines, owner and winemaker Adam Barton had an extensive winemaking career: in McLaren Vale, the Barossa Valley, Coonawarra, the iconic Bonny Doon Vineyard in California and at Reillys Wines in the Clare Valley. He has 6ha of shiraz and 2ha of cabernet sauvignon grown on a stony ridge on the eastern slopes of the region, and sources small batches from other distinguished sites in the Clare and Barossa valleys. The quality of the wines is extraordinarily good and consistent. Exports to the UK, the US and China.

ΨΨΨΨΨ **172° Watervale Riesling 2020** A compelling wine, yet starts a little subdued, revealing candied lemon and orange blossom, with a smidge of creamed honey. Then the palate unfurls with finesse, offering texture, fine acidity and a daikon radish crunch to the finish. Screw cap. 12% alc. **Rating** 95 **To** 2030 $30 JF ✪

ΨΨΨΨΨ **Clare Valley Rosé 2020 Rating** 93 **To** 2022 $24 JF✪
Watervale Riesling 2020 Rating 91 **To** 2030 $24 JF
The Spaniard Clare Valley 2019 Rating 91 **To** 2027 $28 JF

ATR Wines

103 Hard Hill Road, Armstrong, Vic 3377 **Region** Grampians
T 0457 922 400 **www.**atrwines.com.au **Open** Thurs–Sun & public hols 1–5
Winemaker Adam Richardson **Est.** 2005 **Dozens** 4000 **Vyds** 7.6ha
Perth-born Adam Richardson began his winemaking career in 1995, working for Normans, d'Arenberg and Oakridge along the way. He has held senior winemaking roles, ultimately with TWE America before moving back to Australia with wife Eva and children in late 2015. In '05 he had put down roots in the Grampians region, establishing a vineyard with old shiraz clones from the 19th century and riesling, extending the plantings with tannat, nebbiolo, durif and viognier. The wines are exceptionally good, no surprise given his experience and the quality of the vineyard. He has also set up a wine consultancy business, drawing on experience that is matched by few consultants in Australia. Exports to Europe.

ΨΨΨΨΨ **Hard Hill Road Writer's Block Great Western Riesling 2019** This is why we get excited by Grampians riesling! An enduring classic in the making, with impressive intensity from the start. A rich vein of lime cordial, lemon curd, citrus blossom, fresh-cut green apple and wet stone runs deep. Smooth, dry (that tweak of sugar melts into the richness), mouth-watering acidity and a sleek restraint. Quite an accomplishment. Screw cap. 12% alc. **Rating** 96 **To** 2032 $38 JP ✪ ♥
Chockstone Grampians Riesling 2020 Another good reason to look to the Grampians as a serious premium producer of riesling. The grape is so beautifully and expressively in charge, with just a bare minimum of winemaking input. The quality of the fruit is the key. Fragrant aromas of apple blossom, honeysuckle. lemon drop, nashi pear and green apple. Even in its youth it has great powers of persuasion with additional flinty, stony notes on the palate and lip-smacking acidity. Screw cap. 12.5% alc. **Rating** 95 **To** 2027 $25 JP ✪
Chockstone Grampians Shiraz 2019 Fully ripe grapes picked for pepper/ spice overtones to the fruit, matured in used American and French oak. A full-bodied shiraz, full of character and spice; texture, structure and balance all good. Thirty years won't tire it, and it needs 5+ more to open all the secrets lurking in the forest. Screw cap. 14.5% alc. **Rating** 95 **To** 2044 $28 JH ✪
Hard Hill Road Great Western Mule Variation 2018 A blend of nebbiolo, tannat, durif and shiraz in roughly equal proportions, made in a single open fermenter with wild and cultured yeast. Deeply coloured and full bodied, with persistent tannins. The bouquet is exotically spiced, almost into plum pudding, the palate adding black fruits to the equation. The name comes from the Tom Waits album of the same name. Screw cap. 14.5% alc. **Rating** 95 **To** 2045 $45 JH ♥
Hard Hill Road Great Western Petite Sirah 2018 Dense, inky colour all the way to the rim, but a flash of royal purple on the edge as the glass is tilted. The wine is full bodied, yet the tannins have fully resolved and don't actively intrude, nor does the alcohol. A unique and highly successful take on a wine with everlasting life, yet – with appropriate carnivore food – is ready now. Screw cap. 14.5% alc. **Rating** 95 **To** 2040 $50 JH
Chockstone Grampians Rosé 2020 Pretty tea rose in hue, with light, dusty florals, dried raspberry and a wild strawberry bouquet. It's a complex flavour profile, to be sure; textural too, but it also slips down very easily as well. Screw cap. 13.5% alc. **Rating** 94 **To** 2024 $25 JP ✪
Hard Hill Road Close Planted Great Western Shiraz 2018 Love the spice! Not sure if the intensity of the spice can be put down to the close-planted

vineyard (14000 vines/ha), but it's quite a scene stealer. Blue fruits, black cherry, dark chocolate-covered licorice and a touch of jubey pastille sweetness, all with lift and verve. Screw cap. 14.5% alc. **Rating** 94 **To** 2035 $45 JP

Hard Hill Road Great Western The Field 2018 A field blend of 52/22/ 10/9/5/2% shiraz/riesling/nebbiolo/durif/tannat/viognier, with 14 different clones and 3 distinct soil types creating obvious complexity. The contribution of the durif and tannat and the floral brightness of the white grapes is notable. Intense blackberry, ground nutmeg, cassia bark, rose petal, musk. The palate is a lively melange of flavours, textures. A true field blend, an original taste. Screw cap. 14.5% alc. **Rating** 94 **To** 2030 $45 JP ♥

ⵉⵉⵉⵉⵉ **Chockstone Grampians Pinot Gris 2020 Rating** 93 **To** 2025 $25 JH ☺

Atticus Wines
37 Mount View Terrace, Mount Pleasant, WA 6153 **Region** Margaret River
T (08) 9364 3885 **www**.atticuswines.com.au
Winemaker Richard Rowe (Consultant) **Est.** 2005 **Dozens** 7000 **Vyds** 33ha
A very successful venture under the control of CEO Ron Fraser. The wines come from the estate vineyards planted to chardonnay, semillon, sauvignon blanc, shiraz, cabernet sauvignon and merlot. The wines have 3 price levels: at the bottom end, the Chapman Grove range; then the Reserve Range; and, at the top, ultra-premium wines under the Atticus label. Exports to Canada, Hong Kong, Singapore, the Philippines, Thailand, Taiwan and China.

ⵉⵉⵉⵉⵉ **The Finch Collection Margaret River Chardonnay 2018** Opulent fruit is corseted by taut acidity that borders on aggressive. The fruit is wonderfully appealing; salted yellow peach, red apples and rhubarb, but you have to wait to drink it. Give the acid some time to work itself in. Screw cap. 13.2% alc. **Rating** 92 **To** 2032 $40 EL

ⵉⵉⵉⵉ **Chapman Grove Margaret River Sauvignon Blanc Semillon 2020** **Rating** 88 **To** 2022 $22 EL
Reserve Margaret River Chardonnay 2017 Rating 88 **To** 2025 $28 EL
The Finch Collection Margaret River. Red Blend 2018 Rating 88 **To** 2031 $40 EL

Atze's Corner Wines
451 Research Road, Nuriootpa, SA 5355 **Region** Barossa Valley
T 0407 621 989 **www**.atzes.com **Open** Fri–Sat 1–sunset, Sun & public hols 12–5.30
Winemaker Andrew Kalleske **Est.** 2005 **Dozens** 2500 **Vyds** 30ha
The seemingly numerous members of the Kalleske family have widespread involvement in grapegrowing and winemaking in the Barossa Valley. This venture is that of Andrew Kalleske, son of John and Barb. In 1975 they purchased the Atze Vineyard, which included a small block of shiraz planted in '12, but with additional plantings along the way, including more shiraz in '51. Andrew purchases some grapes from the family vineyard. It has 20ha of shiraz, with small amounts of mataro, petit verdot, grenache, cabernet, tempranillo, viognier, graciano, durif, montepulciano, vermentino and aglianico. The wines are all estate-grown and made onsite. The new cellar door opened in 2019, designed to enjoy the the sunset over the 100+yo vineyard. Exports to South Korea, Hong Kong and China.

ⵉⵉⵉⵉⵉ **The Giant Barossa Valley Durif 2018** All the bombastic impact of durif is packed into this deep purple thing of satsuma plum, black cherry and dark fruitcake spice. Licorice, dark chocolate oak and firm, fine, dry tannins bring up a finish of even persistence. Well executed. Screw cap. 14.8% alc. **Rating** 91 **To** 2026 $35 TS

Audrey Wilkinson

750 De Beyers Road, Pokolbin, NSW 2320 **Region** Hunter Valley
T (02) 4998 1866 **www.**audreywilkinson.com.au **Open** 7 days 10–5
Winemaker Xanthe Hatcher **Est.** 1866 **Vyds** 35.33ha
Audrey Wilkinson is one of the most historic and beautiful properties in the Hunter Valley, known for its stunning views and pristine vineyards. It was the first vineyard planted in Pokolbin, in 1866. The property was acquired in 2004 by the late Brian Agnew and has been owned and operated by his family since. The wines, made predominantly from estate-grown grapes, are released in 3 tiers: Audrey Wilkinson Series, Winemakers Selection and Reserve, the latter only available from the cellar door. Exports to the US, Canada, UK, Finland and Czech Republic.

The Ridge Hunter Valley Semillon 2011 Despite the bottle age there is still ample unresolved CO_2 providing aromatic perk, palate lift and an additional layer of protection for the fruit. Lightweight but rapier-like of intensity. Developing from youthful citrus into a late adolescence of quince, buttered toast, quinine, tonic and kinetic. Long and kinetic, unravelling across a stream of talcy acidity jitterbugging down the throat. Will continue to evolve for the better. Screw cap. 11% alc. **Rating** 96 **To** 2028 $80 NG

Reserve Malbec 2009 This has aged very well on re-release, hitting an apogee of tertiary complexity aligned with sprightly freshness, integrated malty oak, mid-palate succulence and impressive length. Aromas of mulch, porcini and wet earth. A core of sweet cherry. A smooth bone of tannin, guiding the fray. Clearly a top site. I'd drink this up sooner rather than later. Screw cap. 13.5% alc. **Rating** 95 **To** 2023 $120 NG

Marsh Vineyard Semillon 2018 Hand picked and fermented cool for fruit and freshness. This is excellent. Tightly coiled, with the kinetic energy of pumice-like mineral and palate-whetting acidity, a force to be reckoned with. Yet as always, this is lightweight. A wonderful paradox that makes semillon in the Hunter so compelling. Nascent and chiselled with citrus scents, talc and staining extract. Wait! Plenty more to come. Screw cap. 12.5% alc. **Rating** 94 **To** 2030 $40 NG

Winemakers Selection Hunter Valley Semillon 2011 Another excellent vintage, making me think that unlike other regions in the country, vintage characteristics here are disparate and less uniform. The wines, arguably more interesting as a result. CO_2, perky and unresolved. Aromas of lemon butter, quince, tangerine, candied citrus zest and toasted white bread. Broader, more open knit and pulpier of feel than The Ridge bottling. Delicious. Long. Utterly convincing. Screw cap. 11% alc. **Rating** 94 **To** 2026 $65 NG

The Lake Hunter Valley Shiraz 2019 Rating 93 **To** 2033 $120 NG
The Lake Hunter Valley Shiraz 2009 Rating 93 **To** 2022 $200 NG
Winemakers Selection Hunter Valley Tempranillo 2014 Rating 93 **To** 2024 $65 NG
Winemakers Selection Hunter Valley Malbec 2019 Rating 93 **To** 2028 $65 NG
Winemakers Selection Hunter Valley Shiraz 2019 Rating 91 **To** 2032 $40 NG

Auld Family Wines

21 Sydenham Road, Norwood, SA 5067 **Region** Barossa Valley
T 0433 079 202 **www.**auldfamilywines.com
Winemaker Simon Adams **Est.** 2018 **Dozens** 7000
The Barossa-based Auld family has been centrally involved with wine for 6 generations; the most recent, Jock and Sam Auld, have founded this new brand. They rightly celebrate their family history, starting with Patrick Auld, who arrived in SA in 1842, purchased 147ha of land at Magill adjacent to Captain Penfold, and began planting in '45, achieving fame for Auldana's wines. Second generation William Patrick Auld in '88 commenced a wine

and spirit business in Adelaide named WP Auld and Sons. Today's wines are branded The William Patrick, Strawbridge and Wilberforce – the last not the name of a family member, but a horse. Patrick Auld was a member of the expedition led by John McDouall Stuart that crossed Australia from south to north for the first time. He (Auld) rode his horse – named Wilberforce – which lived for 37 years. Exports to Hong Kong, the US and the UK.

ŦŦŦŦ **Strawbridge Barossa Valley Cabernet Sauvignon 2017** Cabernet comes to life in the Barossa's cooler seasons, brimming here with redcurrants, red capsicum, sage leaf and menthol. Fine, sappy tannins and tart acidity would both appreciate a little more ripeness, yet confidently hold a long and bright finish that calls for time to soften. Screw cap. 14% alc. **Rating** 89 **To** 2032 $42 TS

Austin's Wines

870 Steiglitz Road, Sutherlands Creek, Vic 3331 **Region** Geelong
T (03) 5281 1799 **www**.austinswines.com.au **Open** By appt
Winemaker Dwayne Cunningham **Est.** 1982 **Dozens** 25 000 **Vyds** 60ha
Pamela and Richard Austin have quietly built their business from a tiny base, and it has flourished. The vineyard has been progressively extended to 60ha. Son Scott (with a varied but successful career outside the wine industry) took over management and ownership in 2008. The quality of the wines is admirable.

ŦŦŦŦŦ **6Ft6 Geelong Rosé 2020** A charming pinot noir-based rosé that passes the tantalising colour test with flying colours in its bright hues of tea-rose pink. Summer berries, acacia, musk, gentle florals. A dusty, cherry-pip tang ignites the palate. There is a great energy here, aided by crisp acidity. Screw cap. 12.5% alc. **Rating** 91 **To** 2025 $25 JP
Moorabool Valley Geelong Pinot Noir 2019 Hot vintage conditions led to fast ripening so the winemaker has worked hard to present a wine moderate in alcohol, balanced in oak and nicely paced. Ripe, sweet, red berry fruit is the star, seasoned with thyme, sage, dark chocolate. Runs long and smooth in tannin. Screw cap. 13.2% alc. **Rating** 91 **To** 2027 $45 JP
6Ft6 King Valley Prosecco NV Sourced from the region most associated with prosecco in Australia and sealed with a screw cap, this super-effervescent bubbly hits the p-spot. Lemon sorbet, apple and pear vibrancy to start is joined by a light nuttiness on the palate. So much energy here with tangy acidity. Good flavour intensity throughout and a bubble that never gives up. Screw cap. 11% alc. **Rating** 91 **To** 2024 $25 JP
Moorabool Valley Geelong Chardonnay 2019 Not an easy vintage, with 9 days of 38+°C in the lead-up to harvest, but the result is a wine with freshness and flavour to burn. Ripe peach, nectarine, lemon citrus and honeysuckle. Crunchy acidity with good depth and textural layering. Screw cap. 13.2% alc. **Rating** 90 **To** 2026 $45 JP
6Ft6 King Valley Geelong Pinot Gris 2020 The 6Ft6 brand regularly over-delivers. Here, a blend of fruit from the King Valley and Geelong displays attractive gris qualities and super-fresh acid drive. Plenty of spiced apple, nashi pear, a dash of honeysuckle, a tickle of lemon rind and ginger across a gently textural background. Screw cap. 13% alc. **Rating** 90 **To** 2025 $25 JP

ŦŦŦŦ **6Ft6 Geelong Chardonnay 2020** **Rating** 88 **To** 2024 $25 JP
6Ft6 Geelong Shiraz 2019 **Rating** 88 **To** 2027 $25 JP

Aylesbury Estate

72 Ratcliffe Road, Ferguson, WA 6236 **Region** Geographe
T 0427 922 755 **www**.aylesburyestate.com.au
Winemaker Luke Eckersley, Damian Hutton **Est.** 2015 **Dozens** 6500 **Vyds** 9ha
Ryan and Narelle Gibbs (and family) are the 6th generation of the pioneering Gibbs family in the Ferguson Valley. When the family first arrived in 1883, they named the farm Aylesbury, after the town in England whence they came. For generations the family ran cattle on

the 200ha property, but in 1998 it was decided to plant 4.2ha of cabernet sauvignon as a diversification of the business. Merlot (2.5ha) followed in 2001, and sauvignon blanc (1.6ha) in '04. In '08 Ryan and Narelle took over ownership and management of the business from Ryan's father, selling the grapes until '15, when the first Aylesbury Estate wines were made. Three years later, Ryan and Narelle purchased the nearby 52 Stones vineyard, adding cooler-climate varieties chardonnay, arneis and gamay to the Aylesbury range. Exports to China.

ᵀᵀᵀᵀᵀ **Q05 Ferguson Valley Gamay 2020** Strawberry, red licorice, fennel flower, camphor, ash and red frog lollies. There is enough spicy nuance to make this more interesting than the bright nose suggests, the tannins almost subliminally wedged into the fine structure. The acidity has a real edge and refreshing lift on the palate. This is firmly in the nouveau style, delivering pleasure and smiles all round. Everything about this is well put together: the packaging, the wine and the price. Screw cap. 14% alc. **Rating** 95 **To** 2025 $30 EL ✪ ♥
The Pater Series Ferguson Valley Cabernet Sauvignon 2018 Dense ruby in colour, the aromatics speak of juniper, cassis, fennel and bay leaf. The palate is saturated in flavour and shaped by omnipresent tannins. Good length of flavour to finish. This is a serious wine, and for the price, very good value. Screw cap. 14.5% alc. **Rating** 95 **To** 2035 $45 EL

ᵀᵀᵀᵀ♀ **The Pater Series Ferguson Valley Chardonnay 2019 Rating** 93 **To** 2027 $45 EL
Q05 Ferguson Valley Arneis 2020 Rating 93 **To** 2025 $30 EL
Waterfall Gully Ferguson Valley Cabernet Sauvignon 2019 Rating 92 **To** 2025 $20 EL ✪

AZ Master Wines   ★★★☆

2/16 Wareham Street, Springvale, Vic 3171 (postal) **Region** Various
T 0456 789 116 **www**.azwines.com.au
Winemaker Various contract **Est.** 2006 **Dozens** 50 000
Awei Lin began sourcing wine in 2006, and exporting with Gapsted Wines in '08. The growth of the business led him to join forces with Zhiming Yi in '15. Derek Fitzgerald, Russell Burns and Richard Langford make the Barossa Valley wines (processed at Elderton, Cooper Burns and Lambert Estate). Oliver Crawford makes the Cabernet Sauvignon (a blend of Coonawarra and Limestone Coast grapes) and Peter Douglas makes the 100% Coonawarra wines at DiGiorgio, the barrels stored there and at Hollicks. Cellar doors are planned for all regions, the first in the Barossa Valley. Exports to China.

ᵀᵀᵀᵀ♀ **808 Barossa Valley Shiraz 2019** This is fully loaded and concocted but overall, the fruit lurking within is very good, albeit slathered with new oak. Full bodied with a cascade of ripe sweet blackberries and plums, awash with licorice and baking spices. Pillars of tannins come gritty and grunty yet there's a density and plushness that softens out the edges. Diam. 15.5% alc. **Rating** 91 **To** 2029 $79 JF
K Barossa Valley Shiraz 2018 A big red wine in a big heavy bottle. These are not positive attributes. Dark, rich and ripe fruits come dripping in licorice and molasses, oak and lots of extract overall. It's full bodied and covered in expansive tannins. Yet the palate has a sheen and it feels smooth, all the way through. Be warned, this is a high-octane red. Diam. 15% alc. **Rating** 90 **To** 2028 $49 JF

ᵀᵀᵀᵀ **005 Eden Valley Riesling 2020 Rating** 88 **To** 2024 $25 JF

B Minor   ★★★★☆

100 Long Gully Road, Healesville, Vic 3777 **Region** Victoria
T 0433 591 617 **www**.bminor.com.au
Winemaker Various **Est.** 2019 **Dozens** 5000
B Minor was originally a small artisan wine brand created in 2010 focusing on producing fresh, creative wines specifically targeting on-premise and specialty retail venues in the US and Australia. Its original philosophy was to create an international brand. In 2020, QiQi Fu

bought out a partner in B Minor and runs the business, enlisting Best's Wines as a contract winemaker. QiQi Fu now principally sells B Minor wines through the B Minor website in addition to Melbourne retailers and restaurants. Exports to China.

♀♀♀♀ Grampians Shiraz 2019 Reveals a vibrant energy which is more than enough to revitalise tired tastebuds. Deep, dense purple. Fresh picked blueberries, black plums, spice, cedar and that irresistible touch of local bush mint/bayleaf. Palate is velvety, ripe, and plush. A mighty smart and lively young shiraz with a big future. Diam. 14.5% alc. **Rating** 95 **To** 2036 $33 JP ○

♀♀♀♀   Heathcote Shiraz 2020 **Rating** 88 **To** 2023 $17 JP ○

Baarmutha Wines   ★★★☆

1184 Diffey Road, Beethworth, Vic 3747 **Region** Beechworth
T (03) 5728 2704 **www**.baarmuthawines.com.au **Open** By appt
Winemaker Vincent Webb **Est.** 2006 **Dozens** 300 **Vyds** 2ha
Vincent Webb is a modern-day Renaissance man. He is a graduate of oenology and viticulture at CSU, but his full-time occupation is scheduler with Ausnet Services. He manages the vineyard and winery with 'plenty of help' from wife Sharon, and their young sons. Family and friends hand-select the fruit at harvest, and small quantities of wine are made using precisely what you would expect: a basket press, open vat fermenters, wild yeast fermentation, and maturation in new and used French oak.

♀♀♀♀ Beechworth Chardonnay 2018 A maker with a minimal-intervention philosophy. Quality fruit is at the heart of this attractive chardonnay dressed in signature Beechworth citrus – grapefruit, lemon – with stone fruit, white flowers and an oyster shell/saline brightness. Fills the mouth. Acidity is just right, tying all the flavours up tight. Luscious from start to finish. Screw cap. 13% alc. **Rating** 92 **To** 2027 $40 JP

 Backline   ★★★☆

169 Douglas Gully Road, Blewitt Spings SA 5171 **Region** McLaren Vale
T 0439 479 758 **www**.backlinewines.com.au
Winemaker Ben Riggs **Est.** 2020 **Dozens** 5500
The Backline label falls under the aegis of Three Kings Wine Merchants, a collaboration between winemaker Ben Riggs, former Wallaby Nathan Sharpe and ex-LVMH marketeer, David Krenich. With no cellar door, sales rely on an online shopping portal, drawing on a broad network of celebrity support. The wines are largely reliant on McLaren Vale and Langhorne Creek sources, marked with salubrious oak and plenty of extract at the pointy end of the hierarchy. (NG)

♀♀♀♀ McLaren Vale Shiraz 2018 A sumptuous, fully loaded shiraz. Scents of black/ maraschino cherry meld with coffee bean, mocha oak, kirsch and bitter chocolate. The grape tannins are firm, warding off the prodigious extract. If one is after a behemoth such as this, it is very well constructed. Tangy on the finish. Diam. 14.5% alc. **Rating** 93 **To** 2034 $50 NG

BackVintage Wines   ★★★★☆

2/177 Sailors Bay Road, Northbridge, NSW 2063 **Region** Various
T (02) 9967 9880 **www**.backvintage.com.au **Open** Mon–Fri 9–5
Winemaker Julian Todd, Nick Bulleid MW, Mike Farmilo (Contract) **Est.** 2003
Dozens 10 000
BackVintage Wines does not own vineyards or a winery. Says Nick Bulleid, 'We buy grapes, manage the fermentation and subsequent maturation. We also blend bulk wine sourced from some of the best winemakers throughout Australia.' The value for money offered by these wines is self-evident and quite remarkable.

Bailey Wine Co

PO Box 368, Penola, SA 5277 **Region** Coonawarra
T 0417 818 539 **www**.baileywineco.com
Winemaker Tim Bailey **Est.** 2015 **Dozens** 750
After two decades living and working in Coonawarra, Tim Bailey decided to take a busman's holiday by establishing his own small wine business. Tim worked at Leconfield for 21 years, and has also worked in the Sonoma Valley of California, travelling through the Napa Valley as well as France. Tim has a simple philosophy: 'Find great growers in the regions and let the vineyard shine through in the bottle.' Thus he sources Clare Valley riesling, Grampians shiraz, Adelaide Hills chardonnay and Coonawarra cabernet sauvignon. Exports to China.

🍷🍷🍷🍷🍷 **Hyde Park Vineyard Grampians Shiraz 2018** Enticing dark purple hue and no denying its DNA – Grampians through and through. While ultimately a savoury drink, it has a core of plump, juicy fruit spiced with cinnamon, pepper and Aussie bush seasoning. Full bodied, the palate lengthened by layers of smoky meaty nuances, roasted hazelnuts and amazingly velvety, tamed tannins. Screw cap. 14% alc. **Rating** 95 **To** 2033 $30 JF ✪

Baileys of Glenrowan

779 Taminick Gap Road, Glenrowan, Vic 3675 **Region** Glenrowan
T (03) 5766 1600 **www**.baileysofglenrowan.com.au **Open** 7 days 10–5
Winemaker Paul Dahlenburg, Elizabeth Kooij **Est.** 1870 **Dozens** 15 000 **Vyds** 144ha
Since 1998 the utterly committed Paul Dahlenburg has been in charge of Baileys and has overseen an expansion in the vineyard and the construction of a 2000t capacity winery. The cellar door has a heritage museum, winery viewing deck, contemporary art gallery and landscaped grounds preserving much of the heritage value. Baileys has also picked up the pace with its muscat and topaque, reintroducing the Winemakers Selection at the top of the tree, while continuing the larger volume Founder series. Casella Family brands purchased the brand and the Glenrowan property from TWE in December 2017. The vineyards and winery have been steadily undergoing conversion to organic since 2011, producing the first full range of certified organic table wines from the 2019 vintage. Baileys had plenty to celebrate for its 150th anniversary in 2020.

🍷🍷🍷🍷🍷 **Founder Series Classic Topaque NV** Baileys turned 150 in '20, celebrating a proud fortified wine history, manifest in this wine of some finesse. Lifted, super-fresh and raisiny, malty in aroma. Filigree-fine on the tongue, with the lasting presence of butterscotch, smoky lapsang souchong tea, licorice block, honey and a touch of Asian spice. Clean as a whistle on delivery. Combines freshness and complexity. Vino-Lok. 17% alc. **Rating** 95 $30 JP ✪
Winemakers Selection Rare Old Topaque NV At home in Glenrowan on the granitic soils of the Warby Ranges, Baileys fortifieds are generally of the lifted and aromatic school. Dense mahogany colour; aromas of spring florals, roses, dried fruits, orange peel and roasted almond are true to form. A fine line of refreshing neutral spirit runs the length of the palate. Rich and textural with crème caramel, walnut brownies, layers of sweet spice, and so much more. Beauty in the glass. 375ml. Vino-Lok. 17.5% alc. **Rating** 95 $75 JP
Winemakers Selection Rare Old Muscat NV A joy to behold. Combines complexity and age with freshness – the hallmark of a top Rare fortified. Aromas of sticky date pudding – so good – dried fruits, grilled hazelnuts and prunes. Smooth. Rolls off the tongue with luscious ease. Clean spirit and well integrated. 375ml. Vino-Lok. 17.5% alc. **Rating** 95 $75 JP

🍷🍷🍷🍷🍷 **Founder Series Classic Muscat NV Rating** 92 $30 JP

Baillieu

Merricks General Wine Store, 3460 Frankston-Flinders Road, Merricks, Vic 3916
Region Mornington Peninsula
T (03) 5989 7622 www.baillieuvineyard.com.au **Open** 7 days 8.30–5
Winemaker Geraldine McFaul **Est.** 1999 **Dozens** 2500 **Vyds** 9ha
Charlie and Samantha Baillieu have re-established the former Foxwood Vineyard, growing chardonnay, viognier, pinot gris, pinot noir and shiraz. The north-facing vineyard is part of the 64ha Bulldog Run property owned by the Baillieus, and is immaculately maintained. The Merricks General Wine Store is a combined bistro/providore/cellar door.

Mornington Peninsula Pinot Noir 2019 There's a lot to like here. At once tangy and juicy, with some tartness and grip to the tannins, but this works off a medium-bodied frame. Layered with cherries, rhubarb, baking spices and infused with smoky woodsy notes. Everything is in its place and while best enjoyed as a young wine, there's enough acidity to give it an edge for short-term cellaring. Screw cap. 13.5% alc. **Rating** 93 **To** 2027 $40 JF

Mornington Peninsula Vintage Brut 2018 **Rating** 88 $35 JF

bakkheia

2718 Ferguson Road, Lowden, WA 6240 **Region** Geographe
T (08) 9732 1394 www.bakkheia.com.au **Open** By appt
Winemaker Michael Edwards **Est.** 2006 **Dozens** 1000 **Vyds** 3ha
This is the retirement venture of Michael and Ilonka Edwards. Michael had 25 years as a clearance diver with the Australian Navy, and then pursued a career in the marine industry. Ilonka had a long-term involvement in the Vogue fashion/food/lifestyle magazines while based in Sydney. They found their way to the Preston Valley in the Geographe region of WA in 2005 and purchased a property that had a patch of cabernet sauvignon planted in 1999. They now have 3ha of grenache, mourvèdre, graciano, tempranillo, cabernet sauvignon, shiraz and malbec; purchasing chardonnay and sauvignon blanc from a neighbour. They have an unusual approach to marketing, starting with the winery name linked to the Roman words for Bacchus and bacchanalian frenzies induced by wine, lots of wine. When the time came to make and sell wine, rather than sell through liquor stores, they set up a membership system. Exports to Singapore.

Cojones Muy Grandes Preston Valley Rosé 2020 Organic grenache, cabernet sauvignon and mourvèdre from the Preston Valley. The rosé is both fine and juicy, with plenty of berry fruit and great length of flavour. Cheesecloth, pomegranate, Turkish delight and raspberry humbug. A lot to like. Screw cap. 12.4% alc. **Rating** 93 **To** 2022 $20 EL **✪**
United & Undaunted Preston Valley Mourvèdre 2018 This has satsuma plum, earthy tannins and wild raspberry. The spice component is dominated by licorice, fennel and aniseed. A core of mulberry on the palate is surrounded by savoury tannin, carrying it over the palate and through the finish. Screw cap. 14.2% alc. **Rating** 93 **To** 2027 $28 EL

Balgownie Estate

Hermitage Road, Maiden Gully, Vic 3551 **Region** Bendigo
T (03) 5449 6222 www.balgownieestatewines.com.au **Open** 7 days 11–5
Winemaker Tony Winspear **Est.** 1969 **Dozens** 10000 **Vyds** 35.28ha
Balgownie Estate is the senior citizen of Bendigo, its original vineyard plantings now 50 years old. The estate also has a cellar door in the Yarra Valley (Yarra Glen), where operations fit in neatly with the Bendigo wines. Balgownie has the largest vineyard-based resort in the Yarra Valley, with over 65 rooms and a limited number of spa suites. In April 2016 a Chinese investment company purchased the Balgownie Bendigo and Yarra Valley operations for $29 million. Exports to the UK, the US, Canada, Fiji, Hong Kong, Singapore, China and NZ.

🍷🍷🍷🍷🍷 Centre Block Bendigo Shiraz 2018 A shiraz rich in Central Victorian charm and honest flavours of its terroir. Buoyant aromas of blackberry, mint, bitter chocolate and earth. Beautifully integrated, everything in its place, with a smooth ride to the finish. Screw cap. 14.2% alc. **Rating** 95 **To** 2030 $65 JP

🍷🍷🍷🍷🍷 Bendigo Cabernet Sauvignon 2018 **Rating** 93 **To** 2026 $45 JP
Bendigo Shiraz 2018 **Rating** 92 **To** 2030 $45 JP
White Label Bendigo Merlot Cabernet Franc 2018 **Rating** 91 **To** 2028 $45 JP

Ballandean Estate Wines   ★★★★

Sundown Road, Ballandean, Qld 4382 **Region** Granite Belt
T (07) 4684 1226 **www**.ballandeanestate.com **Open** 7 days 9–5
Winemaker Dylan Rhymer, Angelo Puglisi **Est.** 1932 **Dozens** 12 000 **Vyds** 34.2ha
A rock of ages in the Granite Belt, owned by the ever-cheerful and charming Angelo Puglisi and wife Mary. Mary has introduced a gourmet food gallery at the cellar door, featuring foods produced by local food artisans as well as Greedy Me gourmet products made by Mary herself. Ballandean Estate can't always escape the unpredictable climate of the Granite Belt. Exports to China.

🍷🍷🍷🍷🍷 Opera Block Granite Belt Shiraz 2018 50th Anniversary of the Opera Block vines. Medium purple. Dark berry/cherry/plum fruit with hints of prune. Tense acidity collides with warm alcohol and firm, fine oak tannins on a finish of medium persistence. There's plenty of potential here, though a screw cap would serve it better in the cellar. ProCork. 14.8% alc. **Rating** 90 **To** 2038 $65 TS

Ballycroft Vineyard & Cellars

1 Adelaide Road, Greenock, SA 5360 **Region** Barossa Valley
T 0488 638 488 **www**.ballycroft.com **Open** 7 days 11–4 by appt
Winemaker Joseph Evans **Est.** 2005 **Dozens** 600 **Vyds** 4ha
This micro-business is owned by Joseph and Sue Evans. Joe's life on the land started in 1984; he later obtained a viticulture degree from Roseworthy. Between '92 and '99 he worked in various capacities at Rockford Wines, and then at Greenock Creek Wines. Joe and Sue are a 2-person band, so would-be visitors to the cellar door would be wise to make an appointment for a personal tasting with one of them. Groups of up to 8 are welcome.

Balnaves of Coonawarra

15517 Riddoch Highway, Coonawarra, SA 5263 **Region** Coonawarra
T (08) 8737 2946 **www**.balnaves.com.au **Open** Mon–Fri 9–5, w'ends 11.30–4.30
Winemaker Pete Bissell **Est.** 1975 **Dozens** 10 000 **Vyds** 74.33ha
Grapegrower, viticultural consultant and vigneron, Doug Balnaves has over 70ha of high-quality estate vineyards. The wines are invariably excellent, often outstanding; notable for their supple mouthfeel, varietal integrity, balance and length – the tannins are always fine and ripe, the oak subtle and perfectly integrated. Coonawarra at its best. Exports to the UK, the US, Canada, Indonesia, South Korea and China.

🍷🍷🍷🍷🍷 The Tally Reserve Cabernet Sauvignon 2018 A magnificent Tally. The fruit has a great depth of flavour and the X-factor that any reserve should. Deep and fragrant, with a brightness of fruit not always obvious in this flagship. Coffee grounds and dark chocolate, studded with mint and hazelnuts. Fuller bodied with fine, gravelly tannins that give texture as much as definition. It needs more time but, wow, it will reward big time! ProCork. 14.5% alc. **Rating** 96 **To** 2043 $100 JF
Shiraz 2019 A lot is packed into this wine, yet it takes everything in its stride and comes out as a more mid-weighted offering. Dark sweet fruits abound. So, too, spices, dark chocolate, coffee grounds and a sprinkle of crushed bay leaves. The tannins have some grit, yet are shapely and ripe. Oak adds some sweet, cedary

seasoning, and is well incorporated. Screw cap. 14.5% alc. **Rating** 95 **To** 2033 $30 JF ✪

Cabernet Sauvignon 2018 All cabernet, and it's marching to its own tune. Hum along to the chorus of pristine flavours of blackberries, mulberries, juniper and baking spices, plus some chocolate flecked with mint. The palate is well contained, with sweet fruit and oak neatly played out. Tannins are lovely – grainy and textural. Screw cap. 14.5% alc. **Rating** 95 **To** 2038 $45 JF

🍷🍷🍷🍷 **The Blend 2018 Rating** 92 **To** 2030 $22 JF ✪

Bangor Vineyard

20 Blackman Bay Road, Dunalley, Tas 7177 **Region** Southern Tasmania
T 0418 594 362 **www.**bangorshed.com.au **Open** 7 days 11–5
Winemaker Tasmanian Vintners **Est.** 2010 **Dozens** 2000 **Vyds** 4ha
Bangor Vineyard's story starts in 1830, when John Dunbabin, convicted of horse stealing, was transported to Van Diemen's Land. Through sheer hard work he earned his freedom and bought his own land, paving the way for 5 generations of farming at Bangor. Today it is a 6200ha property on the Forestier Peninsula in one of the most southerly parts of Tasmania, with 5100ha of native forest, grasslands and wetlands, and 35km of coastline. Both Matt and Vanessa Dunbabin have PhDs in plant ecology and plant nutrition, putting beyond question their ability to protect this wonderful property – until 2000ha were burnt in the 2013 bushfires that devastated their local town of Dunalley and surrounding areas. They established a cellar door in partnership with Tom and Alice Gray from Fulham Acquaculture, also badly affected by the fires. Hence the Bangor Vineyard Shed was born. The vineyard is planted to 1.5ha each of pinot noir and pinot gris, and 1ha of chardonnay. A host of very well-made and sensibly priced wines mark a welcome return to the *Companion*.

Banks Road

600 Banks Road, Marcus Hill, Vic 3222 **Region** Geelong
T (03) 5258 3777 **www.**banksroad.com.au **Open** Fri–Sun 11–5
Winemaker William Derham **Est.** 2001 **Dozens** 2000 **Vyds** 6ha
Banks Road is a family-owned and operated winery on the Bellarine Peninsula. The estate vineyard is adopting biodynamic principles, eliminating the use of insecticides and moving to eliminate the use of all chemicals on the land. The winery not only processes the Banks Road grapes, but also makes wine for other small producers in the area. All in all, an impressive business.

🍷🍷🍷🍷🍷 **Will's Selection Bellarine Peninsula Chardonnay 2016** From 4 rows, enough to produce 2 barrels. Wild-yeast fermented in barrel, with 50% mlf. Gleaming straw green. An interesting chardonnay, relatively early picked, with fresh, light stone fruit first up, then a creamy cashew finish. Travelling well. Screw cap. 12.8% alc. **Rating** 95 **To** 2026 $55 JH

Will's Selection Bellarine Peninsula Pinot Noir 2018 Immediately impresses with that Mediterranean-style garrigue scrub, dried flowers and leafy, lifted aromatic fragrance. Smells of the soil, the bush, of spice and dried herbs, with red cherry and pomegranate. Equally enticing on the palate, with depth and intrigue. Screw cap. 13.6% alc. **Rating** 95 **To** 2026 $55 JP

Soho Road Vineyard Barrique Eight Bellarine Peninsula Pinot Noir 2018 A fragrant and complex bouquet of some delicacy. A wonderful opening gambit, gaining further ground on the palate with wood smoke, forest undergrowth, dark cherry and stylish oak. Lingers long. Screw cap. 13.2% alc. **Rating** 95 **To** 2028 $75 JP

Soho Road Vineyard Bellarine Peninsula Pinot Noir 2018 A walk on the wild side awaits. Intense undergrowth, earth, humus, dried herb aromas. Bold confidence on the palate, peppery with red cherry, pomegranate, savoury tannins and real depth boosted by some fine winemaking attention to detail. Screw cap. 13.2% alc. **Rating** 95 **To** 2026 $40 JP

Soho Road Vineyard Bellarine Peninsula Chardonnay 2018 Carrying plenty of solid oak input, struck flint and biscuity, buttery components that, at times, overshadow the finer aspects of the chardonnay fruit. Complexity is clearly the aim. White nectarine, nougat, grapefruit, baked apple and buttered toast go hand in hand with the oak. Would reward with a little more ageing. Screw cap. 12.4% alc. **Rating** 94 **To** 2025 $40 JP

TTTT **Bellarine Chardonnay 2017 Rating** 89 **To** 2025 $36 JP
Bellarine Pinot Grigio 2019 Rating 89 **To** 2024 $24 JP
Bellarine Shiraz 2018 Rating 89 **To** 2026 $36 JP

Bannockburn Vineyards ★★★★★

92 Kelly Lane, Bannockburn, Vic 3331 (postal) **Region** Geelong
T (03) 5281 1363 **www.**bannockburnvineyards.com **Open** By appt
Winemaker Matthew Holmes **Est.** 1974 **Dozens** 6000 **Vyds** 21.2ha
The late Stuart Hooper had a deep love for the wines of Burgundy, and was able to drink the best. When he established Bannockburn, it was inevitable that pinot noir and chardonnay would form the major part of the plantings, with lesser amounts of riesling, sauvignon blanc, cabernet sauvignon, shiraz and merlot. Bannockburn is still owned by members of the Hooper family, who continue to respect Stuart's strong belief in making wines that reflect the flavours of the (certified organic) vineyard. Exports to Canada, China, Hong Kong, Japan, Singapore and the UK.

TTTTT **Serré 2018** Another top year for Serré, the embodiment of pinot power teamed with refined poise. A rootsy (aka dusty beetroot), red-fruited, hyper-spiced, aromatic entrance. Supremely confident in promise and delivery. So much to take in: forest floor, game, black cherry, smoky cranberry, with a floral interlude of violet and lavender. Tannin weaves its way through to the finish. Screw cap. 13.5% alc. **Rating** 96 **To** 2035 $97 JP
Geelong Chardonnay 2020 Has the groundwork well in place for a long life ahead, with a solid fruit base of citrus, stone fruits, baked biscuit and just a lick of oak spice. Already revealing good balance and a seamless acidity. Screw cap. 13% alc. **Rating** 95 **To** 2030 $67 JP
Geelong Chardonnay 2019 Fresh and crunchy. Nectarine, white peach and grapefruit pith segues beautifully into baked pear tart and almond. A complex youngster, and it's only just starting out. The dry year with an early harvest start has not affected the wine's innate vivacity and charm. Plenty of flavour with restraint, acidity is there but not a feature. Nothing is forced. Screw cap. 13.5% alc. **Rating** 95 **To** 2032 $67 JP
S.R.H. 2017 Deep complex scents of stone fruit, roasted nuts, wild herbs, fennel. Soars with one voice on the palate with complex, layered fruit vying for attention against a rich vein of wood smoke, grilled nuts and refreshing acidity. Screw cap. 13% alc. **Rating** 95 **To** 2033 $77 JP
Geelong Shiraz 2017 This welcomes the drinker with a big burst of whole-bunch intensity: herbal, spicy and peppery. The wow moment continues on the palate and builds, delivering satiny texture, a sleek black-fruit profile and structure. The gentle savoury touches are a bonus. There's a lot to taste and enjoy here. Screw cap. 12.5% alc. **Rating** 95 **To** 2031 $46 JP
De La Terre 2018 Nothing shy about De La Terre. Front and centre with a riot of pinot fruit, full of energy and joie de vivre. The fragrance is all about spices, red and blue berries, forest floor and autumnal shades. Medium bodied, warm and free flowing. Generous in tannin, sporting a sweet spot of confection, licorice and dark chocolate. Screw cap. 13% alc. **Rating** 94 **To** 2030 $67 JP

Barossa Valley Estate ★★★

8 Kraehe Road, Marananga, SA 5352 **Region** Barossa Valley
T (08) 8568 6900 **www.**barossavalleyestate.com **Open** 7 days 10–4.30
Winemaker Ryan Waples **Est.** 1985 **Dozens** 100 000 **Vyds** 180ha

When Barossa Valley Estate was placed in receivership in 2013, a number of Australian wine businesses looked at the opportunity of acquisition, but most observers were surprised when the successful bidder was revealed as NZ-based Delegat, and even more surprised at the price of A$24.7 million. Delegat's economic engine is the Oyster Bay brand, its Sauvignon Blanc centre stage. While Barossa Valley Estate only owns 40ha of shiraz, cabernet merlot, grenache, chardonnay and marsanne, it has extensive contracts with the grapegrowers who were its shareholders when the receiver was appointed. Managing Director Jim Delegat revealed that the acquisition was funded through existing bank facilities even though Delegat had acquired the Hawke's Bay Matariki Group for NZ$8.5 million in Jan '14, this in turn following vineyard acquisitions in '12. The arrival of Delegat has had a dramatic effect; production has increased from 50 000 dozens to 141 500, and the estate vineyards are now almost touching 300ha, many times greater than the 40ha previously owned. Exports to the UK, the US, Ireland, Canada, Singapore, China and NZ.

ŸŸŸŸ **E&E Black Pepper Limited Release Shiraz 2016** A big, bold Black Pepper. Full, vibrant purple red. Deep, dark blackberry and prune fruit meets the full-frontal impact of long ageing in new French oak, making for a savoury and leathery style. Firm, coarse oak tannins conspire with hot alcohol to build a grainy and dry finish. It screams out for time to subsume oak and tannin, but lacks the fruit brightness and body to go the distance. Cork. 15% alc. **Rating** 89 **To** 2028 $100 TS

Barr-Eden Estate   ★★★★

PO Box 117, Nuriootpa, SA 5355 **Region** Barossa Valley
T 0437 091 277 **www.**loveovergold.com.au
Winemaker Contract **Est.** 2014 **Dozens** 400 **Vyds** 6.25ha
Loved by all who knew him, Bob McLean stood large over many parts of the SA wine industry and in 1997 he purchased a block of shiraz in the Eden Valley planted by the Pollner family in 1858, tended by the family for almost 150 years. Bob became very ill, ultimately passing away in April 2015. He was a friend of one of the Barossa's most esteemed grapegrowers, Joel Matschoss, who effectively looked after the vineyard in the last years of Bob's life. In '14 Joel showed the fruit to Pierre-Henri Morel, newly arrived from the Northern Rhône Valley, where he had been Michel Chapoutier's right-hand man. Pierre-Henri was so impressed, he and Joel purchased the fruit, vinified it and Love Over Gold was born. In '16 they created Avenue to Gold from a younger block on the same property. A joint venture followed between Joel, Pierre-Henri, Michael Twelftree and Tim Hower to acquire the property. The plan is to expand the vineyard size and to buy parcels of high-quality Eden Valley fruit, including grenache. Exports to the UK, the US, Canada, France, South Korea, Singapore and China.

ŸŸŸŸŸ **Love Over Gold Mengler's Hill Eden Valley Grenache 2018** From one of South Australia's highest grenache vineyards, this miniscule production of 300 bottles represents a beautifully refined, fragrant and fine-boned grenache. Rose petals, raspberries and wild strawberries embrace grenache's delicate side, intricately framed in powder-fine tannins and the cool, bright morello cherry acidity of this site high atop Mengler's Hill. Diam. 14.3% alc. **Rating** 94 **To** 2026 $35 TS

ŸŸŸŸŸ **Dreams of Gold Mengler's Hill Eden Valley Shiraz 2020** Rating 93 **To** 2035 $35 TS

Barringwood   ★★★★☆

60 Gillams Road, Lower Barrington, Tas 7306 **Region** Northern Tasmania
T 0416 017 475 **www.**barringwood.com.au
Winemaker Josef Chromy Wines (Jeremy Dineen) **Est.** 1993 **Dozens** 3000 **Vyds** 5ha
Barringwood has been producing elegant wines from the ultra-cool climate of northwest Tasmania for over 20 years, the vines planted in 1993. The vineyard is perched on a steep north-facing slope (overlooking the Don valley across to Bass Strait), with one of the longest growing seasons in Tasmania allowing the grapes time to develop complexity while retaining

acidity. Vanessa and Neil Bagot were captivated by the property and purchased Barringwood in 2012. They have developed two new vineyards at Cranbrook and Evandale, with further plantings planned.

🍷🍷🍷🍷 **Blanc de Blanc 2015** A seamless contrast between bright, vibrant chardonnay and a creamier texture and complexity than expected from 4 years on lees. Spicy pear, apple and grapefruit glide long and focused amid brioche, mixed spice and the beginnings of fruit-mince spice. A brilliant finish illuminated by mouth-watering Tasmanian acidity. Barringwood's finest yet. Diam. 11.5% alc. **Rating** 94 $60 TS

🍷🍷🍷🍷 **Pinot Gris 2020 Rating** 92 To 2025 $34 TS
Classic Cuvée 2017 Rating 91 $48 TS

Barristers Block
141 Onkaparinga Valley Road, Woodside, SA 5244 **Region** Adelaide Hills
T (08) 8389 7706 **www**.barristersblock.com.au **Open** 7 days 10.30–5
Winemaker Anthony Pearce, Peter Leske **Est.** 2004 **Dozens** 7000 **Vyds** 18.5ha
Owner Jan Siemelink-Allen has over 20 years in the industry, first as a grapegrower of 10ha of cabernet sauvignon and shiraz in Wrattonbully, then as a wine producer from that region. In 2006 she and her family purchased an 8ha vineyard planted to sauvignon blanc and pinot noir near Woodside in the Adelaide Hills. Exports to the UK, Germany, Vietnam, Malaysia, South Korea, Hong Kong, Singapore and China.

🍷🍷🍷🍷 **The Bully Barossa Wrattonbully Shiraz 2018** Rich, ripe, crimson plum flavours with mint-choc elements. Full bodied and concentrated, drying tannins add their weight mid palate, building a chewy finish. Big wine like this needs a big serve of red meat to allow it to work its best game. Screw cap. 14.4% alc. **Rating** 92 To 2028 $34 TL
Limited Release Aston McLaren Vale Fiano 2020 A little shy to start – field grasses and sea air rising. A good little change of gear in the drinking, still grassy but with a lemon tang and the pithy texture of fresh cut apple. Screw cap. 13.5% alc. **Rating** 91 To 2023 $27 TL

Barwon Ridge Wines
50 McMullans Road, Barrabool, Vic 3221 **Region** Geelong
T 0418 324 632 **www**.barwonridge.com.au **Open** W'ends, public hols & by appt
Winemaker Jack Rabbit Vineyard (Nyall Condon) **Est.** 1999 **Dozens** 900 **Vyds** 3.6ha
In 1999 Geoff and Joan Anson planted chardonnay, shiraz and marsanne at Barwon Ridge, the vines growing slowly (if at all) in the limestone soil. The vineyard nestles in the Barrabool Hills, just to the west of Geelong. Geoff and Joan focus on producing premium fruit; the vineyard is now planted to pinot noir, pinot meunier, shiraz, cabernet sauvignon, marsanne and chardonnay. The wines are made at Leura Park. The vineyard is part of the re-emergence of winemaking in the Barrabool Hills, after the area's first boom from the 1840s to the '80s. The well-written website contains a wealth of information about the history of the region.

🍷🍷🍷🍷 **Chardonnay 2018** This carries an appealing level of flinty complexity in tandem with ripe, fresh peach, citrus and nectarine fruit. A very summery, beachy vibe. The palate is taut and lively with an attractive, biscuity, mealy oak influence and stylish finish. Carries a lovely, self-assured elegance. Screw cap. 13.6% alc. **Rating** 92 To 2025 $29 JP

🍷🍷🍷 **Sparkling 2018 Rating** 89 $37 JP

Basalt Wines
1131 Princes Highway, Killarney, Vic 3283 **Region** Henty
T 0429 682 251 **www**.basaltwines.com **Open** 7 days 10–5
Winemaker Scott Ireland **Est.** 2002 **Dozens** 800 **Vyds** 2.8ha

Shane and Ali Clancey have turned a former potato paddock into a small, but very successful, wine business. In 2002 Shane began planting a multi-clone pinot noir vineyard, plus a small planting of tempranillo. Basalt Wines' grape intake is supplemented by a Drumborg vineyard, including 0.4ha of 26yo MV6 pinot noir and, even more importantly, riesling of the highest quality. Shane is viticulturist, assistant winemaker, wholesaler and runs the cellar door. Ali is involved in various parts of the business, including the small flock of babydoll sheep which graze next to the winery.

The Bream King Tempranillo 2019 The tempranillo fairly jumps with fresh, youthful fruit flavour. A wine with some European sensitivity towards the grape, fine and beautifully balanced, allowing the fruit full reign. Dark cherry, damson plum, wild strawberry and spice. Comes alive with bright acidity and brisk, fine tannins. Screw cap. 13.5% alc. **Rating** 94 **To** 2026 $42 JP

Old Vine Grampians Shiraz 2017 Rating 93 **To** 2031 $55 JP
Great Ocean Road Riesling 2020 Rating 92 **To** 2032 $29 JP
Great Ocean Road Pinot Noir 2019 Rating 91 **To** 2026 $45 JP

Basket Range Wines ★★★★

PO Box 65, Basket Range, SA 5138 **Region** Adelaide Hills
T (08) 8390 1515 **www**.basketrangewine.com.au **Open** By appt
Winemaker Phillip Broderick **Est.** 1980 **Dozens** 250 **Vyds** 8ha
Mary and Phillip Broderick are the owners of this long-standing, but small and little-known winery. It's bigger than a hobby, with the wines available for sale, a Cabernet Sauvignon Merlot Petit Verdot tracking the 4ha plantings of these varieties. The newer plantings of 4ha of clones 777 and MV6 pinot noir are another very different take on his production.

Adelaide Hills Merlot Petit Verdot 2017 An 85/15% duet with long ripening characters set deeply into the fruit – blueberried more than black. Juicy, plump and medium bodied. A peppery savoury note and tannins gather the wine into a really well-balanced, structural and desirable style. Cork. 13% alc. **Rating** 93 **To** 2028 $37 TL
Vineyard Blend Adelaide Hills 2019 This seems an unusual blend, this 40/40/20% cabernet/petit verdot/pinot noir, but it truly reflects the vineyard. A dark-fruited, cabernet-led bouquet to start. It's comforting on the palate, juicy with crimson-berried feels, with a slight gastronomic bitterness that suggests an earthy, leafy character like radicchio, finishing with a great dusting of pepperiness. There's a rustic appeal here that wins you over. Cork. 12.7% alc. **Rating** 92 **To** 2026 $45 TL
Adelaide Hills Cabernet Sauvignon Merlot Petit Verdot 2017 60/35/5% blend. This sings of ripe fruit and vineyard character. There's a backdrop of dried orange dipped in dark chocolate, with the tannins fitting neatly into the palate structure. This wine will go on a good 5- to 10-year journey. Cork. 13% alc. **Rating** 91 **To** 2030 $40 TL
Adelaide Hills Pinot Noir 2019 Fleshy rather than fragrant, shy of overt pinot prettiness but offering a more aperol-like bouquet. Plump on the palate with a delicate bitterness and gentle and rounded mouth-coating tannins. Distinctive pinot expression. Cork. 12.5% alc. **Rating** 90 **To** 2025 $45 TL

Bass Phillip

16 Hunts Road, Leongatha South, Vic 3953 **Region** Gippsland
T (03) 5664 3366 **www**.bassphillip.com **Open** By appt
Winemaker Jean-Marie Fourrier, John Durham **Est.** 1979 **Dozens** 1500 **Vyds** 11ha
Phillip Jones hand crafted tiny quantities of superlative pinot noir which, at its best, had no equal in Australia. Painstaking site selection, ultra-close vine spacing and the very, very cool climate of South Gippsland are the keys to the magic of Bass Phillip and its eerily Burgundian pinots. One of Australia's greatest small producers, they are heading down a new path after Jones announced in May 2020 that he sold the assets (winery, stock and 14ha of vineyards)

to a syndicate led by Burgundian winemaker Jean-Marie Fourrier (who has known Jones for 14 years) and two Singaporeans who already have lucrative wine businesses. The price hasn't been disclosed, but Jones had set a hefty price tag for those who have previously thought it would be a nice business to own.

🍷🍷🍷🍷🍷 **Premium Pinot Noir 2019** Wonderful clarity on display, from the heady aromas to the definition across the palate. A whorl of dark fruits spiced to the max, with wafts of pomegranate, autumnal scents and freshly rolled tobacco. It is definitely in the riper spectrum, yet the palate unfurls with velvety tannins into sweet fruit. Exceptional length and a pleasing, refreshing lift. The pick of the 2019 pinots. ProCork. 14.2% alc. **Rating** 96 **To** 2033 $240 JF
Estate Pinot Noir 2019 Now this certainly entices with its perfume and depth of flavour. Ripe-fruited, spicy, and full of earthiness. The tannins are beautifully shaped, if furry. Fuller bodied, with a refreshing acidity and good persistence. Lovely wine. ProCork. 13.9% alc. **Rating** 95 **To** 2031 $95 JF
Reserve Pinot Noir 2019 The place. The wine. Inextricably linked. But the reserve is no wallflower in 2019: ripe, rich and everything on full display. It has an impressive shape – full bodied, dense and powerful. Lots of tannin, volume and no shortage of flavour. It's packaged well, and ready to drink - it won't live as long as more refined vintages. ProCork. 14.6% alc. **Rating** 95 **To** 2033 $825 JF

Bass River Winery ★★★★
1835 Dalyston Glen Forbes Road, Glen Forbes, Vic 3990 **Region** Gippsland
T (03) 5678 8252 **www.**bassriverwinery.com **Open** Thurs–Tues 10–5
Winemaker Frank Butera **Est.** 1998 **Dozens** 1500 **Vyds** 6ha
The Butera family's 44ha property supports grass-fed beef and olive groves as well as viticulture. Pinot noir, chardonnay, riesling, merlot and cabernet were first planted here in 1998. Both the winemaking and viticulture are handled by father-and-son team Pasquale and Frank. The small production is principally sold through the cellar door, with some retailers and restaurants in the South Gippsland area. Exports to Japan and the UK.

🍷🍷🍷🍷🍷 **1835 Gippsland Pinot Noir 2019** A lovely brightness to the fruit and a plushness to the palate. It starts off teasingly fragrant and offers some cherries and pips, dried herbs and forest-floor appeal. Soft giving tannins, sweet fruit and no reason to keep this a second longer. Screw cap. 13% alc. **Rating** 92 **To** 2025 $50 JF
1835 Gippsland Chardonnay 2019 Mid gold hue. Golden fruit within, from quinces and melons to peaches. Gently spiced, laden with creamy and toasty notes. Not complex but easy to drink. Screw cap. 12.5% alc. **Rating** 90 **To** 2024 $40 JF

Battle of Bosworth ★★★★☆
92 Gaffney Road, Willunga, SA 5172 **Region** McLaren Vale
T (08) 8556 2441 **www.**battleofbosworth.com.au **Open** 7 days 11–5
Winemaker Joch Bosworth **Est.** 1996 **Dozens** 15 000 **Vyds** 80ha
Owned and run by Joch Bosworth (viticulture and winemaking) and partner Louise Hemsley-Smith (sales and marketing), this winery takes its name from the battle that ended the War of the Roses, fought on Bosworth Field in 1485. The vineyards were established in the early 1970s in the foothills of the Mount Lofty Ranges. The vines are fully certified A-grade organic. The label depicts the yellow soursob (*Oxalis pes-caprae*), whose growth habits make it an ideal weapon for battling weeds in organic viticulture. Shiraz, cabernet sauvignon and chardonnay account for 75% of the plantings. The Spring Seed Wine Co wines are made from estate vineyards. Exports to the UK, the US, Canada, Sweden, Norway, Belgium, Hong Kong and Japan.

🍷🍷🍷🍷🍷 **Braden's McLaren Vale Shiraz 2018** This is nestled effortlessly between the regional predeliction for ripeness, power and generosity; and a winemaking hand that is less interventionist than in the past. Palpably natural tannins, soaring florals and well-appointed oak (30% new French). The tannins, grape-skin-pithy, granular and moreish, are particularly impressive. Persuasive, too, toward the 2nd glass. Screw cap. 14.5% alc. **Rating** 94 **To** 2028 $45 NG

πππππ Chanticleer McLaren Vale Shiraz 2018 **Rating** 93 **To** 2027 $45 NG
Best of Vintage McLaren Vale 2018 **Rating** 93 **To** 2030 $50 NG
White Boar 2017 **Rating** 93 **To** 2035 $45 NG
McLaren Vale Cabernet Sauvignon 2019 **Rating** 92 **To** 2027 $28 NG
McLaren Vale Shiraz 2019 **Rating** 91 **To** 2028 $28 NG
McLaren Vale Touriga Nacional 2019 **Rating** 91 **To** 2022 $28 NG

 # Battles Wine

77 Aitken Drive, Winthrop, WA 6150 (postal) **Region** Western Australia
T 0434 399 964 **www.**battleswine.com.au
Winemaker Lance Parkin **Est.** 2018 **Dozens** 850
Battles Wine was started by friends Lance Parkin (winemaker) and Kris Ambrozkiewicz (sommelier, sales) in 2019. Parkin was a winemaker at Houghton in the Swan Valley before the sale to the Yukich family in 2019, at which point the Swan Valley–based component of the Houghton team disbanded and formed their own ventures. Battles focuses on a small collection of tiny-quantity wines from a variety of regions (at this stage, Margaret River, the Great Southern and Geographe) made with great attention to detail, and vineyard provenance top of mind. Ambrozkiewicz (aka Ambro) has a longstanding and intense love of wine, paired with an impressively honed bank of wine knowledge and years of sales experience. (EL)

πππππ Frankland River Shiraz 2020 Spiced mulberry, pomegranate, raspberry, red licorice and pink peppercorn. Szechuan spice, star anise and bucketloads of berries. This is a fete. A party. It's epic. It could do with another year in bottle to help things settle down, but the pedigree of tannin and structure inherent in this wine, along with fruit weight and density, shows it will go the distance and then some. Welcome to WA's new-breed shiraz. It's happening. Screw cap. 14.2% alc. **Rating** 96 **To** 2041 $50 EL ○
Blendaberg Frankland River 2020 43/39/18% riesling/gewürztraminer/pinot grigio, each vinified separately. Buttered sourdough toast, crushed limestone, lime blossom, mandarin pith, juniper and ginger root. Clearly Frankland River, with acidity that gives a structure all of its own. Brine, orange zest and white currants are dragged over the tongue and pulled through into the long finish. Engaging, layered, and not without a shade of mystery. Screw cap. 12.5% alc. **Rating** 94 **To** 2031 $32 EL
Western Australia Shiraz Tempranillo Mourvèdre 2020 An insane vibrant fuschia colour. On the nose and palate, a cavalcade of bright, ripe, stemmy fruits, laden with exotic spice and fine texture. Pomegranate, garden mint, strawberry, star anise, aniseed, red licorice and mulberry take turns on centre stage, guided by saline acidity and chalky tannins. Supple and bouncy, with a bit of chew. Delicious. Screw cap. 14% alc. **Rating** 94 **To** 2028 $35 EL

Bay of Fires

40 Baxters Road, Pipers River, Tas 7252 **Region** Northern Tasmania
T (03) 6382 7622 **www.**bayoffireswines.com.au **Open** Thurs–Mon 10–5 by appt
Winemaker Penny Jones **Est.** 2001
Hardys purchased its first grapes from Tasmania in 1994, with the aim of further developing and refining its sparkling wines, a process that quickly gave birth to House of Arras (see separate entry). The next stage was the inclusion of various parcels of chardonnay from Tasmania in the 1998 Eileen Hardy, then the development in 2001 of the Bay of Fires brand. Bay of Fires has had outstanding success with its table wines: Pinot Noir was obvious, the other wines typically of gold medal standard. Exports to the US, Asia and NZ.

πππππ Sauvignon Blanc 2020 Top-class fruit massaged eloquently by the wonderful texture and harmony of barrel fermentation makes for an exquisite sauvignon. All the varietal markers are on display, yet nothing is jagged or overt, as sauvignon often wants to be. Charged by a citrus core of depth, tension and undeterred vision, carrying a finish of breathtaking line and length. Screw cap. 12.5% alc. Rating 95 To 2030 $46 TS ♥

Riesling 2020 Rating 93 To 2035 $46 TS
Pinot Gris 2020 Rating 93 To 2025 $46 TS
Chardonnay 2019 Rating 92 To 2029 $58 TS
Eddystone Point Chardonnay 2019 Rating 92 To 2027 $32 TS
Eddystone Point Pinot Gris 2020 Rating 92 To 2024 $32 TS
Eddystone Point Riesling 2020 Rating 91 To 2026 $32 TS
Eddystone Point Sauvignon Blanc 2020 Rating 91 To 2023 $32 TS
Eddystone Point Pinot Noir 2019 Rating 91 To 2029 $38 TS
Tasmanian Cuvée Pinot Noir Chardonnay Rosé NV Rating 91 $46 TS
Tasmanian Cuvée Pinot Noir Chardonnay Brut NV Rating 90 $46 TS

Bay of Shoals Wines ★★★★

49 Cordes Road, Kingscote, Kangaroo Island, SA 5223 **Region** Kangaroo Island
T (08) 8553 0289 www.bayofshoalswines.com.au **Open** 7 days 11–5
Winemaker Kelvin Budarick **Est.** 1994 **Dozens** 5000 **Vyds** 15ha
John Willoughby's vineyard overlooks the Bay of Shoals, which is the northern boundary of Kingscote, Kangaroo Island's main town. Planting of the vineyard began in 1994 and it now comprises riesling, sauvignon blanc, savagnin, pinot gris, pinot noir, cabernet sauvignon and shiraz. In addition, 460 olive trees have been planted to produce table olives.

Kangaroo Island Arinto 2020 Florals and salines all in one waft from the glass. Lemons and minerals, too, sherbet aromatics, cut pears, all with a delicate residual sweetness. Refreshing and summery, a lovely twang of grapefruit (with a sprinkle of brown sugar) acidity to finish. Lots of all-round afternoon fun. Screw cap. 10.5% alc. Rating 92 To 2023 $28 TL
Kangaroo Island Riesling 2020 Riesling with the unique addition of some albariño, philosophically matched as the latter thrives in coastal conditions and a sense of salinity, which you do get in this variation. Otherwise, the perfume suggests grapefruit and the palate does all the usual citrus/riesling things. There's a pithy texture and just a tiny note of fruit sweetness lift on the exit. Screw cap. 12.5% alc. Rating 91 To 2023 $28 TL

Bec Hardy Wines ★★★★★

Pertaringa, 327 Hunt Road, McLaren Vale, SA 5171 **Region** McLaren Vale
T (08) 8383 2700 www.bechardy.com.au **Open** By appt
Winemaker Geoff Hardy, Shane Harris **Est.** 2015 **Dozens** 50 000 **Vyds** 2ha
Sixth-generation Bec Hardy and husband Richard Dolan took over ownership of the Pertaringa brand from parents Geoff and Fiona Hardy. Bec is the first female member of the Hardy family to own a vineyard and make wine. Bec and Richard have managed the Pertaringa brand since 2011, the brand celebrating its 40th year in 2020. Export growth of 788% (including 8 years of double-digit growth) resulted in Pertaringa being named Australian Exporter of the Year in 2017 and Regional Exporter of the Year in 2019. The cellar door has been refurbished by renowned interior designer Georgie Shepherd. Exports to Canada, Luxembourg, India, Vietnam, Malaysia, South Korea, Thailand, Singapore, Japan, Taiwan and China.

Pertaringa Tipsy Hill Single Vineyard McLaren Vale Cabernet Sauvignon 2018 Very good, in that salubrious theatre of manicured tannins, preened oak and plucked fruit. An unashamed behemoth, boasting power and precision. Admirably, the regional chord of maritime salinity and black olive-doused tannins is palpable. The varietal persona of verdant herb and currant, forceful. The finish, convincing. Diam. 14.5% alc. Rating 95 To 2033 $150 NG

Pertaringa Yeoman McLaren Vale Shiraz 2018 Rating 92 To 2028 $150 NG

Pertaringa Scarecrow Adelaide Hills Sauvignon Blanc 2020 Rating 91 To 2021 $25 NG

Pertaringa Lakeside Adelaide Pinot Noir 2020 Rating 91 To 2023 $17 NG ✪

Pertaringa Over The Top McLaren Vale Shiraz 2018 Rating 91 To 2026 $40 NG

Pertaringa Adelaide Hills Cabernet Sauvignon 2018 Rating 90 To 2025 $30 NG

Beechworth Wine Estates ★★★★☆

Lot 2 Diffey Road, Beechworth, Vic 3477 **Region** Beechworth
T (03) 5728 3340 **www**.beechworthwe.com.au **Open** By appt
Winemaker Mark Kelly **Est.** 2003 **Dozens** 3200 **Vyds** 8.6ha
John and Joanne Iwanuch describe their estate as a family-run and owned business, with their 4 children participating in all aspects of vineyard life. Situated on the Rail Trail, 4km from Beechworth, they have planted sauvignon blanc, pinot gris, fiano, chardonnay, shiraz, cabernet sauvignon, merlot, tempranillo, sangiovese, tannat, malbec, barbera, nebbiolo and graciano. Exports to Germany.

🍷🍷🍷🍷🍷 **Reserve Chardonnay 2017** A multi-layered chardonnay into which some considered thought has been applied, allowing both the expression of land and winemaker. Delivers almost opulent aromas, rich in cashew, stone fruit, melon and honeyed nougat. The palate is concentrated in fruit flavours, with additional hints of grapefruit and tangelo, together with a lovely, flinty winemaking overlay. Spiced oak, too. A most impressive wine for now and later. Screw cap. 13.3% alc. Rating 95 To 2028 $42 JP

🍷🍷🍷🍷🍷 **Chardonnay 2019** Rating 92 To 2026 $35 JP

Bekkers ★★★★★

212-220 Seaview Road, McLaren Vale, SA 5171 **Region** McLaren Vale
T 0408 807 568 **www**.bekkerswine.com **Open** Thurs–Sat 10–4 or by appt
Winemaker Emmanuelle Bekkers **Est.** 2010 **Dozens** 1500 **Vyds** 18ha
This brings together two high-performing, highly experienced and highly credentialled business and life partners. Toby Bekkers graduated with an honours degree in applied science in agriculture from the University of Adelaide, and over the ensuing years has had broad-ranging responsibilities as general manager of Paxton Wines in McLaren Vale, and as a leading exponent of organic and biodynamic viticulture. Emmanuelle Bekkers was born in Bandol in the south of France, and gained 2 university degrees, in biochemistry and oenology, before working for the Hardys in the south of France, which led her to Australia and a wide-ranging career, including Chalk Hill. Exports to the UK, the US, France and China.

🍷🍷🍷🍷🍷 **McLaren Vale Grenache 2019** A shimmering light ruby. A textural polyglot, incandescent, lit by its delicate shades of fruit as much as its textural precision and savouriness. Nebbiolo meets pinot on the nose. This is what grenache does at the highest calibre. Sandalwood, Darjeeling, bergamot, crushed rose, pomegranate, tamarind and kirsch. Long and gritty in the best sense. Febrile. Tensile. Would love to see it in bigger oak. A beautiful stain on the memory bank. Screw cap. 14.5% alc. Rating 97 To 2026 $90 NG ✪

🍷🍷🍷🍷🍷 **McLaren Vale Syrah 2019** This succinct offering has impressed in the past. This year is no different. Texture, the opus. Nothing about obvious fruit. Hallelujah to that. Carnal aromas of leather, game, sandalwood, something volcanic and a mulchy fecundity. Briary tannins, almost skeletal. Kirsch, a rub of menthol, anise, clove, tamarind and cardamom. Expansive, savoury and long. Fine. Screw cap. 14% alc. Rating 95 To 2028 $120 NG ❤

McLaren Vale Syrah Grenache 2019 A limpid mid-ruby. Dashing aromas of kirsch, freshly grated orange zest, pumice, aniseed, clove and nori. Texture the strike force: scrubby herb and beautifully tuned tannins, sopping up any regional sweetness. Not necessarily to subjugate it, but to make it a more transparent reflection of place. A brilliant offering. Screw cap. 14% alc. **Rating** 94 **To** 2030 $90 NG

Bellarine Estate ★★★★

2270 Portarlington Road, Bellarine, Vic 3222 **Region** Geelong
T (03) 5259 3310 **www**.bellarineestate.com.au **Open** 7 days 11–4
Winemaker Julian Kenny **Est.** 1995 **Dozens** 1050 **Vyds** 10.5ha
This business runs parallel with the Bellarine Brewing Company, also situated in the winery, and the extended operating hours of Julian's Restaurant. It is a popular meeting place. The vineyard is planted to chardonnay, pinot noir, shiraz, merlot, viognier and sauvignon blanc. Exports to the US.

ΥΥΥΥΥ **First Blush Geelong Rosé 2019** Deep salmon hue. Woodsy notes, earth and raspberries indicate a serious bent to the rosé style. The palate confirms, with a depth of fruit flavour, layers of dark fruits, musky strawberry and orange rind with tannic edge and so clean and dry. Screw cap. 13.2% alc. **Rating** 94 **To** 2025 $28 JP ✪

ΥΥΥΥΥ **Two Wives Geelong Shiraz 2019** Rating 93 To 2030 $38 JP
Portarlington Ridge Geelong Chardonnay 2019 Rating 92 To 2025 $25 JP ✪
Portarlington Ridge Geelong Shiraz 2019 Rating 91 To 2025 $25 JP
Phil's Geelong Pinot Noir 2019 Rating 90 To 2025 $40 JP

Bellarmine Wines ★★★★☆

1 Balyan Retreat, Pemberton, WA 6260 **Region** Pemberton
T 0409 687 772 **www**.bellarmine.com.au **Open** By appt
Winemaker Dr Diane Miller **Est.** 2000 **Dozens** 5000 **Vyds** 20.2ha
This vineyard is owned by German residents Dr Willi and Gudrun Schumacher. Long-term wine lovers, the Schumachers decided to establish a vineyard and winery of their own, choosing Australia partly because of its stable political climate. The vineyard is planted to riesling, pinot noir, chardonnay, shiraz, sauvignon blanc and petit verdot. The flagship wines are 3 styles of riesling – dry, off-dry and sweet. Exports to the UK, the US, Germany and China.

ΥΥΥΥΥ **Pemberton Riesling Dry 2020** Single-vineyard from 20+yo vines, fermented in stainless steel to dryness in the pursuit of purity. And pure it surely is. Mandarin pith, citrus frosting, orange blossom and a chalky, sherbet minerality that laces in and out of the fruit. This is beautiful. Light on its feet yet plush, chalky and very long, it is a riesling of understated power and restraint. Di Miller is known for her riesling. This is why. Screw cap. 13.5% alc. **Rating** 95 **To** 2036 $27 EL ✪
Pemberton Riesling Half-dry 2020 The sweetness is undeniable, but the acid has a savoury saline crunch to it. The aromatics are an abundant feast of orange blossom (a character I normally reserve for grüner veltliner), lemon flesh, green apple and white pepper. Curls of garden mint and white pepper colour the edges of the fruit. Screw cap. 12% alc. **Rating** 94 **To** 2036 $27 EL ✪

ΥΥΥΥΥ **Pemberton Pinot Noir 2020** Rating 93 To 2025 $27 EL ✪

Bellbrae Estate ★★★★☆

520 Great Ocean Road, Bellbrae, Vic 3228 **Region** Geelong
T (03) 5264 8480 **www**.bellbraeestate.com.au **Open** See website
Winemaker David Crawford **Est.** 1999 **Dozens** 3000 **Vyds** 7ha
The Surf Coast area of Geelong enjoys a slightly milder climate overall than other areas of the Geelong viticultural region. Being so close to Bass Strait, Bellbrae Estate experiences a maritime influence that reduces the risk of frost in spring and provides more even temperature

ranges during summer – ideal growing conditions for producing elegant wines that retain their natural acidity. Wines are released under the Bellbrae Estate and Longboard labels.

ϙϙϙϙϙ **Longboard Bendigo Pinot Gris 2019** Four months in 2–3yo French barriques contributes significantly to the spice, texture and overall generosity of this gris. On the fuller side with lantana, honeysuckle, baked apple tart, glacé pear and biscuity flavours throughout. Easy early drinking assured. Screw cap. 13% alc. **Rating** 92 To 2024 $28 JP

Longboard Geelong Pinot Noir 2019 A serious pinot noir for the price, in a dark, cherry-scented, lightly herbal style. Aromas of black cherries, bergamot and musk carry through to the palate where earthy, leafy characters roam. Dry cherry-pip tannins bring it to a close. Screw cap. 13.5% alc. **Rating** 92 **To** 2026 $27 JP

Boobs Geelong Chardonnay 2019 A sunny chardonnay to be sure, resplendent in summer stone fruits, spiced apple, nougat and gentle bready/mealy lees. A light savouriness adds to the attraction. Screw cap. 12.5% alc. **Rating** 90 To 2026 $40 JP

ϙϙϙϙ **Longboard Geelong Sauvignon Blanc 2019** **Rating** 89 **To** 2024 $28 JP
Longboard Geelong Chardonnay 2019 **Rating** 89 **To** 2024 $25 JP
Bird Rock Geelong Pinot Noir 2018 **Rating** 89 **To** 2025 $42 JP

Bellebonne ★★★★★

3 Balfour Place, Launceston, Tas 7250 (postal) **Region** Northern Tasmania
T 0412 818 348 **www**.bellebonne.wine
Winemaker Natalie Fryar **Est.** 2015 **Dozens** 600
Bellebonne is the passion project of Natalie Fryar, who spent 14 years as sparkling winemaker for Jansz, establishing herself as one of Australia's top sparkling winemakers and winning the title of 'rosé queen,' while gaining an intimate knowledge of Tasmania's top sparkling sites. She crafts her elegant and sublime Bellebonne cuvées in miniscule quantities from tiny pockets of growers' vines in Tasmania's sparkling epicentre of Piper's River. To finance her first vintage flying solo, she sold a house, worked waitressing shifts and 'bought my cleaner's Ford Festiva and drove it to Tassie with my red Kelpie on the front seat.' She maintains a consulting hand in a number of Northern Tasmania's best sparkling and lends her blending skills to creating her outstanding Abel Gin. Exports to Hong Kong. (TS)

ϙϙϙϙϙ **Natalie Fryar Vintage Rosé 2017** A true execution of talent, masterfully articulating the concentration, character and energy of a powerful vintage. Piper's River pinot noir (100%) declares a dramatic contrast between great depth and the scaffolded frame of acid, phenolic structure and barrel fermentation (6yo oak). The cold winds of Bass Strait whip up energetic structure that holds its drama through a long finish, never for a moment dipping its determined gaze. Diam. 12% alc. Rating 96 $75 TS ✪ ♥

Natalie Fryar Vintage Cuvée 2016 The fruit concentration and tension of Piper's River are wrapped confidently in the signature creaminess and character of partial barrel fermentation. Saline nuances of Bass Strait wash seamlessly with the bright yet perfectly ripe line of cool acidity. For all of its multifaceted complexity, true greatness is defined by precise focus and consummate cohesion on the finish, holding fantastic line and enduring length. Brilliant. Diam. 12% alc. Rating 95 $70 TS

ϙϙϙϙϙ **Bis Rosé NV** **Rating** 93 $40 TS

Bellingham Estate ★★★★☆

59 Bellingham Road, Arthur's Seat, Vic 3936 **Region** Mornington Peninsula
T 0400 821 252 **www**.bellinghamestate.com.au **Open** By appt
Winemaker Richard McIntyre, Jeremy Magyar **Est.** 1991 **Dozens** 400 **Vyds** 1.5ha
In 2007, when Ian Bellingham bought his Arthur's Seat property planted to 1.5ha of pinot noir, he naively thought an hour or so of work each weekend would be enough to keep

everything in shape. As is so often the case, the vines and subsequent wine took over his life. With a background in aeronautical maintenance, Ian left that business behind to concentrate full-time on grape growing. His east–west planted site, quite high by peninsula standards at 220m above sea level, was initially planted about 30 years ago. Ian spent the first few years reworking the vineyards to an exacting standard, eschewing herbicides and pesticides, with all work done by hand. He sources chardonnay from a Main Ridge property and until recently sourced pinot gris, too. Wines are made by Richard McIntyre and Jeremy Magyar at Moorooduc Estate. (JF)

🍷🍷🍷🍷🍷 **The Bellingham Reserve Mornington Peninsula Pinot Noir 2018** It's unclear why this is a Reserve, but it certainly has more depth and fruit weight compared with its sibling. It's composed, with a balance of flavours. The medium-bodied palate is refined, with fine tannins and cleansing acidity in tow. Screw cap. 14% alc. **Rating** 95 **To** 2030 $50 JF

🍷🍷🍷🍷🍷 **Mornington Peninsula Pinot Gris 2018 Rating** 93 **To** 2023 $30 JF
Mornington Peninsula Chardonnay 2017 Rating 92 **To** 2026 $31 JF
Mornington Peninsula Pinot Noir 2018 Rating 90 **To** 2028 $34 JF

Bellwether

14183 Riddoch Highway, Coonawarra, SA 5263 **Region** Coonawarra
T 0417 080 945 **www.**bellwetherwines.com.au **Open** 7 days 12–4
Winemaker Sue Bell **Est.** 2008 **Dozens** 2500
When Constellation decided to sell (or mothball) its large Padthaway winery built by Hardys more than 10 years previously at a cost of $20 million, chief winemaker Sue Bell was summarily retrenched. In quick succession she received a $46000 wine industry scholarship from the Grape & Wine Research Development Council to study the wine industry in relation to other rural industries in Australia and overseas, and its interaction with community and society. She also became Dux of the Len Evans Tutorial, her prize an extended trip through Bordeaux and Burgundy. She decided to stay and live in Coonawarra, and the next stroke of good fortune was that the beautiful stone Glen Roy shearing shed in Coonawarra (built in 1868) came on the market – which these days is her winery and welcoming cellar door. Exports to the UK and Singapore.

🍷🍷🍷🍷🍷 **Wrattonbully Malbec 2018** A malbec pulsating with complex, mouthfilling dark berry/plum fruit, a savoury/earthy regional carpet adding further weight to a wine full of character. Screw cap. 13.8% alc. **Rating** 94 **To** 2030 $30 JH ✪

🍇 Below & Above

43 Eastbrook Road, Eastbrook WA 6260 **Region** Pemberton
T 0414 446 405 **www.**belowandabove.com.au **Open** By appt
Winemaker Bruce Dukes (Contract) **Est.** 2013 **Dozens** 1000 **Vyds** 33ha
The Thella vineyard in Pemberton was purchased by John and Evdokia (aka Kia) Klepec in 2013 and has since been producing wine under the Below & Above label. Winemaker Bruce Dukes has been in charge of winemaking for the past 5 years. The 33ha vineyard is planted to chardonnay, pinot noir and merlot, comprising 6.6ha Gingin chardonnay, a large component of pinot noir (clones 114, 115, 777 and G8V3), 1.2ha of close-planted (1 × 1.5m) 667 pinot, and 181 and Q45v14 merlot clones. The wines are sold with a bit of age (5 years on the merlot, 3 on the pinot and chardonnay). Exports to Singapore and China. (EL)

🍷🍷🍷🍷🍷 **Pemberton Pinot Noir 2018** Very pretty aromatics of black cherry, strawberry, olive tapenade, star anise and something floral … fennel flower. The palate is creamy and fine, the flavours uncurling in the way a flower blooms, unfurling and extending to all corners of the mouth. The tannins are very fine and shapely and licorice-like. It speaks very clearly of Pemberton. A lot to like! Screw cap. 13.5% alc. **Rating** 95 **To** 2031 $38 EL
Pemberton Chardonnay 2018 Complex, toasty aromas shower the glass in yellow peach, curry leaf, red apple skins and guava. The palate follows suit, adding

crushed cashew, creamed macadamia, rosewater and pistachio. Acidity like a ripe lemon, coursing straight down the centre of the palate. There's a lot going on here, and thankfully, the elongated length of flavour gives you every opportunity to experience it. Very smart. Screw cap. 13.4% alc. **Rating** 94 **To** 2031 $38 EL

Ben Haines Wine ★★★★★

342 Rae Street, Fitzroy North, Vic 3068 (postal) **Region** Yarra Valley
T 0417 083 645 **www**.benhaineswine.com.au
Winemaker Ben Haines **Est.** 2010 **Dozens** 4000
Ben Haines graduated from the University of Adelaide in 1999 with a degree in viticulture, waiting a couple of years (immersing himself in music) before focusing on his wine career. An early interest in terroir led to a deliberate choice of gaining experience in diverse regions including the Yarra Valley, McLaren Vale, Adelaide Hills, Langhorne Creek, Tasmania and Central Victoria, as well as time in the US and France. His services as a contract winemaker are in high demand, and his name pops up all over the place. Exports to the US and Asia.

♔♔♔♔♔ **Firelights Grampians Syrah 2019** Dense, dark purple/garnet. Fragrant bush scents, concentrated spice, vanilla pod and peppery red fruits. Strikes a spicy pose, but look further, this wine is complex and elegant, coiled tight in blackberries, blood plum, anise and tilled earth. Seamless integration of oak. And to think it's only starting life. Diam. 13.5% alc. **Rating** 95 **To** 2034 $70 JP
Steels Creek Yarra Valley Pinot Noir 2020 An unusual wine, in that it has an Italian flavour to it, resembling chinotto and Campari with bitter herbs. This makes it refreshing, the palate juicy and tangy. Tannins are in the background adding support and texture, but raspberry-like acidity leads this dance. Diam. 12% alc. **Rating** 94 **To** 2026 $40 JF

♔♔♔♔♕ **Great Western Syrah 2020 Rating** 93 **To** 2030 $40 JP
Red Yarra Valley 2020 Rating 93 **To** 2024 $28 JF
Flowers Flor Yarra Valley Marsanne 2011 Rating 92 **To** 2021 $100 JF
Coldstream Yarra Valley Viognier 2019 Rating 92 **To** 2027 $35 JF
Make A Wilderness Yarra Valley Pinot Noir 2020 Rating 90 **To** 2024 $60 JF

Bendbrook Wines ★★★★

Section 19 Pound Road, Macclesfield, SA 5153 **Region** Adelaide Hills
T (08) 8388 9773 **www**.bendbrookwines.com.au **Open** By appt
Winemaker Leigh Ratzmer **Est.** 1998 **Dozens** 2500 **Vyds** 5.5ha
John and Margaret Struik have established their vineyard on either side of a significant bend in the Angas River that runs through the property, with cabernet sauvignon on one side and shiraz on the other. The name comes from the bend in question, which is indirectly responsible for the flood that occurs every 4–5 years. Exports to Hong Kong.

♔♔♔♔ **Goat Track Adelaide Hills Shiraz 2019** A big, thick, dense shiraz that's spent 10 months soaking in French oak, 20% new. Initially promising a full-bodied approach, the wine is quite relaxed on the palate, with gently spiced plum juices taking centre stage. Screw cap. 14% alc. **Rating** 89 **To** 2026 $58 TL
SL Adelaide Hills Cabernet Sauvignon 2018 Cabernet aromatics are deep and dark berried, weighty even, which fits the entire makeup of this wine. It's thick, full bodied and virtually requires a knife and fork to find your way through. Screw cap. 13.5% alc. **Rating** 89 **To** 2028 $28 TL

Bended Knee Vineyard ★★★★

PO Box 334, Buninyong, Vic 3357 **Region** Ballarat
T (03) 5341 8437 **www**.bendedknee.com.au
Winemaker Peter Roche **Est.** 1999 **Dozens** 250 **Vyds** 1.25ha

Peter and Pauline Roche have 0.5ha each of chardonnay and pinot noir planted at moderately high density, and 0.25ha of ultra-close-planted pinot noir at the equivalent of 9000 vines/ha. Here 4 clones have been used: 114, 115, G5V15 and 777. The Roches say, 'We are committed to sustainable viticulture and aim to leave the planet in better shape than we found it'. Ducks, guinea fowl and chooks are vineyard custodians, and all vine canopy management is done by hand, including pruning and picking. Although production is tiny, Bended Knee wines can be found at some of Melbourne's best restaurants.

 Pinot Noir 2018 A lilting undergrowth, leafy character to this young pinot is most attractive. It sets the scene for bright cranberry, redcurrant fruit, woody spice and sinewy tannins. Accomplished and confident winemaking on display. Screw cap. 13.5% alc. **Rating** 93 **To** 2026 $40 JP
Chardonnay 2019 Hand-picked fruit, pressed as whole bunches, racked to barrel for wild-yeast fermentation and mlf, maturation in French oak barriques (25% new). Heavy scent of toasty vanilla oak hangs over this youngster. The 3 forces at work here – fruit, acid and oak – are yet to fully integrate. Lemon zest, grapefruit juice, quince, veneer and toast with trademark high lemony acidity. Screw cap. 12.5% alc. **Rating** 90 **To** 2025 $40 JP

Bennetts on Bellarine ★★★★

2171 Portarlington Road, Bellarine, Vic 3223 **Region** Geelong
T (03) 8751 8194 **www.**bennettsonbellarine.com
Open Mon, Thurs, Fri, Sun 11–6, Sat 11–9
Winemaker Julian Kenney, Will Derham (Contract) **Est.** 2013 **Dozens** 1950
Owner/vigneron Jamieson Bennett operated hotels in Melbourne when he got the wine bug and moved to the Bellarine Peninsula. The vineyard was planted in 1995 and has been tended by 3 generations of the Bennett family, as portrayed on the winery labels. Sales are primarily through the cellar door, which opened in 2018, designed in rustic tones around the property's 100yo milking shed. Each year from January to Easter the cellar door, with sweeping views across Corio Bay, hosts popular Sunset Sessions with food, wine and music. Wines are made under contract at 2 nearby Peninsula wineries. (JP)

 Geelong Semillon 2020 It's unusual to see semillon grown on the Bellarine Peninsula but given the cool, maritime climate, the Bordeaux grape has made itself at home. Mixes the herbal with the stone fruit and citrus here. With striking acidity, this comes out as a super-bright, tightly coiled youngster that smashes the apple/lime varietal combo on the palate. Screw cap. 12.3% alc. **Rating** 90 **To** 2025 $35 JP
Andresen Vineyard Geelong Sauvignon Blanc 2020 Andresen Vineyard sauvignon blanc is regarded as a reserve-level expression of the grape, combining cool-climate brisk acidity with pristine citrus notes and some winemaking-led nutty mealiness. Brings restraint to a grape that so rarely sees it. Screw cap. 11.6% alc. **Rating** 90 **To** 2025 $40 JP

Beresford Wines ★★★★☆

252 Blewitt Springs Road, McLaren Flat, SA 5171 **Region** McLaren Vale
T (08) 8383 0362 **www.**beresfordwines.com.au **Open** 7 days 10–5
Winemaker Chris Dix **Est.** 1985 **Dozens** 9000 **Vyds** 28ha
This is a sister company to Step Rd Winery in Langhorne Creek, owned and run by VOK Beverages. The estate plantings are shiraz (13ha), cabernet sauvignon (9.3ha), grenache (3ha) and chardonnay (2.7ha), but they account for only a part of the production. Some of the wines offer excellent value. Exports to the UK, Germany, Denmark, Poland, Singapore, Hong Kong and China.

 Limited Release McLaren Vale Cabernet Sauvignon 2018 Superb. Full bodied, but deft and light on its feet. The tannins, ball-bearing precise, alloyed and attenuated, serving to corral currant, sage, black olive, graphite and pencil lead

notes. This is built for the cellar, despite its precocious appeal. I could drink it any time. Screw cap. 14% alc. **Rating** 96 **To** 2033 $80 NG
Estate McLaren Vale Cabernet Sauvignon 2018 Hewn of fruit exclusively from the Beresford Estate Vineyard, in the elevated subregion of Blewitt Springs. Fine tannins, firm and finessed and leafy in the best sense, saline and long-limbed. Fruit intensity of purity and real thrum. Think blackcurrant that remains savoury rather than sweet, a whiff of mint, violet and crushed rock. A potpourri of herbal complexity marks an impressive finish. I'm enjoying this suite from Beresford. Screw cap. 14% alc. **Rating** 94 **To** 2030 $42 NG

♥♥♥♥♡ **McLaren Vale Rosé 2020 Rating** 92 **To** 2021 $20 NG ✪
Barrel Select McLaren Vale G.S.M 2019 Rating 92 **To** 2025 $20 NG ✪
Classic McLaren Vale Cabernet Sauvignon 2018 Rating 92 **To** 2026 $20 NG ✪
Estate McLaren Vale Shiraz 2018 Rating 91 **To** 2026 $42 NG
Limited Release McLaren Vale Shiraz 2018 Rating 91 **To** 2035 $80 NG
McLaren Vale Shiraz 2018 Rating 91 **To** 2028 $30 NG

Best's Wines   ★★★★★

111 Best's Road, Great Western, Vic 3377 **Region** Great Western
T (03) 5356 2250 **www.**bestswines.com **Open** Mon–Sat 10–5, Sun 11–4
Winemaker Justin Purser **Est.** 1866 **Dozens** 25 000 **Vyds** 147ha
Best's winery and vineyards are among Australia's best kept secrets. Indeed the vineyards, with vines dating back to 1866, have secrets that may never be revealed: for example, one of the vines planted in the Nursery Block has defied identification and is thought to exist nowhere else in the world. Part of the cellars too, go back to the same era, constructed by butcher-turned-winemaker Henry Best and his family. The Thomson family has owned the property since 1920, with Ben, the 5th generation, having taken over management from father Viv. Best's consistently produces elegant, supple wines; the Bin No. 0 is a classic, the Thomson Family Shiraz (largely from vines planted in 1867) is magnificent. Very occasionally a pinot meunier (with 15% pinot noir) is made solely from 1868 plantings of those 2 varieties; there is no other pinot meunier of this vine age made anywhere else in the world. Justin Purser brings with him a remarkable CV with extensive experience in Australia, NZ and Burgundy. In the *Wine Companion 2017* Best's was awarded the mantle of Wine of the Year from a field of almost 9000 wines; in 2021 they were Best Value Winery. Exports to the US, Canada, Singapore, Japan, Sweden and China.

♥♥♥♥♥ **Great Western Riesling 2020** The vines are direct descendants of the 1866 plantings in the nursery block. A core of sweet lime-juice essence and spine-tingling acidity makes a wine that follows in the footsteps of its multi-gold-medal-winning predecessors. An indefinite lifespan. Screw cap. 12% alc. **Rating** 96 **To** 2040 $25 JH ✪
Old Vine Great Western Pinot Meunier 2020 A wine of both astonishing history and grace. Part of its great appeal is a delicacy and purity of meunier rarely, if ever, encountered, and at just 12% alcohol. Spring florals, musky spice, leafy underbrush, black cherry, mulberry … the complexities of fruit flavours go on and on. Supple, fleshy tannins and a balance of bright acidity completes one impressive wine. Screw cap. 12% alc. **Rating** 96 **To** 2036 $100 JP
Thomson Family Great Western Shiraz 2019 Best's remains at the top of its game because of wines like this; wines that hold true to the Thomson family's winemaking philosophy, celebrating old vines and its distinguished sites. It all comes together beautifully, perfectly, in Thomson Family Shiraz. Tasted 1 year before release and it's already an elegant and noble wine. Dark berry fruit, hints of sage and cassia bark with gentle leafiness. Oak and tannins, well, they are seamless and supple. A complex life awaits. Screw cap. 14% alc. **Rating** 96 **To** 2042 $250 JP
Bin No. 0 Great Western Shiraz 2019 Vines date back to as far as 1868, the youngest 1992. Right there you have an inkling of what is to come: a stunning concentration of fruit. Impressive, but the supple, savoury tannins are up to the

task of meeting that deep intensity of black fruits, woody spice and violets. What a team for the future. Of course, this is not to forget the vanillan warm-oak component. A wine of history that still stands firm today. Screw cap. 14% alc. **Rating** 96 **To** 2040 $85 JP

Foudre Ferment Great Western Riesling 2020 One of those pure genius moments where the winemaker decides to break in a new foudre intended for red winemaking, with a riesling. The rest is history. Fermentation and maturation on lees in large-format oak broadens the reach of riesling. It's not oaky – it's textural, and fruit characters become way more concentrated: lime cordial, green apple, orange peel. You may never look at riesling in the same way again. Screw cap. 12% alc. **Rating** 95 **To** 2030 $35 JP ✪

Young Vine Great Western Pinot Meunier 2020 Young is a relative term at Best's: Young Vine indicates vines planted in 1970! Vine age certainly plays a role in this gloriously expressive meunier with its wealth of dried flowers, cranberry, lavender, dried herbs, plum and cherry. Quietly complex, modestly so. An earthy, fleshy wine with spicy tannins to contemplate on many levels. Screw cap. 12.5% alc. **Rating** 95 **To** 2032 $45 JP

LSV Great Western Shiraz 2019 Co-fermented with a small amount of viognier, elevating this wine into deliberate Rhône-like territory, the maker admitting to be inspired by the wines of the Old World. This is one decadent, spiced-up, juicy, red-hearted shiraz, pulsing in energy. Bush mint, pepper, anise, red and black cherry, dried raspberry aromas. A light savouriness enhances what is one impressive wine. Screw cap. 14% alc. **Rating** 95 **To** 2032 $35 JP ✪

Great Western Cabernet Sauvignon 2019 Comes fully formed into the world in every respect, and ready to go. So composed and nicely poised with cassis, black olive, plum, well-measured oak and ripe, supple tannins. Hosts a serious density, too, which adds up to one stunning wine for the price. Screw cap. 14.5% alc. **Rating** 95 **To** 2034 $25 JP ✪ ♥

White Gravels Hill Great Western Shiraz 2019 A single-vineyard shiraz off quite distinctive soils of white gravels, including reef quartz on granite bedrock. A decidedly focused and well-structured shiraz that is tight as a coiled spring. Ripe, rich in black and red fruits, spice, well balanced and with budding complexity, it's all set to go. Give it time in the cellar. Screw cap. 14% alc. **Rating** 94 **To** 2032 $45 JP

Hamill Single Vineyard Shiraz 2019 Comes fully formed into the world, combining black/blueberry fruits, sweet spice, baked earth and wood smoke. Warms on the palate, with a depth of fruit intensity and light savouriness. Tasted soon after bottling and already looking a winner. Screw cap. 14% alc. **Rating** 94 **To** 2034 $60 JP

Great Western Nursery Block Dry Red 2020 Old vines and ancient grape varieties combine in a wine of delicacy and elegance. Bright, vibrant fruit aromas of violet, musk, cherry, black tea. The fruit remains focused and a feature on the soft, lighter-bodied, almost sinewy, palate. Give it time, something it's well used to. Screw cap. 12% alc. **Rating** 94 **To** 2030 $45 JP

🍷🍷🍷🍷🍷 **Great Western Pinot Noir 2020** Rating 93 To 2026 $25 JP ✪
Bin No. 1 Great Western Shiraz 2019 Rating 93 To 2032 $25 JP ✪
Great Western Rosé 2020 Rating 92 To 2026 $25 JP ✪
Great Western Sparkling Shiraz 2017 Rating 92 $35 JP ♥

Bethany Wines   ★★★★★

378 Bethany Road, Tanunda, SA 5352 **Region** Barossa Valley
T (08) 8563 2086 **www**.bethany.com.au **Open** Mon–Sat 10–5, Sun 1–5
Winemaker Alex MacClelland **Est.** 1981 **Dozens** 18 000 **Vyds** 38ha
The Schrapel family has been growing grapes in the Barossa Valley for over 140 years, their winery nestled high on a hillside on the site of an old bluestone quarry. Geoff and Rob Schrapel produce a range of consistently well made and attractively packaged wines. Bethany has vineyards in the Barossa and Eden Valleys. Exports to all major markets.

🍷🍷🍷🍷🍷 **East Grounds Barossa Shiraz 2018** The fruits here lean to the red spectrum rather than black. There are more floral notes than you might expect in a regional context, the palate minerally and earthy as well. All added up, this is a very smart, neatly toned, terroir-focused expression. Screw cap. 14.5% alc. **Rating** 95 **To** 2030 $55 TL

First Village Barossa Valley Shiraz 2018 This gets a big tick in value terms, as well as accessible styling. The fruit is bright and primary, fresh and unhindered by oak, even though a small portion of new French was employed. It's a delightfully energetic and rewarding shiraz, offering Barossa pedigree with great approachability. Screw cap. 14.5% alc. **Rating** 94 **To** 2028 $32 TL

GR Reserve Barossa Valley Shiraz 2018 The ultimate Bethany shiraz expression. And with that comes typically a step up in oak use and influence. Old-school, big-boned shiraz in that sense, so you might have to wait a few years for the rich plum flavours to surface through the oak. But it is already beginning this journey, and there's lots to look forward to, if this is your shiraz jam. Cork. 14% alc. **Rating** 94 **To** 2033 $125 TL

Blue Quarry Single Vineyard Barossa Valley Cabernet Sauvignon 2018 Sourced from 2 sites in the Barossa and Eden valleys, there's plenty to love about this cabernet. Its varietal characters are in full swing, with darker berry and blackcurrant fruit, neatly seasoned with spicy French oak – 60% new hogshead barrels and not overwhelmed, thankfully. Sweet fruit to finish, carpeted in fine tannins, yet exiting with flavour intact. Delish. Screw cap. 14% alc. **Rating** 94 **To** 2030 $45 TL

🍷🍷🍷🍷🍷 **Blue Quarry Barossa Grenache 2019** **Rating** 93 **To** 2030 $45 TL
Museum Release Reserve Eden Valley Riesling 2015 **Rating** 92 **To** 2027 $40 TL
First Village Barossa Valley Grenache 2019 **Rating** 92 **To** 2028 $32 TL
Blue Quarry Barrel Select Barossa Valley Shiraz 2018 **Rating** 91 **To** 2028 $45 TL

Bicknell fc   ★★★★★

41 St Margarets Road, Healesville, Vic 3777 **Region** Yarra Valley
T 0488 678 427 **www.**bicknellfc.com
Winemaker David Bicknell **Est.** 2011 **Dozens** 7600 **Vyds** 2.5ha
This is the busman's holiday for Oakridge chief winemaker David Bicknell and partner Nicky Harris (viticulturist). It is focused purely on chardonnay and pinot noir, with no present intention of broadening the range nor the volume of production. Since 2014 all the grapes have come from Val Stewart's close-planted vineyard at Gladysdale, planted in 1988. The partners have leased this vineyard, which will become the total focus of their business. Since 2015 the wines have been labelled Applecross, the name of the highest mountain pass in Scotland, a place that David Bicknell's father was very fond of.

🍷🍷🍷🍷🍷 **Applecross Yarra Valley Chardonnay 2019** A defining feature for this beauty is its tight acid line. It's rather racy, yet it's buffering ginger spice, lemon scents and citrus fruit across the palate. Some creamy/nutty lees add another layer of detail to an otherwise savoury, mouth-watering wine. Screw cap. 13.5% alc. **Rating** 95 **To** 2030 $50 JF

Applecross Yarra Valley Pinot Noir 2019 A light garnet hue, beguiling and belying the flavours here. A whiff of autumnal scents from damp leaves to wood mushrooms and a scattering of Middle Eastern spices. There's freshness throughout but there's certainly structure, though no new oak encumbering. It has a neat, sinewy streak, with tannins stretching across the palate, ending with a tangy chinotto, blood orange flavour and a bright acid line. Mouth-watering. Screw cap. 13.2% alc. **Rating** 95 **To** 2030 $50 JF

Big Easy Radio

11 Stonehouse Lane, Aldinga, SA 5773 **Region** McLaren Vale
T 0437 159 858 **www.**bigeasyradio.com
Winemaker Matt Head **Est.** 2017 **Dozens** 4000 **Vyds** 4ha
Matt Head has ventured far and wide to bring challenging blends (varietal and regional) together in triumph. Moreover, these (most attractive, if left field) wines are all very competitively priced. Exports to Denmark and Japan.

🍷🍷🍷🍷🍷 **Forget Babylon Langhorne Creek Malbec 2019** A luxuriant rich red. Undeniably full bodied. A piste of classy French oak directs flavours of violet, bitter chocolate, lavender, plum and cherry long. A bristle of tannins mark the cheeks and bind everything together in a welcome savoury mould. A plush pleasure zone. Screw cap. 14.5% alc. **Rating** 93 **To** 2026 $32 NG
Perpetual Holidaze McLaren Vale Grenache 2020 A fun wine, straddling an edgy contemporary style, defined by briary tannin, pomegranate scents and a lightness of feel, with the rosewater, kirsch, musk stick and cranberry exuberance of the establishment. Thrills even better with a chill. Screw cap. 14.3% alc. **Rating** 91 **To** 2024 $32 NG
Free Love Rollin' On Langhorne Creek Fiano Vermentino NV A good, even-keeled dry white table wine. The saline pumice-like pucker across the airy finish, the highlight. Quince, fennel, apricot pith and wet-stone riffs. The sort of wine that doesn't get in the way of the moment: the conversation and the food on the plate. Screw cap. 12.5% alc. **Rating** 90 **To** 2022 $25 NG

🍷🍷🍷🍷 **Drink the Sun Rosé 2020 Rating** 88 **To** 2021 $25 NG

Bike & Barrel

PO Box 167, Myrtleford, Vic 3736 **Region** Alpine Valleys
T 0409 971 235
Winemaker Jo Marsh, Daniel Balzer **Est.** 2013 **Dozens** 280 **Vyds** 1.5ha
Brian and Linda Lewis split their vineyard and wine interests in two. One part is a 10ha commercial vineyard, established on undulating free-draining slopes above the valley floor, mainly supplying local wineries with chardonnay, prosecco, pinot noir and tempranillo. For Bike & Barrel they have 1.5ha of pinotage, fiano, schioppettino and refosco dal peduncolo rosso.

Billy Button Wines

11 Camp Street, Bright, Vic 3741 and 61 Myrtle Street, Myrtleford, Vic 3737
Region Alpine Valleys
T (03) 5755 1569 **www.**billybuttonwines.com.au **Open** 7 days 12–6
Winemaker Jo Marsh, Glenn James, Alex Phillips, Megan Wallace **Est.** 2014 **Dozens** 6000
Jo Marsh makes light of the numerous awards she won during her studies for her degree in agricultural science (oenology) at the University of Adelaide. She then won a contested position in Southcorp's Graduate Recruitment Program; she was appointed assistant winemaker at Seppelt Great Western in 2003. By '08 she had been promoted to acting senior winemaker, responsible for all wines made onsite. After Seppelt, she became winemaker at Feathertop, and after 2 happy years decided to step out on her own in '14. She has set up a grower network in the Alpine Valleys and makes a string of excellent wines. Billy Button also shares a cellar door with Bush Track Wines in the heart of Myrtleford.

🍷🍷🍷🍷🍷 **Silver Xenica Alpine Valleys Fiano 2019** The Silver Xenica label denotes the winemaker's favourite parcel of fruit from the vintage. Fiano displays a startling depth of flavour and varietal intensity here, it's easy to see why it stood out to winemaker Jo Marsh. Composed of stone fruits, lime zest, spiced pear, nougat, honeysuckle and hazelnut. The palate runs long, while the textural complexity is off the charts for the variety. More, please! Screw cap. 13% alc. **Rating** 95 **To** 2026 $40 JP

The Beloved Alpine Valleys Shiraz 2018 A deeply coloured young wine with plenty of personality, the result of a lot of obvious love and attention to detail. Super-fragrant and approachable first up, with blackberry, blueberry, wood smoke and aniseed. Proceeds with confidence and effortless balance with lashings of fruit, sage and a touch of undergrowth savouriness winding along a long path of ripe tannins. Screw cap. 14.5% alc. **Rating** 95 **To** 2028 $32 JP ✪

The Affable Alpine Valleys Barbera 2019 An interesting follow-up to the excellent '18 release, with greater ripeness evident, pushing the already plush style into luxuriant territory. Black cherries, wild raspberries, dried herbs and a dusty earthiness greet the drinker, but while the fruit intensity rises in '19, the same degree of medium-bodied structure and fineness is also evident, thanks to some juicy, fresh acidity. Screw cap. 14.5% alc. **Rating** 95 **To** 2026 $32 JP ✪

The Clandestine Alpine Valleys Schioppettino 2019 Jo Marsh is among the most curious and talented winemakers going. Thanks to her intellectual curiosity, we are blessed with wines like this, a rarity whose home is in Italy's northeast. A finely appointed wine of some delicacy and poise. Florals to the fore on the bouquet. Violet, bramble and rose mingle with black cherry, redcurrant and baking spices. Glides across the tongue to an easy conclusion. Compelling in its understatement. Screw cap. 13.5% alc. **Rating** 95 **To** 2026 $32 JP ✪

The Classic Alpine Valleys Chardonnay 2019 This wine aims for complexity and it delivers, with mouthfuls of roasted hazelnuts, lemon butter, honey and yellow peach. Picks up some complex textural elements along the way, nothing too broad, finishing with a very tidy resolve. Screw cap. 13% alc. **Rating** 94 **To** 2028 $32 JP

🍷🍷🍷🍷♀ **The Renegade Alpine Valleys Refosco 2019 Rating** 93 **To** 2026 $32 JP
King Valley Alpine Valleys Rosso 2019 Rating 93 **To** 2024 $22 JP ✪
The Alluring Alpine Valleys Tempranillo 2019 Rating 93 **To** 2027 $32 JP
Drumborg Henty Gewürztraminer 2020 Rating 92 **To** 2025 $27 JP
The Elusive Alpine Valleys Nebbiolo 2018 Rating 92 **To** 2025 $32 JP
The Sojourner Heathcote Lagrein 2020 Rating 92 **To** 2034 $32 JP
The Socialite Alpine Valleys Prosecco 2019 Rating 92 **To** 2023 $32 JP
Zero Dosage Prosecco 2019 Rating 91 **To** 2023 $32 JP
The Versatile Alpine Valleys Vermentino 2020 Rating 90 **To** 2025 $27 JP
The Mysterious Alpine Valleys Malvasia 2019 Rating 90 **To** 2024 $27 JP
The Delinquent Alpine Valleys Verduzzo 2019 Rating 90 **To** 2026 $27 JP
The Dapper Alpine Valleys Durif 2018 Rating 90 **To** 2028 $32 JP

Bimbadgen   ★★★★★

790 McDonalds Road, Pokolbin, NSW 2320 **Region** Hunter Valley
T (02) 4998 4600 **www.**bimbadgen.com.au **Open** 7 days 10–5
Winemaker Richard Done **Est.** 1968 **Dozens** 30 000 **Vyds** 26ha
Bimbadgen's Palmers Lane vineyard was planted in 1968 and the McDonalds Road vineyard shortly thereafter. Both sites provide old-vine semillon, shiraz and chardonnay, with tempranillo a more recent addition. Since assuming ownership in '97, the Lee family has applied the same level of care and attention to cultivating Bimbadgen as they have to other properties in their portfolio. The small but impressive production is consumed largely by the owner's luxury hotel assets, with limited quantities available in the Sydney market. Exports to the UK, Switzerland, Germany, the Netherlands, Japan, Taiwan and China.

🍷🍷🍷🍷🍷 **Signature Hunter Valley Shiraz 2019** Older vines. More oak. Greater ambition. This address pushes very few envelopes, but this is good. Very. The attractive proposition being that it is far more elegant, lithe and layered than its premium-priced siblings. Sour cherry, baking spice, clove, tamarind and varnish. Pliant but detailed, supple and strongly suggestive of the need to age for an additional decade or more. Screw cap. 14.1% alc. **Rating** 95 **To** 2034 $90 NG

ΨΨΨΨΨ Museum Release Signature Palmers Lane Semillon 2015 Rating 93
To 2025 $65 NG
Single Vineyard McDonalds Road Shiraz 2019 Rating 92 To 2028 $50 NG
Single Vineyard Palmers Lane Shiraz 2019 Rating 92 To 2033 $50 NG
Sparkling Blanc de Blancs 2015 Rating 92 $50 NG
Estate Hunter Valley Semillon 2019 Rating 91 To 2027 $25 NG
Estate Hunter Valley Chardonnay 2018 Rating 90 To 2024 $25 NG

Bindi Wines ★★★★★

343 Melton Road, Gisborne, Vic 3437 (postal) **Region** Macedon Ranges
T (03) 5428 2564 **www.**bindiwines.com.au
Winemaker Michael Dhillon, Stuart Anderson (Consultant) **Est.** 1988 **Dozens** 2000
Vyds 6ha
One of the icons of Macedon. The Chardonnay is top-shelf, the Pinot Noir as remarkable
(albeit in a very different idiom) as Bass Phillip, Giaconda or any of the other tiny-production,
icon wines. The addition of Heathcote-sourced shiraz under the Pyrette label confirms Bindi
as one of the greatest small producers in Australia. Exports to the UK, the US and other
major markets.

ΨΨΨΨΨ Quartz Chardonnay 2019 Wow. This made my heart skip a beat. It races
along but not too fast, as it does reveal a complex combo of citrus, lemon balm,
subtle lees influence and a spark of flint. The oak is beautifully integrated, offering
support, as do the grapefruit pith-like phenolics. It's long, pure and simply
sensational. Screw cap. 13% alc. **Rating** 97 **To** 2033 $100 JF ✪ ♥
Dixon Pinot Noir 2019 A blend of fruit off the original vineyard planted in
1988 and the Kaye vineyard planted in 2001. It's morphed into a complete and
compelling wine. Fragrant with florals and warm earth. There's a depth of flavour,
with dark cherries, amaro and bitter Italian herbs that slip across the fuller-bodied
palate. Two key elements here; freshness within and beautiful, plush tannins. What
a wine. Screw cap. 13.5% alc. **Rating** 97 **To** 2034 $65 JF ✪
Original Vineyard Pinot Noir 2019 Its riff is savoury, full of wood smoke,
earthy and autumnal tunes. In the mix, black cherries infused with menthol and
Middle Eastern spices. The palate is an exercise in texture. It is caressed by ribbons
of velvety tannins, bright acidity and a finish that is as long as it is pure. A seamless
wine. Diam. 13% alc. **Rating** 97 **To** 2033 $85 JF ✪
Block 5 Pinot Noir 2019 This is the finest 2019 pinot noir across all regions
that I have tasted. I bow to its elegance, its structure and, indeed, its beauty. It's a
perfect amalgam of fragrance, flavour and shape, with the latter bolstered by plush
tannins covered in raw silk. There's a vitality, an energy that lifts this – it is a wine
unencumbered by obvious winemaking. The site speaks. Time to listen. Diam.
13% alc. **Rating** 97 **To** 2035 $125 JF ✪ ♥

ΨΨΨΨΨ Kostas Rind Chardonnay 2019 The tension in this is fabulous. Taut as a snare
drum, yet intense in flavour. It starts off on a citrus theme, with lemons and a
touch of tangerine, tempered by a layer of nutty, leesy richness – just a smidge –
this is a linear offering. It finishes long and persuasive. A delicious drink. Screw cap.
13% alc. **Rating** 96 **To** 2030 $65 JF ✪
Kaye Macedon Ranges Pinot Noir 2017 This spends an extra 3 years in
bottle and it has the finest structure. There's a restraint, a gentleness, with sweet red
cherries; lightly spiced – think fennel and licorice. Flavours stretch and lengthen
across the medium-bodied palate, before finely chiselled tannins and lithe acidity
take over. The essence of purity right here. Diam. 13.5% alc. **Rating** 96 **To** 2030
$100 JF
Dhillon Col Mountain Heathcote Shiraz 2014 The wine's colour and
freshness belie its age. It has morphed into a complete wine. Fragrant and earthy,
with a dusting of exotic spices – woodsy ones too, with dark fruit certainly in the
picture. Plush, ripe tannins glide effortless across the fuller-bodied palate. Diam.
14% alc. **Rating** 96 **To** 2028 $75 JF ✪

Pyrette Heathcote Shiraz 2019 Alluring purple/black colour. The wine is intense, yet manages a refinement that is the mark of Bindi. Expect an amalgam of savoury flavours with bitumen, licorice and aniseed balls. It's more medium to fuller bodied, with lithe tannins. While there's a richness and depth of flavour that makes you step back, it's all in admiration. Screw cap. 13% alc. **Rating** 95 **To** 2033 $40 JF

Dhillon Col Mountain Heathcote Grenache 2020 The other red under the new Dhillon label is sourced from the same vineyard at Col Mountain. This a fresh, juicy grenache that offers a core of beautiful fruit, yet none of the mawkish confectionary character that can haunt this variety. It is supple, with fine, sandy tannins, buoyant red fruits and a touch of sarsaparilla and sumac. Lip-smackingly delicious. Diam. 13.5% alc. **Rating** 95 **To** 2028 $40 JF

Bird in Hand

Bird in Hand Road, Woodside, SA 5244 **Region** Adelaide Hills
T (08) 8389 9488 **www.**birdinhand.com.au **Open** Mon–Fri 10–5, w'ends & public hols 11–5
Winemaker Kym Milne MW, Dylan Lee, Matteo Malagese **Est.** 1997 **Dozens** 120 000 **Vyds** 29ha
This family-owned business takes its name from a gold mine that prospered nearby during the 19th century. Andrew Nugent and winemaking director Kym Milne MW work together to produce estate wines of high quality. Sustainable initiatives in the vineyard include fertilisers and fungicides being derived from organic sources, and herbicide use has been drastically reduced, with future use moving to zero. The wines are released in 4 tiers: Tribute Series, Nest Egg, Bird in Hand and Two in the Bush. Exports to all major markets.

Bird on a Wire Wines

51 Symons Street, Healesville, Vic 3777 (postal) **Region** Yarra Valley
T 0439 045 000 **www.**birdonawirewines.com.au
Winemaker Caroline Mooney **Est.** 2008 **Dozens** 850
This is the full-time business of winemaker Caroline Mooney. She grew up in the Yarra Valley and has had (other full-time) winemaking jobs in the valley for over 10 years. The focus is on small, single-vineyard sites owned by growers committed to producing outstanding grapes. Having worked at the legendary Domaine Jean-Louis Chave in the 2006 vintage, she has a special interest in shiraz and marsanne, both grown from distinct sites on a single vineyard in the Yarra Glen area. Exports to the UK.

BK Wines

Knotts Hill, Basket Range, SA 5138 **Region** Adelaide Hills
T 0410 124 674 **www.**bkwines.com.au **Open** By appt
Winemaker Brendon Keys **Est.** 2007 **Dozens** 4000
BK Wines is owned by NZ-born Brendon Keys and wife Kirsty. Brendon has packed a great deal into the past decade. He bounced between Australia and NZ before working in California with the well-known Paul Hobbs; he then helped Paul set up a winery in Argentina. Brendon's tagline is 'Wines made with love, not money', and he has not hesitated to confound the normal rules of engagement in winemaking. If he isn't remembered for this, the labels for his wines should do the trick. Exports to Canada, Norway, Italy, France, Cambodia, South Korea, NZ, Japan, Singapore, Hong Kong and China.

♥♥♥♥♥ Ovum Single Vineyard Lenswood Adelaide Hills Pinot Gris 2020 Whole-bunch pressed into a concrete egg with full solids, wild fermented, then 10 months on its lees. The barest of pink blushes. There's spicy white-strawberry aroma, fabulous palate pith and acidity, and that peppery spice holding tight all through the wine. A white wine with intent and inner energy. Synthetic cork. 13.5% alc. **Rating** 94 **To** 2023 $38 TL

ŸŸŸŸŸ Skin n' Bones Single Vineyard Lenswood Adelaide Hills Pinot Noir 2020
Rating 93 To 2025 $38 TL
Swaby Single Vineyard Piccadilly Valley Adelaide Hills Chardonnay 2020
Rating 92 To 2026 $55 TL
Ovum Adelaide Hills Grüner Veltliner 2020 Rating 92 To 2023 $38 TL
The Fall Single Vineyard Adelaide Hills Chardonnay 2020 Rating 91
To 2025 $55 TL
Archer Beau Single Barrel Piccadilly Valley Adelaide Hills Chardonnay
2018 Rating 91 To 2025 $110 TL
Carbonic Adelaide Hills Pinot Noir 2020 Rating 91 To 2022 $32 TL
Remy Single Barrel Lenswood Adelaide Hills Pinot Noir 2018 Rating 90
To 2026 $110 TL

Black & Ginger

563 Sugarloaf Road, Rhymney, Vic 3374 **Region** Great Western
T 0409 964 855 **www**.blackandginger.com.au
Winemaker Hadyn Black **Est.** 2015 **Dozens** 400
This is the venture of 2 friends who met in 2002 after attending the same high school. Hadyn
Black is cellar hand and winemaker, working in the Great Western region. Darcy Naunton
(ginger) is an entrepreneur in Melbourne. Their common interest in wine saw them take a
great leap in 2015 and buy 1t of shiraz from the renowned Malakoff Vineyard in the Pyrenees,
with further vintages following. Hadyn and partner Lucy Joyce purchased a rundown vineyard
in Great Western in late '16, naming the wine Lily's Block after Hadyn's mother, who did
much of the pruning and picking but unfortunately passed away before tasting the wine.

BlackJack Vineyards

3379 Harmony Way, Harcourt, Vic 3453 **Region** Bendigo
T (03) 5474 2355 **www**.blackjackwines.com.au **Open** W'ends & some public hols 11–5
Winemaker Ian McKenzie, Ken Pollock **Est.** 1987 **Dozens** 3000 **Vyds** 6ha
Established by the McKenzie and Pollock families on the site of an old apple and pear orchard
in the Harcourt Valley, BlackJack is best known for very good shiraz. Despite some tough
vintage conditions, BlackJack has managed to produce supremely honest, full-flavoured and
powerful wines, all with an edge of elegance. Exports to China.

Bleasdale Vineyards

1640 Langhorne Creek Road, Langhorne Creek, SA 5255 **Region** Langhorne Creek
T (08) 8537 4000 **www**.bleasdale.com.au **Open** 7 days 10–5
Winemaker Paul Hotker, Matt Laube **Est.** 1850 **Vyds** 45ha
This is one of the most historic wineries in Australia; in 2020 it celebrated 170 years of
continuous winemaking by the direct descendants of the founding Potts family. Not so long
before the start of the 21st century, its vineyards were flooded every winter by diversion of the
Bremer River, which provided moisture throughout the dry, cool growing season. In the new
millennium, every drop of water is counted. The vineyards have been significantly upgraded
and refocused: shiraz accounts for 45% of plantings, supported by 7 other proven varieties.
Bleasdale has completely revamped its labels and packaging, and has headed to the Adelaide
Hills for sauvignon blanc, pinot gris and chardonnay under the direction of gifted winemaker
Paul Hotker. Exports to all major markets.

ŸŸŸŸŸ 18 Year Old Rare Tawny Langhorne Creek NV A mid to deep amber rather
than the heavier tawny expected in a wine of such age. It tells us of the freshness
to follow, a hallmark of the wine, with vibrant baking spice, beautifully delicate
timbered backdrops, the faintest of nutty rancio just appearing. Importantly, no
cloying finish – rather, refreshing, clean and vibrant. Fabulous. Cork. 18.5% alc.
Rating 98 $79 TL ✪ ❤

ŸŸŸŸŸ Adelaide Hills Riesling 2020 Winemaker Paul Hotker has a way with riesling,
far from the centre of the Bleasdale portfolio. There's a tactile feel to the wine that

moves from lime juice painted on the surfaces of the mouth, to mouth-watering acidity. Low yields in this vintage is only part of the story. Screw cap. 11% alc. **Rating** 96 **To** 2030 $30 JH ✪

The Powder Monkey Single Vineyard Langhorne Creek Shiraz 2019
Terroir-defined wine with spot-on ripeness. Fabulously dense, yet not heavy. All manner of savoury complexities here, from nori to cacao richness and bitterness, with the tannins that match those characters in perfect proportion. Will be better in 5 years and has many years ahead of it. Screw cap. 14% alc. **Rating** 95 **To** 2030 $79 TL

Frank Potts Langhorne Creek 2019 A great red blend, 69/17/8/6% cabernet sauvignon/malbec/merlot/petit verdot. Matured for 12 months in 25% new French oak barrels. Understated at first, though very deeply set in its bouquet with the darkest of berries and chocolate, working their layered magic on the palate. The regional imprint of cabernet is in the lead, plump and generous, with masterful integration of tannins. Screw cap. 14% alc. **Rating** 95 **To** 2032 $35 TL ✪

Second Innings Langhorne Creek Malbec 2019 Bleasdale can't put a foot wrong with malbec at whatever price point it chooses. This is flooded with plum varietal fruit, but also has the texture and back-palate structure that many malbecs miss out on. Winemaker Paul Hotker is a wiz. Screw cap. 14% alc. **Rating** 95 **To** 2027 $22 JH ✪ ♥

Generations Langhorne Creek Malbec 2019 Next-level malbec here, with all its varietal expectations fulfilled. Vibrant purple colour, violets and blue/black fruits, a whiff of iodine and a faint sense of Dutch licorice, without its bitterness. All of it swells on the palate, the tannins settling in underneath, fitting neatly with the flow of the wine. Many years ahead of it – decant for now. Screw cap. 14% alc. **Rating** 95 **To** 2028 $35 TL ✪ ♥

16 Year Old Rare Langhorne Creek Verdelho NV Bleasdale's pedigree fortified wine program comes to life with this Verdelho aged for a minimum of 16 years, stored high in the winery in old oak barrels for long, slow evaporation and concentration. Now showing a glossy golden tan, caramel toffee aromas which then join with dark marmalade flavours. The Langhorne Creek climate ensures it's still fresh with balancing acidity. A summer fortified – chill it, cocktail it. Cork. 18.5% alc. **Rating** 95 $79 TL

Wellington Road Langhorne Creek Shiraz Cabernet 2019 A 52/48% blend with shiraz in the lead, yet in classic claret style it's the cabernet that dominates the nose to begin, with vibrant crimson-fruited notes to the fore. In house style, earthy and savoury elements are present through the palate, while a little mint/eucalyptus in the background offers a regional nod, without dominating the elegant fruit expression within. Screw cap. 14% alc. **Rating** 94 **To** 2028 $32 TL

♟♟♟♟♟ **Generations Langhorne Creek Shiraz 2019** **Rating** 93 **To** 2028 $35 TL
Broad-Side Langhorne Creek Shiraz Cabernet Sauvignon Malbec 2019 **Rating** 92 **To** 2028 $22 TL ✪
Wellington Road Langhorne Creek GSM 2020 **Rating** 92 **To** 2026 $32 TL
Wellington Road Langhorne Creek GSM 2019 **Rating** 92 **To** 2028 $32 TL
The Ruby Fig Vintage Fortified SGM 2018 **Rating** 92 **To** 2028 $19 TL ✪
Mulberry Tree Langhorne Creek Cabernet Sauvignon 2019 **Rating** 92 **To** 2026 $22 TL ✪
Adelaide Hills Sauvignon Blanc 2020 **Rating** 91 **To** 2023 $22 TL ✪
Adelaide Hills Pinot Gris 2020 **Rating** 91 **To** 2023 $22 TL ✪
The Wild Fig Langhorne Creek Shiraz Grenache Mourvèdre 2020 **Rating** 91 **To** 2025 $22 TL ✪
Adelaide Hills Chardonnay 2020 **Rating** 90 **To** 2025 $30 TL
Bremerview Langhorne Creek Shiraz 2019 **Rating** 90 **To** 2026 $22 TL
The Wild Plum Langhorne Creek Cabernet Sauvignon Merlot 2019 **Rating** 90 **To** 2025 $20 TL ✪

Blewitt Springs Wine Co

477 Blewitt Springs Road, Blewitt Springs, SA 5171 **Region** McLaren Vale
T 0402 106 240 **www.**blewittspringswineco.com.au **Open** By appt
Winemaker Phil Tabor **Est.** 2017 **Dozens** 500 **Vyds** 7.5ha

It's impossible to do justice to the fast-moving complexity of Phil and Nina Tabor's Blewitt Springs Estate in the confines of this summary. Briefly, Phil's design engineering business in Adelaide became the subject of a bidding war between 2 suitors in 2008; the deal completed at the top of the market. In '13 he worked his first vintage in McLaren Vale and found a mentor in the well-known Phil Christiansen. In '15 he purchased the 40ha Blewitt Springs Estate Vineyard, with 7.3ha of shiraz planted in 3 blocks in 1998, 2005 and '08. First he designed and built the 40t winery, completed in time for the bumper vintage of '17. He had agreed to sell 30t, assuming it would leave him with 8–10t, and swapped/purchased grenache and hatfuls of other varieties. In fact, he was left with 26t, the fermenters full to overflowing. Things returned to normal and 80% of the fruit is sold each year. Concurrently he had begun building the cellar door, renovated a stone bungalow and begun a new house for Nina and him to live in, leaving the bungalow as a luxury B&B. Phil is a hands-on operator and has every intention of doing much of the winemaking and viticulture himself. He has made space in the winery for other winemakers to make one-off wine, and he has learnt by seeing what (and why) they do. The key, however, is his belief in cool fermentation of his red wines, and he won't be changing that.

TTTTT McLaren Vale Shiraz 2019 A lustrous purple hue. Floral aromas. Pulpy of feel. Lithe of briary tannin, with peppery acidity weaving a long thread of bergamot, dried seaweed, blueberry, anise and clove. A joyous, full-bodied wine brimming with life. Screw cap. 14.6% alc. **Rating** 93 **To** 2030 $28 NG
McLaren Vale Tempranillo 2018 This is lashed with vanilla/bourbon American oak and yet, there is a freshness about it. Put that down to the elevated sands of the zone and judicious handling. A dollop of stems in the mix imparts some briar and spice to the tannins, unspooling a weave of sapid cherry, damson plum and baking-spice aromas. The tannins, broad and dusty, corral the full-bodied melee. Screw cap. 14.6% alc. **Rating** 92 **To** 2024 $28 NG

Bloodwood

231 Griffin Road, Orange, NSW 2800 **Region** Orange
T (02) 6362 5631 **www.**bloodwood.biz **Open** By appt
Winemaker Stephen Doyle **Est.** 1983 **Dozens** 4000 **Vyds** 8.43ha

Rhonda and Stephen Doyle are two of the pioneers of the Orange district; 2013 marked Bloodwood's 30th anniversary. The estate vineyards (chardonnay, riesling, merlot, cabernet sauvignon, shiraz, cabernet franc and malbec) are planted at an elevation of 810–860m, which provides a reliably cool climate. The wines are sold mainly through the cellar door and by an energetic, humorous and informatively run mailing list. Bloodwood has an impressive track record across the full gamut of wine styles, especially riesling; all of the wines have a particular elegance and grace. Very much part of the high-quality reputation of Orange. Exports to Malaysia.

TTTTT Schubert 2019 Fine aromas of oatmeal and ginger-spiced biscuit, praline and creamed cashew. The oak and pungent mineral undercurrent serve as a lattice that augurs well for a bright future. Apricot pith, white peach and a hint of marzipan, too. Mid weighted, strident of gait and long of finish. Screw cap. 13% alc. **Rating** 94 **To** 2030 $36 NG

TTTTT Pinot Noir 2019 Rating 92 **To** 2030 $40 NG
Shiraz 2018 Rating 91 **To** 2026 $35 NG

Blue Gables

100 Lanigan Road, Maffra West Upper, Vic 3859 **Region** Gippsland
T (03) 5148 0372 **www**.bluegables.com.au **Open** W'ends 10–5 by appt
Winemaker Alastair Butt, Mal Stewart (sparkling) **Est.** 2004 **Dozens** 1800 **Vyds** 3.7ha
Blue Gables is the culmination of a long-held dream for chemical engineer Alistair and
journalist wife Catherine Hicks. They purchased 8ha of a north-facing hillside slope from
Catherine's father's dairy farm and built a two-storey gabled roof farmhouse, hence the name.
This small vineyard, nestled high above the Macalister Irrigation District in East Gippsland,
was established in 2004 with the planting of the first vines, and continued in '05 with 0.8ha
each of sauvignon blanc, pinot gris and shiraz and 0.4ha of chardonnay. The wines have had
significant success in the Gippsland and Victorian wine shows.

Blue Pyrenees Estate

656 Vinoca Road, Avoca, Vic 3467 **Region** Pyrenees
T (03) 5465 1111 **www**.bluepyrenees.com.au **Open** 7 days 11–5
Winemaker Andrew Koerner, Chris Smales **Est.** 1963 **Dozens** 50 000 **Vyds** 149ha
Forty years after Remy Cointreau established Blue Pyrenees Estate (then known as Chateau
Remy), the business was sold to a small group of Sydney businessmen. Former Rosemount
senior winemaker Andrew Koerner heads the winery team. The core of the business is the
very large estate plantings, most decades old, but with newer arrivals, including viognier.
Blue Pyrenees has a number of programs designed to protect the environment and reduce
its carbon footprint. Blue Pyrenees Estate has been purchased by Glenlofty Wines, forming
the largest producer in the Pyrenees. Exports to China, the US, Japan, Canada and Germany.

🍷🍷🍷🍷🍷 Richardson Reserve Shiraz 2017 A barrel selection of the best wines of what
was a mighty fine vintage, with plenty of hang time for grapes. Given the wine is
named after the larger-than-life late Colin Richardson, who played an important
role in the rebirth of the modern Victorian wine industry, expect a generous-
hearted, highly expressive, complex and cellar-bound shiraz. This still has many
miles to go before it's ready. Diam. 14% alc. **Rating** 95 **To** 2032 $160 JP
Richardson Reserve Cabernet Sauvignon 2017 A wine that expects time
in the cellar, completely in keeping with the philosophy of its namesake, the late
Colin Richardson, who extolled the virtues of ageing Victorian reds. The familiar
scent of the Aussie bush, bay leaf and sage joins dark forest berries, earth and fine
coffee ground, vanillan oak aromas. The firm, tannin-sure palate is enhanced by a
lilting herbal savouriness. Diam. 14% alc. **Rating** 95 **To** 2032 $160 JP
Richardson Shiraz 2018 Matured in new and 2yo French and American oak
for 18 months. Deep, but bright-rimmed colour; blackberry, licorice and tar fill the
full-bodied palate. Built like the late Colin Richardson, with a rumble of tannins
on the long finish. Diam. 14.5% alc. **Rating** 94 **To** 2038 $72 JH

🍷🍷🍷🍷🍷 Luna Chardonnay Pinot Noir NV **Rating** 92 $22 JP ✪
Section One Shiraz 2018 **Rating** 91 **To** 2028 $38 JP
Estate Red 2018 **Rating** 91 **To** 2028 $45 JP
Dry Sparkling Rosé NV **Rating** 91 $28 JP

Blue Range Estate

155 Gardens Road, Rosebud, Vic 3939 **Region** Mornington Peninsula
T (03) 5986 6560 **www**.bluerangeestatewines.com.au **Open** W'ends & public hols 11–4
Winemaker Cosi Melone **Est.** 1987 **Dozens** 5000 **Vyds** 10ha
Established by the De Cicco family in 1987, present owners Cosi and Joe Melone now have
4ha each of chardonnay and pinot grigio, a little over 1ha of shiraz, pinot noir and merlot
making up the remainder. The wines are made onsite by Cosi Melone, and the Blanc de Blanc
won the sparkling wine trophy at Les Concours des Vins du Victoria '10. A feature of the the
cellar door is the older vintages that are available.

♈♈♈♈♈ Mornington Peninsula Pinot Noir 2018 While not overly complex, this is fragrant, juicy and very easy to slurp. Loads of fresh squishy raspberries and poached cherries spiced up with cinnamon. It's lighter framed with supple tannins and neat acidity. In warm weather, I'd be happy to chill this a bit. Screw cap. 13% alc. **Rating** 90 **To** 2025 $25 JF

Blue Rock Wines

PO Box 692, Williamstown, SA 5351 **Region** Eden Valley
T 0419 817 017 **www.**bluerockwines.com.au
Winemaker Zissis Zachopoulos **Est.** 2005 **Dozens** 4000 **Vyds** 15ha
This is the venture of the brothers Zachopoulos: Nicholas, Michael and Zissis, the last with a double degree in viticulture and wine science from CSU. Michael and Nicholas manage the 104ha property, situated in the Eden Valley at an elevation of 475m. Most blocks are northfacing, the slopes providing frost protection with their natural air drainage; the soils likewise rich and free-draining. The vineyards have been planted so far to mainstream varieties, with an ongoing planting program including tempranillo, pinot gris, pinot noir, grenache and mataro. Most of the 450–500t production is the subject of a sales agreement with Grant Burge, but 75t are retained each year to make the Blue Rock wines.

♈♈♈♈ Eden Valley Vineyard Series Riesling 2020 The cool heights of Pewsey Vale have upheld crunch and tension in the concentrated 2020 season. Classic hallmarks of lime, lemon, fig and Granny Smith apple are accented with spice. A wine of line, length and presence, sustained by bright acidity and firm phenolic bite. Screw cap. 12.5% alc. **Rating** 89 **To** 2021 $20 TS

Boat O'Craigo ★★★★☆

458 Maroondah Highway, Healesville, Vic 3777 **Region** Yarra Valley
T (03) 5962 6899 **www.**boatocraigo.com.au **Open** Fri–Sun 10.30–5.30
Winemaker Rob Dolan (Contract) **Est.** 1998 **Dozens** 3000 **Vyds** 21.63ha
Boat O'Craigo is a second-generation family business established by Steve and Margaret Graham in 1998 with the planting of a vineyard at Kangaroo Ground. The elevated site was planted with shiraz, cabernet sauvignon, grenache and viognier. The first vintage was in 2003. A second vineyard in Healesville, purchased in '03, is home to the cellar door. It is bounded by the Graceburn Creek and Black Spur Ranges, with plantings of pinot noir, chardonnay, gewürztraminer, grüner veltliner, pinot gris and sauvignon blanc. Since '15 Travers, Steve and Margaret's eldest son, has run the business. Boat O'Craigo was awarded Dark Horse of the Year in the *Wine Companion 2018*. Exports to Hong Kong and China.

♈♈♈♈♈ First Duke Reserve Yarra Valley Shiraz 2018 A wine of opulence and richness befitting a First Duke. It does have 3% viognier in the mix, adding to its impressive dark purple hue. Black fruits, herbs and woodsy spices are wound together for the base of this savoury, full-bodied red. Cedary, mocha-cream oak adds firm tannins and another layer of gloss throughout. All in all, it stands tall. Screw cap. 13.6% alc. **Rating** 95 **To** 2032 $65 JF

♈♈♈♈♈ Kincardine Single Vineyard Yarra Valley Grenache 2019 **Rating** 93 **To** 2028 $35 JF
Black Spur Single Vineyard Yarra Valley Pinot Noir 2019 **Rating** 90 **To** 2027 $35 JF

Bochara Wines

1099 Glenelg Highway, Hamilton, Vic 3300 **Region** Henty
T (03) 5571 9309 **www.**bocharawines.com.au **Open** Fri–Sun 11–5 or by appt
Winemaker Martin Slocombe **Est.** 1998 **Dozens** 1000 **Vyds** 2.2ha
Planted in 1998, the 2.2ha vineyard includes sauvignon blanc (1ha), pinot noir (0.8ha) and gewürztraminer (0.4ha); varieties all well suited to the cold and sometimes temperamental

Henty climate. The winery's tiny scale means that all operations are done by hand, with wines made onsite by owners Martin Slocombe and Kylie McIntyre. The wines are sold from the rustic cottage at the vineyard, and in restaurants and retailers across south Western Victoria. The Belle Époque label design is taken from a 1901 poster advertising farming land at Bochara.

ŸŸŸŸŸ Pinot Noir 2019 Dark in hue, pretty in scents and softly textured, this young cool-climate pinot offers immediate good drinking with the potential for more ageing. Violets, black and red berries, leafy, sappy and herbal. It presents fresh and lively on the palate with fine tannins and sweet oak spice. Screw cap. 13.6% alc. **Rating** 91 **To** 2028 $32 JP

Boireann ★★★★★

26 Donnellys Castle Road, The Summit, Qld 4377 **Region** Granite Belt
T (07) 4683 2194 **www.**boireannwinery.com.au **Open** Fri–Mon 10–4
Winemaker Brad Rowe **Est.** 1998 **Dozens** 1000 **Vyds** 1.6ha
Boireann is set among the great granite boulders and trees that are so much a part of the Granite Belt. The vineyard is planted to 11 varieties, including 4 that make the Lurnea, a Bordeaux blend; shiraz and viognier; grenache and mourvèdre for a Rhône blend; and a straight merlot. Tannat, pinot noir (French) and sangiovese, barbera and nebbiolo (Italian) make up the viticultural League of Nations. Peter and Therese Stark sold the business in 2017 but worked closely with new managers Brad Rowe and wife Metz; Brad made his first wines in 2018. Exports to Hong Kong and China.

ŸŸŸŸŸ Granite Belt Shiraz 2019 Impeccable ripeness and fine-boned structure make this tiny production the best Queensland wine this year. Impressively full, vibrant purple hue. Dense, inky blackberry, blueberry and satsuma plum fruit, medium bodied and infused with the Granite Belt's cool acidity, completely belying its alcohol. Well-gauged dark chocolate oak leaves the show to top-class fruit, nuanced with black pepper. Fine, mineral tannins carry a long finish. Screw cap. 15% alc. **Rating** 95 **To** 2029 $75 TS
Granite Belt Mourvèdre 2019 Impressive fruit density and definition has been well crafted in this tiny release. Boasting an impressively full vibrant purple hue, it's packed with dense, compact black fruits of all kinds, licorice and high-cocoa dark chocolate oak. Savoury, leathery complexity perfectly captures the signature of the variety. Firm, fine tannins meld neatly with vibrant acidity on a finish of even persistence. One for the cellar. Screw cap. 14.5% alc. **Rating** 94 **To** 2039 $45 TS

ŸŸŸŸŸ Granite Belt Shiraz Viognier 2019 Rating 93 To 2029 $75 TS
The Lurnea Granite Belt 2019 Rating 93 To 2039 $75 TS
Granite Belt Cabernet Sauvignon 2019 Rating 92 To 2039 $45 TS
La Cima Granite Belt Barbera 2019 Rating 90 To 2027 $45 TS

Bondar Wines ★★★★★

148 McMurtrie Road, McLaren Vale, SA 5171 **Region** McLaren Vale
T 0147 888 553 **www.**bondarwines.com.au **Open** Fri–Mon 11–5
Winemaker Andre Bondar **Est.** 2013 **Dozens** 3000 **Vyds** 13.5ha
Husband and wife Andre Bondar and Selina Kelly began a deliberately unhurried journey in 2009, which culminated in the purchase of the celebrated Rayner Vineyard post-vintage '13. Andre had been a winemaker at Nepenthe wines for 7 years, and Selina had recently completed a law degree but was already disillusioned about the legal landscape. They changed focus and began to look for a vineyard capable of producing great shiraz. The Rayner Vineyard had all the answers: a ridge bisecting the land, Blewitt Springs sand on the eastern side; and the Seaview, heavier clay loam soils over limestone on the western side. The vineyard has been substantially reworked and includes 10ha of shiraz, with smaller amounts of grenache, mataro, touriga, carignan, cinsault and counoise. Exports to Hong Kong, the UK, the US and China.

ŸŸŸŸŸ **Rayner Vineyard Shiraz 2019** While I am optimistic about grenache in these parts, I often find the style of shiraz monochromatic. Not in these hands. Despite the heat spikes of a warm year, the sandy blocks across the vineyard thrived. A cool finish to the season, providing perk. All things done right: picking window, use of bunches (20%) and a long extraction. Mostly older wood. A textural tour de force. Violet, blueberry, nori, peppery acidity and a licorella tannin line so fine that it could be threaded through the eye of a needle. A beautiful wine. Screw cap. 14% alc. **Rating** 96 **To** 2032 $45 NG ✪

Adelaide Hills Chardonnay 2019 While I find the array of Mediterranean varieties at this estate compelling, this is exceptional chardonnay from the Hills. Riveting! A core of nougat/cashew/vanilla pod/oatmeal cream, with rims of mineral pungency and a frame flecked by stone-fruit references, sweet and savoury/sour. A thrilling tussle between extract, energy and structural binds. Screw cap. 13% alc. **Rating** 95 **To** 2027 $35 NG ✪ ♥

Rayner Vineyard Grenache 2020 Rosehip, cranberry, pomegranate and wild strawberry. Bracing freshness and a tactile web of diaphanous tannins, reining in any excess. Almost alpine herbal. Granular acidity tows it long. Stunning. Screw cap. 14% alc. **Rating** 95 **To** 2028 $45 NG

ŸŸŸŸŸ **McLaren Vale Grenache Cinsault Rosé 2020** **Rating** 93 **To** 2021 $25 NG ✪
Violet Hour McLaren Vale Shiraz 2019 **Rating** 93 **To** 2028 $28 NG
Higher Springs McLaren Vale Grenache 2020 **Rating** 93 **To** 2027 $45 NG
McLaren Vale Monastrell 2019 **Rating** 93 **To** 2025 $32 NG
McLaren Vale Nero d'Avola 2020 **Rating** 92 **To** 2022 $32 NG
McLaren Vale Fiano 2020 **Rating** 91 **To** 2022 $28 NG

Borrodell Vineyard
★★★★☆

Lake Canobolas Road, Orange, NSW 2800 **Region** Orange
T (02) 6365 3425 **www**.borrodell.com.au **Open** 7 days 11–5
Winemaker Simon Gilbert **Est.** 1964 **Dozens** 20 000 **Vyds** 7ha
Borry Gartrell and Gaye Stuart-Nairne have planted pinot noir, sauvignon blanc, pinot meunier, gewürztraminer and chardonnay adjacent to a cherry, plum and heritage apple orchard and a truffiere. It is a 10-min drive from Orange, and adjacent to Lake Canobolas, at an altitude of 1000m. The wines have been consistent medal winners at regional and small winemaker shows. Exports to China.

Bourke & Travers
★★★☆

PO Box 457, Clare, SA 5453 **Region** Clare Valley
T 0400 745 057 **www**.bourkeandtravers.com
Winemaker David Travers, Michael Corbett **Est.** 1998 **Dozens** 250 **Vyds** 6ha
Owner David Travers' family has been continuously farming in Australia for 157 years. In the 1870s David's great-grandfather, Nicholas Travers, established a vineyard south of Leasingham, between what is now Kilikanoon and O'Leary Walker. However, his son Paul left to establish a large sheep and grazing property near Port Lincoln. Paul's son Gerald (David's father) retains these properties today; David is heavily involved in their operation. He (David) established Bourke & Travers on Armagh Creek in 1996 and planted the first grapes (shiraz) in '98. The Bourke in the brand comes from David's mother's maiden name. The wine portfolio has been increased with a Syrah Rosé, a single-vineyard Grenache and the introduction of 25% whole-bunch fermentation in the Shiraz.

ŸŸŸŸŸ **Single Vineyard Clare Valley Mourvèdre 2019** Captivates with appealing aromas, more fruit-led notes yet plenty of cinnamon and florals. Acid drives the palate and it's a lighter style, supple even, until the raspy tannins kick in. With food it comes into its own. Screw cap. 13.1% alc. **Rating** 90 **To** 2028 $40 JF

Bowen Estate ★★★★

15459 Riddoch Highway, Coonawarra, SA 5263 **Region** Coonawarra
T (08) 8737 2229 **www**.bowenestate.com.au **Open** Mon–Fri 10–5, w'ends 10–4
Winemaker Emma Bowen **Est.** 1972 **Dozens** 12000 **Vyds** 33ha
Regional veteran Doug Bowen presides over one of Coonawarra's landmarks, but he has handed over full winemaking responsibility to daughter Emma, 'retiring' to the position of viticulturist. In May 2015 Bowen Estate celebrated its 40th vintage with a tasting of 24 wines (Shiraz and Cabernet Sauvignon) from 1975 to 2014. Exports to the UK, the Maldives, Sri Lanka, Singapore, China, Japan and NZ.

🍷🍷🍷🍷🍷 **Coonawarra Cabernet Sauvignon 2019** This is on the riper spectrum, but it doesn't stray into OTT territory. There's a lot of flavour, sure, but it comes out complete and balanced. Awash with currants and blackberries, mint chocolates and freshly rolled tobacco. Textural tannins have some poise and the finish is fresh and long. Screw cap. 14.7% alc. **Rating** 95 **To** 2030 $32 JF

🍷🍷🍷🍷🍷 **Coonawarra Shiraz 2019** **Rating** 93 **To** 2030 $32 JF

Bowman's Run ★★★☆

1305 Beechworth-Wodonga Road, Wooragee, Vic 3747 **Region** Beechworth
T (03) 5728 7318 **Open** By appt
Winemaker Daniel Balzer **Est.** 1989 **Dozens** 200 **Vyds** 1ha
Struan and Fran Robertson have cabernet sauvignon, riesling and small plots of shiraz and traminer dating back to 1989. The tiny winery is part of a larger general agricultural holding.

🍷🍷🍷🍷 **Seven Springs Beechworth Riesling 2018** Beechworth does not usually register on the riesling map. Time for a rethink if this is the potential calibre. There's plenty of flavour here, honeysuckle, lime and grapefruit with an attractive chalky texture. Moves along a strong, straight acid line. Screw cap. 12% alc. **Rating** 89 **To** 2026 $30 JP

Box Grove Vineyard ★★★★☆

955 Avenel-Nagambie Road, Tabilk, Vic 3607 **Region** Nagambie Lakes
T 0409 210 015 **www**.boxgrovevineyard.com.au **Open** By appt
Winemaker Sarah Gough **Est.** 1995 **Dozens** 2500 **Vyds** 28.25ha
This is the venture of the Gough family, with industry veteran (and daughter) Sarah Gough managing the vineyard, winemaking and marketing. Having started with 10ha each of shiraz and cabernet sauvignon under contract to Brown Brothers, Sarah decided to switch the focus of the business to what could loosely be called 'Mediterranean varieties'. These days shiraz and prosecco are the main varieties, with smaller plantings of pinot gris, primitivo, vermentino, roussanne, sousão, grenache, nebbiolo, negroamaro, mourvèdre and viognier. Osteria (an Italian word meaning a place that serves wine and food) hosts tastings and meals prepared by visiting Melbourne chefs, by appointment. Exports to the UK and China.

🍷🍷🍷🍷🍷 **Prosecco 2020** Pulses with the kind of light savouriness not often seen in prosecco, built around preserved lemon and acacia together with nashi pear and crunchy apple. Lemon zip and bubble is spot on. Crown seal. 11.2% alc. **Rating** 94 **To** 2024 $25 JP

🍷🍷🍷🍷🍷 **The Weaver Syrah 2018** **Rating** 93 **To** 2030 $45 JP
Late Harvest Viognier 2020 **Rating** 91 **To** 2024 $28 JP
Pinot Gris 2020 **Rating** 90 **To** 2023 $28 JP

Boydell's ★★★★

2 Green Street, Morpeth, NSW 2321 **Region** Hunter Valley
T (02) 4938 5862 **www**.boydells.com.au **Open** Wed–Sun 10.30–5.30
Winemaker First Creek (Liz Silkman) **Est.** 2016 **Dozens** 3000 **Vyds** 9ha

Jane and Daniel Maroulis own and operate 2 businesses on an 80ha property at East Gresford. First is a combined vineyard and luxury accommodation (Boydell's Escape) in a large African safari tent that has attracted much praise in lifestyle/travel media; second is the breeding of cattle. The vineyard is planted to verdelho, chardonnay, shiraz, merlot and pinot noir. Having the wines made by Liz Silkman at First Creek Winemakers was a very wise decision. The name of the winery refers to Charles Boydell, who first took up the land in 1826.

🍷🍷🍷🍷 **Single Vineyard Hilltops Shiraz 2019** A good wine. Succulent. Fresh. Floral. Ripe. Licorice straps, red cherry, mulberry, iodine, tapenade and salumi riffs cascade along a thrum of altitudinal acidity and a ripple of spicy tannins: nicely wrought, fine boned and savoury. Medium bodied of feel despite the alcohol. This is attractive drinking now and across the early to mid term. Screw cap. 14.5% alc. **Rating** 91 **To** 2027 $25 NG

Brand's Laira Coonawarra

14860 Riddoch Highway, Coonawarra, SA 5263 **Region** Coonawarra
T (08) 8736 3260 **www**.brandslaira.com **Open** Mon–Fri 9–4.30, w'ends & public hols 11–4
Winemaker Peter Weinberg, Amy Blackburn **Est.** 1966 **Vyds** 278ha
Three days before Christmas 2015, Casella Family Brands received an early present when it purchased Brand's Laira from McWilliam's. Over the years McWilliam's had moved from 50% to 100% ownership of Brand's and thereafter it purchased an additional 100ha of vineyards (taking Brand's to its present 278ha) and had expanded both the size, and the quality, of the winery. Exports to select markets.

🍷🍷🍷🍷🍷 **One Seven One Cabernet Sauvignon 2018** A very good if powerful vintage, yet this is a classy cabernet that's beautifully modulated and balanced. It has an essential core of lovely fruit – all cassis, mulberries and blackberries – topped with woodsy spices, florals, menthol and choc-mint. The medium body is an exercise in texture from fine-grained, detailed tannins as they head towards a long and pure finish. Elegance comes to mind. Screw cap. 14.5% alc. **Rating** 96 **To** 2028 $80 JF
1968 Vines Cabernet Sauvignon 2018 There's a quality within. A boldness. The fruit has largely stood up to 100% new French oak, aged 20 months. Expect sweet cassis and currants laden with licorice, dried herbs, plus aniseed, rosemary and tar, too. The palate has a velvety texture, savoury, with firm yet furry tannins. Its aim is to hang around for quite some time, yet it's pleasing now. Screw cap. 14.5% alc. **Rating** 95 **To** 2033 $40 JF

🍷🍷🍷🍷🍷 **Old Station Coonawarra Riesling 2020** **Rating** 93 **To** 2025 $20 JF ✪

Brangayne of Orange   ★★★★

837 Pinnacle Road, Orange, NSW 2800 **Region** Orange
T (02) 6365 3229 **www**.brangayne.com **Open** Sun–Fri 11–4, Sat 11–5
Winemaker Simon Gilbert, Will Gilbert **Est.** 1994 **Dozens** 3500 **Vyds** 25.7ha
The Hoskins family (formerly orchardists) moved into grapegrowing in 1994 and have progressively established high-quality vineyards. Brangayne produces good wines across all mainstream varieties ranging, remarkably, from pinot noir to cabernet sauvignon. It sells a substantial part of its crop to other winemakers. Exports to China.

🍷🍷🍷🍷 **Isolde Reserve Chardonnay 2019** A solid chardonnay of depth, plentiful fruit and well-appropriated oak. Nothing pushing the envelope and to be frank, rather conservative. Yet scents of white peach, jasmine, nectarine and vanilla are winning. The acidity: juicy and palpably natural, serving to tow the flavours long. A nice drink. Screw cap. 13% alc. **Rating** 91 **To** 2025 $38 NG
Orange Pinot Noir 2018 Dark cherry, sassafras and woodsy overtones. Orange zest, sandalwood and a firm skirt of tannin, oak, pithy grape and stem. A courageously extracted wine, with more tannic fortitude than most from this region. For the better. Screw cap. 13.5% alc. **Rating** 90 **To** 2025 $38 NG

Orange Shiraz 2018 A well-crafted shiraz that draws on a bow of reductive tension, imparting violet, clove, blueberry and nori scents. The finish, long and peppery. Medium weight, slick and smooth. A bit sweet, to be churlish. Far from complex, but good drinking. Screw cap. 14% alc. **Rating** 90 **To** 2025 $38 NG

Tristan Cabernet Sauvignon Shiraz Merlot 2018 52/28/20% cabernet/shiraz/merlot. Extremely savoury and medium of feel, as with all of these reds. The oak, integrated. The aromas, à point: currant, blueberry, white pepper, anise, clove and sage. The tannins peel across the sapid finish, finishing herbal and just a bit green. Screw cap. 14% alc. **Rating** 90 **To** 2026 $38 NG

Brash Higgins   ★★★★

California Road, McLaren Vale, SA 5171 **Region** McLaren Vale
T (08) 8556 4237 **www**.brashhiggins.com **Open** By appt
Winemaker Brad Hickey **Est.** 2010 **Dozens** 1000 **Vyds** 7ha
Move over TWE's 'vintrepreneurs', for Brad Hickey has come up with 'creator' and 'vinitor' to cover his role (and that of partner Nicole Thorpe) in establishing Brash Higgins. His varied background, including 10 years as head sommelier at some of the best New York restaurants, then a further 10 years of baking, brewing and travelling to the best-known wine regions of the world, may provide some clue. More tangibly, he planted 4ha of shiraz, 2ha of cabernet sauvignon, and grafted 1ha of shiraz to nero d'Avola on his Omensetter Vineyard looking over the Willunga Escarpment. Exports to the US and Canada.

🍷🍷🍷🍷🍷 CHN Willamba Hill Vineyard McLaren Vale Chenin Blanc 2019 An
absolutely delicious wine, utilising a few days on skins and a spontaneous barrel fermentation to glean ample colour, textural and aromatic nourishment. A resinous yellow hue. Think apricot chutney, ginger, tamarind and tangerine. A meld of bright acidity and detailed phenolics service a saline, chewy structural line. Persistent, long and impeccably poised. This is a highly versatile mid-weighted wine of immense character. Screw cap. 13.5% alc. **Rating** 95 **To** 2023 $39 NG

GR/M Co-Ferment McLaren Vale Grenache Mataro 2019 Aromas of dried cherry, tamarind, turmeric and orange zest. Moroccan souk meets Indian bazaar! The tannins, a sandy scrub, are nicely appointed and extracted with confidence. The acidity, dutifully fresh. This is how we should be making wine with these grapes in this country. Period. Screw cap. 14% alc. **Rating** 95 **To** 2025 $39 NG

SHZ Omensetter Vineyard McLaren Vale Shiraz 2018 Cool-climate syrah aromas in the fuller body of a warm-climate shiraz: nori, violet, clove, blueberry, tapenade and salumi. Impressive tannin management incorporating a lick of whole bunches and gentle reduction, imparting a clasp of tension. The barrel work, an addendum. Very fine. Sits well in the mouth, all parts synchronised. Screw cap. 14.5% alc. **Rating** 94 **To** 2026 $42 NG

CBSV Single Vineyard McLaren Vale Cabernet Sauvignon 2018 An exceptional, full-bodied and highly savoury maritime cabernet. Aromas of bitter chocolate, spearmint and a sappy red/blackcurrant riff with a verdant echo of hedgerow lacing the latticework of emery tannin to follow. Saline. Long, precise and auguring well for mid-term patience. A delicious wine. Screw cap. 14.4% alc. **Rating** 94 **To** 2026 $42 NG

🍷🍷🍷🍷🍷 FRNC Clos Antonio Lamento McLaren Vale Cabernet Franc 2020
Rating 93 **To** 2022 $30 NG
R/SM Field Blend McLaren Vale Riesling Semillon 2019 **Rating** 92 **To** 2024 $39 NG
MCC Lennon Vineyard McLaren Vale Mataro Cinsault Carignan 2019 **Rating** 92 **To** 2022 $30 NG
CINS Lennon Vineyard McLaren Vale Cinsault 2020 **Rating** 91 **To** 2022 $37 NG

Brash Road Vineyard   ★★★★☆

PO Box 455, Yallingup, WA 6282 **Region** Margaret River
T 0448 448 840 **www.**brashvineyard.com.au
Winemaker Bruce Dukes (Contract) **Est.** 2000 **Dozens** 1500 **Vyds** 18ha
Brash Vineyard was established in 1998 as Woodside Valley Estate. While most of the grapes were sold to other Margaret River producers, cabernet sauvignon, shiraz, chardonnay and merlot were made, and in '09 the Cabernet Sauvignon and the Shiraz earned the winery a 5-star rating. It is now owned by Chris and Anne Carter (managing partners, who live and work onsite), Brian and Anne McGuinness, and Rik and Jenny Nitert. The vineyard is now mature and produces high-quality fruit.

♟♟♟♟♟ **Single Vineyard Margaret River Sauvignon Blanc 2020** This wine leaves
a trail of medals and trophies in its wake, and it is clear to see why: punchy sauvignon aromatics of gooseberry, cassis, green apple and sugar snap peas fold seamlessly into a textural and layered palate. The resounding impression is one of concentration – this vineyard is known for it. Screw cap. 13.4% alc. **Rating** 94 To 2025 $28 EL ✪
Single Vineyard Margaret River Shiraz 2018 Concentrated cassis and blueberries, raspberry, salted licorice and star anise. Very concentrated, but not overblown. Balanced and supple. Screw cap. 14.1% alc. **Rating** 94 To 2031 $35 EL

♟♟♟♟♀ **Single Vineyard Margaret River Chardonnay 2019 Rating** 92 To 2027
$35 EL
Single Vineyard Margaret River Cabernet Sauvignon 2018 Rating 92
To 2027 $45 EL

Brave Goose Vineyard   ★★★★

PO Box 852, Seymour, Vic 3660 **Region** Central Victoria
T 0417 553 225 **www.**bravegoosevineyard.com.au **Open** By appt
Winemaker Nina Stocker **Est.** 1988 **Dozens** 500 **Vyds** 6.5ha
The Brave Goose Vineyard was planted in 1988 by former chairman of the Grape & Wine Research and Development Corporation, Dr John Stocker and wife Joanne. In '87 they found a property on the inside of the Great Dividing Range, near Tallarook, with north-facing slopes and shallow, weathered ironstone soils. They established 2.5ha each of shiraz and cabernet sauvignon, and 0.5ha each of merlot, viognier and gamay; but made only small amounts under the Brave Goose label. The brave goose in question was the sole survivor of a flock put into the vineyard to repel cockatoos and foxes. Two decades on, Jo and John handed the reins of the operation to their winemaker daughter Nina and son-in-law John Day.

♟♟♟♟♟ **Central Victoria Cabernet Sauvignon 2019** Ah, Central Victoria can most
definitely make excellent, everyday cabernet! Here's strong proof, with a velvety, rich youngster with a lot of love to give. Cassis, dried leaf and loamy earth aromas. Smooth as she goes on the well-structured palate, delivered with easy tannins and drinkability. Screw cap. 14% alc. **Rating** 94 To 2026 $28 JP ✪

♟♟♟♟♀ **Central Victoria Shiraz 2018 Rating** 93 To 2026 $28 JP
Central Victoria Viognier 2019 Rating 90 To 2024 $28 JP

Brave Souls Wine   ★★★☆

12 Clevedon Street, Botany, NSW, 2019 (postal) **Region** Barossa Valley
T 0420 968 473 **www.**bravesoulswine.com.au
Winemaker Julia Weirich and Corey Ryan **Est.** 2017 **Dozens** 3500
The story of Brave Souls and its founder Julia Weirich has a strong Australian can-do air about it, albeit with German beginnings. Julia obtained her German master's degree in industrial engineering and decided she needed to travel but didn't know where to start. She asked her friends, and they all said Australia. From this point on, the story line twisted and turned, first up her lack of fluency (real or imagined) in English, the second being her foray into wine, about which she knew nothing. From a standing start in 2012, and with her tourist visa about

to expire in '13, she noticed a position vacant ad by Fesq & Co. She applied on the basis she had nothing to lose, and 3 interviews later she was marketing coordinator for Fesq. One year earlier she had completed stages WSET 1 to 3. Later she took off for winemaking experience at Bass Phillip, NZ, Burgundy, southern and central Italy and South Africa. Where to next? Back to Australia, where she really wanted to make wine, and to Fesq (which had become like family to her) to take the new role of European Wine Manager, and to Sons of Eden making Brave Souls Wine. And she's studying winemaking with the University of California on its extension program.

Bream Creek   ★★★★★

Marion Bay Road, Bream Creek, Tas 7175 **Region** Southern Tasmania
T 0419 363 714 **www**.breamcreekvineyard.com.au
Winemaker Liam McElhinney **Est.** 1990 **Dozens** 6500 **Vyds** 7.6ha
Until 1990 the Bream Creek fruit was sold to Moorilla Estate, but since then the winery has been independently owned and managed by Fred Peacock, legendary for the care he bestows on the vines under his direction. Fred's skills have seen an increase in production and outstanding wine quality across the range, headed by the Pinot Noir. The list of trophies and medals won is extensive. Fred's expertise as a consultant is in constant demand. Exports to China.

Reserve Pinot Noir 2018 Light red/purple hue. Elegant, spicy red berry fruits are impacted more by the roast nut and dark chocolate influence of French oak than would be expected for just 26% new barrels. All it asks for is time, and it holds the fruit integrity, persistence, fine tannin structure and bright acid line to go the distance. Screw cap. 14% alc. **Rating** 92 **To** 2033 $65 TS
Cabernet Merlot 2019 The record warm 2019 season proved a blessing for cabernet and merlot, producing pristine ripeness of bright, fragrant red berry fruits and a lively, medium red/purple hue. Classy French oak builds more in structure than flavour, refining a confident tannin profile of fine-grained texture. Pretty, bright acidity streams long through an elegant finish. One for the cellar. Screw cap. 14% alc. **Rating** 92 **To** 2039 $36 TS
Vintage Cuvée Traditionelle 2014 A rich, complex sparkling of surprisingly bright, medium straw hue. Pinot noir (65%) delivers red apple and pear, accented by the grapefruit of chardonnay and backed by deep spice becoming toast. Energetic Tasmanian acidity holds the finish with confidence and enduring potential. Diam. 12.5% alc. **Rating** 92 $48 TS
Chardonnay 2019 Value-for-money Tassie chardonnay, loaded with all the tension and cut of the southeast. Crunchy white peach, grapefruit, lime and fig are the main event, supported by the vanilla and cashew nut of spicy French oak. Firm acidity drives a long finish and will appreciate some years to soften. Screw cap. 13.5% alc. **Rating** 91 **To** 2029 $36 TS
Pinot Noir 2019 Medium purple/red. The firm, bony structure of this warm, dry season in concert with the bright acidity of this site define a coiled, savoury and enduring style. Understated dark berry fruits carry through a long finish. Give it time to build flesh and body. Screw cap. 13.5% alc. **Rating** 90 **To** 2034 $42 TS

Bremerton Wines   ★★★★★

15 Kent Town Road, Langhorne Creek, SA 5255 **Region** Langhorne Creek
T (08) 8537 3093 **www**.bremerton.com.au **Open** 7 days 10–5
Winemaker Rebecca Willson **Est.** 1988 **Dozens** 30000 **Vyds** 120ha
Bremerton has been producing wines since 1988. Rebecca Willson (chief winemaker) and Lucy Willson (marketing manager) were the first sisters in Australia to manage and run a winery. With 120ha of premium vineyards (80% of which goes into their own labels), they grow cabernet sauvignon, shiraz, verdelho, chardonnay, sauvignon blanc, malbec, merlot, fiano, graciano and petit verdot. Exports to most major markets.

ŢŢŢŢŢ **Old Adam Langhorne Creek Shiraz 2018** Twenty months maturation in French and American oak. Deep and dark from the outset, the best shiraz of the season is steered into this rich, chewy, chocolatey style, the American oak a necessary element. As is the traditional regional stamp, it is earthy and rich with full-bodied intent, yet not overly weighed down by heavy tannin blocks. Will gather itself more completely over the next decade. Diam. 14.5% alc. **Rating** 96 To 2030 $56 TL **✪**

B.O.V. 2017 Only 4 barrels selected across the traditional regional red program, bringing together a blend of 60/20/20% shiraz/cabernet sauvignon/malbec. The nose is fully engaged in its Aussie claret-like mode, oak entwined, and a faint waft of dark mint chocolate. Dried orange even, if you dwell too long, which is easy to do. Full bodied and layered with fine peppery tannins. Drink it now if you are into heavyweight pleasures, or wait another 5 years to watch it even out and open up further. Diam. 14.5% alc. **Rating** 95 To 2030 $14.50 TL **✪**

Special Release Langhorne Creek Shiraz 2020 No added preservatives. Picked ripe yet still vibrant, aged on full solids for 4–5 months to tease out the natural colours and tannins that enable it to fulfil its total, rich shiraz plum fruit experience without other additions needed. The flavour power is spot-on. Ripe and chewy tannins become part of the concentration on the palate. Neatly done. Satisfying. Screw cap. 15% alc. **Rating** 94 To 2024 $24 TL **✪**

Walter's Reserve Langhorne Creek Cabernet Sauvignon 2016 Matured 20 months in French oak, then 2 years bottle ageing to bring out the best in classical Langhorne Creek cabernet. The nose convinces that it is on the mark, cassis and blackberries, with a regional earthiness and the faintest of palate-edging cabernet bitterness in the tannins. Old-school, big cabernet love here. Diam. 14.5% alc. **Rating** 94 To 2030 $56 TL

Special Release Langhorne Creek Barbera 2019 Powdery dark chocolate, with a layer of crushed crimson, blackberries, seams of savoury spices and fruit flavours on the palate, even a notion of nori seaweed/salines. The variety's natural acidity rocks the finish – while getting there is full of interest. Makes you crave for paté and antipasti treats. Screw cap. 14.5% alc. **Rating** 94 To 2025 $24 TL **✪**

Special Release Langhorne Creek Malbec 2019 With malbec one of Langhorne Creek's finest treats, this sits within the Bremerton Special Release range with a certain pride. To begin, think of the aromas of a dark Negroni, a slice of orange peel included. The flavours follow, without of course the same amaro bitterness, though rich with body and captivating mouth feels. Screw cap. 14.5% alc. **Rating** 94 To 2028 $24 TL **✪**

ŢŢŢŢŢ **Bâtonnage Langhorne Creek Chardonnay 2019** Rating 93 To 2025 $32 TL

Special Release Langhorne Creek Fiano 2020 Rating 93 To 2024 $24 TL **✪**

Bâtonnage Langhorne Creek Shiraz Malbec 2019 Rating 93 To 2030 $32 TL

Special Release Langhorne Creek Grenache 2020 Rating 93 To 2025 $24 TL **✪**

Special Release Langhorne Creek Tempranillo Graciano 2019 Rating 92 To 2024 $24 TL **✪**

Special Release Langhorne Creek Graciano 2019 Rating 92 To 2026 $24 TL **✪**

Special Release Langhorne Creek Mourvèdre 2019 Rating 92 To 2026 $24 TL **✪**

Selkirk Langhorne Creek Shiraz 2019 Rating 91 To 2026 $22 TL **✪**

Special Release Langhorne Creek Lagrein 2018 Rating 91 To 2026 $24 TL

Tamblyn Langhorne Creek Cabernet Shiraz Malbec Merlot 2019 Rating 90 To 2025 $18 TL **✪**

Briar Ridge Vineyard

593 Mount View Road, Mount View, NSW 2325 **Region** Hunter Valley
T (02) 4990 3670 **www**.briarridge.com.au **Open** 7 days 10–5
Winemaker Alex Beckett, Gwyneth Olsen (Consultant) **Est.** 1972 **Dozens** 9500
Vyds 39ha

Semillon and shiraz have been the most consistent performers. Underlying the suitability of these varieties to the Hunter Valley, Briar Ridge has been a model of stability, and has the comfort of substantial estate vineyards from which it is able to select the best grapes. It also has not hesitated to venture into other regions, notably Orange. Alex Beckett has taken over winemaking duties from Gwyn Olsen (Gwyn remains as a consultant). Exports to the UK, Europe and Canada.

Stockhausen Hunter Valley Semillon 2013 A very fine wine from a great year. More life than its Dairy Hill sibling. A chord of unresolved CO_2, even after all these years. It serves to lift the scents of glazed quince, finger lime, buttered toast and pink grapefruit aloft, while a jittery rail of pumice-like acidity splays them broad and long. A gentle chew across the finish for emphasis. Screw cap. 11% alc. **Rating** 95 **To** 2028 $65 NG

Stockhausen Hunter Valley Shiraz 2019 This is a fine '19: extract harnessed by inimitable Hunter savouriness, judicious French oak (17% new) and a steady hand. Plenty of whole berries in the mix to impart a juiciness, floral lift and an effusive joy. Sour cherry, Damson plum, baking spice and vanilla pod. Mid weighted, lithe and long, as the tannins expand with air and the acidity tows the flavours. Delicious. Screw cap. 13.8% alc. **Rating** 95 **To** 2028 $35 NG ✪

Museum Release Dairy Hill Vineyard Hunter Valley Shiraz 2013 A classic. Terracotta, sour cherry, Damson plum, Chinotto and Asian medicinal riffs. The tannins are firm and aptly extracted, with an oaky twigginess as backup. They could be construed as drying. But I see this glass as half full, with a broader and more expansive future in store, based on the prodigious degree of extract that carries the wine and the textual layers that ensue with a work-out in the glass. Screw cap. 13.5% alc. **Rating** 95 **To** 2028 $110 NG

Briar Hill Single Vineyard Hunter Valley Chardonnay 2013 Museum release. Generosity melded with a pungent freshness. White fig, cantaloupe, nectarine and white-peach aromas stretch across a core of nougatine, creamed cashew and vanilla-pod oak. Screw cap. 13% alc. **Rating** 94 **To** 2026 $80 NG

Wrattonbully Fiano 2020 Let's be clear. Fiano is a top-drawer variety. Noble. Tolerant to drought, with a kaleidoscope of stone fruit, fennel, thyme and pungent mineral that transcends any workhorse label. Iterated well in these hands, with proper ripeness, some skin-contact inflection and old barrel-breadth of texture. Among the best to date. Screw cap. 13.5% alc. **Rating** 94 **To** 2024 $28 NG ✪

Dairy Hill Single Vineyard Hunter Valley Semillon 2013 **Rating** 93 **To** 2026 $80 NG

Briar Hill Single Vineyard Hunter Valley Chardonnay 2019 **Rating** 93 **To** 2025 $35 NG

Wrattonbully Viognier 2019 **Rating** 93 **To** 2022 $23 NG ✪

Dairy Hill Single Vineyard Hunter Valley Shiraz 2019 **Rating** 93 **To** 2028 $60 NG

H.R.B. Single Vineyard Hunter Valley Shiraz Pinot Noir 2019 **Rating** 92 **To** 2025 $35 NG

Stockhausen Hunter Valley Chardonnay 2019 **Rating** 92 **To** 2024 $28 NG

Stockhausen Hunter Valley Shiraz 2013 **Rating** 91 **To** 2023 $85 NG

Cold Soaked Cabernet Sauvignon 2018 **Rating** 91 **To** 2023 NG

Brick Kiln

21 Greer Street, Hyde Park, SA 5061 **Region** McLaren Vale
T (08) 8357 2561 **www**.brickiln.com.au
Winemaker Phil Christiansen **Est.** 2001 **Dozens** 1600 **Vyds** 8ha

This is the venture of Malcolm and Alison Mackinnon. They purchased the Nine Gums Vineyard in 2001. It had been planted to shiraz in 1995–96. The majority of the grapes are sold, with a lesser portion contract-made for the partners under the Brick Kiln label, which takes its name from the Brick Kiln Bridge adjacent to the vineyard. Exports to the UK, Canada, China, Hong Kong and Singapore.

ŢŢŢŢŢ Single Vineyard McLaren Vale Shiraz 2017 Aromas of dulce de leche, coconut and bourbon, all due to the 20 months in American oak. Chinese five-spice and game scents, too, with a sweet morello cherry accent echoing from the attack to the forceful, plush finish. Screw cap. 15% alc. **Rating** 91 **To** 2032 $35 NG

Single Vineyard McLaren Vale Shiraz 2016 Open-fermented, basket pressed and matured in American hogsheads (35% new) for 24 months. A classic older-school expression with ample charm and certain virtues. Rich and nourishing. A cornucopia of coffee grind, bourbon caramel and bitter chocolate to vanilla scents, largely derived from the phalanx of oak. Oodles of blackberry and mulberry flavours, too. For those seeking a full-bodied, unabashed expression that harks to a proud past, here is the ticket. Screw cap. 14.9% alc. **Rating** 90 **To** 2032 $35 NG

Brini Estate Wines   ★★★★☆

698 Blewitt Springs Road, McLaren Vale, SA 5171 **Region** McLaren Vale
T (08) 8383 0080 **www.**briniwines.com.au **Open** By appt
Winemaker Adam Hooper (Contract) **Est.** 2000 **Dozens** 8000 **Vyds** 16.4ha
The Brini family has been growing grapes in the Blewitt Springs area of McLaren Vale since 1953. In 2000 John and Marcello Brini established Brini Estate Wines to vinify a portion of the grape production (up to that time it had been sold to companies such as Penfolds, Rosemount Estate and d'Arenberg). The flagship Limited Release Shiraz is produced from dry-grown vines planted in 1947, the other wines from dry-grown vines planted in '64. Exports to Vietnam and China.

ŢŢŢŢŢ Limited Release Single Vineyard McLaren Vale Shiraz 2015 While this does not have the lightness of touch, poise and drinkability of this estate's grenache here, it does have a compelling vinosity and forceful length as a result. Palate-staining, as blue-fruit allusions, lilac, anise, clove and smoked barbecued meat flavours saturate the palate. The oak rests atop the fray without being overt. Its mocha/vanilla notes suit the full-bore style. Screw cap. 14.5% alc. **Rating** 93 **To** 2035 $110 NG

Reserve Single Vineyard McLaren Vale Grenache 2018 Grenache with a serious aura. The sandy nori-soused tannins, saline and gritty are endemic to Blewitt Springs. Attractive aromas of molten raspberry liqueur, Cherry Ripe and a spice mix of tamarind, clove and turmeric. The finish is long, detailed, fresh and impressively intense. Screw cap. 14.5% alc. **Rating** 93 **To** 2027 $50 NG

Stellato Single Vineyard McLaren Vale Grenache 2018 Another poised wine that sits effortlessly in the mouth. Dutiful freshness. Grenache's stamp of briar and Indian-spiced tannins, the spindle tying raspberry, strawberry and wood smoke flavours together. Long and lithe. The seasoned oak, perfect for the weight at hand. Good drinking. Screw cap. 14.5% alc. **Rating** 92 **To** 2025 $35 NG

Estate Single Vineyard McLaren Vale GSM 2018 62/24/14% grenache/shiraz/mourvèdre, the grenache from 55yo vines. Hand-picked fruit from estate vineyards in Blewitt Springs. A relaxed wine that sits easy in the mouth. Crunchy red berries, a whiff of autumnal leaves and sandalwood. A core of darker fruit tones, white pepper and a ferrous burr across the finish. Nice drinking. Screw cap. 14.5% alc. **Rating** 92 **To** 2026 $26 NG

Sebastian Single Vineyard McLaren Vale Shiraz 2018 Regional in a traditional paradigm defined by power, intensity and ripe fruit flavours suggestive of Christmas cake, blueberry, violet, orange rind and kirsch. Baking spice and licorice, too. The tannins, mostly oak, curtail any excess. Screw cap. 14.5% alc. **Rating** 90 **To** 2030 $35 NG

Brinktop Vineyard

66 Brinktop Road, Penna, Tas 7171 **Region** Southern Tasmania
T 0407 224 543 **www.**brinktop.com.au
Winemaker Todd Goebel **Est.** 2017 **Dozens** 600 **Vyds** 8ha
Todd Goebel and Gillian Christian have been growing grapes and producing wine in the Coal
River Valley since 1999, Brinktop their recently established new business. It began with the
purchase of a house that had a 1ha vineyard, and that led to a permanent change in their lives.
In September '17 they moved across the valley to Brinktop, taking with them some select
barrels of pinot noir and tempranillo made by Todd from the 2017 vintage. They adopted the
name Brinktop Killara for one of the wines, Killara being the name of the property when
they purchased it. It's a 65ha property, and they have established 8ha of vines, chiefly selected
clones of pinot noir, then chardonnay, shiraz and a little tempranillo. Vintage 2018 was the
first in the new small winery.

🍷🍷🍷🍷🍷 **Pinot Noir 2018** A spicy, characterful Southern Tasmanian pinot noir, loaded
with white pepper, potpourri and berry compote. Tangy acidity makes for a bright
finish, if a little sweet and sour, well supported by finely crafted tannins. Expressive,
well made and well priced. Screw cap. 13.3% alc. **Rating** 91 **To** 2023 $30 TS

Brokenwood

401-427 McDonalds Road, Pokolbin, NSW 2321 **Region** Hunter Valley
T (02) 4998 7559 **www.**brokenwood.com.au **Open** Mon–Fri 11–5, Sat–Sun 10–5
Winemaker Stuart Hordern, Kate Sturgess **Est.** 1970 **Dozens** 100 000 **Vyds** 64ha
Brokenwood consistently produces excellent wines. Its big-selling Hunter Semillon provides
the volume to balance the limited quantities of the flagships ILR Semillon and Graveyard
Shiraz. Brokenwood purchased the Graveyard Vineyard from Hungerford Hill in 1978 and
has fully rehabilitated the vineyard in a vine-by-vine exercise. There is also a range of wines
coming from regions including Beechworth (a major resource is the Indigo Vineyard),
Orange, Central Ranges, McLaren Vale, Cowra and elsewhere. In 2017 Iain Riggs celebrated
his 35th vintage at the helm of Brokenwood, offering a unique mix of winemaking skills,
management of a diverse business and an unerring ability to keep Brokenwood's high profile
fresh and newsworthy. He also contributed a great deal to various wine industry organisations.
In May 2020 Iain announced his retirement, effective 30 June '20, but he remains on the
board of directors and consults on any issue where his experience will assist. Exports to all
major markets.

🍷🍷🍷🍷🍷 **Graveyard Vineyard Hunter Valley Shiraz 2019** A stellar wine boasting an
intensity of flavour, palate-staining levels of extract and a forensic precision to
the tannins that forces one to swish the wine about the mouth while chewing
every ounce of nourishment from it. Subdued at first, before 2019's ripe kit of
black cherry melds with lilac florals and a long trail of pepper, Indian spice mix
and charcuterie flavours. A venerable wine in the making. Screw cap. 13.5% alc.
Rating 96 **To** 2034 $350 NG
Kats Block Hunter Valley Shiraz 2019 Medium bodied and savoury, in the
Hunter mould of of loamy earth and terracotta, segueing to blue-fruit allusions,
olive, thyme, anise and lilac. Intense yet understated, as are most Brokenwood
wines. The most straight-shooting regional wine of these single blocks. A fine
thrust of fruit across the finish, with chiselled tannins, fine grained and elegant,
guiding it long. Screw cap. 13% alc. **Rating** 95 **To** 2028 $75 NG
Vegas Block Hunter Valley Shiraz 2019 Fermented with 30% whole bunches,
imparting additional tannic lattice and an undercurrent of clove and agave. A
savoury mid-weight wine of exceptional drinkability. It idles in the mouth, plump
and juicy, before reeling off riffs of sour cherry, terracotta, iodine and suede. I have
liked this block in the past and I like it again now, perhaps more so. Screw cap.
13.5% alc. **Rating** 95 **To** 2028 $75 NG
Wildwood Road Margaret River Cabernet Sauvignon 2019 Although
2019 might not quite be in the class of 2018 in this part of the world, this is a

very fine wine nevertheless. A lustrous nose, saturated with cassis, bitter chocolate, blackberry, bouquet garni, scrub and tapenade. A full-bodied palate with the oak a mere adjunct to all that is going on. Firm and attenuated sage-brushed tannins corral the fruit into a savoury whole. Each glass is a kaleidoscope of textural intrigue. Screw cap. 14.5% alc. **Rating** 95 **To** 2035 $100 NG

ILR Reserve Hunter Valley Semillon 2015 Precocious Hunter semillon aromas of lemon candy, talc, buttered toast and lime marmalade. It is an idiosyncrasy of the region that such lightweight, balletic expressions can metastasise into a mouthfeel of creamy breadth and aromas that feign the toastiness of oak with age. Not yet fully mature. The finish, scented with greengage and lemongrass. Screw cap. 11% alc. **Rating** 94 **To** 2028 $100 NG

Verona Vineyard Hunter Valley Shiraz 2019 The most perfumed of these single blocks, with a judicious clench of reduction imparting scents of violet, salumi, nori, clove, licorice allsorts and blueberry. Arguably the most elegant, too, with a cooler-climate feel manifest in peppery tannins and dutiful acidity punching long. The tannin management across these top reds is stellar. Screw cap. 13.5% alc. **Rating** 94 **To** 2027 $100 NG

♟♟♟♟♟ **Wade Block 2 Vineyard McLaren Vale Shiraz 2019** Rating 93 To 2032 $75 NG
Hunter Valley Shiraz 2019 Rating 92 To 2030 $50 NG

Brookland Valley ★★★★★

4070 Caves Road, Wilyabrup, WA 6280 **Region** Margaret River
T (08) 9755 6042 **www.**brooklandvalley.com.au **Open** 7 days 11–5
Winemaker Courtney Treacher **Est.** 1984
Brookland Valley has an idyllic setting, plus its cafe and Gallery of Wine Arts, which houses an eclectic collection of wine, food-related art and wine accessories. After acquiring a 50% share of Brookland Valley in 1997, Hardys moved to full ownership in 2004 and it is now part of Accolade Wines. The quality, value for money and consistency of the wines are exemplary.

♟♟♟♟♟ **Reserve Margaret River Cabernet Sauvignon 2018** Inky, intense, dense and rich. It shows an increase in midnight colour from the other wines that surround it on the bench. On the palate, this is firm, muscular and rippling with flavour; spiced cassis, bramble, red licorice and raspberry at the core. Encasing it is leather strapping, resinous oak, finely textured but impenetrable tannins, yet … it remains supple. Silky. Pure. A powerhouse. Screw cap. 14% alc. **Rating** 96 **To** 2046 $77 EL
Estate Margaret River Cabernet Merlot 2018 As usual, apart from the silky fruit, the texture is the standout here. It is about as slippery as cabernet can get, while still holding shape; silky fine, seamless tannins that seem to pour forth from the fruit. There are no joins in this carbon fibre shell, it is 1 piece. Svelte, streamlined and beautiful. But I swear it used to be cheaper. Screw cap. 14% alc. Rating 95 To 2041 $62 EL

Brookwood Estate ★★★☆

430 Treeton Road, Cowaramup, WA 6284 **Region** Margaret River
T (08) 9755 5604 **www.**brookwood.com.au **Open** Tues–Sat 11–4.30
Winemaker Bronnley Cahill **Est.** 1996 **Dozens** 3500 **Vyds** 5.4ha
Trevor and Lyn Mann established a vineyard in 1996, planting around 1ha each of cabernet sauvignon, semillon, sauvignon blanc, shiraz and chenin blanc. A family enterprise, wines are now made by their daughter Bronnley. Exports to Singapore.

♟♟♟♟♟ **Margaret River Shiraz Cabernet 2018** A mouthful of plummy, plump berry fruit. The length of flavour leaves a little bit to be desired, but it is lovely while it sticks around. Quite delicious. Screw cap. 13.5% alc. **Rating** 90 **To** 2027 $28 EL

ŶŶŶŶ   **Margaret River Chenin Blanc 2020** Rating 88 To 2025 $25 EL
Reserve Small Batch Margaret River Shiraz 2019 Rating 88 To 2027
$45 EL
Margaret River Rosé 2020 Rating 87 To 2022 $25 EL

Brothers at War

274 Laubes Road, Springton, SA 5235 **Region** Barossa Valley
T 0405 631 889 **www.**brothersatwar.com.au **Open** Thurs–Sun 11–5
Winemaker Angus Wardlaw **Est.** 2013 **Dozens** 3500
David Wardlaw was one of the bastions of the Barossa Valley in the second half of the 20th
century, working alongside greats such as Peter Lehmann, John Vickery, Jim Irvine and Wolf
Blass. For son Angus Wardlaw, a life in wine was inevitable, working first (in 2009) at Dorrien
Estate and after 4 years starting at Kirrihill Wines in the Clare Valley. He has a love for all
things Eden Valley. His brother Sam Wardlaw, with a love of all things Barossa, started in the
production side of the business when he worked for Premium Wine Bottlers until '09, when
he was employed by Andrew Seppelt at Murray Street Vineyards, spending the next 6 years
there. Matt Carter's role is mysterious; while he started as a cellar hand at Colonial Wine
for a couple of vintages, he has since moved into civil construction, currently running large
infrastructure projects but returning from time to time to drink plenty of the Brothers at War
wines. Exports to China and Singapore.

ŶŶŶŶŶ   **Single Vineyard Old Vine Barossa Valley Shiraz 2018** Miniscule production
of larger-than-life Lyndoch shiraz. A wine of considerable concentration, drive and
determination. All the black fruits and dark chocolate oak to be expected, with a
spicy whole-bunch overlay. Fine, full tannins rise to the challenge, supporting
a bright finish, elevated to the next level by exceptional line and length. Cork.
14% alc. **Rating** 96 To 2038 $110 TS
Single Vineyard Eden Valley Syrah 2018 Eden Valley shiraz is inherently
more spicy and tangy than the Barossa floor, and 30% whole-bunch fermentation
enhances both virtues. With a full purple hue, there is density here, of spicy
blackberries and black plums. French oak tactically delivers more in firm, fine
tannins than in subtle high-cocoa dark chocolate. Considered, crafted and age-
worthy. Cork. 14% alc. **Rating** 95 To 2038 $80 TS
Single Vineyard Eden Valley Mataro 2019 Clever, innovative winemaking
and a classy result. Fragrant red berry fruit lift and rose petal allure, heightened by
whole bunches. Graceful resolution of fine tannins, bright acidity and impressive
fruit carry. A beautifully fresh and enduring expression of Eden Valley mataro.
Cork. 13.5% alc. **Rating** 95 To 2039 $80 TS
Nothing in Common Eden Valley Riesling 2020 Restraint, purity and
precision denote a riesling of unusual refinement. Tense and honed, with a
streamlined core of lemon, lime and Granny Smith apple carrying through an
electric finish. Heightened, cold night acidity makes for a high-pitched finale that
screams out for time to settle down. This will be one of the longest-lived rieslings
of the harvest. Screw cap. 11% alc. **Rating** 94 To 2040 $35 TS

ŶŶŶŶŶ   **Single Vineyard Eden Valley Grenache 2019** Rating 92 To 2029 $80 TS

Brothers in Arms

Lake Plains Road, Langhorne Creek, SA 5255 **Region** Langhorne Creek
T (08) 8537 3182 **www.**brothersinarms.com.au **Open** By appt
Winemaker Jim Urlwin **Est.** 1998 **Dozens** 25 000 **Vyds** 85ha
The Adams family has been growing grapes at Langhorne Creek since 1891, when the vines
at the famed Metala vineyards were planted. Guy Adams is the 5th generation of the family
to own and work the vineyard, and over the past 20 years has both improved the viticulture
and expanded the plantings. In 1998 they decided to hold back a small proportion of the
production for the Brothers in Arms label; now they dedicate 85ha to it (40ha each of shiraz
and cabernet sauvignon and 2.5ha each of malbec and petit verdot). Exports to the UK, the
US, Canada, Sweden, Denmark, Singapore, South Korea, Malaysia, Hong Kong and China.

ΨΨΨΨΨ **Langhorne Creek Shiraz 2018** Rich plum and ripe blackberry vibes to start, oak ageing providing obvious foundations but not dominating. This fruit has to be some kind of powerful. Full bodied to the max, thick with all the elements entwined. Traditional shiraz swooning seems like the necessary response. Screw cap. 14.7% alc. **Rating** 94 **To** 2028 $45 TL
Langhorne Creek Cabernet Sauvignon 2018 Classical cabernet notes, blackcurrant and raspberry powder in a chocolate framework. The fruit resonates on the palate, while the oak adds its cedar and structural foundations. Big and chewy in a blockbuster style. Screw cap. 14.5% alc. **Rating** 94 **To** 2030 $45 TL

ΨΨΨΨΨ **No. 6 Langhorne Creek Cabernet Sauvignon 2018 Rating** 92 **To** 2028 $22 TL ❂

Brown Brothers ★★★★★

239 Milawa-Bobinawarrah Road, Milawa, Vic 3678 **Region** King Valley
T (03) 5720 5500 **www.**brownbrothers.com.au **Open** 7 days 9–5
Winemaker Joel Tilbrook, Cate Looney, Geoff Alexander, Katherine Brown, Tom Canning, Simon McMillan **Est.** 1889 **Dozens** 1 million **Vyds** 570ha
Brown Brothers draws upon a considerable number of vineyards spread throughout a range of site climates – from very warm to very cool. An expansion into Heathcote added significantly to its armoury. In 2010 Brown Brothers took a momentous step, acquiring Tasmania's Tamar Ridge for $32.5 million. In May '16 it acquired Innocent Bystander and stock from Giant Steps, and with it a physical presence in the Yarra Valley. The premium quality varietal wines to one side, Brown Brothers has gained 2 substantial labels: Innocent Bystander Moscato and Innocent Bystander Prosecco. It is known for the diversity of varieties with which it works, and the wines represent good value for money. Deservedly one of the most successful family wineries – its cellar door receives the greatest number of visitors in Australia. A founding member of Australia's First Families of Wine. Exports to all major markets.

ΨΨΨΨΨ **Patricia Pinot Noir Chardonnay Brut 2014** 78/22% pinot noir/chardonnay, on lees for 6 years. Fruit from the Whitlands Plateau, one of the highest vineyards in Australia, and possessing a rare vitality for a 6yo sparkling. Patricia's signature purity of fruit expression and exhilarating acidity. A persistent, fine bubble. Lemon zest, straw, apple custard and Nice biscuit. Youthful exuberance with grapefruit, citrus, almond meal and a clean creaminess. Cork. 12.5% alc. **Rating** 96 $47 JP ❂
Patricia Chardonnay 2019 The word refined comes to mind with Patricia. Everything is in its place – the result, one presumes, of diligent, thoughtful winemaking. Superfine flavours built around nectarine, citrus, patisserie, biscuit and a surge of tangy acidity. Energy to burn. Should age a treat. Screw cap. 13.1% alc. **Rating** 95 **To** 2029 $45 JP
Patricia Shiraz 2017 From a top vintage, Patricia Shiraz in all of its ripe, sweet, concentrated fruit intensity. A seamless beauty, drinking beautifully now, but with a long road still ahead of it. Lifted, heady aromas (a touch of whole bunch, maybe?) with blue, black and red fruits, violets, wood smoke and gentle spice. Crushed velvet on the tongue, with well-judged oak, tight, well-tuned tannins and lashings of generous fruit. Immerse yourself. Screw cap. 14% alc. **Rating** 95 **To** 2030 $62 JP
Patricia Cabernet Sauvignon 2018 Feel the serenity and the intensity. Patricia is always of the finest quality, a mark of the Brown family's high regard and respect for their late matriarch. Comprised of both sweet and savoury parts, Patricia opens with a full attack of lifted violet, blackcurrant, black plum, cocoa, vanilla and tilled earth. All the pieces fall into place on the palate, across a smooth path of concentrated flavour, with just a hint of the leafy and the savoury. A compelling wine. Screw cap. 14.3% alc. **Rating** 95 **To** 2029 $62 JP
Limited Release King Valley Shiraz Mondeuse Cabernet Sauvignon 2015 Give this wine plenty of air time. A moveable feast that changes each time you return to it. A bit of this – blackberry, plum, woody spices; and a bit of that – sage, bay leaf, pepper, warm, smoky oak. All meld beautifully on the palate. An

inspired combination, tightly constructed, that will continue to age nicely. Don't rush this wine. Screw cap. 14.5% alc. **Rating** 94 **To** 2035 $90 JP

Premium King Valley Prosecco Brut NV A premium prosecco – why not? A drier prosecco than usual, bringing gravitas to the style, with a smarter, tighter line and length. No simple lemonade characters here, but rather some depth in aroma and flavour. Granny Smith apples, grapefruit, pear skin, preserved lemon. Zesty, bright on the palate but settles into a citrus-infused, lemon-tart line of flavour with a waxy mouthfeel. Definitely a step up in poise and elegance for the variety. Agglomerate. 11.5% alc. **Rating** 94 **To** 2026 $25 JP ✪

ⵣⵣⵣⵣⵣ **King Valley Pinot Noir Chardonnay Pinot Meunier NV Rating** 93 $25 JP ✪
Winemaker's Series Heathcote Shiraz 2019 Rating 92 **To** 2027 $30 JP
Sparkling Moscato 2020 Rating 91 **To** 2023 $16 JP ✪
18 Eighty Nine Cabernet Sauvignon 2018 Rating 90 **To** 2024 $19 JP ✪
Cellar Door Release Heathcote Montepulciano 2018 Rating 90 **To** 2023 $25 JP
Sparkling Moscato Rosa 2020 Rating 90 **To** 2023 $16 JP ✪

Brown Hill Estate   ★★★★★

925 Rosa Brook Road, Rosa Brook, WA 6285 **Region** Margaret River
T (08) 9757 4003 **www.**brownhillestate.com.au **Open** 7 days 10–5
Winemaker Nathan Bailey, Angus Pattullo **Est.** 1995 **Dozens** 3000 **Vyds** 22ha
The Bailey family is involved in all stages of wine production, with minimum outside help. Their stated aim is to produce top quality wines at affordable prices, via uncompromising viticultural practices emphasising low yields. They have shiraz and cabernet sauvignon (8ha each), semillon, sauvignon blanc and merlot (2ha each). The quality of the best wines in the portfolio is very good.

ⵣⵣⵣⵣⵣ **Golden Horseshoe Reserve Margaret River Chardonnay 2019** Toasty, chewy and packed with layers of flavour and texture. The saline acid ties it all to a post, the concentrated fruit forms a deep pool of flavour on the tongue. There's a lot to ponder, a lot to like, and thankfully, a whole bottle to drink. Get to it. Screw cap. 13.5% alc. **Rating** 95 **To** 2031 $45 EL
Perseverance Signature Range Margaret River Cabernet Merlot 2018 2018 was potentially the greatest vintage in Margaret River's more than 50-year history. This wine shows why … refreshing acidity countersunk into the perfectly ripe fruit. Very good length of flavour – the tannins exhibit a chewiness and fine grip through a lingering finish. Screw cap. 14% alc. **Rating** 95 **To** 2040 $80 EL
Ivanhoe Reserve Margaret River Cabernet Sauvignon 2018 Medium bodied and red-fruited, pretty in its expression and light on its feet. Claret style, with highly attractive mulberry and raspberry characters laced through the succulent palate. Lovely. Screw cap. 14% alc. **Rating** 94 **To** 2035 $45 EL

ⵣⵣⵣⵣⵣ **Fimiston Reserve Margaret River Shiraz 2018 Rating** 93 **To** 2031 $45 EL
Trafalgar Margaret River Cabernet Merlot 2019 Rating 93 **To** 2027 $28 EL
Bill Bailey Margaret River Shiraz Cabernet 2018 Rating 92 **To** 2035 $85 EL
Hannans Margaret River Cabernet Sauvignon 2019 Rating 92 **To** 2030 $28 EL
Great Boulder Signature Range Margaret River Cabernet Shiraz Merlot Malbec 2018 Rating 92 **To** 2036 $50 EL
Lakeview Margaret River Sauvignon Blanc Semillon 2020 Rating 90 **To** 2023 $26 EL

Brown Magpie Wines   ★★★★☆

125 Larcombes Road, Modewarre, Vic 3240 **Region** Geelong
T (03) 5266 2147 **www.**brownmagpiewines.com **Open** 7 days 11–4 Jan, w'ends 11–4
Nov–Apr
Winemaker Loretta and Shane Breheny, Daniel Greene **Est.** 2000 **Dozens** 5000
Vyds 9ha
Shane and Loretta Breheny's 20ha property is situated predominantly on a gentle, north-facing
slope, with cypress trees on the western and southern borders providing protection against the
wind. Vines were planted over 2001–02, with pinot noir (4ha) taking the lion's share, followed
by pinot gris and shiraz (2.4ha each) and 0.1ha each of chardonnay and sauvignon blanc.
Viticulture is Loretta's love; winemaking (and wine) is Shane's.

🍷🍷🍷🍷🍷 **Paraparap Reserve Single Vineyard Geelong Pinot Noir 2017** A back-to-
normal kind of harvest in 2017 with the indulgence of quite a prolonged ripening
time. The reward is an envious level of depth and concentration of fruit: black
cherry, black tea and potpourri around a green leafiness. Opens up upon a supple
palate. The 2 clones meld into one another producing a gentle opulence. Screw
cap. 14% alc. **Rating** 94 **To** 2029 $60 JP

🍷🍷🍷🍷🍷 **Paraparap Reserve Single Vineyard Geelong Pinot Noir 2018** Rating 93
To 2028 $70 JP
Single Vineyard Geelong Pinot Noir 2018 Rating 93 **To** 2028 $45 JP
Single Vineyard Geelong Shiraz 2018 Rating 93 **To** 2031 $38 JP
Single Vineyard Geelong Pinot Gris 2020 Rating 91 **To** 2024 $30 JP
Single Vineyard Geelong Pinot Grigio 2020 Rating 91 **To** 2023 $30 JP
Single Vineyard Geelong Pinot Gris 2019 Rating 91 **To** 2024 $30 JP
Single Vineyard Geelong Pinot Grigio 2019 Rating 90 **To** 2024 $30 JP
Loretta Blanc de Noir Geelong 2017 Rating 90 $38 JP

Bull Lane Wine Company   ★★★★☆

PO Box 77, Heathcote, Vic 3523 **Region** Heathcote
T 0427 970 041 **www.**bulllane.com.au
Winemaker Simon Osicka **Est.** 2013 **Dozens** 500
After a successful career as a winemaker with what is now TWE, Simon Osicka, together
with viticulturist partner Alison Phillips, returned to the eponymous family winery just within
the eastern boundary of the Heathcote region in 2010. Spurred on by a decade of drought
impacting on the 60yo dry-grown vineyard, and a desire to create another style of shiraz,
Simon and Alison spent considerable time visiting Heathcote vineyards with access to water
in the lead-up to the '10 vintage. After the weather gods gave up their tricks of '11, Bull Lane
was in business. Exports to Denmark and China.

🍷🍷🍷🍷🍷 **Heathcote Shiraz 2019** Runs the gauntlet of aromas and flavours. Fragrant
violet, red fruits, black cherry and musky spice. Flows smoothly and long across an
elegant palate. A well-defined Heathcote shiraz that punches well above its weight.
Screw cap. 14.5% alc. **Rating** 94 **To** 2027 $29 JP ❂

🍷🍷🍷🍷🍷 **Pink Cliffs Heathcote Shiraz 2019** Rating 90 **To** 2029 $35 JP

Buller Wines   ★★★★☆

2804 Federation Way, Rutherglen, Vic 3685 **Region** Rutherglen
T (02) 6032 9660 **www.**bullerwines.com.au **Open** 7 days 10–5
Winemaker Dave Whyte **Est.** 1921 **Dozens** 10 000 **Vyds** 32ha
In 2013, after 92 years of ownership and management by the Buller family, the business was
purchased by Gerald and Mary Judd, a well-known local couple and family with extensive
roots in the North East. They are hands-on in the business and have overseen major
investment in the cellar, storage, operations and, importantly, vineyards. White and sparkling
wines from the King Valley have been added to the range and there is a new restaurant and

refurbished cellar door. Buller celebrates 100 years in 2021. Exports to the UK, Belgium, China, Taiwan, the US, Japan and NZ.

99999 **Calliope Rare Rutherglen Topaque NV** Reveals its age in an olive-edged walnut brown colour and highly concentrated, luscious flavours. Generations of the Buller family laid the foundations for this outstanding fortified. Malt toffee, butterscotch, dried fruits, toasted walnut and almond. Seamless on the palate, effortlessly so, and elevated to the heights of quality and age via lifted aromatics and a beautiful freshness. 500ml. Screw cap. 18% alc. **Rating** 96 $250 JP
Calliope Rare Rutherglen Muscat NV At once delicate and richly concentrated. A wine to sit back and reflect on. Dark malt-biscuit characters, nuts and dried-fruit aromas. Liquid plum pudding in the mouth, raisiny, baking spices, with a touch of balsamic, building in flavour intensity. Smooth, creamy texture. Maintains rare classification status cred with impressive poise. 500ml bottle. Screw cap. 18% alc. **Rating** 95 $250 JP
Calliope Grand Rutherglen Topaque NV Deep walnut brown, with thick, dense sweetness and raisin, toffee, caramel nuttiness. Freshness could be questioned, but what flavour. 500ml Screw cap. 18% alc. **Rating** 94 $150 JP
Calliope Grand Rutherglen Muscat NV Deep amber hues. A more intense and powerful expression and interpretation of grand muscat, a clear indication of the Buller house style. Treacle, dark chocolate, coffee grounds and plum pudding. The palate is dense, with so much sweet richness: salted caramel, vanilla, walnut, butterscotch. Lingers long in the mouth. Screw cap. 18% alc. **Rating** 94 $150 JP

99999 **Calliope Rutherglen Durif 2018** Rating 92 To 2032 $45 JP
Calliope Rare Frontignac NV Rating 92 $250 JP
Calliope King Valley Chardonnay 2018 Rating 90 To 2028 $32 JP
Fine Old Muscat NV Rating 90 $25 JP
Fine Old Tawny NV Rating 90 To 2023 $25 JP

Bundalong Coonawarra   ★★★★

109 Paul Road, Comaum, SA 5277 (postal) **Region** Coonawarra
T 0419 815 925 **www**.bundalongcoonawarra.com.au
Winemaker Andrew Hardy, Peter Bissell **Est.** 1990 **Dozens** 1000 **Vyds** 65ha
James Porter has owned the Bundalong property for many years. In the second half of the 1980s, encouraged by an old shallow limestone quarry on the property, he sought opinions about the suitability of the soil for grapegrowing. In '89 the first plantings of cabernet sauvignon were made, followed by shiraz. The primary purpose of the 65ha vineyard was to supply grapes to major companies. Trial vintages were made in '94 and '96, followed by the first serious vintage in 2008. The strategy has been only to make wine in the very best vintages in Coonawarra.

99999 **Single Vineyard Cabernet Sauvignon 2019** Starts with sweet mulberries, peppermint and redcurrants. It's dry, but there's an appealing sweet spot that gives way to the furry commanding tannins, with oak neatly in place. Its best years are ahead. Screw cap. 14% alc. **Rating** 93 To 2031 $28 JF
Single Vineyard Shiraz 2019 Holding on to the exuberance of youth with bright red plums. Lightly spiced with cinnamon and cedary/charry oak, definitely more savoury accents and a touch sour on the finish. The raspy tannins feel densely packed, yet the palate has some give. Barely fuller bodied. More bottle ageing will reap benefits. Screw cap. 13.5% alc. **Rating** 90 To 2030 $28 JF

Bunnamagoo Estate   ★★★★

603 Henry Lawson Drive, Mudgee, NSW 2850 **Region** Mudgee
T 1300 304 707 **www**.bunnamagoowines.com.au **Open** 7 days 10–4
Winemaker Robert Black **Est.** 1995 **Dozens** 100000 **Vyds** 108ha
Bunnamagoo Estate (on one of the first land grants in the region) is situated near the historic town of Rockley. A 6ha vineyard planted to chardonnay, merlot and cabernet sauvignon has

been established by Paspaley Pearls. The winery and cellar door are located at the much larger (and warmer) Eurunderee Vineyard (102ha) at Mudgee. Exports to the UK, Singapore, Fiji, Papua New Guinea, Indonesia, Hong Kong and China.

🍷🍷🍷🍷 **Shiraz 2019** I like this. Poised, highly regional, generous and good to drink. Nothing is pushed. Plummy sweet fruit, loamy earth and a sachet of spice strewn across the pushy finish. The tannins dusty and lithe, melding with a well-appointed frame of French and American oak. Screw cap. 14% alc. **Rating** 92 **To** 2029 $40 NG
Pinot Gris 2020 Sourced from interstate this vintage, due to the bushfires in Mudgee. A very solid gris, unwinding nicely in the mouth with mid-palate richness, drive and viscosity. Notes of baked apple tart, cinnamon roll and nashi pear reverberate from nose to long, pushy finish. Good drinking. Screw cap. 13% alc. **Rating** 91 **To** 2023 $25 NG

Burge Family Winemakers   ★★★★☆

1312 Barossa Way, Lyndoch, SA 5351 **Region** Barossa Valley
T (08) 8524 4644 **www**.burgefamily.com.au **Open** Thurs–Mon 10–5
Winemaker Derek Fitzgerald **Est.** 1928 **Dozens** 10 000 **Vyds** 10ha
In 2013 Burge Family Winemakers – an iconic producer of exceptionally rich, lush and concentrated Barossa red wines – marked 85 years of continuous winemaking by 3 generations of the family. Burge Family was purchased by the Wilsford Group in November '18; the legacy of the Burge Family will be preserved with no change in wine style. Derek Fitzgerald has stepped into Rick Burge's shoes, having made wine in the Barossa for 14 years. Exports to Hong Kong and China.

🍷🍷🍷🍷🍷 **Draycott Barossa Valley Cabernet Sauvignon 2018** Solid and bold Barossa cabernet, packed with blackcurrants and cassis, met in full force by dense, dark chocolate oak. It holds itself with composure, thanks to a rigid mesh of impressively fine-grained tannins and well-pitched acidity, maintaining confidence and assurance through a long finish. Unashamedly Barossan yet unmistakably cabernet. Patience. Screw cap. 14.5% alc. **Rating** 95 **To** 2038 $50 TS

🍷🍷🍷🍷 **Draycott Barossa Valley Cabernet Shiraz 2018** Rating 93 **To** 2030 $55 TS
The Homestead Barossa Valley Cabernet Shiraz 2018 Rating 92 **To** 2038 $28 TS

Burke & Wills Winery   ★★★★

3155 Burke & Wills Track, Mia Mia, Vic 3444 **Region** Heathcote
T (03) 5425 5400 **www**.wineandmusic.net **Open** By appt
Winemaker Andrew Pattison, Robert Ellis **Est.** 2003 **Dozens** 1200 **Vyds** 1.6ha
After 18 years at Lancefield Winery in the Macedon Ranges, Andrew Pattison moved his operation a few kilometres north in 2004 to set up Burke & Wills Winery at the southern edge of the Heathcote region. The vineyards at Mia Mia comprise 0.6ha of shiraz, 0.6ha of Bordeaux varieties (cabernet sauvignon, petit verdot, merlot and malbec) and 0.4ha of gewürztraminer. He still sources a small amount of Macedon Ranges fruit from his former vineyard; additional grapes are contract-grown in Heathcote. In '17 the winery won the inaugural Premier's Award for Best Victorian Wine with the '15 Vat 1 Shiraz.

🍷🍷🍷🍷 **Vat 1 French Oak Heathcote Shiraz 2018** My, there is a lot going on here. So robust, powerful in a typical Heathcote way and yet so easily approachable. Not intimidating in the least. Deep, impenetrable purple. Licorice, stewed plums, blackberry, violets, dark chocolate, earth. The wine slurps up the oak and then some. Finishes sweet-hearted and warm. Screw cap. 14.2% alc. **Rating** 93 **To** 2031 $36 JP
Mia Mia Heathcote Gewürztraminer 2020 High and cool at 360m, combined with a love of the grape, sees gewürztraminer enjoying a new home in Heathcote. Aromatic rose petal and apple blossom with a good dusting of

Middle Eastern spice. All the lush mouthfeel and flavour you might want is here, with juicy acidity and just a smidge of sweetness. Screw cap. 12.6% alc. **Rating** 91 **To** 2024 $28 JP

The Aristocrat Heathcote 2018 A highly structured wine with tannin and oak power that benefits mightily from decanting. Generous black-fruit intensity, dark chocolate, bush mint and vanilla aromas. Rich and ripe, a strong foundation has been laid out on the palate with cedary oak tannic overlay. Screw cap. 14.5% alc. **Rating** 90 **To** 2028 $32 JP

Mia Mia Heathcote Planter's Blend 2017 Protects its reputation as a fruit-forward, fresh, well-priced red. A light savouriness is well handled alongside the tilled earth, blackberries, spice and firm tannins. Finishes gentle, dry and delicious. Screw cap. 13.5% alc. **Rating** 90 **To** 2024 $25 JP

ϘϘϘϘ Dig Tree Central Victoria Pinot Gris 2019 Rating 88 To 2024 $20 JP

Bush Track Wines

161 Myrtle Street, Myrtleford, Vic 3737 **Region** Alpine Valleys
T 0409 572 712 **www**.bushtrackwines.com.au **Open** Thurs 11–6, Fri–Sat 11–7, Sun 11–6
Winemaker Jo Marsh, Eleana Anderson **Est.** 1987 **Dozens** 550 **Vyds** 8.8ha
Bob and Helen McNamara established the vineyard in 1987, planting shiraz (11 different clones), chardonnay, cabernet sauvignon and sangiovese. They have made small volumes of wines since 2006. Improvement in vineyard practices and the services of Jo Marsh (Billy Button Wines) and Eleana Anderson (Mayford Wines) should secure the future of Bush Track Wines.

ϘϘϘϘϘ Alpine Valleys Sparkling Shiraz 2017 A dense sparkling shiraz. Deep purple, with the scent of its birthplace: acacia flower, alpine herbs, black cherry, spice. Retains some old-style traditions such as a degree of sweetness on the palate and a lively spiciness. The maker, Jo Marsh, was formerly at Seppelt Great Western, home of the style, so rest assured this is one confident, assured and complex sparkling. Crown seal. 14% alc. **Rating** 93 $50 JP

ϘϘϘϘ Ovens Valley Shiraz 2019 Rating 89 To 2025 $32 JP

Buttermans Track

75 Yow Yow Creek Road, St Andrews, Vic 3761 **Region** Yarra Valley
T 0433 649 640 **www**.buttermanstrack.com.au **Open** W'ends 11–5
Winemaker Joel and Gary Trist **Est.** 1991 **Dozens** 600 **Vyds** 2.13ha
I (James) became intimately acquainted with Buttermans Track in the latter part of the 1980s when Coldstream Hills, at that stage owned by my wife Suzanne and myself, purchased grapes from the Roberts family's Rising Vineyard. I had to coax a 3t truck with almost no brakes and almost no engine to tackle the hills and valleys of the unsealed Buttermans Track. Louise and Gary Trist began planting a small vineyard in '91 on a small side road just off the Buttermans Track. Between then and 2003 they established 0.86ha of pinot noir, 0.74ha of shiraz and 0.53ha of sangiovese. The Trist family sold the grapes to Yarra Valley wineries until '08. From that year onwards a small parcel of sangiovese was retained for the Buttermans Track label, which has now extended to include other varieties, son Joel joining Gary in the winery.

Byrne Vineyards

PO Box 15, Kent Town BC, SA 5071 **Region** Lower Murray/Mount Lofty Ranges
T (08) 8132 0022 **www**.byrnevineyards.com.au
Winemaker Mark Robinson, Phil Reedman MW **Est.** 1963 **Dozens** 120 000 **Vyds** 200ha
The Byrne family has been involved in the SA wine industry for 3 generations, with vineyards in the Clare Valley and Riverland. Wine styles include vine-dried, field blends, vegan-friendly wines and regional wines. Exports to the UK, the US, Canada, Germany, Denmark, Sweden, Norway, the Netherlands, Poland, Russia, NZ, Japan and China.

ΨΨΨΫ **Antiquarian Barossa Shiraz 2018** This is no wallflower and despite its obvious oak inputs, this is in good shape. Full of dark fruits, layers of baking spices, woodsy flavouring with licorice and juniper. It's fuller bodied, the tannins are ripe if a little gritty, yet it finishes convincingly. Diam. 14.5% alc. **Rating** 90 **To** 2028 $59 JF

Byron & Harold ★★★★★

57 River Way, Walter Point, WA 6152 (postal) **Region** Great Southern/Margaret River
T 0402 010 352 **www.**byronandharold.com.au
Winemaker Kate Morgan **Est.** 2011 **Dozens** 36 000 **Vyds** 34ha
The owners of Byron & Harold make a formidable partnership, covering every aspect of winemaking, sales, marketing, business management and administration. Paul Byron and Ralph (Harold) Dunning together have more than 65 years of experience in the Australian wine trade, working at top levels for some of the most admired wineries and wine distribution companies. Andrew Lane worked for 20 years in the tourism industry, including in a senior role with Tourism Australia, leading to the formation of the Wine Tourism Export Council. More recently he developed the family vineyard (Wandering Lane). Exports to the UK, Canada, China and NZ.

ΨΨΨΨΨ **The Partners Great Southern Riesling 2020** Tight, bright, savoury and long, this has a curious combination of almost sweet sherbet-like acidity, with powerful fruit that sits firmly on the savoury end of proceedings; like salted preserved lemons and balsamic poached plums. The chalky phenolics tie it all together, weaving structure and cohesion into the wine. Concentrated and muscular with good length of flavour. Screw cap. 12% alc. **Rating** 95 **To** 2036 $40 EL
The Protocol Margaret River Cabernet Sauvignon 2019 The cool 2019 year produced aromatic and nuanced wines in Margaret River. This is one of them. Supple, layered and so pretty – pomegranate, raspberry, red licorice and anise. The tannins are chalky and fine and shape the fruit on its journey across the palate and through to the long finish. Very smart. Screw cap. 14% alc. **Rating** 95 **To** 2036 $55 EL
Gravity Margaret River Cabernet Sauvignon 2019 Savoury red and black fruits, backed by vanilla-pod oak. Uncomplicated, elegant and supple cabernet drinking here that lingers on the palate. Screw cap. 14% alc. **Rating** 94 **To** 2031 $32 EL

ΨΨΨΫ **Rose & Thorns Great Southern Riesling 2020** **Rating** 93 **To** 2031 $32 EL
The Protocol Margaret River Chardonnay 2019 **Rating** 93 **To** 2028 $55 EL
Rags to Riches Margaret River Cabernet Sauvignon 2019 **Rating** 90 **To** 2027 $32 EL

🍇 Cabbage Tree Hill ★★★★

104 Greens Beach Road, Beaconsfield Tas 7270 **Region** Northern Tasmania
T 0407 705 905 **www.**cabbagetreehillwine.com.au **Open** 7 days 11–5
Winemaker Liam McElhinney (Tasmanian Vintners) **Est.** 2013 **Dozens** 500 **Vyds** 2ha
From its home in Beaconsfield on the western Tamar, Cabbage Tree Hill produces a range spanning sparkling, sauvignon blanc, chardonnay, rosé, pinot noir and cabernet sauvignon. Reds are sourced exclusively from well-established estate vines. Contract winemaking is handled by Tasmanian Vintners Pty Ltd (formerly Winemaking Tasmania). Sauvignon blanc, rosé and pinot noir are the standouts. (TS)

ΨΨΨΫ **Tasmania Sauvignon Blanc 2020** Sauvignon on full throttle. Bursting with lemons, gooseberries, passionfruit and lantana. Fresh, lively and vivacious, riding on a bright sunbeam of Tasmanian acidity that carries a long finish until forever. It's not complex or textured, but, blimey, it's pinpoint accurate and oh so energetic. Screw cap. 13% alc. **Rating** 93 **To** 2022 $35 TS
Tasmania Pinot Noir 2018 Aged in oak barrels. Effortless, graceful and unforced, this is a pretty Northern Tasmanian pinot. Red cherry and strawberry tang is delicately fragranced with rose petals and musk. Fine-ground tannins and

bright acid line draw out a finish of lingering harmony. Screw cap. 13.5% alc.
Rating 93 **To** 2028 $45 TS

Tasmania Rosé 2020 Pretty, precise and refreshing, rosé is the ultimate purpose for vibrant, young vine Tassie pinot. Strawberry hull, morello cherries, raspberries, watermelon and guava find tension and style in an energetic acid line. It may not be complex or textured, but it achieves precisely what it sets out to do, with gusto! Screw cap. 12.7% alc. **Rating** 92 **To** 2022 $35 TS

Caillard Wine

5 Annesley Street, Leichhardt, NSW 2040 (postal) **Region** Barossa Valley
T 0433 272 912 **www.**caillardwine.com
Winemaker Dr Phil Lehmann, Andrew Caillard MW **Est.** 2008 **Dozens** 1000

Andrew Caillard MW has had a long and varied career in wine, including vintages at Brokenwood and elsewhere, but has also taken the final step of making his own wine, with the support of wife Bobby. Andrew says the inspiration to make Mataro (and now Shiraz) came while writing the background for Penfolds' The Rewards of Patience tastings. He learnt that both Max Schubert and John Davoren had experimented with mataro, and that the original releases of Penfolds St Henri comprised a fair percentage of the variety. For good measure, Andrew's great (times four) grandfather, John Reynell, planted one of Australia's first vineyards at Reynella, around 1838. Exports to Hong Kong, China, Singapore, South Korea and France.

Barossa Valley Shiraz 2017 I love the elegance and refinement of the cool '17 season in the Barossa when it's sensitively handled and sufficiently ripe. Andrew Caillard and Phil Lehmann nailed it. Unashamedly medium bodied. Fragrant. Spicy. Red-fruited. Vibrant. Refreshing acidity works seamlessly with finely crafted tannins to draw out a long and graceful finish. Bravo. Screw cap. 14.2% alc. **Rating** 93 **To** 2032 $50 TS

Barossa Valley Mataro 2017 It takes some talent to craft mataro that can fly solo as confidently as this. The cool '17 season heightens fragrance and red-berry fruit tang, framed by fine, confident tannins and vibrant acidity that promise great potential. Screw cap. 14.4% alc. **Rating** 92 **To** 2037 $50 TS

Calabria Family Wines

1283 Brayne Road, Griffith, NSW 2680 **Region** Riverina/Barossa Valley
T (02) 6969 0800 **www.**calabriawines.com.au **Open** Mon–Fri 8.30–5, w'ends 10–4
Winemaker Bill Calabria, Emma Norbiato, Tony Steffania, Jeremy Nascimben,
Sam Mittiga **Est.** 1945 **Vyds** 100ha

Calabria Family Wines (until 2014 known as Westend Estate) has successfully lifted both the quality and the packaging of its wines. Its 3 Bridges range is anchored on estate vineyards. The operation is moving with the times, increasing its plantings of durif and introducing aglianico, nero d'Avola and St Macaire (once grown in Bordeaux, and on the verge of extinction, this 2ha is the largest planting in the world). Equally importantly, it is casting its net over the Barossa Valley, Hilltops and King Valley premium regions, taking this one step further by acquiring a vineyard in the Barossa Valley (cnr Light Pass Road/Magnolia Road, Vine Vale) and opening a cellar door/restaurant. Exports to the UK, the US and other major markets, including China.

Francesco Show Reserve Grand Tawny NV Judging by the amber hue and gentle waft of rancio complexity, the average age of the wine here is considerable. High-quality spirit is seamlessly integrated into a fray of spiced date, clove, walnut, tamarind, cinnamon and every other sensorial experience of the Moroccan souk. Complex, long and impeccably realised. Sweet, but far from cloying. Screw cap. 19% alc. **Rating** 96 $45 NG ✪

Reserve Eden Valley Riesling 2019 This is a dainty, intensely flavoured high-country riesling. Aromas of squeezed lime juice, orange verbena, cumquat and quince. The acidity is juicy rather than battery-acid hard. The alcohol, à point. The fruit sweetness, spot on. The phenolics, intact after fermenting pressings only,

serving up a sluice of pucker and detail. Delicious drinking. Screw cap. 11% alc.
Rating 94 To 2028 $30 NG ✪

ŶŶŶŶŶ The Iconic Grand Reserve Barossa Valley Shiraz 2018 Rating 93 To 2030
$175 NG
Alternato Barossa Valley 2018 Rating 93 To 2025 $45 NG
Francesco Show Reserve Grand Liqueur Muscat NV Rating 93 $45 NG
3 Bridges Tumbarumba Chardonnay 2019 Rating 92 To 2027 $25 NG ✪
Elisabetta Barossa Valley Shiraz 2019 Rating 92 To 2028 $45 NG
Saint Petri Barossa Valley Shiraz Carignan 2019 Rating 92 To 2031
$95 NG
Reserve Barossa Valley Cabernet Sauvignon 2017 Rating 92 To 2024
$35 NG
3 Bridges Barossa Valley Grenache 2019 Rating 91 To 2028 $35 NG
Saint Petri Barossa Valley Grenache Shiraz Mataro 2019 Rating 91
To 2027 $95 NG
3 Bridges Reserve Botrytis Semillon 2018 Rating 91 To 2028 $25 NG
Old Vine Barossa Valley Shiraz 2018 Rating 90 To 2028 $30 NG
Pierre d'Amour Syrah 2018 Rating 90 To 2024 $20 NG ✪
Three Bridges Barossa Valley Mourvèdre 2019 Rating 90 To 2028
$35 NG

Campbells ★★★★★

4603 Murray Valley Highway, Rutherglen, Vic 3685 **Region** Rutherglen
T (02) 6033 6000 **www**.campbellswines.com.au **Open** 7 days 10–5
Winemaker Julie Campbell **Est.** 1870 **Dozens** 36 000 **Vyds** 72ha
Campbells has a long and rich history, with 5 generations of the family making wine for over
150 years. There were difficult times: phylloxera's arrival in the Bobbie Burns Vineyard in
1898; the Depression of the 1930s; and premature deaths. But the Scottish blood of founder
John Campbell has ensured that the business has not only survived, but quietly flourished.
Indeed, there have been spectacular successes in unexpected quarters (white table wines,
especially riesling) and expected success with muscat and topaque. Scores of 99 points from
Robert Parker and 100 points from Wine Spectator put Campbells in a special position.
Following the death of Colin Campbell in 2019, daughters Jane and Julie Campbell are now
at the helm, as managing director and head winemaker respectively. A founding member of
Australia's First Families of Wine. Exports to the UK, the US China and other major markets.

ŶŶŶŶŶ Isabella Rare Rutherglen Topaque NV Deep, dark amber, displaying
characterstistic Campbells aromatics, Isabella is a treat for the tastebuds and the
mind, a wine of living history. The aroma is powerfully luscious and concentrated
in plum pudding, orange peel, treacle, raisin. Lush and harmonious to taste, with
hints of Saunders malt, viscous honey and dried fruits, all edged in a clean, lively
spirit. Flows long, hitting the sweet-and-mellow spot. 375ml. Screw cap. 18% alc.
Rating 97 $140 JP ✪
Merchant Prince Rare Muscat NV Mesmerising! Merchant Prince is one of
the most complex tasting experiences you can have. Such is the depth and age of
Campbells fortified stocks; few producers can compete. Dense, deep in colour and
super-concentrated, Merchant Prince seems to pour in slow motion. Molasses,
dried fruits, soaked raisins and toasted nuts meld and weave their way through the
palate, rising in sweet intensity. Clean pair of heels to close. A fortified masterclass.
375ml. Screw cap. 18% alc. Rating 97 $140 JP ✪

ŶŶŶŶŶ Grand Rutherglen Topaque NV Burnished walnut colour. A laid-back
approach, mellow even, with luscious sweetness tempered by cold-tea notes in
tandem with raisined fruit, chocolate panforte and toasted nuts. So much here:
layer upon layer of flavour that fills all senses. But that balance of clean spirit keeps
things tight and fresh. So much class on display. 375ml. Screw cap. 17.5% alc.
Rating 96 $70 JP ✪

Grand Rutherglen Muscat NV Superb fruit is the building block here. The colour of treacle accompanies the scent of fig, dried fruits, nougat and orange peel. As intense as it is in aroma and on the palate, there is an incredible freshness, too, the mark of a great fortified. Layer upon layer of raisiny fruitcake goodness, walnut, quince paste, toffee. All class. Screw cap. 17.5% alc. **Rating** 96 $70 JP ✪

The Barkly Rutherglen Durif 2016 The durif grape loves Rutherglen and the feeling among producers is mutual. The 2016 Barkly is the grape writ large in personality, in alcohol and in boldness. That's the immediate impact. Give it time, let it work through. From the middle palate on it's remarkably finer in detail, textural, warm, even-handed and goes long and clean on the finish. Quite the chameleon. Screw cap. 14.9% alc. **Rating** 95 To 2032 $60 JP

Classic Rutherglen Topaque NV Aromas and flavours are more concentrated here, but the essence of house style, of dried fruits, fruitcake, malt and honey, remains ever-present, together with all-important freshness and liveliness. Traditionally not as intense and luscious as muscat, this Topaque is certainly just as equally and utterly delicious. 500ml. Screw cap. 17.5% alc. **Rating** 95 $40 JP

Classic Rutherglen Muscat NV Quintessential classic in style, with a beautiful line of pure rose oil and dried-fruit aromatics on display throughout. The floral delicacy is a big part of Campbells' understated but concentrated muscat style. Builds layer after layer of flavour, yet remains fresh and vital. This is the blender's art in a glass. 500ml. Screw cap. 17.5% alc. **Rating** 95 $40 JP

Bobbie Burns Rutherglen Shiraz 2018 This release marks the 49th vintage for Bobbie Burns. The secret to its longevity is its honesty, which is nicely expressed here. It is right in the medium-weighted, down to earth, totally accessible, classic Aussie shiraz style. Solid in dark fruits, discreet in oak, awash in tingling, woodsy spice and melded together by fine tannins. Length is assured, the pleasure factor high. Screw cap. 14.5% alc. **Rating** 94 To 2029 $23 JP ✪

♟♟♟♟♟ **The Sixties Block 2019** Rating 93 To 2026 $28 JP
Rutherglen Topaque NV Rating 93 $22 JP ✪
Limited Release Rutherglen Roussanne 2019 Rating 92 To 2024 $25 JP ✪
The Brothers Rutherglen Shiraz 2016 Rating 92 To 2030 $60 JP
Limited Release Rutherglen Durif 2018 Rating 92 To 2033 $28 JP
Rutherglen Muscat NV Rating 92 $22 JP ✪
Sparkling White Trebbiano NV Rating 90 $25 JP

Canobolas-Smith   ★★★★★

Boree Lane, off Cargo Road, Lidster via Orange, NSW 2800 **Region** Orange
T (02) 6365 6113 **www.**canobolassmithwines.com.au **Open** Sat 11–5
Winemaker Murray Smith **Est.** 1986 **Dozens** 1000 **Vyds** 6ha
The Smith family, led by Murray Smith, was one of the early movers in Orange. The vineyard has always been dry-grown, gaining strength from the free-draining clay loam derived from basalt soils. The wines are released under 3 labels, the Strawhouse label from grapes sourced from a vineyard immediately to the north of Canobolas-Smith; the newest label is The Shine, utilising the golden mean enunciated by Pythagoras, and is reserved for very special wines. Exports to Japan.

♟♟♟♟♟ **Shine Reserve Chardonnay 2014** A medium yellow colour with glints of green. A shift away from the overly reductive match-struck style of the recent past, now celebrating both the region's altitudinal freshness and its proclivity for ripeness. In these hands, this richer vintage is amplified by extended time on lees, wild yeast-inflected shiitake/umami accents offsetting teeming stone-fruit flavours, pungent mineral and nourishing barrel work. The touch, deft, but one of flavour, generosity and thrilling length. Screw cap. 14% alc. **Rating** 96 To 2026 $75 NG ✪

Sans Souci Orange Semillon Sauvignon Blanc 2011 This has aged beautifully. Unravelling with time in the glass across riffs of lanolin, quince paste, lemon balm, sour cream, orange verbena, oatmeal and dried straw. Intense and impeccably concentrated for a barrel-fermented style. Juicy acidity and the sting of nettle, driving through the mid palate and pushing exceptionally long. Screw cap. 13% alc. **Rating** 95 **To** 2025 $45 NG

ŸŸŸŸŸ **Wild Yeast Chardonnay 2015 Rating** 93 **To** 2025 $55 NG
Alchemy 2012 Rating 93 **To** 2024 $70 NG
Orange Cabernets 2013 Rating 92 **To** 2023 $45 NG

Cape Barren Wines

123 King William Road, Hyde Park, SA 5061 (postal) **Region** McLaren Vale
T (08) 8267 3292 **www**.capebarren.com.au **Open** By appt
Winemaker Rob Dundon **Est.** 1999 **Dozens** 10 000 **Vyds** 16.5ha
Cape Barren was founded in 1999 by Peter Matthew. He sold the business in late 2009 to Rob Dundon and Tom Adams, who together have amassed in excess of 50 years' experience in winemaking, viticulture and international sales. The wines, including Shiraz and Grenache, are sourced from dry-grown vines between 70 and 125 years old. Chardonnay and grüner veltliner are sourced from the Adelaide Hills. Exports to China, Vietnam, Canada, Malaysia, Singapore, NZ, Denmark, Italy and the Philippines.

ŸŸŸŸŸ **Old Vine Reserve McLaren Vale Shiraz 2018** This is nicely done. While it doesn't pull any contemporary surprises, it is round, rich, fleshy and vinous. Beautiful balance of gushing fruit and nicely positioned oak, conducting the long flow of kirsch, clove, licorice and baking spice flavours. Screw cap. 14.5% alc. **Rating** 95 **To** 2032 $75 NG

ŸŸŸŸŸ **Native Goose McLaren Vale GSM 2019 Rating** 92 **To** 2025 $28 NG
Old Vine McLaren Vale Grenache 2019 Rating 90 **To** 2024 $40 NG

Cape Bernier Vineyard

230 Bream Creek Road, Bream Creek, Tas 7175 **Region** Southern Tasmania
T (03) 6253 5443 **www**.capebernier.com.au **Open** By appt
Winemaker Frogmore Creek (Alain Rousseau) **Est.** 1999 **Dozens** 1800 **Vyds** 4ha
Andrew and Jenny Sinclair took over from founder Alastair Christie in 2014. The vineyard plantings consist of 2ha of pinot noir (including 3 Dijon clones), 1.4ha of chardonnay and 0.6ha of pinot gris on a north-facing slope with spectacular views of Marion Bay. The property is one of several in the region that are changing from dairy and beef cattle to wine production and tourism. Exports to Singapore.

Cape Grace Wines

281 Fifty One Road, Cowaramup, WA 6284 **Region** Margaret River
T (08) 9755 5669 **www**.capegracewines.com.au **Open** 7 days 10–5
Winemaker Dylan Arvidson, Mark Messenger (Consultant) **Est.** 1996 **Dozens** 2000 **Vyds** 6.25ha
Cape Grace can trace its history back to 1875, when timber baron MC Davies settled at Karridale, building the Leeuwin lighthouse and founding the township of Margaret River; 120 years later, Robert and Karen Karri-Davies planted their vineyard to chardonnay, shiraz and cabernet sauvignon, with smaller amounts of cabernet franc, malbec and chenin blanc. Robert is a self-taught viticulturist; Karen has over 15 years of international sales and marketing experience in the hospitality industry. Winemaking is carried out on the property; consultant Mark Messenger is a veteran of the Margaret River region. Exports to Singapore and China.

ŸŸŸŸŸ **Margaret River Chardonnay 2019** If you've ever picked a curry leaf fresh from the plant and crushed it between your fingers, then you know what this wine smells like. Add yellow peach, brine and red apples, and you're there. The flavours on the palate fall in line perfectly with the nose. All things in place. Spicy, exotic, rich, balanced … everything laced up by saline acidity. Screw cap. 12.1% alc. **Rating** 94 **To** 2031 $38 EL

Basket Pressed Margaret River Cabernet Sauvignon 2018 Pungent intensity of blackberry/cassis flavour, and streamlined length though the finish. It extends like a bicep, flexing its regional pedigree and showing the bounty of the vintage. If there was a quibble, it would be the metallic edge to the tannins through the finish, however this is absorbed by the fruit, so it remains minor in the scheme of things. Screw cap. 13.8% alc. **Rating** 94 **To** 2036 $55 EL
Reserve Margaret River Cabernet Sauvignon 2017 2017 was a cool and wet year in Margaret River, and for those who managed their vineyards with care and courage, it was a triumphant year. This wine is elegant and layered, with a supple, medium-bodied claret character. Red berries, salivating, briny acidity and very fine tannins are the making of this wine. Screw cap. 13.8% alc. **Rating** 94 **To** 2036 $85 EL

🍷🍷🍷🍷 **Basket Pressed Margaret River Malbec 2019** **Rating** 90 **To** 2031 $40 EL

Cape Jaffa Wines ★★★★☆

459 Limestone Coast Road, Mount Benson via Robe, SA 5276 **Region** Mount Benson
T (08) 8768 5053 **www**.capejaffawines.com.au **Open** 7 days 10–5
Winemaker Anna and Derek Hooper **Est.** 1993 **Dozens** 10 000 **Vyds** 22.86ha
Cape Jaffa was the first of the Mount Benson wineries. Cape Jaffa's fully certified biodynamic vineyard provides 50% of production, with additional fruit sourced from a certified biodynamic grower in Wrattonbully. Having received the Advantage SA Regional Award in '09, '10 and '11 for its sustainable initiatives in the Limestone Coast, Cape Jaffa is a Hall of Fame inductee. Exports to the UK, Canada, Thailand, the Philippines, Hong Kong, Singapore and China.

🍷🍷🍷🍷🍷 **Epic Drop Mount Benson Shiraz 2019** This is a compelling wine, with dark fruit doused in black pepper, baking spices and a dusting of cocoa. It's fuller bodied and comes with a glossy sheen across the palate, bolstered by ripe, pliant tannins. It's quite delicious. Crack it open now to enjoy its vibrancy, although it will add more complexity in time. Screw cap. 14.5% alc. **Rating** 95 **To** 2030 $29 JF ✪
La Lune Mount Benson Shiraz 2018 A neatly composed wine. Almost gentle at first, with dark fruits, lightly spiced with licorice and wood char via oak. It builds across the palate with textural, sandy tannins and a freshness throughout. It's just the touch of alcohol warmth on the finish pinging this otherwise excellent wine. Diam. 14.8% alc. **Rating** 94 **To** 2030 $60 JF
Upwelling Mount Benson Cabernet Sauvignon 2018 A medium-bodied wine with just the right amount of varietal charm introduced by currants and blackberries, with fresh herbs, but it's also savoury. Tannins are lovely – fine and shapely and overall, this is delicious. Screw cap. 14.5% alc. **Rating** 94 **To** 2033 $29 JF ✪

🍷🍷🍷🍷 **Limestone Coast Shiraz 2019** **Rating** 90 **To** 2025 $20 JF ✪
Mesmer Eyes White & Red Blend Limestone Coast 2019 **Rating** 90 **To** 2024 $29 JF

Cape Landing ★★★★☆

1098 Calgardup Road, Forest Grove, WA 6286 **Region** Margaret River
T 0488 006 169 **www**.capelanding.com.au
Winemaker Bruce Dukes, Remi Guise **Est.** 1998 **Dozens** 2500 **Vyds** 14ha
The current owner, Mark Lewis, purchased the property in 2016 from Cheryl and Larry de Jong, who had established the vineyard in the late 1990s. For many years the vineyard supplied most of its grapes to other wineries in the area. The vineyard is planted to chardonnay, sauvignon blanc, shiraz and cabernet sauvignon. Exports exclusively to the Cayman Islands, and sells into the domestic market here in Australia. Cellar door is currently in the planning. (EL)

🍷🍷🍷🍷🍷 **Reserve Margaret River Cabernet Sauvignon 2019** Very elegant, mineral-laden cabernet. The tannins have a chalkiness that cups the fruit in the mouth.

Cassis, wild raspberry and red currant all vie for space upfront. There is a wild, untamed quality that seems at home on the windswept coastline that frames the Margaret River region. Wow, for a wine to take you places … it's got to be good. Lovely, dusty, earthy, rustic, fine and structured cabernet here. Screw cap. 13.8% alc. **Rating** 95 **To** 2036 $45 EL

Blackwood Margaret River Cabernet Sauvignon 2019 The '19 vintage has a verve and life about it when viewed through the lens of cabernet sauvignon in Margaret River, and this is no exception. Startlingly pure fruit is huddled right at the front of the palate. The tannins are fine and lacy and serve to contain the fruit (as much as it can be) in a willowy shape on the palate. Creamy, intense, but shorter than expected. Screw cap. 14.2% alc. **Rating** 94 **To** 2030 $75 EL

ȲȲȲȲȲ **Blackwood Margaret River Chardonnay 2019 Rating** 93 **To** 2031 $60 EL
Margaret River Sauvignon Blanc 2020 Rating 92 **To** 2024 $28 EL
Reserve Margaret River Chardonnay 2019 Rating 91 **To** 2027 $38 EL
Reserve Margaret River Syrah 2019 Rating 90 **To** 2031 $35 EL
Reserve Margaret River Cabernet Sauvignon 2018 Rating 90 **To** 2027 $45 EL

Cape Mentelle ★★★★★

331 Wallcliffe Road, Margaret River, WA 6285 **Region** Margaret River
T (08) 9757 0888 **www.**capementelle.com.au **Open** 7 days 10–5
Winemaker Frederique Perrin Parker, Coralie Lewis, David Johnson, Ben Cane
Est. 1970 **Dozens** 80 000 **Vyds** 145ha
Part of the LVMH (Louis Vuitton Möet Hennessy) group. Cape Mentelle is firing on all cylinders, with the winemaking team fully capitalising on the extensive and largely mature vineyards, which obviate the need for contract-grown fruit. It is hard to say which of the wines is best; the ranking, such as it is, varies from year to year. That said, Sauvignon Blanc Semillon, Chardonnay, Shiraz and Cabernet Sauvignon lead the portfolio. Exports to all major markets.

ȲȲȲȲȲ **Wallcliffe Margaret River Sauvignon Blanc Semillon 2018** On lees in barrel for 15 months prior to blending. A powerful, statuesque wine. The oak has a big impact both aromatically and on the palate, its final kick is through the finish. Cassis, pear, nectarine and cheesecloth. Put this away for a few years and let it come together. Screw cap. 13% alc. **Rating** 95 **To** 2037 $49 EL

Wallcliffe Margaret River Sauvignon Blanc Semillon 2017 The Wallcliffe has long been one of the class acts in the world of oaked sauvignon blanc semillon blends in Margaret River. The cooler 2017 vintage has predictably produced a fine and taut iteration. Coriander, sugar snap pea, curry leaf, jasmine tea and red apple skins are laced together by salty acidity. All of this is carried on a bed of fine phenolic texture. As usual, the oak plays a dominant role, but this has proven to be absorbed by the fruit over time. Screw cap. 12% alc. **Rating** 95 **To** 2036 $49 EL

Margaret River Chardonnay 2018 A very sophisticated nose, textural, worked and complex. The fruit has a rich, ripe viscosity to it and a fierce salty edge. Red apple skins and tea leaves, salted kelp, slippery ripe yellow peach and a fair whack of curry leaf, brine and preserved lemon. This is happening. A subtle shift in style here, more multifaceted and shimmering, always moving, like dappled sunlight. The best chardonnay under this label to date. Screw cap. 14.5% alc. **Rating** 95 **To** 2031 $55 EL

Wallcliffe Margaret River Merlot Petit Verdot 2017 Dark and dense with secondary characters already forming on the palate. This has leather strapping and exotic spice, putting one in mind of a Bordeaux blend rather than Margaret River. There's a charcuterie/sausage character through the finish. Very attractive and quite unexpected. Will age prodigiously. Screw cap. 14.5% alc. **Rating** 95 **To** 2046 $49 EL

Margaret River Zinfandel 2018 From the near-perfect 2018 vintage springs this intense, oak-driven and concentrated wine. The year has imparted a concentrated ripeness and balance that will stand it in good stead in the cellar.

The evident oak is distracting right now, but will surely mellow over time. A wine with a cult following. Screw cap. 15.5% alc. **Rating** 95 **To** 2045 $65 EL

🍷🍷🍷🍷🍷 **Margaret River Sauvignon Blanc Semillon 2020 Rating** 93 **To** 2025 $26 EL ○
Margaret River Sauvignon Blanc Semillon 2019 Rating 93 **To** 2024 $26 EL ○
Margaret River Rosé 2019 Rating 93 **To** 2023 $28 JH
Trinders Margaret River 2018 Rating 93 **To** 2035 $31 EL
Margaret River Shiraz 2018 Rating 91 **To** 2028 $49 EL
Brooks Margaret River Chardonnay 2020 Rating 90 **To** 2027 $28 EL

Cape Naturaliste Vineyard ★★★★☆

1 Coley Road (off Caves Road), Yallingup, WA 6282 **Region** Margaret River
T (08) 9755 2538 **www.**capenaturalistevineyard.com.au **Open** 7 days 10–5
Winemaker Bruce Dukes, Craig Brent-White, David Moss, Rick Hoile-Mills **Est.** 1997
Dozens 5400 **Vyds** 10.7ha
Cape Naturaliste Vineyard has a long and varied history going back 150 years, when it was a coaching inn for travellers journeying between Perth and Margaret River. Later it became a dairy farm and in 1970 a mining company purchased it, intending to extract nearby mineral sands. The government stepped in and declared the area a national park, whereafter (in '80) Craig Brent-White purchased the property. Bruce Dukes joined Craig as winemaker, initially responsible for the white wines, before red wines were added to the roster. The vineyard is planted to cabernet sauvignon, shiraz, merlot, semillon and sauvignon blanc, and is run on an organic/biodynamic basis with little or no irrigation. Exports to the UK, the US, Canada and China.

🍷🍷🍷🍷🍷 **The Sextant Appassimento Margaret River 2018** Quince, date, blackberry and licorice/anise. This is loaded with flavour, and despite the very high alcohol, doesn't feel alcoholic. Good length of flavour rounds this out, making it clear that it will live for a very long time in the cellar. It is a good example of the style, and will polarise many, but if (very) full-bodied red wine is your proclivity, then try this. Screw cap. 16.5% alc. **Rating** 92 **To** 2036 $160 EL
Single Vineyard Margaret River Cabernet Sauvignon 2018 The typically red-fruited Houghton clone is on show here, the palate is as the nose lays out: saturated with summer raspberry, pomegranate, red licorice and fine tannins. This is a lovely cabernet with a moreish plushness that keeps you coming back for more. Not necessarily a keeper, but a perfect wine in the short/medium term. Screw cap. 13.8% alc. **Rating** 92 **To** 2028 $30 EL

🍷🍷🍷🍷 **Torpedo Rocks Single Vineyard Margaret River Malbec 2018 Rating** 88 **To** 2028 $40 EL

Capel Vale ★★★★★

118 Mallokup Road, Capel, WA 6271 **Region** Geographe
T (08) 9727 1986 **www.**capelvale.com.au **Open** 7 days 10–4
Winemaker Daniel Hetherington **Est.** 1974 **Dozens** 21 000 **Vyds** 52ha
Established by Perth-based medical practitioner Dr Peter Pratten and wife Elizabeth in 1974. The first vineyard adjacent to the winery was planted on the banks of the quiet waters of Capel River. The viticultural empire has since expanded, spreading across Geographe (9ha), Mount Barker (15ha) and Margaret River (28ha). There are 4 tiers in the Capel Vale portfolio: Debut (varietals), Regional Series, Black Label Margaret River Chardonnay and Cabernet Sauvignon and, at the top, the Single Vineyard Wines. Exports to all major markets.

🍷🍷🍷🍷🍷 **Single Vineyard Series Whispering Hill Mount Barker Riesling 2020** With all of the citrus blossom and finesse of the Mount Barker Regional Series Riesling, the game is upped significantly here in the Whispering Hill. The coil of saline acid that is the heart of this wine is surrounded by cushy, plush citrus fruit. The whole

package is ripe, structured, long and lean – what a wine! Screw cap. 12% alc.
Rating 96 To 2041 $33 EL ✪
**Single Vineyard Series The Scholar Margaret River Cabernet Sauvignon
2018** The best estate-grown fruit from the best rows. The nose exudes an
interesting ripe redness (capsicum, tomato, pomegranate). The palate is textured by
fine tannins and layers of ripe fruit character. The quibble is the length of flavour,
which doesn't quite soar as expected. An elegant, savoury and fine wine of salty
succulence and pleasure. Screw cap. 14% alc. **Rating** 94 To 2035 $90 EL

ŸŸŸŸŸ **Regional Series Mount Barker Riesling 2020 Rating** 93 To 2031 $27 EL ✪
Black Label Mallokup Geographe Malbec 2020 Rating 91 To 2031 $35 EL
Regional Series Geographe Rosé 2020 Rating 90 To 2023 $25 EL

Capercaillie Wines ★★★★☆
4 Londons Road, Lovedale, NSW 2325 **Region** Hunter Valley
T (02) 4990 2904 **www**.capercailliewines.com.au **Open** 7 days 10–4.30
Winemaker Lance Mikisch **Est.** 1995 **Dozens** 5000 **Vyds** 5ha
A successful winery in terms of the quality of its wines, as well as their reach outwards from
the Hunter Valley. The Capercaillie wines have generous flavour. Its fruit sources are spread
across South Eastern Australia, although the portfolio includes wines that are 100% Hunter
Valley. Exports to China.

ŸŸŸŸŸ **The Cuillin Chardonnay 2019** Matured for 10 months in oak, with an intense
stirring regime to build textural detail and a creamy breadth. This works well in a
Hunter context, architecting a richly flavoured wine by virtue of ripe fruit, skilful
application of oak and a dutiful beam of tangerine freshness. This is for those
seeking full flavour in a climate of more tensile expressions. This really ripples
across the mouth. Screw cap. 13.5% alc. **Rating** 93 To 2025 $45 NG
Hunter Valley Gewürztraminer 2020 While I assert that a little more alcohol,
flavour and phenolics are positives with this capricious variety, the aromatic
spectrum is spot on: orange blossom, ginger, musk, lychee and rosewater. The
finish, gently astringent and impressively tenacious. Screw cap. 13% alc. **Rating** 92
To 2022 $28 NG
The Cuillin Chardonnay 2020 For those seeking intensely flavoured
chardonnay, flecked with stone- and orchard-fruit scents, mandarin acidity and a
buttress of butterscotch oak across the finish, this is solid. The finish, a slurry of
sweet fruit and grape-skin thickness, a bit stolid and drying. Screw cap. 13.5% alc.
Rating 91 To 2025 $45 NG
The Ghillie 2019 This is an aspirational style, striving for what the Hunter
imparts neither naturally, nor intuitively, at least through a winemaking lens.
The result: mocha, espresso, sweet earthy Hunter scents, clove and oodles of dark
berry fruits. The finish, oaky and sweet. Built for impact over freshness, detail and
grace. Screw cap. 14.5% alc. **Rating** 91 To 2028 $70 NG
Hunter Valley Shiraz 2019 This address pushes ripeness levels higher than the
contemporary zeitgeist, amping the reds into the rich, full-bodied zone. Sweet
cherry, bitter chocolate, polished leather, root spice and cinnamon oak. Age will
tone the fruit down a notch. A solid wine of bold appeal. Screw cap. 14% alc.
Rating 91 To 2028 $38 NG
The Angus Durif 2018 This has opacity in the glass and palate-staining
extract in the mouth. It pushes the envelope, almost to the point of no return,
with a whiff of charred rock, bloodstone, licorice straps and dark plum. Yet the
tannins, granular, detailed and well extracted, serve as a tipping point on the side
of savouriness. Vanilla, coffee grind and mocha layer an OK finish. Screw cap.
15% alc. **Rating** 91 To 2028 $70 NG

ŸŸŸŸ **Hunter Valley Chardonnay 2020 Rating** 89 To 2023 $28 NG
Hunter Valley Verdelho 2020 Rating 88 To 2022 $28 NG

Carillion Wines   ★★★★★

749 Mount View Road, Mount View, NSW 2325 **Region** Hunter Valley
T (02) 4990 7535 **www.**carillionwines.com.au **Open** Thurs–Mon 10–5
Winemaker Andrew Ling **Est.** 2000 **Dozens** 5000 **Vyds** 148ha

In 2000 the Davis family decided to select certain parcels of fruit from their 28ha Davis Family Vineyard in the Hunter Valley, along with the family's other vineyards in Orange (the 30ha Carillion Vineyard) and Wrattonbully (the 90ha Stonefields Vineyard), to make wines that are a true expression of their location. To best reflect this strong emphasis on terroir, the resulting wines were categorised into 3 labels, named after their respective vineyards. In recent years Tim Davis has taken over the reins from his father John, and brought these wines under the Carillion banner. He also launched the Lovable Rogue range of wines, which highlight his keen interest in alternative grape varieties (particularly Italian), as well as exploring innovative and experimental winemaking methods.

🍷🍷🍷🍷🍷 **Aged Release Tallavera Grove Hunter Valley Semillon 2013** A great white-wine vintage. Scents of cumquat and citrus marmalade on buttered toast feign oak. And yet there is none. The low alcohol dictates a light body, yet the flavour intensity and rapier-like length suggest otherwise. The balletic daintiness suggests a style best drunk young. And yet this will last longer than most white wines in the country. Screw cap. 11.5% alc. **Rating** 95 **To** 2028 $45 NG

The Crystals Orange Chardonnay 2014 This museum release has matured very well. All the bells and whistles, with Meursault-like aromas of toasted chestnut, curd, cheesecloth and crème brûlée. Expansive and broad, with age transcending any primary fruit. The finish is a bit tangy and assertive, but the aromas and textural effect are largely quite impressive. The finish, long. I would drink this up. Screw cap. 13% alc. **Rating** 94 **To** 2022 $50 NG

Aged Release Stonefields Arbitrage Wrattonbully Cabernet Merlot Shiraz 2012 This has aged beautifully. The acidity, the caveat. A dense nose of clove and blackberry. The bricking edges in the glass, in complete synchronicity with chords of sweet earth, autumnal leaves, graphite, menthol and pencil shavings. The tannins, unfurling effortlessly across a long finish coated with sage and marjoram. A very nice drink. Screw cap. 14% alc. **Rating** 94 **To** 2028 $55 NG

🍷🍷🍷🍷🍷 **Origins Five Clones Orange Pinot Noir 2019 Rating** 93 **To** 2026 $35 NG
The Feldspars Orange Shiraz 2019 Rating 93 **To** 2025 $50 NG
The Feldspars Orange Shiraz 2015 Rating 93 **To** 2025 $40 NG
Crystals Origin Orange Chardonnay 2019 Rating 92 **To** 2024 $35 NG
Origins Fenestella Hunter Valley Shiraz 2019 Rating 92 **To** 2033 $60 NG
Origins Block 22 Wrattonbully Cabernet Sauvignon 2012 Rating 92
To 2026 $65 NG
Lovable Rogue Lees Stirred Hunter Valley Fiano 2020 Rating 91 **To** 2023
$30 NG
Expressions Hunter Valley Chardonnay 2019 Rating 90 **To** 2024 $25 NG
Origins Block 22 Wrattonbully Cabernet Sauvignon 2018 Rating 90
To 2028 $50 NG
Lovable Rogue Foot Stomped Hunter Valley Sagrantino 2019 Rating 90
To 2024 $30 NG

Carlei Estate | Carlei Green Vineyards ★★★☆

1 Alber Road, Upper Beaconsfield, Vic 3808 **Region** Yarra Valley/Heathcote
T (03) 5944 4599 **www.**carlei.com.au **Open** W'ends 11–6
Winemaker Sergio Carlei **Est.** 1994 **Dozens** 10 000 **Vyds** 2.25ha

Sergio Carlei has come a long way, graduating from home winemaking in a suburban garage to his own (commercial) winery in Upper Beaconsfield; Carlei Estate falls just within the boundaries of the Yarra Valley. Along the way Carlei acquired a bachelor of wine science from CSU, and established a vineyard with organic and biodynamic accreditation adjacent to the Upper Beaconsfield winery, plus 7ha in Heathcote. Contract winemaking services are now a major part of the business. Exports to the US, Singapore and China.

ϙϙϙϙϙ **Carlei Estate Sud Heathcote Shiraz 2019** Already exhibiting plenty of plummy sweet fruits and a happy personality. Or, maybe that should be a vinous personality that will make drinkers happy, one that is ripe and expressive in black/blueberries, a whisper of spice, the odd violet, dark chocolate, and a long laid-back palate. Something for now, with a good chance at ageing, too. Diam. 14.5% alc. Rating 94 To 2026 $59 JP

ϙϙϙϙϙ **Carlei Estate Nord Heathcote Shiraz 2019** Rating 93 To 2032 $59 JP
Green Vineyards Heathcote Shiraz 2019 Rating 93 To 2029 $35 JP

Casa Freschi ★★★★☆

159 Ridge Road, Ashton, SA 5137 **Region** Adelaide Hills
T 0409 364 569 **www.**casafreschi.com.au **Open** By appt
Winemaker David Freschi **Est.** 1998 **Dozens** 2000 **Vyds** 7.55ha
David Freschi is a quality-obsessed vigneron, currently producing single-vineyard wines from 2 vineyards (in the Adelaide Hills and in Langhorne Creek). David Freschi's parents, Attilio and Rosa, planted 2.5ha of cabernet sauvignon, shiraz and malbec in 1972 in Langhorne Creek. David expanded the plantings with 2ha of close-planted nebbiolo in '99. The pursuit of white wines led David to the Adelaide Hills. In '03 he purchased a 3.2ha site at 580m in Ashton and planted chardonnay, pinot gris, riesling and gewürztraminer at 8000 vines/ha, all grown using organic principles. The wines are made at the gravity-fed micro-winery built in '07. Exports to the UK, Singapore, Philippines and Japan.

ϙϙϙϙϙ **Ragazzi Adelaide Hills Chardonnay 2019** Genuine interest in this wine – a blend of clones and parcels from a high Ashton vineyard, whole-bunch pressed, barrel fermented with wild yeast; the wine sat on lees for 9 months. It's deeply layered and expresses poached apple and some orange/mandarin tang, with medium to fuller textures and subtle mineral feel on the finish. Screw cap. 13% alc. Rating 91 To 2025 $30 TL
Langhorne Creek Syrah 2018 Another unique vineyard-specific wine. There's a signature richness in its aromas, generally herbal and floral with a faint note of whole-bunch character on top of dark fruits. Full bodied and structured, the tannins are robust and chewy. Built for the cellar. Cork. 13.5% alc. Rating 90 To 2030 $55 TL
Langhorne Creek Malbec 2018 Vineyard character begins to show itself in this wine. There's a ripeness and richness, a headiness in the aromatics, here with a sense of cooked rhubarb and blueberries rather than red and black fruits. Earthy and rustic, with a mouthful of fine tannins following. Needs a table groaning with rich braised meats. Cork. 13.5% alc. Rating 90 To 2028 $90 TL

ϙϙϙϙ **La Signora Langhorne Creek 2018** Rating 89 To 2040 $45 TL

Casella Family Brands

Wakely Road, Yenda, NSW 2681 **Region** Riverina
T (02) 6961 3000 **www.**casellafamilybrands.com
Winemaker John Casella **Est.** 1969 **Dozens** 12.5 million **Vyds** 5000ha
The fairytale success story for Casella – gifted the opportunity to establish yellow tail as a world brand overnight by Southcorp withdrawing the distribution of (inter alia) its best selling Lindemans Bin 65 Chardonnay in the US – is now almost ancient history. yellow tail will remain the engine room for Casella well into the future, but it has now moved decisively to build a portfolio of premium and ultra-premium wines through its acquisition of Peter Lehmann in 2014; and then Brand's Laira winery, cellar door and the use of the brand name from McWilliam's in '15 – McWilliam's had invested much time and money in expanding both the vineyards and the winery. The Peter Lehmann and Brand's Laira brands will transform the future shape of Casella's business. In December '17 Casella purchased Baileys of Glenrowan. The fact that Casella now has over 5000ha of vineyards spread across Australia is a case of putting its money where its mouth is. It is second only to Treasury Wine Estates in export sales (by value), followed by Pernod Ricard and Accolade. Casella celebrated its 50th anniversary in 2019. Exports to all major markets.

ŶŶŶŶ♀ **Limited Release Cabernet Sauvignon 2018** A rich cabernet boasting welcome restraint, courtesy of well-applied oak and dutiful freshness that curtails any sense of excess while subduing the alcohol. Varietal aromas of cassis, spearmint, black cherry and bouquet garni. The finish, swabbed in oak and rolled in sage. More bona fide grape tannins would be appreciated, but a solid one nonetheless. Screw cap. 14.5% alc. **Rating** 91 **To** 2030 $50 NG

Cassegrain Wines ★★★★

764 Fernbank Creek Road, Port Macquarie, NSW 2444 **Region** Hastings River
T (02) 6582 8377 **www**.cassegrainwines.com.au **Open** Mon–Fri 9–5, w'ends 10–5
Winemaker John Cassegrain (Chief), Alex Cassegrain (Senior) **Est.** 1980 **Dozens** 50 000
Vyds 34.9ha
Cassegrain has continued to evolve and develop. It still draws on the original Hastings River vineyard of 4.9ha, where the most important varieties are semillon, verdelho and chambourcin, with pinot noir and cabernet sauvignon making up the numbers. However, Cassegrain also part-owns and manages Richfield Vineyard in the New England region, with 30ha of chardonnay, verdelho, semillon, shiraz, merlot, cabernet sauvignon and ruby cabernet. Grapes are also purchased from Tumbarumba, Orange, Hilltops, Mudgee and the Hunter Valley. Exports to Japan, China and other major markets.

ŶŶŶŶ♀ **Fromenteau Reserve Chardonnay 2019** A mid straw gold and bright. While it has a certain power thanks to the Tumbarumba fruit and winemaking inputs, this holds its own. Ripe white stone fruit, lots of citrus and leesy flavours of grilled nuts and a smear of lemon curd and vanillan oak. It's full bodied and rich yet doesn't go overboard with the acidity cutting through it all. Screw cap. 13% alc. **Rating** 93 **To** 2027 $60 JF
Hilltops Central Ranges Edition Noir Cabernet Sauvignon 2019 Mid ruby hue. Wafts of cassis and currants, licorice and lots of herbs. Medium bodied with some tangy/tart fruit across the palate. There are woodsy spices and it's somewhat drying on the finish but will be less obvious with hearty fare. Screw cap. 13.5% alc. **Rating** 90 **To** 2028 $35 JF

ŶŶŶŶ **Noble Cuvée NV Rating** 88 **To** 2026 $25 NG

Castelli Estate ★★★★★

380 Mount Shadforth Road, Denmark, WA 6333 **Region** Great Southern
T (08) 9364 0400 **www**.castelliestate.com.au **Open** By appt
Winemaker Mike Garland **Est.** 2007 **Dozens** 20 000
Castelli Estate will cause many small winery owners to go green with envy. When Sam Castelli purchased the property in late 2004, he was intending simply to use it as a family holiday destination. But because there was a partly constructed winery he decided to complete the building work and simply lock the doors. However, wine was in his blood courtesy of his father, who owned a small vineyard in Italy's south. The temptation was too much and in '07 the winery was commissioned. Fruit is sourced from some of the best sites in WA: Frankland River, Mount Barker, Pemberton and Porongurup. Exports to the US, South Korea, Singapore, Japan and China.

ŶŶŶŶŶ **Il Liris Rouge 2018** 66/27/7% cabernet sauvignon/shiraz/malbec. Matured in French oak (70% new). Ferrous, gravel, ironstone, graphite, satsuma plum, raspberry, blood and red licorice. The oak is there, but requires effort to find it among the cavalcade of flavours. The tannins are omnipresent. This is a beast, but a friendly one. A lifetime awaits it, if you have the patience. Otherwise drink it now, it's ready. Vino–Lok. 14.8% alc. **Rating** 97 **To** 2051 $80 EL ◐

ŶŶŶŶŶ **Il Liris Chardonnay 2019** The Il Liris Chardonnay is one of the shining chardonnay lights in the region. Freshly picked and crushed curry leaf, toasted, crushed macadamia and ripe, dripping yellow peach. The acidity on the palate is bright and salty, the texture is shaped by fine phenolics. This is luxurious, but not in a sweet, opulent way. Rather, in a pared-back, 6-star hotel's 'every detail considered' kind of way. Very long. Awesome. Vino-Lok. 12.5% alc. **Rating** 96 To 2036 $70 EL ✪

Frankland River Cabernet Sauvignon 2018 This is a harmonious, powerful and exciting rendition, not only of cabernet sauvignon, but of the Frankland River regional characteristics of the grape. Gravel, ferrous, salted cassis. Licorice. It's a cracker. Supple and dense at once. This will age, too. Buy it and drink it now or when your newborn turns 15. Screw cap. 14.7% alc. **Rating** 96 To 2035 $38 EL ✪

Pemberton Chardonnay 2019 Toasty, spicy oak on the nose and interwoven throughout the palate. Abundant ripe stone fruit in the mouth plays into the hands of salty acid and the cushioning catch of oak. Home run. Screw cap. 13.6% alc. **Rating** 95 To 2030 $34 EL ✪

The Sum Cabernet Sauvignon 2019 This kind of quality for under $20? Bring it on. This is the younger, sweeter, juicier and plumper sibling to the estate cabernet. It has all the regional greatness from Frankland: ferrous, gravel, petrichor and firm tannin structure. But in this context, all of it gently sidles up to bouncy blackcurrant fruit and leaves us with a glass of straight-up pleasure. Cheap doesn't mean 'cheap' – if you want to learn this lesson, start here. Screw cap. 14.7% alc. **Rating** 94 To 2028 $18 EL ✪

🍷🍷🍷🍷🍷 **Great Southern Pinot Noir 2019** Rating 93 To 2029 $34 EL
Frankland River Shiraz 2018 Rating 93 To 2036 $34 EL
The Sum Riesling 2020 Rating 92 To 2028 $18 EL ✪
The Sum Shiraz 2019 Rating 91 To 2026 $18 EL ✪
The Sum Sauvignon Blanc 2020 Rating 90 To 2023 $18 EL ✪
The Sum Rosé 2020 Rating 90 To 2022 $18 EL ✪

Castle Rock Estate   ★★★★★

2660 Porongurup Road, Porongurup, WA 6324 **Region** Porongurup
T (08) 9853 1035 **www**.castlerockestate.com.au **Open** 7 days 10–4.30
Winemaker Robert Diletti **Est.** 1983 **Dozens** 4500 **Vyds** 11.2ha
An exceptionally beautifully sited vineyard (riesling, pinot noir, chardonnay, sauvignon blanc, cabernet sauvignon and merlot), winery and cellar door on a 55ha property with sweeping vistas of the Porongurup Range, operated by the Diletti family. The standard of viticulture is very high, and the vineyard itself is ideally situated. The 2-level winery, set on a natural slope, maximises gravity flow. The rieslings have always been elegant and have handsomely repaid time in bottle; the Pinot Noir is the most consistent performer in the region; the Shiraz is a great cool-climate example; and Chardonnay has joined a thoroughly impressive quartet, elegance the common link. Rob Diletti's excellent palate and sensitive winemaking mark Castle Rock as one of the superstars of WA. Exports to China.

🍷🍷🍷🍷🍷 **A&W Porongurup Riesling 2020** It's like the oak has taken all the top notes off the fruit, but left a rumbling undercurrent of power and depth. The oak has gifted this with a thunderous baritone, yet the delicacy of Porongurup fruit keeps it understated and textural. A deeply quiet, almost introverted riesling yet with an enduring and composed voice. Screw cap. 12.1% alc. **Rating** 97 To 2040 $35 EL ✪

Porongurup Riesling 2020 Simple vinification has produced a far-from-simple wine. This is a superfine, delicate, layered riesling with lacy acidity that courses its way through the fruit. Citrus blossom, ripe citrus, jasmine tea, white pepper, hints of fennel flower and a drop of star anise. Routinely a ridiculous wine for the money. Rob Diletti has a reputation for riesling and this, my friends, is why. Screw cap. 12.4% alc. **Rating** 96 To 2035 $25 EL ✪

Skywalk Porongurup Riesling 2020 The highest RS of Castle Rock's rieslings, at 1.3g/L (hardly sweet!). Textbook white spring blossom aromatics that so define the rieslings from the Porongurup region, rising out of the glass alongside sweet citrus pith and crushed limestone. White pepper, fleshy citrus and saline acid is the story in the mouth, while the unassailable length of flavour is the conclusion. A ridiculously good wine for the money. Screw cap. 12.8% alc. **Rating** 95 **To** 2035 $20 EL ✪

Porongurup Pinot Noir 2019 A recent vertical tasting of Castle Rock pinots back to 2006 showed two things: that they age gracefully, picking up typical earth and mushroom notes along the way; and that there seemed to be more complexity in the younger wines, indicating that they would perform even more favourably in the cellar. This is case in point; vibrant fruit and acid tension on the palate, unfurling to a long and lingering finish. Nuance and finesse here. Screw cap. 13.8% alc. **Rating** 95 **To** 2040 $34 EL ✪

Great Southern Shiraz 2018 At $30, this is the 2nd-most expensive wine that Rob Diletti makes: his wines represent extreme value for money. This is muscular, as we know Mount Barker shiraz can be, yet within those firm tannins lies layers of delicate flavour, like the fine folds underneath a mushroom. The length of flavour further confirms the quality of the fruit. Despite all of these great things, the balance is the ultimate winner here. Screw cap. 13.8% alc. **Rating** 95 **To** 2031 $30 EL ✪

Porongurup Cabernet Sauvignon 2018 Refined, fine-boned, pretty cabernet, shaped by chalky tannins that linger and whip around the palate. The impact of oak is minimal, leaving ample room for cassis to fully unfurl and eddy about. Something utterly satisfying on the palate here. Power without weight. From talented hands comes this quietly elegant wine, grown in a tiny, beautiful little region. And the price: don't start. Screw cap. 13% alc. **Rating** 95 **To** 2030 $25 EL ✪

Diletti Chardonnay 2018 If I had to describe this wine in only a handful of words (imagine that), they would be: classy, glassy, restrained and fine. Gold medal Mount Barker Wine Show '20. Screw cap. 12% alc. **Rating** 94 **To** 2025 $25 EL ✪

🍷🍷🍷🍷 **Porongurup Sauvignon Blanc 2020** **Rating** 93 **To** 2025 $20 EL ✪
Porongurup Chardonnay 2020 **Rating** 90 **To** 2025 $20 EL ✪

Catlin Wines ★★★★★

39B Sydney Road, Nairne, SA 5252 **Region** Adelaide Hills
T 0411 326 384 **www**.catlinwines.com.au
Winemaker Darryl Catlin **Est.** 2013 **Dozens** 2000

Darryl Catlin grew up in the Barossa Valley with vineyards as his playground, picking bush-vine grenache for pocket money as a youngster. Stints with Saltram, the Australian Bottling Company and Vintner Imports followed in his 20s, before he moved on to gain retail experience at Adelaide's Royal Oak Cellar, London's Oddbins and McKay's Macquarie Cellars. Next, he studied for a winemaking degree while working at Adelaide's East End Cellars. Then followed a number of years at Shaw + Smith, rising from cellar hand to winemaker, finishing in 2012 and establishing his own business the following year. Exports to the UK and China.

🍷🍷🍷🍷🍷 **Nellie Margaret Adelaide Hills Chardonnay 2017** Great to have a chardonnay released with time allowed for development, and even then there are fresh, green tinges to the pale gold. Oak has gifted some vanilla spice to the familiar darker stone fruits that tingle a little on the palate as the fresh citrus elements wash in, leaving an even line of acidity and pith. Everything feels really well balanced and in place. Screw cap. 12% alc. **Rating** 95 **To** 2026 $30 TL ✪

Pudding and Pie Adelaide Hills Pinot Noir 2020 Lightly coloured in the glass, highly fragrant and carrying just a little mystery in its savoury offsets – a little nice nebbiolo-like funk. Slightly sour cherry, with an earthy outer layer, Middle Eastern spice notes and a pleasing light grip. It's tasty and moreish. Bang on. Screw cap. 12% alc. **Rating** 95 **To** 2026 $30 TL ✪

ￗￗￗￗￗ The Molly Mae Clare Valley Riesling 2020 Rating 93 To 2028 $20 TL ◐
The Gellert Single Vineyard Adelaide Hills Gamay 2020 Rating 93
To 2025 $30 TL
The Astria Blanc de Blancs Adelaide Hills 2020 Rating 92 $30 TL

Cavalry Wines   ★★★☆

PO Box 193, Nagambie, Vic 3608 **Region** Heathcote
T 0411 114 958 **www.**cavalrywines.com
Winemaker Adam Foster **Est.** 2016 **Dozens** 700 **Vyds** 9.6ha
The vineyard was planted in the 1960s with 5.8ha of shiraz, 2.7ha of cabernet sauvignon and
a field blend of chardonnay, verdelho and riesling. (There was very little planted in Australia
at that time.) The first owner made a little wine for his personal use, but most of the grape
production was used to make excellent grappa, although history doesn't relate how it made
its way to market. More recently the grapes were sold to other wineries, and a major part
continues to be sold. The current owners are Peter Nash, previously an insurance underwriter,
and Josephine Hands, a former teacher. Ardent wine lovers with a history of small investments
in wine, their next step in retirement was to become vignerons – and to put the property in
trust for their grandchildren. They say that they gave their winery its name because it shares
3 boundaries with the Australian Army.

ￗￗￗￗￗ **Rosaria Premium Heathcote Shiraz 2018** A dense young shiraz with the
Heathcote scent of blackberry intensity, Aussie bush and turned earth. A spicy but
subtle palate, medium in weight with the potential to develop further into a wine
of understated elegance. Screw cap. 13.5% alc. **Rating** 91 **To** 2028 $70 JP

ￗￗￗￗ **Christine Heathcote Cabernet Shiraz 2018** Rating 89 To 2028 $38 JP

Cavedon Wines   ★★★★

6047 Mansfield-Whitfield Road, Whitfield, Vic 4870 **Region** King Valley
T 0429 862 808 **www.**cavedonwines.com
Winemaker Gabriel O'Brien **Est.** 2018 **Dozens** 800 **Vyds** 20ha
Like many Italian-Australians in the King Valley, the Cavedon family were originally tobacco
growers before moving into grape growing. Dino Cavedon took up grapes in 1977 planting
in-demand varieties such as riesling, chardonnay, shiraz and merlot. Later, a visit to see family
in Italy saw him return with new enthusiasm for Italian grape varieties and he planted pinot
grigio, barbera and sangiovese for local wine producers. With retirement on his mind and no
obvious succession plan in place, it was decided in 2018 that Dino's daughter, Pia, and son-
in-law, Gabe, would move to the King Valley and carry on his life's work, founding Cavedon
Wines. They produce single-vineyard wines made with minimal intervention in styles well
suited to Mediterranean cuisine, the type of wines they grew up on. (JP)

ￗￗￗￗￗ **King Valley Albariño 2019** The winemaker picked early to capture the grape's
citrus and grapefruit characters with natural acidity, but the bonus is the white
peach, honeysuckle and fig. Albariño can become full-blown and heavy. This
avoids that pitfall nicely. Screw cap. 12% alc. **Rating** 92 **To** 2026 $32 JP
King Valley Gewürztraminer 2019 A picture of understatement and quiet
restraint. Aromatics of potpourri and rose are guided rather than set free. In
conjunction with lychee, lime and spice the result is one delicious, fresh wine.
Screw cap. 11.8% alc. **Rating** 90 **To** 2025 $27 JP
Col Fondo King Valley Prosecco 2019 Made along similar lines to the 2019
Zero Dosage, but retaining the yeast lees of the 2nd fermentation has lifted flavour
and intensity. Baked apple, lemon skin, yeasty brioche and biscuit display a youthful
if raw-like energy. Crown seal. 11% alc. **Rating** 90 **To** 2025 $33 JP

ￗￗￗￗ **King Valley Gewürztraminer 2018** Rating 88 To 2025 $27 JP
Zero Dosage King Valley Prosecco 2019 Rating 88 To 2025 $33 JP

 # Centare

160 Healesville Kooweerup Road, Healesville, Vic 3777 **Region** Yarra Valley
T 0407 386 314 **www**.centarevineyard.com
Winemaker Nicole Esdaile **Est.** 2018 **Dozens** 2000 **Vyds** 5ha
A vineyard originally planted in 1998 on Healesville Kooweerup Road and acquired by
Simon Le in 2018. Nicole Esdale from Wine Network Consulting is the winemaker/ project
manager and Ray Guerin is the consulting viticulturalist, with the wines being made at the
Sunshine Creek facility. New plantings at extremely high density began in November 2020
with aspirations to produce a cabernet blend of the highest quality. The wines will be sold on
the Australian and Chinese markets. Exports to China. (SC)

ŸŸŸŸŸ **Old Block Yarra Valley Cabernet Sauvignon 2019** 7% merlot; open-
fermented with 25 days on skins; 12 months maturation in barriques, 30% new
French. Cedary and leafy on the bouquet initially, some redcurrant and black fruit
appearing as the wine opens up. Still something of a baby, but shows quite classical
Yarra cabernet structure and style. Will undoubtedly benefit from a decent spell in
the cellar. Screw cap. 13.3% alc. **Rating** 93 **To** 2029 $50 SC
Old Block Yarra Valley Chardonnay 2019 Whole-bunch pressed, aged in
French puncheons (30% new) for 10 months. Aromas of citrus – prominent
lemon curd – and touches of nuttiness and nougat, presumably from the oak. Full
bodied in a textural way, but somewhat restrained in flavour, which imparts quite
an elegant feel, accentuated by the freshness on the finish. Attractive now and may
be most enjoyable while it shows these qualities. Screw cap. 13.5% alc. **Rating** 92
To 2025 $40 SC
Old Block Yarra Valley Shiraz 2019 Vines planted in 1998, open-fermented
with around 15% whole bunches, matured in (30% new French, 10% new
American) barriques. Plenty of cool-climate pepper and spice on offer (despite the
warm season) with some vanillan oak character as well. The red berry fruit seems
to not have fully emerged yet, and I think it needs a year or two to show its true
colours. Screw cap. 14% alc. **Rating** 92 **To** 2029 $40 SC

Centennial Vineyards   ★★★★★

'Woodside', 252 Centennial Road, Bowral, NSW 2576 **Region** Southern Highlands
T (02) 4861 8722 **www**.centennial.net.au **Open** 7 days 10–5
Winemaker Tony Cosgriff **Est.** 2002 **Dozens** 10 000 **Vyds** 28.65ha
Centennial Vineyards, jointly owned by wine professional John Large and investor Mark
Dowling, covers 133ha of beautiful grazing land, with the vineyard planted to pinot noir
(7.13ha), chardonnay (6.76ha), pinot gris (4.06ha) and smaller amounts of riesling, pinot
meunier, albariño, tempranillo, grüner veltliner and gewürztraminer. Centennial purchased the
8.2ha Bridge Creek Vineyard in Orange to meet the challenge of the Southern Highlands'
capricious weather. Exports to the UK, the US, Denmark, Singapore, China and South Korea.

ŸŸŸŸŸ **Limited Blanc de Blancs NV** This is by far the top cuvée of this impressive
range. Straight-laced chardonnay. Bready, creamy and luxe, made in the style of
long lees-aged champagnes. Inflections of oyster shell, truffle and iodine. Picks up
steam with air, billowing across the palate while driven long by chalky mineral
crunch and juicy acidity. Very fine. Diam. 12.5% alc. **Rating** 95 $40 NG

ŸŸŸŸŸ **Brut Traditionelle NV Rating** 93 $35 NG
Brut Rosé NV Rating 93 $35 NG
Reserve Single Vineyard Chardonnay 2019 Rating 92 **To** 2027 $39 NG
Winery Block Chardonnay 2019 Rating 91 **To** 2025 $29 NG
Reserve Single Vineyard Albariño 2019 Rating 91 **To** 2025 $29 NG
Reserve Single Vineyard Orange Shiraz Viognier 2018 Rating 91 **To** 2025
$39 NG
Reserve Bridge Creek Rondinella Corvina 2018 Rating 91 **To** 2024
$35 NG
Reserve Single Vineyard Orange Shiraz 2018 Rating 90 **To** 2026 $34 NG

Limited Release Single Vineyard Shiraz 2018 Rating 90 To 2026 $45 NG
RC Limited Release Dolce Classico 2019 Rating 90 To 2026 $39 NG

Ceres Bridge Estate ★★★★★

84 Merrawarp Road, Stonehaven, Vic 3221 **Region** Geelong
T (03) 5271 1212 **www.**ceresbridge.com.au **Open** By appt
Winemaker Scott Ireland, Sam Vogel **Est.** 1996 **Dozens** 400 **Vyds** 7.4ha
Challon and Patricia Murdock began the long, slow and very frustrating process of establishing their vineyard in 1996. They planted 1.8ha of chardonnay in that year, but 50% of the vines died. They persevered by planting 1.1ha of pinot noir in 2000, and replanting in '01. In '05 they signified their intention to become serious by planting shiraz, nebbiolo, sauvignon blanc, viognier, tempranillo and pinot grigio.

🍷🍷🍷🍷🍷 **Paper Mill Chardonnay 2019** The winemaker has risen to the challenge of a hot vintage with a chardonnay that gives every impression of being immune to its effects. Brisk in filigreed acidity with, a palate delivering elegance and precision, it remains cool under pressure. Lemon drop, grapefruit pith, juicy white peach and apple blossom. In for the long haul. Screw cap. 13.5% alc. **Rating** 95 **To** 2031 $30 JP ⊙
Paper Mill Shiraz 2019 In the tradition of Paper Mill shiraz, with another lively adventure. Scented, pure black-cherry pastille, raspberry, pomegranate and ferrous, earthy notes. Supple and succulent, with attractive savouriness and loose-knit tannins, there are strong building blocks in place for a bright future. Screw cap. 13.5% alc. **Rating** 95 **To** 2031 $30 JP ⊙

🍷🍷🍷🍷🍷 **Paper Mill Pinot Noir 2019** Rating 93 To 2027 $30 JP

Chain of Ponds ★★★★

8 The Parade West, Kent Town, SA 5067 **Region** Adelaide Hills/Langhorne Creek
T (08) 7324 3031 **www.**chainofponds.com.au
Winemaker Greg Clack **Est.** 1985 **Dozens** 20 000
It is years since the Chain of Ponds brand was separated from its then 200ha of estate vineyards, which were among the largest in the Adelaide Hills. It does, however, have long-term contracts with major growers. Prior to the 2015 vintage, Greg Clack came onboard as full-time chief winemaker. In May '16 Chain of Ponds closed its cellar door and moved to Project Wine's small-batch processing facility at Langhorne Creek, where it also sources fruit for its budget range. Exports to the UK, the US, Canada, Singapore, Hong Kong, the Philippines, Japan and China.

🍷🍷🍷🍷🍷 **Innocence Adelaide Hills Rosé 2020** Three vineyards/varieties suited to the world of rosé – 47/40% pinot noir/sangiovese from 2 Hills sites, the remaining 13% grenache from Langhorne Creek. Enticing red fruit and petal aromas, with good strawberry flavours, dry and spicy with a mouth-filling textural layer to add a bit of presence. Screw cap. 13% alc. **Rating** 93 **To** 2022 $20 TL ⊙
Corkscrew Road Single Vineyard Adelaide Hills Chardonnay 2019 A single-vineyard iteration (Kuitpo) that has been given the full array of contemporary chardonnay tools – whole-bunch pressed, barrel fermented with both wild and inoculated yeast, matured for 10 months, 6 of those on lees and stirred. All this adds up to a creamy style, more notes of orange than sharper citrus, with some roasted cashew as well. Happy days. Screw cap. 13.7% alc. **Rating** 92 **To** 2025 $35 TL
The Cachet 2018 A 55/45% shiraz/cabernet sauvignon blend from 2 vineyards in the Kuitpo district. This top shelfer is a best barrel selection after separate barrel maturation for 15 months. Cabernet takes a subtle yet pleasing lead on aromas, and carries the structural feels on the palate. It's a big softie of a wine, still immensely juicy and satisfying – even with the mouthful of tannins that rides the final stages. A few more years of resting will see further balance. Screw cap. 14.7% alc. **Rating** 92 **To** 2032 $100 TL

Chalari Wines

14 Slab Gully Road, Roleystone, WA 6111 **Region** Western Australia
T 0404 485 137 **www**.chalariwines.com.au
Winemaker Alexi Christidis **Est.** 2016 **Dozens** 200
Winemaker and proprietor Alexi Christidis explains that the name 'Chalari' reflects his Greek heritage and his father, always one for a cup of coffee or a drink and watching the world go by – the word meaning 'relaxed'. While studying oenology at CSU Alexi decided to make small batches of wine, exemplified by his purchase of 2t of hand-picked riesling from Frankland River, making it in a 5t 'winery' in the Perth Hills, using a low-intervention natural approach.

ŸŸŸŸ̨ **Peel Rosé 2020** Soft mandarin blush in the glass. Layers of phenolic texture on the palate; this has strawberry, orange zest, red apples, lanolin and a hint of red currants. Star anise and aniseed grace the finish. Screw cap. 12.7% alc. **Rating** 90 To 2024 $25 EL

ŸŸŸŸ **Swan Valley Grenache 2020 Rating** 88 To 2025 $30 EL

Chalk Hill

58 Field Street, McLaren Vale, SA 5171 **Region** McLaren Vale
T (08) 8323 6400 **www**.chalkhillwines.com.au
Winemaker Renae Hirsch **Est.** 1973 **Dozens** 20 000 **Vyds** 89ha
The growth of Chalk Hill has accelerated after passing from parents John and Diana Harvey to grapegrowing sons Jock and Tom. Both are heavily involved in wine industry affairs. Further acquisitions mean the vineyards now span each district of McLaren Vale, planted to both the exotic (savagnin, barbera and sangiovese) and mainstream (shiraz, cabernet sauvignon, grenache, chardonnay and cabernet franc). The Alpha Crucis series is especially praiseworthy. Exports to most markets; exports to the US under the Alpha Crucis label, to Canada under the Wits End label.

ŸŸŸŸŸ **Alpha Crucis Old Vine McLaren Vale Grenache 2019** Predominantly 90yo vines in Blewitt Springs, 10% whole-bunch ferment, matured in 3rd-use French oak for 11 months. Brilliant crimson hue: an intensely perfumed bouquet floats into the juicy palate of pomegranate, red cherry and spice. A gorgeous grenache. Superlative length. Screw cap. 14% alc. **Rating** 98 To 2025 $55 JH ✪ ♥
Clarendon McLaren Vale Syrah 2018 A fine example of temperate-grown shiraz. The bouquet pulsates with black cherry, spice, licorice and pepper, the palate opening with a fanfare of dark fruits and finishes with fine-grained tannins. The drinking window is open, and won't close for decades. Screw cap. 14% alc. **Rating** 97 To 2048 $48 JH ✪

ŸŸŸŸŸ **Alpha Crucis McLaren Vale Shiraz 2019** Very smart. Scents of violet, dried seaweed, tapenade and boysenberry are strung across a finessed world of whole-bunch bramble, gently applied oak and maritime acidity. These beautifully positioned structural pillars confer a floating, ethereal feel that magically belies the wine's weight. Ample character, pure fruit and textural precision. Screw cap. 14.5% alc. **Rating** 95 To 2028 $55 NG
Alpha Crucis Adelaide Hills Chardonnay 2019 For such a lean wine, it boasts an uncanny degree of fruit weight and flavour intensity, from nectarine, white peach, fig and rock melon, meandering around a core of lees- and oak-derived vanilla pod and nutty riffs. The acidity, saline and pumice-like, is juicy rather than obtuse. The finish, long. Screw cap. 13% alc. **Rating** 94 To 2028 $55 NG
Alpha Crucis Titan McLaren Vale Shiraz 2019 For the price, this is very hard to top. Even if it were double, it would be impressive. Dark cherry, violet, bitter chocolate, Dutch licorice and clove. Very regional fruit profile, but discernibly noble and far from the madding crowd by virtue of its lithe, slinky tannin profile

and well-applied oak; a welcome belt of savoury restraint. Screw cap. 14.5% alc.
Rating 94 **To** 2028 $30 NG ✪

🍷🍷🍷🍷 McLaren Vale Tempranillo Grenache 2019 **Rating** 92 **To** 2024 $28 NG
McLaren Vale Shiraz 2019 **Rating** 91 **To** 2025 $28 NG
McLaren Vale Barbera 2019 **Rating** 91 **To** 2023 $28 NG
Luna McLaren Vale Shiraz 2019 **Rating** 90 **To** 2024 $22 NG

Chalmers

118 Third Street, Merbein, Vic 3505 **Region** Heathcote
T 0400 261 932 **www.**chalmers.com.au
Winemaker Bart van Olphen, Tennille and Kim Chalmers **Est.** 1989 **Dozens** 10000
Vyds 27ha
Following the 2008 sale of their very large vineyard and vine nursery propagation business,
the Chalmers family has refocused its wine businesses. All fruit comes from the 80ha
property on Mt Camel Range in Heathcote, which provides the grapes for the individual
variety, single-vineyard Chalmers range (Vermentino, Fiano, Greco, Lambrusco, Rosato, Nero
d'Avola, Sagrantino and Aglianico). The entry-level Montevecchio label features blends
and more approachable styles. A second vineyard at Merbein is a contract grapegrower, but
also has a small nursery block housing the Chalmers' clonal selections. In '13 a program of
micro-vinification of the rarer, and hitherto unutilised, varieties from the nursery block was
introduced. In '17 a new winery was commissioned in time for most of that year's vintage, and
from '18 all winemaking was carried out at Merbein. Exports to the UK and Japan.

🍷🍷🍷🍷 Heathcote Pecorino 2020 A fascinating and obscure Italian white grape variety
on the comeback trail in Italy and doing a mighty fine job in Heathcote, too. It's
confidently made and presented here with a strong personality similar to viognier,
built around generous ripeness and alcohol and warm, honeyed, citrus flavours.
High natural acidity moves everything together towards a brisk finish. Screw cap.
14% alc. **Rating** 93 **To** 2025 $31 JP
Heathcote Fiano 2020 Chalmers imported its first fiano vines into the country
in 2002; nearly 20 years later it's becoming a real mover and shaker. A burgeoning
texture and savouriness already in evidence in this youngster, rich in wild herbs,
lemon balm, lime, apple and poached pear. It's all coming together very nicely
indeed with a zingy sea-spray salinity that works the mouth, not to mention the
appetite. Screw cap. 13.5% alc. **Rating** 93 **To** 2025 $35 JP
Heathcote Fiano 2019 Matured 10 months in chestnut botte (Italian wine
barrels). Offers a taste of the exotic. Ginger root, spiced apple, pear skin and
honeysuckle are all long and deep on the bouquet. Acidity is soft, flavours are
intense – preserved lemon, ginger snap, stewed pear, almond nuttiness – together
with a quince-like tartness that is so different from the fiano many of us know.
If this is the result of ageing in chestnut botte, I applaud the move. Screw cap.
13% alc. **Rating** 92 **To** 2028 $35 JP
Heathcote Vermentino 2020 These pioneers of Australian vermentino
understand it so well, keeping it young, fresh and vital. Delicate aromas of
grapefruit, lemon zest, apple and white peach. Keeps the citrus and stone-fruit
theme on the palate with juicy bright acidity. Emerging textural appeal is super-
attractive. Screw cap. 12.8% alc. **Rating** 92 **To** 2024 $27 JP
Dott. Ribolla Gialla 2020 Light straw hue. Delicate aromas of snow pea, apple,
citrus and jasmine. It stretches out on the palate, extending its flavour reach to include
muscat, nougat and dried pear, brought into line nicely by firm acidity. Makes a
striking impression. 500ml. Screw cap. 11.5% alc. **Rating** 92 **To** 2025 $28 JP
Heathcote Nero d'Avola 2020 Nero, as it is increasingly being shortened to,
is one versatile grape. Tasted in youth, this is hard to resist. Fruit-forward, plummy,
cherry sensation with bon-bon confection and floral sub-notes that fills the mouth
with a vibrant energy. In large part, it can be put down to some pretty impressive
and noteworthy tannins that give the wine plenty of bounce and, it must be said,
potential for ageing. Screw cap. 13.4% alc. **Rating** 91 **To** 2025 $27 JP

Heathcote Greco 2020 In a changing climate, this southern Italian white grape is looking like a good find. Mid yellow in colour with the scent of honeysuckle, citrus and apple. Its best work is on the palate, where it really opens up with a generous expanse of pear and apple flavours, biscuity and nicely textural. Bright acidity brings energy. Screw cap. 13.5% alc. **Rating** 90 **To** 2023 $31 JP

Heathcote Greco 2019 Mid yellow hue. A most robust white wine with fig, citrus peel, honeysuckle and wild honey. Almost viognier-like taste. Quite a presence, with texture paramount and riffs of orange blossom, white peach and pear. Fills the mouth with flavour and spice. Screw cap. 13.5% alc. **Rating** 90 **To** 2027 $31 JP

Col Fondo Heathcote Aglianico 2020 Col Fondo is another term for the méthode ancestrale style of sparkling where the wine is not disgorged (sediment removed) after the 2nd fermentation. Palest dusty pink in hue, persistent mousse and an understated and aromatic introduction of red apple, redcurrant and cranberry fruits. A linear, super-dry palate, earthy with dried herbs and oh-so-mouth-puckering clean on the finish. Crown seal. 11.6% alc. **Rating** 90 $35 JP

Montevecchio Heathcote Moscato 2020 Moscato giallo is the grape behind this super-sherbety, lightly fizzy moscato. Like crunching into fat, ripe, sweet table grapes, the flavours ooze sweetness and an intense grapey experience. That's about it, but frankly, that's enough. The essence of moscato is here: clean, fresh, grapey, sweet and light in alcohol. This could be the poster child for the style. Screw cap. 5.5% alc. **Rating** 90 **To** 2023 $24 JP

ΨΨΨΨ **Montevecchio Heathcote Bianco Field Blend 2020** Rating 88 To 2025 $24 JP

Chambers Rosewood   ★★★★★

Barkly Street, Rutherglen, Vic 3685 **Region** Rutherglen
T (02) 6032 8641 **www.**chambersrosewood.com.au **Open** Mon–Sat 9–5, Sun 10–5
Winemaker Stephen Chambers **Est.** 1858 **Dozens** 5000 **Vyds** 50ha
Chambers' Rare Muscat and Rare Muscadelle (previously Topaque or Tokay) are the greatest of all in the Rutherglen firmament and should be treated as national treasures; the other wines in the hierarchy also magnificent. Stephen Chambers (6th generation) comes into the role as winemaker, but father Bill is seldom far away. Exports to the UK, the US, Canada, Belgium, Denmark, China and NZ.

ΨΨΨΨΨ **Rare Rutherglen Muscat NV** The pulse quickens, the muscat colour darkens, the fortified pours a little slower, denser and the flavours intensify. The solera for this fortified has been maintained by Bill Chambers and son Stephen for more than 60 years, exceeding Rare Classification. A wine of immense concentration but also of elegance and freshness, a true indication of a great fortified. And such flavours to discover; of luscious sweet butterscotch, dried fruit, rose oil, roasted almonds, toffeed walnuts, roasted coffee bean delivered fresh and beautifully defined. A world-class tasting experience. 375ml. Screw cap. 17.5% alc. **Rating** 98 $250 JP

ΨΨΨΨΨ **Old Vine Rutherglen Muscat NV** Slowly moving up a notch in age, complexity, depth of flavour and stickiness. Suffice to say, this is a fortified brimming with a seamless beauty and richness of expression. Layers of dried fig, dates, honey cake, toffee and raisin set a fresh and lively pace, aided by neutral spirit. Amazing value. 375ml. Screw cap. 18% alc. **Rating** 95 $25 JP ❂

Old Vine Rutherglen Muscadelle NV Equivalent to the Classic Rutherglen Muscat classification, this amber beauty retains the essence of muscadelle flavour – roasted nuts, tea leaves, malt and toffee – within a smoothly honed, deep, sweet palate of some obvious complexity. The blender's art is right here on display to be celebrated. 375ml. Screw cap. 18% alc. **Rating** 95 $30 JP ❂

Grand Rutherglen Muscadelle NV Oh my … I could inhale the beauty of this muscadelle all day: so mellow, warm, inviting, fuelling the imagination with scents of caramel toffee, roasted salted nuts, prunes and strong roasted coffee. Riveting. And the palate, well, that is no disappointment. Believe it or not, the solera for this wine was established at the same time as the Rare levels of the company's muscat and muscadelle but, in the words of the maker, this wine has been 'driven younger in comparison'. That freshening lifts the intensity of flavour to an astonishing level. 375ml. Screw cap. 18% alc. **Rating** 95 $100 JP

ŶŶŶŶŶ **Rutherglen Muscat NV Rating** 92 $25 JP ✪
Rutherglen Muscadelle NV Rating 92 $25 JP ✪
Sparkling Gouais 2018 Rating 91 $30 JP
3 Vines 2018 Rating 90 **To** 2025 $15 JP ✪

🍇 Chandler Wines   ★★★★

18 Pasteur Ave, Hawthorndene, SA 5051 **Region** Adelaide Hills
T 0434 904 264 **www**.chandlervines.com.au
Winemaker Stefan Chandler **Est.** 2018 **Dozens** 100
Chandler Wines is the small-batch winemaking venture of viticulturist and bud dissection specialist Stefan Chandler, whose day job is in the vineyards of Patritti Wines. He sources fruit from a small number of sites in the Adelaide Hills and McLaren Vale and manages them in his own micro-winery. (TL)

ŶŶŶŶŶ **Adorable Lenswood Adelaide Hills Pinot Noir 2019** Contains 20% whole bunches which feels just about spot-on in the total bouquet. Exudes more than just the classical pinot red-berry combo, with a suggestion of dried choc-dipped orange. More savoury notes to follow, the faintest of amaro bitters and a gentle dusting of tannin on the exit. This edge of darkness is quite alluring. Screw cap. 13% alc. **Rating** 93 **To** 2026 $38 TL
Twisterella Adelaide Hills Chardonnay 2020 Trademark Hills white nectarine to begin. This deepens on the palate, with a honey and nougat-like layer, and later the faintest suggestion of lamb fat. Maybe strange? Certainly interesting. Screw cap. 12.5% alc. **Rating** 90 **To** 2025 $29 TL

Chandon Australia   ★★★★★

727 Maroondah Highway, Coldstream, Vic 3770 **Region** Yarra Valley
T (03) 9738 9200 **www**.chandon.com.au **Open** 7 days 10.30–4.30
Winemaker Dan Buckle, Glenn Thompson, Adam Keath **Est.** 1986 **Vyds** 184ha
Established by Möet & Chandon, this is one of the two most important wine facilities in the Yarra Valley; the tasting room has a national and international reputation, having won a number of major tourism awards in recent years. The sparkling wine product range has evolved with the 1994 acquisition of a substantial vineyard in the cool Strathbogie Ranges and the 2014 purchase of the high-altitude vineyard established by Brown Brothers. These supplement the large intake from the Yarra Valley at various altitudes. Under the leadership of Dan Buckle the high-quality standards have been maintained. Exports to Japan, Thailand, Indonesia, Singapore, South Korea, Malaysia, Vietnam, Philippines, Taiwan and Hong Kong.

Chapel Hill   ★★★★★

1 Chapel Hill Road, McLaren Vale, SA 5171 **Region** McLaren Vale
T (08) 8323 8429 **www**.chapelhillwine.com.au **Open** 7 days 11–5
Winemaker Michael Fragos, Bryn Richards **Est.** 1971 **Dozens** 70 000 **Vyds** 44ha
A leading medium-sized winery in McLaren Vale. In late 2019 the business was purchased from the Swiss Thomas Schmidheiny group – which owns the respected Cuvaison winery in California and vineyards in Switzerland and Argentina – by Endeavour Drinks (part of the Woolworths group). Wine quality is unfailingly excellent. The production comes from estate plantings of shiraz, cabernet sauvignon, chardonnay, verdelho, savagnin, sangiovese and merlot, plus contract-grown grapes. The red wines are not filtered or fined, and there are no tannin or enzyme additions, just SO_2 – natural red wines. Exports to all major markets.

ŶŶŶŶŶ **McLaren Vale Cabernet Sauvignon 2019** McLaren Vale has a long history of producing high-class cabernet, and this is a fine example. Blackcurrant fruit leads, with a retinue of bay leaf and black olive tapenade. The tannins are shapely

though firm, as befits the variety. The colour, too, is exciting. Screw cap. 14.5% alc.
Rating 94 **To** 2039 $33 JH

ㅜㅜㅜㅜ? **The MV McLaren Vale Cabernet Sauvignon 2019** Rating 93 To 2030
$33 NG
Gorge Block McLaren Vale Cabernet Sauvignon 2019 Rating 93 To 2034
$65 NG
Fleurieu Vermentino 2020 Rating 92 To 2022 $20 NG ✪
McLaren Vale Mourvèdre 2019 Rating 92 To 2028 $33 NG
The Parson McLaren Vale Shiraz 2019 Rating 91 To 2026 $18 NG ✪
The MV McLaren Vale Shiraz 2019 Rating 91 To 2025 $33 NG
The Vinedresser McLaren Vale Cabernet Sauvignon 2019 Rating 91
To 2026 $25 NG
The Vinedresser McLaren Vale Shiraz 2019 Rating 90 To 2024 $25 NG

Charles Melton   ★★★★★

Krondorf Road, Tanunda, SA 5352 **Region** Barossa Valley
T (08) 8563 3606 **www.**charlesmeltonwines.com.au **Open** 7 days 11–5
Winemaker Charlie Melton, Krys Smith **Est.** 1984 **Dozens** 12000 **Vyds** 32.6ha
Charlie Melton, one of the Barossa Valley's great characters, with wife Virginia by his side,
makes some of the most eagerly sought à la mode wines in Australia. There are 7ha of
estate vineyards at Lyndoch, 9ha at Krondorf and 1.6ha at Light Pass; the lion's share shiraz
and grenache, and a small planting of cabernet sauvignon. An additional 30ha property was
purchased in High Eden, with 10ha of shiraz planted in 2009 and a 5ha field of grenache,
shiraz, mataro, carignan, cinsault, picpoul and bourboulenc planted in '10. The expanded
volume has had no adverse effect on the quality of the rich, supple and harmonious wines.
Exports to all major markets.

ㅜㅜㅜㅜㅜ **Voices of Angels Adelaide Hills Shiraz 2018** Aged 30 months in 100% new
French oak barrels. By contrast with the might of the Barossa, it may seem
counterintuitive to throw 100% new oak at this spicy Adelaide Hills fruit, but
the marriage here is exemplary. Plush black plum and black cherry fruit sits
comfortably in a finely crafted French oak framework, uniting in a finish of great
line and length. Screw cap. 14% alc. **Rating** 95 **To** 2028 $90 TS
Barossa Valley Sparkling Red NV Disgorged 2020. The luscious black fruits
that characterise Charlie Melton's reds are perfectly suited to sparkling, beautifully
set off by dark chocolate oak, long lees age and powder-fine tannins. Spicy dark
berries of all kinds meet sarsaparilla, fresh licorice straps and black jubes. A long
finish adds alluring savoury nuances of coal steam, pan juices and spice, yet upholds
freshness and vitality at every moment. Confident dosage wraps everything
together harmoniously in a delightful finish. Crown seal. 14% alc. **Rating** 95
$71 TS
Nine Popes 2018 Charlie Melton's flagship is a complex and characterful take
on the classic Barossa blend. The lively, spicy, fragrant mood of grenache leads
out, with strong backing from the black-fruit depth and savoury spice of shiraz.
Concentrated sweet-and-sour berry fruits meet a veritable spice cart of personality.
Dark chocolate oak and plush, finely crafted tannins bring up a long and linear
finish. Screw cap. 14.5% alc. **Rating** 94 **To** 2028 $100 TS

ㅜㅜㅜㅜ? **The Kirche Barossa Shiraz Cabernet Sauvignon 2018** Rating 93 To 2028
$46 TS
The Father In Law Reserve Clare Valley Shiraz 2018 Rating 92 To 2028
$58 TS
Grains of Paradise Barossa Shiraz 2018 Rating 91 To 2028 $90 TS
Barossa Cabernet Sauvignon 2018 Rating 90 To 2028 $58 TS

Charlotte Dalton Wines   ★★★★★

Factory 9, 89–91 Hill Street, Port Elliot, SA 5212 **Region** Adelaide Hills
T 0466 541 361 **www**.charlottedaltonwines.com.au **Open** Fri–Mon 11–3 (7 days
26 Dec–26 Jan)
Winemaker Charlotte Hardy **Est.** 2015 **Dozens** 1200
Charlotte Hardy has been making wines for 20 years, with a star-studded career at Craggy
Range (NZ), Château Giscours (Bordeaux) and David Abreu (California), but has called
SA home since 2007. Her winery is part of her Basket Range house, which has been
through many incarnations since starting life as a pig farm in 1858. Much later it housed
the Basket Range store, and at different times in the past 2 decades it has been the winery
to Basket Range Wines, The Deanery Wines and now Charlotte Dalton Wines. Exports to
the the UK, US, Canada, Sweden and China.

ϙϙϙϙϙ **Project 5255 Langhorne Creek Fiano 2020** Made for a unique
Langhorne Creek collaboration titled Project 5255, giving 3 winemakers
outside of Langhorne Creek the opportunity to create a one-off wine with
Langhorne Creek fruit. Winemaker Charlotte Hardy has been gifted fiano
from Bremerton's vineyard in Langhorne Creek in a low-cropping year.
Fermented slowly over winter in older French barrels, no sulphur added until a
week before bottling in November. A textured style, with oak offering a subtle
wooded nature to the nose, before a delicious lemon-curd-like flavour swirls across
the palate. This is one of the more attention-grabbing fianos witnessed this year.
Screw cap. 13% alc. **Rating** 95 **To** 2024 $35 TL ✪ ❤
Love Me Love You Adelaide Hills Shiraz 2019 Ripe with satsuma plum
notes, and a great dusting of white pepper. Juicy, fleshy, tangy with sticky tannins.
Rolls delightfully through the mouth. Screw cap. 13% alc. **Rating** 95 **To** 2026
$32 TL ✪
A Change Is Coming Adelaide Hills Pinot Noir 2020 As per the
winemaker's approach, this is all about purity of fruit, cherry flesh and pip,
juicy with some peppery spice and fine tannins lingering forever on the finish,
prompting ongoing thirst and the hunger for Chinese roast duck. Screw cap.
13.14% alc. **Rating** 94 **To** 2025 $39 TL

ϙϙϙϙϙ **Grace Adelaide Hills Chardonnay 2019 Rating** 92 **To** 2024 $30 TL

Château Tanunda   ★★★★☆

9 Basedow Road, Tanunda, SA 5352 **Region** Barossa Valley
T (08) 8563 3888 **www**.chateautanunda.com **Open** 7 days 10–5
Winemaker Neville Rowe **Est.** 1890 **Dozens** 150 000 **Vyds** 100ha
This is one of the most historically significant winery buildings in the Barossa Valley, built
from bluestone quarried at nearby Bethany in the late 1880s. It has been restored by John
Geber and family, and a new small-batch basket press has been installed. Château Tanunda
owns almost 100ha of vineyards in Bethany, Eden Valley, Tanunda and Vine Vale, with
additional fruit sourced from a group of 30 growers covering the panoply of Barossa districts.
The wines are made from hand-picked grapes, basket pressed, and are neither fined nor
filtered. There is an emphasis on single-vineyard and single-district wines under the Terroirs
of the Barossa label. The impressive building houses the cellar door, the Grand Cellar (with
over 300 barrels of wine) and the Barossa Small Winemakers Centre, offering wines from
boutique winemakers. The arrival of John's daughter, Michelle Geber, in 2018, has nothing
to do with nepotism and everything to do with her exceptional talent; her CV covers every
aspect of wine and wine business. Exports to all major markets.

ϙϙϙϙϙ **150 Year Old Vines Barossa Semillon 2020** Tense and tight Barossa floor
semillon of neutral nashi pear and lemon definition, built with the structural
support of old French oak barrel maturation. Coiled, taut and restrained, it projects
impressive elegance while delivering enduring persistence. A cellaring special.
Screw cap. 11% alc. **Rating** 94 **To** 2035 $70 TS

ŸŸŸŸŸ **50 Year Old Vines Barossa Cabernet Sauvignon 2018** Rating 93 To 2038
$80 TS
100 Year Old Vines Barossa Shiraz 2018 Rating 91 To 2022 $160 TS

Chatto   ★★★★☆

68 Dillons Hill Road, Glaziers Bay, Tas 7109 **Region** Southern Tasmania
T (03) 6114 2050 **www.**chattowines.com
Winemaker Jim Chatto **Est.** 2000 **Dozens** 1000 **Vyds** 1.5ha
Jim Chatto is recognised as having one of the very best palates in Australia, and has proved to
be an outstanding winemaker. He and wife Daisy long wanted to get a small Tasmanian pinot
business up and running but, having moved to the Hunter Valley in 2000, it took 6 years to
find a site that satisfied all of the criteria Jim considers ideal. It is a warm, well-drained site in
one of the coolest parts of Tasmania, looking out over Glaziers Bay. So far they have planted
8 clones of pinot noir, with a spacing of 5000 vines/ha. This will be a busman's holiday for
some years to come following Jim's appointment as chief winemaker for Mount Pleasant and
Pipers Brook. The '19 crop was lost to bushfire smoke taint, but the many Tasmanian vigneron
friends of the Chatto family have come to the rescue, and while there will be no Isle Black
Label Pinot Noir (estate-based), there will be sufficient Tasmanian-grown pinot noir and
chardonnay to cope with demand.

ŸŸŸŸŸ **Mania Pinot Noir 2019** Jim Chatto's approachable pinot is expertly crafted and
great value. Medium crimson red hue. Alive with spicy red berry fruits beautifully
married with a pretty overlay of exotic spice and sarsaparilla root. Fine, supple
tannins are intricately interwoven with piquant acidity on a long and graceful
finish. Screw cap. 13.6% alc. **Rating** 92 **To** 2022 $37 TS

Cherry Tree Hill   ★★★☆

12324 Hume Highway, Sutton Forest, NSW 2577 **Region** Southern Highlands
T (02) 8217 1409 **www.**cherrytreehill.com.au **Open** 7 days 10–5
Winemaker Anton Balog, Mark Balog **Est.** 2000 **Dozens** 3500 **Vyds** 13.5ha
The Lorentz family, then headed by Gabi Lorentz, began the establishment of the Cherry
Tree Hill vineyard in 2000 with the planting of cabernet sauvignon and riesling. Merlot
and sauvignon blanc followed in '01, and finally chardonnay in '02. Gabi's inspiration was
childhood trips on a horse and cart through his grandfather's vineyard in Hungary. Gabi's son
David is now the owner and manager of the business.

ŸŸŸŸ **Southern Highlands Sauvignon Blanc 2019** This is good. Value, too! While
its more expensive oak-fermented sibling stakes claims of Loire influence, this
is more akin to what one would drink throughout Touraine. Good weight.
Optimally ripe. None of the noxious sweet/sour tanginess and tropical fruit
accents of the worst examples. Rather, honeydew melon, quince, greengage and a
melody of herbal riffs. Balanced nicely by a waft of high-country acidity. A long
effortless finish ensues. The real star of the show. Screw cap. 12.5% alc. **Rating** 89
To 2023 $20 NG

Chimes Estate   ★★★

1a Alexandra Street, South Perth, WA 6151 (postal) **Region** Margaret River
T 0407 435 050 **www.**chimesestate.com.au
Winemaker Philip Thompson, Brett Roberts **Est.** 2001 **Dozens** 400 **Vyds** 3ha
This 30ha property, 13km northeast of the Margaret River township, is located in a valley
surrounded by state forest and dairy farms. In 2001, owners Philip and Margaret Thompson
planted the vineyard to cabernet sauvignon, semillon and sauvignon blanc, alongside an olive
grove. The focus has since shifted to red wine, with 2.5ha of cabernet and 0.5ha of zinfandel.

ŸŸŸŸ **Margaret River Cabernet Merlot 2017** Margaret River saw a cool vintage in
2017, which is evident in aromas of capsicum and sugar snap pea. Alongside, there

are hints of cassis and raspberry. The acidity has a distinct tanginess on the palate. Although this makes the wine refreshing, it's a little on the green side for brilliance. Lovely purity of fruit though. Screw cap. 13% alc. **Rating** 89 **To** 2030 EL

Chris Ringland ★★★★

Franklin House, 6–8 Washington Street, Angaston, SA 5353 **Region** Barossa Valley
T (08) 8564 3233 **www**.chrisringland.com **Open** By appt
Winemaker Chris Ringland **Est.** 1989 **Dozens** 120 **Vyds** 2.05ha
The wines made by Chris Ringland for his eponymous brand were at the very forefront of the surge of rich, old-vine Barossa shiraz wines discovered by Robert Parker in the 1980s. As a consequence of very limited production, and high-quality (albeit polarising) wine, it assumed immediate icon status. The production of 120 dozen does not include a small number of magnums, double magnums and imperials that are sold each year. The addition of 0.5ha of shiraz planted in 1999, joined by 1.5ha planted in 2010, has had little practical impact on availability. Exports to the UK, the US, France, Germany, Spain, South Korea, Japan, Hong Kong and China.

🍷🍷🍷🍷🍷 **CR Barossa Shiraz 2019** Spicy, ripe, succulent and full; classic northwest Barossa. Blackberry, mulberry and blood plum fruit tends toward fruit-mince spice and dark fruitcake, backed confidently by dark chocolate oak. Sweet fruit and warm alcohol is contrasted with firm, balanced tannin support. Bold yet crafted – classic Ringland. Screw cap. 14.5% alc. **Rating** 92 **To** 2025 $30 TS

Chrismont ★★★★☆

251 Upper King River Road, Cheshunt, Vic 3678 **Region** King Valley
T (03) 5729 8220 **www**.chrismont.com.au **Open** 7 days 10–5
Winemaker Warren Proft, Prasad Patil **Est.** 1980 **Dozens** 25 000 **Vyds** 100ha
Arnie and Jo Pizzini's substantial vineyards in the Cheshunt and Whitfield areas of the upper King Valley have been planted to riesling, chardonnay, pinot gris, merlot, barbera, sagrantino, marzemino, arneis, prosecco, fiano, petit manseng, tempranillo, sangiovese and nebbiolo. The La Zona range ties in the Italian heritage of the Pizzinis and is part of the intense interest in all things Italian. In January 2016 the Chrismont Cellar Door, Restaurant and Larder was opened. A feature is the 'floating' deck over the vineyard, which can seat up to 150 people and has floor to ceiling glass looking out over the Black Ranges and King Valley landscape. Exports to the Philippines, Malaysia and Singapore.

Churchview Estate ★★★★★

8 Gale Road, Metricup, WA 6280 **Region** Margaret River
T (08) 9755 7200 **www**.churchview.com.au **Open** Mon–Sat 10–5
Winemaker Dave Longden **Est.** 1998 **Dozens** 25 000 **Vyds** 59ha
The Fokkema family, headed by Spike Fokkema, emigrated from the Netherlands in the 1950s. Business success in the following decades led to the acquisition of the 100ha Churchview Estate in '97, and to the progressive establishment of substantial vineyards (planted to 16 varieties), managed organically. Exports to all major markets.

🍷🍷🍷🍷🍷 **St Johns Limited Release Wild Fermented Margaret River Chenin Blanc 2019** The typicity of chenin is masked here by barrel work and lees stirring, so instead of delivering a 'chenin' experience, this is a texturally complex white, with great length of flavour. All things in place with a lick of salivating salty acid through the finish. Trophy at Margaret River Wine Show 2020. Screw cap. 13% alc. **Rating** 93 **To** 2030 $30 EL
The Bartondale Margaret River Chardonnay 2020 The 2020 vintage in Margaret River was warm and low-yielding, but by all accounts, brilliant. This here has grilled yellow peach, high-impact toasty oak with flambéed almonds and grapefruit. Very rich, a lot going on. Screw cap. 14% alc. **Rating** 92 **To** 2031 $45 EL

The Bartondale Margaret River Chardonnay 2019 This wine shows all the hallmarks of the cool 2019 season – lacy minerality, white stone fruit, saline acid and restraint. The oak plays a dominant role both texturally on the palate and in the flavours that linger after it is gone. Screw cap. 12.5% alc. **Rating** 92 **To** 2028 $45 EL

St Johns Limited Release Margaret River Shiraz Viognier 2019 A fair whack of viognier (15% in a blend where 3-4% is often evident), although the co-ferment has done its flavour-integration job. In this case, the pungent viognier overtakes the shiraz on both the nose and palate, and creates a textural slip – the final indication of its presence. Plenty of flavour has been packed into this wine which overall feels sweet and rich. Screw cap. 15% alc. **Rating** 90 **To** 2031 $30 EL

ΨΨΨΨ **St Johns Limited Release Margaret River Viognier 2019** Rating 89 **To** 2025 $30 EL

St Johns Limited Release Margaret River Cabernet Sauvignon Malbec Merlot 2019 Rating 89 **To** 2027 $35 EL

Cimicky Wines ★★★★☆

100 Hermann Thumm Drive, Lyndoch, SA 5351 **Region** Barossa Valley
T (08) 8524 4025 **www**.cimickywines.com.au **Open** By appt
Winemaker Charles Cimicky, Sam Kurtz, Andrew Aldridge **Est.** 1972 **Dozens** 15 000
Vyds 14.42ha
The Cimicky property was originally settled in Lyndoch in 1842 by early German pioneers. Karl Cimicky purchased the property in 1970, expanding the vineyards and building the imposing Tuscan-style winery, which he named Karlsburg. When Karl retired in the '80s, his son Charles Cimicky and partner Jennie took over the business. The winery was completely refitted and, despite historically keeping an ultra-low profile, they produced a range of highly acclaimed red wines. In 2018 Charles and Jennie sold the business to the Hermann Thumm Drive Property Partnership. Exports to the US, Canada, Switzerland, Germany, Malaysia, Hong Kong and China.

ΨΨΨΨΨ **Reserve Barossa Valley Cabernet Sauvignon 2017** The cool 2017 season in the Barossa elevated cabernet's credentials of black/redcurrant fruit, roasted red capsicum and leaf, even notes of mint. Cassis proclaims ripeness. High-cocoa dark chocolate French oak defines a firm, fine tannin spine, conspiring with tart acidity to make for some astringency which contrasts its sweet fruit mood. Impactful, if not polished. Cork. 14.5% alc. **Rating** 91 **To** 2027 $100 TS

Circe Wines ★★★★☆

PO Box 22, Red Hill, Vic 3937 **Region** Mornington Peninsula
T 0417 328 142 **www**.circewines.com.au
Winemaker Dan Buckle **Est.** 2010 **Dozens** 800 **Vyds** 2.9ha
Circe was a seductress and minor goddess of intoxicants in Homer's *Odyssey*. Circe Wines is the partnership of winemaker Dan Buckle and marketer Aaron Drummond, very much a weekend and holiday venture, inspired by their mutual love of pinot noir. They have a long-term lease of a vineyard in Hillcrest Road, not far from Paringa Estate. Dan says,'It is not far from the Buckle Vineyard my dad planted in the 1980s'. Circe has 1.2ha of vines, half chardonnay and half MV6 pinot noir. They have also planted 1.7ha of pinot noir (MV6, Abel, 777, D2V5 and Bests' Old Clone) at a vineyard in William Road, Red Hill. Dan Buckle's real job is chief winemaker at Chandon Australia. Exports to the UK.

ΨΨΨΨΨ **Mornington Peninsula Chardonnay 2019** Gee this is good. It's refreshing and takes its cue from the savoury book. While it has some grapefruit and lemon zest they act like seasoning to the sulphides, not too much, just for the flint. There's some leesy notes and hazelnut-skin-like oak adding another layer of depth. The palate is smooth and intense where acidity snaps like thin glass and the phenolics are polished. Screw cap. 13.5% alc. **Rating** 93 **To** 2027 $35 JF

Hillcrest Road Vineyard Mornington Peninsula Chardonnay 2019 Razor-sharp and tightly coiled. Smoky, flinty, citrussy and stays on a linear path. While tannins pull on the finish, this is a taut and very good wine that needs more time to evolve. Screw cap. 13.5% alc. **Rating** 93 **To** 2029 $60 JF

Mornington Peninsula Pinot Noir 2019 This is an unusual wine in a way. The flavours are restrained and hard to coax out. The merest hint of autumn leaves, cherry fruit and pips with woodsy spices. Some bitter greens and chinotto add a touch more flavour to the lighter-framed palate. All in all, a refreshing drink-now pinot. Screw cap. 13% alc. **Rating** 90 **To** 2025 $40 JF

Clairault Streicker Wines   ★★★★★

3277 Caves Road, Wilyabrup, WA 6280 **Region** Margaret River
T (08) 9755 6225 **www**.clairaultstreicker.com.au **Open** 7 days 10–5
Winemaker Bruce Dukes **Est.** 1976 **Dozens** 12000 **Vyds** 113ha
This multifaceted business is owned by New York resident John Streicker. It began in 2002 when he purchased the Yallingup Protea Farm and vineyards. This was followed by the purchase of the Ironstone Vineyard in '03 and then the Bridgeland Vineyard. The Ironstone Vineyard is one of the oldest vineyards in Wilyabrup. In April '12 Streicker acquired Clairault, bringing a further 40ha of estate vines, including 12ha now over 40 years old. The two brands are effectively run as one venture. A large part of the grape production is sold to winemakers in the region. Exports to the US, Canada, Norway, Dubai, Malaysia, Singapore, Hong Kong and China.

🍷🍷🍷🍷🍷 **Streicker Ironstone Block Old Vine Margaret River Chardonnay 2019** Perhaps unsurprisingly oak-driven at this very early stage, but the underlying fruit has persistence and quiet concentration that lingers on the palate, determined to outlast the oak. Which it does. Eminently classy and layered, by the time this is released it will be a superstar. Screw cap. 14% alc. **Rating** 96 **To** 2035 $50 EL ✪

Clairault Estate Margaret River Cabernet Sauvignon 2017 Elegant, balanced and fine cabernet from a cool year. The supple fruit is wrapped up in a package of finely gripping tannins, cooling acidity and exotic spice, hinting at both a long future in the cellar and pleasure on the table tonight. Wonderful stuff. Screw cap. 14% alc. **Rating** 96 **To** 2035 $60 EL ✪

Streicker Bridgeland Block Margaret River Fumé Blanc 2019 Cracked coconut, coriander seed, fennel flower, sugar snap peas and graphite against a backdrop of turmeric, saffron, lemon pith and brine. On the palate, this shows just as much of the vineyard as it does the winemaker's hand – the oak and fruit are at constant war with each other for dominance. This needs a year in bottle for the peace treaties to be signed, but life post-signing promises harmony, interest and deliciousness. It has the potential to polarise, but on my page, this is impressive. Screw cap. 13% alc. **Rating** 95 **To** 2032 $30 EL ✪

Clairault Estate Margaret River Chardonnay 2019 Very closed at this very early stage of its obviously long life. Taut acidity that is pure brine; white orchard fruit and thundering length of flavour are all the hallmarks of brilliance. The shutters are pulled right now, but that doesn't mean there's no-one at home. Wait. Screw cap. 13% alc. **Rating** 95 **To** 2037 $45 EL

Streicker Bridgeland Block Margaret River Syrah 2016 A savoury, layered and delicate wine, with complex flavours that continue to emerge over a very long finish. Tannins are pervasive, the spice rack is opened at freshly grated nutmeg, and the fruit is savoury and red. Screw cap. 14% alc. **Rating** 95 **To** 2030 $45 EL

Clairault Margaret River Cabernet Sauvignon 2019 An interesting wine – the flavour is not intensely concentrated, but it is exceedingly long. When you think it has finished, it continues. Cassis, raspberry, bay leaf and violets. There is pepper and saline acid in there, too. Elegant, understated and restrained; a cabernet for the ages. Screw cap. 14.5% alc. **Rating** 95 **To** 2035 $30 EL ✪

🍷🍷🍷🍷🍷 **Clairault Margaret River Sauvignon Blanc Semillon 2020 Rating** 93 **To** 2023 $22 EL ✪

Clairault Margaret River Chardonnay 2019 Rating 93 To 2030 $28 EL
Clairault Margaret River Cabernet Sauvignon Merlot 2019 Rating 93
To 2028 $22 EL ✪
Clairault Halley & Lex Margaret River Cabernet Sauvignon 2018
Rating 91 To 2025 $18 EL ✪
Clairault Halley & Lex Margaret River Sauvignon Blanc 2020 Rating 90
To 2022 $18 EL ✪

 # Clandestine   ★★★★

PO Box 501 Mount Lawley, WA 6050 **Region** Various
T 0427 482 903 **www**.clandestinevineyards.com.au **Open** Not
Winemaker Andrew Vessey (WA), Ben Riggs and Daniel Zuzolo **Est.** 2020 **Dozens** 2000
Owners Nick and Trudy Stacy (ex-Vinaceous Wines) source fruit and winemaking in the key
regions of Margaret River, Mount Barker, Adelaide Hills and McLaren Vale. The new range of
Clandestine wines are vegan-friendly and use minimal sulphites and/or preservatives. Exports
to the UK, the US, Singapore and China. (EL)

🍷🍷🍷🍷 Margaret River Malbec 2019 Matured in French oak barriques for 15 months.
The palate is saturated and dense, although there remains space between the
flavours for thought. Quite something. The vineyard is in a slightly cooler spot,
perhaps the reason for the refreshing acidity that courses its way through the palate.
Red berries, salted tomato and red apple skins to boot – this is spicy and lovely.
Screw cap. 14.5% alc. **Rating** 92 **To** 20230 $28 EL
Margaret River Shiraz 2019 A deep crimson. Fine aromas of boysenberry, dark
cherry, clove, mace and anise, galvanised across the rich palate by a swathe of nicely
tuned oak tannins. The finish, of easygoing punchy length, by virtue of the quality
of the fruit and its tenacity, rather than anything more complicated. Screw cap.
14.5% alc. **Rating** 90 **To** 2025 $28 NG

🍷🍷🍷🍷 Geographe Tempranillo Rosé 2020 **Rating** 88 **To** 2022 $28 EL

Clarence House Wines   ★★★★☆

193 Pass Road, Cambridge, Tas 7170 (postal) **Region** Southern Tasmania
T (03) 6247 7345 **www**.chwine.com.au **Open** By appt
Winemaker Anna Pooley, Justine Pooley **Est.** 1998 **Dozens** 3500 **Vyds** 15ha
Clarence House was built in 1830 at Clarence Vale, Mt Rumney. The house has been kept
in great condition, and in 1998 present owner, David Kilpatrick, began planting vines on a
northeast-sloping block opposite the house. While pinot noir and chardonnay account for
over 8ha of the plantings, the remainder includes pinot blanc and tempranillo.

🍷🍷🍷🍷🍷 Reserve Tasmania Pinot Noir 2020 Judicious fruit selection elevates Clarence
House's Reserve to greater depth and length of black-fruit presence. Black cherries
and blackberries are brushed with white pepper and beetroot. Anna Pooley's
wizardry in the winery intricately marries fine-grained tannins and bright acidity
on a long finish. Elegance meets class in a deliciously age-worthy package. Screw
cap. 13.5% alc. **Rating** 95 **To** 2035 $50 TS
Reserve Tasmania Chardonnay 2018 This is a small price to pay for the
top-tier chardonnay of the house, and the investment buys more wood, but more
importantly the fruit concentration and drive of top barrel selection. White
peach, lemon, grapefruit and fig are woven with spice and the roast cashew nuts
of French oak. Bright acidity focuses a long and full finish. Screw cap. 13.5% alc.
Rating 94 **To** 2026 $40 TS

🍷🍷🍷🍷 Tasmania Chardonnay 2018 **Rating** 92 **To** 2028 $30 TS
Tasmania Pinot Noir 2020 **Rating** 91 **To** 2028 $40 TS

Clarendon Hills   ★★★★★
Brookmans Road, Blewitt Springs, SA 5171 **Region** McLaren Vale
T (08) 8363 6111 **www**.clarendonhills.com.au **Open** By appt
Winemaker Roman Bratasiuk **Est.** 1990 **Dozens** 10 000 **Vyds** 33ha
Age and experience, it would seem, have mellowed Roman Bratasiuk – and the style of his wines. Once formidable and often rustic, they are now far more sculpted and smooth, at times bordering on downright elegance. Roman took another major step by purchasing a 160ha property high in the hill country of Clarendon at an altitude close to that of the Adelaide Hills. Here he has established a vineyard with single-stake trellising similar to that used on the steep slopes of Germany and Austria; it produces the Domaine Clarendon Syrah. He makes up to 20 different wines each year, all consistently very good, a tribute to the old vines. Sons Adam and Alex have joined their father in the business – Adam in the winery, Alex managing the future direction of Clarendon Hills. Exports to the US, Europe and Asia.

Clarnette & Ludvigsen Wines   ★★★★☆
270 Westgate Road, Armstrong, Vic 3377 **Region** Grampians
T 0409 083 833 **www**.clarnette-ludvigsen.com.au **Open** By appt
Winemaker Leigh Clarnette **Est.** 2003 **Dozens** 400 **Vyds** 15.5ha
Winemaker Leigh Clarnette and viticulturist Kym Ludvigsen's career paths crossed in late 1993 when both were working for Seppelt; Kym with a 14ha vineyard in the heart of the Grampians, all but 1ha of chardonnay, 0.5ha of viognier and 0.25ha of riesling planted to rare clones of shiraz, sourced from old plantings in the Great Western area. They met again in 2005 when both were employed by Taltarni. The premature death of Kym in '13 was widely reported, in no small measure due to his (unpaid) service on wine industry bodies. With next generations on both sides, the plans are to continue the business. Exports to China.

🍷🍷🍷🍷🍷 Grampians Riesling 2020 The C&L style, so zesty and lively, remains on top form, as ever. Billson's lime cordial, lemon drop, talc and pear sorbet aromas. Fruit tingle brightness, zingy and citrus-infused, moves across the palate aided by rapier-like acidity. Another reason not to ignore Grampians riesling. Screw cap. 12% alc. Rating 95 To 2027 $28 JP

🍷🍷🍷🍷🍷 Le Grampian Chardonnay 2019 Rating 92 To 2025 $35 JP
Reserve Grampians Shiraz 2018 Rating 92 To 2027 $55 JP
Grampians Tempranillo 2020 Rating 90 To 2025 $28 JP

Clay Pot Wines   ★★★★★
Billy Button Wines, 11 Camp Street, Bright, Vic 3741 **Region** Alpine Valleys
T 0434 635 510 **www**.claypotwines.com.au **Open** 7 days 11–6
Winemaker Glenn James **Est.** 2011 **Dozens** 150
Made by Glenn James, each wine is made in a single clay amphora. Beginning life as a single wine, Pandora's Amphora in 2011 (vermentino fiano moscato giallo), she is now joined by Pyrrha (saperavi) and Taurian (friulano). Sourcing for Pandora moved with Glenn James, beginning in Heathcote, then moving to McLaren Vale with the 2014 and finally finding her home in the Alpine Valleys from 2015. Each wine is just 50 dozen.

🍷🍷🍷🍷🍷 Pyrrha Alpine Valleys Saperavi 2018 It's rare to see the saperavi grape so tamed and, let's face it, looking so elegant. After time in clay amphora there is clearly a transformation of sorts, the grape seems positively relaxed, extolling its fragrant side – all violets, dried herbs, black cherry, mulberry, vanilla pod – and merging its tannin and acidity into a dusty, earthy, well-structured whole. Screw cap. 14% alc. Rating 95 To 2028 $60 JP
Pyrrha Alpine Valleys Saperavi 2017 A striking wine by any measure, on texture, fragrance, tone and control of what is a high-acid grape. Aromatic black fruits, damson plums, earth, briar and violets. An almost seamless melding of all

parties on the palate here, with a bright, peppery spice enlivening things. Wow! Screw cap. 14% alc. **Rating** 95 **To** 2030 $60 JP

♀♀♀♀♀ **Pandora's Amphora 2018 Rating** 91 **To** 2026 $60 JP

Claymore Wines

7145 Horrocks Way, Leasingham, SA 5452 **Region** Clare Valley
T (08) 8843 0200 **www.**claymorewines.com.au **Open** Mon–Sat 10–5, Sun & public hols 11–4
Winemaker Nathan Norman **Est.** 1998 **Dozens** 35 000 **Vyds** 50ha
Claymore Wines is the venture of Anura Nitchingham, a medical professional who imagined this would lead the way to early retirement (which, of course, it did not). The starting date depends on which event you take first: the purchase of the 4ha vineyard at Leasingham in 1991 (with 70yo grenache, riesling and shiraz); the purchase of a 16ha block at Penwortham in '96, and planted to shiraz, merlot and grenache; making the first wines '97; or when the first releases came onto the market in '98. The labels are inspired by U2, Pink Floyd, Prince and Lou Reed. Exports to the UK, Canada, Denmark, Malaysia, Singapore, Taiwan, Hong Kong and China.

♀♀♀♀♀ **You'll Never Walk Alone Premiership 19/20 Clare Valley Cabernet Sauvignon 2018** A barrel selection, with only 2 making the grade for Claymore's top wine. A hefty number, more about winemaking than the fruit from a 60+yo site. Screw cap. 15% alc. **Rating** 90 **To** 2028 $75 JF

♀♀♀♀ **Bittersweet Symphony Clare Valley Cabernet Sauvignon 2018 Rating** 89 **To** 2028 $25 JF

Clonakilla

3 Crisps Lane, Murrumbateman, NSW 2582 **Region** Canberra District
T (02) 6227 5877 **www.**clonakilla.com.au **Open** Mon–Fri 11–4, w'ends 10–5
Winemaker Tim Kirk, Chris Bruno **Est.** 1971 **Dozens** 20 000 **Vyds** 16ha
The indefatigable Tim Kirk, with an inexhaustible thirst for knowledge, is the winemaker and manager of this family winery founded by his father, scientist Dr John Kirk. It is not at all surprising that the quality of the wines is exceptional, especially the Shiraz Viognier, which has paved the way for numerous others but remains the icon. Demand for the wines outstrips supply, even with the 1998 acquisition of an adjoining 20ha property by Tim and wife Lara Kirk, planted to shiraz and viognier. In 2007 the Kirk family purchased another adjoining property, planting another 1.8ha of shiraz, plus 0.4ha of grenache, mourvèdre and cinsault. Exports to all major markets.

♀♀♀♀♀ **Murrumbateman Syrah 2019** This is really astonishing: the flavours, the texture and the depth of this wine without it ever moving much beyond medium bodied. It is not trying to be flash. It's in its own comfort zone, full of florals, ripe fruit and an array of spices. It's an exercise in texture though. Very fine, velvety tannins sashay across the palate, which extends out, adding more fruit flavours, savoury tones and well-integrated oak along the way. Long, decisive and a pleasure to taste. Screw cap. 14% alc. **Rating** 97 **To** 2039 $130 JF ✪ ♥

♀♀♀♀♀ **Canberra District Shiraz Viognier 2019** Some wines have such distinct DNA. This is one of them. It packs so many layers of flavour and depth, yet never moves much beyond medium body. It smells of a souk market; spicy, peppery and exotic. It's replete with dark fruit, wood char and a touch of wintergreen. Raw silk tannins matched to a neat acid line give freshness, vibrancy and a promise it will last some distance yet. Screw cap. 14% alc. **Rating** 96 **To** 2035 $130 JF
Eden Valley Viognier 2020 This is luscious and rich, full of heady aromas of orange blossom and ginger flower. The fuller-bodied palate takes in a hint of white peach, apricot fruit and kernels. Phenolics are beautifully handled. I'd drink this in a heartbeat. Sharing the bottle with friends, of course. Screw cap. 14% alc. **Rating** 95 **To** 2028 $48 JF

O'Riada Canberra District Shiraz 2019 This sings its own tune and it's rather pitch perfect. An array of enticing Middle Eastern spices, pepper too, infusing dark-berried fruit at its core. There's an intensity to the flavours, smoky and seductive. Yet the medium-bodied palate is not overwrought. Beautiful tannins are as textural as a superfine emery board. Screw cap. 14% alc. **Rating** 95 **To** 2033 $45 JF

🍷🍷🍷🍷🍷 **Tasmania Chardonnay 2020 Rating** 93 **To** 2028 $50 JF

Clos Clare

45 Old Road, Watervale, SA 5452 **Region** Clare Valley
T (08) 8843 0161 **www.closclare.com.au Open** W'ends 11–5
Winemaker Sam and Tom Barry **Est.** 1993 **Dozens** 1600 **Vyds** 2ha
Clos Clare was acquired by the Barry family in 2007. Riesling continues to be made from the 2ha unirrigated section of the original Florita Vineyard (the major part of that vineyard was already in Barry ownership). Its red wines come from a vineyard beside the Armagh site. Exports to the UK.

Cloudburst

PO Box 1294, Margaret River, WA 6285 **Region** Margaret River
T (08) 6323 2333 **www.cloudburstwine.com**
Winemaker Will Berliner **Est.** 2005 **Dozens** 450 **Vyds** 1ha
An extremely interesting winery. Will Berliner and wife Alison Jobson spent several years in Australia searching for a place that resonated with them, and on their first visit to Margaret River were immediately smitten, drawn by its biodiversity, beaches, farms, vineyards, community and lifestyle. When they purchased their land in 2004 they hadn't the slightest connection with wine and no intention of ever getting involved. Within 12 months Will's perspective had entirely changed, and in '05 he began planting the vineyard and applying biodynamic preparations, seeking to build microbial life in the soil. They planted the vineyard as if it were a garden, with short rows, and initially planted 0.2ha of each of cabernet sauvignon and chardonnay, and 0.1ha of malbec. By 2020 the vineyard had doubled in size, but without changing the varieties or their proportions. The packaging is truly striking and imaginative. Exports to the US and the UK.

🍷🍷🍷🍷🍷 **Margaret River Cabernet Sauvignon 2018** The complexity of 2018 is on show here in spades: leafy blackberry kirsch on the nose, pastille and black pepper. It's savoury and layered with crushed ants and dry spice, star anise, salted licorice and toasted raspberry. The dense and concentrated palate is backed by very good length. There is a varnish element which distracts from the complex flavours that eddy about, ultimately affecting the tannins and making the experience awkward and not quite together. Screw cap. 13.4% alc. **Rating** 91 **To** 2031 $350 EL

Clover Hill

60 Clover Hill Road, Lebrina, Tas 7254 **Region** Northern Tasmania
T (03) 5459 7900 **www.cloverhillwines.com.au Open** 7 days 10–4.30
Winemaker Robert Heywood, Peter Warr **Est.** 1986 **Dozens** 12 000 **Vyds** 23.9ha
Clover Hill was established by Taltarni in 1986 with the sole purpose of making a premium sparkling wine. It has 23.9ha of vineyards (chardonnay, pinot noir and pinot meunier) and its sparkling wine is excellent, combining finesse with power and length. The American owner and founder of Clos du Val (Napa Valley), Taltarni and Clover Hill has brought these businesses and Domaine de Nizas (Languedoc) under the one management roof, the group known as Goelet Wine Estates. Exports to the UK, the US and other major markets.

🍷🍷🍷🍷🍷 **Cuvée Exceptionnelle Tasmania Blanc de Blancs 2013** Méthode traditionnelle. This has the tension, energy and persistence for a grand journey ahead. Its 6 years on lees have not evolved its bright, medium straw hue, nor primary apple, pear and lemon notes, becoming preserved lemon. Age has just begun to build creaminess and layers of mixed spice, roast almonds, toast, butter and a subtle hint of charcuterie. Diam. 12% alc. **Rating** 94 $65 TS

🍷🍷🍷🍷🍷 **Foudre Tasmania NV Rating** 93 $45 TS
Tasmanian Cuvée Rosé NV Rating 92 $34 TS
Cuvée Exceptionnelle Tasmania Brut Rosé 2016 Rating 92 $65 TS
Vintage Riché Tasmania 2016 Rating 91 $45 TS
Vintage Riché Tasmania 2015 Rating 91 $45 TS

Clyde Park Vineyard   ★★★★★

2490 Midland Highway, Bannockburn, Vic 3331 **Region** Geelong
T (03) 5281 7274 **www**.clydepark.com.au **Open** 7 days 11–5
Winemaker Terry Jongebloed **Est.** 1979 **Dozens** 6000 **Vyds** 10.1ha
Clyde Park Vineyard, established by Gary Farr but sold by him many years ago, has passed through several changes of ownership. Now owned by Terry Jongebloed and Sue Jongebloed-Dixon, it has significant mature plantings of pinot noir (3.4ha), chardonnay (3.1ha), sauvignon blanc (1.5ha), shiraz (1.2ha) and pinot gris (0.9ha), and the quality of its wines is consistently exemplary. Exports to the UK and Hong Kong.

🍷🍷🍷🍷🍷 **Single Block B3 Bannockburn Chardonnay 2020** There's a lot more going on here than your average chardonnay, a deep complexity for one thing. Nougat, honeysuckle, grilled hazelnuts, lemon butter and musky spice, long and smooth across the palate, launch the drinker into another orbit. Hard to believe it's just starting its journey. What a road ahead awaits. Screw cap. 12.5% alc. **Rating** 96 To 2035 $75 JP ✪
Geelong Chardonnay 2020 A complex wine (already) and full of character with distinctive winemaking-led threads. Layers of warm, toasty oak, nougat, almond mealiness and grilled nuts combine with yellow peach, stone fruits and sweet honeysuckle flavours. It's a big mouthful of flavour, well composed and finishing smooth. Screw cap. 12.5% alc. **Rating** 95 To 2031 $45 JP
Geelong Pinot Noir 2020 Another excellent example of the kind of fine-boned and sophisticated expression of pinot noir that Clyde Park celebrates. Forest, wild berries, wood smoke and undergrowth aromas provide insight into what follows. Round and silky in tannins across the palate, effortlessly subtle but with a solid core of flavour. A still-waters-run-deep kind of wine. Screw cap. 13% alc. **Rating** 95 To 2033 $45 JP
Single Block F College Bannockburn Pinot Noir 2020 Works a deeper vein of pinot noir, one where that forces you to pay a little more attention, look a little closer. High-tone perfume of smoky, dark plum, hints of violet and sage. Good intensity and concentration with underlying savoury notes waiting to develop further; and the most supple of tannins. Screw cap. 13.5% alc. **Rating** 95 To 2035 $75 JP
Geelong Sauvignon Blanc 2020 Clyde Park has been a strong believer in the ability of sauvignon blanc to make something seriously exciting in the Geelong region. Its style, ably displayed here, is both fresh and capitvating in herbal intensity but also has citrus, grapefruit and mealy notes. Extends the grape into textural, complex territory. Screw cap. 12.5% alc. **Rating** 94 To 2024 $35 JP
Geelong Pinot Gris 2020 In keeping with Clyde Park winemaking, this is no simple gris. Look closer. Note the restrained yet attractive scent of baked apple, glacé pear, some just-baked biscuit complexity and white nectarine. Next, the drinker moves into a smooth, rolling textural palate which is not only fresh but deep into all manner of complex tastes. Definitely tingles the tastebuds. Screw cap. 13% alc. **Rating** 94 To 2024 $40 JP
Single Block D Bannockburn Pinot Noir 2020 The addition of whole bunches has brought a fine fragrance to this wine and contributed to a mighty firm structure, something that time will no doubt help resolve. A sinewy, linear pinot with raspberry, red-cherry scents and a touch of undergrowth, it cuts a

firm line filled with red fruits and spice through to the end. Still early days for this wine. Screw cap. 13% alc. **Rating** 94 **To** 2034 $75 JP

♚♚♚♚♚ Geelong Shiraz 2020 **Rating** 91 **To** 2030 $45 JP

Coates Wines   ★★★★★

185 Tynan Road, Kuitpo, SA 5172 **Region** Adelaide Hills
T 0417 882 557 **www**.coates-wines.com **Open** W'ends & public hols 11–5
Winemaker Duane Coates **Est.** 2003 **Dozens** 2500
Duane Coates has a bachelor of science, a master of business administration and a master of oenology from the University of Adelaide; for good measure he completed the theory component of the MW program in 2005. Having made wine in various parts of the world, and in SA, he is more than qualified to make and market Coates wines. Nonetheless, his original intention was to simply make a single barrel of wine employing various philosophies and practices outside the mainstream; there was no plan to move to commercial production. The key is organically grown grapes. Exports to the UK and the US.

♚♚♚♚♚ Adelaide Hills The Riesling 2020 An exercise in how to make riesling (too often shrill, battery acid-dry and brittle in this country) into a phalanx of optimally ripe fruit, the sort of juicy acidity that pulls the saliva from the back of the mouth with an elastic cadence and real textural intrigue. Class and complexity, the DNA. Kaffir lime, sure. Better, quince paste, tangerine, lemon meringue and a pungent mineral undercurrent. The older oak, servicing an expansive breadth that stains the cheeks. Thrilling length! Excellent wine. Screw cap. 12% alc. **Rating** 96 **To** 2028 $35 NG ✪ ♥

Adelaide Hills The Reserve Chardonnay 2019 Real vibrato here, as an underlying mineral tension plays off the creamy vanilla-pod oak, subsuming nectarine and melon elements in the name of savouriness. Wild mushroom scents. Dried hay. Nougatine and toasted hazelnuts. As generous as it is tensile. An exceptional mid-weighted chardonnay with no expense spared, built for mid-term ageing. Screw cap. 13% alc. **Rating** 96 **To** 2030 $45 NG ✪ ♥

McLaren Vale The Reserve Syrah 2019 A full-weighted wine with personality masked. A juvenile impatiently waiting to shed the carapace of expectation. Here, oak serves as a bulwark against time, at once preparing for glories ahead, while stultifying immediate gratification. Iodine, wakame, pepper, blue fruits, clove and salumi. Loads of mocha-cedar. Quality oak. Fine-boned and fresh, beneath it all. It just needs time to unleash its inner Cornas. Screw cap. 14% alc. **Rating** 96 **To** 2033 $80 NG

Adelaide Hills The Blanc de Blancs 2016 A pleasure bomb that shifts the paradigm, for the better. Made akin to a great grower champagne. The soft, natural acidity, mitigated with the crescendo of oak and lees. Palate-staining, every crevice of the mouth filled with leesy nourishment. The underlying current is forceful, creamy and endless. A tour de force of Australian fizz. Diam. 12% alc. **Rating** 96 $60 NG ✪ ♥

McLaren Vale The Syrah 2019 This is McLaren Vale meeting the northern Rhône on its own terms. Full bodied, but savoury. Sweetness of obvious fruit, mercifully avoided. The clutch of reduction handled deftly, imparting tension and a sense of freshness across the mid palate. This is how to do it! Dried nori, jamon, tapenade salinity and violets. There's a core of unadulterated blueberry sweetness tempered by clove, cardamom and a skein of peppery acidity threaded long. Screw cap. 14% alc. **Rating** 95 **To** 2028 $30 NG ✪

♚♚♚♚♚ Adelaide Hills The Chardonnay 2019 **Rating** 93 **To** 2027 $35 NG
The Garden of Perfume & Spice Adelaide Hills Syrah 2019 **Rating** 93 **To** 2025 $45 NG
McLaren Vale Langhorne Creek The Shiraz Cabernet 2017 **Rating** 93 **To** 2029 $35 NG

Adelaide Hills The Nebbiolo 2019 Rating 93 To 2027 $45 NG
Adelaide Hills The Pinot Noir 2020 Rating 92 To 2026 $35 NG
Langhorne Creek The Cabernet Sauvignon 2019 Rating 92 To 2032
$35 NG

Cobaw Ridge   ★★★★★

31 Perc Boyers Lane, Pastoria, Vic 3444 **Region** Macedon Ranges
T (03) 5423 5227 **www.**cobawridge.com.au **Open** W'ends 12–5
Winemaker Nelly Cooper, Alan Cooper **Est.** 1985 **Dozens** 1000 **Vyds** 5ha
When the Coopers started planting in the early 1980s there was scant knowledge of the best
varieties for the region, let alone the Cobaw Ridge site. They have now settled on chardonnay
and syrah; lagrein and close-planted, multi-clonal pinot noir are more recent arrivals to thrive.
Cobaw Ridge is fully certified biodynamic, and all winery operations are carried out according
to the biodynamic calendar. Exports to the UK, Poland, Hong Kong, Singapore and Taiwan.

ϒϒϒϒϒ **Chardonnay 2018** Wow. Exquisite wine. There's a lot of flavour here, yet it runs
on the pure energy of its fine acidity. It initially works off a citrus theme, juicy,
tangy and zesty. There's a certain amount of sulphide flint adding another layering
of complexity, but it's not overt. Neither is the oak, which has absorbed this wine
as its own. Leesy, nutty characters add to the palate, which is moreish, savoury and
very complete. Diam. 13.5% alc. **Rating** 96 **To** 2030 $58 JF ✪
Lagrein 2018 Here is Australia's finest lagrein. It smells of warm earth and
ironstone. Black pepper and juniper Alpine herbs and licorice root. It's complex
and detailed, with lithe tannins and chalky acidity. The palate is energised with
excellent fruit flavour, all small berries, with a dusting of cocoa and blood-orange
juice. Yet with all that, it is savoury through and through. And superbly balanced.
Bravo. Diam. 12.7% alc. **Rating** 96 **To** 2028 $80 JF ♥
Chardonnay 2019 Coming off the back of the pristine 2018, this has a deeper
mid straw hue, but is still very fresh and tight. A hint of richer fruit – poached
quinces, finger lime and lemon curd – but this still is kept on a tight leash. The
palate opens up to distinct savoury, flinty and nougat flavours, then a mouth-
watering finish. Diam. 13.5% alc. **Rating** 95 **To** 2029 $60 JF
Il Pinko Rosé 2019 An excellent shiraz rosé that abounds in flavour, texture
and depth. A smidge of barely ripe raspberries, spiced plums and refreshing
watermelon rind. The phenolics are beautifully handled, adding to the overall
texture, and its bright acidity makes for a thirst quencher. Serious rosé, delicious
to drink. Diam. 13.7% alc. **Rating** 95 **To** 2024 $39 JF ♥
Pinot Noir 2019 This smells like autumn. It's smoky and savoury, with blood
orange and hints of rhubarb and damp earth. There's a generosity this vintage,
yet thankfully without the weight. A slight green edge in the mix is the stamp of
Cobaw Ridge, enmeshed into the other flavours like seasoning. Diam. 13.5% alc.
Rating 95 **To** 2032 $60 JF
Pinot Noir 2018 It's always the palate that makes this striking – donned with
silky, velvety tannins and wonderful texture. Of course, there's ripe black cherries
and plums in the mix, too, with an array of baking spices and the distinctive gum
leaf stamp of Cobaw Ridge, which acts like a seasoning. It's supple and juicy, with
fine acidity lengthening out the palate. Diam. 13.7% alc. **Rating** 95 **To** 2030
$58 JF
Syrah 2016 Even with a few years under its belt, the colour, indeed the wine,
is bright and youthful. Deep, dark and penetrating, it's vibrant and lively, even
energising. Full of dark fruit, gun flint, coffee grounds and eucalyptus. While the
tannins hold sway, they are textural, savoury and giving. A lovely wine. Diam.
13.8% alc. **Rating** 95 **To** 2030 $58 JF

Cockfighter's Ghost | Poole's Rock ★★★★☆

576 De Beyers Road, Pokolbin, NSW 2320 **Region** Hunter Valley
T (02) 4993 3688 **www.**cockfightersghost.com.au **Open** 7 days 10–5
Winemaker Xanthe Hatcher **Est.** 1988 **Vyds** 38ha

Cockfighter's Ghost and Poole's Rock were founded in 1988 by the late David Clarke OAM, and acquired by the Agnew family in 2011 (who also own the neighbouring Audrey Wilkinson). The brands have kept separate identities, but are made at the same winery. The Cockfighter's Ghost white wines are sourced from key growers in the Adelaide Hills, the red wines entirely from the Agnew family's Chairman's Vineyard in Blewitt Springs, made by Xanthe Hatcher. Jeff Byrne continues overseeing Poole's Rock, with Chardonnay, Semillon and Shiraz from the Hunter Valley and also some small-batch wines including Pinot Noir from Tasmania. Exports to the US and Canada.

ᵀᵀᵀᵀᵀ **Poole's Rock Hunter Valley Semillon 2007** A medium gold hue and exulting in its early middle age, this is a fine 2007. A bit more to come, too, with careful cellaring. A skittering lightweight frame with pumice-like acidity, tonic mineral underbelly and maturing aromas of citrus marmalade, buttered toast, lemon pastille and quinine. Good length. The joy is in the wine's indelible stamp of place, aged complexities and ease of drinking. Screw cap. 11.6% alc. **Rating** 93 **To** 2025 $75 NG

Poole's Rock Single Vineyard Hunter Valley Chardonnay 2019 This is a huge leap forward from the Premiere cuvée in terms of intensity of fruit, length and the fashion in which the oak hugs the seams of juicy acidity, while serving to focus and direct flavours of white peach, orange verbena, candied lemon and praline. A more complete wine, with fruit and structural latticework in fine synchronicity. Screw cap. 13% alc. **Rating** 93 **To** 2026 $65 NG

Poole's Rock Premiere Adelaide Hills Pinot Noir 2019 Pressed with 30% whole bunch then into French puncheons and matured for 7 months, there's a definite earthiness underneath the familiar pinot fruit suggestions – cherry, strawberry obviously. Its deft woodsy layers add a pleasing complexity as well as well-measured grip on the finish. Nicely done. Screw cap. 13% alc. **Rating** 92 **To** 2028 $40 TL

Poole's Rock Centenary Block Hunter Valley Shiraz 2019 This regime practises a pristine fruit-forward style. Modern and polished. To promote it, too often the acidity is grating. And yet here, while the pH tweaks are likely with us, the earthenware fruit is savoury. The tannins, dusty and broad, subsuming the acidity. The vinous flow of mulberry, anise and clove, impressive. Screw cap. 14% alc. **Rating** 92 **To** 2030 $40 NG

Poole's Rock Hunter Valley Shiraz 2010 This is a good dry table wine, ready to drink. It has the Hunter postcode etched across a nose of sweet red earth, cherry, varnished teak and suede; a savoury finish, defined by a lithe carriage of tannin, moreish and resolved. Far from exuberant, yet of decent length in an understated way. I'd be drinking this with relish. Screw cap. 13.5% alc. **Rating** 92 **To** 2023 $60 NG

Poole's Rock Post Office Hunter Valley Shiraz 2019 Malty, in the best sense. Sweet fecund earth, dark cherry and leather polish mark the Hunter. More complexity derived from aromas of bone broth, clove and violet. A modern reductive style, handled well, aside from the shrill acidity. Again. Good drinking. Screw cap. 14.5% alc. **Rating** 90 **To** 2029 $45 NG

ᵀᵀᵀᵀ **Cockfighter's Ghost Single Vineyard Adelaide Hills Sauvignon Blanc 2020 Rating** 89 **To** 2022 $25 NG

Poole's Rock Premiere Hunter Valley Chardonnay 2019 Rating 89 **To** 2024 $40 NG

Cockfighter's Ghost Single Vineyard Adelaide Hills Pinot Gris 2020 Rating 88 **To** 2023 $25 NG

Coldstream Hills

29-31 Maddens Lane, Coldstream, Vic 3770 **Region** Yarra Valley
T (03) 5960 7000 **www.**coldstreamhills.com.au **Open** Fri–Mon 10–5
Winemaker Andrew Fleming, Greg Jarratt, James Halliday (Consultant) **Est.** 1985
Vyds 100ha
Founded by James Halliday, Coldstream Hills is now a small part of TWE with 100ha of estate
vineyards as its base, 3 in the Lower Yarra Valley and 2 in the Upper Yarra Valley. Chardonnay
and pinot noir continue to be the principal focus; merlot and cabernet sauvignon came
onstream in 1997, sauvignon blanc around the same time, Reserve Shiraz later still. Vintage
conditions permitting, Chardonnay and Pinot Noir are made in Reserve, Single Vineyard
and varietal forms. In addition, Amphitheatre Pinot Noir was made in tiny quantities in
2006 and '13. In '10 a multimillion-dollar winery was erected around the original winery
buildings and facilities; it has a capacity of 1500t. There is a plaque in the fermentation area
commemorating the official opening on 12 October '10 and naming the facility the 'James
Halliday Cellar'. Exports to Singapore, Japan and China.

Reserve Yarra Valley Shiraz 2018 The colour is stunning – dark purple with
a ruby rim. It's floral and spicy. Laced with dark fruits, licorice, pepper and baking
spices, with an undertow of savouriness. Tannins are spot-on, the palate dense, yet
shy of full bodied. Everything rolls out into a harmonious whole. Lovely wine.
Screw cap. 14% alc. **Rating** 95 **To** 2033 $45 JF

Reserve Yarra Valley Cabernet Sauvignon 2019 While still covered in a
youthful gloss – which says more about the brightness and juiciness of fruit – there
is quality and savouriness with this, too. There are fine-grained tannins, cedar and
cigarbox inputs from classy French oak (aged 16 months) and there's a precision
across the palate. It's only just unfurling, so more time in bottle would help. Screw
cap. 13.5% alc. **Rating** 95 **To** 2034 $60 JF

Yarra Valley Pinot Noir 2020 Rating 92 **To** 2028 $35 JF

Collalto

★★★★

Lot 99, Adelaide-Lobethal Road, Lobethal, SA 5241 **Region** Adelaide Hills
T 0429 611 290 **www.**collalto.com.au
Winemaker Revenir (Peter Leske) **Est.** 2006 **Dozens** 630 **Vyds** 8ha
To say this is a business with a difference is a masterly understatement. It has a real vineyard
of 5.5ha of pinot noir and 2.5ha of chardonnay planted in 2001; a real viticulturist (Damon
Koerner), and a real winemaker (Peter Leske). Its owner (who grew up in the Adelaide Hills) is
London-based QC James Drake. Most of the grapes are sold to Petaluma, but enough to make
800–1200 dozen or so a year is held back. The name Collalto describes the high vineyard, and
is also a tribute to their mother Palimira (née Tosolini) whose father came from the village of
that name just north of Udine, in northeastern Italy. Exports to the UK.

Adelaide Hills Pinot Noir 2019 Lots of upfront fruit – black cherry leaning –
with enticing depth of aroma and flavour. Energetic acidity adds vitality to the
palate, but its feet are firmly on the ground, with balanced, light-grained tannin
and an earnest finish. Screw cap. 13.5% alc. **Rating** 94 **To** 2028 $35 TL

Adelaide Hills Chardonnay 2019 Rating 89 **To** 2025 $35 TL

Collector Wines

7 Murray Street, Collector, NSW 2581 **Region** Canberra District
T (02) 6116 8722 **www.**collectorwines.com.au **Open** Thurs–Mon 10–4
Winemaker Alex McKay **Est.** 2007 **Dozens** 6000 **Vyds** 6ha
Owner and winemaker Alex McKay makes exquisitely detailed wines, bending to the dictates
of inclement weather on his doorstep, heading elsewhere if need be. He was part of a talented
team at Hardys' Kamberra Winery and, when it was closed down by Hardys' then new owner
CHAMP, decided to stay in the district. He is known to not speak much, and when he does,

his voice is very quiet. So you have to remain alert to appreciate his unparalleled sense of humour. No such attention is needed for his wines, which are consistently excellent, their elegance appropriate for their maker. Exports to Thailand and Japan.

TTTTT **Tiger Tiger Chardonnay 2018** This is as much a pure expression of cool Tumbarumba fruit as it is of Alex McKay's respectful winemaking – whole-bunch pressed, fermented in French oak, mlf and aged on lees for about 10 months. It's flinty and fine, with pure grapefruit and lemon and a light, leesy, creamy texture. But it's the laser line of acidity that thrills. Screw cap. 12.9% alc. **Rating** 96 To 2030 $38 JF **☉**

Lamp Lit Canberra District Marsanne 2019 Given its youth, this is tight, flinty and lightly aromatic. Bit different on the palate as the flavours have been ramped up, partly via mlf and partly via toasty new French barrels – expect creamed honey and texture. There's some tension between the acidity and the oak, ensuring this will unfurl in time. But today it could slake a thirst. Screw cap. 13.3% alc. **Rating** 95 To 2028 $32 JF **☉**

Reserve Canberra District Shiraz 2018 A pristine and captivating shiraz from every angle. While it appears delicate, with florals and red fruits interspersed with woodsy spices and a whisper of pepper, it's all about refinement. It is also wonderfully savoury. A medium-bodied palate, juicy, with a unison between superfine raw silk tannins and acidity. Complex, compelling and utterly delicious at the same time. Screw cap. 13% alc. **Rating** 95 To 2035 $90 JF

TTTT **Rose Red City Sangiovese 2018** Rating 92 To 2026 $32 JF

Colmar Estate   ★★★★☆

790 Pinnacle Road, Orange, NSW 2800 **Region** Orange
T 0419 977 270 **www.**colmarestate.com.au **Open** W'ends & public hols 10.30–5
Winemaker Chris Derrez, Lucy Maddox **Est.** 2013 **Dozens** 2000 **Vyds** 5.9ha
The inspiration behind the name is clear when you find that owners Bill Shrapnel and his wife Jane have long loved the wines of Alsace: Colmar is the main town in that region. The Shrapnels realised a long-held ambition when they purchased an established, high-altitude (980m) vineyard in May 2013. Everything they have done has turned to gold: notably grafting cabernet sauvignon to pinot noir, merlot to chardonnay, and shiraz to pinot gris. The plantings are now 1.51ha of pinot noir (clones 777, 115 and MV6), 1.25ha of chardonnay (clones 95, 96 and P58), 1.24ha of riesling and lesser quantities of sauvignon blanc, pinot gris and traminer.

TTTTT **Brut 2017** A powerful black-grape-dominant fizz, yet far from heavy. Nor is it sour, in the early-picked Australian vein. Subdued aromas of red cherry underlie billowing notes of biscuit, camomile and cheesecloth, expanding with aeration while really saturating the palate. The finish, long, creamy and seamless. Beautifully integrated on all fronts. Excellent value. Cork. 12% alc. **Rating** 95 $48 NG

TTTT **Block 5 Riesling 2019** Rating 93 To 2026 $35 NG
Chardonnay Pinot Noir 2015 Rating 93 $60 NG
Brut Rosé 2017 Rating 92 $48 NG
Block 6 Riesling 2019 Rating 91 To 2028 $35 NG
Block 2 Chardonnay 2018 Rating 91 To 2026 $45 NG

Comyns & Co   ★★★★☆

Shop 6, 1946 Broke Road, Pokolbin, NSW 2320 **Region** Hunter Valley
T 0400 888 966 **www.**comynsandco.com.au **Open** 7 days 10–4.30
Winemaker Scott Comyns **Est.** 2015 **Dozens** 2000
The stars came into alignment for Scott Comyns in 2018. Having left Pepper Tree Wines in a state of glory at the end of '15, he went out on his own, establishing Comyns & Co with nothing other than his experience as a winemaker for 17 vintages in the Hunter Valley to sustain him. Then Andrew Thomas founded Thomas Wines in the region and Scott joined him as a full-time winemaker, leaving Comyns & Co as a side activity. That has now all

changed, as Missy and Scott have opened a 7-days-a-week cellar door in the Peppers Creek Village, Scott having quit his winemaking role at Thomas Wines.

ŸŸŸŸŸ **Reserve Hunter Valley Shiraz 2019** A classy wine; richer, more intense of flavour and considerably longer than the Estate Shiraz. Floral, with ample iodine and charcuterie scents. A bridge of reduction across the mid palate imparts welcome tension. Nicely played. Pepper, clove and cardamom skitter across a long finish. Screw cap. 13.6% alc. **Rating** 95 **To** 2030 $60 NG
Reserve Hunter Valley Shiraz Pinot Noir 2019 Sappy, savoury, mid weighted, lithe and immensely fresh, despite the palpable extract and ripeness of the vintage. Bing cherry, strawberry and a lightness of being, all pinot. A medicinal varnish note, the riff of the Hunter. Iodine, violet and clove, the eye of shiraz. A sum far greater than these effete parts though. A wine of place. Screw cap. 13% alc. **Rating** 95 **To** 2028 $55 NG
Hunter Valley Pinot Noir Shiraz 2019 A hark to a noble past, steeped in the meld of 2 seemingly incongruous varieties. Lightweight, almost crunchy. Sappy, lifted and lithe. Bing cherry, poached ripe strawberry, orange peel and leather varnish in the background. A straight-up and shameless testimony to what the region did (and still does) exceptionally well. Drink in large draughts! Screw cap. 13% alc. **Rating** 94 **To** 2024 $35 NG

ŸŸŸŸ♀ **Single Vineyard Black Cluster Hunter Valley Shiraz 2019** Rating 93 **To** 2026 $35 NG
Mrs White Hunter Valley Blend 2020 Rating 92 **To** 2022 $28 NG
Hunter Valley Tempranillo 2019 Rating 92 **To** 2023 $35 NG
Hunter Valley Merlot Rosé 2020 Rating 91 **To** 2021 $28 NG

Condie Estate   ★★★★

480 Heathcote-Redesdale Road, Heathcote, Vic 3523 **Region** Heathcote
T 0404 480 422 **www.**condie.com.au **Open** W'ends & public hols 11–5
Winemaker Richie Condie **Est.** 2001 **Dozens** 1500 **Vyds** 6.8ha
Richie Condie worked as a corporate risk manager for a multinational company off the back of a bachelor of commerce degree, but after establishing Condie Estate, completed several viticulture and winemaking courses, including a diploma of winemaking at Dookie. Having first established 2.4ha of shiraz, Richie and wife Rosanne followed with 2ha of sangiovese and 0.8ha of viognier. In 2010 they purchased a 1.6ha vineyard that had been planted in 1990, where they have established a winery and cellar door. Richie says to anyone thinking of going into wine production: 'Go and work in a small vineyard and winery for at least one year before you start out for yourself. You need to understand how much hard physical work is involved in planting a vineyard, looking after it, making the wine, and then selling it.'

ŸŸŸŸ♀ **The Max Shiraz 2017** The Max offers a counter to The Gwen, with fruit picked riper and matured for slightly longer (20 months) in French oak (35% new). The bar is raised here by some smart, precision oak handling and concentration of fruit. This is a rich, generous style of shiraz with a welter of deep, dark forest berries, dates, plums and licorice. Definitely one for the cellar. Screw cap. 14.5% alc. **Rating** 92 **To** 2027 $50 JP
Giarracca Sangiovese 2018 Sangiovese is gaining ground in Heathcote soil. Here, Condie Estate ponders a more complex and deep-fruited expression across a ripe, savoury palate. Classic spiced cherries, bright acid and lithe tannins are in place on the bouquet. The palate is supple and ripe with earthy, leafy notes and a full, mellow charm. Screw cap. 13.5% alc. **Rating** 91 **To** 2026 $30 JP
The Gwen Shiraz 2017 The Gwen differs to The Max principally through the role of 10% seasoned American oak in conjunction with French oak of which 20% is new. That's a fair amount of oak and the show reveals a distinct boot-polish sheen with a savoury spice overlay as a result. Generous in black fruits, plum cake, turned earth, it offers a nice textural ride through to the finish. Screw cap. 14% alc. **Rating** 90 **To** 2025 $30 JP

Cooke Brothers Wines

Shed 8, 89-91 Hill Street, Port Elliot, SA 5212 **Region** South Australia
T 0409 170 684 **www**.cookebrotherswines.com.au **Open** Fri–Mon 11–3
Winemaker Ben Cooke **Est.** 2016 **Dozens** 800

The 3 brothers (eldest to youngest) are: Simon, Jason and Ben. Ben is the partner of Charlotte Hardy, winemaker/owner of Charlotte Dalton Wines. Ben has had a long career in wine: 7 years' retail for Booze Brothers while at university the first time around; 2 vintages at Langhorne Creek 2000–01; and full-time cellar hand/assistant winemaker at Shaw + Smith '03–12 while undertaking 2 degrees externally (wine science and viticulture) at CSU from '04–11. If this were not enough, he had 3 northern Californian vintages at the iconic Williams Selyem winery in '08, '12 and '13. He is now a full-time viticulturist with a vineyard management contracting company that he founded in '12. The elder brothers are not actively involved in the business. Exports to Canada.

ҮҮҮҮҮ **Piccadilly Adelaide Hills Chardonnay 2019** Small-scale and totally attentive winemaking here, just 1 new French puncheon filled with Deanery Vineyard fruit from the Piccadilly Valley, matured for 9 months on full lees. Captivating, ripe stone-fruit aromas and native bush floral fragrance, delicious all the way. Creamily textured, pithy palate grip, with salivating acidity and lengthy finish. Everything good. Screw cap. 13.5% alc. **Rating** 95 **To** 2025 $40 TL

ҮҮҮҮҮ **McLaren Vale Mataro Rosé 2020 Rating** 93 **To** 2023 $30 TL
Adelaide Hills Cabernet Sauvignon 2019 Rating 92 **To** 2026 $35 TL
Langhorne Creek Savagnin 2020 Rating 91 **To** 2023 $30 TL

Cooks Lot

Ferment, 87 Hill Street, Orange, NSW 2800 **Region** Orange
T (02) 9550 3228 **www**.cookslot.com.au **Open** Tues–Sat 11–5
Winemaker Duncan Cook **Est.** 2002 **Dozens** 4000

Duncan Cook began making wines for his eponymous brand in 2002, while undertaking his oenology degree at CSU. He completed his degree in '10 and now works with a number of small growers. Orange is unique in the sense that it has regions at various altitudes; fruit is sourced from vineyards at altitudes that are best suited for the varietal and wine style. Exports to China.

ҮҮҮҮҮ **Iconique Barrique Pinot Noir 2018** This is possibly the finest pinot yet tasted from Orange. Detailed aromas of cherry pith, root spice and bergamot segue a nourishing undertow of autumnal mulch, porcini and umami. The tannins, lithe and diaphanous. Just tactile enough to steer the ship to the light of savouriness. A fine flow of sappy fruit. A bit sweet, to be a pedant. But this is my gripe with virtually all New World pinot and shouldn't deter readers who drink it. Long and energetic. Quite brilliant. Screw cap. 13.5% alc. **Rating** 95 **To** 2025 $50 NG

ҮҮҮҮҮ **Iconique Barrique Chardonnay 2017 Rating** 93 **To** 2026 $50 NG

Coola Road

Private Mail Bag 14, Mount Gambier, SA 5291 **Region** Mount Gambier
T 0487 700 422 **www**.coolaroad.com
Winemaker John Innes **Est.** 2013 **Dozens** 1000 **Vyds** 103.5ha

Thomas and Sally Ellis are the current generation of the Ellis family, who have owned the Coola grazing property on which the vineyard is now established for over 160 years. They began planting the vineyard in the late 1990s with pinot noir, and have since extended the range to include sauvignon blanc, chardonnay, riesling and pinot gris. As the largest vineyard owner in the region, they decided they should have some of the grapes vinified to bring further recognition to the area. If global warming should increase significantly, the very cool region will stand to gain.

ŸŸŸŸŸ **Single Vineyard Mount Gambier Pinot Noir 2017** Very good colour; has excellent varietal expression engendered by a cool vintage in a very cool region. Red and dark cherry fruit has a silky web of spicy/savoury complexity. A really attractive pinot at a giveaway price. Screw cap. 12.5% alc. **Rating** 95 **To** 2030 $28 JH ✪

ŸŸŸŸŸ **Single Vineyard Mount Gambier Chardonnay 2019 Rating** 92 **To** 2029 $22 JH ✪
Single Vineyard Mount Gambier Riesling 2018 Rating 90 **To** 2026 $20 JF ✪

Coolangatta Estate   ★★★★☆

1335 Bolong Road, Shoalhaven Heads, NSW 2535 **Region** Shoalhaven Coast
T (02) 4448 7131 **www**.coolangattaestate.com.au **Open** 7 days 10–5
Winemaker Tyrrell's **Est.** 1988 **Dozens** 5000 **Vyds** 10.5ha
Coolangatta Estate is part of a 150ha resort with accommodation, restaurants, golf course, etc. Some of the oldest buildings were convict-built in 1822. The standard of viticulture is exceptionally high (immaculate Scott Henry trellising) and the contract winemaking is wholly professional. Coolangatta has a habit of bobbing up with medals at Sydney and Canberra wine shows, including gold medals for its mature semillons. In its own backyard, Coolangatta won the trophy for Best Wine of Show at the South Coast Wine Show for 19 out of the show's 20 years.

ŸŸŸŸŸ **Individual Vineyard Wollstonecraft Semillon 2017** A intensely flavoured wine of flinty length and great potential, still tightly furled despite bottle age. A bit of unresolved CO_2 to boot. This stands to age very well. A melody of citrus, gun smoke, spa salts and pungent mineral undertones, from pumice to chalk. The finish, long and strident with a savoury bitter accent. Impressive. Screw cap. 12% alc. **Rating** 93 **To** 2031 $40 NG
Aged Release Individual Vineyard Wollstonecraft Semillon 2019 This has aged very well and is now at its apogee. Lime bitters, buttered toast, quince marmalade and honeydew melon. Again, lacking the racy authority and puckering austerity of expressions from the Hunter, but mouth-coating, flavourful and very ready. Screw cap. 11% alc. **Rating** 91 **To** 2024 $60 NG

Coombe Yarra Valley   ★★★★

673–675 Maroondah Highway, Coldstream, Vic 3770 **Region** Yarra Valley
T (03) 9739 0173 **www**.coombeyarravalley.com.au **Open** Mon, Wed–Sun 10–5
Winemaker Travis Bush **Est.** 1999 **Dozens** 10000 **Vyds** 60ha
Coombe Yarra Valley is one of the largest and oldest family estates in the Yarra Valley. Once home to world famous opera singer Dame Nellie Melba, it continues to be owned and operated by her descendants, the Vestey family. Coombe's wines come from 60ha of vineyards planted in 1998 on the site of some of the original vineyards planted in the 1850s. The renovated motor house and stable block now contain the cellar door, providore, gallery and restaurant which overlook the gardens. Exports to the UK and Japan.

ŸŸŸŸŸ **Tribute Series Pinot Noir 2019** An impressive wine any way you look at it. Beautifully fragrant, all florals and forest floor, with requisite dark cherries and spices. It has a presence but is not a powerful wine – the palate is smooth, supple and the tannins are oh-so slinky. Screw cap. 13.8% alc. **Rating** 95 **To** 2032 $60 JF
Tribute Series Chardonnay 2019 A bit of a yin-and-yang wine, powerful and flavoursome yet has a fine line of acidity tightening everything in its wake. White nectarines spiced with cinnamon, lemon/grapefruit drizzled with creamed honey and nutty lees adding another layer. The oak adds a sensation of sweetness across the rich, textured palate. Screw cap. 13.5% alc. **Rating** 94 **To** 2029 $60 JF

Cooper Burns

494 Research Road, Nuriootpa, SA 5355 **Region** Barossa Valley
T (08) 7513 7606 **www.**cooperburns.com.au **Open** Fri–Mon 11–4
Winemaker Russell Burns **Est.** 2004 **Dozens** 3000
Established in 2004, Cooper Burns was the side project of Mark Cooper and Russell Burns as they worked their winemaking day jobs at Treasury Wine Estates and Torbreck respectively. In '17 they established their winery at Nuriootpa and Russell left Torbreck to work full-time at Cooper Burns. The old homestead garage was renovated in '19 and now serves as the cellar door within the grounds of the winery. Wines produced are Shiraz, Grenache, GSM, Cabernet Sauvignon, Rosé, Riesling and Chardonnay. Exports to the US, Norway and Hong Kong.

ŸŸŸŸŸ **Barossa Valley Grenache Shiraz Mataro 2019** An elegantly medium-bodied blend in which the lead role of grenache is reinforced by carefully judged whole-bunch fermentation. Dark raspberries and fresh strawberries are fragranced with rose petal and musk, underscored by fine-grained tannins that carry a long and eloquent conclusion. Classy Barossa grenache. Screw cap. 14.5% alc. **Rating** 94 To 2024 $30 TS ✪

ŸŸŸŸŸ **Reserve Barossa Valley Shiraz 2018 Rating** 93 To 2033 $150 TS
Reserve Barossa Valley Cabernet Sauvignon 2018 Rating 93 To 2028 $100 TS

Cooter & Cooter

82 Almond Grove Road, Whites Valley, SA 5172 **Region** McLaren Vale
T 0438 766 178 **www.**cooter.com.au
Winemaker James Cooter, Kimberly Cooter **Est.** 2012 **Dozens** 800 **Vyds** 23ha
The cursive script on the Cooter & Cooter wine labels was that of various Cooter family businesses operating in SA since 1847. James comes from a family with more than 20 years in the wine industry. Kimberley is also a hands-on winemaker; her father is Walter Clappis, a veteran McLaren Vale winemaker. Their vineyard, on the southern slopes of Whites Valley, has 18ha of shiraz and 3ha of cabernet sauvignon planted in 1996, and 2ha of old-vine grenache planted in the '50s. They also buy Clare Valley grapes to make riesling.

ŸŸŸŸŸ **McLaren Vale Shiraz 2019** Artisanal and rewarding producer delivering wines of great value, ample fruit and – most importantly, somewhere this warm – properly extracted tannins. Boysenberry, mulberry, licorice and blackberry. Juicy, grapey and pulpy, with the teeming fruit galvanised into a savoury whole by that prized slatey tannic kit, gently briary and herbal. Screw cap. 14% alc. **Rating** 93 To 2028 $25 NG ✪
McLaren Vale Grenache 2020 Of the zeitgeist. Blood plum, orange zest, kirsch and a reductive belt of violet. Acidity, soused in turmeric, tamarind, clove and white pepper, finds an easygoing confluence with spindly tannins. Imminently approachable. Screw cap. 14% alc. **Rating** 92 To 2025 $32 NG

Coppabella of Tumbarumba

424 Tumbarumba Road, Tumbarumba, NSW 2653 (postal) **Region** Tumbarumba
T (02) 6382 7997 **www.**coppabella.com.au
Winemaker Jason Brown **Est.** 2011 **Dozens** 4000 **Vyds** 71.9ha
Coppabella is owned by Jason and Alecia Brown, owners of the highly successful Moppity Vineyards in Hilltops. They became aware of the quality of Tumbarumba chardonnay and pinot noir, in particular the quality of the grapes from the 71ha Coppabella vineyard, when purchasing grapes for Moppity Vineyards. This was the second vineyard established (in 1993) by the region's founder, Ian Cowell, but frost and other problems led him to lease the vineyard to Southcorp, until 2007. The reversion of the management of the vineyard coincided with several failed vintages, and the owner decided to close the vineyard and remove the vines. In October '11, at the last moment, the Browns purchased the vineyard and have since invested heavily in it, rehabilitating the vines and grafting a number of blocks to the earlier

ripening Dijon clones of pinot noir and chardonnay. Coppabella is run as an entirely separate venture from Moppity.

Ϙϙϙϙϙ **The Crest Single Vineyard Pinot Noir 2019** The colour is somewhat dilute and forward yet the wine is fresh. There's a core of sweet, soft and juicy fruit, coated in spices and tethered to ripe tannins. It's not big, but it feels rich and velvety. An autumnal fragrance pops out with some air and the flavours continue to unfurl. Screw cap. 13.5% alc. **Rating** 91 **To** 2024 $35 JF

Corang Estate   ★★★★

533 Oallen Road, Nerriga, NSW 2622 **Region** Southern New South Wales
T 0419 738 548 **www.**corangestate.com.au **Open** By appt
Winemaker Michael Bynon, Alex McKay **Est.** 2018 **Dozens** 1000 **Vyds** 1ha
This is the nascent business of Michael and Jill Bynon. Michael has been in the wine industry in one role or another for 30 years, attending Roseworthy Agricultural College and moving from a marketing career to join the senior corporate ranks. Most impressive of all is that he has passed the master of wine tasting examination. Jill was a linguist and marketing professional, fluent in French, having spent much time in France before moving to Australia from her native Scotland in 2003. It was here that she met Michael, and having bought a bush block and erected a small house, they planted 0.5ha each of shiraz and tempranillo in '18. They also purchase grapes from high-altitude vineyards comparable to that of their own, which is at 600m.

Ϙϙϙϙϙ **Hilltops Shiraz 2019** Floral scented, sweetly fruited, lightly spiced and well priced. You want more? Expect a dash of pepper and cinnamon with charry oak in the mix too, but balanced. There's a whiff of prosciutto so it does have appealing savoury tones to tame the intense fruit. Full bodied, plush tannins and a slightly bitter finish. Screw cap. 14.5% alc. **Rating** 92 **To** 2027 $25 JF ✪
Hilltops Tempranillo 2019 I love the simplicity of this. It's also an utterly delicious drink-now style full of juicy red cherries with a smattering of woodsy spices. The cranberry tartness of the acidity keeps it lively and fresh. Screw cap. 13.5% alc. **Rating** 92 **To** 2025 $25 JF ✪
Reserve Selection Canberra Shiraz 2019 Fabulous dark purple hue. There's a lot to get out of this – the savouriness, the depth of fruit flavour, the general suppleness across the palate. The charry oak lurks in every corner and dries out the finish – hopefully that will dissipate in time. Screw cap. 13.5% alc. **Rating** 90 **To** 2030 $35 JF

Ϙϙϙϙ **Tumbarumba Chardonnay 2019 Rating** 89 **To** 2025 $25 JF

Corduroy   ★★★★

226 Mosquito Hill Road, Mosquito Hill, SA 5214 **Region** Adelaide Hills
T 0405 123 272 **www.**corduroywines.com.au
Winemaker Phillip LeMessurier **Est.** 2009 **Dozens** 320
Phillip and Eliza LeMessurier have moved to the Adelaide Hills, but are continuing the model they originally created in the Hunter under the tutelage of Andrew Thomas at Thomas Wines. In the new environment, they are matching place and variety to good effect.

Ϙϙϙϙϙ **Bonnie's Blend Semillon Chardonnay 2019** Field grass notes to begin. There's nice white stone fruits and subtle texturals with underlying acidity tracking through the palate. Screw cap. 12.8% alc. **Rating** 91 **To** 2025 $30 TL

Ϙϙϙϙ **Single Vineyard Adelaide Hills Chardonnay 2019 Rating** 89 **To** 2025 $30 TL
Single Vineyard Adelaide Hills Pinot Noir 2019 Rating 89 **To** 2025 TL

Coriole ★★★★★

Chaffeys Road, McLaren Vale, SA 5171 **Region** McLaren Vale
T (08) 8323 8305 **www**.coriole.com **Open** Mon–Fri 10–5, w'ends & public hols 11–5
Winemaker Duncan Lloyd **Est.** 1967 **Dozens** 30 000 **Vyds** 48.5ha
While Coriole was established in 1967, the cellar door and gardens date back to 1860, when the original farm houses that now constitute the cellar door were built. The oldest shiraz forming part of the estate plantings was planted in 1917, and since '85, Coriole has been an Australian pioneer of sangiovese and the Italian white variety fiano. More recently, it has planted picpoul, adding to grenache blanc, negroamaro, sagrantino, montepulciano and prosecco. Coriole celebrated its 50th anniversary in 2019, presumably counting from the year of its first commercial wine release. Exports to all major markets.

🍷🍷🍷🍷🍷 **Rubato Reserve McLaren Vale Fiano 2020** This is a superb wine. No two ways about it. Possibly the finest fiano in the country, attesting to the nobility of the variety as much as the promise it shows in the Vale. A monument of mineral pungency, offset by a shimmering veil of tangerine, quince, lemon balm, orange verbena, anise and apricot pith. Ripe. Viscous. Real drive. Phenomenal length. Power, vivacity and weightlessness all at once. Stunning! Screw cap. 13% alc. **Rating** 96 **To** 2024 $50 NG ✪ ♥

Lloyd Reserve McLaren Vale Shiraz 2018 A concentrated wine with an impressive thrust of vinosity. A firm chassis of alloyed tannin and salty acidity corral blue/black-fruit aspersions, smoked-meat barrel-ferment aromas and iodine into a sheath of power and tension. The oak, nestled into the fray. This will live long. Screw cap. 14.3% alc. **Rating** 96 **To** 2035 $110 NG

Vita Reserve McLaren Vale Sangiovese 2019 Very fine! I have been following the ebbs, potholes and flows of sangiovese here for a long time. This, more akin to an elevated expression rather than a grassroots chianti. Depth, vinosity and the edgy carriage of tannins and bright acid crunch that sets apart better wines, all raring. Sapid Bing cherry, thyme, mint and other garden herbs clatter along that jittery thread of tannin. Mocha notes assuage with a dollop of generosity, across a long finish. A confident evolution in full stride. Screw cap. 14.4% alc. **Rating** 95 **To** 2028 $65 NG

The Riesling Block Single Vineyard McLaren Vale Shiraz 2019 This has a noble detail that transcends its Soloist and Estate siblings. Terra Rossa. Meaning, a limestone substrata. A finessed tannic weave is melded to a mineral chord, pulling dark/blue fruits and licorice flavours long. Standard baking spice and cocoa oak. Yet the attraction lies in the texture. Screw cap. 14.3% alc. **Rating** 94 **To** 2032 $60 NG

Estate Grown McLaren Vale Grenache 2019 This is very good bush-vine grenache, acknowledging the need to embed our softer, warm-climatic expressions with tannic mettle derived from a proper extraction regime. Medium bodied, with an explosion of cranberry, blood plum, kirsch, cumquat and pomegranate scents. À point! Savoury and fibrous, the tannic edginess mitigating an inherent pulse of sweet fruit across a long, detailed finish. Just 2 barrels made. Screw cap. 14% alc. **Rating** 94 **To** 2026 $40 NG

🍷🍷🍷🍷🍷 **McLaren Vale Dancing Fig 2019 Rating** 93 **To** 2026 $27 NG ✪
The Soloist Single Vineyard McLaren Vale Shiraz 2019 Rating 93 **To** 2032 $50 NG
Willunga 1920 Single Vineyard McLaren Vale Shiraz 2019 Rating 93 **To** 2033 $110 NG
Pettigala Single Vineyard McLaren Vale Shiraz 2019 Rating 93 **To** 2032 $60 NG
McLaren Vale Montepulciano 2019 Rating 93 **To** 2026 $32 NG
McLaren Vale Nero 2020 Rating 92 **To** 2023 $28 NG
McLaren Vale Piquepoul 2020 Rating 92 **To** 2022 $27 NG
Estate McLaren Vale Shiraz 2019 Rating 92 **To** 2028 $32 NG
McLaren Vale Sangiovese 2019 Rating 92 **To** 2023 $28 NG

McLaren Vale Fiano 2020 Rating 91 To 2024 $27 NG
Redstone McLaren Vale Shiraz 2019 Rating 90 To 2024 $20 NG ✪
Estate McLaren Vale Cabernet Sauvignon 2019 Rating 90 To 2030
$32 NG

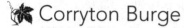

Corryton Burge ★★★★★

161 Murray Street, Tanunda, SA 5352 **Region** Barossa Valley
T (08) 563 7575 **www.**corrytonburge.com **Open** Mon–Fri 12–4, Sat 12–5
Winemaker Trent Burge, Andrew Cockram and Matthew Pellew **Est.** 2020 **Dozens** 4000
A new label with a long history. Siblings Trent (winemaker) and Amelia (marketing) Burge are
6th-generation Barossans. Trent has spent almost 2 decades working in the family vineyards
and winery, creating his Barossa Boy Wines brand; Amelia returned to the business in 2019,
also launching her own Amelia Burge Sparkling Wine range. Their shared enterprise takes
its name from the family's grand 1845 Corryton Park Homestead in Eden Valley. Sourcing
is from the Burge family's 300ha of vines in southern and central Barossa and Adelaide Hills,
and a network of 20 growers as far flung as the Coal River Valley in Tasmania. Their father
Grant Burge plays a mentoring role, and the winemaking team at the family's Illaparra winery
is also acknowledged. With this lineage, it's no surprise the brand has hit the ground running,
appropriately led by a cracking Cabernet Sauvignon, long the hero of the Corryton Park
vineyard. (TS)

🍷🍷🍷🍷🍷 **Percival Norman Barossa Valley Shiraz 2019** There's a lot to love here.
Consummate balance of depth, brightness, succulence and structure, assembled
with care and polish. Pristine black fruits, violets and licorice take the lead, with
the dark chocolate and coffee bean of French oak in rightful second place. Strong,
fine-ground tannins set off impressive endurance. Screw cap. 15% alc. **Rating** 95
To 2039 $45 TS
The Brigadier Barossa Cabernet Sauvignon 2018 The Burge Family's
beautiful and expansive Corryton Park Vineyard in Eden Valley has been the
source of one of Grant Burge's finest cabernets, and it appropriately leads the
new portfolio of his children. The contrast of density and brightness here is
something to behold, reverberating with exact blackcurrant and cassis fruit of
exemplary varietal precision. Wonderful fragrance of violets and rose petals
declares cabernet's floral aspirations. Crafted for the cellar, energised by brilliant
peals of acidity and confident, firm, fine tannins. Benchmark. Screw cap. 14.5% alc.
Rating 95 To 2043 $45 TS

🍷🍷🍷🍷🍷 **Barossa Shiraz 2018** Rating 92 To 2026 $28 TS
Cornelian Bay Tasmania Pinot Noir 2019 Rating 91 To 2029 $45 TS
Barossa Valley Grenache 2020 Rating 91 To 2022 $28 TS
Eden Valley Riesling 2020 Rating 90 To 2022 $28 TS
The Patroness Adelaide Hills Chardonnay 2020 Rating 90 To 2025
$28 TL

Corymbia ★★★★☆

30 Nolan Avenue, Upper Swan, WA 6069 **Region** Swan Valley
T 0439 973 195 **www.**corymbiawine.com.au **Open** By appt
Winemaker Robert Mann, Genevieve Mann **Est.** 2013 **Dozens** 900 **Vyds** 3.5ha
Rob Mann is a 6th-generation winemaker from the second-oldest wine region in Australia.
He was chief winemaker at Cape Mentelle in Margaret River, where he and wife Genevieve
lived. Rob's father had established a family vineyard in the Swan Valley more than 25 years
ago, where they both worked together in Rob's early years as a winemaker. Genevieve worked
as a winemaker in her native South Africa, as well as France, California and South Australia
before meeting Rob and moving to Margaret River in '07 to be winemaker for Howard Park.
Beween them they now have 2 children and 3.5ha in Margaret River and the Swan Valley,
planted to 1.6ha chenin blanc, 0.4ha tempranillo, 0.2ha malbec and 1.3ha cabernet sauvignon.
Exports to Singapore.

🍷🍷🍷🍷 **Margaret River Cabernet Sauvignon 2019** Luminescent ruby with glints of purple and black. It shines as if with its own dense internal light. The telltale ripe and chewy tannin profile handled masterfully by Rob Mann, with pristine fruit and great length of flavour. An exceptionally elegant, powder-fine cabernet, part of the new Margaret River breed. A massive, resounding YES. Screw cap. 13.3% alc. **Rating** 97 **To** 2035 $64 EL **☉**

🍷🍷🍷🍷 **Swan Valley Chenin Blanc 2020** Fruit from Rocket's vineyard. This is pure, pristine, texturally edgy, and layered with all the good things: sheepy lanolin, beeswax, apricots at the height of summer, green apple, crushed limestone and saline acidity. It has rivulets of flavour that course over the tongue … it's brilliant. Finesse and poise from such a warm part of town, very impressive. Screw cap. 12.5% alc. **Rating** 95 **To** 2036 $30 EL **☉**
Rocket's Vineyard Swan Valley Tempranillo Malbec 2019 'Engaging' is an understatement. This is classically structured with dense, chewy tannins that ensconce the ripe and frankly seductive fruit in a blanket of texture. The wine is earthy, layered, glossy and succulent – what an amalgam of emotion and sensation. Yes. Screw cap. 13.9% alc. **Rating** 95 **To** 2035 $42 EL

Coulter Wines

6 Third Avenue, Tanunda, SA 5352 (postal) **Region** Adelaide Hills
T 0448 741 773 **www.coulterwines.com**
Winemaker Chris Coulter **Est.** 2015 **Dozens** 800
Chris Coulter had a 22-year previous life as a chef, but fell in love with wine in the early 1990s and managed to fit in a vintage at Coldstream Hills as a cellar rat. In 2007 he undertook a winemaking degree and secured work with Australian Vintage Limited, gaining large-volume winemaking experience first in Mildura and then at (the then) Chateau Yaldara in the Barossa Valley, remaining there through '14 under Australian Vintage Limited, and thereafter as part of the 1847 winemaking team after its acquisition of the Yaldara site. Coulter Wines was born in the '15 vintage as a side project, making wines from another universe – nothing other than SO$_2$ is added, movements are by gravity and the wine is unfiltered where practicable. He purchases and hand-picks grapes from vineyards mainly in the Adelaide Hills. Exports to Singapore.

🍷🍷🍷🍷 **C1 Adelaide Hills Chardonnay 2020** An immaculate balancing act of bright and vibrant chardonnay fruit with the lightest touch of empathetic oak, finishing with delicious and encouraging, mouth-watering textures. Screw cap. 12.7% alc. **Rating** 95 **To** 2026 $30 TL **☉**

🍷🍷🍷🍷 **C4 Experimental Adelaide Grenache 2020 Rating** 93 **To** 2025 $25 TL **☉**
C2 Adelaide Sangiovese 2020 Rating 93 **To** 2025 $28 TL
C4 Experimental Tempranillo 2020 Rating 93 **To** 2025 $22 TL **☉**

Cowaramup Wines

19 Tassel Road, Cowaramup, WA 6284 **Region** Margaret River
T (08) 9755 5195 **www.cowaramupwines.com.au** **Open** By appt
Winemaker Naturaliste Vintners (Bruce Dukes) **Est.** 1996 **Dozens** 3000 **Vyds** 11ha
Russell and Marilyn Reynolds run a biodynamic vineyard with the aid of sons Cameron (viticulturist) and Anthony (assistant winemaker). Plantings began in 1996 and include merlot, cabernet sauvignon, shiraz, semillon, chardonnay and sauvignon blanc. Notwithstanding low yields and the discipline that biodynamic grapegrowing entails, wine prices are modest. Wines are released under the Cowaramup and Clown Fish labels.

🍷🍷🍷🍷 **Clown Fish Margaret River Sauvignon Blanc Semillon 2020** Gooseberry, sugar snap, jasmine florals and fine chalky phenolics. This is pretty, zesty and energetic – perfect summertime drinking. Screw cap. 13.5% alc. **Rating** 93 **To** 2024 $20 **☉**

Reserve Limited Edition Ellensbrook Margaret River Chardonnay 2018
Matured for 12 months in French oak. Ripe fruit is in concert with salty acid, wrapped in a cloak of soft oak. All things in place, with the added bonus of a bitter phenolic skeleton that gives it structure and interest. Screw cap. 13.5% alc. **Rating** 92 **To** 2027 $30 EL
Clown Fish Margaret River Sauvignon Blanc 2020 Stainless-steel ferment has created a light, bright, juicy and concentrated sauvignon blanc. Pretty, if uncomplicated summer drinking. Screw cap. 13.5% alc. **Rating** 90 **To** 2023 $20 EL ✪

Coward & Black Vineyards

448 Tom Cullity Drive, Wilyabrup, WA 6280 **Region** Margaret River
T (08) 9755 6355 **www.cowardandblack.com.au Open** 7 days 9–5
Winemaker Clive Otto (Contract) **Est.** 1998 **Dozens** 1100 **Vyds** 9.5ha
Patrick Coward and Martin Black have been friends since they were 5 years old. They acquired a property directly opposite Ashbrook and on the same road as Vasse Felix, and began the slow establishment of a dry-grown vineyard; a second block followed 5 years later. In all there are 2.5ha each of cabernet sauvignon and shiraz, and 1.5ha each of chardonnay, semillon and sauvignon blanc. The cellar door is integrated with another of their businesses, The Margaret River Providore, which sells produce from their organic garden and olive grove.

♟♟♟♟♟ **Lady Margo Margaret River Rosé 2020** Hand-picked shiraz, fermented in stainless steel. Soft blush salmon in the glass, the palate floods with watermelon, strawberry, crushed oyster shell and rosewater. The acidity is taut and crunchy, no doubt retained by the earlier pick (evident in the very low alcohol). Pretty, uncomplicated, made for immediate drinking and pleasure. Screw cap. 11.9% alc. **Rating** 91 **To** 2023 $29.95 EL
Margaret River Chardonnay 2019 Struck match and flinty nose, the oak shows it face and sticks around throughout the finish, colouring the experience of the concentrated fruit that came before it. Very worked. Screw cap. 13.7% alc. **Rating** 90 **To** 2025 $35 EL
Winston Margaret River Cabernet Shiraz 2019 Juicy and quite delicious. Lacking in any serious structure or length, this is fine boned and supple – so much so that it almost lends itself towards a slight chill. If ever there was a summer cabernet, this is it. Screw cap. 13.3% alc. **Rating** 90 **To** 2027 $35 EL

♟♟♟♟ **Margaret River Sauvignon Blanc 2020 Rating** 88 **To** 2023 $25 EL
Sweetness & Light Margaret River 2020 Rating 88 **To** 2024 $22 EL

Crabtree Watervale Wines

North Terrace, Watervale, SA 5452 **Region** Clare Valley
T (08) 8843 0069 **www.crabtreewines.com.au Open** 7 days 10.30–4.30
Winemaker Kerri Thompson **Est.** 1984 **Dozens** 5500 **Vyds** 12.1ha
Crabtree is situated in the heart of the historic and iconic Watervale district, the tasting room and courtyard (set in the produce cellar of the original 1850s homestead) looking out over the estate vineyard. The winery was founded in 1984 by Robert Crabtree, who built a considerable reputation for medal-winning riesling, shiraz and cabernet sauvignon. In 2007 it was purchased by an independent group of wine enthusiasts, and the winery firmly continues in the tradition of estate-grown premium wines. Robert remains a shareholder.

♟♟♟♟♟ **Robert Crabtree Shiraz Cabernet 2017** Like a comfy chair, it doesn't take long to settle in and enjoy this full-bodied, archetypal Clare red. It has all the dark fruits and spice, the dark chocolate, the regional mint, the coffee-ground tannins and more to realise all's well. Drinking brilliantly now, but will garner more complexity in time. Screw cap. 14% alc. **Rating** 95 **To** 2032 $50 JF

♟♟♟♟♟ **Robert Crabtree Riesling 2020 Rating** 93 **To** 2030 $45 JF
Grand Clare Valley Muscat NV Rating 93 $35 JF

Watervale Shiraz 2017 Rating 91 To 2027 $32 JF
Watervale Riesling 2020 Rating 90 To 2028 $32 JF

cradle of hills

76 Rogers Road, Sellicks Hill, SA 5174 **Region** McLaren Vale
T 0418 826 206 **www**.cradle-of-hills.com.au **Open** 7 days by appt
Winemaker Paul Smith **Est.** 2009 **Dozens** 800 **Vyds** 6.51ha
Paul Smith's introduction to wine was an unlikely one: the Royal Australian Navy and, in
particular, the wardroom cellar at the tender age of 19. A career change took Paul to the world
of high-performance sports, and he met his horticulturist wife Tracy. From 2005 they travelled
the world with their 2 children, spending a couple of years in Europe, working in and learning
about the great wine regions and about how fine wine is made. Paul secured a winemaking
diploma and they now have 3.46ha of shiraz, 2.67ha of cabernet sauvignon and 0.38ha of
mourvèdre, supplementing this with purchased grenache and mourvèdre.

 # Craft vs Science

John Harris Drive, Nuriootpa, SA 5355 **Region** Barossa Valley
T 0434 027 009 **www**.craftvsscience.com.au
Winemaker Stuart Bloomfield **Est.** 3030 **Dozens** 500
The brand-new first solo pursuit of young winemaker and Dell'uva cellar hand Stuart
Bloomfield, following a dozen vintages in the Barossa, Hunter Valley, Los Caneros, Napa
and NZ. An inaugural release of Grenache, Touriga Naçional and G.S.T. Red Blend landed
in 2021, with Cabernet and Shiraz set to follow. Volumes are tiny, typically just 1 or 2 barrels
of each label, and fruit is sourced in Bethany from mostly young vines of Stuart's parents-
in-law, Rob and Anna Schrapel. Contract-crushed and pressed at Bethany Wines, Stuart
matures his wines in Schrapel's shed. Larger proportions of new oak than usual for young-vine
fruit is seamlessly integrated, thanks to fermentation in barrels – a logistically tricky craft that
Stuart picked up at Provenance Vineyards in the Napa, and seems to have mastered in his first
commercial attempt. Classy labels adorn sensibly lightweight bottles. (TS)

ΨΨΨΨΨ **Barossa Valley Grenache 2020** A crunchy and spicy grenache that
showcases the bright, varietal raspberry and strawberry fruit of the variety. Barrel
fermentation (in 60% new light-toast French oak puncheons and barriques)
provides impressive integration of new oak, even in young-vine fruit. Fine-grained,
powdery tannins and nicely integrated acidity offer balance and poise to a short
finish. Diam. 14.7% alc. **Rating** 90 **To** 2022 $50 TS

ΨΨΨΨ **Barossa Valley Touriga Nacional 2020** Rating 89 To 2025 $50 TS

Craiglee ★★★★★

785 Sunbury Road, Sunbury, Vic 3429 **Region** Sunbury
T (03) 9744 4489 **www**.craigleevineyard.com **Open** 1st Sun each month Feb–Dec
Winemaker Patrick Carmody **Est.** 1976 **Dozens** 2000 **Vyds** 9.5ha
A winery with a proud 19th-century record, Craiglee recommenced winemaking in 1976
after a prolonged hiatus. Produces one of the finest cool-climate shiraz wines in Australia,
redolent of cherry, licorice and spice in the better (warmer) vintages; lighter bodied in the
cooler ones. Mature vines and improved viticulture have made the wines more consistent over
the past 10 years or so.

ΨΨΨΨΨ **Sunbury Shiraz 2017** Pure, unadulterated Craiglee shiraz. Nothing like it. It's
the fragrance, the confluence of dark and red fruit, the grind of black pepper, the
thyme and its savoury nature. It retains a certain elegance and length across the
more medium-bodied palate. Fresh acidity and grainy tannins neatly in tow. Lovely
now, even better in years to come. Screw cap. 13.5% alc. **Rating** 95 **To** 2032
$60 JF

ΨΨΨΨΨ **Sunbury Chardonnay 2019** Rating 93 To 2028 $40 JF
JADV Sunbury Shiraz 2017 Rating 90 To 2025 $45 JF

Craigmoor | Montrose   ★★★★★

Craigmoor Road, Mudgee, NSW 2850 **Region** Mudgee
T (02) 6372 2208 **www**.craigmoor.com.au **Open** Thurs–Mon from 11am
Winemaker Debbie Lauritz **Est.** 1858 **Vyds** 25ha
Established in 1858, Craigmoor is Mudgee's oldest vineyard and winery. The Oatley family
has long owned vineyards in Mudgee and in 2006 they acquired the Montrose winery and
the Craigmoor cellar door and restaurant. Montrose was established in 1974 by Carlo Salteri
and Franco Belgiorno-Nettis, Italian engineers with a love of fine wine. Coincidentally they
were friends of the Oatleys – the 2 families developing their Montrose and Rosemount
wineries almost simultaneously. The cellar door is a 5-min drive from the centre of Mudgee,
surrounded by picturesque vines and gum trees on the banks of Eurunderee Creek.

Craigow   ★★★★

528 Richmond Road, Cambridge, Tas 7170 **Region** Southern Tasmania
T 0418 126 027 **www**.craigow.com.au **Open** W'ends 11–4 or by appt
Winemaker Frogmore Creek (Alain Rousseau), Tasmanian Vintners **Est.** 1989
Dozens 800 **Vyds** 8.75ha
Hobart surgeon Barry Edwards and wife Cathy have moved from being grapegrowers with
only 1 wine to a portfolio of impressive wines – with long-lived Riesling of particular quality,
closely attended by Pinot Noir – while continuing to sell most of their grapes.

🍷🍷🍷🍷🍷 Chardonnay 2019 Terrific Tasmanian chardonnay at a cracking price. Elegant,
honed and energetic, with every detail in the right place. Plucked at the perfect
instant to define precise lemon, fig and white peach. Top-shelf French oak. Just
the right sprinkle of struck-flint complexity. It races to the horizon in a glittering
fanfare of crystalline acidity. Screw cap. 13% alc. **Rating** 95 **To** 2034 $35 TS ✪
Pinot Noir 2019 Characterful, savoury and composed. Bright purple hue. Black
fruits of satsuma plum skin and blackberries meet layers of savoury dried herbs,
confidently supported by fine oak tannins. In time its savoury mood blossoms
magnificently into delightful, spicy berry-fruit allure. A vintage for the cellar.
Screw cap. 13.5% alc. **Rating** 94 **To** 2039 $50 TS

Crawford River Wines   ★★★★★

741 Hotspur Upper Road, Condah, Vic 3303 **Region** Henty
T (03) 5578 2267 **www**.crawfordriverwines.com **Open** By appt
Winemaker John and Belinda Thomson **Est.** 1975 **Dozens** 3000 **Vyds** 11ha
Time flies, and it seems incredible that Crawford River celebrated its 45th birthday in 2020.
Once a tiny outpost in a little-known wine region, Crawford River is now a foremost
producer of riesling (and other excellent wines), originally thanks to the unremitting attention
to detail and skill of its founder and winemaker, John Thomson. His eldest daughter Belinda
has worked alongside her father part-time from '04–11 (full-time between June '05–08) and
has been chief winemaker since '12. She obtained her viticulture and oenology degree in '02
and has experience in Marlborough (NZ), Bordeaux (France), Tuscany (Italy) and the Nahe
(Germany). Between '08 and '16 she was a senior winemaker/technical director of a winery
in Rueda, Spain. Younger daughter Fiona is in charge of sales and marketing. Exports to the
UK and Japan.

🍷🍷🍷🍷🍷 Riesling 2020 Hard to believe this complex, astounding riesling is so, so, very
young. It comes fully formed, in balance, bursting with freshness, purity of
varietal expression and beautiful fruit. And, yes, by usual standards it is riper, with
stone fruits joining lemon drop, grapefruit and baked apple. But it brings added
complexity and texture, which joins with a tingly acidity to produce something
memorable. Screw cap. 13.5% alc. **Rating** 96 **To** 2030 $48 JP ✪
Young Vines Riesling 2020 So youthful, so fresh in a squeezed juice kind of
way. Lemon jelly crystals, lemon drop, grapefruit pith, orange peel, lime blossom,
in scent and on the palate. Nice texture in building phase. But, as usual, the co-star

with equal billing in this production is the crunchy, tangy acidity. Screw cap. 13.5% alc. **Rating** 95 **To** 2031 $35 JP ◐

Museum Release Riesling 2014 Utterly beguiling aromas exhibiting class all the way and, it must be stressed, very much with time on its side. Buttered toast, honey, spiced apple, lemon curd with such impressive concentration, but at the core is a bounty of natural, zesty acidity that lifts the entire tasting experience. Screw cap. 13% alc. **Rating** 95 **To** 2029 $80 JP

Cabernet Sauvignon 2015 Co-winemaker Belinda Thomson has been working on building complexity and density in her cabernet for some time. This 2015 cabernet is the result. Must be considered too early for middle age, such is the taut, coiled profile. Loves a good, long airing before unleashing violets, blackcurrant, tobacco leaf, cedar and red earth. Savoury tannins build a strong foundation. Diam. 14.5% alc. **Rating** 94 **To** 2030 $66 JP

Cabernet Sauvignon 2014 A most youthful 6yo still in the building phase. Henty cabernets are not that common – this lovely aged example gives grounds for more exploration. Dark red, deeply hued. A waft of florals, elevated violet, blackberry leaf, earth and sweet-spiced oak. Resolutely cabernet in structure, with tannic grain and grip, but also elegantly shaped with sustained fruit intensity. Diam. 14% alc. **Rating** 94 **To** 2027 $55 JP

♉♉♉♉♀ **Nektar 2017** Rating 93 **To** 2027 $55 JP
Beta Sauvignon Blanc Semillon 2017 Rating 91 **To** 2024 $34 JP

Credaro Family Estate ★★★★★

2175 Caves Road, Yallingup, WA 6282 **Region** Margaret River
T (08) 9756 6520 **www**.credarowines.com.au **Open** 7 days 10–5
Winemaker Trent Kelly, Paul Callaghan **Est.** 1988 **Dozens** 25 000 **Vyds** 110ha
The Credaro family first settled in Margaret River in 1922, migrating from northern Italy. Initially a few small plots of vines were planted to provide the family with wine in the European tradition. The most recent vineyard acquisition was a 40ha property, with 18ha of vineyard, in Wilyabrup (now called the Summus Vineyard) and the winery has been expanded to 1200t with 300 000L of additional tank space. Credaro now has 7 separate vineyards (150ha in production), spread throughout Margaret River; Credaro either owns or leases each property and grows/manages the vines with its own viticulture team. Exports to the US, China, Singapore and Taiwan.

♉♉♉♉♉ **Kinship Margaret River Chardonnay 2020** Salted pineapple, rockmelon, guava and pawpaw on the nose. The nose suggests a big wine, but this is anything but. On the palate, it is surprisingly delicate, the flavours lingering through into the long finish. Really classy and fine. Screw cap. 12.5% alc. **Rating** 95 **To** 2031 $40 EL

1000 Crowns Margaret River Chardonnay 2019 Ripe summer nectarine, market spice, fennel flower, mandarin pith, all stitched up in a casing of salty acidity, brine and crushed shell. Really smart. Complex and layered, with brilliant length of flavour. Very tight and powerful. Screw cap. 12.5% alc. **Rating** 95 **To** 2031 $65 EL

1000 Crowns Margaret River Cabernet Sauvignon 2018 This is dazzling in its intensity and depth; the perfectly ripe and powerful year is clearly represented. Very dense, concentrated and long. All the hallmarks for ageing are present, but for now it's flamboyantly youthful. Screw cap. 14.5% alc. **Rating** 95 **To** 2041 $100 EL

1000 Crowns Margaret River Shiraz 2019 Aromas of blackberries, star anise and exotic spices. The palate has a concentration of flavour that is very impressive indeed. The tannins are consistently plump and pervasive. This isn't strictly in the 'new wave' of Margaret River shiraz/syrah styles – often silky, red-fruited and slippery – but it makes a strong statement about the potential concentration and density of flavour in the region. Screw cap. 14.5% alc. **Rating** 94 **To** 2035 $75 EL

Kinship Margaret River Cabernet Sauvignon 2019 The tannins are the highlight here – the ripe fruit is ensconced by chalky brick-dust tannins, which shape the wine as it moves through the lingering finish. Brilliant value for money, the structure is key. Impressive. Screw cap. 14% alc. **Rating** 94 **To** 2030 $35 EL

🍷🍷🍷🍷♀ **Kinship Margaret River Cabernet Merlot 2019** Rating 93 To 2031 $40 EL
Kinship Margaret River Shiraz 2019 Rating 92 To 2031 $35 EL
Five Tales Margaret River Cabernet Sauvignon 2019 Rating 92 To 2027 $24 EL ❂
Five Tales Margaret River Sauvignon Blanc 2020 Rating 91 To 2022 $24 EL
Five Tales Margaret River Sauvignon Blanc Semillon 2020 Rating 91 To 2022 $24 EL
Five Tales Margaret River Chardonnay 2020 Rating 91 To 2025 $24 EL
Five Tales Margaret River Pinot Gris 2020 Rating 90 To 2024 $24 EL
Kinship Margaret River Fragola 2019 Rating 90 To 2023 $40 EL

CRFT Wines   ★★★★

45 Rangeview Drive, Carey Gully, SA 5144 **Region** Adelaide Hills
T 0413 475 485 **www.crftwines.com.au** **Open** Fri–Sun 12–5
Winemaker Candice Helbig, Frewin Ries **Est.** 2012 **Dozens** 1000 **Vyds** 1.9ha
Life and business partners NZ-born Frewin Ries and Barossa-born Candice Helbig crammed multiple wine lives into a relatively short period, before giving up secure jobs and establishing CRFT in 2013. Frewin's CV includes Cloudy Bay and the iconic Sonoma pinot noir producer Williams Selyem, among others. Candice is a 6th-generation Barossan. She trained as a laboratory technician before moving to winemaking at Hardys, gaining her degree in oenology and viticulture from CSU and on to Boar's Rock and Mollydooker. The core focus is on small-batch single-vineyard Adelaide Hills pinot noir, chardonnay and grüner veltliner. The Arranmore vineyard was purchased in 2016, gaining NASAA organic certification in 2019, and wines are made with a minimal-intervention approach. Exports to Luxembourg and Singapore.

🍷🍷🍷🍷🍷 **Arranmore Vineyard Adelaide Hills Grüner Veltliner 2020** One of
3 Grüners from this creative Hills couple; 50% whole-bunch pressed with 2 days skin contact, wild fermentation and lees influence. Swelling with white peach and pear, the texture verging on an oiliness, though cut with lines of Meyer lemon and gentle, finishing acidity. Quite delicious, and a definite statement. Screw cap. 13% alc. **Rating** 94 **To** 2024 $30 TL ❂
Longview Vineyard Adelaide Hills Grüner Veltliner 2020 This Macclesfield district variation has subtle green pear notes to begin. There's a wave of tempered minerally acidity as you first sip, more earthy than the others, with lemon/lime elements on the palate. It finishes with mouthfilling texture and complex lingering flavours and textures. Well realised. Screw cap. 13.5% alc. **Rating** 94 **To** 2024 $30 TL ❂
Arranmore Vineyard Piccadilly Valley Adelaide Hills Pinot Noir 2019
Certified organic Piccadilly Valley pinot, with 25% whole bunches. Wild-yeast fermented and everything going for it. Alluring pinot-cherry colour, with a bouquet of fruits (red and darker crimson), poached rhubarb, and intriguing herb and spice notes – almost a touch of sumac. Juicy on the palate, yet with a decent tannin structure and finishing grip. Pinot with well-handled power. Screw cap. 14% alc. **Rating** 94 **To** 2028 $39 TL
Fechner Vineyard Moculta Eden Valley Shiraz 2018 From an old vineyard in the Moculta district of the Eden Valley, this is quite a terroir-focused wine, its fruit spectrum including suggestions of blackberry and fig, with earthy foundations and a spice selection like cumin and coriander seeds. Medium to full bodied, with supportive tannins to add substance to those savoury elements. Let this evolve in the bottle a few hours for extra intrigue. Screw cap. 13.5% alc. **Rating** 94 **To** 2030 $45 TL

ϮϮϮϮϘ The K1 Vineyard Adelaide Hills Grüner Veltliner 2020 Rating 93 To 2024 $30 TL
Whisson Lake Vineyard Piccadilly Valley Adelaide Hills Pinot Noir 2019 Rating 93 To 2028 $39 TL

Crittenden Estate ★★★★★

25 Harrisons Road, Dromana, Vic 3936 **Region** Mornington Peninsula
T (03) 5981 8322 **www**.crittendenwines.com.au **Open** 7 days 10.30–4.30
Winemaker Rollo Crittenden, Matt Campbell **Est.** 1984 **Dozens** 10 000 **Vyds** 4.8ha
Garry Crittenden was a pioneer on the Mornington Peninsula, establishing the family vineyard over 30 years ago and introducing a number of avant-garde pruning and canopy management techniques. Much has changed – and continues to change – in cool-climate vineyard management. Crittenden has abandoned the use of synthetic fertilisers in the vineyard, focusing on biological soil health using natural tools such as compost and cover crops. Pinot noir and chardonnay remain the principal focus at the top tier, but they also produce some remarkable savagnin made under flor in the Jura style. In 2015, winemaking returned to the family vineyard on the Mornington Peninsula in a newly built facility, with son Rollo in charge of the winemaking and general management and daughter Zoe overseeing marketing. Exports to the UK.

ϮϮϮϮϮ Cri de Coeur Mornington Peninsula Chardonnay 2019 This is seamless. It brings together the best flavours – stone fruit, lemon curd, nougatine, grilled nuts and more besides, with acidity leading. It has great energy and drive, length and line. Up there as one of the better Mornington Peninsula chardonnays this vintage. Bravo. Diam. 12.8% alc. **Rating** 96 **To** 2029 $80 JF
Peninsula Pinot Gris 2019 The real deal. Pinot gris as it should be: flavoursome, luscious, textural and brimming with poached pears, grated nashi and loaded with powdered and fresh ginger. Some clotted cream and lemon curd on the palate. Nothing cloying. Quite delicious. Screw cap. 13% alc. **Rating** 95 **To** 2024 $34 JF ✪
Cri de Coeur Sous Voile Mornington Peninsula Savagnin 2016 I've tried this wine several times now over its evolution and the extra time in bottle has made a lot of difference. A bright, burnished amber hue; full of grilled nuts and honeyed fragrances, with quince paste and salty lemons. Complex oxidative aromas and flavours, yet despite its warming 15.8% alcohol, the palate is luscious, silky and well controlled. Diam. 15.8% alc. **Rating** 95 **To** 2026 $80 JF ♥
The Zumma Mornington Peninsula Pinot Noir 2019 An even ebb and flow of pinosity. Dark cherries, woodsy and exotic spices, nori and wood smoke are all here, and more besides. Full bodied with well-plied tannins and a pleasing and abundant depth of flavour. Not too big, just right. Screw cap. 13% alc. **Rating** 95 **To** 2028 $57 JF
Macvin Savagnin NV An equal blend of flor-aged savagnin from 2016 with the variety's grape juice from 2020, then fortified with neutral spirit. It's gorgeous. Mid amber hue, with spiced quinces and raisins. So much in this. A brandy-like flavour, toffee and grilled nuts. Sure, there's sweetness, but it's tempered by the acidity. Glossy texture rounds it out. Diam. 17% alc. **Rating** 95 $90 JF
The Zumma Mornington Peninsula Chardonnay 2019 This has the body and flavours of a riper wine, yet the acidity is tightly cinched so nothing appears over the top. Expect stone fruit with citrus on display and a bit more input from the French oak, more in the toasty, spicy domain, as it's certainly not an oaky wine. Screw cap. 12.5% alc. **Rating** 94 **To** 2028 $57 JF

ϮϮϮϮϘ Peninsula Chardonnay 2019 Rating 93 To 2026 $34 JF
Kangerong Mornington Peninsula Chardonnay 2019 Rating 93 To 2028 $45 JF
Peninsula Pinot Noir 2019 Rating 93 To 2026 $34 JF
Kangerong Mornington Peninsula Pinot Noir 2019 Rating 93 To 2028 $45 JF
Cri de Coeur Mornington Peninsula Pinot Noir 2019 Rating 92 To 2030 $80 JF

Cullarin Block 71 ★★★★

125 Vineyards Road, Lake George, NSW 2581 **Region** Canberra District
T (02) 6226 8800 **www**.cullarin.com.au
Winemaker Celine Rousseau **Est.** 1971 **Dozens** 700 **Vyds** 6.23ha

Dr Edgar Riek was a Canberra-based academic with a brilliant mind and insatiable curiosity, putting him far ahead of contemporary thought. He was largely responsible for the establishment of the National Wine Show, and he and Dr John Kirk of Clonakilla were the first to plant vines in the Canberra District in 1971. Much later Edgar wrote, 'Driving past Lake George, I noticed one spot on the escarpment that was always green, it had its own spring and was warmer in winter than anywhere else in the region. I thought it was the perfect place for my vineyard.' He planted 3.9ha, initially naming the vineyard Cullarin (hence Cullarin Block 71), later Lake George Winery, in recognition of the shed he had built to process 10t of fruit. After he sold the property, another 1.4ha was planted in 1998. Current owner Peter Wiggs also owns the Cote d'Or vineyard in Pokolbin (supplying Andrew Thomas' The Cote Shiraz) and is the majority owner of Eden Road Wines.

🍷🍷🍷🍷🍷 **Canberra District Syrah 2019** 18 months in used French barriques. This wine starts out with the most intriguing and pretty nose of lavender oil, rose petals and jasmine. The medium-bodied palate chimes in with flavours of juicy plums and woodsy spices. It's plush and supple, with shapely tannins that melt into the body of the wine. No overt oak influence. The result is a lovely drink. Screw cap. 13% alc. **Rating** 95 **To** 2030 $50 JF

Cullen Wines ★★★★★

4323 Caves Road, Wilyabrup, WA 6280 **Region** Margaret River
T (08) 9755 5277 **www**.cullenwines.com.au **Open** 7 days 10–4.30
Winemaker Vanya Cullen, Andy Barrett-Lennard **Est.** 1971 **Dozens** 20000 **Vyds** 49ha

A pioneer of Margaret River, Cullen Wines has always produced long-lived wines of highly individual style from the mature estate vineyard. The vineyard has progressed beyond organic to biodynamic certification and, subsequently, has become the first vineyard and winery in Australia to be certified carbon neutral. Winemaking is in the hands of Vanya Cullen, daughter of founders Kevin and Diana Cullen; she is possessed of an extraordinarily good palate and generosity to the cause of fine wine. Exports to all major markets.

🍷🍷🍷🍷🍷 **Vanya Wilyabrup Margaret River Cabernet Sauvignon 2018** Matured in 100% new Taransaud puncheons for 5 months. Unusual for a premium cabernet to spend so little time in oak, but once the wine is in the mouth, the tardis of fruit on the core of the palate reveals a pedigree that defies comprehension and hyperbole. Supple, layered and ridiculously long, this is as close to a spiritual experience as wine can take us. Utterly thought-provoking, speech-stopping cabernet. Elegant in a way that has never previously been explored in Australian cabernet. And that oak? Imperceptible. Screw cap. 13.5% alc. **Rating** 99 **To** 2061 $500 EL ❤

Kevin John Legacy Series Fruit Day Margaret River Chardonnay 2020 Rosewater, pistachio, crushed cashew, yellow peach, flint and cap gun, struck match and salt bush. The saline acid carves a snaking track down the palate, like a lone snowboarder on a freshly groomed run. The length of flavour is interminable, and the impact of the oak is hard to distinguish. This is concentrated, otherworldly, and utterly unique. Bended knee required. Hail Margaret River chardonnay. Screw cap. 13.5% alc. **Rating** 98 **To** 2051 $250 EL

Kevin John 2019 As usual, the Kevin John arrives with an aura about it ... it undulates in the mouth, whipping and changing like Melbourne weather, 4 seasons in one day. It has exotic market spice, ripe orchard fruit, orange blossom, turmeric, saffron curls and saline acid. It's extraordinarily long, incredibly exciting and with phenolic texture that elevates it beyond the excitement that it delivers. Through it all meanders a coastal breeze, keeping it light and airy; the thundering power of Gingin fruit is concealed under many folds of flavour. Screw cap. 13% alc. **Rating** 98 **To** 2041 $127 EL ✪

Diana Madeline 2019 Cassis and red licorice on the nose, bay and salt bush, too. The palate is salty and fine with layers upon layers of spice and texture. The tannins are like finely textured gills, stacked as delicately as the folds in a mushroom. The length of flavour unfurls and extends across the palate, taking so long to fade that this entire tasting note is possible off one sip. The rest are just for pleasure. Drink it now, or in 40+ years from now … both will be possible. Screw cap. 13.5% alc. **Rating** 98 **To** 2061 $140 EL ✪

Diana Madeline 2018 An icon wine from a watershed vintage. This is Margaret River pedigree of the highest order; powdery-fine tannins that shape and caress the perfectly ripe red fruits. The acidity is the driver over the tongue, the layers of flavour and texture seem never-ending. Show stopping. Pure fruit concentration. Blimey. Screw cap. 13% alc. **Rating** 98 **To** 2061 $135 EL ✪

Legacy Margaret River Sauvignon Blanc 2019 It was a cool year for the 2019 vintage, producing mineral, aromatic and very fine wines. This is no exception. Salted edamame, sugar snap, jasmine tea, white currant, green apple skin, juniper berry and salt bush eddy around on the palate, swirling in and out of exotically spiced oak, crushed limestone/talc/basalt/petrichor. Evokes cicadas on a hot afternoon sea breeze, somehow. This is the most profound sauvignon blanc in Australia. Screw cap. 12.2% alc. **Rating** 97 **To** 2035 $100 EL ✪ ♥

Legacy Series Fruit Day Margaret River Malbec 2019 Vibrant green peppercorn, mulberry, raspberry pip and pomegranate. The tannins are uber-fine but absolutely present, lacing the fruit with jasmine tea and bolstered by saline acid. There's an energy here that is underpinned by a rare elegance – malbec is often punchy, vibrant, dense and intense, but seldom elegant like this. Wow. Screw cap. 12.9% alc. **Rating** 97 **To** 2041 $250 EL

♟♟♟♟♟ **Amber 2019** This is easily one of the most exciting Amber releases to date. Bitter orange, citrus zest, saffron and brine, the phenolics are very fine, curling their way in and out of the ever moving fruits on the palate. Balanced, fine and thrilling to drink. Skin contact, amphora ferment, oak-matured sauvignon blanc … who'd have thought it could steal the heart so thoroughly … but it does. Screw cap. 12.5% alc. **Rating** 96 **To** 2031 $39 EL ✪

Mangan East Block Wilyabrup 2019 This has that insane colour that only malbec and petit verdot can achieve: luminescent fuschia. Blackberry, purple jubes, pomegranate and red licorice saturate the tongue, energetically jostling for space on centre stage. The petit verdot rears its head on the finish, introducing lavender, blueberry and red apple skins. Super-concentrated, but still light on its feet. Screw cap. 13.5% alc. **Rating** 95 **To** 2031 $45 EL

Dancing in the Sun Wilyabrup 2018 54/43/3% semillon/sauvignon blanc/verdelho. Salted pineapple, jalapeño, chamomile flower, sugar snap pea, gooseberry, jasmine tea and white currants form the core of this wine. It is salty, savoury and spiced; driven by a strong undercurrent of phenolic structure. It stands to reason that verdelho is a potent if negligible inclusion here, such is the shape of the wine, while the regional marriage of semillon and sauvignon blanc lead the charge. Brilliant length of flavour to finish. Screw cap. 13.5% alc. **Rating** 94 **To** 2031 $25 EL ✪

♟♟♟♟♟ **Mangan Vineyard PF Margaret River Malbec 2018** Rating 93 To 2024 $39 EL

Mangan Vineyard Margaret River Sauvignon Blanc Semillon 2017 Rating 92 To 2022 $29 EL

Late Harvest Margaret River Chenin Blanc 2020 Rating 92 To 2031 $35 EL

Dancing in the Moonlight Wilyabrup Rosé 2020 Rating 92 To 2023 $25 EL ✪

Cumulus Vineyards

1705 Euchareena Road, Molong, NSW 2866 **Region** Orange
T 1300 449 860 **www.**cumulusvineyards.com.au
Winemaker Debbie Lauritz **Est.** 1995 **Dozens** 193 000 **Vyds** 508ha
The 508ha Cumulus vineyard (at 600m above sea level) is one of the largest single estates in
NSW. The wines are made at the Robert Oatley winery in Mudgee and are released under
the Cumulus, Soaring, Climbing, Rolling, Luna Rosa, Block 50, Head in the Clouds, Alte and
Inkberry labels. Exports to most major markets.

♀♀♀♀♀ **Cumulus Luna Rosa Rosado 2020** An eclectic blend of 85/7/4/4% shiraz/
riesling/sangiovese/barbera. Mid coral. Musk stick, sour cherry and dried herb.
Cool-fermented to retain freshness alongside effusive fruit. Palpably dry, easy
drinking, poised and savoury. A don't-think-just-drink proposition. For the price
and vintage challenges, this is very impressive. Screw cap. 12.5% alc. **Rating** 90
To 2021 $13 NG ✪

Cupitt's Estate

58 Washburton Road, Ulladulla, NSW 2539 **Region** Shoalhaven Coast
T (02) 4455 7888 **www.**cupittsestate.com.au **Open** 7 days 11–5
Winemaker Wally Cupitt **Est.** 2007 **Dozens** 7000 **Vyds** 3ha
Griff and Rosie Cupitt run a combined winery and restaurant complex, taking full advantage
of their location on the south coast of NSW. Rosie studied oenology at CSU and has more
than a decade of vintage experience, taking in France and Italy; she also happens to be the
Shoalhaven representative for Slow Food International. The Cupitts have 3ha of vines centred
on sauvignon blanc and semillon, and also source fruit from Hilltops, Canberra District,
Tumbarumba and Orange. Sons Wally and Tom have now joined the business.

♀♀♀♀♀ **Hilltops Nebbiolo 2019** Head and shoulders above everything else. Aromas of
dried rose, sandalwood, tea leaf and woodsy cherry are spot on. Best, the blaze
of expanding sweetness across the mid-palate before it is curtailed from excess
by a twine of beautiful herb-encased tannins. Fine length. Poised, precise and
delicious. Screw cap. 14% alc. **Rating** 93 To 2027 $46 NG
Dusty Dog Hilltops Shiraz 2018 The Rhône-aspirational cool-climate style:
sweet blue-fruit aspersions, violet, clove, tapenade and a meaty umami character.
The finish, a skitter of white pepper and clove, lingers long and a little sweet. Still,
long, detailed and energetic. Plenty to like. Best drunk with youth on its side.
Screw cap. 13.5% alc. **Rating** 92 To 2026 $52 NG
The Pointer Tumbarumba Chardonnay 2019 This is contemporary cool-
climate Aussie chardonnay 101. Smoky, flinty, tensile. A creamy core of leesy build-
up imparts dried hay, cream of wheat and nougatine scents, offsetting the tangy
stone-fruit riffs. The oak, tucking in the seams. Good crunchy length. Screw cap.
13% alc. **Rating** 91 To 2027 $38 NG
The Pointer Tumbarumba Pinot Noir 2019 30% whole bunches and the
rest, whole berries. Wild fermented. The tannins, a douse of turmeric, tamarind,
mescal and orange zest, are briary and elastic as they expand across the palate,
wheeling the strawberry accents in to a table of decorum. Loads of fun. Screw cap.
13.5% alc. **Rating** 91 To 2025 $38 NG
Hilltops Barbera 2019 This was aged in Hungarian wood and has some tannin
as a result. Still plenty of perk. Dark bitter cherry, amaro, root spice and orange
peel. Medium weight and moreish. A highly successful rendition best enjoyed
young. Better, cool. Screw cap. 14% alc. **Rating** 91 To 2023 $38 NG

♀♀♀♀ **Orange Pinot Noir 2019 Rating** 89 To 2024 $40 NG
Hilltops Sangiovese 2019 Rating 88 To 2025 $38 NG

Curator Wine Company ★★★★

28 Jenke Road, Marananga, SA 5355 **Region** Barossa Valley
T 0411 861 604 **www.**curatorwineco.com.au **Open** By appt
Winemaker Tom White **Est.** 2015 **Dozens** 5000 **Vyds** 8ha
This business is owned by Tom and Bridget White, who have made a number of changes in direction over previous years and have now decided to focus on shiraz and cabernet sauvignon from the Barossa Valley, a decision that has been rewarded. The vineyard at Marananga is planted on ancient red soils rich in ironstone and quartzite, and the wines are naturally fermented. Exports to China.

♚♚♚♚♚ **Barossa Valley Shiraz 2019** Tom White has done a fine job of delivering all the power and might of Marananga without sacrificing an iota of brightness or integrity. Brimming with spicy black/blueberries and stewed satasuma plums, its sweet fruit is married harmoniously with high-cocoa dark chocolate and coffee-bean oak. Firm, fine tannins hold a long finish. Diam. 15% alc. **Rating** 94 **To** 2027 $35 TS
Barossa Valley Cabernet Sauvignon 2019 If you love full-bodied cabernet, this is for you. A ripe style of fleshy, spicy black/redcurrants and cassis. Bright acidity, finely structured tannins, vibrant fruit and dark chocolate and coffee oak make for impressive balance, undeterred persistence and considerable integrity. Skilfully executed, delicious and great value. Diam. 15% alc. **Rating** 94 **To** 2029 $35 TS

♚♚♚♚♚ **Marananga Barossa Valley Shiraz 2018 Rating** 92 **To** 2022 $85 TS
Marananga Barossa Valley Cabernet Sauvignon 2018 Rating 92 **To** 2028 $85 TS
White Label Stone Well Vineyard Barossa Valley Shiraz 2018 Rating 91 **To** 2022 $85 TS

Curlewis Winery ★★★★☆

55 Navarre Road, Curlewis, Vic 3222 **Region** Geelong
T (03) 5250 4567 **www.**curlewiswinery.com.au **Open** W'ends 11.30–4
Winemaker Stefano Marasco, Rainer Breit (Consultant) **Est.** 1998 **Dozens** 1000 **Vyds** 2.8ha
Curlewis was established by self-taught winemaker Rainer Breit and Wendy Oliver, who extended the original pinot noir vineyard (now 35yo) with more pinot noir (Pommard clone) and small amounts of chardonnay and arneis. They retired in '11, selling the business to Stefano Marasco and Leesa Freyer. Stefano continues to make the wines using Old World techniques including wild yeast, hot fermentation, post-ferment maceration, prolonged lees contact, neither fining nor filtering the wine. Rainer and Wendy remain part of the Curlewis team as consultants and great friends. Exports to Canada, Sweden, Maldives, Malaysia, Singapore and Hong Kong.

♚♚♚♚♚ **Reserve Geelong Pinot Noir 2017** At 3 years of age this is just starting to spread its wings from the heady perfume of cranberry, wild raspberry and violets through to a strikingly linear palate filling with wild herbs, briar and red-berry intensity. Tannins run long and fine with a lip-smacking clean finish. Screw cap. 13% alc. **Rating** 95 **To** 2027 $70 JP
Reserve Geelong Pinot Noir 2018 A deep colour by Bellarine Peninsula standards with dusty beet aromas of root vegetables, earth, black cherry, cacao. A youngster with a savoury outline and still plenty of room to fill out. Give it time. Those tannins will love you for it. Screw cap. 13% alc. **Rating** 94 **To** 2028 $70 JP

♚♚♚♚♚ **Estate Geelong Pinot Noir 2018 Rating** 93 **To** 2026 $45 JP
Bel Sel Geelong Pinot Noir 2018 Rating 92 **To** 2026 $32 JP
Geelong Syrah 2017 Rating 91 **To** 2027 $40 JP
Bel Sel Geelong Chardonnay 2018 Rating 90 **To** 2027 $32 JP

Curly Flat ★★★★★

263 Collivers Road, Lancefield, Vic 3435 **Region** Macedon Ranges
T (03) 5429 1956 **www.**curlyflat.com **Open** Fri–Mon 12–5
Winemaker Matt Harrop, Ben Kimmorley **Est.** 1991 **Dozens** 6000 **Vyds** 13ha
Founded by Phillip Moraghan and Jenifer Kolkka in 1991, Jenifer has been the sole owner of
Curly Flat since 2017. The focus has always been on the vineyard, a dedicated team ensuring
quality is never compromised. Matt Harrop is now overseeing production. Exports to the UK,
Japan and Hong Kong.

🍷🍷🍷🍷🍷 **Central Macedon Ranges Pinot Noir 2019** Central focuses on the oldest
plantings from 1992 of MV6 made via 40% whole bunches, wild-yeast fermented
and aged in French oak, 27% new, for 16 months. Deep, dark and serious. It's
stern, with an abundance of dark cherries, pips, forest floor and woodsy spices.
Full-bodied, with raw-silk tannins, yet a vitality within as it sashays to a convincing
finish. Screw cap. 13% alc. **Rating** 96 **To** 2034 $53 JF ✪
Western Macedon Ranges Pinot Noir 2019 Fruit comes off vineyards on
the coolest, western blocks. Clones 115 and 144, 17% whole bunches in the wild
ferment and aged in used French oak for 16 months. There's a prettiness, an
alluring fragrance of rose petals that gives way to more obvious cherry nuances.
It's just shy of full bodied, with textural, fine-grained tannins, crunchy acidity and
a moreish element. Compelling wine. Screw cap. 14% alc. **Rating** 96 **To** 2033
$53 JF ✪
Macedon Ranges Chardonnay 2019 Gee, this is sturdy and structured, yet
appealing, with its almond croissant, lemon tart and biscuity inputs. Spicy oak lends
another dimension, as do clotted cream and leesy characters, chasing juicy lemon
and white nectarine. Livewire acidity drives it at every stage. Screw cap. 12.7% alc.
Rating 95 **To** 2030 $46 JF
Macedon Ranges Pinot Noir 2019 A finely tuned offering with everything
in its place. Lots of earthy, truffle aromas, dark fruits mingling with baking spices,
and cedary, charry oak neatly enmeshed into a fuller-bodied frame. Tannins are
plentiful and the acidity lengthens out the palate. Screw cap. 13.5% alc. **Rating** 95
To 2032 $53 JF

Curtis Family Vineyards ★★★☆

514 Victor Harbor Road, McLaren Vale, SA 5171 **Region** McLaren Vale
T 0439 800 484 **www.**curtisfamilyvineyards.com
Winemaker Mark Curtis **Est.** 1973 **Dozens** 10000
The Curtis family traces its history back to 1499 when Paolo Curtis was appointed by
Cardinal de Medici to administer Papal lands in the area around Cervaro. (The name Curtis is
believed to derive from Curtius, a noble and wealthy Roman Empire family.) The family has
been growing grapes and making wine in McLaren Vale since 1973, having come to Australia
some years previously. Exports to the US, Canada, Thailand and China.

🍷🍷🍷🍷🍷 **Martins Vineyard McLaren Vale Shiraz 2018** A beautifully composed wine
that transported me to another realm, following this producer's American-oak-
singed cuvées. Another powerful wine, to be sure, but the relief of whole-berry
pulpiness meshed with skilfully gleaned tannins provides joy. Bergamot, violet,
dark cherry and the cedar scents of the oak cladding all find confluence, while
driving long across the palate. This will age well. Rest assured. Screw cap. 14% alc.
Rating 94 **To** 2030 $150 NG

🍷🍷🍷🍷🍸 **Small Batch Rosé 2020 Rating** 93 **To** 2022 $40 NG
Cavaliere McLaren Vale Cabernet Sauvignon 2018 Rating 93 **To** 2032
$70 NG
Small Batch Grenache 2018 Rating 92 **To** 2024 $60 NG
Small Batch Grenache Shiraz 2019 Rating 92 **To** 2028 $60 NG
Cavaliere McLaren Vale GSM 2019 Rating 90 **To** 2025 $70 NG
Small Batch Tempranillo 2019 Rating 90 **To** 2026 $60 NG

d'Arenberg

58 Osborn Road, McLaren Vale, SA 5171 **Region** McLaren Vale
T (08) 8329 4888 **www**.darenberg.com.au **Open** 7 days 10–5
Winemaker Chester Osborn, Jack Walton **Est.** 1912 **Dozens** 220000 **Vyds** 197.2ha
Nothing, they say, succeeds like success. Few operations in Australia fit this dictum better than d'Arenberg, which has kept its 100+yo heritage while moving into the 21st century with flair and élan. At last count the d'Arenberg vineyards, at various locations, have 37 varieties planted, as well as more than 50 growers in McLaren Vale. There is no question that its past, present and future revolve around its considerable portfolio of richly robed red wines, shiraz, cabernet sauvignon and grenache being the cornerstones. The quality of the wines is unimpeachable, the prices logical and fair. It has a profile in both the UK and the US that far larger companies would love to have. d'Arenberg celebrated 100 years of family grapegrowing in '12 on the property that houses the winery and the iconic cube cellar door and restaurant. A founding member of Australia's First Families of Wine. Exports to all major markets.

🍷🍷🍷🍷🍷 **The Peppermint Paddock Sparkling Chambourcin Graciano NV** No lack of punch, nor froth. Delicious in a carnal sort of way: rhubarb, amaro bitters, ground pepper, dill and sour black cherry, all succulent and savoury as a wonderful meld of poise and mindless joy. Mouthfilling and mercifully, perceivably dry. Twin top. 14% alc. Rating 94 $30 NG ✪

🍷🍷🍷🍷🍷 **The Old Bloke & The Three Young Blondes Shiraz Roussanne Viognier Marsanne 2017** Rating 92 To 2032 $200 NG
The Money Spider Roussanne 2020 Rating 92 To 2024 $21 NG ✪
d'Arry's Original Shiraz Grenache 2018 Rating 92 To 2028 $21 NG ✪
The Athazagoraphobic Cat Sagrantino Cinsault 2018 Rating 92 To 2035 $200 NG
The High Trellis Cabernet Sauvignon 2018 Rating 91 To 2024 $21 NG ✪
The Anthropocene Epoch Mencia 2019 Rating 91 To 2023 $30 NG
The Hermit Crab Viognier Marsanne 2019 Rating 90 To 2023 $18 NG ✪
The Laughing Magpie Shiraz Viognier 2017 Rating 90 To 2026 $30 NG
The Galvo Garage Cabernet Sauvignon Merlot Petit Verdot Cabernet Franc 2017 Rating 90 To 2030 $30 NG

Dabblebrook Wines

69 Dabblebrook Road, Sellicks Hill, SA 5174 **Region** McLaren Vale
T 0488 158 727 **www**.dabblebrookwines.com **Open** By appt
Winemaker Ian Adam **Est.** 2007 **Dozens** 1000 **Vyds** 10ha
Dabblebrook is the seachange occupation of Ian Adam and Libbi Langford. They left Port Douglas after running a waste management business for 20 years, moving south to find what the larger world offered. They had no plans to establish a wine business, but found a property with 5ha of shiraz and 2ha of grenache, planted in 1990. In the early years they grew grapes for d'Arenberg (shiraz and grenache), an arrangement which ran for 5 years. Over the same period Ian worked on the Battle of Bosworth vineyards, gaining experience from Joch Bosworth. In 2011 he decided to make the wine for Dabblebrook; a vintage in the Loire Valley has further cemented his role as a winemaker. The red wines are made with little or no machinery, typically hand-plunged and basket-pressed, with minimal additions. Ian's current CV reads: 'Vigneron, part-time flagpole painter, chandelier cleaner (seasonal) and Doer of Lunch'. Exports to Singapore.

Dal Zotto Wines

Main Road, Whitfield, Vic 3733 **Region** King Valley
T (03) 5729 8321 **www**.dalzotto.com.au **Open** 7 days 10–5
Winemaker Michael Dal Zotto, Daniel Bettio **Est.** 1987 **Dozens** 60000 **Vyds** 46ha
The Dal Zotto family is a King Valley institution; ex-tobacco growers, then contract grapegrowers, they are now 100% focused on their Dal Zotto wine range. Founded by Otto and Elena, ownership has now passed to sons Michael and Christian (and their partners

Lynne and Simone), who handle winemaking and sales/marketing respectively. Dal Zotto is producing increasing amounts of Italian varieties of consistent quality from its substantial estate vineyard; they were the pioneers of prosecco in Australia with the first planting in 1999. The cellar door is in the centre of Whitfield, and is also home to their Trattoria (open weekends). Exports to the UK, UAE, the Philippines, Singapore and China appear to be flying.

♥♥♥♥♥ **L'Immigrante Contro King Valley Shiraz 2016** Released as a 5yo, Contro is just emerging into a complex, fascinating, savoury take on the grape, releasing aromas of wild herbs, black cherries, chocolate and earth. Dark, toasted spices inhabit the palate, so too savoury, dusty tannins and almond/nutty oak. Runs long in the mouth in a velvety stream of spice-laden dark fruits. Screw cap. 15.5% alc. **Rating** 95 **To** 2034 $74 JP

Tabelo Col Fondo King Valley Prosecco 2018 Ah, feel the freshness and vitality of the prosecco grape à la natural. There's a fineness here, together with fruit complexity that you rarely experience with the grape. The vintage, the acidity, seem to hold the clue. White flowers, green apple, orange peel, citrus. Fruit is finely embroidered across the palate, with a light touch of almond mealiness. Acidity is soft, allowing the fruit beautiful and expressive free rein. Crown seal. 12.2% alc. **Rating** 95 **To** 2024 $49 JP

Pucino Col Fondo King Valley Prosecco 2019 A return to the traditional Italian style of prosecco – a revelation when compared to some commercial, sweet styles going. Lightly cloudy lemon colour, with the soft scent of honeysuckle, fresh apple, lemon sorbet and musky florals. Fresh and vital and full of a fine complexity, almost delicate, with a touch of savoury earth. Dry and lemony, with enlivening acidity. A captivating taste experience. Crown seal. 11.3% alc. **Rating** 95 $30 JP ✪

L'Immigrante King Valley Nebbiolo 2015 Like tackling Everest, nebbiolo is a grape that demands a winemaker's respect. Due respect is given here in a fragrant wine replete in purple cherry fruit aromas, violet, dark rose, freshly tilled earth and ferrous minerality. Concentrated and fleshy, it threads in raspberry and anise across a savoury palate firmly set in place, thanks to gently drying tannins. Screw cap. 13.9% alc. **Rating** 94 **To** 2038 $82 JP ♥

♥♥♥♥♀ **Tabelo Col Fondo King Valley Prosecco 2019** **Rating** 93 **To** 2023 $49 JP
King Valley Barbera 2019 **Rating** 92 **To** 2024 $28 JP
Pucino King Valley Prosecco NV **Rating** 92 **To** 2023 $21 JP ✪
King Valley Nebbiolo 2017 **Rating** 91 **To** 2035 $46 JP
King Valley Garganega 2019 **Rating** 90 **To** 2024 $28 JP
King Valley Sangiovese 2019 **Rating** 90 **To** 2024 $28 JP

Dalbosco Wines   ★★★★☆

9 Mt Buffalo Road, Porepunkah, Vic 3740 **Region** Alpine Valleys
T 0437 950 618 **www**.dalboscowines.com.au **Open** By appt
Winemaker Jo Marsh **Est.** 1994 **Dozens** 250 **Vyds** 20ha
The Dalbosco family has been farming in Porepunkah since 1930, and planted the vineyard in 1994 on a sloping site with a northerly aspect offering glorious views towards Mt Buffalo, the soil brown to red loam and shale at depth. Originally predominantly pinot noir and chardonnay (for sparkling), it now has a range of varieties including sauvignon blanc, shiraz, prosecco, friulano with small amounts of refosco and vespolina. Mick Dalbosco graduated from Charles Sturt university in 2001 and started producing wines under the Dalbosco label. As the family business grew, Mick handed over the winemaking reins to Jo Marsh in '14.

Dalfarras   ★★★☆

PO Box 123, Nagambie, Vic 3608 **Region** Nagambie Lakes
T (03) 5794 2637 **www**.dalfarras.com.au **Open** At Tahbilk: Mon–Fri 9–5, w'ends & public hols 10–5
Winemaker Alister Purbrick, Alan George **Est.** 1991 **Dozens** 8750 **Vyds** 20.97ha

The project of Alister Purbrick and artist wife Rosa (née Dalfarra), whose paintings adorn the labels of the wines. Alister is best known as winemaker at Tahbilk (see separate entry), the family winery and home, but this range of wines is intended to (in Alister's words) 'allow me to expand my winemaking horizons and mould wines in styles different from Tahbilk'.

ΨΨΨΨΩ **Prosecco 2020** Explores the delights of the prosecco grape under $20 and it turns out there are many. Lively, persistent bead and mousse. Aromas of lemon sorbet, apple and cut pear. Gathers a full head of steam and zestiness on the palate. Fresh and invigorating in its youth. Cork. 11% alc. **Rating** 90 **To** 2024 $19 JP ✪

ΨΨΨΨ **Pinot Grigio 2020 Rating** 89 **To** 2024 $19 JP ✪

Dalrymple Vineyards

1337 Pipers Brook Road, Pipers Brook, Tas 7254 **Region** Northern Tasmania
T (03) 6382 7229 **www.**dalrymplevineyards.com.au **Open** By appt
Winemaker Peter Caldwell **Est.** 1987 **Dozens** 4000 **Vyds** 17ha
Dalrymple was established many years ago by the Mitchell and Sundstrup families; the vineyard and brand were acquired by Hill-Smith Family Vineyards in late 2007. Plantings are split between pinot noir and sauvignon blanc, and the wines are made at Jansz Tasmania. In '10 Peter Caldwell was appointed, responsible for the vineyard, viticulture and winemaking. He brought with him 10 years' experience at Te Kairanga Wines (NZ) and 2 years with Josef Chromy Wines. His knowledge of pinot noir and chardonnay is comprehensive. In Dec '12 Hill-Smith Family Vineyards acquired the 120ha property on which the original Frogmore Creek Vineyard was established; 10ha of that property is pinot noir specifically for Dalrymple.

ΨΨΨΨΩ **Cottage Block Pipers River Pinot Noir 2019** Pipers River's signature notes of rose petal, rosehip and red cherries take the lead here, with the low-yielding warm season tilting toward spicy blackberries; whole bunches contributing all their exotic lift of potpourri and brambles. Fine tannins coast through a long and dry finish. Screw cap. 14% alc. **Rating** 92 **To** 2029 $64 TS
Pipers River Pinot Noir 2019 Savoury, spicy and black-fruited, uniting the fragrant exotic fanfare of whole bunches with the power of a warm, dry, low-yielding season. Beetroot and bouquet garni are underscored by compact blackberry fruit, carried by firm, fine, drying tannins that promise medium-term life in the cellar. Screw cap. 14% alc. **Rating** 91 **To** 2026 $38 TS
Single Site Swansea Pinot Noir 2017 This warm, north-facing slope in the dry east coast delivers the most savoury, dry and ripe of the 2017 trilogy. Sweet, ripe black cherry and blackberry fruit contrasts mixed spice. Fine tannins make for a style ready to drink in the short term. Screw cap. 13.5% alc. **Rating** 91 **To** 2022 $64 TS
Single Site Coal River Valley Pinot Noir 2018 Already showing some bricking to its hue, this is a vintage characterised by beetroot, sage, thyme and fig, with the remnants of spicy berry fruits holding out on the finish. Finely balanced tannins provide an even close. Screw cap. 14% alc. **Rating** 90 **To** 2021 $64 TS

Dalwhinnie

448 Taltarni Road, Moonambel, Vic 3478 **Region** Pyrenees
T (03) 5467 2388 **www.**dalwhinnie.com.au **Open** 7 days 10–5
Winemaker David Jones **Est.** 1976 **Dozens** 3500 **Vyds** 25ha
David and Jenny Jones make wines with tremendous depth of flavour, reflecting the relatively low-yielding but well-maintained vineyards. The vineyards are dry-grown and managed organically, hence the low yield, but the quality more than compensates. A 50t high-tech winery allows the wines to be made onsite. It's good to see that Dalwhinnie has been acquired by the Fogarty Wine Group. Exports to the UK, the US and China.

ΨΨΨΨΨ **The Eagle Shiraz 2018** The flagship red is a picture of elegance, with underlying strength and precision. Vibrant, dense plum red. Mediterranean spices, dates, blackberries and warm, toasty oak. Lush texture, with supple tannins make it imminently drinkable, but don't be tempted – the best is yet to come. Screw cap. 13.5% alc. **Rating** 95 **To** 2031 $185 JP

Moonambel Shiraz 2018 Strikes a generous pose and colour. There's some pretty smart and attractive oak that is a big part of this wine's appeal. It contributes added gravitas, with wide-ranging influences from prominent spice to a toasty, smoky, mocha overlay. The ripe blackberry, plum, aniseed fruit loves it. Mouth-coating and long. Screw cap. 14.3% alc. **Rating** 95 **To** 2030 $70 JP

Moonambel Cabernet 2018 Classic Pyrenees cabernet all the way, albeit minus the usual level of eucalyptus/bay leaf. A very stylish cabernet (and friends) offering aromas of ripe black fruits, sour cherries, clove and leafy notes. Firm cabernet tannin structure, pulpy and still settling in when tasted 6 months before release. Screw cap. 13.5% alc. **Rating** 94 **To** 2030 $70 JP

♟♟♟♟♀ **Moonambel Chardonnay 2019 Rating** 93 **To** 2028 $50 JP

Dalwood   ★★★☆

700 Dalwood Road, Dalwood, NSW 2335 **Region** Hunter Valley
T (02) 4998 7666 **www**.dalwoodestate.com.au **Open** Long weekends
Winemaker Bryan Currie **Est.** 1828 **Vyds** 23ha

The chain of events making the oldest winery the youngest isn't far removed from the white rabbit appearing out of the magician's hat. George Wyndham was an important figure in the middle of the 19th century. Born in 1801 to a wealthy family, he arrived in Australia in 1823 and promptly set about assembling vast agricultural holdings stretching from Inverell to the Liverpool Plains, the Hunter Valley the centrepiece. He berated the Sydney Agricultural Show for holding the Wine Show in February, and for awarding gold medals that weren't in fact 24-carat gold. In 1904 Penfolds purchased Wyndham Estate and renamed it Dalwood. Declining yields attracted the attention of the bean counters, and in 1967 Penfolds sold the winery and vineyard to Perc McGuigan, but retained the Dalwood brand, leaving McGuigan free to rename it Wyndham Estate. In December 2017 TWE (aka Penfolds) sold the Dalwood brand to Sam and Christie Arnaout (who also own Hungerford Hill and its subsidiaries) and Sweetwater Wines. The synergy of this assemblage is obvious.

♟♟♟♟♀ **Estate Hunter Valley Shiraz 2019** A mid crimson. Medium bodied, highly savoury and of a sassy eminent drinkability. Aromas of polished leather, terracotta, damson plum, five-spice, sassafras and sour cherry. Lithe, detailed and long. An effortless and impressionable wine boasting great fealty to a luncheon-type style and region. Good drinking. Screw cap. 14% alc. **Rating** 92 **To** 2028 $45 NG

Dandelion Vineyards   ★★★★★

PO Box 138, McLaren Vale, SA 5171 **Region** South Australia
T (08) 8323 8979 **www**.dandelionvineyards.com.aut
Winemaker Elena Brooks **Est.** 2007 **Vyds** 124.2ha

Elena Brooks crafts full-bodied wines across South Australia's premium regions: Adelaide Hills, Eden Valley, Langhorne Creek, McLaren Vale, Barossa Valley and Fleurieu Peninsula. She endeavours to draw upon vineyards untempered by over-management, as much as she strives for a softer impact in the winery. As a result, Dandelion wines are increasingly bright, transparent and stamped by a more sensitive oak regime than in the past. Grenache, a strong suit. Exports to all major markets. (NG)

♟♟♟♟♟ **Faraway Tree McLaren Vale Grenache 2019** All the red-fruit allusions of Vale grenache flow in a torrent, wonderfully elevated by the full suite of rose petal, potpourri and incense of expertly deployed whole-bunch fermentation. Finely textured tannins and enticingly tangy acidity provide confident support to a very long finish. Exemplifying a lift and detail often reserved for pinot, this is a sure-fire inclusion in McLaren Vale's A-list. Screw cap. 14.5% alc. **Rating** 96 **To** 2029 $80 TS

Moonrise Kingdom McLaren Vale Shiraz Grenache Petite Sirah 2019 Cast all expectations of grenache blends from your mind, for this is first and foremost a union between full-bodied McLaren Vale shiraz and durif (petite sirah). Full, vibrant purple colour. Engineered around a dense singularity of spicy black plum and licorice, backed confidently by high-cocoa dark chocolate oak and an intricate, rigid tannin scaffold. Loaded with potential and promise. Screw cap. 14.5% alc. **Rating** 95 **To** 2034 $80 TS

♀♀♀♀♀ **Honeypot of the Barossa Roussanne 2020 Rating** 93 **To** 2028 $28 TS
Lionheart of the Barossa Shiraz 2019 Rating 93 **To** 2025 $30 NG
Red Queen of the Eden Valley Shiraz 2018 Rating 93 **To** 2032 $250 NG
Lion's Tooth of McLaren Vale Shiraz Riesling 2019 Rating 93 **To** 2026 $40 NG
Pride of the Fleurieu Cabernet Sauvignon 2019 Rating 93 **To** 2030 $30 NG
March Hare of the Barossa Mataro 2019 Rating 93 **To** 2044 $60 TS
Damsel of the Barossa Merlot 2019 Rating 92 **To** 2039 $30 TS
Menagerie of the Barossa GSM 2019 Rating 91 **To** 2024 $30 NG
Enchanted Garden of the Eden Valley Riesling 2020 Rating 91 **To** 2028 $28 NG
Firehawk of McLaren Vale Shiraz 2018 Rating 91 **To** 2033 $60 TS
Wonderland of the Eden Valley Riesling 2020 Rating 90 **To** 2029 $60 NG
Lioness of McLaren Vale Shiraz 2019 Rating 90 **To** 2026 $30 NG

Dappled Wines ★★★★★

1 Sewell Road, Steels Creek, Vic 3775 **Region** Yarra Valley
T 0407 675 994 **www**.dappledwines.com.au **Open** By appt
Winemaker Shaun Crinion **Est.** 2009 **Dozens** 800
Owner and winemaker Shaun Crinion was introduced to wine in 1999, working for his winemaker uncle at Laetitia Winery & Vineyards on the central coast of California. His career since then has been so impressive I (James) can't cut it short: 2000 Devil's Lair, Margaret River and Corbett Canyon Vineyard, California; '02 Houghton, Middle Swan; '03 De Bortoli, Hunter Valley; '04–06 Pipers Brook, Tasmania; '06 Bay of Fires, Tasmania; '06–07 Williams Selyem, California; '08 Domaine Chandon, Yarra Valley; '10 Domaine de Montille, Burgundy; '09– present Dappled Wines (plus part-time for Rob Dolan). His longer-term ambition is to buy or establish his own vineyard.

♀♀♀♀♀ **Les Verges Single Vineyard Yarra Valley Chardonnay 2019** From the red soil Upper Yarra D'Aloisio Vineyard at Seville. Wild-yeast barrel fermentation in French oak, no additions other than SO$_2$. The bouquet is complex, fruit and oak both contributing, the palate with grapefruit and white peach persisting throughout the long journey. Compelling. Screw cap. 13% alc. **Rating** 97 **To** 2030 $45 JH ✪

♀♀♀♀♀ **Appellation Upper Yarra Valley Pinot Noir 2019** Good depth of colour; the bouquet has fragrant spiced plum and forest berries, the impressive, deeply robed palate following precisely in the tracks of the bouquet. The volume of flavour and mouthfeel suggests even more spicy complexity will follow in the next 2–3 years. Screw cap. 13.5% alc. **Rating** 96 **To** 2030 $30 JH ✪
Champs de Cerises Single Vineyard Upper Yarra Valley Pinot Noir 2019 Hand picked, wild-yeast fermented with 30% whole bunches, SO$_2$ the only addition, the slight turbidity confirming no filtration or fining. A spiced plum bouquet signals a wine of substantial depth and complexity, the texture and structure first class. Diam. 13.5% alc. **Rating** 96 **To** 2030 $45 JH ✪
Appellation Yarra Valley Chardonnay 2019 Hand picked, whole-bunch pressed, wild fermented in French oak, part new. White peach and nectarine are the cornerstones of a supple and creamy chardonnay that sits up and welcomes you. Classic each-way proposition, drink now or later. Screw cap. 13% alc. **Rating** 95 **To** 2029 $30 JH ✪
Fin de la Terre Single Vineyard Yarra Valley Syrah 2019 Hand picked, open-fermented with 100% whole bunches. The high-toned bouquet, with its

bandwidth messaging, reflects the whole-bunch ferment, the light to medium-bodied palate with a display of forest berries, red and black. Delicious early-drinking style. Diam. 13% alc. **Rating** 95 **To** 2030 $45 JH

David Franz

94 Stelzer Road, Stone Well, SA 5352 **Region** Barossa Valley
T 0417 454 556 **www**.david-franz.com **Open** 7 days 11–5
Winemaker David Franz Lehmann **Est.** 1998 **Dozens** 6600 **Vyds** 33.92ha
David Franz (Lehmann) is one of Margaret and Peter Lehmann's sons. He took a very circuitous path around the world before establishing his eponymous winery. Wife Nicki accompanied him on his odyssey and, together with their 3 children, 2 dogs, a mess of chickens and a surly shed cat, all live happily together in their house and winery. The utterly unique labels stem from (incomplete) university studies in graphic design. Exports to the UK, the US, Japan, Hong Kong and China.

David Hook Wines ★★★★

Cnr Broke Road/Ekerts Road, Pokolbin, NSW 2320 **Region** Hunter Valley
T (02) 4998 7121 **www**.davidhookwines.com.au **Open** 7 days 10–4.30
Winemaker David Hook **Est.** 1984 **Dozens** 10000 **Vyds** 8ha
David Hook had over 25 years' experience as a winemaker for Tyrrell's and Lake's Folly, also doing the full Flying Winemaker bit with jobs in Bordeaux, the Rhône Valley, Spain, the US and Georgia. The Pothana Vineyard has been in production for almost 40 years and the wines made from it are given the 'Old Vines' banner. This vineyard is planted on the Belford Dome, an ancient geological formation that provides red clay soils over limestone on the slopes, and sandy loams along the creek flats; the former for red wines, the latter for white.

Old Vines Pothana Vineyard Belford Shiraz 2018 A traditional and mid-weighted wine, showcasing fealty to region and drinkability in spades. Violet, mocha, dark cherry, clove and that fecund earthy scent that is Hunter-inimitable. The mid palate is compressed by the oak. This should age well. Screw cap. 13.5% alc. **Rating** 92 **To** 2033 $65 NG

Hilltops Nebbiolo 2019 A light, frisky easygoing nebbiolo. A pallid mid ruby, this great variety is inherently low in pigments. A carriage of sour cherry, sandalwood, tamarind and strawberry oscillates between a charge of vibrant acidity and a beam of nicely extracted tannins, herbal and lithe. The wine's totem is defined by a winning approachability, versatility and ease of drinking. Screw cap. 13.5% alc. **Rating** 90 **To** 2025 $42 NG

Dawson & James

1240B Brookman Road, Dingabledinga, SA 5172 **Region** Southern Tasmania
T 0419 816 335 **www**.dawsonjames.com.au
Winemaker Peter Dawson, Tim James **Est.** 2010 **Dozens** 1200 **Vyds** 3.3ha
Peter Dawson and Tim James had long and highly successful careers as senior winemakers for Hardys/Accolade Wines. Tim jumped ship first, becoming managing director of Wirra Wirra for 7 years until 2007. Now both have multiple consulting roles. They have long had a desire to grow and make wine in Tasmania, a desire that came to fruition in '10. Exports to the UK and Singapore.

Pinot Noir 2018 Impeccable ripeness at a refreshing 12.6% alcohol. Infused with beautiful, exact red cherry and strawberry fruit. Bright Tasmanian acidity declares structure and endurance as profoundly as finely crafted tannins. Just the right level of whole bunches infuses floral perfume and exotic spice. Impeccably toned oak leaves a long, focused line of fruit purity to finish. Jubilant! Screw cap. 12.6% alc. **Rating** 94 **To** 2033 $78 TS

Chardonnay 2018 **Rating** 93 **To** 2023 $64 TS

DCB Wine

505 Gembrook Road, Hoddles Creek, Vic 3139 **Region** Yarra Valley
T 0419 545 544 **www**.dcbwine.com.au
Winemaker Chris Bendle **Est.** 2013 **Dozens** 1300
DCB is a busman's holiday for Chris Bendle, currently a winemaker at Hoddles Creek Estate, where he has been since 2010. He previously made wine in Tasmania, NZ and Oregon, so he is the right person to provide wines that are elegant, affordable and reward the pleasure of drinking (Chris's aim); the wines also offer excellent value. Exports to the UK and Japan.

Single Vineyard Woori Yallock Chardonnay 2019 Fruit comes off the Lone Star Creek vineyard and the wine is now starting to unfurl to reveal its class. White peach with grapefruit, cinnamon and woodsy spices, a spark of flint, a layer of creamy lees and a fine thread of acidity holding it all in place. Moreish, savoury and delicious in equal measure. Screw cap. 13% alc. **Rating** 93 **To** 2028 $35 JF
Yarra Valley Pinot Noir 2019 While it has some maraschino cherries and pips, it's deep, earthy and flavoursome, largely working off a savoury theme. A youthfulness yet some soul too. The textural palate, with its emery board tannins, is underscored by some meaty reduction. It just works. Screw cap. 13.5% alc. **Rating** 92 **To** 2027 $24 JF ●
Single Vineyard Woori Yallock Pinot Noir 2019 It starts out with some florals, herbs and spices before moving onto a fuller-bodied palate laced with sweetish cherries, black plums, wood char and vanillan oak. A neatly composed wine that is tipped towards savouriness, with grainy tannins and a fresh raspberry-like acidity all the way through. Screw cap. 13.5% alc. **Rating** 92 **To** 2029 $35 JF
Yarra Valley Chardonnay 2019 More savoury than fruity, yet there are flavours of pear and stone fruit. It's nicely shaped even if a bit light, with the merest hint of flint, grilled nuts and spice. Stylish in its own way, a good drink right now and as usual, priced right. Screw cap. 13% alc. **Rating** 91 **To** 2025 $24 JF

De Beaurepaire Wines

182 Cudgegong Road, Rylstone, NSW 2849 **Region** Central Ranges
T 0429 787 705 **www**.debeaurepairewines.com **Open** Wed–Sun 11–5
Winemaker Richard de Beaurepaire, Will de Beaurepaire, Jacob Stein (Contract), Lisa Bray (Contract), Alex Cassegrain (Contract) **Est.** 1998 **Dozens** 12000 **Vyds** 52ha
The large De Beaurepaire vineyard was planted by Janet and Richard de Beaurepaire in 1998 and is situated on one of the oldest properties west of the Blue Mountains, at an altitude of 570–600m. The altitude, coupled with limestone soils and frontage to the Cudgegong River, provides grapes (and hence wines) very different from the Mudgee norm. The vineyard is planted to merlot, shiraz, cabernet sauvignon, pinot noir, petit verdot, viognier, chardonnay, semillon, viognier, verdelho and pinot gris; most of the grapes are sold. Exports to France and Hong Kong.

Coeur d'Or Rylstone Botrytis Semillon 2019 Sumptuous. A prodigious 200g/L RS – even for Sauternes, this is stratospheric. Scents of apricot pith, crystalline ginger, cardamom, rooibos and finger lime. Long and vibrant. Far from cloying. This would suit a bit more oak. Extremely delicious all the same. Screw cap. 14% alc. **Rating** 94 **To** 2032 $50 NG

Leopold Rylstone Shiraz Viognier 2016 Rating 93 To 2026 $60 NG
Henri Rylstone Cabernet Merlot Petit Verdot 2018 Rating 92 To 2035 $40 NG
Le Chevalier Rylstone Merlot Cabernet Petit Verdot 2018 Rating 92 To 2030 $35 NG
Billet Doux Rylstone Semillon Sauvignon Blanc 2017 Rating 91 To 2022 $30 NG
Leopold Rylstone Shiraz Viognier 2009 Rating 90 To 2022 $60 NG

De Bortoli

De Bortoli Road, Bilbul, NSW 2680 **Region** Riverina
T (02) 6966 0100 **www**.debortoli.com.au **Open** Mon–Sat 9–5, Sun 9–4
Winemaker Darren De Bortoli, Julie Mortlock, John Coughlan **Est.** 1928 **Vyds** 367ha
Famous among the cognoscenti for its superb Noble One, which in fact accounts for only
a tiny part of its total production, this winery turns out low-priced varietal wines that are
invariably competently made. They come from estate vineyards, but also from contract-grown
grapes. In June 2012 De Bortoli received a $4.8 million grant from the Federal Government's
Clean Technology Food and Foundries Investment Program. This grant supported an
additional investment of $11 million by the De Bortoli family in their 'Re-engineering Our
Future for a Carbon Economy' project. De Bortoli is a founding member of Australia's First
Families of Wine. Exports to all major markets.

Black Noble NV A blend of aged botrytised semillon, average age 10 years.
Amber, but transparent. Decadent aromas of dried tobacco leaf cum Cuban cigar,
coffee bean, mocha, rancio, date, tamarind and clove. Exotic, but highly individual.
Not fortified, so don't expect the palate-sweeping viscosity of that idiom, despite
a rivalrous degree of palate-staining sweetness and intensity. Screw cap. 17.5% alc.
Rating 93 $52 NG
Noble One Botrytis Semillon 2018 The alcohol, low. The acidity, juicier
and palpably more natural. A gentler approach and easier drinking because of it.
A botrytic parade of dried mango, pineapple chunks, ginger crystals and orange
liqueur. The finish long enough, without the stellar length of great examples. The
poise, exemplary. Apricot marmalade notes linger. The oak beautifully nestled.
Time will tell. Screw cap. 10% alc. **Rating** 93 **To** 2038 $94 NG
Regional Classic Tumbarumba Chardonnay 2019 A chardonnay that
straddles a tight rope of racy acidity and sulphides, the latter just pinching the
finish. But in the midst, intense citrus flavours, lots of lime accents, really juicy and
mouth-watering with moreish savoury inputs. Ultimately, a good drink. Screw cap.
13% alc. **Rating** 90 **To** 2028 $27 JF
Deen De Bortoli Vat 1 Riverina Durif 2018 A deep crimson. Explosive,
packing aromatic punch delivered as violet, blueberry, mulberry, anise, dried
tobacco and oodles of coffee bean/mocha oak. Hedonistic, to be sure. But durif's
tannic mettle and the oak handling ensure that nothing overwhelms the wine's
raw power and joyous drinkability. Screw cap. 15% alc. **Rating** 90 **To** 2026
$16 NG ✪
8 Years Old Fine Tawny NV A more relaxed wine than its older 25yo sibling.
Less complex aromatically, to be sure. More primary and carnal, with mottled
blackberry, volcanic rock, raspberry bon-bon and prune. Yet the seams unfold
effortlessly. The acidity, less shrill. Less ambition and more intuitiveness. With that,
a better and more balanced drink. Screw cap. 18.5% alc. **Rating** 90 $34 NG
Show Liqueur 8 Years Old Muscat NV Date, tamarind, crystalline ginger,
Darjeeling tea, a gentle rancio weld of complexity and ample sweet cushioning.
Nothing hard or shrill. Just a delicious and definitive example of the sort of
fortified wines that fewer people drink but, together with Hunter semillon, are
Australia's inimitable gifts to the wine world. Screw cap. 18% alc. **Rating** 90
$34 NG

Deen Vat 8 Heathcote Hilltops Shiraz 2018 **Rating** 88 **To** 2024 $16 JP ✪
Deen Vat 9 Heathcote Cabernet Sauvignon 2017 **Rating** 88 **To** 2024
$16 JP ✪

De Bortoli (Victoria)   ★★★★★

Pinnacle Lane, Dixons Creek, Vic 3775 **Region** Yarra Valley
T (03) 5965 2271 **www**.debortoli.com.au **Open** 7 days 10–5
Winemaker Stephen Webber, Sarah Fagan, Andrew Bretherton **Est.** 1987 **Dozens** 350 000
Vyds 520ha

Arguably the most successful of all Yarra Valley wineries, not only in terms of the sheer volume of production but also the quality of its wines. It is run by the husband-and-wife team of Leanne De Bortoli and Steve Webber, but owned by the De Bortoli family. The wines are released in 3 quality (and price) groups: at the top Single Vineyard, then Estate Grown and in 3rd place Villages. Small-volume labels increase the offer with Riorret Single Vineyard Pinot Noir, Melba, La Boheme, an aromatic range of Yarra Valley wines and Vinoque, enabling trials (at the commercial level) of new varieties and interesting blends in the Yarra. The BellaRiva Italian varietal wines are sourced from the King Valley, and Windy Peak from Victorian regions including the Yarra, King Valley and Heathcote. The PHI wines are made from the 7.5ha Lusatia Park Vineyard established by the Shelmerdine family in the Yarra Valley, purchased in November '15, and from Heathcote. Exports to all major markets.

ᵀᵀᵀᵀᵀ **Lusatia Chardonnay 2018** A bit like a Ferrari 812 Superfast that can go from zero to 100 in 2.9 seconds, this chardonnay seems to race across the palate, leaving a trail of flavour in its wake. It's pure acidity driving this. Of course there's more in the midst: the citrus, the flint and the smidge of nougatine. A complex, fantastic wine. Screw cap. 12.7% alc. **Rating** 97 **To** 2030 $90 JF ✪

Melba Vineyard Yarra Valley Cabernet Sauvignon 2018 Made only in the best vintages, hand-picked fruit from old vines, destemmed. Fermented on skins for 20 days in 5t vats then gently pressed to a new and used French oak hogshead for 18 months with regular racking. The end result is a beautifully crafted and composed wine. All the beauty of cabernet within, alongside superfine tannins. Elegance with latent power. Diam. 13.5% alc. **Rating** 97 **To** 2038 $160 JF

ᵀᵀᵀᵀᵀ **Melba Amphora Yarra Valley Cabernet Sauvignon 2019** Hand-picked and sorted fruit, destemmed and popped into a 1000L clay vessel. A whopping 150 days on skins followed by another 150 days in used French oak puncheons. This is a beauty. It's savoury, pretty and lighter framed, with wonderful, powdery tannins. Pure, refined and elegant. Bravo. Diam. 13% alc. **Rating** 96 **To** 2034 $80 JF

Melba Reserve Yarra Valley Cabernet Sauvignon 2017 The trio of high-end cabernets are exceptional. This Reserve is an essay in texture and beautiful cabernet flavours. Cassis, warm earth, wood smoke, tar and baking spices. The medium-bodied palate is caressed by cocoa-powder-like tannins and terrific length. Lovely today but will reward more with cellaring. Diam. 13.5% alc. **Rating** 96 **To** 2035 $40 JF ✪

The Estate Vineyard Dixons Creek Yarra Valley Chardonnay 2019 If you had to pick a chardonnay that punches above its weight given its price point, this surely is it. Stamped with Yarra cool, so there's flint and a citrus theme happening. Lemon blossom and juicy tangy fruit across a rather tight and linear palate. It's certainly not lean, as there are dabs of leesy texture and a refreshing saline tang to the finish. Screw cap. 13% alc. **Rating** 95 **To** 2028 $30 JF ✪

Section A5 Yarra Valley Chardonnay 2019 A classy chardonnay that just floats across the palate. It seems light on its feet, offering a hint of flinty reduction, a dash of stone fruit, citrus and ginger spice. It's subtle, a bit of a sleeper, although there's refreshing acidity and enough phenolic grip to add another layer. A very good drink. Screw cap. 12.5% alc. **Rating** 95 **To** 2029 $55 JF

Section A7 Yarra Valley Chardonnay 2019 Wines A5 (vines planted in 1976) and A7 (planted in 1990) are made identically, so site is the feature. A7, for whatever reason, often has the edge, as it does this vintage (by a whisker, I might add). This is refined, long and pure. Complex if delicate flavours and texture, in sync with mouth-watering acidity, a pucker of phenolics on the finish and refreshment writ large. Screw cap. 12.7% alc. **Rating** 95 **To** 2030 $55 JF

PHI Single Vineyard Yarra Valley Chardonnay 2019 It takes a bit of time to open up, so don't chill this within an inch of its life. It starts out a bit reserved: a hint of lemon blossom here, a squirt of lemon juice there and then wham! Everything starts coming together quickly. It's layered with flavour and has a level of complexity. It's also moreish to the very last drop. Screw cap. 12.5% alc. **Rating** 95 **To** 2029 $50 JF

PHI Single Vineyard Yarra Valley Pinot Noir 2019 Lusatia Park vineyard, it's something else. Special, with various blocks finding their way into several wines. This comes off Block C, apparently the darkest-fruited pinot. It has a composure, yet a density of excellent red-shaded, sweet fruit, spicy, juicy and bright. The palate is all about elegance and drive, helped by fine acidity and velvety tannins. Screw cap. 13.7% alc. **Rating** 95 **To** 2033 $50 JF

Riorret Lusatia Park Pinot Noir 2019 There's a decadence about this wine. It's rich and ripe – not too much, as it has a coolness of its Upper Yarra site – but more in the depth and how it feels. All the usual and pleasing flavours are pressed together, then expand across the fuller-bodied palate. Lovely smooth tannins and the finish lingers long. Diam. 13.7% alc. **Rating** 95 **To** 2032 $55 JF

Section A8 Yarra Valley Syrah 2019 The flavours are a little subdued: yes there's a hint of plums, spice and florals, although ultimately it's a savoury wine. The palate shines with a gloss and a buoyancy throughout, with supportive tannins all the way. It's a touch terse on the finish, so come back in another year or so, it'll be smokin'. Screw cap. 14% alc. **Rating** 95 **To** 2035 $55 JF

ȲȲȲȲȲ **The Estate Vineyard Dixons Creek Yarra Valley Gamay 2019** **Rating** 93 **To** 2025 $30 JF

La Boheme Act Four Yarra Valley Syrah Gamay 2019 **Rating** 93 **To** 2025 $22 JF ✪

Rutherglen Estate Sparkling Shiraz Durif NV **Rating** 93 $28 JP

Riorret Balnarring Mornington Peninsula Pinot Noir 2018 **Rating** 92 **To** 2032 $55 JF

Rutherglen Estate Renaissance Shiraz 2019 **Rating** 92 **To** 2029 $50 JP

Rutherglen Estate Renaissance Viognier Roussanne Marsanne 2019 **Rating** 92 **To** 2025 $35 JP

Rutherglen Estate Fiano 2020 **Rating** 91 **To** 2025 $24 JP

The Estate Vineyard Yarra Valley Pinot Noir 2019 **Rating** 91 **To** 2029 $30 JF

Rutherglen Estate Shiraz 2019 **Rating** 91 **To** 2026 $24 JP

La Boheme Act Three Yarra Valley Pinot Gris & Friends 2020 **Rating** 90 **To** 2022 $22 JF

PHI Single Vineyard Heathcote Syrah 2019 **Rating** 90 **To** 2030 $50 JP

Rutherglen Estate Shelley's Block Marsanne Viognier Roussanne 2019 **Rating** 90 **To** 2025 $19 JP ✪

Rutherglen Estate Classic Muscat NV **Rating** 90 $30 JP

The Estate Vineyard Yarra Valley Shiraz 2019 **Rating** 90 **To** 2033 $30 JF

Vinoque Same Same Yarra Valley Pinot Meunier Pinot Noir 2020 **Rating** 90 **To** 2024 $28 JF

Rutherglen Estate Renaissance Durif 2019 **Rating** 90 **To** 2032 $50 JP

King Valley Prosecco NV **Rating** 90 **To** 2022 $22 JP

ȲȲȲȲ **Rutherglen Estate Durif 2019** **Rating** 89 **To** 2026 $24 JP

de Capel Wines   ★★★☆

101 Majors Lane, Lovedale, NSW 2320 **Region** Hunter Valley
T 0419 994 299 **www.**decapelwines.com.au **Open** W'ends by appt
Winemaker Daniel Binet **Est.** 2008 **Dozens** 400 **Vyds** 2.2ha
Owners David and Elisabeth Capel's love of wine and a rural life led them to the purchase of their 11ha property in 2001 at which time the land (previously used for livestock) was mainly cleared, with small patches of remnant vegetation. It wasn't until '08 that they undertook major soil improvements, installed all of the vineyard infrastructure and personally planted 2.2ha of semillon and shiraz under the direction of viticulturist Jenny Bright. They say, 'We are very fortunate to have the support (and muscle) of our close friends and family who put in an amazing effort every vintage and help us to hand-pick every single shiraz and semillon grape that we grow'. It precisely follows the early years (1971–77) of Brokenwood.

ΨΨΨΨ♀ **Gabriela Hunter Valley Shiraz 2019** A warm year withstanding, this is a savoury medium-bodied wine, firmly regional. Damson plum, Asian spice, suede and saddle leather riffs are coaxed long by a curb of cinnamon American oak. Poised and easy drinking. Screw cap. 14% alc. **Rating** 90 **To** 2030 $30 NG

ΨΨΨΨ **Josephine Hunter Valley Semillon 2020 Rating** 88 **To** 2025 $25 NG

De Iuliis   ★★★★★
1616 Broke Road, Pokolbin, NSW 2320 **Region** Hunter Valley
T (02) 4993 8000 **www**.dewine.com.au **Open** 7 days 10–5
Winemaker Michael De Iuliis **Est.** 1990 **Dozens** 15000 **Vyds** 30ha
Three generations of the De Iuliis family have been involved in the establishment of the vineyard. The family acquired a property at Lovedale in 1986 and planted 18ha of vines in '90, selling the grapes from the first few vintages to Tyrrell's but retaining increasing amounts for release under the De Iuliis label. In '99 the land on Broke Road was purchased and a winery and cellar door were built prior to the 2000 vintage. In '11 De Iuliis purchased 12ha of the long-established Steven Vineyard in Pokolbin. Winemaker Michael De Iuliis completed postgraduate studies in oenology at the Roseworthy campus of the University of Adelaide and was a Len Evans Tutorial scholar. He has lifted the quality of the wines into the highest echelon. Exports to the US, Belgium, Italy, Singapore and China.

ΨΨΨΨΨ **Aged Release Hunter Valley Semillon 2014** An exceptional aged release, showcasing the kaleidoscope of buttered toast, lemon curd, cumquat and talc of regional semillon as it transitions from adolescence to the cusp of adulthood. It jitterbugs across the mouth. Febrile, intensely flavoured, despite the overall delicacy and long finish. The only caveat is the brittle acidity. Further age should tone this. Screw cap. 11.2% alc. **Rating** 95 **To** 2029 $45 NG

ΨΨΨΨ♀ **Hunter Valley Chardonnay 2019 Rating** 93 **To** 2026 $25 JH ✿
Limited Release Hunter Valley Chardonnay 2019 Rating 93 **To** 2029 $45 NG
Steven Vineyard Hunter Valley Shiraz 2019 Rating 91 **To** 2029 $45 NG
LDR Vineyard Hunter Valley Shiraz Touriga 2019 Rating 91 **To** 2027 $40 NG
Talga Road Vineyard Hunter Valley Shiraz 2019 Rating 90 **To** 2029 $40 NG
Hunter Valley Shiraz 2019 Rating 90 **To** 2028 $25 NG

De Lisio Wines   ★★★☆
Seaview Road, McLaren Vale, SA 5171 **Region** McLaren Vale
T 0423 146 217 **www**.delisiowines.com.au **Open** By appt
Winemaker Anthony De Lisio **Est.** 2002 **Dozens** 7500
This is the venture of Anthony (Tony) and Krystina De Lisio, focused primarily on McLaren Vale Shiraz and Grenache, the exceptions being a Southern Fleurieu Pinot Grigio and a 4-varietal red blend (Quarterback), which provide the major part of the volume of De Lisio Wines. Tony has many years' experience as a viticulturist and vineyard manager in McLaren Vale, and has been able to source grapes grown just north of McLaren Vale township, at Clarendon, Blewitt Springs, Kangarilla and McLaren Flat. The overall style of the wines is strongly oriented to the US, to which a significant part of the production is exported. The style is achieved through very ripe grapes from low-yielding, mainly old vines, which are open-fermented and barrel aged in predominantly French oak for up to 22 months. Exports to the US, Canada, Denmark, Singapore, Hong Kong and China.

ΨΨΨΨ♀ **Mighty Blue Estate Wandering Stockman McLaren Vale Shiraz Cabernet Sauvignon Grenache Merlot 2015** This works well, in that uber-ripe, oaky and flat-lining sort of way that many rich domestic wines hit after a few years. Mocha oak. Dark cherry, anise, mint and terracotta. A comforting wine with bags of life and a nostalgic halo. Cork. 15% alc. **Rating** 91 **To** 2024 $25 NG

ΨΨΨΨ   **Mighty Blue Estate Henry's Calling McLaren Vale Cabernet Sauvignon**
2016 Rating 88 **To** 2026 $40 NG

Deep Woods Estate   ★★★★★

889 Commonage Road, Yallingup, WA 6282 **Region** Margaret River
T (08) 9756 6066 **www.**deepwoods.wine **Open** Wed–Sun 11–5, 7 days during hols
Winemaker Julian Langworthy, Emma Gillespie, Andrew Bretherton **Est.** 1987
Dozens 30000 **Vyds** 14ha
Deep Woods Estate is a key part of the dynamic wine business of Peter Fogarty that
includes Millbrook in the Perth Hills, Evans & Tate (70% owned), Margaret River Vintners
and extensive vineyard holdings in Wilyabrup and elsewhere in Margaret River, plus in
Smithbrook in Pemberton. The business is the largest producer in WA with 600000 dozen.
There is a similar multifaceted stream in Tasmania, with Tasmanian Vintners (a 50/50% deal
between Peter and Tasmanian businessman Rod Roberts), the acquisition of the outstanding
Lowestoft Vineyard planted in the 1980s with pinot noir in high-density configuration and a
120ha vineyard site at Forcett. Lake's Folly in the Hunter Valley was the first move, Dalwhinnie
in the Pyrenees the most recent acquisition. Exports to Germany, Malaysia, Singapore, Japan
and China.

ΨΨΨΨΨ   **Single Vineyard G5 Margaret River Cabernet Sauvignon 2019** Elegant,
fragrant, medium bodied and silky. This is riddled with cassis, raspberry, licorice,
fennel flower, supple fruit and salivating balance. Will require a decant – the
tannins call 'present' on the roll call. Cellar it with total confidence, but drink
it whenever you want, because it is absolutely beautiful. Screw cap. 14% alc.
Rating 97 **To** 2051 $50 EL ✪
Reserve Margaret River Cabernet Sauvignon 2018 From the original
vineyard planted in '87, the wine matured in new and used French oak for
18 months. This is high-quality, autocratic cabernet, with blackcurrant, earth and
bay leaf on the bouquet and palate alike. Minimalist winemaking allows the fruit
maximum room to speak. Screw cap. 14% alc. **Rating** 97 **To** 2038 $75 JH ✪ ♥
Single Vineyard Margaret River Cabernet Malbec 2019 This is
unbelievably delicious – the malbec adds a backdrop of salty pomegranate,
raspberry and rhubarb to the chorus of cassis and exotic spice. This has a long
cellaring potential, perhaps a touch behind the G5 cabernet from the same vintage,
but boy oh boy … this is going to give you pleasure, right now. Wow. Screw cap.
14% alc. **Rating** 97 **To** 2041 $50 EL ✪

ΨΨΨΨΨ   **Reserve Margaret River Chardonnay 2019** While the 2018 was all about
latent fruit power and ripe concentration, this vintage is defined by intricate
layers of flinty stone fruit and taut minerally acidity. It sings with poise and line,
and doesn't stop for breath. Another astoundingly delicious chardonnay from an
unbroken run. If this isn't on your annual purchase list, it should be. Screw cap.
13% alc. **Rating** 96 **To** 2036 $55 EL ✪
Margaret River Rosé 2020 For the first time, 100% tempranillo from Yallingup
Hills. Handled oxidatively and clearly the product of a warmer, richer year, this
has admirable phenolic structure and shape on the palate, which contains ripe red
berry fruit. Fermented to dry and yet astoundingly generous, this is straight-up
delicious, and far longer and more thought provoking than a rosé has any business
to be. Screw cap. 13% alc. **Rating** 96 **To** 2025 $35 EL ✪ ♥
Harmony Margaret River Rosé 2020 Shiraz, merlot and tempranillo. Juicy,
flavoursome, rollicking red berries and briny acid – this is a little superstar.
Routinely reliable rosé for a really reasonable price. A go-to. Screw cap. 13% alc.
Rating 94 **To** 2023 $15 EL✪
Margaret River Cabernet Sauvignon Merlot 2019 As per usual for the
Deep Woods team, this is a dense, intensely vibrant and cracking cabernet
merlot. Never doubt them, for they are doing brilliant things. Screw cap. 14% alc.
Rating 94 **To** 2030 $35 EL

ŢŢŢŢŢ Margaret River Sauvignon Blanc 2020 Rating 93 To 2022 $20 EL ✪
Ivory Margaret River Semillon Sauvignon Blanc 2020 Rating 93 To 2024
$15 JH ✪
Hillside Margaret River Semillon Sauvignon Blanc 2020 Rating 93
To 2022 $25 EL ✪
Margaret River Chardonnay 2020 Rating 93 To 2027 $20 EL ✪
Hillside Margaret River Cabernet Sauvignon 2019 Rating 93 To 2030
$25 EL ✪
Hillside Margaret River Chardonnay 2020 Rating 92 To 2027 $25 EL ✪

del Rios Wines

2290 Ballan Road, Anakie, Vic 3221 **Region** Geelong
T (03) 5284 1227 **www.**delrios.com.au **Open** Fri 5.30–9.30, W'ends 11.30–5
Winemaker Gus del Rio **Est.** 1996 **Dozens** 5000 **Vyds** 17ha
Gus del Rio, of Spanish heritage, established a vineyard in 1996 on the slopes of Mt Anakie,
northwest of Geelong (chardonnay, pinot noir, cabernet sauvignon, sauvignon blanc, shiraz,
merlot and marsanne). The wines are made onsite in the fully equipped winery, which
includes a bottling and labelling line able to process over 150t. A Spanish-influenced restaurant
opened in 2015. Exports to Hong Kong and China.

ŢŢŢŢŢ Geelong Pinot Noir 2017 We don't see enough bottle-aged pinots. With
3 years behind it, the '17 is just revealing its potential and it's very attractive, in a
wild, autumnal, brooding way. This is a wine that demands your attention and
a plate of something rich and savoury. Forest floor, wild dark berries, baking spices
lead the way into a long intensity based around tomato leaf, dried herbs and black
fruits. Still youthful, with so much more to give. Screw cap. 13.5% alc. **Rating** 95
To 2025 $45 JP
Geelong Marsanne 2017 A ripe, ultra-expressive marsanne released with
bottle age and hence some development. Stunning aromatics rise from the glass,
resplendent in spring florals, honeysuckle, jasmine, spice and wild honey. A waxy,
textural palate follows, building in intensity. Marsanne with attitude and richness.
Screw cap. 13.8% alc. **Rating** 94 To 2025 $32 JP

ŢŢŢŢŢ Geelong Chardonnay 2018 Rating 93 To 2027 $42 JP
Geelong Sauvignon Blanc 2017 Rating 90 To 2024 $28 JP

Delamere Vineyards

Bridport Road, Pipers Brook, Tas 7254 **Region** Northern Tasmania
T (03) 6382 7190 **www.**delamerevineyards.com.au **Open** 7 days 10–5
Winemaker Shane Holloway, Fran Austin **Est.** 1982 **Dozens** 5000 **Vyds** 13.5ha
Delamere was one of the first vineyards planted in the Pipers Brook area. It was purchased by
Shane Holloway and wife Fran Austin and their families in 2007. Shane and Fran are in charge
of viticulture and winemaking. The vineyard has been expanded with 4ha of pinot noir and
chardonnay. Exports to China.

ŢŢŢŢŢ Tasmania Rosé NV 100% pinot noir, articulated in a bright, medium straw hue
and focused red cherry, strawberry hull, pomegranate and pink pepper, contrasting
a savoury, earthy and faintly charcuterie complexity. Varietal flesh and creamy lees
influence unite cool acidity, balanced dosage and fine, subtle tannins on a long
finish. Diam. 13.2% alc. **Rating** 92 To 2021 $35 TS
Tasmania Cuvée 2015 The delicate and elegant lemon of chardonnay and the
crunchy strawberry and red apple of pinot noir characterise the cool Delamere
vineyard. They're contrasted here with the creamy, lactic, funky charcuterie
complexity of fermentation. Perfectly ripe acidity and well-integrated dosage draw
out a long finish. Diam. 12.5% alc. **Rating** 90 $50 TS

Delatite ★★★★

390 Pollards Road, Mansfield, Vic 3722 **Region** Upper Goulburn
T (03) 5775 2922 **www.**delatitewinery.com.au **Open** 7 days 10–5
Winemaker Andy Browning **Est.** 1982 **Dozens** 16 000 **Vyds** 27.25ha
With its sweeping views across to the snow-clad alps, this is uncompromising cool-climate viticulture. Increasing vine age (the earlier plantings were between 1968–82, others between '84–2011) and the adoption of organic (and partial biodynamic) viticulture, have also played a role in providing the red wines with more depth and texture. The white wines are all wild-yeast fermented and as good as ever. In '11 Vestey Holdings Limited, the international pastoral giant, acquired a majority holding in Delatite. Exports to Japan and China.

ŸŸŸŸŸ **Tempranillo 2019** Made with easy drinking in mind. The addition of tempranillo's fellow Spanish red grape, graciano (14%), brings out a sweet plummy, confection fragrance. Red and black cherries fill the palate with licorice and chocolate in support. A medium-bodied example of the grape, all juicy and sweet-fruited with plenty of potential to explore. Screw cap. 12.5% alc. **Rating** 90 To 2024 $45 JP

ŸŸŸŸ **Demelza Cuvée Rosé 2018** **Rating** 89 $50 JP
High Ground Sauvignon Blanc 2020 **Rating** 89 To 2025 $23 JP
Polly's Block Reserve Chardonnay 2018 **Rating** 89 To 2030 $55 JP
Mansfield White Blend 2019 **Rating** 89 To 2024 $28 JP
High Ground Pinot Noir 2019 **Rating** 89 To 2025 $25 JP
Dungeon Gully Malbec Merlot 2018 **Rating** 89 To 2026 $35 JP
Mansfield Red 2018 **Rating** 89 To 2030 $35 JP
Cuvée Gewürz 2018 **Rating** 89 $40 JP
Sauvignon Blanc 2020 **Rating** 88 To 2025 $28 JP
Pinot Noir 2019 **Rating** 88 To 2026 $35 JP

Delinquente Wine Co ★★★★

31 Drayton Street, Bowden, SA 5007 **Region** Riverland
T 0437 876 407 **www.**delinquentewineco.com **Open** By appt
Winemaker Con-Greg Grigoriou **Est.** 2013 **Dozens** 7000
A Hollywood actress once said, 'I don't care what they say about me as long as they spell my name right'. Con-Greg Grigoriou might say, 'I don't care how bad people think my wine labels are as long as they remember them'. Con-Greg grew up on a vineyard in the Riverland and spent a lot of time in wineries with his father and grandfather. He decided to concentrate on southern Italian grape varieties. It's a virtual winery operation, buying fruit from growers who share his vision and having the wine made wherever he is able to find a facility prepared to assist in the making of micro-quantities. Delinquente is getting a lot of airplay from the smart set, and it's no surprise to see production jump from 600 to 7000 dozen. Exports to the UK, the US, Canada, South Korea, Singapore, Japan, Taiwan, Hong Kong and NZ.

ŸŸŸŸŸ **Roko Il Vagabondo Riverland Montepulciano 2020** This is so perky and pleasing with its raspberry sorbet and jelly flavours, a touch of red lollies, too. But don't be fooled – it is not at all sweet, nor one-dimensional. There's a waft of prosciutto, its crisp acidity keeping a tight frame and ripe, rustic tannins holding some sway. A refreshing style that doesn't last long in the glass. Screw cap. 14% alc. **Rating** 91 To 2023 $25 JF
Roxanne the Razor Riverland Negroamaro Nero d'Avola 2020 I dig how these two Italians – negroamaro and nero d'Avola – morph into a juicy and very slurpable drink. It's light on its feet but there's plenty of flavour: squishy raspberries, Mediterranean herbs and refreshing acidity. Bring on summer. Screw cap. 13% alc. **Rating** 90 To 2022 $25 JF

ŸŸŸŸ **Pretty Boy Riverland Nero d'Avola Rosato 2020** **Rating** 88 To 2021 $25 JF
Weeping Juan Riverland Petillant Naturel 2020 **Rating** 88 $25 JF

Della Fay Wines

NR

3276 Caves Road, Yallingup, WA 6284 **Region** Margaret River
T (08) 9755 2747 **www.**kellysvineyard.com.au **Open** By appt
Winemaker Michael Kelly **Est.** 1999 **Dozens** 3000 **Vyds** 6.4ha

This is the venture of the Kelly family, headed by district veteran Michael Kelly. He gained his degree in wine science from CSU before working at Seville Estate and Mount Mary in the Yarra Valley and Domaine Louis Chapuis in Burgundy, then returning to WA and working for Leeuwin Estate and Sandalford. Michael became the long-term winemaker at Fermoy Estate, while he and his family laid the groundwork for their own brand, buying prime viticultural land in Caves Road, Yallingup, in 1999. They have planted cabernet sauvignon, sauvignon blanc, vermentino, nebbiolo, chardonnay, merlot, malbec and petit verdot; they also make Shiraz from Geographe. 'Della Fay' honours the eponymous Kelly family matriarch. Exports to the Netherlands, South Korea, Singapore, Hong Kong and China.

ΨΨΨΨΨ Margaret River Cabernet Sauvignon 2016 While the oak is evident in this wine, the extra years on it mean that things are starting to integrate very nicely indeed. This is soft and plush with really good length of flavour. Plum, mulberry, roasting pan, hints of cassis and plenty of licorice, aniseed and exotic market spice. The shape of the tannins is a real highlight here. Screw cap. 14% alc. **Rating** 94 **To** 2031 $36 EL

Denton

Viewhill Vineyard, 160 Old Healesville Road, Yarra Glen, Vic 3775 **Region** Yarra Valley
T 0402 346 686 **www.**dentonwine.com **Open** By appt
Winemaker Luke Lambert **Est.** 1997 **Dozens** 2500 **Vyds** 31.3ha

Leading Melbourne architect John Denton and son Simon began the establishment of the vineyard with a first stage planting in 1997, completing the plantings in 2004. The name Viewhill derives from the fact that a granite plug 'was created 370 million years ago, sitting above the surrounding softer sandstones and silt of the valley'. This granite base is most unusual in the Yarra Valley, and, together with the natural amphitheatre that the plug created, has consistently produced exceptional grapes. The principal varieties planted are pinot noir, chardonnay and shiraz, with lesser quantities of nebbiolo, cabernet sauvignon, merlot, cabernet franc and petit verdot. Exports to Japan and Hong Kong.

ΨΨΨΨΨ Yarra Valley Nebbiolo 2017 As far as Australian nebbiolo goes, this is rock 'n' roll. It has the tar-and-roses thing going on, with chinotto, blood orange zest and a sprinkling of fresh herbs. The palate is the clincher, though, with oak a background player, simply offering the right support. Ribbons of furry tannins are let loose, while the high-toned acidity weaves everything back into respectful submission. Diam. 13.5% alc. **Rating** 96 **To** 2035 $55 JF ❂

Yellow Chardonnay 2015 Originally 2 barrels were made of this flor wine, one bottled in 2017, and this new 2nd bottling with 4 years under flor. The colour belies its age, and while it's mellowing on the palate, this is incredibly fresh and complex. The acidity is still in the driver's seat. Nutty, with lemon salt and citrus flavours and so tangy. A light flutter of aldehydes add to its umami flavour and a delicate little sweet spot. 500ml bottle. Diam. 12.5% alc. **Rating** 95 **To** 2023 $50 JF

Yarra Valley Pinot Noir 2019 While there's an abundance of richness and flavour, it's all tempered by structure and the wine's overall finesse. It's fuller bodied but not weighty. Ripe fruit, woodsy spices, licorice and menthol bow to fine and chalky tannins. Lots of texture, plenty of enjoyment now and for a few years yet. Diam. 14% alc. **Rating** 95 **To** 2033 $50 JF

Deviation Road

207 Scott Creek Road, Longwood, SA 5153 **Region** Adelaide Hills
T (08) 8339 2633 **www.**deviationroad.com **Open** 7 days 10–5
Winemaker Kate Laurie **Est.** 1999 **Dozens** 8000 **Vyds** 11.05ha

Continuing a 5-generation family winemaking tradition, Hamish and Kate Laurie created their first wine (Pinot Noir) from the 30yo Laurie family–owned vineyard on Deviation Road in 2002. In '04 Hamish and Kate purchased their property at Longwood, which is the current home to 4ha of shiraz and pinot noir, the winery and tasting room. Disgorging equipment from Kate's family's Manjimup winery, originally imported from Champagne, was shipped to the Adelaide Hills in '08 enabling the first Deviation Road traditional method sparkling wine release. Hamish and Kate consistently produce wines that represent the cool-climate terroir of the Adelaide Hills. Exports to the UK, the US and Hong Kong.

ŸŸŸŸŸ **Beltana Adelaide Hills Blanc de Blancs 2014** Opens with aromas of apple and lemon cream streusel bun. With a fine pithy mousse, the palate is compelling, with all the citrus/lemon chardonnay excitement it can muster. This is added to by a subtle aldehydic complexity that expresses itself in a light quinine character. Totally engaging. Always among the finest – this is next level. Diam. 12.5% alc. Rating 97 $95 TL ✪ ❤

ŸŸŸŸŸ **Altair Adelaide Hills Brut Rosé NV** The latest (October 2020) disgorgement of this traditional-method pale-blush beauty reveals riper and richer pinot-oriented strawberry characters, the flavour and expression both precisely delivered with balanced acidity and toned backbone. Exciting drinkability and sophistication all in one glass. Diam. 12.5% alc. Rating 95 $38 TL
Southcote Adelaide Hills Blanc de Noirs 2018 A minimum of 28 months on lees, disgorged February 2021. A palest of blushes hints at its pinot noir origins, as does the initial lift of crunchy strawberry. Softly creamy on the palate, with a fine mousse. This is such an easy, friendly sparkling with just the right amount of berry zing to finish, those white-top strawberry flavours resonating on the finish. Diam. 12.5% alc. Rating 94 $40 TL
Loftia Adelaide Hills Vintage Brut 2017 Traditional method, disgorged September 2020. The latest disgorgement has stayed true to the Loftia line, lifted with lemon skin at the start, then nuances of creamed bun and a bright lemon citrus palate followed by a fine, long finish. The balance is spot-on for this mouth-watering aperitif style. Diam. 12.5% alc. Rating 94 $48 TL

ŸŸŸŸŸ **Mary's Reserve Adelaide Hills Shiraz 2019** Rating 92 To 2028 $65 TL
South Australia Pinot Gris 2020 Rating 90 To 2024 $30 TL

Devil's Cave Vineyard   ★★★★

250 Forest Drive, Heathcote, Vic 3523 **Region** Heathcote
T 0438 110 183 **www.**devilscavevineyard.com **Open** By appt
Winemaker Luke Lomax, Steve Johnson **Est.** 2012 **Dozens** 1200 **Vyds** 0.4ha
This is an acorn and oak story. After retiring from 40+ years of business in Heathcote, Steve and Gay Johnson purchased a property to enjoy their retirement. In 2010 they planted 0.4ha of shiraz, and in '12 Steve asked Luke Lomax (his niece's husband and a winemaker at Yabby Lake and Heathcote Estate) to help with the first vintage of 33 dozen bottles. The camaraderie was such that the Johnsons formed a partnership with Luke and Jade Lomax, and it's been onwards and upwards since, with an impressive collection of gold and silver medals for the Shiraz. The winery's name comes from an adjacent cave known locally as the Devil's Cave. Exports to Thailand.

ŸŸŸŸŸ **Heathcote Shiraz 2019** Each vintage sees a refinement of shiraz at Devil's Cave. Restrained and aromatic in violets, black/blueberries and dried herbs, this young shiraz – tasted 9 months before release – was tightly coiled and focused, a good sign for a bright future. Full bodied with good depth and weight, the palate framed by firm tannins. The thread of regional spice is an attractive reminder of place. Worthy of time in the cellar. Screw cap. 14.5% alc. Rating 92 To 2034 $36 JP
Heathcote Cabernet Sauvignon 2019 Dark, dense purple. Lifted herbals, black fruits, blueberry, bay leaf and regional mineral/iodine aromas. Worthwhile tasting this wine in situ, within sight of the ancient, rust-coloured mineral-rich Cambrian

soils. Firm, in part due to the role of dry tannins. There is plenty of room here for ageing. Give it the time. Screw cap. 14% alc. **Rating** 90 **To** 2036 $32 JP

Devil's Corner   ★★★★☆

The Hazards Vineyard, Sherbourne Road, Apslawn, Tas 7190 **Region** East Coast Tasmania
T (03) 6257 8881 **www.**devilscorner.com.au **Open** 7 days 10–5
Winemaker Tom Wallace, Anthony de Amicis **Est.** 1999 **Dozens** 70 000 **Vyds** 175ha
This is one of the separately managed operations of Brown Brothers' Tasmanian interests,
taking The Hazards Vineyard on the east coast as its chief source – it is planted to pinot noir,
chardonnay, sauvignon blanc, pinot gris, riesling, gewürztraminer and savagnin. The avant-
garde labels mark a decided change from the past and also distinguish Devil's Corner from the
other Tasmanian activities of Brown Brothers. Exports to all major markets.

ΨΨΨΨΨ **Resolution Tasmania Chardonnay 2018** Devil's Corner has grown up, and
this is a very serious Tasmanian chardonnay of larger-than-life proportions. Grand
fruit concentration brims with grapefruit, juicy white peach, spicy fig and wild
lemon. The delicate white blossom fragrance of the bouquet changes up a gear
on the palate, rich and powerful, rumbling with wild honey, ginger, even
toasted sweet corn. Cashew-nut oak unites with high-tensile Tasmanian acidity to
charge a finish of incredible presence and disarming stamina. Screw cap. 13% alc.
Rating 95 **To** 2028 $32 TS ✪
Tasmania Pinot Noir Rosé 2020 Tom Wallace has made quite a splash
with this new and delicious Tassie rosé, and it deserves to be everyone's house
pour this year. The delicacy of pinot noir is captured in a medium, bright salmon
hue and pristine rose petals, morello cherries and strawberry hull. Sensitive barrel
work amplifies wonderfully fine-grained texture and draws out a long finish,
without for a moment interrupting fruit purity or flow. Crystalline Tasmanian
acidity illuminates a brilliant finish. This is my shade of pink. Screw cap. 12% alc.
Rating 95 **To** 2021 $22 TS ✪ ♥

ΨΨΨΨΨ **Tasmania Chardonnay 2020 Rating** 93 **To** 2023 $22 TS ✪
Tasmania Pinot Noir 2019 Rating 92 **To** 2024 $22 TS ✪
Tasmania Mt Amos Pinot Noir 2019 Rating 92 **To** 2034 $65 TS

Devil's Lair   ★★★★★

Rocky Road, Forest Grove via Margaret River, WA 6286 **Region** Margaret River
T (08) 9759 2000 **www.**devils-lair.com
Winemaker Ben Miller, Matt Godfrey **Est.** 1990
Having rapidly carved out a high reputation for itself through a combination of clever
packaging and impressive wine quality, Devil's Lair was acquired by Southcorp in 1996. The
estate vineyards have been substantially increased since, now with sauvignon blanc, semillon,
chardonnay, cabernet sauvignon, merlot, shiraz, cabernet franc and petit verdot, supplemented
by grapes purchased from contract growers. Production has increased from 40 000 dozen to
many times greater, largely due to its Fifth Leg and Dance with the Devil wines. The top-tier
9th Chamber wines are only made in exceptional vintages. Exports to the UK, the US and
other major markets.

ΨΨΨΨΨ **Margaret River Cabernet Sauvignon 2019** Typically pure and speaking in
a clear voice of raspberry, pomegranate, red licorice and exotic spice. The style
has been evolving toward this point at Devil's Lair for years, and it is beautiful
for it. Elegant, long, supple and harmonious. A classical, refined wine from an
understated, cooler vintage – its ageing potential is proven. Screw cap. 14% alc.
Rating 95 **To** 2035 $40 EL
Dance with the Devil Margaret River Chardonnay 2019 The bouquet has
pronounced barrel-fermentation aromas benefiting from a hint of smoky oak, and
the palate takes the baton in a smooth movement. It's easy to take this level of
chardonnay for granted, but that's the gift of a climate that is so reliable for crystal-
clear varietal expression. Screw cap. 13% alc. **Rating** 94 **To** 2025 $25 JH ✪

ΨΨΨΨ♀ **The Hidden Cave Margaret River Chardonnay 2020** Rating 92 To 2028
$20 EL ✪
Dance with the Devil Margaret River Cabernet Sauvignon 2019
Rating 92 To 2030 $30 EL
The Hidden Cave Margaret River Cabernet Shiraz 2018 Rating 92
To 2028 $20 EL ✪
The Hidden Cave Margaret River Semillon Sauvignon Blanc 2020
Rating 91 To 2024 $20 EL ✪

Dewey Station Wines   ★★★

14 Jane Street, Smithfield, SA 5114 **Region** Barossa Valley
T 0476 100 245 **www.deweystationwines.com.au**
Winemaker Stefan Dewey **Est.** 2017 **Dozens** 900
This micro-business (beginning with 135 dozen) has grown, but it's hard to say how much is
still in the tank. Winemaker Stefan Dewey has covered a lot of ground since 2007, all within
the Barossa Valley. He worked in retail, distribution and marketing (enrolling in the wine
marketing course at the University of Adelaide) before taking the ultimate step of beginning
to make wine. He and wife Eleanor share a conviction that wine should be shared with friends
and lots of laughter. Boring, it should not be. But there has to be a limit, and I'll declare my
hand by saying the label designs and production names will only ever gain niche market shares.
But, of course, if you establish that niche, demand drawing supply, the game changes. Exports
to the UK, Japan and South Korea.

ΨΨΨΨ **Anne-Inspired Barossa Valley Shiraz 2018** 50% pressings, 4% whole bunches;
matured for 17 months in 50% new French oak barrels. Powerful black fruits and
black licorice are bolstered by lashings of dark chocolate oak, concluding with
sweet black prunes contrasting with clunky, drying oak tannins. A match for the
heavy bottle. Rich, ripe, raw and ready. Cork. 14.8% alc. **Rating** 89 To 2028
$80 TS

Dexter Wines   ★★★★☆

210 Foxeys Road, Tuerong, Vic 3915 (postal) **Region** Mornington Peninsula
T (03) 5989 7007 **www.dexterwines.com.au**
Winemaker Tod Dexter **Est.** 2006 **Dozens** 1800 **Vyds** 7.1ha
Tod Dexter travelled to the US with the intention of enjoying some skiing; having done
that, he became an apprentice winemaker at Cakebread Cellars, a well-known Napa Valley
establishment. After 7 years he returned to Australia and the Mornington Peninsula, and began
the establishment of his vineyard in 1987; planted to pinot noir (4ha) and chardonnay (3.1ha).
To keep the wolves from the door he became winemaker at Stonier and leased his vineyard to
them. Having left Stonier to become the Yabby Lake winemaker, and spurred on by turning
50 in 2006 (and at the urging of friends), he and wife Debbie established the Dexter label.
The quality of his wines has been impeccable, the Pinot Noir especially so. Exports to the
UAE and Japan.

ΨΨΨΨΨ **Mornington Peninsula Chardonnay 2019** The bright straw-green hue
heralds a beautifully handled wine. The fragrant bouquet of fused fruit and oak is
increased on the harmonious, perfectly balanced palate. There's ultimate detail to
the wine, with white peach all the way through to the finish and aftertaste. Screw
cap. 13.5% alc. **Rating** 97 To 2030 $40 JH ✪

ΨΨΨΨΨ **Black Label Mornington Peninsula Pinot Noir 2018** Don't be fooled by the
lighter hue, as this seduces with its aromatics, largely thanks to 75% whole bunches
in the fermentation, ensuring perfect unison of fruit from a warm, ripe vintage. It's
heady with florals, damp autumn leaves, cherries, rhubarb, cardamom and so much
more. The fuller-bodied palate opens up with all-important plush ripe tannins
and juicy, raspberry-like acidity strutting their stuff. It concludes well and flavours
linger. Screw cap. 13.5% alc. **Rating** 96 To 2031 $90 JF

Mornington Peninsula Pinot Noir 2019 While there's no shortage of flavour, tannin or acidity, Dexter wines tend to be in a tighter, almost lighter frame. As always, the aromas are wonderful wild strawberries and an abundance of cherries, all dusted with Middle Eastern spices including sumac. There's cherry liqueur across the palate and a vibrancy for enjoyment now, yet will reward the patient. Screw cap. 13.5% alc. **Rating** 95 **To** 2030 $60 JF

Di Sciascio Family Wines ★★★★

2 Pincott Street, Newtown, Vic 3220 **Region** Victoria
T 0417 384 272 **www**.dsaswines.com.au
Winemaker Matthew Di Sciascio, Andrew Santarossa **Est.** 2012 **Dozens** 3000
Matthew Di Sciascio's journey through wine has been an odyssey of Homeric proportions. His working life began as an apprentice boilermaker in his father's business. In 1991 he accompanied his father on a trip to Italy, where a shared bottle of wine in the kitchen of his uncle's house sowed the seed that flowered back in Australia. After helping his father and friends with garage winemaking, the vinous pace increased in '97 with vineyard work in the Yarra Valley and enrolment in Dookie Agricultural College's viticultural course. It accelerated further with the establishment of Bellbrae Estate in Geelong and enrolling (in 2002) in the new Deakin University wine and science degree, graduating in '05 as co-dux. In Dec '10 the responsibility for seriously ill parents and a young daughter led to the decision to sell his share of Bellbrae to his financial partners, and (in '12) to start this venture.

♀♀♀♀♀ **D'Sas Heathcote Sangiovese 2019** Perfumed, lithe yet flavoursome. An impressive sangio. All cherries, pips and spices with some dried Mediterranean herbs. The palate is lighter framed even though there's texture from the grainy tannins and plenty of refreshing acidity. Unencumbered by oak. Lunch wine sorted. Screw cap. 14.2% alc. **Rating** 92 **To** 2026 $40 JF

♀♀♀♀ **D'Sas Heathcote Sparkling Shiraz 2018 Rating** 89 $45 JF

Dickinson Estate ★★★★☆

2414 Cranbrook Road, Boyup Brook, WA 6244 **Region** Blackwood Valley
T (08) 9769 1080 **www**.dickinsonestate.com.au
Winemaker Coby Ladwig, Luke Eckersley **Est.** 1994 **Dozens** 6000 **Vyds** 8.52ha
Trevor and Mary Dickinson went from a 20-year life at sea with the Australian Navy to becoming farmers at Boyup Brook in 1987. They learned on the job, initially cropping and breeding sheep for wool, then cattle and fat lambs. In '94 they diversified further, planting shiraz, chardonnay, sauvignon blanc and cabernet sauvignon, and appointing the highly experienced team of Coby Ladwig and Luke Eckersley to make the wines. Exports to the UK and China.

♀♀♀♀♀ **Limited Release Blackwood Valley Shiraz 2019** Black cherry, blackberry and blood plum on the nose. The palate is fleshy, bright and quite delicious – the tannins shape the wine through the cleansing finish. Screw cap. 14.5% alc. **Rating** 93 **To** 2030 $35 EL
Limited Release Blackwood Valley Cabernet Sauvignon 2019 Juicy and succulent cabernet sauvignon. The tannins are very fine, erring towards formless, however this makes for uncomplicated early drinking. Very pretty, all things in place and well constructed. Screw cap. 14.5% alc. **Rating** 90 **To** 2027 $35 EL

♀♀♀♀ **Single Vineyard Blackwood Valley Sauvignon Blanc 2020 Rating** 89 **To** 2023 $18 EL ❂

DiGiorgio Family Wines ★★★★☆

14918 Riddoch Highway, Coonawarra, SA 5263 **Region** Coonawarra
T (08) 8736 3222 **www**.digiorgio.com.au **Open** 7 days 10–5
Winemaker Peter Douglas, Bryan Tonkin **Est.** 1998 **Dozens** 25 000 **Vyds** 353.53ha

Stefano DiGiorgio emigrated from Abruzzo, Italy, in 1952. Over the years, he and his family gradually expanded their holdings at Lucindale to 126ha. In '89 he began planting cabernet sauvignon, chardonnay, merlot, shiraz and pinot noir. In 2002 the family purchased the historic Rouge Homme winery and its surrounding 13.5ha of vines from Southcorp. The plantings have since been increased to almost 230ha, the lion's share to cabernet sauvignon. The enterprise offers full winemaking services to vignerons on the Limestone Coast. Exports to all major markets.

ŸŸŸŸŸ **Francesco Reserve Limestone Coast Cabernet Sauvignon 2012** A shapely and powerful wine, cruising into older age rather well. Excellent colour for starters, savoury fragrance, with wafts of leather and potpourri. The full-bodied palate is being served well by its tannins – still plentiful. Another decade to go on this. Easily. Cork. 13.5% alc. **Rating** 95 **To** 2033 $80 JF

ŸŸŸŸŸ **Coonawarra Cabernet Sauvignon 2018 Rating** 93 **To** 2035 $29 JF
Coonawarra Chardonnay 2019 Rating 90 **To** 2025 $29 JF
Coonawarra Shiraz 2018 Rating 90 **To** 2030 $29 JF
Emporio Coonawarra Merlot Cabernet Sauvignon Cabernet Franc 2018 Rating 90 **To** 2030 $29 JF
Limestone Coast Tempranillo 2019 Rating 90 **To** 2024 $25 JF
Coonawarra Sparkling Merlot 2019 Rating 90 $29 JF

Dinny Goonan   ★★★★☆

880 Winchelsea-Deans Marsh Road, Bambra, Vic 3241 **Region** Geelong
T 0438 408 420 **www.**dinnygoonan.com.au **Open** 7 days Jan, w'ends & public hols Nov–Jun
Winemaker Dinny Goonan, Angus Goonan **Est.** 1990 **Dozens** 1500 **Vyds** 5.5ha
The genesis of Dinny Goonan dates back to 1988, when Dinny bought a 20ha property near Bambra, in the hinterland of the Otway Coast. Dinny had recently completed a viticulture diploma at CSU and initially a wide range of varieties was planted in what is now known as the Nursery Block, to establish those best suited to the area. As these came into production Dinny headed back to CSU, where he completed a wine science degree. Production is focused on shiraz and riesling, with more extensive plantings of these varieties.

ŸŸŸŸŸ **Single Vineyard Riesling 2020** A strong suit with this producer, riesling takes on a wide-ranging complexity in 2020 against a positively zesty exuberance of flavour. A challenging vintage is put to rest. This wine rocks. Fragrant lime citrus, lemon drop, touch of spice, nashi pear running free across a fleshy palate. Tingly acidity. Screw cap. 12.5% alc. **Rating** 95 **To** 2031 $30 JP ❂
Chardonnay 2020 A fine follow-up to the 2019 chardonnay, echoing some of the keen acidity and juicy fruit of that particular vintage. Breaks out with a rush of grapefruit, lemon zest, white peach and signature quince. Firm and tight in structure, with an almond meal smoothness. It's a more restrained, elegant style, the kind that Dinny Goonan does particularly well. Screw cap. 13% alc. **Rating** 94 **To** 2028 $35 JP

ŸŸŸŸŸ **Single Vineyard Shiraz 2019 Rating** 93 **To** 2029 $32 JP

Dirty Three Wines   ★★★★★

64 Cashin Street, Inverloch, Vic 3996 **Region** Gippsland
T 0413 547 932 **www.**dirtythreewines.com.au **Open** Thurs–Mon 11–5.30, 7 days in summer
Winemaker Marcus Satchell **Est.** 2012 **Dozens** 2500 **Vyds** 4ha
The name originates from the 3 friends (and families) who decided to pool their talents in making and marketing wine. Marcus Satchell, Cameron McKenzie and Stuart Gregor were all well known in the nether world of small-volume, high-quality winemaking. Stuart and Cam also had the distraction of Four Pillars Gin in Healesville, a fairytale story of success in its own right. Since then, Marcus and his partner Lisa Sartori have become the sole

owners but the name has been retained, now attributed to the 3 'dirts' that produce their single-vineyard pinots.

♥♥♥♥♥ **The Dirty Chardy Gippsland Chardonnay 2019** The inaugural release under The Dirty label, of course relating to the dirt/soil where the fruit is grown. This has come together well. It's juicy, with a wall of citrus (especially lemon and grapefruit), ginger flower and spice. Oak is very neatly tucked away. It's flinty, with a terrific line of acidity that coats the palate. Just a ripper drink. Screw cap. 13% alc. **Rating** 95 **To** 2029 $39 JF

Dirt One Gippsland Pinot Noir 2019 A deceptive wine, as it's perfumed, quite fine and even subtle. Then the flavours build. Dark cherries, blood orange, earthy, woodsy spices and juniper, with a fleck of fresh herbs and menthol coolness. Sweet, ripe and detailed tannins energise, as does its bright acidity. Entirely convincing and delicious. Screw cap. 14% alc. **Rating** 95 **To** 2030 $60 JF

Aldo Silverwaters Gippsland Shiraz 2019 Named in honour of DTW's co-owner Lisa Satori's father, to celebrate his 80th birthday. Nice tribute, as the wine's terrific. Lots of tannin, yet it imparts texture and savouriness across the medium-bodied palate. Unusual and compelling flavours render it complex, with wood spice, juniper, amaro, lead pencil and dark fruits infused with iodine. Screw cap. 14% alc. **Rating** 95 **To** 2029 $39 JF

Dirt Two Gippsland Pinot Noir 2019 As with Dirt One, this is a highly perfumed pinot and it actually tastes of whole bunches (as in a touch sappy) but only whole berries are in the mix. There's a juiciness to this, blood orange over the cherries and pips, with just a sprinkling of spice. Nicely shaped tannins are firm but not voluminous. There's fresh acidity and good length. Drinkability? Hell yeah. Screw cap. 13% alc. **Rating** 94 **To** 2030 $60 JF

♥♥♥♥♡ **All the Dirts Gippsland Pinot Noir 2019 Rating** 93 **To** 2028 $39 JF
Dirt Three Gippsland Pinot Noir 2019 Rating 93 **To** 2028 $60 JF

Dr Edge   ★★★★☆

5 Cato Avenue, West Hobart, Tas 7000 (postal) **Region** Southern Tasmania
T 0439 448 151 **www**.dr-edge.com
Winemaker Peter Dredge **Est.** 2015 **Dozens** 800 **Vyds** 1.5ha

After working as a winemaker for Petaluma, Peter Dredge moved to Tasmania in 2009, spending 7 years within the Accolade group, becoming chief winemaker at Bay of Fires. He moved proactively to become a consultant and self-employed winemaker to shortcircuit the uncertainty then existing around Accolade and its future. In '15 he sourced a small amount of pinot noir from Joe Holyman of Stoney Rise and Gerald Ellis of Meadowbank to start his own label. He made the wine at Moorilla as a contract client with sole control of the winemaking process. In '15, during vintage, the Ellis family, owners of Meadowbank, approached Pete to form a partnership to relaunch Meadowbank. As part of the deal, Meadowbank have given Pete a sole lease arrangement to 1.5ha, planted evenly between pinot noir, chardonnay and riesling. Exports to the US, Taiwan and China.

♥♥♥♥♡ **East Tasmania Riesling 2020** Bouncing with all the complexity, texture and pyrotechnics of wild fermentation, whole bunches and barrel maturation, this is a unique riesling, foremost and unashamedly of its method. Fresh ginger and ginger beer are accented with vanilla over a core of tense, crunchy lemon and lime. With the highwire acidity and fruit concentration to handle fine phenolic grip, it heightens the tension on a long finish. As idiosyncratic as it is captivating. Screw cap. 12.5% alc. **Rating** 93 **To** 2030 $35 TS

Tasmania Pinot Noir 2020 Pete Dredge's house style is more fruit impact, more exotic nuance, more structural tension, ultimately more 'Edgey'. The herbal potpourri spice of whole bunches contrasts the juicy poached strawberries of carbonic maceration, tensioned with high-pitched Southern Tasmanian acidity and crunchy al dente tannins. It holds every detail with considerable persistence. One for the cellar. Screw cap. 12.5% alc. **Rating** 93 **To** 2030 $55 TS

South Tasmania Chardonnay 2020 Pete Dredge's use of partial whole clusters during fermentation lends a flattering ginger beer character to his white wines, present here in front of chardonnay's grapefruit, lemon and spicy white peach. Tight, glittering, slightly stark acidity coasts long through a finish of determination and endurance. As out there as ever, with a big future before it. Screw cap. 12.5% alc. **Rating** 92 **To** 2030 $55 TS

ΨΨΨΨ   **South Tasmania Riesling 2020 Rating** 89 **To** 2035 $35 TS

Dodgy Brothers ★★★★★

PO Box 655, McLaren Vale, SA 5171 **Region** McLaren Vale
T 0450 000 373 **www.**dodgybrotherswines.com
Winemaker Wes Pearson **Est.** 2010 **Dozens** 2000
This is a partnership between Canadian-born Flying Winemaker Wes Pearson, viticulturist Peter Bolte and grapegrower Peter Sommerville. Wes graduated from the University of British Columbia's biochemistry program in 2008, along the way working at wineries including Château Léoville-Las Cases in Bordeaux. Also in '08 he and his family moved to McLaren Vale, and after working at several wineries, he joined the Australian Wine Research Institute as a sensory analyst. Peter Bolte has over 35 vintages in McLaren Vale under his belt and was the original Dodgy Brother. Peter Sommerville's vineyard provides cabernet sauvignon, cabernet franc and petit verdot for the Dodgy Brothers Bordeaux blend. Exports to Canada.

ΨΨΨΨΨ   **Juxtaposed Old Vine Old Block Sherry Vineyard Blewitt Springs Shiraz 2019** The Blewitt Springs postcode is tattooed across the elevated florals, bouncy blue/boysenberry scents and detailed sandy tannins. Elastic tension here, the fruit reverberating as it pulls the saliva from the back of the mouth while making one hungry. Dried seaweed, olive, salami and a satchel of clove, cardamom and pepper, too. Long and energetic. Lithe and sinuous. Frisky and engaging. Fine. Screw cap. 14.5% alc. **Rating** 96 **To** 2028 $37 NG ✪

Juxtaposed Old Vine Sandy Corner Block Wait Vineyard Blewitt Springs Shiraz 2019 The duo of single-plot Blewitt Springs shiraz wines under this label is exceptional. There is possibly no better expression of upper-echelon warm-climate shiraz at such a price. Premium pedigree. The salient point of differentiation being the riper, coffee grind/mocha elements of this cuvée and its darker-fruit aspersions. Minimal handling is manifest in juicy acidity and moreish precise tannins. Lots of kombu umami elements, conferring warmth and savouriness. A real pulse and fine length. Screw cap. 14.5% alc. **Rating** 96 **To** 2028 $37 NG ✪

Juxtaposed Old Vine McLaren Vale Grenache 2019 A meld of fruit from the subzones that deify elegance when it comes to grenache in the Vale: Blewitt Springs and Clarendon. Savoury overall, with poached strawberry, white pepper and ample spice, strung taut across a briary patina of tannins, sandy and detailed. A spurt of freshness pulls it long. Real pinosity here. Superlative value! Screw cap. 14.3% alc. **Rating** 94 **To** 2025 $29 NG ✪

The Dilemma 2019 There is but a handful of producers that I would make my first call in the Vale. Dodgy Bros is entrenched as one of them. 57/43% cabernets sauvignon/franc each from noble single vineyards. We are clearly in the lap of a warm maritime zone, pulling this classic blend off with aplomb. Particularly in gentle hands, such as these. Piercing currant, bell pepper, spearmint, olive and hedgerow scents, splayed across some pliant sage-doused tannins. Screw cap. 13.9% alc. **Rating** 94 **To** 2028 $29 NG ✪

ΨΨΨΨ♀   **Juxtaposed McLaren Vale Fiano 2020 Rating** 92 **To** 2023 $26 NG
McLaren Vale Shiraz 2019 Rating 92 **To** 2024 $25 NG ✪

DogRidge Wine Company ★★★★

129 Bagshaws Road, McLaren Flat, SA 5171 **Region** McLaren Vale
T (08) 8383 0140 **www.**dogridge.com.au **Open** Mon–Fri 11–5, Sat–Sun 12–4
Winemaker Fred Howard **Est.** 1991 **Dozens** 18 000 **Vyds** 56ha
Dave and Jen Wright (co-owners with Fred and Sarah Howard) had a combined background of dentistry, art and a CSU viticultural degree when they moved from Adelaide to McLaren Flat to become vignerons. They inherited shiraz and grenache vines planted in the early 1940s as a source for Chateau Reynella fortified wines, and their vineyards now range from 2001 plantings to some of the oldest vines in the immediate district. Quality at one end, value-packed at the other end. Exports to Canada, Singapore and Japan.

ΨΨΨΨΨ **Fortified Viognier NV** This is an idiosyncratic concept by virtue of the variety, historically seldom if ever fortified. Excellent! The spirit is high grade and not sticking its alcohol beyond the warm flow of chestnut, apricot pith, orange verbena, molasses and crème Catalan. Very long. Poised. Delicious. Screw cap. 19% alc. **Rating** 95 $25 NG ✪

ΨΨΨΨΨ **MVP McLaren Vale Petit Verdot 2014 Rating** 93 To 2024 $65 NG
The Pup McLaren Vale Cabernet Merlot 2017 Rating 92 To 2023 $20 NG ✪
Most Valuable Player McLaren Vale Cabernet Sauvignon 2013 Rating 92 To 2022 $67 NG
Grand Old Brand New McLaren Vale Shiraz Petit Verdot Cabernet Sauvignon 2014 Rating 92 To 2030 $40 NG
The Pup McLaren Vale GSM 2017 Rating 91 To 2022 $20 NG ✪

DogRock Winery ★★★★☆

114 Degraves Road, Crowlands, Vic 3377 **Region** Pyrenees
T 0409 280 317 **www.**dogrock.com.au **Open** By appt
Winemaker Allen Hart **Est.** 1998 **Dozens** 1000 **Vyds** 6.2ha
This is the venture of Allen (now full-time winemaker) and Andrea (viticulturist) Hart. Having purchased the property in 1998, the planting of shiraz, riesling, tempranillo, grenache, chardonnay and marsanne began in 2000 (0.2ha of touriga nacional added in '16 and arinto and azal in '20). Given Allen's former post as research scientist/winemaker with Foster's, the attitude taken to winemaking is unexpected. The estate-grown wines are made in a low-tech fashion, without gas cover or filtration; the Harts say, 'All wine will be sealed with a screw cap and no DogRock wine will ever be released under natural cork bark'. DogRock installed the first solar-powered irrigation system in Australia, capable of supplying water 365 days a year, even at night or in cloudy conditions.

ΨΨΨΨΨ **Degraves Road Single Vineyard Reserve Pyrenees Shiraz 2019** Warm seasonal ripeness on display here, lashings of fruit and spice that fulfil expectations of 'reserve' quality with its depth and layers of flavour. Pyrenees shiraz with ageing potential plus. Screw cap. 14% alc. **Rating** 95 To 2032 $38 JP
Pyrenees Shiraz 2019 Makes an immediate impact with deep inky hues and intensity of aromas and flavour. Resolutely a Pyrenees shiraz with trademark notes of pepper, Aussie bush and menthol. A very warm growing season has brought out a glorious array of ripe black fruits, heady spice and a relative richness matched with toasty, chocolatey oak and supple tannins. For now or later. Screw cap. 13.5% alc. **Rating** 95 To 2032 $30 JP ✪
Pyrenees Cabernet Sauvignon Shiraz 2019 A 60/40% blend matured for 10 months in French oak (40% new). A brightly coloured, medium-bodied wine with a mix of red and black fruits, spices and fine tannins that have almost casually absorbed the contribution of new oak. The low alcohol is all good. Screw cap. 12.5% alc. **Rating** 95 To 2030 $30 JH ✪
El Rojo 2018 El Rojo – 'the red' – makes a grand entrance, all grenache-style pepper, cherries and baked plum with a confection/blackcurrant bon-bon heart. Moves into savoury, earthy mode and introduces bright, red fruits, pomegranate

and spice among a largely quiet oak component with tannins persistent. Keeps it medium in body and tight. Screw cap. 13.5% alc. **Rating** 95 **To** 2035 $65 JP

♟♟♟♟♟ **El Blanco 2019 Rating** 92 **To** 2026 $38 JP
Pyrenees Grenache 2019 Rating 90 **To** 2028 $30 JP

Domaine A ★★★★☆

105 Tea Tree Road, Campania, Tas 7026 **Region** Southern Tasmania
T (03) 6260 4174 **www**.domaine-a.com.au **Open** Sat–Sun 11–5
Winemaker Conor van der Reest **Est.** 1973 **Dozens** 5000 **Vyds** 11ha
Effective from 1 March 2018 ownership of Domaine A passed from Peter Althaus, its long-term custodian, to Moorilla Estate. There were no changes to existing employees, with Conor van de Reest continuing as winemaker. The inclusion of Domaine A's stock in the sale will be of particular relevance with the opening of Mona's 172-room hotel on the Moorilla property in '22. Mona is Australia's largest private museum showing ancient, modern and contemporary art, founded by philanthropist and collector David Walsh. Exports to Singapore, Japan, Hong Kong and China.

♟♟♟♟♟ **Stoney Vineyard Cabernet Sauvignon 2017** The little brother of Domaine A's iconic cabernet is wonderfully characterful and enduring. Brimming with all the fragrance of the lavender that lines this vineyard, this is a vintage of compact, crunchy blackcurrants backed with a long-enduring framework of firm, fine tannins, dark chocolate oak and lingering acid line. One of the greats. Boasting screw cap for the first time, it's set to live for decades. Screw cap. 13.7% alc. **Rating** 93 **To** 2042 $35 TS

♟♟♟♟ **Stoney Vineyard Pinot Noir 2019 Rating** 89 **To** 2029 $29 TS

Domaine Asmara ★★★★☆

Gibb Road, Toolleen, Vic 3551 **Region** Heathcote
T (03) 5433 6133 **www**.domaineasmara.com **Open** 7 days 9–6.30
Winemaker Sanguine Estate **Est.** 2008 **Dozens** 3000 **Vyds** 12ha
Chemical engineer Andreas Greiving had a lifelong dream to own and operate a vineyard, and the opportunity came along with the global financial crisis. He was able to purchase a vineyard planted to shiraz, cabernet sauvignon, cabernet franc, durif and viognier, and have the wines contract-made. The venture is co-managed by dentist wife Hennijati. The red wines are made from controlled yields of 1–1.5t/acre, hence their concentration. Exports to the UK, Vietnam, Malaysia, Hong Kong and China.

♟♟♟♟♟ **Reserve Heathcote Shiraz 2019** A voluminous, all-stops-out kind of shiraz celebrating richness in keeping with the Asmara house style. Corralling such abundance takes a steady hand, combining the swathes of blackberries, chocolate, minty spice and licorice into a well-structured entity via oak and even-handed tannins. Asmara succeeds. Cork. 15.8% alc. **Rating** 93 **To** 2029 $49 JP
Infinity Heathcote Shiraz 2019 An all-round intense drinking experience, a walk on the other side where fruit ripeness is heading off the charts. The question to be asked is: is it in balance? The answer is in the affirmative. The fruit is allowed to sing a full opera while oak and tannin are definitely in a sympathetic, supporting role. Amid the blackberries, licorice, leather, prune and savouriness a touch of eucalyptus brightens and entices. Cork. 15.8% alc. **Rating** 93 **To** 2028 $88 JP
Private Collection Heathcote Shiraz 2019 Boasts all that we enjoy about Heathcote shiraz from the deepest, darkest colour imaginable and compelling aromas, to the velvety smooth run over the tongue. Cassis is strong in this one, together with a leafy earthiness and chocolatey spice that is quite arresting. Fine tannins follow on cue. Cork. 14.8% alc. **Rating** 92 **To** 2026 $35 JP
Private Reserve Heathcote Durif 2019 Living large and for some time, this durif demands a lot more time in the cellar. A complex opening of blue fruits,

cassis, Dutch licorice, earthy spice aromas with smoky oak. Offers a powerful fruit and sturdy tannin display on the palate. Bold and big boned, it is years away from its best. Put it in the cellar and leave it there for a long while. Cork. 15% alc. **Rating** 91 **To** 2038 $59 JP

🍷🍷🍷🍷   Infinity Heathcote Durif 2019 **Rating** 89 **To** 2038 $98 JP

Domaine Naturaliste   ★★★★★

160 Johnson Road, Wilyabrup, WA 6280 **Region** Margaret River
T (08) 9755 6776 **www.**domainenaturaliste.com.au **Open** 7 days 10–5
Winemaker Bruce Dukes **Est.** 2012 **Dozens** 12000 **Vyds** 21ha
Bruce Dukes' career dates back over 30 years, its foundations built around a degree in agronomy from the University of WA, followed by a master's degree in viticulture and agronomy from the University of California (Davis). A 4-year stint at Francis Ford Coppola's iconic Niebaum-Coppola winery in the Napa Valley followed. Back in WA Bruce worked with a consultancy and contract winemaking business in Margaret River in 2000. His winery was set up to handle small and large amounts of fruit, but it was not until '12 that he made his own wine under the Domaine Naturaliste label. The quality of all the wines is excellent. Exports to the UK, the US, Canada and China.

🍷🍷🍷🍷🍷   Artus Margaret River Chardonnay 2019 Whole-bunch pressed, wild-yeast fermented in new (40%) and used French oak. The bouquet is complex with funky (good) aromas, the palate briefly nodding to the bouquet before moving on to a pure stream of fresh citrus and white peach. The balance and aftertaste are special. Screw cap. 13% alc. **Rating** 97 **To** 2034 $49 JH ✪

🍷🍷🍷🍷🍷   Rachis Margaret River Syrah 2019 Stemmy/sappy/spicy nose that basically jumps out of the glass. While the fruit occupies the midnight end of the spectrum, the pink-peppercorn spice brings it back closer to the middle. This is succulent, fleshy, crunchy … quite gorgeous. A resounding YES, and thoroughly of the 'modern Margaret River way' for shiraz. Bravo. Screw cap. 14% alc. **Rating** 96 **To** 2030 $32 EL ✪

Morus Margaret River Cabernet Sauvignon 2017 Cassis, mulberry, salted black licorice and Szechuan peppercorns. Very long, very dense and lots going on. In his wisdom, my uncle once told me, 'The secret to a good party is too loud, too busy and too dark.' This wine has all the makings of a great party – everything crammed into the bottle with the endurance to go long. Cork. 14% alc. **Rating** 96 **To** 2041 $89 EL

Le Naturaliste Margaret River Cabernet Franc 2018 Dark chocolate, cassis and mulberry adorn the nose here. The palate is huge, concentrated, driven by oak but navigated by sensitive needles of violet, blackberry, licorice and aniseed. The finish is floral, as one expects cabernet franc to be, but it remains a huge wine. The florals are amplified by an engine powered by the sunshine of the 2018 vintage. Cork. 14% alc. **Rating** 96 **To** 2051 $89 EL

Sauvage Margaret River Sauvignon Blanc 2018 Spicy white pepper and nectarine play alongside red apple skins and star anise. This is modern, glossy, seamless winemaking. Nothing but good things to say here, brilliant stuff. Screw cap. 13% alc. **Rating** 95 **To** 2030 $32 EL ✪

Floris Margaret River Chardonnay 2019 Spicy yellow peach, flakes of sea salt and sprinklings of crushed cashew and star anise make for a complex, rich (yet somehow delicate) and precise chardonnay. Glassy texture and very fine phenolic structure places this in top-shelf company. Unbelievable value for money. Screw cap. 13% alc. **Rating** 95 **To** 2031 $30 EL ✪

Discovery Margaret River Cabernet Sauvignon 2018 Perfect weather and yields in '18, the resulting wines standing on the shoulders of their predecessors. The nose here is tempting to say the least – cassis, raspberry and fields of violets and sage. The palate follows obediently, the acidity being the last thing that swoops in and cleans everything up … what a gorgeous wine. Testament to the year, the

hands and the vineyards. Ridiculous price. Screw cap. 14% alc. **Rating** 95 **To** 2030
$24 EL ✪

Discovery Margaret River Sauvignon Blanc Semillon 2020 Salivating
gooseberry, sugar snap pea, jasmine florals and white spice define the nose, the
palate follows suit. This is bouncy and delicious, with brilliant expression of
flavour. The barrel work is almost imperceptible, save for the chalky phenolics
and plush texture on the palate. Lovely. Screw cap. 13% alc. **Rating** 94 **To** 2024
$24 EL ✪

♟♟♟♟♟ **Discovery Margaret River Chardonnay 2019** **Rating** 93 **To** 2028 $24 EL ✪
Discovery Margaret River Syrah 2018 **Rating** 90 **To** 2024 $24 EL

 # Dominic Wines ★★★

8 Kay Ave, Berri, SA 5343 **Region** Riverland
T (08) 8582 5524 **www.dominicwines.com** **Open** Mon–Fri 8.30–5
Winemaker Linley Schultz **Est.** 2004 **Dozens** 2100 **Vyds** 200ha
Third-generation vignerons and producers, the Dominic family estate is based at Berri in
South Australia's Riverland. Post-WWII they planted a simple block with rows of shiraz,
gordo and mourvèdre, supplying to G Gramp and Son (forerunners to Orlando). The list
of varieties expanded with chardonnay and cabernet, while vineyard methods modernised
as well. Son Brian took over the Riverland vineyards in 1992, further expanding until now
the family sources fruit from both their own and grower vineyards in the region as well as
extending their reach to more than 40 growers from Langhorne Creek, Adelaide Hills and
Coonawarra. The portfolio includes Black Label, Evolution, Henry and Lucas and Boundary
Station from Australia, and Edith Sounds from NZ. (TL)

♟♟♟♟ **Adelaide Hills Sauvignon Blanc 2020** Easygoing, tangy and tropical, a dash of
musk aromatic in there too. A short 4-week rest on lees has added some chalky
texture. Nothing too dramatic, yet the citrus-pithy finish does linger well. Screw
cap. 12.5% alc. **Rating** 89 **To** 2023 $18 TL ✪

Dominique Portet ★★★★★

870 Maroondah Highway, Coldstream, Vic 3770 **Region** Yarra Valley
T (03) 5962 5760 **www.dominiqueportet.com** **Open** 7 days 10–5
Winemaker Ben Portet, Tim Dexter **Est.** 2000 **Dozens** 15 000 **Vyds** 9ha
Dominique Portet was bred in the purple. He spent his early years at Chateau Lafite (where
his father was régisseur), and was one of the first Flying Winemakers, commuting to Clos du
Val in the Napa Valley where his brother was also a winemaker. He then spent over 20 years
as managing director of Taltarni and Clover Hill. After retiring from Taltarni, he moved to the
Yarra Valley, a region he had been closely observing since the mid 1980s. In 2000 he found
the site he had long looked for and built his winery and cellar door, planting a quixotic mix
of cabernet sauvignon, sauvignon blanc, merlot, malbec, cabernet franc and petit verdot. Son
Ben is now executive winemaker, leaving Dominique with a roving role as de facto consultant
and brand marketer. Ben himself has a winemaking CV of awesome scope, covering all parts of
France, South Africa, California and 4 vintages at Petaluma. Exports to Canada, India, Dubai,
Hong Kong, Singapore, Malaysia and Japan.

♟♟♟♟♟ **Single Vineyard Yarra Valley Cabernet Sauvignon Malbec 2019** 93/7%
cabernet/malbec. Hand-picked fruit, berry sorted and crushed. On skins for
22 days. Matured 14 months in French oak (30% new). Bright, clear colour; this is
about as good as one could get from the Yarra Valley in a medium-bodied frame,
its purity is wonderful. A drop-dead bargain. Screw cap. 13.5% alc. **Rating** 97
To 2034 $38 JH ✪ ♥

♟♟♟♟♟ **Single Vineyard Yarra Valley Rosé 2020** Hand picked, whole-bunch pressed,
fermented in used French oak, matured for 6 months. Pale salmon pink; a
perfumed spice and blossom bouquet introduces a complex and perfectly balanced
silky palate with a delicious spread of red berry and stone-fruit flavours guarded by
gently cleansing acidity. Screw cap. 13.5% alc. **Rating** 96 **To** 2024 $38 JH ✪ ♥

Fontaine Yarra Valley Chardonnay 2020 This is DP's drink-young chardonnay. It's a beauty and a bargain, full of white stone fruit with layers of citrus and rich, creamy flavours. There's some refinement as the acidity keeps it fresh, lively and on track. One of the best in this style and should be rewarded accordingly. Screw cap. 13% alc. **Rating** 95 **To** 2025 $24 JF ❂

Fontaine Yarra Valley Cabernet Sauvignon 2019 Quite what a classy Yarra Valley cabernet-dominant blend (86/6/5/2/1% cabernet sauvignon/ merlot/cabernet franc/petit verdot/malbec) is doing at this price is beyond me. It is elegant, medium bodied and finely structured, the suite of red/blackcurrant fruits given 12 months in French oak (20% new). Screw cap. 13% alc. **Rating** 95 **To** 2034 $22 JH ❂

 !!!!? **Fontaine Yarra Valley Chardonnay 2019 Rating** 93 **To** 2027 $22 JH ❂
Fontaine Yarra Valley Rosé 2020 Rating 93 **To** 2022 $22 JF ❂

Dorrien Estate

Cnr Barossa Valley Way/Siegersdorf Road, Tanunda, SA 5352 **Region** Barossa Valley
T (08) 8561 2235 **www.**cellarmasters.com.au
Winemaker Nick Badrice **Est.** 1982 **Dozens** 1 million **Vyds** 109.6ha
Dorrien Estate is the physical base of the vast Cellarmasters network – the largest direct sales outlet in Australia. It also makes wine for many producers across Australia at its modern winery, which has a capacity of 14.5 million litres in tank and barrel; however, a typical make of each wine will be little more than 1000 dozen. Most of the wines made for others are exclusively distributed by Cellarmasters. Acquired by Woolworths in May 2011.

!!!!! **Krondorf Symmetry Barossa Shiraz 2018** Woolworths' Pinnacle Drinks makes an arsenal of Barossa shiraz labels (all impressive) and this is the most expensive and the best of them. Compelling depth and lift of high-class glossy black fruits and violet florals. Fine, integrated tannins. Top oak. Fine boned and seamless, it propels long, confident and delicious. Distinguished fruit, skilfully composed. Screw cap. 14.5% alc. **Rating** 95 **To** 2033 $50 TS
Vandemonian Coal River Valley Chardonnay 2019 Tense Tasmanian chardonnay engineered for the long game. Pure lemon and white peach are cut with searing Coal River Valley acidity that draws out a long finish. Cashew nut French oak sits neatly in the background. A pale straw hue proclaims youthful purity. Patience. Screw cap. 12.5% alc. **Rating** 94 **To** 2034 $45 TS

!!!!? **Cat Amongst the Pigeons Fat Cat Eden Valley Riesling 2020 Rating** 93 **To** 2030 $29 TS
Kaleidoscope Tumbarumba Single Vineyard Chardonnay 2019 Rating 93 **To** 2029 $45 JF
Balthazar of the Barossa Marananga Shiraz 2019 Rating 93 **To** 2034 $46 TS
Cat Amongst the Pigeons Fat Cat Barossa Mataro 2018 Rating 93 **To** 2028 $29 TS
Once & Well by Freya Hohnen Margaret River Chardonnay 2019 Rating 92 **To** 2027 $26 EL
Cat Amongst the Pigeons Fat Cat Barossa Grenache 2020 Rating 92 **To** 2025 $29 TS
Mockingbird Lane Hayshed Block Clare Valley Riesling 2019 Rating 91 **To** 2028 $38 JF
Mockingbird Hill Skilly Hills Saw Mill Road Clare Valley Shiraz 2019 Rating 91 **To** 2030 $64 JF
Blood Brother Republic Blewitt Springs McLaren Vale Grenache 2019 Rating 91 **To** 2024 $33 NG
Mockingbird Hill Slate Lane Clare Valley Mataro 2019 Rating 91 **To** 2027 $30 JF
Yarra View Parcel Selection Pinot Noir 2019 Rating 90 **To** 2025 $40 JF
The Ethereal One Fleurieu Malbec 2019 Rating 90 **To** 2023 $21 NG ❂

DOWIE DOOLE

695 California Road, McLaren Vale, SA 5171 **Region** McLaren Vale
T 0459 101 372 **www.**dowiedoole.com **Open** 7 days 10–5
Winemaker Chris Thomas **Est.** 1995 **Dozens** 25 000 **Vyds** 90ha

DOWIE DOOLE was founded in 1995 by Drew Dowie and Norm Doole. They had been connected to the McLaren Vale community for many years as grapegrowers in the region. Vineyard management is now led by champions of sustainable viticulture practices Dave Gartelmann and Drew Dowie. In May '16, with winemaker and managing director Chris Thomas leading a group of like-minded investors, DOWIE DOOLE acquired 35ha of vines of the 53ha Conte Tatachilla Vineyard, book-ended by 50yo bush-vine grenache and grafted (in '12) vermentino, aglianico and lagrein. In October '18, DOWIE DOOLE purchased Possum Vineyard, including its vineyards in Blewitt Springs and 500t winery. Exports to all major markets.

ȲȲȲȲȲ **McLaren Vale Rosé 2020** A gentle coral. Dry, with rosewater, sour cherry, raspberry, rosehip and cranberry scents popping along saline acid rails flecked with pumice. Finishes with a herbal inflection of rosemary, thyme and a twist of orange. This is a refined rosé serving up dangerous drinkability and impressive length. Screw cap. 12.7% alc. **Rating** 93 **To** 2021 $25 NG ✪

Reserve McLaren Vale Shiraz 2018 Another behemoth. A rich mouth-staining red, exhorting power. The oak is easier to take than the all-American Cali Road. Blue/blackberry, vanilla, coffee grind, bitter chocolate, licorice straps and baby back ribs. It takes a Herculean effort to drink a great deal, but it will surely have many fans. Diam. 14.5% alc. **Rating** 93 **To** 2035 $95 NG

C Blanc McLaren Vale Chenin Blanc 2020 As I taste through DOWIE DOOLE's solid suite of white wines, I appreciate the level of acidity; pleasantly fresh, rather than overtly tweaked. Granny Smith apple, lanolin, mint, a melody of citrus and dried pistachio. Supple across the mid palate, with some lees work conferring detail and warmth between the rails of freshness. Screw cap. 12.8% alc. **Rating** 92 **To** 2025 $25 NG ✪

Estate McLaren Vale Merlot 2018 Rich, plump, round and inimitably of the region in its saline warm finish. Baked plum, Christmas cake, violet, hedgerow, olive and vanillan oak scents bustle about the mouth, the oak serving directives. Few surprises here, but poise and generosity in spades. Screw cap. 14% alc. **Rating** 92 **To** 2027 $25 NG ✪

CSM McLaren Vale 2017 Cabernet sauvignon, shiraz and merlot. This is a holdout for the old school of bitter chocolate, coffee-vanilla/bourbon oak and eucalyptus scents. A rich palate of black fruit aspersions and maraschino cherry is corseted by oak tannins that are nevertheless seamlessly integrated. The finish pushes long and heady by virtue of sheer weight and voluminous extract. Screw cap. 14.5% alc. **Rating** 92 **To** 2028 $35 NG

The Architect McLaren Vale Cabernet Sauvignon 2019 Saline olive/salty. The place, undeniable. Sage, tomato bush, graphite and currant. The oak, emphatic and spiky. The acidity, shrill. All shins and elbows at this nascent point. Will settle down with patience and confidence. Diam. 14.5% alc. **Rating** 91 **To** 2032 $80 NG

G&T McLaren Vale Grenache & Tempranillo 2019 A rich slurpy sort of wine, soft and dry, with classic South Australian dark-fruit aspersions, Christmas spice, candied orange rind, anise and vanilla-pod notes oozing from every pore. A bit bristly across the finish, better served with more grape tannins. I would drink this on the cooler side to tone the fruit sweetness down a notch. Screw cap. 13.9% alc. **Rating** 90 **To** 2024 $25 NG

Estate Adelaide Hills Sauvignon Blanc 2020 A solid savvy from the Hills. Fuller bodied, with more ample fruit and attractive texture than most. Greengage, pine, lemon squash, gooseberry and redcurrant scents. Mercifully, no screeching acidity. Nothing overtly sweet/sour. Just a bright flow of dutifully ripe fruit and zesty freshness. Screw cap. 12.4% alc. **Rating** 90 **To** 2021 $20 NG ✪

The Banker McLaren Vale Shiraz 2019 Dark cherry, Dutch licorice, iodine, clove and intense florals, from verbena to violet, the mainstay. A rich and powerful wine, buttressed by ambitious oak and tangy acidity. A risk-averse style, loaded with syrupy blue and dark fruit flavours and packing a punch. There will be plenty of fans who perceive this sort of style as archetypal. Diam. 14.5% alc. **Rating** 90 **To** 2032 $80 NG

Cali Road McLaren Vale Shiraz 2018 I was stunned by the first whiff of this super-charged red. Frankly, I had no idea wines like this are still out there! Unashamed in its brazen black-fruited ripeness and muscularity, with not the slightest pretence of finesse. A phalanx of vanilla/bourbon aromas and mouth-puckering coffee-bean tannins courtesy of 24 months in American oak. This is for those who value power over precision and lightness. Diam. 14.5% alc. **Rating** 90 **To** 2035 $60 NG

B.F.G. McLaren Vale Grenache 2020 Destemmed, with the path set for a ripe, vinous and aromatic grenache. Seville orange, molten raspberry bon-bon and some strewn herb, adding to the gentle tannic composure without quite corralling the billowing sweetness. A generous wine of varietal purity that is, nevertheless, a bit gloppy. Cloying. Needs more structure. Screw cap. 14.4% alc. **Rating** 90 **To** 2025 $30 NG

🍷🍷🍷🍷 **C3 McLaren Vale Chardonnay 2020** **Rating** 88 **To** 2024 $30 NG

Drayton's Family Wines ★★★★☆

555 Oakey Creek Road, Pokolbin, NSW 2321 **Region** Hunter Valley
T (02) 4998 7513 **www**.draytonswines.com.au **Open** Mon–Fri 8–5, w'ends & public hols 10–5
Winemaker Edgar Vales, John Drayton **Est.** 1853 **Dozens** 40 000 **Vyds** 72ha

Six generations of the Drayton family have successively run the family business. It is now in the hands of Max Drayton, and sons John and Greg. The family has suffered more than its fair share of misfortune over the years, but has risen to the challenge. Edgar Vales is the chief winemaker after previous experience as assistant winemaker with David Hook and First Creek Wines. His arrival coincided with the release of a range of high-quality wines. The wines come in part from blocks on the estate vineyards that are over 120 years old and in prime Hunter Valley locations. Exports to Ireland, Bulgaria, Turkey, Vietnam, Malaysia, Indonesia, Singapore, Taiwan and China.

🍷🍷🍷🍷🍷 **Susanne Semillon 2015** A gorgeous aroma, faithful to the region and a contemporary interpretation of its signature variety: buttered toast, quince marmalade, lemon drop, candied orange rind and crystalline ginger, bound to striking mineral detail and pungent crispness. Thrilling length, to boot. Screw cap. 10.4% alc. **Rating** 95 **To** 2030 $60 NG

🍷🍷🍷🍷🍷 **Vineyard Reserve Pokolbin Semillon 2020** **Rating** 92 **To** 2027 $35 NG
Pioneer Series Semillon 2018 **Rating** 92 **To** 2028 $25 NG ✪

Driftwood Estate ★★★★☆

3314 Caves Road, Wilyabrup, WA 6282 **Region** Margaret River
T (08) 9755 6323 **www**.driftwoodwines.com.au **Open** 7 days 10.30–5
Winemaker Kane Grove **Est.** 1989 **Dozens** 18 000 **Vyds** 22ha

Driftwood Estate is a well-established landmark on the Margaret River scene. Quite apart from offering a casual dining restaurant capable of seating 200 people (open 7 days for lunch and dinner) and a mock Greek open-air theatre, its wines feature striking and stylish packaging and opulent flavours. Its wines are released in 4 ranges: Single Site, Artifacts, The Collection and Oceania. Exports to the UK, Canada, Singapore and China.

🍷🍷🍷🍷🍷 **Single Site Margaret River Chardonnay 2019** This is one of 'those' wines. The blindsiding wines that take you by surprise and imprint big on your memory. While the oak is playing a significant role right now, it pales in comparison to the concentrated fruit that lingers behind it. Yellow peach, curry leaf, red apple skins and salty acidity that courses through the very heart of the wine. 2019 was a cooler year, and is one to watch. Wines like this show why. Screw cap. 13% alc. Rating 96 To 2036 $70 EL ✪

Single Site Margaret River Cabernet Sauvignon 2018 This opens with a savoury berry-laden nose characterised by hoisin and anise. Fennel, too. The palate is saturated and ripe, with assertive tannins that shape the wine in the mouth and through the long finish. Classically styled and not breaking any cabernet norms, excellent in its sturdy traditionality. Screw cap. 14.5% alc. **Rating** 95 **To** 2040 $70 EL

Artifacts Margaret River Sauvignon Blanc Semillon 2020 63/33/3/1% sauvignon blanc/semillon/viognier/chardonnay. Matured for 7 months in French oak (33% new). As expected, a dash of viognier has a disproportionate impact on this wine, introducing slippery texture, apricots, juniper, elderflower and hints of star anise. The palate is textural and layered; the oak is evident, yet supportive rather than dominant. Saline acid ties it all together, cleaning up the finish and refreshing the palate. Screw cap. 12.5% alc. **Rating** 94 **To** 2027 $30 EL ✪

ⓉⓉⓉⓉⓉ **Artifacts Margaret River Chardonnay 2020** Rating 93 To 2031 $35 EL
The Collection Margaret River Cabernet Sauvignon 2019 Rating 92 To 2031 $25 EL ✪
Artifacts Margaret River Cabernet Sauvignon 2018 Rating 92 To 2027 $35 EL
Artifacts Margaret River Shiraz 2018 Rating 90 To 2028 $30 EL
Artifacts Margaret River Meritage 2018 Rating 90 To 2031 $35 EL
Artifacts Margaret River Petit Verdot 2018 Rating 90 To 2031 $34 EL

Duke's Vineyard   ★★★★★

Porongurup Road, Porongurup, WA 6324 **Region** Porongurup
T (08) 9853 1107 **www**.dukesvineyard.com **Open** 7 days 10–4.30
Winemaker Robert Diletti **Est.** 1998 **Dozens** 3500 **Vyds** 10ha
When Hilde and Ian (Duke) Ranson sold their clothing manufacturing business in 1998, they were able to fulfil a long-held dream of establishing a vineyard in the Porongurup subregion of Great Southern with the acquisition of a 65ha farm at the foot of the Porongurup Range. They planted shiraz and cabernet sauvignon (3ha each) and riesling (4ha). Hilde, a successful artist, designed the beautiful, scalloped, glass-walled cellar door sales area, with its mountain blue cladding. Great wines at great prices.

ⓉⓉⓉⓉⓉ **Magpie Hill Reserve Riesling 2020** Its power, length and layer upon layer of kaffir lime is wrapped in a pure silver cloak of acidity running through – but never challenging – the fruit. Duke Ranson has every reason to suggest this is one of the best rieslings to come from this jewelled vineyard at the heart of the estate plantings. Screw cap. 13.2% alc. **Rating** 98 **To** 2040 $42 JH ✪ ♥
The First Cab 2019 This is the first vintage, its history dating back to '74 when Duke Ranson tasted a wine made with a clone of cabernet sauvignon he chased for over 40 years to plant. With an entrancing bouquet and a beautifully structured, supremely elegant palate, it is liquid, heart-stopping cassis, handled with great skill. Screw cap. 13.5% alc. **Rating** 98 **To** 2039 $60 JH ✪
Magpie Hill Reserve Shiraz 2019 The colour here is as vibrantly hued as the aromas that waft out of the glass – evident from a foot away. As with the cabernet – this is all things from the Single Vineyard but all things dialled up. Oak. Intensity and voluminous fruit. Gorgeous stuff. Spice and structure. Screw cap. 14% alc. **Rating** 97 **To** 2040 $42 EL ✪
Magpie Hill Reserve Cabernet Sauvignon 2019 As with previous years, this is super-concentrated: amazing that so much flavour can be packed into a glass. Astoundingly powerful fruit, matched by the seamless integration of oak and structure. The tannins are fine, almost subliminal, and hold the fruit in check from start to finish. The natural acidity from both the cooler growing area and vintage is impressively juicy, wrapping up a sensational package. Supple, generous, layered and lingering. What a wine. Screw cap. 13.9% alc. **Rating** 97 **To** 2050 $42 EL ✪

🍷🍷🍷🍷🍷 Single Vineyard Riesling 2020 And what a single-vineyard it is. The scented
bouquet of apple blossom and crushed lime leaves is faithfully replayed on the
light-as-air palate that throws passionfruit and ethereal fruit (not RS) on the
unsuspecting taster's mouth. Screw cap. 13.1% alc. **Rating** 96 **To** 2030 $26 JH ✪
Single Vineyard Shiraz 2019 Cool-climate shiraz, people: get around it! White
pepper, exotic spice and red fruit. Abundance and opulence with restraint. A core
of intense fruit and fine-structured tannins. This is a banger. A beautiful wine that
whistles a tune of purity – what expression! Red licorice to boot. Absolutely yes.
Screw cap. 13.5% alc. **Rating** 95 **To** 2035 $30 EL ✪
Single Vineyard Cabernet Sauvignon 2019 The cooler 2019 vintage has
given rise to this gloriously elegant and layered cabernet. Unbelievably vibrant and
saturated in colour; almost luminescent fuchsia. Pomegranate and raspberry on the
nose – the palate is concentrated and elegant with abundant dark berries and spice,
chalky tannins and a core of pastille fruit. Gorgeous stuff. Screw cap. 13.5% alc.
Rating 95 **To** 2040 $30 EL ✪

🍷🍷🍷🍷🍷 Single Vineyard Rosé 2020 **Rating** 92 **To** 2021 $20 EL ✪

Dune Wine   ★★★★★
PO Box 9, McLaren Vale, SA 5171 **Region** McLaren Vale
T 0403 584 845 **www**.dunewine.com
Winemaker Duncan and Peter Lloyd **Est.** 2017 **Dozens** 1700 **Vyds** 8ha
This is the project of Duncan and Peter Lloyd (of Coriole fame) using fruit sourced from
a single vineyard in Blewitt Springs. The brothers grew up immersed in a world of wine,
olive oil, illegal goat's cheese and great food. Both worked in kitchens from the age of 13
and continued to develop a love of good food and wine. Duncan studied winemaking before
leaving McLaren Vale to work in Tasmania and Margaret River, and then in Chianti and the
Rhône Valley. He returned to McLaren Vale as he couldn't understand why you would want
to live anywhere else. Peter also left the area after university, with eclectic occupations in
France and England. He shares Duncan's views on McLaren Vale, though for now he lives in
Melbourne. Exports to Sweden and Taiwan.

🍷🍷🍷🍷🍷 Blewitt Springs McLaren Vale Shiraz 2019 Fermented with a mix of whole-
bunch, whole-berry and crushed fruit. This really sings; it proclaims its Blewitt
Springs birth with energetic, spicy, savoury notes threaded through predominantly
black fruits, backed and lengthened by fine, but firm, tannins. Remarkable wine.
Screw cap. 14% alc. **Rating** 96 **To** 2034 $26 JH ✪

🍷🍷🍷🍷🍷 Bonaire McLaren Vale Rosé 2020 **Rating** 93 **To** 2020 $26 NG ✪
Pyla McLaren Vale 2019 Rating 93 **To** 2024 $26 NG ✪
Tirari McLaren Vale 2019 Rating 91 **To** 2024 $26 NG

Dutschke Wines   ★★★★☆
Lot 1 Gods Hill Road, Lyndoch, SA 5351 **Region** Barossa Valley
T (08) 8524 5485 **www**.dutschkewines.com **Open** By appt
Winemaker Wayne Dutschke **Est.** 1998 **Dozens** 5000 **Vyds** 15ha
Winemaker and owner Wayne Dutschke set up business with uncle (and grapegrower) Ken
Semmler in 1990 to produce wine. Since then, Dutschke Wines has built its own small
winery around the corner from Ken's vineyard and the portfolio has increased. While Wayne
has now been making small-batch wines for over 20 years, his use of whole-berry ferments,
open fermenters, basket presses and a quality oak regime have all remained the same. He was
crowned Barossa Winemaker of the Year in 2010, inducted into the Barons of Barossa in '13
and is the author of a children's book about growing up in a winery called *My Dad has Purple
Hands*. Exports to the US, Canada, Denmark, Germany, the Netherlands, Taiwan and China.

🍷🍷🍷🍷🍷 Cellar Release Single Barrel St Jakobi Vineyard 75 Block #2 Barossa
Valley 2008 As powerful and profound as any wine I've experienced from
the fabled St Jakobi Vineyard, and proof that Wayne Dutschke is a wizard. It

ripples with spicy blackberries, black cherries, satsuma plums, licorice, prunes and warm spice, propelled by a wonderful torrent of dark chocolate oak. A finish of incredible confidence drifts long, deep and wide, dancing and rumbling with sweet fruit freshness and mesmerising endurance. A case in point that Barossa shiraz can never be judged on numbers, and that in the talented hands of an exceedingly small few, integrity, longevity and profound deliciousness can be attained even toward the very ripe end of the Richter scale. Screw cap. 15.5% alc. **Rating** 97 **To** 2024 $175 TS

ŸŸŸŸŸ **Oscar Semmler Lyndoch Barossa Valley Shiraz 2018** Lyndoch may not be as revered as the fabled parishes of the northern and western Barossa, but this wine alone is a statement that it should be held in equal if not higher regard. Wayne Dutschke exemplifies that wonderful Barossa juxtaposition of sweet, ripe black fruit density and the refinement of crunchy definition, freshness and violet-infused detail. I've been avidly following, buying and cellaring Oscar for decades and I cannot recall such detail, mineral tannin finesse and undeterred persistence. Screw cap. 14.5% alc. **Rating** 96 **To** 2038 $75 TS ✪
Circa Centum by Wayne Dutschke 2018 The exotic spice of these near-100yo vines is highlighted by the triumphant red/blackberry, cherry and plum fruit exuberance of the great 2018 season. Dutschke has captured this spectacle to a level of detail that only he can do, fresh, crunchy and lively, propelled eloquently by fine-grained tannins and luscious, high-cocoa dark chocolate oak. To the cellar! Screw cap. 14.8% alc. **Rating** 96 **To** 2038 $100 TS
Single Barrel Wally's Block God's Hill Road Cellar Release Barossa Valley 2008 Cellar release of miniscule quantities. The freshness and integrity of Wayne Dutschke's Lyndoch shiraz fruit endures, even in the presence of generous alcohol and levels of new oak that would render a mere mortal wine incapacitated. At 13 years of age, sweet satsuma plum and prune fruit carries considerable persistence amid dark chocolate French oak, fine, integrated tannins and warm alcohol. It's at the top of its game, and will go some years yet. Screw cap. 15% alc. **Rating** 94 **To** 2030 $175 TS

ŸŸŸŸŸ **Cellar Release Single Barrel Poplar Holme Block Greenock Road Barossa Valley 2008 Rating** 93 **To** 2023 $175 TS
10 Year Old Barossa Valley Muscat NV Rating 92 $40 TS
22 Year Old Barossa Valley Tawny NV Rating 91 $60 TS

Eagles Rest Wines   ★★★★☆

65 Maxwells Road, Pokolbin, NSW 2320 **Region** Hunter Valley
T 0428 199 888 **www.**eaglesrestwines.com.au **Open** By appt
Winemaker Xanthe Hatcher **Est.** 2007 **Dozens** 1000 **Vyds** 20ha
Eagles Rest has flown under the radar since its establishment in 2007, and still does. The estate is planted to 8ha of chardonnay, 7ha shiraz, 3ha semillon and 2ha verdelho.

ŸŸŸŸŸ **The Wild Place Hunter Valley Semillon 2019** The flagship wine of this superlative suite. The homegrown trope. Semillon, unadorned. Hand picked and crushed, with the resultant pickup of esters and textural detail, compelling. Lemon balm, tonic, spa salts and barley scents of intensity, thrum and thrill. Top tier. Screw cap. 10.5% alc. **Rating** 95 **To** 2030 $28 NG ✪
Maluna Hunter Valley Semillon 2019 A similar dynamic between these 2 semillons as to the 2 chardonnays in the same suite. One, chewier and textually intriguing; the other, a transparent fugue of intensity and weightlessness. This, the latter. Skeletal. Refined. Tonic, citrus zest, grapefruit pulp and a waxy tail. Nascent, still. Loads in store. Prodigious length. Age with immense confidence. Screw cap. 11.5% alc. **Rating** 95 **To** 2034 $35 NG ✪
Maluna Hunter Valley Chardonnay 2019 A more filigreed and linear expression, of superior length to The Wild Place sibling. This said, it does not have the other's chewy, moreish charm. A reticent nose, inferring apricot pith, nougat

and pungent mineral. The finish, extremely long and racy. Nothing shrill or hard. Exceptional integration of all components, punctuated with a brace of oak. A very fine chardonnay, punching far above its weight. Screw cap. 12.5% alc. **Rating** 95 To 2026 $40 NG

ŢŢŢŢŢ The Wild Place Hunter Valley Chardonnay 2019 **Rating** 93 To 2024 $28 NG
The Wild Place Hunter Valley Syrah 2019 **Rating** 93 To 2025 $28 NG
Maluna Block Hunter Valley Shiraz 2019 **Rating** 93 To 2030 $40 NG

Eastern Peake   ★★★★★

67 Pickfords Road, Coghills Creek, Vic 3364 **Region** Ballarat
T (03) 5343 4245 **www**.easternpeake.com.au **Open** 7 days 11–5
Winemaker Owen Latta **Est.** 1983 **Dozens** 2000 **Vyds** 5.6ha
Norm Latta and Di Pym established Eastern Peake, 25km northeast of Ballarat on a high plateau overlooking the Creswick Valley, over 35 years ago. In the early years the grapes were sold, but the 5.6ha of vines are now dedicated to the production of Eastern Peake wines. Son Owen Latta has been responsible for the seismic increase in the quality of the wines. Exports to Canada, Singapore, Japan, and Hong Kong.

Eddie McDougall Wines   ★★★★

801 Glenferrie Road, Hawthorn, Vic 3122 (postal) **Region** Margaret River/King Valley
T 0413 960 102 **www**.eddiemcdougallwines.com.au
Winemaker Eddie McDougall, Lilian Carter **Est.** 2007 **Dozens** 1000
Eddie McDougall is an award-winning winemaker, wine judge, columnist and TV personality. Eddie's winemaking credentials extend over a decade of experience with some of the world's most influential wineries. He has made wines with the likes of Vietti (Barolo), Mas de Daumas Gassac (Languedoc), Deep Woods Estate (Margaret River), Giant Steps (Yarra Valley) and O'Leary Walker (Clare Valley). Eddie holds a bachelor of international business from Griffith University and a postgraduate diploma in wine technology and viticulture from The University of Melbourne. He spearheaded the acquisition of Wairarapa's Gladstone Vineyard in '18, where he took on the role of CEO and chief winemaker. In '13 he was one of 12 elite wine professionals selected for the annual Len Evans Tutorial, regarded as the world's most esteemed wine education program. Exports to NZ, China, Hong Kong, Macau, Singapore, Taiwan, the UK, Philippines and the US.

ŢŢŢŢŢ The Flying Winemaker Margaret River Cabernet Sauvignon 2019
Aromatic, ripe and juicy. Intensely saturated red fruit on the palate – a crowd-pleasing, fleshy wine. Screw cap. 15% alc. **Rating** 90 To 2027 $20 EL ✪

Eden Hall   ★★★★

Cnr Boehms Springs Road and E Lorkes Road, Springton, SA 5235 **Region** Eden Valley
T 0400 991 968 **www**.edenhall.com.au **Open** At Taste Eden Valley
Winemaker Phil Lehmann **Est.** 2002 **Dozens** 7000 **Vyds** 34ha
David and Mardi Hall purchased the historic Avon Brae Estate in 1996. The 120ha property has been planted to cabernet sauvignon (the lion's share, with 11.5ha), riesling (9.3ha), shiraz (8.3ha) and smaller amounts of grüner veltliner and viognier. The majority of the production is contracted to Yalumba, St Hallett and McGuigan Simeon, with 10% of the best grapes held back for the Eden Hall label. Exports to the US, NZ and China.

ŢŢŢŢŢ Reserve Eden Valley Riesling 2020 A contrasting mood to Eden Hall's Springton, the intensity and tension of the season is encapsulated here. Spicy, wild lemon, lime and Granny Smith apple fill an expansive and generous style, holding a finish of considerable drive, persistence and promise. It holds both the richness and breadth for immediate appeal and the cool, focused acid energy to go long. Screw cap. 11.8% alc. **Rating** 94 To 2030 $35 TS

ꭹꭹꭹꭹ Springton Eden Valley Riesling 2020 Rating 89 To 2022 $25 TS
Eden Valley Grüner Veltliner 2020 Rating 89 To 2022 $35 TS
Block 3 Eden Valley Cabernet Sauvignon 2019 Rating 89 To 2034 $40 TS

Eden Road Wines ★★★★☆

3182 Barton Highway, Murrumbateman, NSW 2582 **Region** Canberra District
T (02) 6226 8800 **www**.edenroadwines.com.au **Open** Wed–Sun 11–4.30
Winemaker Celine Rousseau **Est.** 2006 **Dozens** 14000 **Vyds** 5.34ha
The name of this business reflects an earlier time when it also had a property in the Eden
Valley. Now based in the Canberra district, having purchased one of Canberra's oldest vineyards
(est. 1972) and wineries at Dookuna. Syrah, sauvignon blanc and riesling are sourced from
the estate vineyards in Canberra, with chardonnay and pinot noir coming from Tumbarumba.
Viticulturist Thomas Lefebvre is converting the estate vineyards to organic; Rousseau expects
to be making certified organic wines from the 2021 vintage. Exports to the UK and the US.

ꭹꭹꭹꭹꭹ Canberra Syrah 2019 Excellent dark purple hue. Densely packed with flavour,
it's hard to know where to start. Black plums, Dutch salty licorice, fennel and lots
of earthy savouriness. Full bodied with firm tannins in tow. It's structured, with a
ripeness and boldness, but thankfully not oaky. Screw cap. 14.5% alc. **Rating** 94
To 2027 $40 JF

ꭹꭹꭹꭹꭹ Gundagai Sangiovese 2019 Rating 92 To 2025 $40 JF

 # 1837 Barossa ★★★☆

119-131 Yaldara Drive, Lyndoch, SA 5351 **Region** Barossa Valley
T (08) 7200 1070 **www**.1837barossa.com.au **Open** Mon–Sun 11–5
Winemaker Guido Auchli, Peter Gajewski, Ben Cooke **Est.** 1999 **Vyds** 25ha
The ambition of the Swiss tech entrepreneurial Auchli family, 1837 Barossa commemorates
the date on which Colonel William Light named the Barossa. Red wines hail exclusively
from the estate near Lyndoch, while whites are sourced from Eden Valley growers. Viticulture
is overseen by 5th-generation grower Michael Heinrich, with a philosophy of minimal
chemical input. The spectacular estate offers accommodation in its recently refurbished
Barossa Manor, including a restaurant, cellar door and seminar centre. Exports to Europe. (TS)

ꭹꭹꭹꭹꭹ President's Reserve Estate Shiraz Cabernet Sauvignon 2018 Medium,
vibrant purple. A soft, fruit-driven and approachable blend of dark berry/cherry/
plum fruit. Medium persistence and soft tannins make it ready to drink now.
An easy-drinking, quaffing style that doesn't call for too much thought. Cork.
14.5% alc. **Rating** 90 To 2023 $63 TS

1847 | Chateau Yaldara ★★★★☆

Chateau Yaldara, Hermann Thumm Drive, Lyndoch, SA 5351 **Region** Barossa Valley
T (08) 8524 0200 **www**.1847wines.com **Open** 7 days 10–5
Winemaker Chris Coulter, Gabriel Morgan **Est.** 1947 **Dozens** 50000 **Vyds** 100ha
1847 Wines is wholly owned by Chinese group Treasure Valley Wines. The year is
when Barossa pioneer Johann Gramp planted his first vines in the region; there is in fact
no other connection between Gramp and the business he established and that of 1847
Wines, other than the fact that the 80ha estate is in the general vicinity of Gramp's original
plantings. A 1000t winery was built in 2014, handling the core production together with
new varieties and blends. This was underpinned by the acquisition of Chateau Yaldara in '14,
providing a major retail outlet and massively enhanced production facilities. Exports to the US,
Canada, Germany, Morocco, Sri Lanka, Vietnam, Singapore, Taiwan, Hong Kong and China.

ꭹꭹꭹꭹꭹ 1847 Grand Pappy's Barossa Valley Shiraz 2017 Played right, the Barossa's
cooler seasons rank among my favourites. There's a bright, spicy crunch to the best
of '17 Barossa shiraz. This is a refreshingly medium-bodied style laced with red
cherries, greengage plums and a hint of black pepper. Tangy acid line and a fine

tannin grid carry a finish of impressive persistence. Cork. 14.5% alc. **Rating** 95
To 2042 $320 TS

1847 First Pick Barossa Valley Shiraz 2017 Big bottle, big price, big wine.
Chateau Yaldara has set apart its flagship with more impacting oak than the cool
2017 season calls for, making for a long-enduring Barossa shiraz. Medium red/
purple. Spicy black fruits and tangy red berries contrast firm, fine oak tannins.
Give it lots of time. Cork. 14.5% alc. **Rating** 94 To 2042 $480 TS

1847 170 Barossa Valley Shiraz Cabernet Sauvignon 2017 Crafted in the
age-worthy style of the Barossa's classic blends, fusing the blackberries of shiraz
with the blackcurrants of cabernet. The cool 2017 season has furnished vibrant
acidity, interlocking with firm, fine-grained tannins to propel a long and enduring
finish. Cork. 14.5% alc. **Rating** 94 To 2042 $100 TS

Yaldara Reserve Barossa Valley Cabernet Sauvignon 2017 The cool 2017
season heightened the varietal markers of Barossa cabernet, making for an accurate,
leafy style of capsicum and crunchy black/redcurrant fruits. Fine tannins and
vibrant acidity confirm just the right level of ripeness. High-cocoa dark chocolate
oak has been well gauged to meet the mood of the season. One for the long haul.
Screw cap. 14% alc. **Rating** 94 To 2047 $50 TS

ΨΨΨΨΨ **1847 Grand Pappy's Barossa Valley Cabernet Sauvignon Shiraz 2017**
Rating 93 To 2042 $320 TS

1847 Grand Pappy's Barossa Valley Grenache 2017 Rating 92 To 2030
$320 TS

Eisenstone   ★★★★☆

56 Murray Street, Tanunda, SA 5352 **Region** Barossa Valley
T 0417 827 851 **www**.eisenstone.com.au **Open** By appt 10–5
Winemaker Stephen Cook **Est.** 2014 **Dozens** 1000

Stephen Cook took a circuitous route to winemaking: his first occupation on leaving school
in NZ was a 9-year stint with a local bank. The decision to up stakes and travel in SA brought
him into contact with wine and he returned to NZ and completed a bachelor of science
degree and a master's in biochemisty. Even then, he says, not with the intention of becoming
a winemaker. On a whim he called into a small local winery to 'buy a few grapes' and a deal
was struck that he would exchange his time in lieu of payment. 'From the first moment I was
hooked.' He returned to SA and secured the Roseworthy graduate diploma in oenology.
A vintage in California filled his wanderlust; a varied career in the Barossa Valley followed,
working for large wineries, rising steadily up the ranks in a 20-year career. In 2014 he decided
to take a small plunge and embark on Eisenstone, its translation meaning the ironstone soil
on which the early settlers planted their vineyards. He only makes single-vineyard or single-
district shiraz, eschewing all other varieties. He is only interested in high-quality grapes, the
use of top-quality oak the tool to capture the message of the interaction between shiraz and
its particular place. Exports to China, Hong Kong and Malaysia.

Ekhidna   ★★★★

67 Branson Road, McLaren Vale, SA 5171 **Region** McLaren Vale
T 0499 002 633 **www**.ekhidnawines.com.au **Open** 7 days 11–5
Winemaker Matthew Rechner **Est.** 2001 **Dozens** 2000

Matt Rechner entered the wine industry in 1988, spending most of the years since at
Tatachilla in McLaren Vale, starting as laboratory technician and finishing as operations
manager. Frustrated by the constraints of large winery practice, he decided to strike out on
his own in 2001. The quality of the wines has been such that he has been able to build a
winery and cellar door, the winery facilitating the use of various cutting-edge techniques.
Exports to China.

ΨΨΨΨΨ **Rarefied McLaren Vale Shiraz 2016** This is good by virtue of its sheath of
pliant tannins alone, fine grained and spicy. Fine. Otherwise, a typically robust
warm-climate shiraz. Coffee grind/mocha oak, licorice root, clove, pepper and

plentiful dark-fruit accents. Bolshy and long. Screw cap. 14.5% alc. **Rating** 93 **To** 2027 $120 NG

Whole Bunch McLaren Vale Grenache 2017 Shadowing middle age, this is a complex grenache. It has clearly benefited from bottle age. Scents of rosemary, thyme, sandalwood, tamarind and kirsch are splayed across a spindle of crunchy tannins, fibrous and moreish. Long and energetic with a growing sweetness in the glass. Impressive stuff. Screw cap. 14.5% alc. **Rating** 93 **To** 2024 $45 NG

Barrel Ferment McLaren Vale Grenache 2017 The tannins maketh the best wines and here they are: spindly, sandy and refined, directing flavours of raspberry bon-bon, mint, orange zest and mulchy sandalwood long. The acidity, a bit out of step. A heavy hand. Otherwise, a style of great promise. Screw cap. 14.5% alc. **Rating** 92 **To** 2024 $45 NG

2 Mates Your Lucky Day McLaren Vale Shiraz 2019 A lustrous purple. A big wine. But despite the weight and high alcohol, the grape tannins are pulpy and pliant enough as they meld with the oak, corralling blueberry, boysenberry, licorice and lilac notes. The finish, palate-staining across oak-derived riffs of espresso and bitter chocolate. A conventional approach done well. Screw cap. 14.9% alc. **Rating** 91 **To** 2028 $35 NG

She Viper McLaren Vale Cabernet Sauvignon 2017 Despite a reputation for shiraz, the Vale's cabernet is largely so much better. Particularly at this sort of tier. Highly varietal aromas of cassis, sage, tomato bush, bay leaf and hedgerow unwind across a tannic scale, more soprano than bass. Astringent enough to confer a welcome savouriness and saline pucker. Graphite and tapenade to close. Good drinking. Screw cap. 14.5% alc. **Rating** 91 **To** 2026 $30 NG

Rechner McLaren Vale Shiraz 2016 Good drinking for those who like warm-climate shiraz. Akin to opening a closet of a house in which you once lived. The garments may be different, but the feel and smell are the same. Familiarity, in all its cushy warmth, communicated across dark-fruit aspersions, Dutch licorice, clove and bitter chocolate oak. Not my cup of tea, but the fan base will be sated. Screw cap. 14.5% alc. **Rating** 90 **To** 2025 $95 NG

🍷🍷🍷🍷　**She Viper Fleurieu Malbec 2017** **Rating** 88 **To** 2024 $30 NG

Elderslie　★★★★☆

PO Box 93, Charleston, SA 5244 **Region** Adelaide Hills
T 0404 943 743 **www.**eldersliewines.com.au
Winemaker Adam Wadewitz **Est.** 2015 **Dozens** 600 **Vyds** 8ha

Elderslie brings together 2 families with wine in their veins. In their respective roles as winemaker (Adam Wadewitz) and wine marketer (Nicole Roberts), they bring a wealth of experience gained in many parts of the wine world. They each have their partners (Nikki Wadewitz and Mark Roberts) onboard and also have real-life jobs. In 2016 Nicole accepted the position of executive officer of the Adelaide Hills Wine Region, having had brand development roles with 3 of the Hills' leading winemakers: Shaw + Smith, Grosset and The Lane Vineyard. Adam carved out a career at the highest imaginable level, aided by becoming joint dux of the Len Evans Tutorial in 2009. He was senior winemaker at Best's, where he made the '12 Jimmy Watson winner; became the youngest judge to serve as a panel chair at the National Wine Show; and is now senior winemaker for Shaw + Smith and their associated Tolpuddle Vineyard in Tasmania.

🍷🍷🍷🍷🍷　**Hills Blend #2 Adelaide Hills Pinot Meunier Pinot Noir Gamay 2019**
A co-ferment of 40/40/20% pinot noir/meunier/gamay. Seriously fragrant top notes with slate, flint, and leather things happening as well. Lots to contemplate aromatically. And stuff the idea of steering these varieties towards a light-headed red style, this has major concentration and intensity on the palate. Cherry juices lead the fruit feels, while its thick-piled yet soft-touch tannins coat and hold the wine in place. Attention grabbing. Watch this space for further bottle development and follow-up vintages. Screw cap. 13.5% alc. **Rating** 95 **To** 2028 $42 TL

Hills Blend #1 Adelaide Hills Pinot Blanc 2019 Quite a change for pinot blanc by creating a richer, textured, mouthfilling style, similar in many ways to contemporary chardonnay. The nose is different of course, floral and garden herbal, almost a basil note, while the palate resonates with pear compote and woody spices. Quite captivating and definitely fills your cup. Screw cap. 13.5% alc. **Rating** 94 **To** 2026 $42 TL

Elderton   ★★★★★

3-5 Tanunda Road, Nuriootpa, SA 5355 **Region** Barossa Valley
T (08) 8568 7878 **www**.eldertonwines.com.au **Open** Mon–Fri 10–5, w'ends, hols 11–4
Winemaker Julie Ashmead, Brock Harrison **Est.** 1982 **Dozens** 45 000 **Vyds** 65ha
The founding Ashmead family, with mother Lorraine supported by sons Allister and Cameron, continues to impress with their wines. Julie Ashmead (married to Cameron), 5th-generation winemaker at Campbells in Rutherglen, is head of production, overseeing viticulture and winemaking. Elderton has 3 vineyards. Two are in the Barossa Valley – Nuriootpa (Elderton's original estate vineyard, with plantings dating back to 1894, with shiraz, cabernet sauvignon and merlot) and Greenock (originally planted by the Helbig family in 1915, purchased in 2010, consisting of shiraz, grenache, carignan, mourvèdre, cabernet sauvignon, chardonnay and semillon). The 3rd is the Craneford Vineyard in the Eden Valley (planted to shiraz, cabernet sauvignon, riesling and chardonnay). Energetic promotion and marketing in Australia and overseas are paying dividends. Elegance and balance are the keys to these wines. Exports to all major markets.

🍷🍷🍷🍷🍷 **Command Barossa Shiraz 2018** Brooding Barossa shiraz of billowing character. Smoked mettwurst and pan juices. Spicy dark and red berries of all kinds. No small dollop of milk chocolate oak. Quintessential Barossa, replete with generous breadth and enduring length, sustained by fine-ground tannins of considerable endurance. Screw cap. 14.6% alc. **Rating** 95 **To** 2033 $145 TS
Ashmead Barossa Cabernet Sauvignon 2019 Old vines have upheld integrity in crunchy redcurrant and pomegranate fruit, even rosehip lift and red capsicum varietal markers. It holds its ripeness with poise, thanks to a vibrant acid line, joining with confident, medium-grained tannins to sustain a very long aftertaste. Dark chocolate French oak has been well played to build endurance without stealing the limelight. A very strong result for Ashmead in this drought season. Bravo. Screw cap. 14.9% alc. **Rating** 95 **To** 2044 $120 TS

🍷🍷🍷🍷🍷 **Neil Ashmead Grand Tourer Barossa Valley Shiraz 2019** Rating 93 **To** 2039 $60 TS
Ode to Lorraine Barossa Valley Cabernet Shiraz Merlot 2018 Rating 92 **To** 2040 $60 TS

Eldorado Road   ★★★★★

46-48 Ford Street, Beechworth, Vic 3747 **Region** North East Victoria
T (03) 5725 1698 **www**.eldoradoroad.com.au **Open** Fri–Sun 11–5
Winemaker Paul Dahlenburg, Ben Dahlenburg, Laurie Schulz **Est.** 2010 **Dozens** 1500 **Vyds** 4ha
Paul Dahlenburg (nicknamed Bear), Lauretta Schulz (Laurie) and their children have leased a 2ha block of shiraz planted in the 1890s with rootlings supplied from France (doubtless grafted) in the wake of phylloxera's devastation of the Glenrowan and Rutherglen plantings. Bear and Laurie knew about the origins of the vineyard, which was in a state of serious decline after years of neglect. The owners of the vineyard were aware of its historic importance and were more than happy to lease it. Four years of tireless work reconstructing the old vines has resulted in tiny amounts of exceptionally good shiraz; they have also planted a small area of nero d'Avola and durif.

🍷🍷🍷🍷🍷 **Quasimodo Nero d'Avola Shiraz Durif 2018** An unusual blend but, my, does it work a treat! A fragrant and delicious red of an easy presence and impressive balance. Cherry fruit aromas, dark blood plums, sweet oak spice, hints of anise,

chocolate. A soft, engaging wine, supple and ripe in tannins. Screw cap. 13.6% alc.
Rating 95 To 2026 $29 JP ✪ ♥

Comrade Nero d'Avola 2019 After 13 years with the grape, Paul Dahlenburg
knows its well. This is a beautifully composed wine, even in its youth, with a
complex and fragrant aroma of wild herbs, dark cherries, tobacco leaf, wood
smoke and sweet spice. Welcoming and smooth with a savoury feel, it has real
presence. Screw cap. 13.1% alc. **Rating** 95 To 2027 $37 JP

ＹＹＹＹＹ **Beechworth Chardonnay 2019** Rating 92 To 2026 $337 JP
Dreamfields Fiano 2019 Rating 91 To 2025 $33 JP
Beechworth Syrah 2019 Rating 90 To 2029 $37 JP

Eldredge   ★★★☆

Spring Gully Road, Clare, SA 5453 **Region** Clare Valley
T (08) 8842 3086 **www.eldredge.com.au Open** 7 days 11–5
Winemaker Leigh Eldredge **Est.** 1993 **Dozens** 7000 **Vyds** 22.97ha
Leigh and Karen Eldredge established their winery and cellar door in the Sevenhill Ranges at
an altitude of 500m above Watervale. The mature estate vineyard is planted to shiraz, cabernet
sauvignon, merlot, sangiovese, riesling and malbec. Exports to the UK, Singapore and China.

ＹＹＹＹ **Blue Chip Clare Valley Shiraz 2018** A dark, inky and oaky red. Plenty of
oomph with spiced plums and oddly a strong confectionary flavour of red lollies
and vanilla essence. There's a gloss to the full-bodied palate and warmth on the
finish. It's of a style but maybe not blue chip. Screw cap. 14.8% alc. **Rating** 89
To 2027 $30 JF

Eldridge Estate of Red Hill   ★★★★★

120 Arthurs Seat Road, Red Hill, Vic 3937 **Region** Mornington Peninsula
T 0414 758 960 **www.eldridge-estate.com.au Open** Mon–Fri 12–4, w'ends & hols 11–5
Winemaker David Lloyd **Est.** 1985 **Dozens** 1000 **Vyds** 3ha
The Eldridge Estate vineyard was purchased by David and (the late) Wendy Lloyd in 1995.
Major retrellising work has been undertaken, changing to Scott Henry, and all the wines are
estate-grown and made. David also planted several Dijon-selected pinot noir clones (114, 115
and 777), which have been contributing since 2004; likewise the Dijon chardonnay clone 96.
Attention to detail permeates all he does in vineyard and winery. Exports to the US.

ＹＹＹＹＹ **Single Vineyard Pinot Noir 2019** A seductive wine, thanks to its perfume,
slinky texture and lightness of touch. Don't be fooled though, as this has substance.
Raw silk tannins add a quality and depth across the medium-bodied palate, with
seamlessly integrated oak. Expect cherries and pips, wood smoke, florals and the
promise of a lovely drink. Screw cap. 13.5% alc. **Rating** 95 To 2028 $70 JF
Clonal Blend Pinot Noir 2019 Hints of dark cherries, blood orange, woodsy
spices and some charcuterie. This tends to show off more savoury tones. The
tannins feel different, too. But it has the same moreish, satisfying qualities as its
sibling, making for another excellent pinot. Screw cap. 13.5% alc. **Rating** 95
To 2029 $85 JF

ＹＹＹＹＹ **Single Vineyard Chardonnay 2019** Rating 93 To 2027 $60 JF
Wendy Chardonnay 2019 Rating 93 To 2029 $75 JF
MV6 Pinot Noir 2019 Rating 93 To 2029 $75 JF
PTG 2020 Rating 93 To 2025 $35 JF
Single Vineyard Gamay 2019 Rating 92 To 2029 $60 JF
Single Vineyard Fumé Blanc 2020 Rating 90 To 2025 $35 JF

Elgee Park

Merricks General Wine Store, 3460 Frankston-Flinders Road, Merricks, Vic 3916
Region Mornington Peninsula
T (03) 5989 7338 **www.elgeeparkwines.com.au Open** 7 days 8.30–5
Winemaker Geraldine McFaul (Contract) **Est.** 1972 **Dozens** 1500 **Vyds** 4.5ha
The pioneer of the Mornington Peninsula in its 20th-century rebirth, owned by Baillieu
Myer and family. The vineyard is planted to riesling, chardonnay, viognier (some of the oldest
vines in Australia), pinot gris, pinot noir, merlot and cabernet sauvignon. The vineyard is set
in a picturesque natural amphitheatre with a northerly aspect, looking out across Port Phillip
Bay towards the Melbourne skyline.

ŢŢŢŢŢ **Mornington Peninsula Pinot Gris 2019** Light aromatics waft up a mix of
florals, stone fruit with pears a strong point. The same on the palate, with added
creamy/nuttiness and cinnamon. It's juicy, rich, ripe and luscious without feeling
heavy. Very good gris. Screw cap. 14% alc. **Rating** 93 **To** 2024 $35 JF
Mornington Peninsula Cuvée Brut 2016 Spending 44 months on lees has
added creamed honey flavour and nuances across the palate. And much needed,
too, for this is nonetheless racy and tight with an infusion of blossom and citrus.
A very good aperitif style. Diam. 12% alc. **Rating** 91 $50 JF

Elgo Estate

2020 Upton Road, Upton Hill, Vic 3664 **Region** Strathbogie Ranges
T (03) 5798 5563 **www.elgoestate.com.au Open** By appt
Winemaker Grant Taresch, Suzanne Taresch **Est.** 2000 **Dozens** 10000 **Vyds** 100ha
Elgo Estate, owned by the Taresch family, is located high in the hills of the Strathbogie Ranges,
125km northeast of Melbourne, a stone's throw from the southern end of the Heathcote
region. Elgo Estate is committed to sustainable viticulture reflecting and expressing the
characteristics of this cool-climate region. Two distinct wine portfolios via the Allira and Elgo
Estate labels are produced. The wines are 100% estate-grown from their 2 vineyards in the
region, with plantings dating back to the early 1970s. In '12 Elgo purchased the Mount Helen
Vineyard from Robert Kirby. Exports to China.

ŢŢŢŢŢ **Allira Strathbogie Ranges Riesling 2020** Acid hounds will flock to this wine.
The lemon-zesty acidity defines this fine-edged riesling in large part, giving it
tension and energy. It's quite a thing to enjoy in its youth but it's also there for the
journey ahead. Lime, lemon zest, Granny Smith apple, grapefruit all entwined and
beautifully engaged by bracing acidity. This is how Strathbogies' quartz delivers
riesling. So exciting. Screw cap. 13.4% alc. **Rating** 93 **To** 2030 $19 JP ✪

ŢŢŢŢ **Allira Strathbogie Ranges Chardonnay 2020 Rating** 89 **To** 2026 $19 JP ✪

Eling Forest Winery

12587 Hume Highway, Sutton Forest, NSW 2577 **Region** Southern Highlands
T (02) 4878 9155 **www.elingforest.com.au Open** 7 days 10–4
Winemaker Michelle Crockett **Est.** 1987 **Dozens** 4000 **Vyds** 2.5ha
Eling Forest's mentally agile and innovative founder (the late) Leslie Fritz celebrated his 80th
birthday not long after he planted the first vines here in 1987. He celebrated his 88th birthday
by expanding the vineyards, primarily with additional plantings of Hungarian varieties. He
also developed a Cherry Port using spinning cone technology to produce various peach-
based liqueurs, utilising second-class peach waste. In a major change of direction, winemaker
Jeff Aston leased the winery and vineyard in 2012, and produces wines under the Eling Forest
label, and for other local producers. Exports to China.

ŢŢŢŢŢ **Southern Highlands Sauvignon Blanc 2019** This is a sophisticated sauvignon.
Crunchy and herbal, splaying notes of nettle, verdant herb and spearmint across a
crunchy acid carriage. Nothing sweet/sour, a bane of many. Nor, tropical. Just good
carry through, pop and length. Screw cap. 12% alc. **Rating** 91 **To** 2023 $35 NG

Hilltops Tempranillo Rosé 2020 A rich rosé, aligned with a lighter red. Campari, mulled orange and cinnamon stick, musk, cranberry and watermelon. Sapid. Sits nicely in the mouth. Mid weighted and plump. A burst of juicy acidity across the finish tows it to good length. A light phenolic framework imparts a gentle pucker. Drink with food. Screw cap. 13.8% alc. **Rating** 90 **To** 2023 $30 NG

Hilltops Shiraz 2019 A behemoth from a hot vintage that almost got out of hand. Somehow, a semblance of freshness amid the morass of Cherry Ripe, cocoa and vanilla/mocha oak. The tannins, granular and pithy, hailing from the thick grape skins. Almost drinks like an Amarone. Rich, chewy and miraculously, somehow savoury. Best in the short term, with food and on the cooler side. Cork. 15.5% alc. **Rating** 90 **To** 2026 $40 NG

Southern Highlands Sparkling Chardonnay Pinot Noir 2019 Majority chardonnay and a dollop of pinot. Creamy and definitively leesy, with dried straw, brioche, oatmeal and toasted nut scents. Yet the fizz is a little coarse, suggesting either a tank fermentation or transversage rather than disgorgement. A solid fizz. Complex aromas and textures. A bit brittle and yeoman at the finish. Cork. 11.5% alc. **Rating** 90 $40 NG

Ellis Wines

52 Garsed Street, Bendigo Victoria 3550 **Region** Heathcote
T 0401 290 315 **www**.elliswines.com.au **Open** Mon–Sat 10–4
Winemaker Guy Rathjen, Nina Stocker **Est.** 1999 **Dozens** 3000 **Vyds** 54.18ha
Bryan and Joy Ellis own this family business, daughter Raylene Flanagan is the sales manager, and 7 of the vineyard blocks are named after family members. For the first 10 years the Ellises were content to sell the grapes to a range of distinguished producers. However, since then a growing portion of the crop has been vinified. Exports to Hong Kong.

Premium Heathcote Shiraz 2017 It's great to see a premium Heathcote shiraz released with some bottle age. Still, this wine has further cellaring written all over it. The oak remains fresh and assertive, the fruit – a lovely expression of place – is tightly coiled, revealing dark plum, black cherry and bitter chocolate savouriness, but it has a long, long way to go. Complex and beguiling in its infancy. Screw cap. 14.8% alc. **Rating** 95 **To** 2027 $70 JP

Signature Label Heathcote Shiraz 2018 The winemaker recommends opening the wine an hour before tasting. Vigourous decanting certainly opens it up, if earlier drinking is intended. The option of cellaring is even better. Tight-grained, cedary, toasted coconut oak in evidence, with ripe, concentrated blackberry, plum and spice still emerging. Definitely has a power and intensity across the board, in keeping with its warmer northern Heathcote sourcing. Screw cap. 14.8% alc. **Rating** 94 **To** 2030 $40 JP

Signature Label Heathcote Merlot 2017 Rating 90 **To** 2024 $27 JP

Elmswood Estate

75 Monbulk-Seville Road, Seville, Vic 3139 **Region** Yarra Valley
T 0455 997 888 **www**.elmswoodestate.com.au **Open** W'ends 11–5
Winemaker Paul Evans **Est.** 1981 **Dozens** 3000 **Vyds** 7ha
Planted to cabernet sauvignon, chardonnay, merlot, sauvignon blanc, pinot noir, shiraz and riesling on the red volcanic soils of the far southern side of the Yarra Valley. The cellar door operates from 'The Pavilion', a fully enclosed glass room situated on a ridge above the vineyard, with 180° views of the Upper Yarra Valley. It seats up to 110 guests, and is a popular wedding venue. Exports to China.

Yarra Valley Chardonnay 2018 This spends 2 years in French puncheons and by Yarra standards that's a long time. Yet, it has freshness across the fuller-bodied palate even if the finish fades quickly. In the mix, stone fruit, squirts of lemon and zest and pith. It's not overly complex but it is a good drink. Screw cap. 13% alc. **Rating** 90 **To** 2025 $40 JF

Emilian ★★★★☆

PO Box 20 Kalorama, Vic 3766 **Region** Yarra Valley
T 0421 100 648 **www**.emilian.com.au
Winemaker Robin Querre **Est.** 2015 **Dozens** 300
Robin Querre is the 4th generation of a family involved in winemaking since 1897, variously in Saint-Émilion and Pomerol, France. Robin commenced studies in medicine at the University of Bordeaux, but changed to oenology in 1990. He studied under some of the Bordeaux greats (such as Yves Glories, Denis Dubourdieu and Aline Lonvaud), and worked vintages at Chateau Canon and Moueix (under Jean-Claude Berrouet, who was supervising Chateau Petrus), as well as at Rudd Estate in the Napa Valley. This led Robin to work in research, travelling to Australia, Germany, Austria, Switzerland, England, Japan and Israel. He currently works for Laffort Oenology, a private research company based in Bordeaux, developing, producing and selling oenological products to winemakers. He and wife Prue also make small quantities of very good wine in the Yarra Valley.

🍷🍷🍷🍷🍷 Single Vineyard Strathbogie Nebbiolo Rosé 2020 As refreshing as a spring day. This has the right amount of aromatics and flavour, the right amount of freshness and texture and the right amount of acidity and charm to warrant another glass. With friends, another bottle. Top-notch rosé. Screw cap. 12.5% alc. Rating 95 To 2023 $25 JF
Single Parcel Yarra Valley Pinot Noir 2020 While this has the same lightness of touch as its single-vineyard sibling, there's more depth here. Still ethereal, with wafts of spiced cherries, rhubarb and warm earth. Silk-like tannins, a gentle palate, fine acidity and a finish that impresses. Screw cap. 13% alc. Rating 95 To 2026 $35 JF ✪
Single Vineyard Dixons Creek Yarra Valley Pinot Noir 2020 Wow, what a pretty wine. It's delicate and soft, with some sweet cherries, chinotto and spice. Lighter framed, with no hard edges, barely-there tannins and a light veil of acidity. It feels like halfway between a rosé and a pinot noir. Quite a revelation. It's not complex, but it doesn't matter. I could drink a lot of this. Screw cap. 12.5% alc. Rating 94 To 2024 $27 JF ✪

Eperosa ★★★☆

Lot 552 Krondorf Road, Tanunda, SA 5352 **Region** Barossa Valley
T 0428 111 121 **www**.eperosa.com.au **Open** Fri 11–2.30, Sat 11–5 & by appt
Winemaker Brett Grocke **Est.** 2005 **Dozens** 1000 **Vyds** 8.75ha
Eperosa owner and *Wine Companion 2021* Winemaker of the Year Brett Grocke qualified as a viticulturist in 2001 and, through Grocke Viticulture, consults and provides technical services to over 200ha of vineyards spread across the Barossa Valley, Eden Valley, Adelaide Hills, Riverland, Langhorne Creek and Hindmarsh Valley. He is ideally placed to secure small parcels of organically managed grapes, hand-picked, whole-bunch fermented and foot-stomped, and neither filtered nor fined. The wines are of impeccable quality – the use of high quality, perfectly inserted corks will allow the wines to reach their full maturity decades hence. Exports to the UK, the US, Canada and China.

EPIC Negociants ★★★★★

9-11 Claremont Street, South Yarra, VIC 3141 **Region** Various
T 0497 066 200 **www**.epicnegociants.com
Winemaker Andrew Browne **Est.** 2018 **Dozens** 10 000
EPIC Negociants is owned and operated by Andrew Browne, whose family planted the Scotchman's Hill winery in Victoria in 1982. EPIC sources fruit from a number of growers across Australia (and NZ) whose vineyards are certified with one or more of the following accreditations: Australian Certified Organic, Biodynamic (Demeter) or Sustainable Australian Winegrowing. Exports to Singapore, Hong Kong, the UK and the USA. (EL)

🍷🍷🍷🍷🍷 The Apollonian McLaren Vale Cabernet Sauvignon 2019 50% whole bunches works exceptionally well here, imparting an extra degree of tannic precision and savoury brittle to the incorrigible fruit of the region. Cassis, sage, black olive, bay leaf and a sluice of maritime salinity melting into milk chocolate across the pushy finish. Exceptional tannins here. Screw cap. 14.5% alc. **Rating** 95 To 2034 $60 NG

No. 5 The Ridge Margaret River Cabernet Sauvignon 2018 Powdery tannins caress cassis-laden fruit. Juicy and ripe – the perfect representation of Margaret River's incredible '18 vintage. Screw cap. 13.5% alc. **Rating** 95 **To** 2030 $45 EL

The Apollonian McLaren Vale Shiraz 2019 A deep, glossy ruby. Aromas of lilac, wakame, blueberry and barbecued ribs. A sachet of clove and pepper meets the juicy line of acidity, more pertinent to the wine's structure – with this grape in these parts – than the smooth patina of grape tannin and oak. A slick wine. But not a patch on the eponymous cab. Screw cap. 14.5% alc. **Rating** 94 **To** 2030 $60 NG

Ernest Hill Wines

307 Wine Country Drive, Nulkaba, NSW 2325 **Region** Hunter Valley
T (02) 4991 4418 **www**.ernesthillwines.com.au **Open** 7 days 10–5
Winemaker Mark Woods **Est.** 1999 **Dozens** 6000 **Vyds** 12ha
This is part of a vineyard originally planted in the early 1970s by Harry Tulloch for Seppelt Wines; it was later renamed Pokolbin Creek Vineyard, and later still (in '99) the Wilson family purchased the upper (hill) part of the vineyard and renamed it Ernest Hill. It is now planted to semillon, shiraz, chardonnay, verdelho, traminer, merlot, tempranillo and chambourcin. Exports to the US and China.

Cyril Premium Hunter Semillon 2011 At its zenith and ready to drink. The aromatic fireworks and compelling fruit intensity, in stark contrast to the wine's lightweight and balletic mouthfeel. The complexity lies in the dichotomies. Melted butter on toast, quince, citrus marmalade, tonic, quinine and lemon balm scents, all. As the fruit has expanded with bottle age, the finish has lost some verve. Delicious all the same. Screw cap. 35% alc. **Rating** 93 **To** 2022 $11 NG ✪

CEO Cabernet Sauvignon 2018 Full bodied. A quiver of cassis, leather, mulberry, garden herb, sage and that quintessential Hunter scent of terracotta, all bound by a sheath of detailed tannins: fine grained, precise and authoritative. These make the wine, conferring a welcome savouriness while the dutiful freshness pulls the finish to impressive length. A lovely wine. Screw cap. 14% alc. **Rating** 93 To 2026 $40 NG

Alexander Reserve Premium Hunter Chardonnay 2018 This is a richly flavoured chardonnay exuding white fig, cantaloupe, peach and nougat scents. The finish is intense and the flavours lingering long, driven by the extract and hedonism of the fruit. A chardonnay for those seeking the unabashed flavours of yore. Screw cap. 13.5% alc. **Rating** 92 **To** 2023 $40 NG

CEO Shiraz 2017 A greater poise and drinkability than its Shareholders sibling. Scents of wet red earth, sweet cherry, cedar, root spice and clove. The finish, long and relatively effortless but for a clang of unnecessary tangy acidity. Screw cap. 14% alc. **Rating** 92 **To** 2023 $40 NG

Cyril Premium Hunter Semillon 2019 Lightweight and tensile, with a bit more breadth and give than many youthful examples from the region. Scents of lanolin, quince paste, dried hay and lemon drop. Real purity and persuasion to the aromatic spectrum. This is already accessible, but will really hit its straps in a few years. Screw cap. 11.5% alc. **Rating** 91 **To** 2026 $26 NG

Shareholders Shiraz 2018 A full-weighted red with a more refined carapace of tannin than its '17 predecessor, but without its rustic charm and developed complexities. This is still virile and youthful in comparison. Sweet cherry, clove, bergamot, new-car-seat leather and a loamy warmth careen along a lattice of vibrant acidity and the aforementioned tannins. Paradoxically light of feel due to the uncanny freshness. Screw cap. 13.8% alc. **Rating** 91 **To** 2025 $30 NG

Shareholders Shiraz 2017 Medium crimson with bricking edges. The fruit, vivid and still with plenty of life, although veering into tertiary zones. Think cherry, kirsch, anise, clove and hoisin sauce, with that Hunter stamp of sweet red earth, all harnessed by French and American oak, imparting scents of cedar, mocha, bourbon, malt and vanilla. A robust wine, far from the most refined. A bit sweet and clunky at its core, but packing plenty of flavour, verve and the capacity to age a tad further. Screw cap. 13.8% alc. **Rating** 91 **To** 2023 $30 NG

Andrew Watson Reserve Premium Hunter Tempranillo 2018 A well-positioned dry red for the table. Vibrant, mid weighted and versatile, by reckoning of its classical tannic composure and freshness. Not as stiff-upper-lipped as cabernet, but offering more savoury gristle and welcome restraint than shiraz. Succulent red fruits, a smattering of herb and well-nestled oak. Acidity, clearly an obsession here, a bit shrill. Good drinking for now. Screw cap. 13.5% alc. **Rating** 91 **To** 2023 $35 NG

Chicken Shed Chardonnay 2019 An uncluttered mid-weighted chardonnay, brimming with an exuberant melody of stone-fruit flavours, nashi pear and citrus. The acidity, lively and juicy. The gentle oak, an addendum. A wine best enjoyed young in order to capture its esprit. Good drinking. Screw cap. 13% alc. **Rating** 90 **To** 2023 $28 NG

Ernest Schuetz Estate Wines ★★★★

Edgell Lane, Mudgee, NSW 2850 **Region** Mudgee
T 0402 326 612 **www.**ernestschuetzestate.com.au **Open** W'ends 10.30–4.30
Winemaker Liam Heslop **Est.** 2003 **Dozens** 4500 **Vyds** 4.1ha
Ernest Schuetz's involvement in the wine industry started in 1988 at the age of 21. Working in various liquor outlets and as a sales representative for Miranda Wines, McGuigan Simeon and, later, Watershed Wines gave him an in-depth understanding of all aspects of the wine market. In 2003 he and wife Joanna purchased the Arronvale Vineyard (first planted in '91), at an altitude of 530m. When the Schuetzs acquired the vineyard it was planted to merlot, shiraz and cabernet sauvignon, and they have since grafted 1ha to riesling, pinot blanc, pinot gris, zinfandel and nebbiolo. The estate plantings have been complemented by other varieties purchased from other growers. Exports to Vietnam, Hong Kong and China.

♀♀♀♀♀ Family Reserve Single Vineyard Mudgee Chardonnay 2019 A sunny, mid-weighted wine beaming the sort of stone-fruit inflections and tropical accents that many relish. Dried mango, canned peach, nectarine and white fig. An undercurrent of mineral is offset by a core of praline. The 33% new oak, a bit brazen. But there is enough extract and juice to absorb it. Just. Screw cap. 13.9% alc. **Rating** 90 **To** 2025 $30 NG

♀♀♀♀ Family Reserve Single Vineyard Black Mudgee Syrah 2017 Rating 88 **To** 2027 $30 NG

Evans & Tate ★★★★★

Cnr Metricup Road/Caves Road, Wilyabrup, WA 6280 **Region** Margaret River
T (08) 9755 6244 **www.**evansandtate.wine **Open** 7 days 10.30–5
Winemaker Matthew Byrne **Est.** 1970 **Vyds** 12.3ha
The history of Evans & Tate has a distinct wild-west feel to its ownership changes since 1970, when it started life as a small 2-family-owned business centred on the Swan District. Suffice it to say, it was part of a corporate chess game between McWilliam's Wines and the Fogarty Wine Group. Vineyards, brands, a viticultural services business and existing operations encompassing Deep Woods, Smithbrook, Millbrook and Pemberton Estate, plus Selwyn Viticultural Services, will become part of the production facility and other assets of Margaret River Vintners. It is now 100% owned by Fogarty, who previously held 70%. This doubles Fogarty's production to 600000 dozen, cementing its place as the largest producer of WA wine. Exports to all major markets.

♀♀♀♀♀ Single Vineyard Margaret River Chardonnay 2018 This wine is a statement of excellence for Margaret River chardonnay: spicy, rich, saline and very long.

Classy wine and detailed winemaking. Yes please. Screw cap. 13.5% alc. **Rating** 96 To 2030 $35 EL ✪

Redbrook Reserve Margaret River Cabernet Sauvignon 2017 The cooler year has birthed yet another cabernet of delicacy, length and finesse. Matt Byrne's Redbrook Reserve cabernet is worthy of the same praise heaped upon prior vintages. Succulent red fruits and densely packed flavour, held together with fine-knit tannins. Ready to drink now, but with a determined future in the cellar, too – this is what defines the wonder of great Margaret River cabernet. Screw cap. 14% alc. **Rating** 96 **To** 2041 $65 EL ✪

Redbrook Estate Margaret River Chardonnay 2018 Crushed cashew, white peach, briny acidity and silky phenolics on the palate. Seamless, creamy and classy, this is perfectly Margaret River, in a perfect year. Lovely stuff. Screw cap. 13% alc. **Rating** 95 **To** 2030 $40 EL

Redbrook Reserve Margaret River Chardonnay 2018 With all the gold on the bottle it's a wonder it doesn't topple over. Very toasty oak and rich fruit beneath, this bursts upfront but slows down as it extends through the finish. Great length shows the pedigree of the fruit and the year. Winner of 4 trophies and a gold medal, Perth Royal Show '20. Screw cap. 13% alc. **Rating** 95 **To** 2036 $65 EL

Redbrook Margaret River Cabernet Sauvignon 2018 2018 saw the most cabernet franc and malbec ever included in this wine. And to good effect! This is a cracker. Succulent red fruits on the palate, backed by salty spice and a frankly slinky texture. The tannins are shapely and seductive. The whole package is hugely impressive. But not surprising: the Redbrook range of wines rock. Screw cap. 14.5% alc. **Rating** 95 **To** 2035 $40 EL

Metricup Road Margaret River Semillon Sauvignon Blanc 2020 Margaret River absolutely excels at the sem/sauv blend, and this here is why. Concentrated, with both varieties seamlessly dovetailed into each other. Tropical fruit, crushed shell and briny acid. Bravo. Screw cap. 12.5% alc. **Rating** 94 **To** 2027 $35 EL

Single Vineyard Margaret River Cabernets 2019 The blend changes depending on the vintage. In 2019, despite the wine's name, it's actually merlot-led. 52/45/1.5/1.5% merlot/cabernet sauvignon/malbec/cabernet franc. 'Merlot was great in 2019,' says winemaker Matt Byrne. Ten months in a variety of French oak. It leads the charge in this spicy, succulent wine which offers up a balanced feast of fine tannins, plush (but also lean and focused) fruit and salty acid. Cracking value. Screw cap. 14.5% alc. **Rating** 94 **To** 2031 $35 EL

🍷🍷🍷🍷🍸 **Metricup Road Margaret River Rosé 2020 Rating** 92 **To** 2022 $35 EL
Single Vineyard Margaret River Malbec 2019 Rating 92 **To** 2028 $35 EL
Metricup Road Margaret River Pinot Gris 220 Rating 91 **To** 2025 $35 EL

Evoi Wines

529 Osmington Road, Bramley, WA 6285 **Region** Margaret River
T 0437 905 100 **www**.evoiwines.com **Open** 7 days 10–5
Winemaker Nigel Ludlow **Est.** 2006 **Dozens** 10 000
NZ-born Nigel Ludlow has a bachelor of science in human nutrition but, after a short career as a professional triathlete, he turned his attention to grapegrowing and winemaking, with a graduate diploma in oenology and viticulture from Lincoln University, NZ. Time at Selaks was a stepping stone to Flying Winemaking stints in Hungary, Spain and South Africa, before a return as senior winemaker at Nobilo. He thereafter moved to Victoria, and finally to Margaret River. It took time for Evoi to take shape, the first vintage of chardonnay being made in the lounge room of Nigel's house. By 2010 the barrels had been evicted to more conventional storage and since '14 the wines have been made in leased space at a commercial winery. Quality has been exceptional. Exports to the UK, the Caribbean, Norway and Hong Kong.

🍷🍷🍷🍷🍷 **The Luka Margaret River 2018** Brilliant ruby in colour, density and volume are the defining features in the mouth. Aromatically reticent at this stage, the layers and intensity of flavour on the palate suggests it needs further time in bottle. Built for the long haul and excellent for it. Screw cap. 14.5% alc. **Rating** 95 **To** 2045 $80 EL

Reserve Margaret River Malbec 2018 This is serious malbec. Wow. Intense fruit and layers of exotic spice and texture soar across the palate. It is lingering and long, dense and supple, all the while balanced by ripe, chewy acid and structured by firm – yet fine – tannins. Owner/winemaker Nigel Ludlow making a strong case for Margaret River malbec. Savoury, rather than sweet. Screw cap. 14.5% alc. **Rating** 95 **To** 2020 $69 EL

Reserve Margaret River Chardonnay 2019 This is intensely worked and complex, layers of flavour and texture mingle with fruit and spice. Green melon, kiwifruit, yellow peach and guava. Hints of spicy pawpaw through the finish. Quite exotic and fine, the oak playing a significant role in the proceedings. Screw cap. 13.5% alc. **Rating** 94 **To** 2036 $69 EL

♟♟♟♟♟ Margaret River Cabernet Sauvignon 2018 Rating 93 To 2030 $38 EL
Margaret River Fumé Blanc 2019 Rating 93 To 2030 $28 EL

Faber Vineyard   ★★★★☆

233 Haddrill Road, Baskerville, WA 6056 **Region** Swan Valley
T (08) 9296 0209 **www.**fabervineyard.com.au **Open** Fri–Sun 11–4
Winemaker John Griffiths **Est.** 1997 **Dozens** 4000 **Vyds** 4.5ha
John Griffiths, former Houghton winemaker, teamed with wife Jane Micallef to found Faber Vineyard. They have established shiraz, verdelho (1.5ha each), brown muscat, chardonnay and petit verdot (0.5ha each). John says, 'It may be somewhat quixotic, but I'm a great fan of traditional warm-area Australian wine styles, wines made in a relatively simple manner that reflect the concentrated ripe flavours one expects in these regions. And when one searches, some of these gems can be found from the Swan Valley.' Exports to Hong Kong and China.

♟♟♟♟♟ **Reserve Swan Valley Shiraz 2019** The nose has a sweet cola character to it that may induce one to swear there was some American oak in there – but no. It's the sweet, intense fruit from under the Swan Valley sun. The palate is intense and layered, with thundering length of flavour. This is a classically structured and dense wine, and will surely live for decades. Screw cap. 14.5% alc. **Rating** 96 **To** 2036 $84 EL

Swan Valley Liqueur Muscat NV What a glorious wine this is. Extraordinarily opulent. It has a core of salted dried fig, bitter orange and quince that together showcase the heat of the Swan Valley sunshine. After all of that … the finish is cleansing. Layer upon layer of flavour and texture. Cork. 18% alc. **Rating** 96 $60 EL ✪

Grand Liqueur Muscat NV Each vintage, a barrel is chosen and reserved for extended maturation. Deeper and more complex than the Liqueur Muscat, the opulent flavours have a resonance and vibration that move the ground beneath you. Thundering depth and gravitas, shaped by salted fruit and bitter chocolate. Quite stunning. 375ml. Cork. 18% alc. **Rating** 96 $120 EL

Millard Vineyard Swan Valley Shiraz 2019 Intense and muscular, yet supple, a brilliant example of warm-climate shiraz. The finish is laced with aniseed and licorice, the oak rearing its head from the back palate onwards (evident in crushed ants and toasted exotic spices). The fruit proves more than a match for it, though, quashing it in the end. Very young, with great structure. Cork. 14.5% alc. **Rating** 95 **To** 2036 $58 EL

Swan Valley Grenache 2020 Swan Valley grenache is a beautiful thing. Raspberry humbugs, red licorice and apple skins form the foundation of this wine. On the palate it is sinewy and muscular (not a tautology in this instance); the tannins have a shapely finesse through the finish. Excellent grenache from a warm climate – where it belongs. Screw cap. 14.5% alc. **Rating** 95 **To** 2030 $27 EL ✪

Riche Swan Valley Shiraz 2020 The fruit is vibrant and lifted and layered with red fruits and licorice root. The oak has a surprisingly restrained impact on the wine at this time, however it will likely settle in and spread out its sweet wings with further time in the bottle. Quite delicious, with a distinct clove, red licorice,

and aniseed character woven through the finish. Screw cap. 13.5% alc. **Rating** 94
To 2031 $27 EL

ΨΨΨΨΨ Swan Valley Verdelho 2020 Rating 93 To 2027 $24 EL
Frankland River Cabernet Sauvignon 2019 Rating 93 To 2042 $58 EL
Frankland River Malbec 2019 Rating 93 To 2030 $35 EL
Frankland River Cabernet Sauvignon 2018 Rating 92 To 2035 $58 EL
Donnybrook Durif 2019 Rating 92 To 2030 $43 EL
Riche Swan Valley Shiraz 2019 Rating 91 To 2027 $27 EL

Fallen Giants ★★★★★

4113 Ararat-Halls Gap Road, Halls Gap, Vic 3381 **Region** Grampians
T (03) 5356 4252 **www**.fallengiants.com.au **Open** Wed–Sun 10–5
Winemaker Justin Purser **Est.** 1969 **Dozens** 3000 **Vyds** 10.5ha
I (James) first visited this vineyard when it was known as Boroka Vineyard and marvelled at
the location in the wild country of Halls Gap. It wasn't very successful: Mount Langi Ghiran
acquired it in 1998 but by 2013 it had outlived its purpose. It was then that the opportunity
arose for the Drummond family, led by Aaron, to purchase the somewhat rundown vineyard.
They moved quickly; while the '13 vintage was made at Mount Langi Ghiran, thereafter it
was managed under contract by Circe Wines (Aaron Drummond's partnership business with
Dan Buckle) until 2017.

ΨΨΨΨΨ Block 3 Grampians Shiraz 2019 Delivers a sense of completeness and
complexity. Aromas of bramble, dark cherry, blackberry, anise, a touch of Eastern
spices. For all that, it manages to pack in tight, giving a sense of weightlessness in
the mouth, lifted, aromatic and with depth. Hosts an innate beauty that is quite
riveting. Screw cap. 14% alc. **Rating** 95 To 2029 $60 JP

ΨΨΨΨΨ Grampians Shiraz 2019 Rating 93 To 2032 $35 JP
Grampians Cabernet Sauvignon 2019 Rating 92 To 2030 $35 JP

False Cape Wines ★★★★

1054 Willson River Road, Dudley East, SA 5222 **Region** Kangaroo Island
T 0447 808 838 **www**.falsecapewines.com.au **Open** 7 days 11–5
Winemaker Greg Follett, Nick Walker **Est.** 1999 **Dozens** 4000 **Vyds** 30ha
Julie and Jamie Helyar's False Cape Vineyards links 3rd-generation Kangaroo Island farming
with 3rd-generation Langhorne Creek grapegrowers. It is the largest vineyard on Kangaroo
Island with 30ha of vines (shiraz and sauvignon blanc with 10ha each, 6ha of cabernet
sauvignon and lesser amounts of chardonnay, riesling, pinot gris, merlot and pinot noir). The
wines are made by Julie's brother – Greg Follett of Lake Breeze in Langhorne Creek and Nick
Walker of O'Leary Walker makes the Riesling. False Cape is entirely off-grid, completely
relying on solar power; the red grape varieties are dry-grown, free-range turkeys providing
pest control management and sheep are used for weed management during winter. Exports
to Switzerland, Hong Kong and China.

ΨΨΨΨΨ The Captain Kangaroo Island Cabernet Sauvignon 2018 Created as a
reserve style. Concentrated cabernet across the senses, even lines through the
palate, rich flavours, the oak soaked in and integrated. All good. Screw cap. 14% alc.
Rating 94 To 2030 $41 TL

ΨΨΨΨΨ Ship's Graveyard Kangaroo Island Shiraz 2019 Rating 92 To 2028 $27 TL
Montebello Kangaroo Island Pinot Grigio 2020 Rating 91 To 2024
$22 TL
Willson River Kangaroo Island Riesling 2019 Rating 90 To 2024 $22 TL
Silver Mermaid Kangaroo Island Sauvignon Blanc 2020 Rating 90
To 2023 $22 TL
The Captain Kangaroo Island Chardonnay 2019 Rating 90 To 2025
$30 TL

Farmer's Leap Wines

41 Hodgson Road, Padthaway, SA 5271 **Region** Padthaway
T (08) 8765 5155 **www.farmersleap.com Open** 7 days 10–4
Winemaker Renae Hirsch **Est.** 2004 **Dozens** 12000 **Vyds** 357ha
Scott Longbottom and Cheryl Merrett are 3rd-generation farmers in Padthaway. They commenced planting the vineyard in 1995 on the family property and now it has shiraz, cabernet sauvignon, chardonnay and merlot. Initially the majority of the grapes were sold, but increasing quantities held for the Farmer's Leap label have seen production rise. Exports to Canada, Singapore, South Korea, Japan, Taiwan, Hong Kong and China.

🍷🍷🍷🍷🍷 **Padthaway Cabernet Sauvignon 2018** Fragrant with cassis, currants, wafts of cooling mint and dark chocolate. It has a plump palate awash with juicy fruit, ripe tannins and overall is a good drink in the short term. Screw cap. 14.5% alc. **Rating** 91 **To** 2024 $25 JF
Padthaway Shiraz 2018 A deep red/purple hue. Lots of ripe fruit in the mix with woodsy spices, sweet oak and licorice. The full-bodied palate comes coated with firm tannins yet there is a freshness throughout, adding to its appeal. Screw cap. 14.5% alc. **Rating** 90 **To** 2026 $25 JF

Farr | Farr Rising

101 Kelly Lane, Bannockburn, Vic 3331 **Region** Geelong
T (03) 5281 1733 **www.byfarr.com.au**
Winemaker Nick Farr **Est.** 1994 **Dozens** 5500 **Vyds** 13.8ha
By Farr and Farr Rising continue to be separate brands from distinct vineyards, the one major change being that Nick Farr has assumed total responsibility for both labels, leaving father Gary free to pursue the finer things in life without interruption. This has in no way diminished the quality of the Pinot Noir, Chardonnay, Shiraz and Viognier made. Based on ancient river deposits in the Moorabool Valley, the vineyards are in conversion to organic. There are 6 different soils spread across the Farr property, with 2 main types: rich, friable red and black volcanic loam; and limestone, which dominates the loam in some areas. The other soils are quartz gravel through a red volcanic soil, ironstone (called buckshot) in grey sandy loam with a heavy clay base, sandstone base and volcanic lava. The soil's good drainage and low fertility are crucial in ensuring small yields of intensely flavoured fruit. Exports to the UK, Canada, Denmark, Sweden, Hong Kong, Singapore, Taiwan, Maldives, China and Japan.

Feathertop Wines

Great Alpine Road, Porepunkah, Vic 3741 **Region** Alpine Valleys
T (03) 5756 2356 **www.feathertopwinery.com.au Open** By appt
Winemaker Nick Toy **Est.** 1987 **Dozens** 9000 **Vyds** 16ha
Kel Boynton has a beautiful vineyard, framed by Mt Feathertop rising above it. The initial American oak input has been softened in more recent vintages to give a better fruit–oak balance. Kel has planted a spectacular array of 22 varieties, headed by savagnin, pinot gris, vermentino, sauvignon blanc, fiano, verdelho, riesling, friulano, pinot noir, tempranillo, sangiovese, merlot, shiraz, montepulciano and nebbiolo; with smaller plantings of prosecco, pinot meunier, dornfelder, durif, malbec, cabernet sauvignon and petit verdot. Exports to Austria.

Fermoy Estate

★★★★★

838 Metricup Road, Wilyabrup, WA 6280 **Region** Margaret River
T (08) 9755 6285 **www.fermoy.com.au Open** 7 days 10–5
Winemaker Jeremy Hodgson **Est.** 1985 **Dozens** 25000 **Vyds** 27.28ha
A long-established winery with plantings of semillon, sauvignon blanc, chardonnay, cabernet sauvignon and merlot. The Young family acquired Fermoy Estate in 2010 and built a larger cellar door which opened in '13, signalling the drive to increase domestic sales. They are happy to keep a relatively low profile, however difficult that may be given the quality of the wines. Jeremy Hodgson brings with him a first-class honours degree in oenology

and viticulture, and a CV encompassing winemaking roles with Wise Wines, Cherubino Consultancy and, earlier, Plantagenet, Houghton and Goundrey Wines. Exports to Thailand, Fiji, Singapore, Japan and China.

ŶŶŶŶŶ **Reserve Margaret River Chardonnay 2019** As with the Reserve cabernet, the fruit quality in this wine stands up and speaks for itself. Yellow peach, salted cashews and warm roasted spices are at the forefront. Long-lingering flavours are defined once again by the fruit. The winemaking is subtle and has shaped the wine rather than coerced it in any way. Chalky phenolics with a slight bitter edge create some real interest and saliva through the finish. Utterly lovely. Three trophies at the Wine Show of WA '20. Screw cap. 13% alc. **Rating** 96 **To** 2036 $60 EL **☉**

Reserve Margaret River Cabernet Sauvignon 2018 Supple, briny cassis rises up to greet you on first sniff. In a word, pretty. Vibrant. Also joyful. The wine takes a very serious turn on the palate. This is finely structured, shaped by chalky tannins that carry ripe, medium-weight fruit over the tongue and through to the finish. Caresses more than it asserts, making it a subtly spicy, elegant and willowy cabernet, capable of years of grace in the cellar. Brilliant fruit. Screw cap. 14.5% alc. **Rating** 96 **To** 2046 $95 EL

Reserve Margaret River Semillon 2019 At this stage, the sweet, marzipan/crushed coffee oak dominates the wine. However, the fruit has a concentrated jalapeño pungency that suggests it may be up to the task of consuming this mains-size dish of French oak. The brilliant length of flavour further backs up the suspicion that this may yet come up for air. Screw cap. 12.5% alc. **Rating** 95 **To** 2032 $45 EL

Margaret River Chardonnay 2019 In the context of chardonnay, 2019 was a vintage of delicacy, spice, minerality and restraint. In another word, excellent. Grilled stone fruit, salty acid and layers of curry leaf and exotic market spices come together in this sophisticated and expressive wine. There's a sparkly core of purity that is very attractive. Delicious, in a word. Screw cap. 13% alc. **Rating** 94 **To** 2027 $30 EL **☉**

Margaret River Cabernet Sauvignon 2018 Some cabernets are dark and brooding; others, like this one, are red-fruited, succulent and juicy. The tannins are chalky, tightly knit together and chewy, making this a star on the rise. Lovely wine. Screw cap. 14.5% alc. **Rating** 94 **To** 2032 $45 EL

ŶŶŶŶŶ **Margaret River Rosé 2020** **Rating** 93 **To** 2025 $25 EL **☉**
Margaret River Shiraz 2018 **Rating** 92 **To** 2028 $30 EL
Margaret River Cabernet Sauvignon Merlot 2018 **Rating** 92 **To** 2027 $25 EL **☉**
Margaret River Sauvignon Blanc 2019 **Rating** 91 **To** 2025 $25 EL

Ferngrove ★★★★★

276 Ferngrove Road, Frankland River, WA 6396 **Region** Frankland River
T (08) 9363 1300 **www.**ferngrove.com.au **Open** By appt
Winemaker Craig Grafton, Adrian Foot **Est.** 1998 **Vyds** 220ha
For over 20 years, Ferngrove has been producing consistent examples of cool-climate wines across multiple price brackets. The Ferngrove stable includes the flagship Orchid wines, Black Label, White Label and Independence ranges. Ferngrove Vineyards Pty Ltd enjoys the benefits of majority international ownership. Exports to all major markets.

ŶŶŶŶŶ **Dragon Shiraz 2019** Ruby red with glints of pink, this is a veritable fete of flavour and (like the Dragon Cabernet Shiraz) it is comfort and pleasure in a bottle. Perhaps not as complex as some of the very best, but utterly, undeniably beautiful, charming and balanced. Cork. 14% alc. **Rating** 96 **To** 2036 $70 EL **☉**

Dragon Reserve Cabernet Shiraz 2019 Sweet, juicy and plump – there is structure and savoury spice here, but that sweet and comforting fruit is the ruling party. All objections are noted, and overruled. Only satisfaction here. Utterly delicious and will live an age. Screw cap. 14.5% alc. **Rating** 96 **To** 2036 $110 EL

Estate Frankland River Shiraz 2019 95/5% shiraz/malbec. As with most of the premium wines from Ferngrove, this displays an abundance of succulent fruit. It's delicate, soft, structured and long, with so many things to like that it brings a smile to the face. Balance and harmony are the characters that win at the end of the day. Diam. 14.5% alc. **Rating** 95 **To** 2031 $40 EL

Majestic Frankland River Cabernet Sauvignon 2019 Incredibly elegant, supple cabernet, from a region that people are finally starting to clock. Frankland River cabernet is an absolute marvel – this is why. Intensity of fruit, purity of expression and power of a brutish sort, yet all in balance. Pomegranate, cassis, blood and red dirt. The texture is a real standout here: the tannins are slippery, slinky and oh so fine, but like all true power, remain unseen. Screw cap. 14% alc. **Rating** 95 **To** 2035 $38 EL

Independence Great Southern Cabernet Sauvignon 2019 All the body, flesh and structure of cabernet here, while 6% nebbiolo is responsible for the distinctive tannins and the lick of rose petal aromatics. All in all, a juicy, bouncy and joyful execution of 2 unlikely bedfellows. Screw cap. 14% alc. **Rating** 94 **To** 2028 $26 EL ✪

Frankland River Malbec 2019 With 2% cabernet sauvignon. Brilliant intensity of flavour, with retention of elegance besides; quite a cool achievement for malbec (which can often stray towards rambunctious flavour intensity with little restraint). Crunchy acid rounds this out into a thoroughly modern New World interpretation of the style; glossy and spicy and mighty fine. Ridiculous price. Screw cap. 13% alc. **Rating** 94 **To** 2030 $22 EL ✪

🍷🍷🍷🍷⟨ **Diamond Frankland River Chardonnay 2019** **Rating** 92 **To** 2030 $32 EL
Frankland River Shiraz 2019 **Rating** 92 **To** 2025 $22 EL ✪
Frankland River Cabernet Sauvignon 2019 **Rating** 91 **To** 2027 $22 EL ✪

Fetherston Vintners   ★★★★★

1/99a Maroondah Highway, Healesville, Vic 3777 **Region** Yarra Valley
T 0417 431 700 **www**.fetherstonwine.com.au
Winemaker Chris Lawrence **Est.** 2015 **Dozens** 1500
The establishment of Fetherston Vintners in 2015 by Chris Lawrence and Camille Koll was, in hindsight, the logical consequence of their respective careers in wine, food and hospitality. Chris began his career in the kitchen in establishments all over Australia. In '09 he enrolled in the science (oenology) degree with the University of Southern Queensland, graduating in '14 as valedictorian, receiving the Faculty Medal for Science. During his time at Yering Station ('10–14) he worked his way up from junior cellar hand to assistant winemaker. A vintage at Domaine Serene in Oregon's Willamette Valley in '12 gave him further insight into the study of great chardonnay and pinot noir. In '14 he took on the role of winemaker at Sunshine Creek in the Yarra Valley. Camille is Yarra born and bred, growing up in Hoddles Creek. After finishing school, she began a 7-year stint at Domaine Chandon, giving her invaluable insight into professional branding, marketing and customer service. She is now working in hospitality management as her day job. Chris' late grandfather was Tony Fetherston.

🍷🍷🍷🍷🍷 **Yarra Valley Chardonnay 2019** Flinty and a little funky, with grapefruit and lemon flavours mixing it up with some creamy, nutty barrel-ferment flavours. Cedary oak adds a layer, too. Lots in this, yet a tight style and needs food in order to admire it more. Screw cap. 13.4% alc. **Rating** 95 **To** 2029 $38 JF

Yarra Valley Pinot Noir 2019 An ethereal, pretty pinot, with a heady fragrance of red roses, raspberries and woodsy spices. It's lighter framed, with a fineness to its tannins, crunchy acidity and a succulence that makes you return for another sip. Screw cap. 13.5% alc. **Rating** 95 **To** 2027 $38 JF

Field Day   ★★★★☆

RSD1436 Meadows Road, Willunga, SA 5172 **Region** McLaren Vale
T 0428 581 177 **www**.monterrawines.com.au
Winemaker Mike Farmilo, Nick Whiteway **Est.** 2014 **Dozens** 20000 **Vyds** 15ha

Yet another venture by Canadian-born and raised (but long-term McLaren Vale resident) Norm Doole (in partnership with Mike Farmilo and Nick Whiteway). A grapegrower for decades, Norm founded DOWIE DOOLE with Drew Dowie in 1995. Field Day (formerly Loonie Wine Co and before that, Monterra) has been a centre of activity in McLaren Vale in recent years. It flew under the radar when established in 2014, busy with barrel finance and logistics and Norm Doole's mind-spinning roles with the Willunga Basin Water Company, Southern Adelaide Economic Development Board and Boar's Rock. Wines are made from the Adelaide Hills, McLaren Vale, Barossa Valley and Fleurieu Peninsula. Exports to the US, China, Hong Kong, Thaliand and Singapore.

🍷🍷🍷🍷♀ **Monterra Reserve McLaren Vale Shiraz 2018** Greater density and vinosity than the regular shiraz. More floral lift, oak supports and spice elements to offset the blue and dark fruits teeming across the palate. Undeniably full bodied, yet relatively light on its feet for this sort of traditional regional expression. Finishes with tangy acid length. Screw cap. 14.5% alc. **Rating** 91 **To** 2028 $45 NG
Monterra Fleurieu Cabernets 2020 A blend of cabernet sauvignon and cabernet franc showing its blackcurrant and leafy aromatic side in a positive light. The is palate given proper diligence via a mouthful of varietal tannins. At this price, you're onto something. Screw cap. 13.5% alc. **Rating** 91 **To** 2026 $20 TL ✪
Colab and Bloom Adelaide Hills McLaren Vale Tempranillo 2020 Earthy, mineral, savoury elements coating soft plum and black cherry fruits. Varietal tannins wrap the palate, but they are soft and pliable and their texture is a definite part of this wine's expression. Screw cap. 14% alc. **Rating** 91 **To** 2026 $22 TL ✪
Monterra Élevage McLaren Vale Sparkling Red NV Judging by aroma, there is plenty of cabernet in this. Think hedgerow, bell pepper, blackcurrant, licorice, thyme and sage. The green elements provide a welcome lift to toasty oak and the sweetness of the liqueur that glazes a frothy, forceful finish. Twin top. 13.5% alc. **Rating** 91 $55 NG

🍷🍷🍷🍷 **Colab and Bloom Fleurieu Nero d'Avola 2020 Rating** 89 **To** 2025 $22 TL
Colab and Bloom Tempranillo Rosé 2020 Rating 88 **To** 2021 $20 JF
Monterra McLaren Vale Shiraz 2019 Rating 88 **To** 2024 $25 NG

Fighting Gully Road ★★★★★

Kurrajong Way, Mayday Hill, Beechworth, Vic 3747 **Region** Beechworth
T 0407 261 373 **www**.fightinggully.com.au **Open** By appt
Winemaker Mark Walpole, Adrian Rodda **Est.** 1997 **Dozens** 3500 **Vyds** 8.3ha
Mark Walpole (who began his viticultural career with Brown Brothers in the late 1980s) and partner Carolyn De Poi found their elevated north-facing site south of Beechworth in 1995. They commenced planting the Aquila Audax Vineyard in '97 with cabernet sauvignon and pinot noir, subsequently expanding with significant areas of sangiovese, tempranillo, shiraz, petit manseng and chardonnay. In 2009 they were fortunate to lease the oldest vineyard in the region, planted by the Smith family in 1978 to chardonnay and cabernet sauvignon – in fact, Mark shares the lease with long-time friend Adrian Rodda (see A. Rodda Wines). Mark says, 'We are now making wine in a building in the old and historic Mayday Hills Lunatic Asylum – a place that should be full of winemakers!' Exports to Hong Kong.

🍷🍷🍷🍷🍷 **Black Label Smith's Vineyard Beechworth Chardonnay 2018** From vines planted in '78, fermented and matured for 18 months in new and used French oak, partial mlf. The power, intensity and depth of the wine comes from the low yield of these venerable vines. Ripe white nectarine/peach is offset by flinty acidity. Screw cap. 13% alc. **Rating** 97 **To** 2030 $65 JH ✪

🍷🍷🍷🍷🍷 **Beechworth Chardonnay 2019** A strong follow-up to the trophy-winning '18, proving again just how good this region is for chardonnay. A taut and refined style, with layers of citrus – grapefruit, lemon, mandarin rind – nestled among smoky oak and almond meal. A tightly coiled spring on the palate, tense and firm. Feel the energy in the glass. Screw cap. 13% alc. **Rating** 95 **To** 2028 $40 JP ♥

Beechworth Pinot Noir 2019 Medium crimson. Fragrant and high-toned florals join forces with alluring forest berries, thyme and sage. Not an easy year for the region, but it's hard to see this in such a confident youngster, full of life and energy. Tight across the palate, with a lilting tomato leafiness, it's assured of developing further. Screw cap. 13.5% alc. **Rating** 95 **To** 2027 $35 JP ✪ ♥

Black Label La Longa Beechworth Sangiovese 2018 According to the maker, La Longa is a test of patience, with extended time in new and seasoned barriques, followed by more time in large 1600L wooden cask and, finally, bottle ageing before release. Strikes a wild pose, with baked earth, wild thyme, dried herbs, glazed cherries and Szechuan pepper. Supple tannins meld with warm, ripe fruit, but underlying it all is firm, toasty oak. Screw cap. 14% alc. **Rating** 95 **To** 2030 $32 JP ✪

Beechworth Sangiovese 2019 Captures the grape's innate red-cherry and dark-berry flavours beautifully. Bright fruits are enhanced by wild herbs, anise, earth, leafy notes and lithe tannins. Supple and juicy to close. Screw cap. 14% alc. **Rating** 94 **To** 2025 $32 JP

🍷🍷🍷🍷 **Alpine Valleys Aglianico 2017 Rating** 93 **To** 2027 $45 JP
Beechworth Tempranillo 2015 Rating 92 **To** 2027 $32 JP

Finniss River Vineyard ★★★★☆

28 Cadell Street, Goolwa, SA 5214 **Region** Currency Creek
T 0432 546 065 **www.**finnissvineyard.com.au **Open** 7 days 10–4
Winemaker Andrew Hercock **Est.** 1999 **Dozens** 3200 **Vyds** 65.3ha
The Hickinbotham family established several great vineyards, the last of these being that of Finniss River in 1999. The planting mix was good, dominated by 31.3ha of shiraz and 20.9ha of cabernet sauvignon. Between then and February 2015, when Adam and Lauren Parkinson purchased the vineyard, all the grapes were sold, which brought Adam – during his time as general manager of a winery in McLaren Vale, as well as general manager of one of Australia's largest vineyard management companies – into contact with the family and its grapes. Grape sales will remain for the foreseeable future, but the cellar door is the outlet for local sales. Exports to China, the US and Singapore have already been established.

Fire Gully ★★★★

Metricup Road, Wilyabrup, WA 6280 **Region** Margaret River
T (08) 9755 6220 **www.**firegully.com.au **Open** By appt
Winemaker Dr Michael Peterkin **Est.** 1988 **Dozens** 5000 **Vyds** 13.4ha
A 6ha lake created in a gully ravaged by bushfires gave the name. In 1998 Mike Peterkin of Pierro purchased it, and manages the vineyard in conjunction with former owners Ellis and Margaret Butcher. He regards the Fire Gully wines as entirely separate from those of Pierro. The vineyard is planted to cabernet sauvignon, merlot, shiraz, semillon, sauvignon blanc, chardonnay, viognier and chenin blanc. Exports to all major markets.

🍷🍷🍷🍷 **Margaret River Chardonnay 2019** Savoury oak ensconces ripe yellow peach and curry leaf, all balanced by briny acidity. Oak-driven at this inchoate stage, but the fruit has the density to carry this once it has integrated a little more. Just wait, it'll be a cracker. Screw cap. 14% alc. **Rating** 93 **To** 2028 $38 EL

Margaret River Cabernets Merlot 2018 54/23/23% cabernet sauvignon/merlot/cabernet franc. Floral and pretty, this has the telltale crunch from the franc, the plump mid palate from the merlot, and the structure and cassis from the cabernet sauvignon. Lovely wine. Screw cap. 14% alc. **Rating** 93 **To** 2030 $29 EL

🍷🍷🍷 **Margaret River Rosé 2020 Rating** 88 **To** 2022 $35 EL

Firetail

21 Bessell Road, Rosa Glen, WA 6285 **Region** Margaret River
T (08) 9757 5156 **www**.firetail.com.au **Open** 7 days 11–5
Winemaker Bruce Dukes, Peter Stanlake **Est.** 2002 **Dozens** 1000 **Vyds** 4.2ha
Named for the Red-eared Firetail, a bird found only in the southwest corner of WA. Jessica
Worrall and Rob Glass are fugitives from the oil and gas industry. In 2002 they purchased a
historic vineyard in Margaret River that had been planted between 1979 and '81 to sauvignon
blanc, semillon and cabernet sauvignon; they have also planted chardonnay and malbec. Wine
quality is generally excellent.

Margaret River Chardonnay 2020 Creamy, rich and layered with stone fruit,
exotic spice and red apple acidity. A very classy little wine, in very short supply
(just over 100 cases made). Screw cap. 13.7% alc. **Rating** 92 To 2031 $28 EL
Margaret River Sparkling Chardonnay 2016 First disgorgement of this
vintage. Traditional method, partial barrel-fermentation, zero dosage. On lees
for 54 months. Fresh and vibrant, the lees are evident in a cheesecloth backdrop,
providing the stage for the taut citrus fruit to shine. Cork. 11.7% alc. **Rating** 92
$35 EL

First Creek Wines

600 McDonalds Road, Pokolbin, NSW 2320 **Region** Hunter Valley
T (02) 4998 7293 **www**.firstcreekwines.com.au **Open** Mon–Wed 9–6, Thurs–Sat 9–7,
Sun 9–5
Winemaker Liz Silkman, Shaun Silkman, Greg Silkman **Est.** 1984 **Dozens** 60 000
First Creek Wines is the family business of Greg Silkman (managing director and winemaker),
son Shaun Silkman (chief operating officer and winemaker) and Shaun's wife Liz (née Jackson,
chief winemaker). The quality of the wines has been consistently exemplary and there is every
reason to believe this will continue in the years to come. Associated business First Creek
Winemaking Services is the main contract winemaker operating in the Hunter Valley. Exports
to the US, Canada, Ireland, Singapore, Japan and China.

Single Vineyard Black Cluster Semillon 2014 Here, the Black Cluster shows
us a conflation of experience and site, and with that, sensitive winemaking to
express the fruit. Barley sugar, lemon curd, buttered toast. The finish: expansive,
layered, intense and almost powerful in an uncanny way, despite the under-the-
radar low alcohol. Wonderful length. Very fine. Screw cap. 11% alc. **Rating** 95
To 2026 $60 NG
Winemaker's Reserve Hunter Valley Semillon 2011 Museum release. This
is abnormally low of alcohol, even for Hunter semillon. A mere 10%. And yet a
luminescent glint of green and a rifle of flavours, sumptuous and intense: lanolin,
lemon drop, quince and citrus marmalade. A great vintage in these parts, and it
shows. Tensile and long across a jittery carriage of pumice-like freshness, belying
the light weight. Screw cap. 10% alc. **Rating** 94 To 2025 $65 NG

Organic Rosso Puro Hunter Valley Semillon 2017 Rating 93 To 2024 NG
Winemaker's Reserve Hunter Valley Chardonnay 2014 Rating 93 To 2024
$65 NG
Marrowbone Road Hunter Valley Shiraz 2019 Rating 92 To 2027 $60 NG
Hunter Valley Shiraz 2019 Rating 91 To 2025 $25 NG

First Drop Wines

Beckwith Park, Barossa Valley Way, Nuriootpa, SA 5355 **Region** Barossa Valley
T (08) 8562 3324 **www**.firstdropwines.com **Open** Wed–Sat 10–4, Sun 11–4
Winemaker Matt Gant, Anna Higgins **Est.** 2005 **Dozens** 20 000
The First Drop Wines of today has been transformed since its establishment in 2005. It now
has its own winery, part of the old Penfolds winery at Nuriootpa, shared with Tim Smith
Wines. The group of buildings is called Beckwith Park in honour of the man who did so

much groundbreaking work for Penfolds: Ray Beckwith OAM, recipient of the Maurice O'Shea Award, who died in '12, but not before his 100th birthday. The quality of the First Drop wines would have made Ray Beckwith smile in appreciation. Exports to the UK, the US, Canada, Denmark, Japan, Hong Kong and China.

🍷🍷🍷🍷🍷 **The Cream Barossa Valley Shiraz 2018** Matt Gant identifies his best barrels to position The Cream a level above his Fat of the Land single-vineyard wines, elevating this blend above the sum of its parts. Its powerful depth and impact of black fruits, black licorice and the dark chocolate of new French oak are accompanied by heightened definition, coherence, creaminess, lift and persistence. Every element rises in unison, its crescendo holding long and true, promising great things in the cellar. Cork. 15.5% alc. **Rating** 95 **To** 2033 $150 TS

🍷🍷🍷🍷🍷 **Fat of the Land Ebenezer Single Vineyard Barossa Valley Shiraz 2018** **Rating** 93 **To** 2033 $100 TS
Fat of the Land Single Vineyard Greenock Barossa Valley Shiraz 2018 **Rating** 92 **To** 2033 $100 TS

First Foot Forward

6 Maddens Lane, Coldstream, Vic 3770 **Region** Yarra Valley
T 0402 575 818 **www**.firstfootforward.com.au **Open** By appt
Winemaker Martin Siebert **Est.** 2013 **Dozens** 500
Owner and winemaker Martin Siebert's daytime job is at Tokar Estate, where he has been chief winemaker for a number of years. In 2013 he had the opportunity to purchase pinot noir and chardonnay from a mature vineyard in The Patch – high in the Dandenong Ranges on the southern edge of the Yarra Valley. It is cooler and wetter than the floor of the Yarra Valley, so much so that the fruit is consistently picked after Tokar's cabernet sauvignon, reducing the stress that might otherwise have occurred. He says that so long as the fruit is available, he will be purchasing it, adding other wines from the Yarra Valley to broaden the offer to quality-focused restaurants and specialty wine stores around Melbourne.

🍷🍷🍷🍷🍷 **Amphora Ferment Single Vineyard Yarra Valley Sauvignon Blanc 2020** Attention to detail on the sorting table is what makes this an exceptional wine. It's pristine and pure, with a line of juicy acidity. Citrussy and savoury, crisp and crunchy. Love it. Screw cap. 12.8% alc. **Rating** 95 **To** 2025 $25 JF ❂
Upper Yarra Valley Chardonnay 2020 There's a lot to enjoy here: tangy citrus flavours, and lightness of touch across the palate, yet there's texture and definition, too. A very good price for very cool Yarra chardy. Screw cap. 13% alc. **Rating** 95 **To** 2027 $28 JF ❂
Upper Yarra Valley Pinot Noir 2020 While showing the exuberance of youth, this is shaped by raw silk tannins and a smoothness across a light- to medium-bodied palate. It's full of cherries, spice and wild herbs, with refreshing squirts of citrus, especially blood orange and zest. Refreshing, tangy and hard to put down. Screw cap. 13.8% alc. **Rating** 95 **To** 2028 $28 JF ❂
Upper Yarra Valley Chardonnay 2019 A go-to chardonnay that offers the right amount of flavour, juiciness and enjoyment. Full of tangy lemon and grapefruit, with creamed honey and lavender, a savoury palate and mouth-watering acidity. It's linear, but not so tight that it can't be enjoyed now. Screw cap. 13.5% alc. **Rating** 94 **To** 2027 $28 JF ❂

🍷🍷🍷🍷🍷 **Yarra Valley Pinot Noir 2019 Rating** 92 **To** 2025 $28 JF

Fishbone Wines

422 Harmans Mill Road, Wilyabrup, WA 6285 **Region** Margaret River
T (08) 9755 6726 **www**.fishbonewines.com.au **Open** 7 days 10–4.30
Winemaker Stuart Pierce **Est.** 2009 **Dozens** 15 000 **Vyds** 9.1ha
Fishbone Wines' 9.1ha vineyard includes chardonnay, tempranillo and cabernet sauvignon; and 1ha of newer plantings of malbec, vermentino and pinot noir. The Fishbone wines are

created with minimal intervention. The range includes the 'accessible' Blue Label range, single-vineyard Black Label Margaret range and the 'icon' Joseph River wines. The restaurant features a Japanese-inspired menu with a terrace overlooking the property. Exports to the US, Canada, Dubai, Singapore, Taiwan and China.

🍷🍷🍷🍷   **Joseph River Reserve Margaret River Cabernet Sauvignon 2018**
The colour is perfect. The nose is restrained, yet showing characters of cassis, bramble and spice. The palate has a distinct tang that sits adjacent to all expected flavours and characters, leaving a minty/clove sensation through the finish. Some lovely characters, but overall a touch awkward, with a few too many elbows. Screw cap. 14.2% alc. **Rating** 89 **To** 2031 $65 EL

Five Geese

118 Main Road, McLaren Vale, SA 5171 (postal) **Region** McLaren Vale
T 0434 193 308 **www**.fivegeese.com.au
Winemaker Mike Farmilo **Est.** 1999 **Dozens** 5000 **Vyds** 28ha
Sue Trott is devoted to her Five Geese wines, which come from vines planted in 1927 and '65 (shiraz, cabernet sauvignon, grenache and mataro), nero d'Avola a more recent arrival. She sold the grapes for many years, but in '99 decided to create her own label and make a strictly limited amount of wine from the pick of the vineyards, which are run on organic principles. Exports to the UK, South Korea, Singapore and China.

🍷🍷🍷🍷🍷   **Jen's Block Reserve McLaren Vale Cabernet Sauvignon 2017** Hand picked, open-fermented and a meagre 10 days on skins. Why not longer? Cabernet is about real tannin. Yet it all works well in a fairly soft, polished fashion. Cassis, green olive, verdant herb and a scrub of sage-laden tannins. Long and plush. Screw cap. 14.5% alc. **Rating** 93 **To** 2031 $45 NG
The Pippali Old Vine McLaren Vale Shiraz 2017 Hand picked, 7 days on skins, 24 months of maturation in 1st- and 2nd-use French oak. Regional enough, be it the stamp of place or the traditional approach to making wine in these parts, I am unsure. Dark plum, Asian herb, baking spice, anise and spiky acidity. Rich, round and slickly made. Screw cap. 14.5% alc. **Rating** 90 **To** 2027 $35 NG

🍷🍷🍷🍷   **McLaren Vale Shiraz 2017 Rating** 89 **To** 2026 $28 NG

Flametree

Cnr Caves Road/Chain Avenue, Dunsborough, WA 6281 **Region** Margaret River
T (08) 9756 8577 **www**.flametreewines.com **Open** 7 days 10–5
Winemaker Cliff Royle, Julian Scott **Est.** 2007 **Dozens** 20 000
Flametree, owned by the Towner family (John, Liz, Rob and Annie), has had extraordinary success since its first vintage in 2007. The usual practice of planting a vineyard and then finding someone to make the wine was turned on its head: a state-of-the-art winery was built, and grape purchase agreements signed with growers in the region. Show success was topped by the winning of the Jimmy Watson Trophy with its '07 Cabernet Merlot. If all this were not enough, Flametree has secured the services of winemaker Cliff Royle. Exports to the UK, Canada, Indonesia, Malaysia, Singapore, Papua New Guinea, Fiji and Hong Kong.

🍷🍷🍷🍷🍷   **S.R.S. Wallcliffe Margaret River Chardonnay 2019** From a single site, wild-yeast fermented and matured for 10 months in French puncheons (40% new). Intense white peach and pink grapefruit dance a pas de deux on the long palate, creamy cashew oak nuances beating a rhythm in a perfectly judged support role. Screw cap. 13% alc. **Rating** 97 **To** 2032 $65 JH ✪

🍷🍷🍷🍷🍷   **S.R.S. Wilyabrup Margaret River Cabernet Sauvignon 2018** Salty, spicy pomegranate and red raspberry form the base for this medium-bodied cabernet. Supple, pliable and with plenty of flex, this bounces on the palate. It has life, energy, and that classic Margaret River cabernet paradigm of power without weight. The tannins are a standout; chalky and chewy. Screw cap. 14% alc. **Rating** 96 **To** 2046 $85 EL

Jeremy John Margaret River Cabernet Sauvignon Malbec 2018
Sometimes a wine insists you let it finish before you start writing. This takes it long and slow, romancing you with sweet fruit, then whisking you off your feet in a swoop of savoury spice and plush tannin. A lingering, patient and powerful cabernet, capable of a very long life indeed. Screw cap. 14% alc. **Rating** 96 To 2046 $125 EL

Margaret River Chardonnay 2019 Compelling struck-match nose. Silky, viscose palate – rounded almost, shaped by phenolic edge and grip. Flinty and mineral, but with hallmark yellow peach, pink grapefruit and curry leaf. Rounding out in a tight back palate and defined by saline acid. Tremendous value at the price! Screw cap. 13.2% alc. **Rating** 95 To 2030 $29 EL ✪

Margaret River Cabernet Sauvignon 2018 Highly aromatic; a bouquet of cassis, raspberry, aniseed, spicy oak and earthy bramble rises out of the glass. The palate follows suit, resulting in a concentrated, supple and elegant cabernet, the very reason why Margaret River is so successful. Gorgeous wine from a near-perfect vintage. Screw cap. 14% alc. **Rating** 95 To 2036 $45 EL

S.R.S. Karridale Margaret River Sauvignon Blanc 2020 Curried peanuts, pink grapefruit, cleansing palate and bright acid – this is creamy and chewy, the oak a sensitive match to the fruit. The palate moves through a saline finish with flecks of quinine. A really lovely wine with restraint and class. Screw cap. 13% alc. **Rating** 94 To 2030 $33 EL

Margaret River Chardonnay 2020 Salted preserved lemon, yellow peach and brine on the nose. Even at first glance, this has all the concentration and complexity that we have become accustomed to from this label. On the palate, it is both graceful and heady, with flavour packed into every corner of the glass. Screw cap. 13% alc. **Rating** 94 To 2028 $30 EL ✪

♟♟♟♟♟ **Margaret River Sauvignon Blanc Semillon 2020** Rating 93 To 2025 $25 EL ✪
Margaret River Shiraz 2018 Rating 93 To 2028 $29 EL
Margaret River Pinot Rosé 2020 Rating 92 To 2022 $25 EL ✪
Margaret River Cabernet Sauvignon Merlot 2018 Rating 91 To 2028 $30 EL

Flaxman Wines ★★★★★

662 Flaxmans Valley Road, Flaxmans Valley, SA 5253 **Region** Eden Valley
T 0411 668 949 **www.**flaxmanwines.com.au **Open** Sat 11–5, Sun 11.4
Winemaker Colin Sheppard **Est.** 2005 **Dozens** 1200 **Vyds** 2ha
After visiting the Barossa Valley for over a decade, Melbourne residents Colin Sheppard and wife Fi decided on a tree change and in 2004 found a small, old vineyard overlooking Flaxmans Valley, consisting of 90yo riesling, 90yo shiraz and 70yo semillon. The vines are dry grown, hand pruned, hand picked and treated – say the Sheppards – as their garden. Yields are restricted to under 4t/ha and exceptional parcels of locally grown grapes are also purchased. Colin has worked at various Barossa wineries and his attention to detail (and understanding of the process) is reflected in the consistent high quality of the wines. Exports to China.

Flowstone Wines ★★★★★

11298 Bussell Highway, Forest Grove, WA 6286 **Region** Margaret River
T 0487 010 275 **www.**flowstonewines.com **Open** By appt
Winemaker Stuart Pym **Est.** 2013 **Dozens** 1500 **Vyds** 3ha
Veteran Margaret River winemaker Stuart Pym's career constituted long-term successive roles: beginning with Voyager Estate in 1991, thereafter with Devil's Lair, and finishing with Stella Bella in '13, the year he and Perth-based wine tragic Phil Giglia established Flowstone Wines. In '03 Stuart had purchased a small property on the edge of the Margaret River Plateau in the beautiful Forest Grove area, progressively planting chardonnay, cabernet sauvignon, gewürztraminer and more recently touriga. From '17, Flowstone leased a vineyard at Karridale, planted to long-established sauvignon blanc and chardonnay, having previously

purchased part of the crop for its regional wines. The lease puts the vineyard on par with the estate plantings; the best fruit is retained, the balance sold. Thus Queen of the Earth Sauvignon Blanc appeared for the first time in '17, joining the estate chardonnay and cabernet Queens. Exports to the UK and Japan.

ŸŸŸŸŸ **Queen of the Earth Margaret River Sauvignon Blanc 2019** This is sensational. Serious layers of flavour and texture on the palate show a reverence for the variety by Stuart Pym. Long, lean and lithe; this shares guava, lychee, red apple skins, white stone fruit, exotic spice and a distinct oriental leaning of anise and pink peppercorn. Serious stuff. Screw cap. 12.9% alc. **Rating** 97 **To** 2030 $55 EL ✪

ŸŸŸŸŸ **Margaret River Sauvignon Blanc 2019** The palate has a fine textural creaminess that massages the flavour into the mouth rather than asserting it. The characters of salted jalapeño, snow pea and cassis fold seamlessly into the saline acid line. An incredibly elegant and seamless wine – the attention to detail is evident. Very long. Screw cap. 12.5% alc. **Rating** 96 **To** 2027 $32 EL ✪

Queen of the Earth Margaret River Cabernet Sauvignon 2017 Stuart Pym is not afraid of pushing boundaries: 3 years in oak! Well … it's nowhere near as evident in the glass as it should be, thanks to the pedigree of the fruit. Savoury, dense, flavourful and very long, this is built to last. Buy it now, but don't look at it until 2027. Screw cap. 14% alc. **Rating** 96 **To** 2047 $74 EL ✪

Margaret River Gewürztraminer 2019 Intoxicatingly aromatic, spicy and opulent. All the hallmarks of a brilliant Asian food match (lychee, cumin, lemon pith, strawberry, nashi pear and lemongrass) – but the infinitesimal production says it better be great food, too! It's refreshing like a cold pool on a hot day. Screw cap. 13.5% alc. **Rating** 95 **To** 2030 $32 EL ✪

Margaret River Chardonnay 2018 The combination of a ripe and perfect year and the finer, more linear Dijon clones is a good one. Textural, saline and with piercing intensity; this is an absolute joy. Personality and spice with elegance and finesse. Yep, love it. Screw cap. 13% alc. **Rating** 95 **To** 2030 $36 EL

Moonmilk White Margaret River 2020 59/29/8/4% savagnin/viognier/gewürztraminer/sauvignon blanc. Hard to imagine how the low price could repay the work that goes into this tiny quantity of wine (226 cases). Textural, salty, taut and exciting. The floral gewürz and oily viognier make a statement, but it is the edgy savagnin that reins it all in. Chalky phenolics through the finish elevate this into the 'delicious and compelling' category. Screw cap. 13% alc. **Rating** 95 **To** 2024 $22 EL ✪

Moonmilk Margaret River Shiraz Grenache 2019 70/25/5% shiraz/grenache/viognier, vinified separately. Matured 10 months in a combination of old barriques and Cognac barrels (older than 20 years). This wine is brilliant. The complex vinification effort was worth it. Buy it if you can find it. Screw cap. 14% alc. **Rating** 95 **To** 2030 $25 EL ✪

Queen of the Earth Margaret River Chardonnay 2018 18 months in French oak (50% new). The delicate Dijon clone fruit is outdone by the oak in this instance. While this has piercing intensity of fruit, it isn't quite enough to endure through the finish. A beautiful, fascinating, detailed wine made in tiny quantities, in this instance speaking more loudly of oak than of fruit. Screw cap. 13.1% alc. **Rating** 94 **To** 2036 $55 EL

ŸŸŸŸ **Vintage Margaret River Fortified Touriga 2018 Rating** 89 $50 EL

Flying Fish Cove   ★★★★★

3763 Caves Road, Wilyabrup, WA 6280 **Region** Margaret River
T (08) 9755 6600 **www.**flyingfishcove.com **Open** By appt
Winemaker Simon Ding, Damon Easthaugh **Est.** 2000 **Vyds** 25ha
Flying Fish Cove has 2 strings to its bow: contract winemaking for others and the development of its own brand. Long-serving winemaker Simon Ding had a circuitous journey before falling prey to the lure of wine. He finished an apprenticeship in metalwork in 1993. In '96 he

obtained a bachelor of science, then joined the Flying Fish Cove team in 2000. Exports to the UK, the US, Canada and Malaysia.

Forbes & Forbes ★★★

20 Hooper Road, Strathalbyn, SA 5255 **Region** Eden Valley
T 0478 391·304 **www**.forbeswine.com.au **Open** At Taste Eden Valley, Angaston
Winemaker Colin Forbes **Est.** 2008 **Dozens** 1200 **Vyds** 3.2ha
This venture is owned by Colin and Robert Forbes, and their respective partners. Colin says, 'I have been in the industry for a frightening length of time', beginning with Thomas Hardy & Sons in 1974. Colin is particularly attached to riesling and the property owned by the partners in Eden Valley has 2ha of the variety (plus 0.5ha each of merlot and cabernet sauvignon and 0.2ha of cabernet franc). Exports to Japan and China.

🍷🍷🍷🍷🍷 **Cellar Matured Eden Valley Riesling 2011** Wonderful mature Eden Valley riesling. The wet and cool 2011 season furnished layers of apricot, persimmon and spice thanks to the onset of botrytis. These have morphed beautifully with the buttery, nutty, honeyed complexity of a decade of age. Held pristine under screw cap, it's maintained a spine of energetic, cool-vintage acidity that draws out a long, crystalline and still energetic finish. Screw cap. 12.5% alc. **Rating** 95 **To** 2026 $32 TS ✪

🍷🍷🍷🍷 **Alexander Murray Eden Valley Cabernet Sauvignon Merlot Cabernet Franc 2015 Rating** 89 **To** 2025 $32 TS
The Sparkling Alexander Murray Eden Valley 2015 Rating 89 $32 TS

Forest Hill Vineyard ★★★★★

Cnr South Coast Highway/Myers Road, Denmark, WA 6333 **Region** Great Southern
T (08) 9848 2399 **www**.foresthillwines.com.au **Open** 7 days 10.30–5
Winemaker Liam Carmody, Guy Lyons **Est.** 1965 **Dozens** 12000 **Vyds** 36ha
This family-owned business is one of the oldest 'new' winemaking operations in WA and was the site of the first grape plantings in Great Southern in 1965. The Forest Hill brand became well known, aided by the fact that a '75 Riesling made by Sandalford from Forest Hill grapes won 9 trophies. The quality of the wines made from the oldest vines (dry-grown) on the property is awesome (released under the numbered vineyard block labels). Exports to the UK, the US and Finland.

🍷🍷🍷🍷🍷 **Block 1 Mount Barker Riesling 2020** There's only one thing to do while in the presence of a wine such as this: stand aside and allow it to pass. This is statuesque power and grace, with an army of following flavours that trail in its very long wake. Fifty-seven cases. Screw cap. 12.8% alc. **Rating** 98 **To** 2045 $55 EL ✪ ♥

🍷🍷🍷🍷🍷 **Block 8 Mount Barker Chardonnay 2020** Yields were so low in 2019 that this wine wasn't even made. Then 2020 came around – another low-yielding year, producing a tiny quantity. Crushed curry leaf, peach, brine and apple on the nose. On the palate, this is incredibly concentrated and powerful, and although closed right now, it will continue to evolve and unfurl over time. Very impressive. Screw cap. 13% alc. **Rating** 96 **To** 2031 $45 EL ✪
Highbury Fields Riesling 2020 Savoury exotic nose of sesame, soy, citrus pith, creamed honey on buttered toast and graphite. The palate is taut and powerful, the oak coming through on the finish. This is a wine of layering, power, poise and adaptability. Quite astounding for the price. Screw cap. 13% alc. **Rating** 95 **To** 2031 $24 EL ✪
Mount Barker Shiraz 2019 Spicy, lifted and savoury, this is all about berry bramble. The fruit on the palate moves from black cherry to pomegranate, blackberry and raspberry, all embossed with finely inlaid tannins and saline acid. These elements create a tension across the fruit, pulling it all together in a very classy way. Cracking wine and a must-buy for the money. Screw cap. 14% alc. **Rating** 95 **To** 2028 $30 EL ✪

Block 5 Mount Barker Cabernet Sauvignon 2019 This has all of the beauty of the 2018 (ripe fruit, dense tannins, long length of flavour) but also has a delicacy … a space. Remember when exam papers said 'this page has been left intentionally blank'? Well intentional space in a wine allows for time to think, breathe and feel while you drink. This has that. Take your time with it, the tannins are permeating, but the fruit has power. It's all there. Screw cap. 14% alc. **Rating** 95 To 2041 $65 EL

Block 2 Mount Barker Riesling 2020 Like the Block 1, this has fierce intensity of flavour, except through the lens of this wine it has a more wild and untamed nature about it. Brilliant intensity, and definitely a clear expression of Mount Barker riesling. White pepper, clove and anise through the finish. Screw cap. 13% alc. **Rating** 94 To 2035 $36 EL

Mount Barker Cabernet Sauvignon 2019 If Mount Barker had a regional calling card, it would be the inherent muscularity of the wines produced there. At times austere (the whites mainly), but always powerful. This wine is no exception. Dense cassis, red gravel, sea salt, iodine and raspberry, shaped by firm tannins. The long finish reveals the pedigree of the Forest Hill vineyard and hints at the capacity for ageing in the cellar. Not bad for $32! Screw cap. 14% alc. **Rating** 94 To 2036 $32 EL

♟♟♟♟♀ Highbury Fields Cabernet Sauvignon 2019 **Rating** 93 To 2031 $24 EL ✪
Mount Barker Gewürztraminer 2020 **Rating** 92 To 2027 $26 EL
Mount Barker Chardonnay 2020 **Rating** 92 To 2028 $32 EL
Highbury Fields Chardonnay 2020 **Rating** 92 To 2027 $24 EL ✪
Highbury Fields Great Southern Shiraz 2019 **Rating** 92 To 2027 $24 EL ✪
Mount Barker Riesling 2020 **Rating** 91 To 2030 $28 EL
Highbury Fields Sauvignon Blanc 2020 **Rating** 90 To 2023 $24 EL

Forester Estate   ★★★★☆

1064 Wildwood Road, Yallingup, WA 6282 **Region** Margaret River
T (08) 9755 2000 **www.foresterestate.com.au Open** By appt
Winemaker Kevin McKay, Todd Payne **Est.** 2001 **Dozens** 52 000 **Vyds** 33.5ha
Forester Estate is owned by Kevin and Jenny McKay. Winemaker Todd Payne has had a distinguished career, starting in the Great Southern, thereafter the Napa Valley, back to Plantagenet, then Esk Valley in Hawke's Bay, plus 2 vintages in the Northern Rhône Valley, one with esteemed producer Yves Cuilleron in 2008. His move back to WA completed the circle. The estate vineyards are planted to sauvignon blanc, semillon, chardonnay, cabernet sauvignon, shiraz, merlot, petit verdot, malbec and fer. Exports to Switzerland and Japan.

♟♟♟♟♟ Margaret River Sauvignon Blanc 2020 Sweaty complexity on the nose – saffron, curry leaf, sugar snap peas and ripe summer-green capsicum. The palate is texturally layered, with a spicy green jalapeño character that bursts onto the mid-palate scene. Interesting and delicious, complex drinking for the price. Screw cap. 12.5% alc. **Rating** 94 To 2030 $25 EL ✪

♟♟♟♟♀ Yelverton Reserve Margaret River Chardonnay 2018 **Rating** 93 To 2031 $53 EL
Jack out the Box Margaret River Semillon 2019 **Rating** 92 To 2028 $26 EL
Margaret River Cabernet Sauvignon 2018 **Rating** 92 To 2031 $34 EL
Jack out the Box Margaret River Fer 2018 **Rating** 91 To 2028 $41 EL
Margaret River Chardonnay 2019 **Rating** 90 To 2027 $34 EL
Home Block Margaret River Shiraz 2018 **Rating** 90 To 2026 $34 EL
Lifestyle Margaret River Cabernet Merlot 2018 **Rating** 90 To 2026 $24 EL

Forty Paces ★★★★

428 Pipers Creek Road, Pipers Creek, Vic 3444 **Region** Macedon Ranges
T 0418 424 785 **www**.fortypaceswines.com
Winemaker Jason Peasley **Est.** 2001 **Dozens** 100 **Vyds** 0.5ha
Forty Paces has a tiny 0.5ha pinot noir vineyard with MV6, 114, 115 and 777 clones, planted by owner/winemaker Jason Peasley in 2001. Jason has no formal training, but was tutored on the job by Stuart Anderson at Epis in the Macedon Ranges. He follows some organic and/or biodynamic practices in both the vineyard and the winery.

🍷🍷🍷🍷🍷 **Macedon Ranges Pinot Noir 2019** What a lovely, composed and utterly delicious wine. Delicately fragrant, with florals and savoury tones. There's a core of ripe yet lightly spiced fruit, a mere hint of forest floor and oak. What seals the deal across the medium-bodied palate are ribbons of fine, textural tannins. Screw cap. 13.5% alc. **Rating** 95 **To** 2027 $44 JF

Four Sisters ★★★

199 O'Dwyers Road, Tabilk, Vic 3608 **Region** Central Victoria
T (03) 5736 2400 **www**.foursisters.com.au
Winemaker Alan George, Jo Nash, Alister Purbrick **Est.** 1995 **Dozens** 40 000
The 4 sisters who inspired this venture were the daughters of the late Trevor Mast, a great winemaker who died before his time. The business is owned by the Purbrick family (the owner of Tahbilk). It orchestrates the purchase of the grapes for the brand, and also facilitates the winemaking. The production is wholly export-focused, with limited sales in Australia. Exports to all major markets.

🍷🍷🍷🍷🍷 **Central Victoria Shiraz 2018** Keeps true to its Central Victorian identity with generosity, solid shiraz fruit and spice with a touch of the local bay-leaf/eucalyptus character. A friendly, approachable style. Measured, too, with firm structure on display. Smart wine, smart price. Bronze medal Perth Royal Wine Show '20. Screw cap. 14.5% alc. **Rating** 90 **To** 2025 $17 JP ✪
Central Victoria Merlot 2018 Crushed, destemmed, cultured-yeast fermentation, 12 months in mix of new/1–5yo French and American oak. A lot of warm and aromatic merlot fruit on display, nicely handled with sympathetic oak. Ripe cassis, mulberry, stewed plum in this fruit-forward style. Varietal leafiness is a plus as is the sinewy tannin structure. All-round excellent value. Bronze medal Perth Royal Wine Show '20. Screw cap. 14% alc. **Rating** 90 **To** 2023 $17 JP ✪

🍷🍷🍷🍷 **Central Victoria Cabernet Sauvignon 2018 Rating** 89 **To** 2023 $17 JP ✪
Central Victoria Sauvignon Blanc 2020 Rating 88 **To** 2025 $17 JP ✪

Four Winds Vineyard ★★★★

9 Patemans Lane, Murrumbateman, NSW 2582 **Region** Canberra District
T (02) 6227 0189 **www**.fourwindsvineyard.com.au **Open** Thurs–Mon 10–4
Winemaker Highside Winemaking **Est.** 1998 **Dozens** 4000 **Vyds** 11.9ha
Graeme and Suzanne Lunney planted the first vines in '98, moving to the Four Winds property full-time in '99 and making the first vintage in 2000. Daughter Sarah and her husband John now oversee the vineyard and cellar door operations. A distinguished vineyard, selling part of the crop to highly regarded producers, part reserved for its own brand.

🍷🍷🍷🍷🍷 **Kyeema Canberra District Tempranillo 2019** A wine that states its case convincingly, starting with its bright ruby hue. Lots of refreshing raspberries, cherries and red licorice, yet it retains a savoury profile with some meaty/reductive notes. Spot-on, well-defined tannins. Screw cap. 13.4% alc. **Rating** 92 **To** 2027 $37 JF
South Australia Vermentino 2020 There's a lot to like here. Its summery expression, its citrus tang, sea salty and preserved lemon flavours. It's refreshing, uncomplicated and all in all, a delicious drink. Screw cap. 12.9% alc. **Rating** 90 **To** 2023 $28 JF

Canberra District Shiraz 2019 A touch terse and takes its time to open up. Savoury toned with cedary oak infusing the dark fruit. It's laden with baking spices, licorice and flecks of mint. Medium bodied with firm tannins and a slightly dry finish. Screw cap. 13.8% alc. **Rating** 90 **To** 2030 $32 JF

Hard Graft Canberra District Shiraz 2017 On paper, 10 months ageing with up to 30% new French barrels would not seem too much, but the oak dominates even after the wine spends an extra year in bottle. Satsuma plums doused in rosemary, eucalyptus and soy sauce, with wafts of prosciutto and pepper. It's firm across the palate, the tannins hold fast with a radicchio bitterness on the finish. Partner with hearty fare or give it more time. Screw cap. 13.3% alc. **Rating** 90 **To** 2030 $75 JF

 # Fourth Wave Wine

Suite 22, Level 1, OTP house, 10 Bradford Close, Kotara, NSW 2289 **Region** Various
T 1300 778 047 **www.**fourthwavewine.com.au
Winemaker Various **Est.** 2009
Based in the suburbs of Newcastle, Fourth Wave Wine was founded in 2009 by Nicholas and Frances Crampton, boasting wine industry nous; finance and IT skills respectively. Assisted by winemaker and consultant Corey Ryan, Fourth Wave makes wine in 6 countries with a total production of 300 000 dozen bottles packaged under a panoply of brands. A modern-day global negoçiant, if you will. Domestically, brands include Elephant in the Room, Little Giant, Burns and Fuller and Take it to the Grave. While savvy marketing is key to their success, the intrinsic qualities of many of the wines cannot be denied. Exports to China, Canada, South Korea, Malaysia, Singapore, Europe and NZ. (NG)

🍷🍷🍷🍷🍷 **Tread Softly Yarra Valley Pinot Noir 2020** From the Upper Yarra, early picked, wild fermented, matured in used large-format French oak. Woods Crampton steps out of South Australia to fashion this attractively labelled (and vinified) wine. It's not thin or green; the bright, full, clear crimson hue marking a bargain. Screw cap. 12.2% alc. **Rating** 94 **To** 2023 $22 JH ✪

🍷🍷🍷🍷🍷 **Farm Hand One of a Kind McLaren Vale Sangiovese 2019** **Rating** 93 **To** 2024 $22 NG ✪

Farm Hand One of a Kind McLaren Vale Shiraz 2019 **Rating** 91 **To** 2024 $22 NG ✪

Fowles Wine ★★★★☆

Cnr Hume Freeway/Lambing Gully Road, Avenel, Vic 3664 **Region** Strathbogie Ranges
T (03) 5796 2150 **www.**fowleswine.com **Open** 7 days 9–5
Winemaker Victor Nash, Lindsay Brown **Est.** 1968 **Dozens** 80 000 **Vyds** 120ha
This family-owned winery is led by Matt Fowles, with chief winemaker Victor Nash heading the winemaking team. The large vineyard is primarily focused on riesling, chardonnay, shiraz and cabernet sauvignon, but also includes arneis, vermentino, pinot gris, sauvignon blanc, pinot noir, mourvèdre, sangiovese and merlot. Marketing is energetic, with the well-known Ladies who Shoot their Lunch label also available presented in a 6-bottle gun case. Exports to the UK, the US, Canada and China.

🍷🍷🍷🍷🍷 **Upton Run Single Vineyard Strathbogie Ranges Shiraz 2018** The flagship producer that does the 'bogies proud. Tasted 1 month after release and tight as a drum, this benefits from a decant. Still arms and legs but should come together beautifully, exhibiting cool-climate attitude with its heightened spice, pepper and well-structured elegance. A deep, dense wine with intense blackberries, spice, vanilla and sweet soy. Concentrated with ripe tannins. Makes a statement about the premium quality of Strathbogie shiraz. Diam. 14% alc. **Rating** 95 **To** 2032 $125 JP

Ladies who Shoot their Lunch Wild Ferment Shiraz 2018 Machine picked, crushed, destemmed, wild yeast, 10 days on skins, 12 months maturation in 2yo French oak (100%). Another super-generous wild-ferment shiraz of a style that must now be writ in stone for winemaker Lindsay Brown, who blends from a barrel selection. Colour is deep purple-garnet. Boasts a world of baking spices on the bouquet, black berries, stewed plums, baked earth. Upfront and muscular, it launches into an expansive palate highlighted by briar, bay leaf, pepper, dried herbs. Draws in tight thanks to well-knitted tannins. Screw cap. 14% alc. **Rating** 94 To 2027 $35 JP

Upton Run Strathbogie Ranges Cabernet Sauvignon 2018 Cabernet tends to live in the shadow of shiraz in this part of the world. Here, it launches into the super-premium price bracket with gusto, backed by a confident vintage and experienced winemaking. A complex wine that needs further time but already showing attractive earthy, Aussie bush and smoked meats aromas which reflect the source and the year. Clean and well balanced, with a touch of cabernet austerity, it shows restraint and care. Screw cap. 14.6% alc. **Rating** 94 To 2032 $125 JP

ꭹꭹꭹꭹꭹ **Stone Dwellers Strathbogie Ranges Mourvèdre 2019** Rating 93 To 2029 $30 JP
Ladies who Shoot their Lunch Wild Ferment Pinot Noir 2019 Rating 92 To 2025 $35 JP
Stone Dwellers Single Vineyard Strathbogie Ranges Shiraz 2018 Rating 92 To 2030 $30 JP
Stone Dwellers Single Vineyard Strathbogie Ranges Riesling 2020 Rating 90 To 2031 $30 JP
Ladies who Shoot their Lunch Wild Ferment Chardonnay 2019 Rating 90 To 2026 $35 JP

Fox Creek Wines   ★★★★★

140 Malpas Road, McLaren Vale, SA 5171 **Region** McLaren Vale
T (08) 8557 0000 **www**.foxcreekwines.com **Open** 7 days 10–5
Winemaker Ben Tanzer, Steven Soper **Est.** 1995 **Dozens** 35 000 **Vyds** 21ha
Fox Creek has a winemaking history that dates back to 1984 when Helen and Dr Jim Watts purchased a 32ha property in McLaren Vale. The winery has been upgraded to handle the expanded production of Fox Creek, the increase a function of demand for the full-flavoured, robust red wines that make up the portfolio. Part of the estate vineyard dates back to the early 1900s, providing the Old Vine Shiraz that carries the Fox Creek banner. Exports to all major markets.

ꭹꭹꭹꭹꭹ **Old Vine McLaren Vale Shiraz 2019** A brooding wine, yet with a lightness of touch. Notes of coffee bean, dried fig, hoisin sauce and polished leather are piled across a smooth patina of gentle acidity and svelte tannins, growing in stature with air. A very smooth operator for those seeking something quintessentially regional. Screw cap. 14.9% alc. **Rating** 95 To 2032 $68 NG

Reserve McLaren Vale Shiraz 2017 Exactly what the doctor ordered when it comes to premium maritime shiraz. Violet, Asian spice, smoked meats, root spice, cocoa and dark-cherry scents sashay to an old-vine velour. High-quality mocha oak (French/American), gives imminent pleasure while facilitating a long life ahead. Pulsating vinous length. Gently peppery. Rich, just fresh enough and very well done. Screw cap. 14.5% alc. **Rating** 95 To 2035 $90 NG

JSM McLaren Vale Shiraz Cabernet Sauvignon Cabernet Franc 2018 Cabernet franc adds so much to the kit, particularly in this warm-climate blend: a spicy, verdant lift of chilli, spearmint and dill, conferring a degree of refreshment. Otherwise, a salubrious band of cassis, violet, black cherry and anise brushed by well-wrought, sage-doused tannins. A sum far greater than its individual parts! An exercise in poise, effortless drinkability, serious value and great length. Kudos! Screw cap. 14.5% alc. **Rating** 94 To 2028 $29 NG ✪

ꭹꭹꭹꭹꭹ **Limited Release McLaren Vale Grenache 2019** Rating 93 To 2025 $38 NG
Three Blocks McLaren Vale Cabernet Sauvignon 2018 Rating 93 To 2030 $38 NG
Postmaster McLaren Vale GSM 2019 Rating 92 To 2026 $29 NG

Jim's Script McLaren Vale Cabernet Sauvignon Merlot Cabernet Franc
Petit Verdot 2018 Rating 92 To 2028 $29 NG
Vixen Sparkling Red NV Rating 92 $29 NG
McLaren Vale Chardonnay 2020 Rating 91 To 2024 $23 NG ✪
McLaren Vale Shiraz 2018 Rating 91 To 2027 $23 NG ✪
McLaren Vale Vermentino 2020 Rating 90 To 2023 $23 NG
McLaren Vale Merlot 2019 Rating 90 To 2023 $23 NG
Arctic Fox Grand Cuveé NV Rating 90 $29 NG

Foxeys Hangout ★★★★★

795 White Hill Road, Red Hill, Vic 3937 **Region** Mornington Peninsula
T (03) 5989 2022 **www.**foxeys-hangout.com.au **Open** W'ends & public hols 11–5
Winemaker Tony Lee, Michael Lee **Est.** 1997 **Dozens** 14 000 **Vyds** 3.4ha
After 20 successful years in hospitality operating several cafes and restaurants (including one
of Melbourne's first gastropubs in the early 1990s), brothers Michael and Tony Lee planted
their first vineyard in '97 at Merricks North. The venture takes its name from the tale of
2 fox hunters in the '30s hanging the results of their day's shooting in opposite branches of an
ancient eucalypt, using the tree as their scorecard. Michael and Tony also manage the former
Massoni Vineyard at Red Hill established by Ian Home, planting more chardonnay and pinot
noir and opening their cellar door. Michael makes the sparkling wines, Tony (a qualified chef)
makes the table wines and also cooks for the cellar door kitchen.

ΨΨΨΨΨ **Red Lilac Single Vineyard Mornington Peninsula Chardonnay 2019**
A laser beam of acidity leads this tight, persuasive wine. Everything is just so: its
citrus tones, the spice, the layer of creamy lees and nuttiness with some nougatine
flavouring too. A classy chardonnay. Screw cap. 13.5% alc. **Rating** 96 **To** 2030
$50 JF ✪
Mornington Peninsula Shiraz 2019 This has an intensity of flavour and lots
of concentration, followed by ribbons of finely textured tannin. And yet, this is
a neatly composed wine. It is medium bodied and laced with wonderful spice,
especially pepper and dried juniper berries. It's rather elegant. There's a brightness
to the fruit, savoury in outlay and compelling all the way through. Screw cap.
13.5% alc. **Rating** 96 **To** 2030 $45 JF ✪
Mornington Peninsula Chardonnay 2019 There's some generosity to this, but
it's not an opulent wine. It has some flint, lemon and lime blossom. Grapefruit-pith
phenolics neatly shape out the palate and it finishes with a flourish of fine acidity.
It's one of those wines smacked with quality, delicious to drink and requiring no
other thought except enjoyment. Screw cap. 13.5% alc. **Rating** 95 **To** 2027 $38 JF
Kentucky Road Single Vineyard Mornington Peninsula Pinot Gris 2020
Certified biodynamic estate vineyard, and the first gris as a single-vineyard wine
off this slightly north-facing site. It has a delicacy and very good chalky acidity.
Savoury in a way across the palate, with a tonic–quinine texture that's pleasing.
Hints of jasmine and lemon blossom, freshly grated apple and pear sprinkled with
powdered ginger. Long, fine and pure. Nice one. Screw cap. 13% alc. **Rating** 95
To 2025 $45 JF
Field Blend White Single Vineyard Mornington Peninsula 2020 A new
addition and quite a mixed bag, comprising mostly grüner veltliner, with
sauvignon blanc, albariño, chardonnay and vermentino. Enjoy this, for it is a
refreshing, aromatic and lively drink. It's floral and spicy, with a splash of tonic,
without the sweetness of course. The palate has lovely texture, neat phenolics and
finishes light and dry. I could drink a lot of this. Screw cap. 13% alc. **Rating** 95
To 2023 $38 JF
The Red Fox Mornington Peninsula Pinot Noir 2019 Modest colour;
cooking spices frame the bouquet, contributing even more of the palate's message.
In Foxeys' usual style, fine tannins are also centre stage, together with exotic dark
berry fruits. Second place in Foxeys' hierarchy, but nonetheless impressive. Screw
cap. 13.5% alc. **Rating** 95 **To** 2030 $29 JH ✪

Mornington Peninsula Pinot Noir 2019 This steps effortlessly into showcasing regional and varietal characters. It's full of cherries and woodsy spices, blood orange and zest. Plush, ripe tannins caress the medium-bodied palate; the finish lingers and it's just satisfying in every way. Screw cap. 13.5% alc. **Rating** 95 **To** 2029 $38 JF

Scotsworth Farm Single Vineyard Mornington Peninsula Pinot Noir 2019 Dark cherries aplenty, with chinotto, blood orange and zest, earthy with vanilla-pod oak and Indian spices, especially cardamom. Fuller bodied, densely packed tannins, oak and fruit, yet it feels good across the palate. Bright acidity and, dare I say, an energy to it. It does need more time in bottle. Screw cap. 13.5% alc. **Rating** 95 **To** 2033 $70 JF

White Gates Mornington Peninsula Pinot Gris 2020 Part of the certified biodynamic range, fruit from the south-facing vineyard at the winery. This has more weight and flavour compared with its Kentucky Road sibling. It's certainly not a fat gris, but it is full bodied, with more inputs of lemon on poached pears, lime rind, loads of honeysuckle and creamy, leesy nougatine across the palate. Screw cap. 13% alc. **Rating** 94 **To** 2024 $45 JF

Kentucky Road 777 Single Vineyard Mornington Peninsula Pinot Noir 2019 Full colour. Notes of forest floor and dark berries provide a consistent framework for a powerful pinot with a savoury finish. Definite cellaring style, yet to fully open as the tannin extract loosens its grip. Screw cap. 13.5% alc. **Rating** 94 **To** 2029 $70 JH

♟♟♟♟♟ **Mornington Peninsula Rosé 2020** **Rating** 93 **To** 2023 $28 JF
White Gates Single Vineyard Mornington Peninsula Pinot Noir 2019 **Rating** 93 **To** 2027 $70 JF
The Red Fox Mornington Peninsula Shiraz 2019 **Rating** 93 **To** 2027 $30 JF
Mornington Peninsula Pinot Gris 2020 **Rating** 92 **To** 2023 $30 JF

Frankland Estate   ★★★★★

Frankland Road, Frankland, WA 6396 **Region** Frankland River
T (08) 9855 1544 **www**.franklandestate.com.au **Open** Mon–Fri 10–4, public hols & w'ends by appt
Winemaker Hunter Smith, Brian Kent **Est.** 1988 **Dozens** 20 000 **Vyds** 34.5ha
A significant operation, situated on a large sheep property owned by Barrie Smith and Judi Cullam. The vineyard has been established progressively since 1988. The introduction of an array of single-vineyard rieslings has been a highlight, driven by Judi's conviction that terroir is of utmost importance, and the soils are indeed different; the Isolation Ridge Vineyard is organically grown. Frankland Estate has held important International Riesling tastings and seminars for more than a decade. Exports to all major markets.

♟♟♟♟♟ **Isolation Ridge Riesling 2020** Terroir-linked aromas here, a sense of jasmine green tea. The citrus elements are more grapefruit, and with that there's an earthy, spicy side to the palate as well. Trademark acidity is really integrated and comfortable inside the total structure, with its pithy, mineral feels closely connected. A distinctive expression. Screw cap. 13.5% alc. **Rating** 95 **To** 2030 $45 TL ♥

Poison Hill Riesling 2020 Aromas come from the deep, classical limes with hints of darker spice too, subtle cardamom, anise as well. There's a plump fleshiness on the palate, a juicy feel. The flavours suggest lime curd, with acidity neatly incorporated as a foundational layer underneath. Sophisticated and beautifully layered. Screw cap. 13.5% alc. **Rating** 95 **To** 2030 $45 TL

Smith Cullam Syrah 2019 More specific sourcing within the Isolation Ridge vineyard, a section no doubt that brings that little extra va-voom to the way shiraz works here. Enticing floral fragrance as well as a stony, gravelly sense, deliciously attractive and toned on the palate. There's a purity to this wine that enhances all that's on offer. Screw cap. 14.5% alc. **Rating** 95 **To** 2032 $120 TL

Olmo's Reward 2018 A cabernet franc-led blend and showing it, via vibrant redder cherry and mulberry-like aromas, concentrated by sympatico oak. It all comes into focus on the palate; intense yet lifted, energetic and mineral. Even tannins add to an impressive complexity and lingering finish. Screw cap. 14.5% alc. Rating 95 To 2030 $85 TL ♥

Riesling 2020 Totally captivating from the outset. Lime juice, kaffir leaf and the suggestion of something a tad sweeter – palm sugar, even. But this doesn't translate to the palate, which is deliciously zingy and flavourful, those exotic notes echoed. Screw cap. 12.5% alc. **Rating** 94 **To** 2026 $30 TL ✪

Isolation Ridge Syrah 2019 Quite specific vineyard characters here. It definitely smells and tastes of a small addition of viognier, and also some whole bunches employed in the fermentation. So there's perfume and a slight gingery/apricotty note, lip smack and a light chew of tannins, which all make for a quite interesting style. Drinking well now and might just find more and more nuance over the next decade. Screw cap. 14.5% alc. **Rating** 94 **To** 2030 $45 TL

🍷🍷🍷🍷🍷 **Isolation Ridge Riesling 2011 Rating** 93 **To** 2025 $65 TL
Chardonnay 2019 Rating 93 **To** 2026 $30 TL
Rocky Gully Riesling 2020 Rating 92 **To** 2024 $20 TL ✪
Cabernet Sauvignon 2019 Rating 92 **To** 2028 $30 TL

Fraser Gallop Estate   ★★★★★

493 Metricup Road, Wilyabrup, WA 6280 **Region** Margaret River
T (08) 9755 7553 **www.**frasergallopestate.com.au **Open** 7 days 11–4
Winemaker Clive Otto, Ellin Tritt **Est.** 1999 **Dozens** 10000 **Vyds** 20ha
Nigel Gallop began the development of the vineyard in 1999, planting cabernet sauvignon, semillon, petit verdot, cabernet franc, malbec, merlot, sauvignon blanc and multi-clone chardonnay. The dry-grown vines have modest yields, followed by kid-glove treatment in the winery. With Clive Otto (formerly of Vasse Felix) onboard, a 300t winery was built. The wines have had richly deserved success in wine shows and journalists' reviews. Exports to the UK, Sweden, Thailand, Indonesia and Singapore.

🍷🍷🍷🍷🍷 **Palladian Wilyabrup Margaret River Chardonnay 2019** White peach and saline acid are the defining characters here. On the palate, the flavours extend and unfurl into all the far reaches of the mouth and mind; fine chalky phenolics serve to grip and convince a second and third sip. A very special wine. Screw cap. 12% alc. **Rating** 96 **To** 2036 $110 EL

Parterre Wilyabrup Margaret River Cabernet Sauvignon 2018 Reaching heights of near perfection, '18 was a vintage responsible for wines just like this. Supple intensity, concentration of flavour without a gram of weight, the length of flavour possessed only by very healthy, perfectly ripe and balanced grapes. What a gloriously seamless wine, continuing the proud legacy of Parterre. Screw cap. 14% alc. **Rating** 96 **To** 2041 $50 EL ✪

Parterre Wilyabrup Margaret River Semillon Sauvignon Blanc 2019 From the cool '19 vintage, this wine presents salivating graphite and wet-slate characters both on the nose and palate, intermingled with white stone fruit, sweet green sugar snap pea and pink grapefruit. Co-fermented in a combination of older French oak barriques, puncheons and long skinny cigar barrels (these enable better extraction of the thiols from the sauvignon lees), this is a texturally rich yet restrained wine. A recent tasting of the 2013 Parterre shows its ageing potential. Screw cap. 12% alc. **Rating** 95 **To** 2030 $35 EL ✪

Margaret River Chardonnay 2020 This is the very definition of crystalline purity. The oak and fruit interplay is seamless – it is impossible to detangle one from the other. The acidity laces it up with a fine saline thread, and together it courses over the tongue through to a very (very) long finish. Quite remarkable for the price! Extremely classy effort. Screw cap. 13% alc. **Rating** 95 **To** 2029 $26 EL ✪

Palladian Wilyabrup Margaret River Cabernet Sauvignon 2017 The cooler vintage has birthed herbal wines of complexity – of which this is both. The tannins are omnipresent and fine; the fruit is delicate and lingering. This is not the powerhouse one would expect from a flagship wine: it is nuanced and fragrant and all the better for it. Screw cap. 14% alc. **Rating** 95 **To** 2040 $110 EL

Margaret River Semillon Sauvignon Blanc 2020 69/31% Wilyabrup semillon/Karridale sauvignon blanc. A small portion of the semillon was barrel fermented. Pretty, juicy, vibrant and alive. Classy execution has yielded a distinguished, taut and mineral rendition of the classic SSB blend for which Margaret River is so famous. Beautiful. Screw cap. 11.7% alc. **Rating** 94 **To** 2022 $24 EL ✪

Margaret River Cabernet Sauvignon 2018 The nose is intriguingly layered – tobacco leaf, cassis and a brambly raspberry character. The 5% petit verdot contributes a blue-fruited potpourri vibe to the wine, making this a very complex and nuanced little number – exceptional value for money. The palate is thoroughly modern and pure, with structure that is powder fine. Gorgeous. Screw cap. 14% alc. **Rating** 94 **To** 2030 $33 EL

🍷🍷🍷🍷🍷 **Wilyabrup Margaret River Ice Pressed Chardonnay 2020** **Rating** 92 **To** 2031 $34 EL

Frazer Woods Wines ★★★★

3856 Caves Road, Wilyabrup, WA 6280 **Region** Margaret River
T (08) 9755 6274 **www.frazerwoods.com.au**
Winemaker John Frazer, Harrold Osbourne **Est.** 1996 **Dozens** 2000
John Frazer has set up a contract sparkling wine business called the Champagne Shed, although the winemaking is done offsite. He makes the Frazer Woods wines from 2ha of estate-grown shiraz; the white grapes for the pinot chardonnay sparkling are purchased from others. The wines are sold through the Margaret River Wine Cellars and the Witchcliffe Liquor Store.

🍷🍷🍷🍷🍷 **La Cache Blanc de Blanc 2014** On lees 'for an extended period', disgorged May 2014. Complex, textural and layered, this has lemon pith, crushed cashew, plump mousse and a cleansing finish. Not overly complex, but it doesn't break rank once as it glides over the palate. The consistency of texture and flavour is a highlight. Diam. 11.6% alc. **Rating** 92 **To** 2025 $36 EL

La Cache Pinot Noir Chardonnay 2013 Sixty months on lees. Blushed pink/straw/golden in the glass – a difficult colour to pin down exactly. On the nose it has a tahini, cheesecloth, citrus-curd thing going on. The palate has a pleasingly plump mousse that bounces the flavours around the mouth. Enduring length of flavour is a testament to the patience it took to get it this far. Cork. 12.4% alc. **Rating** 91 $36 EL

La Cache Sparkling Rosé 2013 Strawberry and rose petals on the nose, the palate has expansive mousse and a very delicately spicy palate. The finish has a fine phenolic edge to it which gives it some interest, but deviates from the pristine path it was on. Cork. 12.4% alc. **Rating** 91 $36 EL

La Cache Sparkling Shiraz 2008 This has aged shiraz characters of roasted blueberry, quince and a hint of fig. The palate is fresh for its 13 years, with freshly cracked black pepper through the finish. Cork. 12.8% alc. **Rating** 90 $36 EL

Freeman Vineyards ★★★★☆

101 Prunevale Road, Prunevale, NSW 2587 **Region** Hilltops
T 0429 310 309 **www.freemanvineyards.com.au** **Open** By appt
Winemaker Dr Brian Freeman, Xanthe Freeman **Est.** 1999 **Dozens** 5000 **Vyds** 200ha
Dr Brian Freeman spent much of his life in research and education, in the latter with a role as head of CSU's viticulture and oenology campus. In 2004 he purchased the 30yo Demondrille Vineyard and acquired the neighbouring vineyard; 10 years later he acquired a number of other vineyards within a 10km radius. In all he has 22 varieties that range from staples such

as shiraz, cabernet sauvignon, semillon and riesling through to more exotic varieties such as háslevelü and Italian varieties prosecco (glera), sangiovese, nebbiolo and, apparently, Australia's only plantings of rondinella and corvina.

🍷🍷🍷🍷 **Secco Rondinella Corvina 2015** Wonderfully fragrant and displaying an array of complex flavours. Heady, autumnal aromas, panforte, wood smoke, dried porcini and kirsch-soused raisins. The palate is deep and rich, with expansive, fleshy tannins. Lovely texture, with an Italian savoury stamp. An excellent Secco. Screw cap. 14.8% alc. **Rating** 95 **To** 2030 $40 JF

Aged Release Rondinella Corvina Secco 2008 It's a delight to taste an aged release that truly has some age. Too many on the market are barely out of nappies. This is something special. Sure, it's showing off tertiary flavours of Christmas cake and new leather, panforte and potpourri, pomander and dried plums, yet it is astonishingly fresh. Ripe tannins, a smooth palate and a richness to behold. Bravo. Screw cap. 14.5% alc. **Rating** 95 **To** 2028 $90 JF

🍷🍷🍷🍷♔ **Altura Vineyard Nebbiolo 2017 Rating** 91 **To** 2025 $40 JF
Rondo Rosé 2020 Rating 90 **To** 2022 $20 JF ✪
Prosecco 2019 Rating 90 **To** 2022 $23 JF
Dolcino 2019 Rating 90 **To** 2025 $25 JF

Freycinet   ★★★★★

15919 Tasman Highway via Bicheno, Tas 7215 **Region** East Coast Tasmania
T (03) 6257 8574 **www.**freycinetvineyard.com.au **Open** 7 days 10–5 (Oct–Apr), 10–4 (May–Sept)
Winemaker Claudio Radenti, Lindy Bull **Est.** 1979 **Dozens** 9000 **Vyds** 15.9ha
The Freycinet vineyards are situated on the sloping hillsides of a small valley. The soils are brown dermosol on top of Jurassic dolerite; and the combination of aspect, slope, soil and heat summation produces red grapes with unusual depth of colour and ripe flavours. One of the foremost producers of pinot noir, with an enviable track record of consistency – rare in such a temperamental variety. The Radenti (sparkling), Riesling and Chardonnay are also wines of the highest quality. In 2012 Freycinet acquired part of the neighbouring Coombend property from Brown Brothers. The 42ha property extends to the Tasman Highway and includes a 5.75ha mature vineyard and a 4.2ha olive grove. Exports to the UK and Singapore.

🍷🍷🍷🍷 **Riesling 2020** Tasmania showcases riesling's wonderfully exotic side and its high-tensile endurance, but rarely are these united as effortlessly as this. Low yields made for impressive concentration of star fruit, wild lemon and golden kiwifruit. Honed by gloriously crystalline acidity, it glides with consummate control, precision and endurance. One of the greats, it will live forever. Screw cap. 13% alc. **Rating** 95 **To** 2040 $32 TS ✪

Chardonnay 2019 A wonderful, enticing and seamless amalgam of beautiful lemon, white peach and grapefruit, supported delightfully by marzipan and almond oak. Malic acid is beautifully integrated and perfectly ripe, upholding tension and precision, culminating in fantastic, seamless line and length. Gorgeous. Screw cap. 13.5% alc. **Rating** 95 **To** 2029 $45 TS

Shiraz 2018 I could smell the pepper before I even picked up the glass! It stands to reason, from a site of distinctive pepper in pinot, that shiraz would have pepper in spades! Wondrous layers of blackberries, satsuma plums and black cherries framed in fine, confident tannins and wave after wave of black pepper. Nuances of high-cocoa dark chocolate accent an epic finish. Screw cap. 14% alc. **Rating** 95 **To** 2038 $60 TS

Shiraz 2017 In a warm site and ever-warming climate, Claudio Radenti rightly considers shiraz to be 'the next best thing for Freycinet', increasing plantings more than 5-fold in the past 8 years (though still just 1.1ha). If this is what he can conjure in a cool season, he's on to something! Graced with beautifully distinctive white pepper over an elegant core of satsuma plum skin. Powder-fine mineral tannins weave a wonderful web of structure amid vibrant acidity, promising a very long future. Screw cap. 13.4% alc. **Rating** 95 **To** 2042 $60 TS ♥

Pinot Noir 2019 A mighty serious pinot noir. Classy strawberry, blackberry and morello cherry fruit backed with the impressive cracked black pepper signature of the Freycinet site. An excellent frame of medium-grained tannins and vibrant, integrated acidity promises grand endurance. Tense and coiled a year before release, with everything in the right places for a long life, it lingers with excellent line and length. Screw cap. 14% alc. **Rating** 94 **To** 2049 $70 TS

ΨΨΨΨΨ **Wineglass Bay Sauvignon Blanc 2019 Rating** 91 **To** 2021 $28 TS

Frog Choir Wines

At Redgate Winery, Boodjidup Road, Margaret River, WA 6285 **Region** Margaret River
T 0427 777 787 **www.**frogchoir.com **Open** 7 days 11–4.20
Winemaker Naturaliste Vintners (Bruce Dukes) **Est.** 1997 **Dozens** 250 **Vyds** 1.2ha
Kate and Nigel Hunt have a micro-vineyard equally split between shiraz and cabernet sauvignon. It has immaculate address credentials: adjacent to Leeuwin Estate and Voyager Estate; 6km from the Margaret River township. The hand-tended vines are grown without the use of insecticides.

ΨΨΨΨ **Margaret River Cabernet Sauvignon Shiraz 2016** The oak plays a very dominant role here, on both nose and palate. The fruit that sits beneath it is swaddled tight. Clove, arnica and licorice notes are woven across the palate and through the finish to define the lingering impression. After a vigorous work-out in the glass, things start to come together a little more. Screw cap. 13.9% alc. **Rating** 89 **To** 2026 $28 EL

Frogmore Creek

699 Richmond Road, Cambridge, Tas 7170 **Region** Southern Tasmania
T (03) 6248 4484 **www.**frogmorecreek.com.au **Open** 7 days 10–5
Winemaker Alain Rousseau, John Bown **Est.** 1997 **Dozens** 40 000 **Vyds** 55ha
Frogmore Creek is a Pacific Rim joint venture, the owners being Tony Scherer of Tasmania and Jack Kidwiler of California. The business has grown substantially, first establishing its own organically managed vineyard, and thereafter by a series of acquisitions. First was the purchase of the Hood/Wellington Wines business; next was the purchase of the large Roslyn Vineyard near Campania; and finally (in Oct 2010) the acquisition of Meadowbank Estate, where the cellar door is now located. In Dec '12 the original Frogmore Creek vineyard was sold to Hill-Smith Family Vineyards. Exports to the US, Japan, NZ and China.

ΨΨΨΨΨ **Tasmania Cuvée 2017** Méthode traditionnelle. Distinctive blush tint. Mouth-filling and succulent, brimming with spicy wild strawberries, raspberries and red apples, backed by the white citrus crunch of chardonnay. Lees age has lent biscuity, spicy, honeyed complexity. Creamy texture, fine phenolic grip and honeyed dosage find balance if not quite refinement on the finish. Diam. 12.5% alc. **Rating** 91 $45 TS

ΨΨΨΨ **42°S Premier Cuvée Sparkling Rosé NV Rating** 88 $32 TS

Gaelic Cemetery Vineyard ★★★★★

Gaelic Cemetery Road, Stanley Flat, SA 5453 **Region** Clare Valley
T (08) 7081 5955 **www.**gaeliccemeteryvineyard.com **Open** By appt
Winemaker Adam Clay **Est.** 2005 **Dozens** 2000 **Vyds** 16.8ha
Gaelic Cemetery Vineyard was planted in 1996, adjacent to the historic cemetery of the region's Scottish pioneers. Situated in a secluded valley of the Clare hills, the low-cropping vineyard, say the partners, 'is always one of the earliest ripening shiraz vineyards in the region and mystifyingly produces fruit with both natural pH and acid analyses that can only be described as beautiful numbers'. The result is hands-off winemaking. Exports to the UK, the US, Canada, Germany, Singapore, Taiwan, Hong Kong and China.

ＴＴＴＴＴ **Premium Clare Valley Riesling 2019** Upholding a magnificently pale, bright straw-green hue, this is a riesling that is embarking on its long journey, slow and distinguished. Signature lime, lemon and Granny Smith apple are still the theme, with 2 years' age drawing out the first nuances of warm spice and honey. Focused acidity holds a finish of outstanding line and precision, promising great endurance. Screw cap. 11.5% alc. **Rating** 96 **To** 2034 $38 TS ✪

McAskill Clare Valley Riesling 2020 An even progression of refinement and sophistication makes the journey up the Gaelic Cemetery Vineyard riesling tree a thrilling one, and there are great rewards in a little more investment to ascend to the black labels. Accurate lemon, lime and Granny Smith apple. Prominent, tightly clenched acid line. Well-tempered phenolic structure. Great persistence and endurance. 2g/L RS. Screw cap. 12% alc. **Rating** 95 **To** 2035 $45 TS

McAskill Clare Valley Shiraz 2019 Bright and lively blueberry fruit is lifted eloquently by violet fragrance and underlined by pencil-lead-fine chalk mineral structure. Fruit, acidity and tannins embrace triumphantly to define medium-term cellaring potential. It carries medium persistence and will hopefully build in time. Screw cap. 14.5% alc. **Rating** 95 **To** 2031 $55 TS

McAskill Clare Valley Cabernet Malbec 2019 The Clare's signature blend, uniting crunchy red-berried energy and medium weight with chalk mineral tannins of considerable strength and longevity. Redcurrant and cassis aromas are brightened by rose petals, set to a savoury backdrop that speaks malbec. Engineered for the long haul, it loses momentum on the finish, but will hopefully build persistence in time. Screw cap. 13.5% alc. **Rating** 95 **To** 2044 $55 TS

Premium Clare Valley Cabernet Malbec 2018 A beautifully poised, medium-bodied interpretation of Clare's classic blend. Cabernet's redcurrants and red capsicum are graced with the savoury, dried thyme nuances of malbec on a finish of medium persistence. Chalk mineral tannins are shored up by malbec's grip, furnishing medium-term potential. Screw cap. 13.5% alc. **Rating** 94 **To** 2033 $48 TS

ＴＴＴＴＹ **White Hut Clare Valley Riesling 2020** **Rating** 93 **To** 2030 $36 TS
Celtic Farm Clare Valley Shiraz Cabernet 2018 **Rating** 93 **To** 2028 $28 TS
Celtic Farm Clare Valley Riesling 2020 **Rating** 91 **To** 2022 $28 TS

Gala Estate   ★★★★☆

14891 Tasman Highway, Cranbrook, Tas 7190 **Region** East Coast Tasmania
T 0408 681 014 **www**.galaestate.com.au **Open** 7 days 10–4
Winemaker Pat Colombo, Keira O'Brien **Est.** 2009 **Dozens** 5000 **Vyds** 11ha
This vineyard is situated on a 4000ha sheep station, with the 6th, 7th and 8th generations – headed by Robert and Patricia (nee Amos) Greenhill – custodians of the land granted to James Amos in 1821. It is recognised as the 2nd-oldest family business in Tasmania. The 11ha vineyard is heavily skewed to pinot noir (7ha), the remainder planted (in descending order of area) to chardonnay, pinot gris, riesling, shiraz and sauvignon blanc. The main risk is spring frost, and overhead spray irrigation serves 2 purposes: it provides adequate moisture for early season growth and frost protection at the end of the growing season.

ＴＴＴＴＹ **White Label Sauvignon Blanc 2020** The finest sauvignons are built firmly around the citrus end of the ripeness spectrum, with subtle support from the herbal and tropical extremes. This is an exemplar, subtly accented with pretty florals and nuances of spice. A spicy white nectarine fleshiness well counters a tense, tingly acid spine and fine phenolics, completed with just the right lick of RS to avoid any sensation of sweetness. Screw cap. 13% alc. **Rating** 93 **To** 2024 $32 TS

White Label Pinot Gris 2020 A true gris, fleshy, spicy and accurate. Ripe pear is the theme, accented with honey and spice. Well-executed skin contact fills out a medium salmon/straw hue and builds a compelling tension between flesh and phenolic grip. Nicely integrated acidity draws out a very long finish. Screw cap. 12.5% alc. **Rating** 93 **To** 2021 $32 TS

White Label Pinot Rosé 2020 Benchmark Tasmanian rosé of pale, bright salmon hue. A pretty rose petal and rosewater bouquet throws to a wonderful core of fresh strawberries and raspberries, morphing again on the finish to savoury nuances of tomato. Bright, Tasmanian acidity lays out a very long and even finish, completed with just the right touch of sweetness. Screw cap. 12.5% alc. **Rating** 93 **To** 2022 $32 TS

Black Label Emerald Syrah 2019 Black pepper and greengage plum denote a distinctively characterful and exact cool-climate syrah. Firm, fine, dusty tannins speak of Tasmania's dry East Coast, setting a fine-boned mood to a long, dry, savoury finish. Give it time in the deep to build flesh. Screw cap. 13.5% alc. **Rating** 93 **To** 2031 $65 TS

Black Label Pinot Noir 2019 Celebrating all the virtues of East Coast Tasmania pinot, with black plum skin and blackberry fruit, accented with black pepper and brambles. The firm, fine-boned structure of this dry zone scaffolds a rigid tannin shell of considerable endurance. Structure and fruit entangle through a long finish. Screw cap. 13.5% alc. **Rating** 92 **To** 2034 $65 TS

White Label Riesling 2020 Pretty, pristine and precise. A pale straw green hue is a prelude to a riesling of crystalline purity, shot with the hallmarks of lime, lemon and Granny Smith apple, tinted with exotic nuances reminiscent of guava and star fruit. Bright Tasmanian acidity accents a long finish, marked by grainy phenolic grip, which a lick of sweetness is insufficient to calm. Screw cap. 12.5% alc. **Rating** 90 **To** 2025 $37 TS

ㅜㅜㅜㅜ White Label Chardonnay 2020 **Rating** 89 **To** 2024 $32 TS
White Label Pinot Noir 2019 **Rating** 89 **To** 2027 $32 TS

Galafrey ★★★★★

Quangellup Road, Mount Barker, WA 6324 **Region** Mount Barker
T (08) 9851 2022 **www**.galafreywines.com.au **Open** 7 days 10–5
Winemaker Kim Tyrer **Est.** 1977 **Dozens** 3500 **Vyds** 13.1ha
The Galafrey story began when Ian and Linda Tyrer gave up high-profile jobs in the emerging computer industry and arrived in Mount Barker to start growing grapes and making wine, the vine-change partially prompted by their desire to bring up their children in a country environment. The dry-grown vineyard they planted continues to be the turning point, the first winery established in an ex-whaling building (long since replaced by a purpose-built winery). The premature death of Ian at a time when the industry was buckling at the knees increased the already considerable difficulties the family had to deal with, but deal with it they did. Daughter Kim Tyrer is now CEO of the business, with Linda still very much involved in the day-to-day of Galafrey. Exports to Canada and Singapore.

ㅜㅜㅜㅜㅜ Dry Grown Reserve Mount Barker Riesling 2020 Talcy and floral nose, perhaps more so than previous vintages. The palate is intense and focused, searing acidity – an austerity that makes it almost hard, but gosh it's good. Phenolic structure provides a framework from which the fruit clings. There is a saline flick through the finish – crushed oyster shell, creamy, green-apple skin and taut lime pith. Really smart. Screw cap. 12.5% alc. **Rating** 96 **To** 2040 $25 EL ✪

Dry Grown Mount Barker Merlot 2017 This is concentrated and dense with classy layering of flavours and lingering length of flavour. It was a cool vintage in '17 and this is a good representation: fine, elegant and lingering. The nose is redolent of cacao nibs and mulberry … it has intensity and line. A structured and lingering wine, lovely stuff. Screw cap. **Rating** 95 **To** 2025 $30 EL ✪

Dry Grown Mount Barker Müller Thurgau 2020 The 2020 rendition is fermented dry in tank, the vintage giving awesome intensity and purity. Orange peel and turmeric, with saffron and essence of mandarin. It's viscous and rich, and the tannins are powder-fine and grippy. Screw cap. 12% alc. **Rating** 94 **To** 2025 $28 EL ✪

ㅜㅜㅜㅜㅜ Dry Grown Mount Barker Cabernet Franc 2018 **Rating** 93 **To** 2020 $25 EL ✪
Whole Bunch Mount Barker Shiraz 2019 **Rating** 92 **To** 2031 $35 EL

Galli Estate ★★★★☆

1507 Melton Highway, Plumpton, Vic 3335 **Region** Sunbury
T (03) 9747 1444 **www.**galliestate.com.au **Open** 7 days 11–5
Winemaker Alisdair Park **Est.** 1997 **Dozens** 10000 **Vyds** 160ha

Galli Estate has 2 vineyards: Heathcote, which produces the red wines (shiraz, sangiovese, nebbiolo, tempranillo, grenache and montepulciano) and the cooler-climate vineyard at Plumpton in Sunbury, producing the whites (chardonnay, pinot grigio, sauvignon blanc and fiano). All wines are biodynamically estate-grown and made, with wine movements on the new moon. Exports to Canada, Singapore, China and Hong Kong.

🍷🍷🍷🍷🍷 **Adele Sunbury Fiano 2019** Fragrant with honeysuckle, stone fruit, lemon curd and savoury/nutty/leesy flavours, not much, just enough to add an extra layer. It has lovely texture and length, with fine acidity keeping it juicy and lively. Screw cap. 12.5% alc. **Rating** 95 **To** 2024 $40 JF

🍷🍷🍷🍷🍷 **Pamela 2019 Rating** 93 **To** 2029 $60 JF
Lorenzo 2018 Rating 93 **To** 2028 $60 JF
Camelback Sunbury Pinot Grigio 2020 Rating 90 **To** 2023 $22 JF
Camelback Heathcote Montepulciano 2019 Rating 90 **To** 2025 $22 JF

Gapsted Wines ★★★★

3897 Great Alpine Road, Gapsted, Vic 3737 **Region** Alpine Valleys
T (03) 5751 9100 **www.**gapstedwines.com.au **Open** Thurs–Mon 10–5
Winemaker Michael Cope-Williams, Toni Pla Bou, Matt Fawcett **Est.** 1997
Dozens 250000 **Vyds** 256.1ha

Gapsted is the major brand of the Victorian Alps Winery, which started life (and continues) as a large-scale contract winemaking facility. The quality of the wines made for its own brand has led to the expansion of production not only under that label, but also under a raft of subsidiary labels. As well as the substantial estate plantings, Gapsted sources traditional and alternative grape varieties from the King and Alpine valleys. The partners are nearing retirement age and, without family members to step in, put the business up for sale in mid 2021. Exports to Canada, Germany, Norway, Sweden, Russia, UAE, India, Thailand, South Korea, Malaysia, Singapore, Vietnam, Cambodia, Hong Kong, China and Japan.

🍷🍷🍷🍷🍷 **Limited Release Vintage Alpine Valleys Touriga 2018** Durif, the ever reliable multi-tasker, makes for a fabulous vintage fortified retaining its juicy blueberry, black cherry, licorice, violet aromatics and intensity of flavour elevated by attractive brandy spirit. So fresh and complex, I would be strongly tempted to get the cheese platter out right now. But, patience is a virtue with this lovely thing. Screw cap. 18.5% alc. **Rating** 93 $31 JP
Limited Release Alpine Valleys Saperavi 2018 Saperavi (meaning 'dye' in Georgian) always makes a big statement of individuality. Few grapes are as deep in colour – here, black as night – and so ample in tannin and acidity. But look to the fruit flavour: it's crammed with dark forest berries, the aromas of tilled earth and mushroom, of prune and moss. Every time you go back the scene has changed. On the bigger side, sure, but what a mouthful of flavour intensity and drinking pleasure. Screw cap. 14.5% alc. **Rating** 92 **To** 2037 $31 JP
Ballerina Canopy Cabernet Sauvignon 2018 Runs a fine cabernet tannin line throughout, an immediate and attractive feature that reveals not only the identity of the variety but also some sensitive winemaking. A tightly knit youngster bubbling (figuratively, of course) with blackberry, plum, nutmeg spice and earth enlivened with a ripple of tomato leafiness. Sweet-fruited, with blackberry richness and spice, enduring fine tannin structure and balanced, toasted oak. Long. Screw cap. 14.5% alc. **Rating** 91 **To** 2031 $31 JP
Ballerina Canopy Alpine Valleys Durif 2019 Durif calls North East Victoria home and, contrary to common opinion, the grape can present a number of styles from the medium bodied to the rich and ample. This cooler-climate interpretation lies closer to the former. Wood smoke, blue fruits, earth, prune and leather are

strong varietally. It's the spice that draws you in on the palate, so enticing and lingering against a smoky, clove oak backdrop. The variety's prominent tannins remain as ever on guard, but in the background. Screw cap. 14.5% alc. **Rating** 91 **To** 2034 $31 JP

Tobacco Road King Valley Sangiovese Rosé 2020 How fresh and lively is this? Palest pink blush in hue. Pulses with bright acidity, red apple, raspberry and cherry crunch throughout. Little wonder the sangiovese grape is increasingly employed in the service of rosé. Summer fruits from start to finish on the palate with just a light creaminess. Screw cap. 12.5% alc. **Rating** 90 **To** 2024 $16 JP ✪

ŸŸŸŸ **Limited Release Sparkling Pinot Grigio Rosé NV Rating** 88 **To** 2023 $25 JP

Garagiste ★★★★★
72 Blaxland Ave, Frankston South, Vic 3199 **Region** Mornington Peninsula
T 0439 370 530 **www**.garagiste.com.au
Winemaker Barnaby Flanders **Est.** 2006 **Dozens** 2200 **Vyds** 6ha
Barnaby Flanders was a co-founder of Allies Wines (see separate entry) in 2003, with some of the wines made under the Garagiste label. Allies has now gone its own way and Barnaby has a controlling interest in the Garagiste brand. The focus is on the Mornington Peninsula. The grapes are hand-sorted in the vineyard and again in the winery. Chardonnay is whole-bunch pressed, barrel-fermented with wild yeast in new and used French oak, mlf variably used, 8–9 months on lees. Seldom fined or filtered. Exports to the UK, Canada, Norway, Singapore, Japan, Hong Kong and China.

ŸŸŸŸŸ **Terre Maritime Mornington Peninsula Chardonnay 2019** Barnaby Flanders manages to weave magic into his wines. Although a less esoteric explanation is his attention to detail in the vineyard right through to the winemaking. Precise and reasoned. All that combines to a truth: Garagiste crafts some of the finest, most exhilarating wines, from the Peninsula and beyond. Terre Maritime is a case in point. Complex, silky, flinty, flavoursome, long … and the list goes on. Screw cap. 13% alc. **Rating** 97 **To** 2032 $75 JF ✪

ŸŸŸŸŸ **Merricks Mornington Peninsula Chardonnay 2019** A cracking wine that's so flavoursome, yet manages to stay on a tight leash thanks to its acidity. Flinty, smoky and spicy, with lots of grapefruit. The palate is injected with lemon curd and cedary/lemon-balm François Frère fragrance (20% new puncheons). It has length and definition. Complex and thoughtful. Screw cap. 13% alc. **Rating** 96 **To** 2029 $45 JF ✪

Merricks Cuve Béton Mornington Peninsula Pinot Noir 2019 Barnaby Flanders' same exacting standard in the vineyard and winemaking is applied to this compelling wine. The key difference between this and his other pinots is ageing in concrete on lees for 10 months. The palate is extraordinary; the tannins have a completely different shape, round and giving. It's plush and rich in bright fruit, and lightly spiced. An epic, fabulous drink. Screw cap. 13.5% alc. **Rating** 96 **To** 2032 $45 JF ✪

Terre de Feu Mornington Peninsula Pinot Noir 2019 Garagiste's flagship pinot comes out strong: 22 days on 100% whole bunches, fermented wild, as always, and aged in French oak hogsheads, 25% new, for 10 months. It's perfumed and richly flavoured, yet ultimately it's about structure and definition. Somewhat firm and closed, but has all the hallmarks for longevity. Screw cap. 13.5% alc. **Rating** 96 **To** 2035 $75 JF ✪

Le Stagiaire Mornington Peninsula Chardonnay 2020 Fruit from 3 disparate vineyards from Merricks, Balnarring and Tuerong. It's in the drink-me-now zone and neatly balanced. Full of bright citrus flavours, white stone fruit on the verge of ripeness, a spark of flint, smoky, a smidge of leesy texture, and saline, thirst-quenching acidity to close. Screw cap. 13% alc. **Rating** 95 **To** 2027 $30 JF ✪

Mornington Peninsula Aligote 2019 Aligoté is the third (but these days rare) variety of Burgundy. It's like a lemon daquiri without rum's alcohol punch. Savoury, with a dash of lemon/lime flavour, but texture and acidity are the real drivers. Tangy, smoky and super dry on the finish. This is compelling. Screw cap. 13% alc. **Rating** 95 **To** 2026 $35 JF ✪

Balnarring Mornington Peninsula Pinot Noir 2019 A more savoury wine than the Merricks, but made the same. With a lovely composure and softness, it's gently flavoured with cherries, plums, a dash of ginger spice, Dutch licorice and tangy/tart blood orange. Medium bodied; the tannins ripe and friendly. The overall impression is 'drink me now'. Screw cap. 13.5% alc. **Rating** 95 **To** 2030 $45 JF

Merricks Mornington Peninsula Pinot Noir 2019 In a warm vintage that has thrown up lots of inconsistencies across the Peninsula, it's pleasing to find consistencies in quality here. With a beautiful evenness, there's a brightness amid tangy and tart fruit, twigs and earth. It feels cool, and has structure and depth, length and line, good acidity and determined tannins. It's complete. Screw cap. 13.5% alc. **Rating** 95 **To** 2034 $45 JF

🍷🍷🍷🍷🍷 **Tuerong Mornington Peninsula Chardonnay 2019 Rating** 93 **To** 2027 $45 JF
Le Stagiaire Mornington Peninsula Pinot Noir 2019 Rating 93 **To** 2028 $30 JF
Le Stagiaire Mornington Peninsula Pinot Gris 2020 Rating 92 **To** 2024 $30 JF

Garden & Field   ★★★★

PO Box 52, Angaston, SA 5353 **Region** Eden Valley/Barossa Valley
T (08) 8564 2435 **www.**tasteedenvalley.com.au **Open** By appt
Winemaker Peter Raymond **Est.** 2009 **Dozens** 100 **Vyds** 5.6ha
One of those stories that seem to be too good to be true. It is over 100 years since the Schilling family cleared the land of its granite boulders, built cottages from the rocks and planted a vineyard. In the late 1970s the property was sold and when the Vine Pull Scheme was legislated, the new owners were quick to remove the vines. Another decade passed and the property was again on the market. Eventually viticulturist Peter Raymond and wife Melissa purchased it and set about preparing 3.6ha for planting. As they arrived one Saturday morning to begin the long task, they found a group of octogenarian men armed with picks and shovels, there to help plant 3500 vines on what they regarded as holy viticultural land, desecrated by the Vine Pull Scheme. Penfolds now buys most of the grapes for its RWT Shiraz at tip-top prices, but the Raymonds keep enough to make a small amount of wine each year.

🍷🍷🍷🍷🍷 **Gomersal Road Barossa Shiraz 2018** An impressively full, vibrant purple hue heralds a potent, inky, iodine-infused shiraz of impressive stature. Compact, glossy satsuma plum, blackberry and prune fruit defines a singularity of fruit of such integrity and presence that it is completely unperturbed by 26 months in new French oak barrels. A long finish rides on firm, fine tannins. Cork. 14.8% alc. **Rating** 95 **To** 2030 $150 TS

🍷🍷🍷🍷🍷 **Gnadenberg Road Barossa Cabernet Sauvignon Refosco 2018 Rating** 90 **To** 2033 $55 TS

Gartelmann Wines   ★★★★☆

701 Lovedale Road, Lovedale, NSW 2321 **Region** Hunter Valley
T (02) 4930 7113 **www.**gartelmann.com.au **Open** Mon–Sat 9–5, Sun 10–4
Winemaker Liz Silkman, Rauri Donkin **Est.** 1996 **Dozens** 7700
In 1996 Jan and Jorg Gartelmann purchased what was previously the George Hunter Estate – 16ha of mature vineyards, most established by Oliver Shaul in '70. In a change of emphasis, the vineyard was sold and Gartelmann now sources its grapes from the Hunter Valley and

other NSW regions, including the cool Rylstone area in Mudgee. Almost 25 years later, in December 2020, the business was purchased by local chef Matt Dillow, who was already running The Deck cafe based at Gartelmann.

ŸŸŸŸŸ **Joey Mudgee Merlot 2018** Fine merlot. Round and full, but plenty savoury. An earthy swathe of tannins grounds riffs of damson plum and black cherry. The herbal twang has an almost alpine feel to it, imbuing a sense of lightness that belies the alcohol. Good drinking. Screw cap. 14.5% alc. **Rating** 92 **To** 2026 $30 NG
Georg Mudgee Petit Verdot 2017 This rich wine is both quintessentially Australian and evocative of somewhere far cooler: this sort of altitudinal viticulture is seldom found on these shores. Crushed mint, violet, anise, blue and black fruit aspersions and a firm sheath of inky tannin. Savoury and herbal. A bit green. Will age well, transcending the oaky shins and elbows of youth in time. Screw cap. 14% alc. **Rating** 91 **To** 2032 $35 NG
Phillip Alexander Mudgee Cabernet Merlot 2018 As a general rule, Gartelmann wines are savoury, mid weight (despite higher alcohols) and poised. Perhaps a little less American oak would do favours. A potpourri of crushed herb, spearmint, Dutch licorice and blackcurrant. The verdant tannins, nicely aligned with the fruit weight and altitudinal acidity, evince some welcome authority across the back palate. A solid full-bodied cool-climate wine. Screw cap. **Rating** 91 **To** 2028 $30 NG
Diedrich Orange Shiraz 2018 A deep crimson, verging on opaque. A high-octane wine despite hailing from a cool climate. Bitter chocolate, raspberry liqueur, dark cherry and a whiff of vanilla/bourbon. Thickly textured and on the verge of volatile, with a clasp of oak, sharp acidity and smudge of tannins applying a restraining order. For those who like 'em OTT. Screw cap. 15.4% alc. **Rating** 90 **To** 2032 $50 NG

Gatt Wines   ★★★★☆

417 Boehms Springs Road, Flaxman Valley, SA 5235 **Region** Eden Valley
T (08) 8564 1166 **www.gattwines.com Open** Not
Winemaker David Norman **Est.** 1972 **Dozens** 8000 **Vyds** 56.24ha
When you read the hyperbole that sometimes accompanies the acquisition of an existing wine business, about transforming it into a world-class operation, it is easy to sigh and move on. When Ray Gatt acquired Eden Springs, he proceeded to translate words into deeds. As well as the 19.15ha Eden Springs Vineyard, he also acquired the historic Siegersdorf Vineyard (now 21.79ha) on the Barossa floor and the neighbouring Graue Vineyard (15.3ha). The change of name from Eden Springs to Gatt Wines in 2011 was sensible. Exports to Canada, China, Denmark, Finland, France, Germany, Hong Kong, Italy, Japan, South Korea, Macau, Sweden, the US, the UK and Canada.

ŸŸŸŸŸ **Old Vine Barossa Valley Shiraz 2015** A panoply of berry/cherry/plum fruit and licorice melds with layers of dark- and milk-chocolate oak. Supportive acidity and fine, supple tannins pace out a long finish. With everything in the right place, it's ready to drink now and over the next decade. Screw cap. 14.9% alc. **Rating** 93 **To** 2030 $100 TS
Barossa Valley Shiraz 2015 Berry/cherry/plum fruits are lain with a generous sweep of dark- and milk-chocolate oak, backed with a fine splay of fruit and oak tannins and just the right burst of natural acidity. It delivers exactly as expected for a strong vintage on the Barossa floor. Concluding with good length, it's right for drinking now, albeit without the fruit stamina for the long haul. Screw cap. 14.9% alc. **Rating** 92 **To** 2024 $60 TS
High Eden Riesling 2018 The warm 2018 season has built a generous riesling layered with spice and stone fruits, already secondary in its rich layers of honey and ginger nut biscuits. The cool acidity of High Eden swoops in on the finish, energising a long, focused tail and enlivening lemon/lime fruit. Great drinking now, with a few years ahead of it yet. Screw cap. 12.5% alc. **Rating** 91 **To** 2023 $30 TS

High Eden Shiraz 2015 The red berry tang and mixed spice of High Eden contrasts the savoury, charcuterie character of oak age. Layers of supple milk chocolate speak Barossa. Well progressed in its evolution, it concludes long and integrated, albeit without drive, lift or freshness. Screw cap. 14.5% alc. **Rating** 91 **To** 2023 $60 TS

Eden Springs High Eden Cabernet Sauvignon 2016 A savoury, developing cabernet that captures its varietal redcurrant and capsicum signature in this cool, high site. Cedary, high-cocoa dark chocolate oak amplifies its fine tannin profile. Sweet fruit and tangy acidity make for a little sweet-and-sour interplay on the finish, but it nonetheless upholds balance and persistence. Screw cap. 14.5% alc. **Rating** 91 **To** 2026 $40 TS

High Eden Cabernet Sauvignon 2015 Cabernet has long been the hero of Gatt's High Eden Vineyard, here projecting all of its black/redcurrant and capsicum personality in the great 2015 season. 80% new oak is sadly too much, rending it woody and dry, with firm tannins. Fruit carry and acid drive define a long finish. Screw cap. 14% alc. **Rating** 91 **To** 2025 $60 TS

Eden Springs High Eden Riesling 2018 Already progressed to middle age, this is a riesling layered with secondary spice, honey, roast nuts and the beginnings of kerosene. Primary lime and lemon fruit coast through the palate. The tension of High Eden acidity draws out a long and focused finish. Balanced, ripe-fruit phenolic presence is well countered by a lick of residual sweetness. Screw cap. 12% alc. **Rating** 90 **To** 2022 $30 TS

ΨΨΨΨ   **Barossa Valley Cabernet Sauvignon 2015** **Rating** 89 **To** 2021 $60 TS

Gembrook Hill   ★★★★★

Launching Place Road, Gembrook, Vic 3783 **Region** Yarra Valley
T (03) 5968 1622 **www**.gembrookhill.com.au **Open** By appt
Winemaker Andrew Marks **Est.** 1983 **Dozens** 1500 **Vyds** 5ha
Ian and June Marks established Gembrook Hill, one of the oldest vineyards in the southernmost part of the Upper Yarra Valley. The northeast-facing vineyard is in a natural amphitheatre; the low-yielding sauvignon blanc, chardonnay and pinot noir are not irrigated. The minimal approach to winemaking produces wines of a consistent style with finesse and elegance. The unexpected death of Ian in March 2017, and the decision of former winemaker Timo Mayer to concentrate on his own label, left son Andrew Marks in charge of winemaking at Gembrook Hill (and his own label, The Wanderer). Exports to the UK, the US, Denmark, Japan and Malaysia.

ΨΨΨΨΨ   **Yarra Valley Sauvignon Blanc 2019** 50% stainless-steel fermentation, 50% left on the lees for 5 months in used French oak. One of my go-to sauvignon blancs because it's so delicious and refreshing, yet complex and deep. It incorporates texture, with a vibrancy and brightness of fruit. Expect citrus, white pepper, chalky acidity and decent length. Screw cap. 12% alc. **Rating** 95 **To** 2026 $32 JF **☉**

Yarra Valley Chardonnay 2019 Yields were down but quality high, although this wine seems to rise to the occasion no matter the season. Acidity takes charge this vintage, but in between there's grapefruit, barely-ripe white nectarine, a dash of ginger spice and some nutty/leesy influences giving it a flavoursome edge and texture. It's tight across the palate, defining good cellaring potential, yet its countenance makes it easy to enjoy now. Diam. 12.5% alc. **Rating** 95 **To** 2029 $40 JF

Yarra Valley Pinot Noir 2019 Yes, this is unequivocally Yarra Valley, but it is far more distinctive of Gembrook Hill. It's the prettiness, the aromatic allure, the seemingly gentle palate, yet tannins are silky, the acidity just-so, with every element on the same wavelength. Just as Van Morrison sang: 'Wavelength. You never let me down, ah no.' Diam. 13% alc. **Rating** 95 **To** 2033 $40 JF

J.K.M Pinot Noir 2018 Juicy, tangy and moreish, with a core of sweet red cherries, flecked with Middle Eastern spices. The clincher is oh-so-fine tannins and crunchy, perky acidity. Don't rush this. It takes time to make an ethereal statement. Diam. 13% alc. **Rating** 95 **To** 2030 $85 JF

I.J.M. Pinot Noir 2018 This wine has a depth and concentration of flavour although still very much in the pretty Gembrook Hill mould, as it flutters with blood orange, chinotto, forest floor and smoked meats. The palate is pure and fine, with filigreed tannins and a softness and ease too. Diam. 13% alc. **Rating** 95 To 2030 $85 JF

Gemtree Wines   ★★★★★

167 Elliot Road, McLaren Flat, SA 5171 **Region** McLaren Vale
T (08) 8323 0802 **www**.gemtreewines.com **Open** Fri–Tues 11–5
Winemaker Mike Brown, Joshua Waechter **Est.** 1998 **Dozens** 90 000 **Vyds** 123ha
Gemtree Wines is owned and operated by husband and wife team Melissa and Mike Brown. Mike (winemaker) and Melissa (viticulturist) firmly believe it is their responsibility to improve the land for future generations, and the vineyards are farmed organically and biodynamically. Exports to the UK, US, Canada, Sweden, Denmark, Norway, Finland, Japan, China and NZ.

🍷🍷🍷🍷🍷 Small Batch McLaren Vale Marsanne 2020 By far the truest expression of marsanne I have tasted in Australia. Waxy, understated and effortless in a shy, medium-bodied way. Reliant on phenolics more than freshness: as it should be. Ebbs and flows across conversation and with what is on the plate. Lanolin, apricot pith and scents of dried straw before a tatami room is lain. A striking marsanne of immense purity and authenticity. Cork. 13% alc. **Rating** 95 To 2025 $35 NG ✪
Obsidian McLaren Vale Shiraz 2019 Plush. Thick. A salubrious sheen of impeccably poised oak and sensitively extracted grape tannins meld with just enough freshness. Generosity, the calling card. The fruit and arsenal of herb- to spice-inflected flavours sing above the structural frame: black cherry, damson plum, licorice, Asian spice, hoisin and baby back ribs. Slick, long and immensely satisfying. Cork. 14.5% alc. **Rating** 94 To 2036 $100 NG
Ernest Allan McLaren Vale Shiraz 2019 Another rich and powerful wine, bridled by a stern, savoury tannic fibre that tucks in the billowing seams. Iodine, purple fruits, anise and a gentle grind of pepper. The oak, impeccably nestled into the fray. This is a delicious wine that will age well. Cork. 14.5% alc. **Rating** 94 To 2034 $80 NG

🍷🍷🍷🍷🍷 The Phantom Red Blend Ten McLaren Vale 2019 **Rating** 93 To 2032 $80 NG
Small Batch Pet Nat McLaren Vale Grenache 2020 **Rating** 92 $35 NG
Uncut McLaren Vale Shiraz 2019 **Rating** 91 To 2028 $26 NG
Small Batch SBO McLaren Vale Grenache 2020 **Rating** 90 To 2028 $50 NG

Geoff Merrill Wines   ★★★★☆

291 Pimpala Road, Woodcroft, SA 5162 **Region** McLaren Vale
T (08) 8381 6877 **www**.geoffmerrillwines.com.au **Open** Mon–Fri 10–4.30, Sat 12–4.30
Winemaker Geoff Merrill, Scott Heidrich **Est.** 1980 **Dozens** 55 000 **Vyds** 45ha
If Geoff Merrill ever loses his impish sense of humour or his zest for life, high and not-so-high, we shall all be the poorer. The product range consists of 3 tiers: premium (varietal); Reserve, being the older wines, reflecting the desire for elegance and subtlety of this otherwise exuberant winemaker; and, at the top, Henley Shiraz. Exports to all major markets.

🍷🍷🍷🍷🍷 Bush Vine McLaren Vale Shiraz Grenache Mourvèdre 2014 This is drinking very well. Attractive Rhône-inspired aromas: sandalwood, smoked game and a porcini/bracken/bouillon note, earthy and shrouded in umami. Herbal tannins, gently ferrous, ply a straight path across the palate while mollifying shiraz's sweet tendencies, billowing in the background. The finish, tangy. But in all, solid value and very good drinking. Screw cap. 14.5% alc. **Rating** 92 To 2025 $28 NG
Henley McLaren Vale Shiraz 2013 Assuming that this is a museum release given the age, price and bricking deep crimson hue, this has stood up well. Full bodied. Resinous dark cherry, kirsch, dried fruits and orange peel scents curl their

way around a resinous beam of mocha oak, generously applied as is the wont here. The finish is plenty oaky, but is placated by the wine's overall warmth, swirling fruit and generosity. Cork. 14.5% alc. **Rating** 91 **To** 2023 $170 NG

Jacko's McLaren Vale Shiraz 2015 Scents of campfire, vanilla/bourbon and charred cedar. It is the oak, too, that defines the finish with a tannic clang. In the middle lies a core of impressive fruit, aged enough to confer a welcome savouriness manifest as a swathe of iodine, clove, licorice and an Indian to Moroccan souk sachet of spice. The acidity, out of kilter as usual. But plenty to like. Screw cap. 14.5% alc. **Rating** 90 **To** 2025 $30 NG

Geoff Weaver ★★★★★

2 Gilpin Lane, Mitcham, SA 5062 (postal) **Region** Adelaide Hills
T (08) 8272 2105 **www.**geoffweaver.com.au
Winemaker Geoff Weaver **Est.** 1982 **Dozens** 3000 **Vyds** 12.3ha
This is the business of one-time Hardys chief winemaker Geoff Weaver. The Lenswood vineyard was established between 1982 and '88, and invariably produces immaculate riesling and sauvignon blanc and long-lived chardonnays. The beauty of the labels ranks supreme. Exports to the UK, Hong Kong and Singapore.

🍷🍷🍷🍷🍷 **Single Vineyard Adelaide Hills Sauvignon Blanc 2020** To have been able to get these grapes off the Lenswood vineyard (impacted by a disastrous bushfire in December 2019) was a miracle to start with. Geoff Weaver's sauvignon blancs stand alone in their purity and delicacy. As does this iteration, not tempted by wild and exotic aromatics, rather a gently spicy white peach flavour, juicy and absolutely comfortable in its own skin. Screw cap. 12.5% alc. **Rating** 95 **To** 2024 $25 TL ✪

Single Vineyard Adelaide Hills Sauvignon Blanc 2019 A wine that stands tall to show us how great both the Hills and sauvignon blanc can be in Geoff Weaver's gentlemanly hands. The nose and palate are all about well-mannered varietal pungency, gooseberry and ginger, with fabulous, pithy texture and a reverb of exciting flavours on the finish. Simply terrific. Screw cap. 13% alc. **Rating** 95 **To** 2024 $25 TL ✪

Single Vineyard Adelaide Hills Chardonnay 2019 Ripe peachy notes to begin, then more complex elements show their wares on the palate in leesy savoury notes and a crisp apple-like acidity that's long and even. This has a lot more to offer in the coming decade. Screw cap. 13.5% alc. **Rating** 95 **To** 2030 $45 TL

Single Vineyard Adelaide Hills Pinot Noir 2016 Twelve months in French oak barriques, 50% new. The fruit has to be amazing to have relished and celebrated this maturation, and now 5 years on has the first traits of development appearing, too. A rare treat to see this in current-release pinot. Ripe fruit, cherry flesh, subtle woody spices and a sense of gentle earthy tannins. Pinot purity in spades. Screw cap. 13.7% alc. **Rating** 95 **To** 2024 $45 TL

Lenswood Riesling 2020 Working a new way with the riesling in this vintage, the wine was fermented and spent 7 months in old barrels with lees contact, leaving a delicate 5g/L RS in the final wine. The barrel characters offer some cream and spice to the apple and custard apple flavours; the sugars are benign yet textural and in context. Screw cap. 12.5% alc. **Rating** 94 **To** 2025 $30 TL ✪

George Wyndham ★★★★☆

167 Fullarton Road, Dulwich, SA 5065 (postal) **Region** South Eastern Australia
T (08) 8131 2400 **www.**georgewyndham.com
Winemaker Steve Meyer **Est.** 1828 **Dozens** 450000 **Vyds** 75ha
Named in honour of George Wyndham, who planted Australia's first commercial shiraz vineyard in 1830 at Dalwood in the Hunter Valley. Originally Dalwood Wines until 1970, then Wyndham Estate (1970–2015), the wines were renamed George Wyndham in '15. The Bin

range, led by Bin 555 Shiraz, often represents good value for money, as do the 'George' wines (I am George, George the Fixer). At the top is Black Cluster (shiraz) from the Hunter Valley. The wines are made and bottled in the Barossa Valley.

Ghost Rock Vineyard   ★★★★☆

1055 Port Sorrell Road, Northdown, Tas 7307 **Region** Northern Tasmania
T (03) 6428 4005 **www**.ghostrock.com.au **Open** 7 days 11–5
Winemaker Justin Arnold **Est.** 2001 **Dozens** 12000 **Vyds** 30ha
Cate and Colin Arnold purchased the former Patrick Creek Vineyard (planted exclusively to pinot noir in 1989) in 2001. The vineyards, situated among the patchwork fields of Sassafras to the south and the white sands of the Port Sorell Peninsula to the north, now total 30ha: pinot noir (14 clones) remains the bedrock of the plantings, with other varieties including chardonnay, pinot gris, riesling and sauvignon blanc. Ownership has passed to son Justin and his wife Alicia (who runs the cooking school and cellar door). Justin's experience in the Yarra Valley (Coldstream Hills), Margaret River (Devil's Lair) and Napa Valley (Etude) has paid dividends – the business is going from strength to strength, and the capacity of the 100t winery has been tripled. Exports to Japan.

🍷🍷🍷🍷🍷 **Fumé Blanc 2018** Medium straw yellow hue. A complex and strong sauvignon that counters the tension of crunchy wild lemon and spicy gooseberry fruit with the creamy, nutty, vanillan feel of wild oak fermentation. It culminates in a grand finish of enduring persistence, energised by crunchy Tasmanian acidity, promising great things over the coming decade. Screw cap. 13% alc. **Rating** 93 **To** 2030 $34 TS

Oulton Estate Chardonnay 2019 Medium straw yellow. Concentrated grapefruit, lemon, white peach and fig is cut with a tense, firm acid line, jostling with biscuity French oak. All the elements are present, if a little boisterous, just demanding time to calm down and find harmony. It boasts the length and energy to hold for the medium term. Screw cap. 13.5% alc. **Rating** 93 **To** 2027 $52 TS

Oulton XP Pinot Noir 2019 A tinted medium crimson. Juicy strawberries, tangy red cherries, dried thyme and the early beginnings of forest floor. Fine-grained tannins and vibrant acid line hold a long finish. Expressive and balanced Tasmanian pinot. Screw cap. 13.5% alc. **Rating** 93 **To** 2024 $52 TS

Sauvignon Blanc 2020 Unabashed, powerful sauvignon. Rich tinned peas, ripe gooseberries and wild lemons. At once fleshy, generous and textured yet tense and cut with Northern Tasmanian acid drive. Impressive length and presence. For those hankering for sauvignon with more. Screw cap. 13% alc. **Rating** 92 **To** 2022 $30 TS

Chardonnay 2019 Concentration and presence meet tension. Grapefruit and spicy white nectarine meet the bubblegum notes of wild fermentation and lees age. Fruit intensity is countered by tense malic cut on a firm, long finish. Give it a few years to mellow. Screw cap. 13.2% alc. **Rating** 92 **To** 2027 $34 TS

Pinot Gris 2020 Some oak maturation. Signature gris, brimming with extroverted ripe pear, spicy guava, even rockmelon. Cool Tasmanian acidity is backed by phenolic grip on a long finish of fleshy generosity. A luscious and ripe style, ready to drink. Screw cap. 13.8% alc. **Rating** 92 **To** 2021 $30 TS

P3 Rosé 2020 Enticing rosé of medium salmon/copper hue. Fragrant, tense, energetic, refreshing and still juicy, inviting and persistent. All the precocious red berries and cherries of meunier and noir meet the tropical hints of gris. Fleshy fruit sweetness and tangy acidity hold a confident finish. Screw cap. 13% alc. **Rating** 92 **To** 2021 $30 TS

Bonadale Pinot Noir 2019 Medium crimson red. Mulberry and strawberry fruit unite in a palate at once fleshy, spicy and tangy. Fine-grained tannins hold a supple finish of medium persistence. Drink now or in the next few years. Screw cap. 13.5% alc. **Rating** 92 **To** 2024 $52 TS

Giaconda ★★★★★

30 McClay Road, Beechworth, Vic 3747 **Region** Beechworth
T (03) 5727 0246 **www.**giaconda.com.au **Open** By appt
Winemaker Rick Kinzbrunner, Nathan Kinzbrunner **Est.** 1982 **Dozens** 3500 **Vyds** 4ha
These wines have a super-cult status and, given the small production, are extremely difficult
to find; they are sold chiefly through restaurants and via their website. All have a cosmopolitan
edge befitting Rick Kinzbrunner's international winemaking experience. The Chardonnay
is one of Australia's greatest and is made and matured in the underground wine cellar hewn
out of granite. This permits gravity flow and a year-round temperature range of 14–15°C,
promising even more for the future. Exports to the UK, UAE, the US, Canada, Singapore,
Sweden, Norway, Germany, NZ and China.

🍷🍷🍷🍷🍷 **Estate Vineyard Chardonnay 2018** It's so difficult to avoid comparisons with
Montrachet, except to say both have profoundly deep and long palates. Of course,
there's high-quality French oak and the requisite acidity to freshen the finish, but
the ultimate quality lies in the freakish length of the wine. Screw cap. 13.5% alc.
Rating 99 **To** 2038 $130 JH ✪ ❤

🍷🍷🍷🍷🍷 **Warner Vineyard Shiraz 2018** The winemaker believes the '18 sits at the
very top of recent Warner shiraz releases. It's certainly a beauty, and hard to
resist broaching now, such is its complexity and integration. A confident, gently
expressive young shiraz. Middle Eastern spices, tilled earth, bay leaf, Damson
plum, light herbals, dark brooding berries. Warm and inviting, there's a lick of
savouriness on the palate that lifts and catches the tastebuds' attention. That's when
the fun starts. This wine takes you places. Close your eyes … Screw cap. 13.5% alc.
Rating 96 **To** 2036 $79 JP

Estate Vineyard Shiraz 2018 Another restrained beauty from Giaconda, with a
seemingly modest presence until the wine hits the tongue. This is a journey into
the heart of shiraz. Aromas of forest berries, pepper, sage, anise and red earth are
transformed into levels of layered complexity on the palate. Spice is ever-present,
so too wood smoke and leather, with understated, savoury, ripe tannins. Cork.
13.5% alc. **Rating** 96 **To** 2036 $84 JP

Estate Vineyard Pinot Noir 2018 In keeping with past Giaconda pinots, the
'18 opens with a warm generosity and alluring scents of alpine wildflowers, dried
herbs and exotic red fruits including dusty cranberry and pomegranate. A fleshy
palate is well concentrated in fruit and boasts integrated oak and supple tannins
running velvety across the tongue. And still so young. Amazing. Cork. 13.5% alc.
Rating 95 **To** 2034 $84 JP

Giant Steps ★★★★★

314 Maroondah Highway, Healesville, Vic 3777 **Region** Yarra Valley
T (03) 5962 6111 **www.**giantstepswine.com.au **Open** 7 days 11–4
Winemaker Phil Sexton, Steve Flamsteed, Jess Clark **Est.** 1997 **Dozens** 30000 **Vyds** 60ha
In May 2016 the sale by Giant Steps of the Innocent Bystander brand and stock was
completed. The former Innocent Bystander restaurant and shop has been substantially
remodelled to put the focus on the high-quality, single-vineyard, single-variety wines in what
is demonstrably a very distinguished portfolio. Its vineyard resources comprise the Sexton
Vineyard (32ha) in the Lower Yarra and Applejack Vineyard (13ha) in the Upper Yarra; there
is also the Primavera Vineyard in the Upper Yarra under long-term supervised contract and
Tarraford Vineyard in the Lower Yarra under long-term lease. Giant Steps was purchased by
Jackson Family Wines in August 2020. Exports to the UK, the US, Canada, Sweden, Hong
Kong, Singapore, China and NZ.

🍷🍷🍷🍷🍷 **Sexton Vineyard Yarra Valley Chardonnay 2019** A low-yielding site set
on exposed north-facing slopes, Sexton vineyard produces wines of depth and
concentration. There's more richness here than the other 2019 chardonnay releases
from this winery, with stone fruit coming into play on the bouquet and palate and
a more textural feeling. There's width and length to the flavour profile, the oak a

well-integrated component throughout. The finish shows a chalky minerality with real persistence. Screw cap. 13% alc. **Rating** 95 **To** 2029 $60 SC

Yarra Valley Pinot Noir 2020 This hums a mighty fine tune. Starting light and bright with raspberries, red cherries, star anise and a fleck of woodsy spices. It seems almost pretty until the savouriness kicks in. A touch of meaty reduction, lots of tangy acidity, with textural tannins working across a medium-bodied palate. It delivers plenty of flavour, yet it's all well contained. Screw cap. 13.5% alc. **Rating** 95 **To** 2027 $38 JF

Wombat Creek Vineyard Yarra Valley Pinot Noir 2020 Snap. Crackle. Pop. This is brimming with good stuff. Highly perfumed, crunchy fruit flavours and pliable tannins. Thanks to its laser light of natural acidity, it has energy and drive. Screw cap. 13% alc. **Rating** 95 **To** 2029 $65 JF

Tarraford Vineyard Yarra Valley Chardonnay 2019 The lead-up to vintage 2019 in the Yarra was very warm but Tarraford, with its distinctive and cooler microclimate, fared well. The typical minerality that this site provides is its defining character, absorbing 10 months in oak with ease. The fruit is mainly on the citrus spectrum, but it's more the overall structure of the wine that stands out. The palate is juicy but fine, the finish long and crisp. Screw cap. 13% alc. **Rating** 94 **To** 2029 $60 SC

Sexton Vineyard Yarra Valley Pinot Noir 2019 Matured in French oak barriques (25% new) for 8 months, no fining or filtration. Balance is the outstanding quality of this wine. You don't really need to pick it apart, just enjoy the flow of ripe cherry and other typically varietal pinot characters that run through the bouquet and palate. The tannin, although quite light, melds in seamlessly and there's a feeling of freshness on the finish. Screw cap. 13.5% alc. **Rating** 94 **To** 2029 $65 SC

Primavera Vineyard Yarra Valley Pinot Noir 2019 Upper Yarra fruit from this vineyard at Woori Yallock. MV6 and 115 clones, pre-ferment handling; 8 months in French oak barriques (25% new). Soft red fruit, a touch of green herb and a little bit of coffee oak on the bouquet, all nicely in harmony. Quite broad through the palate, and mouthfilling in a way, but holds its shape courtesy of the gently persistent tannins which maintain well through the finish. Screw cap. 13.5% alc. **Rating** 94 **To** 2029 $65 SC

Fatal Shore Coal River Valley Pinot Noir 2019 Some cold soak, some whole-bunch ferment, all matured in French barriques (25% new) for 8 months. Bright, fresh cherry aromas grab your attention on the bouquet, but there are some gamey, greenish notes underneath. Initially seems soft to taste but has a mouthfilling quality and the flavours and the tannin build as it goes along. Give it time in the glass and in the bottle. Screw cap. 13.5% alc. **Rating** 94 **To** 2027 $75 SC

🍷🍷🍷🍷🍷 **Yarra Valley Chardonnay 2020 Rating** 93 **To** 2030 $38 JF
Wombat Creek Vineyard Yarra Valley Chardonnay 2019 Rating 93 **To** 2029 $60 SC
Yarra Valley Rosé 2020 Rating 93 **To** 2023 $25 JF❂
Applejack Vineyard Yarra Valley Pinot Noir 2019 Rating 93 **To** 2029 $65 SC

Gibson   ★★★★☆

190 Willows Road, Light Pass, SA 5355 **Region** Barossa Valley
T (08) 8562 3193 **www.**gibsonwines.com.au **Open** 7 days 11–5
Winemaker Rob Gibson **Est.** 1996 **Dozens** 11 000 **Vyds** 12.4ha
Rob Gibson spent much of his working life as a senior viticulturist for Penfolds, involved in research tracing the characters that particular parcels of grapes give to a wine, which left him with a passion for identifying and protecting what is left of the original vineyard plantings in Australia. He has a vineyard (merlot) in the Barossa Valley at Light Pass, and one in the Eden Valley (shiraz and riesling) and also purchases grapes from McLaren Vale and the Adelaide Hills. Exports to Germany, Taiwan and China.

ŢŢŢŢŢ **Australian Old Vine Collection Barossa Shiraz 2017** The cool 2017 vintage delivers bright, vibrant acidity and crunchy red berry fruits, set to a backdrop of old-vine black fruits (planted 1912–1950s) and subtle exotic spice. A long spell in new French oak barrels has brought resolution and coherence, filled out with high-cocoa dark chocolate. It holds the fruit integrity, structural confidence and persistence to subdue its warm alcohol, set for a strong future. Cork. 14.9% alc. Rating 94 To 2035 $135 TS

ŢŢŢŢŢ **Burkes Hill Eden Valley Riesling 2020** Rating 92 To 2027 $35 TS
Discovery Road Barossa Valley Graciano Rosé 2020 Rating 91 To 2021 $25 TS
Reserve Barossa Shiraz 2018 Rating 91 To 2038 $50 TS
Isabelle Barossa Cabernet Merlot 2018 Rating 91 To 2033 $32 TS
Reserve Barossa Merlot 2018 Rating 90 To 2033 $46 TS

Gilbert Family Wines   ★★★★☆

137 Ulan Road, Mudgee, NSW 2850 **Region** Orange/Mudgee
T (02) 6373 1371 **www**.gilbertfamilywines.com.au **Open** Sun–Thurs 10–4, Fri–Sat 10–5
Winemaker Simon Gilbert, Will Gilbert **Est.** 2004 **Dozens** 18 000 **Vyds** 25.81ha
The Gilbert Family Wine Company was established in 2004 by 5th-generation winemaker Simon Gilbert; 6th-generation Will Gilbert took over the reins in '14. Will draws on extensive Old and New World winemaking experience to push boundaries with different techniques and ideas to make the Gilbert Family wines from Orange and Mudgee. Gilbert + Gilbert wines from the Eden Valley draw from the family history – Joseph Gilbert of Pewsey Vale was the first to plant grapes in the Eden Valley in 1847. Exports to the UK, the US, Canada, Norway, Denmark, Japan, Taiwan, Hong Kong and China.

ŢŢŢŢŢ **Gilbert RS11 Orange Riesling 2019** Some welcome skin contact in the press, imparting a gentle chew, oiliness and a kaleidoscope of additional flavour nuances from tangerine, cumquat and ginger, in addition to kaffir lime, citrus blossom and jasmine. Steely and compact. Latent and composed. A work-out in the glass brings it to life. This is very good domestic riesling. Of thrilling length and just the right dollop of residual. Screw cap. 10.8% alc. Rating 94 To 2032 $36 TS
Gilbert Orange Riesling 2019 Fermented cool in tank, before draining to neutral wood for completion, stirring and élévage on full lees. Tangerine, tonic, bergamot, lemon oil and quinine. Lime, a given. But so much more! 5% fermented on skins. A little malolactic sneaking across the lo-fi controls. The result, excellent. Scintillating, steely length and cut-glass precision. Screw cap. 11.4% alc. Rating 94 To 2032 $28 NG **❂**

ŢŢŢŢŢ **Gilbert L.C.R. Orange Chardonnay 2018** Rating 93 To 2028 $42 NG
Gilbert Orange Riesling 2012 Rating 92 To 2024 $60 NG
Gilbert Sur Lie Orange Sauvignon Blanc 2019 Rating 92 To 2024 $28 NG
Gilbert Orange Chardonnay 2018 Rating 92 To 2024 $30 NG
Gilbert Orange Pinot Noir 2019 Rating 92 To 2026 $32 NG
Gilbert Rosé 2020 Rating 90 To 2022 $24 NG

Gilberts   ★★★★☆

30138 Albany Highway, Kendenup via Mount Barker, WA 6323 **Region** Mount Barker
T (08) 9851 4028 **www**.gilbertwines.com.au **Open** Fri–Mon 10–5
Winemaker Westcape Howe **Est.** 1985 **Dozens** 3000 **Vyds** 9ha
Once a part-time occupation for 3rd-generation sheep and beef farmers Jim and Beverly Gilbert, but now a full-time job and a very successful one. In 2014 the 4th generation, sons Clinton and Matthew, joined the management of the business. The mature vineyard (shiraz, chardonnay, riesling and cabernet sauvignon) coupled with contract winemaking at West Cape Howe, has long produced high class wines. Exports to Canada.

🍷🍷🍷🍷🍷 **JMG Mount Barker Cabernet Shiraz 2018** Punchy cassis from the cabernet is the major player in the glass, an assortment of plump berries from the shiraz is the backdrop. Texture is fine and supple; length of flavour is very good. Oak has a firm grip on the finish, but the fruit is the winner in the end. Screw cap. 14% alc. **Rating** 91 **To** 2027 $25 EL

Mount Barker Riesling 2020 Taut acid and young citrus fruit create a tension on the palate that verges on tart. This is very tightly coiled right now, although the fruit is so delicate, it's unclear whether further time in the bottle is what this wine needs. The clenched fist seems to be made of acid, not fruit. Screw cap. 10% alc. **Rating** 90 **To** 2031 $24 EL

Reserve Mount Barker Shiraz 2018 Sixteen months in 30% new oak. Big, intense, oak-dominated shiraz. The fruit has power but is swathed by the oak, which directs it in a more blocky/bulky direction, rather than, perhaps, allowing it to be a juicier, brighter and fleshier version of itself. It has good length of flavour and a great peppercorn character right in the mid palate. Traditional, rather than modern. Screw cap. 14.5% alc. **Rating** 90 **To** 2035 $40 EL

🍷🍷🍷🍷 **3 Devils Mount Barker Shiraz 2018** **Rating** 89 **To** 2025 $20 EL
Dry Mount Barker Rosé 2020 **Rating** 88 **To** 2021 $20 EL

Gioiello Estate   ★★★★☆

350 Molesworth-Dropmore Road, Molesworth, Vic 3718 **Region** Upper Goulburn
T 0437 240 502 www.gioiello.com.au
Winemaker Scott McCarthy (Contract) **Est.** 1987 **Dozens** 3000 **Vyds** 8.97ha
The Gioiello Estate vineyard was established by a Japanese company and originally known as Daiwa Nar Darak. Planted between 1987 and '96, it accounts for just under 9ha of a 400ha property of rolling hills, pastures, bushland, river flats, natural water springs and billabongs. Now owned by the Schiavello family, the vineyard continues to produce high-quality wines.

🍷🍷🍷🍷🍷 **Mt Concord Upper Goulburn Syrah 2018** A wine to impress with its depth of fruit and elegant expression of place. Intended for a long run in the cellar, it's already exuding a developing complexity. Dark plum, black cherry, leather and sweet oak spice aromas. Fine and layered with long, ripe tannins. Open later rather than sooner. Screw cap. 13.3% alc. **Rating** 95 **To** 2030 $45 JP

🍷🍷🍷🍷🍷 **Upper Goulburn Merlot 2018** **Rating** 91 **To** 2025 $27 JP
Upper Goulburn Syrah 2018 **Rating** 90 **To** 2025 $27 JP
Old House Upper Goulburn Merlot 2018 **Rating** 90 **To** 2028 $45 JP

Gippsland Wine Company   ★★★★

6835 South Gippsland Hwy, Loch, Vic 3945 **Region** Gippsland
T 0477 555 235 www.gippslandwinecompany.com **Open** Fri–Sun 10–5
Winemaker Marcus Satchwell **Est.** 2011 **Vyds** 1.2ha
Mark Heath has worked in some big-name wine companies (mainly in sales and marketing) over the years, but there was always a yearning, a dream to own a vineyard and make wine of his own. It became reality when he and his wife, Jane Taylor, bought a run-down site in 2011 in Loch Village. The appeal of Gippsland was the charm of a region full of owner-operators rather than large-scale businesses. With some hard work, it didn't take long for the north-facing 1.2ha vineyard planted around 1999 to cabernet sauvignon, sangiovese and chardonnay to come back to life. From day one, he secured local winemaker Marcus Satchwell (Dirty Three Wines) to make the wines. Today, Gippsland Wine Company leases 4 other vineyards within a 20km radius from Loch Village, planted to several varieties including riesling, pinot noir, sauvignon blanc and shiraz. A cellar door opened in 2014. (JF)

🍷🍷🍷🍷🍷 **Gustoso 2019** A licorice allsorts blend of cabernet sauvignon, pinot noir, shiraz and sangiovese. It comes together harmoniously, albeit on a lighter frame with surprisingly soft, supple, sweet tannins. A core of juicy ripe fruit, all spiced up with black pepper, wormwood and iodine, and there's a gentleness across the palate. It's a drink-now red. Screw cap. 13.5% alc. **Rating** 94 **To** 2025 $35 JF

ᵀᵀᵀᵀ♀ **Glen Forbes Vineyard Pinot Gris 2019** Rating 93 To 2023 $30 JF
Lochonia & Rhyll Vineyards Syrah 2019 Rating 93 To 2027 $40 JF
Calulu Vineyard Pinot Noir 2019 Rating 91 To 2027 $35 JF

Gisborne Peak

69 Short Road, Gisborne South, Vic 3437 **Region** Macedon Ranges
T (03) 5428 2228 **www.**gisbornepeakwines.com.au **Open** 7 days 11–4
Winemaker Rob Ellis **Est.** 1978 **Dozens** 1800 **Vyds** 5.5ha
Bob Nixon began the development of Gisborne Peak way back in 1978, planting his dream vineyard row by row. The tasting room has wide shaded verandahs, plenty of windows and sweeping views. The vineyard is planted to pinot noir, chardonnay, semillon, riesling and lagrein.

ᵀᵀᵀᵀ♀ **Macedon Ranges Riesling 2020** Straight into a citrus theme with juice and zest, all lemons and limes. Acidity is perky, so it'll hang around a while longer. Screw cap. 12.1% alc. **Rating** 90 To 2027 $40 JF

Glaetzer Wines   ★★★★★

PO Box 824 Tanunda, SA 5352 **Region** Barossa Valley
T (08) 8563 0947 **www.**glaetzer.com
Winemaker Ben Glaetzer **Est.** 1996 **Dozens** 15 000 **Vyds** 20ha
With a family history in the Barossa Valley dating back to 1888, Glaetzer Wines was established by Colin Glaetzer after 30 years of winemaking experience. Son Ben worked in the Hunter Valley and as a Flying Winemaker in many of the world's wine regions before returning to Glaetzer Wines and assuming the winemaking role. The wines are made with great skill and abundant personality. Exports to all major markets.

ᵀᵀᵀᵀᵀ **Amon-Ra Unfiltered Barossa Valley Shiraz 2019** Gloss and polish of superb black fruits, framed in superfine tannins are Ben Glaetzer's hallmarks. He continues to hone his talent at sustaining brightness and freshness, even in northern Barossa shiraz of monumental proportions. This represents one of his finest works yet. Bitter dark chocolate oak holds an enticing finish that ricochets with inky black fruits and licorice. Cork. 15.5% alc. **Rating** 96 To 2034 $100 TS
Anaperenna Barossa Valley 2019 Ben Glaetzer's superpower is upholding glossy brightness and freshness even in the wake of considerable ripeness, all the more impressive in warm drought seasons in the generous northern Barossa. Anaperenna is a showpiece for the modern great Australian blend, brimming in bountiful red and black fruits, backed generously with dark chocolate and coffee-bean new oak. It holds its proportions and considerable alcohol with astonishing confidence, thanks most of all to a bright flash of pure, fresh acidity. Cork. 15.5% alc. **Rating** 95 To 2029 $52 TS

Glaetzer-Dixon Family Winemakers

93 Brooker Avenue, Hobart, Tas 7000 **Region** Southern Tasmania
T 0417 852 287 **www.**gdfwinemakers.com **Open** By appt
Winemaker Nick Glaetzer **Est.** 2008 **Dozens** 2500
History does not relate what Nick Glaetzer's high-profile Barossa Valley winemaker relatives thought of his decision to move to Tasmania in 2005, to make cutting-edge cool-climate styles. Obviously wife Sally approves. While his winemaking career began in the Barossa Valley, he reached into scattered parts of the New World and Old World alike, working successively in Languedoc, the Pfaltz, Margaret River, Riverland, Sunraysia, the Hunter Valley and Burgundy. Exports to the US, Canada, the Netherlands and Singapore.

Glenguin Estate ★★★★★

Milbrodale Road, Broke, NSW 2330 **Region** Hunter Valley
T (02) 6579 1009 **www**.glenguinestate.com.au
Winemaker Robin Tedder MW, Rhys Eather **Est.** 1993 **Dozens** 2000 **Vyds** 5ha
Glenguin Estate was established by the Tedder family, headed by Robin Tedder MW. It is close to Broke and adjacent to Wollombi Brook. The backbone of the production comes from almost 30-year-old plantings of Busby clone semillon and shiraz. Vineyard manager Andrew Tedder, who has considerable experience with organics and biodynamics, is overseeing the ongoing development of Glenguin's organic program.

ΨΨΨΨΨ Glenguin Vineyard Semillon 2017 Lemon buttered toast, finger lime, quince and lemongrass scents are of a purity and sapid intensity, without the shrillness of other regional expressions. Lightweight but extended time on lees has imparted a welcome creaminess. The long flow, precise but effortless. A fine vintage and a lovely wine. Screw cap. 11% alc. **Rating** 95 **To** 2030 $35 NG ✪

ΨΨΨΨΨ Cellar Aged Aristea Shiraz 2009 Rating 93 **To** 2025 $150 NG
Glenguin Vineyard Semillon 2015 Rating 91 **To** 2024 $30 NG

Glenwillow Wines ★★★★

Bendigo Pottery, 146 Midland Highway, Epsom, Vic 3551 **Region** Bendigo
T 0428 461 076 **www**.glenwillow.com.au **Open** Thurs–Mon & public hols 10.30–5
Winemaker Adam Marks **Est.** 1999 **Dozens** 750 **Vyds** 2.8ha
Peter and Cherryl Fyffe began their vineyard at Yandoit Creek, 10km south of Newstead, in 1999. They planted 1.8ha of shiraz and 0.3ha of cabernet sauvignon, later branching out with 0.6ha of nebbiolo and 0.1ha of barbera. Planted on a mixture of rich volcanic and clay loam interspersed with quartz and buckshot gravel, the vineyard has an elevated north-facing aspect, which minimises the risk of frost.

ΨΨΨΨΨ Bendigo Shiraz 2017 Made by the former Bress winemaker, Adam Marks, and carries some of his celebration-of-fruit winemaking style. In this case it's pure, clean and intense, no heaviness or obvious oak, laying out wild berries, black plums, musk and spice with a smidge of pepper. Aromatic and lifted, firm on the finish. Screw cap. 13.7% alc. **Rating** 90 **To** 2024 $28 JP

Golden Grove Estate ★★★★

Sundown Road, Ballandean, Qld 4382 **Region** Granite Belt
T (07) 4684 1291 **www**.goldengroveestate.com.au **Open** 7 days 9–4
Winemaker Raymond Costanzo **Est.** 1993 **Dozens** 4000 **Vyds** 12.4ha
Golden Grove Estate was established by Mario and Sebastian Costanzo in 1946, producing stone fruits and table grapes. The first wine grapes (shiraz) were planted in '72 but it was not until '85, when ownership passed to (CSU graduate) son Sam and his wife Grace, that the use of the property began to change. In '93 chardonnay and merlot joined the shiraz, followed by cabernet sauvignon, sauvignon blanc and semillon. The baton has been passed down another generation to CSU graduate Ray Costanzo, who has lifted the quality of the wines remarkably and has also planted tempranillo, durif, barbera, malbec, mourvèdre, vermentino and nero d'Avola. Its consistent wine show success over recent years with alternative varieties is impressive.

ΨΨΨΨΨ Granite Belt Semillon 2017 A fresh core of accurate lemon and cut grass contrasts all the toasty, spicy, buttery allure of wild-yeast barrel fermentation and bottle age. Holding a bright, medium straw hue and youthful energy, it promises to live long, sustained by focused acid line and enduring persistence. Screw cap. 10.5% alc. **Rating** 92 **To** 2037 $26 TS
Granite Belt Shiraz 2019 Medium, vibrant purple. A compact core of blackberry and dark plum fruit is reticent and closed, framed in a tight, fine tannin web and dark chocolate oak. Nicely crafted and poised, with even flow on a

balanced finish. Give it time to unravel. Screw cap. 14% alc. **Rating** 91 **To** 2034 $28 TS

Granite Belt Durif 2019 Deep, vibrant purple. A sweet, spicy and full durif, lacking nothing in ripeness in spite of early picking due to drought stress. Deep black fruits and dark fruitcake, layered with spice and supported equally by bright acidity and firm, grainy tannins. Screw cap. 13.7% alc. **Rating** 90 **To** 2024 $35 TS

ΨΨΨΨ   **Granite Belt Tempranillo 2019** Rating 89 To 2021 $30 TS

Goldman Wines

11 Ercildoune Street, Cessnock, NSW 2325 (postal) **Region** Hunter Valley
T 0467 808 316 **www**.goldmanwines.com.au
Winemaker Various contract **Est.** 2014 **Dozens** 1500
Owner Callan Goldman grew up in the Hunter Valley, coming into contact with many of the people involved in growing grapes or making wine (or both) in the region. But his real job then and now is working as a civil engineer in northwest WA to fund his various wine production plans. Jo Marsh of Billy Button Wines makes the majority of the impressive portfolio at her new winery in the Ovens Valley.

ΨΨΨΨΨ   **Alpine Valleys Shiraz 2019** Like launching across a field of wildflowers, Alpine Valleys shiraz can certainly put on an aromatic display. Very enticing. Dark, dense purple hue. The aromatics shine on the bouquet together with black cherry, earth and dark chocolate. Full in flavour and presence with just a hint of savoury oak to cap things off. Screw cap. 14.9% alc. **Rating** 91 **To** 2026 $27 JP

ΨΨΨΨ   **Joan Blanc de Blancs Alpine Valleys Chardonnay 2017** Rating 89 $40 JP
Alpine Valleys Chardonnay 2019 Rating 88 To 2025 $27 JP

Gomersal Wines

203 Lyndoch Road, Gomersal, SA 5352 **Region** Barossa Valley
T (08) 8563 3611 **www**.gomersalwines.com.au **Open** Wed–Mon 10–5
Winemaker Barry White **Est.** 1887 **Dozens** 10200 **Vyds** 20.2ha
The 1887 establishment date has a degree of poetic licence. In 1887 Friedrich W Fromm planted the Wonganella Vineyards, following that with a winery on the edge of the Gomersal Creek in '91; it remained in operation for 90 years, finally closing in 1983. In 2000 a group of friends 'with strong credentials in both the making and consumption ends of the wine industry' bought the winery and re-established the vineyard, planting 17ha of shiraz, 2.2ha of mourvèdre and 1ha of grenache. Exports to Switzerland, Iceland, South Korea, Singapore, China and NZ.

ΨΨΨΨΨ   **Clare Valley Riesling 2020** A spot-on drink-now wine with citrussy aromatics moving from lemon to orange and a touch of ginger spice. It's not racy as such, although acidity encases the textural palate flavoured with baked apples. Screw cap. 12.5% alc. **Rating** 92 **To** 2027 $20 JP ○

Goodman Wines

PO Box 275, Healesville, Vic 3777 **Region** Yarra Valley
T 0447 030 011 **www**.goodmanwines.com
Winemaker Kate Goodman **Est.** 2012 **Dozens** 500
Kate Goodman started her winemaking career in McLaren Vale and the Clare Valley, thereafter spending 7 years winemaking at Seppelt in the Grampians. In 2000 she became chief winemaker at Punt Road Wines and remained there until '14, when she left to set up Goodman Wines, leasing a winery together with fellow winemaker Caroline Mooney (of Bird on a Wire). Using some lead time planning, and with the knowledge and approval of Punt Road's owners, she had made wines over the '12 and '13 vintages, all from mature Upper Yarra Valley vineyards. From '17 she is also winemaker for Penley Estate and Zonzo Estate.

Goona Warra Vineyard ★★★★

790 Sunbury Road, Sunbury, Vic 3429 **Region** Sunbury
T (03) 9740 7766 **www.**goonawarra.com.au **Open** By appt
Winemaker Richard Buller, Kirilly Gordon **Est.** 1863 **Dozens** 2500 **Vyds** 5.27ha
A historic stone winery, originally established under this name (meaning black swan) by a 19th-century Victorian premier. Excellent tasting facilities, an outstanding venue for weddings and receptions. A new cellar door opened in August 2020, with construction of a luxury hotel and restaurant due to begin in 2022. Exports to China.

♥♥♥♥♥ **Chairmans Reserve Shiraz 2018** Hand-picked estate fruit, open-fermented, matured for 18 months in French oak. A medium-bodied, perfectly articulated cool climate shiraz with both red and purple fruits sprinkled with spice and pepper. A welcome reappearance for Goona Warra. Cork. 13.5% alc. **Rating** 95 To 2033 $36 JH

♥♥♥♥♡ **Chairmans Reserve Roussanne 2018** **Rating** 92 To 2030 $36 JH

Grace Farm ★★★★☆

741 Cowaramup Bay Road, Gracetown, WA 6285 **Region** Margaret River
T (08) 9384 4995 **www.**gracefarm.com.au **Open** By appt
Winemaker Jonathan Mettam **Est.** 2006 **Dozens** 3000 **Vyds** 8.19ha
Situated in the Wilyabrup district, Grace Farm is the small, family-owned vineyard of Elizabeth and John Mair. It takes its name from the nearby coastal hamlet of Gracetown. Situated beside picturesque natural forest, the vineyard is planted to cabernet sauvignon, chardonnay, sauvignon blanc and semillon with smaller amounts of cabernet franc, petit verdot and malbec. Viticulturist Tim Quinlan conducts tastings (by appointment), explaining Grace Farm's sustainable viticultural practices.

♥♥♥♥♥ **Margaret River Sauvignon Blanc Semillon 2020** Oak is very evident on the nose and palate at this stage, but in time the fruit swells up and overtakes it, a sure sign of a well-executed match. The briny acid that further secures the union is interwoven throughout, making this a very classy proposition indeed. Screw cap. 12.5% alc. **Rating** 94 To 2028 $23 EL
Margaret River Malbec 2018 Fabulous, iridescent colour. The nose has field strawberries, raspberry, green peppercorn and wine gums. The palate has the ripeness and succulence of the '18 vintage, which continues through to the long finish. The tannins exhibit a satisfying grip and chew to them. Quite lovely. Screw cap. 13.5% alc. **Rating** 94 To 2025 $45 EL

♥♥♥♥♡ **Margaret River Cabernet Malbec 2018** **Rating** 93 To 2036 $40 EL
Margaret River Chardonnay 2019 **Rating** 90 To 2031 $35 EL

Gralyn Estate ★★★★

4145 Caves Road, Wilyabrup, WA 6280 **Region** Margaret River
T (08) 9755 6245 **www.**gralyn.com.au **Open** 7 days 10.30–4.30
Winemaker Annette Baxter, Scott Baxter **Est.** 1975 **Dozens** 3000 **Vyds** 4ha
Established by Merilyn and Graham Hutton in 1975, Gralyn Estate has established a good reputation for its wines. The primary focus is on the full-bodied red wines, which are made in a distinctively different style from most from Margaret River, with an opulence reminiscent of some of the bigger wines of McLaren Vale. The age of the cabernet and shiraz vines (45+ years) and the site are significant factors. Lesser amounts of chardonnay and fortified wines are also made. Merilyn and Graham passed the baton to daughter Annette and her partner Scott in 2020.

♥♥♥♥♥ **Reserve Margaret River Cabernet Sauvignon 2013** Coffee-laden oak straddles cassis fruit on the nose. Retains freshness and life on the palate, 7 years on. Cheesecloth and coffee-ground character lingers in the background, perhaps a contribution from the oak. The tannins have an open-weave rusticity about them, the cabernet fruit (from vines planted in '75) has very good length of flavour. Screw cap. 13.2% alc. **Rating** 94 **To** 2027 $120 EL

Artizan Rare Margaret River Muscat NV Rum and raisin on the nose, backed by five-spice, nutmeg, star anise, aniseed and black pepper. This is quite delicious and certainly very complex, but the flavours plateau just when you expect them to reach a crescendo. Very good length of flavour stamps this wine with 'quality', and certainly the luxurious opulence of it is attractive. Screw cap. 18% alc. **Rating** 94 $90 EL

Margaret River Tawny Fortified NV On both the nose and palate this wine expounds the virtues of the tawny style. Bitter rancio characters, date, quince, nutmeg, five-spice, licorice and clove are the calling cards. All things in place and balanced. The finish exhibits a raw pull of tannin that is both distracting and attractive in equal measure. A beautiful wine nonetheless. Screw cap. 19% alc. **Rating** 94 $55 EL

🍷🍷🍷🍷 **Reserve Margaret River Chardonnay 2017** **Rating** 92 **To** 2028 $75 EL

Grampians Estate

1477 Western Highway, Great Western, Vic 3377 **Region** Grampians
T (03) 5354 6245 **www**.grampiansestate.com.au **Open** 7 days 10–5
Winemaker Andrew Davey, Tom Guthrie **Est.** 1989 **Dozens** 2000 **Vyds** 8ha
Graziers Sarah and Tom Guthrie began their diversification into wine in 1989, but their core business continues to be fat lamb and wool production. They acquired the Garden Gully winery at Great Western, giving them a cellar door and a vineyard with 140+yo shiraz and 100+yo riesling. Grampians Estate followed its success of being Champion Small Winery of Show at the Australian Small Winemakers Show for the second year running in '18 by winning the Premier's Trophy for Champion Wine of Victoria in '19. These successes led to a major expansion of the cellar door, with a new cafe and outdoor area. Exports to China.

🍷🍷🍷🍷🍷 **Streeton Reserve Shiraz 2018** A beautifully crafted shiraz exhibiting concentrated spice, pepper and blackberried fruit power. The palate is built around a discreet tannin frame and a solid core of blackberry, plum, kitchen spices and vanilla pod, all in total harmony. Screw cap. 13.5% alc. **Rating** 95 **To** 2032 $75 JP

🍷🍷🍷🍷 **Barrawatta Great Western Shiraz 2017** **Rating** 92 **To** 2032 $50 JP

Grandeur Wellington

201 Blewitt Springs Road, McLaren Flat, SA 5171 **Region** McLaren Vale
T 0414 188 588 **www**.grandeurwellington.com.au **Open** By appt
Winemaker Tony De Lisio, Peter Nicolaidis **Est.** 2010 **Dozens** 12 000 **Vyds** 15ha
Australian winemaking company with over 20 years experience based in McLaren Vale. Backed by Chinese investors and thus far primarily focused on the Chinese market, they are apparently starting to produce wines for local consumption too. Exports to Hong Kong, Vietnam and China.

🍷🍷🍷🍷 **Gen69 McLaren Vale Shiraz 2018** Despite aesthetic alarm bells, this is polished, richly endowed and extremely well made (albeit, to a formula that feels a little outdated). With that, there is nothing wrong with sinking into an armchair that evokes memories of 90s rock. Crushed blue/blackberries. A swab of licorice and tapenade. A creamy velour of milk chocolate oak and massaged tannins. Nothing overt except for the sheen. Manicured and long. A perfect automaton. Cork. 14.8% alc. **Rating** 93 **To** 2033 $45 NG

Gen62 McLaren Vale Cabernet Sauvignon 2018 Another rich steed in the stable, but without the sheen and impeccable manicure of the shiraz. The 18 months in French and American wood is drying out the finish. The fruit is not getting any fresher. Red/blackcurrant, olive and graphite, giving way to a verdant astringency marked by bell pepper, tomato bush and sage. A solid wine best drunk on the earlier side. Cork. 14.5% alc. **Rating** 90 **To** 2025 $35 NG

🍷🍷🍷🍷 Cellar Reserve McLaren Vale Shiraz 2018 Rating 89 To 2028 $90 NG
Cellar Reserve McLaren Vale Cabernet Sauvignon 2018 Rating 88
To 2030 $90 NG

Granite Hills ★★★★★

1481 Burke and Wills Track, Baynton, Vic 3444 **Region** Macedon Ranges
T (03) 5423 7273 **www**.granitehills.com.au **Open** 7 days 11–5
Winemaker Llew Knight, Rowen Anstis **Est.** 1970 **Dozens** 5000 **Vyds** 11.5ha
Granite Hills is one of the enduring classics, having pioneered the successful growing of
riesling and shiraz in an uncompromisingly cool climate. The vineyard includes riesling,
chardonnay, shiraz, cabernet sauvignon, cabernet franc, merlot and pinot noir (the last also
used in its sparkling wine). The Rieslings age superbly, and the Shiraz was the forerunner of
the cool-climate school in Australia. Exports to Japan and China.

🍷🍷🍷🍷🍷 Knight Macedon Ranges Riesling 2020 This charms with its citrus accents
from grapefruit, lemon and tangerine. It has a depth across the palate, juicy, natural
acidity and a purity throughout. A lovely wine now and for quite some time to
come. Screw cap. 12.5% alc. **Rating** 95 To 2032 $27 JF ✪
Tor Macedon Ranges Riesling 2018 Matured for 2 years in bottle before
release. There is a depth of flavour and intensity to Tor. It's exceptionally youthful
but it has touches of baked ricotta, drizzled with lemon sauce, lime zest and
grapefruit pith. The acidity is superfine and the finish is long and satisfying. Screw
cap. 12.5% alc. **Rating** 95 To 2028 $50 JF
Knight Macedon Ranges Grüner Veltliner 2020 This is one very smart
grüner. White pepper, lemon rind, juicy grapefruit and poached pears with
powdered ginger. It has plenty of energy and fine natural acidity zipping across
the palate. Talk about a thirst-quencher. Screw cap. 13% alc. **Rating** 95 To 2024
$27 JF ✪

🍷🍷🍷🍷♀ The Gordon Macedon Ranges 2014 Rating 92 To 2026 $32 JF
Knight Macedon Ranges Shiraz 2017 Rating 91 To 2032 $37 JF
Knight Macedon Ranges Chardonnay 2018 Rating 90 To 2025 $32 JF

Grant Burge ★★★★★

279 Krondorf Road, Barossa Valley, SA 5352 **Region** Barossa Valley
T (08) 8563 7675 **www**.grantburgewines.com.au **Open** 7 days 10–5
Winemaker Craig Stansborough **Est.** 1988 **Dozens** 400000
Grant and Helen Burge established the eponymous Grant Burge business in 1988. It grew
into one of the largest family-owned wine businesses in the valley. In February 2015, Accolade
Wines announced it had acquired the Grant Burge brand and the historic Krondorf Winery.
The 356ha of vineyards remain in family ownership and will continue to supply premium
grapes to the Accolade-owned business. Exports to all major markets.

🍷🍷🍷🍷🍷 Corryton Park Barossa Cabernet Sauvignon 2018 I have long admired
Corryton Park cabernet, less showy and flamboyant than is typical for these parts,
and ultimately more sophisticated. It leads out closed and contemplative, with
a core of crunchy blackcurrant fruit rising on the mid palate and holding with
impressive line and drive. Eloquent, bright acidity and brilliant fine-grained tannins
never drop their gaze long into the finish. A cellaring special. Screw cap. 14.6% alc.
Rating 96 To 2043 $48 TS ✪
Nebu Barossa Cabernet Shiraz 2018 One of the most exciting modern
additions to the extensive Grant Burge portfolio, a cracking rendition that
epitomises the integrity and endurance of the great Australian blend in the
Barossa. Impenetrable in depth and vibrant in hue, contrasting blackcurrant and
blackberry fruit density and a crunch of vibrant energy. Super-fine, commanding
tannins, great fruit drive and high-class French oak make for impressive potential.
Screw cap. 14.5% alc. **Rating** 96 To 2048 $100 TS

Abednego Barossa GSM 2018 Textbook Barossa GSM, intricately and seamlessly assembled by Craig Stansborough, without a detail out of place. Red and dark berry fruits capture this warm season with definition and verve, thanks to a confident spine of vibrant, tangy acidity. Layers of spice are backed eloquently by large- and small-format dark chocolate oak and superfine tannins. Masterfully engineered for the long haul. Screw cap. 14.5% alc. **Rating** 95 **To** 2038 $100 TS

The Holy Trinity Barossa 2018 This aptly named Barossa GSM has ascended magnificently in recent vintages, attaining new heights of spice, detail and intrigue. Exotic and fragrant, it presumably enjoys all the lift and jubilance of whole-bunch inclusion, stimulating crunchy red berry fruits and rhubarb. A long finish embodies poise and life, riding rails of firm, fine tannins and vibrant acid line. A rare GSM for the cellar. Screw cap. 14.5% alc. **Rating** 95 **To** 2038 $48 TS

Balthasar Eden Valley Shiraz 2018 A vibrant purple hue heralds a deep core of compact, crunchy blackberry fruit. Eden Valley spice wafts through a long finish, impeccably directed by finely crafted tannins, backed sensitively by high-cocoa dark chocolate oak. Consummately engineered for the cellar. Screw cap. 14.5% alc. **Rating** 94 **To** 2038 $48 TS

Filsell Old Vine Barossa Shiraz 2018 The hierarchy of shiraz is well established at Grant Burge, and ascending the tree delivers more density of colour, more depth of black fruits and more impacting oak presence. Quintessential Barossa, Filsell unites fruit power with licorice, milk and dark chocolate oak and inimitable nuances of Barossa mettwurst. Medium-grained tannin confidence lays out a long finish that will appreciate medium-term cellaring to integrate. Screw cap. 14.5% alc. **Rating** 94 **To** 2032 $48 TS

🍷🍷🍷🍷🍷 **Miamba Barossa Shiraz 2018 Rating** 93 **To** 2026 $27 TS ✪
Little Kings Barossa GSM 2018 Rating 92 **To** 2025 $27 TS
Cameron Vale Barossa Cabernet Sauvignon 2018 Rating 92 **To** 2033 $27 TS

Grape Farm Winery   ★★★☆

107 McAdams Lane, Moonambel, Vic 3478 **Region** Pyrenees
T (03) 5467 2145 **www**.grapefarmwinery.com.au **Open** Fri–Sun 11–5
Winemaker Heath Stevenson **Est.** 1976 **Dozens** 1000 **Vyds** 3.6ha
Grape Farm Winery was established back in 1976 when the vineyard was acquired by chef Heath and mental health professional Karina Stevenson. They have learnt on the job, carrying all of the vineyard work, Heath the self-taught winemaker. The wines are estate-grown; the low-yielding vineyard managed organically.

🍷🍷🍷🍷🍷 **Bungawa Old Vines Reserve Pyrenees Shiraz 2019** Once tasted, it is evident that a lot of thought has gone into this wine's making. Deep in purple colour, the odd trace of bay leaf, bush mint joins with black cherry, spice and earth aromas. Impressive melding of all of the individual parts, the oak is particularly smart and underplayed, with a light savoury twist to close. Screw cap. 13.5% alc. **Rating** 92 **To** 2029 $55 JP

Pyrenees Merlot 2018 A small splash of 10% cabernet sauvignon was added to this the winery's first (almost) standalone merlot. What a little charmer, well deserving of its new status. Brings forth the grape's plushness and beauty of purity of fruit with a light dusting of spice and oak. Screw cap. 13% alc. **Rating** 92 **To** 2026 $28 JP

Mineshaft Pyrenees 2018 35/25/25/15% cabernet sauvignon/cabernet franc/merlot/shiraz. This well-priced cabernet blend nicely captures the regional qualities of the grapes with stirring Aussie bush, bay leaf aromas intermingling with dark, spiced blackberry, licorice and chocolate. Well balanced with fine-grained tannins and terrific length. Hits the spot. Screw cap. 13.5% alc. **Rating** 91 **To** 2028 $30 JP

🍷🍷🍷🍷 **Pyrenees Shiraz 2018 Rating** 89 **To** 2028 $30 JP
Pyrenees Cabernet Sauvignon 2018 Rating 88 **To** 2025 $30 JP

Graphite Road ★★★★

1163 Graphite Road, Manjimup, WA 6258 **Region** Manjimup
T 0408 914 836 **www**.graphiteroad.com.au **Open** By appt
Winemaker Kim Horton **Est.** 2017 **Dozens** 4250 **Vyds** 9ha
Graphite Road was founded by Bente and Vic Peos, their 3 daughters being the 4th generation of the family involved in the wine industry. From a young age they worked in the vineyard with their parents and share a combined love for wine and food. Graphite Road is the name of the thoroughfare in South Western Australia leading to the township of Manjimup. The road winds through state forests filled with towering Karri trees, crossing the Gairdner River and passing the historic 'One Tree Bridge' on the journey through the scenic natural landscape. Exports to China.

�♀ **Cross Sections Sauvignon Blanc 2020** Straw green aromas of passionfruit, Granny Smith and kiwi mesh on the palate with bright acidity. Refreshing and lifted. Lovely. Screw cap. 13.3% alc. **Rating** 91 **To** 2023 $22 EL ✪
Walker & Wilde Manjimup Chardonnay 2020 Modern, supple, fresh and loaded with stone fruit, brine and gentle minerality. Relatively uncomplicated, vibrant chardonnay with good length of flavour. Screw cap. 13.6% alc. **Rating** 91 **To** 2027 $32 EL

Green Door Wines ★★★★

1112 Henty Road, Henty, WA 6236 **Region** Geographe
T 0439 511 652 **www**.greendoorwines.com.au **Open** Thurs–Sun 11–4.30
Winemaker Ashley Keeffe, Vanessa Carson **Est.** 2007 **Dozens** 1200 **Vyds** 4ha
Ashley and Kathryn Keeffe purchased what was then a rundown vineyard in '06. With a combination of new and pre-existing vines, the vineyard includes fiano, mourvèdre, grenache, verdelho, tempranillo and shiraz. The wines are made in a small onsite winery using a range of winemaking methods, including the use of amphora pots.

♀♀♀♀♀ **Amphora Geographe Tempranillo 2019** Characters of beeswax, Geraldton wax florals, Mariposa plum and red licorice all rise to the fore here. This is a pleasure to drink, as previous vintages have been: layered and complex, fine tannins wrap a core of pure fruit, which lingers through the long finish. Screw cap. 14% alc. **Rating** 95 **To** 2030 $35 EL ✪
Amphora Reserva Geographe Tempranillo 2019 The '18 vintage was exceptional, and as such the fruit here has real concentration and density. The oak is evident and perhaps needs a further year to sink into that plush fruit, but all the layers, angles and elements are present and in place. This is a superstar. Screw cap. 14% alc. **Rating** 94 **To** 2035 $45 EL

♀♀♀♀♀ **Geographe Fiano 2020** **Rating** 93 **To** 2023 $28 EL
Geographe Chardonnay 2019 **Rating** 92 **To** 2027 $35 EL
Spanish Steps Geographe GSM 2019 **Rating** 92 **To** 2025 $25 EL ✪
El Toro Geographe Tempranillo 2019 **Rating** 92 **To** 2027 $25 EL ✪
Amphora Geographe Monastrell 2019 **Rating** 92 **To** 2027 $35 EL
Amphora Geographe Garnacha 2019 **Rating** 91 **To** 2028 $35 EL

 Greenhill ★★★★

1016 Greenhill Road, Summertown, SA 5141 **Region** Adelaide Hills
T (08) 8390 1615 **www**.greenhillwines.com.au **Open** Fri–Sun 10–5 or by appt
Winemaker Paul Henschke **Est.** 2010 **Dozens** 800 **Vyds** 1.5ha
Situated on a former strawberry farm, Greenhill Wines is a winery, vineyard, cellar door and cafe run by Drs Paul and Penny Henschke. Paul is a former AWRI scientist and Affiliate Professor of the University of Adelaide, Penny is a former wheat research scientist. Set in a restored 1880s settlers cottage on a ridge overlooking their estate vines with Piccadilly Valley, Mt Bonython and the Mt George range in the distance, Paul creates a range of estate pinot-based sparkling wines as well as estate and Piccadilly Valley-sourced white and red table wines.

Being a wine microbiologist, Paul likes to exploit yeast in creative ways to enrich flavour complexity. Penny produces a range of Mediterranean foods to complement the wine tasting experience. Direct sales only. (TL)

♟♟♟♟♟ Blanc de Noir Brut 2017 Pinot meunier. From the tiny Summertown estate of Drs Paul and Penny Henschke, with a minimum 18 months on lees and disgorged on demand. This is the epitome of purity, the faintest of apple/aldehyde, all the character and complexity of traditional method sparkling, with lively sherbet brightness on the palate and excellent fine talc mouthfeel. A delicate touch yielding a lovely aperitif wine. Diam. 12% alc. **Rating** 94 $29 TL✪
Brut Rosé 2013 Lightly blushed pinot noir that's spent 6.5 years on lees, delicately expressed and with some earthy, savoury notes now showing in the beginning, but coming to life in the sipping; its bright red fruit flavours irrepressible. Diam. 12% alc. **Rating** 94 $29 TL✪

Greenock Creek Wines   ★★★★

450 Seppeltsfield Road, Marananga, SA 5355 **Region** Barossa Valley
T (08) 8563 2898 **www.**greenockcreekwines.com.au **Open** 7 days 11–5
Winemaker Alex Peel, Peter Atyeo **Est.** 1984 **Dozens** 4000 **Vyds** 22ha
Founders Michael and Annabelle Waugh deliberately accumulated a series of old dryland, low-yielding Barossa vineyards back in the '70s, aiming to produce wines of unusual depth of flavour and character. They succeeded handsomely in this aim, achieving icon status and stratospheric prices in the US, making the opinions of Australian scribes irrelevant. The Waughs retired in 2018 and the business was purchased by a group headed by Sydney-based Jimmy Chen. Peter Atyeo stayed on as assistant winemaker and manager, with Alex Peel (formerly Ross Estate and Yaldara) stepping in as winemaker. Older vineyards were remediated, new sites brought into the fold, and winemaking facilities updated. The wines have been reviewed by the *Companion* for the first time this year. Exports to Asia and the EU.

♟♟♟♟♟ Roennfeldt Road Barossa Valley Cabernet Sauvignon 2016 The roast cashew nut and dark chocolate of new French oak is the focus right now, with a full 3 years in barrel bringing its dry, savoury influence and the beginnings of leathery complexity. Tangy, crunchy red/black berries of impressive concentration arise in time. Fine fruit and oak tannins and powdery acidity entangle on a conclusion of grand persistence. It's charged with all it needs to burst through that brittle oak shell, with sufficient patience. Cork. 14% alc. **Rating** 94 **To** 2041 $250 TS
Barossa Valley Mataro 2020 The savoury, dried sage signature of mataro is well married to the satsuma plums and blackberries of ripe Seppeltsfield, eloquently backed by fine-grained American oak. A long finish of powder-fine tannin and bright acidity carries lingering rhubarb freshness that completely trumps its alcohol. Skilfully composed and great value. Cork. 15% alc. **Rating** 94 **To** 2026 $30 TS✪

♟♟♟♟♟ Seven Acre Barossa Valley Shiraz 2018 Rating 93 **To** 2026 $55 TS
Alices Barossa Valley Shiraz 2019 Rating 90 **To** 2024 $40 TS

Greenstone Vineyards   ★★★★☆

179 Glenview Road, Yarra Glen, Vic 3775 **Region** Yarra Valley/Heathcote
T (03) 9730 1022 **www.**greenstonevineyards.com.au **Open** Thurs–Mon 10–5
Winemaker Han Tao Lau, Sam Atherton, David Li **Est.** 2003 **Dozens** 20000 **Vyds** 39.2ha
In January 2015 the former Sticks Winery (originally Yarra Ridge, established in 1982) was purchased by a group of investors, along with the Greenstone brand and vineyard in Heathcote. The Greenstone vineyard, just north of the Heathcote township at Colbinabbin at the base of the Camel Range, derives its names from the soils on which the 20ha of vines are planted (the lion's share to 17ha of shiraz). The Yarra Valley vineyard is planted mainly to chardonnay (11.7ha) and also includes 4.1ha of pinot noir and smaller plantings of sauvignon blanc, viognier, cabernet sauvignon and petit verdot. Exports to China.

Estate Series Yarra Valley Pinot Noir 2019 An immediately appealing wine starting with wide-ranging aromas: cherries, wood spice, florals, wild herbs and charry oak. It's lighter framed, quite tangy and a little tart which adds to its refreshment. Screw cap. 13.5% alc. **Rating** 92 **To** 2027 $44 JF
Heathcote Sangiovese 2017 Sangiovese co-fermented with 8.5% colorino and 1.5% shiraz, which gets the blood pumping with its energy and brio. Boasts Italian deli aromas of cured meats, dried herbs, almond and black cherries. Shies away from the sweet-fruited in favour of a dry, savoury and dusty sangiovese with mild tannin grip. Close your eyes, a touch of Italy. Screw cap. 15% alc. **Rating** 92 **To** 2024 $34 JP
Estate Series Yarra Valley Chardonnay 2019 While it has a trickle of acidity throughout, this is a softish and easy-to-like wine. Some stone fruit and lemony flavours with just a smidge of texture. Fresh and lively on the finish. Screw cap. 12.5% alc. **Rating** 90 **To** 2025 $45 JF

 Gusto Heathcote Shiraz 2019 Rating 89 **To** 2025 $24 JP
Estate Series Heathcote Shiraz 2018 Rating 89 **To** 2024 $34 JP

GREENWAY Wines ★★★★

350 Wollombi Road, Broke, NSW 2330 **Region** Hunter Valley
T 0418 164 382 **www**.greenwaywines.com.au **Open** W'ends 10–4.30 or by appt (closed Jan)
Winemaker Michael McManus, Daniel Binet **Est.** 2009 **Dozens** 550 **Vyds** 6.5ha
GREENWAY Wines is a small family-owned and operated business. The sustainably managed vineyard is nestled against Wollombi Brook near Broke. The single-vineyard estate wines, only produced in the best vintages, are available from the cellar door and online.

 Favoloso Fiano 2019 Fiano, among the world's greatest white grapes, blossoming in the Hunter. Lanolin, apricot pith, bitter almond and pistachio biscotti scents. Mid weighted and viscous, with a thread of saline freshness galvanising the whole. Punchy drinking. Screw cap. 12.5% alc. **Rating** 91 **To** 2024 $26 NG

Greg Cooley Wines ★★★★★

Lot 1 Main North Road, Clare, SA 5453 **Region** Clare Valley
T (08) 8843 4284 **www**.gregcooleywines.com.au **Open** 7 days 11–4
Winemaker Greg Cooley **Est.** 2002 **Dozens** 3000
Greg Cooley explains, 'All my wines are named after people who have been of influence to me in my 45 years and their influence is as varied as the wine styles – from pizza shop owners, to my greyhound's vet and South Australian author Monica McInerney.' I (James) have to confess that I am taken by Greg's path to glory, because my move through law to wine was punctuated by the part-ownership of 2 greyhounds that always wanted to run in the opposite direction from the rest of the field.

Grey Sands ★★★☆

6 Kerrisons Road, Glengarry, Tas 7275 **Region** Northern Tasmania
T (03) 6396 1167 **www**.greysands.com.au **Open** By appt
Winemaker Penny Jones, Bob Richter **Est.** 1989 **Dozens** 1000 **Vyds** 3.5ha
Bob and Rita Richter began the establishment of Grey Sands in 1989, slowly increasing the plantings to the present total. The ultra-high density of 8900 vines/ha reflects the experience gained by the Richters during a 3-year stay in England, when they visited many vineyards across Europe, as well as Bob's graduate diploma from Roseworthy College. Plantings include pinot noir, merlot, pinot gris and malbec. Exports to the UK.

Glengarry Malbec 2015 Sporting an impressive medium purple hue at almost 6 years of age, this is an enduring take on malbec. Firm, fine tannins and bright acidity unite in equal measure to define a grand future. Blackberry and blackcurrant fruit is accented by a compelling suggestion of spicy, sweet leather. Diam. 12.5% alc. **Rating** 93 **To** 2045 $45 TS

ΥΥΥΥ **Glengarry Tasmania Merlot 2010** **Rating** 89 **To** 2021 $55 TS
The Mattock Glengarry Tasmania 2015 **Rating** 89 **To** 2032 $45 TS

Groom ★★★★☆

28 Langmeil Road, Tanunda, SA 5352 (postal) **Region** Barossa Valley
T (08) 8563 1101 **www**.groomwines.com
Winemaker Daryl Groom, Lisa Groom, Jeanette Marschall **Est.** 1997 **Dozens** 2000
Vyds 27.8ha
The full name of the business is Marschall Groom Cellars, a venture owned by David and Jeanette Marschall and their 6 children, and Daryl and Lisa Groom and their 4 children. Daryl was a highly regarded winemaker at Penfolds before he moved to Geyser Peak in California. Years of discussion between the families resulted in the purchase of a 35ha block of bare land adjacent to Penfolds' 130yo Kalimna Vineyard. Shiraz was planted in 1997, giving its first vintage in '99. The next acquisition was an 8ha vineyard at Lenswood in the Adelaide Hills, planted to sauvignon blanc. In 2000, 3.2ha of zinfandel was planted on the Kalimna Bush Block. Exports to the US.

ΥΥΥΥΥ **Barossa Valley Shiraz 2019** All the might and majesty of the great Kalimna district. Bright purple hue. A compact core of blue fruits of all kinds is brightened by a refreshing acid line and supported by a nicely constructed frame of fine tannins, serving to give poise and precision to a long finish. Long-term potential. Cork. 14.5% alc. **Rating** 95 **To** 2034 $50 TS
Bush Block Barossa Valley Zinfandel 2019 Spicy dark fruitcake and fruit-mince spice proclaim zin. Juicy blackberries and black cherries are well set off by nicely composed acidity and fine-ground tannins; dark chocolate oak an eloquent afterthought. Well played. Cork. 14.5% alc. **Rating** 94 **To** 2039 $30 TS ✪

Grosset ★★★★★

King Street, Auburn, SA 5451 **Region** Clare Valley
T 1800 088 223 **www**.grosset.com.au **Open** 10–5 Wed–Sun (Spring)
Winemaker Jeffrey Grosset, Brent Treloar **Est.** 1981 **Dozens** 11 000 **Vyds** 21ha
Jeffrey Grosset wears the unchallenged mantle of Australia's foremost riesling maker. Grosset's pre-eminence is recognised both domestically and internationally; however, he merits equal recognition for the other wines in his portfolio: Semillon Sauvignon Blanc from Clare Valley/ Adelaide Hills, Chardonnay and Pinot Noir from the Adelaide Hills and Gaia, a Bordeaux blend from the Clare Valley. These are all benchmarks. His quietly spoken manner conceals a steely will. Exports to all major markets. Best Value Winery in the *Wine Companion 2018*. Exports to all major markets.

ΥΥΥΥΥ **G110 Clare Valley Riesling 2019** A new wine and what's it like? Outrageously good. The palate sets it apart as does its savouriness – it's not a fruity clone. It is spicy, with a beeswax note and layered. It has length and line with some phenolic grip, the acidity driving it. It's long, defined and yes, it is an exceptional wine. Screw cap. 12.8% alc. **Rating** 97 **To** 2034 $105 JF ✪

ΥΥΥΥΥ **Polish Hill Clare Valley Riesling 2020** This wine retains the energy and drive of Polish Hill, yet its fruit concentration and ripeness has softened out any hard edges. It's beautifully fragrant, subtle even, and the palate is long and pure with pith-like texture and excellent length. Lovely drink and ready now. Screw cap. 12.9% alc. **Rating** 96 **To** 2030 $65 JF ✪
Alea Clare Valley Riesling 2020 Sometimes, well, often, an off-dry riesling hits the spot. It can be refreshing and lively, yet textural and fulfilling, as this is with its ginger cream and limes, candied citrus and cinnamon spice. A tickle of sweetness rounds out the palate and adds depth, yet the acidity is still very much leading the show. Screw cap. 12.3% alc. **Rating** 95 **To** 2030 $42 JF

Piccadilly Chardonnay 2019 This is smokin'. It has moreish sulphides at play, but it's the bringing together and syncing of all its elements that makes this spot-on. White nectarines, citrus, creamed honey and very spicy, all offset by mouth-watering acidity. It's layered, concentrated and flatteringly fine. Screw cap. 13.5% alc. **Rating** 95 **To** 2029 $75 JF

Gaia Clare Valley 2018 Clare Valley cabernet has its own DNA and once you're hooked, there's no going back. Here's why: mulberries dipped in mint dark chocolate, goji berries, refreshing yet deep and earthy. Currants, sweet and sour cherries, sandy tannins with a slight green edge to the finish. There's a lot going on here. This is still finding its way but it's certainly not lost. Screw cap. 13.7% alc. **Rating** 95 **To** 2035 $90 JF

ΨΨΨΨΫ **Springvale Clare Valley Riesling 2020 Rating** 93 **To** 2029 $47 JF
Apiana Clare Valley Fiano 2020 Rating 93 **To** 2025 $47 JF
Piccadilly Valley Pinot Noir 2019 Rating 93 **To** 2029 $82 JF
Nereus Clare Valley 2018 Rating 90 **To** 2026 $55 JF

Ground to Cloud   ★★★★★

3517 Caves Road, Wilyabrup, WA 6280 **Region** Margaret River
T (08) 9755 6500 **www.**cavesroadcollective.com.au **Open** 7 days 11–5
Winemaker Contract **Est.** 2016
Ground to Cloud is part of the Caves Road Collective, also home to Black Brewing Co and Dune Distilling. The wines are made from the estate vineyard at Wilyabrup and vineyards throughout Margaret River. Visitors can taste wine, craft beer and boutique gin on the deck overlooking the lake, weddings and functions held in the restaurant and gardens.

Grounded Cru   ★★★★☆

49 Ingoldby Road, McLaren Flat, SA 5052 **Region** McLaren Vale
T 0438897738 **www.**groundedcru.com.au **Open** By appt
Winemaker Geoff Thompson, Matt Jackman **Est.** 2015 **Dozens** 18 000
Established as a brand in 2015 with an inaugural release of wines in 2017, Grounded Cru draws fruit from high-quality vineyards in McLaren Vale, Langhorne Creek and the Adelaide Hills, regions that maker Geoff Thompson believes 'talk to each other' due to a complementary patina of mesoclimates, soil types, rainfall, altitude and varying degrees of maritime influence. Thompson was formerly chief winemaker at McPherson Wines in Nagambie. Conversely, his approach at Grounded Cru is one that seeks textural intrigue over obvious fruit, with European styling melded to Australian generosity. The Mediterranean varieties on offer are superlative, boasting poise and savoury tannins laden with briar. Exports to the UK and China. (NG)

ΨΨΨΨΨ **Inc McLaren Vale Cabernet Sauvignon 2018** I have long said how expressive cabernet from the Vale can be. Despite the heat the varietal postcode is undeniable: the maritime salinity, attractive. This is no exception. Svelte and compact, yet copious all at once. Sumptuous aromas of crushed blackcurrant, mint, clove, bay leaf, sage and olive. The tannins keep everything in check and running with a smooth precision. Depth, length, finesse and oomph. A very fine wine. Screw cap. 14.2% alc. **Rating** 95 **To** 2032 $45 NG

Cru McLaren Vale Grenache 2018 A gentle ruby hue, with orange zest, cherry bon-bon and molten strawberry aromas. Fibrous whole-bunch tannins, beautifully detailed, gently scrub the palate of any excess sweetness. This has a pinosity to it, with a thrust of extract and herbal freshness imparting balance and crunchy length. This address is marked by a consistent and indelible style of fine tannin management, complexity and an easygoing deliciousness. Screw cap. 14.1% alc. **Rating** 94 **To** 2024 $28 NG ❂

ΨΨΨΨΫ **Cru McLaren Vale Shiraz 2019 Rating** 93 **To** 2024 $45 NG
Inc McLaren Vale Shiraz 2018 Rating 93 **To** 2030 $50 NG

Cru McLaren Vale Langhorne Creek Cabernet Sauvignon Shiraz Malbec
2018 Rating 92 To 2028 $28 NG
Cru Adelaide Hills Pinot Gris 2020 Rating 91 To 2023 $25 TL
Cru McLaren Vale GSM 2019 Rating 91 To 2024 $28 NG

Grove Estate Wines   ★★★★

4100 Murringo Road, Young, NSW 2594 **Region** Hilltops
T (02) 6382 6999 **www**.groveestate.com.au **Open** 7 days 9.30–4.30
Winemaker Brian Mullany, Tim Kirk, Bryan Martin **Est.** 1989 **Dozens** 4000
Vyds 100ha

Grove Estate Vineyard was re-established in 1989 by Brian and Suellen Mullany on the site where grapes were first planted in Lambing Flat (Young) in 1861 by Croatian settlers who brought vine cuttings with them from Dalmatia. One of the original pickers' huts has been refurbished as the cellar door. Further plantings in '98 were made on their Bit O' Heaven Vineyard, the 2 sites with vastly different soils. The wines are made at Clonakilla by Tim Kirk and Bryan Martin. Exports to China.

🍷🍷🍷🍷🍷 Sommita Hilltops Nebbiolo 2019 A compelling wine that flaunts its varietal
strengths, while remaining true to its connection to land. This is Australian
nebbiolo or, rather, Hilltops nebbiolo. Wafts of spiced cherries, maraschino, too,
floral, a touch of boot polish and dried herbs. The clincher is the tannins. They
feel like raw silk, yet have grip across the medium-bodied palate. With acidity on
the finish, this comes to a resounding conclusion. Screw cap. 14% alc. **Rating** 95
To 2029 $80 JF

🍷🍷🍷🍷🍷 The Italian Hilltops Nebbiolo Sangiovese Barbera Montepulciano Fiano
2019 Rating 90 To 2023 $28 JF

Gumpara Wines   ★★★★

410 Stockwell Road, Light Pass, SA 5355 **Region** Barossa Valley
T 0419 624 559 **www**.gumparawines.net.au **Open** By appt
Winemaker Mark Mader **Est.** 1999 **Dozens** 1000 **Vyds** 21.53ha

In 1856 the Mader family left Silesia to settle in SA, acquiring a 25ha property at Light Pass. Over the generations, farming and fruit growing gave way to 100% grapegrowing; 6 generations later, in 2000, Mark Mader produced the first wine under the Gumpara label. After success with shiraz, Mark branched out into semillon made from a small parcel of almost 90yo estate vines. The portfolio may be small but it's certainly diverse, also with Vermentino, Grenache and a range of fortified wines. The name Gumpara comes from the words 'gum' reflecting the large red gumtrees on the property and 'para', the local Aboriginal word for river. Exports to the US and China.

Gundog Estate   ★★★★★

101 McDonalds Road, Pokolbin, NSW 2320 **Region** Hunter Valley/Canberra District
T (02) 4998 6873 **www**.gundogestate.com.au **Open** 7 days 10–5
Winemaker Matthew Burton **Est.** 2006 **Dozens** 7000 **Vyds** 5ha

Matt Burton makes 4 different Hunter Semillons, and Shiraz from the Hunter Valley, Murrumbateman and Hilltops. The cellar door is located in the historic Pokolbin schoolhouse, next to the old Rosemount/Hungerford Hill building on McDonalds Road. The Burton McMahon wines are a collaboration between Matt Burton and Dylan McMahon of Seville Estate, and focus on the Yarra Valley. In 2016 Gundog opened a second cellar door at 42 Cork Street, Gundaroo (Thurs–Sun 10–5). Exports to the UK.

🍷🍷🍷🍷🍷 Indomitus Rutilus Canberra District Shiraz 2018 Reminiscent of an Etna
red, or lighter southern Rhône. Scant resemblance to shiraz as I know it. The
point? A swaggering Australian iteration of place and style: volcanic smoky/rocky/
mineral freshness driving dark cherry, nori, root spice, a potpourri of Indian spice
and floral scents long and firm. The tannins win me over: expansive, succulent

and saliva-sapping. Thrust of structure and parry of fruit, all Murrumbateman.
A glimpse of the future. Excellent wine. Screw cap. 14.5% alc. **Rating** 96 **To** 2026
$40 NG ✪

Burton McMahon D'Aloisio's Vineyard Yarra Valley Chardonnay 2020
Chalky texture and racy acidity combine to form the backbone to this terrific
wine. It's super-savoury and flinty, with quinine and enough citrus flavours to
satisfy. The palate is tightly wound and time will loosen it up. For now, enjoy its
length and complexity. Screw cap. 12.5% alc. **Rating** 95 **To** 2030 $40 JF

Burton McMahon George's Vineyard Yarra Valley Pinot Noir 2020 A
plusher wine compared with its Syme sibling, and more approachable in this very
youthful stage. A happy combo of sweet, dark fruit, wood smoke, and autumnal
aromas of damp leaves and twigs. Fuller bodied, with shapely tannins and lip-
smacking acidity. Screw cap. 13.5% alc. **Rating** 95 **To** 2030 $40 JF

Burton McMahon Syme on Yarra Vineyard Pinot Noir 2020 There's
a brightness and intensity to the fruit, yet there's also an elegance. Led by red
cherries, blood orange and rind doused in exotic spices. Deceptive, as it feels light
on its feet, but the tannins are svelte, the acidity lively and the finish long. Screw
cap. 13.5% alc. **Rating** 95 **To** 2032 $40 JF

Hunter's Hunter Valley Shiraz 2019 The aromas are classic, reminding me
of my childhood when the moniker 'Hunter River Burgundy' was the misused
norm: cherry, terracotta and a fecund note of wet earth, connoting optimism.
Why? Because this sort of savoury medium-bodied wine, curbed by a skirt of
loamy tannins and a whiff of oak, is so damn drinkable. Poise and length, the
calling cards. Screw cap. 13% alc. **Rating** 95 **To** 2034 $40 NG

Rare Game Hunter Valley Shiraz 2019 An homage to the classic 'Hunter
Burgundy' style pulled off with aplomb. Mid ruby, medium bodied at best. Sappy
and crunchy. Lithe, slender suede-like tannins service a flow of red cherry, plum,
anise, baking spice and lilac. I am tasting this on a 40°C day and it feels refreshing.
Screw cap. 12.9% alc. **Rating** 95 **To** 2032 $70 NG

Marksman's Canberra District Shiraz 2019 Gundog's top Canberra
expression. Christmas spice, licorice straps, salumi, dark cherry, pepper and
an Indian spice sachet of clove and cardamom. A fine thrust of flavour and a
tight weave of chewy tannin, drawn across a spool of bright acidity. Ebbs and
flows. Complexity defined by contrasts of light and shade. Screw cap. 13.5% alc.
Rating 94 **To** 2028 $70 NG

♟♟♟♟♟ **Burton McMahon George's Vineyard Yarra Valley Chardonnay 2019**
Rating 93 **To** 2030 $40 NG
Burton McMahon George's Vineyard Yarra Valley Pinot Noir 2019
Rating 93 **To** 2028 $40 NG
Smoking Barrel Red 2019 Rating 93 **To** 2026 $35 NG
Burton McMahon George's Vineyard Yarra Valley Chardonnay 2020
Rating 92 **To** 2029 $40 JF
Burton McMahon D'Aloisio's Vineyard Yarra Valley Chardonnay 2019
Rating 92 **To** 2028 $40 NG
Indomitus Rosa Hilltops 2019 Rating 92 **To** 2022 $40 NG
Indomitus Albus Hunter Valley Semillon 2018 Rating 91 **To** 2023 $40 NG
Burton McMahon Syme on Yarra Vineyard Pinot Noir 2019 Rating 91
To 2026 $40 NG
Canberra District Shiraz 2019 Rating 91 **To** 2026 $40 NG
Yarra Valley Riesling 2020 Rating 90 **To** 2028 $35 NG

Guthrie Wines   ★★★★

661 Torrens Valley Road, Gumeracha, SA 5253 **Region** Adelaide Hills
T 0413 332 083 **www.**guthriewines.com.au **Open** By appt
Winemaker Hugh Guthrie **Est.** 2012 **Dozens** 1500

Growing up on his family's farm in the Adelaide Hills, Hugh Guthrie developed an early
interest in the wines and vineyards of the region, completing a master of oenology at the

University of Adelaide before working in wineries around Australia and abroad. Most recently he was a winemaker at The Lane Vineyard, winner of many awards for its wines. Wife Sarah looks after the business side of Guthrie, in addition to her day job as an anaesthetist. In 2014 Hugh held his breath, jumped, quit his day job, and became full-time winemaker at Guthrie Wines.

ŦŦŦŦŦ **The Zephyr Pinot Meunier 2020** Party upfront here – vibrant aromatics, cherry crush, a seasoning of sumac and thyme for extra tasting fun. A slight char on the palate brings the senses back to earth. Screw cap. 12.5% alc. **Rating** 92 To 2024 $33 TL

ŦŦŦŦ **The Bright Side Riesling 2020 Rating** 89 To 2024 $26 TL

Haan Estate   ★★★★
148 Siegersdorf Road, Tanunda, SA 5352 **Region** Barossa Valley
T (08) 8562 4590 **www.**haanestate.com.au
Winemaker Daniel Graham (Contract) **Est.** 1993 **Dozens** 5000 **Vyds** 16.3ha
Established in 1993 by the Haan Family, Haan Estate is enjoying a revival under the direction of George Zaal and associate Mingrong Meng of Shanghai. The estate vineyard is planted to shiraz (5.3ha), merlot (3.4ha), cabernet sauvignon (3ha), viognier (2.4ha), cabernet franc (1ha) and malbec, petit verdot and semillon (0.4ha each). Oak use is determined by the vintage and the wines are matured for up to 24 months in new and used barrels and puncheons. The oak undoubtedly plays a role in the shaping of the style of the Haan wines, but it is perfectly integrated and the wines have the fruit weight to carry the oak. Exports to Switzerland, Czech Republic, China and other markets.

ŦŦŦŦŦ **Wilhelmus Barossa Valley 2018** The full suite of cabernet's Bordeaux pals unite seamlessly, fusing blackcurrant and cassis with nuances of roast capsicum and sage. A long spell in French oak leaves a strong mark of cedar and roast cashew nuts, laying out a dusty tannin backdrop to a long finish. Oak and alcohol conspire to clip aromatic expression and lift, but it nonetheless holds the persistence required for the cellar. Cork. 15% alc. **Rating** 92 To 2033 $50 TS

ŦŦŦŦ **Prestige Barossa Valley Merlot 2018 Rating** 89 To 2028 $50 TS

Haddow + Dineen   ★★★★
c/- Bruny Island Cheese Co, 1807 Bruny Island Main Road, Great Bay, Tas 7150
Region Tasmania
T 0412 478 841 **www.**haddowanddineen.com.au **Open** 7 days 9–5
Winemaker Jeremy Dineen, Nick Haddow **Est.** 2017 **Dozens** 800 **Vyds** 2.6ha
This is a collaborative winemaking project involving winemaker Jeremy Dineen and cheesemaker Nick Haddow. Jeremy was Chief Winemaker at Josef Chromy from 2005 to 2020, his knowledge and skill self-evident. Nick Haddow is a cheesemaker and author with a string of awards to his name, but is perhaps best known now for his culinary crusading on SBS' *Gourmet Farmer*. Haddow + Dineen sources from a single vineyard at the mouth of the Tamar River on white quartz gravel with 1.6ha of pinot noir and 1ha of pinot gris. Their wines have no additions other than a small amount of SO$_2$, and are not fined or filtered. They say, 'We value maximum consideration over minimum intervention … for every wine there are a thousand choices [that could be made] or simply employ vigilant inaction.' Exports to Japan and Norway.

ŦŦŦŦŦ **Private Universe Pinot Noir 2019** All the flamboyant exoticism, potpourri fragrance and deep anise of whole-bunch fermentation melds intricately with the red berry fruits of the Tamar. Intricately engineered by Jeremy Dineen, the quartz structure of this austere site defines crystalline tannins that carry a long finish. Potential. Screw cap. 13.5% alc. **Rating** 93 To 2034 $48 TS

ŦŦŦŦ **Grain of Truth Pinot Gris 2019 Rating** 89 To 2021 $48 TS

Hahndorf Hill Winery ★★★★★

38 Pain Road, Hahndorf, SA 5245 **Region** Adelaide Hills
T (08) 8388 7512 www.hahndorfhillwinery.com.au **Open** 7 days 10–5
Winemaker Larry Jacobs **Est.** 2002 **Dozens** 6000 **Vyds** 6.5ha

Larry Jacobs and Marc Dobson, both originally from South Africa, purchased Hahndorf Hill Winery in 2002. Before migrating, Larry had given up a career in intensive care medicine in 1988 when he bought an abandoned property in Stellenbosch and established the near-iconic Mulderbosch Wines. It was purchased at the end of '96 and the pair eventually found their way to Australia and Hahndorf Hill. In 2006, their investment in the winery and cellar door was rewarded by induction into the South Australian Tourism Hall of Fame. Now a specialist in Austrian varieties, they have imported 6 clones of grüner veltliner and 2 clones of St Laurent into Australia and also produce blaufränkisch and zweigelt. In '16 the winery was awarded Best Producer under 100 Tonnes at the Adelaide Hills Wine Show, and their wines too have had trophy and medal success. Exports to the UK, Singapore, Japan and China.

🍷🍷🍷🍷🍷 **White Mischief Adelaide Hills Grüner Veltliner 2020** Small bunches started the ball rolling for a wine with an excellent mouthfeel and a faint white-pepper varietal marker. The length and drive on the finish give the wine serious gravitas. Attention to vinification detail is its own reward. Screw cap. 13% alc. **Rating** 95 To 2023 $24 JH ✪ ♥

GRU Adelaide Hills Grüner Veltliner 2020 A well-defined middle path between a restrained fruit expression and more savoury lines. Typical notes of cut celery and white pepper, subtle citron and Granny Smith apple flavours. An immaculately tempered palate with a dash of spice and grapefruit pithy acidity. Pleasing and complex textures deliver a fulfilling wine on many counts. Screw cap. 12.5% alc. **Rating** 95 To 2025 $29 TL ✪

Reserve Adelaide Hills Grüner Veltliner 2019 A fuller-bodied style with great depth and focus: skin contact, wild ferment in barrel, aged on lees for 10 months, with weekly bâtonnage and released with some bottle age. All of this comes to fruition in the glass. A richly satisfying wine with a sense of tropical fruits and a feel of subtle oiliness, deliciously balanced, with a lingering finish. Screw cap. 13% alc. **Rating** 95 To 2025 $50 TL

Adelaide Hills Rosé 2020 39/26/22/13% tempranillo/shiraz/pinot noir and, uniquely, trollinger. Free-run juices co-fermented to a quite zingy style, lively acidity throughout, a bouquet of garden herbs and crunchy white strawberry bits. A top summer buster. Screw cap. 12.5% alc. **Rating** 95 To 2022 $24 TL ✪

Adelaide Hills Pinot Grigio 2020 Fresh and zesty. Floral and field grassy to begin, with terrific pith and chalkiness in the feels. Familiar Pink Lady apple flavours get a little tickle from faint, spicy musk notes. A gentle tang in the mid palate sends this wine on its summery, refreshing way. Screw cap. 12.5% alc. **Rating** 94 To 2022 $25 TL ✪

Adelaide Hills Shiraz 2018 Interesting vineyard characters: quite aromatic, blueberry to dark plum, and fascinating ultra-dark chocolate with suggestions of orange peel in the background. Plenty of structure, reasonably full bodied with a faint amaro bitters in play in the finish, and quite gastronomic in its appeal. Screw cap. 14.25% alc. **Rating** 94 To 2030 $45 TL

🍷🍷🍷🍷🍸 **Green Angel Late Harvest Grüner Veltliner 2019** Rating 93 To 2025 $35 TL

Blueblood Adelaide Hills Blaufrankisch 2018 Rating 92 To 2028 $45 TL

Hamelin Bay ★★★★

McDonald Road, Karridale, WA 6288 **Region** Margaret River
T (08) 9758 6779 www.hbwines.com.au **Open** 7 days 10–5
Winemaker Richard Drake-Brockman **Est.** 1992 **Dozens** 5000 **Vyds** 23.5ha

The Hamelin Bay vineyard was established by the Drake-Brockman family, pioneers of the region. Richard Drake-Brockman's great-grandmother, Grace Bussell, was famous for her courage when, in 1876, aged 16, she rescued survivors of a shipwreck not far from the mouth of the Margaret River. Richard's great-grandfather Frederick, known for his exploration of the Kimberley, read about the feat in Perth's press and rode 300km on horseback to meet her – they married in 1882. Hamelin Bay's vineyard and winery is located within a few kilometres of Karridale, at the intersection of the Brockman and Bussell Highways, which were named in honour of these pioneering families. Exports to the UK, Canada, Malaysia, Singapore and China.

ǐǐǐǐǐ **Five Ashes Vineyard Margaret River Semillon Sauvignon Blanc 2020** Grassy and pure with a herbal (garden mint, coriander, etc) lift on the mid palate. Perhaps a little more restrained than expected, but texture- and flavour-wise, all things in place. Classy. Screw cap. 12.6% alc. **Rating** 91 **To** 2024 $26 EL
Five Ashes Vineyard Margaret River Chardonnay 2019 While this has attractive stone fruit and spice layers, tart acid hints at an earlier picking window (reinforced perhaps by lower alcohol), which could have been drawn out a touch. The acid on the palate makes an enduring stamp on the tongue and is the final flick of the wrist. Screw cap. 12% alc. **Rating** 90 **To** 2027 $33 EL

Hancock & Hancock   ★★★★☆

210 Chalk Hill Road, McLaren Vale, SA 5171 **Region** McLaren Vale
T (02) 9433 3255 **www.**hancockandhancock.com.au
Winemaker Larry Cherubino, Chris Hancock **Est.** 2007 **Vyds** 8.09ha
Industry doyen Chris Hancock and brother John returned to their family roots when they purchased the La Colline Vineyard in 2007 and began Hancock & Hancock. Chris graduated as dux of the oenology degree at Roseworthy Agricultural College in 1963, taking up immediate employment with the Penfold family. In '76 he joined Rosemount Estate, and after the late Bob Oatley sold it to Southcorp, he stayed on with the business in the upper echelon of management. Bob went on to establish what is now Robert Oatley Margaret River, of which Chris is the deputy executive chairman. Unsurprisingly, Hancock & Hancock wines are distributed by Oatley Family Wine Merchants. Exports to the UK, Hong Kong and China.

Handpicked Wines   ★★★★★

50 Kensington Street, Chippendale, NSW 2008 **Region** Various
T (02) 9475 7888 **www.**handpickedwines.com.au **Open** Mon–Fri 11–10, w'ends 10–10
Winemaker Peter Dillon, Jonathon Mattick **Est.** 2001 **Dozens** 100 000 **Vyds** 83ha
Handpicked Wines is a multi-regional business with a flagship vineyard and winery on the Mornington Peninsula and vineyards in the Yarra Valley, Barossa Valley and Tasmania. They also make wines from many of Australia's leading fine-wine regions. Five of Handpicked's vineyards focus on high-quality pinot noir and chardonnay – 2 in Tasmania's Tamar Valley, Capella Vineyard in the Mornington Peninsula and 2 in the Yarra Valley, including Wombat Creek in the Upper Yarra, the highest elevation vineyard in the valley. Director of winemaking Peter Dillon travels extensively to oversee quality throughout the regions; he and assistant winemaker Jonathon Mattick work closely with a team of viticulturists who manage the vineyards. The cellar door in Sydney's CBD brings the wines together in a stylish retail and hospitality venue. Exports to the US, Canada, the Philippines, South Korea, Cambodia, Malaysia, Singapore, Japan, Taiwan and China.

ǐǐǐǐǐ **Collection Tasmania Pinot Noir 2019** From estate vineyards on either side of the Tamar Valley. Very good colour. The Tamar Valley produces pinot noir with more depth and power than any other Tasmanian district. This wine is a high-quality example, with mouth-coating satsuma plum and morello cherry fruit. Will richly repay prolonged cellaring. Screw cap. 13.5% alc. **Rating** 96 **To** 2034 $60 JH ✪
Auburn Road Vineyard Tasmania Pinot Noir 2019 Tassie pinot. It's something else. It has an intensity, power and so much flavour. And yet, rarely feels heavy or overwrought. This is so perfumed, with florals and autumnal fragrance. It's perfectly framed, highlighting cherry and raspberry accents, woodsy spices

and more besides. Full bodied, with plush, textural tannins. It's complex but not complicated, and this is the inaugural release. Nice one. Screw cap. 12.8% alc. **Rating** 96 **To** 2030 $90 JF

Capella Vineyard Mornington Peninsula Pinot Noir 2019 There's great attention to detail in this wine. It's all on show. Beautifully poised, with everything in place. A heady fragrance, a medium- to fuller-bodied palate layered with cooling red fruits, a fleck of baking spices and a mere hint of wood char acting as a spicy seasoning. To seal the deal, a riff of plush yet fine tannins and light acidity. Screw cap. 13.8% alc. **Rating** 96 **To** 2029 $90 JF

Collection Tasmania Chardonnay 2019 Handpicked has ventured to the Tamar Valley, adding another string to their extensive portfolio. Grapefruit and a hint of mandarin flavours are the cornerstones of a tenacious palate that has excellent natural acidity providing guard rails for a long, focused finish and aftertaste. Screw cap. 12.4% alc. **Rating** 95 **To** 2033 $50 JH

Capella Vineyard Mornington Peninsula Chardonnay 2019 A fleshy and ripe-fruited rendition fitting of the vintage. Layers of white peach, lemon curd and nougatine, with cedary, toasty oak. It's a little flinty, a little tangy and a little flirty. There are neat savoury edges. All in all, it's very moreish. Screw cap. 13.2% alc. **Rating** 95 **To** 2028 $70 JF

Collection Yarra Valley Pinot Noir 2019 This kicks off with a neat display of tangy cherry fruits, fresh basil and a hint of menthol. It's even a touch sappy, giving an impression of whole bunches, but none went into the ferment. It's super refreshing, with a succulence that's appealing. The oak is neatly tucked away, the acidity and tannins in unison and the end is all about harmony. Screw cap. 13.4% alc. **Rating** 95 **To** 2029 $60 JF

Highbow Hill Vineyard Yarra Valley Pinot Noir 2019 The colour is so-so, but not so the wine. It's energising, buoyed by refreshing acidity as much as juicy, tangy fruit. Neatly set into a medium-bodied palate with an array of cherries, raspberries and woodsy spices, with some savoury touches, it's neatly composed and satisfying. Best in youth, but it will hang around for a few years yet. Screw cap. 13.7% alc. **Rating** 95 **To** 2028 $90 JF

Collection Mornington Peninsula Pinot Noir 2019 This is a little ripper. It bounces around with juicy and tangy fruit, refreshing acidity and lithe tannins. There is enough flavour and spice to match a bakery and it has an energising, thirst-quenching quality. Dangerously delicious. Screw cap. 13.2% alc. **Rating** 95 **To** 2029 $60 JF

♀♀♀♀♀ **Collection Mornington Peninsula Chardonnay 2019** Rating 92 To 2028 $50 JF
Collection Yarra Valley Chardonnay 2018 Rating 92 To 2029 $50 JF
Cuvée Tasmania NV Rating 92 $35 JF
Trial Batch Pyrenees Nebbiolo 2018 Rating 91 To 2024 $29 JF
Regional Selections Mornington Peninsula Pinot Gris 2020 Rating 90 To 2024 $26 JF

Hanging Rock Winery ★★★★

88 Jim Road, Newham, Vic 3442 **Region** Macedon Ranges
T (03) 5427 0542 **www.**hangingrock.com.au **Open** 7 days 10–5
Winemaker Robert Ellis **Est.** 1983 **Dozens** 20000 **Vyds** 14.5ha

The Macedon area has proved marginal in spots and the Hanging Rock vineyards, with their lovely vista towards the Rock, are no exception. John Ellis thus elected to source additional grapes from various parts of Victoria to produce an interesting and diverse range of varietals at different price points. In 2011 John's children Ruth and Robert returned to the fold: Robert has an oenology degree from the University of Adelaide, after that working as a Flying Winemaker in Champagne, Burgundy, Oregon and Stellenbosch. Ruth has a degree in wine marketing from the University of Adelaide. Exports to the UK, the US and other major markets.

ŢŢŢŢ **JSE Members Reserve Heathcote Shiraz 2018** A well-modulated wine, right through from the flavours to the tannins. It has all the regional dark fruits and spice and richness, yet offers some refinement. Full bodied, yes, but smooth across the palate. The tannins are ripe and detailed, the oak integrated and overall impressive. Screw cap. 14.5% alc. **Rating** 95 **To** 2033 $45 JF

ŢŢŢŢ **Tarzali Riesling 2020 Rating** 93 **To** 2027 $25 JF ✪
Heathcote Shiraz 2018 Rating 92 **To** 2030 $75 JF
Cambrian Rise Heathcote Shiraz 2019 Rating 90 **To** 2027 $35 JF

Happs   ★★★★☆
575 Commonage Road, Dunsborough, WA 6281 **Region** Margaret River
T (08) 9755 3300 **www**.happs.com.au **Open** 7 days 10–5
Winemaker Erl Happ, Mark Warren **Est.** 1978 **Dozens** 15 000 **Vyds** 35.2ha
One-time schoolteacher, potter and winemaker Erl Happ is the patriarch of a 3-generation family. More than anything, Erl has been a creator and experimenter: building the self-designed winery from mudbrick, concrete form and timber; and making the first crusher. In 1994 he planted a new 30ha vineyard at Karridale to no less than 28 varieties, including some of the earliest plantings of tempranillo in Australia. The Three Hills label is made from varieties grown at this vineyard. Erl passed on his love of pottery to his son Myles, and Happs Pottery now has 4 potters, including Myles. Exports to the US, Denmark, the Netherlands, Malaysia, the Philippines, Vietnam, Hong Kong, China and Japan.

ŢŢŢŢ **Margaret River Viognier 2020** On skins for 4 days, tank fermented with lees stirring. Crystalline fruit on the nose and palate; nashi pear, glacé ginger, green apple, summer apricot and white currant. The palate is viscose and rich, but with line and poise also. A lovely viognier with fine chalky phenolics laced through the mid palate and finish. Really long. Screw cap. 13% alc. **Rating** 94 **To** 2027 $30 EL ✪
Three Hills Margaret River Tannat 2018 Mulberry, aniseed, a touch of arnica, salted Dutch licorice and jasmine tea. On the palate this is balanced, earthy and ripe, with salty acidity that keeps all things on an even keel. A lot to like here, and presumably this will become a graceful, soft, earthy wine in its old age. Screw cap. 13.9% alc. **Rating** 94 **To** 2036 $38 EL
Three Hills Margaret River Sangiovese 2019 Raspberry pip, red licorice, supple, chalky tannins and a lavender flower character through the finish. The flavours don't stop there … pink peppercorn and a slice of prosciutto linger on the palate, compelling another sip. Delicious. Screw cap. 13.8% alc. **Rating** 94 **To** 2031 $38 EL

ŢŢŢŢ **Margaret River Verdelho 2020 Rating** 93 **To** 2024 $22 EL ✪
Three Hills Margaret River Grenache Shiraz Mataro 2018 Rating 93 **To** 2030 $30 JH
Three Hills Margaret River Malbec 2019 Rating 93 **To** 2035 $45 EL
Three Hills Margaret River Petit Verdot 2018 Rating 92 **To** 2031 $38 EL
Three Hills Margaret River Charles Andreas 2018 Rating 90 **To** 2031 $45 EL

Harcourt Valley Vineyards   ★★★☆
3339 Calder Highway, Harcourt, Vic 3453 **Region** Bendigo
T (03) 5474 2223 **www**.harcourtvalley.com.au **Open** Sun 12–4
Winemaker Quinn Livingstone **Est.** 1975 **Dozens** 2500 **Vyds** 4ha
Harcourt Valley Vineyards (planted 1975) has the oldest planting of vines in the Harcourt Valley. Using 100% estate-grown fruit, Quinn Livingstone (2nd-generation winemaker) is making a number of small-batch wines. Minimal fruit handling is used in the winemaking process. The tasting area overlooks the vines, with a large window that allows visitors to see the activity in the winery. Exports to China.

🍷🍷🍷🍷♀ **Barbara's Bendigo Shiraz 2018** Belying its modest price point, this shiraz hails from a top year and shows the kind of fruit concentration and depth we might expect. A lifted dusty, earthy bouquet with blackberry fruits. Brings wild berry fruit and local bush spice with generous flavour to the palate, highlighted by fine tannins and a long finish. Screw cap. 14.9% alc. **Rating** 92 **To** 2028 $25 JP ❍

🍷🍷🍷🍷 **Bendigo Cabernet Sauvignon 2018 Rating** 89 **To** 2025 $25 JP

Hardys   ★★★★★

202 Main Road, McLaren Vale, SA 5171 **Region** McLaren Vale
T (08) 8329 4124 **www**.hardyswines.com **Open** Sun–Fri 11–4, Sat 10–4
Winemaker Nic Bowen **Est.** 1853
The 1992 merger of Thomas Hardy and the Berri Renmano group may have had some elements of a forced marriage, but the merged group prospered over the next 10 years. It was so successful that a further marriage followed in early 2003, with Constellation Wines of the US the groom and BRL Hardy the bride, creating the largest wine group in the world (the Australian arm was known as Constellation Wines Australia or CWA); but it is now part of the Accolade Wines group. The Hardys wine brands are headed by Thomas Hardy Cabernet Sauvignon, Eileen Hardy Chardonnay, Pinot Noir and Shiraz; then the Sir James range of sparkling wines; next the HRB wines, the William Hardy quartet; then the expanded Oomoo range and the Nottage Hill wines. The 'Big Company' slur is ill deserved – these are some of Australia's greatest wines. Exports to all major markets.

🍷🍷🍷🍷🍷 **Eileen Hardy Shiraz 2018** An iconic Australian wine and possibly the best young example tasted. The tannin management, increasingly more refined. Explosive aromas of raspberry bon-bon, bitter chocolate, violet, clove and licorice. Thankfully, though, more than the fruit (guaranteed in these parts), it is the tannic burr that is most provocative. Screw cap. 14.3% alc. **Rating** 96 **To** 2038 $153 NG
Thomas Hardy Cabernet Sauvignon 2017 Excellent dark purple hue. It's deep, rich and complex. More savoury accents among the hint of cassis and currants. Concentrated, with a density across the full-bodied palate, yet the oak is seamlessly integrated, the tannins ripe and plush. A rather polished wine, built for ageing. Screw cap. 14.3% alc. **Rating** 96 **To** 2044 $160 JF
Eileen Hardy Shiraz 2017 The tannins here are increasingly refined and tautly furled by apposite extraction and long maturation in high-quality French oak. Violet lift. Further scents of blueberry, mulberry, clove, pepper grind and nori. The cedar and mocha-laden tension across the finish is this rich wine's totem. Oak, of course, but seamlessly handled, while auguring well for a long unravelling during extended time in the cellar. Screw cap. 14.5% alc. **Rating** 95 **To** 2032 $153 NG
HRB Cabernet Sauvignon 2018 An interregional mesh of grapes, hand picked across exulted cabernet regions Margaret and Frankland Rivers, McLaren Vale and Eden Valley. On paper, highly experimental. In the glass, mission realised. Blackcurrant, a maritime swag of salty olive, dried seaweed and sage-doused tannins, impeccably wrought, attenuated and strident across the mouth. This is high quality. Super value. Immaculate and nestled French oak influence, beautifully positioned to prolong the experience with a bit of age. Screw cap. 14.1% alc. **Rating** 94 **To** 2028 $35 NG

🍷🍷🍷🍷♀ **Basket Pressed Reynella Shiraz 2018 Rating** 93 **To** 2034 $73 NG
Basket Pressed Reynella Grenache 2018 Rating 93 **To** 2025 $73 NG
Tintara McLaren Vale Grenache Shiraz Mataro 2019 Rating 93 **To** 2023 $28 NG
HRB Shiraz 2018 Rating 92 **To** 2028 $35 NG
HRB Pinot Noir 2019 Rating 90 **To** 2027 $35 JF

Hare's Chase

56 Neldner Road, Marananga, SA 5355 **Region** Barossa Valley
T (08) 8431 1457 **www.**hareschase.com
Winemaker Gary Baldwin **Est.** 1998 **Dozens** 5000 **Vyds** 16.8ha
Hare's Chase is the creation of 2 families, headed respectively by Peter Taylor as winemaker, with over 30 vintages' experience and Mike de la Haye as general manager; they own a 100+yo vineyard in the Marananga Valley area of the Barossa Valley. The simple, functional winery sits at the top of a rocky hill in the centre of the vineyard, which has some of the best red soil available for dry-grown viticulture. In 2016 Peter and Mike said, 'After 15 years of developing Hare's Chase, we are starting to believe we may one day give up our day job'. Exports to the US, Canada, Switzerland, Singapore, Hong Kong, Malaysia and China.

🍷🍷🍷🍷 **Marananga Barossa Valley Shiraz 2019** Vibrant, full purple. Dense blackberry and blood plum fruit, licorice and sarsaparilla of considerable presence. High-cocoa dark chocolate and coffee oak rises to the challenge. Firm, fine tannins hold a short finish of warm alcohol. Screw cap. 15.5% alc. **Rating** 89 **To** 2022 $38 TS

Harewood Estate

1570 Scotsdale Road, Denmark, WA 6333 **Region** Denmark
T (08) 9840 9078 **www.**harewood.com.au **Open** Fri–Mon 11–5 (school hols 7 days)
Winemaker James Kellie **Est.** 1988 **Dozens** 15 000 **Vyds** 19.2ha
In 2003 James Kellie, responsible for the contract making of Harewood's wines since 1998, purchased the estate with his wife Careena. A 300t winery was constructed, offering both contract winemaking services and the ability to expand the Harewood range to include subregional wines from across the Great Southern region. Exports to the UK, the US, Denmark, Sweden, Switzerland, Indonesia, Hong Kong, Malaysia, Macau, Singapore, China and Japan.

🍷🍷🍷🍷🍷 **Mount Barker Riesling 2020** This is pretty cool; flavour base of cheesecloth, salty saline acid, citrus pith and green apple skin. The fine, chalky phenolics on the palate elevate this into a very interesting space; softer and rounder than many Mount Barker rieslings, but that regional stamp of coiled acid remains entrenched in the fruit on the mid palate. Screw cap. 12.5% alc. **Rating** 95 **To** 2041 $30 EL ✪
Reserve Denmark Semillon Sauvignon Blanc 2019 Pungently grassy, with a quenching core of gooseberry and passionfruit. This is moreish. The oak is seamlessly countersunk into the concentrated fruit. A very impressive wine, especially for the price. Screw cap. 13% alc. **Rating** 95 **To** 2028 $28 EL ✪
Flux-II Great Southern Pinot Gris 2020 Fruit from Frankland River. Nashi pear, summer florals and a lick of winter stewed apple through the finish. Saline acid and dried apple rings are coupled with orange zest and sherbet. A lot to like here. Not your average pinot gris. Screw cap. 13% alc. **Rating** 95 **To** 2028 $30 EL ✪
Flux-VII Great Southern White Blend 2020 The classic sauvignon blanc/semillon is bookended by gewürz and riesling – this is a proper white blend. All the varieties are like passengers on a carousel, gently bobbing up and down, taking it in turns to go in and out of view. Lovely, lyrical, spicy and refreshing. The gewürztraminer is the last to leave the palate, leaving a wisp of lychee, rosewater and crushed pistachio in its wake. Screw cap. 12.5% alc. **Rating** 95 **To** 2020 $30 EL ✪
Porongurup Riesling 2020 Fleshy, creamy and rounded, this is a beautiful curvy riesling that speaks clearly of place. Some RS is in perfect concert with the fruit and acid, all things coming together in a most pleasurable way. Screw cap. 12.5% alc. **Rating** 94 **To** 2035 $30 EL✪
Denmark Riesling 2020 Very different from Harewood's Mount Barker Riesling, and rightly so. This Denmark iteration is grassy, herbaceous and more floral; the acid sits outside the fruit on the palate, it's not countersunk into it. There is a tingly, sherbet vivacity about this wine. It is more obvious than some of the others in this range, but a brilliant example of why Great Southern rieslings are so great. Screw cap. 12% alc. **Rating** 94 **To** 2036 $30 EL✪

Flux-V Great Southern Pinot Noir 2019 Coffee oak leads the charge on the nose, closely followed by cherry and strawberry. This has spunk and lift on the palate, with a distinct stemmy crunch that gives it an extra layer of crushed green ant interest. Length of flavour is a plus. Screw cap. 14% alc. **Rating** 94 **To** 2025 $30 EL ✪

♀♀♀♀♀ Reserve Great Southern Chardonnay 2019 Rating 92 To 2027 $34 EL
Great Southern Cabernet Sauvignon 2018 Rating 92 To 2028 $21 EL ✪
Denmark Pinot Noir 2020 Rating 90 To 2024 $20 EL ✪

Harkham Winery

266 De Beyers Road, Pokolbin, NSW 2321 **Region** Hunter Valley
T (02) 4998 7648 **www**.harkhamwine.com **Open** W'ends 10–5, Mon–Fri by appt
Winemaker Richard Harkham **Est.** 1985 **Dozens** 1500 **Vyds** 3ha
In 2005 Terry, Efrem and Richard Harkham acquired Windarra estate from the founding Andresen family. They manage the vineyard organically, and practise minimal intervention in the winery, reaching its zenith with the preservative-free Aziza's Shiraz, and the Old Vines Shiraz. Exports to the US, France and Hong Kong.

♀♀♀♀♀ Aziza's Preservative Free Semillon 2019 A shift of the stylistic goalposts of the regional classic, semillon. Often hard in its youth, this iteration has a lusciousness, despite the wine's precocity. Lightweight and high in acidity, abiding by the regional canon. Aromas of lemon drop, orange zest, ginger and cheese rind bounce about a palate that is both juicy, fresh and thirst slaking, drawing the saliva across the back of the mouth with a winning elastic tension. Diam. 11.5% alc. **Rating** 94 **To** 2025 $35 NG

♀♀♀♀♀ Aziza's Preservative Free Chardonnay 2019 Rating 93 To 2023 $35 NG
Aziza's Preservative Free Shiraz 2019 Rating 93 To 2024 $45 NG
Harkham River Burgundy Shiraz 2017 Rating 93 To 2028 $65 NG
Aziza's Preservative Free Rosé 2019 Rating 92 To 2022 $30 NG

Harris Organic

179 Memorial Avenue, Baskerville, WA 6065 **Region** Swan Valley
T (08) 9296 0216 **www**.harrisorganicwine.com **Open** Thurs–Mon 11–4.30
Winemaker Duncan Harris **Est.** 1998 **Dozens** 500 **Vyds** 1.8ha
Owner and winemaker Duncan Harris says Harris is the only organic winery (certified in September 2006) in the Swan Valley. The wines are made from estate vineyards (muscadelle, chenin blanc, chardonnay, pedro ximénez, verdelho, shiraz, malbec and muscat à petit grains blanc and rouge), producing both still and fortified wines. Exports to Canada, Japan and China.

♀♀♀♀♀ Swan Valley Liqueur Muscat NV Luscious, layered and intense in every way, this has concentration and presence. The alcohol threatens to break ranks with the fruit, but is so far kept in check. The bitter chocolate, quince and fig create narrative and interest in the mouth. Screw cap. 18.5% alc. **Rating** 91 $75 EL

♀♀♀♀ Swan Valley Liqueur Port NV Rating 88 $39 EL

Hart & Hunter

Gabriel's Paddock, 463 Deasys Road, Pokolbin, NSW 2325 **Region** Hunter Valley
T (02) 4998 7645 **www**.hartandhunter.com.au **Open** Thurs–Mon 10–4
Winemaker Damien Stevens, Jodie Belleville **Est.** 2009 **Dozens** 2500
This is the venture of winemaking couple Damien Stevens and Jodie Belleville. The grapes are purchased from highly regarded growers within the Hunter. The emphasis is on single-vineyard wines and small-batch processing. Continuing success for the venture led to the opening of a cellar door in late 2014, offering not only the 3 best known Hunter varieties but also experimental wines and alternative varieties.

Hart of the Barossa

Cnr Vine Vale Road/Light Pass Road, Tanunda, SA 5352 **Region** Barossa Valley
T 0412 586 006 **www.**hartofthebarossa.com.au **Open** Fri–Sat 11–4 or by appt
Winemaker Michael Hart, Alisa Hart, Rebekah Richardson **Est.** 2007 **Dozens** 2000
Vyds 6.5ha
The ancestors of Michael and Alisa Hart arrived in SA in 1845, their first address (with
7 children) a hollow tree on the banks of the North Para River. Michael and Alisa personally
tend the vineyard, which is the oldest certified organic vineyard in the Barossa Valley and
includes a patch of 110yo shiraz. The quality of the wines coming from these vines is
exceptional; unfortunately, there is only enough to fill 2 hogsheads a year (66 dozen bottles).
The other wines made are also impressive, particularly given their prices. Exports to Germany,
Hong Kong and China.

Harvey River Estate ★★★☆

Third Street, Harvey, WA 6220 **Region** Geographe
T (08) 9729 2085 **www.**harveyriverestate.com.au **Open** 7 days 10–4
Winemaker Stuart Pierce **Est.** 1999 **Dozens** 20000 **Vyds** 18.5ha
Harvey River Estate has a long and significant tradition of winemaking in WA's southwest.
The Sorgiovanni family have been farming and making wine on the original property since
Guiseppe (Joe) arrived from Italy in 1928. Orchards evolved into a standalone business and
Harvey Fresh went on to become one of WA's largest milk and juice processors. The Harvey
River Estate label was established in 1999, the range of popular varietals designed to be
enjoyed in the short to medium term including Sauvignon Blanc, Chardonnay, Sauvignon
Blanc Semillon, Rose, Merlot, Shiraz, Cabernet Sauvignon. The fruit for these wines is
predominantly from the family-owned vineyards in Geographe. Exports to the US, Canada,
Singapore and China.

🍷🍷🍷🍷🍷 **Geographe Barbera 2020** With 5% dolcetto. This is delicious. Vibrant
red berries, licorice, raspberry, anise and pomegranate. A faint undercurrent of
charcuterie makes it all the more interesting. Fine, natural acid takes it from slurpy
to crunchy; the phenolics structuring, chalky and imperceptible. A brilliant first
release. Screw cap. 14.8% alc. **Rating** 95 **To** 2025 $30 EL ✪

🍷🍷🍷🍷🍷 **Geographe Moscato 2020 Rating** 92 **To** 2023 $30 EL

Haselgrove Wines

187 Sand Road, McLaren Vale, SA 5171 **Region** McLaren Vale
T (08) 8323 8706 **www.**haselgrove.com.au **Open** By appt
Winemaker Alex Sherrah **Est.** 1981 **Dozens** 45000 **Vyds** 9.7ha
Italian-Australian industry veterans Don Totino, Don Luca, Tony Carrocci and Steve Maglieri
decided to purchase Haselgrove 'over a game of cards and couple of hearty reds' in 2008. They
have completely changed the product range, the modern small-batch winery producing the
Legend Series ($90–$150), the Origin Series ($30–$50), the Alternative Series ($24–$26), First
Cut ($23) and the 'H' by Haselgrove Series ($15–$18). Exports to Canada, Germany, Malaysia,
South Korea, Hong Kong, China and NZ.

🍷🍷🍷🍷🍷 **The Lear McLaren Vale Shiraz 2019** Sumptuous and rich. Violet, anise,
molten raspberry liqueur and coffee grind are groomed by impeccably integrated
French oak and ripples of judiciously extracted grape tannins, pithy and tactile.
The piste of flavour is smooth and long. An enjoyable wine, plucked, tweaked
and manicured with great skill. Immense pleasure, here. Screw cap. 14.5% alc.
Rating 95 **To** 2032 $90 NG
Protector McLaren Vale Cabernet Sauvignon 2019 I have a soft spot for
Vale cabernet. It boasts maritime aromas, black olive, oyster shell and soy sauce
salinity. As distinctive – and when good – distinguished as any of the region's
top performing varieties. Cassis and black cherry pulse through the mid palate,
with sage-crusted tannins corralling the impressive finish to great length and a

rewarding savouriness. Tannin management at this top tier is very impressive. Screw cap. 14% alc. **Rating** 95 **To** 2032 $40 NG

🍷🍷🍷🍷🍷 **The Cruth McLaren Vale Shiraz 2019 Rating** 93 **To** 2033 $150 NG
Col Cross Single Vineyard McLaren Vale Shiraz 2019 Rating 93 **To** 2034 $90 NG
Il Padrone McLaren Vale Shiraz 2019 Rating 92 **To** 2028 $45 NG
The Ambassador Single Vineyard McLaren Vale Shiraz 2019 Rating 92 **To** 2031 $90 NG
First Cut McLaren Vale Shiraz 2019 Rating 92 **To** 2026 $23 NG
McLaren Vale Montepulciano 2019 Rating 91 **To** 2024 $26 NG

Hatherleigh Vineyard ★★★★

35 Redground Heights Road, Laggan, NSW 2583 **Region** Southern New South Wales
T 0418 688 794 **www**.nickbulleid.com/hatherleigh
Winemaker Nick Bulleid, Stuart Hordern **Est.** 1996 **Dozens** 240 **Vyds** 1ha
This is the venture of long-term Brokenwood partner and peripatetic wine consultant Nick Bulleid. It has been a slowly, slowly venture, with all sorts of obstacles along the way, with 1ha of pinot noir planted between 1996 and '99, but part thereafter grafted to a better clone, resulting in a clonal mix of MV6 (predominant) with 2 rows of clone 777 and a few vines of clone 115. The wines are made at Brokenwood under the joint direction of Stuart Hordern and Nick, and are available though the website.

🍷🍷🍷🍷🍷 **Pinot Noir 2016** This first appears light on its feet, with an enticing perfume of florals and spicy cherries, it then unfurls with layers of savouriness: crushed coriander seeds, smoky, prosciutto-like flavours and raw silk tannins edge their way across the medium-bodied palate. Not overly complex but offers a spot-on drink now. Screw cap. 14% alc. **Rating** 93 **To** 2026 $43 JF

Hay Shed Hill Wines ★★★★★

511 Harmans Mill Road, Wilyabrup, WA 6280 **Region** Margaret River
T (08) 9755 6046 **www**.hayshedhill.com.au **Open** 7 days 10–5
Winemaker Michael Kerrigan **Est.** 1987 **Dozens** 24000 **Vyds** 18.55ha
Mike Kerrigan, former winemaker at Howard Park, acquired Hay Shed Hill in late 2006 (with co-ownership by the West Cape Howe syndicate) and is now the full-time winemaker. He had every confidence that he could dramatically lift the quality of the wines and has done precisely that. The estate-grown wines are made under the Vineyard and Block series. The Block series showcases the ultimate site-specific wines, made from separate blocks within the vineyard. The Pitchfork wines are made from contract-grown grapes in the region and the KP Wines label is a collaboration between Michael and his daughter Katie Priscilla Kerrigan. Exports to the UK, the US, Denmark, Singapore, Japan, Hong Kong and China.

🍷🍷🍷🍷🍷 **Block 2 Margaret River Cabernet Sauvignon 2018** Matured 18 months in French oak barriques. The nose presents a classical combination of black pepper, plum, raspberry, cassis and mulberry, backed by spiced oak. The palate follows suit and is further ameliorated by the presence of finely grippy tannins which caress the fruit through the lingering finish. Screw cap. 14% alc. **Rating** 95 **To** 2040 $60 EL

Margaret River Sauvignon Blanc Semillon 2020 Aromas of fresh green sugar snap pea, nashi pear and white currant. The palate follows in this vein, with a plush buoyancy to the texture. Showing both restraint and generosity, there is a lot to like. It induces thoughts of dappled shade and warm breezes. The subtle tartness through the finish (no doubt due to earlier picking for that taut acid line) is holding it off an even higher score. Screw cap. 12.5% alc. **Rating** 94 **To** 2023 $22 EL

Block 1 Margaret River Semillon Sauvignon Blanc 2019 Both varieties were picked early and pressed together, then co-fermented in 2nd- and 3rd-use barrels; mlf was blocked and the lees left unstirred. The oak impact is evident on the nose, however the fruit has the requisite intensity to hold its own in this space. Very elegant. Screw cap. 11% alc. **Rating** 94 **To** 2025 $35 EL

🍷🍷🍷🍷♀ **Pitchfork Margaret River Semillon Sauvignon Blanc 2020** Rating 93 To 2022 $17 EL ✪
Margaret River Grenache 2018 Rating 93 To 2030 $30 EL
Margaret River Tempranillo 2019 Rating 93 To 2027 $30 EL
Pitchfork Margaret River Cabernet Merlot 2018 Rating 92 To 2025 $15 EL ✪
Margaret River Malbec 2018 Rating 92 To 2030 $30 EL
Margaret River Chardonnay 2019 Rating 91 To 2028 $28 EL
Morrison's Gift Margaret River Chardonnay 2019 Rating 91 To 2028 $25 EL
KP Naturally Margaret River Chenin Blanc 2020 Rating 91 To 2022 $25 EL
Margaret River Nebbiolo 2019 Rating 91 To 2025 $30 EL
G40 Mount Barker Riesling 2020 Rating 90 To 2031 $25 EL

Hayes Family Wines ★★★★★

102 Mattiske Road, Stone Well, SA 5352 **Region** Barossa Valley
T 0499 096 812 **www.**hayesfamilywines.com **Open** Fri–Sun & public hols 11–5 or by appt
Winemaker Andrew Seppelt **Est.** 2014 **Dozens** 1000 **Vyds** 5ha
Hayes Family Wines is a small family-owned wine producer nestled among organically farmed vineyards in Stone Well on the western ridge of the Barossa Valley. The Hayes family has 25+ years of agriculture and business experience. Shiraz, Grenache, Mataro and Semillon are produced from the old vineyard in Stone Well, and also from Ebenezer and Koonunga in the northern Barossa.

🍷🍷🍷🍷🍷 **V&A Lane Coonawarra Cabernet Sauvignon 2018** A single hogshead of medium-bodied cabernet. Varietal purity and elegance are the calling cards of a high-quality wine. Yes, it's a very good vintage, the grapes reflecting that, but this alone doesn't mean success. Like its Reserve sibling, it's beautifully crafted. Screw cap. 14.2% alc. **Rating** 95 **To** 2038 $50 JH
Reserve Coonawarra Cabernet Sauvignon 2018 A firm, structured cabernet for the long game. Shut up like a trap right now, it leads with firm, fine French oak tannin. Classy oak, albeit difficult to see past it now. Glimpses of blackcurrant fruit occasionally coming up for air. The integrity of the finish confirms its potential, holding medium to good persistence and balance of acidity and fruit, even if those tannins impose for now. All it needs is time – and a lot of it. Screw cap. 14.4% alc. **Rating** 94 **To** 2053 $100 TS

🍷🍷🍷🍷♀ **Hoffmann DV Barossa Valley Shiraz 2019** Rating 93 To 2032 $60 TS
Vineyard Series Ebenezer Barossa Valley Shiraz 2018 Rating 93 To 2033 $50 JH
Stone Well Block 2 Estate Barossa Valley Grenache 2020 Rating 92 To 2025 $40 TS
Regional Series Coonawarra Cabernet Sauvignon 2018 Rating 92 To 2033 $25 TS ✪
Batch No.1 Rare Rutherglen Topaque NV Rating 92 $80 TS
Koonunga Creek Block North Barossa Valley Grenache 2020 Rating 91 To 2022 $40 TS
Barossa Valley Grenache Shiraz 2020 Rating 91 To 2027 $28 TS
Sam's Barossa Valley Grenache 2020 Rating 90 To 2022 $28 TS

Head in the Clouds ★★★★

36 Neate Avenue, Belair, SA 5052 **Region** Adelaide Hills
T 0404 440 298 **www.**headinthecloudswines.com
Winemaker Ashley Coats **Est.** 2008 **Dozens** 300

Head in the Clouds is a family-run microbusiness that, by virtue of its size, is able to lavish attention to detail on sourcing its intake of contract-grown grapes and on the vinification of its wines. The wines are distributed statewide by Glenn Beale.

🍷🍷🍷🍷 **Adelaide Hills Pinot Grigio 2020** With 10% pinot blanc, which punches well above its weight even in this tiny proportion. Savoury senses like fennel and sea air mix with a light honeyed and blossom note to begin. The palate is crisp yet spicy and lifted. Quite moreish. Don't serve it too cold. Screw cap. 12.6% alc. **Rating** 91 To 2023 $20 TL ♻

🍷🍷🍷🍷 **Clare Valley Riesling 2020 Rating** 89 To 2025 $20 TL

Head Wines   ★★★★★

PO Box 58, Tanunda, SA 5352 **Region** Barossa Valley
T 0413 114 233 **www.**headwines.com.au **Open** Feb–Apr by appt
Winemaker Alex Head **Est.** 2006 **Dozens** 6000
Head Wines is the venture of Alex Head. In 1997, he finished a degree in biochemistry from Sydney University. Experience in fine-wine stores, importers and an auction house was followed by vintage work at wineries he admired: Tyrrell's, Torbreck, Laughing Jack and Cirillo Estate. The names of the wines reflect his fascination with Côte-Rôtie in the Northern Rhône Valley. The 2 aspects in Côte-Rôtie are known as Côte Blonde and Côte Brune. Head's Blonde comes from an east-facing slope in the Stone Well area, while The Brunette comes from a very low-yielding vineyard in the Moppa area. In each case, open fermentation (with whole bunches) and basket pressing precedes maturation in French oak. Exports to the UK, Denmark, the Netherlands, Russia, South Korea, NZ and China.

🍷🍷🍷🍷🍷 **Ancestor Vine Barossa Grenache 2019** Kudos to Alex Head for giving these grand old 1858 vines the space to speak eloquently for themselves, unencumbered by oak, alcohol or artefact. A pale to medium vibrant purple hue heralds purity and restraint of wild strawberries, black raspberries and fragrant rosehip. Fine-ground fruit tannins entwine with tangy, high Springton acidity to lay out a long and lively finish. Great potential. Screw cap. 14.5% alc. **Rating** 95 To 2039 $100 TS

The Blonde Barossa Shiraz 2019 Named in honour of limestone bedrock, this is a Barossa shiraz that presents depth and definition with life and space. Crunchy, tangy blackberries and satsuma plums are framed in finely honed tannins and energetic acid line. Dark chocolate French oak rightly leaves the main game to classy fruit. Great length and potential. Screw cap. 14.4% alc. **Rating** 94 To 2039 $50 TS

🍷🍷🍷🍷 **The Brunette Barossa Shiraz 2019 Rating** 93 To 2034 $65 TS
Head Red Barossa Shiraz 2019 Rating 92 To 2024 $25 TS ♻
Old Vine Barossa Shiraz 2019 Rating 92 To 2029 $35 TS

Heartland Wines   ★★★★

The Winehouse, Wellington Road, Langhorne Creek, SA 5255 **Region** Langhorne Creek
T (08) 8333 1363 **www.**heartlandwines.com.au **Open** 7 days 10–5
Winemaker Ben Glaetzer **Est.** 2001 **Dozens** 50 000 **Vyds** 200ha
Heartland is a joint venture of veteran winemakers Ben Glaetzer and Scott Collett. It focuses on cabernet sauvignon and shiraz from Langhorne Creek, with John Glaetzer (Ben's uncle and head winemaker at Wolf Blass for over 30 years) liaising with his network of growers and vineyards. Ben makes the wines at Barossa Vintners. Exports to all major markets.

🍷🍷🍷🍷🍷 **Directors' Cut Langhorne Creek Shiraz 2018** Released very soon after the '17, the vintage difference is noticeable: this '18 has more dark fruits than crimson, the influence of 40% new oak (both French and American), yet is more intricately woven through the palate, adding structure while still allowing those dark, spicy flavours to stick. Neatly balanced and well delivered. Screw cap. 14.5% alc. **Rating** 94 To 2030 $35 TL

Directors' Cut Langhorne Creek Cabernet Sauvignon 2018 Ripe cabernet aromas from the outset. A full-bodied and chocolate-rich palate, fleshy and grapey as well. There's a blueberry and licorice pop to the mid palate as the wine opens with a little time in a decanter. Will gather more interest in its expression over the next 5 years. Screw cap. 14.5% alc. **Rating** 94 **To** 2028 $35 TL

One Langhorne Creek 2018 The self-proclaimed 'apex achievement' in Heartland's Langhorne Creek–focused portfolio, a cabernet-led blend with shiraz. Muscly at the moment (in its pre-release tasting). The core of cabernet blue/ blackberries is poised to unfurl, while the shiraz shows its sweeter fruit feels on the palate and also a touch of rustic flint and char. There's plenty lying below the surface for now that will rise in the next 5–10 years. Screw cap. 14.5% alc. **Rating** 94 **To** 2030 $79 TL

One Langhorne Creek 2016 Heartland calls this wine 'the apex of our achievement' and Langhorne Creek has had extraordinary success with the cabernet/shiraz blend (69/31% here). This is a well-worked synergy: a rich, dark, blackberry crush of aromas to begin, good concentration of fruit, integrated oak influence (12 months in new French and American barrels) and shiraz ripeness giving a sophisticated feel and elite styling. Screw cap. 14.5% alc. **Rating** 94 **To** 2030 $79 TL

ΨΨΨΨΩ **Directors' Cut Langhorne Creek Shiraz 2017** **Rating** 93 **To** 2027 $35 TL
Langhorne Creek Cabernet Sauvignon 2017 **Rating** 93 **To** 2028 $20 TL❂
Langhorne Creek Shiraz 2018 **Rating** 92 **To** 2026 $20 TL❂
Spice Trader Langhorne Creek Shiraz 2016 **Rating** 90 **To** 2024 $17 TL❂
Spice Trader Langhorne Creek Cabernet Sauvignon 2015 **Rating** 90 **To** 2027 $17 TL❂
Spice Trader Langhorne Creek Cabernet Sauvignon Shiraz 2017 **Rating** 90 **To** 2026 $17 TL❂

Heartwines

7-9 Keele Street, Collingwood, Vic 3066 **Region** McLaren Vale/Beechworth
T 0408 432 456 **www**.heartandsoil.com.au
Winemaker Peter Fraser, Tessa Brown, Mark Kelly **Est.** 2015 **Dozens** 800
Melbourne wine importer, distributor and retailer Randall Pollard (and partner Paula Munroe) has friends in many places in the world of wine. Obtaining grapes from the altar of grenache grown on the high sands of Blewitt Springs and having the high priest Peter Fraser make the wine is a feat of no mean dimension. And he's got a few more tricks up his sleeve. Exports to the UK.

ΨΨΨΨΩ **Danger Organic Vines Blewitt Springs Shiraz 2019** This meaty, sumptuously perfumed mid-weighted shiraz is stamped with the zip code of the prized Blewitt Springs sub-zone. Violet and iodine scents lead. Dutch licorice, rosewater and ground pepper/clove notes underlay a punchy stream of blueberry and dark-cherry flavours. Good going toward a second and effortless third glass. Bunchy tannins, embedded nicely into the fray while slaking the thirst. Screw cap. 12.5% alc. **Rating** 93 **To** 2026 $31 NG

Archie Old Bush Vines Blewitt Springs Grenache 2019 Grenache's telltale aroma of kirsch kicks off the melee. Turkish delight, sour-cherry pith, orange zest, too. Some bunchy spice and a scrub of firm sandy tannins – almost volcanic and chamois of feel – splay across a long finish, evincing authority while conferring a welcome savouriness. A delicious wine, although it could do with half a degree more ripeness and warmth. Screw cap. 14% alc. **Rating** 92 **To** 2025 $40 NG

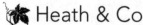 Heath & Co

278 Braeside Road, Finniss, SA 5255 **Region** Currency Creek
T 0400 024 429 **www**.heathandco.com.au
Winemaker David Heath **Est.** 2000 **Dozens** 3100 **Vyds** 6.2ha

Heath & Co is a small family-run vineyard on the banks of the Finniss River on South Australia's Fleurieu Peninsula. Upriver from Currency Creek, where the Finniss flows into the lower Murray and eventually the Southern Ocean, the vineyard covers valley and ridge blocks with a range of soils including alluvial, quartz, and river rock over clay. Established in the early 2000s, with the same legacy plantings as neighbours Salomon Estate and Wirra Wirra, the fruit is certified organic (NASSA 5469) and owners Dave and Hannah Heath profess that tempranillo is their true passion. (TL)

🍷🍷🍷🍷 **Southern Fleurieu Shiraz 2020** Certified organic fruit from the estate's Finniss River vineyard. Encouraging shiraz plumminess and blueberry aromas, with a sense that stems are in play – 50% whole bunches in fact. No oak employed, crafted in a Joven style. Yet this is full bodied with big flavours and structure. The tannins sit in balance, with a perky fruit lift in the finish. Screw cap. 14.5% alc. **Rating** 90 **To** 2026 $35 TL

Heathcote Estate   ★★★★☆

Drummonds Lane, Heathcote, Vic 3523 (postal) **Region** Heathcote
T (03) 5974 3729 **www**.yabbylake.com
Winemaker Tom Carson, Chris Forge, Luke Lomax **Est.** 1999 **Dozens** 5000 **Vyds** 34ha
Heathcote Estate and Yabby Lake Vineyard are owned by the Kirby family of Village Roadshow Ltd. They purchased a prime piece of Heathcote red Cambrian soil in 1999, planting shiraz (30ha) and grenache (4ha). The wines are matured exclusively in French oak. The arrival of the hugely talented Tom Carson as group winemaker has added lustre to the winery and its wines. Exports to the US, the UK, Canada, Sweden, Singapore, Hong Kong and China.

🍷🍷🍷🍷🍷 **Single Vineyard Shiraz 2019** A wine that needs room to move, so break out the decanter. Heathcote shiraz on a higher, finer plane to the usual, boasting tension and refinement. Gorgeous deep purple hue with lifted florals of violet and bramble, spiced-up plums and black cherries. A most complex youngster, still yet to do the full reveal, but with high potential. Long, fine-grained tannins are crying out for time in the cellar. Screw cap. 13.5% alc. **Rating** 95 **To** 2027 $50 JP
Single Block Release Block F Shiraz 2019 Block F brings potency and a deeper concentration of flavour than the standard release. Heathcote's beauty is amplified; its florals, luscious plums and dark berries so fragrant. Well structured with taut tannins, judicious oak on show and plenty of time to kill. This will age very well. Screw cap. 13% alc. **Rating** 95 **To** 2029 $60 JP

Heathvale   ★★★★★

300 Saw Pit Gully Road, via Keyneton, SA 5353 **Region** Eden Valley
T 0407 600 487 **www**.heathvale.com **Open** By appt
Winemaker Trevor March, Tony Carapetis (Consultant) **Est.** 1987 **Dozens** 1200
Vyds 9ha
The origins of Heathvale go back to 1865, when William Heath purchased the property, building the homestead and establishing the vineyard. The wine was initially made in the cellar of the house, which still stands on the property (now occupied by owners Trevor and Faye March). The vineyards were re-established in 1987 and consisted of shiraz, cabernet sauvignon, riesling, sagrantino and tempranillo. Between 2011 and '12 fundamental changes for the better took place – stylish new labels are but an outward sign of the far more important changes to wine style, with the winemaking now under the control of consultant Tony Carapetis (Quattro Mano) and the introduction of French oak. The tempranillo is soon to be planted over to shiraz. Exports to China.

🍷🍷🍷🍷🍷 **Estate Barossa Cabernet Sauvignon 2019** Capturing cabernet of impeccable ripeness and integrity in the challenging drought season of 2019 took tenacity and talent in equal measure. Under the circumstances, this wine is a rare and effortless translation of happy vines. Glorious, polished cassis and blackcurrant declare exacting varietal credentials, impeccably framed in fine-grained tannins, dark chocolate French oak and perfectly judged acidity. It's a delight from the outset, and will only improve over the medium term. Screw cap. 13.3% alc. **Rating** 95 To 2029 $27 TS ✪

The Reward Eden Valley Barossa Shiraz 2019 Trevor March has tended his flagship to a magnificent expression of deep black fruits and licorice, fused to high-cocoa dark chocolate and coffee-bean oak. A long finish of integrity and purpose holds out in spite of the dry warmth of the vintage. Screw cap. 14.8% alc. **Rating** 94 To 2034 $50 TS

Estate Barossa Shiraz 2019 Tended and raised with care and sensitivity, here is an Eden Valley shiraz of presence, fullness and poise. Compact and crunchy, dense blackberry, satsuma plum fruit and licorice take the lead. Oak is sensitively deployed, building structure and persistence more than flavour. Fine-ground tannins furnish a long life. Screw cap. 14.5% alc. **Rating** 94 To 2034 $27 TS ✪

♥♥♥♥♡ **The Witness Eden Valley Riesling 2019** Rating 91 To 2025 $27 TS
The Angry Rabbit Barossa 2019 Rating 91 To 2034 $27 TS

Hedonist Wines ★★★★☆

Rifle Range Road, McLaren Vale, SA 5171 **Region** McLaren Vale
T (08) 8323 8818 **www.**hedonistwines.com.au
Winemaker Walter Clappis, Kimberly Cooter, James Cooter **Est.** 1982 **Dozens** 18 000 **Vyds** 35ha
Walter Clappis has been making wine in McLaren Vale for 40 years, and over that time has won innumerable trophies and gold medals, including the prestigious George Mackey Memorial Trophy with his 2009 The Hedonist Shiraz, chosen as the best wine exported from Australia that year. Daughter Kimberly and son-in-law James Cooter (both with impressive CVs) now support him on the winery floor. The NASAA-certified organic and biodynamic estate plantings of shiraz, cabernet sauvignon, tempranillo and grenache are the cornerstones of the business. Exports include the UK, the US, Canada, Singapore, Thailand and China.

♥♥♥♥♡ **The Hedonist McLaren Vale Shiraz 2019** Aromas of crushed sooty rock, licorice straps, violet, blueberry and clove. A grind of pepper for lift. Salumi, too. A sumptuous wine that does not fall into the mould of a regional caricature. Plenty rich, but plenty fresh. Effortless, lithe and long. Screw cap. 14% alc. **Rating** 92 To 2026 $25 NG ✪

The Hedonist McLaren Vale Cabernet Sauvignon 2019 Plenty to like. Currant, red and black. A sheath of crushed mint, graphite and pencil shaving-clad tannins, pliant enough but soft enough, too, to facilitate early access. Pushy length. An easygoing cab with the hallmarks of something considerably more expensive. Screw cap. 14% alc. **Rating** 92 To 2027 $25 NG ✪

The Hedonist McLaren Vale Sangiovese 2019 Crushed, destemmed fruit spent an impressionable 42 days on skins, suggesting that tannin is the focus. Rightly so, given the frisky edginess of the variety. Dark cherry, lavender, tar, anise and a swab of olive-paste notes, carried long by jittery acidity. The skein of savoury tannins is firm, lithe and highly impressive. Screw cap. 13.5% alc. **Rating** 92 To 2025 $27 NG

♥♥♥♥ **The Hedonist McLaren Vale Sangiovese Rosé 2020** Rating 89 To 2021 $25 NG
The Hedonist McLaren Vale Tempranillo 2020 Rating 89 To 2023 $27 NG
Ecology McLaren Vale Grenache 2020 Rating 88 To 2024 $35 NG

Heemskerk ★★★☆

660 Blessington Road, White Hills, Tas 7258 (postal) **Region** Southern Tasmania
T 1300 651 650 **www.**heemskerk.com.au
Winemaker Marie Clay, Luke Mallaby **Est.** 1975
The Heemskerk brand established by Graham Wiltshire when he planted the first vines in 1965 (in the Pipers River region) is a very different business these days. It is part of TWE, and

sources its grapes from vineyards including the Riversdale Vineyard in the Coal River Valley for riesling; the Lowestoft Vineyard in the Derwent Valley for pinot noir; and the Tolpuddle Vineyard in the Coal River Valley for chardonnay.

🍷🍷🍷🍷 **Coal River Valley Chardonnay Pinot Noir 2014** Bright, pale straw hue. A strong, lively and enduring vintage for Heemskerk, upholding the youthful, bright wild lemon and crunchy Granny Smith apple of Tasmania and underscoring it with brioche complexity and texture of 5+ years lees age. Understated dosage leaves the fanfare to a burst of vibrant acidity. Impressively youthful, with a long future before it. Cork. 12% alc. **Rating** 92 **To** 2034 $60 TS

Heggies Vineyard   ★★★★

Heggies Range Road, Eden Valley, SA 5235 **Region** Eden Valley
T (08) 8561 3200 **www.**heggiesvineyard.com **Open** By appt
Winemaker Teresa Heuzenroeder **Est.** 1971 **Dozens** 15000 **Vyds** 62ha
Heggies was the second of the high-altitude (570m) vineyards established by the Hill-Smith family. Plantings on the 120ha former grazing property began in 1973; the principal varieties are riesling, chardonnay, viognier and merlot. There are also 2 special plantings: a 1.1ha reserve chardonnay block and 27ha of various clonal trials. Exports to all major markets.

🍷🍷🍷🍷 **Eden Valley Cloudline Chardonnay 2020** Great vineyards translate place more profoundly than variety, and there is no mistaking that this is from the home of the wonderful Heggies Riesling. This site perched some 550m above sea level is captured eloquently in the cool nights of 2020. With crunchy lemon, lime, nashi pear and almost ripe white peach, this is a tangy, vibrant chardonnay to drink like a riesling. Cloudline, indeed. Screw cap. 12.5% alc. **Rating** 90 **To** 2022 $24 TS

Heirloom Vineyards   ★★★★★

PO Box 39, McLaren Vale, SA 5171 **Region** Adelaide
T (08) 8323 8979 **www.**heirloomvineyards.com.au
Winemaker Elena Brooks **Est.** 2004
Another venture for winemaker Elena Brooks and her husband Zar. They met during the 2000 vintage and one thing led to another, as they say. Dandelion Vineyards and Zonte's Footstep came along first, and continue, but other partners are involved in those ventures. The lofty aims of Heirloom are 'to preserve the best of tradition, the unique old vineyards of SA, and to champion the best clones of each variety, embracing organic and biodynamic farming'. The quality of the wines has been consistently very good. Exports to all major markets.

🍷🍷🍷🍷🍷 **McLaren Vale Shiraz 2019** Dashing, slick and transfixing. Inky blackberry, black cherry and satsuma plum fruit delivering density with impressive definition, lifted by violet perfume and set to a grand foundation of fresh licorice. Elena Brooks' signature fine-ground tannins carry a long finish. Screw cap. 14.5% alc. **Rating** 96 **To** 2034 $40 TS ✪

A'Lambra Eden Valley Shiraz 2018 In the same heroic, full-bodied style as its '19 siblings, but bringing distinctly savoury and spicy notes into play. Nicely proportioned tannins also bring light and shade; complexity the outcome. Lots to chew on here. Screw cap. 14.3% alc. **Rating** 96 **To** 2038 $80 JH

Assen's Fortalice Adelaide Hills Chardonnay 2019 High-quality fruit is the essence of this wine, establishing its territory from the first sip, finesse joining supple, juicy fruit that slides effortlessly across and along the palate. All class. Screw cap. 12.7% alc. **Rating** 95 **To** 2034 $60 JH

Alcalá McLaren Vale Grenache 2019 Quintessential Vale grenache that ripples with complexity and detail. Rose petals, rhubarb, raspberries, wild strawberries, sage and cherry liqueur. It's framed in magnificent filigree of fine-ground tannins, holding confident focus and determination on a long finish. Screw cap. 14.5% alc. **Rating** 95 **To** 2029 $80 TS

Anevo Fortress McLaren Vale Grenache Touriga Tempranillo 2019
The medium-bodied, effortless, graceful side of grenache is infused in gentle red

berry fruits and a magnificent, powder-fine tannin display. Elena Brooks' blending wizardry is on display in the eloquent exotic spice and dried flowers of touriga and the dark berry fruit depth of tempranillo. The 3 unite seamlessly in a long and distinguished finish. Screw cap. 14.2% alc. **Rating** 95 **To** 2029 $80 TS

ŶŶŶŶ♀ **Alcazar Castle Adelaide Hills Pinot Noir 2020 Rating** 93 **To** 2024 $80 TS
Coonawarra Cabernet Sauvignon 2018 Rating 93 **To** 2038 $40 TS
McLaren Vale Touriga 2020 Rating 92 **To** 2035 $40 TS
Barossa Shiraz 2019 Rating 91 **To** 2025 $40 NG

Helen & Joey Estate   ★★★★

12–14 Spring Lane, Gruyere, Vic 3770 **Region** Yarra Valley
T 1800 989 463 **www.**helenandjoeyestate.com.au **Open** 7 days 10–5
Winemaker Steve Edgerton **Est.** 2011 **Dozens** 25 000 **Vyds** 23.81ha
This is the venture of Helen Xu, who purchased the large Fernando Vineyard on Spring Lane in 2010. It is planted to pinot noir, cabernet sauvignon, merlot, chardonnay, pinot gris, shiraz and sauvignon blanc. Helen's background is quite varied. She has a master's degree in analytical chemistry and was a QA manager for Nestlé for several years. She now owns a business in Shanghai, working with textile ink development together with husband Joey. They currently split their time between China and Australia.

ŶŶŶŶ♀ **Alena Single Vineyard Yarra Valley Chardonnay 2019** The estate's flagship
white and it's a bold style. Ripe peaches, lemon, creamy curd, cinnamon and spicy, smoky vanillan oak flavouring and a touch of nougat. Given the aforementioned, it is by no means a heavy wine, fuller bodied and generous yet the bright acidity keeps this upright. Screw cap. 13% alc. **Rating** 91 **To** 2025 $45 JF
Alena Single Vineyard Yarra Valley Pinot Noir 2019 The colour is somewhat dilute, and while it's not overly complex, it has immediate appeal. Cherries and pips with lots of spices and char via oak. Soft, giving tannins, with a slight green edge. Initially it seems a lightweight, but then it toys with savouriness, returning to more fruit flavours. More for today than for keeping. Screw cap. 13.5% alc. **Rating** 90 **To** 2025 $45 JF

Helen's Hill Estate   ★★★★★

16 Ingram Road, Lilydale, Vic 3140 **Region** Yarra Valley
T (03) 9739 1573 **www.**helenshill.com.au **Open** 7 days 10–5
Winemaker Scott McCarthy **Est.** 1984 **Dozens** 15 000 **Vyds** 53ha
Helen's Hill Estate is named after the previous owner of the property, Helen Fraser. Venture partners Andrew and Robyn McIntosh and Roma and Allan Nalder combined childhood farming experience with more recent careers in medicine and finance to establish and manage the day-to-day operations of the estate. It produces 2 labels: Helen's Hill Estate and Ingram Road, both made onsite. Scott McCarthy started his career early by working vintages during school holidays before gaining diverse and extensive experience in the Barossa and Yarra valleys, Napa Valley, Languedoc, the Loire Valley and Marlborough. The winery, cellar door complex and elegant 140-seat restaurant command some of the best views in the valley. Exports to the Maldives, Hong Kong and China.

ŶŶŶŶŶ **Winemakers Reserve Single Vineyard Yarra Valley Chardonnay 2017**
Hand picked, whole-bunch pressed, fermented in French oak, 35% mlf, matured for 9 months. A selection of the 5 best barrels. Gleaming bright straw green; ravishingly complex and intense grapefruit/white peach flavours, integrated oak adding its voice in the background. A very special wine. Diam. 12.6% alc.
Rating 97 **To** 2029 $100 JH ✪
Winemakers Reserve Single Vineyard Yarra Valley Pinot Noir 2017
A vivid stage for the great '17 vintage, 60% MV6, 20% Pommard and 20% Dijon clone 115. Hand picked, lightly crushed, fermented for 10 days on skins, matured for 10 months in French oak (40% new), this wine is a selection of the 5 best

barrels. A truly lovely pinot, purity and elegance its corner posts, a marriage of intensity and detail, finishing with the opening of the peacock's tail. Diam. 12.5% alc. **Rating** 97 **To** 2032 $100 JH ✪

💯💯💯💯💯 **The Empress Reserve Single Clone Chardonnay 2018** Hand-picked, whole-bunch pressed, fermented in French puncheons (30% new), 30% mlf, matured for 8 months. Bright, light straw-green; has all the elegance and length that puts Yarra Valley chardonnay on a par with Margaret River as the best Australian regions for chardonnay. White peach and nashi pear fruit flavours are dominant, the oak subtle, the acidity fresh. Screw cap. 12.5% alc. **Rating** 96 **To** 2028 $60 JH ✪

First Light Single Clone Yarra Valley Pinot Noir 2017 A single block of MV6, whole-berry ferment (no whole bunches), matured for 11 months in French puncheons (40% new). Very much in the style of the cool vintage; elegant, savoury and very long in the mouth. Wild strawberry/cherry fruit is dusted with spices, dried herbs and cedary oak. A strong sense of place. Screw cap. 12.8% alc. **Rating** 96 **To** 2029 $60 JH ✪

Range View Reserve Single Clone Yarra Valley Pinot Noir 2017 Selectiv'-harvested, lightly crushed, 14 days on skins, matured in French barriques and puncheons (40% new) for 11 months. Rising 4yo, the colour is deep and clear, with some shift towards maturity, but with more to come. This is my style of pinot, with a backdrop of savoury/spicy/foresty nuances to the bright, dark cherry and plum fruit. Screw cap. 12.8% alc. **Rating** 95 **To** 2031 $60 JH ❤

Ingram Road Single Vineyard Yarra Valley Chardonnay 2019 Hand picked, whole-bunch pressed, wild-yeast fermented in French barriques, partial mlf for 8 months. There's a tangy, lively edge to the white-stone-fruit flavour and citrus-tinged acidity. A remarkably good chardonnay at any price, let alone this. While it's ready now, it will age with grace. Screw cap. 12.5% alc. **Rating** 95 **To** 2030 $22 JH ✪

Hill Top Single Vineyard Yarra Valley Syrah 2019 Exceptional colour, vivid crimson/purple on the rim, heralds a perfectly balanced shiraz of medium–plus body. The fruit, oak and tannins are all singing from the same page. Black fruits (both berry and stone fruit) and fine-spun tannins deliver great length. Diam. 14% alc. **Rating** 95 **To** 2039 $35 JH ✪

Old Orchard Single Vineyard Yarra Valley Cabernets 2017 60/20/10/5/5% cabernet sauvignon/merlot/cabernet franc/petit verdot/malbec. The cool '17 vintage will be long remembered in the Yarra Valley for the extreme elegance of both red and white wines. So it is here, with the array of forest/bramble fruits, fine tannins and French oak woven together in a silken chord. Cork. 14.5% alc. **Rating** 95 **To** 2037 $40 JH

Ingram Road Single Vineyard Heathcote Shiraz 2019 Crushed and destemmed, open-fermented, 14 days on skins, matured for 10 months in French oak (10% new). A great example of why Heathcote is regarded as one of the foremost regions in Australia for shiraz. This overflows with supple blackberry fruit, rounded tannins and a clean finish. Exceptional value. Screw cap. 13.7% alc. **Rating** 94 **To** 2034 $22 JH ✪

Lana's Single Vineyard Yarra Valley Rosé 2020 100% cabernet sauvignon. Hand picked, whole-bunch pressed. No time on skins, cold-settled, then fermented in aged barriques for 30 days. Salmon-pink hue; the perfumed bouquet of spiced strawberries heralds a rosé with the lot, with powerful and complex fruit. Very astute winemaking. Screw cap. 12% alc. **Rating** 94 **To** 2022 $28 JH ✪

Old Orchard Single Vineyard Yarra Valley Cabernets 2018 A blend of cabernet sauvignon, cabernet franc, merlot, petit verdot and malbec harvested on the same day and co-fermented, a bold throw. On skins 14 days in an open fermenter, matured for 18 months in French barriques (40% new). A light to medium-bodied blend with blackcurrant, cedar, spice, dried bay leaf and black olive all contributing, along with fine tannins, to a wine of great interest. Diam. 13.7% alc. **Rating** 94 **To** 2030 $40 JH

ŢŢŢŢ♀ **Ingram Road Single Vineyard Yarra Valley Pinot Noir 2019** Rating 93
To 2026 $22 JH ✪
Ingram Road Single Vineyard Yarra Valley Chardonnay 2020 Rating 92
To 2025 $22 JH ✪
Ingram Road Single Vineyard Yarra Valley Sauvignon Blanc 2020
Rating 91 To 2024 $20 JH ✪

Helm ★★★★★

19 Butt's Road, Murrumbateman, NSW 2582 **Region** Canberra District
T (02) 6227 5953 **www.**helmwines.com.au **Open** Thurs–Mon 10–5
Winemaker Ken Helm, Stephanie Helm **Est.** 1973 **Dozens** 5000 **Vyds** 11ha
Ken Helm celebrated his 44th vintage in 2020. Over the years he has achieved many things,
through dogged persistence on the one hand, vision on the other. Riesling has been an
all-consuming interest, ultimately rewarded with rieslings of consistently high quality. He
has also given much to the broader wine community, extending from the narrow focus of
the Canberra District to the broad canvas of the international world of riesling: in '00 he
established the Canberra International Riesling Challenge. He retired as Chairman in '16,
but keeps an active eye on the Challenge. In '14 his youngest child Stephanie (and husband
Ben Osborne, Helm's vineyard manager) purchased Yass Valley Wines, rebranding it as The
Vintner's Daughter (see separate entry). He also persuaded Stephanie to join him as winemaker
at Helm. In '17 Helm completed construction of a separate 40 000L insulated winery with
a double-refrigeration system dedicated to the production of riesling, the old winery now
producing cabernet sauvignon.

ŢŢŢŢŢ **Classic Canberra District Cabernet Sauvignon 2018** In the right vintage,
the intensity of Canberra cabernet is astonishing. It's the combination of
blueberries, cassis and blackberries, moulded to more savoury notes of tapenade,
cedar and tobacco. Given all this, this sits comfortably in a medium-bodied frame,
balanced by refreshing acidity and buoyancy, with precise if determined tannins
and terrific length. Screw cap. 13.5% alc. **Rating** 95 **To** 2028 $50 JF
Premium Canberra District Cabernet Sauvignon 2018 On release, the
Classic is the go-to cabernet while Premium needs to be parked for a few more
years as the oak dominates. It's more solidly built, with densely packed oak-
derived tannins. The fruit is wonderful – squishy, ripe and flavoursome. There's a
smoothness, a richness of texture, gliding across the fuller-bodied palate, laced with
savoury notes, and then the grainy, firm tannins kick in. Powerful and detailed.
Screw cap. 13.5% alc. **Rating** 95 **To** 2030 $90 JF

Hemera Estate ★★★★☆

1516 Barossa Valley Way, Lyndoch, SA 5351 **Region** Barossa Valley
T (08) 8524 4033 **www.**hemeraestate.com.au **Open** 7 days 10–5
Winemaker Jason Barrette **Est.** 1999 **Dozens** 15 000 **Vyds** 22ha
Hemera Estate was originally founded by Darius and Pauline Ross in 1999 as Ross Estate
Wines. The name change came about in 2012 after the business was sold to Winston Wine.
This purchase also saw renewed investment in the winery, vineyard and tasting room, and a
focus on consistently producing high-quality wines. Running very much on an estate basis,
the winery and tasting room are located on the 22ha vineyard in the southern Barossa Valley;
it's primarily planted to shiraz, followed by cabernet sauvignon and 1912 planted grenache,
with smaller plantings of cabernet franc, mataro and tempranillo. Exports to China, Japan,
Thailand and Singapore.

Henschke ★★★★★

1428 Keyneton Road, Keyneton, SA 5353 **Region** Eden Valley
T (08) 8564 8223 **www.**henschke.com.au **Open** Mon–Sat 9–4.30
Winemaker Stephen Henschke **Est.** 1868 **Dozens** 30 000 **Vyds** 100ha
Henschke is the foremost medium-sized wine producer in Australia. Stephen and
Prue Henschke have taken a crown jewel and polished it to an even greater brilliance. Year

on year they have quietly added labels for single vineyards, single varieties or blends. The wines hail from the Eden Valley (the majority), the Barossa Valley or the Adelaide Hills. There's a compelling logic and focus – no excursions to McLaren Vale, Coonawarra, etc. There are now 4 wines from the Hill of Grace Vineyard: the icon itself, Hill of Roses (also shiraz), Hill of Peace (semillon) and Hill of Faith (mataro); the last 2 are only made in exceptional years. Recognition as Winery of the Year in the 2021 *Companion* was arguably long overdue. Exports to all major markets.

🍷🍷🍷🍷🍷 **Hill of Grace Eden Valley 2016** Such effortless grace and caressing elegance, in the presence of commanding endurance that will sustain it for half a century. This is the paradox that defines the legendary fable that is Hill of Grace. The 2016 embodies this: the profound depth of black fruits, bathed in the inimitable fragrance and exotic Chinese five-spice that characterises these old vines, set to tannins more finely textured yet more commanding than ever. Resist the seductive temptations of its youth and drink the 2015 first, because the true spectacle of 2016 is decades away. Vino-Lok. 14.5% alc. **Rating** 99 **To** 2066 $890 TS ♥
Julius Eden Valley Riesling 2020 Filled with citrus and apple blossom on the notably expressive bouquet that leads into a delicious palate, its elfin grace and purity defying the impact of drought. Forget food matching – this lime- and lemon-infused wine has such elegance and balance it sets its own stage. Screw cap. 12% alc. **Rating** 97 **To** 2035 $45 JH ⊘

🍷🍷🍷🍷🍷 **Peggy's Hill Eden Valley Riesling 2020** Delicious riesling in full-on Eden Valley style, lemon blossom aromas swiftly replayed on the juicy yet tightly framed palate. Makes life difficult for the taster such as I, with dozens of wines remaining to be tasted, prohibiting the impulse to swallow just a little bit. Screw cap. 12% alc. **Rating** 96 **To** 2030 $25 JH ⊘
Keyneton Euphonium Barossa 2017 I love the transparency of the Barossa's cooler seasons, in such articulate detail here that all 4 varieties are clearly visible in all their glory. Unashamedly medium bodied, refreshing and enticing, yet in no way underpowered, simplistic or short lived. Crunchy berry fruits, fine-ground tannins and vibrant acidity unite to marvellous effect and outstanding line and length. It takes some skill, dexterity and humility in the winery to allow fruit of such elegance to really sing. A classic Barossa blend with a long future before it. Screw cap. 14.5% alc. **Rating** 95 **To** 2037 $62 TS
Apple Tree Bench Barossa 2017 The combination of fragrance, depth and structure achieved in the Barossa's great shiraz cabernet blends is legendary, and this cool season has given birth to one of the greats. Cabernet's crunchy blackcurrants interlock seamlessly with the spicy blackberries of shiraz. Finely crafted tannins unite with bright, tangy, cool-season acidity to energise a long and enduring finish. A cellaring special. Screw cap. 14.5% alc. **Rating** 95 **To** 2037 $70 TS
Johann's Garden Barossa Valley 2018 You can almost forget the mataro and shiraz in this blend – more than ever this is a gloriously, fragrantly, elegantly, beautifully accurate Barossa grenache. Sumptuous rose petals, red cherries and raspberries are laid in the most enticing bed of caressing, mineral tannins. Mataro and shiraz lend a graceful lift to savoury character, dark berry tints and depth of colour. The seductive side of the Barossa. Vino-Lok. 14.5% alc. **Rating** 95 **To** 2023 $56 TS
Johanne Ida Selma Lenswood Blanc de Noir MD NV A '19 assemblage of reserve pinot noir from 1997 to 2016. Wonderful bright straw hue with a glint of green; it's floral, citrussy and so fresh yet layered with flavour. Nougat, creamed honey and vanilla cream all reined in by fine acidity. Cork. 12% alc. **Rating** 95 $62 JF
Marble Angel Vineyard Cabernet Sauvignon 2018 From a single vineyard in Light Pass, planted late 1970s, this is Australian cabernet through and through, complete with the eucalyptus and menthol of the Australian bush. All the classic varietal hallmarks, too: redcurrants, cassis and cedar. Love the tannins – superfine, powdery and strong. Screw cap. 14.5% alc. **Rating** 94 **To** 2043 $75 TS

ŶŶŶŶ♀ **Louis Eden Valley 2018** Rating 93 To 2025 $33 TS
Giles Adelaide Hills Pinot Noir 2019 Rating 93 To 2024 $55 TS
Stone Jar Eden Valley Tempranillo 2018 Rating 93 To 2030 $50 JF
Adelaide Hills Noble Gewürztraminer 2017 Rating 92 To 2024 $33 TS
The Alan Lenswood Pinot Noir 2017 Rating 92 To 2024 $93 TS
Henry's Seven Barossa 2019 Rating 92 To 2023 $37 TS
The Rose Grower Eden Valley Nebbiolo 2017 Rating 92 To 2027 $50 TS
The Bootmaker Barossa Valley Mataro 2019 Rating 92 To 2034 $37 TS
Croft Adelaide Hills Chardonnay 2019 Rating 91 To 2024 $50 TS
Tappa Pass Vineyard Selection Barossa Shiraz 2018 Rating 91 To 2028 $115 TS
Innes Vineyard Littlehampton Adelaide Hills Pinot Gris 2020 Rating 90 To 2021 $37 TS
Stone Jar Eden Valley Tempranillo 2019 Rating 90 To 2029 $50 TS

Hentley Farm Wines   ★★★★★

Cnr Jenke Road/Gerald Roberts Road, Seppeltsfield, SA 5355 **Region** Barossa Valley
T (08) 8562 8427 **www.**hentleyfarm.com.au **Open** 7 days 11–5
Winemaker Andrew Quin **Est.** 1997 **Dozens** 20 000 **Vyds** 44.7ha
Keith and Alison Hentschke purchased Hentley Farm in 1997, as a mixed farming property with an old vineyard. Keith has thoroughly impressive credentials, having studied agricultural science at Roseworthy, graduating with distinction, later adding an MBA. During the 1990s he had a senior production role with Orlando, before moving on to manage Fabal, one of Australia's largest vineyard management companies. Establishing Hentley Farm might seem all too easy but it required all of his knowledge to create such a great vineyard. A total of 38.2ha were planted between 1999 and 2005. In '04 an adjoining 6.5ha vineyard, christened Clos Otto, was acquired. Shiraz dominates the plantings, with 32.5ha. Situated on the banks of Greenock Creek, the vineyard has red clay loam soils overlaying shattered limestone, lightly rocked slopes and little topsoil. *Wine Companion 2015* Winery of the Year. Exports to the US and other major markets.

ŶŶŶŶŶ **Clos Otto Barossa Valley Shiraz 2018** Barossa shiraz of brooding presence and effortless confidence. Black and red fruits of all kinds, polished and lush. Layers of spice. French oak rises to the challenge, yet sits obediently behind the fruit, flanked in high-cocoa dark chocolate and roast nuts. Finely crafted tannins and vibrant acidity coax out a magnificent finish. One of the greatest yet. Cork. 14.8% alc. **Rating** 96 **To** 2033 $219 TS
H Block Barossa Valley Shiraz Cabernet 2019 The union of shiraz and cabernet brings brightness and confidence to the considerable proportions of Greenock Creek in the drought 2019 season. Blackberries, blueberries and prunes hold long amid black jubes, licorice and high-cocoa dark chocolate French oak. Deep and impenetrable, every crevice filled with inky density, it's confidently scaffolded in heavy tannin artillery to meet its proportions. A show-stopping blend at the big end of the Barossa, with a grand future before it. Cork. 14.8% alc. **Rating** 96 **To** 2039 $187 TS
von Kasper Barossa Valley Cabernet Sauvignon 2019 All the varietal credentials and endurance of cabernet, within the considerable proportions of the Barossa. This is an exact replica of textbook blackcurrant and cassis, with wonderful lift of violets and rosehip. Masterfully crafted tannins of enduring grip and powder-fine texture unite with bright acidity to carry a finish of undeviating line and length. Benchmark Barossa cabernet to bury deep in the cellar. Cork. 14.5% alc. **Rating** 96 **To** 2044 $99 TS
von Kasper Barossa Valley Cabernet Sauvignon 2018 Magnificent, exact, crafted and enduring. Superb blackcurrant/berry fruit is laid out on a fine web of tense tannin structure. Classy cocoa French oak supports a long finish. Superb, bright acid line promises fantastic longevity. One bottle was markedly cork scalped. Reliable closures please. Cork. 14% alc. **Rating** 96 **To** 2043 $99 TS

The Beast Barossa Valley Shiraz 2018 True to its name, this is an inky, brooding thing of deep purple hue. Satsuma plum, blackberry and black cherry fruit of concentrated impact is underscored by licorice and dark chocolate. Fine, confident tannins and lively acid line frame a strong finish and counter the warmth of alcohol. Impressive. Cork. 15% alc. **Rating** 95 **To** 2028 $99 TS

The Beauty Barossa Valley Shiraz 2019 The effect of a sprinkle of co-fermented viognier skins (just 3%) in deepening the colour and introducing a tropical nuance to Barossa shiraz is profound. Deep, vibrant purple in hue and in flavour, this is a powerful, ripe style of inky, black-fruit concentration. High-cocoa dark chocolate oak, firm, refined tannins and warm alcohol stretch out a long and lively finish. Screw cap. 15% alc. **Rating** 94 **To** 2029 $69 TS

H Block Barossa Valley Shiraz Cabernet 2018 Deep purple hue. The crunchy blackcurrant fruit, energetic tannin profile and bright acid line of cabernet is the perfect foil to plush, ripe Barossa shiraz. Dark, tangy blueberry fruits, impressive tannin frame and high-cocoa dark chocolate French oak unite to promise great longevity. Cork. 14.8% alc. **Rating** 94 **To** 2038 $187 TS

♥♥♥♥♀ The Beast Barossa Valley Shiraz 2019 **Rating** 93 **To** 2029 $99 TS
E Block Shiraz 2018 **Rating** 93 **To** 2033 $500 TS
The Quintessential Barossa Valley Shiraz Cabernet 2019 **Rating** 93 **To** 2029 $69 TS
Barossa Valley Shiraz 2019 **Rating** 92 **To** 2029 $35 TS
Clos Otto Barossa Valley Shiraz 2019 **Rating** 92 **To** 2032 $250 TS
The Creation Barossa Valley Shiraz 2018 **Rating** 92 **To** 2028 $187 TS
Barossa Valley Cabernet Sauvignon 2020 **Rating** 91 **To** 2030 $36 TS
The Quintessential Barossa Valley Shiraz Cabernet 2018 **Rating** 90 **To** 2028 $69 TS
The Stray Mongrel Barossa Valley 2020 **Rating** 90 **To** 2025 $36 TS
The Creation Barossa Valley Cabernet Sauvignon 2019 **Rating** 90 **To** 2034 $187 TS
Black Beauty Sparkling Shiraz NV **Rating** 90 $75 TS

Henty Estate   ★★★★★

657 Hensley Park Road, Hamilton, Vic 3300 (postal) **Region** Henty
T 0458 055 860 **www**.henty-estate.com.au
Winemaker Michael Hilsdon **Est.** 1991 **Dozens** 1400 **Vyds** 7ha
Peter and Glenys Dixon hastened slowly with Henty Estate. In 1991 they began the planting of 4.5ha of shiraz, 1ha each of cabernet sauvignon and chardonnay, and 0.5ha of riesling. In their words, 'we avoided the temptation to make wine until the vineyard was mature', establishing the winery in 2003. Encouraged by neighbour John Thomson, they limited the yield to 3–4t/ha on the VSP-trained, dry-grown vineyard. Michael Hilsdon and Matilda McGoon purchased Henty Estate in 2018, their first vintage in '19.

♥♥♥♥♥ Hamilton Chardonnay 2020 Henty Estate is establishing a name for its chardonnay, such is its elegance and Chablis-like presence. Looking smart just months after vintage, with energy in the glass and the arresting aromas of nougat, white flowers, lemon zest and straw. Firm acidity across the palate, grapefruit pith, citrus skin, apple, but a growing, warming spice, too. Mineral tang to close. A natural beauty. Screw cap. 12.4% alc. **Rating** 95 **To** 2028 $30 JP ✪

♥♥♥♥♀ Hamilton Riesling 2020 **Rating** 93 **To** 2030 $30 JP
Edward Shiraz 2018 **Rating** 92 **To** 2026 $45 JP
Hamilton Cabernet Sauvignon 2018 **Rating** 90 **To** 2026 $35 JP

Hentyfarm Wines   ★★★★

250 Wattletree Road, Holgate, NSW 2250 **Region** Henty
T 0423 029 200 **www**.hentyfarm.com.au **Open** By appt
Winemaker Ray Nadeson, Jono Mogg **Est.** 2009 **Dozens** 800

Dr John Gladstones names the Henty GI the coolest climate in Australia, cooler than Tasmania and the Macedon Ranges. This is both bane and blessing, for when it's cold, it's bitterly so. The other fact of life it has to contend with is its remoteness, lurking just inside the South Australian/Victorian border. The rest is all good news, for this region is capable of producing riesling, chardonnay and pinot noir of the highest quality. Seppelt's Drumborg Vineyard focuses on riesling, pinot noir and chardonnay; Crawford River on riesling; both adding lustre to the region. In 2009 Jonathan (Jono) Mogg and partner Belinda Low made several weekend trips in the company of (then) Best's winemaker Adam Wadewitz and his partner Nikki. They were able to buy grapes from renowned Henty grower Alastair Taylor and the first vintage of Chardonnay was made in '09. The portfolio now also includes Riesling, Gewürztraminer, Pinot Gris, Pinot Noir, Pinot Meunier and The Farm Barossa Shiraz. The wines are made by Ray Nadeson at Lethbridge Wines. Exports to China.

ΨΨΨΨ♀ **Henty Pinot Gris 2020** A ripe and juicy pinot gris that arrives fully formed, fresh from bottling. Mixes tropical mango and stone fruits with spiced apple aromas. Soft and supple, it states a strong case for the grape's cool-climate suitability with ginger snap, citrus and crunchy pear that run long across the palate. Easy to get to love. Screw cap. 13.2% alc. **Rating** 90 **To** 2025 $30 JP

ΨΨΨΨ **Henty Chardonnay 2019 Rating** 89 **To** 2027 $30 JP
Henty Pinot Meunier 2018 Rating 88 **To** 2024 $40 JP

Herbert Vineyard ★★★

Bishop Road, Mount Gambier, SA 5290 **Region** Mount Gambier
T 0408 849 080 **www.**herbertvineyard.com.au **Open** By appt
Winemaker David Herbert **Est.** 1996 **Dozens** 550 **Vyds** 1.77ha
David and Trudy Herbert have 1.77ha, planted to pinot noir (1.32ha), with smaller amounts of cabernet sauvignon, cabernet franc, shiraz, pinot gris and merlot. They have built a 2-level (mini) winery overlooking a 1300m² maze, which is reflected in the label logo.

Heritage Estate ★★★★☆

747 Granite Belt Drive, Cottonvale, Qld 4375 **Region** Granite Belt
T (07) 4685 2197 **www.**heritagewines.com.au **Open** 7 days 10–4
Winemaker John Handy **Est.** 1992 **Dozens** 4000 **Vyds** 20ha
Heritage Estate (owned by Robert and Therese Fenwick) has 2 estate vineyards in the Granite Belt: one at Cottonvale (north) at an altitude of 960m, where it grows white varieties; and the other at Ballandean (south), a slightly warmer site, where red varieties and marsanne are planted. Heritage Estate has been a prolific award winner in various Queensland wine shows.

Heritage Wines ★★★☆

399 Seppeltsfield Road, Marananga, SA 5355 **Region** Barossa Valley
T (08) 8562 2880 **www.**heritagewinery.com.au **Open** Mon–Fri 10–5, w'ends 11–5
Winemaker Stephen Hoff **Est.** 1984 **Dozens** 3000 **Vyds** 8.3ha
A little-known winery that deserves a wider audience, for veteran owner/winemaker Stephen Hoff is apt to produce some startlingly good wines. At various times the Riesling (from old Clare Valley vines), Cabernet Sauvignon and Shiraz (now the flag-bearer) have all excelled. The vineyard is planted to shiraz (5.5ha), cabernet sauvignon (2.5ha) and malbec (0.3ha). Exports to the UK, Thailand, Hong Kong, Malaysia and Singapore.

ΨΨΨΨΨ **Barossa Cabernet Sauvignon 2018** Steve Hoff's Heritage Wines have long been a beacon of affordability in Marananga. His cabernet delivers a lot of impact for the price, exemplifying the black fruit, cassis and licorice density of the region, confidently bolstered in equal measure by the coffee bean and high-cocoa dark chocolate influence of American oak. Fine tannins, tangy acidity and a long finish cement its potential. Diam. 14.5% alc. **Rating** 90 **To** 2033 $25 TS

Hesketh Wine Company ★★★★

28 The Parade, Norwood, SA 5067 **Region** South Australia
T (08) 8362 8622 **www**.heskethwinecompany.com.au
Winemaker James Lienert, Keeda Zilm, Andrew Hardy **Est.** 2006 **Dozens** 40 000
Headed by Jonathon Hesketh, this is part of WD Wines Pty Ltd, which also owns Parker
Coonawarra Estate, St John's Road and Vickery Wines (see separate entries). Jonathon spent
7 years as the global sales and marketing manager of Wirra Wirra, and 2.5 as general manager
of Distinguished Vineyards in NZ. He is also the son of Robert Hesketh, one of the key
players in the development of many facets of the SA wine industry. Jonathon says, 'After
realising long ago that working for the man (Greg Trott) was never going to feed 2 dogs,
4 children, 2 cats, 4 chickens and an ever-so-patient wife, the family returned to Adelaide in
early 2006 to establish Hesketh Wine Company'. Exports to all major markets.

🍷🍷🍷🍷 **Jimi's Ferment Limestone Coast Sauvignon Blanc 2019** Inspired by
Sancerre and made by the same recipe, to sophisticated and stunning effect! The
greatest sauvignons are more about mineral tension, structure and drive than
overt fruit. Here, the chalk mineral structure of the Limestone Coast is brilliantly
paired with malic acidity for an incredible finish of undeterred line and length.
Impeccably engineered for the long haul. Screw cap. 12% alc. **Rating** 95 **To** 2034
$35 TS ✪

G.A.R. Great Australian Red 2019 Coonawarra cabernet is a classic partner
with warm-climate South Australian shiraz and this new rendition is set to go
down among the greats. Fragrant, taut and fine-boned, it's packed with spicy,
crunchy berry fruits. An intricate mesh of fruit and oak tannins unites with
vibrant acid drive, setting off a long finish and grand longevity. Screw cap.
14.5% alc. **Rating** 94 **To** 2044 $60 TS

🍷🍷🍷🍷🍸 **Subregional Treasures Ebenezer Barossa Valley Shiraz 2019** **Rating** 92
To 2026 $30 TS
Regional Selections Barossa Valley Negroamaro 2019 **Rating** 92 **To** 2024
$22 TS ✪
Regional Selections Eden Valley Riesling 2020 **Rating** 91 **To** 2025
$20 TS ✪
Subregional Treasures Penola Coonawarra Cabernet Sauvignon 2019
Rating 91 **To** 2029 $30 TS
Regional Selections Adelaide Hills Sauvignon Blanc 2020 **Rating** 90
To 2021 $20 TS ✪
Regional Selections McLaren Vale Fiano 2020 **Rating** 90 **To** 2021 $22 TS

Hewitson ★★★★☆

66 Seppeltsfield Road, Nuriootpa, SA 5355 **Region** Adelaide
T (08) 8212 6233 **www**.hewitson.com.au **Open** Mon, Fri, Sat 11–4.30
Winemaker Dean Hewitson **Est.** 1996 **Dozens** 25 000 **Vyds** 12ha
Dean Hewitson was a winemaker at Petaluma for 10 years, during which time he managed
to do 3 vintages in France and one in Oregon, as well as undertaking his master's at the
University of California, Davis. It is hardly surprising that the wines are immaculately made
from a technical viewpoint. Dean sources 30+yo riesling from the Eden Valley and 70+yo
shiraz from McLaren Vale; he also makes a Barossa Valley mourvèdre from vines planted in
1853 at Rowland Flat, and Barossa Valley Shiraz and Grenache from 60yo vines at Tanunda.
Exports to Europe, Asia and the US.

🍷🍷🍷🍷🍷 **Monopole Mother Vine Barossa Valley Shiraz 2018** A clonal selection from
a single vine planted in 1853, the subsequent plantings necessarily relatively young,
but firing on all cylinders. It is a graceful wine with a silky texture, red and purple
fruits foremost; the tannins superfine, the finish lingering, the aftertaste fresh.
Lovely now or in 20+ years. Diam. 14% alc. **Rating** 97 **To** 2038 $150 JH ✪

ŶŶŶŶŶ **Gun Metal Eden Valley Riesling 2020** Single vineyard. A replay – at an even higher level – of 2019's drought-induced abysmal yields, yet an even better outcome: depth of flavour with refreshing acidity. Screw cap. 12.5% alc. **Rating** 95 To 2030 $28 JH ✪

ŶŶŶŶŶ **Miss Harry Barossa Valley GSM 2018 Rating** 93 To 2028 $28 TS
Old Garden Vineyard Barossa Valley Mourvèdre 2017 Rating 93 To 2027 $88 TS
Barrel 1853 Barossa Valley Shiraz Mourvèdre 2018 Rating 92 To 2022 $450 TS
Private Cellar Barossa Valley Grenache 2018 Rating 92 To 2025 $48 TS

Heydon Estate   ★★★★★

325 Tom Cullity Drive, Wilyabrup, WA 6280 **Region** Margaret River
T (08) 9755 6995 **www**.heydonestate.com.au **Open** 7 days 10–5
Winemaker Mark Messenger **Est.** 1988 **Dozens** 1800 **Vyds** 10ha
Margaret River dentist and cricket tragic George Heydon and wife Mary have been involved in the region's wine industry since 1995. They became 50% partners in Arlewood, and when that partnership was dissolved in 2004 they retained the property and the precious 2ha of cabernet sauvignon and 2.5ha of Gingin clone chardonnay planted in '88. Additional plantings from '95 include Dijon chardonnay clones, sauvignon blanc, semillon, shiraz and petit verdot. The estate is now biodynamic; nearby neighbour Vanya Cullen inspired the decision. Exports to the UK, Singapore and Hong Kong.

Hickinbotham Clarendon Vineyard   ★★★★★

92 Brooks Road, Clarendon, SA 5157 **Region** McLaren Vale
T (08) 8383 7504 **www**.hickinbothamwines.com.au **Open** By appt
Winemaker Chris Carpenter, Peter Fraser **Est.** 2012 **Dozens** 4800 **Vyds** 87ha
Alan Hickinbotham established the vineyard bearing his name in 1971 when he planted dry-grown cabernet sauvignon and shiraz in contoured rows on the sloping site. He was a very successful builder; this is his first venture into wine but his father, Alan Robb Hickinbotham, had a long and distinguished career, which included co-founding the oenology diploma at Roseworthy in '36. In 2012 Clarendon and the stately sandstone house on the property were purchased by Jackson Family Wines; it is run as a separate business from Yangarra Estate Vineyard, with different winemaking teams and wines. The vineyards are undergoing biodynamic conversion. Exports to all major markets.

ŶŶŶŶŶ **Trueman McLaren Vale Cabernet Sauvignon 2019** Flying winemaker Chris Carpenter is well versed in the sort of tannin management that defines his Californian expressions. Here, the piste is not as smooth, with a bit more edge to the framework; a little more greenery to the aromas. For the better. Cassis, pencil lead and dried tobacco leaf, to boot. The finish, long and thrumming; the tannic gristle etching fine grooves of tension with each sip. This will age beautifully. Screw cap. 14.5% alc. **Rating** 97 To 2034 $75 NG ✪ ♥

ŶŶŶŶŶ **The Revivalist McLaren Vale Merlot 2019** This cuvée has shape-shifted. It's a more compact, mid-weighted and savoury experience than previous vintages. Attention to detail is a given here: hand picked, wild fermented and properly extracted. The oak, top-drawer. The tannins, detailed, finely wound, precise and laden with graphite. The length, compelling. Unrivalled by any other merlot but, perhaps, for Blue Poles in Margaret River. Stunning. Screw cap. 13.5% alc. **Rating** 96 To 2032 $75 NG ✪
The Peake McLaren Vale Cabernet Shiraz 2019 The shiraz adds sweetness and breadth to the Bordelais' austerity, imparting black plum, iodine, lilac and anise. The cabernet, clearly the authority with its chiselled countenance of currant, graphite and sage. A delicious meld. Sumptuous without being jammy. Taut, without being hollow. Extremely long. Screw cap. 14.5% alc. **Rating** 96 To 2033 $175 NG

The Nest McLaren Vale Cabernet Franc 2019 The quality of fruit, tannic precision and apposite application of oak under this banner are unequalled in Australia. Nobody else gets it quite as right. The budget and gear help, yet it is the viticulture and sites that are the foundation for everything else. Franc from a warm place, salvaging its sappy cavalcade of tannin, crunch and floral lift. Redcurrant, spearmint and chilli powder lace a finely tuned finish marked by a flourish of garden herb. Kerpow! Screw cap. 13.5% alc. **Rating** 96 **To** 2031 $75 NG ✪ ♥
Brooks Road McLaren Vale Shiraz 2019 A corpulent wine, lush and full. Yet there is nothing jammy about it. Eclipsed by its Bordeaux varietal siblings perhaps, but as far as warm-climate shiraz goes, this is at the apex of the qualitative totem pole. Blue fruits, violet, anise, clove and pepper grind. Some salumi, too. But the tannins are this gorgeous wine's opus. Screw cap. 14.5% alc. **Rating** 95 **To** 2032 $75 NG

Hickinbotham of Dromana ★★★★

194 Nepean Highway (near Wallaces Road), Dromana, Vic 3936
Region Mornington Peninsula
T (03) 5981 0355 **www**.hickinbotham.biz **Open** 7 days 11–5
Winemaker Andrew Hickinbotham **Est.** 1981 **Dozens** 4000 **Vyds** 6ha
After a peripatetic period and a hiatus in winemaking, Hickinbotham established a permanent vineyard and winery base at Dromana. It now makes only Mornington Peninsula wines, drawing in part on estate vineyards (chardonnay, aligoté, taminga, pinot noir, shiraz, cabernet sauvignon, merlot, cabernet franc and ruby cabernet), and in part on contract-grown fruit.

🍷🍷🍷🍷🍷 **Noble Sauvignon Blanc 2017** Medium gold hue; a whorl of intense flavours from burnt orange marmalade and poached saffron pears to a touch of lemon barley water. A slight bitter green edge to the finish, with acidity that balances its sweetness. 500ml bottle. Screw cap. 12.7% alc. **Rating** 90 **To** 2022 $18 JF ✪
Mornington Peninsula Pinot Noir 2016 Don't bother ageing this because it's best now. Plenty of spiced black cherries, strawberry compote and dried herbs. It's lighter bodied, with supple tannins and a fresh finish. Screw cap. 13.5% alc. **Rating** 90 **To** 2022 $45 JF

🍷🍷🍷🍷 **Mornington Peninsula Chardonnay 2017** **Rating** 88 **To** 2022 $30 JF

Hidden Creek ★★★★

Eukey Road, Ballandean, Qld 4382 **Region** Granite Belt
T (07) 4684 1383 **www**.hiddencreek.com.au **Open** Mon & Fri 11–3, w'ends 10–4
Winemaker Andy Williams **Est.** 1997 **Dozens** 1000 **Vyds** 2ha
A beautifully located vineyard and winery at 1000m on a ridge overlooking the Ballandean township and the Severn River Valley. The granite boulder–strewn hills mean that the 70ha property only provides 2ha of vineyard, in turn divided into 3 different blocks planted to shiraz and merlot. Other varieties are sourced from local growers. The business is owned by a group of Brisbane wine enthusiasts. Queensland Winery of the Year, Queensland Wine Awards '18.

🍷🍷🍷🍷🍷 **Unsung Hero Riverland Fiano 2020** Pear, persimmon and apple fruit is polished neatly by a brief spell in barrels, building creamy texture and subtle vanilla nuances. The soft acidity of the Riverland is upheld by blocking mlf, creating a gentle and balanced finish of finesse and carry. This is a lot to pay for Riverland fiano, but it's been well crafted and meets the brief with confidence. Screw cap. 11.1% alc. **Rating** 90 **To** 2021 $45 TS

🍷🍷🍷🍷 **Granite Belt Viognier 2020** **Rating** 89 **To** 2022 $35 TS

Highbank ★★★★☆

Riddoch Highway, Coonawarra, SA 5263 **Region** Coonawarra
T (08) 8736 3311 **www**.highbank.com.au **Open** By appt
Winemaker Dennis Vice **Est.** 1985 **Dozens** 2000 **Vyds** 4ha

Mount Gambier lecturer in viticulture Dennis Vice makes small quantities of single-vineyard chardonnay, merlot, sauvignon and Coonawarra cabernet. The wines are sold through local restaurants and the cellar door, with limited Melbourne distribution. The major part of the grape production is sold. Exports to Japan and China.

🍷🍷🍷🍷🍷 **Family Reserve Single Vineyard Coonawarra Cabernet Sauvignon 2016** Cabernet sauvignon in all its glory, and while it's in the riper spectrum, this is by no means jammy. It's more fresh satsuma plum and blackberry. Laden with flavours from soy sauce and mint chocolate to blackstrap licorice, unfurling over a full-bodied palate to be met by persuasive, plentiful tannins with the texture of cocoa. All in all, impressive. Cork. 15% alc. **Rating** 95 **To** 2033 $89 JF

🍷🍷🍷🍷🍷 **Coonawarra Cabernet Blend 2016** **Rating** 93 **To** 2029 $59 JF

Higher Plane ★★★★★

98 Tom Cullity Drive, Cowaramup, WA 6284 **Region** Margaret River
T (08) 9755 9000 **www**.higherplanewines.com.au **Open** At Juniper Estate, 7 days 10–5
Winemaker Mark Messenger, Luc Fitzgerald **Est.** 1996 **Dozens** 3000 **Vyds** 14.52ha
Higher Plane was purchased by Roger Hill and Gillian Anderson, owners of Juniper Estate, in 2006. The brand was retained with the intention of maintaining the unique and special aspects of the site in the south of Margaret River distinct from those of Wilyabrup in the north. The close-planted vineyard is sustainably farmed using organic principles. Sons Nick and Tom (with winemaking experience in the Yarra Valley) are now running the business. Chardonnay, sauvignon blanc and cabernet sauvignon are the major plantings, with smaller amounts of merlot, shiraz, malbec, petit verdot and verdejo. Exports to Singapore.

🍷🍷🍷🍷🍷 **Margaret River Cabernet Malbec 2018** Ripeness, power and balance, all in equal measure. This is a vibrant beauty, with enough subdued tannins and supple fruit to keep one entertained for some time. Elegant, too. Awesome. Screw cap. 14.1% alc. **Rating** 95 **To** 2041 $28 EL ✪

🍷🍷🍷🍷🍷 **Margaret River Fiano 2020** **Rating** 93 **To** 2025 $28 EL
Margaret River Syrah 2019 **Rating** 93 **To** 2030 $28 EL
Forest Grove Margaret River Chardonnay 2020 **Rating** 92 **To** 2026 $28 EL
Margaret River Malbec 2020 **Rating** 91 **To** 2027 $28 EL

Highland Heritage ★★★★

4759 Mitchell Highway, Orange, NSW 2800 **Region** Orange
T (02) 6363 5602 **www**.highlandheritage.com.au **Open** 7 days 9–5
Winemaker Luke Steel, Mike Degaris (Consultant) **Est.** 1985 **Dozens** 4500 **Vyds** 14.4ha
Owned and operated by the D'Aquino family, the vineyard, restaurant and cellar door are on 125ha located 3km east of Orange, with a heliport offering scenic flights and tours. The vineyard is planted to chardonnay, sauvignon blanc, riesling, pinot noir, merlot, shiraz, cabernet franc and prosecco. At an elevation of 900m, on deep alluvial and rich basalt soils, the cool to cold climate and long growing season produce elegant reds and crisp, clean whites. Exports to Sweden and Finland.

🍷🍷🍷🍷🍷 **Patrono Series Shiraz 2019** A beautifully poised wine with a lovely flow. No jagged edges or extraneous additions. A limpid mid ruby and medium body. A succulent sappy palate exudes red cherry, violet, anise and mace. French and American oak is sublimated by an abundance of fruit and depth of extract, yet still serves to guide the fray long. Finishes a bit sweet without quite enough tannin. I'd drink this on the cooler side as a result. Screw cap. 13.4% alc. **Rating** 93 **To** 2026 $55 NG
Syrah 2019 A light ruby, almost pinotesque. Bright aromas of white pepper, clove, red cherry, violet and five-spice reverberate across a mid-weighted palate, lithe and slinky. Well architected by peppery acidity and gentle tannic latticework serving to pull, guide and propel the wine to crunchy length. Easygoing with ample

charm. Best enjoyed on the earlier side. Screw cap. 13% alc. **Rating** 91 **To** 2023
$32 NG
Estate Generations Shiraz 2019 This mid-weighted shiraz packs grace
and charm, although 18 months in American oak is an odd way to express it
in a climate as ostensibly cool as Orange. Clove, orange zest, ground pepper,
maraschino cherry and lilac meander along a frame of gauzy tannins to the point
of an easygoing evanescence. Clumsy oak across the finish, but a lovely drink all
the same. Screw cap. 13.5% alc. **Rating** 91 **To** 2024 $22 NG ✪

ŸŸŸŸ **Patrono Series Pinot Noir 2019 Rating** 89 **To** 2024 $55 NG

Hill-Smith Estate   ★★★☆

40 Eden Valley Road, Angaston, SA 5353 **Region** Eden Valley
T (08) 8561 3200 **www**.hillsmithestate.com
Winemaker Teresa Heuzenroeder **Est.** 1979 **Dozens** 5000 **Vyds** 12ha
The Eden Valley vineyard sits at an altitude of 510m, providing a cool climate that extends
the growing season; rocky, acidic soil coupled with winter rainfall and dry summers results in
modest crops. The Parish Vineyard in the Coal River Valley of Tasmania was purchased from
Frogmore Creek in 2012.

ŸŸŸŸŸ **Eden Valley Chardonnay 2020** Less is more when it comes to bringing up
Eden Valley chardonnay and the Hill-Smith team have found their groove in
the cool nights of the 2020 harvest. The crunchy, bright, tangy mood of the
Eden is the rightful hero here, in all of its lemon and white peach glory. Wild
fermentation and barrel age have been sensitively played to build subtle texture
without disrupting elegant fruit lines and crystalline acidity. Great value. Screw
cap. 13% alc. **Rating** 91 **To** 2023 $24 TS

ŸŸŸŸ **Eden Valley Chardonnay 2019 Rating** 89 **To** 2022 $24 TS

Hither & Yon   ★★★★☆

17 High Street, Willunga, SA 5172 **Region** McLaren Vale
T (08) 8556 2082 **www**.hitherandyon.com.au **Open** 7 days 11–4
Winemaker Malcom Leask, Richard Leask **Est.** 2012 **Dozens** 10 000 **Vyds** 78ha
Brothers Richard and Malcolm Leask started Hither & Yon in 2012, the Old Jarvie label
added in '16. The grapes are sourced from 78ha of family vineyards at 7 sites scattered
around McLaren Vale. Currently there are 20 varieties, with more to come. Richard
manages the vineyards while Malcolm runs the business. The historic, tiny cellar door in
Willunga has a vintage feel with a café and music events. The Hither & Yon labels feature
the brand's ampersand, with a different artist creating the artwork for each wine. Old Jarvie
(www.oldjarvie.com.au) focuses on blends. Exports to Japan, Taiwan, South Korea, China,
Malaysia, Hong Kong, Singapore, NZ, the UK and Canada.

ŸŸŸŸŸ **Old Jarvie The Enforcer McLaren Vale Shiraz Malbec Mataro 2019**
This blend works very well. Rich, textural and bright. Darker fruit persuasions,
a verdant riff of herb and a ferruginous growl of smoked meat and iodine notes
dousing the firm backbone of tannin. The choice of oak, smart: used 400L French
puncheons. This is compact and dense; yet lithe and strident across the mouth.
An innovative blend that makes for delicious drinking. Screw cap. 14.5% alc.
Rating 94 **To** 2028 $30 NG ✪

ŸŸŸŸŸ **McLaren Vale Shiraz 2020 Rating** 93 **To** 2032 $29 NG
Old Jarvie The Saviour McLaren Vale Grenache Mataro Touriga 2019
Rating 92 **To** 2025 $30 NG
McLaren Vale Grenache Touriga 2020 Rating 92 **To** 2023 $33 NG
McLaren Vale Carignan 2020 Rating 91 **To** 2024 $33 NG
McLaren Vale Muscat Blanc 2020 Rating 91 **To** 2021 $26 NG
McLaren Vale Cabernet Sauvignon 2019 Rating 91 **To** 2025 $29 NG
McLaren Vale Rosé 2020 Rating 91 **To** 2021 $26 NG

McLaren Vale Touriga 2020 Rating 91 To 2025 $33 NG
McLaren Vale Nero d'Avola 2019 Rating 91 To 2023 $33 NG
Leask McLaren Vale Grenache 2019 Rating 90 To 2022 $100 NG
McLaren Vale Grenache Mataro 2020 Rating 90 To 2025 $29 NG
McLaren Vale Aglianico 2018 Rating 90 To 2024 $33 NG

Hobbs Barossa Ranges ★★★★

c/- Vinolokal Wine Bar, 64 Murray Street, Tanunda, SA 5352 **Region** Barossa Valley
T (08) 8563 3935 **www**.hobbsvintners.com.au **Open** Wed–Sun
Winemaker Pete Schell, Chris Ringland (Consultant), Allison and Greg Hobbs
Est. 1998 **Dozens** 1500 **Vyds** 6.2ha
Hobbs Barossa Ranges is the high-profile, if somewhat challenging, venture of Greg and
Allison Hobbs. The estate vineyards revolve around 1ha of shiraz planted in 1905, 1ha planted
in '88, 1ha planted in '97 and 1.82ha planted in 2004; 0.4ha of old white frontignac was
removed in '09, giving space for another small planting of shiraz. The viticultural portfolio is
completed with 0.6ha of semillon planted in the 1960s and an inspired 0.4ha of viognier ('88).
All the wines, made by Peter Schell (at Spinifex), push the envelope. The only conventionally
made wine is the Shiraz Viognier, with a production of 130 dozen. Gregor Shiraz, an
Amarone-style shiraz in full-blooded table-wine mode, and a quartet of dessert wines are
produced by cane cutting, followed by further desiccation on racks. The Grenache comes
from a Barossa floor vineyard; the Semillon, Viognier and White Frontignac from estate-
grown grapes. The Tin Lids wines are made with 'the kids', Sean, Bridget and Jessica. Exports
to the UK, the US, Germany, Singapore, Taiwan and China.

♀♀♀♀♀ **1905 Shiraz 2018** Barossa shiraz of power and might, with volume before detail.
Prunes, blackberry jam and plums unite with licorice in a medium purple thing
of sweet fruit allure. Coffee bean and dark chocolate proclaim the full impact of
a long spell in new French oak. Fine tannins rise to the challenge on a finish of
warm alcohol and generous, expansive fruit. Diam. 14.7% alc. **Rating** 90 **To** 2028
$170 TS

Hoddles Creek Estate ★★★★★

505 Gembrook Road, Hoddles Creek, Vic 3139 **Region** Yarra Valley
T (03) 5967 4692 **www**.hoddlescreekestate.com.au **Open** By appt
Winemaker Franco D'Anna, Chris Bendle **Est.** 1997 **Dozens** 30 000 **Vyds** 33.3ha
The D'Anna family established their vineyard on a property that had been in the family
since 1960. The vines (chardonnay, pinot noir, sauvignon blanc, cabernet sauvignon, pinot
gris, merlot and pinot blanc) are pruned and harvested by hand. A 300t, split-level winery
was built in 2003. Son Franco is the viticulturist and inspired winemaker; he started work
in the family liquor store at age 13, graduating to chief wine buyer by the time he was 21.
He completed a bachelor of commerce at The University of Melbourne before studying
viticulture at CSU. A vintage at Coldstream Hills, then 2 years' vintage experience with Peter
Dredge at Witchmount and, with Mario Marson (ex-Mount Mary) as mentor in '03, has
put an old head on young shoulders. The Wickhams Road label uses grapes from an estate
vineyard in Gippsland as well as purchased grapes from the Yarra Valley and Mornington
Peninsula. Exports to the UK, Denmark, Brazil, Dubai, Japan and China.

♀♀♀♀♀ **Road Block Chardonnay 2018** From an east-facing contoured vineyard that
catches all the morning sun. Perfectly ripened white stone fruit with a quick
squeeze of Meyer lemon. Has been fermented and matured in French oak in such
a way as to leave the gorgeous fruit centre stage, the palate of endless length. Screw
cap. 12.5% alc. **Rating** 98 **To** 2030 $60 JH ♥

♀♀♀♀♀ **Syberia Chardonnay 2018** Perfectly ripened white stone fruit, with a quick
squeeze of grapefruit juice. Whole-bunch pressed to barrel for fermentation and
maturation, yet the fruit retains the limelight. Fantastic length. An outstanding
success in a challenging vintage. Screw cap. 12.8% alc. **Rating** 95 **To** 2028 $60 JH

🍷🍷🍷🍷♀ Wickhams Road Gippsland Chardonnay 2019 Rating 92 To 2024 $19 JF ✿
Wickhams Road Gippsland Pinot Noir 2020 Rating 92 To 2027 $21 JF ✿
Wickhams Road Yarra Valley Pinot Noir 2020 Rating 90 To 2027 $21 JF ✿

Hollick Estates ★★★★★

11 Racecourse Road, Penola, SA 5277 **Region** Coonawarra
T (08) 8737 2318 **www**.hollick.com **Open** 7 days 11–5, public hols 11–4
Winemaker Trent Nankivell **Est.** 1983 **Dozens** 40 000 **Vyds** 87ha
Established in 1983 by the Hollick family, Hollick Estates' vineyard, winery, restaurant and
cellar door overlooks Coonawarra. The estate-grown wines come from 3 vineyards, 2 in
Coonawarra and 1 in nearby Wrattonbully, reflecting the characteristics of each site. The
classic Coonawarra varieties of cabernet sauvignon, shiraz and chardonnay are made, along
with The Nectar (botrytis riesling), barbera and tempranillo. Exports to most major markets.

🍷🍷🍷🍷🍷 The Nectar Coonawarra 2019 Mid gold hue; heady, with saffron poached
pears in honey syrup and sprinkled with fresh herbs and spices. The palate is soft,
easy and unctuous, with dabs of orange marmalade and fresh lemon. The riesling's
acidity coats the sweetness, allowing botrytis flavours to shine. A lovely, gorgeous
and complete wine. 375ml bottle. Screw cap. 10.5% alc. **Rating** 95 **To** 2026
$25 JF ✿
Ravenswood Coonawarra Cabernet Sauvignon 2018 The aromas are so
compelling, it's easy to just smell this, taking in the heady blackcurrants/berries,
charcuterie and a cook's cupboard of baking spices, especially cocoa and star anise.
Of course, there's a seasoning of regional mint/eucalyptus, too. Full bodied, but
there's reticence on the palate, a youthful cabernet character. Tannins are a little
wiry but textural, bolstered by oak. Vital and vibrant now, but time is going to be
a good friend. Screw cap. 14.5% alc. **Rating** 95 **To** 2035 $85 JF

🍷🍷🍷🍷♀ Old Vines Coonawarra Cabernet Sauvignon 2018 Rating 93 To 2028
$36 JF
Wilgha Coonawarra Shiraz 2019 Rating 92 To 2033 $65 JF
Wrattonbully Shiraz 2018 Rating 90 To 2028 $25 JF

Hollydene Estate ★★★★

3483 Golden Highway, Jerrys Plains, NSW 2330 **Region** Hunter Valley
T (02) 6576 4021 **www**.hollydeneestate.com **Open** Mon–Thurs 10–4, Fri 10–9, Sat 9–9,
Sun 9–4
Winemaker Matt Burton **Est.** 1965 **Dozens** 7000 **Vyds** 80ha
Karen Williams has 3 vineyards and associated properties, all established in the 1960s. They
are Hollydene Estate, Wybong Estate and Arrowfield; the latter one of the original vinous
landmarks in the Upper Hunter. The 3 vineyards produce grapes for the Hollydene Estate and
Juul labels. Hollydene also makes sparkling wines from the Mornington Peninsula. Exports to
Germany, Indonesia and China.

🍷🍷🍷🍷♀ Show Reserve Upper Hunter Valley Semillon 2019 I like the dry extract
and sheer juiciness of the '19 vintage in the Hunter: the semillons are typically dry,
introverted and austere; yet more generous and enjoyable young. Notes of dried
hay, lanolin and lemon pith are corralled by a skein of acidity that is both talcy
and juicy, drawing the saliva with each sip and the flavours broad across the palate.
Screw cap. 11% alc. **Rating** 92 **To** 2030 $36 NG

Holm Oak ★★★★☆

11 West Bay Road, Rowella, Tas 7270 **Region** Northern Tasmania
T (03) 6394 7577 **www**.holmoakvineyards.com.au **Open** Thurs–Sun 11–5
Winemaker Rebecca Duffy **Est.** 1983 **Dozens** 15 000 **Vyds** 15ha
Holm Oak takes its name from its grove of oak trees, planted around the beginning of the
20th century and originally intended for the making of tennis racquets. A boutique family

affair, winemaker Rebecca Duffy has extensive winemaking experience in Australia and California; and husband Tim, a viticultural agronomist, manages the vineyard (pinot noir, pinot gris, cabernet sauvignon, chardonnay, riesling and small amounts of merlot, arneis, shiraz and cabernet franc). Cellar door, winery, family home (and a pet pig named Pinot) all co-exist on the vineyard site. Exports to the UK, the US and Japan.

TTTTT **Hot Shot Pinot Noir 2018** Holm Oak's flagship boasts the fruit presence and time to swallow up substantial whole-bunch inclusion, triumphantly emerging from the other side with a core of tangy morello cherry and spicy raspberry fruit. Roast cashew nut notes of French oak assume a rightful support role, highlighting firm, fine tannins that unite with the energy of the Tamar to spell out a very long and exciting future. Screw cap. 13.5% alc. **Rating** 94 **To** 2043 **$130** TS

TTTTT **Pinot Noir 2019 Rating** 90 **To** 2027 **$35** TS

Home Hill ★★★★☆
38 Nairn Road, Ranelagh, Tas 7109 **Region** Southern Tasmania
T (03) 6264 1200 **www**.homehillwines.com.au **Open** 7 days 10–4
Winemaker Catalina Collado **Est.** 1993 **Dozens** 3500 **Vyds** 10.2ha
Terry and Rosemary Bennett planted their first 0.5ha of vines in 1994 on gentle slopes in the beautiful Huon Valley. The plantings have gradually been increased to 10.2ha, including pinot noir, chardonnay, pinot gris and sylvaner. Home Hill has had great success with its exemplary pinot noirs, consistent multi-trophy and gold medal winners in the ultra-competitive Tasmanian Wine Show. Impressive enough but pales into insignificance in the wake of winning the Jimmy Watson Trophy at the Melbourne Wine Awards '15.

TTTTT **Ms Daisy Cuvée 2017** 60/40% pinot noir/chardonnay, tiraged Nov '17, 9.75g/l dosage, disgorged Aug and Oct '19. Palest pink hue, partridge eye; the pinot noir drives a wild strawberry-flavoured wine, the dosage perfectly judged, the length good. Diam. 12.5% alc. **Rating** 95 **$40** JH

Honey Moon Vineyard ★★★★☆
135 Church Hill Road, Echunga, SA 5153 **Region** Adelaide Hills
T 0438 727 079 **www**.honeymoonvineyard.com.au **Open** By appt
Winemaker Jane Bromley, Hylton McLean **Est.** 2004 **Dozens** 800 **Vyds** 1.2ha
Jane Bromley and Hylton McLean planted 0.7ha of pinot noir (clones 777, 114 and 115) and 0.5ha of shiraz (selected from 2 old vineyards known for their spicy fruit flavours). The moon is a striking feature of the landscape, particularly at harvest time when, as a full moon, it appears as a dollop of rich honey in the sky – hence the name. The first vintage was '05, but Jane has been making wine since '01, with a particular interest in Champagne; Hylton is a winemaker, wine science researcher and wine educator with over 20 years' experience.

TTTTT **EBVR Adelaide Hills 2018** EBVR stands for Early Bottled Vintage Red, a fortified take on what used to be known here at Vintage Port. 63% tinta roriz (tempranillo), 31% shiraz and 6% McLaren Vale touriga nacional. Made traditionally, it exudes blackberry-liqueur-meets-chocolate aromatics, with the great art of integrating wood-aged brandy spirit to be virtually invisible. Sweetness is restrained and the fruit chocolate flavours refuse to disappear. Delicious. Diam. 20% alc. **Rating** 96 **$60** TL ✪

TTTTT **Adelaide Hills Pinot Noir 2017 Rating** 93 **To** 2026 **$50** TL
Adelaide Hills Pinot Noir Extra 2018 Rating 92 **To** 2028 **$50** TL
Rosé Brut 2015 Rating 91 **$50** TL
Fancy Adelaide Hills Rosé 2018 Rating 90 **To** 2025 **$26** TL
Adelaide Hills Shiraz 2015 Rating 90 **To** 2024 **$50** TL

HOOSEGG ★★★★★

100 Shiralee Road, Orange, NSW 2800 **Region** Orange
T 0448 983 033 **www**.hoosegg.com
Winemaker Philip Shaw **Est.** 2016
This seems certain to be the last oenological resting place of Philip Shaw, the genius who made the building of the Rosemount Estate empire possible. It was none of his fault that increasing its production from 700000 dozen bottles in 2000 to more than 2 million dozen in 2002 was not even close to being sustainable, nor that (figuratively) the sky should fall down on its new owner (Southcorp) and Rosemount's brand value. Shaw was several jumps in front of the field; he had put in train the purchase of the Koomooloo Vineyard (part in the Orange GI, part in the Central Tablelands), and the following year excised 47ha from Koomooloo for his retirement business, Philip Shaw Wines. In 2015 he passed ownership of Philip Shaw Wines to his sons Daniel and Damien, and built a 50t winery on an ever-smaller block for his ultimate retirement business HOOSEGG.

Horner Wines ★★★★

188 Palmers Lane, Pokolbin, NSW 2325 **Region** Hunter Valley
T 0431 741 203 **www**.hornerwines.com.au **Open** Fri–Sun 110–5 Mon–Thurs by appt
Winemaker Ashley Horner **Est.** 2013 **Dozens** 14500
Ashley and Lauren Horner have a certified organic vineyard planted to chardonnay, viognier and shiraz. Grapes are also sourced from organic vineyards in Orange and Cowra. Ashley had a 14-year career working at Rosemount Estate, Penfolds, Kamberra Estate, Saint Clair (NZ) and Mount Pleasant, ultimately becoming winemaker at Tamburlaine and completing a diploma in wine technology at Dookie College. Lauren has a degree in hospitality/tourism and is now involved in the running of Horner Wines. The move from grapegrowing to winemaking was precipitated by the fall in demand for grape. They sell the wines through www.nakedwines.com.au.

 Family Reserve Shiraz Marsanne 2019 A Hermitage-influenced blend, just 4% marsanne co-fermented. Mid weight, pushing full. Sweet fruit. Blueberry and mulberry, root spice, polished leather, clove and fecund earth. Plenty of flavour and push through the mouth. Not a great deal of real tannin for restraint. Screw cap. 13.9% alc. **Rating** 90 **To** 2026 $29 NG

Houghton ★★★★★

4070 Caves Road, Wilyabrup, WA 6280 **Region** Swan Valley
T (08) 9755 6042 **www**.houghton-wines.com.au **Open** 7 days 11–5
Winemaker Courtney Treacher **Est.** 1836 **Dozens** 43000
Houghton's reputation was once largely dependent on its (then) White Burgundy, equally good when young or 5 years old. In the last 20 years its portfolio changed out of all recognition, with a kaleidoscopic range of high-quality wines from the Margaret River, Frankland River, Great Southern and Pemberton regions to the fore. The Jack Mann and Gladstones red wines stand at the forefront, but to borrow a saying of the late Jack Mann, 'There are no bad wines here'. In November 2019 the Houghton property was sold to the Yukich family, who had acquired part of the property in 1990 and established Oakover Wines. The reunited vineyard has been relaunched as Nikola Estate (see new entry), in honour of Nikola Yukich, who emigrated from Croatia and planted vines in the Swan Valley over 90 years ago. The Houghton brand is retained by Accolade, with the winemaking moved to its Nannup winery in the Blackwood Valley, adjacent to the Frankland River and Margaret River, the sources of most of its grape production. Exports to the UK and Asia.

 Wisdom Margaret River Cabernet Sauvignon 2018 The price of this has gone up recently, now more aligned with the quality of the wine (the new label doesn't hurt, either). This is succulent, plush and vibrant cabernet; the tannins are plump and chewy, the fruit has a jolliness that accompanies serious raspberry, cassis and pomegranate. The tannins are the final confirmation of pedigree: powder-fine and shapely. Gorgeous, statuesque wine. Screw cap. 14% alc. **Rating** 95 **To** 2035 $40 EL

Wisdom Pemberton Pinot Noir 2019 Delicious. Creamy, silky, red fruits and szechuan spice. Some pink peppercorn in there, too. Plump. Screw cap. 13.5% alc. **Rating** 94 **To** 2028 $40 EL

ŶŶŶŶ **Wisdom Pemberton Chardonnay 2019 Rating** 93 **To** 2028 $40 EL
Thomas Yule Frankland River Shiraz 2016 Rating 93 **To** 2036 $95 EL

House of Arras ★★★★★

Bay of Fires, 40 Baxters Road, Pipers River, Tas 7252 **Region** Northern Tasmania
T (03) 6362 7622 **www**.houseofarras.com.au **Open** Thurs–Mon 10–5 by appt
Winemaker Ed Carr **Est.** 1995

The rise and rise of the fortunes of the House of Arras has been due to 2 things: the exceptional skills of winemaker Ed Carr, and its access to high-quality Tasmanian chardonnay and pinot noir. While there have been distinguished sparkling wines made in Tasmania for many years, none has so consistently scaled the heights of Arras. The complexity, texture and structure of the wines are akin to that of Bollinger RD and Krug; the connection stems from the 7–15+ years the wines spend on lees prior to disgorgement. Exports to the UK, the US and Asia.

ŶŶŶŶ **Grand Vintage 2009** 65.9/34.1% chardonnay/pinot noir, aged for 9 years on lees, disgorged Apr '20, the dosage only 2.5g/l. Full straw-yellow hue; layered brioche complexity, powerful drive and length. Australia's answer to Krug. Cork. 12.5% alc. **Rating** 97 $109 JH ✪ ♥

ŶŶŶŶ **Rosé 2008** A tight and incredibly enduring vintage. Pale blush/salmon tint. All the structural integrity, tension and focus of 68% pinot noir. An intricately engineered framework supports a secondary style of long lees age (11 years) and a little more new oak influence than ever before. A vintage for the cellar. Cork. 12.5% alc. **Rating** 96 $122 TS

Museum Release Blanc de Blancs 2004 All the high-tensile structure of Tasmanian chardonnay, with 15 years on lees. At once creamy and silky in texture, tangy and cut in acid line, firm and fine in bitter phenolic structure. This will hold its confidence for another decade yet. The endurance of Tasmanian chardonnay, the class of Arras and the skill of Ed Carr are all on display here. Cork. 12.2% alc. **Rating** 94 $400 TS

Blanc de Blancs NV Aged for 30 months on lees, 8.1g/l dosage, disgorged Mar '20. The balance of stone fruit/apple flavour lights the mouth with precision; long finish and aftertaste. Cork. 12.5% alc. **Rating** 94 $35 JH

ŶŶŶŶ **A by Arras Premium Cuvée NV Rating** 90 $26 TS
Brut Elite NV Rating 90 $61 TS

House of Cards ★★★★★

17/3220 Caves Road, Yallingup, WA 6282 **Region** Margaret River
T (08) 9755 2583 **www**.houseofcardswine.com.au **Open** 7 days 10–5
Winemaker Travis Wray **Est.** 2011 **Dozens** 5000 **Vyds** 12ha

House of Cards is owned and operated by Elizabeth and Travis Wray; Travis managing the vineyard and making the wines, Elizabeth managing sales and marketing. The name of the winery is a reflection of the gamble that all viticulturists and winemakers face every vintage: 'You have to play the hand you are dealt by Mother Nature'. They only use certified organic estate-grown grapes, open-top fermentation, hand plunging and manual basket pressing. It's certainly doing it the hard way, but it must seem all worthwhile when they produce wines of such quality.

ŶŶŶŶ **The Royals Single Vineyard Margaret River Cabernet Sauvignon 2019** Still very closed at this inchoate stage of its life. This wine is very precise and compact, the fruit is clustered on the very middle of the palate and spools out down through the finish. Spiced satsuma plum, cassis, blackberry and raspberry pip. The tannins are silty fine, all of it bound together by sinewy, saline acidity. Screw cap. 13.8% alc. **Rating** 95 **To** 2036 $40 EL

The Royals Single Vineyard Margaret River Cabernet Sauvignon 2018 A cedary/earthy/savoury bouquet translates to a medium- to full-bodied palate, tannins and blackcurrant fruit competing for attention. There's a lot of extract, but it's not harsh. A wine for the patient. Screw cap. 14.2% alc. **Rating** 95 **To** 2038 $40 JH

Black Jack Single Vineyard Margaret River Malbec 2019 Malbec is thriving in Margaret River; the very best expressions show us that poise and elegance can be achieved with this grape. This is all about spiced plum, raspberry, green peppercorn and salted pomegranate. The quality here is evident, and with a further 6 months or so in bottle prior to release, it will be a beauty. Screw cap. 13.7% alc. **Rating** 95 **To** 2031 $48 EL

The Royals Single Vineyard Margaret River Chardonnay 2020 Balanced, textural and concentrated. The oak plays a role currently, however the fruit shows great prowess – it's going to overtake the oak with ease by the time release date rolls around. Great length of flavour shows the pedigree of Gingin clone in Margaret River. Screw cap. 13.5% alc. **Rating** 94 **To** 2031 $48 EL

Dead Man's Hand Margaret River Shiraz 2019 Margaret River saw a cool year in 2019, and so far, the reds that have been released onto the market are showing high spice aromas and detail/nuance on the palate. As does this wine, bolstered by a juicy succulence and bounce from 60% whole bunches. Very attractive. Screw cap. 13.9% alc. **Rating** 94 **To** 2028 $26 EL ✪

Howard Park   ★★★★★

Miamup Road, Cowaramup, WA 6284 **Region** Margaret River
T (08) 9756 5200 **www.**burchfamilywines.com.au **Open** 7 days 10–5
Winemaker Janice McDonald, Mark Bailey **Est.** 1986 **Vyds** 183ha
Over the last 30 or so years the Burch family has slowly acquired vineyards in Margaret River and Great Southern. The Margaret River vineyards range from Leston in Wilyabrup to Allingham in southern Karridale; Great Southern includes Mount Barrow and Abercrombie (the latter acquired in 2014), with Houghton cabernet clones, planted in 1975, all in Mount Barker. At the top of the portfolio are the Howard Park Abercrombie Cabernet Sauvignon and the Allingham Chardonnay, followed by the rieslings, chardonnay and sauvignon blanc; next come pairs of shiraz and cabernet sauvignon under the Leston and Scotsdale labels. The Miamup and the Flint Rock regional ranges were established in 2012. MadFish produces the full range of varietal wines, Gold Turtle the second tier of MadFish. The feng shui–designed cellar door is a must-see. A founding member of Australian First Families of Wines. Exports to all major markets.

♟♟♟♟♟ **Howard Park Mount Barker Riesling 2020** Wow. What a ripper this is. Powerful and intensely concentrated. Scintillating. Titillating. Rippling layers of flavour – I often describe Mount Barker as capable of producing rieslings of muscularity, strength and prowess: this is the very definition. The warmer year is seductive in this context, with the ripe, plush fruit propped up by vertical tent poles of acid. Awesome. Screw cap. 12.5% alc. **Rating** 97 **To** 2041 $34 EL ✪

♟♟♟♟♟ **Howard Park Museum Release Great Southern Riesling 2014** At 7 years old this is teetering on the brink of development, walking on the edge of a canyon of toasted honeysuckle, buttered sourdough, red apple and juniper. Precision and minerality await on the palate, underscored by taut acidity and a torrent of sweet fruit that courses over the palate. Many more years left in the tank. Screw cap. 12% alc. **Rating** 95 **To** 2036 $42 EL

Howard Park Allingham Margaret River Chardonnay 2019 This is very concentrated, with everything clustered up the very front and middle of the palate. The fruit moves on rather quickly, the crushed nuts, toasted oak and saline acid are the lingering memories here. Screw cap. 13% alc. **Rating** 95 **To** 2036 $89 EL

Howard Park Abercrombie Margaret River Mount Barker Cabernet Sauvignon 2018 The 2018 vintage produced wines of untold ripeness and balance and elevated the flavour concentration in almost every variety. This is concentrated and dense. There is a herbal bay/sage component to this wine that creates elegance and interest, the length of flavour very good. Classical cabernet. Minty/menthol. Screw cap. 14% alc. **Rating** 95 **To** 2046 $150 EL

Howard Park ASW Margaret River Cabernet Sauvignon Shiraz 2018 This is typically light, in the style of Howard Park, but has the best balance and concentration of the vintage release. Supple, long and very, very pretty, it speaks primarily of spiced raspberry, red licorice, clove, black tea and pomegranate. Screw cap. 14% alc. **Rating** 95 **To** 2036 $100 EL

ŶŶŶŶŶ **Howard Park Margaret River Chardonnay 2019** Rating 93 To 2035 $58 EL

Jeté Grand Vintage 2015 Rating 93 $48 EL

Howard Park Miamup Margaret River Sauvignon Blanc Semillon 2020 Rating 92 To 2025 $28 EL

Howard Park Flint Rock Great Southern Pinot Noir 2019 Rating 92 To 2027 $28 EL

Howard Park Flint Rock Great Southern Shiraz 2018 Rating 92 To 2031 $28 EL

Howard Park Miamup Margaret River Cabernet Sauvignon 2018 Rating 92 To 2030 $28 EL

Howard Park Leston Margaret River Cabernet Sauvignon 2017 Rating 92 To 2027 $50 EL

Howard Park Scotsdale Great Southern Cabernet Sauvignon 2017 Rating 92 To 2031 $50 EL

Howard Park Margaret River Sauvignon Blanc 2020 Rating 91 To 2025 $31 EL

Howard Park Miamup Margaret River Sauvignon Blanc 2019 Rating 91 To 2023 $28 EL

MadFish Gold Turtle Western Australia Pinot Gris 2020 Rating 91 To 2024 $20 EL ✪

Howard Park Miamup Margaret River Rosé 2020 Rating 91 To 2024 $28 EL

Howard Park Scotsdale Great Southern Shiraz 2017 Rating 91 To 2027 $50 EL

Petit Jeté Brut NV Rating 91 $32 EL

Jeté Brut NV Rating 90 $38 EL

Howard Vineyard   ★★★★☆

53 Bald Hills Road, Nairne, SA 5252 **Region** Adelaide Hills
T (08) 8188 0203 **www**.howardvineyard.com **Open** Wed–Fri 11–4, Sat–Sun 10–5
Winemaker Tom Northcott **Est.** 1998 **Dozens** 6000 **Vyds** 70ha
Howard Vineyard is a family-owned Adelaide Hills winery set among towering gum trees and terraced lawns. Pinot noir, chardonnay, pinot gris and sauvignon blanc are sourced from the 470m altitude Schoenthal 'Beautiful Valley' Vineyard, near Lobethal; Howard's Nairne Vineyard in the warmer Mount Barker district is home to shiraz, cabernet sauvignon and cabernet franc. All the wines are estate-grown. Winemaker Tom Northcott has a bachelor degree in viticulture and oenology from Adelaide University, and has worked vintages in the South of France, Barossa Valley, Western Australia and Tasmania.

ŶŶŶŶŶ **Amos Adelaide Hills Chardonnay 2019** Full-gamut contemporary chardonnay thinking here, all which coalesces into a delicious and complex wine, more pink grapefruit than white peach, though both are in the mix. There's gingery spice, cream biscuit and lemon delicious pudding notes, too. Well crafted and delicious to boot. Diam. 13.2% alc. **Rating** 95 **To** 2028 $50 TL

Adelaide Hills Shiraz 2019 A vibrant purple in the glass, very expressive bouquet of darker rose and spiced satsuma plum, with a spray of fresh kitchen herbs on the palate adding lift. There's some anise spice and black pepper notes as well. Plenty of action in this wine – it keeps the palate tweaked for some time. Screw cap. 13.5% alc. **Rating** 94 To 2028 $35 TL

🍷🍷🍷🍷🍷 Clover Adelaide Hills Pinot Noir 2020 **Rating** 93 To 2026 $35 TL
Block Q Adelaide Hills Sauvignon Blanc 2020 **Rating** 92 To 2024 $25 TL ✪
Adelaide Hills Pinot Gris 2020 **Rating** 92 To 2023 $25 TL ✪
Adelaide Hills Cabernet Franc Merlot Rosé 2020 **Rating** 92 To 2024 $35 TL
Amos Adelaide Hills Pinot Noir 2019 **Rating** 92 To 2030 $60 TL
400 Range Adelaide Hills Sauvignon Blanc 2020 **Rating** 91 To 2023 $20 TL ✪
Adelaide Hills Sparkling Rosé 2019 **Rating** 91 $35 TL
Adelaide Hills Pinot Noir Chardonnay 2020 **Rating** 90 $30 TL

Hugh Hamilton Wines   ★★★★★

94 McMurtrie Road, McLaren Vale, SA 5171 **Region** McLaren Vale
T (08) 8323 8689 **www**.hughhamiltonwines.com.au **Open** 7 days 11–5
Winemaker Nic Bourke **Est.** 1991 **Dozens** 18 500 **Vyds** 21.4ha
In 2014, 5th-generation family member Hugh Hamilton handed over the reins to daughter Mary. She developed the irreverent black sheep packaging. The business continues to embrace both mainstream and alternative varieties, its 85+yo shiraz and 65+yo cabernet sauvignon at its Blewitt Springs vineyard providing the ability to develop the Black label. There have been changes: in the way the vines are trellised, picking and fermenting in small open fermenters, using gravity for wine movements and maturation in high-quality French oak. The cellar door is lined with the original jarrah from Vat 15 of the historic Hamilton's Ewell winery, the largest wooden vat ever built in the Southern Hemisphere. Exports to the UK, the US, Canada, Denmark, Germany, Switzerland, Finland, South Korea, Singapore, Japan and China.

🍷🍷🍷🍷🍷 Black Blood III McLaren Vale Shiraz 2019 A more ethereal, elegant, detailed and fragrant wine than Black Blood I, and even more so than II. This said, it has neither the force of fruit nor the parry of granular tannins that make II special. More diaphanous of structure: flimsy tannins and palpably natural acidity. Kirsch, blackberry, turmeric, bergamot and red-fruit accents, rather than sheer black. And yet this wine expands across a long plume of flavour, belying the heady alcohol. Screw cap. 14.9% alc. **Rating** 95 To 2029 $79 NG
The Ruffian Liqueur Muscat NV Date, orange verbena, cinnamon, molasses and an overall aura of a Moroccan souk. The average age of the blend is modest, rather than extremely old. This promotes freshness amid the morass of exotic sweetness and textural detail. Viscous and generous, yet fresh and impressively long. Screw cap. 18% alc. **Rating** 95 $30 NG ✪

🍷🍷🍷🍷🍷 Black Blood II McLaren Vale Shiraz 2019 **Rating** 93 To 2030 $79 NG
Tonnellerie Boutes McLaren Vale Shiraz 2018 **Rating** 93 To 2027 $50 NG
Black Blood I McLaren Vale Shiraz 2019 **Rating** 92 To 2028 $79 NG
Shearer's Cut McLaren Vale Shiraz 2019 **Rating** 92 To 2024 $30 NG
Tonnellerie Vicard McLaren Vale Shiraz 2018 **Rating** 92 To 2026 $50 NG
Tonnellerie Francois Freres McLaren Vale Shiraz 2018 **Rating** 92 To 2027 $50 NG
Jekyll & Hyde McLaren Vale Shiraz Viognier 2018 **Rating** 92 To 2026 $50 NG
The Oddball McLaren Vale Saperavi 2017 **Rating** 92 To 2026 $150 NG
Ancient Earth McLaren Vale Shiraz 2018 **Rating** 91 To 2028 $50 NG
The Rascal McLaren Vale Shiraz 2018 **Rating** 90 To 2026 $30 NG
Black Ops McLaren Vale Shiraz Saperavi 2019 **Rating** 90 To 2023 $35 NG
Agent Provocateur 2020 **Rating** 90 To 2023 $28 NG
Goldilocks Moscato 2020 **Rating** 90 To 2021 $20 NG ✪

Hugo

246 Elliott Road, McLaren Flat, SA 5171 **Region** McLaren Vale
T (08) 8383 0098 **www**.hugowines.com.au **Open** Mon–Fri 10–5, Sat–Sun 10.30–5
Winemaker Renae Hirsch, Brian Light **Est.** 1982 **Dozens** 8000 **Vyds** 20ha
Hugo came into prominence in the late 1980s with some lovely ripe, sweet reds, which, while strongly American oak–influenced, were outstanding. It picked up the pace again after a dull period in the mid-'90s and has made the most of the recent run of good vintages. The estate plantings include shiraz, cabernet sauvignon, chardonnay, grenache and sauvignon blanc with part of the grape production sold. Exports to Canada.

Johnny's Block McLaren Vale Shiraz 2019 A highly regional blend that pulls few surprises. This said, dark plum and boysenberry flavours are nicely poised. Accents of anise, clove and pepper impart complexity. The oak, a frame of bitter chocolate and cedar. Solid drinking. Screw cap. 14% alc. **Rating** 89 **To** 2025 $45 NG

Humis Vineyard ★★★☆

3730 Heathcote-Rochester Road, Corop, Vic 3559 **Region** Heathcote
T 0419 588 044 **www**.humisvineyard.com **Open** By appt
Winemaker Cathy Branson **Est.** 2011 **Dozens** 800 **Vyds** 13.5ha
Both the wine labels and the letter from Hugh Jones to me giving the background to his and wife Michelle's venture share a battered, old-fashioned typeface. The letter was as interesting for what it didn't say as for what it did, although there was a connection in an improbable way because my mother Muriel's house name was Missy, also Michelle's nickname. The snapshot approach of the website's 'About Us' explains that in 2010, with the wine industry on its knees and a drought in full swing in Heathcote, Hugh saw a dusty paddock running down to a dry Lake Cooper with a 'for sale' sign. The decision was obvious: buy and promise that then very young twins, son Tex and daughter Mallee, wouldn't be too neglected. The ace in the hole was the irrigation water available to the property.

Heathcote Shiraz 2019 Sets a savoury tone from the outset with blackberry, black olive, herb, bay leaf and tilled earth. A lot of presence in the glass, quite muscular, too, but balanced by plush, sweet, spicy fruit and fine tannins. Packs a lot in for the price. Screw cap. 14.7% alc. **Rating** 90 **To** 2026 $25 JP

Hungerford Hill

2450 Broke Road, Pokolbin, NSW 2320 **Region** Hunter Valley
T (02) 4998 7666 **www**.hungerfordhill.com.au **Open** Sun–Thurs 10–5, Fri–Sat 10–6
Winemaker Bryan Currie **Est.** 1967 **Dozens** 22000 **Vyds** 5ha
Sam and Christie Arnaout purchased Hungerford Hill in December 2016, planning to refocus the 50yo label on its Hunter Valley origin, also adding significant new Lower Hunter vineyards at Sweetwater and Dalwood – the oldest continuously operating vineyard in Australia (see separate entries). Hungerford Hill uses these vineyards to bolster its Hunter Valley wines while continuing its more than 20-year association with the cool-climate Tumbarumba and Hilltops regions. Exports to all major markets.

Blackberry Vineyard Hunter Valley Semillon 2013 The 2013 vintage is among the very finest of all semillon vintages. Scintillating aromas of lemongrass, myrtle, curd and tonic. Despite its age, the wine hinges on the cusp of adolescence like a high-wire act, far from full maturity. The salubrious notes are yet to come. But mark my words, the wine's verve, impeccable poise and intensity of fruit assure it. Screw cap. 10.4% alc. **Rating** 96 **To** 2033 $65 NG ✪

Epic Hunter Valley Shiraz 2019 This is classy. Richly flavoured, full of body and laden with the baked sweet earth that defines the Hunter, without any excessive ambition detracting. The oak, classy and well nestled into the fray. Further aromas of clove, bergamot, charcuterie, mulberry, iodine and pepper grind. The finish, long, thickly textured and strident. Impressive gear. Screw cap. 14% alc. **Rating** 94 **To** 2032 $150 NG

ΨΨΨΨ Heavy Metal 2019 Rating 93 To 2031 $55 NG
Tumbarumba Chardonnay 2018 Rating 91 To 2027 $40 JF
Hunter Valley Shiraz 2019 Rating 91 To 2026 $45 NG
Hilltops Corvina 2028 Rating 91 To 2027 $45 JF
Hilltops Shiraz 2019 Rating 90 To 2029 $45 JF
Hilltops Sangiovese 2019 Rating 90 To 2026 $45 JF

Huntington Estate   ★★★★☆

Ulan Road, Mudgee, NSW 2850 **Region** Mudgee
T 1800 995 931 **www**.huntingtonestate.com.au **Open** Mon–Sat 10–5, Sun 10–4
Winemaker Tim Stevens **Est.** 1969 **Dozens** 13 000 **Vyds** 43.8ha
Since taking ownership of Huntington Estate from the founding Roberts family, Tim Stevens
has sensibly refrained from making major changes. The policy of having older vintage wines
available is continuing, making the cellar door a first port of call for visitors to Mudgee. 2019
marked the 30th and final Music Festival, described by ABC Classic FM as one of the best
chamber music festivals in the world. Exports to China.

ΨΨΨΨ **Basket Dried Mudgee Shiraz 2018** The use of American oak, pervasive and
seemingly tattooed on the culture here, works well on this this occasion. Liqueur
cherry bon-bon, mocha, bitter chocolate and dried herb. The oak, forceful, yet
absorbed by the sheer richness and tenacity of everything else going on. The
finish, long and impactful. Screw cap. 15.1% alc. **Rating** 93 To 2028 $75 NG
Mudgee Cabernet Sauvignon 2017 Subdued, highly savoury and mid weight.
Classically sculpted, with a firm bone of tannin defining a gait of restraint, the
wine's capacity to age across the medium term and flavours of currant, varnish,
sweet earth and crushed garden herb. The modest approach befits value and
drinkability in spades. Screw cap. 13.4% alc. **Rating** 91 To 2026 $32 NG
Block 3 Mudgee Cabernet Sauvignon 2016 An apotheosis of toasty oak,
hedonistic ripeness and forceful tannins, saturated with mocha and coffee bean.
Clearly a hot year, with an edge of sûrmaturité (overripeness), aromas of stewed
plum, spearmint, graphite and scorched rock. Yet in French, this is not a negative
but merely a reflection of the conditions. Here, the tannins are the wine's rock.
Its savoury fortress and bulwark against excess. Will age well. Screw cap. 14% alc.
Rating 91 To 2032 $75 NG
Special Reserve Mudgee Chardonnay 2019 A mid-weighted chardonnay,
unfettered by oak or excessive winemaking intervention. As a result, effusive
tangerine, cumquat and stone-fruit flavours, lithe and juicy, are splayed across a
crunchy finish. A gentle curb of vanillan oak directs the melee. A pleasure to drink.
Screw cap. 12.5% alc. **Rating** 90 To 2024 $35 NG
Special Reserve Mudgee Shiraz 2018 Shiraz from these parts drinks as a
savoury, mid-weighted dry red, rather than anything overtly exuberant or sweet of
fruit flavours. Subdued plays on tobacco leaf, iodine, pepper grind and cherry pith.
The tannins, an expansive quilt of briar and clove. Far from a dazzler. But a wine
you are likely to reach for again, as the bottle empties faster than many. Screw cap.
13.8% alc. **Rating** 90 To 2028 $45 NG
Special Reserve Mudgee Cabernet Sauvignon 2017 A traditional and, at
times, iconoclastic estate. The reds, sturdy and earthy, are usually released with a
few years of bottle age up their sleeves to tone and capture the tannic mettle of
the region. Minty. Sweet earthen scents, leather varnish, sassafras, red/blackcurrant
and trussed tomato. Graphite and pencil lead emerge with a swirl. A warm upfront
year. Age should impose greater savouriness and authority. Still nascent. Screw cap.
13.9% alc. **Rating** 90 To 2030 $45 NG

Hurley Vineyard   ★★★★★

101 Balnarring Road, Balnarring, Vic 3926 **Region** Mornington Peninsula
T (03) 5931 3000 **www**.hurleyvineyard.com.au **Open** 1st Fri & w'end each month 11–5
Winemaker Kevin Bell **Est.** 1998 **Dozens** 1100 **Vyds** 3.5ha

It's never as easy as it seems. Despite leading busy city lives, Kevin Bell and wife Tricia Byrnes have done most of the hard work in establishing Hurley Vineyard themselves, with some help from family and friends. Kevin completed the applied science (wine science) degree at CSU, drawing on a wide circle of fellow pinot noir makers in Australia and Burgundy. He has not allowed a significant heart issue to prevent him continuing with his first love.

ҶҶҶҶҶ **Garamond Balnarring Mornington Peninsula Pinot Noir 2019** Garamond is so dutiful. It just seems to fall into place, and yet, it marches to its own beat. It's a very distinctive wine. A mix of sweet-sour tangy cherries, segueing into fleshier fruit flavours and warm spices. It's generous across the palate, with a nice crunch to the acidity tethering shapely, textural tannins. Diam. 14.5% alc. **Rating** 96 **To** 2028 $85 JF

Estate Balnarring Mornington Peninsula Pinot Noir 2019 A riper vintage means there is no Hommage, instead the fruit went into this Estate wine. While certainly plusher and richer in outcome, it is still distinctly Hurley. Lovely aromatics, an array of Middle Eastern spices infusing dark cherries with plush tannins and flow across a full palate. There is still a modicum of elegance and a very high level of delight. Diam. 14.2% alc. **Rating** 95 **To** 2026 $50 JF

Lodestone Balnarring Mornington Peninsula Pinot Noir 2019 Staying true to the site, Kevin Bell needed to bring his fruit in at a higher baumé – anything less would have meant unripe flavours. However, the wine has a generosity and is certainly not warm, despite 14.6% alcohol. A wonderful wine, more suited to short-term drinking. It's imbued with plenty of tannin, moulded over sweet fruit, with some rhubarb and blood orange flavours and a touch of ferrous. Full bodied, deep and earthy. Don't wait. Ready now. Diam. 14.6% alc. **Rating** 95 **To** 2028 $75 JF

Hutton Vale Farm   ★★★★☆

65 Stone Jar Road, Angaston, SA 5353 **Region** Eden Valley
T (08) 8564 8270 **www.**huttonvale.com **Open** By appt
Winemaker Kym Teusner **Est.** 1960 **Dozens** 1500 **Vyds** 27.1ha
John Howard Angas arrived in SA in 1843 and inter alia gave his name to Angaston, purchasing and developing significant farming property close to the still embryonic town. He named part of this Hutton Vale and it is this property that is now owned and occupied by his great-great-grandson John and wife Jan Angas. In 2012, the Angas family and Teusner Wines shook hands on a new partnership arrangement, under which the Angases grow the grapes and Kym Teusner is responsible for the winemaking, sales and marketing of Hutton Vale wines. The vineyards in question first caught Kym's attention when he was at Torbreck and he fulfilled a long-term ambition with the new agreement. Just when the future seemed assured, the vineyards were badly affected by a grass fire in August '14. While much of the vineyard has regenerated, some of the oldest grenache vines were completely destroyed, as were 55 of the magnificent 500yo gum trees that are part of the striking landscape of Hutton Vale. Small quantities of its wines are exported to the UK and China.

ҶҶҶҶҶ **Eden Valley Shiraz 2017** Dense black/blueberry fruit is met evenly by generous high-cocoa dark chocolate and coffee-bean oak. The developing style of this cool vintage lends layers of sweet leather to a long finish. Firm, fine tannins will hold it for the medium-term. Screw cap. 14.7% alc. **Rating** 93 **To** 2032 $75 TS

Eden Valley Cabernet Sauvignon 2017 A savoury and lifted mood typifies the cool 2017 season, exemplified here in fresh bouquet garni. Crunchy, sweet blue/blackberry fruit is backed by supple milk chocolate French oak. An approachable vintage for Eden Valley cabernet, rounded and complete, yet with the fine tannin poise and natural acid line to hold for the medium term. Screw cap. 14.4% alc. **Rating** 92 **To** 2027 $75 TS

ҶҶҶҶ **Eden Valley Grenache Mataro 2017 Rating** 89 **To** 2022 $75 TS

Hutton Wines

PO Box 1214, Dunsborough, WA 6281 **Region** Margaret River
T 0417 923 126 **www.**huttonwines.com
Winemaker Michael Hutton **Est.** 2006 **Dozens** 550
This is another venture of the Hutton family of Gralyn fame, with Michael Hutton, who returned to the Margaret River region in 2005, establishing this micro-business the following year, while continuing his architectural practice. Tiny quantities of semillon sauvignon, chardonnay and cabernet sauvignon are produced; hardly enough to threaten Gralyn.

Idavue Estate

470 Northern Highway, Heathcote, Vic 3523 **Region** Heathcote
T 0429 617 287 **www.**idavueestate.com **Open** W'ends 10.30–5
Winemaker Andrew Whytcross, Sandra Whytcross **Est.** 2000 **Dozens** 600 **Vyds** 5.7ha
Owners and winemakers Andrew and Sandra Whytcross produce award-winning wines; the vineyard managed by Andy, the winery run using normal small-batch winemaking techniques. Shiraz is the flagship wine, with cabernet sauvignon, chardonnay and semillon also grown and made on the estate. The Barrelhouse cellar door is adorned with music paraphernalia and guitars, and regularly holds blues music events.

Blue Note Heathcote Shiraz 2017 Telltale Heathcote hues: so dark and impenetrable. A generous, youthful shiraz with lots of fruit and spice to latch on to from blackberry, mulberry, a touch of tart cranberry, kitchen spices and licorice. Layered oak is well judged, tannins are fine. Plenty to enjoy here at a fair price. Screw cap. 14% alc. **Rating** 94 **To** 2025 $30 JP ◒

Vat 2 Heathcote Shiraz 2017 Rating 93 **To** 2030 $30 JP

 Il Cattivo

65 Bay View Road, Port Elliot, SA, 5212 **Region** Currency Creek
T (08) 7079 1033 **www.**ilcattivo.com.au
Winemaker Anthony Catinari, Richard Bate **Est.** 2017 **Dozens** 1550 **Vyds** 1ha
A new winery venture by property developer Anthony Catinari, whose 2017-planted estate vineyard overlooks Fisherman's Bay at the seaside tourist township of Port Elliot, on the south coast of the Fleurieu Peninsula. The 1ha vineyard is planted to fiano and montepulciano, channelling Anthony's family roots in Italy's Abruzzo region. Additional fruit is sourced from McLaren Vale and the Adelaide Hills, and more plantings of Italian and Spanish varieties, as well as Georgian variety saperavi, are planned. The winemaking is carried out onsite, Anthony has sought training and seeks consultant advice when needed. (TL)

McLaren Vale Grenache 2019 From Blewitt Springs. 10% whole bunches used in a wild fermentation, then pressed into old French hogsheads for 12 months. Familiar grenache bouquet: bush florals, raspberry licorice, with nice underlying earthy notes. Sweet crimson fruit flavours with good acidity/tannin tension and finish. Right in the regional grenache zone. Screw cap. 14.4% alc. **Rating** 92 **To** 2025 $32 TL

In Dreams

3/436 Johnston Street, Abbotsford, Vic 3067 **Region** Yarra Valley
T (03) 8413 8379 **www.**indreams.com.au
Winemaker Nina Stocker **Est.** 2013 **Dozens** 1200
'Hand-crafted wines begin with a dream, the dream of what might be as the first vine is planted.' Nina Stocker sources pinot noir and chardonnay from 3 low-yielding vineyards in the cool Upper Yarra Valley. The cooler microclimate of the area lends itself to traditional winemaking techniques, such as small-batch fermentation and delicate use of French oak, which allow the fruit to express itself. Exports to the UK, Europe and Asia.

ΨΨΨΨ Yarra Valley Pinot Noir 2019 One of those wines that is priced right and delivers plenty of drinking pleasure. Maraschino cherries, stewed rhubarb dotted with anise and dried herbs. It's not a big wine, even if the tannins are a little chewy and grippy, as there's bright acidity keeping it afloat. Screw cap. 13.5% alc. Rating 90 To 2026 $29 JF

Indigo Vineyard ★★★★★

1221 Beechworth-Wangaratta Road, Everton Upper, Vic 3678 **Region** Beechworth
T (03) 5727 0233 **www.**indigovineyard.com.au **Open** 7 days 11–4
Winemaker Stuart Hordern, Marc Scalzo **Est.** 1999 **Dozens** 6000 **Vyds** 46.15ha
Indigo Vineyard has a little over 46ha of vineyards planted to 11 varieties, including the top French and Italian grapes. The business was and is primarily directed to growing grapes for sale to Brokenwood, but since 2004 increasing amounts have been vinified for the Indigo label. The somewhat incestuous nature of the whole business sees the Indigo wines being made at Brokenwood (Marc Scalzo makes the Pinot Grigio). Exports to France.

ΨΨΨΨ Beechworth Pinot Noir 2019 Impressive finesse and elegance on display here, with summer-berry aromas, gentle herbals and undergrowth. Delivers a solid core of bright cherry fruits, potpourri and light spice on a juicy and vibrant palate. Fine-knit tannins complete an impressive picture. Screw cap. 12.8% alc. **Rating** 95 To 2028 $40 JP
Beechworth Shiraz 2018 Another strong example of Beechworth shiraz. Medium-bodied and lovely, rippling with high spice and crunchy, fresh-berried red fruits. Red cherry and plum, cinnamon and graphite. It's all about fragrance, fruit purity and tannins. Seamless. Screw cap. 14% alc. **Rating** 95 To 2028 $36 JP
Beechworth Chardonnay 2019 A shining, bright and breezy citrus-infused chardonnay that lays out why chardonnay is the the grape of the Beechworth region. Boasts a freshness of citrus and stone fruit, gentle florals, flint, crème brûlée texture and a lick of lingering spice. Oak is a background thought, the fruit is the star. One smart vinous package. Screw cap. 12.9% alc. **Rating** 94 To 2025 $36 JP
Secret Village Beechworth Pinot Noir 2018 Boasting the scents of autumn and the veggie patch with red cherry, briar, undergrowth, tomato leaf and nettley herbal overtones. Presents restrained and dry but there is a charm to its texture, a sweet fruit liveliness to the palate that engages. Tasted 5 months before release. Screw cap. 12.5% alc. **Rating** 94 To 2025 $65 JP

ΨΨΨΨ Secret Village Beechworth Chardonnay 2019 Rating 93 To 2026 $50 JP
Secret Village Beechworth Chardonnay 2018 Rating 93 To 2026 $50 JP
Alpine Valleys Beechworth Chardonnay 2018 Rating 92 To 2026 $36 JP
Secret Village Beechworth Viognier 2018 Rating 91 To 2024 $36 JP

Inkwell ★★★★☆

PO Box 33, Sellicks Beach, SA 5174 **Region** McLaren Vale
T 0430 050 115 **www.**inkwellwines.com **Open** By appt
Winemaker Dudley Brown **Est.** 2003 **Dozens** 800 **Vyds** 12ha
Inkwell was born in 2003 when Dudley Brown returned to Australia from California and bought a rundown vineyard on the serendipitously named California Road. He inherited 5ha of neglected shiraz, and planted an additional 7ha to viognier (2.5ha), zinfandel (2.5ha) and heritage shiraz clones (2ha). The 5-year restoration of the old vines and establishment of the new reads like the ultimate handbook for aspiring vignerons, particularly those who are prepared to work non-stop. The reward has been rich. Dudley is adamant that the production will be capped at 1000 dozen; almost all the grapes are sold. Exports to the US and Canada.

ΨΨΨΨ Tangerine McLaren Vale Viogner 2019 A skin-inflected amber expression. Very good it is, too! A moreish phenolic burr corrals viognier's effusive aromas while imparting an umami warmth, savoury and nourishing. Flavours of dried hay and white miso mesh with apricot pith, orange blossom and the curry powder and chutney scents also derived from the skins. Wonderful intensity and life. A zap of volatility for lift. A whole wine, from the attack and middle, to the long, textural finish. Screw cap. 11.6% alc. **Rating** 95 **To** 2026 $26 NG ✪

TTTTT Deeper Well McLaren Vale Shiraz 2012 **Rating** 93 **To** 2026 $100 NG
Deeper Well McLaren Vale Shiraz 2011 **Rating** 93 **To** 2024 $100 NG
Pressure Drop Cabernet Sauvignon 2018 **Rating** 93 **To** 2030 $40 NG
Infidels Primitivo 2018 **Rating** 93 **To** 2026 $30 NG
Blonde on Blonde Viognier 2017 **Rating** 92 **To** 2023 $26 NG
Perfect Day Shiraz 2018 **Rating** 92 **To** 2028 $40 NG
Road to Joy Shiraz Primitivo 2018 **Rating** 92 **To** 2027 $26 NG
Reckoner Cabernet Shiraz 2017 **Rating** 92 **To** 2026 $30 NG
Piece of my Heart Grenache 2017 **Rating** 91 **To** 2022 $30 NG
Pink Cashmere Nouveau Mataro 2019 **Rating** 90 **To** 2023 $30 NG

Innocent Bystander ★★★★

316 Maroondah Highway, Healesville, Vic 3777 **Region** Yarra Valley
T (03) 5999 9222 **www**.innocentbystander.com.au **Open** 7 days 11–9
Winemaker Joel Tilbrook, Cate Looney, Geoff Alexander, Katherine Brown, Tom Canning **Est.** 1997 **Dozens** 49000 **Vyds** 45ha
In April 2016 Brown Brothers and Giant Steps announced that the Innocent Bystander brand (including Mea Culpa) and stock had been sold to Brown Brothers. As part of the acquisition, Brown Brothers purchased the White Rabbit Brewery site adjacent to Giant Steps and this has become the cellar door home of Innocent Bystander. Its business is in 2 completely different wine categories, both fitting neatly together. On one hand is the big volume (confidential) of vintage moscato, the grapes coming from the King Valley; and non-vintage prosecco, similarly sourced. The other side of the business is the premium, high quality Yarra Valley single varietal wines with substantial brand value. Exports to the UK, the US and other major markets.

TTTTT Mea Culpa Yarra Valley Pinot Noir 2019 Turns the volume down and the brooding intensity up. The friendly Yarra Valley cherry/strawberry side is there with a brightness but, so too, a dark lingering power. It has quite the presence, with savoury, sour cherry, black tea, pomegranate, smokehouse and earthy notes. Supple tannins. A sense of intrigue and beauty. Screw cap. 14% alc. **Rating** 95 **To** 2026 $49 JP

TTTTT Yarra Valley Chardonnay 2020 **Rating** 90 **To** 2025 $25 JP

Iron Cloud Wines ★★★★★

Suite 16, 18 Stirling Highway, Nedlands, WA 6009 (postal) **Region** Geographe
T 0401 860 891 **www**.ironcloudwines.com.au
Winemaker Michael Ng **Est.** 1999 **Dozens** 2500 **Vyds** 11ha
In 2003 owners Warwick Lavis and Geoff and Karyn Cross purchased the then-named Pepperilly Estate, which had been planted in 1999 on red gravelly loam soils. Peppermint trees line the Henty Brook, the natural water source for the vineyard. In 2017 Michael Ng, formerly chief winemaker for Rockcliffe, succeeded Coby Ladwig. Exports to China.

TTTTT Rock of Solitude Ferguson Valley Touriga 2019 As is usual for Iron Cloud Wines, this shows brilliant purity of fruit, combined with succulent, chewy tannins that mean the bottle has the propensity to evaporate. Good length of favour rounds it all out. Another cracker here; the earthy finish (arnica, aniseed, clove, freshly turned earth and satsuma plum) elevates it beyond a delicious, gluggable drink and catapults it into the realm of serious. Screw cap. 14.5% alc. **Rating** 95 **To** 2031 $32 EL ✪
Rock of Solitude Ferguson Valley Chardonnay 2020 Majority Dijon clones (95, 96, 277, 76). Hand picked, wild ferment, matured 9 months in French oak (30% new). Impressive winemaking for the price. The clones explain the shape and feel; Dijon acidity is on the citrus spectrum and runs a linear course straight over the palate – often put through some mlf to assist with the acid, which

contributes the crushed nut character here. Nectarine, white peach and cashew. Classy. Screw cap. 13.8% alc. **Rating** 94 **To** 2029 $25 EL ❂

The Alliance Ferguson Valley Chardonnay 2019 Wild fermented in barrel, 9 months in oak (30% new). The oak is very evident at this early stage, but the Gingin clone fruit has great power and intensity on the palate. There's a lot to like here; yellow peach, sea salt, lemon pith, hints of pink grapefruit and jasmine tea. It is rich with these flavours. Perhaps by the time this is released, the oak will have sunk into these characters and it will be more balanced. Screw cap. 13.5% alc. **Rating** 94 **To** 2031 $50 EL

Rock of Solitude Ferguson Valley Cabernet Malbec 2019 The vibrant colour matches the vibrant aromatics, and it matches the vibrant flavours, too. Uncomplicated, unfettered deliciousness. The cabernet brings structure, perfume and crunchiness, while the malbec boosts the perfume and the colour, providing a lush backdrop of purple berry fruits. Pretty awesome stuff for the price. Screw cap. 14% alc. **Rating** 94 **To** 2036 $32 EL

Pepperilly Ferguson Valley Cabernet Shiraz 2019 This is supple, alive and packed to the rafters with bright, summer raspberry, strawberry, mulberry and red licorice. The tannins are very fine, almost willowy, and gently shape the fruit through the finish. Not complex, but utterly delicious in a nouveau way. Screw cap. 14.5% alc. **Rating** 94 **To** 2025 $25 EL ❂

♟♟♟♟♟ **Rock of Solitude Purple Patch Ferguson Valley GSM 2019** Rating 93 To 2028 $32 EL

Rock of Solitude Ferguson Valley Mourvèdre 2018 Rating 93 To 2027 $32 EL

Pepperilly Ferguson Valley Sauvignon Blanc Semillon 2020 Rating 91 To 2025 $35 EL

Ironwood Estate ★★★☆

2191 Porongurup Road, Porongurup, WA 6234 **Region** Porongurup
T (08) 9853 1126 **www.**ironwoodestatewines.com.au **Open** Wed–Mon 11–5
Winemaker Wignalls Wines (Michael Perkins) **Est.** 1996 **Dozens** 2500 **Vyds** 5ha
Ironwood Estate was established in 1996 under the ownership of Mary and Eugene Harma. An estate vineyard of riesling, sauvignon blanc, chardonnay, shiraz, merlot and cabernet sauvignon (in more or less equal amounts) was planted on a northern slope of the Porongurup Range. Exports to Japan and Singapore.

♟♟♟♟♟ **Great Southern Riesling 2020** Succulent, approachable and pure, this has all the regional hallmarks of Porongurup: jasmine florals, citrus pith and juicy acidity, without the final length or phenolic structuring. This does not mean it will not deliver pleasure, though. It's lovely and well put together, with a distinct saline thread running through its core. Screw cap. 12% alc. **Rating** 90 **To** 2028 $28 EL

Irvine

63 Valley Road, Angaston, SA 5353 **Region** Eden Valley
T (08) 8564 1110 **www.**irvinewines.com.au
Winemaker Peter Miles **Est.** 1983 **Dozens** 15000 **Vyds** 111ha
When James (Jim) Irvine established his eponymous winery, he chose a singularly difficult focus for the business: the production of great merlot from the Eden Valley. Throughout the years of establishment, and indeed thereafter, he was a much-in-demand consultant, bobbing up in all sorts of places. Yet when he decided to sell the business in 2014, its potential was greatly increased with the dowry provided by the purchasing Wade and Miles families. In 1867 Henry Winter Miles planted 0.8ha of shiraz. Successive generations of the Miles family had added to the vineyard portfolio from 1967, both acquiring existing vineyards and planting others (Ben's Block vineyard at Penrice is home to 120yo vines). Henry's great-grandson Peter Miles and partner John Wade collectively own 160ha spread through the Barossa and Eden valleys, although only 80ha fall within the new Irvine partnership. Exports to the UK, Switzerland, UAE, Singapore, Malaysia, Japan, Taiwan, Hong Kong and China.

ŸŸŸŸŸ Spring Hill Eden Valley Riesling 2020 Endowed with amiable flesh and spice
while upholding impressive tension and zest, this is an impeccably assembled
riesling at a fantastic price. Picked at precisely the right instant, shot with exact
lime and Granny Smith apple fruit. Fine-tuned phenolic control is tricky at this
level of concentration, calling for a steady hand in both the vines and the winery.
Screw cap. 12.2% alc. **Rating** 94 **To** 2030 $24 TS **✪**

ŸŸŸŸŸ Special Release Eden Valley Grand Merlot 2018 Rating 93 To 2028
$150 TS
The Estate Eden Valley Merlot Cabernet Franc 2019 Rating 92 To 2027
$30 TS
The Estate Barossa Cabernet Sauvignon 2019 Rating 91 To 2029 $30 TS
The Estate Eden Valley Shiraz 2019 Rating 90 To 2029 $30 TS

Itty Bitty Wine Company ★★★☆

PO Box 1146, Balhannah, SA 5242 **Region** Adelaide Hills
T 0414 493 215 **www**.ibwc.com.au
Winemaker Ian Tattersall **Est.** 2013 **Dozens** 160
Ian Tattersall explains he had been interested in wine since the early years of attending medical
school in the '80s, 'Despite being exposed to over-oaked chardonnays, grassy NZ savvies, and
fruit and oak bomb red wines, I developed a passion for the complexity of pinot noir, and the
power of champagnes (particularly enjoying exploring the world of grower champagnes'. In
1995 he built a house on a property in Lenswood that could potentially suit a small vineyard,
but needed more energy and dollars to actually plant the vineyard. He did, however, graduate
from the University of Adelaide graduate diploma of oenology course. Itty Bitty Wine
Company took a further step towards reality with the conversion of a shed on the property to
become a winery facility, self-limiting in size of production at ±150 dozen bottles. There was
a further limitation: the council giving him approval to only process 10t per vintage. He dryly
observes, 'I guess the name is unlikely to need changing for reasons of accuracy'. The main
challenges he found were in procuring super-small winery equipment, but with perseverance,
acquired a little crusher, little fermenters, little presses and little pumps. He even found a label
printer prepared to do business. His current plans are to maintain the status quo, find a
customer base and leave further expansion until partial or full retirement of the stethoscope.
Where he goes from there is written in the sand.

ŸŸŸŸ Adelaide Hills Pinot Noir 2018 Small-scale winemaking. Destemmed, then
20% stems returned. Vinified in 300L lots. Matured in 2–4yo hogsheads for
18 months on lees, stirred regularly. Quite perfumed, with plenty of classic cherry
fruit, and faint orange peel/amaro notes towards the finish. An easy-drinking
$20 pinot. Screw cap. 14.2% alc. **Rating** 89 **To** 2024 $20 TL

J.M. Lentini ★★★

23 Gawley Street, Nuriootpa, SA 5355 **Region** Barossa Valley
T 0412 537 490 **www**.jmlentini.com.au
Winemaker John Lentini **Est.** 2016 **Dozens** 100
Automotive design engineer John Lentini established his eponymous brand in 2016 after
14 years making wines for family and friends in his suburban Melbourne garage. Regular visits
to the Barossa on the back of business trips to Adelaide introduced him to the winemakers and
growers of the region, enabling him to realise his vision to 'make single-vineyard wines that
naturally convey the characteristics of the site and vintage'. His mandate is pure expressions of
shiraz from the cooler sites of the Barossa, in particular the Eden Valley. The range currently
comprises just one wine, with the hope of expanding to showcase the diversity of site
expressions across the Barossa. (TS)

ŸŸŸŸ Eden Valley Syrah 2018 A herbal, savoury and spicy Eden Valley shiraz of fine-
boned tannins and tangy acidity. A touch of whole bunches brings an attractive,
subtle potpourri lift. It concludes a little dried out and tired, lacking fruit vibrancy
and definition. cork. 13.9% alc. **Rating** 89 **To** 2021 $60 TS

Jack Estate   ★★★★

15025 Riddoch Highway, Coonawarra, SA 5263 **Region** Coonawarra
T (08) 8736 3130 **www**.jackestate.com **Open** By appt
Winemaker Conrad Slabber **Est.** 2011 **Dozens** 10000 **Vyds** 201ha
Jack Estate was founded in 2011 by a group of grapegrowers who acquired the large Mildara
Blass winery in Coonawarra. Wines are sourced from the estate vineyards in Coonawarra
(1ha of cabernet sauvignon) and the Murray Darling (200ha). Jack Estate also sources grapes
from neighbouring grapegrowers in Coonawarra and Wrattonbully to complete their 3-tiered
range. Exports to Malaysia, Singapore, the Philippines, Thailand and China.

ŶŶŶŶŶ **Coonawarra Cabernet Sauvignon 2015** Intensely flavoured with chocolate-
coated blackberries, currants, mint leaf lollies and refreshing leafy cabernet nuances.
It's full bodied and rich, with the cedary sweet toasty French oak adding another
layer. Thankfully this stops short of being too ripe and too much. Just. Screw cap.
15% alc. **Rating** 93 **To** 2035 $55 JF
Coonawarra Cabernet Sauvignon 2018 These entry-level wines are OK.
Cabernet is the pick. Varietal yet simple favours, but it's not too soupy or mawkish.
This has some pleasing earthy, savoury flavours to the textural tannins. Screw cap.
14% alc. **Rating** 90 **To** 2025 $25 JF

ŶŶŶŶ **Mythology Coonawarra Shiraz 2015** **Rating** 89 **To** 2027 $55 JF

Jack Rabbit Vineyard   ★★★★

85 McAdams Lane, Bellarine, Vic 3221 **Region** Geelong
T (03) 5251 2223 **www**.jackrabbitvineyard.com.au **Open** 7 days 10–5
Winemaker Nyall Condon **Est.** 2010 **Dozens** 5000 **Vyds** 20ha
Nestled onsite next to the acclaimed Jack Rabbit Restaurant is 1.5ha of pinot noir. Jack
Rabbit Vineyard also owns another 18.5ha of vineyards across The Bellarine, planted on sandy
loam, clay and volcanic-influenced soils, all going in to their range of estate-grown wines.

ŶŶŶŶŶ **The Bellarine Shiraz 2019** Cool-climate savouriness all the way in this super-
spiced shiraz. Dark-fruit expression in plum, black cherry, bramble berry, with
layers of savoury earth and game, graphite, pepper, spice and toasty oak. Fresh and
composed, with pronounced tannins, it should age a treat. Screw cap. 14% alc.
Rating 94 **To** 2029 $45 JP

ŶŶŶŶŶ **The Bellarine Chardonnay 2019** **Rating** 93 **To** 2026 $38 JP

Jackson Brooke   ★★★★☆

126 Beaconsfield Parade, Northcote, Vic 3070 (postal) **Region** Henty
T 0466 652 485 **www**.jacksonbrookewine.com.au
Winemaker Jackson Brooke **Est.** 2013 **Dozens** 500
Jackson Brooke graduated from The University of Melbourne in 2004 with a science degree
and, having spent a summer working at Tarrington Vineyards, went on to study oenology
at Lincoln University in NZ. A vintage at Wedgetail Estate in the Yarra Valley was followed
by stints in Japan, Southern California and then 3 years as assistant winemaker to Ben Portet.
With his accumulated knowledge of boutique winemaking he has abandoned any idea of
building a winery for the foreseeable future, currently renting space at Witchmount Estate.

ŶŶŶŶŶ **Henty Chardonnay 2019** Cool-climate Henty presents a petite, fine-boned
body upon which to build a chardonnay. The maker shows a deft hand with oak,
not overpowering the subtlety but working alongside it. Impressive fruit purity of
citrus, green plum, spiced apple, almond-meal aromas. Smooth and supple across
the palate with creamy fruit flavours, pear and crunchy acidity. Of the less-is-more
school of chardonnay. Screw cap. 12.5% alc. **Rating** 95 **To** 2027 $28 JP **✪**
A.T. Henty Chardonnay 2019 An instantly creamy, buttery and complex
impression. Enticing scent of nougat, honey, biscuit spices. Flavours build in the

mouth, the scene changes to grilled peach, ruby grapefruit, citrus and toasted almonds, drawing into a crisp, savoury finish. All this and still a youngster. Screw cap. 12.5% alc. **Rating** 94 **To** 2027 $48 JP

 G.D. Henty Syrah 2019 Rating 92 **To** 2027 $48 JP

Jackson's Hill Vineyard ★★★☆

Mount View Road, Mount View, NSW 2321 **Region** Hunter Valley
T 1300 720 098 **www.**jacksonshill.com.au **Open** By appt
Winemaker Greg Walls **Est.** 1983 **Dozens** 10000 **Vyds** 10ha
One of the low-profile operations on the spectacularly scenic Mount View Road, making small quantities of estate-grown wine. Sold through the cellar door and Australian Wine Selectors plus exports to China.

ҰҰҰҰҰ Orange Pinot Grigio 2020 Impressive grigio. Optimally ripe, with a swathe of baked apple and nashi pear granita, curbed by a gentle ripple of phenolics and what feels like a lick of oak. Yet the fruit wins out, boasting a lovely flow from attack to long finish. Screw cap. 12.7% alc. **Rating** 91 **To** 2023 $26 NG
Panoramic Langhorne Creek Grenache Shiraz Mourvèdre 2019 A fairly powerful expression of this blend, with a solid bank of flavour and structure that's evenly balanced. It leans to the more robust end of this blend's potential. Screw cap. 14.2% alc. **Rating** 91 **To** 2028 $28 TL
Panoramic Orange Sauvignon Blanc 2019 This mid-weighted sauvignon has an aura of fealty to high country, as much as the textural cogs of precision and purity of fruit. Optimally ripe. Greengage, cantaloupe and a hint of guava, neither straying into the more verdant iterations of the grape, nor the sweet/sour fruity ones. Poised and confident in an easy-drinking guise. Screw cap. 12.8% alc. **Rating** 90 **To** 2022 $26 NG

ҰҰҰҰ Hunter Valley Semillon 2019 Rating 88 **To** 2027 $26 NG
Panoramic Hunter Valley Cabernet Franc 2018 Rating 88 **To** 2022 $28 NG

Jacob's Creek ★★★★☆

2129 Barossa Valley Way, Rowland Flat, SA 5352 **Region** Barossa Valley
T (08) 8521 3000 **www.**jacobscreek.com **Open** 7 days 10–4.30
Winemaker Dan Swincer **Est.** 1973 **Dozens** 5700000 **Vyds** 740ha
Jacob's Creek (owned by Pernod Ricard) is one of the largest-selling brands in the world, and the global success of the base range has had the perverse effect of prejudicing many critics and wine writers who sometimes fail to objectively look behind the label and taste what is in fact in the glass. Exports include the UK, the US, Canada and China, and other major markets.

ҰҰҰҰҰ 1819 The Birth of Johann Barossa Coonawarra Shiraz Cabernet 2018 A blend of monumental promise, declared from the outset in the deepest, vibrant purple hue. Coiled up tight, a powerful core of black fruits calls for considerable time to burst from its shell. French oak offers exacting support, rightly building structure before flavour, setting off superfine, enduring tannins. Line, length and integrity on another plane. Come back in 20 years. Cork. 14.7% alc. **Rating** 97 **To** 2048 $80 TS **◎**

ҰҰҰҰҰ Johann Barossa Valley Shiraz Cabernet 2018 The old vines of the Willandra vineyard on the banks of Jacob's Creek build a powerful blend of spicy, tangy, bright black-fruit presence and grand potential. Old-vine exotic spice is amplified by whole-bunch fermentation. Fruit and oak unite in a tannin frame of all-consuming presence. Outstanding line, length and endurance. Cork. 14.4% alc. **Rating** 96 **To** 2048 $120 TS
Survivor Vine Barossa Shiraz 2016 Barossa survivor vines are at least 70 years of age, uniting here in a quintessential modern shiraz. All the black fruit and dark

chocolate one expects is bathed in a considerable display of tannin: polished, fine and commanding great endurance. Grand testimony to the deep fruit resources and blending wizardy of the JC team. Cork. 14.6% alc. **Rating** 95 To 2042 $110 TS

Limited Release Estate Barossa Valley Riesling 2020 Half fermented and matured for 6 months in seasoned 110L oak octaves makes for a very different take on Jacob's Creek's house style. It delivers all the concentrated lime and lemon fruit and acid tension to be expected, wrapped in folds of brioche, roast almonds and spice, bringing a creaminess to high-tensile structure. It takes quite some talent to achieve this stark juxtaposition with such seamless, effortless grace. Screw cap. 10.5% alc. **Rating** 94 **To** 2028 $50 TS

Organic McLaren Vale Shiraz 2017 A ripe, sweetly-fruited McLaren Vale shiraz of medium purple hue and spicy satsuma plum and blackberry. It swallows new oak, contributing more in firm, fine, drying tannin structure than in high-cocoa dark chocolate flavour. One for the cellar. Cork. 14.7% alc. **Rating** 94 To 2037 $60 TS

🍷🍷🍷🍷♀ **Limited Release Coonawarra Fumé Blanc 2020** **Rating** 92 **To** 2030 $35 TS
Biodynamic McLaren Vale Shiraz 2016 **Rating** 92 **To** 2026 $60 TS
Le Petit Rosé 2020 **Rating** 91 **To** 2021 $18 TS ☉
Jacob Premium Cuvée Vintage Sparkling 2017 **Rating** 91 $30 TS
Reserve Sauvignon Blanc 2020 **Rating** 90 **To** 2021 $18 TS ☉
Nature's Craft Organic Rosé 2020 **Rating** 90 **To** 2021 $20 TS ☉

Jaeschke's Hill River Clare Estate ★★★★★

406 Quarry Road, Clare, SA 5453 **Region** Clare Valley
T (08) 8843 4100 **www**.hillriverclareestate.com.au **Open** 7 days 10–4
Winemaker Steve Baraglia, Angela Meaney **Est.** 1980 **Dozens** 1750 **Vyds** 180ha
The Jaeschke family has been broadacre farming in the Hill River district for over 50 years. In May 2010 they purchased the neighbouring 180ha vineyard established by Penfolds in 1980. It is planted to 16 varieties, including 21.2ha of riesling, the success of which has led to a stream of trophies and gold medals since '13, the first entry in wine shows. The venture began as the idea of daughter Michelle, with the expectation a medal or two. The success led to the use of one of the Atco huts on the property, with a card table set up as a tasting bench – bypassed if you arrive with BYO picnic food, use of the onsite barbecue facilities encouraged. A cellar door grant from PIRSA has led to a substantial facilities upgrade. In March '20, 4 vintages of Riesling ('16 to '19) were available at $18 a bottle, the '15 at $25. If you are a Wine Club member, the price (for a 12-bottle case) is even lower.

James & Co Wines ★★★★

136 Main Street, Rutherglen, Vic 3685 **Region** Beechworth
T 0447 341 373 **www**.jamesandcowines.com.au **Open** Thurs–Mon 11–6
Winemaker Ricky James **Est.** 2011 **Dozens** 750
Ricky and Georgie James intended to buy land in Beechworth and establish a vineyard planted primarily to sangiovese. They say, 'Serendipity led us to Mark Walpole, and we were given the chance to purchase fruit from his Fighting Gully Road Vineyard'. They have set up their home and cellar door in Rutherglen and intend to float between the 2 regions.

🍷🍷🍷🍷♀ **Mornington Peninsula Pinot Grigio 2020** With smoke taint on its doorstep in 2020, James & Co. ventured to the Mornington Peninsula to source its pinot grigio. The maritime climate brings an interesting take on the grape, with a strong sea spray, oyster shell minerality coming through. Lemon, grapefruit pith and quince aromas combine in a tight and vibrant wine that delivers a straight line of acidity, oyster shell, pear drop and nashi pear with exuberant life and crunch. Screw cap. 13% alc. **Rating** 90 **To** 2024 $28 JP

Heathcote Mourvèdre Rosé 2020 James & Co. are well known for their Beechworth Sangiovese Rosé but this year they launch a mourvèdre rosé from Heathcote. Maybe not as savoury as the sangiovese, although there is an inkling

of that on the horizon. It's definitely in keeping with the laid-back James & Co.
approach though, with its mid salmon colour, strawberry, raspberry and potpourri
notes and fruit-first summery feel. Screw cap. 13% alc. **Rating** 90 **To** 2024 $28 JP
Beechworth Sangiovese 2019 A bright young sangiovese full of red cherry,
raspberry liveliness and bounce. Summer berries and anise with layers of spice on
a palate medium in weight and firm in structure. Screw cap. 14% alc. **Rating** 90
To 2025 $36 JP

James Estate   ★★★☆

1142–1210 Hermitage Road, Pokolbin, NSW 2320 **Region** Hunter Valley
T (02) 6547 5168 **www.**jamesestatewines.com.au **Open** Fri–Sun 10–4
Winemaker Giacomo Soldani **Est.** 1997 **Dozens** 10 000 **Vyds** 86ha
James Estate has had an unsettled corporate existence at various times since 1997, but has
now straightened the ship under the ownership of Sydney-based businessman Sam Fayad. The
vineyard is planted to shiraz, cabernet sauvignon, merlot, petit verdot, cabernet franc, semillon,
chardonnay and verdelho.

ＹＹＹＹＹ **Reserve Baerami Vineyard Hunter Valley Shiraz 2019** A step above the
estate bottling in terms of the intensity of the sweet cherry and terracotta flavours.
Savoury and medium of feel, despite the alcohol amping higher than the regional
push toward brisker luncheon styles of yore (at least among the best makers). This
said, the finish is long and scented with mulch, porcini and umami-laden beef
bouillon. Warming. Moreish. A very nice drink. Screw cap. 14.5% alc. **Rating** 91
To 2030 $32 NG

Jansz Tasmania   ★★★★★

1216b Pipers Brook Road, Pipers Brook, Tas 7254 **Region** Northern Tasmania
T (03) 6382 7066 **www.**jansz.com **Open** 7 days 10–4
Winemaker Teresa Heuzenroeder **Est.** 1985 **Dozens** 38 000 **Vyds** 30ha
Jansz is part of Hill-Smith Family Vineyards and was one of the early sparkling wine labels in
Tasmania, stemming from a short-lived relationship between Heemskerk and Louis Roederer.
Its 15ha of chardonnay, 12ha of pinot noir and 3ha of pinot meunier correspond almost
exactly to the blend composition of the Jansz wines. Part of the former Frogmore Creek
Vineyard purchased by Hill-Smith Family Vineyards in December 2012 is dedicated to the
needs of Jansz Tasmania. Exports to all major markets.

ＹＹＹＹＹ **Single Vineyard Vintage Chardonnay 2013** The most emphatic evidence yet
that Piper's River is an exemplar for more than just pinot noir! A year older than
previous releases, yet fresher and more vibrant than ever. This is an exceptional
blanc de blancs and one of the finest from Jansz yet. All the energy and tension
of this cool site is infused in its lively frame and pinpoint precision of lemon fruit.
White peach and pear bring body and intensity, backed magnificently by the
subtle brioche and mixed spice of lees age. Tremendous cut and drive promise a
very long future, charged by a dynamic acid line that melds seamlessly with the
creamy texture of barrel fermentation and long lees age. One of Tasmania's finest
this year. Diam. 12% alc. **Rating** 96 $65 TS ✪ ♥
Late Disgorged 2012 55/45% chardonnay/pinot noir, 7.5 years on lees
(2741 days), disgorged June '20. The result is a very intense wine that is still fresh,
fruit and acidity more obvious than brioche/lees complexity. Remarkable. Diam.
12% alc. **Rating** 96 $56 JH ✪

ＹＹＹＹＹ **Premium Rosé NV Rating** 92 $30 TS
Premium Tasmania Cuvée NV Rating 91 $30 TS
Vintage Rosé 2017 Rating 90 $53 TS

Jarressa Estate Wines ★★★★★

114 Blewitt Springs Road, McLaren Flat, SA 5171 **Region** McLaren Vale
T 0478 517 999 **www.**jarressaestate.com **Open** Fri–Sun 10–4
Winemaker Michael Petrucci, Jarrad White **Est.** 2007 **Dozens** 10 000 **Vyds** 5ha
Proprietor Jarrad White established Jarressa Estate in 2007, taking its name from his childhood home of broadacre cropping and stud cattle at Kadina, north of Adelaide. He is now a 20+-vintage veteran of the wine community, with 10 years working for Penfolds in both Australia and California. Jarressa was initially a hobby venture, making wine to be sold to family and friends, but changed shape after a China-based wine importer shared a bottle of Jarressa. A joint venture was formed, Jarrad making the wine and Li Hui responsible for sales and marketing. It took another significant step with the acquisition of the 5ha Cape Barren Vineyard, prior to this time the wines were made from purchased fruit. Exports to Vanuatu and China.

🍷🍷🍷🍷🍷 **Regional Reveal The Hills McLaren Vale Shiraz 2019** Higher Blewitt sourcing. The siphon of fine-boned cocoa tannins here are savoury and appealing. They galvanise lilac florals, amped blue-fruit allusions, anise and olive, massaging them into a tactile whole. Yet, as persuasive as most of this wine is, it finishes with a burn. Screw cap. 15% alc. **Rating** 93 **To** 2030 $56 NG
Regional Reveal The Flats McLaren Vale Shiraz 2019 Ovaltine oak, licorice straps and anise. Yet, there is floral lift. A strident carriage of long-reaching granular tannins and a palpable sense of care. There is life! While I would prefer more tannin, less alcohol and something a bit more savoury, this is an honest interpretation of a warm place and for that, it deserves just rewards. Screw cap. 15% alc. **Rating** 93 **To** 2032 $56 NG
Regional Reveal The Foothills McLaren Vale Shiraz 2019 Oodles of dark fruit, violet and anise. A big wine, crafted with a sort of hands-off cadence that for me, at least, could use a bit more tannin. This said, the tannins that exist are subtle, finely wrought and long-limbed. Good oomphy drinking. Screw cap. 15% alc. **Rating** 92 **To** 2032 $56 NG

Jarvis Estate ★★★☆

790 Wirring Road, Margaret River, WA 6285 **Region** Margaret River
T (08) 9758 7526 **www.**jarvisestate.com.au **Open** By appt
Winemaker Contract **Est.** 1995 **Dozens** 3000 **Vyds** 8.4ha
Matt and Jackie Jarvis carefully researched the Margaret River region, and in particular the Bramley locality, before purchasing their property, where they now live. It is planted to cabernet sauvignon, shiraz, merlot, chardonnay and cabernet franc (8.4ha). Fruit is grown organically where possible, sheep graze the vineyard in winter. Exports to Ireland, Greece, Taiwan, China and Hong Kong.

🍷🍷🍷🍷🍷 **Margaret River Cabernet Sauvignon 2018** Fruit from 2 estate blocks, planted in '99. Blackberry, leather strap and licorice rise up alongside black cherry and resinous oak. The palate has lovely varietal flavours, the complexity of those flavours the only quibble. Screw cap. 14% alc. **Rating** 90 **To** 2025 $35 EL

Jasper Hill ★★★★★

88 Drummonds Lane, Heathcote, Vic 3523 **Region** Heathcote
T (03) 5433 2528 **www.**jasperhill.com.au **Open** By appt
Winemaker Ron Laughton, Emily McNally **Est.** 1979 **Dozens** 2000 **Vyds** 26.5ha
The red wines of Jasper Hill, crafted by father–daughter team Ron Laughton and Emily McNally, are highly regarded and much sought after. The low-yielding dry-grown vineyards are managed organically and tended by hand. As long as vintage conditions allow, these are wonderfully rich and full-flavoured wines. Emily also purchases fruit from Heathcote for her 2 side projects, creating Lo Stesso Fiano with friend Georgia Roberts, as well as Occam's Razor Shiraz. The family celebrates their 40th vintage in 2021. Exports to the UK, the US, Singapore, China, Japan, Belgium, France and Denmark.

ΨΨΨΨΨ **Lo Stesso Heathcote Fiano 2020** Jasper Hill's Emily McNally's personal label is always thought provoking and edgy. The savoury, textural appeal of the Italian fiano grape is turned up to 11 with a most captivating wine. Poached pear, baked apple, wild honey, a peep of nettle, herb, all rolled into a stunning wine that builds through to the finish. Screw cap. 13.5% alc. **Rating** 95 **To** 2026 $30 JP ✪

Georgia's Paddock Heathcote Shiraz 2019 The first rule with Georgia's is to decant. Splash some air into what is a bigger-than-usual year for the well-known Heathcote shiraz. The '19 needs to stretch. You want those trademark pretty florals to step out from behind the wall of black fruits, rich plums, earth and sweet oak spice. Still as captivating as ever and can only improve. Cork. 15.5% alc. **Rating** 95 **To** 2032 $82 JP

Emily's Paddock Heathcote Shiraz Cabernet Franc 2019 Emily's is traditionally more reserved, and the '19, in particular, benefits from a decant and a splash of air. There is unaccustomed power in this vintage, courtesy of high alcohol, so some of the subtlety of the wine is lost, replaced by a more upfront, bold personality. As the wine moves across the palate, however, there it is, the fine tannin grace, so svelte and lively. And it's still early days for young Emily. Cork. 15.5% alc. **Rating** 95 **To** 2032 $108 JP

Georgia's Paddock Heathcote Nebbiolo 2019 Ah, the alluring scent of nebbiolo, all just-picked roses, red cherry, plum, anise and wild herbs. So striking and inviting, and once in the mouth the flavours continue, to be joined by earthy, mushroom, fennel notes and big, sturdy nebb tannins. Deceptively, you might be tempted to open soon, but resist the urge. This beauty has a long, long way to go. Cork. 14.5% alc. **Rating** 95 **To** 2039 $66 JP

ΨΨΨΨΨ **Georgia's Paddock Heathcote Semillon 2019 Rating** 93 **To** 2026 $45 JP

Jayden Ong   ★★★★

8 Hunter Road, Healesville, Vic 3777 **Region** Yarra Valley
T 0419 186 888 **www.**jaydenong.com **Open** By appt
Winemaker Jayden Ong **Est.** 2010 **Dozens** 1600 **Vyds** 5ha

Jayden Ong, a 1st-generation Eurasian-Australian, was infected by the wine bug working at the Melbourne Wine Room from 2000–06. He has moved with bewildering speed across many facets of the industry since then: wedging in vintages at Curly Flat ('06), Moorooduc Estate ('07) and Allies/Garagiste ('08–09) while completing the CSU oenology course; he also opened Cumulus Inc., a restaurant and bar in Melbourne, with superstar chef Andrew McConnell and business partners; he continues to mentor the Cumulus wine team. He founded what was originally called One Block in '10 with the philosophy of making single-vineyard wines 'from quality individual vineyard sites where the variety grown suits the site', making 100 dozen of his first love – chardonnay – in '10. In '15 he and partner Morgan Ong purchased a small property and home at Mt Toolebewong, 700m above sea level, in the Yarra Valley. In 2021 their new winery and cellar door/bar opened in Healesville. Exports to the UK, Canada, China and Hong Kong.

ΨΨΨΨΨ **Chestnut Hill Mount Burnett Chardonnay 2018** A shot of burnt pineapple, grapefruit, toasty and tasty oak and lemon curd all making their mark immediately. As this continues to blossom, it adds layers of ginger flower, creamed honey and grilled nuts. A flavoursome yet restrained wine, almost tightly wound with lithe acidity to close. Contemplative and compelling. Diam. 13.4% alc. **Rating** 94 **To** 2028 $42 JF

ΨΨΨΨΨ **Chestnut Hill Mount Burnett Sauvignon Blanc 2018 Rating** 93 **To** 2024 $32 JF

Moonlit Forest Day Dreamer Heathcote Fiano Sauvignon Blanc 2020 Rating 92 **To** 2024 $28 JF

La Maison de Ong Lantern Yarra Valley Pinot Noir 2018 Rating 91 **To** 2030 $55 JF

Jeanneret Wines   ★★★★★

Jeanneret Road, Sevenhill, SA 5453 **Region** Clare Valley
T (08) 8843 4308 **www.**jeanneretwines.com **Open** Mon–Sat 10–5 & public hols,
Sun 12–5
Winemaker Ben Jeanneret, Harry Dickinson **Est.** 1992 **Dozens** 18000 **Vyds** 36.5ha
Ben Jeanneret has progressively built the range and quantity of wines he makes at the onsite
winery. In addition to the estate vineyards, Jeanneret has grape purchase contracts with owners
of an additional 20ha of hand-pruned, hand-picked, dry-grown vines spread throughout the
Clare Valley. The Rieslings are very good indeed. Exports to Canada, Belgium, Sweden, South
Korea, Japan and China.

Jericho Wines   ★★★★☆

13 Moore Street, Willunga, SA 5172 (postal) **Region** Adelaide Hills/McLaren Vale
T 0410 519 945 **www.**jerichowines.com.au
Winemaker Neil Jericho, Andrew Jericho **Est.** 2012 **Dozens** 5000
In this venture the whole family is involved. The winemaking team consists of father and son,
Neil and Andrew Jericho. Neil has over 45 years of winemaking experience in Rutherglen,
King Valley and the Clare Valley; and Andrew over 15 years in McLaren Vale working as
senior winemaker for Maxwell Wines and Mollydooker. Andrew obtained his bachelor of
oenology from the University of Adelaide (in 2003) and then moved outside the square for
experience at the highly regarded Grace Vineyard in the Shanxi Province of China. Wife Kaye
is an experienced vintage widow, eldest daughter Sally has marketing and accounting degrees
(she worked for Wine Australia for 10 years). Youngest son Kim was torn between oenology,
hospitality and graphic design; he opted for the latter, hence designing the highly standout
label and Jericho branding. Exports to Singapore and China.

ⓉⓉⓉⓉⓉ **Limited Release Average 24 Years Age Tawny NV** A blend of tawny across
6 barrels that Neil Jericho bought in his early career, along with his own fruit-
cum-tawny that he crafted between regions, growing a family and realising the
importance of the idiom to the Australian wine narrative. Emphasised, surely, by
his experience at Taylor Fladgate in Portugal and later at Campbells and Brown
Brothers. Moroccan souk: date, tamarind and clove. Darjeeling tea. Walnut. Ginger.
Rancio cheesecloth, varnish and nostril stinging lift. Very fine. Cork. 19.8% alc.
Rating 97 $85 NG ✪ ♥

ⓉⓉⓉⓉⓉ **Kuitpo Lockett Vineyard Adelaide Hills Fumé Blanc 2019** Shattering
stereotypes and striking a pose of immense promise and strident energy into
a misbegotten category! Powerful scents of hedgerow, spruce, resin, quince,
cheesecloth, nettle and durian. A rail of new oak, the beam of guidance. Mineral
and thick and gristly and pungent. Long. Palate-staining. Intense. Côtat-like.
Groundbreaking. Diam. 13.5% alc. **Rating** 96 **To** 2027 $42 NG ✪ ♥
Selected Vineyards Adelaide Hills Rosé 2020 A gorgeous colour: faint coral
with a subtle copper hue. Poached strawberry, musk stick and a hint of kirsch pour
along juicy acid rails, pulling the saliva out of the mouth. Crunchy, smoky, gently
tannic and persistent, this is an exceptional rosé, attesting to just how exciting this
category is in Australia. Screw cap. 13.2% alc. **Rating** 95 **To** 2021 $26 NG ✪
The Chase McLaren Vale Shiraz 2018 A deep crimson and a richer style than
the fresher, easier-going wines of Jericho's stable. Judicious oak, the fruit riper (but
still fresh) yet undeniably of the Seaview sub-zone. Violet, clove, blueberry, iodine
and tapenade are pushed to a long peppery finish by a force of personality as
much as the inherent freshness of the wine. Diam. 14.5% alc. **Rating** 95 **To** 2030
$48 NG
**Wait Family Talara Vineyard Blewitt Springs McLaren Vale Grenache
2019** This stands close to the top of the regional totem pole. The tannins,
sandalwood-brushed and wiry, inflected with a briary rasp and additional
complexity from 25% whole bunches. The fruit, lifted by florals and the crunch
of raspberry, pomegranate and rosehip. Tamarind, bergamot and clove, the savoury

portals, underlying. My sole misgiving, the 25% new oak. Larger-format wood, in my view, the better option. Very good, all the same. Diam. 14.5% alc. **Rating** 95 To 2027 $62 NG

♀♀♀♀♀ **Selected Vineyards McLaren Vale GSM 2019 Rating** 93 To 2024
$26 NG ✪
Selected Vineyards Adelaide Hills Fiano 2020 Rating 92 To 2023 $26 NG
Corydon Vineyard Adelaide Hills Syrah 2018 Rating 92 To 2025 $38 TL
Selected Vineyards Adelaide Hills Fumé Blanc 2020 Rating 91 To 2025
$26 NG

Jilyara   ★★★★★
2 Heath Road, Wilyabrup, WA 6280 **Region** Margaret River
T (08) 9755 6575 **www**.jilyara.com.au **Open** By appt
Winemaker Kate Morgan, Laura Bowler **Est.** 2017 **Dozens** 4000 **Vyds** 10ha
Craig Cotterell and partner Maria Bergstrom planted the 9.7ha Jilyara Vineyard in 1995, finishing the task the following year. Until 2017 the crop was sold to other producers in the region, but the game changed that year. They have 6.4ha of cabernet sauvignon, 0.9ha each of malbec and sauvignon blanc, 0.8ha of chardonnay, 0.4ha of merlot and 0.3ha of petit verdot. There are 3 tiers: at the top The Williams' Block duo of Chardonnay and Cabernet Sauvignon (incorporating small amounts of malbec and petit verdot); next comes the Heath Road banner with Chardonnay, Malbec and Cabernet Sauvignon (also including some malbec and petit verdot); the last group is Honeycomb Corner with a Sauvignon Blanc and Cabernet Sauvignon (with some merlot and malbec), the price particularly appealing for the Cabernet. The packaging is very smart, a design-house dream, visually bringing together the local Noongar word of 'Djilyaro' for bee (there is a beehive at each corner of the block). Exports to NZ.

♀♀♀♀♀ **The Williams' Block Margaret River Chardonnay 2019** I love this wine. It is intensely salty, rich, worked, complex and layered. Salted peach, sun-dried kelp (the crispy kind), Dragon Pearl tea, curry leaf, walnuts and pecans. Endlessly interesting, highly worked, intense. It's not for everyone. If you're a fan of gateway Jura, then you might like to give this a burl. Screw cap. 12.5% alc. **Rating** 96 To 2031 $75 EL ✪
The Williams' Block Margaret River Cabernet Sauvignon 2019 As with previous vintages, this is delicious. Layers of exotic spices, salted raspberry and a purebreed succulence that Margaret River seems to achieve with ease. Length of flavour indicates a long cellaring future ahead of it. Screw cap. 14.5% alc.
Rating 95 To 2046 $75 EL

♀♀♀♀♀ **Heath Road Margaret River Malbec 2019 Rating** 93 To 2030 $35 EL
Heath Road Margaret River Cabernet Sauvignon 2019 Rating 92
To 2031 $35 EL
Heath Road Margaret River Chardonnay 2020 Rating 91 To 2028 $35 EL
Honeycomb Corner Margaret River Cabernet Sauvignon 2019
Rating 91 To 2027 $22 EL ✪

Jim Barry Wines   ★★★★★
33 Craig Hill Road, Clare, SA 5453 **Region** Clare Valley
T (08) 8842 2261 **www**.jimbarry.com **Open** 7 days 10–4
Winemaker Tom Barry, Ben Marx, Simon Mussared, Derrick Quinton **Est.** 1959
Dozens 80 000 **Vyds** 380ha
The patriarch of this highly successful wine business, Jim Barry, died in 2004, but the business continues under the active involvement of the 2nd generation, led by the irrepressible Peter Barry; the 3rd generation represented by Peter and Sue Barry's children, Tom, Sam and Olivia. Tom's wife is also called Olivia, and she (Olivia Hoffman) has set a whirlwind pace, graduating with a bachelor of science in commerce from the University of Adelaide, then a master of wine business. Peter purchased the famed Florita Vineyard with his brothers in 1986

(one of the oldest vineyards in the Clare Valley, planted in 1962). The 2nd generation also purchased Clos Clare in 2008 with its high-quality vineyards (see separate entry). Jim Barry Wines is able to draw upon 345ha of mature Clare Valley vineyards, plus 35ha in Coonawarra. In November '16, Jim Barry Wines released the first commercial assyrtiko grown and made in Australia. A founding member of Australia's First Families of Wine. Winery of the Year in the *Wine Companion 2020*. Exports to all major markets.

ΨΨΨΨΨ **Loosen Barry Wolta Wolta Dry Clare Valley Riesling 2017** A magnificent wine. The aromas and flavours are nothing like Clare riesling. And yet it is just that. Beautiful aromatics and delicate flavours from lemon blossom, gardenia to flint and wet stones. Smoky, savoury with squirts of finger lime and a fine layer of ginger cream. Quite ethereal. Texture is its marker. Although the label says it's dry, it feels off-dry, so it has a viscosity, amazing length and definition. Respect. Screw cap. 12.5% alc. **Rating** 98 **To** 2040 $120 JF ✪ ♥

Loosen Barry Wolta Wolta Dry Clare Valley Riesling 2018 This is the second incarnation of this collaborative wine and a very fine follow-up. It's quite savoury with a touch more phenolics adding to its shape. It does have the same texture and off-dry feel that seems to be defining this wine. It's pure, it's energetic, it's something special yet again. Screw cap. 12.5% alc. **Rating** 97 **To** 2038 $120 JF ✪

ΨΨΨΨΨ **Lodge Hill Clare Valley Shiraz 2018** A very impressive wine at this price: the colour deep and bright, the expressive bouquet with earthy/spicy nuances to black fruits. The medium-bodied palate has an extra level of depth aided by supple tannins and a twitch of oak. The value cannot be gainsaid. Screw cap. 14% alc. **Rating** 96 **To** 2038 $25 JH ✪

The McRae Wood Clare Valley Shiraz 2018 The flavours, the savouriness and the feel of this wine are all appealing. Lots of detail with nothing overt. The palate lends itself to cocoa-powder tannins, the oak is integrated and there's a depth of flavour. It comes out as a complete wine. Screw cap. 14% alc. **Rating** 96 **To** 2033 $60 JF ✪

The Armagh Clare Valley Shiraz 2018 This has the smoky, sultry thing going on. It has a richness of flavour and oak, all toasty, with charcuterie and iodine inputs. Yet, the fruit has absorbed the oak, restructuring its DNA to match. Full bodied, without question, the tannins ripe, sweet, luscious and creamy. But this is not overblown – there's a balance and it's so important. It has gravitas. Screw cap. 13.6% alc. **Rating** 96 **To** 2033 $350 JF

The James Clare Valley Cabernet Malbec 2018 This is a mighty wine. Detailed, complex and superbly balanced, with excellent fruit flavours and a savouriness imparted by winemaking and oak. The tannins are quite something, as is the wine overall. Screw cap. 14% alc. **Rating** 96 **To** 2043 $350 JF

Jim's Garden Clare Valley Riesling 2020 A new addition to the Jim Barry riesling portfolio. The slaty, spicy bouquet gives no warning of the intensity of the attack on the palate that continues without hesitation through to the lingering aftertaste. Lime, spice and mineral are the players in a powerful wine. Screw cap. 12% alc. **Rating** 95 **To** 2020 $25 JH ✪

The Florita Clare Valley Riesling 2020 While 2020 is not a vintage to rave about (as in it's certainly not classic Clare), there are rave wines – this being one. Not surprising, given the provenance of this site. Lime and lemon blossom, acidity pared back, but it lacks none of the drive and energy that's part of its DNA. Lovely slippery texture and lime juice adds to its drinking pleasure today. But, of course, this will easily hit the next decade. Screw cap. 12.5% alc. **Rating** 95 **To** 2030 $60 JF

Cellar Release The Florita Clare Valley Riesling 2014 The mid straw-gold hue, the trickle of honey, the baked ricotta aromas and the dab of lime marmalade on buttered toast – ah the alchemy of ageing riesling! It's perfect now, as the acidity is keeping the intense flavours in harmony. Screw cap. 12.1% alc. **Rating** 95 **To** 2024 $70 JF

Clare Valley Assyrtiko 2020 Delicate aromatics at first. A puff of Mediterranean herbs and lemon blossom, but of course all the action is on the palate. Steely, tight and linear, with wet stone and lime juice. The acidity is pure talc and the finish pristine. Lip-smacking and delicious. Screw cap. 12.5% alc. **Rating** 95 **To** 2028 $35 JF ✪

Single Vineyard Kirribilli Coonawarra Cabernet Sauvignon 2019 So fragrant, with the purity of fruit shining through in cassis, blackberries and mulberries. Yes, it has a brightness of youth, but what sets it apart is its lovely tannins and savoury outlook. Elegant and complete. Screw cap. 13.7% alc. **Rating** 95 **To** 2038 $35 JF ✪

The Benbournie Clare Valley Cabernet Sauvignon 2018 An excellent Benbournie that is holding onto its core of bright sweet fruit and dark chocolate, dusted with dried mint. No shortage of tannins from both fruit and oak, with its charry-toasty flavours nonetheless all in check. It has power, depth, terrific length, and yet manages to offer elegance, too. Screw cap. 13.9% alc. **Rating** 95 **To** 2038 $80 JF

Pb Clare Valley Shiraz Cabernet Sauvignon 2018 A blend in unison and surprisingly restrained – in a good way. Sure it has deep flavours, tapenade, spice upon spice to the dark fruits within, but it's not overloaded. Tannins are hazelnut-skin textured, the palate fuller bodied and oak certainly in the mix, adding to a touch of dryness on the finish. Very satisfying regardless. Screw cap. 14% alc. **Rating** 94 **To** 2038 $60 JF

The Cover Drive 2018 Made from estate vineyards in Clare Valley and Coonawarra. Has excellent colour through to the rim, with austere, brooding, dark berry aromas, adding tapenade/bay leaf notes to the flavour mix. Screw cap. 14% alc. **Rating** 94 **To** 2030 $22 JH ✪

🍷🍷🍷🍷🍷 **Single Vineyard McKay's Clare Valley Riesling 2020 Rating** 93 **To** 2028 $35 JF

Watervale Riesling 2020 Rating 93 **To** 2027 $20 JF ✪

Single Vineyard Watervale Shiraz 2019 Rating 93 **To** 2029 $35 JF

Cellar Release The McRae Wood Clare Valley Shiraz 2013 Rating 93 **To** 2028 $70 JF

Lodge Hill Clare Valley Riesling 2020 Rating 92 **To** 2028 $25 JF ✪

JJ Hahn   ★★★★★

Cnr Seppeltsfield Road/Stelzer Road, Stonewell, SA 5352 **Region** Barossa Valley
T (0)8 8562 3300 **www**.jjhahnwineco.com **Open** Mon–Sat 10–4.30, Sun on long w'ends
Winemaker Rolf Binder, Marry Mantzarapis **Est.** 1997 **Dozens** 6000
Established in 1997 as a collaboration with James and Jackie Hahn, who retired in 2010, this is a brand of sibling winemakers Rolf Binder and Christa Deans, alongside sister labels Magpie Estate and formerly also Rolf Binder Wines (recently sold to Accolade Wines). Rolf oversees vineyard management and winemaking, and has extended distribution internationally. Exclusively devoted to red wines, the range celebrates the traditional varieties of shiraz, cabernet sauvignon and merlot. Exports to the UK, Canada, Hong Kong, China and Thailand. (TS)

🍷🍷🍷🍷🍷 **1890s Vineyard Barossa Valley Shiraz 2018** Chinese five-spice, incense and supple tannins tell the story of grand old vines, at once effortlessly enticing and infused with timeless endurance. Top-class American oak sets it off impeccably, heightening its milk chocolate mood. The finish holds to kingdom come. Screw cap. 14% alc. **Rating** 96 **To** 2043 $95 TS

Western Ridge 1975 Planting Barossa Valley Shiraz 2018 Benchmark Barossa shiraz. Rolf Binder has set off the spicy black fruits that characterise the western Barossa with an impressive framework of classy oak structure. Old vines deliver all the density and depth expected, enlivened by a stream of natural acidity that sets a long finish and great potential. Screw cap. 14% alc. **Rating** 95 **To** 2038 $45 TS

🍷🍷🍷🍷🍷 **Stelzer Road Barossa Valley Merlot 2019 Rating** 92 **To** 2024 $30 TS

Reginald Barossa Valley Shiraz Cabernet 2018 Rating 91 **To** 2024 $30 TS

John Duval Wines

PO Box 622, Tanunda, SA 5352 **Region** Barossa Valley
T (08) 8562 2266 **www**.johnduvalwines.com **Open** At Vino Lokal, Tanunda
Winemaker John Duval **Est.** 2003 **Dozens** 8000

John Duval is an internationally recognised winemaker, having been the custodian of Penfolds Grange during his role as chief red winemaker from 1986–2002. He established his eponymous brand in 2003 after almost 30 years with Penfolds and provides consultancy services to clients all over the world. While his main focus is on old-vine shiraz, he has extended his portfolio with other Rhône varieties. John was joined in the winery by son Tim in '16. Exports to all major markets.

🍷🍷🍷🍷🍷 **Integro Barossa Cabernet Sauvignon Shiraz 2017** A full-bodied wine of ultimate coherence and quality, the bouquet setting the signal for the palate to follow. Attention to detail is obvious, especially the handling of tannins and oak. The integration of these components with the blackcurrant fruit is faultless. Cork. 14% alc. **Rating** 98 **To** 2047 $220 JH ♥

🍷🍷🍷🍷🍷 **Eligo The Barossa Shiraz 2018** Eden Valley fruit dominant for the first time. This shiraz achieves definition and detail via grand concentration and enduring structure. Deep wells of black fruits of all kinds, licorice and coal steam are confidently supported by a frame of new French oak tannins. A dry finish reflects a drought year, yet holds pretty good persistence and promise. Cork. 14.5% alc. **Rating** 94 **To** 2033 $130 TS

🍷🍷🍷🍷🍷 **Entity Barossa Shiraz 2019 Rating** 93 **To** 2027 $55 TS

John Kosovich Wines

Cnr Memorial Avenue/Great Northern Highway, Baskerville, WA 6056
Region Swan Valley/Pemberton
T (08) 9296 4356 **www**.johnkosovichwines.com.au **Open** Wed–Mon 10–4.30
Winemaker Anthony Kosovich **Est.** 1922 **Dozens** 2000 **Vyds** 10.9ha

The Kosovich family, headed by Jack Kosovich and his brothers, immigrated from Croatia shortly before the outbreak of World War I. After cutting railway sleepers in the southwest of WA and thereafter in the goldmines of Kalgoorlie, Jack purchased the property in 1922; the first vines planted in that year still grace the entrance to the winery. Cutting railway sleepers by axe made digging the underground cellar seem easy, and a 7m white gum beam cut from a tree felled by Jack in the hills nearby became the supporting structure for the cellar roof; the axe used by Jack to shape the beam hangs from it today. John took over winemaking aged 15 after the death of his father, making fortified wines and rough red wines which remained the staple of the business until the 1960s when John made the then-bold move to change the vineyard to produce white wines. Riesling was the first variety planted, chenin blanc, chardonnay and verdelho followed. In '89 John established a 3.5ha vineyard in Pemberton, changing the face of the business forever, albeit continuing with the magnificent Rare Muscat. The winery was known as Westfield Wines until 2003 when, prompted by John's 50th vintage, the name was changed to John Kosovich Wines. In 1995 John became a member of the Order of Australia for his long contribution to the wine industry and in '04 won the prestigious Jack Mann Medal for services to the WA wine industry; in the same year the winery won the trophy for Best WA Small Producer at the Perth Royal Wine Show. Son Anthony (Arch) took over the winemaking and is looking forward to the 100-year anniversary in '22.

🍷🍷🍷🍷🍷 **Bottle Aged Reserve Swan Valley Chenin Blanc 2015** Toasty and complex, with cheesecloth, savoury preserved lemon, toasted/crushed nuts, apricot, sheepy lanolin and jasmine tea. This is an ever-evolving wine of depth and intensity. I can write long after the wine has been swallowed. For minutes it seems … Screw cap. 13% alc. **Rating** 97 **To** 2036 $48 EL ◊ ♥

🍷🍷🍷🍷🍷 **Reserve Pemberton Cabernet Malbec 2018** Dark, dense and decidedly rustic in both mouthfeel and flavours, this wine has a certain charm that draws you in and holds you close. The length of flavour goes and goes, the surest hallmark of quality. It will have a long future ahead of it, that is another certainty; those tannins verge on prodigious and are well matched to the fruit. Screw cap. 13.5% alc. **Rating** 94 To 2041 $48 EL

🍷🍷🍷🍷🍷 **Swan Valley Fortified Vintage Shiraz 2019** Rating 92 $45 EL

Jones Road ★★★★☆

2 Godings Road, Moorooduc, Vic 3933 **Region** Mornington Peninsula
T (03) 5978 8080 **www.**jonesroad.com.au **Open** W'ends 11–5
Winemaker Travis Bush **Est.** 1998 **Dozens** 6000 **Vyds** 26.5ha
After establishing a very large and very successful herb-producing business in the UK, Rob Frewer and family migrated to Australia in 1997. By a circuitous route they ended up with a property on the Mornington Peninsula, planting pinot noir and chardonnay, then pinot gris, sauvignon blanc and merlot. They have since leased another vineyard at Mt Eliza and purchased Ermes Estate in 2007.

🍷🍷🍷🍷🍷 **Nepean Mornington Peninsula Chardonnay 2019** Pulses with good energy and overall an elegant style. Just the right balance of lemon/grapefruit juice and pith, the oak seamlessly integrated. It's more linear and refreshing as a result. Screw cap. 13.6% alc. **Rating** 95 To 2027 $60 JF

🍷🍷🍷🍷🍷 **Nepean Mornington Peninsula Pinot Noir 2019** Rating 93 To 2029 $60 JF
Mornington Peninsula Pinot Noir 2019 Rating 92 To 2027 $40 JF
Mornington Peninsula Chardonnay 2019 Rating 90 To 2025 $40 JF
Mornington Peninsula Pinot Meunier 2019 Rating 90 To 2026 $35 JF

Jones Winery & Vineyard ★★★★☆

61 Jones Road, Rutherglen, Vic 3685 **Region** Rutherglen
T (02) 6032 8496 **www.**joneswinery.com **Open** Wed–Sun 11–4 or by appt
Winemaker Mandy Jones **Est.** 1860 **Dozens** 3000 **Vyds** 10ha
Jones Winery & Vineyard was established in 1860 and stands as testament to a rich winemaking tradition. Since 1927, the winery has been owned and operated by the Jones family. Two blocks of old vines have been preserved (including 1.69ha of shiraz), supported by further blocks progressively planted between '75 and the present day. Today, Jones Winery & Vineyard is jointly operated by winemaker Mandy Jones, who brought years of experience working in Bordeaux, and her brother Arthur Jones. Together they produce a small range of boutique wines. Exports to France and China.

🍷🍷🍷🍷🍷 **Rare Rutherglen Muscat NV** A special wine by any reckoning, at once delicate and richly concentrated. Glorious dried muscatel scents of rose petal, fig, nougat and orange peel join up on the palate with savoury, nutty, chocolatey richness. Builds across an umami-luscious texture to one long, impressive finish. 500ml. Vino-Lok. 18.5% alc. **Rating** 95 $160 JP
LJ Rutherglen 2018 Low-yielding old-vine shiraz with a little (less than 5%) grenache added. 18 months maturation in oak (70% new French). One for the cellar. Resplendent in a rich coat of cedar mocha-chocolate with pronounced, sturdy tannins. Black fruits, earth, high spice, licorice, with warm texture; it should meld and settle down with time. Screw cap. 13.8% alc. **Rating** 94 To 2030 $75 JP

🍷🍷🍷🍷🍷 **Rutherglen Shiraz 2018** Rating 93 To 2028 $35 JP
Classic Rutherglen Muscat NV Rating 93 $35 JP
Six Generations Durif Vin de Liqueur 2018 Rating 92 $30 JP
Rutherglen Durif 2017 Rating 91 To 2032 $35 JP
Rutherglen Marsanne Roussanne 2018 Rating 90 To 2026 $25 JP
Rutherglen Malbec 2017 Rating 90 To 2032 $35 JP
Sparkling Shiraz NV Rating 90 $38 JP

Josef Chromy Wines   ★★★★☆

370 Relbia Road, Relbia, Tas 7258 **Region** Northern Tasmania
T (03) 6335 8700 **www.**josefchromy.com.au **Open** 7 days 10–5
Winemaker Jeremy Dineen, Ockie Myburgh **Est.** 2004 **Dozens** 40 000 **Vyds** 60ha
Josef Chromy escaped from Czechoslovakia in 1950, arriving in Tasmania 'with nothing but hope and ambition'. A skilled butcher, he established the successful Blue Ribbon meats, the sale of which enabled him to invest in the local wine industry. He went on to own or develop such well-known Tasmanian wine brands as Rochecombe (now Bay of Fires), Jansz, Heemskerk and Tamar Ridge. In 2007, aged 76, Josef launched Josef Chromy wines. The foundation of the business is the Old Stornoway Vineyard, with 60ha of mature vines; the lion's share is planted to pinot noir and chardonnay, with a little pinot gris, riesling and sauvignon blanc, too. Josef has won a string of awards for his services to the Tasmanian wine industry and his wines earn similar respect, rising from strength to strength in recent vintages. Talented and hard-working winemaker Jeremy Dineen handed over the reins to his capable offsider Ockie Myburgh in January 2021. Exports to all major markets. (TS)

ΨΨΨΨΨ ZDAR Sparkling 2008 Brilliantly lively, bright and pale, this contrasts the tension
and zing of chardonnay (54%) with the exuberance of pinot noir that characterises
this upper Tamar site. The backbone of malic acid that defines the Chromy style
imparts a zap of acid drive that suggests incredible potential yet. Diam. 12% alc.
Rating 95 $150 TS
Pinot Noir 2019 Classic Tamar pinot. Blackberry and black cherry fruit with
a savoury backdrop of beetroot. Nicely poised acidity finds harmony with well-
composed fruit and oak tannins. Everything interlocks neatly on a long finish.
Potential. Screw cap. 13.5% alc. **Rating** 94 **To** 2032 $39 TS
Block 115 Pinot Noir 2019 The not-inconsiderable Chromy portfolio
continues to grow outwards and upwards. This single block and single barrel
elevates to higher levels of fragrance, spice, exoticism and complexity. The
potpourri and smoky paprika notes of whole-bunch fermentation leap out from a
core of strawberry and red cherry fruit. Fine tannins and bright acidity draw out
a very long finish. Potential plus. Screw cap. 14% alc. **Rating** 94 **To** 2039 $120 TS
Block 103 Pinot Noir 2019 Epitomising the inimitable character of Chromy's
Relbia vineyard, this block is laden with sour cherries and all the exotic spice and
dried herbs of whole-bunch fermentation. A core of glossy blackberry fruit is well
structured by long-enduring tannins. Screw cap. 13.5% alc. **Rating** 94 **To** 2034
$120 TS

ΨΨΨΨΨ ZDAR Chardonnay 2014 Rating 93 To 2034 $80 TS
ZDAR Pinot Noir 2014 Rating 93 To 2026 $80 TS
Chardonnay 2019 Rating 92 To 2029 $39 TS
Finesse Brut 2016 Rating 92 $48 TS
Tasmanian Cuvée NV Rating 92 $32 TS
DELIKAT SGR Riesling 2019 Rating 91 To 2034 $29 TS
Sparkling Rosé NV Rating 91 $33 TS
Pinot Gris 2020 Rating 90 To 2025 $29 TS

Journey Wines   ★★★★★

2/26 Hunter Road, Healesville, Vic 3777 (postal) **Region** Yarra Valley
T 0427 298 098 **www.**journeywines.com.au
Winemaker Damian North **Est.** 2011 **Dozens** 3000
The name chosen by Damian North for his brand is particularly appropriate given the winding path he has taken before starting (with his wife and 3 children) his own label. Originally a sommelier at Tetsuya's, he was inspired to enrol in the oenology course at CSU, gaining his first practical winemaking experience as assistant winemaker at Tarrawarra Estate. Then, with family in tow, he moved to Oregon's Benton-Lane Winery to make pinot noir, before returning to become winemaker at Leeuwin Estate for 5 years. The wheel has turned full circle as the family has returned to the Yarra Valley, securing 2ha of chardonnay, 2.5ha of

pinot noir and 2ha of shiraz under contract arrangements, and making the wines at Medhurst. Exports to the UK, Singapore, Thailand and China.

JS Wine   ★★★★☆

42 Lake Canobolas Road, Nashdale, Orange, NSW 2800 **Region** Orange
T 0433 042 576 **www**.jswine.com.au **Open** Thurs–Sun 11–5
Winemaker Philip Shaw **Est.** 2016 **Dozens** 2700 **Vyds** 26ha
I simply can't resist quoting the opening to the background information provided: 'Located on the west side of Australia's agricultural province of New South Wales'. JS Wines' estate is about 8km from the centre of Orange, 3 hours' drive from Sydney'. The vineyard and the quality of the wines brings together 3 winemakers who have long-term firsthand knowledge of the Orange region.

Jumy Estate   ★★★★☆

28 Ellsworth Crescent, Camberwell, Vic 3124 (postal) **Region** Yarra Valley/Grampians
T 0433 591 617 **www**.odevine.com.cn
Winemaker Ben Haines **Est.** 2015 **Dozens** 2000
Jumy Estate was founded in 2015 by leading architect Linda Wang and structural engineer Roy Zhang. Highly regarded winemaker Ben Haines' brief is to produce wines that are engaging and distinct, and capture the sense of place. Exports to China.

🍷🍷🍷🍷🍷 **ODE19 Jumy Signature Series Yarra Valley Pinot Noir 2020** This is a lovely, gentle wine, with superfine tannins and a delicacy of flavour. Florals, sweet cherries and plums. It's not the most complex but it is compelling and a delightful drink. Diam. 12% alc. **Rating** 94 **To** 2026 $35 JF

🍷🍷🍷🍷🍷 **ODE19 Jumy Signature Series Grampians Cabernet Merlot 2019** **Rating** 91 **To** 2026 $38 JP
ODE19 Jumy Signature Series Grampians Shiraz 2019 **Rating** 90 **To** 2029 $35 JP

Juniper   ★★★★★

98 Tom Cullity Drive, Cowaramup, WA 6284 **Region** Margaret River
T (08) 9755 9000 **www**.juniperestate.com.au **Open** 7 days 10–5
Winemaker Mark Messenger, Luc Fitzgerald **Est.** 1973 **Dozens** 12000 **Vyds** 19.5ha
Roger Hill and Gillian Anderson purchased the Wrights' Wilyabrup property in 1998, driven by the 25yo vineyard with dry-grown cabernet as the jewel in the crown. They also purchased complementary vineyards in Forest Grove (Higher Plane) and Wilyabrup; the vineyards are sustainably farmed using organic principles. Sons Nick and Tom (formerly a winemaker in the Yarra Valley) are now running the business. The Juniper Crossing and Small Batch wines are sourced from the 3 vineyards, while the Single Vineyard releases are made only from the original vineyard on Tom Cullity Drive. Exports to the UK, the US, Canada, Singapore and Hong Kong.

🍷🍷🍷🍷🍷 **Cornerstone Karridale Chardonnay 2019** In general, 2019 was a cool and wet year in Margaret River. The resulting wines are highly aromatic, finely detailed and nuanced. This wine is the product of the powerful Gingin clone, grown in a cool area in a cool year. This, in combination with blocked mlf, lends a fierceness to the acidity, however the fruit stands up to it: guava, white peach, toasted almonds, brine and pink grapefruit. Outstanding. Screw cap. 13% alc. **Rating** 96 **To** 2036 $70 EL ✪
Cornerstone Wilyabrup Cabernet Sauvignon 2017 The 2017 vintage was a cool, wet one in Margaret River. For those who managed their vineyards with care and courage, it yielded wines of brilliance, clarity, poise and length. Salted black licorice and blackberry on the nose. The dark berry fruits crash together on the palate in a confluence of flavour and energy, coursing across the tongue into a long, restrained finish. Screw cap. 14% alc. **Rating** 96 **To** 2041 $90 EL

Estate Margaret River Aquitaine Rouge 2018 The 2018 vintage was the greatest on record in Margaret River, and was responsible for wines of ripe power, grace, longevity and balance. This wine is no exception. Supple, lithe fruit is framed by fine oak, both of which see it pull away into a long and graceful finish. The saline acidity that courses over the palate keeps things fresh and bright. There is pleasure here. Screw cap. 13.8% alc. **Rating** 96 **To** 2041 $40 EL ✪

Cornerstone Wilyabrup Chardonnay 2020 The nose here is far more citrussy than it is peachy, with layers of brine, graphite, green apple and licks of guava. On the palate it follows in this racy manner. It is restrained, long and very tart (in a scintillating and refreshing kind of way). The warmer year, a high-acid clone and the lack of mlf come together to achieve balance, interest, austerity and class. Screw cap. 13.5% alc. **Rating** 95 **To** 2031 $60 EL

Estate Margaret River Chardonnay 2019 The 2019 vintage was a cool year, one of the coolest, and it was responsible for a tranche of highly aromatic and fine wines. This is no exception. The high-quality oak is centre stage right now, but the length of fruit flavour indicates who will win over time (hint: the fruit). The taut, saline acidity makes this a particular pleasure. Very refined. Screw cap. 12.5% alc. **Rating** 95 **To** 2031 $40 EL

Estate Single Vineyard Margaret River Shiraz 2018 Pungently intense fruit with svelte concentration and brilliant length of flavour. Salted blackberry, licorice, mulberry, satsuma plum and exotic spices. Very classy wine indeed. So long, so layered. Screw cap. 13.9% alc. **Rating** 95 **To** 2031 $40 EL

Crossing Margaret River Cabernet Sauvignon Merlot 2018 Bright, clear crimson-purple; this punches way above its weight from the outset. Supple cassis and persistent – but silky – tannins sketch the outline of a wine with freshness and a balance that will sustain its shape for however long you elect to cellar it. Exceptional value. Screw cap. 14% alc. **Rating** 95 **To** 2030 $20 JH ✪

Cornerstone Karridale Cabernet Sauvignon 2018 The 2018 was a fabulous vintage, near on perfect actually, and Karridale (being in the south) is cooler than many growing areas in the main part of Margaret River. The resulting wine has the aromatics of a cooler subregion, in combination with the formidable power and concentration inherent in the year. Elegant, supple, leafy and long. Impressive. Screw cap. 14% alc. **Rating** 95 **To** 2041 $70 EL

The Tribute Margaret River 2016 Underpinned by very good length of cabernet flavour. The oak feels a little heavy handed at this stage, the lingering impression laced with licorice and star anise. It is succulent, dense and concentrated, no doubt, however the 2016 vintage (brilliant for cabernet sauvignon, yet in many cases defined by tannin and acid) makes a hard stamp on this wine. It will live interminably in the cellar without question. Screw cap. 14% alc. **Rating** 95 **To** 2051 $150 EL

3 Fields Margaret River Chardonnay 2020 The fruit is very restrained right now, but it is already serving up lashings of pawpaw, yellow peach, red apples and the odd curry leaf here and there. The acidity is incredibly quenching and ripe, sprinkling flakes of crunchy sea salt on the fruit. A lot to lust after. Interestingly, the oak is already integrated at this early stage. Very classy. Screw cap. 13.5% alc. **Rating** 94 **To** 2031 $32 EL

Small Batch Margaret River Fiano 2020 Yellow peach fuzz, red apple, nashi pear, strawberry, custard powder and white pepper. The oak is nowhere to be seen, but contributes a supportive structure from which the fruit can hang. A lot to like here! Very smart. Screw cap. 12.5% alc. **Rating** 94 **To** 2025 $27 EL ✪

Small Batch Margaret River Cabernet Sauvignon 2018 It's unfair on other Australian regions that Margaret River can so effortlessly produce cabernet sauvignon with pure varietal definition, coupled with mouthfeel that reassures, not challenges, as cabernet is wont to do. This covers all the bases with blackcurrant and soft tannins, leaving little else to be said. Screw cap. 14% alc. **Rating** 94 **To** 2028 $27 JH ✪

🍷🍷🍷🍷🍷 **Crossing Original White Margaret River Semillon Sauvignon Blanc 2020** **Rating** 93 **To** 2026 $18 EL ✪

Crossing Margaret River Chardonnay 2019 Rating 93 To 2026 $23 JH ✪
3 Fields Margaret River Shiraz 2019 Rating 93 To 2028 $29 EL
Crossing Original Red Margaret River 2019 Rating 93 To 2028 $18 EL ✪
3 Fields Margaret River Sauvignon Blanc Semillon 2019 Rating 92
To 2031 $29 EL
Block 8 Margaret River Shiraz 2016 Rating 92 To 2032 $65 EL
Canvas Margaret River Tempranillo 2019 Rating 91 To 2031 $28 EL
Canvas Margaret River Malbec 2018 Rating 91 To 2031 $32 EL
Botrytis Margaret River Riesling 2019 Rating 91 To 2028 $27 EL
Small Batch Margaret River Cabernet Sauvignon 2019 Rating 90 To 2028
$27 EL

Kaesler Wines

Barossa Valley Way, Nuriootpa, SA 5355 **Region** Barossa Valley
T (08) 8562 4488 **www.**kaesler.com.au **Open** 7 days 11–5
Winemaker Reid Bosward, Stephen Dew **Est.** 1990 **Dozens** 20 000 **Vyds** 36ha
The first members of the Kaesler family settled in the Barossa Valley in 1845. The vineyards date back to 1893, but the Kaesler family ownership ended in 1968. Kaesler Wines was eventually acquired by a small group of investment bankers (who have since purchased Yarra Yering), in conjunction with former Flying Winemaker Reid Bosward and wife Bindy. Reid's experience shows through in the wines, which come from estate vineyards adjacent to the winery, and from 10ha in the Marananga area that includes shiraz planted in 1899. The Small Valley Vineyard wines, made by Stephen Dew, are produced from 49ha in the Adelaide Hills. Exports to all major markets.

🍷🍷🍷🍷🍷 Stonehorse Clare Valley Riesling 2017 It's fresh as a spring day, with the
florals to prove it. A gently spiced, citrussy spread of Meyer lemon with grapefruit
pith. No signs of age, although the palate has softened, the acidity is neat and
while it falls short on the finish, it's a lovely drink. Screw cap. 12.5% alc. **Rating** 94
To 2025 $25 JF ✪
Old Vine Barossa Valley Semillon 2020 Energetic and intense, this is a
concentrated, taut and pristine expression of Barossa floor semillon. Wild lemon
and Granny Smith apple are accented with subtle varietal lanolin notes, cut
with the lively acidity of cool nights that illuminates a bright, long finish. Grand
potential. Screw cap. 11.5% alc. **Rating** 94 To 2035 $25 TS ✪

🍷🍷🍷🍷 Old Bastard Barossa Valley Shiraz 2018 Rating 93 To 2038 $250 TS
Stonehorse Clare Valley Shiraz 2018 Rating 92 To 2028 $25 JF ✪
Stonehorse Clare Valley Chardonnay 2020 Rating 90 To 2024 $25 JF

Kalleske

6 Murray Street, Greenock, SA 5360 **Region** Barossa Valley
T (08) 8563 4000 **www.**kalleske.com **Open** 7 days 10–5
Winemaker Troy Kalleske **Est.** 1999 **Dozens** 10 000 **Vyds** 50ha
The Kalleske family has been growing and selling grapes on a mixed farming property at Greenock for over 140 years. Sixth-generation Troy Kalleske, with brother Tony, established the winery and created the Kalleske label in 1999. The vineyard is planted mainly to shiraz (31ha) and grenache (7ha), with smaller amounts of chenin blanc, semillon, viognier, cabernet sauvignon, mataro, durif, petit verdot, tempranillo and zinfandel. The vines vary in age, with the oldest dating back to 1875; the overall average age is around 50 years. All are grown biodynamically. Exports to all major markets.

🍷🍷🍷 Johann Georg Old Vine Single Vineyard Barossa Valley Shiraz 2018
Old vines deliver impact and depth in this powerful flagship. Inconsistent ripeness
clashes green, leafy, herbal flavours, tart acidity and banana-skin tannins with ripe
components of sweet, jammy feel. This clash makes for an astringent and sour
finish. Screw cap. 14.5% alc. **Rating** 89 To 2038 $175 TS

Karatta Wines

5 Victoria Street, Robe, SA 5276 **Region** Robe
T (08) 8735 7255 **www**.karattawines.com.au **Open** 7 days 10–4
Winemaker Alice Davidson, Richard Bate (Consultant) **Est.** 1994 **Dozens** 4000
Vyds 39.6ha
David and Peg Woods named Karatta Wines after the heritage-listed Karatta House at Robe, built in 1858. In 2016 it was discovered that Peg's family were part owners of the steamer SS *Karatta*, which plied the Southern Ocean between Robe, Kangaroo Island and Adelaide up to the mid-20th century. The original life buoy of the Karatta adorns the tasting room and is the inspiration for new branding, reflecting the maritime influence on the vines and wines. Karatta has 2 vineyards: 12 Mile and Tenison; 12 Mile is less than 10km from the Southern Ocean, the temperature 10–15°C cooler than Coonawarra. Winery and vineyard tours can be arranged by contacting Charles Lawrence 0487 357 254. Exports to the US and Japan.

🍷🍷🍷🍷🍷 Tiny Star Robe 2017 Méthode traditionnelle. Copper hue. Aromas of candied apple and raspberry compote with a smidge of clotted cream and complex aldehydes. The palate is super-tight, savoury and racy. No shortage of acidity here, keeping it very perky. Diam. 12.5% alc. **Rating** 90 **To** 2025 $35 JF

🍷🍷🍷🍷 White 12 Mile Vineyard Robe Field Blend 2020 **Rating** 88 **To** 2023 $20 JF
Griffin Robe Sparkling Shiraz Cabernet NV **Rating** 88 $25 JF

Karrawatta

164 Greenhills Road, Meadows, SA 5201 **Region** Adelaide Hills
T (08) 8537 0511 **www**.karrawatta.com.au **Open** 7 days 11–4
Winemaker Mark Gilbert **Est.** 1996 **Dozens** 6000 **Vyds** 59.25ha
Mark Gilbert is the great-great-great-grandson of Joseph Gilbert, who established the Pewsey Vale vineyard and winery in 1847. Joseph Gilbert had named the property Karrawatta, but adopted Pewsey Vale after losing the toss of a coin with his neighbour. The Karrawatta of today has 12.43ha of vines in the Adelaide Hills, 38.07ha in Langhorne Creek and 8.75ha in McLaren Vale. The vineyards are all hand pruned, the small-batch wines fashioned with minimum intervention. Exports to the US, Canada and Hong Kong.

🍷🍷🍷🍷🍷 Tutelina Langhorne Creek McLaren Vale Adelaide Hills Shiraz 2018 A bold new creation over several years of vineyard focus, taking 5–6 selected rows from Karrawatta's 3 vineyards in 3 regions: 44% Langhorne Creek, 44% McLaren Vale and 12% Adelaide Hills. All shiraz, 17 months in French barriques, 48% new. The fruit has soaked all that up and still comes to the front with massive blackberry flavours and dark spices entwined, all smoothly rounded and complete in its icon-style expression. Out of the box for a first outing. Cork. 14.5% alc. **Rating** 98 **To** 2030 $275 TL ❤

🍷🍷🍷🍷🍷 Ace of Trumps McLaren Vale Shiraz 2019 In-the-zone McLaren Vale shiraz with ripe plum and black fruits, charry elements, crumbled earth all playing a role in a complete expression of variety and region. The palate has energy and medium to full-bodied flow. Plenty to enjoy here. Screw cap. 14.5% alc. **Rating** 94 **To** 2028 $54 TL

🍷🍷🍷🍷🍷 Dairy Block Adelaide Hills Shiraz 2019 **Rating** 93 **To** 2028 $38 TL
The Meddler Langhorne Creek Malbec 2019 **Rating** 93 **To** 2030 $54 TL
Anna's Adelaide Hills Sauvignon Blanc 2020 **Rating** 91 **To** 2023 $30 TL
Joseph Langhorne Creek Shiraz 2019 **Rating** 91 **To** 2028 $54 TL
Anth's Garden Adelaide Hills Chardonnay 2019 **Rating** 90 **To** 2025 $46 TL

KarriBindi

111 Scott Road, Karridale, WA 6288 (postal) **Region** Margaret River
T (08) 9758 5570 **www**.karribindi.com.au
Winemaker Kris Wealand **Est.** 1997 **Dozens** 1500 **Vyds** 32.05ha

KarriBindi is owned by Kevin, Yvonne and Kris Wealand. The name comes from Karridale and the surrounding karri forests, and from Bindi, the home town of one of the members of the Wealand family. In Noongar, 'karri' means strong, special, spiritual, tall tree; 'bindi' means butterfly. The Wealands have established sauvignon blanc (15ha), chardonnay (6.25ha), cabernet sauvignon (4ha), plus smaller plantings of semillon, shiraz and merlot. KarriBindi also supplies a number of high-profile Margaret River wineries. Exports to Singapore and China.

🍷🍷🍷🍷🍷 **Margaret River Sauvignon Blanc 2020** Tank-fermented sauvignon blanc can get a bad rap. But wines like this display all of the pungent virtues of the variety: gooseberry, jalapeño, sugar snap pea, pink grapefruit and ripe (but a little bit sweaty, too) citrus. It's all backed by saline acid, which so often pops its head up in Margaret River. Simple, but pure, this is a brilliant example of sauvignon blanc. Screw cap. 12.5% alc. **Rating** 94 **To** 2025 $20 EL ✪

🍷🍷🍷🍷🍷 **Margaret River Semillon Sauvignon Blanc 2020 Rating** 92 **To** 2023 $20 EL ✪

Kate Hill Wines

21 Dowlings Road, Huonville, Tas 7109 **Region** Southern Tasmania
T 0448 842 696 **www**.katehillwines.com.au **Open** Fri–Mon 11–4
Winemaker Kate Hill **Est.** 2008 **Dozens** 2000 **Vyds** 4ha
When Kate Hill (and husband Charles) came to Tasmania in 2006, Kate had worked as a winemaker in Australia and overseas for 10 years. Kate's wines are made from grapes from a number of vineyards across Southern Tasmania, the aim being to produce approachable, delicate wines. Exports to Singapore.

🍷🍷🍷🍷🍷 **Riesling 2020** A captivating contrast of the tension and cut of Southern Tasmania with the exotic allure of a touch of botrytis. Apricot, frangipani and guava is underlined by a core of lime, lemon and Granny Smith apple. Fruit sweetness unites harmoniously with a line of crystalline acidity on a long finish. Appealing drinking right away, with the stamina to age confidently. Screw cap. 12.2% alc. **Rating** 95 **To** 2030 $32 TS ✪

🍷🍷🍷🍷🍷 **Shiraz 2019 Rating** 93 **To** 2027 $50 TS

Katnook

Riddoch Highway, Coonawarra, SA 5263 **Region** Coonawarra
T (08) 8737 0300 **www**.katnookestate.com.au **Open** Mon–Fri 10–5, w'ends 12–5
Winemaker Dan McNicol **Est.** 1979 **Dozens** 90 000 **Vyds** 198ha
Second in size in the region to Wynns Coonawarra Estate, Katnook has taken significant strides since acquisition by Freixenet, the Spanish cava producer. Once Katnook sold most of its grapes, but it now sells only 10%. The historic stone woolshed in which the second vintage in Coonawarra (1896) was made, and which has served Katnook since 1980, has been restored. Likewise, the former office of John Riddoch has been restored and is now the cellar door; the former stables serve as a function area. Well over half of the total estate plantings are cabernet sauvignon and shiraz; the Odyssey Cabernet Sauvignon and Prodigy Shiraz are the duo at the top of a multi-tiered production. In March 2018 Freixenet announced that Henkell, the Oetker Group's sparkling wine branch, had acquired 50.67% of Freixenet's shares, creating the world's leading sparkling wine group. The brand was sold to Accolade in August 2020. Exports to all major markets.

🍷🍷🍷🍷🍷 **Amara Vineyard Cabernet Sauvignon 2018** From every angle, this is an imposing wine. It spent 18 months in French and American oak, 40% new, boasting a quality of fruit that manages to stand up to this. Deep, rich and ripe with cassis and currants, mint and mocha, olive and new leather. Full bodied, determined tannins define a very firm finish. Screw cap. 14% alc. **Rating** 95 **To** 2033 $55 JF

🍷🍷🍷🍷🍷 **Estate Cabernet Sauvignon 2018 Rating** 93 **To** 2033 $40 JF
The Caledonian Cabernet Shiraz 2018 Rating 91 **To** 2033 $55 JF

Kay Brothers ★★★★★

57 Kays Road, McLaren Vale, SA 5171 **Region** McLaren Vale
T (08) 8323 8211 **www.kaybrothers.com.au Open** 7 days 11–4
Winemaker Duncan Kennedy **Est.** 1890 **Dozens** 10 500 **Vyds** 22ha
A traditional winery with a rich history and just over 20ha of priceless old vines. The red and fortified wines can be very good. Of particular interest is Block 6 Shiraz, made from 125yo vines. Both vines and wines are going from strength to strength. Celebrated its 130th anniversary in 2020. Exports to the US, Canada, China, Hong Kong, Singapore, Thailand, South Korea, the UK, Germany and Switzerland.

ŸŸŸŸŸ **Block 6 McLaren Vale Shiraz 2018** Fine boned. Powerful, sure, but there is a stridency to the fruit rather than a stolidness. Maritime shiraz, at its best, has a cooler side to violet, bergamot, boysenberry, anise and clove scents. The pepper-clad acidity, vibrant and pulling the melee long. The oak, ample, but not exaggerated. Intense, compact, fragrant and ready for the long haul. Screw cap. 14.5% alc. **Rating** 96 **To** 2045 $125 NG
Griffon's Key Reserve McLaren Vale Grenache 2019 A fine example of how the best suitors of grenache in the Vale marry a chiaroscuro of weightlessness with a rich core of fruit intensity. A steer of sandy tannins, a riff of briar and a long pull by the region's maritime freshness. Textbook. Poached strawberry, anise, kirsch, orange peel, cranberry, bergamot and myriad florals. But the tannins are what make me swoon. Screw cap. 14.5% alc. **Rating** 95 **To** 2027 $49 NG

ŸŸŸŸŸ **Hillside McLaren Vale Shiraz 2018 Rating** 93 **To** 2035 $49 NG
Basket Pressed McLaren Vale Grenache 2019 Rating 93 **To** 2024 $30 NG
Basket Pressed McLaren Vale Shiraz 2019 Rating 92 **To** 2028 $30 NG
Ironmonger McLaren Vale 2018 Rating 92 **To** 2032 $35 NG
McLaren Vale Nero d'Avola 2019 Rating 91 **To** 2023 $35 NG
McLaren Vale Grenache Rosé 2020 Rating 90 **To** 2021 $25 NG

Keith Tulloch Wine ★★★★★

989 Hermitage Road, Pokolbin, NSW 2320 **Region** Hunter Valley
T (02) 4998 7500 **www.keithtullochwine.com.au Open** 7 days 10–5
Winemaker Keith Tulloch, Brendan Kaczorowski, Alisdair Tulloch **Est.** 1997
Dozens 10 000 **Vyds** 12.7ha
Keith Tulloch is, of course, a member of the Tulloch family, which has played a leading role in the Hunter Valley for over a century. Formerly a winemaker at Lindemans and Rothbury Estate, he developed his own label in 1997. There is the same almost obsessive attention to detail, the same almost ascetic intellectual approach, the same refusal to accept anything but the best as that of Jeffrey Grosset. In April 2019 the winery became the first Hunter Valley winery to become certified carbon neutral under the National Carbon Offset Standard (NCOS). Exports to the UK.

ŸŸŸŸŸ **Field of Mars Block 2A Hunter Valley Semillon 2018** Pointed aromas of lemon drops, citrus balm and verbena. Indelible scents of dried hay and freshly lain tatami mat. Best, the juicy middle stains the palate before running the scales of pumice, a chalky salinity and pungent mineral length. Fine. Screw cap. 11.25% alc. **Rating** 96 **To** 2035 $50 NG ✪
The Kester Hunter Valley Shiraz 2019 Sumptous and Hunter-savoury. Huge potential. Bing cherry, orange bitters, suede and most impressively, a relaxed, finessed tannic lattice. Firm enough, but detailed, expansive and effortless. The finish is long and plush. Kudos! Screw cap. 14.5% alc. **Rating** 96 **To** 2034 $80 NG
The Kester Hunter Valley Shiraz 2013 A museum release, displaying how well a savoury mid-weighted Hunter shiraz shows with time. A mid brick ruby. Suave. Sophisticated. Polished leather and the avuncular comforts of a fireplace and an armchair. Five-spice, hoisin, duck lacquer. Lots going on. The finish, drying. I wouldn't wait too long for this. At its best now. Screw cap. 13.8% alc. **Rating** 96 **To** 2026 $110 NG

Field of Mars Block 1 Hunter Valley Shiraz 2018 A sumptuous wine. A long keeper. The tension, a jitter of mineral reductive energy and the tannic persuasion of high-quality oak and well-extracted, optimally ripe fruit. Blood stone, bitter chocolate, cherry pith, plum, iodine, anise. Very impressive. Extremely strident and long. Screw cap. 13.9% alc. **Rating** 95 **To** 2033 $90 NG

Museum Release Hunter Valley Semillon 2014 Fruit from '68 plantings on sand. A fast and hot vintage in '14. Lots left in the tank. Lemon drops, dried hay and lemongrass scents career along vibrant acid rails. The finish is long and vinous, but not yet integrated – still a bit 'shins and elbows'. Time will smooth things over. Screw cap. 11.5% alc. **Rating** 94 **To** 2030 $60 NG

Tawarri Vineyard Hunter Valley Shiraz 2019 Fermented wild with a smidgeon of bunches. Maturation in older 600L French wood. Gorgeous! A deft touch and cool aura dictates a medium-bodied and highly savoury expression that still packs some heft. Black cherry, licorice, five-spice and a medicinal riff meanders across the detailed finish. Screw cap. 14.5% alc. **Rating** 94 **To** 2032 $48 NG

ŸŸŸŸ♀ Field of Mars Block 6 & 4 Hunter Valley Chardonnay 2018 Rating 93 **To** 2029 $60 NG
Bainton Vineyard Hunter Valley Shiraz 2019 Rating 93 **To** 2031 $48 NG
McKelvey Vineyard Hunter Valley Shiraz 2019 Rating 93 **To** 2033 $48 NG
MRV Hunter Valley Marsanne Roussanne Viognier 2019 Rating 91 **To** 2025 $38 NG
The Wife Hunter Valley Shiraz 2019 Rating 91 **To** 2028 $68 NG

Kellermeister   ★★★★☆

Barossa Valley Highway, Lyndoch, SA 5351 **Region** Barossa Valley
T (08) 8524 4303 **www**.kellermeister.com.au **Open** 7 days 9.30–5.30
Winemaker Mark Pearce **Est.** 1976 **Dozens** 30 000 **Vyds** 20ha
Since joining Kellermeister from Wirra Wirra in 2009, Mark Pearce has successfully worked through challenging times to ensure the survival of the winery and its brands; and upon the retirement of founders Ralph and Val Jones in late '12, the Pearce family acquired the business. Surrounded by a young, close-knit team, Mark is committed to continuing to build on the legacy that the founders began more than 40 years ago. His winemaking focus is on continuing to preserve Kellermeister's best wines, while introducing new wines made with the intention of expressing the purity of the provenance of the Barossa. Exports to the US, Canada, Switzerland, Denmark, Israel, Taiwan, China and Japan.

ŸŸŸŸ♀ Whiskers Single Vineyard Barossa Valley Grenache 2019 Poached strawberries, ripe raspberries and pretty red cherries unite in a refined and lovely expression of Barossa grenache. Rose petals and musk express its delicate side, while finely textured tannins define upright form and medium-term endurance. Oak is sensitively played to highlight fruit, concluding with medium persistence. Screw cap. 14.5% alc. **Rating** 91 **To** 2027 $45 TS

ŸŸŸŸ The Funk Wagon Barossa GSM 2018 Rating 89 **To** 2022 $35 TS

Kellybrook   ★★★★★

Fulford Road, Wonga Park, Vic 3115 **Region** Yarra Valley
T (03) 9722 1304 **www**.kellybrookwinery.com.au **Open** Thurs–Mon 10–5
Winemaker Stuart Dudine **Est.** 1962 **Dozens** 3000 **Vyds** 8.4ha
The vineyard is at Wonga Park, one of the gateways to the Yarra Valley. A very competent producer of both cider and apple brandy (in Calvados style) as well as table wine. When it received its winery licence in 1970, it became the first winery in the Yarra Valley to open its doors in the 20th century, a distinction often ignored or forgotten.

ŸŸŸŸŸ Willowlake Vineyard Pinot Noir 2019 A light hue belies the depth of flavour within. Sweetly-fruited, with cherries splashed with chinotto, rhubarb compote and whole-bunch tangy/tart flavours. While it has plush tannins and a wave of texture, it's by no means a big wine. Intriguing. Delicious. Screw cap. 13.5% alc. Rating 95 To 2029 $40 JF

Malakoff Vineyard Pyrenees Range Shiraz 2018 A small amount of viognier has found its way into this medium-bodied, fine-featured shiraz. Regional signature bush mint is but a light thread intersecting plum, blueberry, forest berries, cinnamon, prune and white pepper. Tannins are rounded, making for good drinking now. Screw cap. 14.5% alc. **Rating** 94 **To** 2026 $46 JP

ҮҮҮҮҮ **Estate Reserve Yarra Valley Shiraz 2018** Rating 93 To 2026 $35 JF
Yarra Valley Pinot Noir 2019 Rating 92 To 2027 $30 JF
Yarra Valley Cabernet Sauvignon 2018 Rating 92 To 2027 $30 JF

Kelman Vineyard   ★★★★

2 Oakey Creek Road, Pokolbin, NSW 2320 **Region** Hunter Valley
T (02) 4991 5456 **www**.kelmanvineyard.com.au **Open** Thurs–Mon 10–4
Winemaker Xanthe Hatcher **Est.** 1999 **Dozens** 1300 **Vyds** 9ha
Kelman Vineyard is a community development spread over 40ha, with 9ha under vine. The estate is scattered with traditional country cottages and homesteads; vines, olive and lemon groves meander between the dwellings. Named in honour of William Kelman who travelled to Australia with John Busby (father of James Busby) in 1824, marrying John's daughter Katherine on the ship to Australia.

ҮҮҮҮҮ **Hunter Valley Tempranillo 2019** I like few Australian tempranillos. Here is an exception. Mottled cherry, kirsch, mint, beef bouillon, umami warmth and some malty vanillan French oak (35% new) as a backdrop. A long, supine wine to give into due to its earthy charm. Screw cap. 14% alc. **Rating** 91 **To** 2023 $32 NG

ҮҮҮҮ **Hunter Valley Rosé 2020** Rating 89 To 2021 $25 NG
Hunter Valley Sparkling Moscato 2019 Rating 89 $22 NG

Kennedy   ★★★★★

Maple Park, 224 Wallenjoe Road, Corop, Vic 3559 (postal) **Region** Heathcote
T (03) 5484 8293 **www**.kennedyvintners.com.au
Winemaker Glen Hayley, Gerard Kennedy **Est.** 2002 **Dozens** 3000 **Vyds** 29.2ha
Having been farmers in the Colbinabbin area of Heathcote for 27 years, John and Patricia Kennedy were on the spot when a prime piece of red Cambrian soil on the east-facing slope of Mt Camel Range became available for purchase. They planted 20ha of shiraz in 2002. As they gained knowledge of the intricate differences within the site, further plantings of shiraz, tempranillo and mourvèdre followed in '07. The Shiraz is made in small open fermenters, using indigenous yeasts and gentle pigeage before being taken to French oak for maturation. John and Patricia's geologist son Gerard returned to the family business in 2015 and now oversees the winemaking and activities in the vineyard.

ҮҮҮҮҮ **Cambria Heathcote Shiraz 2018** Everything about the beauty of the ancient Cambrian soil and the region's connection to the grape comes together here. It's not showy, far from it. Rather it's a restrained and elegant immersion into a deeply coloured, dark world of serious quality fruit played against a backdrop of sensitive oak and lithe, fine tannins. Screw cap. 14% alc. **Rating** 95 **To** 2028 $38 JP
Pink Hills Heathcote Rosé 2020 A 100% mourvèdre-based rosé, with an established reputation; barrel fermented in old French oak. Pretty light copper in hue, it doesn't stray far from a solid core of ripe summer berries and dusty spice. Dry but not stark, it loosens on the palate with a sweet fruit liveliness, finishing smooth. Screw cap. 13.5% alc. **Rating** 94 **To** 2024 $24 JP ✪

ҮҮҮҮ **Heathcote Shiraz 2018** Rating 93 To 2030 $28 JP

Kensington Wines

1590 Highlands Road, Whiteheads Creek, Vic 3660 **Region** Upper Goulburn
T (03) 5796 9155 **www.**kensingtonwines.com.au **Open** Sun 11–5
Winemaker Nina Stocker, Frank Bonic **Est.** 2010 **Dozens** 15 000 **Vyds** 4ha
This is the venture of husband and wife Anddy and Kandy Xu, born and raised in China but
now residents in Australia. They have created a broad portfolio of wines by sourcing grapes
and wines mostly from regions across Victoria, but also SA. While the primary market is
China (and other Asian countries), the wines have not been made with residual sweetness and
are also sold in Australia. Kandy and Anddy's purchase of the Rocky Passes Vineyard (and
cellar door) in the Upper Goulburn region in 2015 was a significant development in terms
of their commitment to quality Australian wine. Kandy has broadened her own experience
and wine qualifications by completing the WSET diploma and undertaking a vintage at
Brown Brothers. She was co-founder of the Chinese Wine Association of Australia and
continues as the chair. She has translated wine books into Mandarin, including my (James')
Top 100 Wineries of Australia. Exports to China and other Asian countries.

🍷🍷🍷🍷🍷 **Masterpiece Barossa Valley Mataro Shiraz 2018** Mataro takes the lead
here with a wealth of wild berries, dark plum, spice, baked earth and licorice in a
medium-bodied wine of immediate drinking appeal (although further ageing is
definitely on the cards). Runs long on fine, compact tannins. Screw cap. 14.5% alc.
Rating 92 **To** 2026 $68 JP
Heathcote Shiraz 2018 Fifteen months maturation in tank (60%) and French
barrels (20% new). An ultra-ripe expression of Heathcote shiraz rich in a dark,
brooding complexity. Blackberry, dark roasted spices, touch of cedary oak and
baked earth on thick, hearty Heathcote tannins. Screw cap. 15.5% alc. **Rating** 91
To 2030 $35 JP
King Valley Shiraz 2018 The colour is deep and intense, aromas are in the black
cherry, sage, spearmint spectrum with an earthy savouriness. This wine has an exotic
spicy streak with a dried herb and peppery thread running through the palate.
Finishes with long, ripe tannins. Screw cap. 14.5% alc. **Rating** 91 **To** 2026 $58 JP
Goulburn Valley Shiraz 2019 A fresh and lively shiraz, medium in body with
plenty of engaging Goulburn Valley character from the dusty earthiness through
to the scent of bay leaf and Aussie bush. Wears its ripeness well, delivering plum,
black fruits, toasty vanilla, baking spices and cacao. Glides to a smooth finish. Screw
cap. 15% alc. **Rating** 90 **To** 2026 $30 JP

🍷🍷🍷🍷 **Goulburn Valley Chardonnay 2018 Rating** 89 **To** 2025 $18 JP ⬦

🍃 Kerri Greens

38 Paringa Road, Red Hill South, Vic 3937 **Region** Mornington Peninsula
T 0438 219 507 **www.**kerrigreens.com **Open** Sat 11–5, Sun 12–4
Winemaker Tom McCarthy, Lucas Blanck **Est.** 2015 **Dozens** 1000
Kerri Greens (named after a local surf break) is a story of serendipity. It's what happens when
2 young vignerons become colleagues, then friends and now partners in a boutique label
that offers excellence and energising wines. Tom McCarthy (son of local Peninsula producers
Kathleen Quealy and Kevin McCarthy) is the lead winemaker at Quealy Wines these days
and Lucas Blanck (son of winemaker Frederic, from Domaine Paul Blanck in Alsace) is
viticulturist. It just doesn't get any better. Since it began in 2013, Tom and Paul have worked
tirelessly to bring life back to the various vineyards they manage, which form the basis of the
disparate styles. Organics, sustainability and treading gently are important considerations. It's
also a family business strengthened by their wives, Alyce Blanck and Sarah Saxton, who are
very much at the forefront, not just the cellar door. Kerri Greens has its own strong identity.
What's really exciting is that this young quartet is respectful of a wine region that nurtures
them, yet not afraid to shake things up. Bravo. (JF)

🍷🍷🍷🍷🍷 **Ohne Mornington Peninsula Gewürztraminer 2020** Oh my, Ohne is so
good. It's more lemon than lychee, but heady aromas of the variety play true.
Cinnamon, kaffir lime leaves, rosewater and Turkish delight in the mix, but what

sets this apart from many other renditions is that it's not heavy or oily. There is a smidge of texture across the palate, but the fine acidity elevates and tightens, then puts it into cruise control. Screw cap. 12% alc. **Rating** 95 **To** 2026 $28 JF ✪

Foothills Mornington Peninsula Pinot Noir 2020 A more structured offering compared to the Murra wine, all dark cherries, warm earth and some charry/ meaty notes adding another layer of flavour. Full bodied, with grainy ripe tannins, great persistence and a pleasing radicchio-bitter finish. Screw cap. 12.9% alc. **Rating** 95 **To** 2030 $40 JF

Murra Mornington Peninsula Pinot Noir 2019 Fruit off the steep Duke vineyard in Red Hill, with vines edging 30+ years and eschewing herbicides/ synthetic fertilisers. This is a charmer. Rose petals, sweet red cherries and baking spices flow through onto a barely-medium-bodied palate. It's energetic. There's a fineness within, with filigreed tannins and refreshing acidity to close. Screw cap. 13.2% alc. **Rating** 95 **To** 2028 $32 JF ✪

Terrestrial Flowers Mornington Peninsula Blanc de Blancs 2017 The peninsula is generally not my go-to region for sparkling, but this stopped me in my tracks. A super-dry, crisp style, yet among the white floral aromas come wafts of creamed honey, honeycomb and a touch of toasted brioche. The palate is fine, racy and invigorating, with a lemon/lime-juice acid line and persistent bead. Impressive. Alas, just 45 dozen made. Diam. 12% alc. **Rating** 95 $55 JF ♥

Hickson Mornington Peninsula Chardonnay 2019 The longer this lingered in the glass, the better it showed – unfurling and revealing its core of lemon, grapefruit and zest with racy acidity zooming through the palate. It has a hint of creamy, leesy texture adding a layer of savouriness to this terrific drink. Screw cap. 13.2% alc. **Rating** 94 **To** 2029 $42 JF

Lazy Bastard Mornington Peninsula Pinot Noir 2020 This is a drink-now, don't-keep-me pinot noir and it's a ripper, almost thirst quenching. Bright, tangy, upfront fruit of the cherry persuasion with chinotto and crunchy, crackling acidity. It has the pop and juiciness of carbonic maceration and just enough tannin to give it shape and detail. Spot-on. Screw cap. 12.9% alc. **Rating** 94 **To** 2024 $35 JF

Clementina Vendage Tardives Gewürztraminer Pinot Gris 2019 Amber hue, shot with rose gold. Immediately enticing. Saffron-poached quinces, pears in honey, vanilla pod and apricots in syrup, with orange rind and a twist of bitter lemon. It's not overly rich but it has a succulence and a lusciousness, with the sweetness balanced by good acidity and neat phenolics. An excellent VT. 375ml. Screw cap. 14.5% alc. **Rating** 94 **To** 2026 $40 JF

♟♟♟♟♟ **Citrea Mornington Peninsula Riesling 2019** **Rating** 93 **To** 2028 $34 JF
Pig Face Mornington Peninsula Chardonnay 2019 **Rating** 93 **To** 2026 $28 JF
Pinots de Mornington Mornington Peninsula Rosé 2020 **Rating** 93 **To** 2023 $28 JF
Laze Mornington Peninsula Chardonnay 2019 **Rating** 92 **To** 2025 $32 JF

Kerrigan + Berry ★★★★☆

PO Box 221, Cowaramup, WA 6284 **Region** South West Australia
T (08) 9755 6046 **www.**kerriganandberry.com.au **Open** At Hay Shed Hill and West Cape Howe
Winemaker Michael Kerrigan, Gavin Berry **Est.** 2007 **Dozens** 1500
Owners Michael Kerrigan and Gavin Berry have been making wine in WA for a combined period of over 50 years and say they have been most closely associated with the 2 varieties that in their opinion define WA: riesling and cabernet sauvignon. This is strictly a weekend and after-hours venture, separate from their respective roles as chief winemakers at Hay Shed Hill (Michael) and West Cape Howe (Gavin). They have focused on what is important, and explain, 'We have spent a total of zero hours on marketing research, and no consultants have been injured in the making of these wines'. Exports to the UK, Denmark, Singapore and China.

ΨΨΨΨΨ **Mount Barker Margaret River Cabernet Sauvignon 2018** Mount Barker fruit brings the structure and the density, Margaret River the red-fruit succulence and latent power. All things as one here, the perfect example of greatness exceeding the sum of its parts. Muscular in its own way and built for long-term gratification. Screw cap. 14% alc. **Rating** 96 **To** 2045 $60 EL
Mount Barker Great Southern Riesling 2020 Produced from the near-50yo vines on the Langton Vineyard. A wine with intensity and outright power from low yields reflecting the dry season. The mineral framework of lime zest, pith and juice flavours does its job in this classic regional wine. Screw cap. 11.5% alc. **Rating** 95 **To** 2032 $30 JH ◯
Margaret River Chardonnay 2019 From dry-grown Gingin clone in Wilyabrup, early picked to enhance brightness and freshness without compromising varietal expression. Grapefruit leads white peach, with an echo of almond ex-barrel ferment. Will grow with time in bottle. Screw cap. 12% alc. **Rating** 95 **To** 2031 $40 JH

Kilgour Wines ★★★☆

25 McAdams Lane, Bellarine, Vic 3223 **Region** Geelong
T 0448 785 744 **www.**kilgourwines.com **Open** Sat, public hols & by appt
Winemaker Alister Timms **Est.** 1992 **Dozens** 600 **Vyds** 15ha
While this business has roots in the Bellarine Peninsula dating back to 1989, its reappearance in 2017 is a different venture altogether. Anne Timms planted the original vineyard in '89, opening Kilgour Estate. In 2010 she sold the 3.2ha title with the Kilgour Estate winery, the winery label and a separate 2ha of vines to David and Lyndsay Sharp who renamed the business Jack Rabbit. Anne Timms retained 8ha of vines surrounding the Jack Rabbit property and for the next 5 years sold the grapes to other wineries. In '17 she retained part of the crop, with Alister Timms (chief winemaker at Shadowfax) making the Kilgour Wines under contract at Shadowfax.

ΨΨΨΨ **Bellarine Pinot Gris 2020** Presents a well-priced gris with essential ingredients, pears and apples, but also incorporates some extra lovely notes of honeysuckle, glacé fruit and wild honey. Fills the senses, including the long, textural finish. Screw cap. 13% alc. **Rating** 89 **To** 2024 $26 JP
Bellarine Merlot 2019 A super-pretty and elegant merlot that trades heavily on the grape's aromatic, plummy, black cherry and violet-enhanced aromas. Fine and bright with a spicy layer of leafy, dried herbs. It fulfils the price and the point of merlot – to charm the drinker no end. Screw cap. 13% alc. **Rating** 88 **To** 2025 $30 JP

Kilikanoon Wines ★★★★★

30 Penna Lane, Penwortham, SA 5453 **Region** Clare Valley
T (08) 8843 4206 **www.**kilikanoon.com.au **Open** 7 days 11–5
Winemaker Troy van Dulken **Est.** 1997 **Dozens** 100 000 **Vyds** 120ha
Kilikanoon has travelled in the fast lane since winemaker Kevin Mitchell established it in 1997 on the foundation of 6ha of vines he owned with father Mort. With the aid of investors, its 100 000-dozen production comes from 120ha of estate-owned vineyards and access to the best grapes from a total of over 2000ha across SA. Between 2013 and early '14 all links between Kilikanoon and Seppeltsfield were ended; the sale of Kilikanoon's share in Seppeltsfield, together with the sale of Kilikanoon's Crowhurst Vineyard in the Barossa Valley, led to the purchase by Kilikanoon of the winery which it had previously leased, and of the Mount Surmon Vineyard. The small-batch Mr Hyde wines are produced from individual vineyards/blocks in the Clare Valley. Exports to most major markets.

ΨΨΨΨΨ **Kelly 1932 Clare Valley Grenache 2018** This takes no time to reveal its credentials: fresh raspberries and pastilles, warm earth and exotic spices, smoked meats and dried herbs. There is a tinge of very ripe fruit in the mix, too. Fine sandpaper tannins add another textural element across the fuller palate. All in all, there's plenty of enjoyment here. Screw cap. 14.5% alc. **Rating** 95 **To** 2030 $96 JF

ΨΨΨΨ Covenant Clare Valley Shiraz 2018 Rating 93 To 2032 $55 JF
Attunga 1865 Clare Valley Shiraz 2018 Rating 93 To 3033 $250 JF
Oracle Clare Valley Shiraz 2017 Rating 93 To 2032 $96 JF
Prodigal Clare Valley Grenache 2018 Rating 93 To 2028 $33 JF
Blocks Road Clare Valley Cabernet Sauvignon 2018 Rating 93 To 2030 $40 JF
Baudinet Blend Clare Valley GSM 2018 Rating 93 To 2028 $55 JF
Duke Reserve Clare Valley Grenache 2016 Rating 91 To 2028 $55 JF
Killerman's Run Clare Valley GSM 2019 Rating 90 To 2029 $22 JF

Kimbarra Wines   ★★★★☆

422 Barkly Street, Ararat, Vic 3377 **Region** Grampians
T 0428 519 195 **www**.kimbarrawines.com.au **Open** By appt
Winemaker Peter Leeke, Justin Purser, Adam Richardson **Est.** 1990 **Dozens** 180
Vyds 11ha
Peter Leeke has 8.5ha of shiraz, 1.5ha of riesling and 1ha of cabernet sauvignon – varieties that have proven best suited to the Grampians region. The particularly well-made, estate-grown wines deserve a wider audience.

ΨΨΨΨΨ Great Western Shiraz 2019 Once again a challenging vintage has seen well-grown fruit shine, boasting highish alcohols that nevertheless present a pretty harmonious whole. Deep colour, traces of bush mint and sage, black cherry, ripe plum, dark chocolate. A fleshy, smooth middle palate finishes taut. Screw cap. 14.6% alc. **Rating** 95 To 2029 $30 JP ✪
Great Western Riesling 2020 This is one serious riesling, with a penetrating steeliness common to the rieslings of Great Western. A solid core of lemon zest, lime cordial, kaffir lime leaf – tight and coiled – is at the heart of this wines. A good sign for a bright future. It hasn't finished showing us what it's got, not by a long shot. Screw cap. 12% alc. **Rating** 94 To 2030 $30 JP ✪

Kimbolton Wines   ★★★★

29 Burleigh Street, Langhorne Creek, SA 5255 **Region** Langhorne Creek
T (08) 8537 3002 **www**.kimboltonwines.com.au **Open** 7 days 10–4
Winemaker Contract **Est.** 1998 **Dozens** 2000 **Vyds** 55ha
The Kimbolton property originally formed part of the Potts Bleasdale estate. In 1946 it was acquired by Henry and Thelma Case, grandparents of current owners brother and sister Nicole Clark and Brad Case. The grapes from the vineyard plantings (cabernet sauvignon, shiraz, malbec, fiano, carignan and montepulciano) are sold to leading wineries, with small amounts retained for the Kimbolton label. The name comes from a medieval town in Bedfordshire, UK, from which some of the family's ancestors emigrated. Kimbolton opened its cellar door in December '18, constructed from 'a unique mix of high-gloss navy industrial shipping containers' and timber, includes a rooftop viewing platform.

ΨΨΨΨΨ The Rifleman Langhorne Creek Cabernet Sauvignon 2018 Elite selection of fruit here, and a best barrel selection as well. Blackberry and currant notes, with a sense of creaminess as well as subtle choc-mints. It's all playing together with respect and reserve, the finish filled with chewy tannin mouthfeels. Already very smart, but wait a few years and you'll be rewarded. Screw cap. 14% alc. **Rating** 94 To 2030 $60 TL
Special Release The L.G. Langhorne Creek Cabernet Sauvignon 2015 Top-shelf special reserve stuff here. Quite unique, yet very comfortable in its own skin. Classical choc-mint and cassis to begin, no-holds-barred palate concentration, packed with all the flavours. The new oak provides structure and backdrop rather than inhibiting the power of the fruit. Big, chewy, impressive. Cork. 15.5% alc. **Rating** 94 To 2028 $105 TL

ΨΨΨΨΨ Langhorne Creek Shiraz 2018 Rating 93 To 2028 $25 TL ✪
The Rifleman Langhorne Creek Shiraz 2018 Rating 93 To 2030 $60 TL
Bella Monte Sparkling Montepulciano NV Rating 93 To 2025 $38
The Rifleman Adelaide Hills Chardonnay 2019 Rating 91 To 2025 $36 TL
Langhorne Creek Montepulciano Rosé 2020 Rating 91 To 2023 $22 TL ✪
Langhorne Creek Cabernet Sauvignon 2018 Rating 90 To 2028 $25 TL

Kings Landing   ★★★★☆

9 Collins Place, Denmark, WA 6333 (postal) **Region** Great Southern
T 0432 312 918 **www.**kingslandingwines.com.au
Winemaker Coby Ladwig, Luke Eckersley **Est.** 2015 **Dozens** 7000 **Vyds** 9ha
Winemakers Coby Ladwig and Luke Eckersley have spent many years making wines for others, so this is in some ways a busman's holiday. But it's also a serious business, with 9ha of vineyard plantings (3ha of chardonnay and 2ha each of shiraz, riesling and cabernet sauvignon) making this much more than a virtual winery.

ΨΨΨΨΨ **Mount Barker Riesling 2020** If there ever was a region that could produce muscular riesling, it is Mount Barker. This wine has a lip-smacking freshness about it, coupled with that regional coiled acidity and power beyond its weight. Great length of flavour to round it all out. There is a layer of savoury cheesecloth/ parmesan rind in here that makes it all the more interesting. Screw cap. 11.5% alc. **Rating** 94 To 2036 $32 EL
Mount Barker Shiraz 2019 Inky, intense and juicy, this has layers and layers of flavour and texture, all crammed into the glass. It verges on opulent, such is its luxurious intensity of flavour. It has the body of some of the Barossa shiraz of the 2000s: that is to say, big, rich, rounded and ripe. Plenty to grab onto and a lot to like. Salted heirloom tomato, raspberry, red licorice and briny acid. It's a big one. Screw cap. 14.4% alc. **Rating** 94 To 2031 $32 EL

Kirrihill Wines   ★★★★☆

948 Farrell Flat Road, Clare, SA 5453 **Region** Clare Valley
T (08) 8842 1233 **www.**kirrihillwines.com.au **Open** 7 days 11–4
Winemaker Andrew Locke **Est.** 1998 **Dozens** 35000 **Vyds** 600ha
The Kirrihill story started in the late 1990s. The aim was to build a business producing premium wines from temperate vineyards that represent the unique characters of the Clare Valley. Grapes are sourced from specially selected parcels of Kirrihill's 600ha of vineyards. Susan (Susie) Mickan, with vintage experience in Australia, Spain, China and the US, joined Kirrihill as chief winemaker in December 2018. Exports to all major markets.

ΨΨΨΨΨ **E.B.'s The Settler Clare Valley Riesling 2020** Pristine and pure. It starts out subtle, and teases with some white florals, wet stones and daikon radish. Then slowly, more citrus accents, with lemon balm and lime. It's juicy, with superfine acidity lengthening out the palate. Screw cap. 12% alc. **Rating** 95 To 2030 $35 JF ✪
E.B.'s The Pastor Clare Valley Cabernet Malbec 2018 Many of Kirrihill's reds have been hammered with too much oak, and this is not shy either, but somehow it takes everything in its stride. Maybe it's the malbec. Maybe it's magic. There's a buoyancy across the palate, velvety and expansive tannins, lemony acidity and plenty of regional accents. The most restrained of the high-end reds. But still bolshie. Screw cap. 14.5% alc. **Rating** 95 To 2033 $85 JF

ΨΨΨΨΨ **E.B.'s The Peacemaker Clare Valley Shiraz 2018** Rating 93 To 2033 $85 JF
The Partner Series Clare Valley Riesling 2020 Rating 92 To 2028 $29 JF
The Partner Series Clare Valley Shiraz 2018 Rating 92 To 2030 $29 JF
Piccoli Lotti McLaren Vale Nero d'Avola 2019 Rating 91 To 2022 $27 NG

KJB Wine Group

Region McLaren Vale
T 0409 570 694
Winemaker Kurt Brill **Est.** 2008 **Dozens** 800 **Vyds** 20ha
KJB Wine Group Pty Ltd is the venture of Kurt Brill, who began his involvement in the wine industry in 2003, largely through the encouragement of his wife Gillian. He commenced a marketing degree through the University of Adelaide but switched to the winemaking degree at CSU in '08, finally graduating in '19. Fruit is sourced from growers in different parts of McLaren Vale, made in small volumes with sales along the eastern seaboard of Australia. Kurt also has international winemaking experience gained in Bordeaux and Fleurie, France. Exports to the UK and Denmark.

ＹＹＹＹＹ **Land of the Vines McLaren Vale Shiraz 2019** A strong regional wine of the older school: dark-fruit allusions, anise, clove, pepper grind, dry-aged meat and lashings of malty oak. This said, the grape tannins are shapely, saline and properly extracted, conferring authority and an uncanny savouriness amid the teeming fruit and oaky phalanx. A waft of volatility services perk and aromatic lift. The length, long and gritty. This has lots of personality and that is a virtue. Screw cap. 14.5% alc. **Rating** 92 **To** 2029 $28 NG
Land of the Vines Rocco McLaren Vale GSM 2019 Medium weight despite the alcohol, this is a gently extracted wine relying on an arsenal of new American and seasoned French wood for its tannins. The mid palate is sweet and plush, showcasing notes of molasses, Turkish delight, sour cherry and cranberry. The finish, a bit tangy but pleasingly long. A solid wine. Screw cap. 14.5% alc. **Rating** 90 **To** 2026 $26 NG

ＹＹＹＹ **Land of the Vines McLaren Vale Cabernet Sauvignon 2019** **Rating** 88 **To** 2029 NG

Knappstein

2 Pioneer Avenue, Clare, SA 5453 **Region** Clare Valley
T (08) 8841 2100 **www.**knappstein.com.au **Open** 7 days 10–4
Winemaker Michael Kane, Mike Farmilo (Consultant) **Est.** 1969 **Dozens** 75 000 **Vyds** 114ha
Knappstein's full name is Knappstein Enterprise Winery, reflecting its history before being acquired by Petaluma, then part of Lion Nathan, followed by Accolade. After a period of corporate ownership, Knappstein has now come full circle and is back in private ownership, purchased in 2019 by Yinmore Wines. Despite these corporate chessboard moves, wine quality has remained excellent. The wines are produced from the substantial mature estate Enterprise, Ackland, Yertabulti and The Mayor's vineyards. Exports to all major markets.

ＹＹＹＹＹ **Mayors Vineyard Clare Valley Shiraz 2019** After a 3-year hiatus (the last vintage was 2015) the Mayor's back. An abundance of flavour has been packed into this, highlighting its unique regional tones. Accents of black fruits infused with dark chocolate and mint, plus lots of earthy elements such as twigs and Aussie bush. Full bodied, masses of tannin and it's not shy. Yet it's still finding its way – very youthful and primary, bold and sassy. Screw cap. 14.5% alc. **Rating** 93 **To** 2033 $53 JF
Enterprise Single Vineyard Clare Valley Cabernet Sauvignon 2018
Yes it is ripe, as per vintage conditions, but it is also a very contained wine. Not overwrought. Deep, dark and rich with plump cassis and currants injected with bitter chocolate and mint, plus sweet cedary oak. Full bodied, with no shortage of tannins. Its best years are yet to come. Screw cap. 14.2% alc. **Rating** 93 **To** 2033 $53 JF
Insider Clare Valley Riesling 2020 This is good. Really good. A mix of pristine citrus fruit and perky acidity carry the fuller flavours of lemon curd and creamed honey. It's mostly textural, with a lick of sweetness rounding out the palate. Screw cap. 12.5% alc. **Rating** 92 **To** 2030 $30 JF

Enterprise Vineyard Clare Valley Riesling 2020 This has tension like a balloon on the verge of bursting. It's intense, with lots of lemon zest and juice; a touch estery, with a hint of tropical fruit. But it's super-dry with puckering acidity. More time. Definitely. Screw cap. 12% alc. **Rating** 91 **To** 2030 $38 JF

Insider Clare Valley Shiraz Malbec 2019 Richly flavoured and ripe of fruit, with savoury inputs, especially via malbec. The tannins are plump yet chewy. Tangy raspberry acidity on the finish just means a barbecue is essential. Screw cap. 14.5% alc. **Rating** 91 **To** 2026 $30 JF

Ackland Single Vineyard Watervale Riesling 2020 While it has some Watervale florals and warm-slate aromas, it's a touch reticent, offering a squirt of lime juice and zest plus lemon salts. The acidity is certainly upfront yet the palate broadens out. Pleasant but not as 'wow' as this label can often be. Screw cap. 12% alc. **Rating** 90 **To** 2028 $38 JF

ŢŢŢŢ **Clare Valley Shiraz 2018 Rating** 89 **To** 2026 $22 JF

Knee Deep Wines

22 Rathay Street, Victoria Park, WA 6100 **Region** Margaret River
T (08) 9755 6776 **www**.kneedeepwines.com.au
Winemaker Kate Morgan **Est.** 2000 **Dozens** 5000
Perth surgeon and veteran yachtsman Phil Childs and wife Sue planted their property in Wilyabrup in 2000 to chardonnay, sauvignon blanc, semillon, chenin blanc, cabernet sauvignon and shiraz. The name was inspired by the passion and commitment needed to produce premium wine and as a tongue-in-cheek acknowledgement of jumping in, 'boots and all', during a testing time in the wine industry, the grape glut building more or less in tune with the venture. The reins have now passed to the Holden family, Matt and Clair Holden having worked alongside the Childs family for 5 years. Exports to Germany.

ŢŢŢŢŢ **Birdhouse Margaret River Chardonnay 2020** 72/28% Gingin/Clone 5. Wild ferment in barrel, matured for 10 months in French oak (28% new). Red apples, white peach and a slice of nectarine. This is pretty, layered and almost tropical, but very fine. The acidity that courses in and out of the fruit is saline and laces it all together. Screw cap. 12% alc. **Rating** 93 **To** 2028 $39 EL

Birdhouse Margaret River Cabernet Sauvignon 2019 Intensely dark and structured, this has all the Margaret River hallmarks that make cabernet so great here. Whether or not the wine needed a little lashing of shiraz remains to be seen (we will never know), such is the purity of cassis and wild raspberry that are alternately woven through the fine tannins and briny acidity present in this wine. Lovely stuff, for sure. Screw cap. 14% alc. **Rating** 93 **To** 2036 $35 EL

Margaret River Sauvignon Blanc Semillon 2020 Gooseberry, crunchy apple, gentle talc and a whiff of fresh-cut grass. All things in place. This is pure, layered and very pretty. A lot to like! Screw cap. 12% alc. **Rating** 91 **To** 2025 $24 EL

Birdhouse Margaret River Shiraz 2019 Pretty, creamy, juicy and dark. The oak is evident, but plays a supporting structural role rather than dominating. The fruit is ripe but not overdone, and the flavours hover over the blackberry-cream-pie space. Supple and modern with a finish that has been sprinkled with aniseed, clove and black pepper. Screw cap. 14% alc. **Rating** 91 **To** 2027 $35 EL

Margaret River Cabernet Sauvignon 2019 A savoury, lean and structured cabernet sauvignon with a stemmy green crunch on the mid palate. This is often seen as a negative, but in the context of this glass, it has a herbal bay/sage sort of vibe and brings added complexity and texture to the experience. It is filtered through a melange of berries and spice. Pretty cool drinking for $24. Screw cap. 13.5% alc. **Rating** 91 **To** 2027 $24 EL

Margaret River Rosé 2020 98/2% shiraz/sauvignon blanc. 'Tempting' was the first thing that came to mind – and stayed. A sweeter style and very appealing for it. Raspberry, strawberry and other red berries are balanced by saline acid that brings the picture together. A lovely wine with many angles of enjoyment. Screw cap. 12% alc. **Rating** 90 **To** 2022 $24 EL

Birdhouse Margaret River Malbec 2019 Perfumed and spicy, littered with red/black forest fruits. The palate has a delicious approachability, the only quibble is the length of flavour, peaking at 'moderate'. The tannins are fine and pleasantly grippy, shaping the wine as it courses over the tongue. Jubilant stuff, here. Screw cap. 13.5% alc. **Rating** 90 **To** 2027 $35 EL

🍷🍷🍷🍷 **Margaret River Sauvignon Blanc 2020** Rating 89 To 2021 $24 EL

Koerner Wine   ★★★★☆

935 Mintaro Road, Leasingham, SA 5452 **Region** Clare Valley
T 0408 895 341 **www**.koernerwine.com.au **Open** By appt
Winemaker Damon Koerner **Est.** 2014 **Dozens** 4000 **Vyds** 60ha
Brothers Damon and Jonathan (Jono) Koerner grew up in the Clare Valley but flew the coop to work and study in other parts of Australia and abroad. The substantial vineyards had been owned and managed by their parents, Anthony and Christine Koerner, for 35 years, but they have passed ownership and management of the vineyards on to their sons. While the major part of the crop is sold to other wineries, in 2016 Damon made 11 wines. A major point of difference from other Clare Valley wineries is the use of synonyms for well-known varieties, as well as adopting Australian name usage, turning the world upside down with left-field winemaking practices. Exports to the UK, the US, Canada, Belgium, the Netherlands, South Korea, Singapore and Japan.

🍷🍷🍷🍷🍷 **Parish Riesling 2020** A gentle, elegant wine that is subtle at first, even subdued. It slowly reveals some ginger lemon tea, lemon blossom, gardenia and wet pebbles. The palate is smooth and textural, with mouth-watering acidity. Beautifully modulated and a real surprise. Diam. 11.5% alc. **Rating** 95 **To** 2026 $45 JF
Gullyview Riesling 2020 The trio of rieslings from 2020 offer differences as much as similarities. Of the latter, it is texture. This is lovely. Superfine palate with honeycomb, ginger tea and lemon curd. The acidity is soft and rolls around the palate. It lingers and it's fabulous. Diam. 12.2% alc. **Rating** 95 **To** 2026 $45 JF

🍷🍷🍷🍷♀ **Vivian Red Wine 2019** Rating 93 To 2030 $50 JF
Mammolo Sciacarello 2020 Rating 93 To 2023 $40 JF
Rolle Vermentino 2020 Rating 92 To 2024 $45 JF
Pigato Vermentino 2020 Rating 91 To 2023 $30 JF
Grace Riesling 2020 Rating 90 To 2025 $45 JF

K1 Wines by Geoff Hardy   ★★★★☆

159 Tynan Road, Kuitpo, SA 5172 **Region** Adelaide Hills
T (08) 8388 3700 **www**.winesbygeoffhardy.com.au **Open** 7 days 11–4
Winemaker Geoff Hardy, Shane Harris **Est.** 1980 **Dozens** 20 000 **Vyds** 43ha
Geoff Hardy's great-great-grandfather, the original Thomas Hardy, first planted grapes in SA in the 1850s and was one of the founding fathers of the Australian wine industry. In 1980, Geoff left the then family company, Thomas Hardy & Sons, to make his own way with wife Fiona. In 1986 they purchased an old dairy farm in the Kuitpo area of the southern Adelaide Hills and planted out the first vineyard in the Kuitpo region in 1987. K1 Wines by Geoff Hardy also includes the Hand Crafted range of wines, sourced from premium regions across SA, and the entry-level GMH range. Exports to Canada, Sweden, Finland, India, Malaysia, South Korea, Indonesia, Thailand, Vietnam, Japan, Taiwan and China.

🍷🍷🍷🍷♀ **K1 by Geoff Hardy Adelaide Hills Cabernet Sauvignon 2018** Everything here feels settled into itself, with integrated oak and a reserved sense to the wine. Its earthy, olive savoury elements add more serious tones to the palate and the tannins are quite comfortably placed in the overall expression. Screw cap. 14.5% alc. **Rating** 93 **To** 2030 $45 TL
Hand Crafted by Geoff Hardy Montepulciano 2019 This monte exudes an attractive fragrance to begin; potpourri led by sage and thyme, the fruit more in line with blueberry and mulberry rather than anything blacker. The tannins

kick in with force mid palate, but the fruit and savoury matrix is powerful enough to generate its own impressive wave of flavours. Screw cap. 13.7% alc. **Rating** 92 To 2028 $30 TL

K1 by Geoff Hardy Adelaide Hills Pinot Noir 2019 There's a nice little edge of flint and whole-bunch woodiness here, with plenty of cherry fruit flavour. The palate is softly gripped by gentle spicy tannins. Screw cap. 12.5% alc. **Rating** 91 To 2025 $45 TL

Hand Crafted by Geoff Hardy McLaren Vale Shiraz 2019 Sourced from long-term Vale growers, matured for 20 months in 20% new French hogshead barrels. Rich with the big crimson fruits of the region and its earthy, mineral middle-palate powers. Screw cap. 14.5% alc. **Rating** 90 To 2028 $30 TL

K1 by Geoff Hardy Adelaide Hills Shiraz 2018 Eighteen months in 30% new French barrels. Dark berry and plum compote with a heap of anise, licorice-like spice flavours entwined. Chewy yet suits the weight of the fruit and oak seasoning. Diam. 14.5% alc. **Rating** 90 To 2030 $45 TL

GMH Adelaide Hills Cabernet Sauvignon 2019 From a new red label range, this is quite a perky cabernet with plenty of varietal aromatic elements on show: black fruits, mint-choc, bay leaf, followed by a well-captured cabernet palate of the same notes, with obvious but finely cast varietal tannins. Decent value. Cork. 13.5% alc. **Rating** 90 To 2028 $25 TL

Hand Crafted by Geoff Hardy Adelaide Hills Tannat 2018 A big wine in every sense. Older barrels for 20 months of maturation have allowed all the built-in power elements to integrate, the fruit dark and rich, almost chocolate pudding-esque, the expected tannins rounded and rich. Heavyweight wine territory. Screw cap. 15% alc. **Rating** 90 To 2030 $30 TL

� **Hand Crafted by Geoff Hardy Adelaide Hills Grüner Veltliner 2020** **Rating** 89 To 2023 $25 TL

🍇 Koomilya ★★★★

Amery Road, McLaren Vale SA 5171 **Region** McLaren Vale
T (08) 8323 8000 **www**.koomilya.com.au **Open** By appt
Winemaker Stephen Pannell **Est.** 2015 **Dozens** 2000 **Vyds** 13ha

The Koomilya vineyard is wedged between the original Upper Tintara vineyard planted in 1862, and the Hope Farm or Seaview vineyard established in the early 1850s. It includes 13ha of vineyards, thought to have been first planted in the 1850s. More than 15ha of native bush and scrub, with a creek line that flows through the heart of the property, all have a moderating influence on the microclimate of the property. Stephen Pannell first experienced the fruit from this vineyard when he made the Jimmy Watson trophy–winning 1995 Eileen Hardy Shiraz, a major component of which was sourced from the Koomilya JC Block. Seventeen years later in 2012, Stephen and wife Fiona bought the property and have embarked on rejuvenating it with organic farming, weeding the native bush and removing olive trees to create biochar to return as charcoal to the soil. Plantings of new varieties have followed, with a small set of wines created to specifically reflect the location, accent and circumstances of the seasons throughout each particular vintage. Exports to the UK, the US, Sweden and Singapore. (TL)

♏♏♏♏♏ **McLaren Vale Shiraz 2017** This is a most distinctive shiraz in the greater regional context, exuding a powerful mix of black fruits with the smells of Australian bush enveloping the fruits. The palate is dense, not with oak but with rich, savoury licorice and definite earthy, mossy, roasted root vegetable notes in there as well. And with all that, there's still a medium-bodied flow through the mouth. Which should be open in awe at the exit because of how astoundingly good this wine is! Screw cap. 14% alc. **Rating** 98 To 2030 $70 TL ✪ ♥

Koonara ★★★★

44 Church Street, Penola, SA 5277 **Region** Coonawarra
T (08) 8737 3222 **www.**koonara.com **Open** Mon–Thurs 10–5, Fri–Sat 10–6, Sun 10–4
Winemaker Peter Douglas **Est.** 1988 **Dozens** 10000 **Vyds** 9ha
Trevor Reschke planted the first vines on the Koonara property in 1988. Peter Douglas, formerly Wynns' chief winemaker before moving overseas for some years, has returned to the district and is consultant winemaker. After 10 years of organic viticulture practises, Koonara's vineyards in Coonawarrra were certified organic in 2017. Since '13 Koonara have leased and managed the Kongorong Partnership Vineyard in Mount Gambier, which had previously sold its grapes to Koonara. Exports to Russia, Malaysia and China.

🍷🍷🍷🍷🍷 **Emily May Mount Gambier Pinot Noir Rosé 2020** Pale rose gold hue; it's soft and light, full of squishy red berries, strawberries with some vanilla cream plus a snip of fresh herbs. You'd call this a gentle rosé and it doesn't disappoint. Screw cap. 11% alc. **Rating** 92 **To** 2022 $20 JF
Angel's Peak Coonawarra Shiraz 2019 Lots of bright upfront fruit packed with black pepper and juniper, mint and tapenade. Very flavoursome. The palate is ripe and generous although the tannins and oak feel a bit raw. Time will take care of that. Screw cap. 14% alc. **Rating** 91 **To** 2030 $25 JF

Kooyong ★★★★☆

PO Box 153, Red Hill South, Vic 3937 **Region** Mornington Peninsula
T (03) 5989 4444 **www.**kooyongwines.com.au **Open** At Port Phillip Estate
Winemaker Glen Hayley **Est.** 1996 **Dozens** 13000 **Vyds** 41.11ha
Kooyong, owned by Giorgio and Dianne Gjergja, released its first wines in 2001. The vineyard is planted to pinot noir (26.64ha), chardonnay (10.35ha) and, more recently, pinot gris (3ha) and a little shiraz (0.97ha). In July '15, following the departure of Sandro Mosele, his assistant of 6 years, Glen Hayley, was appointed to take his place. The Kooyong wines are made at the state-of-the-art winery of Port Phillip Estate, also owned by the Gjergjas. Exports to the UK, Canada, Belgium, the Netherlands, Singapore, Hong Kong, Japan and China.

🍷🍷🍷🍷🍷 **Farrago Single Block Mornington Peninsula Chardonnay 2019** It's a little shy at first, then gains confidence, starting to strut its stuff, delivering white peach and grapefruit, spiced up with ginger and a fleck of fresh herbs. The palate has depth and generosity, with the oak flavouring an interplay. Yet fine acidity keeps it tight, as moreish sulphides kick in, adding a savoury edge and a lingering finish. Screw cap. 13.5% alc. **Rating** 95 **To** 2028 $60 JF

🍷🍷🍷🍷🍷 **Estate Mornington Peninsula Chardonnay 2019** Rating 93 To 2028 $42 JF
Estate Mornington Peninsula Pinot Noir 2019 Rating 93 To 2033 $48 JF
Ferrous Single Block Mornington Peninsula Pinot Noir 2019 Rating 93 To 2032 $75 JF
Clonale Mornington Peninsula Chardonnay 2020 Rating 92 To 2025 $34 JF
Faultline Single Block Mornington Peninsula Chardonnay 2019 Rating 92 To 2028 $60 JF
Beurrot Mornington Peninsula Pinot Gris 2020 Rating 91 To 2024 $32 JF
Haven Single Block Mornington Peninsula Pinot Noir 2019 Rating 91 To 2033 $75 JF
Meres Single Block Mornington Peninsula Pinot Noir 2019 Rating 90 To 2029 $75 JF
Estate Mornington Peninsula Shiraz 2019 Rating 90 To 2027 $44 JF

Kooyonga Creek ★★★☆

2369 Samaria Road, Moorngag, Vic 3673 **Region** North East Victoria
T (03) 9629 5853 **www.**kooyonga.com.au **Open** Fri–Sun 11–5 or by appt
Winemaker Luis Simian **Est.** 2011 **Dozens** 5000 **Vyds** 7.5ha

When you read the name of this winery, you expect to find it somewhere on or near the Mornington Peninsula. In fact it's a very long way to North East Victoria, where Barry and Pam Saunders planted 7.5ha of vineyards on their farm and released the first wines under the name Kooyonga Chapel in 2003. They planted a sensibly focused range of 1.6ha each of shiraz, cabernet sauvignon, chardonnay and sauvignon blanc, with merlot recently grafted over to tempranillo.

♀♀♀♀♀ Cabernet Sauvignon 2017 A warm, earthy cabernet to curl up with. A wine without pretence, just good old-fashioned richness of blackberry, plum, earth, leather and a central core of sweet spice. Yes, it's big for a cabernet but not unwieldy, courtesy of smooth, far-reaching tannins. Screw cap. 14.5% alc. **Rating** 91 **To** 2030 $20 JP ✪

Krinklewood Biodynamic Vineyard   ★★★★
712 Wollombi Road, Broke, NSW 2330 **Region** Hunter Valley
T (02) 6579 1322 **www**.krinklewood.com **Open** Mon–Thurs 12–4, Fri–Sun 10–4
Winemaker Valentina Moresco, PJ Charteris (Consultant) **Est.** 1981 **Dozens** 7500
Vyds 20ha
Krinklewood is a family-owned certified biodynamic organic winery. Every aspect of the property is managed in a holistic and sustainable way; Rod Windrim's extensive herb crops, native grasses and farm animals all contribute to biodynamic preparations to maintain healthy soil biology. The small winery is home to a Vaslin Bucher basket press and 2 Nomblot French fermentation eggs, a natural approach to winemaking. Exports to Hong Kong.

♀♀♀♀♀ Basket Press McLaren Vale Broke Fordwich Shiraz 2019 Boasting an admirable biodynamic certification, these wines are far better today than they were even a year or 2 ago. Indigenous fermentation in eggs. Bing cherry, violet, licorice and clove – all gently mid weighted and savoury – is meshed with sensitive oak influence and a reductive pull. The acidity, a little brittle. Screw cap. 14.2% alc. **Rating** 93 **To** 2028 $60 NG
Broke Fordwich Shiraz 2019 My favourite wine of this Krinklewood suite by virtue of its inimitable and unabashed regional imprint: on the fullish side of medium but savoury, earthy and dense of extract, all at once. Asian five-spice and lacquer scents meld with poached plum, violet and kirsch. Anise and clove hang off a well-appointed oak frame. Nothing excessive, although on the riper side. Delicious drinking. Screw cap. 14% alc. **Rating** 93 **To** 2028 $40 NG
Basket Press Broke Fordwich Chardonnay 2019 Mid weighted with ample stone-fruit scents billowing across a lees-derived pungency and a creamy core of oatmeal and nougat. Well-appointed vanillan oak seams direct the fray. Screw cap. 13% alc. **Rating** 92 **To** 2026 $45 NG
Broke Fordwich Chardonnay 2019 An acidity-chasing level of alcohol in a region as warm as the Hunter, yet flavour does not feel compromised. Lightweight, dry and versatile. Jubey lemon oil, apricot pith and dried hay notes sashay along a gentle beam of cedar oak and a core of vanilla cream and cashew. Good drinking. All the better for its generous flavours and attainable aspirations. Screw cap. 12.6% alc. **Rating** 92 **To** 2024 $35 NG
Spider Run White Broke Fordwich 2019 This sits nicely in the mouth, conferring a mineral tension as much as a chord of lemon balm, oatmeal biscuit, pink grapefruit and apricot pith, strung across a fret board of brisk acidity and gentle phenolic chew. Lightweight but packing ample flavour. A good pulse from fore to aft. Screw cap. 12.2% alc. **Rating** 92 **To** 2025 $40 NG
Vat 48 Orange Cabernet Merlot 2017 Sappy. Herbal. A meld of bitter chocolate and spearmint, interplayed with creme de cassis, terracotta and dried sage. A flavourful mouthful, given focus by a firm weave of grape tannin spooled over a spindle of smart oak. Medium, savoury and good drinking. Akin to a Chinon from a very ripe vintage. Screw cap. 14% alc. **Rating** 92 **To** 2026 $45 NG

♀♀♀♀ Francesca Rosé 2020 Rating 88 **To** 2021 $35 NG
Wild Red 2019 Rating 88 **To** 2023 $28 NG

Kurtz Family Vineyards

731 Light Pass Road, Angaston, SA, 5353 **Region** Barossa Valley
T 0418 810 982 **www**.kurtzfamilyvineyards.com.au **Open** By appt
Winemaker Steve Kurtz **Est.** 1996 **Dozens** 3000 **Vyds** 18.1ha
The Kurtz family vineyard is at Light Pass. It has 9ha of shiraz, the remainder planted to chardonnay, cabernet sauvignon, semillon, sauvignon blanc, petit verdot, grenache, mataro and malbec. Steve Kurtz has followed in the footsteps of his great-grandfather Ben Kurtz, who first grew grapes at Light Pass in the 1930s. During a career working first at Saltram and then at Foster's until 2006, Steve gained invaluable experience from Nigel Dolan, Caroline Dunn and John Glaetzer, among others. Exports to the US, Germany, Malaysia and China.

TTTTT **Boundary Row Barossa Valley Cabernet Sauvignon Shiraz 2017** Eden Valley cabernet brings mint, leaf, fragrant lift and bright acid drive to dark-berry-fruited Light Pass shiraz. Dark chocolate oak and finely structured tannins provide measured support. Line and length offer appeal for those who appreciate a minty style. Screw cap. 14% alc. **Rating** 90 **To** 2027 $28 TS

Kyneton Ridge Estate

517 Blackhill Road, Kyneton, Vic 3444 **Region** Macedon Ranges
T 0408 841 119 **www**.kynetonridge.com.au **Open** W'ends & public hols 11–5
Winemaker Contract **Est.** 1997 **Dozens** 1200 **Vyds** 4ha
Established by John Boucher and partner Pauline Russell in the shadow of Blackhill Reserve, an ideal environment for pinot noir and chardonnay vines. They maintain traditional processes but new facilities have recently been introduced to enhance the production process for the sparkling wines. The additional production capacity gives the opportunity to source additional suitable quality parcels of shiraz and cabernet sauvignon from Macedon and Heathcote. Kyneton Ridge was purchased by Angela and Andrew Wood in late '19.

TTTTT **The John Boucher Heathcote Sparkling Shiraz NV** Minimum 2 years on lees. A very good sparkling shiraz, leading with an excellent dark purple hue. There are no hard edges, although there are certainly layers of tannin, all ripe and fleshy. Dark fruit, licorice, umami/Vegemite with a sweet edge from the dosage. Well balanced. Diam. 14.5% alc. **Rating** 93 $35 JF
Macedon Pinot Noir Chardonnay 2013 Méthode traditionnelle. Mid straw hue. Lots of lovely creamy mousse and wafts of nougat and creamed honey. It has a certain level of complexity, which is expected given its age, yet there's a freshness and bright acidity pulling it together. This is flavoursome and very good. Diam. 13.2% alc. **Rating** 92 $35 JF

TTTT **Reserve Macedon Ranges Pinot Noir 2019 Rating** 88 **To** 2028 $40 JF

L.A.S. Vino

PO Box 361 Cowaramup, WA 6284 **Region** Margaret River
www.lasvino.com
Winemaker Nic Peterkin **Est.** 2013 **Dozens** 800
Owner Nic Peterkin is the grandson of the late Diana Cullen (Cullen Wines) and the son of Mike Peterkin (Pierro). After graduating from the University of Adelaide with a master's degree in oenology and travelling the world as a Flying Winemaker, he came back to roost in Margaret River with the ambition of making wines that are a little bit different, but also within the bounds of conventional oenological science. The intention is to keep the project small. Exports to the UK, Belgium, Sweden, Dubai, Singapore, Japan and China.

TTTTT **CBDB Margaret River Chenin Blanc Dynamic Blend 2019** From the cooler 2019 vintage, this brings cheesecloth, rind and preserved lemon on the nose, all of which pave the way for nashi pear and saline acid. This is a texturally complex and layered wine of poise and personality. Length of flavour is long and bang on point. Some wines have a charm and an intrigue that compel a 2nd (and 3rd) glass. This is one. Cork. 13.5% alc. **Rating** 96 **To** 2030 $50 EL ✪

Albino PNO Margaret River Rosé 2019 This is a seriously structured, textured, leesy rosé, with layers that continue to reveal themselves even as the volume fades. Like the Doppler effect, you can hear it coming and you can hear it going, too … intriguing to say the least. Cheesecloth, red berries, lanolin, Geraldton wax, citrus-rind acidity and a salty, pithy vibe through the finish. Epic food wine. Diam. 13% alc. **Rating** 95 **To** 2025 $45 EL

Wildberry Springs Margaret River Chardonnay 2019 If you're a fan of L.A.S. Vino you'll know better than to expect something specific of a new wine. This has a complex array of flavours: honeydew melon, sour cream, tangelo, brine, yellow peach … there's oat and sourdough and pineapple and the list could go on and on. Beneath it all, classy phenolics shape the wine through the long finish, hinting at the pedigree here. Screw cap. 13.5% alc. **Rating** 95 **To** 2036 $75 EL

La Kooki Wines

12 Settlers Retreat, Margaret River, WA 6285 **Region** Margaret River
T 0447 587 15 **www**.lakookiwines.com.au
Winemaker Eloise Jarvis, Glenn Goodall **Est.** 2017 **Dozens** 335
Except for the fact that the proprietors of La Kooki have accumulated 42 years of winemaking between them, there would be little or nothing to say about a winery that has a small wine portfolio. Two detailed A4 sheets cover the conception and birth of La Kooki's Rosé, one stating the quantity made as 114 dozen, the other 250 dozen. Either way, you'd better be quick, because it's an unusual wine.

🍷🍷🍷🍷🍷 **Boya Margaret River Chardonnay 2020** Sit – there is a story here. Karridale fruit is fermented wild in barrel (20% new), with stones collected from the local coast. 'Boya' means 'stones' in the local Wadandi language. The barrels are periodically rolled, agitating the stones within, stirring the lees and creating layers of phenolic complexity. White peach, fennel flower, white pepper, brine, crushed macadamia and suggestions of curry leaf. On the palate, the pristine and formidable saline acid infuses a staunch backbone, which spools out through a long finish. Screw cap. 12.6% alc. **Rating** 96 **To** 2036 $65 EL ❂

🍷🍷🍷🍷🍷 **Right Side of Racy Margaret River Chardonnay 2019 Rating** 93 **To** 2027 $38 EL
Ten Foot Ferguson Valley Tempranillo 2019 Rating 92 **To** 2027 $25 EL ❂
Carbonic Blanc Margaret River Verdelho 2020 Rating 90 **To** 2021 $25 EL

La Linea ★★★★☆

36 Shipsters Road, Kensington Park, SA 5068 (postal) **Region** Adelaide Hills
T (08) 8431 3556 **www**.lalinea.com.au
Winemaker Peter Leske **Est.** 2007 **Dozens** 4000 **Vyds** 6.64ha
La Linea is a partnership between experienced wine industry professionals Peter Leske (ex-Nepenthe) and David LeMire MW. Peter was among the first to recognise the potential of tempranillo in Australia and his knowledge of it is reflected in the 3 wine styles made from the variety: a dry rosé, a dry red blended from several Adelaide Hills vineyards, and Sureno, made in select vintages from specific sites at the southern end of the Hills. The pair pioneered mencia – the red variety from northwest Spain – in the Hills. They also produce the off-dry riesling 25GR (25g/l RS) under the Vertigo label. Exports to the UK.

🍷🍷🍷🍷🍷 **Adelaide Hills Mencia 2019** Only a handful are crafting this variety at the moment, hopefully more will see its pleasantries. Cherry and dusty white pepper, a most desirable palate weight and flow. Very distinctive tannins that start in the juice then rise and gently pucker. Encourages follow-up pours. I'll have mine with a char-grilled steak and bearnaise. Screw cap. 13% alc. **Rating** 95 **To** 2025 $29 TL ❂ ♥

🍷🍷🍷🍷🍷 **Adelaide Hills Tempranillo Rosé 2020 Rating** 92 **To** 2023 $24 TL ❂
Adelaide Hills Tempranillo 2019 Rating 91 **To** 2026 $27 TL
Vertigo 25GR Adelaide Hills Riesling 2020 Rating 90 **To** 2025 $24 TL

La Prova ★★★★★

102 Main Street, Hahndorf, SA 5245 **Region** Adelaide Hills
T (08) 8388 7330 **www.**laprova.com.au **Open** 1st w'end of the month 11–5 or by appt
Winemaker Sam Scott **Est.** 2009 **Dozens** 5000

Sam Scott's great-grandfather worked in the cellar for Max Schubert and passed his knowledge down to Sam's grandfather. It was he who gave Sam his early education. Sam enrolled in business at university, continuing the casual retailing with Booze Brothers – which he'd started while at school – picking up the trail with Baily & Baily. Next came wine wholesale experience with David Ridge, selling iconic Australian and Italian wines to the trade. This led to a job with Michael Fragos at Tatachilla in 2000 and since then he has been the 'I've been everywhere' man, working all over Australia and in California. He moved to Bird in Hand winery at the end of '06, where Andrew Nugent indicated that it was about time he took the plunge on his own account and this he has done. Exports to the UK and Singapore.

🍷🍷🍷🍷🍷 **Colpevole Adelaide Hills Nebbiolo 2018** All the mysteries of nebbiolo unveiled here. There's a faint petrichor note and roast root vegetables to start, then some cherry. As expected, a complete wraparound of varietal tannins coat the mouth, but allow the fruit and savoury weave to remain true to the finish. Stylish and very moreish. Screw cap. 14.1% alc. **Rating** 96 **To** 2030 $45 TL ✪

Adelaide Hills Pinot Grigio 2020 Orchard florals suggest a pretty wine, and this is that. But the energy here is astounding, with fabulous grapefruit-like acidity and pith. It's already exciting the palate in that sense, yet there's an underlying layer of apple turnover flavour as well, bringing even more joy. Screw cap. 12.5% alc. **Rating** 95 **To** 2023 $26 TL ✪

Adelaide Hills Nebbiolo Rosato 2020 Pink with copper tinges. The nose is a little earthy, along with its red fruits, and then you get a rush of crunchy, zingy red and white berries, a peppery spice and salivating finish, leaving the palate thirsty for more and more. Fantastic rosé. Screw cap. 12.8% alc. **Rating** 95 **To** 2024 $26 TL ✪ ♥

Limestone Coast Dolcetto 2020 You've got to love a wine with aromas that strike you with as much personality as this. Crushed blueberry, with handfuls of kitchen herbs, and a distinctive dark-berried sweet spot on the palate, textured up with pith and lightly puckery tannins. Heaps of energy, and just a little twist of darker amaro bitters to finish. Smashing. Screw cap. 13.5% alc. **Rating** 95 **To** 2026 $26 TL ✪

Adelaide Hills Fiano 2020 There's a slate-like note to begin, mineral to the nose, with Winemaker Sam Scott's signature skill of creating vibrant lift as well as textural foundations. Lemon fruit and pith first, then a blanched nut mouthfeel. Salines, often typical in the variety, season the palate as the wine lingers. Screw cap. 13.5% alc. **Rating** 94 **To** 2023 $28 TL ✪

Adelaide Hills Sangiovese 2019 Wild-yeast fermented, over a month on skins, the search for 'grippy tannins' kept under tight control. Pickled cherry, spice and finely etched tannins on the long, well-balanced palate add up to a wine that will fervently embrace virtually any Italian dish. Screw cap. 14% alc. **Rating** 94 **To** 2026 $26 JH ✪

🍷🍷🍷🍷🍷 **McLaren Vale Nero d'Avola 2019 Rating** 93 **To** 2025 $26 TL ✪
Rusco Adelaide Hills Barbera 2019 Rating 92 **To** 2028 $35 TL

Lake Breeze Wines ★★★★☆

Step Road, Langhorne Creek, SA 5255 **Region** Langhorne Creek
T (08) 8537 3017 **www.**lakebreeze.com.au **Open** 7 days 10–5
Winemaker Greg Follett **Est.** 1987 **Dozens** 20 000 **Vyds** 90ha

The Folletts have been farmers at Langhorne Creek since 1880, and grapegrowers since the 1930s. Part of the grape production is sold, but the quality of the Lake Breeze wines is exemplary, with the red wines particularly appealing. Exports to the UK, the US, Canada, Switzerland, Denmark, Germany, Peru, Singapore, Hong Kong, Japan and China.

ŶŶŶŶŶ Langhorne Creek Cabernet Sauvignon 2019 The epitome of signature Langhorne Creek cabernet. The quality of the fruit is evident from the outset. It's matured for 20 months in French oak, 40% new, yet this is subservient to the black/blueberry aromas and flavours, some regional dark choc-mint adding a tiny whiff behind. Everything knits together perfectly and the varietal tannin structures lie in exact tune with the whole. When it works so well, wines like this just come alive. Screw cap. 14% alc. **Rating** 97 **To** 2031 $29 TL ✪ ♥

ŶŶŶŶŶ Langhorne Creek Rosato 2020 While you might think this kind of rosé is just a fun summer splash, the reality is that 50% of the grenache base for the wine comes from 90yo vines. Aged without oak for 2–3 months on its lees, it displays all the expected white-tipped strawberry flavours, with strikingly next-level spice and pithiness. Worthy of reward. Screw cap. 13% alc. **Rating** 95 **To** 2024 $19 TL ✪

Section 54 Langhorne Creek Shiraz 2019 The portion of old-vine fruit from the region's traditional flood plains plays a major role in this wine, revealed in a sophisticated, mature style of shiraz. Plums and spice, bright and lifted, with some French oak influence providing a calm and secure foundation underneath, the rich tannins tightening everything. An absolute pleasure to drink. Screw cap. 14.5% alc. **Rating** 95 **To** 2028 $28 TL ✪

Arthur's Reserve Langhorne Creek Cabernet Sauvignon Malbec Petit Verdot 2018 The best 12 barrels of cabernet sauvignon, with 5/2% malbec/petit verdot. Such a dark, powerfully layered wine with thick, plush tannins across the palate. Fruit and oak, which (at 90% new French) plays its part with great respect to everything else around it, finding a fulfiling harmony. You won't find many wines of such traditional style and excellence at this price – anywhere. Screw cap. 14% alc. **Rating** 95 **To** 2032 $48 TL ♥

Old Vine Langhorne Creek Grenache 2020 The vibrant garnet colour is the first thing that grabs attention. The rest is all about the rustic appeal of grenache: cherry flesh and skins, crumbled dry earth, and a lively palate where the fruit, spice and tannins are pretty energetic. Makes your mouth stand to attention. Lick-your-lips good. Screw cap. 14.5% alc. **Rating** 94 **To** 2028 $29 TL ✪

ŶŶŶŶŶ Reserve Langhorne Creek Chardonnay 2019 Rating 92 **To** 2026 $28 TL
Bernoota Langhorne Creek Shiraz Cabernet 2019 Rating 92 **To** 2030 $25 TL ✪
Bullant Langhorne Creek Cabernet Merlot 2019 Rating 92 **To** 2026 $19 TL ✪
Langhorne Creek Vermentino 2020 Rating 91 **To** 2023 $19 TL ✪
Bullant Langhorne Creek Shiraz 2019 Rating 90 **To** 2025 $19 TL ✪
Langhorne Creek Malbec 2019 Rating 90 **To** 2028 $28 TL

Lake Cairn Curran Vineyard ★★★☆

'Park Hill', Leathbridge Road, Welshman's Reef, Vic 3462 **Region** Bendigo
T 0419 339 097 **www.**lakecairncurranvineyard.com.au **Open** By appt
Winemaker Sarah Ferguson, Moorooduc Estate (Richard McIntyre), Kilcnum Wines (David Cowburn) **Est.** 1987 **Dozens** 800 **Vyds** 5.4ha
When Ross and Sarah Ferguson purchased what is now known as Lake Cairn Curran Vineyard in 1999, they acquired not only the vineyard (chardonnay, pinot noir and shiraz), but also a slice of history, evoked by the beautiful labels. The Park Hill homestead dates back to the establishment of the Tarrengower Run in the 1840s, and the mudbrick cellar door is located adjacent to the homestead, overlooking the Cairn Curran Reservoir and Loddon River Valley. Notwithstanding that, Sarah has a wine science (oenology) degree from CSU, and having worked several vintages at Moorooduc Estate, makes small batches of wine at the newly renovated onsite winery. However, Rick McIntyre will continue to make the major table wine releases, David Cowburn of Kilchurn the sparkling wines.

ŶŶŶŶŶ Shiraz 2017 A bit of a charmer that's easy to cosy up to, especially with the fleck of black pepper that dots the wine. It's a regional marker and it's not over the top, rather it works in nicely with the black and red fruits, woodsy spice and medium-bodied plushness of the shiraz. Screw cap. 13.5% alc. **Rating** 90 **To** 2026 $22 JP

Lake Cooper Estate   ★★★★☆

1608 Midland Highway, Corop, Vic 3559 **Region** Heathcote
T (03) 9387 7657 **www**.lakecooper.com.au **Open** W'ends & public hols 11–5
Winemaker Paul Boulden, Richard Taylor **Est.** 1998 **Dozens** 11 224 **Vyds** 34ha
Lake Cooper Estate is a substantial venture in the Heathcote region, set on the side of
Mt Camel Range with panoramic views of Lake Cooper, Greens Lake and the Corop
township. In 2019 plans for the construction of a 300t winery, cellar door, restaurant and
accommodation were announced, with a complete overhaul of winemaking practices by the
highly experienced Paul Boulden and Richard Taylor. Viticulturist Shane Bartel will oversee
new plantings of shiraz and grenache and a move towards sustainable practices in the vineyard.
Exports to China.

ΨΨΨΨΨ **Well Rhapsody Reserve Heathcote Shiraz 2019** More restrained in taste
than the packaging would suggest. A tannin-taut, well-structured young red built
for distance not speed, with coiled fruits, earthy spices and a pinch of savouriness
all in waiting. Heathcote and Australian Shiraz trophies, Australian International
Wine Challenge '20. Diam. 14.5% alc. **Rating** 95 **To** 2032 $100 JP
Well Reserve Heathcote Cabernet Sauvignon 2019 As always, the deep
Heathcote hues are a standout. A lovely expression of place. Ripe blackberry, dark
cherry, a dusty leafiness and smoky Aussie bush. A fine line of tannin runs the
length of the palate. Excellent concentration of fruit. A picture of elegance in the
glass. Diam. 14.5% alc. **Rating** 94 **To** 2032 $40 JP

ΨΨΨΨΨ **Well Bin 1962 Heathcote Shiraz 2019 Rating** 93 **To** 2030 $40 JP

Lake George Winery   ★★★★☆

173 The Vineyards Road, Lake George, NSW 2581 **Region** Canberra District
T (02) 9948 4676 **www**.lakegeorgewinery.com.au **Open** Thurs–Sun 10–5
Winemaker Nick O'Leary, Anthony McDougall **Est.** 1971 **Dozens** 2000 **Vyds** 8ha
Lake George Winery was established by legend-in-his-own-lifetime Dr Edgar Riek, who
contributed so much to the Canberra District and the Australian wine industry. It has now
passed into the hands of Sarah and Anthony McDougall, and the 47yo dry-grown chardonnay,
pinot noir, cabernet sauvignon, semillon and merlot plantings have been joined by shiraz,
tempranillo, pinot gris, viognier and riesling. The winemaking techniques include basket
pressing and small-batch barrel maturation.

ΨΨΨΨΨ **Pinot Noir 2018** This sits snugly in come-and-drink-me-now territory. And it
has layers and beauty too. Poached cherries and rhubarb, spiced with cinnamon
and the orange myrtle of chinotto. The palate is a lesson in elegance – cool and
refreshing, with lithe tannins, all light and bright. Screw cap. 13% alc. **Rating** 95
To 2026 $35 JF **✪**
Shiraz 2019 The same lightness of touch as the pinot noir. A fantastic purple-
red hue entices, as does the palate. A neat mix of sweet-berried fruit, woodsy
spices and oak char give it a savoury edge with grainy, fine tannins. Overall, very
satisfying. Screw cap. 13.5% alc. **Rating** 95 **To** 2028 $35 JF **✪**

Lake's Folly   ★★★★★

2416 Broke Road, Pokolbin, NSW 2320 **Region** Hunter Valley
T (02) 4998 7507 **www**.lakesfolly.wine **Open** 7 days 10–4 while wine available
Winemaker Rodney Kempe **Est.** 1963 **Dozens** 4500 **Vyds** 13ha
The first of the weekend wineries to produce wines for commercial sale, long revered for its
Cabernet Sauvignon and nowadays its Chardonnay. Just as they should, terroir and climate
produce a distinct wine style. Lake's Folly no longer has any connection with the Lake
family, having been acquired some years ago by Perth businessman Peter Fogarty. Peter's
family company previously established the Millbrook Winery in the Perth Hills and has
since acquired Deep Woods Estate and Evans & Tate in Margaret River, Smithbrook Wines
in Pemberton and Dalwhinnie in the Pyrenees, so is no stranger to the joys and agonies

of running a small winery. Peter has been an exemplary owner of all the brands, providing support where needed but otherwise not interfering.

🍷🍷🍷🍷🍷 **Hunter Valley Cabernets 2019** A beautiful wine of exquisite detail and perfume. Currant, mulberry, violet, mulch, mint, graphite, anise and black olive. Sage-rolled tannins, impeccably hewn of sinew and fine grained oak. Delicate, sappy and mellifluous. So measured. So classy. Dangerously easy to drink already, it reminds me of a great Chinon. I feel guilty spitting it. Screw cap. 12.5% alc. **Rating** 97 **To** 2032 $80 NG ✪ ♥

🍷🍷🍷🍷🍷 **Hill Block Chardonnay 2020 Rating** 93 **To** 2025 $90 NG
Hunter Valley Chardonnay 2020 Rating 93 **To** 2027 $80 NG

Lamont's Winery ★★★★
85 Bisdee Road, Millendon, WA 6056 **Region** Swan Valley
T (08) 9296 4485 **www.**lamonts.com.au **Open** Thurs–Sun 10–5 (Swan Valley)
Winemaker Digby Leddin **Est.** 1978 **Dozens** 7000 **Vyds** 2ha
Corin Lamont, daughter of the late Jack Mann, oversees the making of wines in a style that would have pleased her father. Lamont's also boasts a superb restaurant run by granddaughter Kate Lamont. The wines are going from strength to strength, utilising both estate-grown and contract-grown (from southern regions) grapes. Another of Lamont's restaurants in Perth is open for lunch and dinner Mon–Fri, offering food of the highest quality, and is superbly situated. The Margaret River cellar door is open 7 days 11–5 for wine tasting, sales and lunch.

🍷🍷🍷🍷🍷 **White Monster 2019** Creamy, crushed nuts (macadamia, walnut, cashew), yellow peach, salty acid and plush mouthfeel. A satisfying and full-bodied wine. Ultimately the impact of mlf and oak may divide the room, but for those who seek it, this hits the spot. And with a name such as 'White Monster' it is fairly clear what lies in wait. Screw cap. 13.5% alc. **Rating** 94 **To** 2028 $45 EL
Swan Valley Shiraz 2019 Winner of Best Shiraz trophy at Swan Valley Wine Show 2020. This wine made an impression on the judging table for its modern approach to juicy fruit, which is at the very centre of the wine. It is wrapped by firm tannins and loads of exotic spice, making it a delicious and balanced expression of warm-climate shiraz. It repeats this performance today in the glass. A ripper. Screw cap. 14.5% alc. **Rating** 94 **To** 2031 $35 EL

🍷🍷🍷🍷🍷 **Black Monster 2017 Rating** 93 **To** 2031 $55 EL
Navera NV Rating 93 $35 EL
Liqueur Verdelho NV Rating 91 **To** 2031 $35 EL

Landaire ★★★★
Riddoch Hwy, Padthaway, SA 5271 **Region** Padthaway
T 0417 408 147 **www.**landaire.com.au **Open** Thurs–Sun 11–4
Winemaker Pete Bissell **Est.** 2012 **Dozens** 2000 **Vyds** 200ha
David and Carolyn Brown have been major grapegrowers in Padthaway for 2 decades, David having had a vineyard and farming background, Carolyn with a background in science. Landaire has evolved from a desire, after many years of growing grapes at their Glendon Vineyard, to select small quantities of the best grapes and have them vinified by Pete Bissell, chief winemaker at Balnaves. It has proved a sure-fire recipe for success. Exports to the UK, Hong Kong and China.

🍷🍷🍷🍷🍷 **Padthaway Chardonnay 2019** This is one of those wines that defies its location: it's a finer rendition to many others in the region. Then again, Pete Bissell (ex-Balnaves) made this. Still young, but he recently retired and so this is his last chardonnay for Landaire. What a fitting send off. It's refined, elegant, a mix of white stone fruit, citrus and all lightly spiced. The palate is supple, soft, textural and delicious. Screw cap. 12% alc. **Rating** 95 **To** 2026 $37 JF

ŶŶŶŶŶ Padthaway Estate Eliza Blanc de Blancs 2018 Rating 91 $48 JF
Padthaway Single Vineyard Shiraz 2018 Rating 90 To 2030 $40 JF
Padthaway Cabernet Sauvignon 2017 Rating 90 To 2033 $40 JF

Landhaus Estate   ★★★★☆

102 Main Street, Hahndorf, SA 5245 **Region** Barossa Valley/Adelaide Hills
T 0418 836 305 **www**.landhauswines.com.au **Open** Thurs–Mon 11–5
Winemaker Shane Harris **Est.** 2002 **Dozens** 15 000 **Vyds** 1ha
John, Barbara and son Kane Jaunutis purchased Landhaus Estate in 2002, followed by 'The
Landhaus' cottage and 1ha vineyard at Bethany. Bethany is the oldest German-established town
in the Barossa (1842) and the cottage was one of the first to be built. Kane has worked vintages
for Mitolo and Kellermeister, as well as managing East End Cellars, one of Australia's leading
fine-wine retailers. John brings decades of owner/management experience and Barbara
20 years in sales and marketing. Rehabilitation of the estate plantings and establishing a grower
network have paid handsome dividends. Exports to China, Canada, Taiwan and Singapore.

ŶŶŶŶŶ Barbara Enchanting Barossa Valley Shiraz 2018 From 77yo vines in a single
vineyard in Bethany, the elegant mood of the district lends detail and poise to all
the ripe black-fruit depth and exotic spice of old-vine shiraz. Fine-boned tannins
are intricately framed in the bright acidity of cool nights, effortlessly swallowing up
new French oak. It concludes long and balanced, with a fleshy allure that beckons
early drinking. Diam. 14.6% alc. **Rating** 94 To 2026 $96 TS

ŶŶŶŶŶ From The Den Penance Barossa Valley Cabernet Sauvignon 2017
Rating 93 To 2032 $88 TS
From The Den Rekindled Barossa Valley Shiraz Cabernet Sauvignon
2017 Rating 92 To 2025 $64 TS
Adelaide Hills Grüner Veltliner 2020 Rating 91 To 2022 $20 TS ❍

Lane's End Vineyard   ★★★★☆

885 Mount William Road, Lancefield, Vic 3435 **Region** Macedon Ranges
T (03) 5429 1760 **www**.lanesend.com.au **Open** By appt
Winemaker Howard Matthews, Kilchurn Wines **Est.** 1985 **Dozens** 400 **Vyds** 2ha
Pharmacist Howard Matthews and family purchased the former Woodend Winery in 2000,
with 1.8ha of chardonnay and pinot noir (and a small amount of cabernet franc) dating back
to the mid-1980s. The cabernet franc has been grafted over to pinot noir and the vineyard
is now made up of 1ha each of chardonnay and pinot noir (five clones). Howard has been
making the wines for over a decade.

ŶŶŶŶŶ Macedon Ranges Pinot Noir 2019 There's no doubt this will be more refined
in another year or so. Yet it is gloriously rich and ripe for drinking now. Heady
aromas, dark fruits, layered with spices, pepper, eucalyptus, chinotto and blood
orange zest, all in unison across the full-bodied palate. Tannins are plush velvet
and so moreish. Resistance is futile. Screw cap. **Rating** 95 To 2029 $48 JF

Lange Estate   ★★★★

633 Frankland–Cranbrook Road, Frankland River, WA 6396 **Region** Frankland River
T 0438 511 828 **www**.langestate.com.au **Open** By appt
Winemaker Liam Carmody, Guy Lyons **Est.** 1997 **Dozens** 7000 **Vyds** 20ha
The eponymous Lange Estate is owned and run by the family: Kim and Chelsea, their children
Jack, Ella and Dylan, together with parents Don and Maxine. The vineyard is situated in
the picturesque Frankland River, tucked away in the far northwestern corner of the Great
Southern. The vineyard, with an elevation of almost 300m and red jarrah gravel loam soils,
produces wines of great intensity. Exports to China.

ŶŶŶŶŶ Fifth Generation Frankland River Cabernet Sauvignon 2019 People talk
about 'wine being made in the vineyard', and to a certain extent this is true. But

when you put good fruit in the hands of talented craftspeople, you get this. Exotic spices imbue the nose with a density and seriousness, the fruit on the palate lives up to that expectation too. Serious, structural, concentrated and long – bitter chocolate laces the finish. This is a beautiful, long-lived wine. Screw cap. 14.5% alc. **Rating** 96 **To** 2040 $50 EL ⊘

Fifth Generation Frankland River Shiraz 2019 This 2019 shows the strength of the vintage in Frankland River. It is concentrated and lively, with layers of fruit flavours, structured by fine tannins which drag the fruit across the palate into the long and unfurling finish. Beautiful today and likely beautiful for different reasons in 15–20 years. Screw cap. 14.5% alc. **Rating** 95 **To** 2041 $50 EL

Providence Road Frankland River Cabernet Sauvignon 2019 This is the middle child between the big Fifth Generation cabernet, and the little TSR cabernet. The fruit here is verging on opulent and luxurious, the tannins and acidity keeping everything in check. Harmony and balance are the key words – not at all what we know of middle children. Lovely wine, a lot to like. Screw cap. 14% alc. **Rating** 95 **To** 2030 $32 EL ⊘

TSR Frankland River Cabernet Sauvignon 2019 This is the juicy, supple and vibrant younger sibling to the Fifth Generation cabernet sauvignon. Bouncy fruit and chewy tannins pave the way for pleasure here. Brilliant drinking for the price. Screw cap. 14% alc. **Rating** 94 **To** 2028 $23 EL ⊘

ŸŸŸŸŸ **Providence Road Frankland River Shiraz 2019 Rating** 93 **To** 2031 $32 EL
Providence Road Frankland River Chardonnay 2019 Rating 92 **To** 2029 $32 EL
Providence Road Frankland River Riesling 2020 Rating 91 **To** 2033 $32 EL

Langmeil Winery ★★★★☆

Cnr Langmeil Road/Para Road, Tanunda, SA 5352 **Region** Barossa Valley
T (08) 8563 2595 **www**.langmeilwinery.com.au **Open** 7 days 10–4
Winemaker Paul Lindner **Est.** 1996 **Vyds** 33.12ha
Langmeil Winery, owned and operated by the Lindner family, is home to what may be the world's oldest surviving shiraz vineyard, The Freedom 1843. It was planted by Christian Auricht, a blacksmith who fled religious persecution in his native Prussia and sought a new life for his family in Australia. The historic, now renovated, site was once an important trading post and is also the location of the Orphan Bank Vineyard. This plot of shiraz vines, originally planted in the '60s, was transplanted from the centre of Tanunda to the banks of the North Para River in 2006. Exports to all major markets.

ŸŸŸŸŸ **Three Gardens Viognier Marsanne Roussanne 2020** Ripe nectarine and grapefruit are brushed with subtle lemon blossom aromatics and subtly underscored with the hazelnut cream nuances of partial barrel maturation. A finish of medium length is braced with a little more firm phenolic grip than it needs, but nonetheless a good result for the price. Screw cap. 13% alc. **Rating** 90 **To** 2022 $20 TS ⊘

Black Beauty Barossa Malbec 2019 More about easy-drinking Barossa appeal than it is about varietal distinction, and none the less for it. Vibrant purple/red hue. Crunchy, sweet berry/cherry/plum fruit is the start, middle and end game, nicely supported by crunchy tannins and vibrant acid line. An appealing Barossa quaffer. Screw cap. 14.5% alc. **Rating** 90 **To** 2024 $30 TS

ŸŸŸŸ **Valley Floor Barossa Shiraz 2018 Rating** 89 **To** 2028 $30 TS
Three Gardens Barossa GSM 2019 Rating 89 **To** 2024 $20 TS

 # Lannister ★★★☆

2/141 Sir Donald Bradman Drive, Hilton, SA 5033 **Region** McLaren Vale/Riverland
T 0433 188 319 **www**.lannister.com.au
Winemaker Goe Difabio **Est.** 2012 **Dozens** 550 **Vyds** 10ha

Drawing on a vast multitude of South Australian regions as far afield as the Murraylands, Limestone Coast, McLaren Vale and Barossa and Clare valleys, with 4 production facilities, the Lannister wines are almost exclusively focused on export. Judging by the website and extraordinarily high pricing, the focal market appears to be China. There is no collective cellar door. The Caudo, Di Fabio and Bent Creek labels also fall under the same export aegis. (NG)

🍷🍷🍷🍷🍷 **Clare Valley Riesling 2020** Lovely varietal and regional character of citrus blossom, wet stones, lemon zest and juice, plus fresh herbs and leafy greens adding another dimension. Pleasant and approachable, with enough zip to the acidity to confidently gather some age. Screw cap. 12% alc. **Rating** 90 **To** 2025 $26 JF

Lark Hill   ★★★★☆
31 Joe Rocks Road, Bungendore, NSW 2621 **Region** Canberra District
T (02) 6238 1393 **www**.larkhill.wine **Open** Thurs–Mon 11–4
Winemaker Dr David Carpenter, Sue Carpenter, Chris Carpenter **Est.** 1978
Dozens 6000 **Vyds** 12ha
The Lark Hill vineyard is situated at an altitude of 860m, offering splendid views of the Lake George escarpment. The Carpenters have made wines of real quality, style and elegance from the start, but have defied all the odds (and conventional thinking) with the quality of their pinot noirs in favourable vintages. Significant changes have come in the wake of son Christopher gaining 3 degrees – including a double in wine science and viticulture through CSU – and the organic/biodynamic certification of the vineyard and wines in 2003. Lark Hill planted the first grüner veltliner in Australia in 2005 and in 2011 purchased 1 of the 2 Ravensworth vineyards from Michael Kirk, with plantings of sangiovese, shiraz, viognier, roussanne and marsanne.

Larry Cherubino Wines   ★★★★★
3462 Caves Road, Wilyabrup, WA 6280 **Region** Western Australia
T (08) 9382 2379 **www**.larrycherubino.com **Open** 7 days 10–5
Winemaker Larry Cherubino, Andrew Siddell, Matt Buchan **Est.** 2005 **Dozens** 8000
Vyds 120ha
Larry Cherubino has had a particularly distinguished winemaking career, first at Hardys Tintara, then Houghton and thereafter as consultant/Flying Winemaker in Australia, NZ, South Africa, the US and Italy. He has developed numerous ranges, including top-tier Cherubino, single-vineyard range The Yard and the single-region Ad Hoc label. The range and quality of his wines is extraordinary, the prices irresistible. The runaway success of the business has seen the accumulation of 120ha of vineyards, the appointment of additional winemakers and Larry's own appointment as director of winemaking for Robert Oatley Vineyards. Exports to the UK, the US, Canada, Ireland, Switzerland, Hong Kong, South Korea, Singapore, China and NZ.

🍷🍷🍷🍷🍷 **Cherubino Budworth Riversdale Vineyard Frankland River Cabernet Sauvignon 2018** Great colour, deep but vivid crimson/purple. Cedary French oak and blackcurrant fruit are joined at the hip by superb tannins that reflect the day-by-day assessment of the must during the latter weeks of maceration. The mouth-watering savoury aftertaste is the coup de grace for this great cabernet. Screw cap. 14% alc. **Rating** 98 **To** 2043 $175 JH ✪ ♥
Cherubino Dijon Karridale Chardonnay 2019 Fermented and matured for 10 months in new and 1yo French oak. The elegance and detail of the perfectly balanced mix of white peach, pink grapefruit and quality oak reflects the marriage of the Dijon clones and quality oak. The length and balance are immaculate. Screw cap. 13% alc. **Rating** 97 **To** 2030 $45 JH ✪
Cherubino Margaret River Chardonnay 2019 Rich and layered on the nose, with crushed nuts, salted peach and preserved lemon. Marzipan, nougat, nashi pear, brine and loads of creamy softness on the palate, no doubt thanks to partial mlf. Delicious. 'Oh yum' was muttered aloud while tasting this, not a common

occurrence. Length of flavour shows this will continue to evolve gracefully for years. Screw cap. 13.5% alc. **Rating** 97 **To** 2036 $65 EL ☉

Cherubino Frankland River Cabernet Sauvignon 2018 An iridescent ruby in the glass. Saturated in flavour and packed with fine, chalky tannins that provide substance and structure for the sweet fruit. There is so much going on here that 2nd and 3rd sips are needed. The tannins and the fruit are generous, chewy and expansive. This bottle could evaporate in a moment. A ruminating wine and a showpiece for Frankland River pedigree. Screw cap. 13.5% alc. **Rating** 97 **To** 2041 $75 EL ☉

♥♥♥♥♥ **Cherubino Great Southern Riesling 2020** Piercing intensity on the palate which spears the tongue with acid, citrus fruit and blossom. It then glides over the rest of the mouth leaving bursts of flavour in its wake. Stopping short of fearsome (only just) this has latent power and structure to spare. It will evolve for decades in your cellar. Screw cap. 12.5% alc. **Rating** 96 **To** 2041 $35 EL ☉

Cherubino Frankland River Shiraz 2019 The fruit has a plush succulence that crouches on the core of the palate. Savoury tannins shape and guide the fruit through a long finish. It has thundering intensity and a jet stream of length behind it. All things in place for a very long life ahead, but it's tight and closed right now. Perhaps, for all its layers, this is how it should be. Screw cap. 14% alc. **Rating** 96 **To** 2041 $55 EL ☉

Pedestal Margaret River Cabernet Sauvignon 2018 From vineyards in Wilyabrup, matured in French oak for 12 months. It ticks all the boxes with its cassis fruit on the one hand, firm cabernet tannins on the other, providing all-up balance. Exceptional value for a wine with an extended drinking window of opportunity. Screw cap. 14% alc. **Rating** 96 **To** 2033 $25 JH ☉

Cherubino Porongurup Riesling 2020 Fleshy, soapy and elegant, flaunting the aromatic calling cards of the Porongurup region: spring blossoms, crushed limestone and pithy citrus. The palate follows in exactly this manner, talcy phenolics kick in toward the finish and redirect the wine to a very long, lingering close. Screw cap. 12.2% alc. **Rating** 95 **To** 2035 $40 EL

The Yard Riversdale Frankland River Riesling 2020 Hand picked from the Riversdale Vineyard. It only takes the first sip for the treasure cave of intense lime juice to unroll in waves of flavour that keep coming on each retaste. A classic each-way bet: now, and in 7 or so years as the depth of the wave grows and changes both in flavour (toast) and feel. Screw cap. 12% alc. **Rating** 95 **To** 2033 $25 JH ☉

Laissez Faire Riesling 2020 Porongurup can express a very particular character in its rieslings; they are talcy and chalky (both in texture and flavour), with a distinct floral nose (jasmine and stephanotis are the most oft observed) and the acidity is intricately woven in and out of the fruit. This has all of those characteristics, which steer it in a most regal and beautiful direction. Very, very long length of flavour. Screw cap. 12.4% alc. **Rating** 95 **To** 2041 $29 EL ☉

Cherubino Gingin Wilyabrup Chardonnay 2019 The 60% new oak imparts a bonfire of toast and complexity on the nose; flint, cap gun and lots of work. The palate is super-dense and intense, with pink grapefruit, yellow peach, curry leaf and crushed cashews. All the good things are here, coupled with explosive power and line: typical of the Gingin clone in Margaret River. A super-smart wine from a cool and brilliant vintage. Screw cap. 13.1% alc. **Rating** 95 **To** 2036 $49 EL

Cherubino Willows Vineyard Rosé 2020 Grenache's salivating boiled lolly character wafts out of the glass. Generous, expansive fruit on the palate, yet it retains poise and restraint as it glides over the tongue. Good length of flavour means it finishes as it started, with elegance and supple fruit … all in the pursuit of pleasure. After all – isn't that why we drink rosé? Screw cap. 13.5% alc. **Rating** 95 **To** 2025 $40 EL

Laissez Faire Syrah 2019 Hand-picked fruit, matured in oak for 10 months. Minimal additions. Very pretty nose, laced with red berries, star anise, szechuan peppercorn and red licorice. The palate follows suit and is silky, layered and dense! So remarkably dense. Weightless too, though … quite a brilliant wine. Screw cap. 14% alc. **Rating** 95 **To** 2030 $39 EL

Laissez Faire IV 2019 72/13/12/3% shiraz/grenache/mataro/counoise. Delicious balance of red varieties here. It's muscular and supple at once, focused only on delivering pleasure. Which it does. Big glass, please. Screw cap. 13.9% alc. **Rating** 95 **To** 2030 $29 EL ✪

Pedestal Vineyard Elevation Margaret River Cabernet Sauvignon 2018 With 18/9% cabernet franc/malbec. 12 months in oak, further 12 months in bottle prior to release. Cassis, blackberry and mulberry laced with arnica and black licorice. There is a resinous midnight backdrop to all of this, which pushes concentration and power. Pretty remarkable for the price. Screw cap. 13.9% alc. **Rating** 95 **To** 2030 $32 EL ✪

Ad Hoc Avant Gardening Frankland River Cabernet Sauvignon Malbec 2018 Frankly, this is stunning. Texturally like velvet, the fruit is concentrated and pure, reaching into every corner of the mouth. Satsuma plum, raspberry, pink peppercorn, pomegranate and beetroot. Really, really brilliant drinking, at a preposterous price. Screw cap. 14.5% alc. **Rating** 95 **To** 2031 $22 EL ✪

Cherubino Pannoo Vineyard Porongurup Pinot Noir 2019 Smoky, meaty and laced with aniseed, the palate overtakes the aromatics with black cherry and a sweet, creamy vanilla pod character that creates a sumptuousness there. Good length of flavour to close shows the strength of the cool vineyard site. More brawn than finesse. Screw cap. 13% alc. **Rating** 94 **To** 2028 $65 EL

Laissez Faire Foudre Porongurup Pinot Noir 2019 This is lovely. Supple, stemmy, spicy fruit that sings with strawberry, raspberry pip and hints of watermelon. The spice component consists of star anise, fennel and finely ground pepper. Through the finish, a sweet pastry flavour emerges, along with saline acidity and strawberry leaf. Screw cap. 13.5% alc. **Rating** 94 **To** 2027 $44 EL

Cherubino Margaret River Cabernet Sauvignon 2018 Everyone understands that cabernet is a variety with a particular proclivity for oak, however there is such a thing as too much. Here, the succulent red fruits that so show the pedigree of Margaret River in this close to perfect vintage are almost suffocated by oak. There is no doubt as to the quality, but one wonders why it was necessary. Good length of flavour shows its capacity for ageing, but this is not for now. Age it with confidence for 25+ years. Screw cap. 14.5% alc. **Rating** 94 **To** 2046 $75 EL

🍷🍷🍷🍷🍷 **The Yard Channybearup Pemberton Sauvignon Blanc 2020** Rating 92 To 2032 $25 EL ✪
Pedestal Margaret River Sauvignon Blanc 2020 Rating 92 To 2025 $25 EL ✪
Pedestal Margaret River Semillon Sauvignon Blanc 2020 Rating 92 To 2028 $25 EL ✪
Laissez Faire Porongurup Chardonnay 2019 Rating 92 To 2027 EL
Laissez Faire Pinot Noir 2019 Rating 92 To 2025 $39 EL
Cherubino Beautiful South Red Wine 2018 Rating 92 To 2030 $40 EL
Uovo Cabernet Nebbiolo 2018 Rating 92 To 2031 $60 EL
Cherubino Riversdale Vineyard Shiraz Malbec 2018 Rating 92 To 2030 EL
Folklore Classic White 2020 Rating 91 To 2024 $13 EL ✪
Apostrophe Possessive Reds' Frankland River 2019 Rating 91 To 2025 $16 EL ✪
Ad Hoc Wallflower Great Southern Riesling 2020 Rating 90 To 2031 $21 EL ✪
Laissez Faire Arneis 2019 Rating 90 To 2027 $34 EL
The Yard Riversdale Frankland River Cabernet Sauvignon 2018 Rating 90 To 2027 $35 EL

Latta

67 Pickfords Road, Coghills Creek, Vic 3364 **Region** Macedon Ranges
T 0408 594 454 **www**.lattavino.com.au **Open** By appt
Winemaker Owen Latta **Est.** 2012 **Dozens** 1500
This is the culmination of a long-standing desire of Owen Latta to make wines from small plantings in the Pyrenees, Grampians and Macedon regions. Eastern Peake, owned by the Latta family, makes wine from the Ballarat region, and the rationale was to avoid confusing the nature of the 2 operations. He says he has empathy with the growers he works with from when he and his father were themselves contract grapegrowers for others. The degree of that empathy is fortified by the fact that the growers have been known to the Latta family for over 15 years. The wines are, to put it mildly, unconventional.

Laughing Jack

194 Stonewell Road, Marananga, SA 5355 **Region** Barossa Valley
T (08) 8562 3878 **www**.laughingjackwines.com.au **Open** By appt
Winemaker Shawn Kalleske **Est.** 1999 **Dozens** 5000 **Vyds** 38.88ha
The Kalleske family has many branches in the Barossa Valley. Laughing Jack is owned by Shawn, Nathan, Ian and Carol Kalleske, and Linda Schroeter. The lion's share of the vineyard is planted to shiraz, with lesser amounts of semillon and grenache. Vine age varies considerably, with old dry-grown shiraz the jewel in the crown. A small part of the grape production is taken for the Laughing Jack Shiraz. As any Australian knows, the kookaburra is also called the laughing jackass, and there is a resident flock of kookaburras in the stands of blue and red gums surrounding the vineyards. Exports to Malaysia, Hong Kong and China.

Limited Two Barossa Valley Shiraz 2018 Shawn Kalleske's flagship is a selection of his best 2 barrels. A quintessential and benchmark take on Greenock, built around a singular core of red/blackberry fruits. It's locked into a strong lattice of firm, fine, mineral fruit and oak tannins, illuminated by a bright beacon of natural acidity. Every nuance moves forward in unison, marking out a very long finish. One bottle was subtly cork scalped. Cork. 14.5% alc. **Rating** 96 **To** 2048 $150 TS

Moppa Hill Gold Seam Barossa Valley Cabernet Sauvignon 2018 Serious Barossa cabernet, coiled, tense and enduring. Deep, vibrant purple. Impeccably varietal: tiny, crunchy black/redcurrants, blackberries and cassis. Top-class French oak deployed confidently yet with the utmost care. Bright, natural acid line and fantastic persistence make for a cellaring special. Screw cap. 14.5% alc. **Rating** 96 **To** 2048 $40 TS ✪

Moppa Hill Block 6 Barossa Valley Shiraz 2018 Shawn Kalleske has achieved wonderful balance and poise in the warm '18 season, upholding all the deep, dark, brooding power of Barossa shiraz and – vitally – energising it with fantastic natural acidity and fine, polished tannins. The result is a delight to behold; an enticing core of compact blackberries, satsuma plums and fresh licorice. Dark chocolate oak is but an afterthought. This is what we love about Barossa shiraz! Screw cap. 14.5% alc. **Rating** 95 **To** 2033 $40 TS

Carl Albert Moppa Block Barossa Valley Shiraz 2018 There is a delightful detail here uncharacteristic of the far western Barossa, with a lifted violet air and layers of mixed spice. This high site also lends a measured tone to the palate, streamlined, focused and guided equally by energetic natural acidity and fine-boned, powdery, well-controlled tannins. Great potential. Cork. 14.5% alc. **Rating** 95 **To** 2043 $95 TS

Greenock Barossa Valley Shiraz 2018 Full, vibrant purple. The plush, sweet fruit and milk-chocolate core that signifies Greenock is scaffolded masterfully in a web of firm tannins, both fruit- and oak-derived. Red and blue fruits of all kinds abound, set to a bright line of natural acidity that keeps everything on track through a long finish. Engineered for the long haul with Shawn Kalleske precision. Screw cap. 14.5% alc. **Rating** 94 **To** 2038 $50 TS

Old Vine Moppa Barossa Valley Grenache 2018 Shawn Kalleske's attentive, hand-made approach brings the sensitivity to let grenache shine. Structured, savoury and serious, understated berry fruits are accented by tomato and sage, with a core of sweet fruit lingering long through well-gauged dark chocolate French oak and a beautiful splay of fine, confident tannins. Proper grenache, with an exciting future before it. Cork. 14.5% alc. **Rating** 94 **To** 2033 $65 TS

🍷🍷🍷🍷🍷 Jack's Barossa Valley GSM 2018 **Rating** 93 **To** 2028 $25 TS **○**
Jack's Barossa Valley Shiraz 2018 **Rating** 90 **To** 2025 $25 TS

Laurel Bank ★★★★

130 Black Snake Lane, Granton, Tas 7030 **Region** Southern Tasmania
T (03) 6263 5977 **www.**laurelbankwines.com.au **Open** By appt
Winemaker Greer Carland **Est.** 1986 **Dozens** 1700 **Vyds** 3.5ha
Laurel Bank was established by Kerry Carland in 1986 but deliberately kept a low profile by withholding release of most of its early wines. When the time came, Kerry entered the Hobart Wine Show in '95 and won the trophy for Most Successful Tasmanian Exhibitor. The moderate slope of the north-facing vineyard overlooking the Derwent River has 2 radically different soil types: one high vigour, the other low. Intelligent matching of variety and soil has led to a natural balance and (relative) ease of canopy management – and balanced wines.

🍷🍷🍷🍷🍷 **Sauvignon Blanc 2020** A blend of earlier- and later-picked parcels (a week apart) contrasting pretty, sweet passionfruit tropicals with sage and thyme. Pale straw-green hue. A focused core of lemon and Granny Smith apple carries long and true, guided by bright acidity and well-handled phenolic grip. A little barrel fermentation has built texture and length without interrupting purity. Top class and top value. Screw cap. 12.8% alc. **Rating** 94 **To** 2025 $25 TS **○**
Cabernet Merlot 2019 Ripeness is the game for Tasmanian cabernet, and vine age and diligent viticulture have made all the difference here. A full, vibrant purple/red hue announces a blend of presence and varietal integrity. Blackcurrants and cassis of impressive density are backed by coffee bean and dark chocolate French oak, vibrant acidity and impressively fine tannins. Crafted, complete, compelling. Screw cap. 14.2% alc. **Rating** 94 **To** 2034 $39 TS

🍷🍷🍷🍷🍷 Riesling 2019 **Rating** 90 **To** 2027 $25 TS

Leasingham ★★★★☆

PO Box 57, Clare, SA 5453 **Region** Clare Valley
T 1800 088 711 **www.**leasingham-wines.com.au
Winemaker Matt Caldersmith **Est.** 1893
Leasingham has experienced death by a thousand cuts. First, its then owner, CWA, sold its Rogers Vineyard to Tim Adams in 2009. CWA then unsuccessfully endeavoured to separately sell the winemaking equipment and cellar door, while retaining the winery. In January '11 Tim Adams purchased the winery, cellar door and winemaking equipment, making the once-proud Leasingham a virtual winery (or brand). The quality of the wines has not suffered. Exports to the UK and Canada.

🍷🍷🍷🍷🍷 **Classic Clare Cabernet Sauvignon 2018** This appears riper, richer and warmer than the 14% alcohol suggests. But no denying its sense of place. Lots of intense flavours from blackberries, currants and mulberries, with espresso coffee to dark chocolate infused with mint. And yes, lots of toasty, cedary oak. Mouth-coating tannins and overall, a solid wine. Screw cap. 14% alc. **Rating** 94 **To** 2033 $79 JF

🍷🍷🍷🍷🍷 Classic Clare Shiraz 2018 **Rating** 91 **To** 2032 $78 JF

Leconfield

15454 Riddoch Highway, Coonawarra, SA 5263 **Region** Coonawarra
T (08) 8323 8830 **www.**leconfieldwines.com **Open** 7 days 11–4
Winemaker Paul Gordon, Greg Foster **Est.** 1974 **Dozens** 25 000 **Vyds** 43.7ha
Sydney Hamilton purchased the unplanted property that was to become Leconfield in 1974, having worked in the family wine business for over 30 years until his retirement in the mid '50s. When he acquired the property and set about planting it he was 76 and reluctantly bowed to family pressure to sell Leconfield to nephew Richard in '81. Richard has progressively increased the vineyards to their present level, over 75% dedicated to cabernet sauvignon – for long the winery's specialty. Exports to most major markets.

♟♟♟♟♟ **Coonawarra Cabernet Sauvignon 2019** The tune is Coonawarra but its melody is Leconfield. A riff of blackberries and satsuma plums, mint and menthol tempered by woodsy spices, and the oak just so. All flavours flow through to a palate just shy of full bodied. There's an elegance within, refreshing acidity and perfectly framed emery board tannins to close. Screw cap. 14.5% alc. **Rating** 95 To 2036 $36 JF
Coonawarra Cabernet Franc 2019 All hail cabernet franc. So under-appreciated as a varietal, and yet Leconfield knows how to weave some magic. Aromatics to swoon over and the sweetly-fruited core comes packaged in spice, potpourri and fresh bay leaves, with a savoury overlay. It enjoys a plushness, a softness across the palate, complete with fine tannins. Gorgeous now, but will garner more complexity in time. Screw cap. 14.5% alc. **Rating** 95 To 2034 $30 JF ✪

♟♟♟♟♟ **Coonawarra Cabernet Merlot 2018** Rating 93 To 2026 $26 JF ✪
McLaren Vale Shiraz 2019 Rating 92 To 2032 $26 JF
Coonawarra Reserve Shiraz 2019 Rating 92 To 2034 $30 JF
Coonawarra Merlot 2019 Rating 92 To 2028 $26 JF
La Sevillana Coonawarra Rosé 2020 Rating 91 To 2022 $26 JF
Coonawarra Chardonnay 2019 Rating 90 To 2025 $26 JF

Leeuwin Estate

Stevens Road, Margaret River, WA 6285 **Region** Margaret River
T (08) 9759 0000 **www.**leeuwinestate.com.au **Open** 7 days 10–5
Winemaker Tim Lovett, Phil Hutchison, Breac Wheatley **Est.** 1974 **Dozens** 50 000
Vyds 160ha
This outstanding winery and vineyard is owned by the Horgan family, founded by Denis and Tricia, who continue their involvement, with son Justin Horgan and daughter Simone Furlong joint chief executives. The Art Series Chardonnay is, in my (James') opinion, Australia's finest example based on the wines of the last 30 vintages. The move to screw cap brought a large smile to the faces of those who understand just how superbly the wine ages. The large estate plantings, coupled with strategic purchases of grapes from other growers, provide the base for high-quality Art Series Cabernet Sauvignon and Shiraz; the hugely successful, quick-selling Art Series Riesling and Sauvignon Blanc; and lower priced Prelude and Siblings wines. Exports to all major markets.

♟♟♟♟♟ **Art Series Margaret River Chardonnay 2018** Benchmark pedigree Margaret River chardonnay from the perfect 2018 vintage. Kaffir leaf, ocean spray, nectarine, yellow peach, custard apple and white peach are the start. Saffron curls, vanilla pod and freshly grated nutmeg frame saline acidity, crouched and coiled. Length of flavour extends across the palate in an endless procession of texture and complexity. All of the power, grace and excellence of previous years is here, amplified. Screw cap. 13.5% alc. **Rating** 98 To 2051 $126 EL ✪ ♥
Art Series Margaret River Cabernet Sauvignon 2017 Wow. Silky smooth aromas of red berries, grey minerality (granite, graphite, etc) and breaths of ocean air whispered about. The palate is exactly as the nose promises, elegant and refined. Length of flavour is where this really kicks into gear, extending seamlessly across

the palate, lingering and swirling in its profile. Beautiful, classical cabernet from a cool vintage. What a pleasure this is. Screw cap. 13.5% alc. **Rating** 97 **To** 2041 $70 EL ✪

🍷🍷🍷🍷🍷 **Art Series Margaret River Shiraz 2018** The same layers of complexity and spice as the 2017, with all the ripe fruit and power hallmarks of the 2018 vintage. Bouncy and chewy, the tannins are woven into the fruit. Fruit, oak, acid and tannins are integrated and elegant, showing cohesion and harmony from the get-go. Cool-climate elegance is the lasting impression of this wine, as is the fine, chalky tannin profile that ultimately carries the fruit over the course of the palate. Very detailed. Margaret River can be responsible for seriously beautiful shiraz – this is one. Screw cap. 14% alc. **Rating** 96 **To** 2031 $42 EL ✪

Prelude Vineyards Margaret River Cabernet Sauvignon 2018 In case you missed it, '18 may be the greatest cabernet and chardonnay vintage in living memory in Margaret River. So goes it for the Prelude: sheer density of fruit and rippling length of flavour are the calling cards. Bargain at the price. Screw cap. 13.5% alc. **Rating** 96 **To** 2035 $35 EL ✪

Art Series Margaret River Riesling 2020 Lime blossom, coriander, hints of lychee and spring blossom. Galangal, kaffir leaf. The Indian Ocean makes a briny impact on the juicy acidity. Sesame seed. Green apple and talc. Incredibly pretty and bright, but soft, too. This has precision, but not a retina-burning laser like Great Southern iterations. Plushness and plumpness is the order of the day. Low yields, small bunches and small berries. Supple. Subtle. Screw cap. 12% alc. **Rating** 94 **To** 2036 $35 EL

Prelude Vineyards Margaret River Chardonnay 2019 The cooler '19 vintage produced saline acid which is fine and tight. Almond meal and cashew initially; the mid palate and beyond shows attractive exotic spice complexity and great length of flavour. Green pistachio, yellow peach and brine. Regular lees stirring has built texture, but it is the intensity of fruit that makes this great: the Leeuwin chardonnay DNA is evident from the first mouthful. Screw cap. 13.5% alc. **Rating** 94 **To** 2027 $36 EL

🍷🍷🍷🍷🍷 **Margaret River Rosé 2020 Rating** 93 **To** 2021 $28 EL
Siblings Margaret River Sauvignon Blanc 2020 Rating 92 **To** 2023 $23 EL ✪
Pinot Noir Chardonnay Brut 2018 Rating 91 $23 EL ✪

Lenton Brae Wines   ★★★★☆

3887 Caves Road, Margaret River, WA 6285 **Region** Margaret River
T (08) 9755 6255 **www**.lentonbrae.com **Open** 7 days 10–5
Winemaker Edward Tomlinson **Est.** 1982 **Vyds** 7.3ha
The late architect Bruce Tomlinson built a strikingly beautiful winery (heritage-listed by the Shire of Busselton) that is now in the hands of winemaker son Edward (Ed), who consistently makes elegant wines in classic Margaret River style. A midwinter (French time) trip to Pomerol in Bordeaux to research merlot is an indication of his commitment. Exports to the UK.

🍷🍷🍷🍷🍷 **Wilyabrup Margaret River Semillon Sauvignon Blanc 2020** A distinctly cassis-driven nose and palate, with wisps of juniper, jasmine tea and red apple skin. The palate morphs into layers of vanilla pod, lychee and brine. A really restrained expression of the blend. Screw cap. 13.5% alc. **Rating** 92 **To** 2024 $22 EL ✪

Lady Douglas Margaret River Cabernet Sauvignon 2019 2019 was a cool and wet vintage in Margaret River, but it has proven to be capable of producing aromatic wines of poise, structure and delicacy. At this stage, this wine is closed and speaks more of tannin and structure than it does of fruit succulence. Perhaps it will soften in time. Screw cap. 14% alc. **Rating** 91 **To** 2031 $38 EL

Wilyabrup Margaret River Cabernet Sauvignon 2019 The fruit is brilliant, that is evident, but the tannins gobble it up completely. They overtake the sweet berries, and grip them with an iron fist. A touch challenging at this stage, but will come together in time. Screw cap. 14.5% alc. **Rating** 90 **To** 2036 $80 EL

Leo Buring

Sturt Highway, Nuriootpa, SA 5355 **Region** Eden Valley/Clare Valley
T 1300 651 650
Winemaker Tom Shanahan **Est.** 1934
Between 1965 and 2000 Leo Buring was Australia's foremost producer of rieslings, with a rich legacy left by former winemaker John Vickery. After veering away from its core business into other varietal wines, it has now refocused on riesling. Top of the range are the Leopold Derwent Valley and the Leonay Eden Valley rieslings, supported by Clare Valley and Eden Valley rieslings at significantly lower prices, and expanding its wings to Tasmania and WA.

ŸŸŸŸŸ **Leonay Eden Valley Riesling 2020** Another epic chapter in the odyssey that is Leonay, possessing an effortless purity, precision and endurance that appear nothing short of supernatural here. All the lemon, lime and Granny Smith apple hallmarks of the greats are here in full measure, but rather than swaying to the tropical mood of the season, it upholds breathtaking dignity, even tilting toward white pepper. Concentration meets elegance. Acid line is mesmerising, driving a finish that holds undeterred and undiminished for a full 45 seconds. Screw cap. 11.5% alc. **Rating** 97 **To** 2045 $40 TS ✪ ♥

ŸŸŸŸŸ **Eden Valley Dry Riesling 2020** Exotic allusions, intense concentration and bright acid drive make this a quintessential expression of 2020 in the Eden Valley. Glimpses of frangipani and kiwifruit dart about a tense core of pure lime, lemon and Granny Smith apple. It holds drive and presence through a long finish, sustained by enduring acidity, with the concentration and confidence to quash very subtle phenolic structure. What a wine, what a price! Screw cap. 11.5% alc. **Rating** 94 **To** 2027 $20 TS ✪

ŸŸŸŸŸ **Clare Valley Dry Riesling 2020 Rating** 90 **To** 2026 $20 JF ✪

Leogate Estate Wines

1693 Broke Road, Pokolbin, NSW 2320 **Region** Hunter Valley
T (02) 4998 7499 **www.**leogate.com.au **Open** 7 days 10–5
Winemaker Mark Woods **Est.** 2009 **Dozens** 30 000 **Vyds** 127.5ha
Since purchasing the substantial Brokenback Vineyard in 2009 (a key part of the original Rothbury Estate, with the majority of vines over 50 years old), Bill and Vicki Widin have wasted no time. Initially the Widins leased the Tempus Two winery but prior to the '13 vintage they completed the construction of their own winery and cellar door. They have also expanded the range of varieties, supplementing the long-established 30ha of shiraz, 25ha of chardonnay and 3ha of semillon with between 0.5 and 2ha of each of verdelho, viognier, gewürztraminer, pinot gris and tempranillo. They have had a string of wine show successes for their very impressive portfolio. In '16 Leogate purchased a 61ha certified organic vineyard at Gulgong (Mudgee) planted to shiraz, cabernet sauvignon and merlot. Leogate has an impressive collection of back-vintage releases available on request. Exports to the UK, the US, Malaysia, Hong Kong and China.

ŸŸŸŸŸ **Museum Release Creek Bed Reserve Hunter Valley Semillon 2013** A stellar vintage for the Hunter. The whites are particularly lauded and rightly so. This is an effortless meld of chewiness and pungent mineral freshness. Nectarine, quince, beeswax, fennel, finger lime and a regional hint of lemon drop. Pulpy, intense and impressively long, pummelling the cheeks while staining the throat. Screw cap. 11.5% alc. **Rating** 96 **To** 2032 $50 NG ✪

ŸŸŸŸŸ **Museum Release Creek Bed Reserve Hunter Valley Semillon 2014** A fine vintage by virtue of consistent ripening and extract, yet not quite up to the complexity and subdued energy of the '13. This said, an easier wine to grasp, perhaps. Waxy and full. White peach, wasabi, white pepper and a pumice-like glint to the chalky acidity. Long and very fine. Screw cap. 11% alc. **Rating** 96 **To** 2028 $50 NG ✪

The Basin Reserve Hunter Valley Shiraz 2019 An east-facing site, imbuing the freshness and detail that warmer plots can't convey. This said, unabashedly powerful. But lifted, floral and taut. Judicious French oak positions the fruit, while providing structural latticework. More savoury. Altogether finer, better structured and transmitting of site to glass. Long. The Hunter postcode stamped across riffs of terracotta and polished leather. Blue/black-fruit aspersions, anise, clove, green olive and pepper grind. Screw cap. 14.5% alc. **Rating** 96 **To** 2038 $110 NG

Museum Release Western Slopes Reserve Hunter Valley Shiraz 2013 Varnish, violet, brambly dark-berry aspersions and, my oh my, those sumptuous, gritty tannins that mark this overlooked vintage, at least for reds. The weightier fruit and warmer feel of this cuvée suit the terser tannic meld. Iodine, black pepper, clove and an Indian potpourri of other spice is layered through a very long finish. Thoroughly impressive. Screw cap. 14% alc. **Rating** 96 **To** 2026 $150 NG

Brokenback Vineyard Hunter Valley Gewürztraminer 2019 The Hunter spools few high-quality expressions of this grape across its humid climate, but perhaps it should try more. The aromas are bang on: grape spice, lychee, orange blossom and crystalline ginger. The palate could be a bit more unctuous and chewy, but that is being churlish. Mid weighted, highly versatile and very good drinking. An unexpected beauty. Screw cap. 13% alc. **Rating** 95 **To** 2024 $22 NG ✪

Vicki's Choice Reserve Hunter Valley Chardonnay 2018 The Übermensch. The fugue of flavour and generosity sought by those weaned on chardonnay of the past. Tastes almost Californian. And yet, with an indelible imprint of skilful winemaking, drawing peach, ginger spice, vanilla pod, cinnamon and nectarine across a pungent skein of jittery minerality. Dense and ample. Long and impressionable. Screw cap. 13.8% alc. **Rating** 95 **To** 2026 $70 NG

Creek Bed Reserve Hunter Valley Chardonnay 2017 A fully loaded chardonnay. Packed and ready to please. All in the here and now. Generous. Vanilla-pod oak, dried mango, canned pineapple and a melody of exuberant stone-fruit scents. The finish is layered and directed by satisfying and well-appointed ginger-spiced oak pillars. For those seeking flavour, here lies the shrine. Screw cap. 13.5% alc. **Rating** 95 **To** 2025 $38 NG

Malabar Reserve Hunter Valley Shiraz 2019 Violet, blueberry pie, dark molten cherry, anise and mocha. Creamy, rich and salubrious, with a dichotomous tension. Turkish ballet dancer. The earthiness of the Hunter, in a modern, ripe vein befitting the Brokenback Vineyard. Mercifully, not reductive. The flow, smooth and long. Largely used French oak, imparting cedar and vanilla. Far from resolved. Yet the densely concentrated fruit only suggests integration. Given the quality of components, I wish the style were a little lighter with more grape tannin. Delicious all the same. Screw cap. 14.5% alc. **Rating** 95 **To** 2038 $70 NG

Museum Release The Basin Reserve Hunter Valley Shiraz 2013 I like this because of the tannins, a pithy corset of grapey nourishment, firm and authoritative. While this vintage is renowned for whites, I like the structural latticework of the reds. Medium bodied. Lifted with florals and bitters, but subdued by virtue of extract and a herbal edge. Think boysenberry, dark cherry, coffee bean and bay leaf. Tactile, chewy and very savoury. Almost Italian in terms of composure. A lovely wine. Screw cap. 14% alc. **Rating** 95 **To** 2025 $150 NG

Western Slopes Reserve Hunter Valley Shiraz 2019 Despite the warmer western plot, there is a welcome litheness. A pulpy, floral, dense and powerful wine, with just enough freshness. Just! Lilac, boysenberry, kirsch, varnish, tapenade and salumi. Sweet and sappy across the finish. A bit hot on my Adam's apple. Heady personality. Lacks the tension and earthy Hunter personality of the other cuvées. The richest of the bunch. Screw cap. 14.5% alc. **Rating** 94 **To** 2035 $110 NG

ⓎⓎⓎⓎⓎ **Black Cluster Hunter Valley Shiraz 2019** Rating 93 **To** 2032 $30 NG
Brokenback Vineyard Hunter Valley Shiraz 2019 Rating 93 **To** 2031 $40 NG

Museum Release Brokenback Hunter Valley Shiraz 2011 Rating 93
To 2028 $145 NG
Creek Bed Reserve Hunter Valley Chardonnay 2018 Rating 92 To 2025
$38 NG
Brokenback Vineyard Hunter Valley Pinot Gris 2020 Rating 92 To 2023
$27 NG
Brokenback Vineyard Hunter Valley Shiraz 2018 Rating 92 To 2030
$40 NG
Museum Release Brokenback Vineyard Hunter Valley Semillon 2013
Rating 92 To 2023 $70 NG
Brokenback Vineyard Hunter Valley Chardonnay 2018 Rating 91 To 2023
$26 NG
Brokenback Vineyard Hunter Valley Chardonnay 2017 Rating 91 To 2022
$26 NG

Lerida Estate

87 Vineyards Road, Lake George, NSW 2581 **Region** Canberra District
T (02) 4848 0231 **www.leridaestate.com.au Open** 7 days 10–5
Winemaker Jacob Law **Est.** 1997 **Dozens** 10 000 **Vyds** 11.69ha
Lerida Estate owes a great deal to the inspiration of Dr Edgar Riek; it is planted immediately
to the south of Edgar's former Lake George vineyard. Lerida is planted mainly to pinot noir,
with pinot gris, chardonnay, shiraz, merlot and cabernet franc and viognier also onsite. Michael
and Tracey McRoberts purchased Lerida in 2017 and significant expansion is underway.
They have leased a 20yo shiraz vineyard (4ha) in the heart of Murrumbateman and shiraz
has overtaken pinot noir as the predominant variety produced. The Glen Murcutt–designed
winery, barrel room, cellar door and restaurant have spectacular views over Lake George.
Exports to China.

ꜸꜸꜸꜸꜸ Cullerin Canberra District Chardonnay 2019 This seems delicate at first, too
shy to reveal much. It unfurls to offer stone fruit and citrus, ginger and woodsy
spices plus a floral lift. Soft across the palate yet with a succulence throughout,
zippy acidity cutting through the creamy, nutty lees. There's also a buttered
popcorn/yeasty character sneaking through, not unpleasant, just there. A lovely
drink now rather than a keeper. Screw cap. 13% alc. **Rating** 93 **To** 2025 $38 JF
Josephine Canberra District Pinot Noir 2019 This has enough heady
aromatics to lure you in. The flavours are confirmed on the palate, with the right
ratio of sweet cherry fruit to spice and a touch of mint. It's soft and plush with
squishy, ripe tannins. The oak regime has backed off this year and the wine's all the
better for it. A lovely drink. Screw cap. 13.3% alc. **Rating** 93 **To** 2026 $75 JF
Canberra District Shiraz 2019 Not shy on the colour or flavour front this
vintage. A melange of ripe sweet plums and blackberries, peppered and spiced
with a dusting of toasty oak then an even flow across the full-bodied palate.
And with its plush, ripe tannins, this turns out ready to pour. Screw cap. 14.2% alc.
Rating 91 **To** 2026 $28 JF
Hilltops Tempranillo 2019 A lighter- to medium-bodied wine, best drunk now.
Dark cherries, cola and sarsaparilla. The tannins are subdued for the variety but it's
a fresh and inviting wine. Screw cap. 13.5% alc. **Rating** 90 **To** 2025 $28 JF

Lethbridge Wines

74 Burrows Road, Lethbridge, Vic 3222 **Region** Geelong
T (03) 5281 7279 **www.lethbridgewines.com Open** Mon–Fri 11–3, w'ends 11–5
Winemaker Ray Nadeson, Maree Collis **Est.** 1996 **Dozens** 10 000 **Vyds** 7ha
Lethbridge was founded by scientists Ray Nadeson, Maree Collis and Adrian Thomas.
In Ray's words, 'Our belief is that the best wines express the unique character of special
places'. As well as understanding the importance of terroir, the partners have built a unique
strawbale winery, designed to recreate the controlled environment of cellars and caves in
Europe. Winemaking is no less ecological: hand-picking, indigenous-yeast fermentation, small

open fermenters, pigeage (foot-stomping) and minimal handling of the wines throughout the maturation process are all part and parcel of the highly successful Lethbridge approach. Ray also has a distinctive approach to full-blown chardonnay and pinot noir. There is also a contract winemaking limb to the business. Exports to the UK, the US, Denmark, Russia, Singapore, Thailand, Japan, Hong Kong and China.

ΨΨΨΨΨ **Dr Nadeson Riesling 2020** After time away from sourcing riesling from Henty, Ray Nadeson is back with a new source from the region and renewed zip in his winemaking step. You can understand why. The energy on display is thrilling; rapier-like acidity matched with a quiet depth of fruit intensity. Lemon zest, lime, apple, nougat saline and don't forget the spice. All humming along in off-dry unison. And still so, so young. Screw cap. 9.7% alc. **Rating** 95 **To** 2026 $35 JP ✪

Allegra 2018 Lethbridge's flagship chardonnay, capable of stopping you in your tracks. With fineness, concentration of fruit and judicious winemaking, this is one of Geelong's best expressions of the grape. Citrus to the fore on the bouquet, with grapefruit, lemon, white nectarine and almond-meal notes. Fine lined throughout with a tantalising theme of bush herbs and lemon thyme. Bright, crystalline freshness to close. Screw cap. 13.8% alc. **Rating** 95 **To** 2026 $90 JP

Pinot Noir 2019 Ray Nadeson writes some of the most lyrical wine labels going. His hope with this wine is to reveal tannins that feel 'like you are melting into a soft cushion'. Well, they are certainly supple. A big proponent of whole-bunch fermentation, his '19 is striking in its structure and force of personality, with an imposing herbal imprint, chocolate cherry and red berries. Balance of oak/fruit/tannin is impressive, but the sustained length is that and more. Screw cap. 13.5% alc. **Rating** 95 **To** 2028 $48 JP

Mietta Pinot Noir 2018 Following on from a strong '17 vintage comes another top year. A rousing, lifted aromatic bouquet fills the glass, all red berries, pomegranate, cranberry, lapsang souchong and exotic spice. A wine still in its infancy, with slow reveals of sweet fruit, dried herbs, bitter chocolate and savoury earth. A fine tannin structure exudes an elegance. Everything in its place and just waiting on time. Screw cap. 13.5% alc. **Rating** 95 **To** 2027 $90 JP

Chardonnay 2019 A savoury, mealy style of chardonnay, a nice contrast to the top-tier Allegra. Plenty of barrel ferment complexity, together with almond, nougat, pear and lovely spiciness. Melds beautifully on the palate with quince, grilled nuts and mandarin rind. Harmonious oak. Quite the complex number for a wine so young. Screw cap. 14% alc. **Rating** 94 **To** 2025 $48 JP

Malakoff Vineyard Shiraz 2019 What a charmer. The vineyard's red ferrous soils bring a natural balance and elegance, upon which sit layers of purple/red fruits, blackberry leaf, sour cherry, briar, pepper and earth. Medium in body, fine in texture, with ripe cherry tannins, it finishes with an Italian-style dryness. Screw cap. 14% alc. **Rating** 94 **To** 2026 $48 JP

ΨΨΨΨΨ **The Bartl Chardonnay 2019** **Rating** 93 **To** 2027 $55 JP
Pinot Gris 2020 **Rating** 92 **To** 2026 $35 JP

Leura Park Estate   ★★★★☆

1400 Portarlington Road, Curlewis, Vic 3222 **Region** Geelong
T (03) 5253 3180 **www.**leuraparkestate.com.au **Open** Thurs–Sun 10–5, 7 days Jan
Winemaker Darren Burke **Est.** 1995 **Dozens** 3000 **Vyds** 20ha
Leura Park Estate's vineyard is planted to chardonnay (50%), pinot noir, pinot gris, sauvignon blanc, riesling, shiraz and cabernet sauvignon. Owners David and Lyndsay Sharp are committed to minimal interference in the vineyard and have expanded the estate-grown wine range to include Vintage Grande Cuvée. The next step was the erection of a winery for the 2010 vintage, leading to increased production and ongoing wine show success.

ΨΨΨΨΨ **Bellarine Peninsula Pinot Noir 2019** A most convincing young pinot noir with cranberry, raspberry, stewed plums and a hint of leafy complexity amid spice, vanilla and wood smoke. Impressive tannin structure is long, deep and balanced, bringing added fineness to the fruit expression. Quite an all-round delicate pinot noir, but with substance for further ageing. Screw cap. 12.5% alc. **Rating** 94 **To** 2028 $45 JP

ŸŸŸŸŸ **Bellarine Peninsula Sauvignon Blanc 2019** Rating 92 To 2023 $30 JP
Bellarine Peninsula Chardonnay 2019 Rating 92 To 2028 $35 JP
Bellarine Peninsula Shiraz 2018 Rating 91 To 2026 $45 JP
Vintage Grande Blanc de Blanc 2020 Rating 90 $38 JP

Lienert Vineyards   ★★★★

Artisans of Barossa, 16 Vine Vale Road, Tanunda, SA 5352 **Region** Barossa Valley
T (08) 8524 9062 **www**.lienert.wine **Open** 7 days 9–5
Winemaker James Lienert **Est.** 2001 **Dozens** 5000 **Vyds** 100ha
Lienert Vineyards is a partnership between brothers John and James Lienert, who have converted the family's farmland on the Barossa Valley's western ridge from cropping to vineyards, planting the first vines in the distinctive terra rossa soils in 2001. John manages the vineyard, which also supplies fruit to a number of Barossa wineries. James makes wines under the Lienert Vineyards and Jack West labels from selected blocks. Exports to Singapore.

ŸŸŸŸŸ **Sieben Klon Barossa Valley Shiraz 2019** Greengage plum and raspberry fruit leads out elegant and bright, defining a shiraz of refreshing elegance for western Barossa. Fine tannin profile and bright acidity make for an elegantly poised palate, though falling a little short. Screw cap. 14.5% alc. **Rating** 92 **To** 2027 $45 TS

Lightfoot & Sons   ★★★★★

717 Calulu Road, Bairnsdale, Vic 3875 **Region** Gippsland
T (03) 5156 9205 **www**.lightfootwines.com **Open** Mon–Fri 11–5
Winemaker Alastair Butt, Tom Lightfoot **Est.** 1995 **Dozens** 10 000 **Vyds** 29.3ha
Brian and Helen Lightfoot first established a vineyard of predominantly pinot noir and shiraz, with some cabernet sauvignon and merlot, on their Myrtle Point farm in the late '90s. The soils were found to be similar to that of Coonawarra, with terra rossa over limestone. In the early days, most of the grapes were sold to other Victorian winemakers, but with the arrival of Alistair Butt (formerly of Brokenwood and Seville Estate) and sons Tom and Rob taking over the business around 2008 (Tom in the vineyard and cellar, Rob overseeing sales and marketing), the focus has shifted to producing estate wines. Cabernet and merlot have since been replaced with more chardonnay, some gamay and pinot grigio, but pinot noir retains the top spot, with half of all plantings. (TS)

ŸŸŸŸŸ **Myrtle Point Vineyard Gippsland Chardonnay 2019** While the colour is a mid straw gold, it's fresh and a pretty smart wine. White stone fruit, splashes of citrus and lots of spices, but the real pleasure is the palate. Fuller bodied, with a silky, slippery texture. Screw cap. 13.6% alc. **Rating** 95 **To** 2026 $30 JF ❂
Home Block Gippsland Chardonnay 2018 Gee, these chardonnays pack a lot of flavour! This is full of delicious nougatine, honeycomb cream lees and umami characters. Lots of fleshy, ripe stone fruit, with ginger spice and smoky oak that's integrated while the palate fans out. It feels rich and ripe, but acidity tightens it all up. Nice one. Screw cap. 12.5% alc. **Rating** 95 **To** 2026 $55 JF

ŸŸŸŸŸ **Myrtle Point Vineyard Gippsland Pinot Noir 2019** Rating 93 To 2032 $30 JF
Gippsland Pinot Noir Shiraz 2019 Rating 90 To 2026 $40 JF

Lillypilly Estate   ★★★★☆

47 Lillypilly Road, Leeton, NSW 2705 **Region** Riverina
T (02) 6953 4069 **www**.lillypilly.com **Open** Mon–Sat 10–5.30, Sun by appt
Winemaker Robert Fiumara **Est.** 1982 **Dozens** 11 000 **Vyds** 27.9ha

Botrytised white wines are by far the best offering from Lillypilly, with the Noble Muscat of Alexandria unique to the winery. These wines have both style and intensity of flavour and can age well. Their table wine quality is always steady – a prime example of not fixing what is not broken. Exports to the UK, the US, Canada and China.

🍷🍷🍷🍷🍷 **Family Reserve Noble Blend 2018** Among Australia's better sweet unfortified iterations. A botrytised jingle of candied mango, spiced pineapple and citrus marmalade. The acidity, palate-staining high. The wine's effusive flavour profile is balanced with its vivacity, such that despite the thrumming fruit flavours and hedonistic sweetness, it comes across as long, drinkable and almost savoury. Screw cap. 12% alc. **Rating** 93 **To** 2030 $36 NG

Noble Harvest 2019 Vermetino and Muscat; the sort of varieties that we can look forward to as a stronger and eventual dominant presence in this field. Tangerine, turmeric and tamarind spice, offset by quince, nashi pear and grape spice. The envelope of acidity encases the RS, imparting an almost savoury finish of crunchy length. Screw cap. 12% alc. **Rating** 92 **To** 2030 $30 NG

Noble Blend 2019 Largely sauvignon. Exuberance. Cumquat, tangerine and an underlying greengage pungency. Plenty sweet, but a jitterbug of texture almost sublimates the sweetness with an uncanny freshness and tangy length. Screw cap. 12% alc. **Rating** 91 **To** 2030 $32 NG

limefinger   ★★★★

18 Edwards Rd, Polish Hill River, SA 5453 **Region** Clare Valley
T 0417 803 404 **www.**limefingerwine.com.au **Open** Sat–Sun 11–4
Winemaker Neil Pike **Est.** 2020 **Dozens** 400 **Vyds** 0.5ha
Winemaker Neil Pike has been part of the Clare Valley wine scene for 40 years and helped create and craft the success of Pikes Wines. He decided in January 2020 to retire from that juggernaut so the next generation could take over. It was time, but he wasn't finished with riesling. 'I truly love making wine, riesling in particular, and I certainly love drinking riesling. So limefinger is good fun.' Just 2 rieslings are made, one sourced from a vineyard he's long admired in Watervale, the other from the 500 vines planted at his home property in Polish Hill River. The rieslings are only available via limefinger's website or mailing list. (JF)

🍷🍷🍷🍷🍷 **The Learnings Watervale Riesling 2020** The limefinger label is Neil Pike's retirement project. The wine is indeed full of limes, but more kaffir leaves with Meyer lemon juice. While it's tangy and juicy, with superfine acidity, it has a softness and approachability, too. Lemon drops and a mouth-watering freshness. Glad he hasn't really retired. Screw cap. 12% alc. **Rating** 95 **To** 2030 $37 JF

Lindeman's (Coonawarra)   ★★★★★

Level 8, 161 Collins Street, Melbourne, Vic 3000 (postal) **Region** Coonawarra
T 1300 651 650 **www.**lindemans.com
Winemaker Brett Sharpe **Est.** 1965
Lindeman's Coonawarra vineyards have assumed a greater importance than ever thanks to the move towards single-region wines. The Coonawarra Trio of Limestone Ridge Vineyard Shiraz Cabernet, St George Vineyard Cabernet Sauvignon and Pyrus Cabernet Sauvignon Merlot Malbec are all of exemplary quality.

🍷🍷🍷🍷🍷 **Coonawarra Trio Limestone Ridge Vineyard Shiraz Cabernet 2018** An excellent rendition this vintage, with its 73/27 shiraz/cabernet split. If anything, it's almost a pared-back wine, full bodied for sure, yet with refinement, too. Expect dark plums and cassis, cedary oak and a sprinkle of mint. But the tannins, wow – supple and velvety. Screw cap. 13.7% alc. **Rating** 96 **To** 2033 $70 JF ✪

Coonawarra Trio St George Vineyard Cabernet Sauvignon 2018
This vintage has handed out an impressive Coonawarra Trio and one of the best St George wines. Of course, this is destined to garner more complexity

in time, but it's hard not to open it now and enjoy its youthful exuberance. A classy interplay of sweet and savoury, well-pitched oak, with distinct regional choc/eucalypt/mint flavours acting as seasoning across the shapely palate. Exemplary tannins and a persistent finish. Screw cap. 14.5% alc. **Rating** 96 To 2035 $70 JF ❂

Coonawarra Trio Pyrus Cabernet Sauvignon Merlot Malbec 2018 This is in tip-top form, starting with its enticing dark purple/red hue. A cascade of dark, sweet fruit come liberally fragrant, with baking spices and choc-mint. They follow through on a full-bodied yet neatly contained palate that offers up beautiful cocoa-like tannins. Screw cap. 13.9% alc. **Rating** 95 **To** 2038 $70 JF

Lindeman's (Hunter Valley)

Level 8, 161 Collins Street, Melbourne, Vic 3000 (postal) **Region** Hunter Valley
T 1300 651 650 **www**.lindemans.com
Winemaker Wayne Falkenberg, Brett Sharpe **Est.** 1843
Just when I expected it least, Lindeman's has produced some seriously good wines from the Hunter Valley, and one half of the Lindeman's winemaking or marketing side (without talking to the other half) has exhumed some of the Bin number systems that were used in the glory days of the 1960s, admittedly without total consistency. Thus for white wines, 50 or 55 were the last 2 digits used for what was named Riesling, 70 for what was named White Burgundy, and 75 for what was called Chablis; with the shiraz-based wines, the last 2 digits were 00, 03 or 10. The most famous were the 1965 Claret and Burgundy releases Bin 3100 and Bin 3110, the most famous Chablis 1967 Bin 3475.

Lindenderry at Red Hill

142 Arthurs Seat Road, Red Hill, Vic 3937 **Region** Mornington Peninsula
T (03) 5989 2933 **www**.lindenderry.com.au **Open** W'ends 11–5
Winemaker Barnaby Flanders **Est.** 1999 **Dozens** 1000 **Vyds** 3.35ha
Lindenderry at Red Hill is a sister operation to Lancemore Hill in the Macedon Ranges and Lindenwarrah at Milawa. It has a 5-star country house hotel, conference facilities, a function area, day spa and restaurant on 16ha of gardens. It also has a little over 3ha of vineyards, planted equally to pinot noir and chardonnay 20 years ago. Notwithstanding the reputation of the previous winemakers for Lindenderry, the wines now being made by Barney Flanders are the best yet. He has made the most of the estate-grown grapes, adding cream to the cake by sourcing some excellent Grampians shiraz.

🍷🍷🍷🍷🍷 **Mornington Peninsula Chardonnay 2019** Once the funky, flinty reduction takes a back seat, the stone fruit, vanilla-pod oak and citrus tones mingle upfront. Neat acidity keeps everything tidy. Screw cap. 13% alc. **Rating** 90 **To** 2028 $45 JF
Mornington Peninsula Pinot Noir 2019 A lighter offering, yet plenty of enticing aromatics. Florals, black cherries and powdered ginger on the nose, with the palate taking up chinotto and cardamom. Integrated oak adds shape and woodsy spices. Just the sinewy tannins need to settle in. Screw cap. 13% alc. **Rating** 90 **To** 2027 $45 JF

Lino Ramble

11 Gawler Street, Port Noarlunga, SA 5167 **Region** McLaren Vale
T 0409 553 448 **www**.linoramble.com.au **Open** W'ends 12–5
Winemaker Andy Coppard **Est.** 2012 **Dozens** 3500
After 20 years of working for other wine companies, big and small, interstate and international, Andy Coppard and Angela Townsend say, 'We've climbed on top of the dog kennel, tied a cape around our necks, held our breaths, and jumped'. And if you are curious about the name (as I was), the story has overtones of James Joyce's stream of consciousness mental rambles. Exports to Canada and Japan.

Lisa McGuigan Wines

2198 Broke Road, Pokolbin, NSW 2320 **Region** Various
T 0418 424 382 **www**.lisamcguiganwines.com **Open** Thurs–Mon 11–5
Winemaker Liz Silkman, Lisa McGuigan **Est.** 2010 **Dozens** 10000
Lisa McGuigan is a 4th-generation member of a famous Hunter Valley winemaking dynasty,
started many decades ago by Perc McGuigan and more recently (and perhaps more famously)
led by Brian McGuigan. In 1999 Lisa started Tempus Two from her garage, and under the
McGuigan-Simeon (now Australian Vintage) umbrella, the volume rose to 250000 dozen
before she left in 2007 to start a retail wine business. In '10 she turned full circle, starting her
own business in the Hunter Valley and using the winemaking skills of Liz Silkman, whom she
had headhunted for Tempus Two, and who is now also chief winemaker at First Creek Wines.
Lisa opened her cellar door in December '19. Located within the Blaxland's complex on
Broke Road, the VAMP venue and wine room brings together wine, oysters, art and fashion.

Velvet Yarra Valley Pinot Noir 2019 Strawberry, red cherry and kirsch notes.
Mulled wine, too, with a whiff of clove, sassafras, orange peel and root spice.
Mocha/vanilla wood is noticeable but certainly not dominant, melding with the
bright acidity as a structural carriage, guiding the flavours long. Cork. 13.5% alc.
Rating 92 **To** 2027 $60 NG
Claudius Hemp Platinum Collection Hunter Valley Chardonnay 2019
Oak and tank fermented, before an infusion of hemp to impart 'a nutty finish'.
Otherwise, a stock standard contemporary domestic chardonnay. Cantaloupe
and white fig. Stone fruits, too. Creamy and nicely oak inflected, with hints of
nougatine and cashew. There is a herbal bitterness to this, marking the finish.
Not unattractive. Presumably the hemp. Mid weighted, round and of solid length.
Screw cap. 13.5% alc. **Rating** 90 **To** 2025 $35 NG

Platinum Collection Hunter Valley Grüner Veltliner 2019 Rating 89
To 2024 $35 NG

Livewire Wines

PO Box 369, Portarlington, Vic 3223 **Region** Geelong
T 0439 024 007 **www**.livewirewines.com.au
Winemaker Anthony Brain **Est.** 2011 **Dozens** 1000
Anthony Brain started working life as a chef, but in the late 1990s 'took a slight bend into
the wine industry'. He started gathering experience in the Yarra Valley, and simultaneously
started oenology studies at CSU. Margaret River followed, as did time in SA before a return
to the Yarra, working at De Bortoli from 2003 to '07 (undertaking vintages in the Hunter,
King and Yarra valleys). Five vintages as winemaker at Bellarine Estate followed, giving him
'a platform and understanding of the Geelong region and the opportunity to learn more
about sites, viticulture and winemaking decisions'. It hasn't prevented him from foraging far
and wide.

Bellarine Peninsula Pinot Noir 2018 Moves away from the perky and fruity
to venture down a savoury road, embedded with exotic and musky spice, dusty
beetroot, tilled earth, black cherry and anise. A herbal thread runs deep, cutting the
edges on the palate and providing the structure. Screw cap. 12.6% alc. **Rating** 89
To 2025 $32 JP
Valley of the Moon Arinto 2019 Riverland fruit. An impressive amount
of work involved in the winery here for such a relatively modest price. This
Portuguese white grape comes out the other side waxy and soft in texture with
honeysuckle, pear, ginger and a preserved lemon/savoury twist. Some generous
flavour across the board. Screw cap. 12.4% alc. **Rating** 88 **To** 2024 $27 JP
RxV Riesling Viognier 2019 A 50/50 blend of riesling and viognier that spent
5 months on skin. Skin contact delivers a rich, golden colour to this wine. The
scent of fruit orchards with apricot, Golden Delicious apples, honeysuckle and
jasmine. The wine is generous in concentrated flavour and phenolic texture but
also delivers freshness. Screw cap. **Rating** 88 **To** 2023 $36 JP

Valley of the Moon Tempranillo 2019 A striking, fresh tempranillo that translates the grape's vibrancy into one enjoyable, easy-drinking wine. Fruit-proud, it exudes ripe black cherries, berries, red licorice and spicy aromas. To taste, it shows its dark, earthy, spicy side with light, savoury tannins. Made to drink young. Screw cap. 13.2% alc. **Rating** 88 **To** 2023 $27 JP

Liz Heidenreich Wines

PO Box 783, Clare, SA 5453 **Region** Clare Valley
T 0407 710 244 **www.**lizheidenreichwines.com
Winemaker Liz Heidenreich **Est.** 2018 **Dozens** 2000 **Vyds** 6ha
In 1866 Liz Heidenreich's great-great-grandfather Georg Adam Heidenreich, a Lutheran minister, was sent from Hamburg to the Barossa Valley to provide religious care and instruction for those living in the parish of Bethany. In 1936 Liz Heidenreich's grandfather planted vines at Vine Vale; those vines are still in production, still owned and managed by the Heidenreich family. After 15 years as an intensive care nurse, Liz decided to follow her family heritage and enrolled in a post-graduate winemaking degree course at the University of Adelaide. After working in many different winemaking regions in Australia and abroad, she says her spiritual wine homes are the Barossa and Clare valleys. The red wines she makes are from the family-owned old vines in the Barossa Valley, while her other focus of riesling comes from the Clare Valley, more particularly O'Leary Walker, where she makes small parcels of fruit and also undertakes the contract winemaking of Peter Teakle wines. Exports to China.

Barossa Valley Shiraz 2018 Made in a more restrained style, eschewing overripe fruit. It's a lovely wine. More red fruit upfront, with orange juice freshness; earthy with red licorice and smells of joss sticks. Fuller-bodied tannins, quite pliant, with a succulence that makes it very appealing. Screw cap. 14.3% alc. **Rating** 95 **To** 2030 $30 JF ✪
Barossa Valley Grenache 2019 Very nice wine. Deep, earthy, awash with dark fruits, woodsy spices and oak flavour, which needs to settle. Full bodied and savoury, with sandpaper-fine tannins and excellent length. This is going to hang around for some time. Compelling now though, if you let it breathe. Screw cap. 14.3% alc. **Rating** 95 **To** 2033 $30 JF ✪
Watervale Clare Valley Riesling 2020 A pure and pristine riesling. Gentle. It slips in some florals, chalky acidity and lime zest. A bit more comes out in time. Lemony bath salts and wet stones. It has a quiet presence. A lovely drink. Screw cap. 11.7% alc. **Rating** 94 **To** 2029 $24 JF ✪

Lloyd Brothers

34 Warners Road, McLaren Vale, SA 5171 **Region** McLaren Vale
T (08) 8323 8792 **www.**lloydbrothers.com.au **Open** 7 days 11–5
Winemaker Ross Durbidge **Est.** 2002 **Dozens** 10 000 **Vyds** 42.4ha
Lloyd Brothers Wine and Olive Company is owned and operated by David and Matthew Lloyd, 3rd-generation McLaren Vale vignerons. Their 25ha estate overlooks the township, and is planted to 20ha shiraz, 2.5ha bushvine grenache and 1ha bushvine mataro (plus 18.9ha of sauvignon blanc, chardonnay, pinot gris and shiraz in the Adelaide Hills). The shiraz planting allows the creation of a full range of styles, including Rosé, Sparkling Shiraz, Fortified Shiraz and Estate Shiraz, along with the White Chalk Shiraz, so named because of the white chalk used to mark each barrel during the classification process. Exports to the UK.

McLaren Vale Grenache Shiraz Mourvèdre 2019 Each variety fermented and aged separately for 14 months in seasoned French wood, including some barriques. A swathe of bitter chocolate and oak-derived vanillans meld with blue fruits, kirsch, anise and clove. Expansive and luxuriant, as much as it is taut and energetic. A complex juxtaposition, with firm, briary tannins to conclude. Screw cap. 14.5% alc. **Rating** 95 **To** 2028 $35 NG ✪

Western Block 2 McLaren Vale Shiraz 2019 Rating 93 **To** 2035 $45 NG
White Chalk McLaren Vale Shiraz 2016 Rating 93 **To** 2035 $70 NG

Lobethal Road Wines

2254 Onkaparinga Valley Road, Mount Torrens, SA 5244 **Region** Adelaide Hills
T (08) 8389 4595 **www**.lobethalroad.com **Open** Thurs–Mon 11–5
Winemaker Michael Sykes **Est.** 1998 **Dozens** 7500 **Vyds** 10.5ha

Dave Neyle and Inga Lidums bring diverse, but very relevant, experience to the Lobethal Road vineyard; the lion's share planted to shiraz, with smaller amounts of chardonnay, tempranillo, sauvignon blanc, graciano, pinot gris and roussanne. Dave has been in vineyard development and management in SA and Tasmania since 1990. Inga has 25+ years' experience in marketing and graphic design in Australia and overseas, with a focus on the wine and food industries. The property is managed with minimal chemical input. Exports to the UK and Switzerland.

Adelaide Hills Sauvignon Blanc 2020 From the spiritual home (in Australia) of elegant, fine-boned sauvignon blanc springs this pretty little thing. Juniper berry, white currant, hints of cassis, green apple, white pear and sugar snap peas. The palate is whippy, persistent, deceptively concentrated and very long. Compelling wine for the price. Screw cap. 12% alc. **Rating** 93 **To** 2024 $25 EL ✪

Adelaide Hills Pinot Gris 2020 The acidity (assuming due to elevated sites) gives a little zing on the palate, while the summer nashi pears, sugar snap peas and juniper berry flesh out things around it. The oak is felt from the mid palate onwards which does distract a bit, but otherwise a lovely wine with good length. Screw cap. 13.1% alc. **Rating** 92 **To** 2025 $25 EL ✪

Adelaide Hills Chardonnay 2020 Very pure, cool-climate chardonnay. Aromas of fresh vanilla pod, juniper berry, white peach and a dash of mulberry make for a lithe and delicate wine. Good length of flavour finishes this off. Quite lovely. Screw cap. 13.4% alc. **Rating** 91 **To** 2027 $25 EL

Adelaide Hills Pinot Noir 2019 Very detailed, with medicinal, crushed-ant characters on both the nose and palate, backed by pink berry fruit and held together by fine, salty acidity. On the piquant side of the street, with lingering length of flavour. Screw cap. 11.8% alc. **Rating** 91 **To** 2027 $25 EL

Adelaide Hills Shiraz 2018 Matured for 12 months in seasoned French oak barriques. This is a cool-climate iteration with lush summer mulberry sprinkled with ground white pepper. Fine, pretty and savoury, all told, with good length of flavour to round it out. There is a very attractive Rhône reduction here that adds an extra dimension of interest. Screw cap. 14.2% alc. **Rating** 90 **To** 2028 $25 EL

Maja Blanc de Blancs 2017 Matured on lees for 36 months, disgorged December 2020. Bright straw; delicate curls of lemon curd and oyster shell float out of the glass. On the palate it is fine and wispy again, the phenolics taking on a gently bitter edge through the finish. Quite lovely in all other respects. Diam. 12.3% alc. **Rating** 90 $50 EL

Local Weirdos

144A Bulwer Street, Perth WA 6000 (postal) **Region** Swan Valley
T 0413 355 451 **www**.localweirdos.wine
Winemaker Sam Jorgensen **Est.** 2020 **Dozens** 450 **Vyds** 3.2ha

An idea born of 5 mates with a shared love of wine: Sam Jorgensen, Dave Cosford, Larry Jorgensen, Charles Stewart and Matthew Stewart. They are focused on 2 core principles at this stage: minimally messed with wines picked from vineyards that have been treated the same, and from the Swan Valley. The Swan has a long and rich history that has for many years fallen out of favour with the general public but is currently experiencing a resurgence of popularity, thanks to producers like these guys, ensuring that the wines are listed at premium venues around the state – a big move for the Valley. The Local Weirdos represent the younger generation of the Swan Valley who are pushing boundaries and making wines that suit the modern palate, using very old techniques like the Georgian qvevri-fermented and aged Chateau da Swan Grenache. (EL)

Turbulent Juice Swan Valley Semillon 2020 Burnt amber in the glass, this has the sexy sway of skin on the nose – orange zest, mandarin pith, jasmine tea, rockmelon, cloves, fennel flower, cracked pepper, cinnamon sticks. Without putting everything on the shelf into the trolley, hopefully it will be sufficient to say that these complex fruit flavours are wedged between layers of bitter tannins and briny acid. Yes. Diam. 11.6% alc. **Rating** 94 **To** 2027 $40 EL

Chateau da Swan Qvevri Grenache 2020 Fermented and matured in a 1000L Georgian qvevri. Zero additions. Bouquet garni of all spice, coriander seed, mustard, orange zest and green olive. These are sprinkled across raspberry and black cherry. Red licorice and star anise cluster on the palate and send out little shooting stars of acidity into every corner of the mouth. Cleansing yet grippy, this is an amalgam of texture and experience. So Old World that it's new again, made by a group of young wine fanatics in the Swan. Not a traditional grenache by any means. An important wine. Glorious. Challenging. Exciting. Diam. 13.1% alc. **Rating** 94 **To** 2025 $45 EL

🍷🍷🍷🍷🍷 **Big Valley Bombo Swan Valley Semillon Grenache 2020** **Rating** 92 **To** 2023 $35 EL

Lofty Valley Wines

110 Collins Road, Summertown, SA 5141 **Region** Adelaide Hills
T 0400 930 818 **www.**loftyvalleywines.com.au **Open** Wends by appt
Winemaker Peter Leske **Est.** 2004 **Dozens** 400 **Vyds** 3ha
Medical practitioner Dr Brian Gilbert began collecting wine when he was 19, flirting with the idea of becoming a winemaker before being pointed firmly in the direction of medicine by his parents. Thirty or so years later he purchased a blackberry- and gorse-infested 12ha property in the Adelaide Hills, eventually obtaining permission to establish a vineyard. Chardonnay (2ha) was planted in 2004 and 1ha of pinot noir in '07, both on steep slopes.

🍷🍷🍷🍷🍷 **Steeped Single Vineyard Adelaide Hills Pinot Noir 2019** Piccadilly Valley fruit with one-third whole bunch and 30% in new French oak. Fruit intensity is right there from the start, classic cherry notes then with a more individual feel in a Chinese braise with five-spice kind of space, associated woody elements and light grip heading to the exit. Has some appeal. Screw cap. 13.5% alc. **Rating** 91 **To** 2025 $40 TL

🍷🍷🍷🍷 **Ascent Single Vineyard Adelaide Hills Chardonnay 2019** **Rating** 89 **To** 2025 $35 TL
Lattitude Adelaide Hills Sparkling 2017 **Rating** 89 $50 TL

Logan Wines

1320 Castlereagh Highway, Apple Tree Flat, Mudgee, NSW 2850 **Region** Mudgee
T (02) 6373 1333 **www.**loganwines.com.au **Open** 7 days 10–5
Winemaker Peter Logan, Jake Sheedy **Est.** 1997 **Dozens** 50 000
Logan is a family-owned and operated business with an emphasis on cool-climate wines from Orange and Mudgee. Owner and head winemaker Peter Logan majored in biology and chemistry at Macquarie University, moving into the pharmaceutical world working as a process chemist. In a reversal of the usual roles, his father encouraged him to change careers and Peter obtained a graduate diploma in oenology from the University of Adelaide in 1996. The winery and tasting room are situated on the Mudgee vineyard in Apple Tree Flat. Exports to the EU, Japan and other major markets.

🍷🍷🍷🍷🍷 **Ridge of Tears Orange Shiraz 2018** This is very good. Aromatic and pulpy. Despite the clear intensity of flavour, extract of fruit and weight, this is deft of detail and light on its feet. Detailed, transparent and boasting the clarity of 970m elevation. Scents of mace, rhubarb, saddle leather, salumi and lilac. The acidity, bright and juicy, tows the tail long. The belt of reduction across the mid palate, applied with poise and drinkability in mind. Approachable already. Will also age with grace. Screw cap. 14% alc. **Rating** 95 **To** 2030 $50 NG

🍷🍷🍷🍷🍷 Vintage M Orange Cuvée 2017 Rating 93 $40 NG
Weemala Orange Pinot Gris 2020 Rating 92 To 2024 $20 NG ⊙
Clementine Orange Pinot Gris 2019 Rating 92 To 2024 $25 NG ⊙
Weemala Mudgee Tempranillo 2019 Rating 92 To 2026 $20 NG ⊙
Weemala Orange Riesling 2019 Rating 91 To 2027 $20 NG ⊙
Weemala Orange Pinot Noir 2020 Rating 90 To 2025 $20 NG ⊙
Ridge of Tears Mudgee Shiraz 2018 Rating 90 To 2028 $50 NG
Clementine Blushing Minnie Orange Pinots 2019 Rating 90 To 2022
$25 NG

 # Lone Star Creek Vineyard ★★★★

75 Owens Rd, Woori Yallock VIC, 3139 **Region** Yarra Valley
T 0414282629 **www.**lonestarcreekwines.com.au
Winemaker Franco D'Anna **Est.** 1997 **Dozens** 800 **Vyds** 22ha
The Lone Star Creek vineyard was established in 1997 by Robin Wood and Gillian Bowers, who are primarily contract growers; 2017 was the first vintage under their own label. Pinot noir (52%), pinot gris (23%), chardonnay (15%), sauvignon blanc (5%) and syrah (5%) are planted. Situated on the border of Woori Yallock and Hoddle's Creek, the cool-climate upper Yarra fruit was sold to wineries including Hoddle's Creek Estate, so when the time came to start producing wine under the Lone Star Creek Vineyard label, enlisting Hoddle's Creek's own Franco D'Anna as winemaker must have seemed an obvious choice. The vineyard is not subject to strictly organic management, but the philosophy with both the viticulture and winemaking is one of minimal intervention throughout the entire process. The current range of wines are very moderately priced, all things considered. (SC)

🍷🍷🍷🍷🍷 Chardonnay 2019 Wild-yeast fermented, 9 months on lees in new and used French oak barriques. Has complexity on the bouquet, with grilled nuts, stone fruit, vanilla and some chalky minerality all part of the picture. It gives the impression of being a little lean on the palate, but the texture and acidity propel it along and it sustains well on the finish. Cool-climate elegance on show, you could say. Screw cap. 12.5% alc. Rating 93 To 2029 $24 SC ⊙
Pinot Noir 2020 It seems reds, pinot noir particularly, come loaded with acid and a lighter frame this vintage. This is simply made but it's a little beauty. A core of tangy juicy fruit, super fragrant and so juicy with shy tannins. A light red to enjoy in its youth. Spot-on. Screw cap. 12.5% alc. Rating 93 To 2025 $28 JF
Red 2020 60% pinot noir, all destemmed and 40% syrah with 25% whole bunches, fermented separately. It's part of the light dry red movement in the Yarra. This is just right. Savoury yet juicy, light and bright with enough textural tannins and lively acidity to go another round. Or three. Screw cap. 13% alc. Rating 93 To 2025 $27 JF ⊙
Sauvignon Blanc 2019 Barrel fermented and aged on lees in older French barriques for around 6 months prior to bottling. Really interesting and attractive combination of smoky/flinty characters and almost tropical fruit on the bouquet. Brisk with acidity and racy along the palate, but textural as well, from the oak maturation. Likely to be even better with a little more time in the bottle. Great value. Screw cap. 12% alc. Rating 92 To 2025 $20 SC ⊙
Chardonnay 2020 Lots of zest appeal here, taking off with all manner of citrus flavours and lemon blossom florals too. There's texture with some lees influence imparting grilled nuts and creamy curd. A shapely wine with soft acidity gently leading it to the finishing line. Screw cap. 12.5% alc. Rating 92 To 2026 $25 JF ⊙
Pinot Gris 2020 A lovely copper/pink blush; lots of crunchy red apples and pears too. Spicy with a squirt of lemon juice throughout. While it has texture, it's quite a tight gris. Screw cap. 12.5% alc. Rating 92 To 2023 $22 JF ⊙
Pinot Gris 2019 Some skin contact and lees ageing in oak. Distinctly bronze-pink in colour, almost like a pale rosé. Pear and red apple on the bouquet and something that makes me think of green mango. Quite generous in flavour and mouthfilling without being sweet-fruited; the soft acidity keeps things tight

and provides the freshness on the finish. Deftly made and very good drinking. Screw cap. 12.5% alc. **Rating** 92 **To** 2025 $22 SC ✪

Pinot Noir 2019 Nine months in new (25%) and used French barriques. Sappy, sour cherry notes the main theme as you take a first sniff, oak spice and some twiggy forest-floor characters in the background. Sweet red-berried fruit is the introduction on the palate, but it develops a more structural feeling as it goes along, finishing with surprisingly firm tannin. I'd give this a year or so to find its feet. Screw cap. 13% alc. **Rating** 92 **To** 2029 $27 SC

Syrah 2019 Grapes are 75% crushed/destemmed, 25% whole bunch, all open-fermented. Looks good in the glass – bright, intense crimson right to the edge. A panoply of cool-climate shiraz aromas here, including both sweet and peppery spice, capsicum, sour cherry, dry wood and a hint of mezcal. Soft and finely boned on the palate, it will benefit from time to flesh out, but it won't need ages in the cellar. Screw cap. 13% alc. **Rating** 91 **To** 2029 $27 SC

Lonely Shore ★★★★

18 Bavin Street, Denmark, WA 6333 (postal) **Region** Denmark
T 0418 907 594 **www.**lonelyshore.com.au
Winemaker Liam Carmody **Est.** 2014 **Dozens** 200 **Vyds** 2ha

Liam Carmody's grandmother (Freda Vines) was the author of a historical novel published in 1958, telling the story of early settlement on the south coast of WA. Liam graduated from Curtin University in 2003, since working in Sonoma, California, NZ, France, South Africa and the Mornington Peninsula before settling in Denmark and taking up a full-time winemaking role at Forest Hill. Thus Lonely Shore is very much a busman's holiday. The grapes come from the dry-grown DeiTos Vineyard near Manjimup.

🍷🍷🍷🍷🍷 **DeiTos Vineyard Pinot Noir 2020** As is usual for this vineyard, the fruit is on the darker end of the spectrum: mulberry, black licorice, black cherry and exotic spice. The palate is structured, tannic and a wee bit grungy, propped up by a stemmy, bunchy character mid palate that lifts it way up. The acidity is cooling and woven through the finish. Another very smart release from Lonely Shore. Screw cap. 13.5% alc. **Rating** 95 **To** 2031 $35 EL ✪

Long Gully Estate ★★★★

100 Long Gully Road, Healesville, Vic 3777 **Region** Yarra Valley
T (03) 9510 5798 **www.**longgullyestate.com **Open** Fri–Sun 10–5
Winemaker Hamish Smith **Est.** 1982 **Dozens** 3500 **Vyds** 22ha

Established by Reiner and Irma Klapp in the 1980s, a declining Long Gully Estate was purchased in 2018 by the Magdziarz family (owners of nearby Warramunda) in partnership with Vin Lopes. Significant investment in the vineyards, cellar door and the winery followed, with winemakers living onsite in tents during the 2019 vintage and relying on fruit from Warramunda and elsewhere for both the 2019 and 2020 vintages. Plantings of chardonnay, pinot noir, cabernet sauvignon, sauvignon blanc, riesling, shiraz, merlot and viognier have been rescued, with further pinot noir and cabernet added in 2019. 2021 represents the first vintage from estate fruit under the new owners, and the first year wines have been submitted to the *Companion* in almost a decade. Exports to the UK, Switzerland, Singapore and China. (TS)

🍷🍷🍷🍷🍷 **Single Vineyard Yarra Valley Shiraz 2019** A vibrant purple/black hue immediately entices, as do the savoury aromas. Dark plums are all spiced up with licorice and the palate has some energy. It's a neatly contained wine, with raw silk tannins providing some grip to the finish. The acidity is bright and this feels good. Screw cap. 14% alc. **Rating** 92 **To** 2028 $38 JF

Yarra Valley Chardonnay 2020 A chardonnay in a skinny jeans phase, coming across a bit tight and lean. There are dabs of lemon juice and zest, appealing chalky acidity and a hint of texture. While more stuffing would help, it is refreshing, with a distinct lemon/saline tang on the finish. Screw cap. 12.5% alc. **Rating** 90 **To** 2026 $38 JF

Yarra Valley Rosé 2020 A pastel pink/copper hue; lots of bright fruit flavours from nectarines and plums, some raspberry lollies and a whisper of spice. Juicy, textural and quite a bit of body, with a sensation of sweetness on the finish, yet neat acidity too. Screw cap. 13.5% alc. **Rating** 90 **To** 2022 $28 JF

ϼϼϼϼ   **Single Vineyard Yarra Valley Pinot Noir 2020 Rating** 88 **To** 2026 $38 JF

Longline Wines   ★★★★★
PO Box 131, McLaren Vale, SA 5171 **Region** McLaren Vale/Adelaide Hills
T 0415 244 124 **www**.longlinewines.com.au
Winemaker Paul Carpenter **Est.** 2013 **Dozens** 800
The name reflects the changing nature of the Carpenter family's activities. Over 40 years ago Bob Carpenter gave up his job as a bank manager to become a longline fisherman at Goolwa; this was in turn replaced by a move to McLaren Vale for farming activities. Son Paul graduated from the University of Adelaide and began his professional life as a cereal researcher for the university, but a vintage job at Geoff Merrill Wines at the end of his university studies led him to switch to winemaking. Over the next 20 years he worked both locally and internationally, in the Rhône Valley and Beaujolais and at Archery Summit in Oregon. Back in Australia he worked for Hardys and Wirra Wirra, and is currently senior winemaker at Hardys Tintara. Together with partner Martine, he secures small parcels of outstanding grapes from 4 grower vineyards of grenache and shiraz (3 vineyards in McLaren Vale, the 4th in the Adelaide Hills).

Longview Vineyard   ★★★★★
154 Pound Road, Macclesfield, SA 5153 **Region** Adelaide Hills
T (08) 8388 9694 **www**.longviewvineyard.com.au **Open** Wed–Sun 11–4, Mon–Tues by appt
Winemaker Michael Sykes, Paul Hotker **Est.** 1995 **Dozens** 20 000 **Vyds** 59ha
With a lifelong involvement in wine and hospitality, the Saturno family has been at the helm of Longview since 2007. Plantings of barbera, grüner veltliner, riesling, pinot noir and new clones of chardonnay and pinot grigio were added to the existing shiraz, cabernet sauvignon, nebbiolo and sauvignon blanc. A new cellar door and kitchen was unveiled in '17, adding to 16 accommodation suites, a popular function room and unique food and wine events in the vineyard. Exports to the UK, Ireland, Canada, Denmark, Finland, Hungary, Germany, Singapore, Thailand, Hong Kong and China.

ϼϼϼϼϼ   **The Piece Shiraz 2018** The elite wine of the Longview family, with the best blocks separately vinified with 15% whole bunches included. Sophisticated shiraz weaving together dark fruit with a subtle baked-blackberry-pie note. Balanced, structured oak and tannins in play, every element in harmony as the wine lifts with energy and interest in the finish, yet with a sense of reserved manners at every turn. Diam. 14.5% alc. **Rating** 95 **To** 2030 $90 TL ♥

Macclesfield Grüner Veltliner 2020 One of the leading Adelaide Hills proponents of this variety, here deciding on free-run juice only, with lees returned later to soften and enrich the otherwise crisply structured palate. There's a slate-like sense to start, grapefruit and green pear, then add a dash of varietally typical white pepper, with an interesting parsnip-like line in the exit. Plenty to be captivated by. Screw cap. 12.5% alc. **Rating** 94 **To** 2024 $30 TL ✪

Nebbiolo Rosato 2020 An all-nebbiolo pinkie with the palest of copper hues, focusing on one of Longview's major varietal assets. The fragrance here is so captivating – orange peel and cut white strawberry tops, reverbing in the mouth with exciting tang, a peppery spice energy, and penetrating acidity. Mouth freshener of the highest calibre. Screw cap. 13% alc. **Rating** 94 **To** 2022 $26 TL ✪

Macclesfield Cabernet Sauvignon 2019 A new range from the Longview crew offers more defined vineyard block selection, here matched with a gentle winemaking approach that allows this cabernet to be a little more reserved, yet totally on point, varietally speaking. The cabernet senses are there, black fruits, a note of cassis, a faint backdrop of mint and dark chocolate, all collected and steered forward by obvious but sensitively structured cabernet tannins. This drinks well now and will delight further over a decade. Screw cap. 14% alc. **Rating** 94 **To** 2030 $45 TL

Fresco 2020 A light-hearted spring/summer red created from 80/16/4% nebbiolo/pinot nero/barbera, fragrant, with crushed berries, a smatter of spice on the palate and the finest of tannin pinches to handle snacking, pizzas and pasta. A great example of a youthful, lighter-handled red wine that hits all the style and trend boxes. Screw cap. 14% alc. **Rating** 94 **To** 2023 $32 TL

ƷƷƷƷƷ **Saturnus Nebbiolo 2019** Rating 93 To 2030 $50 TL
Macclesfield Syrah 2019 Rating 92 To 2028 $45 TL
Queenie Adelaide Hills Pinot Grigio 2020 Rating 91 To 2023 $23 TL ◐
LV Shiraz Cabernet Sauvignon 2018 Rating 91 To 2030 $24 TL

 # Lost Farm Wines

527 Glynburn Road, Hazelwood Park, SA 5063 **Region** Tasmania
T (08) 8397 7100 **www**.lostfarmwines.com.au
Winemaker Richard Angove **Est.** 2018 **Dozens** 2000
Fifth-generation South Australian winemaker and grape grower Richard Angove fell in love with the Tamar Valley while working vintage in 2008, but it took him a decade to realise his ambition to work with a small group of growers to produce wines in the region. Sparkling, pinot noir and a stunning chardonnay are made from well-established vineyards in the Tamar Valley. (TS)

ƷƷƷƷƷ **Tasmania Chardonnay 2019** Sophisticated Tasmanian chardonnay, confidently uniting the struck-flint complexity of fermentation with classy French oak cashew nut notes and the cool tension of lemon and white peach. The creamy texture of barrel work harmonises with crystalline acidity, well-married to fruit concentration and body. It holds every detail through an enduring finish. Screw cap. 13.5% alc. **Rating** 96 **To** 2029 $42 TS ◐

ƷƷƷƷƷ **Tasmania Pinot Noir Chardonnay 2015** Rating 91 To 2021 $48 TS

 # Lost Penny

538 Carrara Hill Road, Ebenezer, SA 5355 **Region** Barossa Valley
T 0418 857 094 **www**.lostpennywines.com **Open** By appt
Winemaker Carol Riebke **Est.** 2017 **Dozens** 650 **Vyds** 32.6ha
Sixth-generation Barossan winemaker and grapegrower couple Carol and Nick Riebke bottle shiraz, cabernet sauvignon and grenache primarily from their estate vineyard in Ebenezer, passed down through Nick's family since the late 1800s (and in which an 1891 penny was recently discovered). Carol learnt her craft under Barossa winemaking legend John Glaetzer before establishing their family brand. 'We're gamblers!' Nick admits. 'It's the risk, the anticipation and the intrigue about what the next season will bring that keep us coming back for more!' Exports to Switzerland. (TS)

ƷƷƷƷƷ **Money Garden Barossa Valley Cabernet Sauvignon 2018** From an estate vineyard in Ebenezer, matured 18 months in French oak barrels. Medium purple red. Ripe black/redcurrant and cherry fruit is accented by varietal notes of leaf and capsicum. French oak lends both nutty dark chocolate backing and firm, fine tannin structure, sitting disjoint currently but all in the right places for medium-term development. It concludes with even line and length. Diam. 14% alc. **Rating** 90 **To** 2032 $30 TS

ƷƷƷƷ **Almond Row Barossa Valley Shiraz 2018** Rating 89 To 2022 $30 TS

Lou Miranda Estate

1876 Barossa Valley Way, Rowland Flat, SA 5352 **Region** Barossa Valley
T (08) 8524 4537 **www**.loumirandaestate.com.au **Open** Mon–Fri 10.30–4, w'ends 11–4
Winemaker Angela Miranda **Est.** 2005 **Dozens** 20 000 **Vyds** 23.29ha
Lou Miranda's daughters Lisa, Angela and Victoria are the driving force behind the estate, albeit with continuing hands-on involvement from Lou. The jewels in the crown of the estate plantings are 0.5ha of mourvèdre planted in 1897 and 1.5ha of shiraz (and a tiny 0.14ha grenache) planted in 1907. The remaining vines have been planted gradually since '95, the varietal choice widened by cabernet sauvignon, merlot, chardonnay and pinot grigio. Exports to all major markets.

 ## Lowboi

PO Box 40, Denmark, WA 6333 **Region** Great Southern
T 0438 849 592 **www**.lowboiwines.com.au
Winemaker Guy Lyons **Est.** 2017 **Dozens** 400 **Vyds** 3.5ha
In 2017 winemaker Guy Lyons (Forest Hill) and his wife bought the Springviews vineyard on the south side of the dramatically beautiful Porongurup range in Great Southern and created their brand, Lowboi. Planted in 1985, the vineyard orientation is east–west and was established as a dry-grown site, although irrigation was added in 2020 due to constant water pressure in the area. The soils are layered laterite gravels with loam and weathered granite. Planted on the south-facing slope is riesling and Gingin clone chardonnay. Their grüner veltliner comes from the Lyons family farm in Mount Barker. The 'Lowboi' name originates from the farm Lyons' mother grew up on in the Great Southern shire of Tambellup. (EL)

🍷🍷🍷🍷🍷 **Porongurup Riesling 2020** The year 2020 was a warm, generous vintage, but thanks to the cool aspect of the site this is exploding with spring florals, citrus blossom and green apple. The palate is laced with fine, talcy phenolics. All coiled power and grace. Epic length. What a wine. Screw cap. 12.5% alc. **Rating** 96 To 2040 $36 EL ✪

Porongurup Chardonnay 2018 There is something very special about the Springviews vineyard site, and this wine. Flinty, fine, cool-climate chardonnay here, with layers of curry leaf, brine, citrus pith, white peach, nectarine, cap gun and fennel flower. The phenolics have a jasmine tea character to them, and cradle the fruit in the cups of their hands, all the way across the palate and into a long finish. Screw cap. 13% alc. **Rating** 96 To 2036 $40 EL ✪

Mount Barker Grüner Veltliner 2020 Densely packed with flavour and showing the Mount Barker muscle, this is concentrated, dense and long, with a swathe of exotic spice and grilled citrus fruit. Another firm statement of talent for winemaker Guy Lyons. Screw cap. 12.5% alc. **Rating** 95 To 2031 $32 EL ✪

Lowe Wines

327 Tinja Lane, Mudgee, NSW 2850 **Region** Mudgee
T (02) 6372 0800 **www**.lowewine.com.au **Open** 7 days 10–5
Winemaker Dr Tim White, David Lowe **Est.** 1987 **Dozens** 15 000 **Vyds** 11.5ha
The Tinja property has been in the Lowe family for 5 generations; vines were first planted here in the 1970s. The 11.5ha of certified organic/biodynamic vineyards are unirrigated and untrellised. The focus is 'gutsy' red wine, from shiraz, merlot and zinfandel planted in the '90s – the zin producing what Ned Goodwin MW describes as Australia's 'finest example'. Fruit is also sourced from growers in other regions for the entry-level Dragonfly range. A Chef-Hatted restaurant (The Zin House), an extensive permaculture/market garden and a large events pavilion look out over scenic farmland. (TS)

🍷🍷🍷🍷🍷 **Mudgee Cabernet Sauvignon 2018** A sizzle of volatility imparts verve. Mulberry and hedgerow; mocha and coffee-bean tannin from the oak. Most impressionable, a layer of pulpy grape extract, Ribena-like, buffering the substantial finish with fine-grained tannin, attenuated and lithe. A bit rustic, but plenty in store. Cork. 14.3% alc. **Rating** 95 To 2030 $50 NG

Organic Mudgee Zinfandel 2018 A variety seldom seen in these parts, but after working extensively in California, I can unequivocally state that this is the finest example on these shores. Fecund apricot scents dance with ripe cherry and plum, maraschino cherry, olive and licorice. The swathe of tannins are dusty and pliant. The bristle of oak a guide, rather than a hurdle. Not hard. Plush and unashamed. Cork. 15.1% alc. **Rating** 95 **To** 2028 $95 NG

 **Block 8 Organic Mudgee Shiraz 2018 Rating** 93 **To** 2032 $35 NG
Block 5 Reserve Mudgee Shiraz 2018 Rating 93 **To** 2030 $75 NG
Red Gold Mudgee 2018 Rating 92 **To** 2023 $30 NG
Block 5 Organic Shiraz 2018 Rating 91 **To** 2028 $75 NG

Lowestoft ★★★★☆

680 Main Road, Berriedale, Tas 7011 **Region** Tasmania
T (08) 9282 5450 **www**.fogarty.wine **Open** By appt
Winemaker Liam McElhinney **Est.** 2019 **Dozens** 1250 **Vyds** 3ha
The premium Tasmanian brand of WA-based Fogarty Wine Group, Lowestoft is Tasmania's most exciting new label this year. The group purchased the 3ha Lowestoft vineyard and historic house at Berriedale near Mona just north of Hobart in 2019. Its impressive inaugural release from the same year encompasses sourcing from across Southern Tasmania and the Tamar Valley. Substantial plantings on 2 properties at Forcett and Richmond in the Coal River Valley bring the group's holdings to some 200ha, making this Tasmania's second-largest vineyard owner. Winemaking is conducted at Tasmanian Vintners (formerly Winemaking Tasmania), the state's biggest contract facility, in which the group purchased a 50% share. Lowestoft is a worthy newcomer to Fogarty's lauded suite of boutique wineries across Western Australia, Lake's Folly in the Hunter Valley and Dalwhinnie in the Pyrenees. (TS)

ŸŸŸŸŸ **Tasmania Chardonnay 2019** Launching Tasmania's most exciting new premium label, the Fogarty Group sure has hit the ground running. This is pitch-perfect chardonnay that embraces the generosity of a warm season and frames it intricately in crystalline acidity, top-class oak and just the right whiff of struck-flint reduction. Masterfully assembled and a joy to taste for the first time. Screw cap. 13% alc. **Rating** 96 **To** 2027 $65 TS ✪

ŸŸŸŸŸ **Single Vineyard Tasmania Pinot Noir 2019 Rating** 93 **To** 2034 $85 TS
La Maison Tasmania Pinot Noir 2019 Rating 92 **To** 2039 $175 TS

LS Merchants ★★★★★

163 Treeton Road North, Cowaramup, WA 6284 **Region** Margaret River
T 0492 962 348 **www**.lsmerchants.com.au **Open** Mon–Sat 10.30–4.30, Sun 10.30–6
Winemaker Dylan Arvidson **Est.** 2017 **Dozens** 7000
LS Merchants was started by Dylan Arvidson and his partner Taryn in 2017. Arvidson was born in Blenheim NZ, raised in Geelong, Victoria and moved to Margaret River in 2009 to work at Juniper Estate. LS Merchants is focused on making wine from many different regions in Western Australia (Margaret River, their base, the Great Southern and Geographe). While Arvidson adheres to a minimalist winemaking approach he does not identify as a 'natural winemaker', rather allowing wild fermentation to occur where possible and pushing wine grapes and styles in many different directions. There is plenty of variety in the LS Merchants portfolio, but they are bound together by his clean, bright and expressive winemaking style. (EL)

ŸŸŸŸŸ **470 Frankland River Shiraz 2019** Hoo boi. This is why Frankland River is making a name for itself; intensely inky, yet gravelly and textured. Salty red licorice, raspberry and full to bursting with titillating characters of brine, ferrous, kelp, red dirt, clear skies and vast vistas. OK – the red dirt, sky and vistas aren't included, but like all great wine – it's taking me there. The Frankland River shiraz style oozes pedigree … already. What a future lies in wait. Screw cap. 14.2% alc. **Rating** 95 **To** 2036 $45 EL

Margaret River Cabernet Sauvignon 2018 Cassis, ferrous, blood and plum, with lashings of raspberry, red apple skins and pink peppercorn. On the palate the wine is slinky and shapely, the tannins moulding the fruit through a long finish. Impressive 3rd release from a near-perfect vintage. Screw cap. 14% alc. **Rating** 95 To 2030 $45 EL

Margaret River Chardonnay 2020 Where the 2019 was racy, mineral and fine, this is concentrated, punchy and again – mineral. We can thank 2020 for the power; it was a warmer year, lower yielding, but by all accounts brilliant. As is this. Screw cap. 13.4% alc. **Rating** 94 To 2031 $37 EL

Margaret River Chardonnay 2019 The cooler year has created a wine of tension and nuttiness. This is both voluminous and focused at once, perhaps owing to the clonal blend (Gingin for explosiveness, Dijon for line). The acidity has a saltiness to it that will ensure evaporation of the bottle. Screw cap. 12.7% alc. **Rating** 94 To 2030 $37 EL

Margaret River Chenin Blanc 2019 Initially this drinks more like a flinty, funky chardonnay than a chenin, until the waxy mid palate kicks in – then it's all chenin sailing. Hints of summer florals and sheepy tufts pop up here and there, but it's the briny acid that really calls out the variety. Screw cap. 13.6% alc. **Rating** 94 To 2031 $30 EL ✪

Margaret River Vermentino 2020 OK, this is delicious. All the components are playing harmoniously here – the acidity is ripe and salty and the oak is seamlessly punched into the fruit, which speaks of nashi pear, crunchy green apples, summer florals and Asian spice ... there's a lot to like here. The phenolics are the final box ticked – chalky, fine and shapely. What a cracker. Screw cap. 12.9% alc. **Rating** 94 To 2026 $30 EL ✪

ŦŦŦŦŦ Red Blend 2020 Rating 93 To 2026 $30 EL
Margaret River Chenin Blanc 2020 Rating 92 To 2031 $30 EL
Frankland River Pinot Gris 2020 Rating 92 To 2025 $30 EL
Hoi Polloi Margaret River Cabernet Malbec 2019 Rating 91 To 2026 $25 EL

Lyons Will Estate ★★★★

60 Whalans Track, Lancefield, Vic 3435 **Region** Macedon Ranges
T 0412 681 940 **www**.lyonswillestate.com.au **Open** 2nd and 4th w'end of each month 11–5 or by appt
Winemaker Oliver Rapson, Renata Morello **Est.** 1996 **Dozens** 1000 **Vyds** 5.2ha
Oliver Rapson (with a background in digital advertising) and Renata Morello (a physiotherapist with a PhD in public health) believe the Macedon Ranges has the best of both worlds: less than an hour's drive to Melbourne, ideal for pinot and chardonnay and still sparsely settled. The property had 2ha of vines planted in 1996: pinot noir and chardonnay. Over time they have extended the pinot noir to 2ha and the chardonnay to 1.2ha, also planting 1ha each of riesling and gamay. Oliver makes the Pinot Noir and Chardonnay, Renata the Riesling and Gamay.

ŦŦŦŦŦ Macedon Ranges Chardonnay 2019 A very tight wine for a warm vintage, even in Macedon. A touch more fruit flavour would help. No shortage of acidity, it's mouth-watering and fresh. Linear and long with wafts of lemon blossom, a mere smidge of citrus and nougatine. There's a tangy juiciness and a desperate need for food to match. It will develop in a few years. Diam. 13% alc. **Rating** 92 To 2030 $42 JF

ŦŦŦŦ Macedon Ranges Gamay 2019 Rating 89 To 2025 $40 JF

M. Chapoutier Australia ★★★★☆

141-143 High Street, Heathcote, Vic 3523 **Region** Pyrenees/Heathcote
T (03) 5433 2411 **www**.mchapoutieraustralia.com **Open** W'ends 10–5 or by appt
Winemaker Michel Chapoutier **Est.** 1998 **Dozens** 8000 **Vyds** 48ha

M. Chapoutier Australia is the eponymous offshoot of the famous Rhône Valley producer. The business focuses on vineyards in the Pyrenees, Heathcote and Beechworth with collaboration from Ron Laughton of Jasper Hill and Rick Kinzbrunner of Giaconda. After first establishing a vineyard in Heathcote adjacent to Jasper Hill, Chapoutier purchased the Malakoff Vineyard in the Pyrenees to create Domaine Terlato & Chapoutier (the Terlato & Chapoutier joint venture was established in 2000; Terlato still owns 50% of the Malakoff Vineyard). In '09 Michel Chapoutier purchased 2 neighbouring vineyards, Landsborough Valley and Shays Flat; all these are now fully owned by Tournon. (Tournon consists of Landsborough Valley and Shays Flat estates in the Pyrenees and Lady's Lane Estate in Heathcote.) Exports to all major markets.

ΨΨΨΨΨ **Tournon Lady's Lane Vineyard Heathcote Shiraz 2018** Svelte but plush, solid in shiraz personality for the now, while keeping something in reserve for later. Lady's Lane does come with quite a dual personality. Blue fruits, dark berries and plums. Smooth across the palate, it's also lightly savoury. Keep looking and you see something different each time. Cork. 14.5% alc. **Rating** 95 **To** 2032 $50 JP
Domaine Terlato and Chapoutier L-Block Pyrenees Shiraz 2016 Plenty of concentration and interest here, with ripe blood plums, wild berries, earth and chocolate. At times elemental and fresh, this 5yo is still being formed, meshing savoury, toasty, spiced oak. A work in progress and looking good. Cork. 14% alc. **Rating** 94 **To** 2030 $80 JP

ΨΨΨΨΨ **Domaine Terlato and Chapoutier S-Block Pyrenees Shiraz 2016** **Rating** 92 **To** 2028 $60 JP
Tournon Shays Flat Vineyard Pyrenees Shiraz 2017 **Rating** 91 **To** 2027 $30 JP
Tournon Landsborough Vineyard Pyrenees Chardonnay 2019 **Rating** 90 **To** 2027 $30 JP
Tournon Landsborough Vineyard Pyrenees Viognier 2019 **Rating** 90 **To** 2026 $30 JP
Tournon Mathilda Victoria Viognier Marsanne 2019 **Rating** 90 **To** 2025 $15 JP ♻
Domaine Terlato and Chapoutier Lieu-Dit Malakoff Pyrenees Shiraz 2017 **Rating** 90 **To** 2032 $40 JP
Tournon Landsborough Vineyard Pyrenees Grenache Shiraz Touriga 2017 **Rating** 90 **To** 2024 $30 JP

Mac Forbes ★★★★★

Graceburn Wine Room, 11a Green Street, Healesville, Vic 3777 **Region** Yarra Valley/ Strathbogie Ranges
T (03) 9005 5822 **www**.macforbes.com **Open** Thurs–Sat 12–11, Sun–Mon 12–7
Winemaker Hannah Hodges **Est.** 2004 **Dozens** 8000 **Vyds** 13ha
Mac Forbes cut his vinous teeth at Mount Mary, where he was winemaker for several years before heading overseas in 2002. He spent 2 years in London working for Southcorp in a marketing liaison role, then travelled to Portugal and Austria to gain further winemaking experience. He returned to the Yarra Valley prior to the '05 vintage, purchasing grapes to make his own wines. He has a 2-tier portfolio: first, the Victorian range, employing unusual varieties or unusual winemaking techniques; and second, the Yarra Valley range of multiple terroir-based offerings of chardonnay and pinot noir. Exports to the UK, the US, Canada, Norway, Thailand, Singapore, Hong Kong and China.

Macaw Creek Wines ★★★★

Macaw Creek Road, Riverton, SA 5412 **Region** Mount Lofty Ranges
T (08) 8847 2657 **www**.macawcreekwines.com.au **Open** By appt
Winemaker Rodney Hooper **Est.** 1992 **Dozens** 8000 **Vyds** 10ha
The property on which Macaw Creek Wines is established has been owned by the Hooper family since the 1850s, but development of the estate vineyards did not begin until 1995.

The Macaw Creek brand was established in '92 with wines made from grapes from other regions. Rodney Hooper is a highly qualified and skilled winemaker with experience in many parts of Australia and in Germany, France and the US. The wines are certified organic and free of preservatives. Exports to Canada, Sweden, Norway, the Netherlands, Finland and China.

ŸŸŸŸŸ **Mount Lofty Ranges Cabernet Shiraz 2017** Matured 18 months in a range of oaks, adding some lovely background cedar and spice notes. The fruit aromatics and flavours are true to form, a blackberry and cassis lift to begin, with riper plum flowing onto the palate. Given the power and the fruit here, the tannin feel is proportionately spot on. Great value. Screw cap. 14% alc. **Rating** 95 **To** 2030 $21 TL ✪

ŸŸŸŸŸ **Reserve Mount Lofty Ranges Shiraz Malbec 2018 Rating** 93 **To** 2027 $35 TL
Basket Pressed Clare Valley Shiraz 2018 Rating 92 **To** 2027 $21 TL ✪
Organic Mount Lofty Ranges Riesling 2019 Rating 91 **To** 2026 $18 TL ✪

McGlashan's Wallington Estate ★★★★☆

225 Swan Bay Road, Wallington, Vic 3221 **Region** Geelong
T (03) 5250 5760 **www**.mcglashans.com.au **Open** Thurs–Sun & public hols 11–5, 7 days in Jan
Winemaker Robin Brockett (Contract) **Est.** 1996 **Dozens** 2500 **Vyds** 12ha
Russell and Jan McGlashan began the establishment of their vineyard in 1996. Chardonnay (6ha) and pinot noir (4ha) make up the bulk of the plantings, the remainder shiraz and pinot gris (1ha each). The wines are made by Robin Brockett, with his usual skill and attention to detail. The cellar door offers food and music, with 4 cottages offering vineyard accommodation.

ŸŸŸŸŸ **Bellarine Peninsula Chardonnay 2019** Displays Bellarine Peninsula sunny, pine/lime citrus characters, a strong calling card and very attractive. Mixes it up on the palate with green apple, white peach and mealy French oak. A supple chardonnay, creamy and generous in flavour. Screw cap. 13.5% alc. **Rating** 90 **To** 2026 $38 JP
Bellarine Peninsula Rosé 2020 Ah, the joy of a young rosé boasting all of the vibrancy of acidity and fruit captured just months before you broach the bottle. It's all here, nicely encapsulated in strawberry parfait, raspberry bon-bon, cranberry and musk florals, with a real zingy acidity. Screw cap. 12.5% alc. **Rating** 90 **To** 2023 $32 JP
Bellarine Peninsula Pinot Noir 2019 A very approachable, drink-me style that is in keeping with the previous '18 release. Some bright, delicious fruit on display in the red cherry spectrum, with sweet spice. A year in French oak has imparted balance and a light dusting of spice and texture. Screw cap. 13% alc. **Rating** 90 **To** 2026 $34 JP
Bellarine Peninsula Shiraz 2019 A move up in intensity, concentration and the role of 18 months in French and American oak, imparting robust tannins and toasty vanilla spice. For the Geelong region this is a hearty take on shiraz with blackberry, plum, dark chocolate and savouriness. Screw cap. 13.5% alc. **Rating** 90 **To** 2029 $45 JP

ŸŸŸŸ **Single Stave Bellarine Peninsula Chardonnay 2019 Rating** 89 **To** 2025 $32 JP
Bellarine Peninsula Pinot Grigio 2020 Rating 89 **To** 2025 $32 JP

McGuigan Wines ★★★★☆

447 McDonalds Road, Pokolbin, NSW 2320 **Region** Hunter Valley
T (02) 4998 4111 **www**.mcguiganwines.com.au **Open** 7 days 9.30–5
Winemaker Thomas Jung **Est.** 1992 **Dozens** 4.3 million **Vyds** 2000ha
McGuigan Wines is an Australian wine brand operating under parent company Australian Vintage Ltd. McGuigan represents 4 generations of Australian winemaking and, while its roots are firmly planted in the Hunter Valley, its vine holdings extend across SA, from the

Barossa Valley to the Adelaide Hills and the Eden and Clare valleys, into Victoria and NSW. McGuigan Wines' processing facilities operate out of 3 core regions: the Hunter Valley, Sunraysia and the Barossa Valley. Exports to all major markets.

McHenry Hohnen Vintners ★★★★★

5962 Caves Road, Margaret River, WA 6285 **Region** Margaret River
T (08) 9757 7600 **www.**mchenryhohnen.com.au **Open** 7 days 10.30–4.30
Winemaker Jacopo Dalli Cani **Est.** 2004 **Dozens** 7500 **Vyds** 50ha

The McHenry and Hohnen families have a long history of grapegrowing and winemaking in Margaret River. They joined forces in 2004 to create McHenry Hohnen with the aim of producing wines honest to region, site and variety. Vines have been established on the McHenry, Calgardup Brook and Rocky Road properties, all farmed biodynamically. Exports to the UK, Singapore, Japan and China.

♟♟♟♟♟ **Hazel's Vineyard Margaret River GSM 2019** Hazel's vineyard was only planted in 1999 and already this smacks of pedigree. Let's start at the finish: this is a ripping wine. It has both radiant and pretty fruit on nose and palate. Firm, structuring tannins pervade every aspect of the experience and the oak serves to hold it altogether in an unseen way. This is delicious and serious. Brilliant winemaking and craftsmanship. What a pleasure. Screw cap. 14.5% alc. **Rating** 97 To 2035 $40 EL **☼**

Rolling Stone Margaret River 2017 85/5/5/5% cabernet sauvignon/malbec/merlot/petit verdot from the biodynamically farmed Hazel's Vineyard (certified from 2021 vintage). 16 months in French oak (40% new). Savoury, oak-driven and structured tannins are the standout feature here; shapely, finely knit and supple. They provide a frame from which the red berries and exotic spice can hang. Long and rippling, this is a wine of savoury succulence and longevity. Screw cap. 14.1% alc. **Rating** 97 **To** 2046 $135 EL **☼**

♟♟♟♟♟ **Calgardup Brook Vineyard Margaret River Chardonnay 2019** This is perhaps my favourite (by a whisker) of these 2 single-vineyard chardonnays. It has a bitter phenolic kick through the finish that adds a layer of sparkle, interest and excitement to the wine and creates a salty undulation through the finish. It moves in a dappled way, this wine. I like it. Screw cap. 13.3% alc. **Rating** 96 **To** 2036 $65 EL **☼**

Hazel's Vineyard Margaret River Cabernet Sauvignon 2018 Savoury, textured and very long, this is not the succulent red-fruited explosion of Margaret River cabernets (neither a good nor bad thing, just an observation). It has the layered complexity we often find in Bordeaux, with a plumply satisfying core of cassis and redcurrant. Not overt, but restrained, with willowy tannins. Cellar or drink – both will bring immense pleasure. Screw cap. 14% alc. **Rating** 96 **To** 2041 $70 EL **☼**

Hazel's Vineyard Margaret River Chardonnay 2019 White spice, nectarine, coastal spray and crushed macadamia on the nose. The palate is where the mlf is evident; it creates a creamy, buttery texture that sits alongside the pink grapefruit and mandarin pith. Blossom and red apple skin round out the palate, the saline acidity forms curls of sensation as it fades. Screw cap. 13.3% alc. **Rating** 95 **To** 2036 $65 EL

Burnside Vineyard Margaret River Chardonnay 2019 From the oldest vines (planted 1981) the Burnside is the smoothest, most cohesive, most consistent of McHenry Hohnen's 3 single-vineyard chardonnays. This consistency on the palate breeds richness somehow, with mlf building density and resonance. Screw cap. 13.3% alc. **Rating** 95 **To** 2036 $65 EL

Laterite Hills Margaret River Chardonnay 2019 After a reticent bouquet, this springs into life on the palate with its clear-as-a-bell white peach/grapefruit varietal signature. French oak is little more than a shadow in the background, development potential unlimited. Screw cap. 13.3% alc. **Rating** 95 **To** 2034 $40 JH

Hazel's Vineyard Margaret River Syrah 2019 It seems these guys can't do any wrong at the moment. Layered, spicy, slightly reductive (in a good and engaging way), stemmy, juicy and delicious. Briny acid and red fruits. Savoury, structured and quite exciting, with the salted heirloom tomato character that so excites in shiraz/syrah. Screw cap. 14% alc. **Rating** 95 **To** 2038 $40 EL

Hazel's Vineyard Margaret River Zinfandel 2019 Wow – what a nose! An abundant spread of forest fruits; mulberry, raspberry, blackberry, five-spice and clove. Licorice and cocoa. The texture on the palate is chalky, the tannins soft but omnipresent. This is a cracker of a wine with balance, elegance and spice. It's got plushness and depth too, though. Screw cap. 14.2% alc. **Rating** 95 **To** 2030 $50 EL

Margaret River Marsanne Roussanne 2020 61% marsanne fermented in seasoned oak, 39% roussanne pressed to concrete egg. Matured separately on lees for 6 months prior to blending. The best examples of this Rhône blend can have a biscuity dryness that offsets the typically rich and opulent fruit characters of both varieties. And so here. Balanced and long, both components are stitched together with a thread of saline acidity. Screw cap. 13% alc. **Rating** 94 **To** 2031 $40 EL

♚♚♚♚♔ **Margaret River BDX 2019 Rating** 93 **To** 2031 $40 EL

McKellar Ridge Wines ★★★★☆

2 Euroka Avenue, Murrumbateman, NSW 2582 **Region** Canberra District
T 0407 482 707 **www**.mckellarridgewines.com.au **Open** W'ends 10–4
Winemaker John Sekoranja, Marina Sekoranja **Est.** 2005 **Dozens** 800 **Vyds** 5.5ha
Dr Brian Johnston established McKellar Ridge in 2005 and after 10 years decided it was time to retire. John and Marina Sekoranja worked with Brian for 12 months before purchasing the winery in July '17. Brian continued to provide support as winemaking consultant during vintage while John and Marina completed bachelor of wine science degrees at CSU. The change has seen an increase in the number of wines available, including from Tumbarumba.

♚♚♚♚♚ **Canberra District Shiraz 2019** There's such restraint across these reds, without losing any flavour. They are a joy to taste. A spot-on, cool-climate shiraz. It's full of red fruits, pepper and baking spices. Toasty oak is neatly integrated and the wine is actually earthy and savoury. Everything flows easily across its medium-bodied palate: it's buoyant, with wonderfully grainy tannins. Could drink this by the bucketload. Screw cap. 13.3% alc. **Rating** 95 **To** 2029 $45 JF

Canberra District Shiraz Viognier 2019 An exuberant purple/black hue, largely thanks to 3% viognier. It's altogether a fleshier and more dense wine compared with the straight Shiraz, but equally compelling. Nine months in French oak, 20% new, has an impact on the palate weight and tannins, but by and large, the core of dark, sweet, ripe fruit holds its own. More time to soften the tannins is certainly needed. Screw cap. 13.5% alc. **Rating** 95 **To** 2034 $50 JF

McLaren Vale III Associates ★★★★☆

McLaren Vale Visitor Centre, 796 Main Road, McLaren Vale, SA 5171
Region McLaren Vale
T 1800 501 513 **www**.mclarenvaleiiiassociates.com.au **Open** Mon–Fri 9–5, Sat–Sun 10–4
Winemaker Campbell Greer **Est.** 1999 **Dozens** 12000 **Vyds** 34ha
McLaren Vale III Associates is a very successful boutique winery owned by Mary and John Greer and Reg Wymond. An impressive portfolio of estate-grown wines allows them control over quality and consistency, and thus success in Australian and international wine shows. The cellar door is currently under reconstruction; wines can be tasted at the McLaren Vale Visitor Centre in the meantime. Exports to Hong Kong, Singapore and China.

♚♚♚♚♔ **The Descendant of Squid Ink Shiraz 2019** A solid wine blending an older-school approach with a more contemporary reductive edge: aromas of boysenberry, anise, clove and Dutch licorice. Some reductive handling promotes more contemporary notes of lilac florals, iodine and tapenade. The finish, a clang

of oak tannins, is a bit clumsy. Nevertheless, plenty of appeal. Screw cap. 14.5% alc.
Rating 91 To 2026 $43 NG
The Album Reserve Shiraz 2019 This is possibly the better wine of this (more
expensive) tier. 30% whole bunch imparts some briary complexity. The oak, as
always, a tannic gong across the finish like the crescendo of a heavy-metal anthem.
Fun then. Clumsy now. Blue/black fruits and a lead solo of anise. A peppery finish
of substantial length. Screw cap. 14.5% alc. Rating 91 To 2030 $80 NG
Black Bay Shiraz 2019 The name is derived from the cracking Black Bay
of Biscay soils. An old-school take-no-prisoners expression, lashed with new
American and French oak seasoning. Bumptious texture and rich in boysenberry,
black cherry, anise and clove flavours. Round and plush, the tannins are well-
managed for this sort of older-fashioned style, mitigating the oak that has been
thrown at it. Decent drinking. Screw cap. 14.5% alc. Rating 90 To 2032 $75 NG

McLeish Estate ★★★★★

462 De Beyers Road, Pokolbin, NSW 2320 **Region** Hunter Valley
T (02) 4998 7754 **www**.mcleishestatewines.com.au **Open** 7 days 10–5
Winemaker Andrew Thomas (Contract) **Est.** 1985 **Dozens** 8000 **Vyds** 17.3ha
Bob and Maryanne McLeish have established a particularly successful business based on estate
plantings. The wines are of consistently high quality, and more than a few have accumulated
show records leading to gold medal–encrusted labels. The quality of the grapes is part of the
equation; the other, the skills of winemaker Andrew Thomas. Over the years, there have been
many trophies and medals, the majority won in the Hunter Valley and Sydney wine shows.
Exports to the UK, the US and Asia.

♟♟♟♟♟ **Hunter Valley Semillon 2011** I tasted this alongside the delicious '09.
I expected this to be the better wine and perhaps it is. Time may show it up. Yet
currently, it remains a bit of a Dorian Gray. Inured against advancement and real
generosity by tonic water CO_2, still unresolved; lemongrass acidity, pumice and
a whiff of quinine, verdant herb and buttered toast development, the latter still
struggling to escape the structural carapace. Be a little more patient. Screw cap.
11.1% alc. Rating 95 To 2026 $80 NG
Hunter Valley Semillon 2009 A museum release that continues to drink very
well, vindicating Hunter semillon as the longest ageing of any Australian white
and certainly the country's most inimitable style. A lightweight balletic nature
juxtaposed with a rapier-like attack of lanolin, buttered toast, lemon squash, quince
paste and citrus marmalade notes of an uncanny intensity. Long. Optimal drinking,
but far from done. Screw cap. 11% alc. Rating 95 To 2024 $125 NG

♟♟♟♟♀ **Reserve Hunter Valley Shiraz 2019** Rating 92 To 2026 $65 NG
Hunter Valley Shiraz 2019 Rating 91 To 2026 $35 NG

McPherson Wines ★★★★

199 O'Dwyer Road, Nagambie, Vic 3608 **Region** Nagambie Lakes
T (03) 9263 0200 **www**.mcphersonwines.com.au
Winemaker Jo Nash **Est.** 1968 **Dozens** 500 000 **Vyds** 262ha
McPherson Wines is, by any standards, a substantial business. Made at various locations from
estate vineyards and contract-grown grapes, they represent very good value across a range
of labels. Winemaker Jo Nash has been at the helm for many years and co-owner Alistair
Purbrick (Tahbilk) has a lifetime of experience in the industry. Quality is unfailingly good.
Exports to all major markets.

♟♟♟♟♀ **Don't tell Gary Shiraz 2019** What's not to like? Deep and expressive purple
hues. Ripe blueberry, blackberry vibrancy and punch with licorice strap, chocolate
and warm, spiced oak. Generous and cuddly. Jo Nash certainly knows her shiraz.
Screw cap. 14.5% alc. Rating 92 To 2027 $24 JP ❂
Bella Luna Fiano 2020 Fiano is kicking goals at a number of price points. Here
is a great-value example that exudes personality+. The grape's signature apple

and fleshy pear combines with quince, lemon rind and grapefruit pith. A gently textured palate finishes with bright acid crunch. Plenty to enjoy here for $19. Screw cap. 12% alc. **Rating** 90 **To** 2024 $19 JP ✪

ᵠᵠᵠᵠ **MWC Shiraz Mourvèdre 2018 Rating** 89 **To** 2024 $22 JP
Pickles McPherson Sauvignon Blanc 2020 Rating 89 **To** 2025 $15 JP ✪
La Vue Riesling 2020 Rating 88 **To** 2024 $19 JP
Catriona McPherson Chardonnay 2020 Rating 88 **To** 2024 $15 JP ✪
MWC Pinot Gris 2019 Rating 88 **To** 2025 $22 JP
Laneway Shiraz 2018 Rating 88 **To** 2024 $19 JP
Aquarius Sangiovese 2020 Rating 88 **To** 2023 $19 JP

Madman's Gully   ★★★★

31 Newbound Lane, Beechworth Vic 3747 **Region** Beechworth
T 0425 774 660 **www**.madmansgullywines.com.au
Winemaker Jo Marsh **Est.** 2009 **Dozens** 180 **Vyds** 0.4ha
The name Madman's Gully is attributed to the antics of a naked Scotsman protecting his claim on the 1850s goldfields, which produced much of the riches on which Beechworth was built. Fiona Wigg has a background in agricultural science, accumulating many years of practical experience as a viticulturist, first with Southcorp Wines and later working as a consultant and educator. During Fiona's time as a vineyard manager at Seppelt Great Western she developed an interest in elegant, cool-climate shiraz, which led to the search for a suitable vineyard site of her own. With husband Ross she established a small patch of shiraz vines in 2009 on the edge of the old Madman's Gully goldfield above Beechworth. Sited at 580m above sea level on a gentle north-facing slope, the vineyard comprises a mix of French clones on rootstock. (JP)

ᵠᵠᵠᵠᵠ **Beechworth Syrah 2018** Whether you call it syrah or shiraz, the effect is the same. This is a spice-fuelled, berry-charged expression of the grape from a cool region that captivates. A charge of lifted aromatics, red and blue berries, bramble, mocha-coffee grounds, chocolate with a hint of pepper. All are effortlessly assembled with integrated oak tannins. Dances to a lively beat. Screw cap. 13.3% alc. **Rating** 93 **To** 2027 $38 JP
Beechworth Syrah 2019 After the aromatic 2018 vintage, we see a more robust, dark-fruited, intense kind of syrah with succulent black cherries, black olive-brine savouriness, violets and woodsy oak spice. Oak is more of a feature in this wine, tannins, too. Screw cap. 13.4% alc. **Rating** 92 **To** 2030 $38 JP

Magpie Estate   ★★★★☆

Rolf Binder, Cnr Seppeltsfield Road/Stelzer Road, Stonewell, SA 5352
Region Barossa Valley
T (08) 8562 3300 **www**.magpieestate.com **Open** At Rolf Binder
Winemaker Rolf Binder, Noel Young **Est.** 1993 **Dozens** 16 000 **Vyds** 16ha
A partnership between 2 Rhône-philes: Barossa winemaker Rolf Binder and UK wine impresario Noel Young. Fruit is sourced from a group of select growers, with the acquisition of the Smalltown Vineyard in Ebenezer providing estate-grown fruit from the 2017 vintage. Each fruit batch is kept separate, giving the winemakers more blending options. The intent is to make wines that have a sense of place and show true Barossa characters, wines that are complex with a degree of elegance. The winemaking style is focused on minimal intervention, with an aversion to massive extract and over-oaked wines. Rolf and Noel say they have a lot of fun making these wines but they are also very serious about quality. Exports to the UK, Canada, Denmark, Poland, Finland, Singapore and Taiwan.

ᵠᵠᵠᵠᵠ **The Fakir Barossa Valley Grenache 2019** Bright, crunchy and refined. An eloquently medium-bodied and exact Barossa grenache, all about spicy, tangy berry/cherry fruit, graced in pretty, powder-fine fruit tannins. Oak, alcohol and artefact all refreshingly downplayed. Enticingly crafted. Screw cap. 14% alc. **Rating** 93 **To** 2025 $30 TS

Small Town Barossa Valley Shiraz 2019 There's a succulent, rich and fleshy breadth to Rolf Binder's reds, exemplified here in a generous and enticing take on Ebenezer. Packed with licorice and black fruits of all descriptions. The fine, fluffy tannins of pressings unite with dark- and milk-chocolate oak and tangy acidity to bring definition to a luscious and long finish. Screw cap. 14% alc. **Rating** 92 **To** 2024 $25 TS ✪

The Good Luck Club Barossa Valley Cabernet Sauvignon 2018 As much Barossa as it is cabernet, brimming with fleshy blue/blackberry fruits. Its varietal personality peeks through in crunchy red berry fruits, confirmed on a finish of tangy acidity and finely textured tannin grip. Dark chocolate oak completes a generous, persistent and deliciously immediate cabernet. Screw cap. 13.5% alc. **Rating** 92 **To** 2023 $30 TS

The Malcolm Barossa Valley Shiraz 2017 Generous, ripe and spirity, contrasting with the cool 2017 season, making for a sweet and sour effect. Spicy, stewy berry fruits edge toward prune. Fine tannin structure draws out a long finish of rich, luscious dark chocolate, showcasing classy new oak. It concludes with spirity alcohol warmth. Cork. 15.5% alc. **Rating** 91 **To** 2027 $195 TS

Rag & Bone Eden Valley Riesling 2020 Encapsulating the full concentration of the 2020 harvest, this is a rich and ripe Eden Valley riesling of medium straw-green hue. Kaffir lime and fig venture into the tropical realm of guava and even passionfruit. The bracing acidity of the season marks out a long and tense finish, impacted by phenolic bitterness on the close. Screw cap. 12.5% alc. **Rating** 90 **To** 2025 $30 TS

The Scoundrel Barossa Valley Grenache Shiraz 2019 Characterful, spicy, succulent and immediate. Exotic lift of Middle Eastern spice. A core of sweet, juicy, ripe mulberry and blackberry. Tangy acidity and fine tannins bring up a long finish. The quintessential barbecue quaffer with the versatility to handle both red and white meats. Screw cap. 14% alc. **Rating** 90 **To** 2022 $30 TS

ŶŶŶŶ **The Black Craft Barossa Valley Shiraz 2019 Rating** 89 **To** 2025 $35 TS

Main & Cherry ★★★★

Main Road, Cherry Gardens, SA 5157 **Region** Adelaide Hills
T 0431 692 791 **www.**mainandcherry.com.au **Open** By appt
Winemaker Michael Sexton **Est.** 2010 **Dozens** 2500 **Vyds** 4.5ha

Michael Sexton grew up on the property and graduated in oenology from the University of Adelaide in 2003. Grapes from the existing shiraz plantings were sold to other wineries but in '10 the first single-vineyard Shiraz was made and the Main & Cherry brand name chosen. Since then plantings of bushvine grenache and mataro have been made. The business has grown with the purchase of an established vineyard in Clarendon planted to 2.4ha of shiraz and 0.9ha of grenache (the plantings at the Cherry Gardens Vineyard consist of 0.8ha shiraz and 0.2ha each of mataro and grenache). Exports to Vietnam and China.

ŶŶŶŶŶ **Clarendon McLaren Vale Shiraz 2019** From winemaker Mike Sexton's family estate vineyard in the higher eastern slopes of the region. Made gently – foot trodden, hand plunged, basket pressed, older oak – to allow a finer expression to come to the surface. Crimson-fruited, subtly compoted with warm spices, lip-smacking fine tannins and all up, deliciously realised. Diam. 14.3% alc. **Rating** 94 **To** 2028 $50 TL

ŶŶŶŶ **McLaren Vale Sangiovese 2020 Rating** 89 **To** 2025 $26 TL
Gökotta 2020 Rating 88 **To** 2024 $28 TL

Main Ridge Estate ★★★★★

80 William Road, Red Hill, Vic 3937 **Region** Mornington Peninsula
T (03) 5989 2686 **www.**mre.com.au **Open** W'ends & public hols 11–5
Winemaker James Sexton **Est.** 1975 **Dozens** 1200 **Vyds** 2.8ha

Quietly spoken and charming, Nat and Rosalie White founded the first commercial winery on the Mornington Peninsula. It has an immaculately maintained vineyard and equally meticulously run winery. In December 2015, ownership of Main Ridge Estate passed to the Sexton family, following the retirement of Nat and Rosalie after 40 years. Tim and Libby Sexton have an extensive background in large-scale hospitality, first in the UK, then with Zinc at Federation Square, Melbourne, and at the MCG. Son James Sexton is completing the bachelor of wine science at CSU. Nat continues as a consultant.

ŸŸŸŸŸ   **The Acre Mornington Peninsula Pinot Noir 2019** Good energy and vibrancy here, felt across the palate. It starts out with requisite sweet cherry and pips, tangy plums, too, folded into the savouriness of cedary oak, cinnamon and aniseed. The tannins are textural, the acidity is charged and it's as juicy as all get-out. Screw cap. 14.5% alc. **Rating** 95 **To** 2029 $85 JF
Half Acre Mornington Peninsula Pinot Noir 2019 Made identically to its full Acre sibling, yet this usually has an added layer; not so much weight, but the texture and tannin are completely different. This is savoury and shapely. Dark spices, cherries, cool autumnal, leafy aromas and chinotto. The palate enjoys some buoyancy as the acidity drives the finish. It has depth and complexity to warrant cellaring, yet makes a compelling argument to drink now. Diam. 14% alc. **Rating** 95 **To** 2030 $95 JF

Majella
★★★★★

Lynn Road, Coonawarra, SA 5263 **Region** Coonawarra
T (08) 8736 3055 **www.**majellawines.com.au **Open** 7 days 10–4.30
Winemaker Bruce Gregory, Michael Marcus **Est.** 1969 **Dozens** 30 000 **Vyds** 60ha
The Lynn family has been in residence in Coonawarra for over 4 generations, starting as storekeepers, later graduating into grazing. The Majella property was originally owned by Frank Lynn, then purchased in 1960 by nephew George, who ran merinos for wool production and prime lambs. In '68 Anthony and Brian (the Prof) Lynn established the vineyards, since joined by Peter, Stephen, Nerys and Gerard. Bruce Gregory has been at the helm for every wine made at Majella. The Malleea is one of Coonawarra's classics, The Musician one of Australia's most outstanding red wines selling for less than $20 (having won many trophies and medals). The largely fully mature vineyards are principally shiraz and cabernet sauvignon, with a little riesling and merlot. Exports to the UK, Canada and Asia.

ŸŸŸŸŸ   **GPL68 Coonawarra Cabernet Sauvignon 2016** The flagship red coming off vines planted in 1968. It is majestic. A perfect interplay of fruit and savouriness and integrated oak imparts a self-assuredness. It's full bodied but not a blockbuster. The tannins are ripe and exquisite and the finish long. Screw cap. 14.5% alc. **Rating** 96 **To** 2036 $130 JF
Coonawarra Cabernet Sauvignon 2018 A defining feature of this wine is how complete it appears, even in youth. It bodes well for long-term enjoyment, too. A synergy of flavour and textures from blackcurrants, mint, toasty and cedary wood, and more besides. Finely chiselled tannins and cleansing acidity slink across the full-bodied palate. Screw cap. 14.5% alc. **Rating** 95 **To** 2036 $35 JF ✪
The Malleea Coonawarra 2016 55/45% cabernet sauvignon/shiraz, from Majella's oldest plantings, in 1971 and 1968 respectively. And respectfully. Ripe fruit dons mocha, mint, baking spices, vanillan and cedary oak. Full-bodied and deep across the palate, with plush tannins and a creaminess, too. Excellent wine. Screw cap. 14.5% alc. **Rating** 95 **To** 2033 $80 JF

ŸŸŸŸŸ   **Coonawarra Shiraz 2018 Rating** 92 **To** 2031 $35 JF
The Musician Coonawarra Cabernet Shiraz 2019 Rating 91 **To** 2027 $19 JF ✪
Coonawarra Sparkling Shiraz 2019 Rating 91 $40 JF

Malcolm Creek Vineyard   ★★★★

33 Bonython Road, Kersbrook, SA 5231 **Region** Adelaide Hills
T 0404 677 894 **www.**malcolmcreekwines.com.au **Open** By appt
Winemaker Peter Leske, Michael Sykes **Est.** 1982 **Dozens** 800 **Vyds** 2ha
Malcolm Creek was the retirement venture of Reg Tolley, who decided to upgrade his
retirement by selling the venture to Bitten and Karsten Pedersen in 2007. The wines are
invariably well made and develop gracefully; they are worth seeking out, and are usually
available with some extra bottle age at a very modest price. However, a series of natural
disasters have decimated Malcolm Creek's production in recent years: '11 cabernet sauvignon
not harvested due to continuous rain; '14 chardonnay not produced because of microscopic
yield following rain and wind at flowering; and the '15 vintage truncated by bushfire and
smoke taint. Exports to the UK, the US, Denmark, Malaysia and China.

🍷🍷🍷🍷🍷 **Adelaide Hills Sauvignon Blanc 2019** A personal take on Hills sauvignon.
Rather than go for the popular, vibrant and upfront tropical fruit and herbal
stylings, this is more textured, gentler on the senses, fuller bodied and sedate. Has
its merits as a dry, unoaked yet meaningful style. Screw cap. 12.5% alc. **Rating** 90
To 2023 $25 TL
Ashwood Estate Adelaide Hills Chardonnay 2019 Whole-bunch pressed,
partially barrel fermented then 10 months in 15% new oak. All the right moves
here for expressive chardonnay, though the oak impresses itself upon the fruit to
begin, with some apple and stone-fruit suggestions vying for attention on the
palate. Screw cap. 13.5% alc. **Rating** 90 **To** 2024 $30 TL

Mandala   ★★★★★

1568 Melba Highway, Dixons Creek, Vic 3775 **Region** Yarra Valley
T (03) 5965 2016 **www.**mandalawines.com.au **Open** Mon–Fri 10–4, w'ends 10–5
Winemaker Charles Smedley, Don Pope **Est.** 2007 **Dozens** 10 500 **Vyds** 29ha
Mandala is owned by Charles Smedley, who acquired the established vineyard in 2007. The
vineyard has vines up to 25 years old, but the spectacular restaurant and cellar door complex is
a more recent addition. The vineyards are primarily at the home base in Dixons Creek, with
chardonnay (9.1ha), pinot noir (6.1ha), cabernet sauvignon (4.4ha), sauvignon blanc (2.9ha),
shiraz (1.7ha) and merlot (0.4ha). There is a separate 4.4ha vineyard at Yarra Junction planted
entirely to pinot noir with an impressive clonal mix. Exports to China.

🍷🍷🍷🍷🍷 **Yarra Valley Fumé Blanc 2020** The inaugural release, made from hand-picked
fruit, whole clusters pressed to old oak, wild fermented and aged 9 months. It's a
really good outcome. Cunchy citrussy flavours, passionfruit pith, pine needle and
basil coolness are matched to a more textural palate. Plenty of acidity ensures a
delicious drink right now. Screw cap. 12.6% alc. **Rating** 95 **To** 2023 $30 JF ✪
The Mandala Compass Yarra Valley Chardonnay 2019 There's a
lusciousness and a depth to this, yet acidity is in charge. This means the white
stone fruit, honeycomb, nougatine and sweetish oak flavours can be enjoyed
without it feeling heavy. It's complex, savoury and the finish is long. Screw cap.
12.2% alc. **Rating** 95 **To** 2029 $80 JF

🍷🍷🍷🍷🍷 **Yarra Valley Shiraz 2019 Rating** 93 **To** 2027 $30 JF
The Prophet Yarra Valley Pinot Noir 2019 Rating 92 **To** 2029 $60 JF
Yarra Valley Chardonnay 2020 Rating 91 **To** 2026 $30 JF
Yarra Valley Rosé 2020 Rating 90 **To** 2022 $25 JF
The Mandala Butterfly Yarra Valley Cabernet Sauvignon 2018 Rating 90
To 2030 $60 JF
Late Disgorged Blanc de Blancs 2010 Rating 90 $60 JF

Mandalay Road ★★★★

254 Mandalay Road, Glen Mervyn via Donnybrook, WA 6239 **Region** Geographe
T (08) 9732 2006 **www**.mandalayroad.com.au **Open** 7 days 11–5
Winemaker Peter Stanlake, John Griffiths **Est.** 1997 **Dozens** 600 **Vyds** 4.2ha
Tony and Bernice O'Connell left careers in science and education to establish plantings of
shiraz, chardonnay, zinfandel and cabernet sauvignon on their property in 1997 (followed by
durif).A hands-on approach and low yields have brought out the best characteristics of the
grape varieties and the region.

🍷🍷🍷🍷🍷 **Geographe Durif 2019** Very pretty, floral and saturated in dark forest fruits.
The tannins on the palate are soft and shapely, giving the whole thing an air of
opulence. The quibble is that it's over sooner than is desired, but it is delicious
while it lasts. A truly lovely example of the variety. Screw cap. 13.4% alc.
Rating 94 **To** 2031 $30 EL ✪

🍷🍷🍷🍷🍷 **Top Block Geographe Zinfandel 2018 Rating** 93 **To** 2030 $30 EL
Geographe Riesling 2020 Rating 92 **To** 2028 $20 EL ✪
Geographe Chardonnay 2019 Rating 90 **To** 2028 $30 EL

Mandoon Estate ★★★★☆

10 Harris Road, Caversham, WA 6055 **Region** Swan District
T (08) 6279 0500 **www**.mandoonestate.com.au **Open** 7 days 10–5
Winemaker Ryan Sudano, Lauren Pileggi **Est.** 2009 **Dozens** 10000 **Vyds** 50ha
Mandoon Estate, headed by Allan Erceg, made a considerable impression with its wines
in a very short time. In 2008 the family purchased a site in Caversham in the Swan Valley.
Construction of the winery was completed in time for the first vintage in '10. They have also
purchased 20ha in Margaret River. Winemaker Ryan Sudano has metaphorically laid waste
to Australian wine shows with the quality of the wines he has made from the Swan Valley,
Frankland River and Margaret River.

🍷🍷🍷🍷🍷 **Reserve Margaret River Chardonnay 2019** Salty, saline, fine and yet rich,
all the beauty of Margaret River chardonnay in a sentence (and a glass). Really
good length of flavour, the acidity giving a tangy jolt of excitement that pierces
the heart of the ripe orchard fruit. The cooler '19 vintage has birthed a wine
of nuance and restraint, both of which look good here. Screw cap. 13% alc.
Rating 96 **To** 2036 $59 EL ✪
Reserve Research Station Margaret River Cabernet Sauvignon 2016
Buoyant red berries, pink peppercorn and exotic Asian spices like star anise. The
palate is succulent, fine and plush … this is modern and silky, with charm and
beauty for days. A gorgeous, poetic cabernet made in a style that is becoming
more and more uniquely Australian. True pleasure, seamless balance. One trophy
and 7 gold medals so far. Screw cap. 14% alc. **Rating** 96 **To** 2050 $84 EL
Old Vine Shiraz 2018 At below $30 this is an unassailable proposition. Justifies
Swan Valley's reputation for old-vine shiraz. Great depth and intensity of flavour,
which in the hands of Ryan Sudano is also coupled with restraint. A core of berry
fruits is ensconced in spice, cooling acid and clever oak handling. Don't miss it.
Screw cap. 14.5% alc. **Rating** 95 **To** 2030 $30 EL ✪
Reserve Frankland River Shiraz 2017 Floral, potpourri, blackberry and anise.
This is endlessly interesting on the nose, suggestions of arnica nestled into the
black-fruit spectrum. The palate is decidedly salty; all flavour directed towards the
red-fruit corner, but with sprinklings of sea salt crackled over the top. An elegant
wine of fine structure for all the brawny characters that define it. Screw cap.
14.5% alc. **Rating** 95 **To** 2035 $55 EL
Old Vine Grenache 2019 If you don't get excited by the prospect of Swan
Valley grenache, we need to talk. In the hands of winemaker Ryan Sudano, this is
possessed of both supple, bouncy raspberry fruit, and muscular, structuring tannins.
The wine in the mouth is frankly delicious, and wears its alcohol with ease. On
reflection, there is a jasmine tea note on the palate that is very attractive, too.

Likely a long life ahead of it. Gold medal Swan Valley Wine Show '20. Screw cap.
14.5% alc. **Rating** 95 **To** 2032 $30 EL ✪

Margaret River Sauvignon Blanc 2020 Pungent aromas of Cape gooseberry,
cassis, juniper and sprinklings of exotic spice to boot. The fine phenolics create
interest and direction, steering the wine through the long finish. Screw cap.
12.5% alc. **Rating** 94 **To** 2025 $23 EL ✪

Block 1895 Verdelho 2020 From the oldest verdelho block in WA, planted in
1895 by the Roe family. A touch of sweat and funk on the nose, but the palate is
tight as a drum. Lean and savoury citrus characters underpinned by white pepper
and spice. Passionfruit. The finish draws out into a linger, a curl and a waft. Lovely
stuff. Lyrical, almost. Screw cap. 13% alc. **Rating** 94 **To** 2031 $28 EL ✪

Old Vine Grenache 2018 Fruit from the Sita vineyard planted 1955. Matured
in seasoned French oak. Savoury and structured, this has redcurrants, raspberry and
mulberry, with licorice and fennel through the finish. More muscular and gnarly
than it is juicy and sweet, this is an altogether more serious grenache than many.
Screw cap. 14.5% alc. **Rating** 94 **To** 2028 $30 EL ✪

Surveyors Red 2018 Grenache, syrah, mataro. Sweet berry fruits and satsuma
plum on the nose lead the way for the flavours in the mouth, which obediently
follow suit. Supple tannins create shape on the palate. This is a spicy, delicious and
satisfying rendition of the blend. Definitely worth crossing the road for. Screw cap.
14.5% alc. **Rating** 94 **To** 2030 $28 EL ✪

🍷🍷🍷🍷 **Surveyors White 2020 Rating** 93 **To** 2031 $20 EL ✪
Margaret River Cabernet Merlot 2017 Rating 93 **To** 2031 $30 EL

Mandurang Valley Wines ★★★★

77 Fadersons Lane, Mandurang, Vic 3551 **Region** Bendigo
T (03) 5439 5367 **www**.mandurangvalleywines.com.au **Open** W'ends & public hols 11–5
Winemaker Wes Vine, Steve Vine **Est.** 1995 **Dozens** 2500 **Vyds** 3ha
Wes and Pamela Vine planted their first vineyard at Mandurang in 1976 and started making
wine as a hobby. Commercial production began in '93, and an additional vineyard was
established in '97. Wes (a former school principal) became full-time winemaker in '99. Son
Steve has progressively taken greater responsibility for the winemaking, while Wes is spending
more time developing export markets. Pamela manages the cellar door cafe. Exports to China.

🍷🍷🍷🍷 **Bendigo Riesling 2019** Aromas of lime blossom, preserved lemon and
grapefruit feature in this dry, steely riesling. The palate has a reserved waxy quality,
supple and textural, with citrus, honeysuckle and apple notes – and what spice.
Don't overchill. Screw cap. 12.4% alc. **Rating** 92 **To** 2026 $22 JP ✪

Bendigo Brut Rosé 2018 Pretty salmon pink with a copper tinge. Boasting
plenty of flavour in the acacia, cherry and spice spectrum. Bottle fermented with
just a light touch of autolysis, the real charm here is the vinous flavour and bright,
bubbly personality. Simple but delicious drinking. Diam. 12.8% alc. **Rating** 90
To 2023 $28 JP

Old Vine Bendigo 2017 A traditional Aussie red that delivers a sturdy, dark-
fruited wine with plenty of tannic power. Briar, baked earth, herb-infused
mulberry and blackberry aromas. Ripe fruit is more than a match for the level of
new, spiced oak. Nicely tied together with chalky tannins. Screw cap. 14.3% alc.
Rating 90 **To** 2027 $40 JP

🍷🍷🍷🍷 **Bendigo Shiraz 2016 Rating** 89 **To** 2027 $30 JP
Bendigo Merlot 2018 Rating 88 **To** 2026 $26 JP
Bendigo G.S.M 2017 Rating 88 **To** 2027 $26 JP
Bendigo Malbec 2019 Rating 88 **To** 2026 $28 JP

Manser Wines

c/- 3 Riviera Court, Pasadena, SA 5042 (postal) **Region** Adelaide Hills
T 0400 251 168 **www**.manserwines.com.au
Winemaker Phil Christiansen **Est.** 2015 **Dozens** 1000 **Vyds** 6ha

Phil Manser has a long history of involvement in the wine industry in various parts of the world and has now teamed up with brother Kevin and father Bernie to run the family vineyard. The vineyard was established by Tim James, a skilled winemaker with senior winemaking and management roles at Hardys and Wirra Wirra. He planted the vineyard to 4 clones of shiraz, planted randomly throughout the vineyard in 1997, a common practice in France. The Mansers acquired the property in 2015, Tim remaining an enthusiastic spectator during vintage. They also source fruit from a 65yo vineyard in Blewitt Springs and a 3rd vineyard on the McMurtrie Mile which feeds their One Mad Moment range. Contract winemaker Phil Christiansen looks after the destinies of a considerable number of vineyards throughout McLaren Vale.

ㅇㅇㅇㅇ **Block 4 Adelaide Hills Shiraz 2018** From a distinguished site on the border between Adelaide Hills and McLaren Vale, planted by Tim James with 4 clones of shiraz; acquired by the Manser family in '15. There's a spectacular black-fruited core to the wine, with very good mouthfeel and length. No SO_2 added, suggesting a careful watch is needed if the wine is cellared. Screw cap. 14.5% alc. **Rating** 94 To 2033 $55 JH

ㅇㅇㅇㅇ **One Mad Moment McLaren Vale Shiraz Grenache 2019** Rating 89 To 2027 $30 NG

Mansfield Wines

201 Eurunderee Lane, Mudgee, NSW 2850 **Region** Mudgee
T (02) 6373 3871 **www**.mansfieldwines.com.au **Open** Thurs–Tues & public hols 10–5
Winemaker Bob Heslop, Ian McLellan **Est.** 1975 **Dozens** 1500 **Vyds** 5.5ha

Ian McLellan and family purchased Mansfield Wines from his cousin Peter Mansfield in late 1997. The original plantings, which included chardonnay, frontignac, sauvignon blanc, cabernet sauvignon, merlot and shiraz, were removed, to be replaced by a Joseph's coat patchwork of savagnin, vermentino, petit manseng, parellada, tempranillo, touriga, zinfandel and tinta cão, supported by grenache, mourvèdre and pedro ximénez. Sousão and carignan are more recent arrivals.

ㅇㅇㅇㅇㅇ **Monastrell 2018** A delicious wine. Full bodied and burly, with a ferrous tannic mettle that champions balance over dryness, and a sumptuous flow of flavour. Aromas of smoked meat, dark cherry, clove, blood, game, espresso and black volcanic rock. The oak, French and American, a mere adjunct. There is a lot of mass packed into the glass but there is nothing sweet or jammy about it. Screw cap. 14% alc. **Rating** 91 To 2025 $21 NG ✪

ㅇㅇㅇㅇ **Mudgee V.P. 2005** Rating 88 $25 NG
Firetail 2017 Rating 88 To 2024 $21 NG

Many Hands Winery

2 Maxwells Road, Coldstream, Vic 3770 **Region** Yarra Valley
T 0400 035 105 **www**.manyhandswinery.com.au **Open** Fri–Mon 10–5
Winemaker Tony Indomenico **Est.** 2010 **Dozens** 1000 **Vyds** 2.6ha

Owners Jennifer Walsh and Tony Indomenico were looking for a tree change when in 2010 they came across a 2.6ha vineyard that had been planted in 1982 to 6 mainstream varieties, but not always looked after. The first task was to rehabilitate the vineyard and thereafter build a restaurant offering Italian food reflecting Tony's Sicilian heritage. The restaurant opened in '17 and has been well received.

ㅇㅇㅇㅇㅇ **Yarra Valley Cabernet Sauvignon Cabernet Franc 2019** Excellent and alluring bright purple/black hue. But oh the fragrance! Mulberries and curry leaves, wine pastilles and violets, turmeric and crushed coriander seeds. It's heady. The palate is wonderfully restrained, working off medium bodied and sweetly-fruited, with slightly dusty tannins. A lovely drink. Diam. 13.5% alc. **Rating** 95 **To** 2033 $45 JF

Manyara Wines ★★★★☆

380 Onkaparinga Valley Road, Balhannah, SA 5242 **Region** Adelaide Hills
T 0427 900 658 www.manyarawines.net.au **Open** By appt
Winemaker Darryl Catlin **Est.** 1994 **Dozens** 1500 **Vyds** 7.5ha
Manyara Wines, a family-owned and -operated vineyard and winery, was established on fertile land once used to breed and train thoroughbred race horses. The altitude of the Adelaide Hills brings low night-time temperatures and rainfall, and both have a positive influence on grape growing. Simon Roe grew up among vineyards in the Riverland, his grandfather, Jack Neilson, was a winemaker at Hardys. Contemplating a return to Australia after 20 years in South East Asia, Simon and wife Melissa knew they had found their future at Manyara, which they purchased in August 2014. The vines on the property were planted in 1994, and are carefully hand-tended to make the single-vineyard wines. Exports to Cambodia, Singapore, Thailand, Vietnam and Myanmar.

Marchand & Burch ★★★★★

PO Box 180, North Fremantle, WA 5159 **Region** Great Southern
T (08) 9336 9600 www.burchfamilywines.com.au
Winemaker Janice McDonald, Pascal Marchand **Est.** 2007 **Dozens** 2000 **Vyds** 8.46ha
A joint venture between Canadian-born and Burgundian-trained Pascal Marchand and Burch Family Wines. Grapes are sourced from single vineyards and, in most cases, from single blocks within those vineyards (4.51ha of chardonnay and 3.95ha of pinot noir, in each case variously situated in Mount Barker and Porongurup). Biodynamic practices underpin the viticulture in the Australian and French vineyards, and Burgundian viticultural techniques have been adopted in the Australian vineyards (e.g. narrow rows and high-density plantings, Guyot pruning, vertical shoot positioning and leaf and lateral shoot removal). Exports to the UK, the US and other major markets.

 Mount Barker Chardonnay 2019 Aromas of curry leaf, struck match and yellow peach to start, following through on the palate. The edges of the fruit have a creamy underside, characterised by crushed cashew and white spice. Long and rich, this has quenching acid (no doubt from the elevated vineyards from which this fruit was sourced) and long, unfurling flavours to close. Star anise and wafts of fennel flower. Screw cap. 13% alc. **Rating** 95 **To** 2036 $78 EL
Mount Barrow Mount Barker Pinot Noir 2019 A very restrained nose leads in to a compact and very long palate. The cherry and spice flavours don't provide flourish or flamboyance on the palate; rather they forge, very seriously, across a predetermined track, straight through to a long finish. Structurally serious and so dense as to almost be sturdy, this is in need of some ageing in order for it to show its significant potential. Screw cap. 13.5% alc. **Rating** 95 **To** 2031 $54 EL
Villages Rosé 2020 Blackberry cream pie, strawberry and clove. Really great intensity on the palate – there's a lot of flavour here, and good length too. Screw cap. 13% alc. **Rating** 94 **To** 2025 $26 EL ✪

Marcus Hill Vineyard ★★★★

560 Banks Road, Marcus Hill, Vic 3222 (postal) **Region** Geelong
T (03) 5251 3797 www.marcushillvineyard.com.au
Winemaker Chip Harrison **Est.** 2000 **Dozens** 1000 **Vyds** 3ha
In 2000, Richard and Margot Harrison, together with 'gang-pressed friends', planted 2ha of pinot noir overlooking Port Lonsdale, Queenscliff and Ocean Grove, a few kilometres from Bass Strait and Port Phillip Bay. Since then chardonnay, shiraz, more pinot noir, and 3 rows of pinot meunier have been added. The vineyard is run with minimal sprays, and the aim is to produce elegant wines that truly express the maritime site.

🍷🍷🍷🍷🍷 **Bellarine Peninsula Pinot Noir 2018** Some confident and assured winemaking ability on display here. Quite exciting. It gives the air of delicacy but deep waters are at play. Bright cherry red in the glass, forest floor, wild strawberries, wild herbs and a hint of spicy musk. Turns serious on the palate, sinewy and concentrated with brilliant clarity of fruit and fine tannins. Screw cap. 13.8% alc. **Rating** 93 To 2025 $34 JP

Bellarine Peninsula Pinot Meunier 2018 Heady with florals – irresistible – and the sweet scent of summer berries, musk, fruit tingle confection and a touch of exotic spice and dried herbs. Smooth, ripe tannins add to the appeal. It fully deserves its own moment rather than being blended. Delicious. Screw cap. 13.5% alc. **Rating** 93 To 2026 $34 JP

Bellarine Peninsula Chardonnay 2019 A stylish chardonnay that combines superfine nectarine, stone fruits and citrus with some skilful seasoning from new French oak. Enjoys concentration and weight with bright acidity. Screw cap. 12.8% alc. **Rating** 90 To 2027 $34 JP

Margan

1238 Milbrodale Road, Broke, NSW 2330 **Region** Hunter Valley
T (02) 6579 1317 **www.**margan.com.au **Open** 7 days 10–5
Winemaker Andrew Margan, Nicole Wilson **Est.** 1997 **Dozens** 25 000 **Vyds** 96ha
Andrew Margan, following in his late father's footsteps, entered the wine industry over 20 years ago working as a Flying Winemaker in Europe, then for Tyrrell's. The growth of the Margan family business over the following years has been the result of unremitting hard work and a keen understanding of the opportunities Australia's most visited wine region provides. They have won innumerable awards in the tourism sector, against competition in the Hunter Valley, across NSW and Australia. The next generation looks similarly set to cover all bases when their parents retire: eldest son Ollie is finishing a double degree in winemaking and viticultural science at the University of Adelaide; daughter Alessa is studying communications at UTS while working in wine and food PR; and younger son James is enrolled in economics at The University of Sydney. Andrew has continued to push the envelope in the range of wines made, without losing focus on the varieties that have made the Hunter famous. He planted barbera in 1998 and has since progressively added mourvèdre, albariño, tempranillo and graciano; the vineyards are in conversion to organic. Exports to the UK, the US, Sweden and Canada.

🍷🍷🍷🍷🍷 **Aged Release Francis John Hunter Valley Semillon 2016** Aged in bottle for 5 years before release. Sleek and pure. Uncluttered with lees handling or riper inflections of more contemporary expressions. Silty acidity reigns over lemon zest, cheesecloth, grapefruit and grassy herbal notes. Still unfurling. Time will tell. Screw cap. 11% alc. **Rating** 93 To 2030 $50 NG

White Label Fordwich Hill Hunter Valley Shiraz 2019 A welcome confluence of 50yo vines, 12 months in (1st to 3rd pass) French barriques, volcanic loams and plenty of destemmed whole berries to impart a pulpy, lively jubiness to the fruit, all accentuated by a violet lift. Licorice straps and lavender notes, too. This is a benchmark medium-bodied Hunter red, drinking akin to a luncheon claret. Just what the region does well. Screw cap. 13.5% alc. **Rating** 93 To 2034 $50 NG

Aged Release Timbervines Hunter Valley Shiraz 2017 Inimitable Hunter nose of fecund earthy loams, terracotta, blue fruits, lilac, polished leather and suede. Smart! Reductive handling is apparent but sublimated by the gushing fruit. Medium bodied, compact, savoury and fresh. A stellar year! This is a very good drink, with plenty left up its sleeve. Screw cap. 14% alc. **Rating** 93 To 2034 $75 NG

White Label Timbervines Hunter Valley Tempranillo Graciano Shiraz 2019 This is good. Tempranillo's abominable performance on these shores is cushioned by the virtuosity of the other 2 varieties. A confluence of pulpy blue fruits, rhubarb to amaro scents, orange zest and a ginger spiciness plying the long, granular finish. The oak, well nestled. A sassy wine, with a visceral, gulpable appeal. Screw cap. 14% alc. **Rating** 92 To 2026 $40 NG

White Label Saxonvale Hunter Valley Mourvèdre 2019 A light to mid ruby, with an attractive luminescence. Herbal aromas of pine, fennel, lavender, thyme and dried tobacco enmesh a core of red berry succulence. The tannins, ferrous and savoury, unwind nicely while operating as welcome signposts to a place of poise and sappy length. The warm vintage has benefited this late-ripening variety. Mourvèdre, far from the archetype, but a delicious iconoclast as the only one produced in the region. Screw cap. 14% alc. **Rating** 92 **To** 2027 $50 NG

White Label Saxonvale Hunter Valley Shiraz Mourvèdre 2019 This field blend was the last-picked plot of fruit (owing, presumably, to the later-ripening nature of mourvèdre which constitutes 15% of the blend). Blueberry, lavender, a dried herbal potpourri and kirsch notes rally along a gentle burr of ferrous grape and barrique cedar tannins. Screw cap. 14% alc. **Rating** 91 **To** 2029 $40 NG

White Label Ceres Hill Hunter Valley Barbera 2019 A medium ruby, bright and shimmering in the glass. A reductive rubbery hint soon gives way to dark cherry, raspberry bon-bon and rosewater. On the lighter side of mid weight. Truer to barbera's high acidity: low tannin ratio than in the past, with a supple vibrant finish pushing the flavours long and crunchy. The oak, a mere addendum. A good lunchtime quaff. Screw cap. 13.5% alc. **Rating** 91 **To** 2024 $40 NG

Marion's Vineyard ★★★★☆

361 Deviot Road, Deviot, Tas 7275 **Region** Northern Tasmania
T (03) 6394 7434 **www**.marionsvineyard.com.au **Open** 7 days 11–5
Winemaker Cynthea Semmens **Est.** 1979 **Dozens** 3500 **Vyds** 8ha

Marion's Vineyard was established by young Californian couple Marion and Mark Semmens, backyard winemakers in their home state, who purchased a 14ha rundown apple orchard on the Tamar River in 1980. They had seen the property on a holiday trip to Tasmania the year before, knew instantly that it would make a great vineyard site and returned home to sell their house and possessions that wouldn't come with them. With blood, sweat and tears they planted 4ha of chardonnay, pinot noir, cabernet and müller-thurgau, subsequently doubling the size. Daughter Cynthea left Tasmania to ultimately obtain a wine marketing degree from Roseworthy and an oenology degree from CSU. She travelled the world undertaking vintages, gaining invaluable experience. Back in Australia she worked for Tatachilla and Hardys Tintara when she met husband-to-be winemaker David Feldheim. They returned to Tasmania in 2010, Cynthea contract-making Marion's Vineyard wines and establishing their own small business Beautiful Isle Wines in '13. In '19, Marion, Cynthea, David and Nick (Cynthea's brother) jointly bought Mark's share of Marion's Vineyard, fulfilling a long-desired succession plan.

🍷🍷🍷🍷🍷 **Syrah 2018** Shiraz is a highlight of Marion's vineyard, with more scheduled to be planted in the coming years. With a vibrant purple hue, this is a pepper-laden, medium-bodied style of satsuma plum skin and blackberry fruit. Fine-boned tannins contain some promise for the medium term. Screw cap. 12.7% alc. **Rating** 90 **To** 2028 $50 TS

🍷🍷🍷🍷 **Chardonnay 2019 Rating** 89 **To** 2024 $40 TS
Cabernet Sauvignon 2018 Rating 88 **To** 2033 $50 TS

Marq Wines ★★★★★

860 Commonage Road, Dunsborough, WA 6281 **Region** Margaret River
T (08) 9756 6227 **www**.marqwines.com.au **Open** Fri–Sun & public hols 10–5
Winemaker Mark Warren **Est.** 2011 **Dozens** 2500 **Vyds** 1.5ha

Mark Warren has a degree in wine science from CSU and a science degree from the University of WA; to complete the circle, he is currently lecturing in wine science and wine sensory processes at Curtin University, Margaret River. He also has 27 years' experience in both the Swan Valley and Margaret River, and his current major commercial role is producing the extensive Happs range as well as wines under contract for several other Margaret River brands. When all of this is added up, he is responsible for 60 to 70 individual wines each year, now including wines under his own Marq Wines label. A quick look at the list – Vermentino,

Fiano, Wild & Worked Sauvignon Blanc Semillon, Wild Ferment Chardonnay, Rose, Gamay, Tempranillo, Malbec, and Cut & Dry Shiraz (Amarone style) − points to the underlying philosophy: an exploration of the potential of alternative varieties and unusual winemaking methods by someone with an undoubted technical understanding of the processes involved.

ŸŸŸŸŸ **DNA Margaret River Cabernet Sauvignon 2018** In a truly great vintage like '18, it is right to expect excellence. This is concentrated, layered and bursting at the seams with flavour. The palate is a bounty of seamlessly countersunk oak, succulent fruit, exotic spice and slinky tannins. Major yes, here. Screw cap. 14.3% alc. **Rating** 96 **To** 2035 $35 EL ✿

Wild Ferment Margaret River Chardonnay 2019 Winemaker (and owner) Mark Warren has got a reputation for making interesting, affordable and high-quality wines − a lusty combination. This wine is no exception. Here, cap gun/flint/funk exist alongside yellow peach, red apple skins and the telltale curry leaf − all of it stitched up by briny acidity and fine phenolics. A lot to like, especially at the price. Screw cap. 12.9% alc. **Rating** 95 **To** 2031 $30 EL ✿

Margaret River Fiano 2019 Whole-bunch pressed, 3 months in 4yo oak with regular bâtonnage. White pepper, white peach, nectarine and honeydew melon. This has the benefit of being both rich and refreshing at once, thanks to the taut acid that curls its way through the fruit. Phenolics provide shape and structure in the mouth. This is a cracker. Screw cap. 13.2% alc. **Rating** 95 **To** 2025 $25 EL ✿

Margaret River Vermentino 2020 The alcohol indicates an early pick, so the expectation is a crunchy, crispy vermentino. We are well met. Zingy, sherbety acid and orchard fruit so pretty and light that it is almost lyrical. One could consume quite a bit of this without noticing. Quite delicious. An excellent match for a seafood barbecue in summer. Screw cap. 12.1% alc. **Rating** 95 **To** 2023 $25 EL ✿

Margaret River Tempranillo 2019 Lifted violets and raspberry on the nose; lashings of sweet fruit and salted pomegranate on the palate. Lovely balance between oak, fruit and acid. A graceful and attractive medium-bodied tempranillo with a bounty of exotic spice, sprinkled over chalky tannins. Screw cap. 14.2% alc. **Rating** 95 **To** 2028 $30 EL ✿

Margaret River Semillon Sauvignon Blanc Verdelho 2020 75/15/10% semillon/sauvignon blanc/verdelho. Wild ferment in tank. Tropical, ripe and laden with graphite phenolics, this is an atypical spin on the trad SSB blend. A lot to touch and feel here, with bucket loads of concentrated flavour that rolls over the tongue in waves. Impressive. Screw cap. 13.3% alc. **Rating** 94 **To** 2027 $22 EL ✿

DNA Margaret River Cabernet Sauvignon 2017 Ruby hue. This is a picture of concentration and density. The length of flavour further reinforces the quality of the fruit here. The 2017 growing season was cool and wet, but the only mark that this has left on the wine is a spicy layer of interest and secondary flavour. The fruit is ripe, the oak is evident but well judged. All things in place. Screw cap. 14.3% alc. **Rating** 94 **To** 2036 $35 EL

Margaret River Malbec 2019 Raspberry leaf tea, red licorice, anise and pink peppercorn. The palate has tannins that are fine, soft, plump − they create a boudoir vibe − like freshly fluffed pillows. The acidity runs counter to this, keeping the wine balanced and taut. The length of flavour beyond that draws out into an elongated close. Brilliant stuff. Restraint and interest at once. Bravo. Screw cap. 14.1% alc. **Rating** 94 **To** 2030 $30 EL ✿

ŸŸŸŸŸ **Cut and Dry Margaret River Shiraz 2019 Rating** 93 **To** 2031 $4 EL ✿
Cabernet Franc Margaret River 2019 Rating 93 **To** 2027 $25 EL ✿

Mary's Myth ★★★★

144 Johnsons Road, Balhannah, SA 5242 **Region** South Australia
T 0447 608 479 **www.**marysmyth.com.au
Winemaker Alister McMichael **Est.** 2018 **Dozens** 550
This is the as-yet small venture of 3 childhood friends: Alister McMichael, Evan Starkey and Millie Haigh. Alister grew up in the Adelaide Hills in the late 1990s and after finishing his studies headed to the Mosel Valley to absorb Old World treatment of riesling. His return was

not to Australia, but the northern Canterbury district of NZ where for 6 months he was exposed to minimalistic vinification approaches plus biodynamic/organic inputs. Then he was off again, this time to the very cool Finger Lakes of Upstate New York. While the primary purpose was, of course, to continue the pursuits of riesling, he also observed the making of pinot noir and cabernet franc in such an unlikely environment. Finally back in the Adelaide Hills, Mary's Myth was conceived; the name inspired by the discovery that each of their grandmother's names was Mary.

🍷🍷🍷🍷♀ **The Gift Adelaide Hills Shiraz 2018** A barrel of shiraz was gifted to the MM crew who then added their finishing flourishes. It's ripe, intense, warm-hearted and juicy shiraz with a tang of satsuma plum on the palate. Oak adds spice but not timber, sitting into a medium- to full-bodied style, a delicate orange/amaro-like edge on the finish giving it a distinctive note. Cork. 14.5% alc. **Rating** 93 **To** 2028 $40 TL
Clare Valley Riesling 2020 A unique riesling, utilising a specific Austrian yeast and kept on its light lees for 4 months, together encouraging a citrus-like sugar candy note, somewhere between musk sticks and lemon sherbet, with a delicate honeysuckle feel too. Palate texture is more familiar, with a soft pithy feel. Different, yes. And attractive because of it. Screw cap. 12.5% alc. **Rating** 92 **To** 2025 $22 TL **☉**
Langhorne Creek Cabernet Sauvignon 2019 Natural ferment, aged for 12 months in new French oak. The colour has a welcome ruby tone, suggesting a medium-bodied style, and that it is. Familiar regional red/blueberry aromatics and flavours with earthy, almost-charred roast root vegetable savoury offsets and pliable tannins. Screw cap. 14.4% alc. **Rating** 91 **To** 2026 $35 TL
Langhorne Creek Shiraz 2019 Natural ferment, matured in French oak for a year, one-third new. Good deep shiraz plum and blackberried characters. Tannins sit neatly in the frame, providing length and palate foundations. Screw cap. 14.5% alc. **Rating** 90 **To** 2025 $35 TL

Massena Vineyards   ★★★★☆

26 Sturt Street, Angaston, SA 5353 **Region** Barossa Valley
T 0408 821 737 **www**.massena.com.au **Open** By appt
Winemaker Jaysen Collins **Est.** 2000 **Dozens** 5000 **Vyds** 4ha
Massena Vineyards draws upon 1ha each of mataro, saperavi, petite sirah and tannat at Nuriootpa, also purchasing grapes from other growers. It is an export-oriented business, although the wines can also be purchased by mail order, which, given both the quality and innovative nature of the wines, seems more than ordinarily worthwhile. Exports to the US, Canada, France, Switzerland, Denmark, South Korea, NZ, Hong Kong and China.

🍷🍷🍷🍷♀ **The Moonlight Run 2019** Realising its aspiration of a 'soft, slurpy' southern Rhône style, this is a juicy, fruity and engaging GMS. Glossy red fruits of old bush-vine grenache are seamlessly melded with the savoury spice of whole-bunch mataro and the black licorice and satsuma plum of shiraz. Fine, supple tannins lend just the right amount of grip to steady the finish. Screw cap. 14.5% alc. **Rating** 91 **To** 2023 $35 TS

🍷🍷🍷🍷 **The Twilight Path 2019 Rating** 89 **To** 2022 $30 TS

Massoni

30 Brasser Avenue, Dromana, Vic 3936 **Region** Pyrenees/Mornington Peninsula
T (03) 5981 0711 **www**.massoniwines.com **Open** By appt 10–4.30
Winemaker Adam Dickson **Est.** 1984 **Dozens** 30000 **Vyds** 277.5ha
Massoni is a substantial business owned by the Ursini family, and it is a venture with 2 completely distinct arms. In terms of vineyard and land size, by far the larger is the GlenKara Vineyard in the Pyrenees (269ha). It also has 8.5ha on the Mornington Peninsula where Massoni started and where it gained its reputation. In 2012 Massoni purchased the former Tucks Ridge/Red Hill winemaking facility at Dromana. Exports to China.

ŶŶŶŶ♀ **Mornington Peninsula Chardonnay 2018** Strikes out confidently with
the aroma of pear, melon, flinty sulphides and stone fruit. The palate is packing
similar summery fruits but delves a little deeper with some nutty, mealy, grapefruit
elements and smooth texture. There's a lot happening in the glass here. Great value
on display. Screw cap. **Rating** 90 **To** 2024 $25 JP

ŶŶŶŶ **Pyrenees Shiraz 2015 Rating** 89 **To** 2026 $25 JP

Maverick Wines

981 Light Pass Road, Vine Vale, Moorooroo, SA 5352 **Region** Barossa Valley
T 0402 186 416 **www.**maverickwines.com.au **Open** By appt
Winemaker Ronald Brown **Est.** 2004 **Dozens** 6000 **Vyds** 33ha
This is the business established by highly experienced vigneron Ronald Brown. It has
evolved, now with 7 vineyards across the Barossa and Eden valleys, all transitioned into
biodynamic grape production. The vines range from 40 to almost 150 years old, underpinning
the consistency and quality of the wines. Exports to NZ, France, Russia, Thailand, Japan
and China.

ŶŶŶŶŶ **Trial Hill Eden Valley Shiraz 2018** Ronald Brown is a wizard in the vineyard.
Such cool-climate mood and powder-fine elegance are rarely found even at this
altitude of the Barossa. White pepper and violets dance over a crunchy palate of
delectable black cherry and satsuma plum fruit. Tannin, acidity and fruit harmonise
effortlessly, testimony to happy vines in perfect balance and peace. Diam. 13.5% alc.
Rating 97 **To** 2043 $180 TS
The Maverick Barossa Shiraz Cabernet Sauvignon 2018 The Maverick is
living, breathing proof of the adage that the best wines are made in the vineyard
and polished in the winery. To capture such depth, character and seamless
composure with such space and grace is the holy grail of Australia's definitive
blend. Shiraz and cabernet unite as one, as pitch-perfect red and black fruits
join with fine-ground tannins in a finish of mesmerising line and length. Diam.
13% alc. **Rating** 97 **To** 2038 $320 TS ♥

ŶŶŶŶŶ **Ahrens' Creek Barossa Valley Cabernet Sauvignon 2018** Fragrance,
brightness, elegance and endurance are the refreshing themes here. Is it the
aromatic rose petal aromatics that make this so enticing, or the crunchy redcurrant
and cassis fruit that pops on the palate; the powder-fine tannins or bright acidity
that draw out an epic finish? It might take another glass to decide! Diam. 13% alc.
Rating 96 **To** 2038 $150 TS ♥
Barossa Shiraz 2019 It's impossible to pigeonhole wine on its alcohol (never
trust a number) but so refreshing to experience a Barossa shiraz with the fragrant
violet lift, medium-bodied elegance and crunchy red cherry fruit brightness to
prove that vineyard balance does not demand high octane to achieve delightfully
complete ripeness. A measured hand in the oak barrel hall sets off a delicious wine
of fine-boned frame and jubilant persistence. This is the kind of Barossa shiraz that
wins heart. Not least mine. Screw cap. 13.5% alc. **Rating** 95 **To** 2034 $50 TS
Barossa Ridge Barossa Valley Shiraz 2018 With impeccable ripeness,
refreshingly low alcohol and enticingly fine-grained structure, this is a beautiful
expression of grand old vines. I love the way it seamlessly juxtaposes the depth
of blackberry, licorice and dark chocolate with the vibrancy of natural acidity
and graceful, effortless tannins. Masterfully grown and crafted. Diam. 13% alc.
Rating 95 **To** 2033 $150 TS
Trial Hill Eden Valley Grenache 2019 It's cool and high up at Trial Hill in
Pewsey Vale, gently coaxing out the delicate and pretty side of grenache. Think
elegant red fruits, cherries and strawberries, with subtle rose petal accents. A world
away from the all too often warm, jammy generosity of Barossa floor grenache, this
is a more contemplative style of tangy, bright acid line and powder-fine tannins. It
leads out reserved, rising to a pinotesque crescendo on a grand finish. Its finest days
are yet to come. Diam. 14% alc. **Rating** 95 **To** 2029 $150 TS

Ahrens' Creek Barossa Valley Shiraz 2018 The spicy, leathery allure and potpourri exoticism of ancient vines is gracefully elevated through careful, extended barrel maturation. A core of spicy red berry fruits hovers long and supple through a tail of fine-grained tannins and tangy acidity. Diam. 13% alc. **Rating** 94 **To** 2028 $150 TS

Barossa Valley Cabernet Sauvignon Merlot 2019 A proper cabernet merlot. Accurate, defined, vibrant and enduring. Signature, crunchy red/blackcurrants are lifted by wonderful rosehip fragrance, energised equally by confident, fine-grained tannin webbing as tangy, bright acidity. Cool-climate references are refreshing in this warm, dry Barossa season. Bravo! Screw cap. 14% alc. **Rating** 94 **To** 2039 $50 TS

Ahrens' Creek Barossa Valley Mourvèdre 2019 A brand new release, in response to the calibre of the season, celebrating the savoury mood of mourvèdre in appealing layers of tomato, paprika, even curry powder. The bright, medium-bodied mood that characterises Maverick is epitomised in crunchy red berry fruits, tangy acidity and well-polished fine-grained tannins. Oak rightfully leaves the main act to expressive, varietal fruit personality. Diam. 14% alc. **Rating** 94 **To** 2029 $150 TS

🍷🍷🍷🍷🍷 **Barossa GSM 2019** Rating 93 To 2024 $50 TS
Barossa Ridge Barossa Valley Cabernets 2018 Rating 92 To 2028 $150 TS
Ahrens' Creek Barossa Valley Grenache 2019 Rating 90 To 2022 $150 TS

Max & Me ★★★★☆

Eden Valley Hotel, 11 Murray Street, Eden Valley, SA 5235 **Region** Eden Valley
T 0403 250 331 **www.**maxandme.com.au **Open** 7 days 12–5
Winemaker Philip Lehmann **Est.** 2011 **Dozens** 900 **Vyds** 10.22ha
Max is the name of a German shepherd/whippet cross purchased by Phil Lehmann from the RSPCA pound and who introduced Phil to his wife-to-be Sarah during a visit to the Barossa. A dog lover from way back, she fell in love with Max; Phil made it clear she wouldn't get Max unless she married him (Phil). Phil had previously purchased the Boongarrie Estate (on Keyneton Road, at an elevation of 430–460m) with 5.25ha of shiraz and 4.97ha of cabernet sauvignon. They converted the vineyard to (non-certified) organic management, with no herbicides and only copper/sulphur sprays. The benefits are self-evident, reflected in the high quality of the wines made since '11. Sarah manages direct wine sales. The future is for modest growth, planting riesling and grenache.

🍷🍷🍷🍷🍷 **Woodcarvers Vineyard Mirooloo Road Eden Valley Riesling 2020** High-toned blossom/flower scents fill the bouquet. The palate is juicy with Rose's lime juice and crisp, clear acidity to give balance now and join forces with the fruit as the wine gains texture and complexity with prolonged cellaring. Screw cap. 12.9% alc. **Rating** 96 **To** 2032 $30 JH ✪

🍷🍷🍷🍷 **High Eden Eden Valley Barossa Pinot Noir 2020** Rating 89 To 2025 $45 TS

Maxwell Wines ★★★★☆

Olivers Road, McLaren Vale, SA 5171 **Region** McLaren Vale
T (08) 8323 8200 **www.**maxwellwines.com.au **Open** 7 days 10–5
Winemaker Kate Petering, Mark Maxwell **Est.** 1979 **Dozens** 30 000 **Vyds** 40ha
Maxwell Wines has carved out a reputation as a premium producer in McLaren Vale, making some excellent red wines in recent years. The majority of the vines on the estate were planted in 1972, including 19 rows of the highly regarded Reynella clone of cabernet sauvignon. The Ellen Street shiraz block in front of the winery was planted in '53. In a region abounding with first-class restaurants (and chefs), Maxwell has responded to the challenge with extensive renovations to the restaurant and cellar door. Kate Petering, formerly chief winemaker at Mount Langi Ghiran, was appointed head winemaker in March '19. Exports to all major markets.

🍷🍷🍷🍷🍷 **Fresca McLaren Vale Grenache 2020** A delicious, unadulterated grenache without the clutter: neither oak, lengthy maceration nor any obvious adornment. A transparent mid ruby. Refined scents of red pastille, cherry bon-bon, Seville orange and riffs of briar, pepper and clove nestling amid a gentle tannic rasp. Drink this chilled and with gusto. Screw cap. 12.5% alc. **Rating** 92 **To** 2023 $28 NG
Kangaroo Island Shiraz 2019 Medium bodied and immensely savoury. A cool aura manifest as scents of white pepper, dill, fennel, clove and redcurrant. This is far from the South Australian norm and all the more intriguing because of it. Drinks akin to a wine from the Grampians, or thereabouts. This is good drinking. Lithe and spicy. Solid length. Screw cap. 14% alc. **Rating** 91 **To** 2024 $32 NG
Ellen Street McLaren Vale Shiraz 2018 This delivers what many expect of the region: a full-bodied and glossy shiraz, oozing sumptuously across the palate. Rich of dark fruit, clove, anise and vanilla pod accents, the latter derived from 18 months spent in mostly French oak. The finish all espresso, bitter chocolate and American oak bourbon, with a clang of tannins across the roof of the mouth for punctuation. Screw cap. 14.5% alc. **Rating** 90 **To** 2028 $42 NG
Silver Hammer McLaren Vale Shiraz 2018 A lustrous deep ruby. The first impression: cocoa and vanilla/bourbon American oak. French oak in there, too. Plenty of dark-fruit aspersions in the midst, but this address is very reliant on barrels (new and old) for the salubrious effect that they seek. Sometimes, overdone. Here, just about right. For those seeking a smooth rummage of fruit that melts into a malty sheath of oak, here is your wine. Fine value, to boot. Screw cap. 14.5% alc. **Rating** 90 **To** 2024 $24 NG

🍷🍷🍷🍷 **Clan Wine Club Malbec 2019** **Rating** 89 **To** 2024 $36 NG
Four Roads McLaren Vale Grenache 2019 **Rating** 88 **To** 2024 $32 NG

Mayer ★★★★★

66 Miller Road, Healesville, Vic 3777 **Region** Yarra Valley
T (03) 5967 3777 **www**.timomayer.com.au **Open** By appt
Winemaker Timo Mayer **Est.** 1999 **Dozens** 2000 **Vyds** 3ha
Timo Mayer, also winemaker at Gembrook Hill Vineyard, teamed with partner Rhonda Ferguson to establish Mayer on the slopes of Mt Toolebewong, 8km south of Healesville. The steepness of those slopes is presumably 'celebrated' in the name given to the vineyard (Bloody Hill). Pinot noir has the lion's share of the high-density vineyard, with smaller amounts of shiraz and chardonnay. Mayer's winemaking credo is minimal interference and handling, and no filtration. The Empire of Dirt wines are a collaboration between son Rivar Ferguson-Mayer and UK importer Ben Henshaw. Exports to the UK, France, Germany, Denmark, Sweden, Singapore and Japan.

🍷🍷🍷🍷🍷 **Yarra Valley Syrah 2020** It's a chiaroscuro wine. Light and shade. Ripe and less so. It's also super-refreshing, with oodles of pepper, juniper, umeboshi (salted plums) and red berries. The whole bunches add some complexing Italian digestif, bitter herb and orange notes. There's also crunchy acidity, sinewy tannins and a fair amount of energy. Diam. 13.5% alc. **Rating** 95 **To** 2028 $55 JF
Yarra Valley Merlot 2020 Of course this is made with 100% whole bunches in the ferment. It's Timo Mayer's style. It works, as there's a juiciness matched to more savoury flavours. It's surprisingly not stalky or sappy from the whole bunches, so there's obviously good ripeness here. I could drink a lot of this. Yup. Merlot. But not as you know it. Diam. 13% alc. **Rating** 95 **To** 2026 $50 JF
Yarra Valley Cabernet 2020 There's such a vibrancy and deliciousness here (via the 100% whole-bunch ferment), not a green twig flavour at all. A delicate wrap of cassis, blackcurrants, pepper and baking spices with more tangy/tart pink grapefruit and fresh umeboshi. Tannins are in tow, acidity too, and it finishes fresh and convincing. Diam. 13.5% alc. **Rating** 94 **To** 2028 $55 JF

🍷🍷🍷🍷🍷 **Bloody Hill Villages Coldstream Syrah 2020** **Rating** 93 **To** 2027 $36 JF
Bloody Hill Villages Healesville Pinot Gris 2020 **Rating** 92 **To** 2024 $32 JF
Bloody Hill Villages Healesville Sauvignon Blanc 2020 **Rating** 90 **To** 2026 $32 JF

Mayford Wines

★★★★★

6815 Great Alpine Road, Porepunkah, Vic 3740 **Region** Alpine Valleys
T (03) 5756 2528 **www**.mayfordwines.com **Open** By appt
Winemaker Eleana Anderson **Est.** 1995 **Dozens** 1000 **Vyds** 3.9ha

The roots of Mayford go back to 1995, when Brian Nicholson planted a small amount of shiraz, chardonnay and tempranillo. Further plantings of shiraz, tempranillo, cabernet sauvignon and malbec have increased the vineyard to 3.9ha, with more plantings planned. In their words, 'In-house winemaking commenced shortly after Brian selected his seasoned winemaker bride in 2002'. Wife and co-owner Eleana Anderson was a Flying Winemaker, working 4 vintages in Germany while completing her wine science degree at CSU (having earlier obtained an arts degree). Vintages in Australia included one at Feathertop (also at Porepunkah), where she met Brian. Initially, Eleana was unenthusiastic about tempranillo, which Brian had planted after consultation with Mark Walpole, Brown Brothers' viticulturist. But since making the first vintage in '06, she has been thoroughly enamoured of the variety. Eleana practises minimalist winemaking, declining to use enzymes, cultured yeasts, tannins and/or copper. Exports to Singapore.

🍷🍷🍷🍷🍷 **Porepunkah Shiraz 2018** Another exciting journey into cool-climate shiraz territory, exuding both strength and intensity, but with a fine touch. Scent of blackberries, generous spice and earth. Starts with a bang flavour-wise, all ripe, a no-beg-your-pardon confidence, but then slides irresistibly into an embrace of violet, dark chocolate and warm, woodsy spice. Screw cap. 13.9% alc. **Rating** 95 To 2032 $44 JP

Ovens Crossing Porepunkah Tempranillo Cabernet Sauvignon 2018 Do yourself a favour and make this a keeper. While everything is in its place and nicely so, it's still got a way to go, which is the winemaker's intention. It is made with longevity in mind, hence the firm tannin structure and the noted involvement of vanillan oak wrapped around some classy, generous black fruits, spice and wild herbs. The middle palate sings a mighty tantalising song. Screw cap. 13.9% alc. **Rating** 95 To 2032 $55 JP

Porepunkah Tempranillo 2019 This is a smart tempranillo, delivering a fine-grained elegance. Ripe, dark fruits lead by black cherry envelope the senses. Red licorice, violets and herbs add a fragrant touch on the palate, nicely entwined by savoury tannins. This wine is definitely heading in the direction of super-complexity. Keep it ageing a little longer, if you can. Screw cap. 13.9% alc. **Rating** 95 To 2034 $42 JP ❤

🍷🍷🍷🍷🍷 **John Warwick Chardonnay 2019** **Rating** 93 To 2027 $42 JP

Maygars Hill Winery

★★★★☆

53 Longwood-Mansfield Road, Longwood, Vic 3665 **Region** Strathbogie Ranges
T 0402 136 448 **www**.maygarshill.com.au **Open** By appt
Winemaker Contract **Est.** 1997 **Dozens** 900 **Vyds** 3.2ha

Jenny Houghton purchased this 8ha property in 1994, planting shiraz (1.9ha) and cabernet sauvignon (1.3ha). The name comes from Lieutenant Colonel Maygar, who fought with outstanding bravery in the Boer War in South Africa in 1901 and was awarded the Victoria Cross. In World War I he rose to command the 8th Light Horse Regiment, winning yet further medals for bravery. The 100th anniversary of Lieutenant Colonel Maygar's death was in 2017. The Shiraz and Cabernet Sauvignon, both in Reserve and standard guise, have been consistently excellent for a number of years. In mid-2021, the winery was sold to established vineyard owners from North East Victoria. Exports to China.

🍷🍷🍷🍷🍷 **Shiraz 2019** An excellent follow-up to the superb '18 shiraz, with concentration and style. Deep purple hue. Still youthful and in development mode, but sporting typical 'bogies balance and structure. Sweet, ripe black cherry, bracken, abundant woody spices and baked earth. The palate has a dense but smooth texture, with a touch of lasting elegance. Screw cap. 14% alc. **Rating** 95 To 2027 $30 JP ✪

Reserve Cabernet Sauvignon 2019 A distinctive cabernet described by the maker as an 'elegant' version of the standard cabernet, with a percentage of whole bunches added to the ferment. Matured in American and French oak for 16 months, it has slurped up the oak, retaining a cedary sheen. A deep, dark world of violets, cassis, briar and wild forest berries. Light savouriness on the palate. Supple and, yes, elegant. Bring out the decanter with this one. Screw cap. 13% alc. Rating 95 To 2029 $42 JP

Cabernet Sauvignon 2019 Sings loudly where it hails from, a telltale bay-leaf/eucalyptus thread very much in evidence. It is without doubt an attractive feature, a potent sense of Central Victorian terroir. Good varietal intensity, too: cassis and black cherry, dried bay leaf, a touch of peppermint, violet, leafy. Sinewy mouthfeel. Fine, edgy tannins are quite pronounced, providing structure and potential for further ageing. Screw cap. 13% alc. **Rating 94 To 2029 $30 JP ©**

mazi wines ★★★★

5 Wilbala Road, Longwood, SA 5153 **Region** McLaren Vale
T 0406 615 553 **www**.maziwines.com.au
Winemaker Alex Katsaros, Toby Porter **Est.** 2016 **Dozens** 1500
Lifelong friends Toby Porter and Alex Katsaros always talked about making wine together as an adjunct to their day jobs in wine. Toby has been a winemaker at d'Arenberg for 15+ years and Alex had 10 years' experience working with alternative varieties here and abroad. They decided to only make rosé, and more power to them in doing so. McLaren Vale is the sole source for their grapes, focusing on grenache, but they are happy to work with bush-vine mataro. The aim is to produce fresh wines with vibrant fruit, normally by crushing and pressing the grapes for a cool ferment in stainless steel, but maturation in old French oak can (and has) been used to build palate complexity without sacrificing fruit. The derivation of the name is as simple as that of their raison d'être – it is Greek for together. Exports to the US, Singapore and Hong Kong.

🍷🍷🍷🍷🍷 **Limited Release McLaren Vale Rosé 2020** A superb rosé from grenache and mourvèdre, whole-bunch pressed and partly barrel fermented. An eddy of creamy red fruits, spiced oatmeal and white peach pith notes segue to a chewy, ferrous mid palate. No wonder given the varieties at hand and savvy oak handling. Medium bodied, but rich for the idiom. Bone dry, herbal and winningly savoury. A thirst-slaking burst of freshness follows, towing it long. I'd be drinking this with richer dishes. This is as good as rosé gets. Cork. 13% alc. Rating 95 To 2024 $44 NG ♥

🍷🍷🍷🍷🍸 **McLaren Vale Grenache Rosé 2020** Rating 92 To 2022 $25 NG ©

Mazza Wines ★★★★

PO Box 480, Donnybrook, WA 6239 **Region** Geographe
T (08) 9201 1114 **www**.mazza.com.au
Winemaker Contract **Est.** 2002 **Dozens** 1000 **Vyds** 4ha
David and Anne Mazza were inspired by the great wines of Rioja and the Douro Valley, and continue a long-standing family tradition of making wine. They have planted the key varieties of those 2 regions: tempranillo, graciano, bastardo, sousão, tinta cão and touriga nacional. They believe they were the first Australian vineyard to present this collection of varieties on a single site and I am reasonably certain they are correct. Exports to the UK.

🍷🍷🍷🍷🍷 **Geographe Touriga Nacional 2018** Delicious. Exciting. Savoury, layered and complex, this has oodles of mulberry, blackberry, raspberry and red licorice. It's both salty and sweet, with juicy acid firmly entrenched between the two, providing balance, finesse and depth. Not enough can be said in favour of this wine. It has great length of flavour, and evolution across the palate, too. A superstar from a brilliant vintage. Screw cap. 14.5% alc. Rating 96 To 2031 $32 EL ©

Geographe Touriga Nacional Sousao 2017 Mulberry, satsuma plum, earthy tannins and a plush, savoury character that is very much 'not from here'. This has a cleansing acid line that keeps the dense, fresh fruit in check, while the suggestion of blood, ferrous, salted licorice and charcuterie make for very interesting drinking indeed. Balanced, exciting and quite delicious. Screw cap. 14% alc. **Rating** 94 To 2031 $32 EL

♈♈♈♈♉ Geographe Bastardo Rosé 2020 Rating 93 To 2022 $28 EL
Geographe Tempranillo 2018 Rating 91 To 2030 $30 EL

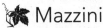 # Mazzini

12 Albert Terrace Belmont, Vic 3216 (postal) **Region** Geelong
T 0448 045 845 **www**.mazziniwines.com.au
Winemaker Ray Nadeson, Duncan Lowe **Est.** 2016 **Dozens** 400
Mazzini Wines was established in 2016 by Paul and Karen Marinelli after fostering strong connections with the Geelong wine industry over the last decade. Mazzini Wines doesn't boast the usual winery, vineyard and cellar door but rather operates as a form of négociant/wine merchant, sourcing fruit from some of the region's most promising individual vineyards and utilising the skills of experienced local winemakers Ray Nadeson and Duncan Lowe. The colourful Mazzini wine labels are a nod to Paul's Italian heritage and the name of his Nonno's street in Mola di Bari in Puglia, Italy. The wines are intended to reflect the hands-on and pure approach to the produce he grew up admiring in his family. (JP)

♈♈♈♈♉ Geelong Pinot Noir 2019 Wild-yeast fermentation with 10% whole bunches, matured in new and used French oak. A wonderful showcase for Geelong pinot noir, mixing boldness of fruit and presence in the glass with nuance and complexity. Glossy and deep in colour. Fragrant in raspberry, red cherry, violets and anise. A full, exciting mouthful of flavour with everything in its place, running smooth and long. Screw cap. 13.1% alc. **Rating** 92 To 2026 $33 JP

♈♈♈♈ Single Vineyard Geelong Chardonnay 2020 Rating 88 To 2024 $33 JP
Single Vineyard Geelong Pinot Gris 2020 Rating 88 To 2025 $30 JP
Single Vineyard Geelong Shiraz 2019 Rating 88 To 2028 $30 JP

Meadowbank Wines

652 Meadowbank Road, Meadowbank, Tas 7140 **Region** Southern Tasmania
T 0439 448 151 **www**.meadowbank.com.au **Open** By appt
Winemaker Peter Dredge **Est.** 1976 **Dozens** 800 **Vyds** 52ha
In 1976 Gerald and Sue Ellis picked the first grapes from their large Glenora property at the top end of the Derwent River from vines planted 2 years earlier by the previous owner. There have been 4 major expansions since, most recently a 10ha planting of pinot noir, chardonnay, syrah and gamay in 2016, lifting the total to 52ha, the major part as fully mature vines. Meadowbank supplies grapes to 6 or so small wineries and also leases 32ha to Accolade. Peter Dredge, having been intimately associated with the vineyard for 6 years, formed a partnership with the Ellis family (Gerald, Sue, daughter Mardi and her husband, Alex Deane) to relaunch Meadowbank. The wines are made by Peter at his contract winemaking facility from the portion of vineyard set aside for the Meadowbank wines. Exports to South East Asia, China and Taiwan.

♈♈♈♈♉ Chardonnay 2020 All the tension and presence of this historic estate high in the Derwent Valley. Impressive concentration of lemon, grapefruit and white peach, evenly supported by cashew nut French oak. A grand finish of focus and endurance rides on a laser beam of cool, crystalline acidity. Long-term prospects. Screw cap. 12.5% alc. **Rating** 95 To 2037 $50 TS
Pinot Noir 2020 A jubilant celebration of elegant, young pinot! Fresh, vibrant, primary and crunchy. Bountiful red cherries, poached strawberries and raspberries, elevated by the fragrant rose petal, potpourri and dried herb of nicely moderated whole-bunch fermentation. A long finish is charged equally by tangy morello cherry acidity as silky, fine-ground tannins. The quintessential lunchtime pinot. Screw cap. 13% alc. **Rating** 94 To 2028 $55 TS

Medhurst

24–26 Medhurst Road, Gruyere, Vic 3770 **Region** Yarra Valley
T (03) 5964 9022 **www.medhurstwines.com.au Open** Thurs–Mon & public hols 11–5
Winemaker Simon Steele **Est.** 2000 **Dozens** 6000 **Vyds** 12ha
The wheel has come full circle for Ross and Robyn Wilson. In the course of a very distinguished corporate career, Ross was CEO of Southcorp when it brought the Penfolds, Lindemans and Wynns businesses under its banner. Robyn spent her childhood in the Yarra Valley, her parents living less than a kilometre away from Medhurst. The vineyard is planted to low-yielding sauvignon blanc, chardonnay, pinot noir, cabernet sauvignon and shiraz vines. The winery focuses on small-batch production and also provides contract winemaking services. The visual impact of the winery has been minimised by recessing the building into the slope of land and locating the barrel room underground. The building was recognised for its architectural excellence at the Victorian Architecture Awards. The arrival of Simon Steele (his loss much mourned by Brokenwood) has enhanced the already considerable reputation of Medhurst.

🍷🍷🍷🍷🍷 **Estate Vineyard Chardonnay 2020** Wowee. This is a bit of rock'n'roll. All citrus tones, with flint, fennel and daikon. It's complex and savoury, with lots of texture. Brilliant acidity wraps it up tightly. Moreish and utterly delicious. Screw cap. 13% alc. **Rating** 96 **To** 2032 $44 JF ✪
Reserve Yarra Valley Chardonnay 2019 Reserve in name and reserved in nature. It takes time to coax out the flavours hiding within: nougatine, lemon zest and citrus, lemon curd and a dusting of oak. Seemingly light on, but it is more about restraint here. The chalky acidity renders the palate long and takes it into the future. This is a sleeper at the moment. Give it time to wake up. Screw cap. 13.2% alc. **Rating** 96 **To** 2032 $90 JF
Reserve Yarra Valley Cabernet 2018 This shares similar DNA to the estate cabernet and that means elegance, but this just has the X-factor, so important for a Reserve. Here it has a bit more flavour and depth, albeit in a finely tuned offering. There are waves of flavour: red and blackcurrants, fennel and fresh tobacco, with cedary oak, all rolled into a harmonious whole. Tannins are lovely, fine yet ripe. Acidity brings a freshness to a lovely wine. Alas, a paltry 30 dozen made. Screw cap. 13% alc. **Rating** 96 **To** 2033 $90 JF
Estate Vineyard Rosé 2020 A pastel pink copper blush entices. Lightly spiced and delicately flavoured with redcurrants and a squeeze of blackberries. There's some texture and savouriness, a succulence and juiciness. It's refreshing to the very last drop and the joy continues. Top rosé. Screw cap. 13% alc. **Rating** 95 **To** 2023 $25 JF ✪
Estate Vineyard Pinot Noir 2020 The aromas and flavours packed into this wine are head spinning. Sweet black cherries take on a Middle Eastern array of spices, with sumac and chinotto. There's a succulence across the medium-bodied palate, tannins with the texture of raw silk and a vibrancy to the acidity. This is quite something. Screw cap. 13% alc. **Rating** 95 **To** 2032 $50 JF
Estate Vineyard Cabernet Sauvignon 2018 It would be easy to overlook this in other company. That would be a shame. It's finely chiselled and pure. There's a balance of flavours, completely absorbing 40% new oak. It's medium bodied and lithe, with powdery, light tannins and elegance writ large. Screw cap. 13% alc. **Rating** 95 **To** 2030 $60 JF
YRB 2020 50/50% pinot noir/shiraz, hand picked and destemmed fruit, eventually ending up in used French puncheons for 8 months. A wine that makes you want to take the day off and enjoy a long lunch. It has a gorgeous perfume and the palate delivers juicy and bright cherries and plums, all spiced up. It's vibrant, refreshing and feels light, with a gentle tow to its tannins. Screw cap. 13.5% alc. **Rating** 95 **To** 2027 $44 JF

🍷🍷🍷🍷🍷 **Estate Vineyard Yarra Valley Shiraz 2019 Rating** 93 **To** 2033 $60 JF

Meerea Park ★★★★★

Pavilion B, 2144 Broke Road, Pokolbin, NSW 2320 **Region** Hunter Valley
T (02) 4998 7474 **www**.meereapark.com.au **Open** 7 days 10–5
Winemaker Rhys Eather **Est.** 1991 **Dozens** 10000
This is the project of Rhys and Garth Eather, whose great-great-grandfather, Alexander
Munro, established a famous vineyard in the 19th century, known as Bebeah. While the
range of wines chiefly focuses on semillon and shiraz, it extends to other varieties (including
chardonnay) and also into other regions. Meerea Park's cellar door is located at the striking
Tempus Two winery, owned by the Roche family, situated on the corner of Broke Road and
McDonald Road. It hardly need be said that the quality of the wines, especially with 5 years'
cellaring, is outstanding. Exports to the UK, the US, Canada, Singapore and China.

ΨΨΨΨΨ **Alexander Munro Individual Vineyard Aged Release Hunter Valley
Semillon 2011** A wine of structural mettle and fealty to the region. The
mantle of ageability, so integral to variety and region, is intact. A dichotomous
mesh of balletic finesse and body, with cumquat marmalade, quince, lemon balm
and buttered toast riffs of semillon breaching middle age, rather than senility.
Exceptional. Screw cap. 11% alc. **Rating** 96 **To** 2028 $80 NG ♥
Indie Individual Vineyard Hunter Valley Marsanne Roussanne 2019
This is exceptional. Such promise, suggesting more of these great Rhône varieties
should be planted in the region. Sumptuous and savoury, with pear, marzipan,
dried straw and cheesecloth scents billowing across a full-weighted palate; sewn
by a thread of mineral between seams of smart oak. I'd like more phenolics, but
excellent all the same. Screw cap. 13% alc. **Rating** 96 **To** 2030 $30 NG ✪
Alexander Munro Individual Vineyard Hunter Valley Semillon 2015 An
aged release, the juvenile shins and elbows shed for more mature, relaxed and
subtle complexities. Light bodied but rich of flavour. Less sherbet and citrus; more
lanolin, lemon balm, buttered toast and quince, the acidity palpably absorbed by
the wine's expansive gait and effortless, long glide. Screw cap. 11% alc. **Rating** 95
To 2028 $50 NG
Hell Hole Individual Vineyard Hunter Valley Shiraz 2019 Fascinating how
these individual-vineyard iterations ebb and flow in such expert hands. This feels
like the Hunter of my youth: sarsaparilla, varnish, molten cherry, anise, polished
leather and something saddle-bound and rustic. Yet clean. Savoury. Relaxed. Of
a place. Full, according to the alcohol on the label, yet feels mid weighted, with a
firm, tannic bind to the food on the table. Screw cap. 14% alc. **Rating** 95 **To** 2032
$60 NG
Terracotta Individual Vineyard Hunter Valley Shiraz 2019 The syrah
moniker suggests a cool climate, yet this remains a distinctively loamy-textured and
savoury Hunter wine. As 20% whole bunch, it imparts a gentle scrub of cardamom
to tamarind-soused tannins, galvanising chinotto, varnish and black-cherry aromas.
Yet the oak is what sets this wine apart: wielded with a deft hand, it sublimates
sweetness and leads to a long, precise finish. Screw cap. 14.5% alc. **Rating** 94
To 2030 $70 NG
BLACK Hunter Valley Shiraz 2018 Unlike so many prestige cuvées, this
eschews a riper harvest window and overt oak for a relatively savoury expression
of place and refinement, despite the largesse of extract and high-quality fruit that
comes from a best-of-the-best barrel culling. The oak, new and used, is easily
absorbed. Blueberry, mulberry and violet. A sweet mid palate chafed by a bridge
of tannins. The flow is long and classy. A bit sweet, to be churlish, but this will age
well. Screw cap. 14% alc. **Rating** 94 **To** 2032 $300 NG

ΨΨΨΨΨ **Terracotta Individual Vineyard Hunter Valley Semillon 2016** Rating 93
To 2030 $35 NG
Indie Individual Vineyard Hunter Valley Roussanne 2019 Rating 93
To 2025 $30 NG
Alexander Munro Individual Vineyard Hunter Valley Shiraz 2018
Rating 93 **To** 2032 $110 NG

Late Harvest Hunter Valley Semillon 2019 Rating 91 To 2024 $25 NG
The Aunts Individual Vineyard Hunter Valley Shiraz 2019 Rating 91
To 2025 $35 NG
XYZ Hunter Valley Shiraz 2019 Rating 90 To 2026 $25 NG

 Memento Wines

60 Melvilles Road, Rutherglen, Vic 3685 **Region** Rutherglen
T www.memento-wines.com.au
Winemaker Jonathon Thompson **Est.** 2017 **Dozens** 640
The story of Memento Wines is in large part the story of Roy Dempsey (1930–2010), the
late grandfather of winemaker Jonathon 'Jono' Thompson. Dempsey left school at the age of
14 in 1944 to work with his father in the famous Burgoynes vineyard in Rutherglen, and
devoted the next 66 years to working the vineyards and wineries of the region, often with his
young grandson by his side. Young Jono followed in his footsteps, first in viticulture and then
in winemaking at Rutherglen Estates before going on to work extended stints in California
and in Italy at Alberto Antonini's Poggiotondo in Chianti. In 2015 he rejoined Rutherglen
Estates. Two years later he teamed up with business partners, Kirby and Luke Heyme, to form
Memento Wines. A working winery is now being established on the same land where Jono's
grandfather Roy dabbled in winemaking in a shed, producing wines for family and friends.
And so, the Dempsey wine story turns full circle. (JP)

ΨΨΨΨΩ **King Valley Riesling 2018** An off-dry style but unfortunately not indicated
on the label. Sourced from Whitlands, one of the highest subregions in the
country at 800m elevation, we see a lovely purity of cool–climate fruit. Fragrant
white flowers, lime cordial, lemon and grapefruit. Moves with grace across the
palate. Zesty acidity with fruit-tingly sweetness. Screw cap. 12.5% alc. **Rating** 92
To 2026 $32 JP
Rutherglen Shiraz Durif 2018 Both grape varieties putting on a show,
championing a style which deserves more attention. Shiraz (with pelourin)
is in fact parent to durif, so it's a nice fit. Lovely, expressive wine highlighting
dark chocolate, plum, dark berries and a world of sweet spice. Dense and supple
with well-honed tannins, it's good to go now. Screw cap. 14.7% alc. **Rating** 92
To 2030 $30 JP

ΨΨΨΨ **Beechworth Merlot Cabernet Sauvignon 2017** Rating 89 To 2026 $25 JP
Beechworth Sangiovese 2018 Rating 89 To 2025 $25 JP
Yarra Valley Pinot Noir 2017 Rating 88 To 2025 $38 JP

Merindoc Vintners

PO Box 77, Tooborac, Vic 3522 **Region** Heathcote
T (03) 5433 5188 **www**.merindoc.com.au
Winemaker Steve Webber, Sergio Carlei, Bryan Martin **Est.** 1994 **Dozens** 1800 **Vyds** 35ha
Stephen Shelmerdine has been a major figure in the wine industry for over 25 years, like his
family (who founded Mitchelton Winery) before him, and has been honoured for his many
services to the industry. Substantial quantities of the grapes produced are sold to others; a
small amount of high-quality wine is contract-made. The Merindoc and Willoughby Bridge
wines are produced from the 2 eponymous estate vineyards in Heathcote. Exports to China.

ΨΨΨΨΩ **Merindoc Heathcote Riesling 2019** Soft acidity (yes, it's a thing) makes a
big impression here, contributing delicious approachability while also acting as a
launch pad for a lively citrus intensity. Apple blossom, jasmine, lime cordial, freshly
cut apple. Juicy and spicy. Screw cap. 11.5% alc. **Rating** 93 To 2026 $27 JP **O**
Merindoc Heathcote Shiraz 2018 From a single 1.6ha block at Tooborac at
the southern entry to the Heathcote region. The area's granitic soils come into
play, contributing a natural balance and depth to the wine. Lingering cracked
pepper and spice, black fruits, dusty road/earth. Slurped up its 17 months in
French oak barriques to produce an all-round charmer wrapped up in sinewy

tannins and impressive regional credentials. Screw cap. 14.2% alc. **Rating** 93
To 2028 $49 JP

Willoughby Bridge Heathcote Sangiovese 2018 Accomplished and
confident in delivery, sangiovese is proving to be just as at home in Heathcote as
shiraz. A similar varietal fruit range, too, from blackberry, black cherry and plum,
but it's that light herbal/caper infusion that indicates the variety. Plays out across
a textural background with a gently savoury personality on show. Screw cap.
13% alc. **Rating** 91 To 2028 $33 JP

Merindoc Heathcote Viognier 2019 A bit of a strong suit at Merindoc on
the southern border and across the entire Heathcote wine region, viognier laps
up the warmth and gives back in kind with spice, musk, apple and citrus on a lush
palate with crunchy acid freshness. Super-smart youngster. Screw cap. 13.5% alc.
Rating 90 To 2025 $27 JP

Willoughby Bridge Heathcote Vermentino 2019 Another solid vermentino
from this Heathcote producer who is moving more and more into Mediterranean
grape varieties. Gently spiced poached pear, apple, white nectarine fruit with
a dusty, earthy overlay. There's almost a wild honey character peeking through,
too. Chalky texture and nice balance throughout. Screw cap. 12% alc. **Rating** 90
To 2025 $27 JP

Willoughby Bridge Heathcote Montepulciano 2018 Lively garnet red. Kind
of quiet to start with: black cherry, subtle spice and a touch of potpourri. More
forceful to taste with plenty of berry goodness, liberal spice, licorice strap and
some Italian-esque prune and light savouriness. It's a relatively simple wine but the
enjoyment factor is high. Screw cap. 13.7% alc. **Rating** 90 To 2025 $33 JP

Merindoc Heathcote Sparkling Shiraz 2018 One of the lighter, prettier and
more aromatic sparkling reds on the market, it brings together a fine texture and
a slightly drier approach, which is bound to find it good acceptance as both an
aperitif and with food. Damson plums, raspberry and gentle spice and savouriness.
Clean, fresh and youthful. Diam. 13% alc. **Rating** 90 $39 JP

ȲȲȲȲ   **Merindoc Heathcote Chardonnay 2019** Rating 89 To 2025 $27 JP
Heathcote Pinot Grigio 2019 Rating 89 To 2023 $27 JP
Willoughby Bridge Heathcote Shiraz 2018 Rating 89 To 2027 $35 JP
Willoughby Bridge Heathcote Albariño 2019 Rating 88 To 2024 $27 JP
Heathcote Blanc de Blancs 2018 Rating 88 $39 JP

Mérite Wines   ★★★★

PO Box 167, Penola, SA 5277 **Region** Wrattonbully
T 0437 190 244 **www**.meritewines.com
Winemaker Mike Kloak **Est.** 2000 **Dozens** 2000 **Vyds** 40ha
Mérite Wines was established in 2000. It was the end of Mike Kloak and Colleen Miller's
protracted search for high-quality viticultural land, with a particular focus on the production of
merlot utilising recently released clones that hold the promise of producing wine of a quality
not previously seen. However, it's not a case of all eggs in the same basket; malbec, cabernet
sauvignon and shiraz have also been planted. It was not until '13 that the first small amount of
wine was made (most of the grapes were, and will continue to be, sold to other winemakers).

ȲȲȲȲȲ   **Wrattonbully Merlot Rosé 2020** Refreshing as a spring or summer's day.
Either way, this is delicious. A pale ruby with a copper tinge. It's tangy with
clementine and cranberries, lightly spiced, and the lemony acidity leaves a crisp
finish. Screw cap. 13.4% alc. **Rating** 93 To 2023 $24 JF ❂

Merricks Estate   ★★★★

Thompsons Lane, Merricks, Vic 3916 **Region** Mornington Peninsula
T (03) 5989 8419 **www**.merricksestate.com.au **Open** 1st w'end of month, every
w'end in Jan
Winemaker Simon Black (Contract) **Est.** 1977 **Dozens** 2000 **Vyds** 4ha

Melbourne solicitor George Kefford, with wife Jacky, runs Merricks Estate as a weekend and holiday enterprise. It produces distinctive, spicy, cool-climate shiraz, which has accumulated an impressive array of show trophies and gold medals. As the current tasting notes demonstrate, the fully mature vineyard and skilled contract winemaking by Simon Black are producing top class wines. Exports to Hong Kong.

ΨΨΨΨΩ **Mornington Peninsula Chardonnay 2019** A rich and flavoursome style, almost old-school but not outdated. Yellow peaches and poached pears drizzled with cream. Really spicy, all cinnamon and peppery. The oak is making an impact both in flavour and in the shape of the wine – almost too much, but the acidity ensures everything is in place. Screw cap. 13.5% alc. **Rating** 90 **To** 2026 $40 JF

ΨΨΨΨ   **Mornington Peninsula Shiraz 2016 Rating** 88 **To** 2025 $34 JF

 # mesh   ★★★★

40 Eden Valley Road, Angaston SA 5353 **Region** Eden Valley
T (08) 8561 3200 **www.**meshwine.com
Winemaker Robert Hill-Smith, Jeffrey Grosset **Est. Dozens** 2000 **Vyds** 12ha
Celebrating its 20th anniversary in 2022, mesh is the profound yet unlikely weaving together of the skills, knowledge and ideas of 2 names arguably more obsessive about South Australian riesling than any other: Robert Hill-Smith (5th-generation custodian of Yalumba) and Clare Valley legend Jeffrey Grosset. Their simple mandate is to champion Eden Valley riesling in a single wine. Fruit is sourced from 2 vineyards planted in 1944 and 1982 at 425m elevation. Hill-Smith and Grosset each vinify the same fruit separately, hand picked from alternate rows on the same day. The final blend is determined collaboratively post-vintage, 'amid lively debate'. The result is as legendary as its story anticipates, though unfairly (yet perhaps inevitably) never seems to enjoy quite the limelight enjoyed by Hill-Smith and Grosset's own rieslings. (TS)

ΨΨΨΨΨ **Classic Release Eden Valley Riesling 2015** A cool January produced an ideal balance of flavour and natural acidity. A fantastically youthful and dynamic 6yo riesling, upholding a vibrant, youthful, pale straw-green hue. Lime, lemon and Granny Smith apple have but begun their evolution to almond meal, spice and honey. Crystalline acidity sustains impressive line, persistence and energy. One of the greats for the cellar. Screw cap. 12% alc. **Rating** 95 **To** 2032 $38 TS

ΨΨΨΨΩ **Eden Valley Riesling 2020 Rating** 92 **To** 2025 $32 TS

Mewstone Wines   ★★★★★

11 Flowerpot Jetty Road, Flowerpot, Tas 7163 **Region** Southern Tasmania
T 0425 253 218 **www.**mewstonewines.com.au **Open** Thurs–Mon 11–4.30
Winemaker Jonathan Hughes **Est.** 2011 **Dozens** 5000 **Vyds** 3.6ha
Brothers Matthew and Jonathan (Jonny) Hughes established Mewstone Vineyard on the banks of the D'Entrecasteaux Channel in the tiny hamlet of Flowerpot in 2011. The vineyard is planted on a former cherry orchard, the original 2ha since expanded to 3.6ha consisting mainly of pinot noir (2ha) with 0.7ha each of riesling and chardonnay and a tiny 0.2ha of shiraz. Jonny is the winemaker in this family venture; he studied winemaking in NZ before working in Langhorne Creek, Central Otago, Mornington Peninsula, Barolo, Hunter Valley and Okanagan Valley in British Columbia. Heading home to Tasmania, Jonny worked in various roles within the local wine industry before settling in as the assistant winemaker at Moorilla Estate for 7 years. With the vineyard established to produce the single-site Mewstone wines, the brothers have embarked on a second label, Hughes & Hughes, which focuses on Tasmania as a whole. Purchasing quality grapes from other local vineyards, this label uses slightly unconventional winemaking techniques that Jonny encountered on his world travels. Small-batch production means he can put maximum effort in. Best New Winery in the *Wine Companion 2019*. Exports to Singapore, China and Italy.

ΨΨΨΨΨ **Hughes & Hughes Lees Aged Chardonnay 2019** From a single vineyard in the Coal River Valley, wild-yeast fermented in barrel, 100% mlf, matured on lees for 10 months. The power and intensity of the wine is remarkable, as is its funky complexity. Grapefruit is in the saddle, white stone fruit close by. A compelling wine. Screw cap. 13.9% alc. **Rating** 98 **To** 2032 $45 JH ✪

ŦŦŦŦŦ **Hughes & Hughes 25% Whole Bunch Pinot Noir 2019** As the name suggests, this single-vineyard pinot was fermented with 25% whole bunches, the remainder destemmed whole berries, matured in French oak for 10 months. Excellent colour; the bouquet is riddled with exotic spices, the powerful black cherry palate with forest floor notes and abundant tannins. Longevity is assured. Screw cap. 13.2% alc. **Rating** 96 **To** 2034 $45 JH ✪

ŦŦŦŦŶ **Hughes & Hughes Pinot Gris 2020 Rating** 93 **To** 2022 $30 TS
Hughes & Hughes Riesling 2020 Rating 92 **To** 2030 $30 TS
D'Entrecasteaux Channel Chardonnay 2019 Rating 92 **To** 2024 $60 TS
Hope Pinot Noir 2018 Rating 92 **To** 2043 $125 TS
Hughes & Hughes Chardonnay 2020 Rating 91 **To** 2025 $35 TS
Hughes & Hughes Lees Aged Chardonnay 2020 Rating 91 **To** 2030 $45 TS
D'Entrecasteaux Channel Riesling 2019 Rating 90 **To** 2034 $50 TS

Mia Valley Estate   ★★★☆

203 Daniels Lane, Mia Mia, Vic 3444 **Region** Heathcote
T (03) 5425 5515 **www.miavalleyestate.com.au Open** 7 days 10–5
Winemaker Norbert Baumgartner, Pamela Baumgartner, Nick Baumgartner **Est.** 1999
Dozens 1000 **Vyds** 3.2ha
Norbert and Pam Baumgartner both had indirect connections with wine, and a direct interest in drinking it. In 1998, after many years of searching for the right property, they discovered 40ha with softly undulating land and the Mia Mia (pronounced mya-mya) Creek running through it. They produced their first vintage, from 1.6ha of shiraz and cabernet, in their garage in 2002. Over the years they have built a winery, doubled plantings and grafted some vines over to riesling and malbec. Along the way Norbert completed winemaking and viticulture courses. They then contended with the '09 bushfires, the '11 rains, floods and disease, a '12 vintage more than they could handle, '14 decimated by frosts and late '15 and '16 severe drought. Are they giving up? No sign of it so far. They have been joined in the winery and vineyards by son Nick. Exports to the UK, the US, Japan and China.

ŦŦŦŦ **Barrel Select Heathcote Shiraz 2018** An abundance of fruit and oak here in equal proportion. Solid, full bodied and chunky, with a wealth of ripe fruits and toasty oak. Boasts a smooth, weighty presence in the glass. Earth, leather, roast meat and prune highlight a definite savoury bent, too. Screw cap. 14.5% alc. **Rating** 89 **To** 2028 $40 JP
Mia Mia Heathcote Shiraz Cabernet Sauvignon 2018 The classic Aussie blend remains alive and well and offering a ripe, generous barrel selection. There is a definite sense of place on display, of Aussie bush, bay leaf, roasted spices, plums moving into a rich, deep palate with cabernet tannins helping to drive structure and energy. Screw cap. 14.5% alc. **Rating** 89 **To** 2030 $45 JP
Heathcote Cabernet Malbec 2018 In keeping with the Mia Valley Estate style of generous, sweet-fruited, well-oaked reds, the cabernet malbec fits a lot of everything in, including juicy blackberry, vanilla pod, dark chocolate, licorice and choc-mint/spearmint spice. Baked earth and leather savouriness give an Old World feel. Screw cap. 13.5% alc. **Rating** 89 **To** 2026 $30 JP
Luta Heathcote Shiraz 2018 Celebrates generosity, unabashed and large, but it carries quite well. A more powerful expression of Heathcote shiraz than we normally get to see. Blackberry, Aussie bush, red earth, spice, savoury notes. The presence of woody, smoky, nutty oak makes a show on the palate. Warm alcohol finish. Screw cap. 15.9% alc. **Rating** 88 **To** 2028 $30 JP
Ziggy Heathcote Shiraz 2018 Another larger-than-life shiraz from this maker. Brings together ultra-ripe, robust fruit flavour – sweet plums, glacé cherry, dark chocolate panforte – to make a wine with a lot of presence but little grace. Screw cap. 15.8% alc. **Rating** 88 **To** 2030 $30 JP

Miceli ★★★★

60 Main Creek Road, Arthurs Seat, Vic 3936 **Region** Mornington Peninsula
T (03) 5989 2755 **www**.miceli.com.au **Open** W'ends 11–5, public hols by appt
Winemaker Anthony Miceli **Est.** 1991 **Dozens** 3000 **Vyds** 5.5ha
This may be a part-time labour of love for general practitioner Dr Anthony Miceli, but that
hasn't prevented him from taking the venture very seriously. He acquired the property in 1989
specifically to establish a vineyard, planting 1.8ha in '91, with subsequent plantings of pinot
gris, chardonnay and pinot noir. Between '91 and '97 Anthony completed the wine science
course at CSU; he now manages both vineyard and winery. Miceli is one of the top producers
of sparkling wine on the peninsula.

🍷🍷🍷🍷🍷 **Olivia's Mornington Peninsula Chardonnay 2018** Strikes a balance between
lemon and white-nectarine flavours, with winemaking inputs of creamy lees and
oak spice. While it's not particularly refined, it has a neat acid line and comes
together well. Screw cap. 13.9% alc. **Rating** 90 **To** 2027 $40 JF

Michael Hall Wines ★★★★★

103 Langmeil Road, Tanunda, SA 5352 **Region** Mount Lofty Ranges
T 0419 126 290 **www**.michaelhallwines.com **Open** Fri–Sat 11–5 or by appt
Winemaker Michael Hall **Est.** 2008 **Dozens** 2500
For reasons no longer relevant (however interesting) Michael Hall was once a jewellery valuer
for Sotheby's in Switzerland. He came to Australia in 2001 to pursue winemaking – a lifelong
interest – and undertook the wine science degree at CSU, graduating as dux in '05. His vintage
work in Australia and France is a veritable who's who of producers: in Australia with Cullen,
Giaconda, Henschke, Shaw + Smith, Coldstream Hills and Veritas; in France with Domaine
Leflaive, Meo-Camuzet, Vieux Telegraphe and Trevallon. He is now involved full-time with
his eponymous brand and the wines are as impressive as his experience suggests they should
be. Exports to the UK and the US.

🍷🍷🍷🍷🍷 **Piccadilly and Lenswood Adelaide Hills Chardonnay 2019** Two blocks in
Lenswood and Piccadilly Valley provide excellent fruit, wild barrel fermented and
matured for 11 months in oak, of which 25% was new. The fruit remains the main
focus, delicious white nectarine flavours of the utmost purity, delicately spicy and
textured, with energy to spare in the exit. Superb. Screw cap. 13.7% alc. **Rating** 96
To 2027 $50 TL ✪
Adelaide Hills Pinot Noir 2019 Hidden power is a key here, the stalks from
47% whole bunch inclusion providing spice to lift the vitality of the pinot fruit,
forest notes sitting in the wings. Give this some air and a swish in the decanter
now and invest in a few for the cellar – it's a cracker now and will improve for
10 years. Screw cap. 13.4% alc. **Rating** 95 **To** 2031 $50 TL
Flaxman's Valley Eden Valley Syrah 2019 Quite restrained to begin, earthy/
dusty notes adding a grounding for the black cherry/berry compote aromas
to take their time. Delicious weight on the palate, the ripeness spot on, a fine
balancing act with 20% whole bunches and 20% new oak over 20 months.
Everything here in the right place. Cellaring should prompt further pleasures.
Screw cap. 14.2% alc. **Rating** 95 **To** 2031 $50 TL
Sang de Pigeon Adelaide Hills Chardonnay 2019 Wild-yeast fermented in
barrel. Matured on lees for 11 months in a good percentage of new French oak,
which has given some gingery spice over to the wine in a good way, without
dominating the citrus and white nectarine fruit senses. Finishes with a vibrant
upward lift. Screw cap. 13.6% alc. **Rating** 94 **To** 2026 $30 TL ✪
Mount Torrens Adelaide Hills Syrah 2018 Sourced from the Mt Torrens
district, 14 months in French oak. The nose swirls with blackberry liqueur notes.
The palate is similarly rich in flavour, with a fine chalky tannin coating securing a
long, opulent finish. Screw cap. 14.1% alc. **Rating** 94 **To** 2028 $50 TL

🍷🍷🍷🍷🍷 **Barossa Valley Roussanne 2020 Rating** 91 **To** 2025 $40 TL
Adelaide Hills Sauvignon Blanc 2020 Rating 90 **To** 2024 $38 TL
Sang de Pigeon Adelaide Hills Pinot Noir 2019 Rating 90 **To** 2026 $32 TL

Michel Marie ★★★★★

PO Box 204, Yenda, NSW 2681 **Region** Riverina
T 0411 718 221 **www**.michelmarie.co
Winemaker Sam Brewer **Est.** 2013 **Dozens** 250 **Vyds** 21ha
Michel and Marie Nehme married in 1969 and migrated to Australia, ultimately moving to
the Riverina to bring up their children, including daughter Julie. In the 1980s, after the De
Bortoli success of Noble One in 1982, the family decided to only grow botrytis semillon
from the 21ha vineyard, selling the grapes until 2013. Michel took great delight in being
named the King of Rot but tragedy loomed when he developed pancreatic cancer. With
bittersweet timing, the '15 and '16 vintages of the Botrytis Semillon made for them by friend
and neighbour Sam Brewer (of Yarran Wines) both won gold medals at the Royal Melbourne
Wine Awards '18, the '16 emerging with the trophy. One week after Julie Nehme came back
home with the trophy, her father succumbed to cancer. De Bortoli won a silver medal at
the same show. Both the '15 and '16 are for sale online, with the '13 museum stock in small
quantity and not for sale. Exports to China.

Michelini Wines ★★★☆

213 Great Alpine Road, Myrtleford, Vic 3737 **Region** Alpine Valleys
T (03) 5751 1990 **www**.micheliniwines.com.au **Open** 7 days 10–5
Winemaker Matt Kilby **Est.** 1982 **Dozens** 12000 **Vyds** 80ha
The Michelini family are among the best-known grapegrowers of the Buckland Valley in
North East Victoria. Having migrated from Italy in 1949, they originally grew tobacco,
diversifying into vineyards in '82. The main vineyard, on terra rossa soil, is at an altitude of
300m, mostly with frontage to the Buckland River. The Devils Creek Vineyard was planted
in '91 on grafted rootstocks with merlot and chardonnay taking the lion's share. A vineyard
expansion program has seen the plantings reach 60ha.

🍷🍷🍷🍷 **Sparkling Merlot NV** Like its table-wine counterpart, its sparkling form looks
quite aromatic and restrained with black and red berries, spice, earthiness and a
sweet, pastille/jubey quality across the palate. Lots of energy here. Diam. 14% alc.
Rating 89 $25 JP

Mike Press Wines ★★★★

PO Box 224, Lobethal, SA 5241 **Region** Adelaide Hills
T (08) 8389 5546 **www**.mikepresswines.com.au
Winemaker Mike Press **Est.** 1998 **Dozens** 12000 **Vyds** 22.7ha
Mike and Judy Press established their Kenton Valley Vineyards in 1998, when they purchased
34ha of land in the Adelaide Hills at an elevation of 500m. They planted mainstream cool-
climate varieties (merlot, shiraz, cabernet sauvignon, sauvignon blanc, chardonnay and pinot
noir) intending to sell the grapes to other wine producers. Even an illustrious 43-year career
in the wine industry did not prepare Mike for the downturn in grape prices that followed
and that led to the development of the Mike Press wine label. They produce high-quality
sauvignon blanc, chardonnay, rose, pinot noir, merlot, shiraz, cabernet merlot and cabernet
sauvignon, which are sold at mouth-wateringly low prices.

🍷🍷🍷🍷🍷 **Single Vineyard Adelaide Hills Pinot Noir Rosé 2020** Estate-grown fruit.
Very bright fuchsia colour. The bouquet surges out of the glass, all strawberries,
fresh and poached. The palate moves onto another plane, powerful and arresting.
A pinot noir masquerading as a rosé. The price is downright ludicrous. Screw cap.
12% alc. **Rating** 94 **To** 2023 $13 JH ✪
Jimmy's Block Single Vineyard Adelaide Hills Shiraz 2018 A single-
vineyard, single-block variation that is a step up from the producer's standard estate
shiraz, named after the favourite parcel of his (vineyard manager) son. The nose is
classic cooler-climate blueberry to crimson plum with a display of peppery spice,
all spilling into the palate with plenty of brightness and vitality, backed in with
good upright structure and length. Very smart at this rate. Screw cap. 14% alc.
Rating 94 **To** 2026 $16 TL ✪

🍷🍷🍷🍷♀ Single Vineyard Adelaide Hills Merlot 2018 Rating 93 To 2026 $13 TL ❂
Single Vineyard Adelaide Hills Pinot Noir 2018 Rating 92 To 2025 $17 TL ❂
Single Vineyard Adelaide Hills Shiraz 2018 Rating 92 To 2033 $15 JH ❂
Single Vineyard Adelaide Hills Sauvignon Blanc 2020 Rating 91 To 2022 $12 TL ❂

Miles from Nowhere ★★★★

PO Box 128, Burswood, WA 6100 **Region** Margaret River
T (08) 9264 7800 **www**.milesfromnowhere.com.au
Winemaker Frederique Perrin, Gary Stokes **Est.** 2007 **Dozens** 20 000 **Vyds** 46.9ha
Miles from Nowhere is one of the 2 wineries owned by Franklin and Heather Tate. Franklin returned to Margaret River in 2007 after working with his parents establishing Evans & Tate from 1987 to 2005. The Miles from Nowhere name comes from the journey Franklin's ancestors made over 100 years ago from Eastern Europe to Australia: upon their arrival, they felt they had travelled 'miles from nowhere'. The plantings include petit verdot, chardonnay, shiraz, sauvignon blanc, semillon, viognier, cabernet sauvignon and merlot, spread over 2 vineyards planted over 20 years ago. Exports to the UK, the US, Canada, Asia and NZ.

🍷🍷🍷🍷♀ Margaret River Sauvignon Blanc 2020 Grassy and pure on the nose, the palate follows suit with a complexing chalky phenolic structure that engages and creates interest in the mouth. The acid leaves a lingering saline impression through to the finish, with some crushed shell and lemon pith for good measure. Screw cap. 12.6% alc. **Rating** 91 To 2024 $18 EL ❂
Margaret River Sauvignon Blanc Semillon 2020 Typically grassy on the nose with a floral, talcy, ashy perimeter. The sauvignon blanc (60%) packs a tidy little punch, and the balance of semillon elevates the texture to almost chewy. With no oak or lees to speak of, this is pure and taught with a fine, salty acid line defining the finish. Pretty brilliant value for money here. Screw cap. 13.2% alc. **Rating** 91 To 2024 $18 EL ❂

🍷🍷🍷🍷 Best Blocks Margaret River Chardonnay 2019 Rating 89 To 2027 $32 EL

Millbrook Winery ★★★★★

Old Chestnut Lane, Jarrahdale, WA 6124 **Region** Perth Hills
T (08) 9525 5796 **www**.millbrook.wine **Open** Wed–Mon 10–5
Winemaker Adair Davies **Est.** 1996 **Dozens** 10 000 **Vyds** 8ha
Millbrook is situated in the historic town of Jarrahdale, southeast of Perth. Located at the picturesque Chestnut Farm, the property backs on to the Serpentine River and is nestled among jarrah forests. Chestnut Farm dates back to the 19th century, when the original owner planted an orchard and grapevines in 1865, providing fruit to the local timber-millers in Jarrahdale. In 1996 Chestnut Farm and Millbrook Winery were bought by Peter and Lee Fogarty, marking the family's first entry into the wine business. Together with their children John, Mark and Anna they planted the vineyard. In 2001 a state-of-the-art winery was completed, including a restaurant. In addition to the 8ha estate, Millbrook draws on vineyards in prime locations across WA for sauvignon blanc, vermentino, fiano, chardonnay, tempranillo, grenache, mourvèdre and pedro ximénez. Exports to Malaysia, Hong Kong, Singapore, China and Japan.

🍷🍷🍷🍷🍷 Estate Shiraz Viognier 2019 3% viognier. Plush, velvety shiraz fruit is ensconced by plump tannins, the whole experience being one of pleasure and comfort. Acid and balance are judged with care and accurate detail. This is a beautiful wine, punching well above its weight. Screw cap. 14.5% alc. **Rating** 95 To 2041 $40 EL
Limited Release Chardonnay 2019 The nose is satisfyingly creamy and rich – toasted oak, curry leaf and salted yellow peach. The palate is intensely concentrated with nuts galore and saline acid. Load up a Burgundy glass – this is on the richer side of things, so do not approach if Chablis is more your style. Screw cap. 14.5% alc. **Rating** 94 To 2027 $50 EL

Regional Range Perth Hills Viognier 2020 Sweet spiced apple, ginger, pepper, mandarin pith, summer apricot and jasmine tea. The palate is fat, slippery and oily, with apricot marmalade and cloudy apple juice in equal measure. The length of flavour is very good, however the intensity of florals and ripe orchard fruit mean this will likely be consumed within 5 years of release – and that will be ok. Because it is delicious. Screw cap. 14% alc. **Rating** 94 **To** 2031 $40 EL

� **Single Vineyard Geographe Chardonnay 2020 Rating** 93 **To** 2028 $35 EL
Regional Range Geographe Grenache Shiraz Mourvèdre 2020 Rating 93 **To** 2026 $25 EL **◯**
Regional Range Geographe Tempranillo 2019 Rating 93 **To** 2027 $25 EL **◯**
Limited Release Pedro Ximénez NV Rating 93 $60 EL
Margaret River Fiano 2020 Rating 92 **To** 2023 $25 EL **◯**
Single Vineyard Frankland River Shiraz 2019 Rating 92 **To** 2031 $35 EL
Regional Range Margaret River Sauvignon Blanc 2020 Rating 91 **To** 2023 $25 EL
Regional Range Geographe Rosé 2020 Rating 90 **To** 2023 $25 EL

Millon Wines
★★★★☆

48 George Street, Williamstown, SA 5351 **Region** Eden Valley
T (08) 8524 6691 **www.**millonwines.com.au
Winemaker Angus Wardlaw **Est.** 2013 **Dozens** 20 000
Millon Wines has 3 vineyards: one in the Eden Valley, the second in the Barossa Valley and the third in the Clare Valley. Winemaker Angus Wardlaw, with a degree in wine science from CSU and experience in the Clare Valley as winemaker at Kirrihill Wines, 'believes the Eden Valley is the future of the Barossa' (see separate entry for his family business, Brothers at War). He makes the Millon wines with a minimalist approach.

Milton Vineyard
★★★★☆

14635 Tasman Highway, Swansea, Tas 7190 **Region** East Coast Tasmania
T (03) 6257 8298 **www.**miltonvineyard.com.au **Open** 7 days 10–5
Winemaker John Schutz, Anna Pooley, Justin Bubb **Est.** 1992 **Dozens** 11 000 **Vyds** 19.8ha
Michael and Kerry Dunbabin have one of the most historic properties in Tasmania, dating back to 1826. The property is 1800ha, meaning the vineyard (9ha of pinot noir, 6ha pinot gris, 1.5ha chardonnay, 1ha each of gewürztraminer and riesling, plus 10 rows of shiraz) has plenty of room for expansion.

♐♐♐♐ **Pinot Gris 2020** Varietal pear and Golden Delicious apple fruit contrasts the tension of grapefruit and lemon, energised by racy Tasmanian acidity. Phenolic grip defines a firm finish. Screw cap. 13.3% alc. **Rating** 89 **To** 2024 $28 TS

 # Miners Ridge
★★★★☆

135 Westgate Rd, Armstrong, Vic 3377 **Region** Grampians
T 0438 039 727 **www.**minersridge.com.au **Open** By appt
Winemaker Adam Richardson **Est.** 2000 **Dozens** 450
Andrew and Katrina Toomey established Miners Ridge Wines in 2000 after many years growing grapes in the Great Western region for other wineries. They decided to take small parcels of their finest fruit and craft a range of wines to reflect their 17ha vineyard site at Armstrong, enlisting experienced local winemaker Adam Richardson (ATR Wines) as their contract winemaker. Their vineyard, nestled on a gentle ridge in the foothills of Victoria's Grampians, takes its name from Chinese gold miners who worked the area's goldfields in the mid 1800s. (JP)

♐♐♐♐♐ **A.T. Grampians Shiraz 2018** Comes with an impressive wine show record at the 2020 Western Victorian Wine Challenge picking up trophy for Best Shiraz, Best Single Vineyard Wine of Show and Best Wine of Show. Ripe loganberry, black cherry, bakery spices, chocolate, dusty oak with an almost quiet restraint and finesse. Carries its 14.5% alcohol very well. Integrated tannins, velvety in texture and with a long finish. Wine of the show indeed! Screw cap. **Rating** 95 **To** 2031 $35 JP ✪

🍷🍷🍷🍷♀ **A.T. Grampians Shiraz 2019 Rating** 92 **To** 2029 $35 JP
Grampians Shiraz 2018 Rating 90 **To** 2026 $25 JP

Ministry of Clouds   ★★★★★

765 Chapel Hill Road, McLaren Vale, SA 5171 **Region** McLaren Vale
T 0417 864 615 **www.**ministryofclouds.com.au **Open** By appt
Winemaker Julian Forwood, Bernice Ong **Est.** 2012 **Dozens** 5000 **Vyds** 9.6ha
Bernice Ong and Julian Forwood say, 'The name Ministry of Clouds symbolises the relinquishing of our past security and structure (ministry) for the beguiling freedom, independence and adventure (clouds) inherent in our own venture'. I doubt whether there are 2 partners in a relatively young wine business with such extraordinary experience in sales and marketing of wine, stretching back well over 20 years. They bypassed owning vineyards or building wineries, instead headhunting key winemakers in the Clare Valley and Tasmania for riesling and chardonnay respectively, and the assistance of Tim Geddes at his winery in McLaren Vale, where they make the red wines. In 2016 they took the plunge and purchased part of the elevated Seaview block adjacent to Chapel Hill, Samuels Gorge, Coriole and Hardys' Yeenunga Vineyard, with 7ha of shiraz and 2ha of cabernet sauvignon. They have enlisted the very experienced Richard Leaske to help manage the vineyard. Exports to the UK, Sweden, Malaysia, Singapore, Hong Kong, South Korea and Thailand.

🍷🍷🍷🍷🍷 **Clare Valley Riesling 2020** Despite the searing dryness of this mid-weight wine, the extract and compelling vinosity are winning. Low yields, evidently. The extract absorbs the tensile acidity, making for a compact juiciness. Austere in its youth, but far from shrill. Pithy lime, quince, anise, spa salts and pink grapefruit. Stony. Pumice-like. Thirst-slaking and long. Screw cap. 12.4% alc. **Rating** 95 **To** 2032 $32 NG ✪
Tasmania Chardonnay 2019 A fantastic nose reminiscent of cooler hands in Burgundy and the Jura: cheesecloth, lanolin and a hint of stone fruits. The mineral carapace, impressive. The acidity, juicy and natural. The structure, the totem. Presumably malolactic happened a bit by virtue of the minimalist handling. But not much, suggested by its chiselled precision.Stellar wine in the making. Screw cap. 12.9% alc. **Rating** 94 **To** 2029 $48 NG
McLaren Vale Grenache 2019 I have criticised earlier vintages of this wine as abstemious and ascetic. Grenache, after all, is a later ripener equipped with joyous fruit and (when made well) a jittery kit of briary tannins to confer a whiff of savouriness. And so it goes. Lots of whole-berry florals and juby red-fruit riffs. Complex hints of orange rind, sassafras, turmeric and clove, to boot. Warmth and mineral tannic rasp as an effortless whole. Delicious. Screw cap. 14.2% alc. **Rating** 94 **To** 2025 $38 NG

🍷🍷🍷🍷♀ **McLaren Vale Shiraz 2019 Rating** 93 **To** 2026 $32 NG
McLaren Vale Tempranillo Grenache 2019 Rating 93 **To** 2025 $32 NG
McLaren Vale Picpoul 2020 Rating 92 **To** 2022 $35 NG

Minnow Creek   ★★★☆

42 Frontenac Avenue, Panorama, SA 5041 (postal) **Region** McLaren Vale
T 0404 288 108 **www.**minnowcreekwines.com.au
Winemaker Tony Walker **Est.** 2005 **Dozens** 1600
Tony Walker spent 6 years as winemaker at Fox Creek, after 2 previous vintages in Beaujolais and Languedoc. He founded Minnow Creek in 2005, not with any fanfare of (marketing) trumpets, but simply to make very good wines that reflected their place and their variety, the Lopresti family providing many of the grapes for the best red wines of Minnow Creek.

🍷🍷🍷🍷🍷 **McLaren Vale Shiraz 2018** A deep lustrous crimson. Scents of campfire, violet, anise, a swab of black olive and molten blue/dark-fruit accents bode well. Cherry bon-bon at the core. Mocha/bitter-chocolate oak influence, too. A highly regional but unashamedly rich wine, a paean to generosity and flavour, yet balanced and energetic. Will win many fans. Screw cap. 14.5% alc. **Rating** 92 **To** 2026 $29 NG
The Silver Minnow Langhorne Creek Pinot Gris 2020 A mid-weighted and highly textural gris. Drawing on the complexity that 40% barrel fermentation bestows, notes of nashi pear granita, quince, ripe apple and jasmine are galvanised by a judicious meld of oak and phenolics. A creamy core of leesy nougatine provides a well-judged counterpoint. Flavour, balance and versatility in spades. Screw cap. 13.5% alc. **Rating** 91 **To** 2022 $21 NG ❂

Mr Barval Fine Wines ★★★★★

7087 Caves Road, Margaret River, WA 6285 **Region** Margaret River
T 0481 453 038 **www**.mrbarval.com **Open** 7 days 11–5
Winemaker Robert Gherardi **Est.** 2015 **Dozens** 1300
Robert Gherardi was born with wine in his blood. As a small boy he'd go to Margaret River to pick grapes with 3 generations of his extended Italian family. The grapes were taken to his grandmother's suburban backyard to begin the fermentation, followed by a big lunch or dinner to celebrate the arrival of the new vintage to be. Nonetheless, his first degree was in marine science and biotechnology; while completing the course he worked in an independent wine store in Perth. Having tasted his way around the world in the bottle, at age 25 he enrolled in the full oenology and viticulture degree. This led to employment at Moss Wood for 4 years, then Brown Hill Estate as assistant winemaker and finally to Cullen for 3 years. Vanya Cullen encouraged him to travel to Barolo and work with Elio Altare for 3 harvests over a 5-year period. This included moving to Barolo with his wife and children to experience the full 4 seasons of viticulture and winemaking. He returns to Italy each year for his boutique travel business, with customised tours of Barolo, Valtellina and further north. And so he arrived at the name for his winery: Margaret River, Barolo and Valtellina. Exports to Singapore and Hong Kong.

🍷🍷🍷🍷🍷 **Riserva Margaret River Cabernet Sauvignon 2018** The pedigree of the Margaret River 2018 vintage is clearly on show here. Ripe and brambly cassis, silky tannins and a dense, viscous texture. There's a lot going on here. Loaded with salted red fruits, exotic spice, savoury tannins and all shaped by generous chewy texture, drawing out to a long finish. Screw cap. 13.9% alc. **Rating** 95 **To** 2041 $80 EL
Vino Rosso 2019 Merlot, petit verdot and malbec. Whole berries, wild-yeast fermented, basket pressed to 3yo oak and matured for 21 months. Smells like red snakes, jubes, red licorice and other delicious lollies. The palate is made far more serious by finely structuring, chalky tannins and a swathe of subtle, spicy oak. The briny acid cleans it all up. So much to love, most of all the bouncy texture, which demands another sip. Screw cap. 14.5% alc. **Rating** 95 **To** 2028 $29 EL ❂
Margaret River Cabernet Merlot 2018 The 21 months in oak is evident, but it doesn't dominate the fruit in any way. Savoury red fruits are bound together by a judicious sprinkling of black pepper, star anise and licorice. This almost feels Old World. Screw cap. 14.2% alc. **Rating** 94 **To** 2030 $40 EL

🍷🍷🍷🍷🍷 **Mistral Margaret River 2020 Rating** 92 **To** 2028 $29 EL
Nebbia Margaret River 2020 Rating 92 **To** 2028 $35 EL
Margaret River Chardonnay 2020 Rating 90 **To** 2028 $40 EL

Mr Riggs Wine Company ★★★★★

169 Douglas Gully Road, McLaren Flat, SA 5171 **Region** McLaren Vale
T 1300 946 326 **www**.mrriggs.com.au **Open** Mon–Fri 9–5
Winemaker Ben Riggs **Est.** 2001 **Dozens** 20 000 **Vyds** 7.5ha

With over a quarter of a century of winemaking experience, Ben Riggs is well established under his own banner. Ben sources the best fruit from individual vineyards in McLaren Vale, Clare Valley, Adelaide Hills, Langhorne Creek, Coonawarra and from his own Piebald Gully Vineyard (shiraz and viognier). Each wine expresses the essence of not only the vineyard but also the region's terroir. The vision of the Mr Riggs brand is unpretentious and personal: 'To make the wines I love to drink'. He drinks very well. Exports to the US, Canada, Denmark, Sweden, Germany, the Netherlands, Switzerland, Singapore, NZ, Hong Kong and China.

ΨΨΨΨΨ **The Gaffer McLaren Vale Shiraz 2018** Has all one could wish for in a wine that speaks so clearly of its place, yet does so without bombast. The colour is bright, the bouquet with aromas of plum, spice and dark chocolate, the medium-bodied palate in total synchrony. Screw cap. 14.5% alc. **Rating** 95 **To** 2043 $25 JH ✪

The Chap 2014 Malty oak scents. Cedar, leaf, licorice and cigar box, too. Dark plum. Asian spice. There is an umami breadth to this, imparted by a bit of bottle age. The tannins are resolving nicely, yet with plenty of strength and sinew left to carry this to a rewarding maturity. Diam. 14.5% alc. **Rating** 95 **To** 2035 $100 NG

Montepulciano d'Adelaide 2019 Predominantly Adelaide Hills–grown fruit from one of the earliest growers of this increasingly exciting variety. There's a captivating purity to this beautifully medium-weight wine, with lingering cherry cola-esque aromas and flavours. An even coat of tannins is balanced by prominent fruit. A delicious drink, and one of the higher achievers in this class. Screw cap. 14.5% alc. **Rating** 94 **To** 2028 $30 TL ✪

ΨΨΨΨΩ **Mrs Pinot Gris 2020 Rating** 93 **To** 2025 $22 TL ✪
Burnt Block McLaren Vale Shiraz 2018 Rating 93 **To** 2034 $50 NG
JFR McLaren Vale Shiraz 2018 Rating 93 **To** 2036 $50 NG
Woodside Adelaide Hills Sauvignon Blanc 2020 Rating 92 **To** 2023 $22 TL ✪
Piebald Adelaide Hills Syrah 2019 Rating 92 **To** 2027 $30 TL
The Magnet McLaren Vale Grenache 2019 Rating 91 **To** 2025 $30 NG
Mr Brightside Preservative Free McLaren Vale Shiraz 2020 Rating 90 **To** 2022 $22 NG
Outpost Coonawarra Cabernet 2019 Rating 90 **To** 2033 $25 JF

Mistletoe Wines ★★★★★

771 Hermitage Road, Pokolbin, NSW 2320 **Region** Hunter Valley
T (02) 4998 7770 **www**.mistletoewines.com.au **Open** 7 days 10–5
Winemaker Scott Stephens **Est.** 1989 **Dozens** 5000 **Vyds** 5.5ha
Mistletoe Wines, owned by Ken and Gwen Sloan, can trace its history back to 1909, when a vineyard was planted on what was then called Mistletoe Farm, before disappearing. The Sloans have long since created a winery business here to stay. All wine is made onsite. Ken and Gwen still live at the winery, both working 7 days a week with no intention of retiring. Son Robert is the viticulturist and assistant winemaker, daughter Cassandra runs the cellar door with Gwen and granddaughter Natane. The quality and consistency of these wines is irreproachable, as is their price. Exports to China.

ΨΨΨΨΨ **Grand Reserve Hunter Valley Shiraz 2019** Crushed, destemmed, open-fermented, matured for 16 months in new and used French oak. Another very good vintage, the picking decision spot on, leaving a skein of freshness running through the perfectly balanced, medium-bodied palate. Blackberry, plum and a regional whisper of earth provide all the flavour one could wish for, the tannins lining up in measured support. Screw cap. 13.5% alc. **Rating** 96 **To** 2040 $75 JH ✪

Reserve Hunter Valley Semillon 2019 Hand picked, whole-bunch pressed, a short maturation in tank on gross lees after a cold ferment. Gleaming straw green; the lemon-scented bouquet leads into a generously flavoured palate, with lemon curd and Meyer lemon fruit flavours extended by the backbone of acidity. Now or later enjoyment. Screw cap. 12.2% alc. **Rating** 95 **To** 2030 $25 JH ✪

Grand Reserve Hunter Valley Shiraz 2018 The style of wine here is richly flavoured, albeit far from the modern reductively massaged styles that have bifurcated the region. The French oak choice, cedar and malt. Steeped in terracotta, Bing cherry, polished leather and anise scents, unravelling across a mid-weighted gait. Archetypal Hunter. The savouriness and the tannic roll out, inimitably of place. Long finish with plenty of time up its sleeve. Worth celebrating. Screw cap. 13.5% alc. **Rating** 94 **To** 2033 $75 NG

ŸŸŸŸ♀ **Museum Release Reserve Hunter Valley Semillon 2011** Rating 93
To 2023 $35 NG
Home Vineyard Hunter Valley Shiraz 2018 Rating 93 To 2032 $40 NG
Grand Reserve Hunter Valley Shiraz 2014 Rating 93 To 2031 $85 NG
Reserve Tumbarumba Pinot Noir 2018 Rating 92 To 2027 $35 NG
Hunter Valley Pinot Noir Shiraz 2018 Rating 92 To 2026 $32 NG
T-Rose Hunter Valley 2019 Rating 91 To 2022 $24 NG
Hilltops Sangiovese 2018 Rating 91 To 2025 $27 NG
Home Vineyard Hunter Valley Semillon 2019 Rating 90 To 2027 $24 NG
Hunter Shiraz 2019 Rating 90 To 2028 $27 NG

Mitchell ★★★★

246 Hughes Park Road, Sevenhill via Clare, SA 5453 **Region** Clare Valley
T (08) 8843 4258 www.mitchellwines.com **Open** 7 days 11–5
Winemaker Andrew Mitchell, Simon Pringle **Est.** 1975 **Dozens** 15 000 **Vyds** 70ha
One of the stalwarts of the Clare Valley, established by Jane and Andrew Mitchell, producing long-lived rieslings and cabernet sauvignons in classic regional style. The range now includes very creditable semillon, grenache and shiraz. A lovely old stone apple shed is the cellar door and upper section of the upgraded winery. Children Angus and Edwina are now working in the business, heralding generational changes. Over the years the Mitchells have established or acquired 70ha of vineyards on 4 excellent sites, some vines over 60 years old; all are managed organically, with biodynamic composts used for over a decade.

ŸŸŸŸ♀ **Kinsfolk Shiraz 2016** There's a vivacity belying its age and the colour is full of brightness. Nothing heavy-handed here, it's highly perfumed and medium framed, yet the tannins hold some sway. A really pleasing drink now, but it'll go on for some time yet. Screw cap. 13% alc. **Rating** 91 **To** 2028 $40 JF
Kinsfolk Grenache 2019 Bright ruby hue. A pretty wine with florals, potpourri, raspberries, red licorice and warm spices. The palate is soft, there's some give to the tannins, but they are playing second fiddle to the juicy acidity. Screw cap. 13.5% alc. **Rating** 91 **To** 2025 $40 JF

Mitchell Harris Wines ★★★★★

38 Doveton Street North, Ballarat, Vic 3350 **Region** Pyrenees
T (03) 5331 8931 www.mitchellharris.com.au **Open** Sun–Mon 11–5, Tues–Thurs 11–9, Fri–Sat 11–11
Winemaker John Harris **Est.** 2008 **Dozens** 2300
Mitchell Harris Wines is a partnership between Alicia and Craig Mitchell and Shannyn and John Harris. John, the winemaker, began his career at Brown Brothers, then spent 8 years as winemaker at Domaine Chandon in the Yarra Valley, cramming in Northern Hemisphere vintages in California and Oregon. The Mitchell and Harris families grew up in the Ballarat area and have an affinity for the Macedon and Pyrenees regions. While the total make is not large, a lot of thought has gone into the creation of each of the wines, which are sourced from the Pyrenees, Ballarat and Macedon regions. In 2012 a multipurpose space was created in an 1880s brick workshop and warehouse providing a cellar door, bar and education facility. Exports to Switzerland.

ŸŸŸŸŸ **Sabre 2017** 54/46% pinot noir/chardonnay. Tiraged October 2017, disgorged October 2020. 4 g/l dosage. Cool Macedon Ranges and Henty climates bring the full force of refined elegance and striking natural acidity to this new vintage Sabre.

One of the finer, restrained sparkling wines going around of some delicacy. White flowers, grapefruit, stone fruits and honey nougat aromas evolve on an equally delicate palate, firm in structure and a long aftertaste. Cork. 11% alc. **Rating** 95 $50 JP ♥

Sabre Rosé 2017 Attractive salmon-pink hue. Cranberry nougat, strawberry, toasted hazelnut aromas lead into a long and focused rosé of substance and complexity. Cool acidity of the cool regions bring crunch to the palate and a long finish. Cork. 11% alc. **Rating** 95 $60 JP ♥

ŸŸŸŸŸ **Pyrenees Sauvignon Blanc Fumé 2020 Rating** 93 **To** 2027 $28 JP
Blanc #1 2020 Rating 93 $30 JP
Wightwick Vineyard Ballarat Chardonnay 2019 Rating 93 **To** 2030 $32 JP
Ballarat & Macedon Ranges Pinot Noir 2019 Rating 93 **To** 2026 $40 JP
Pyrenees Sangiovese 2020 Rating 92 **To** 2027 $28 JP
Pyrenees Rosé 2020 Rating 90 **To** 2025 $28 JP
Sabre Ratafia Pinot Noir NV Rating 90 $25 JP
Curious Winemaker Pyrenees Shiraz 2020 Rating 90 **To** 2027 $30 JP
Pyrenees Cabernet Sauvignon 2019 Rating 90 **To** 2031 $32 JP

Mitchelton   ★★★★★

Mitchellstown via Nagambie, Vic 3608 **Region** Nagambie Lakes/Heathcote
T (03) 5736 2222 **www.**mitchelton.com.au **Open** 7 days 10–5
Winemaker Andrew Santarossa **Est.** 1969 **Dozens** 35 000 **Vyds** 139ha
Mitchelton was founded in 1969 by Ross Shelmerdine, named after the explorer Thomas Mitchell, who passed by here. Ross had a splendid vision for the striking winery, restaurant, now-iconic observation tower and surrounding vineyards. Owned by Gerry Ryan OAM (founder of Jayco) since 2012, Mitchelton is a destination in its own right, with music concerts 'on the green' hosting such varied luminaries as Dame Kiri Te Kanawa and Jimmy Barnes; a hotel and spa also opened in 2018. Wine quality has remained consistent over the years, particularly of the top-tier shiraz. Mitchelton has estate vineyards in both Nagambie and Heathcote and purchases fruit from growers across Victoria. Exports to China, Singapore, Indonesia, South Korea and Vietnam.

ŸŸŸŸŸ **Spring Single Block Heathcote Shiraz 2018** The Spring block on the Mitchelton Toolleen vineyard enjoys a siginficant limestone and greenstone basalt influence. The result is beautiful, lifted aromatics of violets, dried herbs, wild blackberries and Asian spice. The palate is fruit-driven, fleshy and quite high in tannin, with subtle oak influence. Another keeper from this site. Screw cap. 14.6% alc. **Rating** 95 **To** 2032 $50 JP

Estate Grown Heathcote Shiraz 2018 The full suite of Heathcote attractions on display here from the rich, dense black fruits, the hint of gumleaf/spearmint and lively woodsy spice to the smooth-as texture and fine tannins, all generously proportioned. Plenty to like and enjoy right here and still with so much potential. Screw cap. 14.4% alc. **Rating** 95 **To** 2028 $40 JP

Print Shiraz 2018 The company flagship, with a Heathcote focus these days, garnering the region's strengths – deep intensity of colour and fruit power – but definitely presenting a greater elegance than some of its competitors. Blackcurrant, red plums, licorice, woodsy spice. There's a balance of key elements across the palate, an almost mineral-like fineness to the tannins and smart oak handling. Bit of a quiet achiever. Screw cap. 14.8% alc. **Rating** 95 **To** 2032 $90 JP

Heathcote Collection Shiraz 2018 Winemaker Andrew Santarossa captures the richness and intrigue of the region's No. 1 grape very well, pursuing a plush, modern, oak-driven style requiring extensive time in bottle. Dark berries, plum cake, aniseed, dark chocolate panforte and savoury, spicy oak, with firm tannins. Looking a treat now and still a long way to go. Cork. 14.5% alc. **Rating** 95 **To** 2031 $45 JP

ΨΨΨΨΨ Single Vineyard Marsanne 2020 Rating 93 To 2032 $25 JP
Single Vineyard Toolleen Heathcote Shiraz 2018 Rating 93 To 2030
$50 JP
Single Vineyard Chardonnay 2020 Rating 92 To 2025 $25 JP ○
Preece Grenache Rosé 2020 Rating 92 To 2023 $20 JP ○
Blackwood Park Riesling 2020 Rating 91 To 2026 $25 JP
Single Vineyard Roussanne 2020 Rating 90 To 2026 $25 JP
Single Vineyard Nagambie Shiraz 2019 Rating 90 To 2026 $25 JP
Single Vineyard Nagambie Cabernet Sauvignon 2019 Rating 90 To 2027
$25 JP

Mitolo Wines   ★★★★☆

141 McMurtrie Road, McLaren Vale, SA 5171 **Region** McLaren Vale
T (08) 8323 9304 **www**.mitolowines.com.au **Open** Thurs–Mon 10–5
Winemaker Ben Glaetzer **Est.** 1999 **Dozens** 40 000
Mitolo had a meteoric rise once Frank Mitolo decided to turn a winemaking hobby into a
business. In 2000 he took the plunge into the commercial end of the business, inviting Ben
Glaetzer to make the wines. Split between the Jester range and single-vineyard wines, Mitolo
began life as a red wine–dominant brand but now produces a range of varietals. In November
'17 Mitolo opened their $3 million tasting room, restaurant and event space with a flourish.
Exports to all major markets.

ΨΨΨΨΨ Savitar McLaren Vale Shiraz 2018 Super-premium shiraz postcode 101:
judicious extraction conferring tannic prowess; presumably some whole-berry
work imparting floral/iodine lift and a joyous pulpy mid palate; barrel-ferment
smoked-meat aromas and a skein of pepper, tapenade and clove-doused freshness.
This is a bumptious warm-climate shiraz that nevertheless boasts the aromatic
synergy and structural latticework of an expression from somewhere cooler. Very
good. Screw cap. 14.5% alc. **Rating** 95 To 2030 $89 NG
Serpico McLaren Vale Cabernet Sauvignon 2019 Hand picked and placed
in drying crates to undergo appassimento; this elevates tannins while concentrating
fruit in a shift of the phenolic makeup, imparting a firm, ferrous savouriness.
Unabashedly big, yet far from jammy, as a welcome result. Asian spice, blood stone,
bitter amaro and cherry pith, with a verdant echo of cabernet in the background.
Screw cap. 15.5% alc. **Rating** 94 To 2032 $89 NG

ΨΨΨΨΨ Of the Wind Adelaide Hills Chardonnay 2020 Rating 93 To 2024 $49 NG
Angela McLaren Vale Shiraz 2018 Rating 93 To 2025 $39 NG
7th Son McLaren Vale 2018 Rating 93 To 2025 $39 NG
Jester McLaren Vale Grenache 2019 Rating 92 To 2024 $25 NG ○
Jester McLaren Vale Cabernet Sauvignon 2019 Rating 92 To 2027
$25 NG ○
G.A.M. McLaren Vale Shiraz 2018 Rating 91 To 2030 $59 NG
Jester McLaren Vale Shiraz 2019 Rating 90 To 2025 $25 NG
Jester McLaren Vale Malbec 2019 Rating 90 To 2025 $25 NG

Molly Morgan Vineyard   ★★★★

496 Talga Road, Rothbury, NSW 2320 **Region** Hunter Valley
T (02) 4930 7695 **www**.mollymorgan.com
Winemaker Usher Tinkler **Est.** 1963 **Dozens** 2000 **Vyds** 7.66ha
Established by the Roberts family in 1963, later acquired by a syndicate headed by Andrew
Simon of Camperdown Cellars fame. Molly Morgan focuses on estate-grown wines from
vines up to 50+ years old (the semillon planted in 1963, shiraz and chardonnay following in
stages through to '97). The vineyard is named after an exceptionally resourceful woman who
was twice convicted and sent to NSW, married 3 times (the last time when she was 60, her
husband aged 31). Out of this improbable background she emerged as a significant benefactor
of the sick, earning the soubriquet 'Queen of the Hunter'.

ΨΨΨΨΨ **MoMo Hunter Valley Semillon 2019** Youthful Hunter semillon personified: lemongrass, tonic, barley sugar and citrus balm. Broader than most examples, in the best sense. Approachable given the warm year, although I'd wait at least a couple of years. A fine skein of acidity, pulpy fruit and an uncluttered juicy palate of considerable length, auguring well for a very bright future. A beautifully measured wine. Screw cap. 11% alc. **Rating** 93 **To** 2031 $25 NG ✪

MoMo Hunter Valley Rosé 2019 Shiraz. A very bright, deep and attractive coral colour. Sappy. Intensely flavoured, despite the moderate alcohol. Rich, even. This level of intensity is clearly a skill at this address, belying the wine's inherent lightness of being. Poached strawberry, thyme, orange blossom and roseship. A highly versatile rosé that is far from the Provençal mock-ups of the madding crowd. Screw cap. 12.2% alc. **Rating** 92 **To** 2022 $25 NG ✪

MoMo Hunter Valley Shiraz 2019 Another uncluttered wine boasting fealty to region and an an easygoing drinkability. Simply put, there is nothing bothering my palate when I taste. Moreover, it tastes of the the sweet Hunter earth. Terracotta, even. Poached cherries, polished leather and a verdant lilt of herb, to boot. Mid weighted, energetic enough and truly exceptional value. Screw cap. 13.5% alc. **Rating** 92 **To** 2026 $25 NG ✪

MoMo Hunter Valley Chardonnay 2019 This suite of wines have an intuitive feel about them. They reflect their provenance and fruit without fuss and seemingly, without winemaking tomfoolery. Scents of apricot pith, white fig, honeydew melon and a creamy core of nougatine melded with toasted nuts. This lightweight chardonnay boasts an intensity of flavour and transparency, dealing a hand of mellifluous drinkability. Screw cap. 11.9% alc. **Rating** 91 **To** 2024 $25 NG

Montalto

★★★★★

33 Shoreham Road, Red Hill South, Vic 3937 **Region** Mornington Peninsula
T (03) 5989 8412 **www**.montalto.com.au **Open** 7 days 11–5
Winemaker Simon Black **Est.** 1998 **Dozens** 12 000 **Vyds** 47ha
John Mitchell and family established Montalto in 1998, but the core of the vineyard goes back to '86. It is planted to pinot noir, chardonnay, pinot gris, riesling, shiraz, tempranillo and sauvignon blanc. Intensive vineyard work opens up the canopy, with yields of 3.7–6.1t/ha. Wines are released in 3 ranges: the flagship Single Vineyard, Montalto estate wines and Pennon Hill. Montalto leases several external vineyards that span the peninsula, giving vastly greater diversity of pinot noir sources and greater insurance against weather extremes. There is also a broad range of clones adding to that diversity. Montalto has hit new heights with its wines from these blocks. Exports to the Philippines and China.

ΨΨΨΨΨ **Single Vineyard The Eleven Mornington Peninsula Chardonnay 2019** A refined, elegant style and lip-smackingly delicious. It's the acidity, it's the drive, it's the length. It works off a citrus theme with grapefruit, lemon and mandarin, with a dab of smoky, flinty reduction and enough spicy oak and creamy lees to add some extra seasoning. Linear and pure. Excellent wine. Screw cap. 13% alc. **Rating** 96 **To** 2030 $60 JF ✪

Single Vineyard Tuerong Block Mornington Peninsula Chardonnay 2019 OK. Fans of funk and smoky reduction, here you go. From a warmer site, this is racy, juicy and so tangy. Lots of grapefruit, lemon and white nectarine flavours, with a decent showering of spice and zest. There is so much packed into this, yet everything is kept on a tight leash. Moreish, savoury and compelling. Screw cap. 13% alc. **Rating** 95 **To** 2030 $60 JF

Pennon Hill Mornington Peninsula Shiraz 2019 I've said it elsewhere that 2019 is a terrific shiraz vintage on the peninsula. Here's another wonderful example. It's really savoury, with some meaty reduction, but there is certainly a core of good fruit, spiced up with herbs and tapenade. Textural tannins, ripe yet raspy, hold sway on the fuller-bodied palate. Looks great now and even better with food. Screw cap. 13.6% alc. **Rating** 95 **To** 2030 $34 JF ✪

Estate Mornington Peninsula Shiraz 2019 There's more volume to this compared with the Pennon Hill shiraz, but similar traits. This is also savoury, deep and rich with charcuterie and meaty reduction, just enough for some seasoning. Full bodied, with glossy, ripe, fleshy fruit. Big, slightly gritty tannins. Quite a commanding wine. Screw cap. 13.5% alc. **Rating** 95 **To** 2032 $50 JF

ϓϓϓϓϓ **Estate Mornington Peninsula Chardonnay 2019 Rating** 93 **To** 2028 $45 JF
Estate Mornington Peninsula Pinot Gris 2019 Rating 93 **To** 2023 $36 JF

Montara ★★★★★

76 Chalambar Road, Ararat, Vic 3377 **Region** Grampians
T (03) 5352 3868 **www**.montarawines.com.au **Open** First Fri each month 11–late or by appt
Winemaker Simon Fennell **Est.** 1970 **Dozens** 3000 **Vyds** 19.2ha
Montara gained considerable attention for its pinot noirs during the 1980s and continues to produce wines of distinctive style under the ownership of no less than 6 siblings of the Stapleton family. As I (James) can attest from several visits over the years, the view from the cellar door is one of the best in the Grampians region. Simon Fennell, with an extensive winemaking history, including assistant winemaker at Best's Wines, and with direct knowledge of the Grampians region, has replaced long-serving winemaker Leigh Clarnette. Exports to the US, Canada, Indonesia, Taiwan, Hong Kong and China.

ϓϓϓϓϓ **Home Block Single Vineyard Grampians Pinot Noir 2019** Grampians getting its pinot act together big time right here. It's there from the start with solid red/garnet colour and a bouquet dripping in fragrant, ripe red cherry fruits, wild strawberries, musk, bracken and spice. Fills the mouth with glorious sweet-fruited flavours and ripe tannins. A precise pinot with verve! Champion Pinot Noir at the Western Victorian Wine Challenge 2020. Screw cap. 12.5% alc. **Rating** 95 **To** 2026 $45 JP
Chalambar Road Grampians Pinot Noir 2018 A complex, concentrated Chalambar Road, deserving of serious contemplation and a lot more time in bottle before broaching. Deep red hues. A reserved bouquet, still tight like the palate, with emerging blackberries, dusty cocoa, earth and Aussie bush scents. Finely textured with dense tannins against a core of medium-weight black fruits and well-judged oak. Screw cap. 14.5% alc. **Rating** 95 **To** 2028 $70 JP

ϓϓϓϓϓ **Grampians Shiraz 2019 Rating** 92 **To** 2026 $25 JP
Grampians Riesling 2020 Rating 90 **To** 2028 $25 JP
Grampians Cabernet Sauvignon 2018 Rating 90 **To** 2026 $25 JP

Monty's Leap ★★★★

45821 South Coast Highway, Kalgan, WA 6330 **Region** Albany
T 0407 424 455 **www**.montysleap.com.au **Open** Tues–Thurs 10–5, Fri–Sat 10–10, Sun 10–7
Winemaker Castle Rock (Robert Diletti) **Est.** 1996 **Dozens** 3000
Hospitality and IT professionals Phil Shilcock and Michelle Gray purchased the former Montgomery's Hill in October 2017 and launched the Monty's Leap brand. They had long shared the dream of owning a vineyard and restaurant, and jumped at the opportunity when Montgomery's came up for sale. The mature vineyard (planted in 1996–97 by founders Pamela and Murray Montgomery) is planted on the banks of the Kalgan River, 16km northeast of Albany.

ϓϓϓϓϓ **The Mulberry Block Great Southern Chardonnay 2019** Cool-climate finesse here; nashi pear, green apple skin, white nectarine, white pepper, restraint and line. Quietly spoken, polite and even contrite, this is a pretty little thing – willowy and almost lyrical. The phenolics have a quartz-like character. If you don't pay attention, you'll miss it, and that would be a shame. Screw cap. 13% alc. **Rating** 92 **To** 2030 $40 EL

River Hawk Single Vineyard Great Southern Shiraz 2019 Blackberry, licorice and raspberry form both the nose and palate here. Very pretty and juicy, this has a finely woven tannic profile that laces up the fruit and shapes the experience on the palate. Screw cap. 14% alc. **Rating** 92 **To** 2028 $35 EL

Single Vineyard Great Southern Cabernet Sauvignon 2019 Supple red fruits and fine powdery tannins are the calling cards of this wine. The oak is subtle, yet firmly entrenched in the fruit, contributing shape to the tannins through the finish. Screw cap. 14% alc. **Rating** 92 **To** 2031 $35 EL

Great Southern Appleshed Red 2019 Cabernet franc, cabernet sauvignon, merlot and a small dash of shiraz. Matured for 10 months in French oak (10% new). This is a vibrant and juicy blend with lip-smacking red berries (raspberry and mulberry), lashings of licorice, aniseed and freshly ground back pepper. Plenty to like, especially at the price. Screw cap. 14.2% alc. **Rating** 91 **To** 2027 $20 EL ❂

♀♀♀♀ The Sailor Single Vineyard Cabernet Sauvignon Shiraz 2018 **Rating** 89 **To** 2031 $35 EL

Moores Hill Estate   ★★★★☆

3343 West Tamar Highway, Sidmouth, Tas 7270 **Region** Northern Tasmania
T (03) 6394 7649 **www.**mooreshill.com.au **Open** 7 days 10–5
Winemaker Julian Allport **Est.** 1997 **Dozens** 5000 **Vyds** 7ha
The Moores Hill Estate vineyard (owned by winemaker Julian Allport and Fiona Weller plus Tim and Sheena High) consists of pinot noir, riesling, pinot gris and chardonnay, with a very small amount of cabernet sauvignon and merlot. The vines are located on a northeast-facing hillside, 5km from the Tamar River and 30km from Bass Strait. Moores Hill became Tasmania's first 100% solar-powered winery in 2017, the wines all made onsite.

♀♀♀♀♀ Pinot Gris 2020 Top-class gris. Pretty, pale straw/salmon hue. Textbook pear (fresh and glacé) of supple, slippery texture is juxtaposed with the Tamar's lemon tang. Judicious oak builds texture without flavour. It finishes long, accented with mixed spice, honey and just the right level of phenolic bite. Screw cap. 13.5% alc. **Rating** 94 **To** 2023 $35 TS

♀♀♀♀♀ Chardonnay 2019 **Rating** 93 **To** 2026 $40 TS
Méthode Blanc de Blancs NV **Rating** 93 $45 TS
Riesling 2020 **Rating** 92 **To** 2035 $35 TS
Pinot Noir 2019 **Rating** 90 **To** 2023 $40 TS

Moorilla Estate   ★★★★☆

655 Main Road, Berriedale, Tas 7011 **Region** Southern Tasmania
T (03) 6277 9900 **www.**moorilla.com.au **Open** Fri–Mon 12–6
Winemaker Conor van der Reest **Est.** 1958 **Dozens** 11 000 **Vyds** 15.36ha
Moorilla Estate was the second winery to be established in Tasmania in the 20th century, Jean Miguet's La Provence beating it to the punch by 2 years. However, through much of the history of Moorilla Estate, it was the most important winery in the state, if not in size then as the icon. Magnificently situated on a mini-isthmus reaching into the Derwent River, it has always been a must-visit for wine lovers and tourists. Production is around 160t/year, sourced entirely from the vineyards around Moorilla and its St Matthias Vineyard (Tamar Valley). The winery is part of an overall development said by observers (not Moorilla) to have cost upwards of $150 million. Its raison d'être is the establishment of an art gallery (Mona) that has the highest atmospheric environment accreditation of any gallery in the Southern Hemisphere, housing both the extraordinary ancient and contemporary art collection assembled by Moorilla's owner, David Walsh, and visiting exhibitions from major art museums around the world. Exports to South Korea, Hong Kong, Singapore and Taiwan.

♀♀♀♀♀ Muse St Matthias Vineyard Syrah 2016 The signature white pepper of cool-climate shiraz leads the way through aromas and flavours of black plum. Medium purple/red. Age has begun its evolution toward leather and earth, framed in finely textured tannins. It concludes with good persistence, promising medium-term life in the cellar. Screw cap. 14.1% alc. **Rating** 92 **To** 2026 $54 TS

Muse St Matthias Vineyard Sauvignon 2018 Intense and powerful, ricocheting with fresh lantana, frangipani and lemon squash. The vanilla presence of part fermentation and 9 months maturation in oak barrels rises to the occasion, cut with a tense finish of malic acid drive that promises medium-term potential. It concludes long and a touch sweet. Anything it lacks in grace it makes up for in impact. Screw cap. 13.8% alc. **Rating** 91 **To** 2028 $29 TS

Moorooduc Estate ★★★★★

501 Derril Road, Moorooduc, Vic 3936 **Region** Mornington Peninsula
T (03) 5971 8506 **www**.moorooducestate.com.au **Open** 7 days 11–5
Winemaker Dr Richard McIntyre, Jeremy Magyar **Est.** 1983 **Dozens** 6000 **Vyds** 14ha
Richard McIntyre has taken Moorooduc Estate to new heights, having completely mastered the difficult art of gaining maximum results from wild-yeast fermentation. Starting with the 2010 vintage, there was a complete revamp of grape sources and hence changes to the tiered structure of the releases. These changes were driven by the simple fact that the McIntyre vineyard could only yield 1500 dozen, and by leasing additional Mornington Peninsula vineyards the business was able to expand to the 5000–6000 dozen produced annually. The entry-point wines under the Devil Bend Creek label remain principally sourced from the Osborn Vineyard; the mid-priced Chardonnay and Pinot Noir are now sourced from multiple sites. The single-vineyard Robinson Pinot Noir and Chardonnay, Garden Vineyard Pinot Noir and McIntyre Shiraz are priced a little below the ultimate 'Ducs' (The Moorooduc McIntyre Chardonnay and Pinot Noir). Exports to the UK, the US and Hong Kong.

🍷🍷🍷🍷🍷 **Robinson Vineyard Chardonnay 2019** There's always a lot of class to this chardonnay. It has flavour aplenty, yet everything is reined in by fine and tight acidity. It's also flinty, spicy and tangy. The oak is a mere part of the overall profile, not at all dominating. Long, pure and utterly refreshing. Screw cap. 13% alc. **Rating** 96 **To** 2029 $60 JF ❂

The Moorooduc McIntyre Chardonnay 2019 This is so bound to the Moorooduc Estate DNA, there's no point unravelling it. It sits comfortably even in a warmer vintage. There's a neat confluence of stone fruit and citrus, moreish sulphides, savoury notes and more besides. Screw cap. 13.5% alc. **Rating** 95 **To** 2027 $80 JF

Robinson Vineyard Pinot Noir 2019 A glass of this at the end of a day and all would seem well with the world. There's a lot to relish and consider, but it never feels forced or over the top. It's a fine mesh of sweet cherries, a dusting of cinnamon, cedar wood and dried herbs. The palate is the thing. Finely tuned with beautiful, silky tannins and a freshness that makes you pour another glass, to consider the state of affairs. Screw cap. 14% alc. **Rating** 95 **To** 2028 $60 JF

The Moorooduc McIntyre Pinot Noir 2019 As the flagship pinot noir, this lives up to its reputation. It's a whorl of the darkest cherries, covered in baking spices, a fleck of mint and an overlay of savoury inputs, the French oak neatly integrated. It builds on the palate, full bodied but not unwieldy. Mouthfilling and generous, with the plushest tannins, ripe and sweet. Very satisfying and approachable now. Screw cap. 13.5% alc. **Rating** 95 **To** 2029 $80 JF

Garden Vineyard Pinot Noir 2019 Here's a wine that could slake a thirst. Bright, poppy fruit, nicely spiced and so perfumed. Works off a more medium-bodied frame, tannins have some pull, but it's all about the juiciness and lip-smacking tang at the moment. It's not their most complex wine but it is one of the most interesting and delicious to drink. In a way, this is the outlier in the pinot range as all the fruit is fermented as whole bunches. It works a treat in this warmer vintage. Screw cap. 13.5% alc. **Rating** 94 **To** 2026 $60 JF

🍷🍷🍷🍷 **Chardonnay 2019 Rating** 93 **To** 2025 $40 JF
Pinot Gris 2019 Rating 93 **To** 2024 $40 JF

Pinot Noir 2019 Rating 93 To 2027 $40 JF
McIntyre Vineyard Shiraz 2019 Rating 92 To 2030 $60 JF
Pinot Gris On Skins 2019 Rating 91 To 2023 $40 JF

Moppity Vineyards   ★★★★★

Moppity Road, Young, NSW 2594 (postal) **Region** Hilltops
T (02) 6382 6222 **www**.moppity.com.au
Winemaker Jason Brown **Est.** 1973 **Dozens** 30 000 **Vyds** 66.54ha

Jason Brown and wife Alecia, with backgrounds in fine-wine retail and accounting, purchased Moppity Vineyards in 2004 when it was already 31 years old. Initially they were content to sell the grapes to other makers, but that changed with the release of the '06 Shiraz, which won top gold in its class at the London International Wine & Spirit Competition. In Nov '09 the '08 Eden Road Long Road Hilltops Shiraz, made from Moppity Vineyards grapes, won the Jimmy Watson Trophy. These awards are among a cascade of golds for its shiraz wines, Riesling, Tumbarumba Chardonnay and Cabernet Sauvignon. Production (and sales) have soared and all the grapes from the estate are now used for the Moppity Vineyards brand. The Lock & Key range provides exceptional value for money. Moppity has also established Coppabella, a separate venture, in Tumbarumba. Exports to the UK and China.

ΨΨΨΨΨ **Estate Hilltops Shiraz 2019** This reveals a core of black plums, cherry liqueur, earthy and warm, with soy sauce and licorice. It's rich and full bodied, with oak in check, savouriness throughout, supportive tannins and frankly, a bargain. Screw cap. 14% alc. **Rating** 95 To 2032 $35 JF ✪

ΨΨΨΨΨ **Reserve Hilltops Shiraz 2018 Rating** 93 To 2030 $80 JF
Reserve Hilltops Cabernet Sauvignon 2018 Rating 93 To 2033 $80 JF
Estate Hilltops Cabernet Sauvignon 2018 Rating 90 To 2030 $35 JF

Morambro Creek Wines   ★★★★

Riddoch Highway, Padthaway, SA 5271 **Region** Padthaway
T (08) 8723 1065 **www**.morambrocreek.com.au
Winemaker Ben Riggs **Est.** 1994 **Dozens** 30 000 **Vyds** 178.5ha

The Bryson family has been involved in agriculture for more than a century, moving to Padthaway in 1955 as farmers and graziers. From the '90s they have progressively established large plantings of shiraz (88.5ha), cabernet sauvignon (47.5ha), chardonnay (34.5ha) and sauvignon blanc (8ha). The Morambro Creek and Mt Monster wines have been consistent winners of wine show medals. Exports to the UK, the US and other major markets.

ΨΨΨΨΨ **Padthaway Cabernet Sauvignon 2019** For a young cabernet, there is no harm cracking this open now. Sure it will last some distance but it has a core of really lovely fruit, all cassis and blackberries spiced with pepper and cinnamon, plus cedary, toasty oak. It's full bodied with persuasive tannins and built for ageing, but those aromas will suck you right in. Screw cap. 14.5% alc. **Rating** 93 To 2030 $35 JF

Padthaway Shiraz 2018 This is just sitting right. No shortage of dark fruits interspersed with savoury meaty nuances, the oak well-integrated and memory-foam tannins adding more volume. It certainly has a density and concentration of flavours but it's not over the top. It's good now and will be for a while longer. Screw cap. 14.5% alc. **Rating** 92 To 2028 $35 JF

Jip Jip Rocks Padthaway Shiraz 2019 Lots of ripe juicy fruit to the fore, nicely spiced, and the oak tucked in well. Nothing is out of place. It's great value and a pleasing drink. Screw cap. 14.5% alc. **Rating** 90 To 2024 $23 JF

Jip Jip Rocks Padthaway Shiraz Cabernet 2019 Take this to a barbecue and I guarantee everyone will want a glass. Why? Bright berries and spicy fruit with a savoury pulse and enough volume to please. Fresh and lively, yet balanced by some decent tannins. Screw cap. 14.5% alc. **Rating** 90 To 2026 $23 JF

Mordrelle Wines

411 River Road, Hahndorf, SA 5243 **Region** Adelaide Hills
T 0448 928 513 **www**.mordrellewines.com.au **Open** By appt
Winemaker Martin Moran **Est.** 2010 **Dozens** 2000
Based in Hahndorf in the beautiful Adelaide Hills, Mordrelle Wines is owned by Martin Moran together with his wife Michelle and her family, David and Jane Dreckow. The Mordrelle portfolio sources fruit from their own small vineyard in the nearby village of Mylor, as well as pinot noir, syrah, sauvignon blanc, grüner veltliner and a few styles of chardonnay from other Adelaide Hills locations. A special focus has been bottle-fermented Blanc de Blancs with extended time on lees from 5 to 10 years. Martin has also worked on viticulture research projects in Langhorne Creek and (tapping into his Argentinian roots) has made Malbec from there as well as a regional trophy-winning Barbera and other varieties. Mordrelle's labels are created from original artworks painted by Jose Luis Moran, Martin's late father. Exports to Denmark and China. (TL)

ΨΨΨΨΨ Blanc de Blanc Late Disgorged Chardonnay 2011 Traditional method blanc de blancs with just 6 months on lees when first released. Disgorged on demand, so with a crown seal closure it's still fresh, while starting to develop a lovely balance in line with its aged characters. Green apple with lemon flavours, vibrant acidity, good fruit through the palate. Smart, tasty wine. Crown seal. 12% alc. **Rating** 94 **To** 2023 $110 TL
Basket Press Adelaide Hills Pinot Noir 2019 One of 2 pinots from this stable, here from the Norton Summit district and displaying a darker fruit colour and profile than its Lenswood sibling. The cherry vibe is blacker, there's a note of dark fruit and nut chocolate with a touch of mint; and a richer, more complex nasal and palate aroma across the whole wine. A tad more structure than the Lenswood pinot. Both adorable, by the way. Screw cap. 14% alc. **Rating** 94 **To** 2028 $40 TL
Basket Press Langhorne Creek Shiraz 2019 Fruit from a single vineyard, traditionally made, 15 months in oak. Amazingly intense royal purple colour in the glass. The oak appears first on the nose. There's a heap going on here with dark fruits and berries, a fabulous shot of licorice and further spices through the palate. It's all held in place by the tannins, presentable yet pliable. Intense yet with an artisan touch. Screw cap. 14.5% alc. **Rating** 94 **To** 2030 $45 TL
Clone 1654 Adelaide Hills Syrah 2015 One of 3 clonal shiraz releases from a small block in the Mylor village district – and needs to be considered in the context of all 3 to fully be appreciated. This is the more common/benchmark SA shiraz clone, with darker fruits and more exotic spices on show, anise and vanilla. The oak impact is darker as well, though not overdone. More familiar traditional shiraz character in a medium to fuller-bodied variation of the 3. Screw cap. 14% alc. **Rating** 94 **To** 2028 $40 TL
Langhorne Creek Cabernet Sauvignon 2018 Top Langhorne Creek cabernet with terrific and immmediate varietal notes, its cassis, berry, faint floral and mint aromatics setting the scene for a pleasing drinking vibe from start to finish. The flavour is rich, with a suggestion of blackberry pie, classic cabernet grip and tannins kept neatly in check. Well done. Screw cap. 14.5% alc. **Rating** 94 **To** 2030 $35 TL
The Gaucho Limited Edition Langhorne Creek Malbec 2019 A single row from a single vineyard of Langhorne Creek's notable red variety. Vinified with traditional attention and aged in oak for 15 months. The colour is insanely intense, the nose swelling with mulberry, mocha, and spiced-berry pie, as well as the variety's trademark violet and earthiness. All this is echoed as you sip, wrapped in medium to full body and fluffy tannins. Crafting malbec to such a top-shelf style is brave and, in this case, most pleasing. Screw cap. 14.5% alc. **Rating** 94 **To** 2030 $85 TL

ΨΨΨΨΨ Basket Press Langhorne Creek Barbera 2019 Rating 93 **To** 2028 $35 TL
Clone 1125 Adelaide Hills Syrah 2015 Rating 92 **To** 2028 $40 TL

Clone 1127 Adelaide Hills Syrah 2015 Rating 92 To 2028 $40 TL
Adelaide Hills Sauvignon Blanc 2019 Rating 91 To 2024 $30 TL
Gran Reserva Adelaide Hills Chardonnay 2017 Rating 91 To 2026 $50 TL
Lenswood Adelaide Hills Pinot Noir 2019 Rating 91 To 2026 $35 TL
Langhorne Creek Shiraz Cabernet Sauvignon Malbec 2018 Rating 91
To 2026 $25 TL
Reserva Adelaide Hills Chardonnay 2018 Rating 90 To 2026 $40 TL

Morgan Simpson ★★★★

PO Box 39, Kensington Park, SA 5068 **Region** McLaren Vale
T 0417 843 118 **www.**morgansimpson.com.au
Winemaker Richard Simpson **Est.** 1998 **Dozens** 1200 **Vyds** 17.1ha
Morgan Simpson was founded by SA businessman George Morgan (since retired) and
winemaker Richard Simpson, who is a graduate of CSU. The grapes are sourced from the
Clos Robert Vineyard, planted to shiraz (9ha), cabernet sauvignon (3.5ha), mourvèdre (2.5ha)
and chardonnay (2.1ha), established by Robert Allen Simpson in 1972. Most of the grapes are
sold, the remainder used to provide the reasonably priced, drinkable wines for which Morgan
Simpson has become well known: they are available through their website.

🍷🍷🍷🍷🍷 **Barcore McLaren Vale Shiraz Mataro 2017** $20 buys a nourishing, rich
mouthful of wine that is admirably savoury. A ferrous mataro burr across the back
end. Loads of anise, sassafras, salami, violet and black cherry, but the firm plane
of tannin makes this a winning ticket. Screw cap. 14.8% alc. **Rating** 92 **To** 2025
$20 NG ✪

Row 42 McLaren Vale Cabernet Sauvignon 2018 A relaxed and full-
bodied maritime cab. Saline and lithe tannins, palpably firm enough to rally the
morass of flavours, draw a gentle bow of tension across cassis, olive, dried sage
and a potpourri of anise and scrub. Screw cap. 15.4% alc. **Rating** 92 **To** 2026
$20 NG ✪

Basket Press McLaren Vale Shiraz 2018 A take-no-prisoners sort of wine.
For some, out of hand; for others, a rich, old-fashioned regional red that draws
on the Vale's propensity for prodigious ripeness while tucking it under vanilla/
bourbon seams of American oak. It has its charms. Boysenberry, molten raspberry,
biter chocolate and a sizzle of volatility that confers lift while indicating that
the envelope has been pushed hard. Screw cap. 15.7% alc. **Rating** 90 **To** 2024
$22 NG

🍇 Morlet Wines ★★★☆

205 Clews Rd, Cowaramup, WA 6284 **Region** Margaret River
T (08) 9385 6665 **www.**morletwines.co.au
Winemaker Dylan Arvidson, Japo Dalli Cani **Est.** 2001 **Dozens** 500 **Vyds** 5ha
Owners Nigel Morlet and Philippa Lamont purchased the property in Cowaramup in 2001.
Planted to the small vineyard are chardonnay, zinfandel, merlot and petit verdot. Morlet Wines
is possibly the only producer in the area which is focused on zinfandel. From this grape they
make a pet nat, a rosé and a dry table wine. They also make a reserve zinfandel and a port.
Sold within Australia. (EL)

🍷🍷🍷🍷🍷 **Margaret River Chardonnay 2020** White peach, red apple and a hint of curry
leaf in there. On the palate this is concentrated, zingy and bright. The oak kicks
in through the finish leaving a spicy, sandalwood character on the palate. The fruit
pulls up sooner than expected, but while it is there it is moreish, concentrated and
quite delicious. Screw cap. 13.1% alc. **Rating** 91 **To** 2029 $33 EL

🍷🍷🍷🍷 **Pink Zin Margaret River 2020** Rating 88 To 2023 $33 EL

Morris

★★★★★

Mia Mia Road, Rutherglen, Vic 3685 **Region** Rutherglen
T (02) 6026 7303 **www**.morriswines.com **Open** Mon–Sun 10–4
Winemaker David Morris **Est.** 1859 **Dozens** 100 000 **Vyds** 96ha
One of the greatest of the fortified winemakers, ranking an eyelash behind Chambers
Rosewood. Morris has changed the labelling system for its sublime fortified wines with a
higher-than-average entry point for the (Classic) Liqueur Muscat; Topaque and the ultra-
premium wines are being released under the Old Premium Liqueur (Rare) label. The art of
these wines lies in the blending of very old and much younger material. These Rutherglen
fortified wines have no equivalent in any other part of the world (with the honourable
exception of Seppeltsfield in the Barossa Valley). In July 2016 Casella Family Brands acquired
Morris after decades of uninterested ownership by Pernod Ricard.

♟♟♟♟♟ **Old Premium Rare Topaque NV** A masterclass from Australia's greatest fortified
maker, David Morris, right here. The depth of complexity and intensity lays bare
the art of the blender and the depth and quality of the source material. Dried
fruit, malt, fruitcake, caramel toffees, licorice, roasted hazelnut and so much more
infused in an enveloping umami warmth. 500ml. Screw cap. 17.5% alc. **Rating** 98
$90 JP ✪
Old Premium Rare Liqueur Rutherglen Muscat NV A rich baroque tapestry
of aromas and flavours of great complexity. Immense concentration and depth on
display but realised with real grace and elegance. The superlatives flow but they are
needed. Plum pudding, chocolate, coffee bean, walnut and fruit peel combine with
toasty elements and dried dates, all smoothy honed and lifted by neutral spirit. The
finish stays with you. 500ml. Screw cap. 17% alc. **Rating** 97 $90 JP ✪

♟♟♟♟♟ **Cellar Reserve Grand Liqueur Rutherglen Topaque NV** Deep, dark
molasses in hue. Lifted and fresh aromas – a key to quality in aged fortifieds – of
fruitcake, roasted nuts, cold tea and coffee grounds. So smooth across the palate;
and complex, aided by a low-strength neutral spirit which allows the aged flavours
to soar. 500ml. Screw cap. 17.3% alc. **Rating** 96 $50 JP ✪
Cellar Reserve Grand Liqueur Rutherglen Muscat NV Varied vine ages
in play here, planted in 1965, 1974, 1982 and 2002, contributing varying degrees
of flavour complexity. When combined with age, neutral spirit and judicious
blending, they smash it out of the park! What a stunner. A rich, velvety fabric
of fig, butterscotch, toffee, walnut, panforte. Flavours go and go. Astoundingly
complex and, importantly, fresh. 500ml. Screw cap. 17.3% alc. **Rating** 96 $50 JP ✪
Cellar Reserve Grand Tawny NV If master blender David Morris can't get
drinkers interested in tawny fortifieds then the style is lost. Here, he invites the
eye in warm walnut brown tones and the nose with the scent of malt/toffee,
roasted almond and raisin. The invitation is delivered with great flavour, warmth
and chocolate/coffee/malt generosity edged in clean, fresh spirit. Lingers like mad.
500ml. Screw cap. 19% alc. **Rating** 95 $50 JP
Old Premium Rare Rutherglen Tawny NV A liqueur tawny with
concentrated raisin, toffee, coffee, balsamic and nutty characters aplenty. Drenches
the mouth in concentrated flavour, a powerfully persuasive wine to make you
wonder why you don't buy this kind of vinous history more often. 500ml. Screw
cap. 20% alc. **Rating** 95 $90 JP
Classic Rutherglen Topaque NV Manages to combine elegance and freshness
with a richness of flavour, not an easy task. A lovely delicacy pervades this wine, of
freshly roasted coffee beans, mocha, golden syrup, honey and that thread of cold
tea so emblematic of the grape and style. A mix of age, clean neutral spirit here
and, always, the seamless Morris style. What value! 375ml. Screw cap. 17.5% alc.
Rating 95 $25 JP ✪
Classic Rutherglen Muscat NV A vibrant, fresh example of the classic style.
Golden brown in hue, lifted fragrance of nougat, orange peel, toffee and dark malt
biscuit. That sweet maltiness runs deep on the palate with a luscious intensity.

Silken palate texture. A top quality classic classification statement. 500ml. Screw cap. 17.5% alc. **Rating** 94 $25 JP ❂
Black Label Rutherglen Muscat NV What a steal. Amazing quality right here. The wealth and depth of the Morris fortified solera system is evident even at the entry-level muscat. Butterscotch, dried fruits, honey and a hint of rose petal combine with a luscious palate with developing nuttiness. Sweetness freshened nicely by the neutral spirit. 500ml. Screw cap. 17.3% alc. **Rating** 94 $20 JP ❂

🍷🍷🍷🍷🍷 **Sparkling Shiraz Durif NV Rating** 93 $20 JP ❂
Rutherglen VP Vintage 2008 Rating 93 $25 JP ❂
Classic Rutherglen Tawny NV Rating 92 $25 JP ❂
Bin 158 Rutherglen Durif 2017 Rating 90 To 2030 $27 JP

Moss Brothers

8 Wattle Place, Margaret River, WA 6285 **Region** Margaret River
T 0402 010 352 **www.**mossbrotherswines.com.au
Winemaker Rory Parks **Est.** 1984 **Dozens** 7000 **Vyds** 16.03ha
This is the reincarnation of the Moss Brothers brand, though not its vineyards, which were acquired by Amelia Park in 2015. It is a parallel business to Trove Estate. Paul Byron and Ralph Dunning are the major forces in both ventures, both with extensive whole-of-business expertise across Australia. Exports to the US and China.

🍷🍷🍷🍷🍷 **Fidium Margaret River Cabernet Sauvignon 2019** Highly aromatic and very pretty, laden with cassis, raspberry and pomegranate. Totally supple and elegant. The oak is there in a supportive and structuring manner, but is almost imperceptible. Delicious. Screw cap. 14% alc. **Rating** 96 To 2041 $55 EL ❂
Fidium Margaret River Sauvignon Blanc 2020 Barrel fermented and matured for 6 months. Elegant, restrained and very classy, this has layers upon layers of nashi pear, green apple, kiwifruit, jasmine tea and sugar snap pea. Quite gorgeous, and thanks to the oak, likely great for a number of years. Screw cap. 12.5% alc. **Rating** 94 To 2026 $40 EL

🍷🍷🍷🍷🍷 **Moses Rock Margaret River Sauvignon Blanc 2020 Rating** 93 To 2024 $28 EL
Moses Rock Margaret River Chenin Blanc 2020 Rating 93 To 2031 $28 EL
Fidium Margaret River Malbec 2019 Rating 93 To 2031 $45 EL
Fidium Margaret River Chardonnay 2019 Rating 92 To 2031 $45 EL
Fidium Margaret River Shiraz 2019 Rating 92 To 2030 $45 EL

Moss Wood

926 Metricup Road, Wilyabrup, WA 6284 **Region** Margaret River
T (08) 9755 6266 **www.**mosswood.com.au **Open** By appt
Winemaker Clare Mugford, Keith Mugford **Est.** 1969 **Dozens** 11 000 **Vyds** 18.14ha
Widely regarded as one of the best wineries in the region, producing glorious chardonnay, power-laden semillon and elegant cabernet sauvignon that lives for decades. Moss Wood also owns RibbonVale Estate, the wines treated as vineyard-designated within the Moss Wood umbrella. Exports to all major markets.

🍷🍷🍷🍷🍷 **Wilyabrup Margaret River Cabernet Sauvignon 2018** Rippling layers of flavour and texture here. So long that it carries itself over the palate and through into the finish … what a finish! Pedigree and happenstance have collided to create a legend. The 2018 will go down as one of the greatest Moss Wood cabernets ever made, alongside the 2001. Screw cap. 14.5% alc. **Rating** 98 To 2061 $160 EL ❂
Ribbon Vale Margaret River Cabernet Sauvignon 2018 We live in hallowed times: the '18 cabernets from Margaret River are being released into the wild … there's never been a better time to be alive. Concentrated, fine, pedigree cabernet with explosive, low-down torque that drags the flavours over the palate

into the interminably long finish. Epic. Will live as long as you do. Screw cap. 14.5% alc. **Rating** 97 **To** 2050 $77 EL ✪

🍷🍷🍷🍷🍷 **Wilyabrup Margaret River Semillon 2020** Although vinified à la Hunter Valley – clear juice with multiple yeasts, bottled straight after cold fermentation – the result is a universe away from young Hunter semillon. It has striking depth to its supple lemongrass and white peach fruit flavours, lengthened and balanced by demure acidity. Screw cap. 14.2% alc. **Rating** 96 **To** 2035 $44 JH ✪

Ribbon Vale Elsa Margaret River 2019 Wow. Ok, so a new breed of barrel-aged sauvignon blanc is here. Intense and rich, rounded, complex and viscous in texture. The tannins (yes, tannins – despite only an hour on skins) are ripe and chewy; they frame the soft citrus fruit in a pillow of texture. Sauvignon blanc can be edgy – this is not. Semillon can be grassy – this is not. Keith has managed to capture the attributes of both varieties, with none of the obviousness. What a wonder. Screw cap. 12.5% alc. **Rating** 96 **To** 2025 $76 EL ❤

Wilyabrup Margaret River Chardonnay 2019 The 2019 vintage was a cool one in Margaret River, and the best wines exhibit a cool restraint and delicacy that works alongside the natural latent power of the grape. In this instance, the opulent, luxurious style of chardonnay that Moss Wood is known for is somewhat tempered by the cool season. Very pretty, very soft, and with hints of butter menthol, yellow peach, white pepper and fennel flower. Graceful, elegant and svelte. Screw cap. 14% alc. **Rating** 96 **To** 2036 $89 EL

Wilyabrup Margaret River Pinot Noir 2018 Moss Wood pinot noir has developed a reputation over the years for its capability to age gracefully in the cellar. Here, through the lens of the near-perfect 2018 vintage, the pristine and piercingly intense fruit shows longevity and pedigree, in wonderful balance with all aspects of its makeup. Screw cap. 14% alc. **Rating** 96 **To** 2048 $77 EL

Ribbon Vale Margaret River Merlot 2018 Pretty, succulent red fruits are all wrapped up in fine, shapely tannins. Supple, lithe and elegant. A beautiful wine. Screw cap. 14% alc. **Rating** 96 **To** 2041 $77 EL

Wilyabrup Margaret River Cabernet Sauvignon 2017 The 2017 vintage is responsible for cabernets of incredible poise and layering. This is not a thundering power piece, rather an intricately detailed and mesmerising wine, with fine folds of flavour: bay leaf, raspberry, star anise, sage, hints of fennel, pomegranate and pink peppercorn. This is pure, floral, pretty, and very long. Moss Wood has proven its capability for graceful ageing and this will be no exception. Screw cap. 14% alc. **Rating** 96 **To** 2046 $152 EL

Amy's Margaret River 2019 The 2019 vintage in Margaret River was cool and wet, producing wines of concentrated, high aroma and vibrancy. This is all of that, with layers of nuance on the palate. It is very restrained and long; unfurling, petal by petal, rather than revealing itself all at once. Elegant and classy to the very end. A ripper. Buy it and cellar it with confidence, or drink its beauty tonight – both viable options. Screw cap. 13.5% alc. **Rating** 95 **To** 2041 $45 EL

Ribbon Vale Vineyard Margaret River Botrytis Semillon 2018 The fruit has piercing intensity of flavour on the tongue; ginger spice, Italian mountain herbs, white pepper, stone fruit, apple and pear blossom, crunchy sea salt flakes and something else dry and salty in there … dried kelp perhaps. This is an ever-moving, complex, layered and diaphanous wine of great length. Highly recommended. 375ml bottle. Screw cap. 10.5% alc. **Rating** 95 **To** 2036 $65 EL

Mount Avoca   ★★★★☆

Moates Lane, via Vinoca Road, Avoca, Vic 3467 **Region** Pyrenees
T (03) 5465 3282 **www**.mountavoca.com **Open** 7 days 11–4
Winemaker David Darlow **Est.** 1970 **Dozens** 15000 **Vyds** 23.46ha
A winery that has long been one of the stalwarts of the Pyrenees region, owned by 3rd-generation Matthew Barry. The estate vineyards (shiraz, sauvignon blanc, cabernet sauvignon, chardonnay, merlot, cabernet franc, tempranillo, lagrein and viognier) are certified

organic, as is the winery. The Moates Lane range of wines are partly or wholly made from contract-grown grapes. Exports to China, the US, NZ, Singapore and South Korea.

🍷🍷🍷🍷🍷 **Estate Old Vine Pyrenees Shiraz 2019** Shiraz is the great strength of this Pyrenees producer, the grape that really sets the pulse racing. Give this old-vine rendition some air and watch it lift. Supple and dense in sweet-fruited blackberries, blood plums, earth, chocolate. Goes long. Screw cap. 14.5% alc. **Rating** 95 To 2031 $38 JP

🍷🍷🍷🍷🍷 **Estate Pyrenees Shiraz 2019 Rating** 93 To 2030 $28 JP
Estate Pyrenees Cabernet Sauvignon 2019 Rating 93 To 2026 $38 JP
Estate Pyrenees Chardonnay 2019 Rating 91 To 2026 $38 JP
The Calling Pyrenees Shiraz 2017 Rating 90 To 2031 $85 JP

Mount Benson Estate ★★★★

329 Wrights Bay Road, Mount Benson, SA 5275 **Region** Mount Benson
T 0417 996 796 **www.**mountbensonestate.com.au **Open** 7 days 10–5 Sept–Jun
Winemaker Contract **Est.** 1988 **Dozens** 800 **Vyds** 24.2ha
The future of Mount Benson isn't easy to foresee. Both climate and soil offer rich rewards for those who understand the extreme differences between the 4 seasons (for humans as well as vines). The newly installed owners of Mount Benson Estate have one obvious advantage: husband Brian Nitschinsk served for 39 years in the Australian Navy, retiring as a commander engineer. Figuratively, Mount Benson (a puny rise measured in only tens of metres) has one foot in the Southern Ocean and one foot on the ground, so Brian should feel right at home. Wife Carolyn was a secondary school teacher specialising in art and visual communication. Thus, the cold windswept landscape of winter is something they will be able to cope with. The legacy of 2 generations of the founding Wehl family has already demonstrated the ability of the vineyard to produce shiraz of exceptional quality, cabernet sauvignon not far behind.

🍷🍷🍷🍷🍷 **Rosé of Syrah 2019** 55/45% shiraz/cabernet sauvignon, vinified separately, resting in picking bins before fermentation, creating the full, bright crimson/ purple hue. The bouquet and palate are pure cherry sarsaparilla, the potential for excess weight dealt with by the wine's crisp acidity. Screw cap. 13.6% alc. **Rating** 90 To 2022 $25 JH

Mt Duneed Estate ★★★★

65 Pettavel Road, Waurn Ponds, Vic 3216 **Region** Geelong
T (03) 5266 1244 **www.**mtduneedestate.com.au **Open** Tues–Sun 11.30–5 (summer) Thurs–Sun 11.30–5 (winter)
Winemaker Rob Dolan **Est.** 2014 **Dozens** 9000 **Vyds** 5ha
Visitors to Mt Duneed Estate may find the winery looks familiar – it was previously owned and run by Pettavel Winery. Four families purchased Mt Duneed Estate in 2012. They leased the winery to Scotchmans Hill for a short time before fully taking over its running and wine production in 2014. Experienced winemaker Rob Dolan (of Rob Dolan Wines) is at the helm, overseeing 3 ranges of wines, each offering a range of grape varieties from different locations. (JP)

🍷🍷🍷🍷🍷 **Single Vineyard Yarra Valley Pinot Noir 2017** Moves up in sophistication and complexity to the standard release, presenting a picture of quiet elegance. Perfumed, dried flowers with a raspberry, plum fruit aroma and tobacco leaf. Keeps things bright while also revealing a dark, forest floor/earthy, smoky oak side. Screw cap. 13.5% alc. **Rating** 92 To 2025 $45 JP
Single Vineyard Heathcote Shiraz 2017 So Heathcote, down to its cassis and leafy dried characters, including the scent of Aussie bush and rich, red earth. Soft and plush, too. The palate moves up in structure and tannin presence as you taste through. This wine won't mind a bit more bottle age. Screw cap. 14% alc. **Rating** 91 To 2028 $45 JP

ΨΨΨΨ   Single Vineyard Yarra Valley Chardonnay 2016 Rating 88 To 2023 $45 JP
Yarra Valley Pinot Noir 2019 Rating 88 To 2025 $21 JP

Mount Eyre Vineyards ★★★★

173 Gillards Road, Pokolbin, NSW 2320 **Region** Hunter Valley
T 0438 683 973 **www.**mounteyre.com **Open** At Garden Cellars, Hunter Valley Gardens
Winemaker Andrew Spinaze, Mark Richardson, Michael McManus **Est.** 1970
Dozens 3000 **Vyds** 25ha
This is the venture of 2 families whose involvement in wine extends back several centuries
in an unbroken line: the Tsironis family in the Peleponnese, Greece; and the Iannuzzi family in
Vallo della Lucania, Italy. Their largest vineyard is at Broke, with a smaller vineyard at Pokolbin.
The 3 principal varieties planted are chardonnay, shiraz and semillon, with smaller amounts of
merlot, chambourcin, verdelho, fiano and nero d'Avola.

ΨΨΨΨΨ   **Three Ponds Holman Hunter Valley Nero d'Avola 2019** This is highly
varietal, melding sassafras, pickled cherry, candied orange zest and lavender with
a regional breadth across the mid palate and that quintessential Hunter loaminess.
Full bodied but savoury enough. I just wish this was hand picked, especially at the
price. A dusty belt of tannins helps to tuck it all in. A long finish achieved due to
the force of personality. Screw cap. 14.6% alc. **Rating** 92 **To** 2023 $45 NG
Three Ponds Hunter Valley Shiraz 2019 Very Hunter, expressing an earthy
warmth and scents of dried cherry pith, anise and terracotta. Succulent. A richer
expression from a very warm vintage, balanced by lithe tannins and savoury
integrity. A good drink. Screw cap. 14.5% alc. **Rating** 92 **To** 2026 $40 NG
Monkey Place Creek Hunter Valley Shiraz 2019 A vintage of considerable
extract and heft, yet uncanny precision. The going is good! Medium bodied,
savoury and bright. Perhaps a bit too bright, with tangy acidity towing flavours
of red and dark cherry, suede and varnish to good length. 12.9% alc. **Rating** 90
To 2022 $25 NG

Mount Horrocks ★★★★★

The Old Railway Station, Curling Street, Auburn, SA 5451 **Region** Clare Valley
T (08) 8849 2243 **www.**mounthorrocks.com **Open** W'ends & public hols 10–5
Winemaker Stephanie Toole **Est.** 1982 **Dozens** 3500 **Vyds** 9.4ha
Owner/winemaker Stephanie Toole has never deviated from the pursuit of excellence in the
vineyard and winery. She has 3 vineyard sites in the Clare Valley, each managed using natural
farming and organic practices. The attention to detail and refusal to cut corners is obvious in
all her wines. The cellar door is in the renovated old Auburn railway station. Exports to the
UK, China, and other major markets.

ΨΨΨΨΨ   **Watervale Riesling 2020** Wow. This is so good it's hard to put down. Beautiful
poise and yet quite energising. A heady mix of white flowers, quince and lemon/
lime, with a biscuity flavour, too. The acidity is fine and pure, gliding along
the palate to a most resounding finish. Screw cap. 13% alc. **Rating** 96 **To** 2030
$38 JF ✪
Alexander Vineyard Clare Valley Shiraz 2018 Excellent, full crimson/purple
colour. A wine that is all about high-quality shiraz picked at precisely the right
moment. Equal amounts of blackberry and plum drive the bouquet and medium-
bodied palate with consummate ease, oak and tannins in dutiful support. Screw
cap. 14% alc. **Rating** 96 **To** 2038 $50 JH ✪
Alexander Vineyard Clare Valley Shiraz 2019 Excellent purple/black hue.
In a way a commanding wine, yet it has alluring perfume, and a wave of spices
over black fruit. Full bodied, deep, earthy and complex. Ribbons of tannins strung
through, a touch raspy (presumably from toasty oak) but either way, it offers a solid
drink today, or more refinement in a few years. Screw cap. 14% alc. **Rating** 95
To 2032 $48 JF

ҮҮҮҮ Clare Valley Semillon 2020 Rating 93 To 2029 $38 JF
Clare Valley Nero d'Avola 2019 Rating 92 To 2024 $40 JF
Cordon Cut Clare Valley Riesling 2020 Rating 91 To 2027 $42 JF

Mount Langi Ghiran Vineyards ★★★★★

80 Vine Road, Bayindeen, Vic 3375 **Region** Grampians
T (03) 5354 3207 **www**.langi.com.au **Open** 7 days 10–5
Winemaker Adam Louder, Darren Rathbone **Est.** 1969 **Dozens** 45 000 **Vyds** 65ha
A maker of outstanding cool-climate peppery shiraz, crammed with flavour and vinosity,
and very good cabernet sauvignon. The shiraz has long pointed the way for cool-climate
examples of the variety. The business was acquired by the Rathbone family group in 2002.
The marketing is integrated with the Yering Station and Xanadu Estate wines, a synergistic
mix with no overlap. Wine quality is exemplary. Exports to all major markets.

ҮҮҮҮҮ Mast Grampians Shiraz 2019 A vinous ode to the late, great innovative
winemaker Trevor Mast, who promoted the kind of cool-climate shiraz we now
so enjoy. This is all about the quality of the fruit, the light pepper and swirling
spice, anise, wild raspberries, cassis. It moves with precision on the palate, elegant
and supple. Screw cap. 14.8% alc. **Rating** 96 **To** 2038 $90 JP ♥
Langi Grampians Shiraz 2019 The Swiss clone, planted in 1969 and still on
its own roots, is at the heart of this impressive flagship shiraz. It has a deep vein
of ripeness of dark plum, aniseed, sage, lifted wood spices and blackberries. Taut
across the palate in structure but velvety in flavour, it raises the question of when
to drink. The answer: not just now, if possible. Screw cap. 14.8% alc. **Rating** 96
To 2034 $200 JP
Cliff Edge Grampians Shiraz 2019 A range of clones lend character to the
delicious complexity in this wine. You have to wonder about their powerful role.
Deep, dense purple. A beautifully elegant expression of concentrated spice, pepper
and black-hearted shiraz. Revels in lifted aromatics of violet and woodsy spice,
anise and chocolate, with a surge of fine tannins and vanillan oak through to the
finish. Screw cap. 14.5% alc. **Rating** 95 **To** 2032 $35 JP ✪
Cliff Edge Grampians Cabernet Sauvignon Merlot 2019 The cabernet
comes off old vines planted in 1974 in Great Western and, wow, what a
contribution they make! Brilliant, deep-hued purple. A powerfully good aroma
of concentrated fruit and spice: blackberry, boysenberry, musky sweet aromatics,
pepper and violets. It resonates across the tongue, the 2 grapes in complete unison.
Tannins run deep but fine, through to the finish. Screw cap. 14.5% alc. **Rating** 95
To 2032 $35 JP ✪
Talus Grampians Cabernet Sauvignon 2019 For those who haven't as
yet discovered the beauty of Grampians cabernet sauvignon, here is an ideal
opportunity. A wine of poise and elegance that absorbs 66% new oak. A rich
embroidery of flavours, from cassis, bush mint and leafy cabernet characters and
licorice through to dusty cacao, nicely interspersed with savoury oak, weaves a
wonderful wine. Screw cap. 14.5% alc. **Rating** 95 **To** 2034 $60 JP

ҮҮҮҮ Billi Billi Pinot Gris 2020 Rating 93 To 2023 $20 JH ✪
Talus Grampians Shiraz 2019 Rating 93 To 2034 $60 JP ✪
Cliff Edge Grampians Riesling 2020 Rating 92 To 2025 $25 JP ✪
Cliff Edge Grampians Pinot Gris 2020 Rating 90 To 2024 $25 JP
Billi Billi Shiraz 2018 Rating 90 To 2023 $20 JP ✪

Mt Lofty Ranges Vineyard ★★★★★

Harris Road, Lenswood, SA 5240 **Region** Adelaide Hills
T (08) 8389 8339 **www**.mtloftyrangesvineyard.com.au **Open** Fri–Sun & public hols 11–5
Winemaker Peter Leske, Taras Ochota **Est.** 1992 **Dozens** 3000 **Vyds** 4.6ha
Mt Lofty Ranges is owned and operated by Sharon Pearson and Garry Sweeney. Nestled high
in the Lenswood subregion of the Adelaide Hills at an altitude of 500m, the very steep north-
facing vineyard (pinot noir, sauvignon blanc, chardonnay and riesling) is pruned and picked by

hand. The soil is sandy clay loam with a rock base of white quartz and ironstone, and irrigation is kept to a minimum to allow the wines to display vintage characteristics.

ᵀᵀᵀᵀᵀ **S&G Lenswood Chardonnay 2019** The fruit has to be immaculate to deliver at this level. And it does – more grapefruit flavours, acidity and accompanying pith on the palate, adding a keen tension to typical white stone-fruit notes. Deliciously crafted. Screw cap. 13.2% alc. **Rating** 95 **To** 2027 $85 TL

S&G Lenswood Pinot Noir 2019 The top shelf of 3 pinots, from the best 2 rows in the Lenswood vineyard. No new oak. Attractive cherry (almost liqueur) preliminaries, with superfine tannins coating the palate. The flavours are tight and mineral, with just a subtle stalky whole-bunch vibe going on. All very good. Screw cap. 13.2% alc. **Rating** 95 **To** 2029 $85 TL

Late Disgorged Lenswood Méthode Traditionelle Pinot Noir Chardonnay 2013 Complex traditional method characters from start to finish. Lightly toasty and bready with autolysis notes, then a slow rise of chardonnay citrus flavours come into play, providing palate excitement and extra-sensory interest with a fine talc texture. Balance is well achieved, the flavour length captivating. Cork. 11.5% alc. **Rating** 95 **To** 2025 $95 TL

Home Block Lenswood Riesling 2020 A fabulous expression of this variety. High-toned white orchard florals and cut yellow and green citrus fruits, with brilliant acidity and pithy minerality in the mouth. It's even spicy, with length, line and glorious tangy flavour retention. A real riesling pleasure. Screw cap. 12.5% alc. **Rating** 94 **To** 2026 $30 TL ✪

Aspire Lenswood Chardonnay 2019 From a warmer section of this Lenswood estate block, picked earlier to retain more edge and tension. Just 25% new oak in play, not pushing into this lovely white nectarine-fruited version, just adding a supportive creamy layer with a light spice on the finish. All up very tasty. Screw cap. 13% alc. **Rating** 94 **To** 2026 $55 TL

S&G Adelaide Hills Shiraz 2019 As with all the S&G range, there's a more savoury, mineral style developing; the nose is more earthy and there's a note of button mushroom on the palate as well. Only 1yo oak in the making, and the tannins are quite prominent, while a lift of tart plums echoes on the finish. Micro-terroir-specific and best appreciated in that context. Screw cap. 13.5% alc. **Rating** 94 **To** 2028 $85 TL

ᵀᵀᵀᵀᵧ **Aspire Lenswood Pinot Noir 2019 Rating** 92 **To** 2028 $55 TL
Old Gum Block Adelaide Hills Shiraz 2019 Rating 92 **To** 2028 $35 TL
Aspire Adelaide Hills Shiraz 2019 Rating 91 **To** 2028 $55 TL
Not Shy Lenswood Pinot Noir Rosé 2020 Rating 90 **To** 2022 $24 TL

Mount Majura Vineyard ★★★★★

88 Lime Kiln Road, Majura, ACT 2609 **Region** Canberra District
T (02) 6262 3070 **www**.mountmajura.com.au **Open** 7 days 10–5
Winemaker Dr Frank van de Loo **Est.** 1988 **Dozens** 5000 **Vyds** 9.3ha

Vines were first planted in 1988 by Dinny Killen on a site on her family property that had been especially recommended by Dr Edgar Riek; its attractions were red soil of volcanic origin over limestone, with reasonably steep east and northeast slopes providing an element of frost protection. The tiny vineyard has been significantly expanded since it was purchased in '99. Blocks of pinot noir and chardonnay have been joined by pinot gris, shiraz, tempranillo, riesling, graciano, mondeuse and touriga nacional. Much attention has been focused on tempranillo, with 6 clones planted: D8V12, D8V13, CL770, T306, requena and tinta roriz. Three single-site tempranillos (Rock Block, Dry Spur and Little Dam) are more recent arrivals. The Mount Majura flagship remains the Canberra District Tempranillo, with volume and quality cementing its place. All the grapes used come from these estate plantings. One of the star performers in the Canberra District.

ᵀᵀᵀᵀᵀ **Little Dam Canberra District Tempranillo 2019** The most complete, structured and compelling of the single-site wines. Its own distinct personality comes through with a whorl of dark fruits, tarry and earthy, licorice root and a smidge of sarsaparilla. It's very savoury with exceptional tannins – ripe, textural, with a graininess akin to raw silk, the acidity bright and the finish long. Screw cap. 14.5% alc. **Rating** 96 **To** 2033 $65 JF ✪

Dry Spur Canberra District Tempranillo 2019 A neat confluence of juicy, tangy and tart fruit, with flavours of juniper, charcuterie and woodsy spices. The tannins are embedded with a fine sandy/grainy texture and the mouth-watering acidity demands a plate of jamon. Lovely wine. Screw cap. 14.5% alc. **Rating** 95 **To** 2030 $65 JF

Canberra District Tempranillo 2019 It's such a distinctive tempranillo, distinctly Mount Majura. This reveals a quiet confidence at first. The splash of red berries, the hint of sarsaparilla and the dusting of spices, all enticing. The flavours build across the palate – tangy raspberry-like acidity an interplay with arrowhead-shaped tannins. Screw cap. 14.5% alc. **Rating** 95 **To** 2033 $48 JF

🍷🍷🍷🍷♀ **TSG Canberra District Tempranillo Shiraz Graciano 2018** **Rating** 93 **To** 2030 $38 JF
Rock Block Canberra District Tempranillo 2019 **Rating** 93 **To** 2033 $65 JF
Canberra District Chardonnay 2019 **Rating** 91 **To** 2027 $29 JF

Mount Mary   ★★★★★

Coldstream West Road, Lilydale, Vic 3140 **Region** Yarra Valley
T (03) 9739 1761 **www.**mountmary.com.au
Winemaker Sam Middleton **Est.** 1971 **Dozens** 4500 **Vyds** 18ha
Mount Mary was one of the foremost pioneers of the rebirth of the Yarra Valley after 50 years without viticultural activity. From the outset they produced wines of rare finesse and purity. Today its star shines brighter than that of any of the 169 producers in the Yarra Valley. The late founder, Dr John Middleton, practised near-obsessive attention to detail long before that phrase slid into oenological vernacular. He relentlessly strove for perfection and all 4 of the wines in the original Mount Mary portfolio achieved just that (within the context of each vintage). Charming grandson Sam Middleton is equally dedicated. An all-encompassing recent tasting of every vintage of these 4 wines left me in no doubt he is making even better wines since assuming the winemaker mantle in June 2011. In '08 Mount Mary commenced a detailed program of vine improvement, in particular assessing the implications of progressively moving towards a 100% grafted vineyard to provide immunity from phylloxera. Part involved a move to sustainable organic viticulture and ongoing use of straw mulch to retain as much moisture as possible in the vineyard. Winery of the Year in the *Wine Companion 2018*. Exports to the UK, the US, Denmark, Hong Kong, Singapore, South Korea and China.

🍷🍷🍷🍷🍷 **Yarra Valley Quintet 2019** A quintet of 44% cabernet sauvignon, 30% merlot, 16% cabernet franc and 5% each of malbec and petit verdot, all in harmony. Heady aromatics, the fruit pristine and lightly spiced. But it's the medium-bodied palate that really woos: focused and seamless with superfine yet detailed tannins. Of course it has the beauty and charm of youth but age will send this to another level. Did I mention elegance? Tick. Cork. 13% alc. **Rating** 98 **To** 2039 $165 JF ✪ ♥
Yarra Valley Chardonnay 2019 There must be some magic dust landing on Mount Mary, or rather, its chardonnay site. Latterly, this has just been rockin' it. No different this year: a pristine, refined and ultra-elegant wine. A harmonious offering of citrus and light, creamy leesy flavours, spice and vanilla-pod oak. The succulence via acidity ensures it lingers long. I got goosebumps tasting this. Screw cap. 13% alc. **Rating** 97 **To** 2035 $120 JF ✪

🍷🍷🍷🍷🍷 **Yarra Valley Pinot Noir 2019** The light ruby hue belies the whorl of intense flavour. Pretty aromatics. It bursts out with raspberries and cherries, then richer strawberry compote infused with bitter herbs, cloves and sarsaparilla. French oak is neatly tucked away, but acts as a support, while superfine tannins glide across a lighter- to medium-bodied frame. A beautiful and beguiling wine. Cork. 13% alc. **Rating** 96 **To** 2035 $165 JF

Yarra Valley Triolet 2019 65/25/10% sauvignon blanc/semillon/muscadelle. Often nervy and tight on release, this is taut, linear and refreshingly dry. It does open up to reveal its savouriness, although there's a touch of lemon meringue pie, without the sweetness of course. It's mouth-watering, complex, compelling and unique. Screw cap. 13% alc. **Rating** 95 **To** 2033 $105 JF

Marli Russell by Mount Mary RP2 2019 The combination of 55/20/20/5% grenache/shiraz/mourvèdre/cinsault in this warmer vintage has brought out the best of each to make a harmonious, singularly focused wine. While there's a plushness to the fruit, and even an intensity of flavour, it's rather restrained, with a medium-bodied palate at best. A flutter of exotic spices, fine, grainy tannins and a succulence throughout make this a delicious wine. Screw cap. 13% alc. **Rating** 95 **To** 2029 $75 JF

Marli Russell by Mount Mary RP1 2019 45/45/10% marsanne/roussanne/clairette. The mid straw gold colour indicates some development, as do the ripe flavours. A mix of stone fruit, quince, nougatine and bitter lemon with some phenolic grip, so the finish is wonderfully crisp and dry, almost brittle. Screw cap. 13% alc. **Rating** 94 **To** 2030 $55 JF

Mount Monument Vineyard

1399 Romsey Road, Romsey, Vic 3434 **Region** Macedon Ranges
T 0410 545 646 **www**.mountmonumentwines.com
Winemaker Ben Rankin **Est.** 2008 **Dozens** 800 **Vyds** 2.3ha
Mount Monument nestles into the shoulder of Mount Macedon, one of Australia's coolest wine regions. At 600m the volcanic silica soils are host to the chardonnay, pinot noir and riesling planted many years prior to its acquisition by Nonda Katsalidis. Under viticulturist John Heitmann, the vineyard is managed with minimal chemical intervention, and utilises organic and biodynamic inputs.

Riesling 2019 Hand picked and whole-bunch pressed, fermented naturally and aged in old oak. This rizza rocks. It has lemon blossom and lime-juice freshness. A textural palate with the merest hint of creaminess is met by very fine acidity. It has a gentle persuasion and lingers. Delicious. Alas, a mere 25 dozen made. Screw cap. 12% alc. **Rating** 95 **To** 2029 $45 JF

Chardonnay 2018 At first, there appears to be a lot of winemaking artefact – the toasty, spicy oak, nutty leesy flavours and a clotted-cream malo character, but then they fall neatly into line. Stone fruit and citrus come to the fore, joined by some lemony saline freshness and just-picked herbs. The fine acidity is what elevates this and puts it into overdrive. It's energising. Screw cap. 12.3% alc. **Rating** 95 **To** 2028 $45 JF

Pinot Noir 2018 This just teases with its vibrant, sweet red cherries and pips, woodsy spices and overall succulence working across its more medium-bodied palate. But it is compelling. The flavours build and linger, with hazelnut skins-esque tannins pinched by a slight green/stemmy grip on the finish. Screw cap. 14% alc. **Rating** 94 **To** 2030 $45 JF

Mt Pilot Estate

208 Shannons Road, Byawatha, Vic 3678 **Region** North East Victoria
T 0419 243 225 **www**.mtpilotestatewines.com.au **Open** By appt
Winemaker Marc Scalzo **Est.** 1996 **Dozens** 600 **Vyds** 13ha
Lachlan and Penny Campbell have planted shiraz (7ha), cabernet sauvignon (3ha), viognier (2ha) and durif (1ha). The vineyard is planted on deep, well-drained granitic soils at an altitude of 250m near Eldorado, 20km from Wangaratta and 35km from Beechworth. Exports to Singapore.

Reserve Viognier 2017 This smart viognier is definitely worthy of your attention, striking the always delicate balance between richness of fruit and brightness of acidity in the grape. Baked apple, nougat, orange peel, earthy, toasted spice and nuts fill the senses with a deep complexity. It works beautifully on the palate, getting the textural tone and pitch just right. Juicy acidity whets the appetite. Screw cap. 13.7% alc. **Rating** 95 **To** 2027 $35 JP ✪

Reserve Shiraz 2017 The burgeoning Eldorado area of North East Victoria is one to watch, with its stunning, dark-hued red wines sporting a rich intensity of fruit. A thoughtful and polished shiraz, the inclusion of a splash of viognier bringing delightful, lifted aromatics. Violet, ripe blackberry, dark chocolate, turned earth. For all of its apparent richness, it is quite elegant, with a strong foundation of firm, savoury tannins. Screw cap. 14.4% alc. **Rating** 94 **To** 2030 $40 JP

♟♟♟♟♟ **Estate Grown Cabernet Sauvignon 2017 Rating** 93 **To** 2029 $30 JP
Shiraz 2017 Rating 90 **To** 2027 $27 JP

Mount Pleasant ★★★★★

401 Marrowbone Road, Pokolbin, NSW 2320 **Region** Hunter Valley
T (02) 4998 7505 **www**.mountpleasantwines.com.au **Open** Thurs–Mon 10–4
Winemaker Adrian Sparks **Est.** 1921 **Vyds** 88.2ha
The glorious Elizabeth and Lovedale Semillons are generally commercially available with 4 to 5 years of bottle age; they are treasures with a consistently superb show record. Mount Pleasant's individual vineyard wines, together with the Maurice O'Shea memorial wines, add to the lustre of this proud name. The appointment of Jim Chatto as group chief winemaker in 2013 and the '14 vintage – the best since 1965 – has lifted the range and quality of the red wines back to the glory days of Maurice O'Shea, who founded Mount Pleasant and proved himself one of Australia's great winemakers. Winery of the Year in the *Wine Companion 2017*. Exports to all major markets.

♟♟♟♟♟ **1880 Vines Old Hill Vineyard Hunter Valley Shiraz 2018** This is a wine of ascetic, aptly reductive tension. Eking out visceral pleasure over the cerebral is a challenge right now. But it is often the way with youthful wine this good. The transparent, fine-boned, chalky and tensile structural pillars serve as a path into a bright future. For now, think lilac, cherry pip, bergamot and crunchy red berries. Wonderful chewy length. Expands. A truly excellent wine. Takes time to calibrate to its elastic cadence. Somehow reminiscent of fine youthful Burgundy. Screw cap. 13.5% alc. **Rating** 97 **To** 2040 $135 NG ✪

Maurice O'Shea Hunter Valley Shiraz 2018 An utterly stupendous wine, in the same league as Penfolds 1962 Bin 60A. This O'Shea has the complexity of a great tapestry woven centuries ago when time was of no consequence. The sky, the soil and the fruit coalesce into an entity that throbs with intensity and a never-ending kaleidoscope of blackberry, earth and leather flavours. Screw cap. 13.5% alc. **Rating** 99 **To** 2040 $250 JH ✪ ♥

Mount Stapylton Wines ★★★☆

1212 Northern Grampians Road, Laharum, Vic 3401 **Region** Grampians
T 0429 838 233 **www**.mts-wines.com
Winemaker Leigh Clarnette **Est.** 2002 **Dozens** 300 **Vyds** 1.5ha
Mount Stapylton's vineyard is planted on the historic Goonwinnow Homestead farming property at Laharum, on the northwest side of the Grampians, in front of Mt Stapylton. In 2017 the vineyard lease was purchased from founder Howard Staehr by the Staehr family and is now being run as an addition to their mixed farming enterprise.

♟♟♟♟♟ **Grampians Shiraz 2019** A wine of widespread appeal that gifts approachability and further potential for ageing. Generous Grampians hallmarks of elevated spice, intense black fruits and medium-bodied elegance. Unctuous mouthfeel and fine-grained tannins are a big attraction. Everything is in its place. Screw cap. 14% alc. **Rating** 91 **To** 2029 $38 JP

♟♟♟♟ **Grampians Rosé 2020 Rating** 89 **To** 2025 $24 JP

Mount Terrible ★★★★

289 Licola Road, Jamieson, Vic 3723 **Region** Central Victoria
T (03) 5777 0703 **www**.mountterriblewines.com.au **Open** By appt
Winemaker John Eason **Est.** 2001 **Dozens** 350 **Vyds** 2ha
John Eason and wife Janene Ridley began the long, slow (and at times very painful) business of establishing their vineyard just north of Mt Terrible in 1992 – hence the choice of name. In 2001 they planted 2ha of pinot noir (MV6, 115, 114 and 777 clones) on a gently sloping, north-facing river terrace adjacent to the Jamieson River. DIY trials persuaded John to have the first commercial vintage in '06 contract-made. He has since made the wines himself in a fireproof winery built on top of an underground wine cellar. John has a sense of humour second to none, but must wonder what he has done to provoke the weather gods, alternating in their provision of fire, storm and tempest. Subsequent vintages have provided some well-earned relief. Exports to the UK.

🍷🍷🍷🍷🍷 **Jamieson Pinot Noir 2018** Not a shy pinot by any stretch. Solid red colour and boasting an intense fragrance of sage, thyme, macerated spiced cherries and oak. The oak, a mix of Francois Freres and Sirugue, medium toasted, takes centre stage, providing tannin structure, warm texture and woody spice. Fortunately the fruit is up to the challenge. Screw cap. 13.5% alc. **Rating** 95 **To** 2030 $45 JP

Mount Trio Vineyard ★★★★☆

2534 Porongurup Road, Mount Barker WA 6324 **Region** Porongurup
T (08) 9853 1136 **www**.mounttriowines.com.au **Open** By appt
Winemaker Gavin Berry, Andrew Vesey, Caitlin Gazey **Est.** 1989 **Dozens** 3500
Vyds 8.5ha
Mount Trio was established by Gavin Berry and wife Gill Graham (plus business partners) shortly after they moved to the Mount Barker area in late 1988, Gavin to take up the position of chief winemaker at Plantagenet, which he held until 2004, when he and partners acquired the now very successful and much larger West Cape Howe. They have increased the estate plantings to 8.5ha with pinot noir (3.4ha), riesling (3.3ha), shiraz (1ha) and chardonnay (0.8ha). Exports to the UK, Denmark and China.

🍷🍷🍷🍷🍷 **Porongurup Riesling 2020** A piercingly pretty and plump riesling with layers of sweet citrus fruit, gentle exotic spice and citrus florals. The 6g/l RS is tucked so neatly away into the folds of flavour that it simply amplifies the deliciousness, rather than presenting in an obvious way. Hard to imagine a more quenching wine in the heat of summer. Screw cap. 12.5% alc. **Rating** 94 **To** 2031 $23 EL
Great Southern Shiraz 2019 Fresh and peppery cool-climate syrah. Layers of black fruit flavours are shaped by fine tannins and a distinct licorice character that cools everything down. Remarkably elegant drinking for $23. Bravo. Screw cap. 13.5% alc. **Rating** 94 **To** 2028 $23 EL

🍷🍷🍷🍷🍸 **Porongurup Pinot Noir 2019 Rating** 92 **To** 2028 $23 EL **⊘**
Great Southern Sauvignon Blanc 2020 Rating 90 **To** 2022 $18 EL **⊘**
Great Southern Pinot Noir 2020 Rating 90 **To** 2026 $18 EL **⊘**
Home Block Porongurup Pinot Noir 2019 Rating 90 **To** 2028 $35 EL
Great Southern Cabernet Merlot 2018 Rating 90 **To** 2028 $18 EL **⊘**

Mount View Estate ★★★★☆

Mount View Road, Mount View, NSW 2325 **Region** Hunter Valley
T (02) 4990 3307 **www**.mtviewestate.com.au **Open** Mon–Sat 10–5, Sun 10–4
Winemaker Scott Stephens **Est.** 1971 **Dozens** 5000 **Vyds** 16ha
Mount View Estate's vineyard was planted by the very knowledgeable Harry Tulloch almost 50 years ago; he recognised the quality of the red basalt volcanic soils of the very attractive hillside site. Prior owners John and Polly Burgess also purchased the adjoining Limestone Creek Vineyard in 2004 (planted in 1982), fitting it seamlessly into Mount View Estate's

production. The quality of the wines is outstanding. The business changed hands in '16, now owned by a Chinese national with no further details available. Exports to China.

ΨΨΨΨ℧ **Flagship Hunter Valley Shiraz 2019** Modern styling, positioned just right. Fresh, detailed and far from reductive, an anathema. Mulberry, blueberry, licorice, fecund raspberry, sweet leather and clove. The oak, an addendum. Just a bit sweet. More extraction would help it along. Screw cap. 14% alc. **Rating** 93 **To** 2033 $85 NG

Museum Release Reserve Hunter Valley Semillon 2016 A delicious release. Not the stellar '13, or the rich '14. Yet good drinking all the same. Inimitable aromas of lemon curd, buttered toast and truffled scrambled eggs. The mid palate, a bit hollow. A bit soft. The finish, a little short. And yet there is ample joy manifest as an aged example of a grape that produces the most unique of all Australian white wine. Screw cap. 11% alc. **Rating** 92 **To** 2024 $65 NG

Reserve Hunter Valley Shiraz 2019 I like the stylising: modern and polished, far from the revamp of the classic Hunter luncheon style gaining traction. Yet also far from the pit of reduction, monochromatic aromas and glossy textures, into which so many in this region fall. Blueberry, iodine and vanillan oak. A swab of anise, clove and alternate spice. Polished. Yet the tannins, refined. The acidity, not overwrought. The pulse, long. Good drinking. Screw cap. 14% alc. **Rating** 91 **To** 2028 $45 NG

Reserve Hunter Valley Petite Sirah 2019 A sturdy grape imparting an inky density of colour, ferruginous tannins and acidity, marked by a dried herbal undercurrent. Tobacco leaf, dark-fruit allusions, mocha oak and strewn herb. A firm swathe of tannins, tattooing authority across the finish while subjugating sweetness in the name of savouriness. I like this. Screw cap. 13.5% alc. **Rating** 90 **To** 2029 $45 NG

Mountadam   ★★★★☆

High Eden Road, Eden Valley, SA 5235 **Region** Eden Valley
T 0427 089 836 **www**.mountadam.com.au **Open** By appt
Winemaker Phil Lehmann **Est.** 1972 **Dozens** 30 000 **Vyds** 148ha
Founded by the late David Wynn for the benefit of winemaker son Adam, Mountadam was (somewhat surprisingly) purchased by Möet Hennessy Wine Estates in 2000. In 2005, Mountadam returned to family ownership when it was purchased by David and Jenni Brown from Adelaide. David and Jenni have worked to bring the original Mountadam property back together with the purchase of Mountadam Farm in 2007 and the High Eden Vineyard from TWE in '15, thus reassembling all of the land originally purchased by David Wynn in the late 1960s. Phil Lehmann stepped into the role of chief winemaker in 2019, with extensive experience in the Barossa and Eden valleys at Peter Lehmann, Yalumba, Teusner, WD Wines and his own label Max & Me. Exports to the UK, Canada, France, Switzerland, Poland, Hong Kong and China.

ΨΨΨΨΨ **Eden Valley Cabernet Sauvignon 2018** Cabernet was evidently in a happy place high in the Mountadam vineyard in '18, displaying an integrity, balance and concentration that can only come from long, slow ripening. It's at once varietal and generous, with a textbook array of red/blackcurrants, cassis, roast capsicum and cedar trailing all the way to the distant horizon. Ripe, fine, confident tannins and seamless, bright acidity guarantee longevity. For all it represents, this is a bargain. Screw cap. 15% alc. **Rating** 95 **To** 2038 $28 TS ❁

ΨΨΨΨ℧ **Eden Valley Chardonnay 2019 Rating** 93 **To** 2032 $28 TS
High Eden The Red 2018 Rating 93 **To** 2030 $40 TS
Eden Valley Riesling 2020 Rating 92 **To** 2023 $28 TS
High Eden Estate Chardonnay 2019 Rating 92 **To** 2029 $40 TS
Eden Valley Pinot Gris 2020 Rating 92 **To** 2022 $28 TS
Eden Valley Shiraz 2018 Rating 92 **To** 2033 $28 TS
Patriarch High Eden Shiraz 2018 Rating 92 **To** 2026 $40 TS
Five-Fifty Eden Valley Pinot Noir Rosé 2020 Rating 91 **To** 2024 $20 TS ❁

Five-Fifty Barossa Cabernet Sauvignon 2018 Rating 91 To 2023 $20 TS ✪
High Eden The Red 2017 Rating 90 To 2037 $40 TS

Mulline ★★★★★

19/33 Fisher Parade, Ascot Vale, Vic 3032 (postal) **Region** Geelong
T 0402 409 292 **www**.mulline.com
Winemaker Ben Mullen **Est.** 2019 **Dozens** 1000
This is the venture of Ben Mullen and business partner Ben Hine, the derivation of the winery
name self-evident. Ben Mullen grew up in the Barossa Valley and studied oenology at the
University of Adelaide, graduating in 2012. His journey thereafter was in the purple, working
at Yarra Yering, Oakridge, Torbreck and Leeuwin Estate, Domaine Dujac in Burgundy in
'13 (lighting a fire for pinot noir and chardonnay), Craggy Range in NZ ('15), coming back
to Geelong as winemaker for Clyde Park in '17–18. Here he made the wine that won the
Shiraz Trophy at the National Wine Show (for the '17 vintage) and the Geelong Trophy at
the Australian Pinot Noir Challenge. Ben Hine also came from SA, and worked in hospitality
for many years before obtaining his law degree; he is working full-time as a lawyer. When
they met, it was he who took the running in creating the brand and the business structure
behind it. In wine terms, this means a range of single-vineyard wines at the top, backed by the
Geelong region range (and no wines from elsewhere). Exports to the UK.

ⵯⵯⵯⵯⵯ Single Vineyard Portarlington Chardonnay 2020 A smart chardonnay that
distances itself from fruit-driven, ultra-clean styles, preferring a more complex
restraint. Aromas of lemon, fig and rockpool are subdued. Texture plays a big
role here too, so there's tart citrus acidity and pithy grapefruit, lemon zest and
green apple. A slow burn of flavour build-up and length. Give it time. Screw cap.
13% alc. **Rating** 95 **To** 2028 $50 JP
Single Vineyard Sutherlands Creek Chardonnay 2020 Another interesting
study in structure – and the relationship between texture and acidity – from
Mulline winemaker Ben Mullen. Quite a philosophical question to ponder as you
delve into this chardonnay, juicy and crisp in nectarine, white peach, grapefruit and
quince. Good line and length on the palate, courtesy of rapier-like acidity. Taut but
plenty of flavour in reserve. Screw cap. 13% alc. **Rating** 95 **To** 2028 $50 JP
Single Vineyard Sutherlands Creek Pinot Noir 2020 Moorabool Valley
fruit, even though just bottled when tasted, is in fine form indeed, revealing good
depth and concentration. Lifted, fragrant and pure, with the subtlest oak and
confident handling. Sweet raspberry, dusty red cherry, musk, bramble and bracken
glide across the palate. An exciting early start to a wine that will shine. Screw cap.
12% alc. **Rating** 95 **To** 2027 $50 JP
Single Vineyard Drysdale Pinot Noir 2020 Enticing solid red colour.
Delicious red berry scents, dried flowers, violet, wild herbs. A tight, focused young
pinot that is approachable now in its pristine prettiness but really warrants extra
time. Juicy palate, fleshy ripe tannins complete a wine still developing. Screw cap.
12.5% alc. **Rating** 94 **To** 2026 $50 JP

ⵯⵯⵯⵯⵦ Single Vineyard Sutherlands Creek Fumé Blanc 2020 Rating 93 To 2025
$50 JP
Single Vineyard Portarlington Pinot Noir 2020 Rating 91 To 2026 $50 JP
Single Vineyard Anakie Riesling 2020 Rating 90 To 2025 $35 JP

Munari Wines ★★★★★

1129 Northern Highway, Heathcote, Vic 3523 **Region** Heathcote
T (03) 5433 3366 **www**.munariwines.com **Open** 7 days 11–5
Winemaker Adrian Munari **Est.** 1993 **Dozens** 3000 **Vyds** 6.9ha
Established on one of the original Heathcote farming properties, Ladys Creek Vineyard is
situated on the narrow Cambrian soil strip 11km north of the town. Adrian Munari has
harnessed traditional winemaking practices to New World innovation to produce complex,
fruit-driven wines that marry concentration and elegance. Wines are produced from estate

plantings of shiraz and cabernet sauvignon. Plantings of merlot, cabernet franc and malbec have recently been grafted to sangiovese. Exports to the UK and China.

ỸỸỸỸỸ Ladys Pass Heathcote Shiraz 2018 Unlike some Heathcote makers, Munari does not do formidable or statuesque. Its raison d'être is far more egalitarian. In a good year like 2018, Lady's Pass shines with utter approachability and fruit-forward expression that celebrates the quality of its fruit. Finely perfumed, flavoured and velvety textured, it shows another side to the region's favourite grape. Diam. 14.5% alc. **Rating** 95 **To** 2035 $45 JP

The Gun Picker Heathcote Shiraz Cabernet 2018 This traditional Aussie blend is a fine follow-up wine to the 2016 vintage. Its strength remains in a plethora of lifted Aussie scents and flavours, of wild bush mint, briar, fresh earth and dried herbs. The varieties are harmonious on the palate, joined by vanillan oak and lively tannins. A strong vintage for the region has delivered an impressive wine. Diam. 13.8% alc. **Rating** 94 **To** 2032 $35 JP

ỸỸỸỸỸ India Red Heathcote Cabernet Sauvignon 2018 **Rating** 92 **To** 2028 $30 JP

Murdoch Hill ★★★★★

260 Mappinga Road, Woodside, SA 5244 **Region** Adelaide Hills
T (08) 7200 5018 **www**.murdochhill.com.au **Open** Thurs–Mon 11–4
Winemaker Michael Downer **Est.** 1998 **Dozens** 5000 **Vyds** 17.3ha
A little over 20ha of vines have been established on the undulating, gum tree–studded countryside of Charlie and Julie Downer's 60yo Erika property, 4km east of Oakbank. In descending order of importance, the varieties planted are sauvignon blanc, shiraz, cabernet sauvignon and chardonnay. Son Michael, with a bachelor of oenology degree from the University of Adelaide, is winemaker. Exports to the UK, the US, Canada, Sweden, Norway, the Netherlands, the UAE, Hong Kong, China, Taiwan and Singapore.

ỸỸỸỸỸ The Rocket Limited Release Adelaide Hills Chardonnay 2020 A best vineyard and best barrel selection from the Piccadilly Valley, whole-berry pressed, wild fermented and matured 10 months in more than 50% new oak. In estate style, this is as elegant a chardonnay as you could imagine, with all the elements interwoven, no spikes, no edges. A whiff of oak at the start, but that's it, no other intrusion. The whole is all the parts treated equally. Let it find greater style over the next 2–5 years. Screw cap. 13.5% alc. **Rating** 96 **To** 2026 $85 TL

Adelaide Hills Sauvignon Blanc 2020 The aromatic bouquet has a suite of nettle, herb and fresh-cut-grass notes that play directly to the lively and fresh palate, there picked up with gooseberry and citrus fruit. The finish is clean and brightly polished, the wine at its best now. Screw cap. 12% alc. **Rating** 95 **To** 2022 $24 JH ✪

The Tilbury Adelaide Hills Chardonnay 2020 Fermented in barrel and matured 9 months in 30% new oak, not that you see it bossing the fruit in any way. Tighter fruit, with a sway of grapefruit flavour and pith. Watch this develop more completely through the end of 2021 and for the next few years. Screw cap. 12.5% alc. **Rating** 95 **To** 2028 $48 TL

The Surrey Single Vineyard Piccadilly Valley Pinot Meunier 2020 Very pretty to start, with crushed red fruits. The stems are entwined but not distracting. A whiff of flint as well. All this slips into the mouth, juicy as all get-out, with a heap of peppery spice to season the palate. Has loads of drinkability, appeal and table manners. Screw cap. 12% alc. **Rating** 95 **To** 2025 $40 TL

The Phaeton Piccadilly Valley Adelaide Hills Pinot Noir 2020 All the woody herbal and spice elements of the region and variety, with a unique nub of lifted fragrance and sweet cherry right in the core of the palate, in a style that has developed over the years with a waft of wood smoke. All of this makes for a mighty fine expression. Screw cap. 13% alc. **Rating** 95 **To** 2028 $48 TL

Apollo Piccadilly Valley Pinot Noir 2020 Fragrant and lifted to begin, crimson fruits and foresty, sappy underlines, elegant flow across the palate with a delicate earthy, woody spice. Nothing extravagant, nothing out of place either. Serene. Screw cap. 13% alc. **Rating** 95 **To** 2028 $85 TL

Adelaide Hills Pinot Noir 2020 Perfume lifts from the glass, earthy, spicy and a delicate aperol note. The palate is in the winemaker's preferred style, juicy and gently flowing, light to medium weight, a soft grip to finish. Ethereal is the word. Screw cap. 13% alc. **Rating** 94 **To** 2026 $30 TL ✪

♥♥♥♥♀ **Adelaide Hills Chardonnay 2020 Rating** 93 **To** 2025 $30 TL
The Sulky Adelaide Hills Riesling 2020 Rating 92 **To** 2025 $32 TL
The Landau Single Vineyard Oakbank Adelaide Hills Syrah 2019
Rating 92 **To** 2028 $48 TL
Limited Release Vis-a-Vis Adelaide Hills Cabernet Franc 2020 Rating 92
To 2025 $36 TL
Adelaide Hills Shiraz 2019 Rating 91 **To** 2028 $30 TL

Murray Street Vineyards ★★★★

37 Murray Street, Greenock, SA 5360 **Region** Barossa Valley
T (08) 8562 8373 **www**.murraystreet.com.au **Open** 7 days 10–5
Winemaker Ben Perkins **Est.** 2001 **Dozens** 20 000 **Vyds** 105ha
Murray Street Vineyards was founded in 2001 and quickly established itself as a producer of exceptionally good wines. The current winemaker is Ben Perkins, who grew up a stone's throw away in Greenock. The 2 brands of Murray Street and MSV carry the flag, MSV the senior brand.

♥♥♥♥♀ **Greenock Estate Barossa Valley Cabernet Sauvignon 2018** Powerful
Barossa cabernet. Distinct varietal etchings of cassis, red/blackcurrants, roast capsicum and cedar. Full, rich and ripe, yet tangy and lively. Dark chocolate French oak rises boldly to the occasion, building fine-grained tannin presence for medium-term cellaring. Diam. 14.5% alc. **Rating** 93 **To** 2033 $50 TS

♥♥♥♥ **Gomersal Barossa Valley Shiraz 2018 Rating** 89 **To** 2023 $50 TS

Murrumbateman Winery ★★★★

131 McIntosh Circuit, Murrumbateman, NSW 2582 **Region** Canberra District
T 0432 826 454 **www**.murrumbatemanwinery.com.au **Open** 7 days 10–5
Winemaker Bobbie Makin **Est.** 1972 **Dozens** 3500 **Vyds** 4ha
Draws upon 4ha of estate-grown sauvignon blanc and shiraz. It also incorporates an à la carte restaurant and function room, together with picnic and barbecue areas.

♥♥♥♥ **Sangiovese 2019** Appealing varietal aromas and flavours – the cherries, the pips,
the spice and the amaro twang comes together well. Lighter framed with supple tannins. A touch sweet, yet it has an appealing charred radicchio bitterness to the finish. Screw cap. 13.6% alc. **Rating** 89 **To** 2023 $25 JF

MyattsField Vineyards ★★★★☆

Union Road, Carmel Valley, WA 6076 **Region** Perth Hills
T (08) 9293 5567 **www**.myattsfield.com.au **Open** Fri–Sun & public hols 11–5
Winemaker Josh Davenport, Rachael Davenport, Josh Uren **Est.** 1997 **Dozens** 4000
Vyds 4.5ha
MyattsField Vineyards is owned by Josh and Rachael Davenport. Both have oenology degrees and domestic and Flying Winemaker experience, especially Rachael. In 2006 they decided they would prefer to work for themselves. They left their employment, building a winery in time for the '07 vintage. Their vineyards include cabernet sauvignon, merlot, petit verdot, shiraz and chardonnay. They also purchase small parcels of grapes from as far away as Manjimup. Exports to Singapore and Taiwan.

♥♥♥♥♀ **Durif 2019** A flamboyantly full-bodied wine, with a consistent drive and
evolution of flavour over the palate; morphing from black cherries laced with

bitter chocolate, through to blood plum, salted licorice and a host of other flavours. The tannins are plump and chewy and while very present, they provide structure and direction. The alcohol is fully entrenched and as such, imperceptible. Screw cap. 15% alc. **Rating** 95 **To** 2036 $30 EL ❂

Vermentino 2020 Crunchy, crisp and frisky, with plenty of go. Nashi pear, saline acid and a cleansing finish come together to create this decidedly Euro-style vermentino. You know when a wine takes you places in your mind that it's doing its job well. Screw cap. 13.4% alc. **Rating** 94 **To** 2023 $22 EL ❂

🍷🍷🍷🍷🍷 **Cabernet Sauvignon Merlot Cabernet Franc 2018** Rating 91 To 2028 $26 EL

Joseph Myatt Reserve 2018 Rating 91 To 2031 $45 EL

Mylkappa Wines

Mylkappa Road, Birdwood, SA 5234 **Region** Adelaide Hills
T (08) 8568 5489 **www.**mylkappawines.com.au
Winemaker Kirrihill Wines (Donna Stephens) **Est.** 1998 **Dozens** 2100 **Vyds** 36.3ha
Having left the Adelaide Hills in 1988 with their 3 children, Patricia and Geoff Porter returned 10 years later to purchase an old dairy farm at Birdwood. Since then the entire family has worked tirelessly to progressively establish a large vineyard planted to chardonnay, sauvignon blanc, 2 clones of pinot noir and pinot gris. Much of the grape production is sold to other Adelaide Hills makers.

Myrtaceae ★★★★☆

53 Main Creek Road, Main Ridge, Vic 3928 **Region** Mornington Peninsula
T (03) 5989 2045 **www.**myrtaceae.com.au **Open** W'ends & public hols 12–5
Winemaker Julie Trueman **Est.** 1984 **Dozens** 350 **Vyds** 2ha
John Trueman (viticulturist) and wife Julie (winemaker) purchased their Mornington Peninsula hinterland property near Arthurs Seat in 1984. Chardonnay (0.6ha) was planted in '98, and the initial plantings of cabernet were replaced with pinot noir (0.4ha) in '99. Just one Chardonnay and one Pinot Noir are made each year from the estate grapes, a Rosé made from pinot is a more recent addition. Meticulous viticulture using Scott Henry trellising is used to maximise sunlight and airflow at this cool, elevated site. Extensive gardens surround the winery.

🍷🍷🍷🍷 **Mornington Peninsula Pinot Noir 2017** A pale ruby with an advanced hue, although still fresh enough. It's delicate, with hints of cherries, woodsy spices and iodine meeting up with soft, easy tannins. There's appeal here, given its lighter frame and gentleness, but drink up. Screw cap. 13.5% alc. **Rating** 89 **To** 2023 $35 JF

Naked Run Wines

8305 Horrocks Righway, Sevenhill, SA 5453 **Region** Clare Valley/Barossa Valley
T 0408 807 655 **www.**nakedrunwines.com.au
Winemaker Steven Baraglia **Est.** 2005 **Dozens** 1500
Naked Run is the virtual winery of Jayme Wood, Bradley Currie and Steven Baraglia; their skills ranging from viticulture through to production, and also to the all-important sales and marketing (and not to be confused with Naked Wines). Riesling and shiraz are sourced from Clare Valley, grenache from the Williamstown area of the Barossa Valley and shiraz from Greenock. Exports to China.

🍷🍷🍷🍷🍷 **The First Clare Valley Riesling 2020** Pristine, pure and very classy. A beautifully balanced wine of lemon blossom, tangerine and a hint of bath salts, plus beeswax and an array of spices. It's flavoursome, almost textural, as there's a succulence across the palate. Ultimately though, this is all about refinement, with the acidity present yet delicate. Screw cap. 11.5% alc. **Rating** 96 **To** 2030 $24 JF ❂

Place in Time Sevenhill Clare Valley Riesling 2016 Revealing the right amount of aged characters, from lime marmalade on buttered toast to baked ricotta and lemon curd. It's in the complex zone, with some weight and richness throughout. The acidity is still at the forefront, though, so it's lively, frisky even. An excellent, compelling wine. Alas, just 64 dozen made. Screw cap. 12% alc. **Rating** 96 **To** 2028 $40 JF ✪

Hill 5 Clare Valley Shiraz Cabernet 2019 Apparently the aim of this wine is to let the fruit be the hero. Well that has been achieved. It is so delicious and lively, with red plums, blackberries, currants and a flutter of baking spices. It's juicy, medium bodied, with textural tannins and enjoyment stamped all over it. Oh, and a bargain too! Screw cap. 14% alc. **Rating** 95 **To** 2027 $24 JF ✪

The Aldo Barossa Valley Grenache 2019 Fruit from winemaker Steve Baraglia's family vineyard, planted by his grandfather 80 years ago. It's made in a juicy, fresh style, but not at all simple. Quality shines through. Heady aromatics, all cherry and sarsaparilla, with lots of earthiness and a dash of pepper so it's not tutti-frutti. It's slinky across the medium-bodied palate, to the point where the grainy tannins kick in and the glass empties. Screw cap. 14% alc. **Rating** 95 **To** 2027 $24 JF ✪

ȳȳȳȳȳ **BWC Barossa Valley Shiraz 2018 Rating** 93 **To** 2026 $28 JF
Der Zweite Clare Valley Riesling 2020 Rating 91 **To** 2028 $28 JF

Nannup Estate ★★★★☆

Lot 25 Perks Road, Nannup, WA 6275 **Region** Blackwood Valley
T (08) 9756 2005 **www**.nannupestate.com.au
Winemaker Ryan Aggiss (Contract) **Est.** 2017 **Dozens** 5000 **Vyds** 14.43ha
Nannup Estate is owned by Mark Blizzard and family. The vineyard sits high on the granite ridges of the Blackwood River escarpment. During the growing season the vines enjoy long hours of sunshine followed by moderate coastal breezes in the afternoons and cool evenings – idyllic growing conditions. Abundant water, granite loam soils and low frost and disease pressure all contribute to reliable quality and consistent vintages. The first 6ha of vines were planted in 1998, with subsequent plantings in 2000 and '06. The vineyard now comprises almost 14.5ha of cabernet sauvignon, merlot, chardonnay, tempranillo and malbec. Exports to China.

ȳȳȳȳȳ **Phillip Stanley Reserve Chardonnay 2018** The nose is full of red apple skin, crushed cashew, yellow peach and briny acid. Oak is impactful, but already well on its way to merging with the fruit. Packaging is classy and expensive, Indigenous artwork on the label from Delvine Pitjara – all things that reflect the care in the bottle. Screw cap. 13% alc. **Rating** 95 **To** 2035 $51 EL

Phillip Stanley Cabernet Sauvignon 2018 The Indigenous artwork by Delvine Pitjara that graces this label is brilliant. The wine is impressive too – densely concentrated fruit, tightly knit tannins and plenty of flavour that forges a path through the finish. The acidity keeps the ripe fruit in check; all things in harmonious place in this wine. Screw cap. 14% alc. **Rating** 95 **To** 2035 $51 EL

Firetower Cabernet Sauvignon 2019 With 5% malbec. Matured 16 months in French oak (28% new). Floral, red-fruited and extraordinarily pretty. While it isn't overly complex, it is balanced, supple and totally delicious. Screw cap. 14.5% alc. **Rating** 94 **To** 2036 $38 EL

Rolling Hills Cabernet Sauvignon 2019 95/5% cabernet sauvignon/malbec. Matured for 16 months in French oak (28% new). This is layered and finely textured, with oodles of cassis, pomegranate, redcurrant and mulberry. Very elegant, with cooling acidity through the finish. Screw cap. 14.5% alc. **Rating** 94 **To** 2036 $38 EL

ȳȳȳȳȳ **Rolling Hills Chardonnay 2020 Rating** 93 **To** 2028 $38 EL
Firetower Tempranillo Rosé 2020 Rating 92 **To** 2024 $30 EL
Firetower Sauvignon Blanc 2020 Rating 91 **To** 2025 $30 EL
Rolling Hills Tempranillo 2019 Rating 90 **To** 2028 $38 EL

Nannup Ridge Estate   ★★★★☆

128 Perks Road, Cundinup, Nannup, WA 6275 **Region** Blackwood Valley
T (08) 9286 2202 **www**.nannupridge.com.au
Winemaker Bruce Dukes **Est.** 1998 **Dozens** 4000 **Vyds** 16ha
The business is owned by the Fitzgerald brothers, who purchased the then unplanted property
from the family that had farmed it since the early 1900s. They established 16ha of mainstream
varieties backed by a (then) grape sale agreement with Houghton and Constellation. They
still regard themselves as grape growers but have successful wines skilfully contract-made by
celebrated winemaker Bruce Dukes. Terrific value is par for the course. Exports to China.

Narkoojee   ★★★★★

220 Francis Road, Glengarry, Vic 3854 **Region** Gippsland
T (03) 5192 4257 **www**.narkoojee.com **Open** 7 days 10.30–4.30
Winemaker Axel Friend **Est.** 1981 **Dozens** 5000 **Vyds** 13.8ha
Narkoojee, originally a dairy farm owned by the Friend family, is near the old gold-mining
town of Walhalla and looks out over the Strzelecki Ranges. The wines are produced from
the estate vineyards, with chardonnay accounting for half the total. Former lecturer in civil
engineering and extremely successful amateur winemaker, Harry Friend, changed horses in
1994 to take joint control of the vineyard and winery with son Axel, and they haven't missed
a beat since; their skills show through in all the wines. Exports to China.

ŸŸŸŸŸ **Tumbarumba Chardonnay 2018** Another reminder of how good fruit from
Tumbarumba is, with this morphing into a yin-and-yang wine. It's flavoursome
with stone fruit, lemon curd and a leesy, nutty richness. Yet its fine acidity, linearity,
length and freshness keep it reined in. Screw cap. 12.5% alc. **Rating** 95 **To** 2028
$27 JF ✪

ŸŸŸŸŸ **Gippsland Cabernet Sauvignon 2018 Rating** 92 **To** 2028 $29 JF
Four Generations Gippsland Merlot 2018 Rating 91 **To** 2030 $43 JF
Lily Grace Gippsland Chardonnay 2019 Rating 90 **To** 2024 $29 JF
The Athelstan Gippsland Merlot 2018 Rating 90 **To** 2027 $29 JF
Reserve Maxwell Gippsland Cabernet 2018 Rating 90 **To** 2031 $40 JF

Nashdale Lane Wines   ★★★★☆

125 Nashdale Lane, Nashdale, NSW 2800 **Region** Orange
T 0458 127 333 **www**.nashdalelane.com **Open** 7 days 11–5
Winemaker Nick Segger, Tanya Segger **Est.** 2017 **Dozens** 6000 **Vyds** 24ha
Nashdale Lane began as a dream following Nick and Tanya Segger's brief working holiday
on a tiny vineyard in Tuscany in 2001, setting in motion a long search for a suitable patch of
their own. The dream became reality in '17 with the purchase of an 18yo vineyard in Orange.
At first the winemaking was contracted out, but these days Nick and Tanya are hands–on in
both the winery and cellar door, the latter set up in a refurbished apple packing shed on the
property. The vineyard is planted mainly to chardonnay, shiraz, pinot gris and sauvignon blanc,
with smaller amounts of riesling, pinot noir, tempranillo and arneis. Visitors to Nashdale Lane
can stay in luxury cabins set among the vines. Exports to the UK.

ŸŸŸŸŸ **Orange Fumé Blanc 2019** Barrel-fermented sauvignon blanc, with a portion
handled in tank. This pungent, gently mid-weighted and impressive expression
coaxes both freshness and complexity from the barrel work, transcending most
domestic expressions. Bright acidity and deft oak corral notes of durian, nettle,
greengage and guava into a firm phalanx of intensity and length. Screw cap.
12.5% alc. **Rating** 93 **To** 2023 $35 NG
Legacy Orange Rosé 2019 Aged in French oak for 12 months, the colour is a
coppery light ruby. Wild fermented with full mlf, the ambition is palpable. Sapid
cherry, sandalwood, wood smoke and rhubarb scents are pushed and pulled by oak
tannins and bright altitudinal acidity. A complex rosé that deserves a place at the
table. Screw cap. 12.5% alc. **Rating** 91 **To** 2022 $45 NG

Legacy Orange Shiraz 2019 This kicks off well: violet, cardamom, iodine, tapenade and a whiff of charcuterie. Northern Rhône aspirational, with a reductive clutch of tension handled with aplomb. Sure, the mid palate could have a bit more cushion and the yields need consideration. Yet this is savoury, mid weighted, fresh, aromatically attractive and of solid length. Screw cap. 13.5% alc. **Rating** 91 **To** 2024 $65 NG
Orange Chardonnay 2019 A blowsy, attractive, medium-bodied chardonnay brimming with concentrated flavour. Rewarding in an age when so many of us want more of it! White peach, nectarine, nougatine, creamed cashew and some vanilla-pod oak pillars provide direction. Loosely knit, but not lacking poise or focus. Richly flavoured and rewarding. Screw cap. 13% alc. **Rating** 90 **To** 2023 $35 NG

Nepenthe   ★★★★

93 Jones Road, Balhannah, SA 5242 **Region** Adelaide Hills
T (08) 8398 8899 **www**.nepenthe.com.au **Open** 7 days 10–5
Winemaker James Evers **Est.** 1994 **Dozens** 44 000 **Vyds** 93ha
Nepenthe quickly established its reputation as a producer of high-quality wines, but founder Ed Tweddell died unexpectedly in 2006 and the business was purchased by Australian Vintage Limited the following year. The winery was closed in '09 and winemaking operations transferred to McGuigan Wines (Barossa Valley). The Nepenthe winery has since been purchased by Peter Leske and Mark Kozned, and provides contract winemaking services via their Revenir venture. Nepenthe has 93ha of close-planted vines in the Adelaide Hills, with an exotic array of varieties. Exports to all major markets.

 Altitude Adelaide Hills Pinot Gris 2020 Classical pear and apple to begin, orchard florals as well. A 6-week stint on lees has imparted some creamy texture to the palate, with the pomme fruits and a dash of citrus continuing throughout. Perfectly acceptable and good value. Screw cap. 13.5% alc. **Rating** 92 **To** 2023 $20 TL ✪
Altitude Adelaide Hills Sauvignon Blanc 2020 All the good sauvignon blanc feels in here, tropical fruits, passionfruit, a smattering of lime. What attracts, too, is a well-tempered palate that doesn't rely on simplistic acidity, but rather finds a satisfying textural feel. Screw cap. 13.6% alc. **Rating** 90 **To** 2023 $20 TL ✪

New Era Vineyards   ★★★★☆

PO Box 391, Woodside SA 5244 **Region** Adelaide Hills
T 0413 544 246 **www**.neweravineyards.com.au
Winemaker Robert Baxter, Iain Baxter **Est.** 1988 **Dozens** 1500 **Vyds** 15ha
The New Era vineyard is situated over a gold reef that was mined for 60 years until 1940, when all recoverable gold had been extracted. The vineyard was mostly contracted to Foster's and now includes shiraz, pinot noir, cabernet sauvignon, tempranillo, merlot, saperavi, sangiovese, touriga nacional, nebbiolo, nero d'Avola and chardonnay. Much of the production is sold to other winemakers in the region. The small amount of wine made has been the subject of favourable reviews. Exports to Singapore.

 Adelaide Hills Grüner Veltliner 2020 Devastated by the December 2019 Hills bushfires, 2t of grüner fruit was donated to New Era by the Saturno lads at Longview Vineyard in Macclesfield. One portion went to tank for a crisp and crunchy vibe, the other underwent wild fermentation in barrels for a richer element, then blended together. This is a delicate, pithy, yellow-citrus-natured wine. The variety's trademark white pepper is there in the background, while other attractive notes pop out as well – a grapefruit tang offset by a faint honey cornflake. A brilliant mouth-watering finish. What a success. Screw cap. 12.5% alc. **Rating** 94 **To** 2024 $25 TL ✪

♀♀♀♀♀ **Adelaide Hills Tempranillo 2019 Rating** 93 **To** 2028 $33 TL
Limestone Coast Dolcetto Rosé 2020 Rating 91 **To** 2022 $25 TL

Newbridge Wines

18 Chelsea Street, Brighton, Vic 3186 (postal) **Region** Bendigo
T 0417 996 840 **www**.newbridgewines.com.au **Open** At Newbridge Hotel, Newbridge
Winemaker Mark Matthews **Est.** 1996 **Dozens** 300 **Vyds** 1ha

The Newbridge property was purchased by Ian Simpson in 1979, partly for sentimental family history reasons and partly because of the beauty of the property situated on the banks of the Loddon River. It was not until '96 that Ian decided to plant shiraz. Up to and including the 2002 vintage the grapes were sold to several local wineries. Ian retained the grapes and made wine in '03, and lived to see that and the following 2 vintages take shape before his death. The property is now run by his son Andrew, the wines contract-made by Mark Matthews, supported by Andrew.

Bendigo Shiraz 2018 A 50/50% blend of French and American oak barrels are a fine accompaniment for the generous, ripe (but never overpowering) fruit on display here. A warm and engaging wine combining upfront blackberries, licorice, choc-mint, bush mint with a long thread of savouriness along the lines of undergrowth, mushroom and smoked meats. A vivid expression of the region and its style of shiraz. Screw cap. 14% alc. **Rating** 91 **To** 2026 $25 JP

Ngeringa

119 Williams Road, Mount Barker, SA 5251 **Region** Adelaide Hills
T (08) 8398 2867 **www**.ngeringa.com **Open** By appt
Winemaker Erinn Klein **Est.** 2001 **Dozens** 3000 **Vyds** 5.5ha

Erinn and Janet Klein say, 'As fervent practitioners of biodynamic wine growing, we respect biodynamics as a sensitivity to the rhythms of nature, the health of the soil and the connection between plant, animal and cosmos. It is a pragmatic solution to farming without the use of chemicals and a necessary acknowledgement that the farm unit is part of a great whole.' It is not an easy solution and the Kleins have increased the immensity of the challenge by using ultra-close vine spacing of 1.5m × 1m, necessitating a large amount of hand-training of the vines plus the use of a tiny crawler tractor. Lest it be thought they have stumbled onto biodynamic growing without understanding wine science, they teamed up while studying at the University of Adelaide in 2000 (Erinn – oenology, Janet – viticulture/wine marketing) and then spent time looking at the great viticultural regions of the Old World, with a particular emphasis on biodynamics. The JE label is used for the basic wines, Ngeringa only for the very best (NASAA Certified Biodynamic). Exports to Belgium, Norway, Japan, Hong Kong and China.

Summit Vineyard Adelaide Hills Pinot Noir 2019 Enticing mid crimson. Attractive pinot noir fruit, spice and savoury elements in the aromatic lifts. All those complexities reverberate on the palate in a harmonious lively weave, with just the right amount of peppery tannin to wrap it all together. Really evocative. Cork. 13% alc. **Rating** 95 **To** 2028 $55 TL

Iluma Vineyard Adelaide Hills Syrah 2019 Rating 91 **To** 2028 $65 TL

Nick Haselgrove Wines

281 Tatachilla Road, McLaren Vale, SA 5171 **Region** Adelaide
T (08) 8383 0886 **www**.nhwines.com.au **Open** By appt
Winemaker Nick Haselgrove **Est.** 1981 **Dozens** 9000

After various sales, amalgamations and disposals of particular brands, Nick Haselgrove now owns The Old Faithful (the flagship), Blackbilly, Clarence Hill, James Haselgrove and The Wishing Tree brands. Exports to the US, China, Hong Kong and Singapore.

Clarence Hill Reserve McLaren Vale Cabernet Sauvignon 2018 Good maritime cabernet with the telltale scent of brine melding nicely with the varietal suite of blackcurrant, bouquet garni and a swab of black olive tapenade. Full weighted, with a clutch of well-defined tannins (both oak and grape) keeping everything in a gear that flows to a warm textural finish of detail and poise. Diam. 14.5% alc. **Rating** 93 **To** 2032 $65 NG

James Haselgrove Futures McLaren Vale Shiraz 2018 Among the more ambitious cuvées at this estate, this is up there with the best. The coconut-chipped oak lends a tannic curb to teeming black-fruit references, iodine and scrubby menthols. Pushed, sure; but within the realms of possibility and balance for those who like 'em rich in bitter chocolate. Diam. 14.5% alc. **Rating** 92 **To** 2030 $70 NG

Clarence Hill Reserve McLaren Vale Shiraz 2018 Lilac and varnish scents, with flavours of seaweed and anise merging with blue/dark-fruit references. A core of sweet liqueur segues to a toasty recipe of French/American oak, all paving the way to a smooth glide across a comparatively long finish. Diam. 14.5% alc. **Rating** 92 **To** 2028 $65 NG

The Old Faithful McLaren Vale Shiraz 2017 This wine is barrel aged for a whopping 40 months, so its vintage is always behind other releases. Clearly a mission statement of sorts, suggesting faith in the old-vine material as much as a bent toward a powerful, oak-driven style that few others champion. This is far more restrained than recent experiences. Still, capacious. Still oozing mocha, bitter chocolate, clove, cherry amaro and varnish from every pore. Just fresher. Less desiccated. Better. Diam. 14.5% alc. **Rating** 92 **To** 2033 $75 NG

The Old Faithful Cafe Block McLaren Vale Shiraz 2017 Forty months in French wood, the startling statistic. A better wine than recent vintages. Suave. Paradoxically fresh, creamy and sort of light on its feet despite the heft. But one cannot escape the clench of mocha cedar oak across the back end, clanging across a field of Hoisin sauce, five-spice, sweet cherry, pepper and clove. Diam. 14.5% alc. **Rating** 92 **To** 2033 $75 NG

The Old Faithful McLaren Vale Grenache 2019 Handled more akin to shiraz than grenache, with 18 months in French oak puncheons. The best wine of this top tier. The drying finish strongly suggests less time in older, larger porous oak would be advised. Aromas of kirsch, bramble and cranberry. The finish, spicy and relatively fresh despite the obtuse woody finish. Good material. Simply needs a defter touch. Diam. 14.5% alc. **Rating** 92 **To** 2029 $75 NG

ҬҬҬҬ **Clarence Hill Adelaide Cabernet Sauvignon 2018** **Rating** 89 **To** 2025 $18 NG ✪
Clarence Hill McLaren Vale Shiraz 2018 **Rating** 88 **To** 2030 $40 NG

Nick O'Leary Wines ★★★★★

149 Brooklands Road, Wallaroo, NSW 2618 **Region** Canberra District
T (02) 6230 2745 **www**.nickolearywines.com.au **Open** By appt
Winemaker Nick O'Leary **Est.** 2007 **Dozens** 12 000 **Vyds** 11ha
At the ripe old age of 28, Nick O'Leary had been involved in the wine industry for over a decade, working variously in retail, wholesale, viticulture and winemaking. Two years earlier he had laid the foundation for Nick O'Leary Wines, purchasing shiraz from local vignerons (commencing in 2006); riesling following in '08. His wines have had extraordinarily consistent success in local wine shows and competitions since the first vintages, and are building on that early success in spectacular fashion. At the NSW Wine Awards '15, the '14 Shiraz was awarded the NSW Wine of the Year trophy, exactly as the '13 Shiraz was in the prior year – the first time any winery had won the award in consecutive years.

ҬҬҬҬҬ **Tumbarumba Chardonnay 2019** Oh my. This is fabulous. It sparkles in the glass and lights up the palate. It's heady, with the right amount of flinty, smoky sulphides and lovely citrus flavours – grapefruit and lemon, zest and pith. There's tension across the palate, mainly an interplay between toasty oak and creamy lees flavours and acidity. It's tight and will continue to unfurl beautifully over the next few years. Screw cap. 13% alc. **Rating** 96 **To** 2029 $32 JF ✪

Heywood Canberra District Shiraz 2019 Seriously. This is too good to be true, especially at this price. A highly perfumed, floral and spicy wine. The palate is assured and medium bodied, dotted with beautiful fruit flavours, superfine tannins and length to behold. Elegant and refined. Screw cap. 13.5% alc. **Rating** 96 **To** 2029 $35 JF ✪

Bolaro Canberra District Shiraz 2019 This is made almost identically to the Heywood shiraz (bar the extra 5% whole bunches, capped at 35% here). Both wines are really an expression of their site. This is obviously different yet equally compelling. It's more plush, with darker fruit, more woodsy spices and pepper. The palate is full bodied, with shapely, grainy yet denser tannins and the acidity is bright and encompassing. It is also incredibly vibrant and, quite frankly, rather sexy. Screw cap. 13.5% alc. **Rating** 96 **To** 2035 $58 JF ✪ ♥

Canberra District Shiraz 2019 This has found its groove. It offers everything one could want from a cool-climate shiraz: perfume, juicy fruit, the right seasoning of pepper, spice, oak, tangy acidity and a freshness throughout. Terrific wine and excellent value. Screw cap. 13.5% alc. **Rating** 95 **To** 2029 $30 JF ✪

Nick Spencer Wines   ★★★★★

11 Loch Street, Yarralumla, ACT 2600 (postal) **Region** Gundagai
T 0419 810 274 **www.**nickspencerwines.com.au
Winemaker Nick Spencer **Est.** 2017 **Dozens** 2500
No winemaker's career starts newborn with receiving a degree in oenology at the University of Adelaide. The desire to make wine comes well before the inception to the studies. Some string the process out, others don't even undertake the process. Nick Spencer didn't procrastinate. In the early years he worked for Rosemount Estate, Coldstream Hills, Madew Wines and Tertini. He won the biggest wine show trophy in 2009: the Jimmy Watson; in '11 he was a Len Evans Tutorial scholar and in '14 was a finalist in the Young Gun of Wine and a finalist in the Gourmet Traveller Winemaker of the Year. He has travelled extensively through France, NZ and California, and in '14 made wine in Khakheti in Georgia. Having lead the team at Eden Road for 7 years, he finally moved to establish his own business in '17. His 2 regions of interest are Tumbarumba and Gundagai – adjoining but very different. The quality of his wines from Gundagai make him the captain of that ship.

🍷🍷🍷🍷 **Tumbarumba Chardonnay 2019** Tumbarumba and chardonnay. Two
wonderful words working in unison. This is all flinty and fine, citrussy and spicy, with a touch of white stone fruit. The palate is linear and long, with hints of leesy/creamy flavours giving some extra depth; so, too, cedary oak and toasty notes. Savoury, moreish and fabulous. Screw cap. 12.5% alc. **Rating** 95 **To** 2028 $40 JF

Gundagai Medium Dry Red 2019 60/20/10/5/5% shiraz/cabernet/malbec/ tempranillo/touriga, fermented separately and aged in used French oak puncheons. This is really getting its DNA established. It is medium bodied and dry, although there's an abundance of ripe fruits. Tangy and slightly sinewy this vintage, but so refreshing. Loads of baking spices, with bitter herbs, lithe acidity and neat tannins to close. Screw cap. 13% alc. **Rating** 95 **To** 2030 $35 JF ✪

Hilltops Malbec 2019 Mighty malbec, albeit a cool rendition. While a touch more ripeness would add to the flavour profile, this is a lovely wine, compelling actually. Awash with tangy fruit, morello cherries, juniper berries and green peppercorns, with radicchio bitterness like an Italian aperitif. It's ridiculously refreshing, unencumbered by new oak. And most importantly, the tannins are ripe. Screw cap. 12.5% alc. **Rating** 95 **To** 2028 $55 JF

🍷🍷🍷🍷🍸 **Tumbarumba Grüner Veltliner 2019 Rating** 90 **To** 2024 $35 JF

Night Harvest   ★★★★

PO Box 921, Busselton, WA 6280 **Region** Margaret River
T (08) 9755 1521 **www.**nightharvest.com.au
Winemaker Bruce Dukes, Ben Rector, Simon Ding **Est.** 2005 **Dozens** 2000
Vyds 300ha

Andy and Mandy Ferreira arrived in Margaret River in 1986 as newly married young migrants. They soon became involved in the construction and establishment of new vineyards, as well as growing vegetables for the local and export markets. Their vineyard-contracting business expanded quickly when the region experienced its rapid growth in the late '90s, so the vegetable business was closed, and they put all their focus into wine. They were involved in the establishment of about 300ha of Margaret River vineyards, many of which they continue to manage today (Brash Vineyard and Passel Estate are among the 18 estates that fall into this category). As their fortunes grew, they purchased their own property and produced their first wines in 2005. Harvesting is a key part of their business, and currently they harvest fruit from over 100 sites. Hence the Night Harvest brand was born, and Butler Crest was added as a premium label. Exports to the US and the UK.

🍷🍷🍷🍷🍷 **John George Margaret River Cabernet Sauvignon 2018** Earthy cassis and salted licorice are the first aromas to rise from the glass; in the mouth the wine performs just as the nose has laid out. The tannins really dominate the palate, they are omnipresent and grippy. This will continue to evolve for some time in the cellar, but if early drinking is desired, then a decant (for an hour or 2 at least) is recommended. Screw cap. 13.5% alc. **Rating** 92 **To** 2036 $40 EL

🍃 Nikola Estate ★★★★

148 Dale Road, Middle Swan, WA 6056 **Region** Swan Valley
T (08) 9374 8050 www.nikolaestate.com.au **Open** Thurs–Mon 10–5
Winemaker Damien Hutton, Daniel Charter **Est.** 2019 **Vyds** 56ha
While the Nikola brand may be new to the Swan Valley, the Yukich family behind it is anything but. To start at the end in 2019, Houghton Estate in the Swan Valley (vineyards, historic cellar door, est. 1836, and the winemaking facility) was purchased by brothers Graeme and Kim Yukich (3rd generation) from the private equity Carlyle Group, forming what is now the Nikola Estate. Winemaker Damian Hutton has moved from a long history at Millbrook (Fogarty Group) to assume the mantle at Nikola. Looking further back in time prior to the current state of play, the first acquisition of Houghton property by the Yukich family occurred in 1989 (45ha sold to Mark Yukich, 2nd generation) which precipitated the formation of Oakover Wines in the 1990s. Prior to that, the Yukich Brothers wine company was formed in 1953 by Nikola Yukich. (EL)

🍷🍷🍷🍷🍷 **Chenin Blanc 2020** Apricot, honeydew melon, cap gun, struck match, white pepper, green apple and pear are structured and shaped by fine waxy phenolics and supported by subtle oak. A lot to like here, from a region that has had grapes in the ground since 1829. Screw cap. 13% alc. **Rating** 94 **To** 2031 $35 EL
Verdelho 2020 Fruit from the Swan Valley (as the oldest wine region in WA, and the first place that verdelho was planted, this should proudly be on the front label!). Fresh and pure, this has lashings of nashi pear, exotic white spice, cooling saline acid and an irrepressibly silky texture. A lot to love here. Screw cap. 12% alc. **Rating** 94 **To** 2027 $25 EL ✪
Tempranillo 2020 Succulent yet tannic, this has brilliant length of flavour, confirming the multilayered approach of the palate. Raspberry, cassis, tobacco leaf, sage, pepper, jasmine tea and blueberries. Very impressive. Screw cap. 14.5% alc. **Rating** 94 **To** 2031 $30 EL ✪

🍷🍷🍷🍷🍷 **Shiraz 2019 Rating** 93 **To** 2031 $35 EL
Shiraz 2019 Rating 92 **To** 2031 $25 EL ✪
Sauvignon Blanc 2020 Rating 91 **To** 2025 $25 EL

Nine One Six ★★★★

916 Steels Creek Road, Steels Creek, Vic 3775 (postal) **Region** Yarra Valley
T (03) 5965 2124 www.nineonesix.com.au
Winemaker Ben Haines **Est.** 2008 **Dozens** 200 **Vyds** 2ha
In 2008 John Brand and Erin-Marie O'Neill purchased their 8ha property in the Yarra Valley, including 2ha of well-performing vines that had been planted in 1996. One year on, the Black

Saturday bushfires destroyed their home and everything in it, as well as part of the vineyard. They rebuilt their lives and home, reinvesting in wine and vineyard alike. Their focus now is on pinot noir alone and in understanding the impact of subtle differences in the soil and subsoil on the wines they produce, vinifying and bottling small segments of the vineyard separately. 'Each bottle is protected by various mechanisms to ensure product integrity, and serial number validation entitles collectors to future pre-release allocations.' The brand evolved from 916 to Nine One Six in 2020.

♟♟♟♟♟ **Yarra Valley Pinot Noir 2019** While the bottle has some heft, not so the pristine wine within. Heady with florals, a touch of star anise, fennel and blood orange with a waft of forest floor. Sweet plums and cherries mingle and linger. Don't be fooled by its apparent gentleness and lightness across the palate, as the fine tannins and bright acidity lengthen out the finish. A lovely wine. Diam. 12% alc. **Rating** 94 **To** 2027 $60 JF

919 Wines ★★★★

39 Hodges Road, Berri, SA 5343 **Region** Riverland
T 0408 855 272 **www**.919wines.com.au **Open** Wed–Sun & public hols 10–5 & by appt
Winemaker Eric Semmler **Est.** 2002 **Dozens** 2500 **Vyds** 17ha
Eric and Jenny Semmler have been involved in the wine industry since 1986 and have a special interest in fortified wines. Eric made fortified wines for Hardys and worked at Brown Brothers. Jenny has worked for Strathbogie Vineyards, Pennyweight Wines and St Huberts. They have planted micro-quantities of varieties for fortified wines: palomino, durif, tempranillo, muscat à petits grains, tinta cão, shiraz, tokay and touriga nacional. They use minimal water application, deliberately reducing the crop levels, and are certified organic. In 2011 they purchased the 12.3ha property at Loxton they now call Ella Semmler's Vineyard. Exports to Sweden.

♟♟♟♟♟ **Vintage 2020** A fortified blend of mostly durif and touriga nacional with a splash of tinta cão. No oak. Excellent dark purple. A confluence of vibrant bramble fruit, kirsch and Middle Eastern spices. Sure there's a richness, a sweetness across the palate but there's also decent tannins and weight, it's all well modulated and the neutral spirit is in balance. Nice one. Screw cap. 18.5% alc. **Rating** 91 $65 JF

Nintingbool ★★★★

56 Wongerer Lane, Smythes Creek, Vic 3351 (postal) **Region** Ballarat
T 0429 424 399 **www**.nintingbool.com.au
Winemaker Peter Bothe **Est.** 1998 **Dozens** 600 **Vyds** 2ha
Peter and Jill Bothe purchased the Nintingbool property in 1982 and built their home in '84, using bluestone dating back to the gold rush. They established an extensive Australian native garden and home orchard but in '98 diversified by planting pinot noir, with a further planting the following year lifting the total to 2ha. Ballarat is one of the coolest mainland regions and demands absolute attention to detail (and a warm growing season) for success.

♟♟♟♟♟ **Pinot Noir 2018** In the style of previous releases with its distinctive firm, linear structure and cool, leafy herbals, but showing more depth of flavour and intensity. The 2018 year seems to have been very kind. Brambly, dark berry fruits, wood smoke, earth notes, deep spice, with a spray of fine tannins from edge to edge. A work of some complexity. Screw cap. 13.8% alc. **Rating** 95 **To** 2027 $35 JP ✪

♟♟♟♟♟ **Shiraz 2018 Rating** 92 **To** 2028 $27 JP

Nocton Vineyard ★★★★

373 Colebrook Road, Richmond, Tas 7025 **Region** Southern Tasmania
T (03) 6260 2688 **www**.noctonwine.com.au **Open** Thurs–Mon 10–4, Tues–Wed by appt
Winemaker Frogmore Creek (Alain Rousseau) **Est.** 1998 **Dozens** 12 500 **Vyds** 36ha

Nocton Vineyard is the reincarnation of Nocton Park. After years of inactivity (other than the ongoing sale of the grapes from what is a first-class vineyard) it largely disappeared. Wines are released under the Nocton Vineyard and Willow (Reserve) labels. The quality across the 2 labels is very good. Exports to the US, Hong Kong and China.

🍷🍷🍷🍷🍷 **Tasmania Chenin Blanc 2020** A juxtaposition of the tropical exuberance of chenin and the energetic tension of the Coal River Valley. Alluring – if unexpected – sweet blackcurrant juice and golden kiwifruit are scored with a deep cut of enduring and perfectly ripe acidity, guiding a long finish. As idiosyncratic as it is enticing. Screw cap. 12.5% alc. **Rating** 92 **To** 2027 $50 TS
Estate Pinot Noir 2019 Depth of blood plum, spicy blackberry and black pepper, even black pastilles and licorice. It's laced with savoury nuances of beetroot and sage, built around a rigid frame of powdery oak and fruit tannins. A solid Tassie pinot of deep colour and impact, if not grace. Screw cap. 13.5% alc. **Rating** 90 **To** 20329 $32 TS

🍷🍷🍷🍷 **Storm Bay Sauvignon Blanc 2019 Rating** 89 **To** 2021 $25 TS
Sauvignon Blanc 2019 Rating 89 **To** 2025 $29 TS
Tasmania Chardonnay 2019 Rating 89 **To** 2021 $29 TS
Storm Bay Pinot Noir 2019 Rating 89 **To** 2024 $25 TS

Nocturne Wines   ★★★★☆

PO Box 111, Yallingup, WA 6282 **Region** Margaret River
T 0477 829 844 **www.**nocturnewines.com.au
Winemaker Alana Langworthy, Julian Langworthy **Est.** 2007 **Dozens** 1300 **Vyds** 8ha
Alana and Julian Langworthy were newly minted winemakers when they met in SA over 15 years ago and set up a small winery project called Nocturne Wines. The intention was to make small quantities of project wines as an adjunct to their day jobs as employed winemakers. The enlightened Peter Fogarty, owner of WA's fastest growing wine business (Fogarty Family Wines), raised no objection to Nocturne Wines when he appointed Julian chief winemaker in 2011. Nocturne has been able to buy the Sheoak Vineyard (former Jimmy Watson–producing vineyard – Harvey River Bridge 2010), with its 4ha of mature cabernet sauvignon vines, but Nocturne wines are still produced in modest quantities. The flood of show awards will, indeed, be enhanced by the arrival of Nocturne alongside Deep Woods Estate. The SR range explores Margaret River's subregions; the 2019 SR Rosé was awarded Best Rosé in the 2021 *Wine Companion*. Exports to the UK.

🍷🍷🍷🍷🍷 **Sheoak Vineyard Margaret River Cabernet Sauvignon 2019** In a line-up of wines that were often double and triple the price (and more), the Sheoak single-vineyard cabernet stood out. No wonder this sells out in a nanosecond each year. Ridiculous price for the quality. Supple, pristine and densely packed with sweet fruit from every angle, this is long and dark and layered and awesome. The oak is almost imperceptible, but the wine's structure and tannins ensure a long future. We'll all be old by the time this fades. Screw cap. 14% alc. **Rating** 97 **To** 2051 $53 EL

🍷🍷🍷🍷🍷 **Tassell Park Vineyard Margaret River Chardonnay 2019** We're starting to know what to expect from the Langworthy duo and this wine: flinty curry leaf, yellow peach, brine, crunchy acid and good length of flavour. This vintage is no exception, although perhaps a slightly leaner iteration due to the cooler year. Crushed macadamia and cashew are laced through the finish … awesome. Yes. (Try decanting it for extra pleasure). Screw cap. 13% alc. **Rating** 96 **To** 2036 $53 EL ✪
Treeton SR Chardonnay 2019 Creamy cashew and ripe citrus nose, the palate has a searing line of shaley, minerally acid that courses over the very centre of the tongue. The mid palate onwards plumes into a concentrated and rich cloud of flavour. The fruit spectrum is very much in the yellow peach, white nectarine and pink grapefruit space. Engaging, chalky phenolics through the finish. Textbook brilliance. Screw cap. 13% alc. **Rating** 95 **To** 2027 $30 EL ✪

Carbunup SR Sangiovese Nebbiolo Rosé 2020 The previous vintage was awarded Best Rosé at the *Halliday Wine Companion* Awards Australia in August, and deservedly so. Aromatically, this is all about laid-back red-berry spice. Pomegranate, shale, mineral and graphite characters and white pepper. The palate has full and generous flavour, full texture and full concentration. The grip it exhibits is an extra layer of sass and charm. Really good length of flavour, which moves through to creamy in the lingering and morphing finish. Pleasure here. Also bottled in magnum. Screw cap. 13% alc. **Rating** 95 **To** 2022 $30 EL ✪

Yallingup SR Cabernets 2019 This is not just a playground for cassis, it welcomes a gentle leafy, herbal note, fennel flower and raspberry into play. Overseeing it all are firm yet fine tannins, fencing it all in, drawing all the flavours out onto the field for a long finish. All components get along harmoniously. Pretty magnificent stuff, given the price. Screw cap. 14% alc. **Rating** 95 **To** 2036 $36 EL

Norfolk Rise Vineyard

Limestone Coast Road, Mount Benson, SA 5265 **Region** Mount Benson
T (08) 8768 5080 **www**.norfolkrise.com.au
Winemaker Alice Baker **Est.** 2000 **Dozens** 20 000 **Vyds** 130ha
Norfolk Rise Vineyard is by far the largest and most important development in the Mount Benson region. It is owned by privately held Belgian company G and C Kreglinger, which was established in 1797. In early 2002 Kreglinger acquired Pipers Brook Vineyard and has since maintained the separate brands of Pipers Brook and Norfolk Rise. There are 46 blocks of sauvignon blanc, pinot gris, pinot noir, shiraz, merlot and cabernet sauvignon, allowing a range of options in making the 6 single-variety wines in the portfolio. The business has moved from the export of bulk wine to bottled wine, which gives significantly better returns to the winery. Exports to the US, Canada, Europe and Asia.

🍷🍷🍷🍷🍷 **Limestone Coast Shiraz 2019** A sprinkling of black pepper and bold fruit distinguishes this well-priced red. It's supple with shapely tannins and a certain vivacity that makes it appealing. A red to enjoy now, without any more thought. Screw cap. 14.5% alc. **Rating** 90 **To** 2024 $19 JF ✪

Norton Estate

758 Plush Hannans Road, Lower Norton, Vic 3401 **Region** Western Victoria
T (03) 5384 8235 **www**.nortonestate.com.au **Open** Fri–Sun & public hols 11–4
Winemaker Best's Wines **Est.** 1997 **Dozens** 1200 **Vyds** 5.66ha
In 1996 the Spence family purchased a rundown farm at Lower Norton and, rather than looking to the traditional wool, meat and wheat markets, trusted their instincts and planted vines on the elevated, frost-free, buckshot rises. The surprising vigour of the initial planting of shiraz prompted further plantings of shiraz, cabernet sauvignon and sauvignon blanc, plus a small planting of an American variety also called Norton. The vineyard is halfway between the Grampians and Mt Arapiles, 6km northwest of the Grampians region, and has to be content with Western Victoria, but the wines show regional Grampians character and style.

🍷🍷🍷🍷🍷 **Arapiles Run Shiraz 2019** Wears its Grampians regional identity proudly with prominent spice – cinnamon, nutmeg, bay leaf and pepper – which is well suited to the ripe, sweet-berried fruit. The palate is lively, brisk in tannin and juicy. Should age a treat. Screw cap. 14% alc. **Rating** 94 **To** 2029 $30 JP ✪

🍷🍷🍷🍷🍷 **Sauvignon Blanc 2020 Rating** 90 **To** 2023 $25 JP

Nova Vita Wines

11 Woodlands Road, Kenton Valley, SA 5235 **Region** Adelaide Hills
T (08) 8356 0454 **www**.novavitawines.com.au **Open** Wed–Sun 11–5
Winemaker Mark Kozned **Est.** 2005 **Dozens** 20 000 **Vyds** 49ha
Mark and Jo Kozned's 30ha Woodlands Ridge Vineyard is planted to chardonnay, sauvignon blanc, pinot gris and shiraz. They subsequently established the Tunnel Hill Vineyard, with

19ha planted to pinot noir, shiraz, cabernet sauvignon, sauvignon blanc, semillon, verdelho, merlot and sangiovese. The name Nova Vita reflects the beginning of the Kozned's new life, the firebird on the label coming from their Russian ancestry – it is a Russian myth that only a happy or lucky person may see the bird or hear its song. They are building a new winery and cellar door at the Woodlands Ridge Vineyard. In the meantime, the majority of the wines are made at Revenir. Exports to the US, Finland, Thailand, Singapore and China.

🍷🍷🍷🍷🍷 **Firebird Adelaide Hills Cabernet Sauvignon 2018** Sourced from an estate vineyard in the far northern districts of the Hills, settled and rested for close to 2 years in a range of new and older, small and larger oak vessels. This offers an attractive, gentile style of cabernet, unmistakably blackcurrant, with a subtle roasted red capsicum layered into it. The flavours weave well together, the palate quite lively and the tannins relaxed; a faint bitterness built into the finish of this medium-bodied style. Screw cap. 14.5% alc. **Rating** 94 **To** 2028 $30 TL ☻

🍷🍷🍷🍷🍷 **Firebird Adelaide Hills Pinot Gris 2020** Rating 92 To 2024 $20 TL ☻
Firebird Adelaide Hills Rosé 2020 Rating 90 To 2022 $20 TL ☻
Firebird Adelaide Hills Pinot Noir 2019 Rating 90 To 2024 $30 TL

Nugan Estate ★★★★

580 Kidman Way, Wilbriggie, NSW 2680 **Region** Riverina
T (02) 9362 9993 **www.**nuganestate.com.au **Open** Mon–Fri 9–4
Winemaker Daren Owers **Est.** 1999 **Dozens** 300 000
Nugan Estate arrived on the scene like a whirlwind. It is an offshoot of the Nugan Group headed by Michelle Nugan (until her retirement in Feb 2013), inter alia the recipient of an Export Hero Award in '00. The wine business is now in the energetic hands of Matthew Nugan. Exports to Denmark, Finland, Ireland, the UK, the US, Canada, NZ, Japan and Brazil.

🍷🍷🍷🍷🍷 **La Brutta Zinfandel Petite Sirah 2018** Two varieties that punch in the heavyweight division on their own, let alone as a tag team, so you can expect muscle and extroverted character. Masses of dark plum-like fruit, heaps of baking spice and vanilla, and chewy oak on the palate. Not for the faint-hearted, yet somewhat loveable in a gentle giant way. Screw cap. 14.5% alc. **Rating** 90 **To** 2028 $28 TL
Alfredo Frasca's Lane Vineyard King Valley Sangiovese 2019 It's a happy marriage of the sangiovese grape and the King Valley here, one where the former's natural red berries, herbs and woodsy spice shine. Easy all the way across the palate, so much so, it can easily be enjoyed right now. It wouldn't mind a short time in the cellar, either. Screw cap. 13.5% alc. **Rating** 90 **To** 2026 $26 JP

🍷🍷🍷🍷 **Manuka Grove Vineyard Riverina Durif 2017** Rating 89 To 2026 $26 NG
Frasca's Lane Vineyard King Valley Chardonnay 2019 Rating 88 To 2024 $22 JP

O'Leary Walker Wines ★★★★★

7093 Horrocks Highway, Leasingham, SA 5452 **Region** Clare Valley/Adelaide Hills
T 1300 342 569 **www.**olearywalkerwines.com **Open** Mon–Sat 10–4, Sun & public hols 11–4
Winemaker David O'Leary, Nick Walker, Jack Walker, Luke Broadbent **Est.** 2001
Dozens 20 000 **Vyds** 45ha
David O'Leary and Nick Walker together had more than 30 years' experience as winemakers working for some of the biggest Australian wine groups when they took the plunge in 2001 and backed themselves to establish their own winery and brand. Initially the principal focus was on the Clare Valley with 10ha of riesling, shiraz and cabernet sauvignon the main plantings; thereafter attention swung to the Adelaide Hills where they now have 35ha of chardonnay, cabernet sauvignon, pinot noir, shiraz, sauvignon blanc and merlot. The vineyards were certified organic in 2013. O'Leary Walker also has a cellar door in the Adelaide Hills at 18 Oakwood Road, Oakbank at the heritage-listed former Johnson Brewery established in 1843 (7 days 11–4). Exports to the UK, Ireland, Canada, UAE, Asia and Japan.

🍷🍷🍷🍷🍷 **Polish Hill River Armagh Shiraz 2018** Very good colour through to the rim; the bouquet has a complex array of licorice and tantalising warm spices. The palate is full bodied and intense, yet so balanced it doesn't muffle a classic Clare Valley shiraz filled with blackberry and black cherry fruit. Screw cap. 14.5% alc. **Rating 97 To 2038 $35 JH ✪**

🍷🍷🍷🍷🍷 **Claire Reserve Polish Hill River Shiraz 2018** The colour is a deep, dark garnet. Yes, lots of oak flavouring – all cedary and smoky – yet it's enmeshed into the full-bodied wine. Expect a bomb of flavour from blackberries, plums, aniseed balls and bay leaves, with a savoury overlay. A voluptuous palate, pillars of steadfast tannins and a guarantee that this will hold together for many years yet. Screw cap. 14.5% alc. **Rating 96 To 2038 $110 JF**

Claire Reserve Clare Valley Shiraz 2016 Hailing from 100yo vines, the concentration is literally breathtaking. You can sense the power on the swarthy/leathery/black fruit of the bouquet, the palate doubling down on all that goes before. Its future will be measured in decades not years – needs the optimism of matriarch Claire Marie O'Leary. Screw cap. 14.5% alc. **Rating 96 To 2066 $110 JH**

Polish Hill River Armagh Cabernet Sauvignon 2018 Cabernet in Clare takes on its own meaning, its own structure and flavour (providing the producer gets it right). It's right on, here. Everything is in its place, from dark spiced fruits, spread of mint chocolate, woodsy spices and tannins. There's a freshness, too, refreshing acidity and smooth tannins. Screw cap. 14% alc. **Rating 96 To 2030 $35 JF ✪**

🍷🍷🍷🍷🍷 **Oakbank Adelaide Hills Chardonnay 2020 Rating 92 To 2025 $30 TL**
Watervale Riesling 2020 Rating 91 To 2026 $25 JF
Polish Hill River Riesling 2020 Rating 90 To 2025 $30 JF
Oakbank Adelaide Hills Sauvignon Blanc 2020 Rating 90 To 2024 $25 TL
Oakbank Adelaide Hills Pinot Noir 2020 Rating 90 To 2025 $35 TL

Oakdene ★★★★★

255 Grubb Road, Wallington, Vic 3221 **Region** Geelong
T (03) 5256 3886 **www.**oakdene.com.au **Open** 7 days 10–4
Winemaker Robin Brockett, Marcus Holt **Est.** 2001 **Dozens** 8000 **Vyds** 32ha
Bernard and Elizabeth Hooley purchased Oakdene in 2001. Bernard focused on planting the vineyard (shiraz, pinot gris, sauvignon blanc, pinot noir, chardonnay, merlot, cabernet franc and cabernet sauvignon) while Elizabeth worked to restore the 1920s homestead. Much of the wine is sold through the award-winning Oakdene Restaurant and cellar door. The quality is exemplary, as is the consistency of that quality; Robin Brockett's skills are on full display. A new vineyard (11km from Oakdene) planted in '17 (to shiraz, pinot noir, pinot gris, chardonnay, sauvignon blanc, merlot, riesling, cabernet franc and cabernet sauvignon) has increased the plantings from 12ha to 32ha. Export to Switzerland and Hong Kong.

🍷🍷🍷🍷🍷 **Liz's Single Vineyard Bellarine Peninsula Chardonnay 2019** This wine has a reputation for generosity of flavour and the 2019 vintage doesn't disappoint. Arrives with a bang! Take a long inhale of all that stone fruit, dried peach, orange peel, honeysuckle and pear. Keep that thought, because there's more to behold on the palate and this time it comes with delicious texture and length. Coastal saline sea-spray notes hover, providing added zing. Screw cap. 13.6% alc. **Rating 95 To 2028 $35 JP ✪**

Bellarine Peninsula Chardonnay 2019 Fermented and matured for 10 months in new and used French barriques. Gleaming straw-green hue. The quality of the fruit is obvious; the wine already in the saddle; the gait smooth and supple; white stone fruit, citrussy acidity and creamy cashew in harmony. Screw cap. 13.4% alc. **Rating 94 To 2029 $24 JH ✪**

Peta's Single Vineyard Bellarine Peninsula Pinot Noir 2019 Deep purple/garnet colour. Intense and savoury in aromas of Thai herbs, anise, wood smoke, black cherry. Runs a touch wild and savoury across the tongue in shades of cherry cola, rhubarb and sage, with notes of smoke. A light dusting of spice throughout helps fuel the wine's energy. Screw cap. 13.7% alc. **Rating** 94 **To** 2027 $43 JP

🍷🍷🍷🍷🍷 **Ly Ly Single Vineyard Bellarine Peninsula Pinot Gris 2020** Rating 93 To 2025 $28 JP
William Single Vineyard Bellarine Peninsula Shiraz 2019 Rating 93 To 2031 $43 JP
Bellarine Peninsula Sauvignon Blanc 2020 Rating 92 To 2023 $23 JP ✪
Jessica Single Vineyard Bellarine Peninsula Sauvignon 2020 Rating 91 To 2023 $28 JP
Bellarine Peninsula Rosé 2020 Rating 91 To 2024 $23 JP ✪
Kristen Sparkling Blanc de Blancs 2017 Rating 91 $35 JP
Yvette Sparkling Pinot Noir Chardonnay 2016 Rating 91 $35 JP
Bellarine Peninsula Pinot Grigio 2020 Rating 90 To 2023 $23 JP
Bellarine Peninsula Pinot Noir 2019 Rating 90 To 2026 $24 JP
Bellarine Peninsula Shiraz 2019 Rating 90 To 2026 $13.20 JP ✪

Oakover Wines ★★★★

14 Yukich Close, Middle Swan, WA 6056 **Region** Swan Valley
T (08) 9374 8000 **www.oakoverwines.com.au Open** Wed–Sun 11–4
Winemaker Daniel Charter **Est.** 1929 **Dozens** 15 000 **Vyds** 27ha
Oakover Wines is a family-operated winery located in the Swan Valley. Formerly part of Houghton, in 1990 it came under the Yukich family's control as Oakover Estate. Prominent Perth funds manager Graeme Yukich and his family have been involved in the region since Nicholas Yukich purchased his first block of land in 1929. In 2002 Oakover Estate became Oakover Wines and is now the 3rd-largest winery in the Swan Valley. Oakover's White Label brand is currently sold in over 500 independent liquor outlets in WA and Vic, with expansion into NSW and Qld planned. Exports to India and China.

🍷🍷🍷🍷🍷 **Shiraz 2019** 70/30% Perth Hills/Swan Valley. As expected, this is juicy, vibrant and energetic with a smooth core of purple fruits wrapped in spicy tannin. There is a lot of pleasure here for the price. Screw cap. 14% alc. **Rating** 91 **To** 2026 $16 EL ✪

🍷🍷🍷🍷 **Chenin Blanc 2020** Rating 89 To 2024 $16 EL ✪
Sauvignon Blanc Semillon 2020 Rating 88 To 2022 $16 EL ✪

Oakridge Wines ★★★★★

864 Maroondah Highway, Coldstream, Vic 3770 **Region** Yarra Valley
T (03) 9738 9900 **www.oakridgewines.com.au Open** 7 days 10–5
Winemaker David Bicknell, Tim Perrin **Est.** 1978 **Dozens** 35 000 **Vyds** 61ha
Winemaker David Bicknell has proved his worth time and again as an extremely talented winemaker. At the top of the Oakridge brand tier is 864, all Yarra Valley vineyard selections, only released in the best years (Chardonnay, Pinot Noir, Syrah, Cabernet Sauvignon); next is the Oakridge Vineyard Series (the Chardonnay, Pinot Noir and Sauvignon Blanc come from the cooler Upper Yarra Valley; the Shiraz, Cabernet Sauvignon from the Lower Yarra); and the Over the Shoulder range, drawn from all of the sources available to Oakridge (Pinot Grigio, Chardonnay, Pinot Noir, Cabernet Merlot). The estate vineyards are Oakridge Vineyard, Hazeldene Vineyard and Henk Vineyard. Exports to the UK, the US, Canada, Sweden, Norway, Fiji, Singapore, Hong Kong, Indonesia and China.

🍷🍷🍷🍷🍷 **864 Single Block Release Drive Block Funder & Diamond Vineyard Yarra Valley Chardonnay 2019** It might have a smidge more volume and ripeness compared with the exemplary 2017, but this is a very fine follow up. The same DNA. It's about harnessing the power. Expect citrus, flint and form. Length, precision and a mineral drive. The devil is in the details, according to winemaker Dave Bicknell. This wine is the embodiment – indeed the reward – of that. Screw cap. 14% alc. **Rating** 97 **To** 2030 $90 JF ✪ ♥

ϘϘϘϘϘ Vineyard Series Willowlake Yarra Valley Chardonnay 2019 All the chardonnays in the Vineyard Series are made identically, so capturing the essence of the place is paramount. This is so good. Flinty, fine, citrussy, long and pure. An ethereal style, yet so much going on. It's hard to pick a favourite in this range. They are all expressive. Today it's Willowlake, tomorrow … who knows? Screw cap. 13.2% alc. **Rating** 96 **To** 2030 $44 JF ✪

Vineyard Series Henk Yarra Valley Chardonnay 2019 A north-facing vineyard at Woori Yallock in the Upper Yarra. It comes with no shortage of flavour or drive. Lemon blossom, struck match, ginger spice and savoury, leesy notes. Feeling fuller and richer on the palate at first, it is pulled through a tight vortex by a silk-thread of acidity. Compelling and equally delicious. Screw cap. 13.3% alc. **Rating** 96 **To** 2029 $44 JF ✪

864 Single Block Release Aqueduct Block Henk Vineyard Yarra Valley Pinot Noir 2019 The 864 Single Block wines are the pinnacle of the Oakridge range. They have the X-factor. Once again, pinot noir from the Henk vineyard rises to the occasion this vintage. If feels effortless. Perfect amalgam of aromas and flavours. The textural tannins are so velvety soft, yet add shape, with flashes of raspberry acidity throughout. Screw cap. 14.3% alc. **Rating** 96 **To** 2035 $90 JF ❤

864 Single Block Release Close Planted Block Oakridge Vineyard Yarra Valley Syrah 2019 Well, syrah has certainly earned its place at the top tier this vintage. Fruit off the close-planted site (5200 vines/ha) at Oakridge, mostly destemmed, with 20% whole bunches in the ferment. Matured 10 months in 10% new French puncheons, harnessing the elements into a complete wine. It's wonderfully savoury, spicy and smoky, with plentiful grainy, textural tannins. It's full bodied, but there's no excess here. Screw cap. 13.7% alc. **Rating** 96 **To** 2034 $90 JF

Vineyard Series Hazeldene Yarra Valley Chardonnay 2019 The winemaking of all the Vineyard Series chardonnays is the same: hand-picked, whole bunches pressed directly to French puncheons, natural fermentation and aged 10 months on lees. It's not so much a recipe, but a means of extracting and holding on to the differences of each site. This the most accessible in the range, and immediately satisfying. An assortment of citrus, white nectarine, ginger spice and chalky acidity. Screw cap. 13.2% alc. **Rating** 95 **To** 2029 $44 JF

Vineyard Series Barkala Yarra Valley Chardonnay 2019 Pristine and pure. Flinty, spicy, citrussy and the peppery flavour of new-season ginger spun into gossamer threads of flavour across the palate. There's depth here, but it is still tightly wound and needs more time. Screw cap. 13.6% alc. **Rating** 95 **To** 2030 $44 JF

Vineyard Series Prices Road Yarra Valley Chardonnay 2019 A lot of depth across the palate, a richness with grilled nuts and creamy lees making an impression into poached quince and citrus flavours. A hint of toasty oak, and a lemon bath salts sensation to the acidity. Great energy and drive. Screw cap. 13.3% alc. **Rating** 95 **To** 2029 $44 JF

Garden Gris Yarra Valley 2019 The 2nd offering of this textural, lightly tannic and thoroughly appealing gris. It's a beauty. Cloudy pastel ruby and smells of watermelon and rind, Turkish delight and freshly pickled Japanese ginger in red shiso. It's refreshing and obviously phenolic, but all neatly played. The natural acidity adds to its succulence as it finishes dry and brimming with life. Screw cap. 11.6% alc. **Rating** 95 **To** 2025 $30 JF ✪

Yarra Valley Rosé 2020 A trio of pinots noir, meunier and gris fermented in old casks makes for a fab rosé with a very pale pastel copper hue. There's texture, flavour and a dry finish. In between, dabs of spicy red fruits, lemon zest and unripe pear, as in crunchy and textural. It's a top-notch rosé. Screw cap. 12.5% alc. **Rating** 95 **To** 2023 $30 JF ✪

Vineyard Series Oakridge Yarra Valley Shiraz 2019 A superb purple/black hue, the same colour as the plums and berries at the core of this shiraz. But it's most definitely savoury; spicy and peppery with very nicely controlled smoky reduction woven across the bouquet and palate. Full bodied, with determined

tannins and a wonderful sense of clarity throughout. Screw cap. 14.1% alc.
Rating 95 To 2032 $44 JF

Light Dry Red Yarra Valley 2020 With the Yarra Valley cornering the Light
Dry Red market, here's another ripper and it won't break the budget. 50/50%
pinot/shiraz. Loaded with bright, poppy fruit doused in pepper, spice and all things
nice. It's just shy of medium bodied, with crunchy acidity and grainy tannins.
Fitting the style brief brilliantly, it eschews any serious intent, other than crafting a
delicious drink. Screw cap. 14% alc. Rating 95 To 2026 $30 JF ✪

Yarra Valley Pinot Noir 2019 A similar feel or DNA to the Light Dry Red and
you know what that means? It's a delicious drink. Full of bright, juicy cherries and
pips, laced with woodsy spices and a dash of Angostura bitters. Smoky and sultry,
too. Just shy of full bodied, textural and plush, with slightly grainy tannins. Lively
and fresh. Get into this now. Screw cap. 14% alc. Rating 94 To 2026 $30 JF ✪

Vineyard Series Oakridge Yarra Valley Cabernet Sauvignon 2019 A
very classy cabernet with a riff of cassis, currants and almost-ripe blackberries
spiced to the max, with touches of wintergreen. It is balanced and cooling across
its medium-bodied palate with, crunchy acidity to snap it closed. A modern-day
claret, perhaps. Screw cap. 12.7% alc. Rating 94 To 2033 $44 JF

Local Vineyard Series Blanc de Blancs 2015 Fifty-two months on lees and
disgorged February 2020. A very smart fizz. It flirts with flint and citrus, baked
biscuit and grilled nuts. And the flavours build across the palate: white nectarine,
citrus and lemon curd with more complex aged characters of nougat and
shortbread. Neat acidity ensures the volume isn't cranked to up too high. Moreish
and satisfying. Diam. 12.5% alc. Rating 94 $55

🍷🍷🍷🍷♀ **Vineyard Series Willowlake Yarra Valley Sauvignon 2019** Rating 93
To 2025 $30 JF

Local Vineyard Series Hazeldene Vineyard Yarra Valley Pinot Gris 2020
Rating 93 To 2025 $30 JF

Meunier 2020 Rating 93 To 2025 $30 JF

Vineyard Series Hazeldene Yarra Valley Pinot Noir 2019 Rating 93
To 2027 $44 JF

Vineyard Series Prices Road Yarra Valley Pinot Noir 2019 Rating 93
To 2028 $44 JF

Oakway Estate   ★★★★☆

575 Farley Road, Donnybrook, WA 6239 **Region** Geographe
T (08) 9731 7141 **www**.oakwayestate.com.au **Open** W'ends 11–5
Winemaker Tony Davis **Est.** 1997 **Dozens** 1500 **Vyds** 2ha
Ria and Wayne Hammond run a vineyard, beef cattle and sustainable blue-gum plantation
in undulating country on the Capel River in the southwest of WA. The grapes are grown
on light gravel and loam soils that provide good drainage, giving even sun exposure to the
fruit and minimising the effects of frost. The vineyard is planted to shiraz, merlot, cabernet
sauvignon, nero d'Avola, malbec, muscat, sauvignon blanc, vermentino and chardonnay, and
the wines have won a number of medals.

🍷🍷🍷🍷🍷 **Los Ninos Single Vineyard Geographe Malbec 2018** Wildly aromatic nose:
Mariposa plum, raspberry and licorice. The palate follows exactly, making this a
succulent, delicious little number which for the price (especially for the price)
should not be missed. Should you have the patience to wait, layers of flavour
and texture will unfurl themselves in the glass. Screw cap. 13.5% alc. Rating 95
To 2030 $28 EL ✪

Il Sardo Single Vineyard Vermentino 2020 Pretty! White melon, spring
florals and green apple and pear. The palate is vibrant and energetic with a line
of citric acid that courses over the middle of the palate. Plugs you in and zaps
you (in a good way). Energising and delicious. Screw cap. 12.3% alc. Rating 94
To 2021 $25 EL ✪

Il Vino Rosato 2020 100% Nero d'Avola. Now we're talking … flavour: this is
intense and moving to full concentration. Pretty salmon onion-skin colour. Red

berry, szechuan peppercorn, red licorice and spice. The palate is plump and plush, with plenty of succulence and bounce. Well crafted, with some creamy characters on the mid palate for interest, bolstered by fine phenolics through the finish. Great effort. Super-saline tang. Screw cap. 12.2% alc. **Rating** 94 **To** 2021 $25 EL **☉**

Il Siciliano Single Vineyard Nero d'Avola 2019 A juicy and vibrant nose reminiscent of purple wine gums, black licorice and red snakes – all appealing things. The palate delivers all the plush comfort promised by the nose. A sobering flick of acid and tannins through the finish brings it into a more balanced space. Lovely wine, full of pleasure. Another example of Geographe bringing home the (alternative red) bacon. Screw cap. 14.6% alc. **Rating** 94 **To** 2025 $28 EL **☉**

Oates Ends   ★★★★★

22 Carpenter Road, Wilyabrup, WA 6280 **Region** Margaret River
T 0401 303 144 **www**.oatesends.com.au **Open** By appt
Winemaker Cath Oates **Est.** 1999 **Dozens** 2000 **Vyds** 11ha

Cath Oates returned home to Margaret River after an international winemaking career spanning 15 years. The wines are made from the family Wilagri Vineyard, planted in 1999 and now owned and managed by viticulturist brother Russ Oates. Oates Ends is the culmination of both of their respective experience and wine philosophies. The vineyard is run on sustainable farming principles (Cath is also chair of AGW's Sustainability Advisory Committee). Sheep are a big part of the vineyard program with winter mowing a given and they are increasingly being relied upon for leaf plucking during the growing season. The name comes from the shed wine made for family and friends in the early 2000s from the ends of the rows the harvesters missed and acknowledges the importance of family farming traditions. Exports to Canada and Singapore.

♀♀♀♀♀ Margaret River Cabernet Sauvignon 2018 Cath Oates' vineyard is in Wilyabrup, oft regarded as the heartland of Margaret River. The nose is savoury and spiced, laden with raspberry, Cherry Ripe, cassis and violets. The acidity exerts a taut mineral presence over the mouth: it swoops in and captures the soul. Fine, elegant cabernet; the perfect example of what sensitive winemaking, good vineyards and a brilliant vintage can do. Screw cap. 14% alc. **Rating** 96 **To** 2036 $50 EL **☉**

Margaret River Tempranillo 2020 Amaro, Italian mountain herbs, garden mint, and freshly diced fennel are the backdrop to purple violets and sweet cherry fruit on the nose. The fruit sweeps across the palate, leaving a trail of fresh summer raspberries in its wake. Pure, cleansing and quite alluring, the small component of seasoned American oak fleshes out the finish. Beautiful. Modern. Slinky. Fresh. Yes. Screw cap. 13.5% alc. **Rating** 95 **To** 2025 $30 EL **☉**

Margaret River Cabernet Sauvignon 2017 The cooler 2017 vintage has birthed a wine of savoury spice, leather strapping, cassis and bramble. Tasted side by side with the lauded 2018, the 2017 lens reveals more restraint, less volume, and a heightened sense of minerality in the finish. The verdict? A supple, lingering and refined cabernet with a much softer voice than its younger sibling. It whispers, rather than shouts. Screw cap. 14% alc. **Rating** 94 **To** 2038 $50 EL

♀♀♀♀♀ Margaret River Semillon Sauvignon Blanc 2020 Rating 93 **To** 2030 $25 EL **☉**

Ochota Barrels   ★★★★★

Merchants Road, Basket Range, SA 5138 **Region** Adelaide Hills
T 0400 798 818 **www**.ochotabarrels.com
Winemaker Taras Ochota **Est.** 2008 **Dozens** 900 **Vyds** 0.5ha

Taras Ochota has been a talisman for a new generation of Australian winemakers, creating with wife Amber an exciting portfolio of wines from small, beloved Adelaide Hills blocks as well as neighbouring districts such as McLaren Vale. After completing his oenology degree at Adelaide University he followed a varied path making wines for many of Australia's top producers, as well as being a consultant winemaker in Sweden and Italy over 20 years, with Amber in a range of technical and marketing roles beside him. They set up Ochota Barrels in 2008 and garnered much more than a cult following. Tragically, Taras died in October 2020. The 2021 vintage was managed by Amber, with assistance of Taras' dad Yari and Louis Schofield, as well as long-time winemaking mentor Peter Leske. Exports to the UK, the US, Canada, Denmark, Norway, Sweden, Ukraine, Hong Kong, NZ, the Netherlands, Singapore, Germany and Japan. (TL)

🍷🍷🍷🍷🍷 **Control Voltage +5VOV Chardonnay 2020** Sourced from a single vineyard in the Piccadilly Valley, with focused terroir expression. Smells of delicate bath powders one moment, soft lime and mint gels the next. Totally seductive. The palate is energised and mineral, with subtle lemon zest and Pink Lady apple suggestions, tonic quinine and spice. Has fabulous thrust and a mouth-watering finish. A bloody marvel. Cork. 13.6% alc. **Rating** 96 **To** 2026 $60 TL ✪
Impeccable Disorder Pinot Noir 2020 In the style of its house and winemaker, this pinot grabs a surge of early-harvest energy and drives it with intense focus. Heaps of power, a throb of underlying acidity, powdered-thyme and violet scents to begin and on the palate. Lots to love here. Impressive every step of the way. And then some. Cork. 12.1% alc. **Rating** 95 **To** 2028 $80 TL

🍷🍷🍷🍷♀ **Slint Chardonnay 2020 Rating** 93 **To** 2025 $40 TL
Surfer Rosa Sangiovese Grenache 2020 Rating 93 **To** 2023 $25 TL ✪
A Sense of Compression Grenache 2020 Rating 92 **To** 2027 $92 TL
From the North Mourvèdre 2020 Rating 92 **To** 2027 $40 TL
A Forest Pinot Noir 2020 Rating 91 **To** 2025 $40 TL
The Mark of Cain Pinot Meunier 2020 Rating 91 **To** 2026 $40 TL
Where's The Pope Syrah 2020 Rating 91 **To** 2024 $40 TL
Weird Berries in the Woods Gewürztraminer 2020 Rating 90 **To** 2022 $35 TL

Old Plains   ★★★★

71 High Street, Grange, SA 5023 (postal) **Region** Adelaide Plains
T 0407 605 601 **www**.oldplains.com
Winemaker Domenic Torzi, Tim Freeland **Est.** 2003 **Dozens** 4000 **Vyds** 12ha
Old Plains is a partnership between Tim Freeland and Dom Torzi, who have acquired some of the last remaining small parcels of old-vine shiraz, grenache and cabernet sauvignon in the Adelaide Plains region. Wines made from these vines are sold under the Old Plains label. Pinot gris, riesling and a sparkling pinot noir/chardonnay are sourced from the Adelaide Hills and sold under the Longhop brand. Exports to the US and Denmark.

🍷🍷🍷🍷🍷 **Terreno Old Vine Adelaide Plains Grenache 2019** Delightful steerage of fruit from 60yo vines in 3 restored vineyard blocks. Traditional winemaking with 15% whole bunch and old-fashioned basket pressing has wrought a neatly layered raspberry/plum fruit concoction here, with dusty tannins and a long finish. Simple yet magic. Screw cap. 14.5% alc. **Rating** 94 **To** 2026 $35 TL
Longhop Adelaide Plains Cabernet Sauvignon 2017 No heavy-handed winemaking needed to showcase the cabernet aromas and fruit power here, in what was an unusually (and beneficially) cool year for this variety in this place. All the varietal thrills – blackcurrant, blackberry and some plum fruitcake notes, with a fulfilling palate and tannin-supported structure. Great value. Screw cap. 14.5% alc. **Rating** 94 **To** 2026 $20 TL ✪

🍷🍷🍷🍷♀ **Power of One Old Vine Adelaide Plains Shiraz 2018 Rating** 92 **To** 2026 $35 TL
Longhop Old Vine Adelaide Plains Grenache 2020 Rating 92 **To** 2024 $20 TL ✪
Longhop Adelaide Hills Riesling 2020 Rating 90 **To** 2024 $24 TL

🍇 Olive Hills Estate

3221 Murray Valley Highway, Rutherglen, Vic 3685 **Region** Rutherglen
T 0438 561 331 **www.**olivehills.com.au **Open** 7 days 10–4
Winemaker Ross Perry, Harry Perry **Est.** 1999 **Dozens** 2000 **Vyds** 15ha
The Perry family brought a historic piece of Rutherglen wine history back to life when they purchased the neglected Olive Hills mansion and 202ha of land in 1997. The original site, including vineyards, was developed by Scottish immigrant Hugh Fraser in 1886, but had long been left to time and decay. Ross and Kay Perry bought the heritage-listed house and land and set about returning it to its former glory, including vineyards and wine production. Ross had studied winemaking at Charles Sturt University, while Kay had experience in marketing and sales. Their sons, Harry and Joe, have also embraced the life, with Harry studying winemaking, and Joe planning future studies in viticulture. In 2020, the 2 sons launched a new wine range, Climb The Tower Wines, which reflects their life playing in the mansion's tower. Olive Hills Estate capitalises on its history and location by becoming a setting for weddings and functions. (JP)

🍷🍷🍷🍷♀ **Rutherglen Shiraz Malbec 2017** A meeting of 2 great minds. Why don't we see more blends of shiraz and malbec? Looking fresh and composed for a 3yo wine, resplendent in licorice, black cherry fruits, earth, cherry liqueur and attractive musky florals. Clearly enjoyed its 2 years in new French oak. Long, clean finish. Screw cap. 14.5% alc. **Rating** 93 **To** 2025 $80 JP
Rutherglen Durif 2019 The winemaker presents this wine as an ageing proposition first and foremost, noting the role of the grape's prominent tannins. It would be a shame to go early, although there are some lovely dark fruits of the forests at play here with woodsy spice, vanillan oak and dark chocolate. A slice of savouriness adds considerable interest. Screw cap. 14.5% alc. **Rating** 92 **To** 2033 $35 JP
Rutherglen Cabernet Sauvignon 2017 A father-and-son team (Ross and Harry Perry) working in Rutherglen, who do seem to like their reds on the big and cuddly side. Cabernet strikes out with deep concentration and richness, embracing a generous heart of sweet fruit. A wide, encompassing fruit call: purple berries, bramble, cassis and stewed plum. Smoky, baked earth, truffle on the palate. Leathery, ripe tannins. Definitely strikes a warm region pose. Screw cap. 14.5% alc. **Rating** 90 **To** 2025 $56 JP

🍷🍷🍷🍷 **du Cluse 2017** **Rating** 89 **To** 2027 $35 JP

Oliver's Taranga Vineyards ★★★★★

246 Seaview Road, McLaren Vale, SA 5171 **Region** McLaren Vale
T (08) 8323 8498 **www.**oliverstaranga.com **Open** 7 days 10–4
Winemaker Corrina Wright **Est.** 1839 **Dozens** 10 000 **Vyds** 90ha
William and Elizabeth Oliver arrived from Scotland in 1839 to settle in McLaren Vale. Six generations later, members of the family are still living on the Whitehill and Taranga farms. The Taranga property has 15 varieties planted (the lion's share to shiraz and cabernet sauvignon, with lesser quantities of durif, fiano, grenache, mataro, merlot, sagrantino, tempranillo, mencia, vermentino and white frontignac). Corrina Wright (the Oliver family's first winemaker) makes the wines. In 2021 the family celebrates 180 years of grapegrowing. Exports to the UK, the US, China, Singapore, Hong Kong, Denmark and Finland.

🍷🍷🍷🍷🍷 **HJ McLaren Vale Shiraz 2018** A deep crimson. Violet, blueberry, black cherry, anise, boysenberry and nori scents curl their way around a pillar of toasty mocha oak. While apparent, it is far from obtuse, operating as a welcome signpost to the wine's warmth, richness and cavalcade of flavours. Long and generous, without being loud. Screw cap. 14.5% alc. **Rating** 95 **To** 2033 $80 NG
M53 McLaren Vale Shiraz 2016 A deep crimson. A waft of quintessential warm-climate shiraz scents: freshly polished leather, varnish, dark-fruit aspersions, coffee grind, cedar and blueberry and cream. Avuncular. Like sinking into a worn armchair. The new French hogsheads are buried by the sheer depth of fruit and

extract. Powerful, sure. But not too heavy. The natural tannins, massaged. A smooth ride with a long road ahead. Screw cap. 14.5% alc. **Rating** 95 **To** 2036 $180 NG

Small Batch McLaren Vale Mencia 2020 This shows great promise. So much so, that it is already gulpable in large drafts! Boasting cool-climate syrah-like florals, white pepper, iodine, chilli and a sappy verdant note, this feels barely mid weighted as it edges its way around the mouth. Balletic, even. Impeccably ripe. Immaculate poise. Minimal ageing in older French wood. The clutch, just right. Screw cap. 14% alc. **Rating** 94 **To** 2024 $35 NG

 Small Batch McLaren Vale Fiano 2020 Rating 93 To 2025 $37 NG
DJ McLaren Vale Cabernet Sauvignon 2019 Rating 93 To 2022 $30 NG
Small Batch McLaren Vale Grenache 2020 Rating 92 To 2024 $32 NG
Small Batch McLaren Vale Brioni's Blend 2019 Rating 92 To 2022 $32 NG
The Hunt for Mrs Oliver Sparkling Fiano 2018 Rating 92 $48 NG
Chica McLaren Vale Mencia Rosé 2020 Rating 91 To 2021 $27 NG
McLaren Vale Shiraz 2019 Rating 91 To 2022 $30 NG
Small Batch McLaren Vale Vermentino 2020 Rating 90 To 2023 $27 NG

Oparina Wines ★★★★☆

126 Cameron Road, Padthaway, SA 5271 **Region** Padthaway
T 0448 966 553 **www**.oparina.com.au
Winemaker Phil Brown, Sue Bell **Est.** 1997 **Dozens** 500 **Vyds** 44ha
Oparina is the venture of Phil and Debbie Brown (along with father Terry and the three third-generation Brown children). Phil grew up in the Padthaway region on the family farm, moving to the Barossa Valley to study and then teach agriculture. He returned to the family farm (with newly planted vineyards) in 1998, simultaneously enrolling in (and completing) an oenology degree. The majority of the grapes are sold, shiraz and cabernet sauvignon finding their way into top-tier wines such as Penfolds Bin 389, Bin 707 and St Henri. Family and community commitments limited the amount of time he could devote to winemaking and in '14 Sue Bell of Bellwether Wines was contracted to make the wines, with input from Phil. Further vineyard plantings were made in '16 with small blocks of less traditional varieties.

Oranje Tractor ★★★★☆

198 Link Road, Albany, WA 6330 **Region** Great Southern
T (08) 9842 5175 **www**.oranjetractor.com **Open** Sun 11–5 or by appt
Winemaker Rob Diletti, Pamela Lincoln **Est.** 1998 **Dozens** 1000 **Vyds** 3ha
The name celebrates the 1964 vintage orange-coloured Fiat tractor acquired when Murray Gomm and Pamela Lincoln began the establishment of the vineyard. Murray was born next door, but moved to Perth to work in physical education and health promotion. Here he met nutritionist Pamela, who completed the wine science degree at CSU in 2000, before being awarded a Churchill Fellowship to study organic grape and wine production in the US and Europe. The vineyard has been certified organic since 2005.

 Albany Merlot 2018 Savoury and driven by tannins, this is a modestly plump and delicately structured wine of great interest. Perhaps not the typical dense merlot, this does have a cavalcade of salted red fruits which are held together by fine-grained, lacy tannins. A cool-climate expression of the grape, quite lovely. Screw cap. 12.5% alc. **Rating** 92 **To** 2028 $27 EL

Orlando ★★★★

Barossa Valley Way, Rowland Flat, SA 5352 **Region** Barossa Valley
T (08) 8521 3111 **www**.pernod-ricard-winemakers.com
Winemaker Ben Thoman **Est.** 1847 **Dozens** 10000 **Vyds** 14ha
Orlando is the parent who has been separated from its child, Jacob's Creek (see separate entry). While Orlando is over 170 years old, Jacob's Creek is little more than 45 years old. For what

are doubtless sound marketing reasons, Orlando aided and abetted the separation, but the average consumer is unlikely to understand the logic and, if truth be known, is unlikely to care.

ȲȲȲȲȲ **Centenary Hill Barossa Shiraz 2016** The fragrant, exotic spice of century-old Barossa vines is something to behold, heightened magnificently by carefully gauged whole-bunch fermentation. Classy, polished dark chocolate oak sits just below the fruit at every moment throughout a finish of incredible persistence and undeviating line. Quite phenomenal. Screw cap. 14.8% alc. **Rating** 97 **To** 2038 $70 TS ☻

ȲȲȲȲȲ **Jacaranda Ridge Coonawarra Cabernet Sauvignon 2016** Quintessential Coonawarra cabernet of power and promise. Deep wells of blackcurrant, blackberry and cassis take on strong licorice reflections in 2016, generously bolstered by rich coffee bean and high-cocoa dark chocolate oak. Masterfully assembled, a veritable army of fine tannins carry the finish very straight and long. Cork. 14.5% alc. **Rating** 96 **To** 2046 $65 TS ☻

ȲȲȲȲȲ **Steingarten Eden Valley Riesling 2020 Rating** 93 **To** 2028 $50 TS
Hilary Adelaide Hills Chardonnay 2019 Rating 93 **To** 2027 $35 TS
Lawson's Padthaway Shiraz 2015 Rating 93 **To** 2040 $75 TS
Bungalow Barossa Valley Cabernet Sauvignon 2015 Rating 93 **To** 2025 $35 TS
Cellar 13 Barossa Valley Grenache 2019 Rating 92 **To** 2024 $35 TS
Lyndale Adelaide Hills Chardonnay 2019 Rating 91 **To** 2026 $50 TS
Printz Shed Northern Barossa Shiraz 2018 Rating 90 **To** 2033 $35 TS

 # Otherness ★★★★

20A Park Road, Angaston, SA 5353 (postal) **Region** Barossa Valley
T 0499 819 044 **www.**otherness.com.au
Winemaker Marco Cirillo, Ian Hongell, Neil Pike, Dan Standish, Grant Dickson
Est. 2016 **Dozens** 500
Otherness is an exciting collaboration between South Australian winemakers and musician, restauranteur and wine man Grant Dickson. Well loved for his eclectic wine list in his former life at the Barossa's beloved FermentAsian, Dickson is intimately connected with the surrounding wine regions and their makers. Each cuvée is crafted by a different winemaker, representing a who's-who list of local producers. Unusually and significantly for a contract-making arrangement, each maker is declared and celebrated on the label. (TS)

ȲȲȲȲȲ **Verthandi Tasmania Riesling 2020** German rieslings were always my choice at (Otherness owner Grant Dickson's) FermentAsian restaurant, so no surprise that he's produced a stunning off-dry style himself. Made by John Hughes at Rieslingfreak, the tension of Tamar acidity is perfectly countered with residual sweetness. Spicy lime, wild lemon and crunchy Granny Smith apple fruit holds impressive drive and persistence. Tantalising now, it will live for decades. Screw cap. 9.4% alc. **Rating** 94 **To** 2040 $55 TS

ȲȲȲȲȲ **440 Barossa Valley Cabernet Sauvignon 2017 Rating** 92 **To** 2027 $55 TS

Ottelia

2280 V&A Lane, Coonawarra, SA 5263 **Region** Coonawarra
T 0409 836 298 **www.**ottelia.com.au **Open** Thurs–Mon 10–4
Winemaker John Innes **Est.** 2001 **Dozens** 8000 **Vyds** 9ha
John and Melissa Innes moved to Coonawarra intending, in John's words, to 'stay a little while'. The first sign of a change of heart was the purchase of a property ringed by red gums and with a natural wetland dotted with Ottelia ovalifolia, a native water lily. They still live in the house they built there. John worked as winemaker at Rymill Coonawarra while Melissa established a restaurant. After 20 years, John left Rymill to focus on consultancy work throughout the Limestone Coast and to establish and run Ottelia. Exports to Malaysia, Thailand, Singapore, Japan and China.

🍷🍷🍷🍷 **Padthaway Graciano 2019** A welcome new addition to the Ottelia range. The wine is expressive of the variety – the pepper, the warm, woodsy baking spices, the soft fruit and grainy tannins. It's satisfying and such a good drink – best in the short term. Screw cap. 13.4% alc. **Rating** 93 **To** 2024 $28 JF

Coonawarra Shiraz 2019 There's obviously new oak in this, adding to the smoky, charry nuances and some tannin structure. It's rich and ripe, deep and earthy. Lots of black pepper and licorice over the black plums with some bitter herbs. Full bodied with steadfast tannins, yet all in all, a solid offering. Screw cap. 14.1% alc. **Rating** 92 **To** 2029 $28 JF

Coonawarra Cabernet Sauvignon 2018 A ripe vintage yet this has a cool stamp on it. A decent mix of violets, lavender, fresh tomato leaves and mint to the cassis and currant flavours. Medium bodied with firm tannins, buoyant and good acid drive to the finish. Screw cap. 13.8% alc. **Rating** 91 **To** 2030 $36 JF

Limestone Coast Sangiovese 2019 Given its lighter frame and unpretentious outlook, this works. It starts out with florals and light red fruits with Mediterranean herbs but is in the savoury and soft realm. Raw feel to the tannins in a sangio way, with neat acidity. Earthy with a hint of leather. A perfect bistro wine. Screw cap. 13.8% alc. **Rating** 91 **To** 2024 $28 JF

Limestone Coast Pinot Gris 2020 A gris groove, with pears and baked apples all spiced up with cinnamon and fennel. Soft acidity and texture across a fuller palate, think lemon curd infused with honeysuckle. Lovely drink. Screw cap. 12.8% alc. **Rating** 90 **To** 2021 $22 JF

Limestone Coast Pinot Gris 2019 A gentle, soft gris with freshly cut pears and apples, all lightly spiced with a touch of creaminess across the palate. Refreshing and rewarding. Screw cap. 12.7% alc. **Rating** 90 **To** 2022 $22 JF

Out of Step   ★★★★★

6 McKenzie Avenue, Healesville, Vic 3777 (postal) **Region** Yarra Valley
T 0419 681 577 **www**.outofstepwineco.com
Winemaker David Chatfield, Nathan Reeves **Est.** 2012 **Dozens** 2000

Out of Step is the micro virtual winery of David Chatfield and Nathan Reeves. Nathan is currently in Tasmania on a sabbatical from the business, while David continues to work on the label as well as helping to look after the vineyards at Oakridge. Along the way they have variously chalked up experience at Stella Bella (Margaret River), Lusatia Park (now owned by De Bortoli), Sticks Yarra Valley and Vinify (California). Their initial foray was a Sauvignon Blanc from the acclaimed Willowlake Vineyard (Yarra Valley), a Chardonnay from Denton View Hill Vineyard (Yarra Valley) and a Nebbiolo from the Malakoff Vineyard in the Pyrenees. Exports to Singapore, Hong Kong and China.

Ox Hardy   ★★★★☆

207 Whitings Road, Blewitt Springs, SA 5171 **Region** McLaren Vale
T (08) 8362 8622 **www**.oxhardywines.com.au **Open** By appt
Winemaker Andrew Hardy **Est.** 2018 **Dozens** 2000 **Vyds** 45ha

It's difficult to overstate the importance of this winery. Its unbroken family line goes back to 1850 and Andrew's great-great-grandfather Thomas Hardy, oft described as the father of the SA wine industry. The interwoven links between the family and the eponymous Hardys Wines have seen an unbroken history of supply of grapes to and from the epicentre of wine production under the Thomas Hardy name for 167 years. How much by design or chance is immaterial, but some of the best vineyards in McLaren Vale and its surrounds have remained in the hands of members of the family outside the corporate structure. One such is the Upper Tintara Vineyard, established by Dr AC Kelly in 1861, purchased by Thomas Hardy in '71. In '91 he expanded the plantings with shiraz, now called Ancestor Vines, and the vineyard has been the prime source of Hardys' Eileen Hardy for 48 years. Small amounts of shiraz were made by Andrew and his late father Bob as a hobby. Since 2008 each vintage has been 70 dozen (other than '09 and '11 declassified); the '08 released in June '19, with subsequent vintages to be an ongoing annual release. Exports to Hong Kong, the UK and Singapore.

ΨΨΨΨΨ **Slate McLaren Vale Shiraz 2019** A glossy deep purple, brimming with life. Pulpy. Grapey. Effusive of violet, mace, blueberry, molten raspberry, nori and Seville orange scents. The tannins, detailed and moreish, grape skinsy and nourishing. They serve as this delicious wine's orb around which everything else revolves. Long, sappy and just firm enough. Screw cap. 14.5% alc. **Rating** 94 **To** 2026 $80 NG

ΨΨΨΨΨ **1891 Ancestor Vines Upper Tintara Vineyard McLaren Vale Shiraz 2012** **Rating** 93 **To** 2028 $225 NG
McLaren Vale Grenache 2020 **Rating** 91 **To** 2023 $38 NG

Paisley Wines   ★★★★

158 Horns Road, Angaston, SA 5353 **Region** Barossa Valley
T 0491 377 737 **www.**paisleywines.com.au
Winemaker Derek Fitzgerald **Est.** 2017 **Dozens** 1800 **Vyds** 5ha
Derek Fitzgerald made wines for nearly 20 years in WA, Langhorne Creek and the Barossa Valley before gentle persuasion by wife Kirsten led to the decision to make wine on their own account. The 3 varieties produced are classic Barossa: grenache, mataro and shiraz. Derek has winkled out some small parcels of grapes from long-proven vineyards up to 70 years old. Adelaide Hills Fiano completes the range.

ΨΨΨΨΨ **Cashmere Eden Valley Riesling 2020** Classic Eden Valley hallmarks of fresh lime, lemon and Granny Smith apple are enriched by the generosity of the low-yielding 2020 harvest in the depth and breadth of custard apple, poached pear and nutmeg. The tension of cool nights draws out a long finish of vibrant acid line. Screw cap. 12% alc. **Rating** 93 **To** 2025 $28 TS
Clurichaun Single Vineyard Barossa Valley Mataro 2018 Mataro in all its glory, celebrating a vivid contrast between depth of blackberry and plum fruit and the savoury allure of dried herbs, fresh leather and spice. Oak steps up, elevating firm, fine-grained, furry, unfined tannins and drawing out a long finish dried by warm alcohol. Everything holds its place confidently. Screw cap. 15% alc. **Rating** 93 **To** 2028 $45 TS
Linen Adelaide Hills Fiano 2020 Cleverly crafted fiano, judiciously deploying barrels, solids and bâtonnage to build character and texture, while crucially upholding varietal integrity in this subtle grape. Nashi pear and grapefruit are well supported by creamy texture and almond meal character. Cool, bright acidity and well-judged phenolic bite provide just the right level of tension to a long finish. Screw cap. 12.5% alc. **Rating** 92 **To** 2022 $25 TS ❂
Kelpie Eden Valley Shiraz 2019 The glossy, black fruit depth of the Eden Valley is heightened here in black jubes, black cherries and blueberries. Firm, fine tannins underscore a finish of even flow and persistence. A shard of powdery acidity dominates on the end, demanding time to soften and calm. Screw cap. 14.9% alc. **Rating** 92 **To** 2034 $45 TS
Maeve Single Vineyard Barossa Valley Shiraz 2018 The impact and power of Koonunga Hill are solidly framed in the flavour and structure of French and American oak barrels. Spicy, ripe dark berry/cherry/prune and licorice fruit leads out, slightly contracted in the wake of long barrel maturation. Warm alcohol and firm oak tannins conspire on a firm, dry finish. Screw cap. 14.8% alc. **Rating** 91 **To** 2026 $60 TS

ΨΨΨΨ **Turntable Barossa Valley GSM 2018** **Rating** 89 **To** 2028 $25 TS

Palmer Wines   ★★★★☆

1271 Caves Road, Dunsborough, WA 6281 **Region** Margaret River
T (08) 9756 7024 **www.**palmerwines.com.au **Open** 7 days 10–5
Winemaker Mark Warren, Bruce Dukes, Clive Otto **Est.** 1977 **Dozens** 6000 **Vyds** 51.39ha
Steve and Helen Palmer have mature plantings of cabernet sauvignon, sauvignon blanc, shiraz, merlot, chardonnay and semillon, with smaller amounts of malbec and cabernet franc. Recent vintages have had major success in WA and national wine shows.

ΨΨΨΨΩ **Purebred by Marc Warren Sauvignon Blanc 2019** Sweaty thiol funk on the nose. This is concentrated passionfruit, mushroom, sugar snap pea and gooseberry all jumbled into one. On the palate it is flavoursome and bouncy – the acidity courses through the fruit leaving a salty trail in its wake. Screw cap. 12.3% alc. **Rating** 92 **To** 2024 $27 EL

Margaret River Amour Rosé 2020 Unoaked grenache rosé. Soft blush pink in the glass, This has a fine phenolic thread that works its way through the forest of raspberry, pomegranate, rosewater and brine. Balanced, supple and long. Screw cap. 13.3% alc. **Rating** 92 **To** 2024 $30 EL

Margaret River Sauvignon Blanc Semillon 2019 Concentrated tropical fruits and crushed nuts. The saline acidity weaves its way through the fruit. Very fresh and punchy. Screw cap. 12.1% alc. **Rating** 91 **To** 2024 $37 EL

Margaret River Malbec 2019 Matured for 13 months in French oak (33% new). Vibrant, intense and saturated flavour; blackcurrant pastille, raspberry and nutmeg. The acidity is juicy and ripe, reminiscent of red apples. Screw cap. 14.3% alc. **Rating** 91 **To** 2031 $35 EL

ΨΨΨΨ **Krackerjack Bin 117 Sauvignon Blanc Semillon 2019 Rating** 88 **To** 2021 $20 EL

Purebred by Bruce Dukes Cabernet Sauvignon 2015 Rating 88 **To** 2030 $44 EL

Paracombe Wines ★★★★

294b Paracombe Road, Paracombe, SA 5132 **Region** Adelaide Hills
T (08) 8380 5058 **www**.paracombewines.com **Open** By appt
Winemaker Paul Drogemuller **Est.** 1983 **Dozens** 15 000 **Vyds** 22.1ha

Paul and Kathy Drogemuller established Paracombe Wines in 1983 in the wake of the devastating Ash Wednesday bushfires. The winery is located high on a plateau at Paracombe, looking out over the Mount Lofty Ranges, and the vineyard is run with minimal irrigation and hand pruning to keep yields low. The wines are made onsite, with every part of the production process through to distribution handled from there. Exports to the UK, Canada, Denmark, Sweden, Luxembourg, Singapore and China.

ΨΨΨΨΩ **Adelaide Hills Pinot Blanc 2020** Lots to like here, from an alluring aroma that carries multiple suggestions, sea spray and white citrus blossom among them. It all flows onto the palate in a neatly balanced, fresh, savoury and saline style that begs for the company of top-shelf seafood. Screw cap. 11% alc. **Rating** 93 **To** 2022 $23 TL ✪

The Reuben 2016 The epitome of Australian bordeaux blending: 37/32/23/6/2% cabernet sauvignon/merlot/cabernet franc/malbec/shiraz. A well-woven, understated yet classic aromatic introduction, similarly expressed on the palate. Complex and confident, a distinctive energy and freshness as well. Recommended at such an attractive price. Screw cap. 14.6% alc. **Rating** 93 **To** 2026 $25 TL ✪

Adelaide Hills Shiraz 2016 Well crafted and balanced evenly, with classic cool-climate spice over dark fruits. Medium to full bodied, settled into its skin with 5 years of age on it, the 30% new oak integrated. And great value. Screw cap. 14.6% alc. **Rating** 92 **To** 2026 $25 TL ✪

Caretaker Adelaide Hills Cabernet Sauvignon 2017 This is a nothing-but-the-truth kind of cabernet sauvignon, leafy, herbal, fragrant to start, with a delicious, medium-weighted palate, blackberry/currant notes, with an almost creamy texture. Tannins are soft and supportive. Nothing too complex, yet nothing out of place either. Screw cap. 14% alc. **Rating** 92 **To** 2028 $65 TL

Adelaide Hills Malbec 2016 A single-vineyard small-production wine. There's an immediate aromatic statement here: black cherries, typical varietal violet florals, earthy spice, crumbled rich soil, all of those elements flowing into the palate with added structure from alcohol and tannin. A big wine that will suit lamb and beef barbecues over charcoal. Screw cap. 14.8% alc. **Rating** 92 **To** 2028 $30 TL

ΨΨΨΨ   Adelaide Hills Riesling 2020 Rating 89 To 2026 $21 TL
Adelaide Hills Viognier 2019 Rating 89 To 2025 $35 TL
Adelaide Hills Gruner V5 2019 Rating 89 To 2023 $23 TL
Adelaide Hills Red Ruby 2020 Rating 89 To 2022 $21 TL
Dimenticato Adelaide Hills Shiraz 2017 Rating 89 To 2027 $50 TL
Melrose Shiraz 2017 Rating 89 To 2025 $35 TL

Paradigm Hill   ★★★★☆

26 Merricks Road, Merricks, Vic 3916 **Region** Mornington Peninsula
T 0408 039 050 **www**.paradigmhill.com.au **Open** W'ends 12–5
Winemaker Dr George Mihaly **Est.** 1999 **Dozens** 1500 **Vyds** 4.2ha
Dr George Mihaly (with a background in medical research, biotechnology and pharmaceutical
industries) and wife Ruth (a former chef and caterer) realised a 30-year dream of establishing
their own vineyard and winery, abandoning their previous careers to do so. George had all
the necessary scientific qualifications and built on those by making the 2001 Merricks Creek
wines, moving to home base at Paradigm Hill in '02. The vineyard, under Ruth's control,
is planted to 2.1ha of pinot noir, 0.9ha of shiraz, 0.82ha of riesling and 0.38ha of pinot gris.
Exports to the US, Germany, Singapore and China.

ΨΨΨΨΩ   **Adesso Mornington Peninsula Pinot Noir 2019** The most charming pinot
in the range, thanks to its perfume and flavours of spiced cherries, plums, orange
peel and a certain minty undertone. It's refreshing and close to lighter framed,
although the tannins hold some sway. It finishes convincingly. Screw cap. 13.9% alc.
Rating 92 To 2029 $79 JF
L'ami Sage Mornington Peninsula Pinot Noir 2019 A surprisingly delicate
rendition in a way, with a faint scent of rose petals, earth and cinnamon, moving to
a core of sweet cherries. The palate is soft, easy and almost fades away before the
oak tannins kick in, adding some shape and grit. Drink this in its youth as that's
the appeal. Screw cap. 13.8% alc. **Rating** 91 To 2028 $69 JF

ΨΨΨΨ   Mornington Peninsula Pinot Gris 2020 Rating 89 To 2024 $55 JF

Paradise IV   ★★★★★

45 Dog Rocks Road, Batesford, Vic 3213 (postal) **Region** Geelong
T (03) 5276 1536 **www**.paradiseivwines.com.au
Winemaker Douglas Neal **Est.** 1988 **Dozens** 800 **Vyds** 3.1ha
The former Moorabool Estate was renamed Paradise IV for the very good reason that it
is the site of the original Paradise IV Vineyard, planted in 1848 by Swiss vigneron Jean-
Henri Dardel. It is owned by Ruth and Graham Bonney. The winery has an underground
barrel room and the winemaking turns around wild-yeast fermentation, natural mlf, gravity
movement of the wine and so forth. Exports to China.

Paralian Wines   ★★★★☆

21 Eden Terrace, Port Willunga, SA 5171 **Region** McLaren Vale/Adelaide Hills
T 0413 308 730 **www**.paralian.com.au **Open** By appt
Winemaker Skye Salter, Charlie Seppelt **Est.** 2018 **Dozens** 450
Charlie Seppelt and Skye Salter have covered many miles and worked in many places since
they met in 2008 working the vintage at Hardys Tintara in McLaren Vale. By the time they
took the plunge and established Paralian Wines in '18 they had accumulated 46 vintages
between them, working for others. The name is a noun for someone who lives by the sea.
Charlie's first exposure to McLaren Vale was as a vintage casual at d'Arenberg and it was
vinous love at first sight. He and Skye headed off overseas, a high point undertaking vintage
in Burgundy. He headed back to Australia, she went on to the Languedoc, seemingly ideal,
but found it as depressing as Burgundy had been inspirational. They agreed McLaren Vale,
and in particular Blewitt Springs, was the place they wanted to make grenache and shiraz with
high fragrance and brightness, grenache joining pinot noir as a high-class wine to be enjoyed

young or much later. No fining or additions are used other than SO₂ and little requirement for new oak. Watch this space.

🍷🍷🍷🍷🍷 **Marmont Vineyard McLaren Vale Grenache 2020** A stellar vintage in these parts: extract and freshness, a holy duopoly. Fragrant, febrile, mid-weighted of feel, despite the concentration and totem of juicy tannins. Spindly, detailed and drenched in tamarind, turmeric and clove, akin to the sensations of a souk. This is like sucking on an orange mulled with sour cherry and exotica. Long and gorgeous. Value! I am pouring another glass, one-handed, as I finish the note. Screw cap. 14% alc. **Rating** 96 **To** 2027 $42 NG ✪

🍷🍷🍷🍷🍷 **Blewitt Springs McLaren Vale Grenache Shiraz 2020 Rating** 93 **To** 2025 $36 NG

Paringa Estate   ★★★★★

44 Paringa Road, Red Hill South, Vic 3937 **Region** Mornington Peninsula
T (03) 5989 2669 **www**.paringaestate.com.au **Open** 7 days 11–5
Winemaker Lindsay McCall, Jamie McCall **Est.** 1985 **Dozens** 15 000 **Vyds** 30.5ha
Schoolteacher-turned-winemaker Lindsay McCall became known for an absolutely exceptional gift for winemaking across a range of styles but with immensely complex pinot noir and shiraz leading the way. The wines have an unmatched level of success in the wine shows and competitions that Paringa Estate is able to enter; the limitation being the relatively small production of the top wines in the portfolio. His skills are no less evident in contract winemaking for others. But time has passed and son Jamie joined the winemaking team in 2012, after completing winemaking and viticulture at the University of Adelaide, Waite Campus. He was put in charge of winemaking at Paringa Estate in '17 following 5 home vintages and one in Oregon, focusing on pinot noir. Exports to the UK, Denmark, Ukraine, Singapore, Japan, Hong Kong and China.

🍷🍷🍷🍷🍷 **The Paringa Single Vineyard Shiraz 2019** Vying for top spot as the finest The Paringa to date, it manages to harness overall power through a prism of elegance. Awash with black ripe plums and satsuma, too. Incredibly spicy, with pepper and cardamom in the mix, the oak merely playing backup. Full bodied, with precision tannins, some grainy texture and great persistence. Wow. Screw cap. 14% alc. **Rating** 96 **To** 2034 $80 JF

Estate Shiraz 2019 Outrageous colour – wonderful deep purple, with a rich red rim. This is magnificent. Dark fruits infused with black pepper, woodsy spices and juniper set the flavour profile. The full-bodied palate is complex and detailed. Oak adds another layer of depth, yet there's a controlled vibrancy and freshness throughout. Screw cap. 14% alc. **Rating** 96 **To** 2033 $50 JF ✪

The Paringa Single Vineyard Chardonnay 2019 While the Estate chardonnay works off a racy, linear theme and offers more class, The Paringa is all power. More of everything in this. More malty oak, mlf, lots of barrel ferment flavours, a density across the palate and lots of reduction – funky and flinty sulphides loved by many. As its power has been harnessed, it's behaving. Just. Screw cap. 13.5% alc. **Rating** 95 **To** 2029 $80 JF

Estate Chardonnay 2019 This is good. Really good. Eschewing mlf has resulted in a racy wine with layers of flavour, initially of the citrus persuasion. Grapefruit, lemon and a touch of mandarin, plus a decent smattering of spices. Savoury, moreish, a touch of flint and mouth-watering acidity. It gives more and more with each sip. Screw cap. 13.5% alc. **Rating** 95 **To** 2029 $45 JF

Robinson Vineyard Pinot Noir 2019 Deep, rich and voluptuous. An amalgam of black cherries, kirsch, wood spice and menthol, but it's most definitely in the savoury spectrum. Full bodied, with firm tannins, yet there's some squishy texture across the palate and lively acidity throughout. Impressive. Screw cap. 13.5% alc. **Rating** 95 **To** 2032 $80 JF

Estate Pinot Noir 2019 A defining feature of this vintage (apart from lower yields) is accessibility in the wines. Here the Estate offers plushness, personality and satisfaction. Expect juniper and red cherries, with a sprinkling of baking spices infused into a fuller-bodied style. Smooth, supple tannins sashay across the palate. Screw cap. 13.5% alc. **Rating** 95 **To** 2029 $65 JF

Peninsula Shiraz 2019 A vibrant garnet/purple hue; a core of ripe plums, with a flash of cloves, cinnamon, all warm spices and florals. The palate is savoury, with an appealing succulence bolstered by supple tannins and terrific freshness. It seems vintage '19 suits shiraz from this region. Screw cap. 13.5% alc. **Rating** 95 **To** 2029 $29 JF ☉

ŶŶŶŶ♀ **The Paringa Single Vineyard Pinot Noir 2017 Rating** 93 **To** 2030 $100 JF
The Paringa Single Vineyard Pinot Noir 2019 Rating 92 **To** 2033 $100 JF

Parker Coonawarra Estate ★★★★★

15688 Riddoch Highway, Penola, SA 5263 **Region** Coonawarra
T (08) 8737 3525 **www.parkercoonawarraestate.com.au Open** 7 days 10–4
Winemaker James Lienert, Andrew Hardy, Keeda Zilm **Est.** 1985 **Dozens** 30 000
Vyds 20ha
Parker Coonawarra Estate is at the southern end of Coonawarra, on rich terra rossa soil over limestone. Cabernet sauvignon is the dominant variety (17.45ha), with minor plantings of merlot and petit verdot. It is now part of WD Wines, which also owns Hesketh Wine Company, St John's Road, Vickery Wines and Ox Hardy. Production has risen substantially since the change of ownership. Exports to all major markets.

ŶŶŶŶŶ **Kidman Block 2019** A lovely shiraz from a lovely vintage. Excellent dark garnet with a shot of purple. Deep, earthy, savoury flavours wash over black plums and cherries. Fuller bodied, with beautiful tannins – plush, ripe and velvety soft. A long persistent finish completes a compelling wine. Screw cap. 14.5% alc. **Rating** 96 **To** 2034 $65 JF ☉

S.B.W. Simpatico McLaren Vale Coonawarra Shiraz Cabernet Sauvignon 2019 The most complete and balanced wine of the SBW range this vintage. Excellent dark garnet, flushed with purple. It's a deliciously savoury wine, although spiced-up dark fruits are at its core. Fuller bodied and plush, with lightly drying tannins and great persistence. Screw cap. 14.5% alc. **Rating** 95 **To** 2034 $65 JF

ŶŶŶŶ♀ **Terra Rossa Shiraz 2019 Rating** 93 **To** 2029 $34 JF
95 Block 2018 Rating 93 **To** 2038 $65 JF
S.B.W. Evita Coonawarra Barossa Valley Shiraz Malbec 2019 Rating 93 **To** 2028 $34 JF
Terra Rossa Merlot 2019 Rating 91 **To** 2028 $34 JF

Passel Estate ★★★★

655 Ellen Brook Road, Cowaramup, WA 6284 **Region** Margaret River
T (08) 9717 6241 **www.passelestate.com Open** 7 days 10.30–5
Winemaker Bruce Dukes **Est.** 1994 **Dozens** 1500 **Vyds** 6.7ha
Wendy and Barry Stimpson were born in England and South Africa respectively and, during numerous visits to Margaret River over the years, fell in love with the region's environment. They made Margaret River home in 2005 and in '11 purchased and expanded the vineyard, which is planted to shiraz, cabernet sauvignon and chardonnay. Viticulturist Andy Ferreira manages the vineyard with sustainable practices, keeping yields restricted to 6.5–7t/ha. The very talented and highly experienced contract winemaker Bruce Dukes is responsible for the wines. Exports to Singapore and Hong Kong.

ŶŶŶŶŶ **Lot 71 Reserve Margaret River Cabernet Sauvignon 2016** Plush and velvety, the relatively late release has catapulted this into a delicate balance of both age and freshness. It's ready to go now, although the hallmarks for ageing are there as well. Satsuma plums, briny acid and fine, shapely tannins. Screw cap. 14% alc. **Rating** 95 **To** 2036 $96 EL

Margaret River Sauvignon Blanc 2019 20% barrel fermented in new French oak, 80% in stainlesss steel, blended post-fermentation, then left on lees and stirred fortnightly for 5 months until bottling. The nose has a really attractive corporeal funk to it – reminiscent of skin after an ocean swim. The palate is delicate and fine, the oaked component providing a plush bed of texture on which the delicate fruit lingers. Complex layers of texture elevate this to serious. Screw cap. 13% alc. **Rating** 94 **To** 2030 $30 EL ✪

Passing Clouds   ★★★★☆

30 Roddas Lane, Musk, Vic 3461 **Region** Macedon Ranges
T (03) 5348 5550 **www.**passingclouds.com.au **Open** 7 days 10–5
Winemaker Cameron Leith **Est.** 1974 **Dozens** 5500 **Vyds** 5ha

Graeme Leith and son Cameron undertook a monumental change when they moved the entire operation that started way back in 1974 in Bendigo to its new location at Musk, near Daylesford. The vines at Bendigo had been disabled by ongoing drought and all manner of pestilence, and it was no longer feasible to continue the business there. However, they still have a foot in Bendigo courtesy of their friends, the Adams at Rheola. Graeme has now left the winemaking in the hands of Cameron, instead using his formidable skills as a writer. Cameron and wife Marion have made a coup with the establishment of a new train stop (and dedicated platform) at the Passing Clouds cellar door and winery at Musk. The venture is the result of a collaboration between Passing Clouds, Spa Country Railway and the Victorian Regional Development Wine Growth Fund. The development has led to the incorporation of a restaurant (open Mon–Fri) and structured tastings built around the food. Exports to all major markets.

🍷🍷🍷🍷🍷 **Estate Macedon Ranges Chardonnay 2019** It has some verve yet is luscious and inviting. Rich, ripe stone fruit and ginger spice, clotted cream and honey with tangy acidity. Lots going on and a lot to like. Screw cap. 13% alc. **Rating** 93 **To** 2028 $47 JF
Serpentine Bendigo Shiraz 2019 Fruit is sourced from a single block within the Serpentine vineyard. This is no wallflower. Packed with flavour – all plums, blackberry jam, licorice, coffee grounds and charry oak. Full bodied and assertive; deep and earthy with fleshy, plump tannins. There's a gloss to this – partly from the alcohol but thankfully everything falls into place, and convincingly so. Screw cap. 15% alc. **Rating** 93 **To** 2034 $53 JF
Bendigo Shiraz 2019 Smells of the Aussie bush with its eucalyptus and paperbark aromas – not too much, just enough for enjoyment and a desire to be in such a location. Enmeshed within are flavours of red plums, baking spices and gritty tannins. A good drink in anyone's book. Screw cap. 14.8% alc. **Rating** 93 **To** 2032 $34 JF
Bendigo Riesling 2020 Expect balm and blossom aromas, yet quite a fruity palate at first with white peach, lemon juice and zest. Softish acidity but enough to guide the gentle sweetness on the finish. A lovely drink. Screw cap. 11.6% alc. **Rating** 92 **To** 2026 $34 JF
Graeme's Shiraz Cabernet 2019 A plush, very ripe offering from this vintage yet it holds its own. Blackberries and blueberries, sweetly-fruited and dabbed with cloves, eucalyptus and licorice, which all work across the full-bodied palate. Ripe tannins and a generosity that allows for immediate appeal. Screw cap. 15% alc. **Rating** 90 **To** 2030 $34 JF
The Angel 2019 Cabernet sauvignon. Teems with all manner of blackberry accents from fresh fruit, compote to jam. It's a riper offering but it doesn't go entirely overboard. Tannins have some grit, with a bitter edge. While it finishes with some alcohol warmth, overall this is rather stern and somewhat closed. Best to cellar for a few more years. Screw cap. 14% alc. **Rating** 90 **To** 2034 $53 JF

Patina ★★★★★

109 Summerhill Lane, Orange, NSW 2800 **Region** Orange
T (02) 6362 8336 **www**.patinawines.com.au **Open** Fri–Mon 11–5
Winemaker Gerald Naef **Est.** 1999 **Dozens** 2500 **Vyds** 3ha

Gerald Naef's home in Woodbridge in California was surrounded by the vast vineyard
and winery operations of Gallo and Robert Mondavi. It would be hard to imagine a more
different environment than that provided by Orange. Gerald and wife Angie left California
in 1981, initially establishing an irrigation farm in northwest NSW; 20 years later they moved
to Orange and by 2006 Gerald was a final-year student at wine science at CSU. He set up a
micro-winery at the Orange Cool Stores, his first wine the trophy-winning '03 Chardonnay.

🍷🍷🍷🍷🍷 **Museum Release Orange Cabernet Merlot 2006** Of all museum releases
here (and I've tasted a few), this is by far the best. A digestible luncheon claret:
impeccably poised, medium bodied and immensely savoury. A bow of nourishing
tannin, massaged with bottle age and well-appointed oak, drawn taut by high-
country freshness. The fruit, bright and rich as it fades into a halcyon senescence.
Plum, Asian medicine, tea leaf, currant, mint, tobacco and graphite. A beautiful
wine at its apogee. Cork. 13.5% alc. **Rating** 96 **To** 2027 $65 NG ✪
Museum Release Reserve Orange Chardonnay 2004 This has plenty of
merit. The aromas, rather brilliant: toasted hazelnut, orange verbena, truffle and
cheesecloth. The palate, still brimming with life and good crunchy length. I'd take
advantage of the opportunity to drink a fine domestic chardonnay with this sort
of age, knitted to a producer with the moxie to show it. Screw cap. 12.3% alc.
Rating 94 **To** 2024 $65 NG

🍷🍷🍷🍷🍷 **Sticky Tea Orange Riesling 2018 Rating** 93 **To** 2027 $25 NG ✪
Reserve Orange Chardonnay 2017 Rating 93 **To** 2028 $55 NG
Scandalous Orange Riesling 2017 Rating 92 **To** 2027 $25 NG ✪
Orange Chardonnay 2018 Rating 91 **To** 2026 $35 NG

Patrick of Coonawarra ★★★★☆

Cnr Ravenswood Lane/Riddoch Highway, Coonawarra, SA 5263 **Region** Coonawarra
T (08) 8737 3687 **www**.patrickofcoonawarra.com.au **Open** 7 days 10–5
Winemaker Luke Tocaciu **Est.** 2004 **Dozens** 5000 **Vyds** 93.5ha

Patrick Tocaciu (who died in 2013) was a district veteran, with prior careers at Heathfield
Ridge Winery and Hollick Wines. Wrattonbully plantings (almost 55ha) cover all the
major varieties, while in Coonawarra the low-yielding Home Block (cabernet sauvignon) is
supplemented by a second vineyard of 17.5ha of cabernet and smaller amounts of riesling and
sauvignon blanc. Patrick of Coonawarra also carries out contract winemaking for others. Son
Luke, with a degree in oenology from the University of Adelaide and vintage experience in
Australia and the US, has taken over in the winery.

🍷🍷🍷🍷🍷 **Home Block Cabernet Sauvignon 2015** There's no doubting the quality here,
although spending 2 years in French and American barriques, 50% new, makes
a strong statement. A riper style, with plush tannins – but some grip, too. While
it will continue to age well, start enjoying it now, while it has a balance of fruit.
Screw cap. 13.8% alc. **Rating** 95 **To** 2030 $45 JF

🍷🍷🍷🍷🍷 **Two Blocks Riesling 2020 Rating** 92 **To** 2030 $25 JF ✪
Cabernet Sauvignon 2016 Rating 92 **To** 2028 $29 JF
P Series by Patrick Limestone Coast Rosé 2020 Rating 91 **To** 2022
$19 JF ✪
Two Blocks Cabernet Sauvignon 2018 Rating 90 **To** 2030 $32 JF

Patritti Wines

13–23 Clacton Road, Dover Gardens, SA 5048 **Region** Adelaide
T (08) 8296 8261 **www**.patritti.com.au **Open** Mon–Sat 9–5 (7 days Dec)
Winemaker James Mungall, Ben Heide **Est.** 1926 **Dozens** 190 000 **Vyds** 16ha
A family-owned business with impressive vineyard holdings of 10ha of shiraz in Blewitt Springs and 6ha of grenache at Aldinga North. The surging production points to success in export and also to the utilisation of contract-grown as well as estate-grown grapes. Patritti is currently releasing wines of very high quality at enticing prices and a range of lesser-quality wines at unfathomably low prices. The JPB Single Vineyard celebrates Giovanni Patritti, who arrived in Australia in 1925; he sold his wines under the 'John Patritti Brighton' label. Exports to the UK, Sweden, Germany, Poland, India, Vietnam and China.

Marion Vineyard Adelaide Grenache Shiraz 2018 From one of the last genuine urban vineyards in Adelaide, in the Marion council district, and vinified nearby in Patritti's suburban winery. This wine's sourcing and story is as exciting as the wine in the glass. A 90/10% grenache/shiraz blend from old vines, with 6 months in a range of new (10%) and older oak, 60/40% American/French. Plenty of just-out-of-the-oven baking spice aroma to begin, hot cross bun, energetic crimson fruits, with a bath of rich, earthy tannins on the palate. So much to love about this wine. Cork. 14.5% alc. **Rating** 94 **To** 2028 $40 TL

JPB Single Vineyard Shiraz 2019 **Rating** 93 **To** 2030 $70 TL
Merchant Adelaide Hills Pinot Grigio 2020 **Rating** 92 **To** 2022 $25 TL ❂
Lot Three Single Vineyard McLaren Vale Shiraz 2019 **Rating** 92 **To** 2029 $40 TL
Merchant McLaren Vale Shiraz 2019 **Rating** 91 **To** 2027 $25 TL
Blewitt Springs Estate Eden Valley Riesling 2020 **Rating** 90 **To** 2023 $18 TL ❂
Adelaide Hills Vermentino 2019 **Rating** 90 **To** 2022 $24 TL
Merchant McLaren Vale Grenache Shiraz Mourvèdre 2019 **Rating** 90 **To** 2025 $25 TL
Adelaide April Red 2020 **Rating** 90 **To** 2022 $24 TL

Paul Conti Wines

529 Wanneroo Road, Woodvale, WA 6026 **Region** Greater Perth
T (08) 9409 9160 **www**.paulcontiwines.com.au **Open** Tues–Sat 11–5
Winemaker Jason Conti **Est.** 1948 **Dozens** 4000 **Vyds** 11ha
Third-generation winemaker Jason Conti has assumed control of winemaking, although father Paul (who succeeded his own father in 1968) remains involved in the business. Over the years Paul challenged and redefined industry perceptions and standards. The challenge for Jason is to achieve the same degree of success in a relentlessly and increasingly competitive market environment, and he is doing just that. There are 4 estate vineyards; 3 in Greater Perth, in Carabooda (chenin blanc), at the homestead property in Woodvale (nero d'Avola), and in Mariginiup (shiraz), and one in Wilyabrup in Margaret River (planted to chardonnay, sauvignon blanc, muscat à petit grains, malbec, cabernet sauvignon and shiraz). Exports to Malaysia.

Lorenza Sparkling Chenin Blanc NV Pretty and floral – all the lovely chenin-y things are there; lanolin, citrus fruits, summer apricots and waxy texture. The phenolics are fine and serve to cradle the fruit, contributing to the already plump mouthfeel. Fabulous aperitif-style chenin. Cork. 12.5% alc. **Rating** 95 $25 EL ❂
Tuart Block Chenin Blanc 2020 Pure and fine, the palate has a satisfying textural complexity before extending into the long finish. Overall, this is almost simple in its expression of chenin, but absolutely true to the variety. White pepper through the finish. Trophy Swan Valley Wine Show 2020. Screw cap. 13.5% alc. **Rating** 94 **To** 2030 $18 EL ❂

Margaret River Chardonnay 2020 **Rating** 93 **To** 2028 $25 EL ❂
Pemberton Pinot Noir 2020 **Rating** 91 **To** 2025 $25 EL
Nero d'Avola 2019 **Rating** 91 **To** 2027 $20 EL ❂

Paul Nelson Wines ★★★★★

14 Roberts Road, Denmark, WA 6333 (postal) **Region** Great Southern
T 0406 495 066 **www**.paulnelsonwines.com.au **Open** School hols 11–5
Winemaker Paul Nelson **Est.** 2009 **Dozens** 1500 **Vyds** 2ha
Paul Nelson started making wine with one foot in the Swan Valley, the other in the Great
Southern, while completing a bachelor's degree in viticulture and oenology at Curtin
University. He then worked successively at Houghton in the Swan Valley, Goundrey in Mount
Barker, Santa Ynez in California, South Africa (for 4 vintages), hemisphere-hopping to the
Rheinhessen, 3 vintages in Cyprus, then moving to a large Indian winemaker in Mumbai
before returning to work for Houghton. He has since moved on from Houghton and (in
partnership with wife Bianca) makes small quantities of table wines.

ΨΨΨΨΨ **Karriview Vineyard Denmark Chardonnay 2018** Curry leaf, grilled yellow
peach, brine, red apple skin, salted stone-fruit succulence. This is viscous and
rich with a cool-climate saline line of acid straight down the centre of the
palate. Really impressive length of flavour. Minerality and crushed shell alongside
thundering depth of flavour and juicy acid. Screw cap. 13.5% alc. **Rating** 97
To 2035 $65 EL ✪ ♥
Loam Frankland River Syrah 2019 Elegant, fine, restrained and frothing with
red fruits and exotic spice. The persistent length of flavour ultimately defines
this wine, although it is the most supple and delicate syrah made in the region.
Interesting, often the most expensive wines have the most oak thrown at them …
this has been made with a light hand, the oak seamlessly and imperceptibly
countersunk into the fruit. Cork. 13.5% alc. **Rating** 97 To 2041 $95 EL ✪

ΨΨΨΨΨ **Karriview Vineyard Denmark Pinot Noir 2018** Sour red cherry and field
strawberry at the height of summer meander out of the glass, backed by spicy,
freshly ground nutmeg. On the palate, pomegranate underpins a tight line of acid
that courses over the tongue, and the tannins prop up the fine fruit, keeping it
all in line. This is restrained and exciting. Shapely tannins ultimately define this
savoury pinot noir, capable of gracefully evolving for decades. Screw cap. 13.5% alc.
Rating 96 To 2041 $65 EL ✪

ΨΨΨΨΨ **Nodus Tollens Geographe Arneis 2020 Rating** 93 To 2027 $30 EL
Army of Grapes Riesling 2020 Rating 90 To 2025 $20 EL ✪

Paul Osicka ★★★★★

Majors Creek Vineyard at Graytown, Vic 3608 **Region** Heathcote
T (03) 5794 9235 **www**.paulosickawines.com.au **Open** By appt
Winemaker Simon Osicka **Est.** 1955 **Vyds** 13ha
The Osicka family arrived from Czechoslovakia in the early 1950s. Vignerons in their own
country, their vineyard in Australia was the first new venture in central and southern Victoria
for over half a century. With the return of Simon Osicka to the family business, there have
been substantial changes. Simon held senior winemaking positions at Houghton, Leasingham,
and as group red winemaker for Constellation Wines Australia, interleaved with vintages in
Italy, Canada, Germany and France, working at the prestigious Domaine Jean-Louis Chave for
the '10 vintage. The fermentation of the red wines has changed from static to open fermenters
and French oak has replaced American. Extensive retrellising of the 65yo estate plantings
is now complete. Installation of a conveyor belt enables 100% berry sorting and eliminates
pumping; installation of new vats is another improvement. Paul Osicka, Simon's father, passed
away in 2019 after 50 vintages and over 60 years of involvement in the vineyards. Exports to
Denmark.

ΨΨΨΨΨ **Heathcote Majors Creek Vineyard Shiraz 2019** The maker reported low
yields from small bunches and tiny berries in 2019, evident in the concentration
of fruit flavour here. The big man, Simon Osicka, delivers nuance like few others,
the juxtaposition of black cherry and fennel here, the dollop of lilting spice and

anise there, and all the while a quiet, driving power and intensity, but also elegance. A wine for contemplation in a COVID-weary world. Screw cap. 14.5% alc. Rating 95 To 2034 $35 JP ✪

Moormbool Heathcote Shiraz 2019 A most individual shiraz, one that is both plummy and cherry-laden but also dark and savoury, blending both worlds through 18 months in seasoned French oak vats. Ripe cherry, bracken, woody spices, moving into a thick, velvety density, kept in check by savoury tannins. Screw cap. 14.5% alc. Rating 95 To 2034 $50 JP

Majors Creek Vineyard Heathcote Cabernet Sauvignon 2019 Cabernet sauvignon has always been a strength at Paul Osicka Wines, often taking a starring role in many vintages. Clearly, resolutely cabernet from the outset, with restrained fruit and a tight focus on structure and tannins that go and go. It's still early days, with assured blackcurrant, wild berries, toasted spices and baked earth which are set to shine for some time. Screw cap. 14.5% alc. Rating 95 To 2032 $35 JP ✪

Paulett Wines   ★★★★☆

752 Jolly Way, Polish Hill River, SA 5453 **Region** Clare Valley
T (08) 8843 4328 **www**.paulettwines.com.au **Open** 7 days 10–5
Winemaker Neil Paulett, Jarrad Steele **Est.** 1983 **Dozens** 35 000 **Vyds** 79.5ha
The Paulett story is a saga of Australian perseverance, commencing with the 1982 purchase of a property with 1ha of vines and a house, promptly destroyed by the terrible Ash Wednesday bushfires the following year. Son Matthew joined Neil and Alison Paulett as a partner in the business some years ago; he is responsible for viticulture on the property holding, much expanded following the purchase of a large vineyard at Watervale. The winery and cellar door have wonderful views over the Polish Hill River region, the memories of the bushfires long gone. Exports to the UK, Denmark, Germany, Singapore, Malaysia, China and NZ.

 Polish Hill River Riesling 2020 Pristine, linear and tight. Flavours of lemon, lime, even grapefruit in the mix, with wafts of wet stone and ginger powder. It's long and energising, the acidity ensuring it lengthens out and lingers long. Screw cap. 12.5% alc. Rating 95 To 2028 $30 JF ✪

Polish Hill River Aged Release Riesling 2016 Mid straw hue but not overtly showing much age. The aromas do though, and it's drying on the finish. However, there's lovely toasty notes, with brioche and butter slathered with lime marmalade. Depth across the palate, with baked ricotta drizzled in a spicy lemon glaze. While the palate feels rich and almost voluminous, the tight acid lines come in and makes short shrift of that. Screw cap. 12.8% alc. Rating 94 To 2025 $75 JF

 Pauletts 109 Clare Valley Riesling 2020 Rating 93 To 2030 $90 JF
Polish Hill River Late Harvest Riesling 2020 Rating 92 To 2027 $25 JF ✪
Polish Hill River Shiraz 2018 Rating 91 To 2028 $30 JF
Alison Botrytis Riesling 2020 Rating 91 To 2026 $30 JF

Paulmara Estates   ★★★★☆

144 Seppeltsfield Rd, Nuriootpa, SA 5355 **Region** Barossa Valley
T 0417 895 138 **www**.paulmara.com.au **Open** By appt
Winemaker Jason Barrette **Est.** 1999 **Dozens** 650 **Vyds** 13ha
Born to an immigrant Greek family, Paul Georgiadis grew up in Waikerie, where his family had vineyards and orchards. His parents worked sufficiently hard to send him first to St Peters College in Adelaide and then to Adelaide University to do a marketing degree. He became the whirlwind grower-relations manager for Southcorp, and one of the best-known faces in the Barossa Valley. Paul and wife Mara established a vineyard in 1995, currently planted to shiraz, sangiovese, mataro, nero d'Avola and cabernet sauvignon. Part of the production is sold, and the best shiraz makes the Syna Shiraz ('syna' being Greek for together).

Syna Barossa Shiraz 2017 The concentrated black-fruit density and impact that defines Marananga finds a tangy drive in the cool 2017 season. Firm French oak sits before the fruit in both nutty flavour and firm tannin grip. It holds the persistence and structural integrity to hold out until fruit and oak ultimately unite. Cork. 14.5% alc. **Rating** 94 **To** 2037 $60 TS

🍷🍷🍷🍷♀ **MARAnanga Barossa Valley Shiraz 2019 Rating** 92 **To** 2034 $30 TS

Paxton

68 Wheaton Road, McLaren Vale, SA 5171 **Region** McLaren Vale
T (08) 8323 9131 **www**.paxtonvineyards.com **Open** 7 days 10–5
Winemaker Dwayne Cunningham, Kate Goodman (Consultant) **Est.** 1979
Dozens 32 000 **Vyds** 82.5ha

David Paxton is of one Australia's most successful and respected viticulturists, with a career spanning over 40 years. He started his successful premium grower business in 1979 and has been involved with planting and managing some of the most prestigious vineyards in McLaren Vale, Barossa Valley, Yarra Valley, Margaret River and Adelaide Hills for top global wineries. There are 6 vineyards in the family holdings in McLaren Vale: Thomas Block (25ha), Jones Block (22ha), Quandong Farm (18ha), Landcross Farm (2ha), Maslin (3ha) and 19th (12.5ha). All are certified organic and biodynamic, making Paxton one of the largest biodynamic producers in Australia. The vineyards have some of the region's oldest vines, including the 125yo EJ shiraz. His principal focus is on his own operations in McLaren Vale with Paxton Wines, established in '98 as a premium shiraz, grenache and cabernet producer. The cellar door sits on Landcross Farm, a historic 1860s sheep farm in the original village consisting of limestone houses and shearing shed. Exports to the UK, the US, Canada, Denmark, France, Germany, Sweden, the Netherlands, Russia, Finland, Japan, Malaysia, Singapore, Hong Kong, Taiwan and China.

🍷🍷🍷🍷🍷 **Quandong Farm Single Vineyard McLaren Vale Shiraz 2019** The first Paxton vineyard to adopt a biodynamic regime. The complex bouquet has sweet dark berry fruits, spice and wood smoke (not bushfire) aromas, and a medium- to full-bodied palate that stays light on its feet in a wealth of licorice, juniper and savoury, earthy notes. Screw cap. 14% alc. **Rating** 96 **To** 2034 $30 JH ❂

🍷🍷🍷🍷♀ **EJ McLaren Vale Shiraz 2018 Rating** 93 **To** 2030 $100 NG
NOW McLaren Vale Shiraz 2020 Rating 91 **To** 2024 $25 NG
McLaren Vale Graciano 2020 Rating 91 **To** 2024 $30 NG
McLaren Vale Pinot Gris 2020 Rating 90 **To** 2023 $22 NG
McLaren Vale Rosé 2020 Rating 90 **To** 2022 $22 NG

Payne's Rise

10 Paynes Road, Seville, Vic 3139 **Region** Yarra Valley
T (03) 5964 2504 **www**.paynesrise.com.au **Open** Thurs–Sun 11–5
Winemaker Franco D'Anna (Contract) **Est.** 1998 **Dozens** 2000 **Vyds** 5ha

Tim and Narelle Cullen have progressively established 5ha of cabernet sauvignon, shiraz, pinot noir, chardonnay and sauvignon blanc since 1998. They carry out all the vineyard work. Tim is also a viticulturist for a local agribusiness. Narelle is responsible for sales and marketing. The contract-made wines have won both gold medals and trophies at the Yarra Valley Wine Show since '10, echoed by success at the Victorian Wines Show. Exports to China.

🍷🍷🍷🍷♀ **Mr Jed Yarra Valley Pinot Noir 2020** A very pale ruby but it belies the flavours within. Juicy tangy cherries, chinotto and pink grapefruit all lightly spiced. It is on the leaner side and the tannins somewhat sinewy but should settle in. Super-refreshing as it is. Screw cap. 12.5% alc. **Rating** 91 **To** 2030 $35 JF
Yarra Valley Chardonnay 2020 It's tightly coiled and doesn't want to give too much away. Certainly lots of citrus is woven through, with a smidge of nougatine with creamy curd lees flavours. The palate is taut and refined with refreshing acidity that is doing the muscle work. A bit more time to settle will do wonders. Screw cap. 12.5% alc. **Rating** 90 **To** 2028 $30 JF

Peccavi Wines

1121 Wildwood Road, Yallingup Siding, WA 6282 **Region** Margaret River
T 0404 619 861 **www**.peccavi-wines.com **Open** By appt
Winemaker Bruce Dukes, Remi Guise **Est.** 1996 **Dozens** 6000 **Vyds** 16.5ha

Jeremy Muller was introduced to the great wines of the world by his father when he was young and says he spent years searching New and Old World wine regions (even looking at the sites of ancient Roman vineyards in England), but did not find what he was looking for until one holiday in Margaret River. There he found a vineyard in Yallingup that was available for sale and he did not hesitate. He quickly put together an impressive contract winemaking team and appointed Colin Bell as viticulturist. The wines are released under 2 labels: Peccavi for 100% estate-grown fruit (all hand-picked) and No Regrets for wines with contract-grown grapes and estate material. The quality of the wines is very good, reflecting the skills and experience of Bruce Dukes. Exports to the UK, Canada, Sweden, Malaysia, Singapore, Japan, Hong Kong and South Korea.

99999 **Estate Margaret River Merlot 2018** We're taught to seek bitter cocoa and mulberry in merlot, but outside of Bordeaux, those characters rarely assert themselves with any conviction. Until now. There is a new clone in Margaret River from Bordeaux – Clone 181. The first thing that hits you is the structure. The tannins serve not only to shape the powerful (textbook) fruit, but they assert themselves so obviously that they become the hallmark of the wine. There is no doubt this is the greatest merlot in Australia. Prove me wrong. Screw cap. 14% alc. **Rating** 98 **To** 2051 $150 EL ✪ ♥

99999 **Margaret River Cabernet Sauvignon 2018** A savoury, oak-driven and tannic wine, built for long-haul cellaring rather than short-term enjoyment. The length of flavour shows what an experienced winemaker (Bruce Dukes) can do with great fruit. At this stage, the nose, palate and finish are dominated by oak, however there is no doubt as to its quality. Buy it and quickly intern it in the cellar before you are tempted to prematurely open a bottle. Not a typical Margaret River cabernet. Screw cap. 14.5% alc. **Rating** 95 **To** 2046 $75 EL
Margaret River Chardonnay 2018 Rich, textural and piled high with ripe orchard fruits. This is the power and density of the Gingin clone. Great length of flavour. A layered and almost opulent wine with acid that creates a nervy tension on the palate. Premier cru stuff, here. Screw cap. 13% alc. **Rating** 94 **To** 2030 $65 EL

99999 **No Regrets Margaret River Cabernet Merlot 2020** **Rating** 91 **To** 2028 $26 EL

Peel Estate

290 Fletcher Road, Karnup, WA 6176 **Region** Peel
T (08) 9524 1221 **www**.peelwine.com.au **Open** 7 days 10–5
Winemaker Will Nairn, Mark Morton **Est.** 1973 **Dozens** 4000 **Vyds** 4ha

Peel's icon wine is the Shiraz, a wine of considerable finesse and with a remarkably consistent track record. Every year till 2019 Will Nairn held a Great Shiraz Tasting for 6yo Australian shiraz, pitting Peel Estate (in a blind tasting attended by 100 or so people) against Australia's best; it was never disgraced. The wood-matured Chenin Blanc is another winery specialty. Exports to the UK and China.

99999 **Old Vine Zinfandel 2018** With 16% alcohol and a back label that states 'Wimps beware!' you know what you're getting yourself into … On the palate this is far softer and rounder than expected, the alcohol presents itself after the wine has gone – one could breathe fire. For lovers of the variety, this is plush, ripe and very succulent. Licorice, quince, date, mulberry, raspberry, chocolate and fig. Screw cap. 16% alc. **Rating** 93 **To** 2031 $50 EL

Peerick Vineyard ★★★★

Wild Dog Track, Moonambel, Vic 3478 **Region** Pyrenees
T (03) 5467 2207 **www.peerick.com.au Open** W'ends & public hols 11–4
Winemaker Chris Jessup, Mount Langhi Ghiran (Dan Buckle) **Est.** 1990 **Dozens** 2000
Peerick is the venture of Chris Jessup and wife Meryl. They have mildly trimmed their
Joseph's coat vineyard by increasing the plantings to 5.6ha and eliminating the malbec
and semillon, but still grow cabernet sauvignon, shiraz, cabernet franc, merlot, sauvignon
blanc and viognier. Quality has improved as the vines have reached maturity. Exports to NZ.

 Pyrenees Shiraz 2019 A dash (3%) of viognier definitely makes an impression
in the almost iridescent purple colour. It's there in the lifted aromatics, too, floral
and striking together with blackberry, plum and licorice. The palate belies the
high-ish alcohol. Yes, there is a generosity of fruit and quiet underlying oak, but
it all sits mid weighted with structure and a solid backbone. Smart winemaking.
Screw cap. 14.9% alc. **Rating** 92 **To** 2027 $30 JP
Pyrenees Cabernet Sauvignon 2018 Peerick is located on harsh and thirsty
soils with little top soil and plenty of shale and quartz. The result, as seen here, is
medium bodied with an almost mineral-like tangy mouthfeel and easy balance.
It suits cabernet well, allowing a gentle, leafy earthiness and vibrant red berries to
shine. Oak is handled just so, promoting the fruit to the centre stage. Screw cap.
13.5% alc. **Rating** 90 **To** 2026 $30 JP
The Mang Pyrenees 2019 A single-vineyard blend of hand-picked
43/42/10/5% merlot/cabernet sauvignon/shiraz/cabernet franc. Wild-yeast
fermentation, 15% whole bunches in closed fermenters. Matured for 12 months
in French oak (30% new). Intended to be approachable in its youth and still have
something in reserve for later on. Inviting plummy, sweet-fruited cherry, raspberry,
red licorice and leafy notes. Good concentration on the palate, fleshy and velvety
over the tongue with dry tannins. Screw cap. 13.8% alc. **Rating** 90 **To** 2026 $40 JP

Pembroke ★★★☆

191 Richmond Road, Cambridge, Tas 7170 **Region** Tasmania
T (03) 6278 3808 **www.**pembrokewines.com.au **Open** Most w'ends
Winemaker Contract **Est.** 1980 **Dozens** 200 **Vyds** 1.3ha
The Pembroke vineyard was established in 1980 by the McKay and Hawker families. Still
owned by them, it is now one of the oldest vineyards in the Coal River Valley area, and is
planted to pinot noir.

 Tasmania Pinot Noir 2019 Vibrant purple hue. The black-fruit presence of
the Coal River Valley contrasts with the rigid framework of French oak. Spicy
blackberries and mulberries take on fruitcake spice, backed by fine oak tannin
grip that calls for time to integrate. It holds the fruit integrity and acid line to go
the distance. A long finish is accented with notes of bouquet garni. Screw cap.
13.8% alc. **Rating** 92 **To** 2029 $65 TS

Penfolds ★★★★★

30 Tanunda Road, Nuriootpa, SA 5355 P16 **Region** Barossa Valley
T (08) 8568 8408 **www.penfolds.com Open** 7 days 10–5
Winemaker Peter Gago **Est.** 1844
Penfolds is the star in the crown of Treasury Wine Estates (TWE) but its history predates the
formation of TWE by close on 170 years. Its shape has changed in terms of its vineyards, its
management, its passing parade of great winemakers and its wines. There is no other single
winery brand in the New or the Old World with the depth and breadth of Penfolds. Retail
prices range from less than $20 to $950 for Grange, which is the cornerstone, produced every
year, albeit with the volume determined by the quality of the vintage, not by cash flow. There
is now a range of regional wines of single varieties and the Bin Range of wines that includes
both regional blends and (in some instances) varietal blends. Despite the very successful

Yattarna and Reserve Bin A Chardonnays, and some impressive rieslings, this remains a red wine producer at heart. Exports to all major markets.

ΨΨΨΨΨ **Yattarna Bin 144 Chardonnay 2018** An ultra-cool climate blend of Tasmania, Tumbarumba and Adelaide Hills fruit wastes no time in setting the terms of engagement with a wine of infinite class. The flinty/smoky aromas introducing an almost painful intensity on the mercurial palate, a celebration of white-fleshed stone fruits. It has made light work of 8 months in 100% new French oak. Struts its stuff without a care in the world. Screw cap. 13% alc. **Rating** 99 **To** 2033 $175 ✪ ❤
Grange Bin 95 2016 Penfolds nailed the great 2016 vintage, making a wine that is perfect in every way. The blend of 97% shiraz and 3% cabernet sauvignon comes from the Barossa Valley, McLaren Vale, Clare Valley and Magill Estate in Adelaide, in that order, and as usual spent 18 months in new American hogsheads. Its detail is superb, with light and shade allowing blackberry and plum fruit pride of place, but there's also flashes of spice and licorice. It's as mouth-watering with the last taste as the first, and 7.3g/l of acidity leaves the mouth fresh. Cork. 14.5% alc. **Rating** 99 **To** 2066 $950 JH
Reserve Bin A Adelaide Hills Chardonnay 2019 Hand picked, whole-bunch pressed, part direct to barriques for wild ferment and 100% mlf, the balance via tank for brief settling before 8 months in French oak (80% new). A beautifully detailed chardonnay, white peach and pink grapefruit plus supple creamy cashew run through the very long palate. Rubs shoulders with the best in the land. Screw cap. 13% alc. **Rating** 98 **To** 2030 $125 JH ✪
Bin 707 Cabernet Sauvignon 2018 From McLaren Vale, Coonawarra, Barossa Valley, Wrattonbully, Robe and Adelaide Hills, the oak from America (100% new), and 18 months' worth at that. Can cabernet sauvignon ever be seductive? Not if it's compared to pinot noir or modern grenache. But if approached on its own terms, the answer here is yes. Penfolds' wizardry with tannins coats the mouth with as much opulent red fruit and warm vanillan oak, each of the 3 components balancing the others. It's a triumph in the context of the vintage. Climate change casualty? No way. Cork. 14.5% alc. **Rating** 98 **To** 2048 $650 JH
RWT Bin 798 Barossa Valley Shiraz 2018 This full-bodied shiraz spent 16 months in French hogsheads (64% new, 36% 1yo). The red winemaking team at Penfolds has the game by the throat here. It's flashy, it's opulent, its depth of black fruits and surrounds of oak and tannins sweep away any resistance. But beware of the pea and thimble trick – it needs at least 10 years to let you come up for air. Cork. 14.5% alc. **Rating** 97 **To** 2053 $200 JH
Bin 169 Coonawarra Cabernet Sauvignon 2018 This is a close relative of RWT Bin 798 – single region and 100% French oak – and is dramatically different from Bin 707. This is a purist's cabernet, turning its face on the mastery of the regional blending that is the birthmark of the Penfolds red wine style. Vive la différence. Tannin is the heartbeat here, cassis and olive tapenade wrapped around the tannin, not vice versa. A roasted side of baby lamb is the way to go. Cork. 14.5% alc. **Rating** 97 **To** 2043 $360 JH

ΨΨΨΨΨ **Bin 51 Eden Valley Riesling 2020** The low yield and cool conditions from Jan through to harvest have resulted in a wine humming with the full box and dice of citrus blossoms and flavours; perfectly poised acidity promises a long future. Top class wine. Screw cap. 12% alc. **Rating** 96 **To** 2030 $40 JH ✪
St Henri Shiraz 2017 The cool and late vintage kissed the wine on both cheeks, making the classic maturation in 50yo vats doubly welcome. A glimpse of the future is the use of fruit from Port Lincoln joining the Barossa Valley, McLaren Vale, and Eden Valley in the blend. This has none of the hardness that sometimes gives an edge to St Henri, purity stepping in to its sculpted palate. Includes 3% cabernet sauvignon. Screw cap. 14.5% alc. **Rating** 96 **To** 2047 $135 JH
Bin 389 Cabernet Shiraz 2018 This '20 release marks the 60th anniversary of Bin 389. It is a 57/43% blend from McLaren Vale, Barossa Valley, Padthaway, Coonawarra, Robe and Wrattonbully, matured in American hogsheads (38% new). A perennial favourite of mine, though the price does cause me to blink. It has

great colour, and a supple mouthfeel that invests the wine with a hint of elegance, underlined by the fluid, flawless balance, the length a given. Screw cap. 14.5% alc. Rating 96 To 2040 $100 JH

Bin 150 Marananga Barossa Valley Shiraz 2018 A relatively recent addition to the Penfolds red wine line up, the impact of the first release ('08) still fresh in my mind. A relentless fusion of ripe berry fruits, earth and licorice, packed with ripe tannins and new oak (25% each French and American). From the heart of the valley floor, and proud of it. Screw cap. 14.5% alc. Rating 95 To 2038 $100 JH

Bin 128 Coonawarra Shiraz 2018 Twelve months maturation in French hogsheads (26% new) resulted in a wine with a vivid yet deep crimson-purple hue that duly delivered on the promise of its colour. A light-year away from the style of the '80s, American oak providing more flavour than the fruit. Now there's a velvety-smooth abundance of plum, blackberry compote and spice couched in soft, but persistent, tannins. Screw cap. 14.5% alc. **Rating** 94 **To** 2038 $60

Bin 407 Cabernet Sauvignon 2018 From Coonawarra, Padthaway, Wrattonbully, McLaren Vale, Barossa Valley and Robe, matured for 12 months in French (21% new) and American hogsheads (9% new). The warm vintage was mitigated in part by the major Limestone Coast components. Medium to full-bodied, with pronounced blackcurrant varietal fruit expression framed by sage and bay leaf, and appropriately firm cabernet tannins that add both texture and structure. Give it as much time as possible, however accessible it is now. Screw cap. 14.5% alc. **Rating** 94 **To** 2038 $110 JH

🍷🍷🍷🍷♀ **Bin 311 Chardonnay 2019** Rating 93 To 2025 $50 JH
Bin 23 Tasmania Adelaide Hills Henty Pinot Noir 2019 Rating 93 To 2030 $50 JH
Bin 28 Kalimna Shiraz 2018 Rating 92 To 2028 $50 JH
Bin 138 Barossa Valley Shiraz Grenache Mataro 2018 Rating 91 To 2028 $60 JH

Penfolds Magill Estate   ★★★☆

78 Penfold Road, Magill, SA 5072 **Region** Adelaide
T (08) 8301 5569 **www.**penfolds.com **Open** 7 days 9–6
Winemaker Peter Gago **Est.** 1844 **Vyds** 5.2ha
This is the birthplace of Penfolds, established by Dr Christopher Rawson Penfold in 1844. His house is still part of the immaculately maintained property that includes 5.2ha of precious shiraz vines used to make Magill Estate Shiraz and the original and subsequent winery buildings, most still in operation or in museum condition. In May 2015 Penfolds unveiled the redevelopment of Magill Estate with the opening of a new cellar door (where visitors can taste Grange by the glass) and Magill Estate Kitchen, a casual dining environment with a grazing menu built on local and fresh ingredients and meant for sharing. The much-awarded Magill Estate Restaurant, with its panoramic views of the city, remains a temple for sublime food and wine matching. Exports to all major markets.

🍷🍷🍷🍷🍷 **Magill Estate Shiraz 2018** The only single-vineyard wine in the entire Penfolds lineup, spending 17 months in French (24% new) and American hogsheads (18% new). This vintage has a far greater weight and personality than this often shy, understated wine. Red and black cherry fruit, spice and rounded – indeed polished – tannins give the wine a regal air. Cork. 14.5% alc. **Rating** 96 **To** 2038 $150 JH

Penley Estate   ★★★★★

McLeans Road, Coonawarra, SA 5263 **Region** Coonawarra
T (08) 8736 3211 **www.**penley.com.au **Open** 7 days 10–4
Winemaker Kate Goodman, Lauren Hansen **Est.** 1988 **Dozens** 48 000 **Vyds** 111ha
In 1988 Kym, Ang and Bec Tolley joined forces to buy a block of land in Coonawarra – Penley Estate was underway, the amalgamation of a 5th-generation wine family Penfold and

Tolley. In 2015 Ang and Bec took full ownership of the company. They have made a number of changes, welcoming general manager Michael Armstrong and, even more importantly, appointing Kate Goodman as winemaker. Behind the scenes Ang's husband David Paxton, one of Australia's foremost viticulturists, has been working as a consultant, with improvements in vineyard performance already evident. In December '17, Penley also opened a cellar door in the main street of McLaren Vale. Exports to all major markets.

🍷🍷🍷🍷🍷 **Helios Coonawarra Cabernet Sauvignon 2019** Despite the hefty 1.6kg bottle, this wine is anything but weighty. An excellent dark garnet hue, it's resplendent with pure cabernet aromas and flavours. A latent power and beauty at the same time, with exceptional tannins, long and finely chiselled. Cork. 14.5% alc. **Rating** 97 **To** 2044 $150 JF ❂

🍷🍷🍷🍷🍷 **Chertsey Coonawarra 2018** A 3-way bet of 70/20/10% cabernet sauvignon/merlot/cabernet franc. They must be magic numbers, because this is an enchanting outcome. The aromas are like perfume: all floral, blackberries and exotic spices. But it is the palate that really puts on the charm. Medium bodied, exquisite tannins and vivacious, yet elegant throughout. Screw cap. 14% alc. **Rating** 96 **To** 2033 $75 JF ❂
Eos Coonawarra Shiraz Cabernet Sauvignon 2018 There's a certain power and depth built into this. Awash with dark fruit and darker spices, fuller bodied, with a gloss and a shine to the tannins that make it appealing. It's going to age superbly. Cork. 13.5% alc. **Rating** 95 **To** 2038 $100 JF
Steyning Coonawarra Cabernet Sauvignon 2018 This 100% cabernet will evolve superbly, a hallmark of this majestic variety. But it is also approachable now, with the appealing freshness of bright dark fruit. It's lightly scented, delicately spiced with powdery tannins and finishes long. Screw cap. 14% alc. **Rating** 95 **To** 2033 $75 JF

🍷🍷🍷🍷🍷 **Phoenix Coonawarra Cabernet Sauvignon 2019** **Rating** 93 **To** 2027 $20 JF ❂
Tolmer Coonawarra Cabernet Sauvignon 2019 **Rating** 93 **To** 2033 $30 JF
Project VIII Shiraz Cabernet Sauvignon 2020 **Rating** 92 **To** 2025 $50 JF
Project E Coonawarra Cabernet Sauvignon 2020 **Rating** 92 **To** 2033 $50 JF

Penna Lane Wines   ★★★★

Lot 51 Penna Lane, Penwortham via Clare, SA 5453 **Region** Clare Valley
T 0403 462 431 **www**.pennalanewines.com.au **Open** Fri–Sun 11–5
Winemaker Peter Treloar, Steve Baraglia **Est.** 1998 **Dozens** 4500 **Vyds** 4.37ha
Penna Lane is located in the beautiful Skilly Valley, 10km south of Clare. The estate vineyard (shiraz, cabernet sauvignon and semillon) is planted at an elevation of 450m, which allows a long, slow ripening period, usually resulting in wines with intense varietal fruit flavours.

🍷🍷🍷🍷🍷 **Clare Valley Shiraz 2018** No shortage of anything in this red, starting with its deep, dark garnet hue. Expect soused black plums dripping with mint chocolate and licorice plus a kitchen cabinet full of spices. Full bodied, yet the tannins are plump and expansive, the palate silky and aside from the slightly warm finish, this hits the spot. Screw cap. 14.5% alc. **Rating** 92 **To** 2028 $28 JF
Skilly Valley Riesling 2020 A pared-back style with an invitation to drink it now. Delicate florals, ginger spice and citrus are the main players. The palate is light with juicy acidity. Screw cap. 12.5% alc. **Rating** 91 **To** 2028 $28 JF

Penny's Hill   ★★★★☆

281 Main Road, McLaren Vale, SA 5171 **Region** McLaren Vale
T (08) 8557 0800 **www**.pennyshill.com.au **Open** Mon–Sat 10–5, Sun 11–5
Winemaker Alexia Roberts **Est.** 1988 **Dozens** 60 000 **Vyds** 44ha

Founded in 1988 by Tony and Susie Parkinson, Penny's Hill produces high-quality shiraz (Footprint and The Skeleton Key) from its close-planted McLaren Vale estate, also the source of the Edwards Road Cabernet Sauvignon and The Experiment Grenache. Malpas Road and Goss Corner vineyards complete the estate holdings, providing fruit for Cracking Black Shiraz and Malpas Road Merlot. White wines (The Agreement Sauvignon Blanc and The Minimalist Chardonnay) are sourced from 'estates of mates' in the Adelaide Hills. Also includes the Black Chook and Thomas Goss Brands. Penny's Hill cellars are located at the historic Ingleburne Farm, which also houses the award-winning The Kitchen Door restaurant and Red Dot Gallery. Noted for its distinctive 'red dot' packaging. Exports to Canada, the US, China, Malaysia, Thailand, NZ, South Korea and Germany.

Peos Estate

1124 Graphite Road, Manjimup, WA 6258 **Region** Manjimup
T (08) 9772 1378 **www.peosestate.com.au Open** By appt
Winemaker Willow Bridge (Kim Horton) **Est.** 1996 **Dozens** 13 000 **Vyds** 37.5ha
The Peos family has farmed in the west Manjimup district for almost a century, the 3rd generation of 4 brothers developing the vineyard from 1996. There are over 37ha of vines including shiraz, merlot, chardonnay, cabernet sauvignon, sauvignon blanc, pinot noir and verdelho.

ŸŸŸŸŸ Four Kings Single Vineyard Manjimup Shiraz 2019 Smelling this elicited a smile, such is the vibrancy and potent intensity of the aromatics: blackberry, violets, fennel flower, licorice. The palate is juicy, fleshy and almost bouncy – the tannins have a jolly chew about them that trampolines the flavours around the mouth. Once gone, the wine leaves a satisfying, cleansing aftertaste. Screw cap. 14.5% alc. Rating 95 To 2027 $32 EL ✪

Four Kings Single Vineyard Manjimup Pinot Noir 2020 Pure and silky, this has loads of creamy cherry fruit that teeters on the front of the palate. It topples onto the tongue in a crash of red licorice, peppercorn, crunchy redcurrants, olive, black tea and fennel flower. Unfurling flavours through the finish reveal more intricacies as time goes on. Who says WA can't do pinot? Screw cap. 14% alc. Rating 94 To 2031 $32 EL

Four Aces Single Vineyard Manjimup Shiraz 2019 Anise, blackberry, licorice and ripe raspberry. On the palate this falls in line, showing the depth of fruit that the aromas hinted at. At this stage, the presence of oak is still very evident, contributing a resin/cigar box character to the dense fruit. While it's closed right now, the concentration of fruit shows how it will evolve. Give it some time either in the cellar or the decanter. Screw cap. 14% alc. Rating 94 To 2036 $40 EL

Four Aces Single Vineyard Manjimup Cabernet Sauvignon 2019 Concentrated and dense blackberry fruit sings against a backdrop of dried herbs and exotic spice. Density is the order of the day, spooling out into layers of lingering flavour. Super-smart cabernet, here. Screw cap. 14.5% alc. Rating 94 To 2031 $40 EL

ŸŸŸŸŸ Four Aces Single Vineyard Manjimup Chardonnay 2020 Rating 92 To 2028 $35 EL

Four Aces Single Vineyard Manjimup Pinot Noir 2020 Rating 92 To 2031 $45 EL

Four Kings Single Vineyard Manjimup Cabernet Sauvignon 2019 Rating 92 To 2031 $32 EL

Pepper Tree Wines

86 Halls Road, Pokolbin, NSW 2320 **Region** Hunter Valley
T (02) 4909 7100 **www.peppertreewines.com.au Open** Mon–Fri 9–5, w'ends 9.30–5
Winemaker Dylan Thompson **Est.** 1991 **Dozens** 50 000 **Vyds** 172.1ha
Pepper Tree is owned by geologist Dr John Davis. It sources the majority of its Hunter Valley fruit from its Davis Family Vineyard at Mt View, but also has premium vineyards at Orange,

Coonawarra and Wrattonbully. The highly credentialled Gwyn Olsen ('12 Dux, Advanced Wine Assessment Course, AWRI; '14 Young Winemaker of the Year, Gourmet Traveller WINE; '15 Rising Star of the Year, Hunter Valley Legends Awards; and '15 Len Evans Tutorial Scholar) was appointed winemaker in '15. Exports to the UK, Canada, Denmark, Finland, Singapore, the US and China.

🍷🍷🍷🍷🍷 **Single Vineyard Premium Reserve Alluvius Hunter Valley Semillon 2010** A stunning bright yellow, glinted with green. Lightweight. Balletic, even. Fine bones of pumice-like acidity juxtaposed against a thrust of intense flavour. Perhaps the finish is not as long as it once was, although for this sacrifice, one reaps a high level of aromatic complexity: buttered white toast, quince and lime marmalade, lemon drop and barley water. Delicious drinking. I wouldn't wait much longer. Screw cap. 11% alc. **Rating** 94 **To** 2023 $75 NG

Limited Release Orange Shiraz 2019 A shimmering ruby with purple edges transmitting vibrancy and joy across the aromatic spectrum: iodine, boysenberry, pepper grind, clove and smoked meat, all given levity by soaring violet florals. The reductive handling, savvy. The finish, long and effortless. Screw cap. 13.8% alc. **Rating** 94 **To** 2024 $35 NG

Limited Release Red Hill Hunter Valley Shiraz 2019 A mid-weighted luncheon red in the traditional style of the Hunter, with a contemporary sheen. All in French oak (20% new) with a seasoning of 30% whole bunches, helping to attenuate the tannins, while imparting a dash of spicy complexity. Nicely construed. Plenty of red fruit, earth, cinnamon and spice, but structurally furled around the pillar of oak at its core. I'd give this an aggressive decant. Expands nicely in the glass, with the tannins pliant and just tactile enough, coaxing the fruit long. A lovely drink. Screw cap. 13.5% alc. **Rating** 94 **To** 2028 $40 NG

🍷🍷🍷🍷🍷 **Limited Release Tallavera Hunter Valley Shiraz 2010** Rating 93 To 2025 $70 NG

Limited Release The Pebbles Wrattonbully Shiraz Viognier 2018 Rating 93 To 2028 $35 NG

Premium Reserve Single Vineyard Block 21A Wrattonbully Cabernet Sauvignon 2018 Rating 93 To 2032 $60 NG

Premium Reserve Calcare Single Vineyard Coonawarra Cabernet Sauvignon 2018 Rating 93 To 2032 $45 NG

Single Vineyard Elderslee Road Reserve Wrattonbully Cabernet Sauvignon 2018 Rating 93 To 2020 $45 NG

Premium Reserve Calcare Single Vineyard Coonawarra Cabernet Sauvignon 2010 Rating 93 To 2025 $75 NG

Single Vineyard Strandlines Grand Reserve Wrattonbully Cabernet Shiraz 2018 Rating 93 To 2030 $60 NG

Coquun Premium Shiraz Blend Hunter Valley Shiraz 2010 Rating 92 To 2024 $130 NG

Single Vineyard Reserve The Gravels Wrattonbully Shiraz Viognier 2018 Rating 92 To 2024 $45 NG

Museum Release Single Vineyard Strandlines Wrattonbully Shiraz Cabernet 2010 Rating 92 To 2024 $90 NG

Limited Release Coonawarra Rosé 2020 Rating 91 To 2021 $30 NG

🌿 Peppergreen Estate

13 Market Place, Berrima, NSW 2577 **Region** Southern Highlands
T (02) 4877 1070 **www.**peppergreenestate.com.au **Open** Wed–Mon 10–5
Winemaker Balog Brothers (Contract), Kiri Irving (Contract) **Est.** 2016 **Dozens** 3750
Vyds 16ha
Established in 2016 with a cellar door in the bucolic Southern Highlands town of Berrima, Peppergreen Estate's proprietary vineyard is tucked away in nearby Canyonleigh at 700m elevation, complete with olive oil processing and a high-quality restaurant that serves 'modern French' cuisine. Pinot noir, shiraz, riesling and chardonnay are all grown on the

estate's holdings as the owners endeavour to appropriate ideal grape varieties to the cool climate of the region, while acknowledging the encroaching influence of global warming. As it stands, the traditionally crafted sparkling wines show promise, having spent extended time on lees to impart a toasty complexity and creamy generosity to the twang of the cooler zone. (NG)

ꝐꝐꝐꝐꝐ **Single Vineyard Southern Highlands Pinot Gris 2019** A wine of considerable viscosity despite the lowish alcohol. Textural and pliant, relying on a chewiness more than any acidity for its structural composure. It reminds me of a white Rhône, as much as oily gris from Alsace. Asian pear, marzipan and dried-straw scents billow along to a convincing finish, just a bit hot. Screw cap. 12.9% alc. **Rating** 90 **To** 2024 $30 NG

ꝐꝐꝐꝐ **Southern Highlands Chardonnay 2018 Rating** 89 **To** 2024 $35 NG
Orange Cabernet Sauvignon 2018 Rating 89 **To** 2025 $35 NG
Southern Highlands Pinot Noir 2018 Rating 88 **To** 2023 $45 NG

Petaluma ★★★★★

254 Pfeiffer Road, Woodside, SA 5244 **Region** Adelaide Hills
T (08) 8339 9300 **www**.petaluma.com.au **Open** 7 days 10–5
Winemaker Mike Mudge, Amy Hickling, Dave Horne **Est.** 1976 **Dozens** 130 000
Vyds 240ha

The Petaluma range has been expanded beyond the core group of Croser sparkling, Clare Valley Riesling, Piccadilly Valley Chardonnay and Coonawarra Merlot. Newer arrivals of note include Adelaide Hills Viognier and Shiraz. The plantings in the Clare Valley, Coonawarra and Adelaide Hills provide a more than sufficient source of estate-grown grapes for the wines. A new winery and cellar door opened in 2015 on a greenfield site with views of Mount Lofty. In '17 Petaluma (along with all wine brands owned by Lion Nathan) was acquired by Accolade. Exports to all major markets.

ꝐꝐꝐꝐꝐ **Hanlin Hill Clare Valley Riesling 2020** An austere style, but impressive, with its steely drive and length. It starts out a bit shy, with a hint of florals and dried herbs, but opens up to quite a generous palate for a Clare Valley riesling. As expected, lots of citrussy flavours of lemon and zest, tangerine too. The acidity appears soft yet refreshing. Screw cap. 13.5% alc. **Rating** 95 **To** 2030 $36 JF
Piccadilly Valley Chardonnay 2019 A richer house style. The oak and fruit have found harmony, with senses of seaside airs as well. The peach/nectarine stone-fruit flavours swell on the palate. The balance is right, with a subtle vanilla essence note on the finish. This carries the flag for old-school/traditional chardonnay lovers. Screw cap. 14.2% alc. **Rating** 95 **To** 2026 $54 TL
B&V Vineyard Adelaide Hills Shiraz 2018 An intense dark colour. Masses of rich shiraz fruit, with the oak woven through to start – but not to add timber, more a dark set of Asian spices, anise and nutmeg among it. These dwell on the palate before a wave of sticky tannins wash in, providing a foundation for a long, rich finish. Screw cap. 14% alc. **Rating** 95 **To** 2028 $54 TL
Evans Vineyard Coonawarra 2015 85/15% cabernet sauvignon/merlot, cold soaked then fermented on skins for 2 weeks, matured in new French oak for 20 months. The new oak impacts on both the flavour and texture. Needs time to integrate, as it surely will over the next 5+ years. Great potential. Screw cap. 14.5% alc. **Rating** 95 **To** 2040 $73 JH
Croser Piccadilly Valley Pinot Noir Chardonnay 2015 Disgorged Nov '20. The fruit shows its class on the nose here, with a faint background aldehyde note for interest. The citrus-focused palate hits a straight line, supporting creamy apple-bun characters that arise along with its excellent mouthfeel. Par excellence. Diam. 14% alc. **Rating** 95 $40 TL

ꝐꝐꝐꝐꝐ **Coonawarra Merlot 2018 Rating** 93 **To** 2034 $77 JF
Croser Late Disgorged 2006 Rating 93 $67 TL
Croser Non Vintage Adelaide Hills Rosé NV Rating 93 $30 TL

Evans Vineyard Coonawarra 2016 **Rating** 92 **To** 2032 $77 JF
White Label Coonawarra Shiraz 2019 **Rating** 91 **To** 2029 $30 JF
White Label Dry Coonawarra Rosé 2020 **Rating** 90 **To** 2022 $29 JF
Adelaide Hills NV **Rating** 90 $30 TL

Peter Drayton Wines ★★★★

Ironbark Hill Vineyard, 694 Hermitage Road, Pokolbin, NSW 2321
Region Hunter Valley
T (02) 6574 7085 **www**.pdwines.com.au **Open** 7 days 10–5
Winemaker Damien Stevens, Peter Drayton **Est.** 2001 **Dozens** 20000 **Vyds** 16.5ha
Owned by Peter and Leesa Drayton. The estate plantings include shiraz, chardonnay, semillon,
cabernet sauvignon, tempranillo, merlot, verdelho and tyrian. Peter is a commercial/industrial
builder, so constructing the cellar door was a busman's holiday. The vineyard features an
atmospheric function venue and wedding chapel set among the vines, with events organised
and catered for by Enzo Weddings. Exports to Vietnam, Hong Kong and China.

ΨΨΨΨ♀ **Anomaly Hunter Valley Montepulciano 2020** A sturdy, thick-skinned variety
from the wilds of Abruzzo. It is tough! But coupled with the judicious decision to
ferment as whole berries with minimal extraction, the result is uncannily joyous!
Vivid florals set the pace. A ferrous mid-palate is glossed with a cushy feel by
assorted blue fruit and an amaro bitterness. The finish, firm and long. What's not
to like? This is a delicious victory over a torrid year. Raise your glass! Screw cap.
13% alc. **Rating** 92 **To** 2022 $36 NG
Anomaly King Valley Arneis 2020 A very good arneis. Far from shy and
confidently drawing on the dry extract of a warm year, this rich dry white exudes
scents of white peach, ripe apple and Asian pear, driven long by sheer force of
flavour and personality. Screw cap. 14% alc. **Rating** 91 **To** 2022 $30 NG
Wildstreak Hunter Valley Cabernet Franc 2019 A delicious full-bodied
franc, displaying the variety's attractive verdant aromas: hedgerow, chilli, spearmint
and violet. An undercarriage of redcurrant plies the mid palate, with a firm line
of grape tannin and a buffering of acidity towing the finish. Screw cap. 14% alc.
Rating 91 **To** 2024 $32 NG
Anomaly Hunter Valley Vermentino 2020 Vermentino is a great Italian
indigene with its heart in Sardinia and soul, Liguria. An attractive nose of nashi
pear gelato, jasmine and lemon verbena. On the lighter side of mid weighted
and palpably dry, this easy-drinking expression concludes with a saline burst of
freshness. Easy to like. Screw cap. 12% alc. **Rating** 90 **To** 2022 $30 NG
Anomaly King Valley Saperavi 2019 A glossy crimson, glowing with life.
Aromatic fireworks, from lilac, anise, molten raspberry and blackberry jam. Yet
this fully loaded wine is packed with extract and the sort of tannic mettle that
mitigates any sense of excess or overt sweetness. Delicious. Satisfying drinking all
round. Screw cap. 14% alc. **Rating** 90 **To** 2022 $36 NG

ΨΨΨΨ Wildstreak Hunter Valley Shiraz 2019 **Rating** 89 **To** 2026 $32 NG

Peter Lehmann ★★★★★

Para Road, Tanunda, SA 5352 **Region** Barossa Valley
T (08) 8565 9555 **www**.peterlehmannwines.com **Open** By appt
Winemaker Nigel Westblade, Tim Dolan, Brett Smith, Brooke Blair **Est.** 1979
Dozens 750000
The seemingly indestructible Peter Lehmann (the person) died in June 2013, laying the seeds
for what became the last step in the sale of the minority Lehmann family ownership in the
company. The Hess Group of California had acquired control in '03 (leaving part of the capital
with the Lehmann family) but a decade later it became apparent that Hess wished to quit its
holding. Various suitors put their case forward but Margaret Lehmann (Peter's widow) wanted
ongoing family, not corporate, ownership. Casella thus was able to make the successful bid in
November '14, followed by the acquisition of Brand's Laira in December '15. Exports to the
UK, the US, Canada and China.

ŸŸŸŸŸ **Wigan Eden Valley Riesling 2016** Wigan is king of Eden Valley riesling and yet again one of the top releases of the year. Still a magnificent straw green at just 5yo, it's at that magic moment where primary and secondary characters unite in equal measure. All the fresh lime and Granny Smith apple of youth, backed by rising buttery, spicy, roast almond maturity. Brilliant acid line charges an astonishing finish that lasts for 30 seconds. Yes, I timed it! For all it represents, this might just be the bargain of the year. Screw cap. 11% alc. **Rating** 97 **To** 2031 $35 TS ✪

VSV Valley View Road Barossa Valley Shiraz 2018 This is a great example of the Barossa Valley at its best, marrying elegance with high-definition shiraz. The palate is long, balanced, and, above all else, fresh. Screw cap. 14.5% alc. **Rating** 97 **To** 2038 $60 JH ✪

Stonewell Barossa Shiraz 2017 Lehmann's depth of reach into Barossa's finest sites is in evidence here, upholding the style and greatness of its flagship, even in a cooler season. A magnificently full, vibrant purple hue, it's packed with compact, dense, crunchy, bright black fruits of all kinds, dressed in a gown of finely woven tannins. High-cocoa dark chocolate French oak has been perfectly tuned to the season. Integrity and persistence define great longevity. Screw cap. 14.5% alc. **Rating** 97 **To** 2042 $100 TS ✪

ŸŸŸŸŸ **Margaret Barossa Semillon 2015** An impossibly pale straw green. Shot with cut grass, fresh lemon, Granny Smith apple skin. Building preserved lemon, buttered toast and subtle nutmeg. Crystalline acidity electrifies an exceedingly long finish. The Hunter is king of dry semillon and Margaret is its only true rival. Screw cap. 10.3% alc. **Rating** 96 **To** 2035 $35 TS ✪ ❤

H&V Eden Valley Riesling 2020 Pitch-perfect Eden Valley riesling of impeccable precision. Textbook lime, lemon and Granny Smith apple. This low-yielding season has delivered fantastic concentration, and all the energy of cool nights is captured in shimmering acidity. The skill of the Lehmann team in managing phenolics is exemplified in 2020, making this one of the rieslings of the vintage. Captivating from the outset and it will live long, if you can keep your hands off it! Screw cap. 11% alc. **Rating** 95 **To** 2030 $25 TS ✪

Mentor Barossa Cabernet 2017 The cooler vintages yield the most exciting Barossa cabernets. This is a season packed with density and definition in a compact core that encapsulates the full spectrum of varietal hallmarks of cassis, blackcurrant, capsicum, tobacco, coffee bean and cedar. True to the season, it's already evolving into the savoury spectrum of sweet roast capsicum, yet holds the integrity, stamina and firm, fine, mineral tannins to age long. Another truly great Mentor. Screw cap. 14.5% alc. **Rating** 95 **To** 2037 $45 TS

8 Songs Barossa Shiraz 2017 Impressive full purple hue for this cool season. The plush red fruits and supple milk-chocolate feel that define 8 Songs are lifted by pretty notes of rhubarb and white pepper. Bright acidity and fine-grained, confident tannins make this a vintage for the cellar. Screw cap. 14.5% alc. **Rating** 94 **To** 2037 $45 TS

The Bond Barossa Grenache 2018 Graceful and accurate Barossa grenache in an enticingly medium-bodied guise. Alluring signature raspberry, poached strawberry and rhubarb fruit is the focus, sensitively and subtly supported by seasoned French oak, building more in texture than flavour. Finely crafted tannins carry a long finish. The definition of Barossa grenache. Screw cap. 14% alc. **Rating** 94 **To** 2025 $25 TS ✪

H&V Barossa Valley Cabernet Sauvignon 2019 H&V has been an exciting tier for Lehmann from the outset, and this is a very strong release. A crunchy and compelling cabernet of impressively full, vibrant purple hue. Bright blackcurrant and cassis fruit takes a rightful lead, confidently backed by a chassis of firm, fine tannins, engineered to go the distance. Screw cap. 14.5% alc. **Rating** 94 **To** 2034 $25 TS ✪

ŸŸŸŸŸ **Masterson Barossa Shiraz 2016 Rating** 93 **To** 2046 $1000 TS
H&V Eden Valley Pinot Gris 2020 Rating 92 **To** 2021 $25 TS ✪
Portrait Eden Valley Riesling 2020 Rating 90 **To** 2023 $18 TS ✪

Pewsey Vale Vineyard ★★★★☆

Eden Valley Road, Eden Valley, SA 5353 **Region** Eden Valley
T (08) 8561 3200 **www.**pewseyvale.com **Open** By appt
Winemaker Louisa Rose **Est.** 1847 **Dozens** 20 000 **Vyds** 65ha
Pewsey Vale was a famous vineyard established in 1847 by Joseph Gilbert. It was appropriate that when the Hill-Smith family began the renaissance of the Eden Valley plantings in 1961, it should do so by purchasing Pewsey Vale and establishing 50ha of riesling. In '77 the Riesling also finally benefited from being the first wine to be bottled with a Stelvin screw cap. While public reaction forced the abandonment of the initiative for almost 20 years, Pewsey Vale never lost faith in the technical advantages of the closure. A quick taste (or better, a share of a bottle) of 5–7yo Contours Riesling will tell you why. Exports to all major markets.

♀♀♀♀♀ **Prima 23GR Single Vineyard Estate Eden Valley Riesling 2020** Sweet wine is more about acidity than sugar, and early harvest upholds impressive vibrancy in Prima. Purity of lime and Granny Smith apple linger long, with cool, high, natural acidity triumphing over gentle sweetness. Just the thing for spicy fusion action, now or later. Screw cap. 9.5% alc. **Rating** 93 **To** 2030 $28 TS
The Contours Museum Reserve Single Vineyard Estate Eden Valley Riesling 2016 An enticing secondary style of toast, roast almonds, butter and wild honey over a core of preserved lemon and lime. It concludes long and spicy, guided by a focused line of bright acidity. A touch of reductive burnt rubber on opening quickly blows off. Screw cap. 12.5% alc. **Rating** 92 **To** 2026 $38 TS
Single Vineyard Estate Eden Valley Riesling 2020 A perpetual star in accessible, affordable riesling, this historic vineyard and legendary label deserve a place in every home entertainer's repertoire. Lime, Granny Smith apple and spice assume their usual positions. This dry, low-yielding season has lent a salty feel to its gentle acid line, making this a vintage for short-term drinking. Screw cap. 12.5% alc. **Rating** 91 **To** 2024 $26 TS

Pfeiffer Wines ★★★★★

167 Distillery Road, Wahgunyah, Vic 3687 **Region** Rutherglen
T (02) 6033 2805 **www.**pfeifferwines.com.au **Open** Mon–Sat 9–5, Sun 10–5
Winemaker Chris Pfeiffer, Jen Pfeiffer **Est.** 1984 **Dozens** 20 000 **Vyds** 33ha
Family-owned and run, Pfeiffer Wines occupies one of the historic wineries (built in 1885) that abound in North East Victoria, which makes it worth a visit on this score alone. In 2012 Chris Pfeiffer was awarded an Order of Australia Medal (OAM) for his services to the wine industry. Both hitherto and into the future, Pfeiffer's Muscats, Topaques and other fortified wines are a key part of the business. The arrival of daughter Jen, by a somewhat circuitous and initially unplanned route, has dramatically lifted the quality of the table wines, led by the reds. Chris Pfeiffer celebrated his 40th vintage in '13, having well and truly set the scene for supremely gifted daughter Jen to assume the chief winemaking role in due course. Exports to the UK, the US, Canada, Belgium, Hong Kong, Singapore and China.

♀♀♀♀♀ **Rare Rutherglen Topaque NV** A muscadelle of unusual age averaging 25 years old, with world-class silken, supple qualities and complexity. Here, the fortified blender's art reaches its pinnacle. Immense concentration is on display and yet it is still so fresh, thanks to sensitive fortification using neutral spirit. Cold-brew coffee, dark chocolate, malt biscuit, dried fruits and more. Luscious, umami texture, with treacle-like richness that sticks to the sides of the mouth. Glorious! 500ml. Screw cap. 17.5% alc. **Rating** 97 $123 JP
Rare Rutherglen Muscat NV The blender's art moves up a notch with Rare. Only the best barrel samples from the best parcels of base wine from the best vintages make the grade. Average age here is 25 years. The colour is darker again, a warm walnut. The wine is thicker, slower to move around the glass, stickier. Coffee grounds, soused raisins, rum-and-raisin chocolate, orange peel and toasted hazelnuts, beautifully alive. A rare taste to savour. 500ml. Screw cap. 17.5% alc. **Rating** 97 $123 JP ◯

ΨΨΨΨΨ **Rare Rutherglen Tawny NV** Average age is 25 years. A selection of classic Portuguese and French grape varieties. A stunning fortified by any measure from a master blender on the rise, Jen Pfeiffer. A rich collaboration of fruit concentration, age and spirit that maintains impressive complexity of walnut, toffee, dried fruits and mandarin peel entwined in a seamless teaming with warm, enduring spirit. 500ml. Screw cap. 20% alc. **Rating** 96 $95 JP

Grand Rutherglen Topaque NV A wine that reveals the bounty and beauty of age, the accumulation of wines put down year after year, decade after decade to build an invaluable repository. Amber hued. The aroma and flavours of malt biscuit, tea leaves, fruit-and-nut chocolate and toffee fill the senses. The texture is silken, with layers of flavour, nuts and leather. While sweet, it is not overly so, retaining a clean, fresh finish. 500ml. Screw cap. 17.5% alc. **Rating** 96 $84 JP

Grand Rutherglen Muscat NV Average age is 18–20 years, with some of the winery's oldest parcels included in the blend. The level of intensity feels like it has tripled between Classic and Grand. The amber colour is a clue, the depth of aromas and flavours seals it. Raisin cake, rich toffee, a splash of treacle here, a smidge of rose oil there. The key, as always, is the degree of freshness the maker has brought to the blend, to lift and enhance the aged batches of wines. Perfect. 500ml. Screw cap. 17.5% alc. **Rating** 96 $84 JP

Christopher's Rutherglen VP 2018 Deep purple hue. The 5 Portuguese varieties bring lifted aromatics of rose, violet, black cherry, raspberry – so pretty – which become entwined on the palate in rich layers of spice, licorice and chocolate with a brandy twist. Intense but not heavy. Quite the opposite. It's way, way too early to even contemplate opening. Give it 10 years at least. Screw cap. 18.5% alc. **Rating** 96 $30 JP ✪

Seriously Fine Pale Dry Apera NV Jen Pfeiffer keeps the dry apera fires burning, an art on the wane in Australia. Seriously good apera, so complex, fresh, alive and super-dry. Almond kernel, tart green apple, salted citrus, orange peel. That salty tang is irresistible. Finishes long and clean, lip-smackingly so. 500ml. Screw cap. 16% alc. **Rating** 95 $29 JP ✪

Classic Rutherglen Topaque NV With an average age of 13 years, the progression of flavour intensity starts to become more noticeable, concentrated, yet, importantly, there is also a sense of youthful freshness. Mahogany coloured with sweet golden syrup, salted caramel, orange peel and nougat aromas. The sweetness is cut nicely by spiced, toasted nuts. Clean spirit makes it shine. Excellent value. 500ml. Screw cap. 17.5% alc. **Rating** 95 $29 JP ✪

Classic Rutherglen Muscat NV Combining freshness with age, Classic is lively in dried fig, orange peel, aromatic bergamot and malt. Bright and lively in neutral spirit, yet can retreat into some hidden depths of a quiet intensity. 500ml. Screw cap. 17.5% alc. **Rating** 95 $29 JP ✪

Seriously Nutty Medium Dry Apera NV For those who like their apera with less of the desert-dry salty lemony tang and more of the salted nuts and vanillan oak sweetness, Seriously Nutty fits the bill. The key still remains freshness, which is here in spades. It retains an attractive lightness, a honeyed, spiced character which is warming and long. 500ml. Screw cap. 21.5% alc. **Rating** 95 $50 JP

Rutherglen Topaque NV Trademark topaque characters here, from the scent of cold tea and butterscotch through to honey cake. A top introduction to the fortified classification system with this entry-level topaque that shows good balance of flavour and freshness. 500ml. Screw cap. 17.5% alc. **Rating** 94 $20 JP ✪

ΨΨΨΨφ **Tempranillo 2019 Rating** 92 **To** 2026 $27 JP
Durif 2017 Rating 91 **To** 2031 $33 JP
Classic Rutherglen Tawny NV Rating 91 $20 JP ✪
Rutherglen Muscat NV Rating 91 $19 JP ✪
Seriously Pink Apera NV Rating 91 $20 JP ✪
Funky Pi.G Pinot Grigio 2019 Rating 90 **To** 2025 $22 JP
Winemakers Selection Rutherglen Shiraz 2018 Rating 90 **To** 2028 $30 JP

Phaedrus Estate   ★★★★☆

220 Mornington-Tyabb Road, Moorooduc, Vic 3933 **Region** Mornington Peninsula
T (03) 5978 8134 **www**.phaedrus.com.au **Open** W'ends & public hols 11–5
Winemaker Ewan Campbell, Maitena Zantvoort **Est.** 1997 **Dozens** 3000 **Vyds** 2.5ha
Since Maitena Zantvoort and Ewan Campbell established Phaedrus Estate, they have gained a
reputation for producing premium cool-climate wines. Their winemaking philosophy brings
art and science together to produce wines showing regional and varietal character with
minimal winemaking interference. The vineyard includes 1ha of pinot noir and 0.5ha each of
pinot gris, chardonnay and shiraz.

♟♟♟♟♟ **Single Vineyard Reserve Mornington Peninsula Pinot Noir 2019** Just
when you think there's too much flavour, too much of a good time in a glass, it
all falls into place. This has opulence aplenty, thanks to plush ripe fruit, with a full-
bodied palate caressing velvety tannins. It has drive on the finish and the result is
an empty glass in hand. Screw cap. 13.9% alc. **Rating** 95 **To** 2028 $45 JF
Mornington Peninsula Shiraz 2019 Sultry, smoky reduction is interspersed
with ripe fruit here and it works brilliantly. Super-fragrant, with really cool-climate
flavours, even in this warmer vintage: violets, pepper, iodine and bay leaves. It's
compelling, with shapely tannins and some grunt, too, yet it just falls a tad short –
a minor quibble though, as it's a ripper. Screw cap. 13.5% alc. **Rating** 94 **To** 2033
$28 JF ✪

♟♟♟♟♀ **Mornington Peninsula Fiano 2020** Rating 92 **To** 2023 $26 JF
Mornington Peninsula Pinot Noir 2019 Rating 92 **To** 2027 $28 JF
Sparkling Pinot Noir Chardonnay NV Rating 90 $45 JF

Philip Shaw Wines   ★★★★☆

100 Shiralee Road, Orange, NSW 2800 **Region** Orange
T (02) 6362 0710 **www**.philipshaw.com.au **Open** 7 days 11–5
Winemaker Daniel Shaw **Est.** 1989 **Dozens** 25 000 **Vyds** 47ha
Philip Shaw, former chief winemaker of Rosemount Estate and then Southcorp, first became
interested in the Orange region in 1985. In '88 he purchased the Koomooloo Vineyard and
began extensive plantings. The varieties include shiraz, merlot, pinot noir, sauvignon blanc,
cabernet franc, cabernet sauvignon and viognier and the vineyard is in conversion to organic.
Philip has handed the reins to sons Daniel and Damian to concentrate on his HOOSEGG
wines. Exports to the UK, Norway, Finland, the Philippines, Indonesia, Hong Kong, China
and NZ.

♟♟♟♟♀ **No. 6 Orange Chardonnay 2015** This has matured to a calm adolescence,
shedding the youthful jangle of shins and elbows. More left in the tank. The
aromas serve as a retina into high-quality chardonnay's possibilities, particularly
when honed in classy wood with extended lees handling: white fig, peach, oatmeal
biscuit, curry powder, cashew and dried hay. Crunchy. Mellifluous. Solid length.
Screw cap. 12.6% alc. **Rating** 93 **To** 2025 $75 NG
No. 3 Orange Shiraz 2018 This distinctly cool-climate shiraz is synonymous
with the sort of light/mid-weighted, aromatic and effusively vibrant luncheon
syrah from a litany of communes in the northern Rhône. Crozes? A little less
acidity here. A deep ruby, with crackling precision and aromas of ground pepper,
mace, clove tapenade, dried seaweed and violet. A carnal burr of smoked meats
underlying it all. Pulpy. Defined emery tannins. Cagey with energy. A very good
drink. Cork. 13.5% alc. **Rating** 93 **To** 2025 $75 NG
No. 8 Orange Pinot Noir 2019 This is a mid-weighted and sturdy pinot.
Mescal and Indian spice scents mark the use of whole clusters, imparting
complexity and a carriage of fibrous tannins. Red cherry and rhubarb notes, too.
Dense for the category, with the force of personality driving a sappy finish of
moderate length. Screw cap. 13.2% alc. **Rating** 92 **To** 2025 $45 NG
No. 8 Orange Pinot Noir 2018 A translucent mid ruby. Smudgy aromas of
cherry cola to sarsaparilla. Orange zest and some forest floor – porcini to wet

leaves. A tangerine/cardamom riff suggests the use of some whole bunches, segueing to a spiky tannic frame. A solid if not simple pinot, with a long savoury finish. Screw cap. 13% alc. **Rating** 92 **To** 2025 $45 NG

Pink Billy Saignée Orange 2018 This flavoursome, dry and mid-weighted rosé is delicious. Bridling a full-flavoured impact of musk stick, pomegranate, watermelon, tangerine and orange blossom to ginger spice scents; with a jittery frame of pungent mineral, cool-climate energy and a curb of 'skinsy' texture. Ample flavour and freshness all in one. Screw cap. 13.5% alc. **Rating** 91 **To** 2021 $28 NG

The Architect Orange Chardonnay 2019 A fascinating juxtaposition against the ambitious styling of the '18 just tasted, this is more of a straight shooter. But I like the barrel of honeydew melon, green and red apple and the waft of tangerine tanginess. A gentle flintiness imparts some tension. A warm year, to be sure, but this is very well handled and, at the price, a flavoursome winner. Screw cap. 12.8% alc. **Rating** 90 **To** 2023 $24 NG

The Architect Orange Chardonnay 2018 A limpid light yellow with green edges draws one in. The first draw is a pungent one, with lees-derived hints of curd, lime splice and raw oats. The second is more fruit driven, with an emphasis on white peach. A holster of cashew and nougatine parlays some generosity. A well-built chardonnay straddling a contemporary tension with ample flavour. Screw cap. 13% alc. **Rating** 90 **To** 2024 $24 NG

🍷🍷🍷🍷 **The Wire Walker Orange Pinot Noir 2019** **Rating** 88 **To** 2023 $24 NG

Philippa Farr ★★★★★

PO Box 271, Wonthaggi, Vic 3995 **Region** Gippsland
T 0438 326 795 **www**.philippafarr.com.au
Winemaker Philippa Farr **Est.** 2012 **Dozens** 250 **Vyds** 0.5ha
This is take 3 for the Farr family, father Gary and brother Nick having shown the way. Growing up at Bannockburn, surrounded by vines and sheep, Philippa was exposed to fine wine from an early age. In 2003 she undertook the vintage at Brokenwood, and after completing the first year of a bachelor of wine science degree, she returned to work at Brokenwood full-time, studying part-time, until the completion of the '05 vintage. She says that 'just to ensure her childhood upbringing on a sheep farm was not her true passion, she followed a farming career in the following years in Gippsland'. She also took time to complete vintages at Bellvale, Domaine Dujac, By Farr and Purple Hen. After 4 years living in Gippsland, Philippa made her first Pinot Noir from half a ha of high-density planted pinot.

Piano Piano ★★★★☆

852 Beechworth-Wangaratta Road, Everton Upper, Vic 3678 **Region** Beechworth
T (03) 5727 0382 **www**.pianopiano.com.au **Open** By appt
Winemaker Marc Scalzo **Est.** 2001 **Dozens** 1500 **Vyds** 4.6ha
'Piano piano' means 'slowly slowly' in Italian, and this is how Marc Scalzo and wife Lisa Hernan have approached the development of their business. Marc has a degree in oenology from CSU, many years' practical experience as a winemaker with Brown Brothers and vintage experience with Giaconda, John Gehrig and in NZ with Seresin Estate and Delegat's. In 1997 they planted 2.6ha of merlot, cabernet sauvignon, tempranillo and touriga nacional on their Brangie Vineyard in the King Valley; they followed up with 1.2ha of chardonnay ('06) and 0.8ha of shiraz ('08) on their Beechworth property.

🍷🍷🍷🍷🍷 **Henry's Block Beechworth Shiraz 2018** A good year brings forth another strong Henry's Block, velvety in texture, balanced in delivery, with an intense core of blackberries, licorice, smoky cigar box. And spice. What spice! Will age gracefully. Screw cap. 13.9% alc. **Rating** 95 **To** 2028 $42 JP

🍷🍷🍷🍷🍷 **Sophie's Block Beechworth Chardonnay 2019** **Rating** 92 **To** 2024 $42 JP

Pierro ★★★★★

Caves Road, Wilyabrup via Cowaramup, WA 6284 **Region** Margaret River
T (08) 9755 6220 **www**.pierro.com.au **Open** 7 days 10–5
Winemaker Dr Michael Peterkin **Est.** 1979 **Dozens** 10 000 **Vyds** 7.85ha
Dr Michael Peterkin is another of the legion of Margaret River medical practitioner-vignerons; for good measure, he married into the Cullen family. Pierro is renowned for its stylish white wines, which often exhibit tremendous complexity; the Chardonnay can be monumental in its weight and texture. That said, its red wines from good vintages can be every bit as good. Exports to the UK, Denmark, Belgium, Russia, Malaysia, Indonesia, Hong Kong, Singapore and Japan.

🍷🍷🍷🍷🍷 **Margaret River Chardonnay VR 2017** A staggeringly complex wine with layer upon layer of flavour and texture, all working in concert with each other to achieve one goal: excellence. The waves of flavour ripple across the mouth and seep into the soul. Exceptional. Screw cap. 14% alc. **Rating** 97 **To** 2041 $120 EL ✪

🍷🍷🍷🍷🍷 **L.T.C. Semillon Sauvignon Blanc 2020** 50/41/9% sauvignon blanc/semillon/chardonnay. Although '20 has been rough in many ways. in WA vineyards it was warm, early and brilliant quality – a silver lining to what was otherwise a blindside year. This is concentrated and focused; completely balanced and refreshing. A stunning rendition of the LTC, the acidity is juicy and chewy. With the ability to age gracefully in the cellar, this is a cracker. Screw cap. 13.5% alc. **Rating** 96 **To** 2030 $35 EL ✪

Margaret River Chardonnay 2019 Some wines demand a minute before you can put words to them. This has tremendous length of flavour, such is the quality of the fruit, that it just forges on and on. Suffice to say, the full mlf style has helped accentuate creamy, powerful fruit, and seamlessly applied oak caresses it through the finish. This is very pure – crystalline in fact – but it is very young right now. Screw cap. 13.5% alc. **Rating** 96 **To** 2039 $105 EL

Nunc Tempus Est Margaret River Chenin Blanc 2018 From a tiny plot of chenin, this is the first varietal bottling. Hand picked and sorted, whole-bunch pressed, fermented in stainless steel and left on ferment lees for 6 months. Dry. Spicy, fine, and bang-on classical chenin. The palate has apricot and pear, littered with Geraldton wax florals and white pepper. There is an extraordinarily exciting interplay of acid and fruit, which comes together to leave an impression of clove/star anise at the end. Screw cap. 14% alc. **Rating** 95 **To** 2035 $35 EL ✪

Reserve Margaret River Cabernet Sauvignon Merlot 2017 Up to 40 days on skins and matured in French oak for 18 months (60% new). For all the work in the winery, the fruit was clearly very gently handled, with judicious tannin extraction. Medium-bodied, supple, and texturally constructed of fine silk. Densely packed with berry flavour, and corseted by exotic spice, this is a supremely elegant wine. Screw cap. 14% alc. **Rating** 95 **To** 2036 $90 EL

🍷🍷🍷🍷 **Margaret River Cabernet Sauvignon Merlot L.T.Cf. 2017** **Rating** 93 **To** 2030 $46 EL

Pig in the House **NR**

Balcombe Road, Billimari, NSW 2804 **Region** Cowra
T 0427 443 598 **www**.piginthehouse.com.au **Open** Fri–Sun 11–5 by appt
Winemaker Antonio D'Onise **Est.** 2002 **Dozens** 3000 **Vyds** 25ha
Jason and Rebecca O'Dea established their vineyard (7ha shiraz, 6ha cabernet sauvignon, 5ha merlot, 4.5ha chardonnay and 2.5ha sauvignon blanc) on a block of land formerly used as home for 20 free-range pigs – making any explanation about the name of the business totally unnecessary. Given its prior use, one would imagine the vines would grow lustily, and it is no surprise that organic certification has been given by Biological Farmers of Australia. The O'Deas have in fact taken the process several steps further, using biodynamic preparations

and significantly reducing all sprays. The wines made are good advertisements for organic/ biodynamic farming. Exports to Japan and China.

ŸŸŸŸŸ **Organic Rosé 2019** A light coral with copper edges. A great colour! A textural and expansive palate, boasting a multitude of layers. Poached strawberry, orange zest, a twine of dried herbs and musk notes barrel long down the throat. This is impressive: dry and really thirst slaking. I am unsure when this was released, but it is drinking very well. Screw cap. 13% alc. **Rating** 92 **To** 2022 $25 NG ✪
Organic Shiraz 2019 A lithe and powerful wine that builds across the palate while managing – only just – to restrain notes of root spice, dark cherry, menthol, clove and lilac from slipping to the wrong side of the savoury/sweet divide. I'd be drinking this over the short term. Screw cap. 14.5% alc. **Rating** 91 **To** 2024 $25 NG

Pike & Joyce ★★★★★

730 Mawson Road, Lenswood, SA 5240 **Region** Adelaide Hills
T (08) 8389 8102 **www.**pikeandjoyce.com.au **Open** 7 days 11–4
Winemaker Steve Baraglia, Andrew Kenny **Est.** 1998 **Dozens** 5000 **Vyds** 18.5ha
This is a partnership between the Pike family (of Clare Valley fame) and the Joyce family, related to Andrew Pike's wife, Cathy. The Joyce family have been orchardists at Lenswood for over 100 years and also have extensive operations in the Riverland. Together with Andrew they have established a vineyard planted to sauvignon blanc (5.9ha), pinot noir (5.73ha), pinot gris (3.22ha), chardonnay (3.18ha) and semillon (0.47ha). The wines are made at the Pikes' Clare Valley winery. Exports to the UK, China and other major markets.

ŸŸŸŸŸ **The Kay Reserve Adelaide Hills Chardonnay 2019** High-toned. The fruit dominates here. The barrel-ferment characters remain present, but soak deliciously into balance, allowing just a touch of gingery oak spice into the mix. Everything delicious. Screw cap. 13% alc. **Rating** 95 **To** 2028 $65 TL
Beurre Bosc Adelaide Hills Pinot Gris 2020 Lovely familiar varietal pear and apple aromas. There's a little squeeze of lemon over the same fruit profile on the palate, giving a note of acidity. A medium-bodied palate, structured by a small portion of barrel ferment and a dash of peppery spice on the finish. Tasty and well crafted. Screw cap. 13% alc. **Rating** 94 **To** 2023 $25 TL ✪
Clonal Selection MV6 Adelaide Hills Pinot Noir 2020 One of a trio of clonal variations, MV6, 114 and 777, each vinified separately to showcase their differences. All were matured for 7 months in oak, but only the MV6 saw a little (18%) new oak, which added an extra peppery spice to the pinot palate. The fruit is deliciously perky and the total feels well mannered and elegant. Screw cap. 14% alc. **Rating** 94 **To** 2030 $50 TL

ŸŸŸŸŸ **Ceder Adelaide Hills Riesling 2020 Rating** 92 **To** 2028 $30 TL
Epice Adelaide Hills Gewürztraminer 2020 Rating 92 **To** 2023 $30 TL
Separe Adelaide Hills Grüner Veltliner 2020 Rating 92 **To** 2023 $25 TL ✪
Les Saignees Adelaide Hills Dolcetto Pinot Noir Rosé 2020 Rating 92 **To** 2023 $25 TL ✪
Vue du Nord Adelaide Hills Pinot Noir 2020 Rating 92 **To** 2025 $32 TL
Innesti Adelaide Hills Nebbiolo 2019 Rating 91 **To** 2030 $40 TL
Descente Adelaide Hills Sauvignon Blanc 2020 Rating 90 **To** 2023 $25 TL
Sirocco Adelaide Hills Chardonnay 2019 Rating 90 **To** 2025 $32 TL

Pikes ★★★★★

233 Polish Hill River Road, Sevenhill, SA 5453 **Region** Clare Valley
T (08) 8843 4370 **www.**pikeswines.com.au **Open** 7 days 10–4
Winemaker Andrew Pike **Est.** 1984 **Dozens** 50 000 **Vyds** 130ha
Pikes is a family affair, established in the 1980s by Andrew, Neil and Cathy Pike with support from their parents Merle and Edgar. A generation on, Neil Pike has retired after 35 years as chief winemaker and Andrew's sons Jamie and Alister have come on board (Jamie to oversee sales and marketing, Alistair to run the craft brewery that opened in '14). The award-winning

Slate restaurant opened in '18, alongside a new tasting room. Riesling inevitably makes up half of all plantings; shiraz, cabernet, sangiovese, pinot grigio and tempranillo dominate the other half. Pikes' flagship wines are the Merle Riesling and EWP Shiraz, named after Merle and Edgar, and only made in exceptional vintages. Exports to Hong Kong, China, Canada, Ireland, Singapore, Poland, Japan, Sweden, Malaysia, Taiwan, NZ, the UK, Cyprus, the Philippines, France and the US. (TS)

ΨΨΨΨΨ **The Merle Clare Valley Riesling 2020** Pikes' flagship, but also a Clare Valley flagship. It's not often a 6-month-old riesling can be described as luscious, but that's the impact of this wine. It's citrus focused, of course, and it also has keynote acidity, but it's the honeyed mouthfeel and flavour that hits the jackpot. Screw cap. 12% alc. **Rating** 98 **To** 2035 **$52** JH ✪ ♥

ΨΨΨΨΨ **Traditionale Clare Valley Riesling 2020** Elegance is the cornerstone of this lovely riesling, with a flawless serenade of citrus allsorts, its spine of acidity a contradiction in terms, because it's almost sweet – an illusion, of course. An each-way proposition for now or later consumption. Screw cap. 12% alc. **Rating** 96 **To** 2035 **$25** JH ✪

The E.W.P. Clare Valley Shiraz 2018 While Pikes' flagship shiraz has some years ahead of it, gee it's compelling now. Quite floral and heady with garam marsala, licorice and a touch of charry oak. A core of perfectly ripe fruit leads the way across the more medium-bodied palate; but it's savoury through and through, with shapely tannins and requisite long finish. Screw cap. 13.5% alc. **Rating** 95 **To** 2033 **$72** JF

ΨΨΨΨ♀ **Hills & Valleys Clare Valley Riesling 2020** Rating 93 To 2026 $20 JF ✪
Eastside Clare Valley Shiraz 2018 Rating 93 To 2026 $27 JF ✪
The Hill Block Clare Valley Cabernet 2019 Rating 93 To 2034 $75 JF
The Hill Block Clare Valley Cabernet 2018 Rating 93 To 2030 $72 JF
Homage Clare Valley Cabernet Malbec 2019 Rating 93 To 2026 $27 JF ✪
Gill's Farm Clare Valley Mourvèdre 2019 Rating 93 To 2027 $27 JF ✪
The Assemblage Clare Valley Shiraz Mourvèdre Grenache 2018 Rating 92 To 2025 $25 JF ✪
Los Companeros Clare Valley Shiraz Tempranillo 2018 Rating 92 To 2026 $22 JF ✪
Olga Emmie Clare Valley Riesling 2020 Rating 91 To 2025 $25 JF
Valley's End Clare Valley Sauvignon Blanc Semillon 2020 Rating 91 To 2023 $22 JF ✪
Luccio Clare Valley Fiano 2020 Rating 91 To 2023 $24 JF
Luccio Clare Valley Sangiovese Rosé 2020 Rating 90 To 2021 $24 JF
The Dogwalk Clare Valley Cabernet 2018 Rating 90 To 2026 $22 JF
Luccio Clare Valley Sangiovese 2019 Rating 90 To 2024 $24 JF
Gill's Farm Clare Valley Mourvèdre 2020 Rating 90 To 2025 $27 JF

Pimpernel Vineyards ★★★★★

6 Hill Road, Coldstream, Vic 3770 **Region** Yarra Valley
T 0407 010 802 **www.**pimpernelvineyards.com.au **Open** Fri–Sun 10–4
Winemaker Damien Archibald, Mark Horrigan **Est.** 2001 **Dozens** 3000 **Vyds** 6ha
Lilydale-based cardiologist Mark Horrigan's love affair with wine started long before he had heard about either the Yarra Valley or his family's links, centuries ago, to Condrieu, France. He is a direct descendant of the Chapuis family, his ultimate ancestors buried in the Church of Saint-Étienne in 1377. In a cosmopolitan twist, his father came from a Welsh mining village, but made his way to university and found many things to enjoy, not the least wine. When the family moved to Australia in 1959, wine remained part of everyday life and, as Mark grew up in the '70s, the obsession passed from father to son. In 2001 he and wife Fiona purchased a property in the Yarra Valley on which they have built a (second) house, planted a vineyard, and erected a capacious winery designed by WA architect Peter Moran. In the course of doing so they became good friends of near-neighbour the late Dr Bailey Carrodus; some of the delphic labelling of Pimpernel's wines is pure Carrodus. Exports to the UK and Singapore.

Pindarie ★★★★☆

946 Rosedale Road, Gomersal, SA 5352 **Region** Barossa Valley
T (08) 8524 9019 **www.**pindarie.com.au **Open** 7 days 11–5
Winemaker Peter Leske **Est.** 2005 **Vyds** 36ha
Owners Tony Brooks and Wendy Allan met at Roseworthy College in 1985. Tony was the
6th generation of farmers in SA and WA, and was studying agriculture; NZ-born Wendy was
studying viticulture. On graduation Tony worked overseas managing sheep feedlots in Saudi
Arabia, Turkey and Jordan; Wendy worked for the next 12 years with Penfolds, commencing
as a grower liaison officer and working her way up to become a senior viticulturist. She also
found time to study viticulture in California, Israel, Italy, Germany, France, Portugal, Spain
and Chile, working vintages and assessing vineyards for wine projects. In 2001 she completed
a graduate diploma in wine business. The cellar door and the Grain Store cafe (winner
of Australian tourism awards in '13 and '14 as well as Hall of fame for SA Tourism) has
panoramic views. Exports to Taiwan and China.

ŸŸŸŸŸ **Schoff's Hill Barossa Valley Cabernet Sauvignon 2019** A contrast of the
less-ripe end of the cabernet spectrum of leafy/grassy/green capsicum tension
with the full alcohol and cassis character of ripeness. To its credit, fine-ground
tannins and balanced acidity both display impeccable ripeness, well supported by
dark chocolate French oak. Skilful winemaking has made something impressive
and varietally accurate of drought-season fruit. Screw cap. 15% alc. **Rating** 92
To 2029 $35 TS

ŸŸŸŸ **Small Block Barossa Valley Montepulciano 2019 Rating** 89 To 2026
$32 TS

Pinelli Wines ★★★★☆

30 Bennett Street, Caversham, WA 6055 **Region** Swan District
T (08) 9279 6818 **www.**pinelliwines.com.au **Open** Mon–Sat 9–5, Sun & public hols 10–5
Winemaker Robert Pinelli, Daniel Pinelli **Est.** 1980 **Dozens** 17 000 **Vyds** 9.78ha
Domenic and Iolanda Pinelli emigrated from Italy in the mid-1950s, and it was not long
before Domenic was employed by Waldeck Wines, then one of the Swan Valley's more
important wineries. With the benefit of 20 years' experience gained with Waldeck, in '80 he
purchased a 2.8ha vineyard that had been established many years previously. It became the
site of the Pinelli family winery, cellar door and home vineyard, subsequently significantly
expanded, with cabernet sauvignon, colombard, merlot and shiraz. Son Robert graduated
with a degree in oenology from Roseworthy in 1987, and has been the winemaker at
Pinelli for over 20 years. His brother Daniel obtained a degree in civil engineering from the
University of WA in '94, but eventually the lure of the family winery became too strong, so he
joined his brother in '02, and obtained his oenology degree from CSU in '07. He graduated
with distinction, and was awarded the Domaine Chandon Sparkling Wine Award for best
sparkling wine production student.

ŸŸŸŸŸ **Grand Tawny NV** Easily the standout tawny from the Swan Valley this year:
balanced, rich, supple, viscous and long, with each component in harmony with
the others and alcohol hidden. This has salivating, salty sweetness, tempered by
refreshing acidity and surrounded by characters of quince, date, nutmeg, star anise
and licorice. A beautiful wine. Truly. Screw cap. 18.5% alc. **Rating** 95 $55 EL

ŸŸŸŸŸ **Reserve Verdelho 2020 Rating** 93 To 2026 $18 EL **❸**
Reserve Durif 2019 Rating 91 To 2031 $32 EL

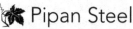 Pipan Steel ★★★★★

583 Carrolls Road, Mudgegonga, Vic 3737 **Region** Alpine Valleys
T 0418 679 885 **www.**pipansteelwines.com.au
Winemaker Paula Pipan, Daniel Balzer **Est.** 2008 **Dozens** 225 **Vyds** 0.4ha
For Paula Pipan and Radley Steel, it's been a long journey in search of a dream of bringing
their girls up in the country on a vineyard. The vineyard would not be planted to just any

grape variety, it had to be nebbiolo. The couple were – are – passionate about the grape that hails from Piedmont, Italy. Their search for suitable land took them to the Hunter Valley, Margaret River, Italy and ended on a hillside of decomposed granite soil in Mudgegonga in North East Victoria in the foothills of the Australian Alps. And so Pipan Steel was born. Under the sponsorship of Tyrrell's Wines winemaker, Andrew Spinaze, Paula was accepted into the wine degree at Charles Sturt University. Radley, a sports medicine practitioner, moved his practice to North East Victoria and became the viticulturist. Three nebbiolo clones were sourced from Gruppo Matura in Italy and planted in east-west oriented rows down the hillside, which drops from 410m to 390m. Each clone is vinified separately, and each wine spends time in large, seasoned French oak for 2 years and then another year in bottle before release. (JP)

IX Alpine Valleys Nebbiolo 2016 Clone 9 is said to produce generous, perfumed wines. This is the clearly the clone that celebrates the fruity side of nebbiolo, the floral side, too. The aromas are charged with an energy: briar, rose, forest berries, cherry, cranberry and dark spice. Soft and textured and generous in flavour with approachable tannins, it sings. Screw cap. 14.2% alc. **Rating** 95 To 2031 $45 JP

III Alpine Valleys Nebbiolo 2016 Blend 3 is a blend of clone 7 (44%), clone 9 (23%) and clone 10 (33%). All the individual strengths of the clones are brought together and the result is probably a little predictable: the whole is greater than the sum of its parts. The delicacy and structural strength of the grape is maintained, while III also invests heavily in flavour, savouriness and potential for ageing. Screw cap. 14.1% alc. **Rating** 95 To 2032 $45 JP

X Alpine Valleys Nebbiolo 2016 Rating 93 To 2032 $45 JP
VII Alpine Valleys Nebbiolo 2016 Rating 92 To 2030 $45 JP

Pipers Brook Vineyard ★★★★★

1216 Pipers Brook Road, Pipers Brook, Tas 7254 **Region** Northern Tasmania
T (03) 6382 7555 **www.**kreglingerwineestates.com **Open** By appt
Winemaker Luke Whittle **Est.** 1974 **Dozens** 70 000 **Vyds** 176.51ha
The Pipers Brook empire has almost 200ha of vineyard supporting the Ninth Island, Pipers Brook and Kreglinger labels with the major focus, of course, being on Pipers Brook. Fastidious viticulture and a passionate winemaking team along with immaculate packaging and enterprising marketing create a potent and effective blend. Pipers Brook operates a cellar door at the winery and is owned by Belgian-owned sheepskin business Kreglinger, which has also established the large Norfolk Rise Vineyard at Mount Benson in SA (see separate entry). Exports to the UK, the US and other major markets.

Kreglinger Brut de Blancs 2016 A bright, pale straw hue reflects the understated grace of delicate white pear and lemon fruit. The subtle complexity of 3+ years on lees lends more in silky texture than in complexity of flavour. Salty acidity and invisible dosage are perfectly integrated for a seamless finish. Cork. 12.5% alc. **Rating** 95 $65 TS

Kreglinger Brut Rosé 2016 Ultra-pale salmon hue. An effortless marriage between the cool acidity of Pipers River, the creamy texture of 3+ years on lees, fine-grained tannins and perfectly gauged dosage, capturing the character and restraint of Pipers River. A gorgeous rosé that confirms Kreglinger's place in Tasmania's A-league. Cork. 12.5% alc. **Rating** 95 $75 TS

Riesling 2020 The exotic personality of Northern Tasmanian riesling is expressed here with impressive refinement, control and determination yet approachability – a difficult contrast to capture. A focused core of lemon, lime and Granny Smith apple is subtly nudged by loquat, mandarin and spice. Beautifully ripe acidity flows effortlessly through a long finish, with just the right hint of sweetness. Screw cap. 12% alc. **Rating** 94 To 2032 $35 TS

Kreglinger Vintage Brut 2016 A compelling change of mood for Kreglinger: more elegant, more detailed, more precise, more beautiful. Crunchy red apple and lemon are accented with subtle spice, a hint of white pepper and the beginnings of the toasty complexity of lees development (3+ years). Great potential. Cork. 12.5% alc. **Rating** 94 $55 TS

Ninth Island Sparkling Rosé NV The smartest bargain sparkling rosé is back on form in '19. There's nothing else within miles of this price with such elegance, character, texture and polish. Pipers River pinot takes the lead in signature rose petal, strawberry hull and raspberry, with precise balance of flesh and tension. Acidity, dosage and phenolics marry seamlessly with the texture that only méthode traditionnelle can produce. I love this cuvée. Cork. 12.5% alc. **Rating** 94 $25 TS ○

ŸŸŸŸŸ Sauvignon Blanc 2020 Rating 93 To 2030 $35 TS
Tasmania Sparkling 2017 Rating 93 $45 TS
Chardonnay 2019 Rating 92 To 2026 $45 TS
Reserve Pinot Noir 2019 Rating 92 To 2034 $60 TS
New Certan Pinot Noir 2019 Rating 92 To 2029 $95 TS
Kreglinger Brut NV Rating 92 $35 TS
Ninth Island Riesling 2020 Rating 90 To 2022 $25 TS

Pirramimma   ★★★★

Johnston Road, McLaren Vale, SA 5171 **Region** McLaren Vale
T (08) 8323 8205 **www**.pirramimma.com.au **Open** Mon–Fri 10–4.30, w'ends & public hols 10.30–5
Winemaker Geoff Johnston **Est.** 1892 **Dozens** 50 000 **Vyds** 91.5ha
A long-established family-owned company with outstanding vineyard resources, which it is using to full effect. A series of intense old-vine varietals includes semillon, sauvignon blanc, chardonnay, shiraz, grenache, cabernet sauvignon and petit verdot, all fashioned without over-embellishment. Wines are released in several ranges: Pirramimma, Stock's Hill, White Label, ACJ, Katunga, Eight Carat and Gilded Lilly. Exports to all major markets.

ŸŸŸŸŸ **McLaren Vale Cabernet Sauvignon 2018** This is good, attesting yet again to the quality of cabernet from the Vale. A saline nose of anise, cassis, sage, saltbush and black olive tapenade. Fine. The mid-palate, expansive and layered by better oak tannins and firm and juicy grape ones. Check. The finish is tight, but not harsh. The billowing extract augurs well for a bright future. Screw cap. 14.6% alc. **Rating** 93 **To** 2032 $35 NG

Alexander Campbell Johnston 2017 48/21/11/8/6/6% cabernet/shiraz/petit verdot/tannat/merlot/malbec. Opaque. A fine nose dominated by the pencil lead, graphite, sage and molten cassis of warm-climate cabernet. The other varieties serve their master, offering nuanced inflections of tannin, colour, acidity, mid-palate plushness and aromatics. A sumptuous wine of considerable power juxtaposed against a winning restraint. The extended time in oak, attenuating the tannins nicely. Cork. 14.6% alc. **Rating** 93 **To** 2030 $100 NG

Vineyard Select McLaren Vale Primitivo 2018 This is a delicious full-bodied wine. Highly varietal, affirming this Puglian grape's great promise in the zone. Pulpy, with aromas of maraschino cherry, blue fruits, anise and orange zest. The tannins, pliant but far from forceful. Dusty and terracotta of feel yet, while relatively subtle, there is a severity to the oak. A green harshness, detracting from what could have been an excellent wine. As it stands, still a very good one. Screw cap. 14.5% alc. **Rating** 93 **To** 2023 $40 NG

Digby McLaren Vale Rare Old Fortified NV A modern tawny, if 'modern' is applicable for a wine as smoking-room-esque as this. A razor-sharp whiff of volatile rancio stings the nostril hairs. A good sign. Acidity, an obtuse blade. Riffs on walnut, washed rind, date and souk-like rubs for lamb and pigeon pastilla. The length, scented and endless. Just breathe deeply and indulge. Fortified is among the few world-class Australian categories. This, a very good example. Cork. 18.5% alc. **Rating** 93 $100 NG

Stock's Hill McLaren Vale GSM 2018 A delicious GSM, full weighted without being heavy. The wine ably promotes grenache's kirsch-scented generosity, ethereal feel and spice mix of aromas. The oak, a gentle beam across the wine's mid-drift, corralling the fruit as much as staving it off, just enough for the wine to find poise, regional probity and a zone of drinkability. Screw cap. 14.5% alc. **Rating** 92 To 2026 $25 NG ✪

Ironstone Old Bush Vine McLaren Vale Grenache 2016 There is plenty of joy here. Far from the regional zeitgeist of fine-boned febrile expressions, this is amped. Oozing Christmas cake spice, dried orange peel, fig and molten raspberry liqueur, a harness of Ovaltine oak brings a sense of decorum. The finish, long and forceful. The tangy acidity, an unnecessary distraction. But plenty of charm and chutzpah. Screw cap. 14.8% alc. **Rating** 91 To 2029 $70 NG

Vintage Fortified Shiraz 2018 Aromas of old wood, eucalyptus and pine resin echo across a forcefield of saturated raisin, mulberry and Christmas cake spice. Myriad dried fruits, clove, rum, bitter chocolate and molasses, to boot. The finish long, a bit varnishy and rustic, with some volatile perk. Yet what is not to like? Resinous, layered and intense. A wine that tastes as if it was made both 100 years ago and yesterday. Screw cap. 18.5% alc. **Rating** 91 $30 NG

Geoffrey McLaren Vale 12 Year Old Liqueur NV I like this by virtue of its fiery raisiny fortitude. Seville Orange marmalade, date and tangerine. The spirit, unresolved and a bit obtuse, but the personality is winning. This will go with mature washed rinds and unpasteurised blue cheeses. Cork. 19.5% alc. **Rating** 91 $40 NG

McLaren Vale Aged Tawny NV Exceptional value for money. Five-spice, date, tamarillo, turmeric, cardamom, clove, star anise and tamarind. Essentially, imagine walking through a Moroccan souk jet lagged; and then, a glass of this to resuscitate body and mind. The acidity is shrill. But there is enough pleasure here without being too much of a pedant. Screw cap. 19.5% alc. **Rating** 90 $25 NG

♥♥♥♥ **French Oak McLaren Vale Adelaide Hills Chardonnay 2018** Rating 88 To 2024 $30 NG
1892 McLaren Vale Shiraz 2018 Rating 88 To 2026 $30 NG
Sparkling Shiraz NV Rating 88 $25 NG

Pizzini ★★★★★

175 King Valley Road, Whitfield, Vic 3768 **Region** King Valley
T (03) 5729 8278 www.pizzini.com.au **Open** 7 days 10–5
Winemaker Joel Pizzini **Est.** 1980 **Dozens** 30000 **Vyds** 85ha
The Pizzini family have been grapegrowers in the King Valley for over 40 years. Originally much of the then riesling, chardonnay and cabernet sauvignon grape production was sold, but since the late '90s the focus has been on winemaking, particularly from Italian varieties. Pizzini's success has enabled an increase in vineyard holdings to 85ha, with 30ha of sangiovese, 20ha of pinot grigio, 13ha of prosecco, 2.5ha each of brachetto, arneis and verduzzo and 2ha of colorino. Exports to the UK and Japan.

♥♥♥♥♥ **Per gli Angeli 2011** Per gli Angeli is Italian for 'for the angels'. This fortified trebbiano is not made every year and is made in the labour-intensive Vin Santo style, with grapes dried on straw mats. Looks and smells like a young muscat, amber in colour and deliciously aromatic with aromas of fig, raisin, nougat, vanilla. Covers the palate in smooth, golden syrup, mocha coffee – so creamy, so intense. 375ml. Screw cap. 14% alc. **Rating** 95 $75 JP

Pietra Rossa King Valley Sangiovese 2018 Sangiovese is a natural in the King Valley. Here's the evidence. Rich, glossy red hue. Bright, ripe black cherry, raspberry, plum and spice aromas jump. Takes a serious turn on the palate with texture, depth of flavour, light savouriness and smoky, toasty oak tannins, tapering lean and dry into the finish. Screw cap. 13.8% alc. **Rating** 94 To 2028 $28 JP ✪

King Valley Nebbiolo 2016 A nebbiolo made with serious intent and hence released with some bottle age. Tight and coiled, so consider a good decant. As usual, a lifted, aromatic, charming bouquet of cherry, dried herbs, violet and potpourri. It's a real feature of Pizzini nebbiolo. Fine line through the palate, those nebbiolo savoury tannins are tamed, but only just. Mandarin skin, red berries and undergrowth all held in a tight tannin embrace. Just waiting … Screw cap. 13.8% alc. **Rating** 94 **To** 2032 $55 JP

🍷🍷🍷🍷♀ **Forza di Ferro King Valley Sangiovese 2018 Rating** 92 **To** 2030 $55 JP
Il Soffio Prosecco Rosé NV Rating 92 **To** 2022 $28 JP
Nonna Gisella King Valley Sangiovese 2019 Rating 91 **To** 2026 $22 JP ❂
La Volpe King Valley Nebbiolo 2019 Rating 91 **To** 2027 $28 JP

🍇 Place of Changing Winds ★★★★★

Waterloo Flat Road, Bullengarook, Vic 3437 **Region** Macedon Ranges
www.placeofchangingwinds.com.au **Open** By appt
Winemaker Remi Jacquemain, Robert Walters, Tom Trewin **Est.** 2012 **Dozens** 1000
Vyds 3.1ha

This extraordinary high-density vineyard is slotted between Mount Macedon and Mount Bullengarook. It's the brainchild of the committed and obsessive Robert Walters, the founder of importer Bibendum, boasting a dazzling array of boutique wine luminaries in its portfolio. Through his many connections and much research comes Place of Changing Winds, known as Warekilla in the local Wurundjeri language. It's a rocky site at 500m elevation, surrounded by forest. The whole farm covers 33ha but vines comprise just 3.1ha, planted to 44000 vines. A high-density site of pinot noir and chardonnay, ranging from 12500 to 33000 vines/ha: there is nothing like this in Australia, or even in Burgundy (where 10000 vines is deemed high density). No expense has been spared. The site is organically certified and the level of detail is nothing short of extraordinary. Robert also sources syrah and marsanne from Heathcote, through a long-term relationship with a grower at Colbinabbin. Exports to France, Sweden, Spain, the UK, Malaysia and Singapore. (JF)

🍷🍷🍷🍷🍷 **Clos de la Connerie Pinot Noir 2019** This has the darkest hue and fruit profile in the pinot range, yet shares the same core of fruit-derived sweetness, bolstered by oak. Dark cherries, plums, mint and some whole-bunch flavouring to the fore. The palate is supple, with fine filigreed tannins. In time, this just might prove to be the jewel in the crown. Diam. 12.5% alc. **Rating** 96 **To** 2032 $85 JF
High Density Pinot Noir 2019 This is a wine of definition. It's ripe but cool, long and pure, with fine tannins and a freshness throughout. Yes, there are sweet fruit flavours within, such as cherries and juniper, plus spice and mint, but they are almost incidental or, rather, the backup. Bravo. Diam. 12.5% alc. **Rating** 96 **To** 2033 $130 JF
Bullengarook Chardonnay 2019 Quite a deep yellow/straw hue yet it has clarity. I'm not overly fond of new Stockinger oak for chardonnay in particular, as it can often impart a bitter character, but the richness of fruit has tamed that and all else besides. Full bodied and flavoursome with hints of stone fruit, flint, ginger spice and a layer of creamy lees. Let's be clear: this is not a fruit-driven wine – it's savoury and textural. The flavours build, and while it feels substantial, there's a freshness to the acidity cutting through. Diam. 12.5% alc. **Rating** 95 **To** 2028 $52 JF
Between Two Mountains Pinot Noir 2019 At first this is shy and delicate. It unfurls to reveal lightly spiced cherries, wafts of menthol and dried herbs with more complex savoury flavours, pips and woodsy spices. But texture is the thing: medium bodied, with fine tannins, smooth and lithe. Diam. 12.5% alc. **Rating** 95 **To** 2029 $60 JF

🍷🍷🍷🍷♀ **Colbinabbin Vineyard Heathcote Syrah 2019 Rating** 93 **To** 2032 $48 JF
Tradition Pinot Noir Syrah 2019 Rating 92 **To** 2027 $40 JF

Plan B Wines

Freshwater Drive, Margaret River, WA 6285 **Region** Great Southern/Margaret River/Geographe
T 0413 759 030 **www**.planbwines.com
Winemaker Vanessa Carson **Est.** 2003 **Dozens** 40 000 **Vyds** 20ha
Plan B is owned and run by wine consultant Terry Chellappah 'between rocking the bass guitar and researching bars'. He says he is better at one than the other. Plan B has been notably successful, with significant increases in production. Winemaker Vanessa Carson has made wine in Margaret River and Frankland Valley, as well as in Italy and France. Exports to all major markets.

DR Great Southern Riesling 2020 Spritzy bath salts, talcy florals and plenty of lime pith make for a big mouthful of wine. This is rich and slippery, and if it wasn't for the dry designation on the back label, you'd swear it had some sweetness in there. Good length of ripe flavour and bright acid makes for a very easy-drinking riesling. Screw cap. 13% alc. **Rating** 92 **To** 2031 $30 EL

TV Ferguson Valley Tempranillo Viognier 2019 Plenty of dense juicy flavour, but the inclusion of viognier is an odd choice – it buffs the rusticity of the tempranillo tannins, glossing over their charm. Despite it, this is quite a delicious, commercial style. Screw cap. 14% alc. **Rating** 91 **To** 2027 $33 EL

OD Frankland River Riesling 2020 Fermentation arrested to leave 16.81g/l RS, hence the OD in the label: Off Dry. Pretty, soapy florals on the nose, the palate is delicate, round and plump. Uncomplicated pleasure awaits, certainly a smart match to spicy foods. Screw cap. 11% alc. **Rating** 90 **To** 2029 $25 EL

Solo Margaret River Sangiovese 2018 Juicy red fruit is wrapped in a blanket of structuring tannin – this does not scream 'sangiovese', but it is well put together and quite delicious. Screw cap. 14% alc. **Rating** 90 **To** 2028 $30 EL

Plantagenet

45 Albany Highway, Mount Barker, WA 6324 **Region** Mount Barker
T (08) 9851 3111 **www**.plantagenetwines.com **Open** 7 days 10–4.30
Winemaker Luke Eckersley, Chris Murtha **Est.** 1968 **Dozens** 30 000 **Vyds** 126ha
Plantagenet was established by Tony Smith, who continues to be involved in its management over 45 years later, notwithstanding that it has been owned by Lionel Samson & Son for many years. He established 5 vineyards: Bouverie in 1968 (sold in 2017), Wyjup in '71, Rocky Horror 1 in '88, Rocky Horror 2 in '97 and Rosetta in '99. These vineyards are the cornerstones of the substantial production of the consistently high-quality wines that have always been the mark of Plantagenet: highly aromatic Riesling, tangy citrus-tinged Chardonnay, glorious Rhône-style Shiraz and ultra-stylish Cabernet Sauvignon. Exports to the UK, Canada, the US, Japan, South Korea and China.

Tony Smith Mount Barker Shiraz 2018 Only made in exceptional years. Densely packed with concentrated, reverberating fruit that ripples across the tongue and through to the long finish. There is oak here, but it is swamped by the fruit which allows nothing to stand in its way. An exceptional wine of muscular definition and streamlined length of flavour. A very impressive first release: bravo. Screw cap. 14.5% alc. **Rating** 97 **To** 2046 $150 EL ✪

Lionel Samson Mount Barker Cabernet Sauvignon 2018 Salted cassis and blackberry pie on the nose and palate. This is supple and elegant and although concentrated, it doesn't have the palate weight of the shiraz. This is not a bad thing, just interesting. Elegance and longevity live here side by side. A masterful first release, and quite delicious now or in decades to come. Screw cap. 14% alc. **Rating** 97 **To** 2056 $150 EL ✪

Wyjup Collection Mount Barker Cabernet Sauvignon 2018 Single-vineyard cabernet with a distinctly inky countenance – this is wall to wall flavour that dives deep into the palate and soars long. Margaret and Frankland Rivers may take all the limelight for cabernet, but there are a handful of premium producers in Mount Barker doing the subregion very proud indeed, this being one of them. You can taste the sunshine here, but the cool nights are evident in the bright acidity, rounding this out to a very balanced yet intense wine that is built for the long haul. Screw cap. 14% alc. **Rating** 96 **To** 2051 $80 EL

Wyjup Collection Mount Barker Riesling 2020 Picked at night, fermented to dry, left on lees in tank for 3 months prior to bottling. Unbelievably tempting nose of ripe fleshy citrus (lime and lemon), green-apple skin and fine white spice. The palate is taut and saline, with just a lingering curl of flavour left on the palate in the end. Ethereal, but joyful, too. Screw cap. 13% alc. **Rating** 95 **To** 2035 $45 EL

Angevin Great Southern Riesling 2020 Fruit from Mount Barker. This is powder fine and racy with concentrated fruit power. Quite an astoundingly beautiful and pure wine of poise, line and length. Screw cap. 11% alc. **Rating** 95 **To** 2036 $32 EL ☉

Wyjup Collection Mount Barker Pinot Noir 2019 Red cherry, sarsaparilla, black pepper, bay leaf, sage and szechuan peppercorns. The palate is both structurally stemmy and creamy; the layers of flavour tucked away into the folds of texture. The acid provides a cooling flourish throughout, embossed flush into the fruit. An elegant, structural and sophisticated pinot noir. Screw cap. 12.5% alc. **Rating** 95 **To** 2031 $70 EL

Wyjup Collection Mount Barker Shiraz 2018 Densely packed with flavour from every angle, this is seriously silky, seriously flavoursome and very long. An impressive wine which leads with red forest fruits and closes with the same. The acid and tannins are thick as thieves. The question is, is this too big, rich, or obvious? A beautiful wine, but could benefit from a whisker of restraint. Screw cap. 14.5% alc. **Rating** 94 **To** 2036 $80 EL

♀♀♀♀♀ **Normand Great Southern Pinot Noir 2020** Rating 92 **To** 2031 $40 EL
Wyjup Collection Mount Barker Chardonnay 2019 Rating 91 **To** 2027 $70 EL

Poacher's Ridge Vineyard ★★★★★

1630 Spencer Road, Narrikup, WA 6326 **Region** Mount Barker
T (08) 9857 6066 **www.**poachersridge.com.au **Open** Fri–Sun 10–4
Winemaker Robert Diletti **Est.** 2000 **Dozens** 1000 **Vyds** 6.9ha
Alex and Janet Taylor purchased the Poacher's Ridge property in 1999. It had previously been used for cattle grazing. The vineyard includes shiraz, cabernet sauvignon, merlot, riesling, marsanne, viognier and malbec. Winning the Tri Nations 2007 merlot class against the might of Australia, NZ and South Africa with its '05 Louis' Block Great Southern Merlot was a dream come true. And it wasn't a one-time success – Poacher's Ridge Merlot is always at, or near, the top of the tree. Exports to Singapore and Japan.

♀♀♀♀♀ **Great Southern Riesling 2020** The fruit here has that intense muscularity that riesling from the region can have; it speaks of lychee, red apple, sea salt, nutmeg, citrus pith and white nectarine, all backed by fine, chalky phenolics. A lot going on, good length of flavour and a satisfying eucalyptus spritz through the finish, making it savoury as well as concentrated. Brilliant. Screw cap. 12.8% alc. **Rating** 94 **To** 2036 $28 EL ☉

Great Southern Marsanne 2020 A shining example of marsanne in WA. It's fine, with a pluming back palate that seems to expand with volumes of flavour as time goes by. It is richly layered and builds upon itself. Ultimately dry and built around a core of acid and phenolics. For lovers of this grape, you must try this. It has a proven track record for ageing gracefully, too. Screw cap. 13.5% alc. **Rating** 94 **To** 2031 $26 EL ☉

♀♀♀♀♀ **Great Southern Shiraz 2019** Rating 93 **To** 2031 $35 EL

Poachers ★★★★☆

431 Nanima Road, Springrange, NSW 2618 **Region** Canberra District
T (02) 6230 2487 **www**.poacherspantry.com.au **Open** 7 days 9.30–5
Winemaker Will Bruce **Est.** 1998 **Dozens** 3500 **Vyds** 20ha
Poachers Vineyard, owned by the Bruce family, shares its home with the Poachers Pantry, a renowned gourmet smokehouse. The quality of the wines is very good. The northeast-facing slopes, at an elevation of 720m, provide some air drainage and hence protection against spring frosts.

🍷🍷🍷🍷🍷 **Canberra District Syrah 2019** This is a bit subtle and slinky, yet shows off its spiced cherry, berry, pips and peppered flavours well. The acidity is a bit jangly, but there's a juiciness within. It's very easy to sip away, thanks to a refined, barely medium-bodied palate, covered in lacy tannins. Screw cap. 13% alc. **Rating** 94 To 2029 $30 JF ✪

🍷🍷🍷🍷🍷 **Canberra District Tempranillo 2019 Rating** 91 **To** 2027 $30 JF

Pt. Leo Estate ★★★★

3649 Frankston-Flinders Road, Merricks, Vic 3916 **Region** Mornington Peninsula
T (03) 5989 9011 **www**.ptleoestate.com.au **Open** 7 days 11–5
Winemaker Tod Dexter (Consultant) **Est.** 2006 **Dozens** 600 **Vyds** 20ha
Pt. Leo Estate is owned by one of Australia's wealthiest families, headed by octogenarian John Gandel and wife Pauline. They have donated countless millions of dollars to charity, and 30 years ago they purchased 20ha of land on the wild side of the Mornington Peninsula, building several houses for the exclusive use of family. Over the ensuing years they added parcels of land, created a lake at the entrance of the property, and in 2006 planted a 20ha vineyard. It is now also the site of a major sculpture park, populated by some very large pieces, and many smaller. A cellar door and restaurant opened in October '17. A second fine dining restaurant, Laura, opened in March '18. Both restaurants are managed by Ainslie Lubbock (ex Attica and The Royal Mail Hotel), with chef Phil Wood (ex Rockpool) and head sommelier Andrew Murch (ex Rockpool and Stokehouse).

🍷🍷🍷🍷🍷 **Mornington Peninsula Pinot Rosé 2020** An attractive copper-tinged pink. This is really spicy, almost peppery, with some crab apple, candied floss flavour and tangy red fruits too. There's lovely texture, freshness and neat acidity keeping everything on track. Screw cap. 13% alc. **Rating** 91 **To** 2022 $34 JF
Mornington Peninsula Pinot Gris 2020 There are enough varietal flavours to please here, with freshly cut nashi pears, poached pears topped with cinnamon and lemon cream, a little yeasty too. The palate is shapely yet well contained, for a gris. Stays fresh to the last drop. Screw cap. 13.5% alc. **Rating** 90 **To** 2022 $34 JF
Mornington Peninsula Pinot Noir 2019 Already some forward bricking to the mid garnet hue; lots of autumnal aromas of mulch and leaves with strong blood orange, chinotto and amaro flavours. The medium-bodied palate fleshes out with stewed fruits and enough tannin to add shape, but it's a drink-early offering. Screw cap. 14% alc. **Rating** 90 **To** 2024 $46 JF

Pokolbin Estate ★★★★☆

McDonalds Road, Pokolbin, NSW 2321 **Region** Hunter Valley
T (02) 4998 7524 **www**.pokolbinestate.com.au **Open** 7 days 9–5
Winemaker Xanthe Hatcher **Est.** 1980 **Dozens** 2500 **Vyds** 15.7ha
Pokolbin Estate has a very unusual, but very good, multi-varietal, multi-vintage array of wines always available for sale. The Riesling is true riesling, not misnamed semillon, the latter being one of their best wines, and wines under screw cap going back 6 or 7 vintages, and single-vineyard offerings to boot, are available.

🍷🍷🍷🍷🍷 **Phil Swannell Semillon 2013** Possibly the finest vintage for semillon in my lifetime, 2013 boasts concentration of fruit and a relaxed stridency, imparting freshness and detail without any severity. The wines are effortlessly poised, incredibly juicy and have drunk well across their lifetimes. No exception here. At its zenith: lemon butter, toast, Seville orange and hibiscus roll long across the mouth. Delicious. Screw cap. 11.4% alc. **Rating** 95 **To** 2024 $30 NG ❂

ŢŢŢŢ♀ **Phil Swannell Semillon 2009 Rating** 93 **To** 2024 $60 NG
Limited Release Reserve Hunter Valley Shiraz 2014 Rating 93 **To** 2027 $80 NG
Hunter Valley Riesling 2019 Rating 91 **To** 2027 $30 NG
North South Hunter Valley Shiraz 2016 Rating 90 **To** 2026 $30 NG

Pontifex Wines   ★★★★

PO Box 161, Tanunda, SA 5352 **Region** Barossa Valley
T 0418 811 066 **www**.pontifexwines.com.au
Winemaker Peter Kelly **Est.** 2011 **Dozens** 2000 **Vyds** 7ha
Sam Clarke is the son of David and Cheryl Clarke, founders of Thorn-Clarke Wines, a leading Barossa Valley winery (see separate entry). Thus it was easy for the family to meet Sam and wife Helen's wish to buy a 6ha slice of shiraz planted in 1991. For good measure, Peter Kelly (Thorn-Clarke's winemaker) is the winemaker for the venture. After 6 years, Pontifex (as the new venture was named on its birth in 2011) planted a ha of mourvèdre and grenache on the rich Bay of Biscay soils of the Krondorf district. They also purchase old-vine grenache. Exports to China.

ŢŢŢŢ♀ **Barossa Valley Shiraz 2018** Blackberry, blueberry and blood plum fruit is subtly lifted by sensitive inclusion of a dash of viognier. Finely structured tannins seamlessly unite fruit and French oak. It loses momentum on the finish, but lacks nothing in balance and integration. Screw cap. 14.5% alc. **Rating** 91 **To** 2025 $35 TS

 Ponting   ★★★★

169 Douglas Gully Road, Blewitt Spings, SA 5171 **Region** McLaren Vale
T 0439 479 758 **www**.pontingwines.com.au
Winemaker Ben Riggs **Est.** 2020 **Dozens** 9500
The Ponting label falls under the aegis of Three Kings Wine Merchants, a collaboration between winemaker Ben Riggs and the former Australian cricket captain, Ricky Ponting. A tensile Chardonnay and a soon to be-released Pinot Noir, hewn of cooler-climate Tasmanian fruit as an homage to the cricketing Taswegian's involvement, are exceptions to the South Australian sourcing pervasive across the lineup: an Adelaide Hills Sauvignon Blanc, a McLaren Vale Shiraz, a Langhorne Creek Cabernet and at the pointy end, the Ponting 366 cuvée, a blend of Shiraz from the Vale and Cabernet from Coonawarra. (NG)

ŢŢŢŢ♀ **Pioneer Tasmania Chardonnay 2019** A crunchy and bright Tamar Valley chardonnay of lemon, lime and Granny Smith apple fruit. Medium straw hue. Accents of spice provide interest to a focused palate of citrus vitality. With verve, energy and acid drive, it will age long and confident. Screw cap. 13% alc. **Rating** 92 **To** 2027 $28 TS
366 McLaren Vale Coonawarra Shiraz Cabernet Sauvignon 2017 A ridiculously heavy bottle adding a solid amount to the price. Opaque. All to script: high octane, with a reductive sash conveying tension to bitter chocolate, blue- and dark-fruit allusions, seaweed, cherry bon-bon and a curb of vanillan oak. Good pushy length. Tangy hot finish. This will please many. Diam. 14.5% alc. **Rating** 92 **To** 2032 $125 NG
The Pinnacle McLaren Vale Shiraz 2017 A collaborative effort with the cricketer. Rich. The reductive clutch eased from the regional norm. Dutch licorice, iodine, violet, ample Cherry Ripe and blue fruits are corralled by a skein of oak-derived tannin; towed to decent length by balanced acidity. Screw cap. 14.5% alc. **Rating** 91 **To** 2026 $25 NG

ŢŢŢŢ   **Mowbray Boy Tasmania Pinot Noir 2019 Rating** 89 **To** 2021 $33 TS

Pooley Wines ★★★★★

Butcher's Hill Vineyard, 1431 Richmond Road, Richmond, Tas 7025
Region Southern Tasmania
T (03) 6260 2895 **www.**pooleywines.com.au **Open** 7 days 10–5
Winemaker Anna Pooley, Justin Bubb **Est.** 1985 **Dozens** 8500 **Vyds** 12.48ha
Three generations of the Pooley family have been involved in the development of Pooley Wines, although the winery was previously known as Cooinda Vale. Plantings have now reached almost 13ha in a region that is warmer and drier than most people realise. In 2003 the family planted pinot noir and pinot grigio (with more recent plantings of pinot noir and chardonnay) at Belmont Vineyard, a heritage property with an 1830s Georgian home and a (second) cellar door in the old sandstone barn and stables. Exports to the UK, the US and Sweden.

♙♙♙♙♙ **Margaret Pooley Tribute Single Vineyard Tasmania Riesling 2020** A monumental Tasmanian riesling in which every detail has been intricately placed to fulfil its manifesto of grand character and profound endurance. A core of impeccable, spicy wild lemon is nuanced by stone-fruit exotics. Epic acidity, skin-contact phenolics, lees texture and RS unite in a crystalline display of glittering energy that promises decades in the cellar. Breathtaking line and length in the presence of profound fruit concentration confirm one of Tasmania's finest rieslings of the vintage. Margaret would be proud indeed. Screw cap. 12% alc. **Rating** 97 To 2050 $75 TS ✪ ♥

♙♙♙♙♙ **Coal River Valley Riesling 2020** From the estate Butcher's Hill and Cooinda Vale Vineyards, whole-bunch pressed and fermented with a specialised (riesling) yeast. A lovely wine that delicately paints the mouth with its kaffir lime juice flavours, cosseted with layered, harmonious acidity. Great length too. Screw cap. 12% alc. **Rating** 96 To 2033 $39 JH ✪
Butcher's Hill Single Vineyard Chardonnay 2019 A triumphant accord between Anna Pooley's talents in the winery and Hannah McKay's in the vineyard. Captivating struck flint hovers over a tense core of lemon, grapefruit and Beurre Bosc pear. Fig fleshes out mid-palate concentration. Classy cashew nut and vanillan oak sits just below the fruit, pushing it both upwards and outwards. A cellaring special. Screw cap. 13.9% alc. **Rating** 95 To 2032 $65 TS
Coal River Valley Pinot Grigio 2020 Proper grigio and my favourite this year. Tense, crunchy, determined. A native Tasmanian. Windswept mettle. Precise, signature, spicy pear, both ripe and crunchy. Wild lemon tension. Coal River acidity and skin phenolics embrace triumphantly on a bracing and lingering finish. Rare endurance. Screw cap. 13% alc. **Rating** 95 To 2030 $36 TS ♥

♙♙♙♙♙ **Butcher's Hill Single Vineyard Riesling 2020 Rating** 93 To 2030 $65 TS
Cooinda Vale Single Vineyard Chardonnay 2019 Rating 93 To 2039 $65 TS
Coal River Valley Pinot Noir 2020 Rating 92 To 2033 $46 TS
J.R.D. Single Vineyard Syrah 2019 Rating 92 To 2039 $110 TS

Poonawatta ★★★★★

1227 Eden Valley Road, Flaxman Valley, SA 5235 **Region** Eden Valley
T 0448 031 880 **www.**poonawatta.com.au **Open** By appt
Winemaker Andrew Holt, Christa Deans, Harry Mantzarapis **Est.** 1880 **Dozens** 1800
Vyds 4ha
The Poonawatta story is complex, stemming from 0.8ha of shiraz planted in 1880. When Andrew Holt's parents purchased the Poonawatta property, the vineyard had suffered decades of neglect and the slow process of restoration began. While that was underway, the strongest canes available from the winter pruning of the block were slowly and progressively dug into the stony soil, establishing the Cuttings Block over 7 years, and the yield is even lower than that of the 1880 Block. The Riesling is produced from a separate vineyard planted by the Holts in the 1970s. Grenache was planted in 2019. Exports to France, the US, Canada, Malaysia, China and Denmark.

🍷🍷🍷🍷 **The 1880 Eden Valley Shiraz 2015** Typical bright crimson-purple hue of good depth. A seriously wonderful wine, full bodied yet so well balanced and structured it seems lighter. Blackberry, spice and licorice flavours fill the supple palate. This is right up there with the best in the family. Cork. 14.6% alc. **Rating** 98 **To** 2050 $110 JH

The 1880 Eden Valley Shiraz 2018 From drought to rain to more rain to drought! 2.6t picked 20 Apr, 3 of 7 barrels declassified. Bright crimson-purple. In that deceptive guise: full bodied and powerful, yet it's not obvious. The family blackberry base has juicy/spicy highlights, the tannins woven through the fruit and oak. Tasted not long after bottling, but makes light of it. For release '22, and regular customers will jump for it. The alcohol, incidentally, is perfect. Cork. 14.5% alc. **Rating** 97 **To** 2050 JH

🍷🍷🍷🍷 **The 1880 Eden Valley Shiraz 2017** A very wet spring led to extensive bunch thinning, but still 5.2t picked 1 May, 20% free-run drained off, 11 of 13 barriques declassified, 50L lost at bottling, only 530 bottles actually made (not 1965 as per label). Yes, it's distinctly savoury, but also spicy, and with thrust to the palate. The colour is typical, bright crimson-purple, and the wine has plenty to dwell on. Cork. 14.5% alc. **Rating** 95 **To** 2045 JH

Insurance Block Eden Valley Shiraz 2018 There is vast diversity across Poonawatta's extensive range of single-vineyard shiraz, and this is a standout for value and class. Deep and vibrant in both hue and palate, it captures impressive blackberry, black cherry and black plum fruit, confidently supported by acid verve, firm, fine tannins and classy French oak (rightly in that order). Screw cap. 14% alc. **Rating** 94 **To** 2033 $42 TS

🍷🍷🍷🍷 **The Eden Riesling 2020 Rating** 93 **To** 2027 $35 TS
The Cuttings Eden Valley Shiraz 2017 Rating 90 **To** 2032 $55 TS

Port Phillip Estate ★★★★★

263 Red Hill Road, Red Hill, Vic 3937 **Region** Mornington Peninsula
T (03) 5989 4444 **www**.portphillipestate.com.au **Open** 7 days 11–5
Winemaker Glen Hayley **Est.** 1987 **Dozens** 7000 **Vyds** 21.04ha
Port Phillip Estate has been owned by Giorgio and Dianne Gjergja since 2000. The ability of the site to produce outstanding syrah, pinot noir and chardonnay, and very good sauvignon blanc, is something special. In July '15, following the departure of winemaker Sandro Mosele, his assistant of 6 years, Glen Hayley, was appointed to take his place. The futuristic, multi-million-dollar restaurant, cellar door and winery complex, designed by award-winning Wood/Marsh Architecture, overlooks the vineyards and Westernport Bay. Exports to Canada and China.

🍷🍷🍷🍷 **Balnarring Pinot Noir 2019** While medium bodied at best, with smooth and supple tannins, this packs a lot of flavour and depth. Floats between florals, spicy dark cherries and heady forest-floor aromas. Oak is neatly integrated. It's compelling, complex, lithe and a lovely drink. Screw cap. 13.5% alc. **Rating** 95 **To** 2033 $39 JF

🍷🍷🍷🍷 **Balnarring Chardonnay 2019 Rating** 93 **To** 2029 $37 JF
Red Hill Pinot Noir 2019 Rating 93 **To** 2029 $39 JF
Morillon Single Block Chardonnay 2019 Rating 92 **To** 2029 $54 JF
Morillon Single Block Pinot Noir 2019 Rating 91 **To** 2032 $61 JF
Red Hill Chardonnay 2019 Rating 90 **To** 2028 $37 JF
Salasso Rosé 2020 Rating 90 **To** 2022 $26 JF
Quartier Pinot Noir 2019 Rating 90 **To** 2027 $27 JF

Portsea Estate ★★★★☆

7 Pembroke Place, Portsea, Vic 3944 **Region** Mornington Peninsula
T (03) 5984 3774 **www**.portseaestate.com **Open** By appt
Winemaker Tim Elphick **Est.** 2000 **Dozens** 3500 **Vyds** 4ha

Noted filmmaker Warwick Ross and sister (silent partner) Caron Wilson-Hawley have moved fast and successfully since their first vintage in 2004. Starting out with the luxury of having the first 7 vintages made at Paringa Estate by Lindsay McCall and team, Portsea Estate has since built an onsite winery and hired Tim Elphick, who has a wealth of cool-climate winemaking experience. Warwick's 2013 film *Red Obsession* was highly rated by film critics around the world. It takes an inside look at the Chinese fascination for the greatest wines of Bordeaux.

🍷🍷🍷🍷🍷 **Estate Pinot Noir Rosé 2020** Pastel pink hue and appealing in all ways. The right amount of spice, red fruits and zest. The tangy acidity tempered by lovely texture. A dry, refreshing finish warrants another glass. Or two. Screw cap. 13.1% alc. **Rating** 90 **To** 2022 $32 JF

🍷🍷🍷🍷 **Estate Pinot Gris 2019 Rating** 88 **To** 2023 $32 JF
Back Beach Pinot Noir 2019 Rating 88 **To** 2024 $30 JF

Precious Little Wine

Peninsula Providore, 2250 Bull Creek Road, Tooperang, SA 5255 **Region** South Australia **T** 0417 212 514 **www.**preciouslittlewine.com.au **Open** Mon–Fri 10–4, Sat–Sun 11–4 **Winemaker** Marty O'Flaherty **Est.** 2016 **Dozens** 600
Precious Little is the side project of mates Marty O'Flaherty and Adam Smith. Ex-chef Marty is winemaker for Atkins Family and Fox Gordon Wines, having cut his winemaking teeth at Zilzie in Victoria before working across SA and as far afield as Piedmont. Clare Valley boy Adam has 20 years of experience as an independent viticultural consultant and a grower liaison officer, now enjoying the challenge of seeking out exciting parcels for Marty to transform into small-batch wines. Wines can be tasted at the nearby Peninsula Providore.

🍷🍷🍷🍷🍷 **Marananga Barossa Valley Nero d'Avola 2019** Delicious Barossa nero. Signature licorice and satsuma plum, even a hint of sarsaparilla and ginger, with lingering spice lifted by French oak. Refreshingly medium bodied yet perfectly ripe. Vibrant acidity dances with finely textured tannins, concluding dry and fine. Screw cap. 13.5% alc. **Rating** 92 **To** 2024 $30 TS
Marananga Barossa Valley Shiraz 2018 Spicy and herbal, this is an unusually (yet refreshingly) savoury Marananga shiraz, defined by vibrant acidity and layers of spice. It is nonetheless ripe and harmonious, with a core of medium-bodied black fruits. Fine tannins sit neatly within a long finish. Screw cap. 14.5% alc. **Rating** 91 **To** 2028 $40 TS

Pressing Matters

665 Middle Tea Tree Road, Tea Tree, Tas 7017 **Region** Southern Tasmania **T** (03) 6268 1947 **www.**pressingmatters.com.au **Open** By appt 0408 126 668 **Winemaker** Samantha Connew **Est.** 2002 **Dozens** 2600 **Vyds** 7.3ha
Greg Melick wears more hats than most people manage in a lifetime. He is a major general (the highest rank in the Australian Army Reserve) a top level barrister (senior counsel) and has presided over a number of headline special commissions and inquiries into subjects as diverse as cricket match fixing and the Beaconsfield mine collapse. More recently he became deputy president of the Administrative Appeals Tribunal and chief commissioner of the Tasmanian Integrity Commission. Yet, if asked, he would probably nominate wine as his major focus in life. Having built up an exceptional cellar of the great wines of Europe, he has turned his attention to grapegrowing and winemaking, planting almost 3ha of riesling at his vineyard in the Coal River Valley. It is on a perfect north-facing slope, and the Mosel-style rieslings are making their mark. His multi-clone pinot noir block (just over 4ha) is also striking gold. Exports to the US, Singapore and Hong Kong.

🍷🍷🍷🍷🍷 **R139 Tasmania Riesling 2020** Pristine dessert riesling of crystalline structure, pitch-perfect purity and jubilant persistence. Acidity is the game for all sweet wines, declaring its greatness here in an icepick of frozen wild lemon and lime juice. Boiled lolly sweetness (139g/L RS) has been perfectly gauged to almost (but not quite) meet it in the middle, which is just as it should be. Great persistence and never-ending endurance. Screw cap. 8.5% alc. **Rating** 95 **To** 2050 $36 TS

R69 Riesling 2020 There aren't nearly as many medium-sweet rieslings made in Tasmania as there ought to be, which makes the good ones all the more important. Delightfully fragrant, pure and crystalline. Lemon blossom, frangipani, lime juice and a shake of white pepper. RS (69g/L) lends a boiled sweets feel to a long, zesty, limedrops finish. A shard of icy acidity guarantees it will live forever – if you can possibly keep your hands off it. Screw cap. 9.7% alc. **Rating** 94 **To** 2050 $39 TS

R9 Riesling 2020 Rating 93 **To** 2035 $39 TS
R0 Riesling 2020 Rating 92 **To** 2035 $39 TS
Pinot Noir 2019 Rating 90 **To** 2022 $36 TS

Primo Estate ★★★★★

McMurtrie Road, McLaren Vale, SA 5171 **Region** McLaren Vale
T (08) 8323 6800 **www**.primoestate.com.au **Open** 7 days 11–4
Winemaker Joseph Grilli, Daniel Grilli, Tom Garrett **Est.** 1979 **Dozens** 30 000
Vyds 34ha
Joe Grilli has always produced innovative and excellent wines. The biennial release of the Joseph Sparkling Red (in its tall Italian glass bottle) is eagerly awaited, the wine immediately selling out. The vineyard includes plantings of colombard, shiraz, cabernet sauvignon, riesling, merlot, sauvignon blanc, chardonnay, pinot gris, sangiovese, nebbiolo and merlot. Also highly regarded are the vintage-dated extra virgin olive oils. Exports to all major markets.

Joseph The Fronti NV Always delicious, muscat's telltale grapey spice, lychee and orange blossom scents are effusive, morphing into an elixir of rancio/walnut, dried tobacco and peat aromas, bridging a resinous viscosity and dutiful freshness that are more compelling with the virtues of age. The finish, infinite. Screw cap. 19.5% alc. **Rating** 96 $50 NG ❂

Joseph d'Elena Clarendon Pinot Grigio 2020 Rating 93 **To** 2024 $35 NG
Joseph Sparkling Red NV Rating 92 $96 NG
Shale Stone McLaren Vale Shiraz 2019 Rating 90 **To** 2028 $21 NG ❂

Prince Albert ★★★★

100 Lemins Road, Waurn Ponds, Vic 3216 **Region** Geelong
T 0412 531 191 **www**.princealbertvineyard.com.au **Open** By appt
Winemaker Fiona Purnell, David Yates **Est.** 1975 **Dozens** 350 **Vyds** 2ha
The original Prince Albert vineyard operated from 1857 to 1882, and was re-established on the same site by Bruce Hyett in 1975 (Bruce passed away in Feb 2013, aged 89). In '07 Dr David Yates, with a background based on a degree in chemistry, purchased the pinot-noir-only venture. David is committed to retaining certified organic status for Prince Albert, and sees no reason to change the style of the wine, which he has always loved. Exports to the UK.

Geelong Pinot Noir 2015 Clones MV6 and D4V2 employed here in this dark, well-detailed pinot. Fruits of the forest, black tea, dried herb and musk. A beguiling, lifted palate, remarkably youthful and fresh for a 5yo wine. Fine in tannin line and long on the finish. Screw cap. 14.3% alc. **Rating** 94 **To** 2027 $46 JP

Principia ★★★★★

139 Main Creek Road, Red Hill, Vic 3937 **Region** Mornington Peninsula
T (03) 5931 0010 **www**.principiawines.com.au **Open** By appt
Winemaker Darrin Gaffy **Est.** 1995 **Dozens** 750 **Vyds** 3.5ha
Darrin Gaffy's guiding philosophy for Principia is minimal interference, thus the vines (3ha of pinot noir and 0.5ha of chardonnay) are not irrigated and yields are restricted to 3.75t/ha or less. All wine movements are by gravity or by gas pressure, which in turn means there is no filtration, and both primary and secondary fermentation are by wild yeast. 'Principia' comes from the word 'beginnings' in Latin. Exports to Japan and Hong Kong.

ŸŸŸŸŸ **Mornington Peninsula Chardonnay 2019** There's a great deal of attention and care across the Principia range, with chardonnay in the lead this vintage. Moreish and savoury, yet initially working off a citrus theme – lemon balm, curd and zest. There's a succulence, then texture across the refined palate, with flinty, fine acidity. Gosh, it's really hard to put down. So I didn't. Screw cap. 13.6% alc. **Rating** 95 **To** 2029 $45 JF

Altior Mornington Peninsula Pinot Noir 2019 The flagship red. A barrel selection, matured in 70% new French oak, which has certainly settled into the body of the wine. Good concentration, with cranberries, morello and red cherries, blood orange and lots of spice, too. Despite all this, it is certainly tightly wound, almost austere, with a firm tannic hold. Not a bad thing at all, as time will be its friend. Screw cap. 13.7% alc. **Rating** 95 **To** 2030 $60 JF

Kindred Hill Mornington Peninsula Pinot Noir 2019 It's bright, tight and almost lean yet full of fragrance, all autumnal with mulch and chinotto. The medium-weighted palate feels sinewy at first with ripe/unripe fruit tang. The acidity is showing itself strongly while stern tannins offer support. A bit nervy at the moment, but refreshing. It's a very good wine and time will no doubt alter its outcome for the better. Screw cap. 13% alc. **Rating** 94 **To** 2030 $60 JF

ŸŸŸŸŸ **Mornington Peninsula Pinot Noir 2019 Rating** 93 **To** 2027 $45 JF

Printhie Wines ★★★★★

208 Nancarrow Lane, Nashdale, NSW 2800 **Region** Orange
T (02) 6366 8422 **www**.printhiewines.com.au **Open** Mon–Fri 3–5, Sat–Sun 11–5
Winemaker Drew Tuckwell **Est.** 1996 **Dozens** 25 000 **Vyds** 32ha
Owned by the Swift family. The next generation, Edward and David, have taken over (from Jim and Ruth Swift) to guide the business into its next era. In 2016 Printhie clocked up 10 years of commercial wine production and the vineyards are now reaching a good level of maturity at 25 years. The 32ha of estate vineyards are planted at varying elevations between 630 and 1000m above sea level. Winemaker Drew Tuckwell has been at Printhie for a decade and has over 20 years of winemaking experience in Australia and Europe. Exports to China.

Project Wine ★★★★

83 Pioneer Road, Angas Plains, SA 5255 **Region** South Australia
T (08) 8537 0600 **www**.projectwine.com.au
Winemaker Peter Pollard **Est.** 2001 **Dozens** 155 000
Originally designed as a contract winemaking facility, Project Wine has developed a sales and distribution arm that has rapidly developed markets both domestic and overseas. Located in Langhorne Creek, it sources fruit from most key SA wine regions, including McLaren Vale, Barossa Valley and Adelaide Hills. The diversity of grape sourcing allows the winery to produce a wide range of products under the Tail Spin, Pioneer Road, Parson's Paddock, Bird's Eye View and Angas & Bremer labels. Exports to the UK, NZ, Switzerland, Canada, Japan and China.

ŸŸŸŸŸ **Angas & Bremer Langhorne Creek Shiraz 2018** Big, rich, old-school shiraz that's spent 18 months maturing in American oak, 25% new. It's a testament to the fruit involved that it stands up to the sweet vanilla/spice barrel impact. In the end, that's the style and for the price, what you see is what you get. Screw cap. 14.8% alc. **Rating** 92 **To** 2026 $25 TL

 # Protero ★★★★★

60 Olivers Road, McLaren Vale SA 5171 **Region** Adelaide Hills
T (08) 8323 8000 **www**.protero.com.au **Open** By appt
Winemaker Stephen Pannell **Est.** 1999 **Dozens** 3000 **Vyds** 13.2ha
Stephen and Fiona Pannell first discovered the nebbiolo growing outside Gumeracha in the northern Adelaide Hills in 2004 – it had been planted by Rose and Frank Baldasso in 1999. The vineyard, on a western-facing slope, is home to 5 clones of nebbiolo that Stephen has

worked with since 2005. Surrounded by native bush, twice in 20 years the vineyard has been surrounded by fire and twice it has survived (including a week after the Pannells bought the property in December 2019). They have since removed chardonnay, pinot noir, merlot and viognier from the vineyard and planted barbera, dolcetto, gewürztraminer, pinot gris and riesling. Nebbiolo remains a passion, but Stephen poses the questions each year: what is Australian nebbiolo? How does it translate? 'We shouldn't attempt to replicate the wines of Piedmont, but rather create a unique style of nebbiolo that speaks of our place.' (TL)

ŶŶŶŶŶ **Gumeracha Adelaide Hills Nebbiolo 2018** You might just want to stay with the aromas forever and a day, captivating, lifted, generous in their mix of dried orange, garden rose beds, leaf stem and petal, followed by a completely different savoury, mineral, amaro bitters-toned palate. Nebbiolo tannins as expected, fitting comfortably into the matrix. A fascinating, long-term journey ahead. Screw cap. 14% alc. **Rating** 96 **To** 2030 $38 TL ❂

Gumeracha Capo Adelaide Hills Nebbiolo 2018 Nebbiolo's paler garnet colour is immediately in the zone, the aromas lifted, with a black cherry, leather and terracotta-like earthiness. Once all of these meld on the palate, the wine becomes intently more about its savoury and sweet-umami elements, the variety's tannins wrapping up with a gentle force and subtle bitterness. Something special here. Screw cap. 14.5% alc. **Rating** 96 **To** 2030 $80 TL

ŶŶŶŶŶ **Adelaide Hills Grigio Nero Pinots 2020** **Rating** 93 **To** 2025 $28 TL

Provenance Wines ★★★★★

100 Lower Paper Mills Road, Fyansford, Vic 3221 **Region** Geelong
T (03) 5222 3422 **www.**provenancewines.com.au **Open** 7 days 11–5 summer,
Thurs–Mon 11–5 winter
Winemaker Scott Ireland, Sam Vogel **Est.** 1997 **Dozens** 6500 **Vyds** 14.2ha
In 1997 when Scott Ireland and partner Jen Lilburn established Provenance Wines, they knew it wouldn't be easy starting a winery with limited capital and no fixed abode. The one thing the business had was Scott's 20+ years' experience operating contract wine services in the Hunter Valley, Barossa, Coonawarra, Mudgee, Clare Valley, Yarra Valley and Tasmania. He says he met so many dedicated small winemakers that he was hooked for life. In 2004 Scott moved to Austins & Co as winemaker while continuing to grow the Provenance business, developing key relationships with growers in Geelong, the ultra-cool Macedon, Ballarat and Henty. in 2016 Sam Vogel, Scott's long-term assistant winemaker, stepped up to join the business as a partner and they took a long-term lease of 25% of the Fyansford Paper Mill, refurbishing the heritage-listed 1870s local bluestone buildings, providing excellent cellaring conditions. Exports to Malaysia and Hong Kong.

ŶŶŶŶŶ **Ballarat Chardonnay 2019** The perfect introduction to Ballarat chardonnay for those new to its significant charms. So fine but so full of depth, too, deceptively so. Grapefruit, lime, wax flowers, almond nut, grilled white peach. Quietly goes about its work on the palate establishing authority with filigree-fine acid structure and balance throughout. Screw cap. 13.3% alc. **Rating** 95 **To** 2029 $52 JP

Geelong Chardonnay 2019 Dry and warm to hot conditions aside, winemaker Scott Ireland has turned out another stunner of a chardonnay, full of flavour, intensity and character. Runs the gamut from Golden Delicious apple, nectarine, quince and white peach to grilled nuts, with preserved lemon savouriness. Quite the mouthful of flavour, but all the while, nicely restrained. Screw cap. 13.2% alc. **Rating** 95 **To** 2029 $52 JP

Henty Chardonnay 2019 There's a power here, a linear beauty, built around a purity of fruit and structure. It demands further time in bottle to explore the citrus, lime, peach, nectarine, dried herb, mealy complexity already evident and waiting to fully reach resolution. A succulent palate, with lemony acidity guiding this journey. Screw cap. 13.3% alc. **Rating** 95 **To** 2029 $52 JP

Henty Pinot Noir 2018 Winemaker Scott Ireland's signature aromatics are all over this impressive youngster, with wild herbs, potpourri, violets, earth and, yes,

red berries – alive and vibrant. Fills the mouth with flavour and doesn't let go. Beauty, form and persistence. Screw cap. 13.5% alc. **Rating** 95 **To** 2027 $52 JP
Geelong Pinot Noir 2018 A spirited pinot performance from a strong vintage. Deeply coloured. Very fruit-focused bouquet with an undercurrent of dried herbs and winter greens. Runs deep on the palate, perfectly poised, sprinkled with spice, a touch of smoke and controlling, even-handed tannins. Screw cap. 13.5% alc. **Rating** 95 **To** 2027 $52 JP ♥
Ballarat Pinot Noir 2018 Hand-picked fruit, 50% whole bunch, wild-yeast open fermentation, 11 days on skins, mlf, 10 months in French barriques (30% new). Still early days for this pinot; tight and slowly yielding to time in bottle. Emerging deep dark aromas of tilled earth, forest floor, wild blackberries and herbs. Gathering itself together on the palate around a solid core of spice and black cherry, the sinewy tannins yet to fully meld. A dark, brooding pinot in the making. Screw cap. 13.5% alc. **Rating** 94 **To** 2027 $52 JP

🍷🍷🍷🍷🍷 **Ironstone Geelong Shiraz 2018 Rating** 93 **To** 2028 $52 JP
Henty Riesling 2020 Rating 92 **To** 2032 $30 JP
Henty Pinot Gris 2020 Rating 92 **To** 2024 $30 JP
Western Districts Rosé 2020 Rating 92 **To** 2025 $25 JP ✪
Geelong Shiraz 2019 Rating 91 **To** 2025 $36 JP
Golden Plains Pinot Noir 2019 Rating 90 **To** 2025 $32 JP

Punch ★★★★★

10 Scott Street, St Andrews, Vic 3761 **Region** Yarra Valley
T 0424 074 234 **www**.punched.com.au **Open** W'ends 12–5
Winemaker James Lance **Est.** 2004 **Dozens** 1800 **Vyds** 3.25ha
In the wake of Graeme Rathbone taking over the brand (but not the real estate) of Diamond Valley, James Lance and his wife Claire leased the vineyard and winery from James' parents, David and Catherine Lance, including the 0.25ha block of close-planted pinot noir. In all, Punch has 2.25ha of pinot noir (including the close-planted), 0.8ha of chardonnay and 0.4ha of cabernet sauvignon. When the 2009 Black Saturday bushfires destroyed the crop, various grapegrowers called offering assistance, which led to the purchase of the grapes used for that dire year and the beginning of the 'Friends of Punch' wines. Exports to Singapore and China.

🍷🍷🍷🍷🍷 **Lance's Vineyard Close Planted Pinot Noir 2018** Open-fermented with wild yeast, 13 months in French oak, 50% new. Yarra Valley pinot royalty with much history – always a pleasure to taste. Gamey and brooding at this stage of its life. The fruit is yet to fully emerge it seems, from the concentration and complexity of the dense texture, the tannin and the oak, but the underlying dark plum and cherry characters are there. This needs time in the cellar to unfold and flourish. Screw cap. 13.5% alc. **Rating** 95 **To** 2033 $90 SC

🍷🍷🍷🍷🍷 **Lance's Vineyard Chardonnay 2018 Rating** 93 **To** 2025 $45 SC
Lance's Vineyard Cabernet Sauvignon 2018 Rating 93 **To** 2038 $45 SC
Lance's Vineyard Pinot Noir 2018 Rating 92 **To** 2028 $55 SC

Punt Road ★★★★★

10 St Huberts Road, Coldstream, Vic 3770 **Region** Yarra Valley
T (03) 9739 0666 **www**.puntroadwines.com.au **Open** 7 days 10–5
Winemaker Tim Shand, Travis Bush **Est.** 2000 **Dozens** 20 000 **Vyds** 65.61ha
Punt Road is owned by the Napoleone family, 3rd-generation fruit growers in the Yarra Valley. Their vineyard in Coldstream is one of the most historic sites in Victoria, first planted to vines by Swiss immigrant Hubert De Castella in 1860. The Napoleone Vineyard was established on the property in 1987. Chief winemaker Tim Shand joined the winery in 2014 and has established a reputation for consistent quality of all the Punt Road wines. The 2 main ranges are Punt Road and Airlie Bank, plus a small production of single-vineyard 'Block' wines, only available at cellar door, made only in the best vintages. Exports to the US, UK, Canada, Sweden, Denmark, Singapore, China and Sri Lanka.

🍷🍷🍷🍷 **Block 1 Yarra Valley Pinot Noir 2019** A barrel selection from Block 1 of the Napoleone vineyard, all MV6, 5% whole bunches. Matured in French barriques, 30% new. This has come together seamlessly. Subtle in a way, could initially be overlooked. It takes time to blossom. The palate is refined and supple, with smooth and silky tannins. Screw cap. 13% alc. **Rating** 95 **To** 2029 $85 JF
Block 13 Napoleone Vineyard Yarra Valley Merlot 2019 Punt Road's merlot is usually a companion to its cabernet, but this vintage dictated a separate bottling as a cellar door-only release. It's lovely and complete, combining precise pockets of flavour from mulberries, Angelina plums to dried herbs, eucalyptus and earthy aromas. Tannins are stylishly fine, but with enough substance to hold everything in check, with a twang of soursob on the finish. Screw cap. 13% alc. **Rating** 95 **To** 2032 $40 JF

🍷🍷🍷🍷♀ **Yarra Valley Pinot Noir 2020 Rating** 92 **To** 2025 $32 JF
Airlie Bank Yarra Valley Pinot Noir 2020 Rating 91 **To** 2023 $22 JF ❂
Napoleone Vineyard Yarra Valley Shiraz 2019 Rating 91 **To** 2027 $32 JF

Pure Vision Organic Wines ★★★☆

PO Box 258, Virginia, SA 5120 **Region** Adelaide Plains
T 0412 800 875 **www**.purevisionwines.com.au
Winemaker Joanne Irvine, Ken Carypidis **Est.** 2001 **Dozens** 18 000 **Vyds** 55ha
The Carypidis family runs 2 brands: Pure Vision and Nature's Step. The oldest vineyards were planted in 1975; organic conversion began in 2009. Growing grapes under a certified organic regime is much easier if the region is warm to hot and dry, conditions unsuitable for botrytis and downy mildew. You are still left with weed growth (no herbicides are allowed) and powdery mildew (sulphur sprays are permitted), but the overall task is much simpler. The Adelaide Plains, where Pure Vision's vineyard is situated, is such a region. Ken Carypidis has been clever enough to secure the services of Joanne Irvine as co-winemaker. Exports to Singapore, Hong Kong and China.

🍷🍷🍷🍷♀ **White Organic Pinot Gris 2019** A little skin contact plus 6 months on lees has given this wine some body and spruiked the pear flavours with a dash of spice, supporting a leisurely flow and finish. Screw cap. 12.5% alc. **Rating** 91 **To** 2024 $25 TL

Purple Hands Wines ★★★★★

Artisans Wine Room, 64 Murray Street, Tanunda, SA 5352 **Region** Barossa Valley
T 0401 988 185 **www**.purplehandswines.com.au
Winemaker Craig Stansborough **Est.** 2006 **Dozens** 3000 **Vyds** 14ha
This is a partnership between Craig Stansborough, who provides the winemaking know-how and an 8ha vineyard of shiraz (northwest of Williamstown in a cooler corner of the southern Barossa), and Mark Slade, who provides the passion. Don't ask me (James) how this works – I don't know – but I do know they are producing outstanding single-vineyard wines (the grenache is contract-grown) of quite remarkable elegance. The wines are made at Grant Burge, where Craig is chief winemaker. Exports to the UK, China, Hong Kong and the Philippines.

🍷🍷🍷🍷🍷 **Planta Circa Ancestor Vine Barossa Valley Shiraz 2019** Capturing such lift of violet fragrance in warm-climate shiraz is a skill at which the southern Barossa is particularly adept. Old-vine exotic spice and supple, slippery tannins back a stunning core of blackberry/cherry fruit. A sense of measured confidence in fruit, alcohol and oak is resounding proof that less is always more in the Barossa. Brilliant work from Craig Stansborough. Diam. 14.1% alc. **Rating** 96 **To** 2034 $80 TS
Old Vine Barossa Valley Grenache 2019 Old bush vines, 35% whole bunch, matured in used puncheons for 10 months. The wine is medium bodied and perfectly balanced, the flavours of red and purple fruit held in a gently savoury net of fine tannins. It's akin to a high-quality Rhône wine with no confection, and will live for years. Screw cap. 14% alc. **Rating** 96 **To** 2029 $30 JH ❂

After Five Wine Co. Single Vineyard Barossa Valley Shiraz 2019 A delightful, deep, vibrant purple hue and enticing depth of black cherry, satsuma plum, blackberry and fresh licorice straps define the essence of Williamstown shiraz. Fine-grained tannins, high-cocoa dark chocolate French oak and nicely poised acidity all assume their rightful positions. It will age for the medium term, if you can possibly keep your hands off! Screw cap. 14.5% alc. **Rating** 95 **To** 2032 $45 TS

Barossa Valley Shiraz 2018 From the Stansborough vineyard in Williamstown, this is signature southern Barossa shiraz of density and definition, at a party-friendly price. Fantastic accuracy of blackberry, blueberry and black cherry fruit is the hero. Whole bunches and oak have been sensitively played to elevate the fruit profile. Bright acidity and fine tannins draw out a long finish. Screw cap. 14% alc. **Rating** 94 **To** 2028 $30 TS ✪

♥♥♥♥♀ **Colours of the South Adelaide Pinot Gris 2020** Rating 93 **To** 2022 $25 TS ✪
After Five Wine Co. Single Vineyard Barossa Valley Serata 2019 **Rating** 93 **To** 2027 $45 TS
Colours of the South Barossa Valley Pinot Blanc 2020 Rating 92 **To** 2022 $25 TS ✪
Barossa Valley Mataro Shiraz Grenache 2019 Rating 92 **To** 2026 $30 TS

Pyren Vineyard ★★★★

Glenlofty-Warrenmang Road, Warrenmang, Vic 3478 **Region** Pyrenees
T (03) 5467 2352 www.pyrenvineyard.com
Winemaker Leighton Joy, Brock Alford **Est.** 1999 **Dozens** 10 000 **Vyds** 28.3ha
Brian and Leighton Joy have 23ha of shiraz, 5ha of cabernet sauvignon and 1ha malbec, cabernet franc and petit verdot on the slopes of the Warrenmang Valley near Moonambel. Yield is restricted to between 3.7t and 6.1t/ha. Exports to the UK and China.

♥♥♥♥♥ **Union 2019** Not the easiest of vintages and yet Union comes through with flying colours again, this time with malbec in the lead role with cabernet. Vibrant and fresh in purple hues, it bursts out in high florals, plum, black cherry, blueberry and light herbals. Seamless to taste and, while firm in structure, it remains effortlessly light on its feet. Diam. 14% alc. **Rating** 95 **To** 2034 $60 JP

♥♥♥♥♀ **Reserve Syrah 2019** Rating 93 **To** 2032 $60 JP
Pyrenees Cabernet 2019 Rating 93 **To** 2030 $60 JP
Little Ra Ra Roopa Pyrenees 2020 Rating 91 **To** 2025 $30 JP
Earthscape Shiraz 2018 Rating 90 **To** 2028 $35 JP

Quarisa Wines ★★★★

743 Slopes Road, Tharbogang, NSW 2680 (postal) **Region** South Australia
T (02) 6963 6222 www.quarisa.com.au
Winemaker John Quarisa **Est.** 2005
John Quarisa has had a distinguished career as a winemaker spanning over 20 years, working for some of Australia's largest wineries including McWilliam's, Casella and Nugan Estate. He was also chiefly responsible in 2004 for winning the Jimmy Watson Trophy (Melbourne) and the Stodart Trophy (Adelaide). John and Josephine Quarisa have set up a very successful family business using grapes from various parts of NSW and SA, made in leased space. Production has risen in leaps and bounds, doubtless sustained by the exceptional value for money provided by the wines. Exports include the UK, the US, Canada, Sweden, Denmark, Finland, Poland, Russia, Malaysia, Indonesia, Thailand, Singapore, NZ, Japan, Hong Kong and China.

♥♥♥♥♀ **Mrs Q Adelaide Hills Sangiovese 2019** Full-tilt sangio here. Dark plums, anise, black olive tapenade all throw their lot into this satisfying expression. The variety's typical tannins are well managed within the whole matrix. Screw cap. 14.5% alc. **Rating** 90 **To** 2027 $19 TL ✪

Quartz Hill Vineyard

65 Lillicur West Road, Lamplough, Vic 3352 (postal) **Region** Pyrenees
T (03) 5465 3670 **www**.quartzhillwines.com.au **Open** W'ends & by appt
Winemaker Darrin Gaffy, Owen Latta **Est.** 1995 **Dozens** 600 **Vyds** 4.15ha

Quartz Hill was established in 1995, with Shane and Michelle Mead relocating from
Melbourne to run their vineyard in '99. After growing grapes for other wine labels for many
years, the first Quartz Hill wine came onto the market in '09. Winemaking is a family effort,
with brother Darrin Gaffy from Principia on the Mornington Peninsula (see separate entry)
as winemaker, and all winemaking processes performed traditionally, by hand. Grenache and
touriga have recently been added to the shiraz, viognier and mencia plantings. A new cellar
door and winery, built from straw bales, opened in 2021.

Pyrenees Syrah 2018 A wine that is easy to get into, such are its welcoming
ways. It is a deep red/purple colour, gentle in aromas that are all about bright
red fruits, savoury spice and pepper overtones. It's smooth and subtle to taste.
Everything is nicely in place for good drinking now, or later if you are patient.
Screw cap. 13.8% alc. **Rating** 91 **To** 2026 $38 JP

Pyrenees Mencia 2018 Rating 88 **To** 2025 $28 JP

Quattro Mano

PO Box 189, Hahndorf, SA 5245 **Region** Barossa Valley
T 0430 647 470 **www**.quattromano.com.au **Open** By appt
Winemaker Anthony Carapetis, Christopher Taylor, Philippe Morin **Est.** 2006
Dozens 2500 **Vyds** 3.8ha

Anthony Carapetis, Philippe Morin and Chris Taylor have collective experience of over
50 years working in various facets of the wine industry, Philippe as a leading sommelier for
over 25 years, and presently as Director of French Oak Cooperage, Anthony and Chris as
winemakers. The dream of Quattro Mano began in the mid-1990s, becoming a reality in
2006 (it's unclear how 3 equals 4). They produce an eclectic range of wines, tempranillo the
cornerstone. It's an impressive, albeit small, business. Exports to the US and Japan.

La Reto Barossa Valley Tempranillo 2018 From one of the Barossa's older
plantings of tempranillo, this is a bright purple-tinted thing that unites considerable
fruit presence with the firm, medium-grained tannin structure and complexity of
long oak age. Spicy blackberries and mulberries are backed by dried herbs. Oak
heightens its savoury profile, albeit quashing fruit lift, while lending leathery, gamey
allusions that linger long. Screw cap. 14.5% alc. **Rating** 91 **To** 2028 $28 TS

Quealy Winemakers

62 Bittern-Dromana Road, Balnarring, Vic 3926 **Region** Mornington Peninsula
T (03) 5983 2483 **www**.quealy.com.au **Open** 7 days 9–5
Winemaker Kathleen Quealy, Tom McCarthy **Est.** 1982 **Dozens** 8000 **Vyds** 8ha

Kathleen Quealy and Kevin McCarthy were among the early waves of winemakers on
the Mornington Peninsula. They challenged the status quo – most publicly by introducing
Mornington Peninsula pinot gris/grigio (with great success). Behind this was improvement
and diversification in site selection, plus viticulture and winemaking techniques that allowed
their business to grow significantly. The estate plantings are 2ha each of pinot noir, pinot gris
and friulano, as well as smaller plots of riesling, chardonnay and moscato giallo. Their leased
vineyards are established on what Kathleen and Kevin consider to be premium sites for pinot
gris and pinot noir. These are now single-vineyard wines: Musk Creek, Campbell & Christine
and the newer Tussie Mussie Vineyard. Son Tom stepped up as head winemaker in 2019.
Lucas Blanck manages the certified organic estate vineyards; the leased vineyards are moving
towards 100% organic management. Exports to Japan, China and Taiwan.

Pinot Grigio 2020 It has the spice, the crunchy pear, the saline, lemony tang and
crisp natural acidity to seal it with a big grigio stamp of approval. So refreshing
and delicious. Screw cap. 12.9% alc. **Rating** 95 **To** 2024 $35 JF ✪

Tussie Mussie Vineyard Late Harvest Pinot Gris 2019 Starting off with a gorgeous burnished copper/orange hue, it gets better. Burnt toffee, lemon brittle and cardamom-infused crème brûlée plus apricot jam. And yet, the acidity lifts the rich flavours, tempers the sweetness and lets the silky luscious texture continue. Superb. Screw cap. 11.5% alc. **Rating** 95 **To** 2026 $35 JF ✪

Turbul Friulano 2019 Mid gold hue, like an autumn sun. Strong quinine flavour, angostura bitters on poached quince. Peach fuzz tannins, chewy and ripe, but these phenolics work well, creating the body and texture of the wine. Smoky, with some red fruits, too. It gives more with each sip. Slippery texture, honeyed and rich. At its best without chilling the life out of it. Diam. 13.9% alc. **Rating** 95 **To** 2026 $40 JF

Lina Lool Amber 2019 This is an elixir. Golden Delicious apples, quince, spice, pink grapefruit with lemon/lime acidity. A complex wine with beautifully handled phenolics. It gave me goose bumps. Screw cap. 13.2% alc. **Rating** 95 **To** 2026 $35 JF ✪

KKO1 Pinot Noir 2019 Dark, sweet fruits, chinotto, licorice root, lots of spices and florals. Nicely layered flavours, with ribbons of tannin to what is quite a structured wine, yet with a plushness throughout. There's a tanginess, a juiciness and energy to this. A fitting tribute from all sides. Screw cap. 13.4% alc. **Rating** 95 **To** 2030 $40 JF

Seventeen Rows Pinot Noir 2019 The most structured of the Quealy pinot noirs. Full bodied, good concentration, with ripe, plush tannins and sweet, spicy fruit. Savoury notes shine through with hazelnut skins, black olives, an earthiness and iodine. It leaves an impression. Screw cap. 12.9% alc. **Rating** 95 **To** 2030 $65 JF

Campbell & Christine Pinot Noir 2019 Smells of the Mornington Peninsula in autumn. Damp earth, woodsy and mushroom, spiked with tangy cherries. It's a lovely wine. Juicy and zesty and framed by its medium-bodied palate and velvety tannins. A delicious drink. Screw cap. 13% alc. **Rating** 94 **To** 2029 $45 JF

🍷🍷🍷🍷🍷 **Pobblebonk Field Blend 2020** **Rating** 93 **To** 2024 $35 JF
Musk Creek Pinot Gris 2020 **Rating** 92 **To** 2024 $35 JF
Tussie Mussie Pinot Gris 2019 **Rating** 91 **To** 2024 $30 JF
Musk Creek Pinot Noir 2019 **Rating** 90 **To** 2024 $40 JF

 Quid Pro Quo

520 Milbrodale Road, Broke, NSW 2330 **Region** Broke Fordwich
www.qpq.com.au **Open** By appt
Winemaker John Emmerig **Est.** 2012 **Dozens** 500 **Vyds** 56ha
By day, lawyer John Emmerig is a managing partner in a global law firm and an adjunct professor of law. Yet 2 other passions fuel another side to him – art (he's a renowned painter and Archibald prize finalist), and of course wine. His foray into the latter began in 2012 when he completed a short winemaking course. Initially based in Canberra and making wine from locally purchased fruit, he and wife Jane moved to Sydney for work and sought a property closer than the country's capital. In 2015, they bought 56ha in Broke Fordwich. From 2016, and with a strong eye to climate change, they wasted no time in planting varieties such as nero d'Avola, negroamaro, fiano, touriga, primitivo, sangiovese and gamay, alongside Hunter stalwarts such as semillon, shiraz and chardonnay. Smoke taint thwarted their first vintage from the Hunter so all the wines this year are from the Canberra region. A new onsite winery is expected to be completed in 2022. (JF)

🍷🍷🍷🍷🍷 **Canberra District Cabernet Merlot 2018** A 51/49 split that has come together well for a more approachable style. The brightest hue of all the reds; a whiff of florals, then cassis and currants all spiced up with menthol, baking spices and wood char. While there's a plushness, the palate weight is medium, with gritty tannins neatly tucked in. Screw cap. 13.7% alc. **Rating** 91 **To** 2028 $40 JF
Canberra District Cabernet Sauvignon Merlot 2018 An approachable style. The brightest hue of all the reds; a whiff of florals, then cassis and currants all

spiced up with menthol, baking spices and wood char. While there's a plushness, the medium-weight palate has gritty tannins neatly tucked in. Screw cap. 13.7% alc. **Rating** 91 **To** 2028 $40 JF

Canberra District Shiraz Viognier 2018 This is full of plums and spice, florals and dried herbs. It's not complex but it is pleasant. The palate is on the lighter side of medium bodied, the tannins have some shape and texture, with a slight grip to the finish. Screw cap. 13.9% alc. **Rating** 90 **To** 2027 $40 JF

ᵀᵀᵀᵀ   **Canberra District Sangiovese 2018 Rating** 88 **To** 2022 $34 JF

Quiet Mutiny

10 Elaine Cresecent, West Hobart, Tas, 7000 (postal) **Region** Tasmania
T 0410 552 317 **www**.quietmutiny.wine
Winemaker Greer Carland **Est.** 2017 **Dozens** 400
Owner and winemaker Greer Carland grew up on the Laurel Bank family property, learning to prune vines at an early age. She completed her oenology degree at the University of Adelaide in 2000 and, after a few years of international vintages in Chile, France and the US and a short stint in WA, she returned to Tasmania in '04. For the next 12 years she worked with Julian Alcorso at Winemaking Tasmania, also making the Laurel Bank wines. In '16 she left to focus on making the family wines at Laurel Bank and to start her own label. She intends to secure land and establish a vineyard for Quiet Mutiny with her viticulturist husband Paul Smart.

ᵀᵀᵀᵀ♀   **Charlotte's Elusion Riesling 2020** Pretty, pure, elegant and floral. A wonderfully accurate and graceful Derwent Valley riesling of medium straw hue and lemon blossom and frangipane fragrance. A core of cool lemon and red apple is accented with exotic notes of guava and pomegranate. Fine acidity draws out a long finish, with some phenolic bite from partial skin contact. Screw cap. 12% alc. **Rating** 92 **To** 2027 $38 TS

Venus Rising Pinot Noir 2019 Spicy, complex and black-fruited, this is a pinot that confidently fuses crunchy blackberry fruits and beetroot with the savoury, dried thyme overlay of whole-bunch fermentation and the subtle cashew-nut grip of a touch of new French oak. Firm, fine tannins bring up a dry finish of medium persistence. Screw cap. 13.5% alc. **Rating** 91 **To** 2026 $48 TS

Quin Wines

785 Seppeltsfield Road, Seppeltsfield SA 5355 **Region** Barossa Valley
T 0407 363 842 **www**.quinwines.com.au
Winemaker Andrew Quin **Est.** 2018 **Dozens** 500 **Vyds** 7.2ha
The story of Quin Wines and of Andrew and Skye Quin has a feeling of what was meant to be. It all happened so logically, and quickly, you have to draw breath for a moment. Andrew and Skye met at high school in Melbourne, and travelled the world before settling in the Barossa Valley. Andrew's journey started in his grandmother's garden as young boy, which led to the study of horticulture and, eventually, viticulture and winemaking. After consolidating his knowledge at wineries in Victoria and Sonoma, California, he mixed travel and work in the French Languedoc region. After his return to Australia, a chance visit to Hentley Farm in 2008 led to his appointment as chief winemaker for the relatively newly minted brand. It's been forwards and upwards in quick succession. Andrew and Skye have opened the Barossa's latest high-end accommodation, Cambourne Boutique Accommodation. It was the 2014 purchase of the 7.2ha Cambourne Vineyard that has allowed him to have fun, winning a slew of trophies at the Barossa Wine Show '18. The balance of the production from the vineyard is sold. In between all of that they have 3 (very loud) children.

ᵀᵀᵀᵀᵀ   **Eden Valley Shiraz 2019** Great vibrancy of colour in a medium to full purple hue. Impeccably defined, compact blackberry, blueberry and satsuma plum fruit drive long through the palate. A fine, rigid tannin chassis has been intricately engineered for the long haul. It holds line, length and integrity on the finish. Screw cap. 14.5% alc. **Rating** 94 **To** 2034 $55 TS

🍷🍷🍷🍷 Barossa Valley Shiraz 2019 Rating 93 To 2028 $55 TS
Malakoff Vineyard Pyrenees Nebbiolo 2019 Rating 93 To 2024 $55 NG
Barossa Valley Grenache 2019 Rating 90 To 2024 $55 TS

R. Paulazzo

852 Oakes Road, Yoogali, NSW 2680 **Region** Riverina
T 0412 696 002 **www.rpaulazzo.com.au**
Winemaker Rob Paulazzo **Est.** 2013 **Vyds** 12ha
Rob Paulazzo began winemaking in 2000 and covered a lot of ground before establishing his eponymous Riverina business. In Australia he worked for McWilliam's and Orlando, in NZ for Giesen. He also completed 4 vintages in Burgundy, plus vintages in Tuscany, the Napa Valley and Niagara Peninsula (Canada). In addition to the family's vineyard, established over 80 years ago, Rob also sources fruit from Hilltops, Tumbarumba, Orange and Canberra District.

Ravens Croft Wines ★★★☆

274 Spring Creek Road, Stanthorpe, Qld 4380 **Region** Granite Belt
T (07) 4683 3252 **www.**ravenscroftwines.com.au **Open** Fri–Sun & public hols 10.30–4.30
Winemaker Mark Ravenscroft **Est.** 2002 **Dozens** 1000 **Vyds** 1.5ha
Mark Ravenscroft was born in South Africa and studied oenology there. He moved to Australia in the early '90s, and in '94 became an Australian citizen. His wines come from estate plantings of verdelho, pinotage and albariño, supplemented by contract-grown grapes from other vineyards in the region. The wines are made onsite.

🍷🍷🍷🍷 **The Waagee Granite Belt 2018** Cabernet and friends rise to the vibrant, cool heights of the Granite Belt. Medium vibrant purple hue. Accurate, crunchy black/redcurrant fruit is energised by prominent high-altitude acidity that will appreciate some years to soften. Medium-grained tannins and good persistence guarantee it will go the distance. Nicely managed oak lets the fruit be the star. Screw cap. 14% alc. **Rating** 92 To 2038 $60 TS

🍷🍷🍷🍷 **Granite Belt Petit Verdot 2019** Rating 89 To 2034 $45 TS

Ravensworth ★★★★★

312 Patemans Lane, Murrumbateman, ACT 2582 **Region** Canberra District
T (02) 6226 8368 **www.**ravensworthwines.com.au
Winemaker Bryan Martin **Est.** 2000 **Dozens** 2000 **Vyds** 2.6ha
Winemaker, vineyard manager and partner Bryan Martin (with dual wine science and winegrowing degrees from CSU) has a background in wine retail, food and beverage experience in the hospitality industry and teaches part-time. He is also assistant winemaker to Tim Kirk at Clonakilla, after 7 years at Jeir Creek. Judging at wine shows is another string to his bow. Ravensworth's organically managed vineyard is mainly planted to shiraz (4 clones, including Best's and Tahbilk), riesling (3 Geisenheim clones) and sangiovese (3 clones) with lesser amounts of white varieties.

🍷🍷🍷🍷🍷 **A Long Way Around Margaret River Chenin Blanc 2020** This is wonderful, a wine that defies the odds. Imagine ambrosia. It's a cross between a lemon daiquiri and shiso pickled ginger. It tastes like spiced ginger and fresh ginger in a black tea weakly sweetened with honey – this is obviously dry but the fruit weight lends itself to that sensation. Peppery too. Lovely texture, the phenolics beautifully handled and acidity paramount in harnessing those tannins and energy of this wine. Respect. Screw cap. 12.5% alc. **Rating** 95 To 2026 $28 JF ✪
Estate Shiraz Viognier 2019 Sometimes, a wine just feels calm, balanced. Nothing overt, with the edges smooth, such as this lovely wine with its 4% viognier, co-fermented. A core of ripe fruit and spices, with layers of savouriness, but it's not fruity at all. Medium bodied, supple, with textural tannins and lots of detail throughout. Finishes long and pure. Screw cap. 13.5% alc. **Rating** 95 To 2028 $45 JF

Estate Sangiovese 2019 This is fabulous. Savoury, tangy, refreshing and thoughtful. Dark cherries, spicy, with some woodsy influence, but it's the tannins that are spot-on, Italianate in shape and texture, finishing with fine acidity. Screw cap. 13% alc. **Rating** 95 **To** 2028 $40 JF

The Long Way Around Frankland River Gewürztraminer 2020 The colour is of Turkish delight and so too the aromas and flavours. It's a Middle Eastern extravaganza with musk, rose petals and lemon oil. The palate is soft and textural, until the chewy tannins kick in. They're like fine sandpaper, and there's blood-orange acidity travelling along for the ride, too. Screw cap. 13% alc. **Rating** 94 **To** 2026 $28 JF ✪

The Long Way Around Tasmania Pinot Noir 2020 This is stonkingly good. It's quite ethereal. Perfumed, cherry accented, lightly spiced, fresh basil and pine needles with an autumnal/earthy fragrance. Fine tannins and acidity coat the palate. It's almost a pared-back Tassie pinot, yet still retains great purity. Screw cap. 13% alc. **Rating** 94 **To** 2028 $36 JF

♟♟♟♟♟ **The Long Way Round Bianco 2020** **Rating** 93 **To** 2025 $27 JF ✪
Hilltops Nebbiolo 2019 **Rating** 91 **To** 2026 $42 JF
The Long Way Round Tinto 2020 **Rating** 90 **To** 2023 $27 JF

Redbank   ★★★★

1597 Snow Road, Milawa, Vic 3678 **Region** King Valley
T (08) 8561 3200 **www**.redbankwines.com **Open** 7 days 10–5
Winemaker Dave Whyte **Est.** 2005 **Dozens** 33 000 **Vyds** 20ha
The Redbank brand was for decades the umbrella for Neill and Sally Robb's Sally's Paddock. The brand was aquired by Hill-Smith Family Vineyards in 2005, leaving the Robbs with the winery, surrounding vineyard and the Sally's Paddock label. Local winegrowers – the Ross, Judd and Murtagh families – purchased the brand in August 2018 and have launched a new cellar door venture under the umbrella of Milawa Providore. Redbank purchases grapes locally from the King Valley and Whitlands as well as further afield. Exports to all major markets.

♟♟♟♟♟ **Sunday Morning King Valley Pinot Gris 2019** As far as pinot gris goes, this is light on the aromatics and spice usually associated with the variety. What it does have is a charming delicacy, magnifying the grape's Granny Smith apple, Packham pear and citrus qualities; and a gentle savouriness. With texture and linear acidity, it packs a lot into a small package. Screw cap. 12.7% alc. **Rating** 91 **To** 2025 $25 JP
King Valley Pinot Grigio 2019 King Valley and pinot grigio were made for each other. The cool region enhances acidity and gives the variety a quiet intensity. Look to the subtlety here and don't over-chill. Nettle, hay, hints of honeysuckle, green apple and lemon peel. Keeps the fruit intensity going aided by racy acidity right to the end. Defines the grape nicely. Screw cap. 13% alc. **Rating** 91 **To** 2025 $25 JP

♟♟♟♟ **Ellora Brut Cuvée King Valley Chardonnay Pinot Noir 2014** **Rating** 89 $24 JP
Victoria Chardonnay 2019 **Rating** 89 **To** 2024 $17 JP ✪
Central Victoria Shiraz 2018 **Rating** 89 **To** 2026 $17 JP ✪
King Valley Prosecco 2019 **Rating** 89 **To** 2023 $25 JP
King Valley Sauvignon Blanc 2019 **Rating** 88 **To** 2024 $17 JP ✪
King Valley Chardonnay 2019 **Rating** 88 **To** 2024 $25 JP
Victoria Pinot Grigio 2019 **Rating** 88 **To** 2023 $17 JP ✪
Emily King Valley Chardonnay Pinot Noir NV **Rating** 88 $15 JP ✪

Redgate   ★★★★★

659 Boodjidup Road, Margaret River, WA 6285 **Region** Margaret River
T (08) 9757 6488 **www**.redgatewines.com.au **Open** 7 days 10–4.30
Winemaker David Dowden **Est.** 1977 **Dozens** 5500 **Vyds** 18ha

Founder and owner of Redgate, the late Bill Ullinger, chose the name not simply because of the nearby eponymous beach, but also because – so it is said – a local farmer (with a prominent red gate at his property) had run an illegal spirit still 100 or so years ago, and its patrons would come to the property and ask whether there was any 'red gate' available. True or not, Redgate was one of the early movers in the region, and now has close to 20ha of mature estate plantings (the majority to sauvignon blanc, semillon, cabernet sauvignon, cabernet franc, shiraz and chardonnay, with smaller plantings of chenin blanc and merlot).

ΨΨΨΨΨ Ullinger Reserve Margaret River Sauvignon Blanc 2020 From one angle, the aromatics are dominated by asparagus, sugar snap pea and cassis. From another, this is riddled with spicy green jalapeño, white pepper and coriander. The palate is juicy and plush, the oak serving to boost textural complexity rather than leave flavour artefact. Screw cap. 13% alc. **Rating** 95 **To** 2030 $25 EL ✪

Margaret River Sauvignon Blanc Semillon 2020 Once you've identified the scent in this wine as being green jalapeño, it is challenging to see much else. Despite how that may sound, it is a positive trait, and serves to distinguish this vineyard from its regional neighbours. Taut, spicy drinking here, with seriously concentrated fruit. Hard to know what food to match it with … perhaps drink it solo? Screw cap. 13.5% alc. **Rating** 95 **To** 2028 $23 EL ✪

Ullinger Reserve Margaret River Cabernet Sauvignon 2017 The nose is interesting and has stopped me in my tracks more than once in the process of writing this note. It has the same pungency possessed by the semillon, in which I saw green jalapeño – in this I see the pure, perfumed essence of cassis. On the palate it is exactly as the nose has promised; dense, intense and packed with flavour. Uncomplicated, pure. Screw cap. 14.6% alc. **Rating** 95 **To** 2041 $65 EL

Margaret River Semillon 2020 The nose here could be described in a number of ways, but once you smell green jalapeño, it is impossible to unsmell it. It's all the better for it. Spicy salsa verde, coriander and green apple aromas introduce the flavours on the palate. All things fall into place. This is a cracking wine; pungent, concentrated and salivatingly saline. Yes. Screw cap. 13% alc. **Rating** 94 **To** 2027 $25 EL ✪

Margaret River Cabernet Sauvignon 2018 Neither the high alcohol nor the long time in oak can suppress the pure cassis character of this wine. Raspberry pip and red licorice nestle together on the palate, while saline acid and fine tannins bring up the rear. Somewhat uncomplicated in the presentation of flavours, but extremely attractive and with good length of flavour. Screw cap. 15.1% alc. **Rating** 94 **To** 2036 $38 EL

Margaret River Cabernet Sauvignon 2017 As we have come to expect from this producer, the nose here is pungently pure and bright, laden with cassis, plum and raspberry. On the palate the tannins are earthy and fine, cupping the fruit and softening the whole affair. A lot to love here, and the cooler vintage from whence it came has done nothing to reduce the punch of the fruit. Intense and bright. Screw cap. 14.6% alc. **Rating** 94 **To** 2031 $38 EL

ΨΨΨΨΨ Margaret River Cabernet Franc 2018 Rating 92 **To** 2030 $40 EL

RedHeads Wine

258 Angaston Road, Angaston, SA 5353 **Region** South Australia
T (08) 8562 2888 **www**.redheadswine.com **Open** Fri 12–7, w'ends 11–5
Winemaker Alex Trescowthick, Darren Harvey **Est.** 2003 **Dozens** 25 000 **Vyds** 8ha
RedHeads was established by Tony Laithwaite in McLaren Vale and has since moved to the Barossa Valley. The aim was to allow winemakers working under corporate banners to produce small-batch wines. The team 'liberates' premium parcels of grapes from large companies 'a few rows at a time, to give them the special treatment they deserve and to form wines of true individuality and character. It's all about creating wines with personality, that are made to be enjoyed.' Exports to most major markets.

ΨΨΨΨ **Nobs and Snobs South Australia Cabernet Malbec 2019** Headed up with familiar cabernet nasals, leaning more to the earthier side of the fence with the violet florals of the malbec keen to make a presence. Both varieties find a mutual direction, medium to fuller bodied, tannins well integrated into the palate so as not to knock out the flavours. Screw cap. 14% alc. **Rating** 89 **To** 2028 $30 TL

Redman ★★★★☆

14830 Riddoch Highway, Coonawarra, SA 5263 **Region** Coonawarra
T (08) 8736 3331 **www.**redman.com.au **Open** Mon–Fri 9–5, w'ends 11–4
Winemaker Bruce Redman, Daniel Redman **Est.** 1966 **Dozens** 18 000 **Vyds** 34ha
Redman has been making wine in Coonawarra for over 110 years – and Coonawarra cabernet for 50 years. Brothers Bruce (winemaker) and Mal (general manager) and Bruce's sons Dan (winemaker and marketer) and Mike (assistant winemaker and cellar hand), represent the 4th and 5th generations of the family business. Their prestige cuvée is The Redman, a blend of cabernet sauvignon, shiraz and merlot. Exports to China, the UK, Japan, Taiwan and South Korea.

ΨΨΨΨΨ **The Redman 2010** The colour, the brightness of flavour and the fruit bely its age, although there are certainly tertiary flavours within. Lovely cedar box and baking spices, ironstone and warm bitumen. The tannins are perfectly poised, with excellent acidity, and the finish long and pure. A stunning The Redman with a few more years ahead of it yet. Cork. 14.5% alc. **Rating** 96 **To** 2030 $80 JF

ΨΨΨΨ♀ **Coonawarra Cabernet Sauvignon Merlot 2018 Rating** 93 **To** 2033 $35 JF
Coonawarra Cabernet Sauvignon 2018 Rating 92 **To** 2035 $33 JF
Coonawarra Shiraz 2018 Rating 90 **To** 2030 $22 JF

Reillys Wines ★★★★

Cnr Leasingham Road/Hill Street, Mintaro, SA 5415 **Region** Clare Valley
T (08) 8843 9013 **www.**reillyswines.com.au **Open** 7 days 10–4
Winemaker Justin Ardill **Est.** 1994 **Dozens** 25 000 **Vyds** 115ha
Established in 1993 by Justin and Julie Ardill. Justin hand made the first vintage in '94 on the verandah of the heritage-listed Reillys Cottage – built in 1856 by Irish shoemaker Hugh Reilly from local slate – which today serves as their cellar door and restaurant. Justin continues to use the same traditional winemaking techniques of prolonged open fermentation, hand plunging and barrel maturation. The wines are made from estate vineyards (the oldest planted in 1919). Exports to Canada, Malaysia, Singapore, NZ, Hong Kong and China.

ΨΨΨΨ♀ **Museum Release Watervale Riesling 2017** In a short time, this has garnered some aged qualities: baked ricotta, lime marmalade and lemon curd. It's neatly composed and the palate understated. Screw cap. 12.5% alc. **Rating** 93 **To** 2024 $40 JF
Dry Land Clare Valley Tempranillo 2019 Excellent dark garnet hue and bright; while it has a richness from dark cherries, red licorice and sarsaparilla flavours, it has a vibrancy too. It's medium bodied with persistent tannins and very fresh, juicy and well contained. It helps that, by Reillys' standards, the alcohol is restrained. Screw cap. 14% alc. **Rating** 93 **To** 2026 JF
Moon Vine Limited Release Barossa Valley Shiraz 2018 Deep, dark and menacing. A wave of richness from fruit and oak comes rushing through, working across the full-bodied palate. Expect brown spices, dark chocolate and rolled tobacco in the mix with expansive, gritty tannins and warmth on the finish. Screw cap. 16% alc. **Rating** 90 **To** 2028 JF

Reis Creek Wines ★★★☆

1 Lyndoch Valley Road, Barossa Valley SA 5351 **Region** Barossa Valley
T (08) 7007 3068 **www.**reiswines.com.au **Open** Wed–Sun 10–5
Winemaker Jim Jin **Est.** 2009 **Dozens** 20 000 **Vyds** 65ha

This substantial business is owned by Jim Jin, who arrived in SA to study oenology at the University of Adelaide in 2008. Jim created Reis Creek in 2009, and the nature of the business changed significantly with the purchase of a 65ha vineyard from Leo Pech, a 4th-generation member of one of the leading grapegrowing families in the Barossa Valley. Exports to China.

ŶŶŶŶŶ **Chairman Barossa Valley Shiraz 2018** Vibrant, full purple hue. Glossy black cherry and succulent blackberry fruits triumph over the high-cocoa dark chocolate and coffee bean presence of new French oak. Finely structured tannins carry a finish that's clipped slightly by warm alcohol, but the fruit holds its integrity with confidence. Cork. 15.5% alc. **Rating** 90 **To** 2023 $110 TS

Renzaglia Wines   ★★★★★
38 Bosworth Falls Road, O'Connell, NSW 2795 **Region** Central Ranges
T (02) 6337 5756 **www**.renzagliawines.com.au **Open** By appt
Winemaker Mark Renzaglia, Sam Renzaglia **Est.** 2017 **Dozens** 2500 **Vyds** 3ha
American Mark Renzaglia and his Australian wife Sandy planted their first vineyard in 1997 (1ha of chardonnay, cabernet sauvignon and merlot), Mark making small quantities of his own wines while working as a vineyard manager and winemaker at Winburndale Wines for 11 years. The original plantings now make up the estate Bella Luna Vineyard, to which shiraz, viognier, tempranillo and grenache have been added in recent years. Mark also manages a vineyard in the middle of the famous Mount Panorama race circuit and has access to the grapes from the 4ha Mount Panorama Estate. Son Sam has since joined the business too, and a new winery and cellar door have been constructed. Exports to the US.

ŶŶŶŶŶ **Mount Panorama Estate Chardonnay 2019** These Renzaglia wines are proving a revelation, with the engineering of flavour and structural architecture as finessed as the packaging. No shortage of ripe fruit flavours, with dried mango, white peach and nectarine strung across a chassis of salubrious oak, impeccably integrated, imparting riffs on hazelnut, truffle, nougat and chestnut. A masterstroke of ripe fruit, sexy oak, pungent mineral and mouth-watering freshness. Generosity far from the madding crowd. A very fine wine. Screw cap. 13% alc. **Rating** 96 **To** 2028 $50 NG ✪

Mount Panorama Estate Cabernet Sauvignon 2018 This is exceptional cool-climate cabernet, somehow transcending the green edges of its blended sibling to showcase a sheath of impeccably tuned tannins, ripe and juicy. This makes all the difference! Spearmint, blackcurrant, olive, chilli, bay leaf and a swathe of firm, saliva-sapping tannins driving a long finish. Already delicious, its precocity belies the depth and longevity herein. Screw cap. 13.8% alc. **Rating** 96 **To** 2035 $50 NG ✪ ♥

Mount Panorama Estate Shiraz 2018 A cool-climate display of Australia giving a nod to the luncheon wines of the northern Rhône. Crozes, perhaps. Blueberry, kelp, charcuterie, violet and an anchovy/tapenade salinity splayed across a long finish, driven by gentle but palpable tannins and a stream of juicy acidity. The tannins, to be churlish, could be firmer. Nevertheless, a delicious wine best in the earlier to mid term. Screw cap. 13.9% alc. **Rating** 94 **To** 2026 $50 NG

Bella Luna Vineyard Cabernet Sauvignon Merlot 2018 An after-dinner biscuit meld of chocolate and mint. Yet, as is the wont at this address, the structural latticework is impeccably engineered; the tannins, detailed and ripe. The oak, smart. Verdant herb, bell pepper, a smear of black olive, cassis and bouquet garni. This will age very well, eventually sublimating the minty sweetness into something more nourishing and savoury. Screw cap. 13.5% alc. **Rating** 94 **To** 2032 $50 NG

ŶŶŶŶŶ **Stone Wall Riesling 2019** Rating 93 **To** 2025 $30 NG
Shiraz 2018 Rating 92 **To** 2023 $23 NG ✪
Cabernet Sauvignon 2018 Rating 92 **To** 2025 $23 NG ✪
Wahluu Blanc de Blancs 2017 Rating 91 $50 NG

Reynella   ★★★★

202 Main Road, McLaren Vale, SA 5161 **Region** McLaren Vale/Fleurieu Peninsula
T 1800 088 711 **www**.reynellawines.ocm.au **Open** Sun–Fri 11–4, Sat 10–4
Winemaker Matt Caldersmith **Est.** 1838
John Reynell laid the foundations for Chateau Reynella in 1838; over the next 100 years the
stone buildings, winery and underground cellars, with attractive gardens, were constructed.
Thomas Hardy's first job in SA was with Reynella; he noted in his diary that he would be
able to better himself soon. He did just that, becoming by far the largest producer in SA by
the end of the 19th century; 150 or so years after Chateau Reynella's foundations were laid,
CWA (now Accolade Wines) completed the circle by making it its corporate headquarters,
while preserving the integrity of the Reynella brand in no uncertain fashion. Exports to all
major markets.

Ricca Terra   ★★★★☆

PO Box 305, Angaston, SA 5353 **Region** Riverland
T 0411 370 057 **www**.riccaterra.com.au
Winemaker Ashley Ratcliff **Est.** 2017 **Dozens** 10000 **Vyds** 80ha
The Ricca Terra venture of Ashley and Holly Ratcliff was decades in the making. Ashley
began his journey in wine in 1992 when he joined Orlando as a viticulturist, thereafter
moving to Yalumba where he remained until 2016. During this time he obtained a bachelor
of applied science, a master's degree in marketing and became a graduate of the AWRI sensory
evaluation course. In his 15 years with Yalumba he was winery manager for the vast Riverland
winery and technical manager (viticulture). He was the recipient of 4 major state and federal
industry awards, all focusing on viticulture in drought-prone regions. So when he and Holly
purchased an 8ha vineyard in the Riverland it presented the opportunity to plant varieties
pushing the envelope, such as the rare planting of an ancient Balkan variety slankamenka bela.
There are now 80ha of varieties, mainly selected for the climate, grown with surface mulches,
soil moisture monitoring probes and smart viticultural practices. The wines are made using
all of the cutting edge techniques, hand picked into half-tonne bins and chilled for 12 hours
before transfer to the winery in the Barossa Valley. Ricca Terra means rich earth in Italian.
Exports to the UK, the US, Canada and Belgium.

🍷🍷🍷🍷🍷 **Bullets Before Cannonballs 2020** A blend of tempranillo, lagrein, aglianico
and shiraz, percentages unknown, but I'm assuming the former is dominant as it's
full of red licorice and cola, with v-shaped tannins (that start with some volume
and then taper to a precise end point). This just works. Plump, fleshy, very savoury,
with some meaty reduction adding to its shape alongside charred radicchio
bitterness on the finish; yet its core is all juicy, ripe fruit. Screw cap. 14.8% alc.
Rating 95 To 2025 $23 JF

🍷🍷🍷🍷⚇ **Soldiers' Land 90 Year Old Vines Grenache 2020** Rating 91 To 2024
$30 JF
Colour of Calmness Rosé 2020 Rating 90 To 2021 $23 JF
Small Batch Nero d'Avola 2020 Rating 90 To 2024 $27 JF

Richard Hamilton   ★★★★☆

439 Main Road, McLaren Vale, SA 5171 **Region** McLaren Vale
T (08) 8323 8830 **www**.richardhamiltonwines.com **Open** Mon–Fri 10–5, w'ends &
public hols 11–5
Winemaker Paul Gordon, Greg Foster **Est.** 1972 **Dozens** 25000 **Vyds** 40.46ha
Richard Hamilton has outstanding estate vineyards, some of great age, all fully mature. An
experienced and skilled winemaking team has allowed the full potential of those vineyards to
be realised. The quality, style and consistency of both red and white wines has reached a new
level; being able to keep only the best parcels for the Richard Hamilton brand is an enormous
advantage. Exports to the UK, the US, Canada, Denmark, Sweden, Germany, Belgium,
Malaysia, Vietnam, Hong Kong, Singapore, Japan, China and NZ.

ŸŸŸŸŸ **Centurion McLaren Vale Shiraz 2019** A sumptuous expression. Floral. Purple/ blue-fruit allusions, with a sachet of clove, pepper and anise scattered across a long, juicy, uncluttered finish. Almost pulpy. The vinosity clear. While I'd like to see no new oak and more bona fide grape tannin, this is a delicious wine. Screw cap. 14.5% alc. **Rating** 93 **To** 2032 $75 NG

Ghost Hill Single Vineyard McLaren Vale Shiraz 2019 A brooding heavyweight with an attractive lightness of touch. Boysenberry, dark cherry, raspberry liqueur, lilac, clove, smoked meats and mace barrel across a rich palate, defined by a peppery skein of acidity. Firm toasty oak pillars are still dominant. Finishes with a saline lick and drying oak, marked by mocha and bitter chocolate. The oak will integrate, given the wine's sheer extract. Time needed. Screw cap. 14.5% alc. **Rating** 92 **To** 2032 $38 NG

Burton's Vineyard Old Bush Vine McLaren Vale Grenache Shiraz 2019 Aromas of kirsch, cranberry and rosehip. Some carob, clove, orange zest and turmeric, too. The tannins are skeletal, briary and brisk, just as they should be – the best aspect of this wine. The fruit, otherwise, still reticent and needing to build with time and your patience. Screw cap. 14.5% alc. **Rating** 92 **To** 2026 $40 NG

Hut Block McLaren Vale Cabernet Sauvignon 2018 At this meagre price, the wine is stellar. Vale cabernet 101. Think cassis, spearmint, a smear of black olive, sage and sea spray salinity dousing the juicy finish. Lovely drinking with varietal and regional pedigree intact. Screw cap. 14.5% alc. **Rating** 92 **To** 2023 $22 NG ✪

Lot 148 McLaren Vale Merlot 2019 A delicious medium-bodied wine, brimming with life and a succulence of fruit that has drawn me back for another whiff before penning this note. Damson plum, verdant herb, a sappy minty lift and a perfect proportion of oak to promote an effusive drinkability. The tannins, tactile enough to confer poise; gentle enough to promote imminent pleasure. Screw cap. 14% alc. **Rating** 91 **To** 2023 $22 NG ✪

Colton's McLaren Vale G.S.M. 2019 Amen! A solid wine offering value. I like the subdued ferrous nose, underlain by a carnal whiff of smoked meat and iodine; and the way the tannins are built in. Just enough of everything to placate the typical Australian ripeness while keeping proceedings strapped to a metre of savouriness. I smile at the open weave of easygoing red/dark fruit. I take umbrage, just a little, at the tangy finish. Screw cap. 14.5% alc. **Rating** 90 **To** 2024 $22 NG

ŸŸŸŸ **Little Road McLaren Vale Shiraz 2019 Rating** 89 **To** 2024 $22 NG
The Coonawarrior Coonawarra Cabernet Sauvignon 2018 Rating 88 **To** 2025 $17 JF ✪

RidgeView Wines   ★★★★★

273 Sweetwater Road, Pokolbin, NSW 2320 **Region** Hunter Valley
T (02) 6574 7332 **www.**ridgeview.com.au **Open** Wed–Sun 10–5
Winemaker Darren Scott, Gary MacLean, Mark Woods **Est.** 2000 **Dozens** 3000 **Vyds** 9ha
Darren and Tracey Scott have transformed a 40ha timbered farm into a vineyard with self-contained accommodation and a cellar door. The greater part of the plantings are 4.5ha of shiraz; cabernet sauvignon, chambourcin, merlot, pinot gris, viognier and traminer make up a somewhat eclectic selection of other varieties.

ŸŸŸŸŸ **Museum Release Generations Reserve Hunter Valley Semillon 2013** Arguably the finest Hunter semillon vintage of my drinking lifetime. Of these museum releases, the '07 has the flare, big charisma and an incongruous Euro appeal. The 2013, however, reverts to the tensile drive so fidelitous to the local turf. Lanolin, nettle, bath salts, lemon zest and a bare whiff of toast. Loads of speed. The shift into an aged gear will bring a marvellous wine. All that is required is patience. Screw cap. 11.4% alc. **Rating** 96 **To** 2033 $65 NG ✪

Museum Release Generations Reserve Hunter Valley Semillon 2007 This has aged brilliantly. For some, unrecognisable perhaps from the citric verve of youthful expressions. Yet the degree of aged complexity is riveting. Dried hay, raw honey, buttered toast, quinine and apricot pith. This, aside from the acidity, has an uncanny resemblance to aged white Rhône. A beautiful wine, far from the conventional norm, aged or otherwise. Compelling intensity and length. A stunning wine. Screw cap. 11% alc. **Rating** 96 **To** 2024 $40 NG ✪

Museum Release Generations Reserve Hunter Valley Semillon 2016 A wine into late adolescence. Spa salts, talc, oyster shell mineral, lemon balm and chalk. Still restrained. Pink grapefruit. A hint of toast, but not much. The acidity, fine boned rather than tart. Soft, but palpable enough for the style. Gangly. Shins and elbows like an unwieldy teen, but such kinetic energy. Simply a matter of time before it expands and explodes. Screw cap. 11% alc. **Rating** 94 **To** 2030 $40 NG

Hunter Valley Verdelho 2018 Possibly the most sophisticated verdelho I have ever tasted. And no, that is not a backhanded put-down. This is very good. Almost exceptional. Taut, mineral and nicely oily, a textural carapace that restrains varietal tendencies toward tropical exuberance. The finish long and effortless. Wonderful persistence. An excellent food wine. All about texture. More European than Australian. Plenty of traction left. Screw cap. 12.9% alc. **Rating** 94 **To** 2025 $25 NG ✪

🍷🍷🍷🍷🍷 **Impressions Effen Hill Vineyard Hunter Valley Shiraz 2019** **Rating** 93 **To** 2034 $45 NG

Impressions Single Vineyard Hunter Valley Chardonnay 2018 **Rating** 92 **To** 2023 $35 NG

Impressions Effen Hill Vineyard Hunter Valley Shiraz 2016 **Rating** 92 **To** 2028 $45 NG

Impressions Hunter Valley Shiraz 2011 **Rating** 92 **To** 2026 $65 NG

Museum Release Impressions Single Vineyard Hunter Valley Chardonnay 2015 **Rating** 90 **To** 2023 $60 NG

Rieslingfreak ★★★★★

103 Langmeil Road, Tanunda, SA 5352 **Region** Clare Valley
T 0439 336 250 **www**.rieslingfreak.com **Open** Sat 11–4 or by appt
Winemaker John Hughes, Belinda Hughes **Est.** 2009 **Dozens** 7500 **Vyds** 40ha

The name of John Hughes' winery leaves no doubt about his long-term ambition: to explore every avenue of riesling, whether bone-dry or sweet, coming from regions across the wine world, albeit with a strong focus on Australia. The wines made from his Clare Valley vineyard offer dry (No. 2, No. 3, No. 4 and No. 10), off-dry (No. 5 and No. 8), sparkling (No. 9) and fortified (No. 7) styles. Exports to the UK, the US, Canada and Hong Kong.

🍷🍷🍷🍷🍷 **No. 2 Polish Hill River Riesling 2020** From the Polish Hill River. Bright straw green, it's an utterly delicious wine which has aromas and flavours that seem to change in quick succession, with Meyer lemon, white peach and Granny Smith apple in full song. Its mouthfeel and the length of the finish are both exceptional. Screw cap. 12% alc. **Rating** 97 **To** 2033 $37 JH ✪

🍷🍷🍷🍷🍷 **No. 6 Clare Valley Aged Release Riesling 2015** Ah, the joy of riesling as it garners age! Heady, with toasted and buttered brioche, spread with lime marmalade. It's still very fresh, bright and even a touch austere, with puckering acidity. It is starting to dry out on the finish, so best to enjoy this sooner rather than later. Screw cap. 12% alc. **Rating** 96 **To** 2023 $42 JF ✪

No. 4 Eden Valley Riesling 2020 Does this riesling know how to charm, or what? It's a delight! All heady, with florals, citrus flavours, stone fruit and tangy acidity in tow, yet there's texture too. The finish is refreshingly dry. It incorporates the allure of the region, the decisiveness of the variety and the expertise of its maker. Screw cap. 12% alc. **Rating** 95 **To** 2030 $27 JF ✪ ♥

🍷🍷🍷🍷🍷 **No. 3 Clare Valley Riesling 2020** **Rating** 93 **To** 2030 $27 JF ✪

No. 5 Clare Valley Off-dry Riesling 2020 **Rating** 90 **To** 2027 $27 JF

Rikard Wines   ★★★★☆

279 Old Canobolas Road, Nashdale, NSW 2800 **Region** Orange
T 0438 847 353 **www**.rikardwines.com.au **Open** By appt
Winemaker William Rikard-Bell **Est.** 2015 **Dozens** 850 **Vyds** 1ha
William Rikard-Bell's first job as winemaker was at Canobolas Smith in Orange. After
interludes in Bordeaux, Mudgee and the Hunter, he returned to Orange and purchased a
10ha block on Mt Canobolas with his wife Kimberley. They have planted 5000 pinot noir
and chardonnay vines at 1050m above sea level. More chardonnay and pinot will be planted
in the future, and possibly some riesling. The vines are close planted, with narrow rows and a
low cordon height. The grapes are hand picked, the small-batch wines made using traditional
Old World techniques. A winery and bottling line was completed in February 2020.

🍷🍷🍷🍷🍷 **Black Label Orange Chardonnay 2019** A stellar wine, with bright acidity and
pungent mineral weaving a thread of apricot pith, jasmine, orange verbena and
nougat. Yet it is the acidity, juicy and saliva-sapping, that makes this wine. Screw
cap. 12.8% alc. **Rating** 94 **To** 2028 $65 NG

🍷🍷🍷🍷🍷 **Orange Chardonnay 2019 Rating** 93 **To** 2026 $40 NG
Orange Shiraz 2019 Rating 93 **To** 2028 $60 NG
Black Label Orange Pinot Noir 2019 Rating 92 **To** 2025 $75 NG
Orange Riesling 2020 Rating 91 **To** 2028 $30 NG

Rill House Vineyard   ★★★★

O'Leary's Lane, Spring Hill, Vic 3444 **Region** Macedon Ranges
T 0414 235 062 **www**.rillhouse.com
Winemaker Matt Harrop, Loic Le Calvez **Est.** 1986 **Dozens** 500 **Vyds** 2.4ha
The Rill House Vineyard was planted in 1986 in a natural amphitheatre on the edge of
the Wombat State Forest, with a natural spring (rill) that runs through the property. At
650m above sea level, it is one of the coolest sites in the region, and is managed using organic
and biodynamic practices. Exports to France.

🍷🍷🍷🍷🍷 **My Deer Bride Chardonnay 2019** Tightly wound around a line of high-
voltage acidity, so it is superfine, linear and guaranteed to light up your palate.
Racy citrus and lemon curd. Sulphides add some depth. While there's an
impression of texture via oak, lees and malolactic fermentation, this is a livewire.
Screw cap. 13% alc. **Rating** 93 **To** 2030 $60 JF
Dashing Red Fox Pinot Noir 2019 A nice composure here, with pepper and
dried herbs strewn across roasted beetroot with an earthy rhubarb flavour too.
Reduction accentuates the charry oak, and the tannins are a little raspy. But the
end result is a savoury offering with a refreshing tangy tartness to the acidity. Screw
cap. 13% alc. **Rating** 91 **To** 2032 $68 JF
Well Groomed Goose Fumé Blanc 2019 Pristine flavours of white stone fruit
and grapefruit hold sway, with brisk acidity in tow plus smoky, spicy oak. Although
sulphides clip the finish, the overall savouriness appeals. Screw cap. 12.5% alc.
Rating 90 **To** 2025 $42 JF

Riposte   ★★★★★

PO Box 256, Lobethal, SA 5241 **Region** Adelaide Hills
T 0412 816 107 **www**.timknappstein.com.au
Winemaker Tim Knappstein **Est.** 2006 **Dozens** 14 000
Tim Knappstein is a 3rd-generation vigneron, his winemaking lineage dating back to 1893
in the Clare Valley. He made his first wines at the family's Stanley Wine Company and
established his own wine company in the Clare Valley in 1976. After the sale of that company
in '81, Tim relocated to Lenswood in the Adelaide Hills to make cool-climate wines led by
pinot noir and chardonnay. His quest has now been achieved with consistently excellent wines
reflected in the winery's 5-star rating since the *Wine Companion 2012*. Exports to the UK,
the US, Canada, Switzerland, Denmark, Germany, Indonesia, Japan, Hong Kong and China.

🍷🍷🍷🍷 **The Sabre Adelaide Hills Pinot Noir 2019** The bright, clear crimson colour signals a highly fragrant bouquet and an incisive, precisely detailed palate, with its display of red and dark cherry fruit evident from start to finish. Pure fruit, but also has texture and length. Screw cap. 13% alc. **Rating** 95 **To** 2030 $38 JH

The Cutlass Single Vineyard Adelaide Hills Shiraz 2019 Adelaide Hills and shiraz are having a public love affair, exemplified by this wine's brightly flavoured pepper, spice and cherry fruits, on a very complex palate that's just within medium-bodied bounds. Its 50% whole-bunch fermentation adds fine, savoury tannins to the long finish. Screw cap. 13.5% alc. **Rating** 95 **To** 2027 $28 JH ✪

Rising ★★★★

Yow Yow Rising, St Andrews, Vic 3761 **Region** Yarra Valley
www.risingwines.com.au
Winemaker Anthony Fikkers **Est.** 2017 **Dozens** 2500
Anthony Fikkers crafts wines that express the power of the Rising Vineyard, while also coaxing out the elegance that the Yarra Valley is renowned for. Anthony's philosophy of minimal intervention but maximum attention to detail allows each of the wines to fully express its origins.

🍷🍷🍷🍷 **Yarra Valley Gamay 2020** If you like flavour and crunch from whole bunches, then this will please but there are some green elements infiltrating: stemmy notes, peppercorns and fresh herbs. There is also juicy, tangy blood orange and a dusty finish. Screw cap. 13% alc. **Rating** 91 **To** 2027 $33 JF

Risky Business Wines ★★★★

PO Box 6015, East Perth, WA 6892 **Region** Various
T 0457 482 957 **www**.riskybusinesswines.com.au
Winemaker Andrew Vesey **Est.** 2013 **Dozens** 8900
The name Risky Business is decidedly tongue-in-cheek because the partnership headed by Rob Quenby has neatly side-stepped any semblance of risk. The grapes come from vineyards in Great Southern and Margaret River that are managed by Quenby Viticultural Services. Since the batches of wine are small, the partnership is able to select grapes specifically suited to the wine style and price. So there is no capital tied up in vineyards, nor in a winery – the wines are contract-made. In 2018 Risky Business expanded its operations to Victoria's King Valley, making Italian-style Prosecco, Grigio and Sangiovese. Exports to Japan and China.

🍷🍷🍷🍷 **King Valley Prosecco NV** So easy to get to love. Simple enjoyment assured with delicious lemon sorbet, citrus, fresh cut apple and harmonious slurpy, bright acidity. Does the grape proud. Crown seal. 10.5% alc. **Rating** 95 **To** 2023 $25 JP ✪

Margaret River Cabernet Sauvignon 2019 The 2019 vintage will forever fall in the shadow of the exceptional 2018, however many of the cabernets that have presented themselves over the past 6–12 months of releases have shown an energy, a structure and a distinct blackness that speaks volumes about their inherent quality. This is no exception. It possesses all the beauty and intrigue that the '19 cabernets exhibit, and it finishes with a long tendril of luscious, ripe, pure cassis fruit. Quite beautiful, and certainly impressive for the price. Screw cap. 14.5% alc. **Rating** 94 **To** 2031 $25 EL ✪

Frankland River Shiraz Tempranillo Grenache 2019 Quite delicious – juicy, almost slurpy, and with an abundance of red berries. Chalky tannins shape the back palate, and guide it through the finish. Better-than-average pizza wine. Find it. Screw cap. 14.5% alc. **Rating** 94 **To** 2027 $25 EL ✪

🍷🍷🍷🍷 **Margaret River Shiraz Tempranillo Grenache 2019** **Rating** 93 **To** 2027 $25 EL ✪

Frankland River Malbec 2019 **Rating** 92 **To** 2025 $25 EL ✪

RiverBank Estate

126 Hamersley Road, Caversham, WA 6055 **Region** Swan Valley
T (08) 9377 1805 **www**.riverbankestate.com.au **Open** 7 days 10–5
Winemaker Digby Leddin **Est.** 1988 **Dozens** 4500 **Vyds** 12ha
RiverBank Estate was first planted on the fertile banks of the Swan River in 1988 and has
grown to encompass 12ha of mature, low-yielding vines (18 varieties), the wines made onsite.
The property was purchased by the Lembo family in 2017 and has been rebranded into
3 wine ranges: On The Run, Rebellious and Eric Anthony. RiverBank was named Winery
of the Year 2019 by Ray Jordan and Best Small Cellar Door in the Swan Valley 2019 by
Peter Forrestal of *Gourmet Traveller*. Winemaker Digby Leddin spent 2 decades with Lamont's
Winery before joining RiverBank in '17. Exports to Azerbaijan, Maldives and China.

ŸŸŸŸŸ **Eric Anthony Swan Valley Shiraz 2018** Highly aromatic forest fruits, blood
plum and star anise. The palate is medium bodied, fleshy and supple, with fine
tannins and great length. Not strictly classical in style, but not exactly modern,
either. A lovely wine. Gold medal Blackwood Valley and WA Boutique wine
shows '20. Screw cap. 14.7% alc. **Rating** 95 **To** 2030 $35 EL ✪
Eric Anthony Cabernet Malbec 2018 83% cabernet sauvignon from Margaret
River with 17% malbec from Donnybrook. 18 months in French oak. Both
varieties are sourced from areas that show their best qualities, coming together in
spectacular fashion here. This is succulent and ripe, verging on rambunctious, with
loads of flavour encased in furry yet firm tannins. Trophy at Blackwood Valley and
WA Boutique wine shows '20. Screw cap. 14.5% alc. **Rating** 94 **To** 2036 $35 EL

ŸŸŸŸ♀ **Rebellious Swan Valley Tempranillo 2018** **Rating** 93 **To** 2027 $25 EL ✪
Rebellious Swan Valley Verdelho 2020 **Rating** 92 **To** 2024 $25 EL ✪
Eric Anthony Pemberton Chardonnay Pinot Noir 2017 **Rating** 91 $35 EL

Riversdale Estate

222 Denholms Road, Cambridge, Tas 7170 **Region** Southern Tasmania
T (03) 6248 5555 **www**.riversdaleestate.com.au **Open** 7 days 10–5
Winemaker Nick Badrice **Est.** 1991 **Dozens** 9000 **Vyds** 37ha
Ian Roberts purchased the Riversdale property in 1980 while a university student. He says
he paid a record price for the district. The unique feature of the property is its frontage to
the Pittwater waterfront, which acts as a buffer against frost and also moderates the climate
during the ripening phase. It is a large property with 37ha of vines and one of the largest olive
groves in Tasmania, producing 50 olive-based products. Five families live permanently on the
estate, providing all the labour for the various operations, which also includes luxury French
Provincial-style cottages overlooking the vines. A cellar door and French bistro opened in
Jan '16. Wine quality is consistently good and can be outstanding.

Rob Dolan Wines

21-23 Delaneys Road, South Warrandyte, Vic 3134 **Region** Yarra Valley
T (03) 9876 5885 **www**.robdolanwines.com.au **Open** 7 days 10–5
Winemaker Rob Dolan, Adrian Santolin **Est.** 2010 **Dozens** 30 000 **Vyds** 25ha
Rob Dolan has been making wine in the Yarra Valley for over 30 years and knows its
every nook and cranny. In 2011 he was able to purchase the Hardys Yarra Burn winery
at an enticing price. It is singularly well equipped and, in addition to making the excellent
Rob Dolan wines there, he conducts an extensive contract winemaking business. Business is
booming, production having doubled, with exports driving much of the increase. Exports to
the UK, the US, Canada, Malaysia, Singapore, Hong Kong, Thailand and China.

ŸŸŸŸ♀ **White Label Yarra Valley Chardonnay 2019** A confluence of savouriness,
flinty and ripe fruit on show. It's moreish with peaches and citrus, tangy acidity
with leesy, creamy flavours enhancing the palate. There's persistence and a good
feel to this. Screw cap. 13.5% alc. **Rating** 91 **To** 2027 $32 JF

Black Label Yarra Valley Chardonnay 2019 A lot of flavour packed into this rewarding wine. Lemon glaze over peaches, creamed honey drizzled on honeydew and toasty oak sets the scene. It's fleshy and ripe and the acidity keeps everything in check. Nice one. Screw cap. 13.7% alc. **Rating** 90 **To** 2027 $28 JF

Signature Series Yarra Valley Pinot Noir 2019 Awash with dark fruit, toasty cedary oak and a bolder imprint. Full bodied and intense with layers of fruit over spices, raspy tannins over acidity. A burly wine that is still coming together, the oak not quite integrated. Time will tell. Screw cap. 13.5% alc. **Rating** 90 **To** 2030 $80 JF

White Label Yarra Valley Shiraz 2019 This leads with the savoury flavours that suit shiraz so much: the spice, the pepper, the cured meats, the warm bitumen and the coffee grounds, altogether appealing. Of course there's juicy dark fruit, smoky toasty oak and firm tannins to be found. It's very drying on the finish but with hearty fare that would be less obvious. Screw cap. 14% alc. **Rating** 90 **To** 2028 $38 JF

Signature Series Yarra Valley Cabernet Sauvignon 2019 This needs time. Deep dark garnet wafts of blackberries and ripe currants, cloves and cinnamon with lots of woodsy, cedary, toasty oak. Sweet fruit across the full-bodied palate, tannins sinewy and firm. Leave this in the cellar for a few more years. Screw cap. 14% alc. **Rating** 90 **To** 2032 $80 JF

Robert Oatley Margaret River ★★★★★

3518 Caves Road, Wilyabrup, WA 6280 **Region** Margaret River
T (08) 9750 4000 **www.**robertoatley.com.au **Open** 7 days 10.30–4.30
Winemaker Larry Cherubino **Est.** 2006 **Vyds** 155ha

Robert Oatley Wines, founded by the late Robert (Bob) Oatley AO BEM in 2006, is a family-owned winery led by his eldest son Sandy Oatley who, with his father, brother and sister, planted the first Oatley vineyards in the late 1960s. The trio of labels celebrates Bob Oatley's vision with the Signature Series, particular vineyard sites with Finisterre, and the best of the best barrels under The Pennant. Focusing on wines from Margaret River (and Great Southern) and McLaren Vale, the business now bases itself in the Margaret River, with a vineyard and cellar door on Caves Road in the heart of the region. Exports to the UK, the US, Canada and China.

♟♟♟♟♟ **The Pennant Margaret River Chardonnay 2019** Toasty oak and spicy struck-match characters waft out of the glass. This has all the frills: yellow peach, brine, red apple skin, curry leaf and crushed salted cashews. The palate follows suit with a mouth-watering flick of acid that lashes across the tongue. If the wine had a sound effect it would be a whip crack. Screw cap. 12.5% alc. **Rating** 96 **To** 2036 $90 EL

Signature Series Margaret River Cabernet Sauvignon 2018 This is first-class Margaret River cabernet at an economy price. It has elegance and poise, the cassis and black-olive flavours fresh and detailed, the crisp tannins likewise. The colour, too, is bright and clear. Screw cap. 13.5% alc. **Rating** 95 **To** 2033 $24 JH ✪

Finisterre Margaret River Cabernet Sauvignon 2018 Fruit from Wilyabrup. 18 months in new and used French oak. Classic bay leaf, sage, cassis and thyme are held together by spicy, resinous oak. The fruit on the palate has density and weight; the tannins are upfront, finely knit and pervasive. Robust cabernet with all the hallmarks of a long future before it. Screw cap. 14% alc. **Rating** 95 **To** 2035 $45 EL

The Pennant Frankland River Cabernet Sauvignon 2017 Pungently savoury on the nose, reminiscent of tomato sauce – it has that salted tomato, sweet fruit vibe going on. Statuesque palate, all redcurrant and blackberries. Red gravel, kelp, brine and a density that is part of the calling card of Frankland River cabernet. The tannins through the finish have a metallic cast, the wine wraps up with licorice and aniseed; curls of star anise the lingering puffs of flavour. Screw cap. 14% alc. **Rating** 94 **To** 2041 $105 EL

The Pennant Margaret River Cabernet Sauvignon 2017 Salty, savoury and moving to secondary flavours already. This feels aged beyond its years at this point, although the savoury spice and firm structure are not without their charms. Dense texture and cohesion on the palate, clove and star anise to finish. Screw cap. 14% alc. **Rating** 94 **To** 2036 $105 EL

ⓎⓎⓎⓎⓎ **Signature Series Great Southern Riesling 2020** Rating 90 To 2027 $24 EL
Signature Series Margaret River Chardonnay 2018 Rating 90 To 2026 $24 EL

Robert Stein Vineyard ★★★★★

Pipeclay Lane, Mudgee, NSW 2850 **Region** Mudgee
T (02) 6373 3991 **www.**robertstein.com.au **Open** 7 days 10–4.30
Winemaker Jacob Stein, Lisa Bray **Est.** 1976 **Dozens** 20000 **Vyds** 18.67ha
While 3 generations of the family have been involved since Robert (Bob) Stein began the establishment of the vineyard, the chain stretches even further back, going to Bob's great-great-grandfather, Johann Stein, who was brought to Australia in 1838 by the Macarthur family to supervise the planting of the Camden Park Vineyard. Bob's son Drew and grandson Jacob have now taken over winemaking responsibilities. Jacob has worked vintages in Italy, Canada, Margaret River and Avoca and, more particularly, in the Rheingau and Rheinhessen regions of Germany. Since his return, one success has followed another. Exports to Germany, Hong Kong, Singapore and China.

ⓎⓎⓎⓎⓎ **Half Dry Mudgee RS 15 Riesling 2019** Among the few truly world-class rieslings of its ilk in Australia. The acidity, mouth-watering and juicy, driving flavours of Rose's lime, ginger, pink grapefruit and other citrus, very long. A balletic wine, lightweight and ethereal, straddling a tightrope of structural clarity and precision, firm and brisk as the acidity sweeps the residual sweetness into a palpably dry finish; the sweetness balancing the acidity. Some hot-vintage chewiness adding to the textural mantle. An example of how acidity and sweetness synchronise; one best served by an equal dose of the other. Screw cap. 11.5% alc. **Rating** 95 **To** 2032 $45 NG

ⓎⓎⓎⓎⓎ **Reserve Mudgee Riesling 2019** Rating 93 To 2025 $50 NG
Reserve Mudgee Shiraz 2018 Rating 93 To 2029 $50 NG
The Kinnear Mudgee Shiraz Cabernet 2017 Rating 93 To 2027 $90 NG
Reserve Mudgee Cabernet Sauvignon 2018 Rating 93 To 2030 $60 NG
Mudgee Cabernet Sauvignon 2018 Rating 92 To 2025 $35 NG
Mudgee Riesling 2020 Rating 91 To 2025 $30 NG
Mudgee Shiraz 2018 Rating 91 To 2024 $40 NG
Reserve Mudgee Chardonnay 2019 Rating 90 To 2025 $40 NG

Robin Brockett Wines ★★★★★

43 Woodville St, Drysdale, Vic 3222 (postal) **Region** Geelong
T 0418 112 223 **www.**robinbrockettwines.com
Winemaker Robin Brockett **Est.** 2013 **Dozens** 400
Robin Brockett is chief winemaker at Scotchmans Hill, a position he has held for over 30 years, making consistently very good wines through the ebbs and flows of climate. In 2013 he took the first steps towards the realisation of a 35-year dream of making and selling wines under his own label. He put in place an agreement to buy grapes from the Fenwick (2ha) and Swinburn (1ha) vineyards, and in '13 made the first wines.

ⓎⓎⓎⓎⓎ **Swinburn Vineyard Bellarine Peninsula Chardonnay 2019** Robin Brockett has sourced some lovely fruit off limestone soils at Wallington for this smart, complex, young chardonnay. Struck flint, white peach, grapefruit and pear. As enticing as the bouquet is, it's the palate that seals the deal, smooth in texture, concentrated in fruit, with just a hint of grilled nuts. Bright, fine finish. Screw cap. 13.5% alc. **Rating** 95 **To** 2029 $40 JP
Fenwick Vineyard Bellarine Peninsula Pinot Noir 2018 A dramatic counterpoint to the Swinburn Vineyard Pinot Noir, with an immediate and lifted

aromatic bouquet demanding your attention. So evocative of violets, potpourri, baking spice, black cherry and more. The palate delivers a juicy, crunchy texture now, with the promise of a bright future courtesy of ripe tannins and an overall high quality. Screw cap. 13.5% alc. **Rating** 95 **To** 2028 $42 JP

♀♀♀♀♀ **Swinburn Vineyard Bellarine Peninsula Pinot Noir 2018** Rating 91 To 2026 $42 JP

Rochford Wines ★★★★★

878-880 Maroondah Highway, Coldstream, Vic 3770 **Region** Yarra Valley
T (03) 5957 3333 **www**.rochfordwines.com.au **Open** 7 days 9–5
Winemaker Kaspar Hermann, Kelly Healey **Est.** 1988 **Dozens** 20 000 **Vyds** 26ha
This Yarra Valley property was purchased by Helmut Konecsny in 2002; he had already established a reputation for pinot noir and chardonnay from the family-owned Romsey Park Vineyard in the Macedon Ranges (sold in '10). Since '10, Helmut has focused on his Yarra Valley winery and vineyards. In addition to the cellar door, the property has 2 restaurants, a retail shop and an expansive natural amphitheatre and observation tower – a showpiece in the region. Exports to the US and China.

♀♀♀♀♀ **Hill Road Single Vineyard Yarra Valley Syrah 2019** A compelling wine as it's totally savoury. OK, there's a hint of dark plums and a fragrance of violets, but that's it. Umami to the max here. Expect iodine, warm stones, wood smoke and cured meats, with an array of exotic spices. Lithe tannins and refreshing acidity seal the deal. Screw cap. 13% alc. **Rating** 95 **To** 2029 $48 JF
la Gauche Yarra Valley Cabernet Sauvignon 2019 The colour is good, the bouquet full of promise that is duly delivered by the medium-bodied palate, cassis riding high, superfine tannins sealing the deal. Great value. Screw cap. 13.3% alc. **Rating** 95 **To** 2034 $29 JH ❂

♀♀♀♀♀ **Premier Single Vineyard Yarra Valley Pinot Noir 2020** Rating 93 To 2030 $130 JF
Premier Single Vineyard Upper Yarra Valley Chardonnay 2020 Rating 92 To 2029 $100 JF
L'Enfant Unique Single Vineyard Yarra Valley Pinot Noir 2020 Rating 92 To 2033 $85 JF
Isabella's Single Vineyard Yarra Valley Cabernet Sauvignon 2019 Rating 91 To 2034 $80 JF
Yarra Valley Chardonnay 2020 Rating 90 To 2027 $38 JF
Isabella's Single Vineyard Yarra Valley Chardonnay 2020 Rating 90 To 2026 $75 JF
Yarra Valley Pinot Gris 2020 Rating 90 To 2022 $30 JF
Yarra Valley Rosé 2020 Rating 90 To 2021 $30 JF

RockBare ★★★★☆

62 Brooks Road, Clarendon, SA 5157 **Region** South Australia
T (08) 8383 7459 **www**.rockbare.com.au
Winemaker Shelley Torresan **Est.** 2000 **Vyds** 29ha
The RockBare journey, which began in late 2000, took a new direction recently when 2 multi-generational wine families came together in partnership: the Jackson family from California and the Melbourne-based Valmorbida family. Their combined focus will create a distinctive expression on the diverse wine regions across SA and those varieties that make them famous. Winemaker Shelley Torresan heads a team that sources grapes from family-owned vineyards and also well-regarded growers. Many of these loyal growers have been involved with RockBare for the past 18 years, committed to representing the very best of SA and being part of the now bigger RockBare family. Exports to most major markets.

Rockcliffe ★★★★☆

18 Hamilton Road, Denmark, WA 6333 **Region** Great Southern
T (08) 9848 1951 **www**.rockcliffe.com.au **Open** 7 days 11–5 or by appt
Winemaker Elysia Harrison, Mike Garland, Neil Miles **Est.** 1990 **Dozens** 30 000
Vyds 11ha

The Rockcliffe winery and vineyard business, formerly known as Matilda's Estate, is owned
by citizen of the world Steve Hall. The wine ranges echo local surf place names, headed by
Rockcliffe itself but extending to Third Reef and Quarram Rocks. Over the years, Rockcliffe
has won more than its fair share of trophies and gold and silver medals in wine shows. Exports
to the UK, Canada, Malaysia, Singapore, Thailand, Japan, Taiwan and China.

ΨΨΨΨΨ **Third Reef Great Southern Shiraz 2019** Powerfully structured and intensely
flavoured – this is why we love Frankland River shiraz! Here, it expresses with
cooling, mineral acidity, gravelly tannins and a lush red fruit opulence at its heart.
Impressive. Screw cap. 14.5% alc. **Rating** 95 **To** 2031 $35 EL
Reserve Great Southern Shiraz 2019 Intense, stemmy and stalky, with
brambly raspberry-bush characters on the palate. Plenty of blackberry fruit laced
through the palate; the alcohol does leave a trail of clove/aniseed on the tongue
once the fruit ebbs away. There is intensity and concentration here for those who
seek it. Screw cap. 14.9% alc. **Rating** 94 **To** 2036 $100 EL

ΨΨΨΨΨ **Third Reef Great Southern Riesling 2020 Rating** 91 **To** 2031 $25 EL

Rockford ★★★★★

131 Krondorf Road, Tanunda, SA 5352 **Region** Barossa Valley
T (08) 8563 2720 **www**.rockfordwines.com.au **Open** 7 days 11–5
Winemaker Robert O'Callaghan **Est.** 1984

Rockford can only be described as an icon, no matter how overused that word may be. It
has a devoted band of customers who buy most of the wine through the cellar door or mail
order (Robert O'Callaghan's entrancing annual newsletter is like no other). Some wine is sold
through restaurants and there are 2 retailers in Sydney and 1 each in Melbourne, Brisbane and
Perth. Whether they will have the Basket Press Shiraz available is another matter; it is as scarce
as Henschke Hill of Grace (but less expensive). Exports to Canada, Switzerland, Vietnam,
Singapore, Japan, Fiji, NZ, Thailand, Malaysia, Hong Kong and China.

Rogers & Rufus ★★★☆

40 Eden Valley Road, Angaston, SA 5353 **Region** Barossa Valley
T (08) 8561 3200 **www**.rogersandrufus.com
Winemaker Sam Wigan **Est.** 2009

This is a decidedly under-the-bedcover partnership between Robert Hill-Smith and his
immediate family, and Rupert and Jo Clevely – Rupert is the former Veuve Clicquot director
in Australia but now runs gastro pub group Geronimo Inns in London. Late in 2008 the Hill-
Smiths and Clevelys decided (in their words) 'to do something fun together with a serious dip
at Euro-styled dry and savoury delicate rosé using 3 site-specific, old, low-yielding, dry-grown
grenache sites from the Barossa floor'.

ΨΨΨΨΨ **Grenache of Barossa Rosé 2020** With its pretty, pale salmon hue and
understated pear and strawberry hull nuances, Rogers & Rufus defines the elegant
end of the Barossa Valley rosé continuum. Primary and graceful, it carries refined
and subtle acidity and just the right level of delicate phenolic tension. For those
who appreciate that less is indeed more with rosé. Screw cap. 12% alc. **Rating** 91
To 2021 $23 TS

 # Rogue Vintner

324 Koornang Road, Carnegie, Vic 3163 (postal) **Region** Various
T 0423 216 632 **www**.roguevintner.com
Winemaker Matt Herde **Est.** 2019 **Dozens** 1500
A multi-regional wine brand created and led by wine marketer Matt Herde. Regions for the
2019 red and white wines include Langhorne Creek, McLaren Vale, the Great Southern and
Margaret River. Exports to the US, Canada, Sweden and South Korea. (EL)

🍷🍷🍷🍷 **Gone Rogue Mish Mash White 2019** 75/20/5% riesling/pinot gris/viognier.
This is aromatic, layered and almost toasty with loads of taut, salty acidity. Simple,
but delicious. Screw cap. 12.5% alc. **Rating** 89 **To** 2023 $25 EL

Rogues Lane Vineyard

370 Lower Plenty Road, Viewbank, Vic 3084 (postal) **Region** Heathcote
T 0413 528 417 **www**.rogueslane.com.au
Winemaker Wild Duck Creek (Liam Anderson) **Est.** 1995 **Dozens** 240 **Vyds** 3.2ha
Philip Faure grew up in South Africa and studied agriculture at Stellenbosch University. After
migrating to Australia and spending some time in the IT industry, Philip found his way to
Heathcote, purchasing Rogues Lane Vineyard in 2015. The low-yielding vineyard, planted in
1995 and made up of 95% shiraz and 5% malbec, has seen 'an enormous amount of work'.
Philip produced his first wine in '17.

🍷🍷🍷🍷🍷 **Reserve Heathcote Shiraz 2018** A vibrant and deeply coloured shiraz in
keeping with the regional style, oozing toasted spices, blackberry, bramble and
briar. Sweet mocha oak makes an appearance on the palate, polishing the fruit and
supple tannins. Finishes smooth and long. Screw cap. 15% alc. **Rating** 90 **To** 2030
$55 JP

Rojomoma

16 Sturt Road, Nuriootpa. SA 5355 **Region** Barossa Valley
T 0421 272 336 **www**.rojomoma.com.au **Open** By appt
Winemaker Bernadette Kaeding, Sam Kurtz **Est.** 2004 **Dozens** 800 **Vyds** 5.4ha
Winemaker Sam Kurtz is a 6th-generation Barossan with over 30 vintages behind him.
Together with his partner Bernadette Kaeding, he purchased a vineyard in 1996, complete
with 1.49ha of then 110yo dry-grown grenache planted in 1886. Shiraz, cabernet sauvignon,
petit verdot and tempranillo have since been added. Grapes from the old and new plantings
were sold to Rockford, Chateau Tanunda, Spinifex and David Franz until 2004, when they
began making wine under the Red Art label. Bernie is also an author and photographer; her
art is displayed at the winery. Exports to the UK, China and Malaysia.

🍷🍷🍷🍷🍷 **Wild Scarlet Barossa Valley Shiraz Cabernet 2018** Impressively full, vibrant
purple hue. There's real personality and character here. All the depth and sweet
fruits of the Ebenezer vines are nicely lifted by the spicy fragrance of some whole
bunches, well set off by finely structured tannins. It delivers a lot for the price.
Screw cap. 14.1% alc. **Rating** 91 **To** 2025 $25 TS

🍷🍷🍷🍷 **Wild Scarlet Barossa Valley Shiraz 2018** **Rating** 89 **To** 2024 $25 TS
Red Art Barossa Cabernet Sauvignon 2016 **Rating** 89 **To** 2028 $38 TS

Rolf Binder

Cnr Seppeltsfield Road/Stelzer Road, Tanunda, SA 5352 **Region** Barossa Valley
T (08) 8562 3300 **www**.rolfbinder.com **Open** Mon–Sat 10–4.30, Sun on long weekends
Winemaker Rolf Binder, Christa Deans, Harry Mantzarapis **Est.** 1955 **Dozens** 28 000
Vyds 110ha
A winery steeped in family tradition and Barossa history, Rolf Binder and sister Christa Deans
are following their father's philosophy, using primarily estate-grown fruit from their own

vineyards located in various districts of the Barossa. A vineyard acquisition in the Vine Vale area has provided the family with centenarian shiraz vines planted in the 1890s, in fact parent vines to the Hanisch Shiraz. In 2019 Rolf and Christa celebrated 25 consecutive vintages, surely a unique record achievement for a brother/sister winemaking team. The brand was acquired by Accolade Wines in March 2021. Exports to all major markets.

ŸŸŸŸŸ **Heysen Barossa Valley Shiraz 2018** Binder's fabled Heysen vineyard has delivered a fantastic and characterful Barossa shiraz in 2018, brilliantly capturing tremendous depth without sacrificing brightness or definition. Crunchy black fruits of all kinds play to a backdrop of fresh licorice straps, wonderfully bright acidity and fine tannin confidence. Good value. Screw cap. 14% alc. **Rating** 96 To 2033 $75 TS ✪
Veritas Winery Bull's Blood Barossa Valley Shiraz Mataro Pressings 2018 From estate-grown bush vines planted in the 1880s, this signature blend has won a rightful place in Barossa folklore. As idiosyncratic as its name and label, this has long been one of Rolf Binder's most consistent and impressive performers. All the power and stature of pressings amplify the exotic allure of old vines. Ripe, fleshy black fruits of all kinds are impeccably framed in generous tannins, courtesy of the Mataro pressings, lively acidity and classy dark chocolate oak. It's larger than life, without a step out of place. Screw cap. 14% alc. **Rating** 95 To 2028 $65 TS
Hanisch Barossa Valley Shiraz 2018 There's power here. More alcohol, more oak and more tannin than the Heysen. Binder's big boy locks its brooding black fruits in a cage of splintery, sweet American oak that imposes a little now but promises to settle in time. Great line and length will sustain it in the cellar just as long as the cork holds out. Cork. 14.5% alc. **Rating** 94 To 2038 $150 TS
Heinrich Barossa Valley Shiraz Mataro Grenache 2018 Deep and brooding black fruits and licorice of an impressive harvest of Barossa shiraz are surrounded by the savoury personality of very old-vine mataro and the spicy approachability of grenache. Dark chocolate oak and fine tannins unite them seamlessly, drawing out a long finish of considerable polish and joy! Delicious. Screw cap. 14% alc. **Rating** 94 To 2025 $45 TS

ŸŸŸŸŸ **Barossa Valley Cabernet Sauvignon 2018** Rating 93 To 2033 $30 TS
Barossa Valley Shiraz 2019 Rating 90 To 2022 $25 TS

Rollick Wines ★★★☆

Region Barossa Valley
T 0416 866 384 **www**.rollickwines.com.au
Winemaker Jack Weedon **Est.** 2019 **Dozens** 500
Established in 2018 by Barossa couple Jack Weedon and Tash Hayes, Rollick Wines is named, labelled and marketed in anticipation of a good time. With 12 years' experience across Australia, NZ, France and Italy (including 7 at Henschke), Jack looks after winemaking, while Tash's background in marketing 'makes the rest of the magic happen'. (TS)

ŸŸŸŸŸ **First Step Riverland Fiano 2020** Pale straw green. Spicy nashi pear and lemon unite in a clean, youthful style. Three hours skin contact and bâtonnage lend gentle texture and a touch of phenolic grip. It concludes with medium persistence, drawn out by bright acidity. Simple yet well crafted. Accurate, appealing and ready for fusion-cuisine action. Screw cap. 12.5% alc. **Rating** 90 To 2021 $25 TS

ŸŸŸŸ **Folly Eden Valley Riesling 2020** Rating 89 To 2025 $28 TS

Ros Ritchie Wines ★★★★☆

Magnolia House, 190 Mount Buller Road, Mansfield, 3722 **Region** Upper Goulburn
T 0444 588 276 **www**.rosritchiewines.com **Open** Fri 5–8, w'ends & public hols 11–4
Winemaker Ros Ritchie **Est.** 2008 **Dozens** 2000 **Vyds** 7ha
Ros Ritchie was winemaker at the Ritchie family's Delatite winery from 1981 to 2006, but moved on to establish her own winery with husband John in '08 on a vineyard near

Mansfield. They became shareholders in Barwite Vineyards in '12 (planted to chardonnay, pinot noir, riesling and pinot gris) and in '14 established their new winery there. Apart from gewürztraminer (grown at Dead Man's Hill Vineyard), they work with local growers, foremost the Kinlock, McFadden, Timbertop and Baxendale vineyards, the last planted by the very experienced viticulturist Jim Baxendale (and wife Ruth) high above the King River Valley. All vineyards are managed with minimal spray regimes. The cellar door is located at the historic Magnolia House at Mansfield, open on select weekends, hosting seasonal wine dinners and special events.

ŸŸŸŸŸ **Barwite Vineyard Riesling 2020** Incredible value right here. So young and yet revealing so much in readiness for a long life ahead. A jasmine and spring blossom fragrance, teeming with lemon sorbet, green apple and a gently spicy lift. A kind of slatey minerality inhabits the palate in league with fast-paced chalky acidity. In a difficult year, out pops a stunner. Screw cap. 13% alc. **Rating** 95 **To** 2030 $26 JP ✪

ŸŸŸŸŸ **Upper Goulburn Pinot Gris 2020 Rating** 93 **To** 2026 $26 JP ✪
Barwite Vineyard Riesling 2019 Rating 92 **To** 2033 $26 JP
Upper Goulburn Pinot Grigio 2020 Rating 92 **To** 2025 $22 JP ✪
Upper Goulburn Pinot Grigio 2019 Rating 90 **To** 2025 $22 JP
Baxendale's Vineyard Cabernet Sauvignon 2018 Rating 90 **To** 2028 $27 JP
Sandy Creek Vineyard Tempranillo 2018 Rating 90 **To** 2026 $27 JP

Rosabrook Margaret River Wine   ★★★★

1390 Rosa Brook Road, Rosabrook, WA 6285 **Region** Margaret River
T (08) 9368 4555 **www**.rosabrook.com.au
Winemaker Severine Logan, Brian Fletcher **Est.** 1980 **Dozens** 12 000 **Vyds** 25ha
The original Rosabrook estate vineyards were established between 1984 and '96. In 2007 Rosabrook relocated its vineyard to the northwestern end of the Margaret River wine region, overlooking Geographe Bay and the Indian Ocean. Warm days and cool nights, influenced by the ocean, result in slow, mild-ripening conditions. Exports to the UK, Sweden, Dubai, Japan, Hong Kong and China.

ŸŸŸŸŸ **Single Vineyard Estate Cabernet Sauvignon 2018** Elegant cabernet, full to bursting with raspberry, pink peppercorn and pomegranate. The layers of flavour and spice have space between them – the concentration of flavour does not extend to weight, meaning this is light on its feet, yet with impressive power and length, too. Screw cap. 14.5% alc. **Rating** 94 **To** 2036 $45 EL
Single Vineyard Estate Cabernet Sauvignon 2017 Lifted and bright, with a purity on the mid palate that makes it incredibly quenching and delicious. Cassis, redcurrant and aniseed form the base, while spicy tannins and plump texture are the decorations. The acidity is filigreed into the fruit. A lovely wine. Screw cap. 14% alc. **Rating** 94 **To** 2036 $45 EL
Tempranillo 2018 Silky and juicy aromatics of raspberry, mulberry, hints of violet and vanilla pod. Quite delicious. Perfect ripeness is marbled throughout this wine, the tail speaking of succulent forest fruits and red berries. The flavour complexity stops short of cascading, but in terms of satisfaction and beauty – this is spot on. Screw cap. 14% alc. **Rating** 94 **To** 2027 $26 EL ✪

ŸŸŸŸ **Cabernet Merlot 2019 Rating** 89 **To** 2027 $20 EL

Rosby   ★★★☆

122 Strikes Lane, Mudgee, NSW 2850 **Region** Mudgee
T 0419 429 918 **www**.rosby.com.au **Open** 7 days 10–4
Winemaker Tim Stevens **Est.** 1995 **Dozens** 1500 **Vyds** 8ha
Gerald and Kay Norton-Knight have shiraz and cabernet sauvignon established on what is a truly unique site in Mudgee. Many vignerons like to think that their vineyard has special qualities, but in this instance the belief is well based. The vineyard is situated in a small valley

with unusual red basalt over a quartz gravel structure, encouraging deep root growth, making the use of water far less critical than normal. Tim Stevens of Huntington Estate has purchased some of the ample production and makes the Rosby wines. A rammed-earth cellar door has recently been completed at Rosby and there is an art gallery and sculpture garden onsite, too.

ŶŶŶŶŶ Mudgee Cabernet Sauvignon 2018 A deep crimson, the edges glimpsing the first signs of development. A stomping full-bodied cabernet that pushes few envelopes, while offering up plenty of flavour. Vanilla/bourbon oak tannins mark the roof of the mouth and serve as a corset of restraint, directing blackcurrant, menthol, crushed sage, sweet earth, tapenade and notes of mulch to a bolshy finish of good length. Shan't disappoint. Screw cap. 14.1% alc. **Rating** 91 **To** 2027 $30 NG

Rosenthal Wines

24 Rockford Street, Denmark, WA 6333 **Region** Great Southern
T 0432 312 918 **www**.rosenthalwines.com.au
Winemaker Luke Eckersley, Coby Ladwig **Est.** 2001 **Dozens** 35 000 **Vyds** 40ha
The original Rosenthal Vineyard (Springfield Park) was established in 1997 just north of Manjimup, by Dr John Rosenthal. In 2012 Coby Ladwig and Luke Eckersley acquired the business and relocated it to Mount Barker. Both have a sound knowledge of vineyards throughout the southwest of WA. The fruit for Rosenthal wines is sourced from their leased vineyard in Mount Barker, plus growers in Frankland River and Pemberton. Exports to the UK, India, the Philippines and China.

ŶŶŶŶŶ The Marker Great Southern Shiraz 2019 Supple raspberry and mulberry on the nose, peppered with sprinklings of star anise and licorice. On the palate, this has very fine tannins, and although the oak is very much present, it is balanced by vibrant and powerful fruit, making its wood work a secondary player in the end. Lovely, and will continue to gracefully evolve over the next 10 or so years. Screw cap. 14.5% alc. **Rating** 94 **To** 2031 $40 EL
Collector Mount Barker Cabernet Sauvignon 2019 Incredibly attractive flavours of red raspberry, pomegranate, salted tomato and star anise, however it all ends far too soon. This is really beautiful, but the length of flavour is a major quibble. Screw cap. 14.2% alc. **Rating** 94 **To** 2031 $90 EL

ŶŶŶŶŶ Richings Frankland River Shiraz 2019 Rating 93 **To** 2036 $60 EL
Richings Frankland River Cabernet Sauvignon 2019 Rating 93 **To** 2031 $60 EL
The Marker Great Southern Riesling 2020 Rating 91 **To** 2032 $35 EL
The Marker Pemberton Chardonnay 2020 Rating 91 **To** 2025 $40 EL
Richings Pemberton Chardonnay 2020 Rating 91 **To** 2027 $60 EL
Collector Mount Barker Chardonnay 2019 Rating 91 **To** 2027 $90 EL
Richings Mount Barker Riesling 2020 Rating 90 **To** 2030 $35 EL

Rosily Vineyard

871 Yelverton Road, Wilyabrup, WA 6284 **Region** Margaret River
T (08) 9755 6336 **www**.rosily.com.au **Open** 7 days 11–5 Dec–Jan
Winemaker Mick Scott **Est.** 1994 **Dozens** 6000 **Vyds** 12.28ha
Ken Allan and Mick Scott acquired the Rosily Vineyard site in 1994 and the vineyard was planted over 3 years to sauvignon blanc, semillon, chardonnay, cabernet sauvignon, merlot, shiraz, grenache and cabernet franc. The first crops were sold to other makers in the region, but by '99 Rosily had built a 120t capacity winery. It has gone from strength to strength, all of its estate-grown grapes being vinified under the Rosily Vineyard label, the wines substantially over-delivering for their prices. The vineyard was certified organic (ACO) in May 2017.

ŶŶŶŶŶ Reserve Margaret River Chardonnay 2018 2018 was one of the greatest vintages in Margaret River's history, creating wines of power, grace and balance. This certainly has the fruit concentration and intensity of the vintage; white peach, red apples, curry leaf, crushed cashew, almond meal, sea salt and hints of jasmine tea. The oak is impactful at this stage, but it will only integrate further into the cushion of ripe fruit. Screw cap. 13% alc. **Rating** 95 **To** 2031 $55 EL

ŸŸŸŸŸ **Margaret River Chardonnay 2020 Rating** 93 **To** 2030 $28 EL
Margaret River Chardonnay 2019 Rating 93 **To** 2025 $28 EL
Reserve Margaret River Cabernet Sauvignon 2017 Rating 92 **To** 2031 $55 EL
Margaret River Cabernet Sauvignon 2018 Rating 90 **To** 2031 $28 EL

Ross Hill Wines   ★★★★★

134 Wallace Lane, Orange, NSW 2800 **Region** Orange
T (02) 6365 3223 **www**.rosshillwines.com.au **Open** 7 days 10.30–5
Winemaker Luke Steele **Est.** 1994 **Dozens** 25 000 **Vyds** 18.2ha
Peter and Terri Robson planted chardonnay, merlot, sauvignon blanc, cabernet franc, cabernet sauvignon and pinot noir on north-facing slopes of the Griffin Road Vineyard in 1994. In 2007 their son James and his wife Chrissy joined the business and the Wallace Lane Vineyard (pinot noir, sauvignon blanc and pinot gris) was planted. The vines are now mature and the winery was NCOS Certified Carbon Neutral in '13. The Barrel & Larder School of Wine and Food (WSET Levels 1 and 2) operates from the extended cellar door. Exports to Germany, Singapore, Hong Kong and China.

ŸŸŸŸŸ **Pinnacle Series Griffin Road Vineyard Orange Sauvignon Blanc 2019**
Among the better sauvignons in the country, more suggestive of the pungent mineral notes of the Loire's better examples than wines from the New World. Aromas of nettle, redcurrant and gooseberry. The plume of acidity, juicy and saliva-sapping, bringing the wine to life as much as forcing one to reach for the next glass. This is benchmark. Screw cap. 12.7% alc. **Rating** 95 **To** 2025 $30 NG ✪

ŸŸŸŸŸ **Pinnacle Series Griffin Road Vineyard Orange Chardonnay 2019**
Rating 93 **To** 2026 $40 NG
Pinnacle Series Single Vineyard LT Orange Chardonnay 2019 Rating 93 **To** 2031 $70 NG
Founders Reserve Orange Merlot 2019 Rating 92 **To** 2029 $80 NG
Pinnacle Series Griffin Road Vineyard Orange Cabernet Sauvignon 2019 Rating 92 **To** 2029 $45 NG
The Griffin Orange Cabernet Sauvignon Merlot Cabernet Franc 2017 Rating 92 **To** 2031 $95 NG
Orange Tempranillo 2019 Rating 92 **To** 2025 $25 NG ✪
Pinnacle Series Wallace Lane Vineyard Orange Pinot Noir 2019 Rating 91 **To** 2027 $45 NG
Pinnacle Series Griffin Road Vineyard Orange Cabernet Franc 2019 Rating 90 **To** 2028 $50 NG

Rouleur   ★★★★☆

80 Laurens Street, North Melbourne, Vic 3051 **Region** Yarra Valley/McLaren Vale
T 0419 100 929 **www**.rouleurwine.com **Open** By appt
Winemaker Matthew East **Est.** 2015 **Dozens** 2500
Owner Matt East's interest in wine began at an early age while he was growing up in the Yarra Valley and watching his father plant a vineyard in Coldstream. Between February 1999 and December 2015 his day job was in sales and marketing, culminating in his appointment in '11 as national sales manager for Wirra Wirra (which he had joined in '08). Following his retirement from that position, he set in motion the wheels of Rouleur. He lives in Melbourne, with the Yarra in easy striking distance for sourcing fruit and making wine (at Yering Farm in Coldstream). He also makes wines from McLaren Vale, with that fruit cold-freighted to Coldstream. Back in Melbourne he has transformed a dilapidated milk bar in North Melbourne into his inner-city cellar door. Exports to Hong Kong, Singapore and Switzerland.

ŸŸŸŸŸ **Yarra Valley Pinot Gris et al 2020** A wonderful white. Aromatic, texturally bold, flamboyant and damn easy to drink, especially with food. Mandarin, cumquat, musk, rosewater and Moroccan souk. Pithy, detailed and tannic, with a saline and pumice-like finish. But poised and measured, with nothing excessive in fruit or structure. Delicious! Screw cap. 12.2% alc. **Rating** 96 **To** 2024 $34 NG ✪ ♥
Arlo's Upper Yarra Valley Pinot Noir 2019 A mid-weight wine with sour cherry, rosehip and sassafras riffs. Whole-bunch briary tannins provide textural relief, savouriness, depth and precision. There is nothing particularly green about them, aside from their chiffon-like veil of restraint that curtails the fruit. Skeletal, with just enough fruit hanging off very fine bones. Delicious domestic pinot at a great price. Diam. 13.5% alc. **Rating** 95 **To** 2028 $43 NG
McLaren Vale Shiraz 2019 A sumptuous shiraz made in a restrained style. This dichotomy alone infers intrigue and complexity. 20% whole bunch, wild ferment (as is standard at this address) and largely neutral wood. Sensible. Blueberry, lilac florals, iodine, salumi, tapenade and a skein of peppery acidity punctuate a plush finish. Delicious drinking. Screw cap. 14.4% alc. **Rating** 95 **To** 2028 $32 NG ✪
McLaren Vale Grenache 2019 Superlative grenache. Mid weight, with that febrile friskiness more reminiscent of elevated Gredos than, say, the Southern Rhône. Briary pithy tannins, tactile and firm, corral an almost ethereal veil of bright red fruits, from raspberry and cranberry to pomegranate, orange zest and bergamot. Pliant, expansive, savoury and long. Great value. Screw cap. 14.3% alc. **Rating** 95 **To** 2023 $32 NG ✪

ŸŸŸŸ♀ **Strawberry Fields Yarra Valley Pinot Meunier 2020** **Rating** 93 **To** 2025 $34 NG
Whole Bunch McLaren Vale Mataro 2019 **Rating** 93 **To** 2026 $34 NG
Yarra Valley Chardonnay 2020 **Rating** 92 **To** 2027 $32 NG
Yarra Valley Pinot Noir 2019 **Rating** 92 **To** 2027 $29 NG
Ronda McLaren Vale Nero d'Avola 2019 **Rating** 92 **To** 2024 $32 NG

Rowlee ★★★★

19 Lake Canobolas Road, Nashdale, NSW 2800 **Region** Orange
T (02) 6365 3047 **www.**rowleewines.com.au **Open** 7 days 11–5
Winemaker Nicole Samodol, James Manny **Est.** 2000 **Dozens** 7000 **Vyds** 8ha
Rowlee's vineyard (chardonnay, pinot noir, gewürztraminer, riesling, sauvignon blanc, pinot gris and Italian varieties arneis and nebbiolo) was planted 20 years ago by Nik and Deonne Samodol in the high-altitude (950m) cool climate of Orange. Their daughter, Nicole Samodol, and her partner James Manny 'combine European wine growing heritage with New World practices' to make the wines in 3 ranges: Rowlee, Single Vineyard and R-Series. The wines are available from the cellar door, specialist wine retailers and restaurants.

ŸŸŸŸ♀ **Orange Fumé Blanc 2019** A fine mid-weighted Loire-inspired sauvignon, partially barrel fermented for complexity, breadth and focus. Rapier-like intensity, with extended lees handling conferring additional detail to riffs of gooseberry, nettle, guava and a melody of citrus. A long and punchy finish. Screw cap. 12.5% alc. **Rating** 93 **To** 2024 $40 NG
R-Series Orange Chardonnay 2019 This is a richer expression from finer parcels of fruit embellished with newer French oak, albeit flintier and more tensile. Sumptuous aromas of hazelnuts, tatami and cream give way to a bumptious palate layered with stone fruit accents. Impressive. Screw cap. 14% alc. **Rating** 93 **To** 2028 $65 NG
Orange Arneis 2019 An autumnal fruit bowl, with nashi pear, bitter almond and ripe apple scents melding with jasmine, hay and orange blossom. A sluice of cool-climate acidity, juicy and natural feeling, tows it all long. Effortless drinking! A mid-weighted wine of savoury appeal that will prove versatile at the table. Screw cap. 13% alc. **Rating** 92 **To** 2023 $35 NG

R-Series Orange Pinot Noir 2019 A richer, more suave expression than its less-expensive pinot siblings. Aged in classy French barriques for 9 months, there is a mocha accent to fecund cherry, strawberry and clove. Contrasts of lighter shades sashaying with dark. Supple texture and packed with flavour, before a work-out in the glass reveals an undercarriage of savoury tannins that will transport this wine into a promising future. Screw cap. 14% alc. **Rating** 92 **To** 2027 $65 NG
Central Ranges Cabernet 2019 I like this. Minty and bitter-chocolate accented, clearly Australian. Cassis, hedgerow and anise, too. The tannins are measured, directing the fruit without being too astringent. A simple, sassy, mid-weighted table wine delivering ample pleasure and versatility. Screw cap. 13.5% alc. **Rating** 90 **To** 2024 $35 NG
Orange Chardonnay 2019 Hand picked, barrel fermented and aged on lees in the same French wood for 10 months. Regular stirring is evident in the creamy mouthfeel, redolent of nougat and cashew. Nectarine, white peach and citrus scents follow through on the fullish palate. The oak, well integrated. The flow, uninterrupted. A wine that bridles a safe approach and a bit of derring-do. Screw cap. 14% alc. **Rating** 90 **To** 2025 $40 NG

ΨΨΨΨ   **Single Vineyard Orange Pinot Noir 2019** Rating 89 **To** 2024 $50 NG
Single Vineyard Orange Nebbiolo 2019 Rating 89 **To** 2024 $60 NG
Single Vineyard Orange Riesling 2019 Rating 88 **To** 2028 $35 NG

Rudderless   ★★★★☆

Victory Hotel, Main South Road, Sellicks Beach, SA 5174 **Region** McLaren Vale
T (08) 8556 3083 **www.**victoryhotel.com.au **Open** 7 days
Winemaker Peter Fraser **Est.** 2004 **Dozens** 550 **Vyds** 2ha
It's a long story how Doug Govan, owner of the Victory Hotel (circa 1858), came to choose the name Rudderless for his vineyard. The vineyard is planted on 2 levels (in 1999 and 2003) to a complex mix of shiraz, graciano, grenache, malbec, mataro and viognier. It surrounds the hotel, which is situated in the foothills of the Southern Willunga Escarpment as it falls into the sea. The wines are mostly sold through the Victory Hotel, where the laidback Doug keeps a low profile.

ΨΨΨΨΨ   **Sellicks Hill McLaren Vale Shiraz 2019** A solid portion (50%) of whole berries in the ferment, imparting a pulpy energy to the wine. And yet there is a brood of black rock mineral, salumi, tapenade and clove/black-pepper riffs, meandering along a skeletal beam of well-wrought, sooty tannins. Nicely rustic. The tannins are firm, gritty and very impressive as they pull the saliva forth. Reminds me of an avant-garde wine from the Languedoc. Rich but not jammy. Nothing out of place. Screw cap. 14% alc. **Rating** 94 **To** 2027 $35 NG
Sellicks Hill McLaren Vale Grenache 2019 Hand picked, sorted and destemmed, but plenty of whole-berry, pulpy jive. Energy! Extracted with aplomb, as is the Peter Fraser signature. Maturation in older French wood, the way it should be with this effusive variety. Kirsch, bramble, orange zest, clove and turmeric scents skitter along a fibrous web of briary tannin. Delicious. Screw cap. 14% alc. **Rating** 94 **To** 2025 $35 NG

ΨΨΨΨ♀   **Sellicks Hill McLaren Vale Malbec 2019** Rating 92 **To** 2026 $35 NG

Ruggabellus   ★★★★★

PO Box 32, Stockwell, SA 5355 **Region** Barossa Valley
T 0412 773 536 **www.**ruggabellus.com.au
Winemaker Abel Gibson **Est.** 2009 **Dozens** 1000
Abel Gibson arrived in the Barossa Valley as a 2-year-old in 1975, his father on the way to becoming senior viticulturist for Penfolds, and absorbed the 150yo history of the Valley. It was almost inevitable that between 1990 and '92, Abel, then in his late teens, would flirt with university studies (including wine science at Roseworthy) then decided he wanted nothing more to do with it. Between '93 and 2000 he spent winters skiing and snowboarding, riding

thousands of kilometres on a bicycle around NZ and Tasmania, then 20000km around Australia in a '74 VW Kombi, and travelling through Central America, discovering its 3000+yo civilisations, all of this funded by seasonal employment. Simply because it was easy, when he returned home in '01 he took a vintage job at Penfolds, which did nothing to light his fire. In '02 he was offered a position at Rockford, and at the age of 27 he finally found what he had been looking for. An '03 vintage in Spain at Campo de Borja was followed by the '04 vintage with Charles Melton, before he finally joined his father's winery over the next 3 years. The next decisive step was a 3-year stint at Spinifex, cementing all of the pieces of his prior experience into a coherent whole, and laying the ground for his small-batch winemaking, linked to specific plots of old vines. Exports to the UK, the US and Japan.

Rymill Coonawarra

Riddoch Highway, Coonawarra, SA 5263 **Region** Coonawarra
T (08) 8736 5001 **www**.rymill.com.au **Open** 7 days 11–5
Winemaker Shannon Sutherland **Est.** 1974 **Dozens** 50000 **Vyds** 140ha
The Rymills are descendants of John Riddoch and have long owned some of the finest Coonawarra soil, upon which they have grown grapes since 1970. In 2016 the Rymill family sold the winery, vineyards and brand to a Chinese investor. The management, vineyard and winery teams have remained in place and new capital has financed moves to improve the vineyards and winery. Winemaker Shannon Sutherland has experience in the Napa Valley, Beaujolais, Canada and Marlborough, as well as Great Western and the Hunter Valley in Australia. The winery building also houses the cellar door and art exhibitions, which, together with viewing platforms over the winery, make it a must-see destination for tourists. Exports to all major markets.

🍷🍷🍷🍷🍷 **The Surveyor Cabernet Sauvignon 2018** It's somewhat eyebrow-raising to have 'certified sustainable' stamped on a bottle which comes in at 50g shy of 2kg. That isn't sustainable. However, the wine is excellent. Deep, rich and powerful. It has a vibrancy, it's floral and full of beautiful fruit. Full bodied, with a plushness and an abundance of ripe tannins. The length is superb. The most complete and balanced Surveyor to date. Diam. 14.6% alc. **Rating** 96 **To** 2038 $90 JF
Classic Release Cabernet Sauvignon 2018 This is pure Coonawarra, showing plenty of class. Cassis and blackcurrants are inflected with tobacco, mint and woodsy spices. It's more medium bodied, very fresh and lively. Tannins are pitch-perfect – ripe, savoury and slightly grainy. It feels nicely polished, but not fabricated. Screw cap. 14.2% alc. **Rating** 95 **To** 2033 $32 JF ✪

🍷🍷🍷🍷 **CF Cabernet Franc 2020 Rating** 91 **To** 2025 $25 JF
MC2 Coonawarra Merlot Cabernet Sauvignon Cabernet Franc 2019 Rating 90 **To** 2025 $20 JF ✪
PV Coonawarra Petit Verdot 2020 Rating 90 **To** 2026 $25 JF

Saddler's Creek

Marrowbone Road, Pokolbin, NSW 2320 **Region** Hunter Valley
T (02) 4991 1770 **www**.saddlerscreek.com **Open** 7 days 10–5
Winemaker Brett Woodward **Est.** 1989 **Dozens** 6000 **Vyds** 10ha
Saddler's Creek is a boutique winery that is little known outside the Hunter Valley, but has built a loyal following of dedicated supporters. It came onto the scene over 25 years ago with some rich, bold wines, and maintains this style today. Fruit is sourced from the Hunter Valley and Langhorne Creek, with occasional forays into other premium regions.

🍷🍷🍷🍷🍷 **Alessandro Reserve Chardonnay 2019** A delicious wine, constructing the vanilla-cedar lattice from the oak in just the right measure, while architecting it with the mineral pungency of the high country. White peach, fig, honeydew and nougatine at the core. A wonderful thrust of intense fruit rivalled by a parry of juicy freshness, pulling it all to very impressive length. Precision and juiciness, personified. Screw cap. 13.8% alc. **Rating** 95 **To** 2027 $45 NG

🍷🍷🍷🍷🍺 **Bluegrass Langhorne Creek Cabernet Sauvignon Shiraz 2018** Rating 92
To 2028 $45 NG
Tumbarumba Pinot Noir 2018 Rating 90 To 2024 $36 NG
Saddlier's Hilltops Tempranillo 2019 Rating 90 To 2024 $36 NG

Sailor Seeks Horse   ★★★★★

Port Cygnet Winery, 60 Lymington Road, Cygnet, Tas 7112 **Region** Southern Tasmania
T 0418 471 120 **www**.sailorseekshorse.com.au **Open** W'ends 11–4 or by appt
Winemaker Paul Lipscombe, Gilli Lipscombe **Est.** 2010 **Dozens** 1500 **Vyds** 6.5ha
While I was given comprehensive information about the seriously interesting careers of
Paul and Gilli Lipscombe, and about their vineyard, I am none the wiser about the highly
unusual and very catchy name. The story began in 2005 when they resigned from their
(unspecified) jobs in London, did a vintage in Languedoc and then headed to Margaret River
to study oenology and viticulture. While combining study and work, their goal was to learn
as much as possible about pinot noir. They worked in large, small, biodynamic, conventional,
minimum- and maximum-intervention vineyards and wineries – Woodlands, Xanadu, Beaux
Freres, Chehalem and Mt Difficulty, all household names. By '10 they were in Tasmania
working for Julian Alcorso's Winemaking Tasmania (now Tasmanian Vintners) and found a
derelict vineyard that had never cropped, having been abandoned not long after being planted
in '05. It was in the Huon Valley, precisely where they had aimed to begin – the coolest district
in Tasmania. They are working as winemakers for celebrated Home Hill Winery and manage
Jim Chatto's vineyard in Glaziers Bay. Exports to the UK, the US and Singapore.

St Aidan   ★★★★☆

754 Ferguson Road, Dardanup, WA 6236 **Region** Geographe
T (08) 9728 3007 **www**.saintaidan.com.au **Open** Mon–Tues & Thurs–Fri 11–4,
w'ends & public hols 11–5
Winemaker Mark Messenger (Contract) **Est.** 1996 **Dozens** 1500 **Vyds** 2.6ha
Phil and Mary Smith purchased their property at Dardanup in 1991, a 20-min drive from the
Bunbury hospital where Phil works. They first ventured into Red Globe table grapes, planting
1ha in 1994–2005, followed by 1ha of mandarins and oranges. With this experience, and with
Mary completing a TAFE viticulture course, they extended their horizons by planting 1ha
each of cabernet sauvignon and chardonnay in '97, 0.5ha of muscat in '01, and semillon and
sauvignon blanc thereafter.

🍷🍷🍷🍷🍷 **Geographe Tempranillo 2019** Pure red berries and juicy succulence for days.
The fine, chalky and shapely tannins hold this off being slurpy … that guilt-
ridden, delicious space that reds can sometimes move towards. This makes a
fabulous case for modern tempranillo. Screw cap. 14% alc. **Rating** 95 To 2025 $25
EL ✪
Geographe Sauvignon Blanc Semillon 2020 Pale straw in colour, aromas of
lemon citrus mingle with white florals, green guava and nashi pear. The palate has
a juicy, chewy acid backbone, partnered with a gently plump viscosity. There is
chalky phenolic finesse that elevates this wine into excellence. Purity, with brilliant
intensity and concentration of flavour. Yes! Screw cap. 13.9% alc. **Rating** 94
To 2023 $20 EL ✪

🍷🍷🍷🍷🍺 **Ferguson Cabernet Sauvignon 2018** Rating 92 To 2030 $35 EL
Zena Liqueur Muscat NV Rating 90 $35 EL

Saint & Scholar   ★★★★☆

Maximilian's Restaurant, 15 Onkaparinga Valley Road, Verdun, SA 5245
Region Adelaide Hills
T (08) 8388 7777 **www**.saintandscholar.com.au **Open** Wed–Sun 11–5
Winemaker Stephen Dew **Est.** 2018 **Dozens** 12 000 **Vyds** 50ha

Owned by Ed Peter, Dirk Wiedmann and Reid Bosward, Saint & Scholar is a substantial newcomer with 50ha of shiraz, pinot noir, pinot gris, chardonnay and sauvignon blanc. It has also recently opened a large cellar door in Maximilian's Restaurant in Verdun. Winemaker Stephen Dew is the Saint, Reid Bosward (winemaker at Kaesler) is the Scholar. Stephen Dew has worked vintages at Domaine Prieuré-Roch owned by Henri-Frédéric Roch, a co-director of Domaine de la Romanée-Conti (by virtue of the Roch family ownership of 50% of Domaine). Henri-Frédéric was a natural winemaker and having tasted Roch's wines in his winery in Burgundy, I (James) can attest that his wines reflect his beliefs. Reid Bosward has worked 30 harvests over 25 years in Bordeaux (the Lurton family), Minervois, Moldova, South Africa and Spain. He is the Scholar and absolutely not a natural winemaker, just a very good one. Exports to all major markets.

🍷🍷🍷🍷🍷 **Saving Grace Adelaide Hills Shiraz 2018** A richer and plusher style on the nose. Lovely shiraz flavours without excessive show-off extras on the palate, allowing some sweeter, exotic spice notes to lift. Easy drinkability. Screw cap. 14.5% alc. **Rating** 92 **To** 2025 $45 TL
Adelaide Hills Pinot Shiraz 2018 Pretty aromatics to start, crushed crimson fruits with a dusty, leafy backdrop. Juicy and spicy in the sipping, decent medium-weighted structure and line with a mineral feel through the palate. A drink-now style, yet still with presence. Screw cap. 14% alc. **Rating** 90 **To** 2025 $30 TL

St Hallett ★★★★★

St Hallett Road, Tanunda, SA 5352 **Region** Barossa Valley
T (08) 8563 7000 **www**.sthallett.com.au **Open** 7 days 10–5
Winemaker Helen McCarthy **Est.** 1944 **Dozens** 210 000
St Hallett sources all their grapes from within the Barossa GI and is synonymous with the region's icon variety – shiraz. Old Block is the ultra-premium leader of the band (using old-vine grapes from Lyndoch and Eden Valley), supported by Blackwell (Greenock, Ebenezer and Seppeltsfield). The winemaking team continues to explore the geographical, geological and climatic diversity of the Barossa, manifested through individual processing of all vineyards and single-vineyard releases. In 2017 St Hallett was acquired by Accolade. Exports to all major markets.

🍷🍷🍷🍷🍷 **Planted 1919 Eden Valley Shiraz 2015** This new flagship sings the virtues of a single site in the soothing voice of ancient Eden Valley vines. In spite of the massive bottle, this is not part of the 'bigger is better' brigade. Breathtakingly fresh and pure at 6 years old, the glorious 2015 season unites wonderful rose petal fragrance with tangy morello cherry fruits, a backdrop of bright acidity and superb, fine-ground tannins. Grand testimony to Toby Barlow's sensitivity and considerable talent. Diam. 14.6% alc. **Rating** 97 **To** 2040 $450 TS

🍷🍷🍷🍷🍷 **Higher Earth Eden Valley Syrah 2018** St Hallett's deep reach into the great sites of the Eden Valley and its blending wizardry forge an exquisite take on this great vintage. At once concentrated and vibrant, spice-laden and enduring. Impeccably constructed tannins draw out a finish of pinpoint detail and lingering persistence. Screw cap. 14.5% alc. **Rating** 96 **To** 2038 $60 TS ❂
Mighty Ox Barossa Shiraz 2018 True to name, the mighty northern Barossa comes alive with depth and impact. Yet, crucially, this boasts the lift, detail and precision that set the modern St Hallett apart. Full, vibrant purple, it brims with crunchy blackberries, black cherries and satsuma plums, laced with exotic spice. Refreshing acidity and enduring fine-grained tannins complete a long finish. Cork. 14.8% alc. **Rating** 96 **To** 2048 $210 TS
Single Vineyard Mattschoss Barossa Shiraz 2018 The exotic spice of old vines unites with the fragrance of this cool, high site to produce a signature Eden Valley shiraz brimming with character, amplified by whole-bunch fermentation. Potpourri and spice of all kinds make way for a core of crunchy black/blueberry fruit, impeccably supported by dark chocolate French oak. Fine tannins will see it out for the medium term. Screw cap. 14.3% alc. **Rating** 95 **To** 2033 $55 TS

Single Vineyard Dawkins Eden Valley Shiraz 2018 Wonderful purity of enticing black cherry, raspberry and blood plum fruit launches from a vibrant purple hue. Layers of classic Eden Valley spice flow through a very long finish. Classy French oak resolves fine tannins and lends a backdrop of high-cocoa dark chocolate. One for the cellar. Screw cap. 14.5% alc. **Rating** 95 **To** 2038 $55 TS
Butcher's Cart Barossa Shiraz 2018 St Hallett delivers impressively at every price point of Barossa shiraz, and character, depth and polish find a compelling synergy here. Crunchy dark berry fruits glide long into the finish, energised by vibrant acidity and beautifully composed tannins. Expertly crafted, with lots of joy thrown in along the way. Screw cap. 14.5% alc. **Rating** 94 **To** 2028 $39 TS
Blackwell Barossa Shiraz 2018 Blackwell assumes a unique place in the St Hallett hierarchy, embodying the density and impact of the northern Barossa in waves of blackberry and satsuma plum fruit and licorice. Fantastic hue of full, vibrant purple. Dark chocolate oak lurks in the background. Quintessential modern Barossa shiraz in all its glory. Screw cap. 14.5% alc. **Rating** 94 **To** 2033 $54 TS

🍷🍷🍷🍷 Faith Barossa Shiraz 2019 Rating 92 To 2025 $24 TS ✪

St Huberts

Cnr Maroondah Highway/St Huberts Road, Coldstream, Vic 3770 **Region** Yarra Valley
T (03) 5960 7096 **www**.sthuberts.com.au **Open** By appt
Winemaker Greg Jarratt **Est.** 1966 **Vyds** 20.49ha
The St Huberts of today has a rich 19th-century history, not least in its success at the 1881 Melbourne International Exhibition, which featured every type of agricultural and industrial product. The wine section alone attracted 711 entries. The Emperor of Germany offered a Grand Prize, a silver gilt epergne, for the most meritorious exhibit in the show. A St Huberts wine won the wine section, then competed against objects as diverse as felt hats and steam engines to win the Emperor's Prize, featured on its label for decades thereafter. Like other Yarra Valley wineries, it dropped from sight at the start of the 20th century, was reborn in 1966 and, after several changes of ownership, became part of what today is TWE. The wines are made at Coldstream Hills but have their own, very different, focus. St Huberts is dominated by cabernet and the single-vineyard roussanne. Its grapes come from warmer sites, particularly the valley floor (part owned and part under contract).

🍷🍷🍷🍷 Yarra Valley Cabernet Sauvignon 2018 One of those wines that just falls into place. A medium-bodied cabernet with lots of varietal satisfaction. It's savoury, flitting with spicy oak, tapenade and gum leaves and the tannins textural and lightly raspy. Screw cap. 13% alc. **Rating** 93 **To** 2030 $35 JF
The Stag Cool Climate Victoria Pinot Noir 2019 This always offers good value at this price point. It is lively and bright, kicking off with a core of juicy cherry fruit. A good dash of baking spices and licorice with dried herbs in the mix. The tannins are svelte and it feels cool and refreshing. Screw cap. 13.5% alc. Rating 91 To 2025 $25 JF
Yarra Valley Chardonnay 2020 Lots of flavour here, without going sideways. Some citrus and stone fruit with vanilla-pod oak and woodsy spices come to the fore. Fuller bodied with requisite leesy creaminess across the palate. Screw cap. 13.5% alc. **Rating** 90 **To** 2025 $27 JF

St Hugo

2141 Barossa Valley Way, Rowland Flat, SA 5352 **Region** Barossa Valley
T (08) 8115 9200 **www**.sthugo.com **Open** Fri–Mon 10.30–4.30
Winemaker Peter Munro **Est.** 1983 **Dozens** 50000 **Vyds** 57ha
This is a standalone business within the giant bosom of Pernod Ricard, focused on the premium and ultra-premium end of the market, thus differentiating it from Jacob's Creek. It is presumably a substantial enterprise, even though little information about its size or modus operandi is forthcoming. Exports to the UK, Singapore, NZ and China.

ΨΨΨΨΨ **Barossa Shiraz 2018** An impressive vintage for St Hugo, leading out with a full, vibrant purple hue. A deep, compact yet bright core of crunchy blackberries, black cherries and satsuma plum hails a great vintage in the Barossa. High-cocoa dark chocolate French oak has been strategically and expertly deployed for long-term endurance. Impressive promise. Screw cap. 14.5% alc. **Rating** 95 **To** 2043 $50 TS
Coonawarra Cabernet Sauvignon 2018 Varietally exact and consummately engineered for the long haul, this is a quintessential St Hugo of might and poise. Deep, ripe black/redcurrants and cassis mark out a long palate, accented with sage and impeccably braced with classy French oak and a mouth-filling splay of fine tannins. Bright acidity completes a long finish. Screw cap. 14.7% alc. **Rating** 95 **To** 2043 $50 TS
Barossa Coonawarra Cabernet Shiraz 2018 Barossa shiraz serves to both build and tone Coonawarra cabernet, united seamlessly in a tightly coiled structure of great promise. Crunchy, focused, compact black fruits are intricately supported by a multicultural mix of oak, laying out a long finish of high-cocoa dark chocolate and coffee bean. A cellaring special. Screw cap. 14.2% alc. **Rating** 95 **To** 2038 $50 TS

ΨΨΨΨΨ **Eden Valley Riesling 2020 Rating** 92 **To** 2030 $40 TS
Barossa Grenache Shiraz Mataro 2019 Rating 90 **To** 2024 $50 TS

St John's Road ★★★★

1468 Research Road, St Kitts, SA 5356 **Region** Barossa Valley
T (08) 8362 8622 **www.**stjohnsroad.com **Open** By appt
Winemaker James Lienert, Andrew Hardy, Keeda Zilm **Est.** 2002 **Dozens** 12 000
Vyds 20ha
St John's Road, part of WD Wines Pty Ltd (which also owns Hesketh Wine Company, Parker Coonawarra Estate and Vickery Wines), brings together the highly experienced winemaking team of James Lienert (formerly of Penfolds, plus vintages in the US, Germany and NZ), Keeda Zilm (O'Leary Walker and Vickery Wines) and Andrew Hardy (over 35 years of winemaking in SA, plus Bordeaux and California; Andrew has recently launched the Ox Hardy label). Wines are sourced from the estate Resurrection Vineyard in Ebenezer, and from high-quality local vineyards. Exports to the UK, the EU and Asia.

ΨΨΨΨ **Peace of Eden Riesling 2020** Elegant, immediate and affordable. The ripeness of the season is expressed in guava and star fruit, over a core of classic lime and Granny Smith apple. The bright tension of the cool nights draws out a long finish. It takes a little phenolic grip and saltiness in its stride. Screw cap. 12% alc. **Rating** 89 **To** 2023 $22 TS

St Johns Vineyards ★★★★☆

283 Yelverton North Road, Yelverton, WA 6281 **Region** Margaret River
T (08) 9417 5633 **www.**stjohnsbrook.com.au **Open** By appt
Winemaker Andrew Dawson **Est.** 1997 **Dozens** 70 000 **Vyds** 100ha
St Johns Vineyards (previously Latitude 34 Wine Co) was established in 1997 with their first vineyards in the Blackwood Valley (83ha), followed in '98 by the St Johns Brook Vineyard in Yallingup (37ha). A 1200t winery with temperature-controlled wine storage was built in 2004. The wines are released under the St Johns Brook, Optimus, The Blackwood and Crush labels. Exports to Thailand, China, the UK, Poland and Hong Kong.

ΨΨΨΨΨ **St Johns Brook Reserve Margaret River Cabernet Sauvignon 2018** Ripe, powerful cabernet, punctuated by layers of red berries. Exotic spice is tucked into the folds of flavours, working in concert over the tongue, steered by firm tannins through a long finish. There's a no-nonsense vibe to this wine. It's not simple, but it's not complicated. The length of flavour tells us everything we need to know about the quality of the fruit. Screw cap. 14.5% alc. **Rating** 95 **To** 2036 $50 EL
St Johns Brook Reserve Block 8 Margaret River Cabernet Sauvignon 2018 Powerful, beautiful cabernet with all of the succulent fruits on show:

pomegranate, raspberry, cassis, redcurrant and satsuma plum, backed by salted licorice and aniseed. There is a floral note here, too … of the fennel flower kind. This gets the same score as the Reserve for different reasons: this is the seductive, plush, inviting one of the pair. Beautiful. Screw cap. 14.5% alc. **Rating** 95 To 2036 $50 EL

🍷🍷🍷🍷🍷 St Johns Brook Reserve Margaret River Chardonnay 2019 Rating 93 To 2031 $50 EL
Optimus The Terraces Blackwood Valley Shiraz 2018 Rating 93 To 2036 $100 EL
St Johns Brook Recolte Margaret River Sauvignon Blanc Semillon 2020 Rating 92 To 2024 $24 EL ✪
St Johns Brook Reserve Margaret River Shiraz 2018 Rating 92 To 2031 $50 EL
St Johns Brook Single Vineyard Margaret River Chardonnay 2019 Rating 91 To 2027 $34 EL
St Johns Brook Single Vineyard Margaret River Cabernet Sauvignon 2018 Rating 91 To 2028 $34 EL
Optimus The Terraces Block 3 Cabernet Sauvignon 2018 Rating 91 To 2036 $100 EL
St Johns Brook Single Vineyard Margaret River Shiraz 2018 Rating 90 To 2027 $34 EL
The Blackwood El Toro Rojo Blackwood Valley Shiraz Tempranillo 2019 Rating 90 To 2025 $34 EL

St Leonards Vineyard   ★★★★

St Leonards Road, Wahgunyah, Vic 3687 **Region** Rutherglen
T 1800 021 621 **www.**stleonardswine.com.au **Open** Thurs–Sun 10–5
Winemaker Nick Brown, Chloe Earl **Est.** 1860 **Dozens** 3500 **Vyds** 12ha
An old favourite, relaunched in late 1997 with a range of premium wines cleverly marketed through an attractive cellar door and bistro at the historic winery on the banks of the Murray. It is run by Eliza Brown (CEO), sister Angela (online communications manager) and brother Nick (vineyard and winery manager). They are perhaps better known as the trio who fulfil the same roles at All Saints Estate. Exports to the US, the Philippines, Hong Kong and China.

🍷🍷🍷🍷🍷 Hip Sip Muscat NV The name, the Japanese-inspired 'tattoo' label and the whole groovy hip-flask package offers a re-imagining of muscat. Expect a lightness, a savouriness, revealing the floral charm of the grape. Rose petal, honeysuckle, fig, nougat, dried-fruit aromas, fresh and lively. Rose oil to the fore, emphasising a smooth palate with chewy sweet toffee and golden syrupy sweetness. Young, fruity and delicious. Brown muscat picked ripe, crushed and macerated for up to 3 days, pressed, fortified with grape spirit and matured in large barrels. 350ml. Vino-Lok. 17.5% alc. **Rating** 90 $22 JP

🍷🍷🍷🍷 Moscato 2019 Rating 89 To 2023 $22 JP
The Keep Tawny Fortified NV Rating 89 $22 JP
Pinot Gris 2020 Rating 88 To 2024 $28 JP

Salomon Estate   ★★★★☆

Braeside Road, Finniss, SA 5255 **Region** Southern Fleurieu
T 0417 808 243 **www.**salomonwines.com **Open** By appt
Winemaker Bert Salomon, Simon White **Est.** 1997 **Dozens** 7000 **Vyds** 12.1ha
Bert Salomon is an Austrian winemaker with a long-established family winery in the Kremstal region, not far from Vienna. He became acquainted with Australia during his time with import company Schlumberger in Vienna; he was the first to import Australian wines (Penfolds) into Austria, in the mid-1980s, and later became head of the Austrian Wine Bureau. He was so taken by Adelaide that he moved his family there for the first few months of each

year, sending his young children to school and setting in place an Australian red winemaking venture. He retired from the Bureau and is now a full-time travelling winemaker, running the family winery in the Northern Hemisphere vintage and overseeing the making of the Salomon Estate wines. Exports to all major markets.

🍷🍷🍷🍷🍷 **Governor Fleurieu Shiraz Cabernet Sauvignon 2018** Shiraz is made for cabernet in these parts. Even at a young age in a big bottle, the divide is invisible. Salomon's savoury style sings in layers of dried herbs and a glimpse of eucalyptus, carried by a core of dark, crunchy berry fruits. Powder-fine tannins will appreciate some years to tuck into its folds. Magnum. Diam. 14.5% alc. **Rating** 92 **To** 2036 $60 TS

Finniss River Braeside Vineyard Fleurieu Peninsula Cabernet Sauvignon 2018 Bert Salomon has managed to bottle a real sense of Australiana, replete with scents of the bush, bay and tomato leaf. Cabernet upholds its voice with grace and truth, with red/blackcurrants flying on a fine-woven carpet of powdery tannins. Sensitively toned oak cements medium to long-term promise. Screw cap. 14.5% alc. **Rating** 92 **To** 2038 $36 TS

Finniss River Sea Eagle Vineyard Fleurieu Peninsula Shiraz 2018 Impressive colour: deep and vibrant. Slick, spicy dark berry fruits of all persuasions and a dusting of oregano are boosted by a hit of charry oak. The 2 are yet to marry, but give them time. Firm, fine-grained tannins, tangy acidity and good persistence will get it there. Screw cap. 14.5% alc. **Rating** 90 **To** 2033 $40 TS

Saltram ★★★★☆

Murray Street, Angaston, SA 5353 **Region** Barossa Valley
T (08) 8561 0200 **www**.saltramwines.com.au **Open** 7 days 10–5
Winemaker Alex MacKenzie **Est.** 1859 **Dozens** 150 000
There is no doubt that Saltram has taken strides towards regaining the reputation it held 30 or so years ago. Grape sourcing has come back to the Barossa Valley for the flagship wines. The red wines, in particular, have enjoyed great show success over the past decade with No. 1 Shiraz and Mamre Brook leading the charge. Exports to all major markets.

🍷🍷🍷🍷🍷 **No. 1 Barossa Shiraz 2017** Cool years like these bless the Barossa with brightness, definition, integrity and endurance. Saltram has captured all the focus and poise of the season while upholding incredible black fruit density. Epic tannins entwine with magnificent natural acidity. High-class French oak sits just behind the fruit at every moment of a very long finish. Screw cap. 14.5% alc. **Rating** 97 **To** 2047 $100 TS ✪

🍷🍷🍷🍷🍷 **The Journal Old Vine Barossa Shiraz 2017** A graceful dignity, space and a multifaceted complexity set apart these centenarian Eden Valley vines from Saltram's Barossa shiraz blends. Age lifts fragrance and exotic spice, while altitude brightens the vibrant acid flow of this cool harvest. Crunchy dark and red berry fruits are granted space and grace by large-vat maturation. Fine, mineral tannins glide through a finish of good if not outstanding length. Screw cap. 14% alc. **Rating** 96 **To** 2042 $175 TS

Pepperjack Premium Cut Barossa Cabernet Shiraz 2018 Richard Mattner unites the big-gun regions of SA to celebrate the quintessential Aussie blend. It rejoices in all there is to love about the past, present and future of Australian winemaking. A deep core of blackcurrant and blackberry fruit stretches tall and long, upheld by a fine splay of intricate tannins and bright acidity. Outstanding line and unwavering persistence make for one of the best reds at this price on the shelves today. Screw cap. 14.5% alc. **Rating** 96 **To** 2038 $40 TS ✪

Mr Pickwick's Particular Tawny NV Incredible depth and age are proclaimed in a magnificently savoury and complex tawny. Roast nuts, dried fruits and spice of all kinds flow into dark chocolate, caramel, fruit-mince spice and warm hearth. Long age has concentrated acidity, bringing liveliness amid judicious sweetness on a finish of monumental carry. Cork. 19.5% alc. **Rating** 96 $75 TS ✪

Pepperjack Barossa Cabernet Sauvignon 2019 A core of glossy, crunchy blackcurrant fruit is backed by licorice and high-cocoa dark chocolate oak. Varietal definition and endurance are captured in an exciting interplay between bright acidity and confident, fine-grained tannin that coast effortlessly through a long finish, promising great things in a decade. Screw cap. 14.5% alc. **Rating** 94 To 2037 $30 TS ✪

♟♟♟♟♟ **Pepperjack Adelaide Hills Padthaway Chardonnay 2019 Rating** 93 To 2026 $27 TL ✪
Pepperjack Barossa Shiraz Cabernet 2019 Rating 93 To 2034 $30 TS
Mamre Brook Barossa Cabernet Sauvignon 2018 Rating 92 To 2038 $38 TS
Pepperjack Barossa Shiraz 2018 Rating 91 To 2024 $30 TS
Pepperjack McLaren Vale Barossa Grenache 2019 Rating 91 To 2023 $25 NG
Pepperjack Scotch Fillet Graded McLaren Vale Shiraz 2019 Rating 90 To 2028 $50 NG

Sam Miranda of King Valley   ★★★★

1019 Snow Road, Oxley, Vic 3678 **Region** King Valley
T (03) 5727 3888 **www**.sammiranda.com.au **Open** 7 days 10–5
Winemaker Sam Miranda **Est.** 2004 **Dozens** 25 000 **Vyds** 55ha
Sam Miranda, grandson of Francesco Miranda, joined the family business in 1991, striking out on his own in 2004 after Miranda Wines was purchased by McGuigan Simeon. The Myrrhee Estate vineyard is at 450m in the upper reaches of the King Valley. This is where the varieties for Sam Miranda's Signature Range of wines are sourced, each with the name of the nearest town or named district. In 2016 Sam Miranda purchased the Oxley Estate vineyard on Snow Road with 40ha of vines to be reworked over coming years. Exports to the UK, Sweden and Fiji.

♟♟♟♟♟ **Estate Vineyard Sangiovese 2016** The real strength in Sam Miranda winemaking lies in its approach to Italian varieties. There is an innate understanding. Sangiovese is a case in point, with a natural savouriness and almost casual approach which belies the effort on display, such is the balance of black fruits and wild herbs with hints of anise and tilled earth. The palate is soft and supple, but there's also substance, enough for continued ageing. Screw cap. 13% alc. **Rating** 94 To 2027 $60 JP

♟♟♟♟♟ **Girls Block Cabernet Franc Merlot Cabernet Sauvignon 2018 Rating** 93 To 2031 $55 JP
Estate Vineyard Nebbiolo 2015 Rating 92 To 2029 $65 JP
Single Vineyard Tempranillo 2019 Rating 92 To 2027 $40 JP
Super King Sangiovese Cabernet 2019 Rating 91 To 2029 $30 JP

Samson Tall   ★★★★

219 Strout Road, McLaren Vale, SA 5171 **Region** McLaren Vale
T 0488 214 680 **www**.samsontall.com.au **Open** 7 days 10–5
Winemaker Paul Wilson **Est.** 2016 **Dozens** 500
Paul Wilson and Heather Budich purchase grapes from local growers, making the wine in a small winery on their property. The cellar door is a small church built in 1854, the winery and church (with a small historic cemetery) surrounded by gardens and a vineyard. Paul has learned his craft as a winemaker well; all of the wines are well made and the grapes well chosen.

♟♟♟♟♟ **McLaren Vale Grenache 2019** A svelte expression of an uncanny lightness, extrapolated with palpable respect for arguably the finest variety of the region. A winning approach that does not necessarily guarantee old bones, but ensures a joyous ride from youth to middle age. Sour cherry, pomegranate, cranberry, bergamot, thyme, lavender and kirsch. Grenache meets pinot. A splay of impeccably hewn tannins, spindly, herbal and moreish, brings a huge smile to this Rhône lover. Screw cap. 14.5% alc. **Rating** 96 **To** 2025 $30 NG ✪

Hatwell Vineyard McLaren Vale Grenache 2019 A stunning wine! Cherry skin, raspberry bon-bon, mint, thyme, rosemary and a slew of other iterations of dried herb. Dense, incredibly compact and firm, yet air in the glass eases the fray into a sheer pleasure zone. Screw cap. 13.8% alc. **Rating** 95 **To** 2026 $60 NG

🍷🍷🍷🍷🍷 **McLaren Vale Shiraz 2019** Rating 93 To 2025 $30 NG
McLaren Vale Tempranillo 2019 Rating 92 To 2024 $30 NG

Samuel's Gorge   ★★★★☆

193 Chaffeys Road, McLaren, SA 5171 **Region** McLaren Vale
T (08) 8323 8651 **www**.gorge.com.au **Open** 7 days 11–5
Winemaker Justin McNamee, Riley Harrison **Est.** 2003 **Dozens** 5000 **Vyds** 10ha
After a wandering winemaking career in various parts of the world, Justin McNamee became a winemaker at Tatachilla in 1996, where he remained until 2003, leaving to found Samuel's Gorge. He established his winery in a barn built in 1853, part of the old Seaview Homestead. The historic property was owned by Sir Samuel Way, variously Chief Justice of the South Australian Supreme Court and Lieutenant Governor of the state. The grapes come from small contract growers spread across the ever-changing (unofficial) subregions of McLaren Vale and are basket-pressed and fermented in old open slate fermenters lined with beeswax. Exports to the UK, Canada, NZ and China.

🍷🍷🍷🍷🍷 **Kaleidoscope Horizons Grenache Graciano Tempranillo 2018** Sour cherry, kirsch, thyme, olive, rosemary and lavender bound to a wave of tannic persuasion – both classy oak and grape-derived – that maketh the wine. After all, these are deeply, unashamedly Mediterranean inspired. The tannins are the pillar of poise, restraint and direction. Long, firm and yet unabashedly rich. Cork. 14.5% alc. **Rating** 94 **To** 2026 $75 NG

McLaren Vale Mourvèdre 2019 I have enjoyed this wine in the past, feeling that it has evolved into something even more savoury, ferruginous and satisfying. Mourvèdre, a wonderful grape so suited to the region, is done justice. Full bodied to be sure, but a carapace of iron-clad tannins allows red- and black-fruit aspersions to unravel subtly. No jamminess, but a whiff of game and myriad herbal notes transpire across a bow of tension: thyme, tobacco, root spice and olive tapenade. Bravo! Screw cap. 14.5% alc. **Rating** 94 **To** 2026 $40 NG

🍷🍷🍷🍷🍷 **McLaren Vale Grenache 2019** Rating 93 To 2025 $40 NG
Mosaic of Dreams Grenache Shiraz Mourvèdre 2018 Rating 93 To 2026 $75 NG
McLaren Vale Tempranillo 2020 Rating 93 To 2027 $40 NG
McLaren Vale Graciano 2019 Rating 93 To 2026 $40 NG
Comet Tail Sparkling Shiraz 2017 Rating 91 To 2028 $50 NG

Sandalford   ★★★★★

3210 West Swan Road, Caversham, WA 6055 **Region** Margaret River/Swan Valley
T (08) 9374 9374 **www**.sandalford.com **Open** 7 days 10–5
Winemaker Hope Metcalf **Est.** 1840 **Dozens** 60000 **Vyds** 106.5ha
Sandalford is one of Australia's oldest and largest privately owned wineries. In 1970 it moved beyond its original Swan Valley base, purchasing a substantial property in Margaret River that is now the main source of its premium grapes. Wines are released under the 1840 (Swan Valley), Element, Winemakers, Margaret River and Estate Reserve ranges with Prendiville Reserve at the top. Exports to all major markets.

🍷🍷🍷🍷🍷 **Estate Reserve Wilyabrup Vineyard Margaret River Shiraz 2018** Gorgeous nose – all raspberry, blackberry, clove, peppercorn and licorice. The palate follows in exactly this manner; lively, succulent and statuesque. A beautiful wine. Screw cap. 14.5% alc. **Rating** 95 **To** 2030 $35 EL ✪

1840 Swan Valley Cabernet Merlot 2018 This is salty, supple and full to the brim with succulent berry fruits. A lively, silky and very balanced wine. The heat of the summer sun that beats down on the vines in the Swan Valley is almost invisible in this glass. Complete pleasure, here. Screw cap. 14.5% alc. **Rating** 95 **To** 2035 $50 EL

Estate Reserve Wilyabrup Vineyard Margaret River Chardonnay 2019 Matured on lees for 8 months in French oak (30% new). Savoury, spicy oak encases ripe yellow peach, orchard fruits and hints of curry leaf. The acidity that laces it all together is distinctly saline, making this a classical Margaret River chardonnay. The cool '19 vintage has laid a delicate imprint. Screw cap. 12.5% alc. **Rating** 94 **To** 2028 $35 EL

Prendiville Reserve Margaret River Chardonnay 2019 Rich, toasty and flavoursome, this paces up and down the peach and nectarine aisle, stalking the fruit section for more to add to the collection; pawpaw, guava, white currant, red apples and more. The acid is succulent and juicy on the palate. This is fuller than expected for the cool year from whence it came. Not nuanced, but layered. Screw cap. 13.5% alc. **Rating** 94 **To** 2036 $75 EL

Prendiville Reserve Margaret River Shiraz 2018 Significant oak influence – the fruit is almost up to the task, but it needs more time to integrate to gain full enjoyment and satisfaction. Good length of flavour says this has plenty of years ahead of it. Screw cap. 14.5% alc. **Rating** 94 **To** 2035 $120 EL

Prendiville Reserve Margaret River Cabernet Sauvignon 2018 The oak sits astride the fruit on the nose – all leather strapping, star anise, black pepper and other dark, spicy things. Powerful cassis, blackberry and raspberry on the palate, but these fruits feel book-ended by oak at this stage. All the hallmarks required for ageing exist here, so likely it will achieve some harmony over time. Screw cap. 14.5% alc. **Rating** 94 **To** 2046 $120 EL

ŸŸŸŸŸ **Margaret River Sauvignon Blanc Semillon 2020** **Rating** 93 **To** 2024 $22 EL ✪
1840 Swan Valley Chenin Blanc 2020 **Rating** 93 **To** 2031 $30 EL
Estate Reserve Margaret River Sauvignon Blanc Semillon 2020 **Rating** 92 **To** 2024 $25 EL ✪
1840 Swan Valley Shiraz 2018 **Rating** 92 **To** 2030 $50 EL
Estate Reserve Wilyabrup Vineyard Margaret River Cabernet Sauvignon 2018 **Rating** 92 **To** 2030 $45 EL
Estate Reserve Margaret River Verdelho 2020 **Rating** 91 **To** 2025 $25 EL
Margaret River Shiraz 2019 **Rating** 90 **To** 2025 $22 EL

Sandhurst Ridge   ★★★★☆

156 Forest Drive, Marong, Vic 3515 **Region** Bendigo
T (03) 5435 2534 **www**.sandhurstridge.com.au **Open** 7 days 11–5
Winemaker Paul Greblo **Est.** 1990 **Dozens** 3000 **Vyds** 7.3ha

The Greblo brothers (Paul is the winemaker, George the viticulturist) began the establishment of Sandhurst Ridge in 1990, planting the first 2ha of shiraz and cabernet sauvignon. Plantings have increased to over 7ha, principally cabernet and shiraz but also a little merlot, nebbiolo and sauvignon blanc. As the business has grown, the Greblos have supplemented their crush with grapes grown in the region. Exports to Malaysia, Taiwan and China.

ŸŸŸŸŸ **Bendigo Cabernet Sauvignon 2019** A smart young Bendigo cabernet (in contrast to the high-octane '18 shiraz from this maker), revealing balance and harmony across the board. Varietally strong with dusty, earthy aromas and blackberry freshness. Medium bodied, a balanced tannin presence and well structured. Screw cap. 14% alc. **Rating** 91 **To** 2026 $32 JP
Reserve Bendigo Shiraz 2018 A distinctly Bendigo feel to this shiraz with its open, bush mint, Aussie bush characters across the palate. They join black fruits, licorice, terracotta and nutty oak. Deceptively powerful. Screw cap. 14.4% alc. **Rating** 90 **To** 2028 $50 JP

Sanguine Estate ★★★★★

77 Shurans Lane, Heathcote, Vic 3523 **Region** Heathcote
T (03) 5433 3111 **www**.sanguinewines.com.au **Open** W'ends & public hols 10–5
Winemaker Mark Hunter **Est.** 1997 **Dozens** 15000 **Vyds** 26ha
The Hunter family – parents Linda and Tony, their children Mark and Jodi and their respective partners Melissa and Brett – have 21.5ha of shiraz and a 'fruit salad block' of chardonnay, viognier, verdelho, merlot, tempranillo, petit verdot, lagrein, nebbiolo, grenache, cabernet sauvignon and cabernet franc. Low-yielding vines and the magic of the Heathcote region have produced Shiraz of exceptional intensity, which has received rave reviews in the US and led to the 'sold out' sign being posted almost immediately upon release. With the ever-expanding vineyard, Mark has become full-time vigneron and winemaker, and Jodi has taken over from her father as CEO and general manager. Exports to China.

🍷🍷🍷🍷🍷 **Progeny Heathcote Shiraz 2019** It is clear that we have here a shiraz specialist who pays close attention to style and quality at every price point. A $25 shiraz, Progeny hits above its weight in complexity and fruit vibrancy, all with just a relatively light dusting of oak (9 months in French oak and only 10% new). A serious wine, deep, impenetrable 'Heathcote purple' in hue. Hits high notes of violets, blackberry, briar, bramble and spice. Oak is ne'er to be seen but its warm, textural affect on the palate is. A hint of mint gives you a glimpse of the local terroir. Delicious. Screw cap. 14.8% alc. **Rating** 95 **To** 2028 $25 JP ✪
Inception Heathcote Shiraz 2018 There's an open generosity to this wine. The high alcohol aids the delivery; so too some powerfully persuasive fruit. In its youth, everything is laid out: concentrated blackberry, dark chocolate, dried herbs and a toastiness across a full-bodied but well-structured winescape. Enjoyable, yes, but still in assembly phase. Wait a while longer. Screw cap. 14.9% alc. **Rating** 95 **To** 2032 $40 JP

🍷🍷🍷🍷🍷 **Heathcote Cabernets 2019 Rating** 93 **To** 2027 $25 JP ✪
Heathcote Tempranillo 2019 Rating 91 **To** 2024 $30 JP
Kindred Heathcote Shiraz 2018 Rating 90 **To** 2025 $18 JP ✪

Santa & D'Sas ★★★★

2 Pincott Street, Newtown, Vic 3220 **Region** Various
T 0417 384 272 **www**.santandsas.com.au
Winemaker Andrew Santarossa, Matthew Di Sciascio **Est.** 2014 **Dozens** 9000
Santa & D'Sas is a collaboration between the Santarossa and Di Sciascio families. Andrew Santarossa and Matthew Di Sciascio met while studying for a bachelor of applied science (wine science). Wines are released under the Valentino label (fiano, sangiovese and shiraz), dedicated to Matthew's father; the remaining wines simply identify the region and variety. Exports to China.

🍷🍷🍷🍷🍷 **King Valley Prosecco NV** A confident, assured prosecco, clean and bright, persistent in mousse and nicely encapsulating the grape's lively green apple, pear, musky florals and aromatics. Super-brisk through to the finish. Crown seal. 11% alc. **Rating** 93 **To** 2021 $24 JP ✪
Valentino King Valley Fiano 2019 Mitchelton winemaker, Andrew Santarossa, presents a strong case for Fiano under his separate joint-project label with a full-bodied, ripe, spiced-apple-and-pear wine, big on texture and personality. Screw cap. 13.3% alc. **Rating** 91 **To** 2023 $45 JP

Santarossa Wine Company ★★★★☆

1 The Crescent, Yea, Vic 3717 (postal) **Region** Yarra Valley/Heathcote
T 0419 117 858 **www**.betterhalfwines.com.au
Winemaker Andrew Santarossa **Est.** 2007 **Vyds** 16ha
Santarossa Vineyards started out as a virtual winery business owned and run by 3 brothers of Italian heritage. It is now solely owned by winemaker Andrew and wife Megan

Santarossa. Yarra Valley wines appear under the Better Half label, while the Sea Glass range (www.seaglasswines.com.au) explores the many different terroirs of the Mornington Peninsula.

ŸŸŸŸŸ **Sea Glass Mornington Peninsula Chardonnay 2019** Flinty and very tight, letting some citrus flavours through, with a dash of spice and woodsy, cedary oak, quality by the taste of it. It is intense and focused, incredibly fresh and vibrant, with a juicy sluicing of acidity. Screw cap. 13.3% alc. **Rating** 95 **To** 2028 $45 JF

ŸŸŸŸŸ **Sea Glass Single Vineyard Merricks Mornington Peninsula Chardonnay 2019 Rating** 93 **To** 2033 $70 JF
Sea Glass Single Vineyard Balnarring Mornington Peninsula Pinot Noir 2019 Rating 90 **To** 2028 $70 JF

Santolin Wines   ★★★★☆

c/- 21-23 Delaneys Road, South Warrandyte, Vic 3134 **Region** Yarra Valley
T 0402 278 464 **www.**santolinwines.com.au
Winemaker Adrian Santolin **Est.** 2012 **Dozens** 1000
Adrian Santolin grew up in Griffith, NSW, and has worked in the wine industry since he was 15. He moved to the Yarra Valley in 2007 with wife Rebecca, who has worked in marketing roles at various wineries. Adrian's love of pinot noir led him to work at wineries such as Wedgetail Estate, Rochford, De Bortoli, Sticks and Rob Dolan Wines. In '12 his dream came true when he was able to buy 2t of pinot noir from the Syme-on-Yarra Vineyard, increasing production in '13 to 4t, split between chardonnay and pinot noir. The Boy Meets Girl wines are sold through www.nakedwines.com.au. Exports to the UK, the US and Hong Kong.

ŸŸŸŸŸ **Cosa Nostra Yarra Valley Arneis 2020** Reminiscent of a spring garden full of white flowers and oregano. The palate has a delicacy and joy with soft acidity and a hint of lemon. A lovely rendition. Screw cap. 12.3% alc. **Rating** 93 **To** 2023 $25 JF ❂
Gruyere Yarra Valley Pinot Noir 2019 Floral and fragrant. Spicy and smoky. An appealing pinot that starts out pretty and gives an impression of lightness and ripeness. Sweet cherry fruit, blood orange and a juiciness throughout eventually meet up with raw silk tannins and fine acidity. It feels ready now, rather than a keeper. That's not a bad thing. Screw cap. 14.5% alc. **Rating** 92 **To** 2027 $42 JF
Gladysdale Yarra Valley Chardonnay 2019 Slow off the mark, more a long-distance runner it seems. Flavours build, moving from citrus to stone fruit, fig to creamed honey. The palate fills out with richness and leesy influences plus well-handled phenolics. Then wham! A sprint home with its acidity. Screw cap. 13.5% alc. **Rating** 91 **To** 2027 $40 JF
Gladysdale Yarra Valley Pinot Noir 2019 While its Gruyere sibling comes from the Lower Yarra Valley, Gladysdale comes from the cooler Upper Yarra and it shows. Smoky with obvious whole bunches adding mulch fragrance while a skein of sweet cherry and plums wraps around flavours of blood orange, woodsy, savoury spices, with tannins neatly in tow. A very different outcome to its sibling and that's the point. Screw cap. 14.5% alc. **Rating** 91 **To** 2027 $42 JF
Cosa Nostra Yarra Valley Pinot Noir 2019 With its calling card stamped with 'drink me now', enjoy the core of juicy ripe sweet fruit, the dash of oak spices, herbs and ultimate refreshment. Tannins are lithe and fit neatly within the lighter-framed palate. Screw cap. 14% alc. **Rating** 90 **To** 2025 $32 JF

ŸŸŸŸ **Cosa Nostra Heathcote Nero d'Avola 2019 Rating** 88 **To** 2024 $28 JF

Sapling Yard Wines   ★★★★

56 Wallace Street, Braidwood, NSW 2622 **Region** Canberra District
T 0410 770 894 **www.**saplingyard.com.au **Open** Fri–Sat 11–5.30
Winemaker Carla Rodeghiero, Malcolm Burdett **Est.** 2008 **Dozens** 1800 **Vyds** 1.2ha
Carla Rodegheiro and Andrew Bennett work full-time in the pharmaceutical clinical research and building industries respectively. Carla started out as a microbiologist working as a locum

in hospitals in Australia and London. While in London, she also worked evenings in a wine bar in Carnaby Street where she tasted a 1993 Mount Langi Ghiran Shiraz and vowed to one day make a wine of similar remarkable quality. In '97 she began a wine science degree at CSU, completing the last residential term in 2004 (with 9-week-old daughter Mia in tow), having worked vintages in the Hunter Valley, Orange, Macedon Ranges and Willamette Valley, Oregon. In '08 Carla and Andrew planted a 1.2ha vineyard at Braidwood to pinot noir, riesling, pinot blanc and tempranillo but they also continue to source their best grapes from the Canberra District.

ȚȚȚȚ **The Curmudgeon Canberra District Shiraz 2019** This has come together well and is intensely flavoured. Loads of blackcurrants and plums, awash with baking spices, pepper and crushed mint. Viognier (3%) is making a mark, too – floral with a touch of apricot. There's also a savoury layer, a smoked meat flavour that's appealing. Full bodied, rich and satisfying with ripe, plump tannins yet everything converges to a defined finish. Screw cap. 13.5% alc. **Rating** 93 **To** 2029 $45 JF

Entrechat Canberra District Sparkling 2018 65/35% pinot noir/chardonnay, 2 years on lees. A hint of camomile, lemon blossom and a touch of buttered toast with citrussy flavours. It's not overly complex but it is fresh, lively, savoury and delicious. Zork SPK. 12.5% alc. **Rating** 93 $38 JF

Sassafras Wines ★★★★

20 Grylls Crescent, Cook, ACT 2614 (postal) **Region** Canberra District
T 0476 413 974 **www.**sassafraswines.com.au
Winemaker Paul Starr, Nick O'Leary **Est.** 2013 **Dozens** 720
Paul Starr and Tammy Braybrook brought unusual academic knowledge with them when they established Sassafras Wines. Tammy has a science degree, has worked as an economist and is now an IT professional and part-time florist. Paul has a PhD in cultural studies and intended to be an academic in humanities before a detour into environment work in government. Tammy knew Mark Terrell, of Quarry Hill, and the pair ended up working in the Terrell Vineyard with pruning and vintage work, leading to local college courses in winemaking. Paul worked at Eden Road cellar door on weekends for 4 years. History is an interest for both, and when thinking of heading in an altogether new wine direction, they read about what they describe as the ancestral method of making sparkling wine using the original yeast and fermentable sugar to create the mousse, bypassing disgorgement altogether.

ȚȚȚȚ **Salita Sagrantino 2018** It's always a pleasure to try this sagrantino. Yes. It's true. This manages to massage its mighty tannins, the texture of astringent persimmons, into place so that all the flavours amalgamate. Deep, rich plum fruit, salted plums too, amaro, aniseed and a strong ironstone note work across the palate. There is volume but it's not an outrageously massive wine, helped by the reasonable 13.5% alcohol. In between the tannin build up, chunks of sopressa will work. Screw cap. 13.5% alc. **Rating** 93 **To** 2028 $30 JF

Savaterre

929 Beechworth-Wangaratta Road, Everton Upper, Vic 3678 **Region** Beechworth
T (03) 5727 0551 **www.**savaterre.com **Open** By appt
Winemaker Keppell Smith **Est.** 1996 **Dozens** 2500 **Vyds** 8ha
Keppell Smith embarked on a career in wine in 1996, studying winemaking at CSU and (at a practical level) with Phillip Jones at Bass Phillip. He has established 8ha of chardonnay and pinot noir (close-planted at 7500 vines/ha), shiraz and sagrantino on the 40ha Savaterre property, at an elevation of 440m. Organic principles govern the viticulture and the winemaking techniques look to the Old World rather than the New. Smith's stated aim is to produce outstanding individualistic wines far removed from the mainstream. Exports to France, UAE and Singapore.

SC Pannell

60 Olivers Road, McLaren Vale, SA 5171 **Region** McLaren Vale
T (08) 8323 8000 **www**.pannell.com.au **Open** Thurs–Mon 11–5
Winemaker Stephen Pannell **Est.** 2004 **Dozens** 15000 **Vyds** 9ha
The only surprising piece of background is that it took (an admittedly still reasonably youthful) Steve Pannell and wife Fiona so long to cut the painter from Constellation/Hardys and establish their own winemaking and consulting business. Steve radiates intensity and his extended experience has resulted in wines of the highest quality, right from the first vintage. The Pannells have 2 vineyards in McLaren Vale, the first planted in 1891 with a precious 3.6ha of shiraz. The future for the Pannells is limitless, the icon status of the label already well established. See also new entries Koomilya and Protero. Exports to the UK, the US, Sweden, Singapore and China.

🍷🍷🍷🍷🍷 **Smart Clarendon Grenache 2019** Intense aromas of molten cherry liqueur, orange amaro, bergamot and cranberry. A fine vinous pulse, drawing the fore with the aft. Long attenuated filigreed tannins, sandy to be sure, but very fine. This is exceptional grenache that, with a few others, sets the regional high tone. Screw cap. 14.5% alc. **Rating** 96 **To** 2026 $60 NG ✪

McLaren Vale Shiraz Grenache 2018 This is very good. The sort of warm-climate expression that I enjoy drinking: full bodied, sure, but pulpy and almost ethereal, with a slake of saline briary tannins suggesting whole bunches in the mould. The tannins make the wine, steering notes of rosehip, bergamot, kirsch, sassafras, orange zest, cranberry and lilac about the mouth. A spurt of maritime freshness, towing it long. Screw cap. 14.5% alc. **Rating** 95 **To** 2025 $40 NG

Old McDonald McLaren Vale Grenache 2019 Pinot with a Mediterranean vibe. Full, but feels ethereal. Firm, but feels svelte. A mid ruby at best. Succulent. A meld of fecund raspberry, root spice, clove, cranberry and rosehip, drawn at the waist by a firm skein of saline, puckering tannin, sandy and pumice-like. The founder of the contemporary grenache zeitgeist. Fine. Screw cap. 14% alc. **Rating** 95 **To** 2026 $60 NG

McLaren Vale Aglianico 2019 A grape that I love as much as grenache. Almost. Not in terms of its pinosity melded with Mediterranean accents, but because of its unbridled ferruginous structure and Neapolitan air. Think Diego Maradona in his prime. Bitter chocolate, cherry pith and amaro riffs. But the defining aspect is the long, thirst-slaking bind of palate-defining, tannic architecture. Australia has not traditionally done this. And here it is! Why were we not planting this 100 years ago? Screw cap. 14% alc. **Rating** 95 **To** 2030 $40 NG ♥

Merrivale McLaren Vale Shiraz 2019 A lustrous crimson. Elevated aromas of boysenberry, clove, nori and Christmas cake are slung over a carriage of finely wrought spicy tannins, firm enough to engage the food at hand, while being juicy enough to chew. Finishes long, precise, fresh and sappy, marked by a ferrous burr that augurs well for cellaring. Screw cap. 13.5% alc. **Rating** 94 **To** 2030 $40 NG

🍷🍷🍷🍷🍷 **Langhorne Creek Montepulciano 2019 Rating** 91 **To** 2023 $30 NG
Dead End McLaren Vale Tempranillo 2019 Rating 90 **To** 2022 $28 NG

Scarborough Wine Co

179 Gillards Road, Pokolbin, NSW 2320 **Region** Hunter Valley
T (02) 4998 7563 **www**.scarboroughwine.com.au **Open** 7 days 9–5
Winemaker Ian Scarborough, Jerome Scarborough **Est.** 1985 **Dozens** 25000 **Vyds** 47ha
Ian Scarborough honed his white winemaking skills during his years as a consultant, and has brought all those skills to his own label. He makes 3 different styles of chardonnay: the Blue Label is a light, elegant, Chablis style for the export market; a richer barrel-fermented wine (Yellow Label) is primarily directed to the Australian market; the third is the White Label, a cellar-door-only wine made in the best vintages. The Scarborough family also acquired a portion of the old Lindemans Sunshine Vineyard (after it lay fallow for 30 years) and have planted it with semillon and (quixotically) pinot noir.

♀♀♀♀♀ **The Obsessive The Cottage Vineyard Hunter Valley Semillon 2019**
Lower alcohol, but no less intensely flavoured because of it. Subdued notes of
lemon balm, pink grapefruit pith and spa salts curl around a chalky beam of acidity.
Despite the youthful restraint, the length is anything but subtle. This will age very
well. Screw cap. 10% alc. **Rating** 93 **To** 2034 $30 NG
The Obsessive Old North Vineyard Hunter Valley Shiraz 2017 A rich
wine. Plenty oaky, as is the wont here (yet mercifully not reductive, my peeve in
the region). Oak-driven aromas of cedar and vanilla segue to pickled dark cherry,
wakame, clove, anise and mace. A vibrato of peppery acidity and a clench of oak,
to finish. This rich expression will age nicely across the medium term. Screw cap.
14.1% alc. **Rating** 91 **To** 2029 $60 NG

Schild Estate Wines

1095 Barossa Valley Way, Lyndoch, SA 5351 **Region** Barossa Valley
T (08) 8524 5560 **www**.schildestate.com.au **Open** W'ends 10–4
Winemaker Scott Hazeldine **Est.** 1998 **Dozens** 40000 **Vyds** 134ha
Ed Schild is a Barossa Valley grapegrower who first planted a small vineyard at Rowland Flat
in 1952, steadily increasing his vineyard holdings over the next 50 years to their present level.
The flagship wine is made from 170+yo shiraz vines on the Moorooroo Vineyard. Exports
to all major markets.

♀♀♀♀♀ **Edgar Schild Reserve Old Bush Vines Barossa Valley Grenache 2019**
Textbook Barossa grenache. A bright and vibrant young thing that champions
primary fruit focus and varietal integrity of poached strawberries, raspberries and
red cherries. Astutely downplayed oak leaves the structural role to powder-fine
fruit tannins. Hints of rhubarb and thyme lend complexity to a finish of medium
persistence. Screw cap. 14.5% alc. **Rating** 94 **To** 2024 $36 TS

♀♀♀♀♀ **Barossa Valley Grenache 2019** Rating 90 To 2023 $45 TS

Schoolhouse Wines

4 Nelson Street, Stepney, SA 50969 **Region** Coonawarra
T (08) 8362 6135 **www**.cwwines.com **Open** Mon–Fri 9–5
Winemaker Ben Wurst **Est.** 2020 **Dozens** 5000
Schoolhouse is the top brand of the large wine enterprise CW Wines, a business with a
host of local and SA labels. Coonawarra shiraz and cabernet sauvignon are Schoolhouse's
mainstays, with a Limestone Coast sauvignon blanc featuring in the 2nd-tier Headmaster
range. The wines are crafted by Ben Wurst, who has worked in the region for close to
20 years. (JF)

♀♀♀♀♀ **Coonawarra Cabernet Sauvignon 2018** Excellent dark garnet with a shot
of purple; fragrant with blackberries and mulberries and brown spices. The fruit
has admirably soaked up the significant oak. There's a vibrancy and vitality here
offering immediate drinking pleasure, its firm tannins and refreshing acidity will
also help this to age well. Diam. 14.5% alc. **Rating** 93 **To** 2033 $80 JF
Headmaster Coonawarra Shiraz 2019 It starts out solidly with a core of ripe
fruit, densely packed with flavour from licorice and lashings of oak to a subtle
sprinkling of pepper. Youthful and vibrant with steadfast tannins and an evenness
across the fuller-bodied palate. Screw cap. 14.5% alc. **Rating** 91 **To** 2029 $55 JF
Coonawarra Shiraz 2018 It has a density and richness with the oak having an
impact both in aroma and flavour. However, the richness of sweet fruit and spices
with the full-bodied palate are able to corral everything in place. Diam. 14.5% alc.
Rating 91 **To** 2028 $80 JF

Schubert Estate ★★★★

26 Kensington Road, Rose Park, SA 5067 **Region** Barossa Valley
T (08) 8562 3375 **www.**schubertestate.com **Open** Mon–Fri 11–5
Winemaker Gary Baldwin **Est.** 2000 **Dozens** 4200 **Vyds** 14ha
Founders Steve and Cecilia Schubert have sold their business to Mrs Sofia Yang and Mrs Lin
Tan, a sale that has been implemented over a 3-year period. It was agreed that the Schuberts
would guide the new owners into the business as they came to grips with running a small but
ultra-successful high-end wine business. They aim to continue making the Gooseyard Block
and the Gander on the premises with plans for a larger winery and to have other wines in an
expanded portfolio contract-made elsewhere. In 2016 Schubert Estate opened a cellar door
in Adelaide in a renovated stone villa. Exports to Germany, Malaysia, South Korea, Hong
Kong and China.

ŸŸŸŸ **Marananga Barossa Valley Viognier 2019** The luscious apricot and fig
of viognier meets the toasty, coffee and milk chocolate personality of French
oak. A supple style that tactically deploys well-handled phenolics to define its
finish. A toasty wine and a little tired for its age. Screw cap. 13.5% alc. **Rating** 89
To 2021 $25 TS

Schwarz Wine Company ★★★★★

PO Box 779, Tanunda, SA 5352 **Region** Barossa Valley
T 0417 881 923 **www.**schwarzwineco.com.au **Open** At Vino Lokal, Tanunda
Winemaker Jason Schwarz **Est.** 2001 **Dozens** 5000
The economical name is appropriate for a business that started with 1t of grapes making
2 hogsheads of wine in 2001. Shiraz was purchased from Jason Schwarz's parents' vineyard in
Bethany, the vines planted in 1968; the following year half a tonne of grenache was added,
once again purchased from the parents. In '05, grape sale agreements with another (larger)
winery were terminated, freeing up 1.8ha of shiraz and 0.8ha of grenache. From this point on
things moved more quickly: in '06 Jason formed a partnership (Biscay Road Vintners) with
Peter Schell of Spinifex, giving them total control over production. Exports to the UK, the
US, France, Denmark, Singapore, Japan and China.

ŸŸŸŸŸ **The Grower Barossa Valley Shiraz 2019** An impressively full, vibrant purple
hue heralds a carefully blended shiraz that unites the districts of the central Barossa
Valley. Judicious deployment of whole bunches and seasoned French oak upholds
a resolute focus on classy blackberry, black cherry and satsuma plum fruit, nuanced
with black pepper and violets. Finely textured tannins and bright acidity carry a
finish of impressive line, length and potential. Great value. Screw cap. 14.2% alc.
Rating 95 To 2034 $30 TS ✪
The Schiller Single Vineyard Barossa Valley Shiraz 2018 The deep, exotic
spice, black and red berry fruits and supple, slippery tannins of ancient 1881 vines
are confidently backed by high-class dark chocolate and coffee-bean French oak.
Fruit and oak duck and swoop long through the finish, neither competing nor
integrating, but setting into a comfortable stand-off that only calls for time to
settle. Screw cap. 14.8% alc. **Rating** 95 To 2033 $80 TS

ŸŸŸŸŸ **Meta Barossa Shiraz 2019 Rating** 93 To 2029 $38 TS
Barossa Valley Rosé 2020 Rating 91 To 2021 $25 TS
The Grower Barossa Valley GSM 2019 Rating 91 To 2027 $30 TS

Scion ★★★☆

74 Slaughterhouse Road, Rutherglen, Vic 3685 **Region** Rutherglen
T (02) 6032 8844 **www.**scionwine.com.au **Open** 7 days 10–5
Winemaker Rowly Milhinch **Est.** 2002 **Dozens** 2500 **Vyds** 4.85ha
Self-taught winemaker Rowly Milhinch is a descendant of GF Morris, one of Rutherglen's
most renowned vignerons of the mid-19th century. Rowly aspires to make contemporary
wines 'guided by a creative interpretation of traditional Rutherglen varietals, Durif a specialty'.

The wines are made from the estate Linlithgow Vineyard and the revitalised 1.48ha Terravinia Vineyard managed by Rowly.

♀♀♀♀♀ **Muscat X NV** Rowly Milhinch goes outside the traditional muscat mould to create what he describes as a 'bridge between wine and spirits.' Gleaming rose gold. Earth, orange peel, prune, raisins in wild honey. Elevates the grape's aromatic rose-oil characters to a new high. Light on its feet, young, fresh, grapey and sweet. The new muscat has arrived. Screw cap. 17.2% alc. **Rating** 93 $55 JP
Rutherglen Viognier 2019 It's not easy getting the delicate balance of viognier right. One false step and you are in oily, blowsy, overripe territory. No false steps here. On point and singing, the wine is both citrus and stone-fruit ripe, generous in flavour and middle-palate texture but also, importantly, runs clean and juicy fresh with lemony acidity. Screw cap. 13.3% alc. **Rating** 92 **To** 2026 $36 JP
After Dark Rutherglen Durif 2018 Another Rowly original interpretation of a fortified that is clearly different – the label boasts an After Dark Negroni recipe – a single-vintage fortified that makes durif the star. Dusty cacao chocolate, allspice, blueberry compote with a herbal edge. A mix of the Italian-style bitter savouriness and sweetness, the whisker of sugar accentuating its fortified credentials. Screw cap. 17.2% alc. **Rating** 92 $29 JP
Rutherglen Durif 2019 A warm and aromatic young durif from the home of the variety. It looks deep and powerful like many, but floats like a cloud. Plenty of ripe, dark berries on show, dark chocolate and earth but then it lifts, elevated by high spice and pretty aromatics. Screw cap. 13.6% alc. **Rating** 91 **To** 2027 $38 JP

♀♀♀♀ **Skins 2019 Rating** 89 **To** 2025 $45 JP
Rutherglen Rosé 2020 Rating 89 **To** 2024 $28 JP
Stems Durif 2018 Rating 89 **To** 2026 $45 JP
Rutherglen Syrah 2018 Rating 88 **To** 2027 $36 JP

Scorpo Wines   ★★★★★

23 Old Bittern–Dromana Road, Merricks North, Vic 3926
Region Mornington Peninsula
T (03) 5989 7697 **www**.scorpowines.com.au **Open** 1st w'end each month or by appt
Winemaker Paul Scorpo **Est.** 1997 **Dozens** 6000 **Vyds** 17.3ha
Paul Scorpo has a background as a horticulturist/landscape architect, working on major projects ranging from private gardens to golf courses in Australia, Europe and Asia. His family has a love of food, wine and gardens, all of which led to them buying a derelict apple and cherry orchard on gentle rolling hills between Port Phillip and Western Port bays. They have established pinot noir (10.4ha), pinot gris and chardonnay (3.2ha each) and shiraz (0.5ha). Exports to Japan.

♀♀♀♀♀ **Eocene Single Vineyard Chardonnay 2019** Tight as a drum, shot with racy acidity. And no shortage of very flinty sulphides, which would be too much funky reduction, if not for the weight and richness of fruit to balance. Complex, assured, rich, textural, savoury and compelling. Screw cap. 14% alc. **Rating** 96 **To** 2029 $75 JF ✪
Mornington Peninsula Shiraz 2019 This is almost black, with a shot of red/purple. It's not a wallflower. There are plenty of steadfast grainy tannins reined in by a ribbon of acidity. Smells great, tastes even better: black cherries, exotic spices plus sumac, the flavours are intense and satisfying. It opens up more and more, revealing a gloss across the full-bodied palate. Screw cap. 14% alc. **Rating** 95 **To** 2033 $50 JF

♀♀♀♀♀ **Aubaine Mornington Peninsula Chardonnay 2019 Rating** 93 **To** 2027 $32 JF
Noirien Mornington Peninsula Pinot Noir 2020 Rating 93 **To** 2027 $32 JF
Mornington Peninsula Pinot Gris 2018 Rating 92 **To** 2022 $35 JF
Eocene Single Vineyard Pinot Noir 2019 Rating 92 **To** 2032 $80 JF

Scotchmans Hill   ★★★★★

190 Scotchmans Road, Drysdale, Vic 3222 **Region** Geelong
T (03) 5251 3176 **www**.scotchmans.com.au **Open** 7 days 10.30–4.30
Winemaker Robin Brockett, Marcus Holt **Est.** 1982 **Dozens** 50 000 **Vyds** 40ha
Established in 1982, Scotchmans Hill has been a consistent producer of well-made wines
under the stewardship of long-term winemaker Robin Brockett and assistant Marcus Holt.
The wines are released under the Scotchmans Hill, Cornelius, Jack & Jill and Swan Bay
labels. A change of ownership in 2014 has resulted in significant vineyard investment. Exports
to Asia.

♀♀♀♀♀ **Bellarine Peninsula Shiraz 2018** 15% whole bunches, wild fermentation,
10 months in French oak. A highly expressive, fragrant and complex bouquet
carries onto the savoury/spicy palate with wild blackberry, licorice and black
peppercorn flavours. The tannins are very good, adding to texture and length.
Screw cap. 14.5% alc. **Rating** 98 **To** 2040 $42 JH ✪

♀♀♀♀♀ **Cornelius Airds Vineyard Bellarine Peninsula Chardonnay 2018** For one
so young, this chardonnay is loaded with character and complexity. A strong start
to a long life, for sure. Bellarine maritime brightness evident from the start, with
a burst of pristine stone fruits, citrus, almond biscotti. Dances across the palate,
marrying judicious oak handling, purity of fruit, brisk acidity, concentration and
balance. It's got it all. Screw cap. 13% alc. **Rating** 95 **To** 2028 $75 JP
Cornelius Single Vineyard Bellarine Peninsula Chardonnay 2018 Intense
and mouth-filling, composed of white stone fruits, citrus, grilled nuts, almond
meal and spice. Super-fresh on the palate, bright in personality, with a pronounced
and attractive grapefruit pithiness and spiced apple coming into play, with layers
of sherbet-like acidity. Puts a tang in chardonnay's step now, with the promise of
ageing well. Screw cap. 13% alc. **Rating** 95 **To** 2028 $75 JP
Cornelius Kincardine Vineyard Bellarine Peninsula Chardonnay 2018
What a difference a vineyard can make! The Cornelius Kincardine presents a
very different chardonnay face to its sister, Cornelius Sutton, being more obvious
in texture, oak and weight. Mealy, bruised apple, peach skin, nougat, stone fruits
indicate a wine in search of complexity. Mission accomplished on the palate.
Resonates long. Screw cap. 13.5% alc. **Rating** 95 **To** 2028 $75 JP
Cornelius Kirkcaldy Vineyard Bellarine Peninsula Pinot Noir 2018
Destemmed fruit, cold soaked for 5 days, wild-yeast fermented then mlf and
15 months in French oak puncheons (one-third new). A densely packed pinot
with all the flavour you need but also a fineness, a delicacy. Red fruits, dark
cherries, spice-dusted oak. Fine, close-knit tannins bring freshness, purpose and the
potential for further ageing. Screw cap. 13.5% alc. **Rating** 95 **To** 2027 $72 JP
Cornelius Norfolk Vineyard Bellarine Peninsula Pinot Noir 2018 Quite
an accomplished single-vineyard pinot. Early days, but there is a developing
thread of complexity built around classic dark cherry, kirsch, dried herbs and
flowers. Appears immediately delicate and fine in tannin and personality, but it's a
blind, behind which is a serious work in progress. Impressive balance and flavour
penetration at work. Screw cap. 13.5% alc. **Rating** 95 **To** 2028 $72 JP
Cornelius Strathallan Vineyard Bellarine Peninsula Syrah 2018 A single-
vineyard expression of shiraz that works blueberries in among dark summer fruits,
blackcurrant bon-bon confection, undergrowth and powerful spice. Fresh and
juicy across the palate, highlighting the wine's youth. Toasty oak is still settling in.
Should evolve nicely. Screw cap. 14% alc. **Rating** 95 **To** 2028 $75 JP
Mount Bellarine Shiraz 2019 Single-vineyard shiraz built to last. Complex too,
with purple/blackberries, grated ginger, cola and licorice across the aroma and
palate, framed by chocolatey oak and drawn in tight by pronounced dusty tannins.
Give it time. Screw cap. 14% alc. **Rating** 94 **To** 2031 $35 JP

♀♀♀♀♀ **Bellarine Peninsula Sauvignon Blanc 2020 Rating** 93 **To** 2025 $30 JP
Cornelius Single Vineyard Bellarine Peninsula Pinot Gris 2019 Rating 92
To 2026 $38 JP

Cornelius Spray Farm Vineyard Bellarine Peninsula Syrah 2018
Rating 92 To 2027 $75 JP
Cornelius Airds Vineyard Bellarine Peninsula Blanc de Blanc 2016
Rating 92 $60 JP
Cornelius Single Vineyard Bellarine Peninsula Sauvignon 2019 Rating 91
To 2025 $35 JP
Jack & Jill Bellarine Peninsula Chardonnay 2019 Rating 91 To 2025 $30 JP
Bellarine Peninsula Chardonnay 2019 Rating 91 To 2026 $42 JP
Bellarine Peninsula Pinot Noir 2019 Rating 91 To 2026 $42 JP
Cornelius Armitage Vineyard Bellarine Peninsula Pinot Noir 2018
Rating 91 To 2026 $72 JP
Mount Bellarine Chardonnay 2019 Rating 90 To 2026 $35 JP

Seabrook Wines

1122 Light Pass Road, Tanunda, SA 5352 **Region** Barossa Valley
T 0427 224 353 **www.**seabrookwines.com.au **Open** Thurs–Mon 11–5
Winemaker Hamish Seabrook **Est.** 2004 **Dozens** 3000 **Vyds** 10.1ha
Hamish Seabrook is the youngest generation of a proud Melbourne wine family once
involved in wholesale and retail distribution, and as leading show judges of their respective
generations. Hamish too, is a wine show judge but was the first to venture into winemaking,
working with Best's and Brown Brothers in Victoria before moving to SA with wife Joanne.
In 2008 Hamish set up his own winery on the family property in Vine Vale, having previously
made the wines at Dorrien Estate and elsewhere. Here they have shiraz (4.4ha), cabernet
sauvignon (3.9ha) and mataro (1.8ha), and also continue to source small amounts of shiraz
from the Barossa, Langhorne Creek and Pyrenees. Exports to Hong Kong and China.

The Merchant Barossa Valley Shiraz 2018 Dense, deep and compact.
High-cocoa dark chocolate and coffee-bean oak orbits a compact singularity
of blackberry, satsuma plum and licorice. Firm tannins and nicely poised acidity
hold a long finish with the integrity and brightness to go the distance. Screw cap.
14.5% alc. **Rating** 94 To 2033 $40 TS
The Chairman Great Western Shiraz 2018 The fine-grained mineral
structure of Great Western provides a wonderful lattice to support fruit of
satsuma plum, blackberry and licorice depth. Accents of pepper declare regional
distinctiveness, eloquently underlined with dark chocolate French oak. Screw cap.
14.5% alc. **Rating** 94 To 2033 $50 TS

Lineage Langhorne Creek Shiraz 2018 Rating 93 To 2033 $22 TS ✪

Sedgley & Sons

181 Coolart Road, Hastings, Vic 3915 **Region** Mornington Peninsula
T 0428 178 849. **www.**sedgleyandsons.com.au
Winemaker Rick McIntyre **Est.** 2014 **Vyds** 0.8ha
The name harks back to a 19th-century family business in Gawler, SA. Now it's a modern-
day boutique wine brand focusing on pinot noir. The Sedgley family bought Creadon Farm
in 2014, which features an established garden, quince orchard and luxury holiday rental
homestead. Importantly, the 0.8ha of pinot noir vines are about 25 years old. The wine is
made by Richard McIntyre and Jeremy Magyar at Moorooduc Estate. (JF)

Creadon Park Mornington Peninsula Pinot Noir 2018 A savoury-accented
offering although there's the telltale spiced cherries and blood-orange flavours. Just
shy of medium bodied. Textural tannins and light charry oak add some grip, yet
there's a suppleness throughout. Screw cap. 13% alc. **Rating** 91 To 2025 $32 JF
Creadon Park Mornington Peninsula Pinot Noir 2019 Pale ruby with some
bricking to the rim. There's no shortage of aromatics and flavour though, ranging
from red cherries, rhubarb and radishes, with a kick of black pepper and baking
spices. Yet this is lighter framed with sweet pliable tannins and neat acidity. It's a
lovely drink-now option. Screw cap. 14% alc. **Rating** 90 To 2024 $32 JF

Sedona Estate ★★★★

182 Shannons Road, Murrindindi, Vic 3717 **Region** Upper Goulburn
T 0432 435 180 **www**.sedonaestate.com.au **Open** Wed–Sun & public hols 11.30–5
Winemaker Paul Evans **Est.** 1998 **Dozens** 2500 **Vyds** 5.5ha
Sedona Estate, established by Paul Evans (a trained commercial pilot) and Sonja Herges
(from Germany's Mosel Valley), is located in the picturesque Yea Valley, gateway to Victoria's
high country. The unique combination of abundant sunshine, cool nights and low rainfall
in this elevated wine region provides a true cool climate for growing premium-quality fruit.
Sangiovese (the vines sourced from Yarra Yering) and carménère were added to the existing
plantings of cabernet sauvignon, merlot and shiraz in 2017. Exports to China.

ΨΨΨΨΨ **Reserve Yea Valley Shiraz 2017** Only produced in exceptional years, this
Reserve Shiraz casts a large shadow of oak, American in particular, with toasted
coconut, cedar, leather and earth. It's joined by ripe blackberries, plums and
high spice. More brocade than silk. What it lacks in subtlety, it makes up for in
commanding presence. Screw cap. 14% alc. **Rating** 90 **To** 2030 $40 JP
Yea Valley Cabernet Sauvignon 2016 A highly expressive cabernet with
a character-defining degree of woody herbs and spice. Blackberry, blueberry,
savoury wet earth and a fistful of Aussie bush herbs and dark spices. Solid wine
for the price. Silver medal London Wine Competition '20. Screw cap. 13.5% alc.
Rating 90 **To** 2026 $26 JP
Yea Valley Sangiovese 2019 With cuttings from the late Dr Bailey Carrodus,
Sedona has fashioned a delicious sangiovese highlighting the grape's abundant red-
and black-cherry charm. Earth, cacao powder join with macerated raspberries,
plums and an attractive cherry-kirsch warmth on the palate. Warm oak and
smooth tannins seal the easy-drinking deal. Screw cap. 13% alc. **Rating** 90
To 2024 $30 JP

ΨΨΨΨ **Reserve Yea Valley Cabernet Sauvignon 2018 Rating** 89 **To** 2028 $40 JP

See Saw ★★★☆

4 Nanami Lane, Orange, NSW 2800 **Region** Orange
T (02) 6364 3118 **www**.seesawwine.com
Winemaker Justin Jarrett **Est.** 1995 **Dozens** 10 000 **Vyds** 152ha
Justin and Pip Jarrett have been growing grapes in Orange for over 25 years. Their approach
to farming is sustainable with a focus on leaving a positive environmental legacy across their
3 high-elevation vineyards (between 700m and 900m). The wines are organically grown and
made with as little intervention as possible. Fulcra is the ultra-premium label, made from small
parcels of the best fruit. Exports to the US, Sweden and Taiwan.

ΨΨΨΨΨ **Fulcra Orange Chardonnay 2019** Despite the restrained alcohol, the aromas
are intense: dried mango, canned peach and nectarine. Almost botrytic. The palate,
rich, soft and creamy. Slippery, almost. Not a shy style. A meld of cool-climate
clarity with ambitions that deliver flavour and a salubrious texture, over the usual
tensile freshness. Screw cap. 12.5% alc. **Rating** 92 **To** 2026 $80 NG

ΨΨΨΨ **Organic Orange Shiraz 2019 Rating** 89 **To** 2024 $25 NG

Semprevino ★★★★

271 Kangarilla Road, McLaren Vale, SA 5171 **Region** McLaren Vale
T 0417 142 110 **www**.semprevino.com.au
Winemaker Russell Schroder **Est.** 2006 **Dozens** 800
Semprevino is the venture of Russell Schroder and Simon Doak, who became close friends
while at Monash University in the early 1990s – studying mechanical engineering and science
respectively. Russell is the prime mover, who, after working for CRA/Rio Tinto for 5 years,
left on a 4-month trip to Western Europe and became captivated by the life of a vigneron.
Returning to Australia, he enrolled in part-time wine science at CSU, obtaining his wine

science degree in 2005. Between '03 and '06 he worked vintages in Italy and Victoria, coming under the wing of Stephen Pannell at Tinlins (where the Semprevino wines are made).

ŶŶŶŶŶ McLaren Vale Shiraz 2019 This meets all expectations for a regional shiraz at this price: a glossy, deep crimson segueing to exuberant aromas of lilac, blueberry, boysenberry, nori, tapenade and some smoked meat. Pulpy and lively, with some reductive tension, gentle acidity and a skein of lithe tannin wafting about the seams, while curtailing any sense of heat or excess. A very good shiraz. Screw cap. 14.4% alc. **Rating** 93 **To** 2028 $35 NG

McLaren Vale Pinot Grigio 2020 Grigio can be exciting. A relatively neutral variety, this dry, medium-bodied expression has been picked on flavour with additional textural intrigue imparted by 4 weeks of post-fermentation lees handling. Nashi pear, Granny Smith apple and jasmine notes gush along gentle acid rails. Finishes long, textural and juicy. Screw cap. 13.5% alc. **Rating** 90 **To** 2023 $22 NG

Sentio Wines   ★★★★★

23 Priory Lane, Beechworth, Vic 3437 (postal) **Region** Various
T 0433 773 229 **www**.sentiowines.com.au
Winemaker Chris Catlow **Est.** 2013 **Dozens** 800
This is a winery to watch. Owner/winemaker Chris Catlow was born (1982) and raised in Beechworth and says, 'A passion for wine was inevitable'. He drew particular inspiration from Barry Morey of Sorrenberg, working there in his late teens. He completed a double-major in viticulture science and wine science at La Trobe University, working with Paringa Estate, Kooyong and Portsea Estate from 2006–13. Here Sandro Mosele led him to his fascination with the interaction between place and chardonnay; Chris in turn worked with Benjamin Leroux in Burgundy during vintage in '13, '14 and '16.

Seppelt   ★★★★★

36 Cemetery Road, Great Western, Vic 3377 **Region** Grampians
T (03) 5361 2239 **www**.seppelt.com.au **Open** 7 days 10–5
Winemaker Adam Carnaby/Clare Dry **Est.** 1851 **Vyds** 620ha
Seppelt once had dual, and very different, claims to fame. The first was as Australia's foremost producer of both white and red sparkling wine, the former led by Salinger, the latter by Show Sparkling and Original Sparkling Shiraz. The second claim, even more relevant to the Seppelt of today, was based on the small-volume superb red wines made by Colin Preece from the 1930s through to the early '60s. These were ostensibly Great Western–sourced but – as the laws of the time allowed – were often region, variety and vintage blends. Two of his labels (also of high quality) were Moyston and Chalambar, the latter recently revived. Preece would have been a child in a lolly shop if he'd had today's viticultural resources to draw on, and would have been quick to recognise the commitment of the winemakers and viticulturists to the supreme quality of today's portfolio. Ararat businessman Danial Ahchow has leased the cellar door and surrounds, including the underground drives. Winemaker Clare Dry took over from Adam Carnaby from the 2021 vintage.

ŶŶŶŶŶ Drumborg Vineyard Riesling 2020 Gleaming straw-green hue is a come-on, the blossom-filled bouquet picking up the story. The palate changes gear to a bright, fresh and crisp interplay between mineral acidity and hints of passionfruit. Dyed-in-the-wool cellar-worthy, its greatest years stretch long into the future. Screw cap. 11.5% alc. **Rating** 95 **To** 2040 $40 JH

St Peters Grampians Shiraz 2019 Even in its youth, St Peters brings a sense of poise and elegance. The '19 has an added degree of refinement, oak seems more measured than in the past, the fruit more composed. The vintage rates highly with winemakers in the region. Restrained aromas of earthy spice, plums, blackberries and a hint of bay leaf. Smooth and subtle in the mouth – it's early days – with depth. Screw cap. 14.5% alc. **Rating** 95 **To** 2033 $80 JP

Arrawatta Hill Single Vineyard Limited Release Great Western Shiraz 2019 Immediate poise and elegance with the celebration of Grampians' black/blueberry forthright fruitiness, baking spice and some pretty smart oak. A solid depth of fruit flavour with a touch of local pepper on the palate goes hand in hand with precise, fine tannins, wrapping up in a long, juicy finish. Full of promise. Screw cap. 14.5% alc. **Rating** 95 **To** 2029 $90 JP

🍷🍷🍷🍷 **Chalambar Grampians Heathcote Shiraz 2019 Rating** 92 **To** 2026 $27 JP
Original Sparkling Shiraz NV Rating 90 $27 JP

Seppeltsfield   ★★★★★

730 Seppeltsfield Road, Seppeltsfield, SA 5355 **Region** Barossa Valley
T (08) 8568 6200 **www**.seppeltsfield.com.au **Open** 7 days 10.30–5
Winemaker Fiona Donald, Charlie Seppelt, Matthew Pick, Henry Slattery **Est.** 1851
Dozens 50 000 **Vyds** 1500ha
The historic Seppeltsfield property and its bounty of old fortified wines was originally established by the Seppelt family in 1851. Later acquired by Foster's Group (now Treasury Wine Estates), Seppeltsfield returned to private ownership in 2007 with Warren Randall now owning in excess of 90% of its capital. Randall, former sparkling winemaker for Seppelt Great Western in the 1980s, has led a revival of Seppeltsfield, gradually restoring the heritage-listed property. The estate's 1888 gravity cellar is back in full operation and a tourism village has been established. Randall has also slowly pieced together the largest premium, privately owned vineyard holding in the Barossa – enabling Seppeltsfield to complement its treasure trove of fortifieds with table wine releases. The 100 Year Old Paras have no parallel anywhere else in the world and the conjunction of 100 years of devoted stewardship (think former cellarmaster James Godfrey) and climate/terroir/varieties have had an outcome that can never, ever, be duplicated. Exports to the UK, China, South East Asia, Hong Kong, Scandinavia, South Korea, Japan, Canada and the US.

🍷🍷🍷🍷🍷 **100 Year Old Para Vintage Tawny 1921** If persistence, longevity, complexity and concentration are the ultimate marks of greatness, Para is in a league all of its own. In this bottle, 100 summers and 100 winters have amassed an explosive power, sheer viscosity and mesmerising complexity impossible to articulate in words. A drop is all it takes to transport you into its universe where time stands still and you are held in suspended animation for minutes. Utterly transfixing. Cork. 21.7% alc. **Rating** 99 $700 TS ♥
Para Tawny 2000 The legendary fortified outfit of Seppeltsfield achieves epic levels of complexity even in single-vintage blends. All the profound power, detail and impeccable balance we've come to expect, but what truly sets off the millennium vintage is line and length that hover unwavering for more than 60 seconds. Absolutely splendid. Screw cap. 20.8% alc. **Rating** 97 $88 TS ✪
Para Rare Tawny NV 170 years of legendary history and masterful expertise are woven into the intricate fabric of this phenomenal blend, not to mention one of the finest colletions of old blending material in the country. Its flavour allusions would fill a page, and then some, so I won't even start. Exquisite detail of grand old age, seamlessly united with younger material and perfectly integrated spirit. A mesmerising finish holds undeterred for 90 seconds and counting! Screw cap. 20.2% alc. **Rating** 97 $75 TS ✪

🍷🍷🍷🍷🍷 **Para Grand Tawny NV** A fantastically affordable introduction to the grand old age and fabled mystique that surround Seppelt Para. Incredible depth of savoury allure is the signature of old age. Monumental persistence. A little spirity by contrast with its big brothers, yet, as always, a benchmark for its category. Screw cap. 20.9% alc. **Rating** 94 $38 TS

🍷🍷🍷🍷🍷 **No. EC4 Cabernet Sauvignon Shiraz 2018 Rating** 90 **To** 2033 $45 TS

Serafino Wines ★★★★★

Kangarilla Road, McLaren Vale, SA 5171 **Region** McLaren Vale
T (08) 8323 0157 **www.**serafinowines.com.au **Open** Mon–Fri 10–4.30, w'ends &
public hols 10–4.30
Winemaker Charles Whish **Est.** 2000 **Dozens** 30 000 **Vyds** 121ha
After the sale of Maglieri Wines to Beringer Blass in 1998, Maglieri founder Serafino (Steve)
Maglieri acquired the McLarens on the Lake complex originally established by Andrew
Garrett. The operation draws upon over 120ha of shiraz, cabernet sauvignon, chardonnay,
merlot, semillon, barbera, nebbiolo, sangiovese, and grenache; part of the grape production
is sold. Serafino Wines has won a number of major trophies in Australia and the UK, Steve
Maglieri awarded a Member of the Order of Australia in January 2018. Exports to the UK,
the US, Canada, Hong Kong, Malaysia and NZ.

🍷🍷🍷🍷🍷 **McLaren Vale GSM 2019** Strikingly deep, bright-rimmed hue. The 83/14/3%
blend works to perfection, with the red fruits of grenache doing all the lifting,
shiraz providing a dab of plum coupled with silky tannins. Truly delicious. Screw
cap. 14.5% alc. **Rating** 96 **To** 2030 $28 JH ✪
Reserve McLaren Vale Grenache 2019 A seriously structured and textured
grenache à la Rhône Valley, and an each-way bet for cellaring and drinking
sooner rather than later. While red fruits are the core of the wine, its notes of earth
and spice provide complexity of a high order. Screw cap. 14.5% alc. **Rating** 95
To 2032 $45 JH

🍷🍷🍷🍷 **Bellissimo Fiano 2020** Rating 92 To 2022 $25 NG ✪
Terremoto McLaren Vale Syrah 2017 Rating 92 To 2026 $120 NG
McLaren Vale GSM 2020 Rating 92 To 2025 $28 NG
Sorrento McLaren Vale Chardonnay 2020 Rating 91 To 2022 $20 NG ✪

Serengale Vineyard ★★★★

1168 Beechworth-Wangaratta Road, Everton Upper, Vic 3678 **Region** Beechworth
T 0428 585 348 **www.**serengalebeechworth.com.au **Open** Fri–Sun 11–4 or by appt
Winemaker Gayle Taylor **Est.** 1999 **Dozens** 1000 **Vyds** 7ha
Gayle Taylor and Serena Abbinga established their business in 1999. Gayle had worked in the
wine industry for over 20 years, while Serena was seeking to return to North East Victoria
after many years living and working in inner city Melbourne. A 3-year search culminated in
the acquisition of a 24ha property in the Everton Hills. In the first years they concentrated
on planting the 7ha vineyard, with 2.6ha of merlot, 1.2ha chardonnay, 1ha each of cabernet
sauvignon, shiraz and pinot gris, and 0.2ha of prosecco. In '15 the winery was completed, and
the first vintage made. While Gayle is winemaker and Serena estate manager, their hands-on
approach means there's a fair degree of job sharing.

🍷🍷🍷🍷 **Beechworth Shiraz 2017** A shiraz revealing the complexity of a little bottle age.
It changes in the glass in a fascinating way; get the decanter ready. At once dark
plums, blackberry, toasted spice, milk chocolate aromas, then a savoury left turn,
with turned earth and leather. A warm and inviting texture with hearty tannins.
Screw cap. 13.6% alc. **Rating** 93 **To** 2027 $42 JP

🍷🍷🍷 **Birds On The Hill Beechworth Shiraz 2018** Rating 89 To 2026 $32 JP

Serrat ★★★★★

115 Simpsons Lane, Yarra Glen, Vic 3775 **Region** Yarra Valley
T (03) 9730 1439 **www.**serrat.com.au
Winemaker Tom Carson, Kate Thurgood **Est.** 2001 **Dozens** 1000 **Vyds** 3.5ha
Serrat is the family business of Tom Carson (after a 12-year reign at Yering Station, now
running Yabby Lake and Heathcote Estate for the Kirby family) and wife Nadège. They have
close planted (at 8800 vines/ha) 0.8ha each of pinot noir and chardonnay, 0.4ha of shiraz and
a sprinkling of viognier. Most recent has been the establishment of an esoteric mix of 0.1ha

each of malbec, nebbiolo, barbera and grenache. The vineyards are undergoing organic conversion. As well as being a consummate winemaker, Tom has one of the best palates in Australia and a deep understanding of the fine wines of the world, which he and Nadège drink at every opportunity (when they aren't drinking Serrat). Viticulture and winemaking hit new heights with the 2014 Yarra Valley Shiraz Viognier named *Wine Companion 2016* Wine of the Year (from a field of 8863 wines). Exports to Hong Kong and China.

🍷🍷🍷🍷🍷 **Yarra Valley Shiraz Viognier 2020** It's little wonder these wines sell out. They're priced so well for the quality offered. This wine a case in point. Firstly there's a vibrancy and freshness. It is awash with intense flavours, with black pepper, cinnamon and sarsaparilla infusing the sweetest cherries. It's hedonistic. It's full bodied, with plush and expansive tannins. Rather majestic. Screw cap. 14% alc. **Rating** 97 **To** 2035 $45 JF ⊘

🍷🍷🍷🍷🍷 **Yarra Valley Grenache Noir 2020** This is gorgeous. It's really, really hard to put down. The aromas are intoxicating, with their musk and red fruits, the dash of sarsaparilla, red licorice and cinnamon. The medium-bodied palate has intense, sweet fruit swooshing across it, with sandy tannins and neat acidity dutifully following. Another glass, please. Screw cap. 14% alc. **Rating** 96 **To** 2028 $45 JF ⊘
Yarra Valley Chardonnay 2020 A very chic chardonnay. It is reserved but soon charms: lemon blossom and dried herbs, grapefruit and lemon, with a shimmer of nougat/lees/oak flavour. The palate is juicy, succulent and its fine line of acidity strings everything together. Screw cap. 13% alc. **Rating** 95 **To** 2030 $45 JF
Yarra Valley Pinot Noir 2020 It smells of autumn. Strong aromas of mulch, porcini and poached rhubarb. It's wildly aromatic and appears to have a lot of whole-bunch character, yet a modest 20% in the ferment. It's also brimming with red cherries, chinotto, blood orange and its zest, plus a ferrous note. Sweet fruit and an intensity across the palate, the tannins ripe yet steadfast. Autumn's the best season. Screw cap. 13% alc. **Rating** 95 **To** 2035 $45 JF

🍷🍷🍷🍷🍷 **Fourre-Tout Yarra Valley 2020 Rating** 91 **To** 2026 $30 JF
Yarra Valley Nebbiolo 2020 Rating 91 **To** 2025 $45 JF

Sevenhill Cellars   ★★★★

111c College Road, Sevenhill, SA 5453 **Region** Clare Valley
T (08) 8843 5900 **www**.sevenhill.com.au **Open** 7 days 10–5
Winemaker Will Shields **Est.** 1851 **Dozens** 25 000 **Vyds** 96ha
One of the historical treasures of Australia; the oft-photographed stone wine cellars are the oldest in the Clare Valley and winemaking has been an enterprise within this Jesuit province since 1851. All the wines reflect the estate-grown grapes from old vines. Notwithstanding the difficult economic times, Sevenhill Cellars has increased its vineyard holdings from 74ha to 96ha and, naturally, production has risen. Exports to Switzerland, South Korea, Indonesia, Malaysia, Papua New Guinea, Singapore, NZ, Hong Kong and China.

🍷🍷🍷🍷🍷 **St Francis Xavier Single Vineyard Riesling 2020** An austere style yet intensely flavoured. Lemon sherbet, wet stones, dried herbs and lots of lemon peel and grapefruit flavours. Very dry with some phenolics on the finish, all add rather than detract, so there's plenty to consider. Screw cap. 12.5% alc. **Rating** 92 **To** 2030 $40 JF
Inigo Clare Valley Riesling 2020 This lays on the regional charm with lemons and limes, both with blossom and flavour. It's zippy and refreshing with talc-like acidity racing across the palate to a dry and convincing finish. Screw cap. 12% alc. **Rating** 90 **To** 2030 $25 JF
Inigo Clare Valley Cabernet Sauvignon 2018 Dark purple/garnet hue. Lots of cassis and mulberries within, infused with woodsy spices, mint and earthiness. A brightness across the palate with firm-fisted tannins in tow. It has a bit of grunt but it's not quite in overdrive. Screw cap. 14.5% alc. **Rating** 90 **To** 2030 $28 JF

Seville Estate

65 Linwood Road, Seville, Vic 3139 **Region** Yarra Valley
T (03) 5964 2622 **www.**sevilleestate.com.au **Open** 7 days 10–5
Winemaker Dylan McMahon **Est.** 1972 **Dozens** 8000 **Vyds** 12ha

Seville Estate was founded by Dr Peter and Margaret McMahon in 1972. After several changes of ownership, Yiping Wang purchased the property in early 2017. Yiping is a wine retailer in the Guangxi province of China. Yiping's supportive yet hands-off approach has allowed winemaker and general manager Dylan McMahon (grandson of founder Peter McMahon) to steer the ship. The estate has expanded to encompass the neighbouring vineyard and property (formerly Ainsworth Estate). This extra land has allowed for replanting original vine material grafted onto rootstock to preserve the original 1972 clones and safeguard the future of this unique property. Seville Estate also has luxury accommodation with the original homestead and 3 self-contained apartments. Exports to the US, Canada and China.

ŶŶŶŶŶ **Reserve Yarra Valley Chardonnay 2020** The X-factor is definitely stamped on this, warranting its Reserve label. A structured and detailed chardonnay that hits all the high notes. A perfect balance of grapefruit, woodsy spices, vanilla-pod oak, savouriness and nutty leesy flavours. The skein of acidity wraps up tightly, adding its own mouth-watering quality. Screw cap. 12.8% alc. **Rating** 96 **To** 2032 $90 JF

Yarra Valley Pinot Noir 2020 A beautiful wine that pleases from the moment it is poured, with its bright hue, heady aromas and very fine palate. Expect wild strawberries and cherries, a flutter of dried herbs and woodsy spices, with exceptional tannins appearing light yet smooth. The palate is sheer elegance. Screw cap. 13.2% alc. **Rating** 96 **To** 2032 $45 JF ❂

Dr McMahon Yarra Valley Shiraz 2018 This flagship shiraz comes via hand-picked fruit, 100% whole bunches, wild fermented and matured 10 months in 2 new French oak puncheons. While it's not a blockbuster, it is built to age. The oak is overt, needing to settle, so it's somewhat smoky and meaty. Yet allowing it to breathe reveals a core of dark fruit, all spicy and peppery, with textural, slightly drying tannins. It is savoury, complex and will reward the patient drinker. Screw cap. 13% alc. **Rating** 96 **To** 2038 $175 JF

Yarra Valley Chardonnay 2020 You know what the problem is with this wine – it vanishes too quickly in the glass. That's because it's so moreish, savoury and threaded with fantastic acidity and flavour. It's citrussy, with dashes of lemon and grapefruit, and a fine layer of creamy lees adding some volume. A cracking wine. Screw cap. 12.5% alc. **Rating** 95 **To** 2030 $45 JF

Single Vineyard Series Seville Pinot Noir 2020 A neatly composed and very agreeable pinot. It's in the red-fruit spectrum, lightly spiced with lithe tannins and a good energy across the palate. It's just shy of medium bodied, bright and fresh, with tangy acidity. Cooling and moreish. Nice drop. Screw cap. 13.5% alc. **Rating** 95 **To** 2027 $38 JF

Old Vine Reserve Yarra Valley Shiraz 2019 There's a fragrance of florals and red fruits right upfront, but it's tempered by savoury inputs from sulphides, juniper, lead pencil and charcuterie. Firm, tannins and acidity hold forth, but will soon melt into its medium-bodied frame. Screw cap. 13.5% alc. **Rating** 95 **To** 2035 $90 JF

Old Vine Reserve Yarra Valley Cabernet Sauvignon 2019 Excellent crimson hue, delicate aromas and flavours, and while there's a splash of cassis and currants, it's very savoury. Licorice, warm earth, a hint of cigar box and cedary oak – not much. This is definitely on the reserved side. Screw cap. 13% alc. **Rating** 94 **To** 2030 $90 JF

ŶŶŶŶŶ **Off-Dry Yarra Valley Riesling 2019** **Rating** 93 **To** 2026 $38 JF
Yarra Valley Shiraz 2019 **Rating** 93 **To** 2029 $45 JF
Sewn Little Red Yarra Valley 2019 **Rating** 93 **To** 2026 $27 JF ❂
Yarra Valley Riesling 2019 **Rating** 91 **To** 2026 $38 JF
Single Vineyard Series Seville Chardonnay 2020 **Rating** 91 **To** 2025 $38 JF

Single Vineyard Series Gruyere Chardonnay 2020 Rating 91 **To** 2025 $38 JF

Single Vineyard Series Coldstream Pinot Noir 2020 Rating 91 **To** 2027 $38 JF

Yarra Valley Blanc de Blancs 2017 Rating 91 $55 JF

Sew & Sew Wines ★★★★

97 Pennys Hill Road, The Range, SA 5172 **Region** Adelaide Hills/McLaren Vale
T 0419 804 345 **www**.sewandsewwines.com.au **Open** By appt
Winemaker Jodie Armstrong **Est.** 2015 **Dozens** 3500
Winemaker and viticulturist Jodie Armstrong has worked in the wine industry for more than 20 years. She sources grapes from the vineyards that she manages, her in-depth knowledge of these vineyards allowing her to grow and select premium fruit. She makes the wines in friends' wineries 'where collaboration is a source of inspiration'. Exports to Denmark, Canada and Fiji.

♟♟♟♟ **Sashiko Series Adelaide Hills Chardonnay 2019** No oak employed here, so what you see is all about the fruit, which is a bit of a fruit salad of pear, white nectarine and some honeydew melon. Lees stirring while in tank has offered a subtle nutty/creamy palate texture. Simple, unadorned and transparent in its style. Screw cap. 13.5% alc. **Rating** 89 **To** 2025 $25 TL

Sashiko Series McLaren Vale Shiraz 2018 Big robust Vale shiraz with a dark chocolate note, and while there's 20% new American oak employed, it doesn't make any major impact. The wine is dark and deep and will satisfy drinkers with a taste for that set of characters. Screw cap. 14% alc. **Rating** 89 **To** 2026 $25 TL

Shadowfax ★★★★★

K Road, Werribee, Vic 3030 **Region** Geelong/Macedon Ranges
T (03) 9731 4420 **www**.shadowfax.com.au **Open** 7 days 11–5
Winemaker Alister Timms **Est.** 2000 **Dozens** 10000 **Vyds** 28ha
Once an offspring of Werribee Park and its grand mansion, Shadowfax is now very much its own master. It has 10ha of mature vineyards at Werribee; plus 5ha of close-planted pinot noir, 5ha of chardonnay and 2ha of pinot gris at the Little Hampton Vineyard in Macedon; and 3ha of pinot noir, 2ha of chardonnay and 1ha of gewürztraminer elsewhere in Macedon. Alister Timms, with degrees in science (The University of Melbourne) and oenology (University of Adelaide) became chief winemaker in '17 (replacing long-serving winemaker Matt Harrop). Exports to the UK, the US and China.

♟♟♟♟♟ **Little Hampton Pinot Noir 2019** Such a solid performer. It's wonderfully fragrant; all florals, exotic spices, cherries and cola. Unencumbered by new oak flavour (aged in used French hogsheads and puncheons), it's all about the purity of fruit and drive across a fuller-bodied palate. It's laced with velvety tannins and the finish is long as it is fresh. Screw cap. 13% alc. **Rating** 96 **To** 2033 $65 JF ✪

K Road Shiraz 2019 The dark crimson hue is delightful, and it gets better from there as the flavours unfurl. Purple plums, currants dipped in cocoa and flecked with herbs and tapenade. Very complex. Full bodied and, while aged in 50% new French puncheons, the oak isn't demanding – it adds to the savouriness and grainy tannins. Screw cap. 14% alc. **Rating** 96 **To** 2035 $45 JF ✪

Midhill Chardonnay 2019 A classy chardonnay, stamped with regional cool. This means there's grapefruit, lime and zest, with fresh ginger and allspice throughout. A fine thread of acidity weaves across the palate, which opens up to reveal richer flavours of creamy lees and nougatine. Screw cap. 13% alc. **Rating** 95 **To** 2029 $50 JF

Straws Lane Macedon Ranges Pinot Noir 2019 A captivating wine, flaunting its high-and-cool credentials. Tight but not mean, precise tannins, with the texture of raw silk and refreshing acidity that washes through. It's an austere style, long and pure. One to watch. Screw cap. 13% alc. **Rating** 95 **To** 2033 $50 JF

Macedon Ranges Pinot Noir 2019 This is just lovely. Fragrant, cherries and spices galore, with the tannins soft and giving. It's ready now and will delight with or without food. Screw cap. 13% alc. **Rating** 94 **To** 2028 $34 JF

♟♟♟♟♟ **Macedon Ranges Chardonnay 2019 Rating** 92 **To** 2028 $34 JF
Minnow Carignan 2019 Rating 91 **To** 2026 $24 JF
Minnow Grenache Mataro 2020 Rating 90 **To** 2024 $24 JF

Sharmans ★★★★

Store 148, Invermay Road, Invermay, Tas 7250 **Region** Northern Tasmania
T (03) 6343 0773 **www**.sharmanswines.com.au **Open** Thurs–Fri 11–5.30, Sat 11–2
Winemaker Jeremy Dineen, Ockie Myburgh **Est.** 1986 **Dozens** 2500
When Mike Sharman planted the first vines at Relbia in 1986, he was the pioneer of the region and he did so in the face of a widespread belief that it was too far inland and frost-prone. He proved the doomsayers wrong, helped by the slope of the vineyard draining cold air away from the vines. In 2012 the property was acquired by local ophthalmologist Ian Murrell and his wife Melissa, a Launceston-based interior designer. The grounds and vineyards have been developed and renovated, the original residence now a cellar door and al fresco area, the picturesque grounds enhanced by award-winning landscaper Chris Calverly.

♟♟♟♟♟ **Tasmania Sauvignon Blanc 2020** Pretty sauvignon, plucked in the perfect instant and assembled with care and precision. A fragrant air of lantana over a core of crunchy lemon and lime, subtly accented with exotic notes of guava. Refreshing, crystalline acidity pierces a long and energetic finish. Screw cap. 12.6% alc. **Rating** 93 **To** 2025 $28 TS
Tasmania Pinot Noir 2019 Testimony to site and craft, this is a precise expression of Relbia pinot, beautifully assembled and fantastically priced. Crunchy blackberries and blood plums are neatly framed in fine-boned tannins, set off with just the right sprinkle of whole-bunch herbs. Fruit and oak tannins unite confidently on a long finish, honed for medium-term cellaring. Screw cap. 13.3% alc. **Rating** 93 **To** 2027 $30 TS
Tasmania Blanc de Blanc 2015 Relbia is more famous for its pinot noir, which usually takes the lead in Josef Chromy's sparkling (in whose capable hands this cuvée is also made), but this demonstrates that chardonnay can also produce fizz of character, tension and endurance. A pale straw hue proclaims freshness and cut. A core of lemon, grapefruit and spicy white peach is well endowed with the biscuit, brioche, crème caramel and creamy texture of long lees age. Crunchy, crystalline acidity (presumably some malic) elongates a persistent and dynamic finish, well balanced with integrated dosage. Diam. 12.5% alc. **Rating** 93 $60 TS
Tasmania Pinot Gris 2020 Accurate gris, wrapped in spicy pear, lemon and wild honey. Tense acidity and bitter phenolic grip unite on a long finish, well contrasting taut lemon with oily, succulent ripe pear. Screw cap. 13.8% alc. **Rating** 92 **To** 2022 $30 TS

♟♟♟♟ **SGR Tasmania Riesling 2020 Rating** 89 **To** 2030 $30 TS

Shaw + Smith ★★★★★

136 Jones Road, Balhannah, SA 5242 **Region** Adelaide Hills
T (08) 8398 0500 **www**.shawandsmith.com **Open** 7 days 11–5
Winemaker Martin Shaw, Adam Wadewitz **Est.** 1989 **Vyds** 56ha
Cousins Martin Shaw and Michael Hill Smith MW already had unbeatable experience when they founded Shaw + Smith as a virtual winery in 1989. In '99 Martin and Michael purchased the 36ha Balhannah property, building the superbly designed winery in 2000 and planting more sauvignon blanc, shiraz, pinot noir and riesling. It is here that visitors can taste the wines in appropriately beautiful surroundings. The 20ha Lenswood Vineyard, 10km northwest of the winery, is mainly planted to chardonnay and pinot noir. Exports to all major markets.

𝒴𝒴𝒴𝒴𝒴 **M3 Adelaide Hills Chardonnay 2020** The first thing that strikes you is an elegance that is so fundamental to the style and respectful to the elite fruit within. The faintest of oak lifts adds a complexity to start, but the energy and concentration of the fruit become the prime focus on the palate. It's all about chardonnay's finest flavours and a vibrant acidity to drive it long into the future. Screw cap. 13.5% alc. **Rating** 98 **To** 2030 $49 TL ✪ ♥

𝒴𝒴𝒴𝒴𝒴 **Adelaide Hills Sauvignon Blanc 2020** A lightness of touch now marks this wine, less wild-tropical-fruit punch and more grapefruit/citrus, both aromatic partners creating a superbly balanced aromatic pattern that is enhanced by a short maturation on lees to develop the most delicious, powdery mouthfeel. Always a style leader, now offering next-level varietal sophistication. Screw cap. 12.5% alc. **Rating** 96 **To** 2023 $29 TL ✪ ♥

Balhannah Vineyard Adelaide Hills Shiraz 2018 From the home vineyard at Shaw + Smith's Balhannah winery and cellar door, there's a stunningly attractive ripeness to this wine, dark blue and purple fruit notes with kitchen herbal tweaks adding a heightened gastronomic appeal – dark mint, fennel and rocket pepperiness. Delicious medium-bodied structurals and fine tannins provide an equally sophisticated mouthfeel and finish. Superb wine. Screw cap. 14% alc. **Rating** 96 **To** 2030 $93 TL

Adelaide Hills Riesling 2020 From a high Lenswood vineyard, half whole-bunch pressed, half crushed. The blend sat on lees for 4 months to develop a delicate Granny Smith/Pink Lady apple textural pithiness that fits perfectly with those same fruit flavours and pure orchard floral aromatics. Delicious, mouth-awakening, aperitif styling. Screw cap. 11.5% alc. **Rating** 95 **To** 2028 $33 TL ✪ ♥

M3 Adelaide Hills Chardonnay 2019 The clear expression of on-point ripe peach and nectarine fruits is this wine's calling card. A delicate little wrap of oak adds the spice of ginger-nut biscuit with the swell of an appealing creaminess; subtle acidity holds it in balance all the way. Fruit, oak, spice and tang – the whole varietal experience. Screw cap. 13.5% alc. **Rating** 95 **To** 2030 $49 TL

Lenswood Vineyard Adelaide Hills Chardonnay 2019 From Shaw + Smith's 500m-high Lenswood vineyard, fondly nurtured to showcase the finer chardonnay elements. A warm and dry ripening season has yielded ripe peach and nectarine notes to begin, flint and wet stone characters offsetting fruit richness with earthy support. The palate is all about sculpted chardonnay luxury. A wealth of flavour is toned by natural acidity, crafted with a calm balance and superbly steady trajectory. Screw cap. 13.5% alc. **Rating** 95 **To** 2028 $93 TL

Lenswood Vineyard Adelaide Hills Pinot Noir 2019 This wine is so delicate to start that you could miss its genuine class at first. That would be a shame, because what lies beneath is most beguiling and has every chance of awakening into something very, very special over the next few years. Fragrant with violet notes and blueberries, puckered with gentle savoury spice and acidity. And these are just the first layers beginning to unfold. Be patient. Decant for now. Screw cap. 13.5% alc. **Rating** 95 **To** 2030 $93 TL

Adelaide Hills Pinot Noir 2020 An initial delicate waft of pinot-cherry aromas lifting out of a more grounded, charry base. Soon, a hidden intensity gathers steam, with fruit and woody savouries combining on the palate, announcing blueberry-toned flavours mostly. Evenly finished, balance critical. Encourages 2nd and 3rd pours without asking. Screw cap. 13% alc. **Rating** 94 **To** 2028 $49 TL

Adelaide Hills Shiraz 2019 There's an alluring mix of fruit and flint in the aromatics, offering an early hint of the balanced earthiness and plum-fruit flavours sitting very comfortably together across the whole length of the palate. Fine, white peppery notes from the tannins add a savoury element on the finish. Screw cap. 13.5% alc. **Rating** 94 **To** 2030 $49 TL

Shaw Wines

34 Isabel Drive, Murrumbateman, NSW 2582 **Region** Canberra District
T (02) 6227 5827 **www.**shawwines.com.au **Open** 7 days 10–5
Winemaker Graeme Shaw, Jeremy Nascimben **Est.** 1999 **Dozens** 12 000 **Vyds** 28ha
Graeme and Ann Shaw established their vineyard (cabernet sauvignon, merlot, shiraz, semillon
and riesling) in 1998 on a 280ha fine wool–producing property established in the mid-
1800s and known as Olleyville. It is one of the largest privately owned vineyard holdings
in the Canberra area. Their children are fully employed in the family business, Michael as
viticulturist and Tanya as cellar door manager. Exports to Vietnam, Singapore, Thailand, the
Philippines, South Korea, Hong Kong and China.

🍷🍷🍷🍷 **Estate Canberra Shiraz 2018** No shortage of flavour here, yet it retains a
composure while working off a medium- to fuller-bodied palate. Expect red and
black plums, a fair pinch of woodsy spices and pepper with eucalypt. It's a savoury
offering really, with grainy tannins in tow and a freshness that gives immediate
drinking appeal. Screw cap. 14% alc. **Rating** 92 **To** 2028 $34 JF
Reserve Merriman Canberra District Cabernet Sauvignon 2018 An
explosion of flavours from mint and blackberries, currants and menthol with
lashings of oak in the mix. There's a vibrancy and juiciness across the full-bodied
palate, with gritty yet shapely tannins and while a tad firm, it has appeal. Built to
be better in a few years. Screw cap. 14% alc. **Rating** 92 **To** 2032 $65 JF
Winemakers Selection Canberra Cabernet Sauvignon 2018 Showing its
cool credentials with mint and herbs slinking around blackberries, currants and
woodsy spice. It has a refreshing appeal with tannins aplenty, hovering between
savoury and fruit flavours. Screw cap. 14% alc. **Rating** 90 **To** 2025 $20 JF ✪

🍷🍷🍷 **Estate Canberra Cabernet Shiraz 2018 Rating** 89 **To** 2031 $34 JF
Winemakers Selection Canberra Shiraz 2018 Rating 88 **To** 2026 $20 JF

Shepherd's Hut

PO Box 194, Darlington, WA 6070 **Region** Porongurup
T (08) 9299 6700 **www.**shepherdshutwines.com
Winemaker Rob Diletti **Est.** 1996 **Dozens** 2000 **Vyds** 15.5ha
The shepherd's hut that appears on the wine label was one of four stone huts used in the
1850s to house shepherds tending large flocks of sheep. When WA pathologist Dr Michael
Wishart (and family) purchased the property in 1996, the hut was in a state of extreme
disrepair. It has since been restored, still featuring the honey-coloured Mount Barker stone.
Riesling, chardonnay, sauvignon blanc, shiraz and cabernet sauvignon have been established.
The business is now owned by son Philip and wife Cathy, who also run a large farm of mainly
cattle. Most of the grapes are sold to other makers in the region, but those retained make
high-quality wine at mouth-watering prices thanks to the skill of winemaker Rob Diletti.

🍷🍷🍷🍷 **Porongurup Pinot Noir 2019** This wine has made a local name for itself for its
low price, high quality and small quantity – it sells out each vintage. In the glass
it is vibrantly pink tinged. The palate is silky and fine with spice to spare. Pretty
red and pink berry, raspberry lolly aromatics and an appealing creamy texture that
is one and the same with the fruit. Good length of flavour. Screw cap. 13.2% alc.
Rating 94 **To** 2023 $27 EL ✪

Sherrah Wines

148 McMurtrie Road, McLaren Vale SA 5171 **Region** McLaren Vale
T 0403 057 704 **www.**sherrahwines.com.au **Open** Fri–Mon 11–5
Winemaker Alex Sherrah **Est.** 2016 **Dozens** 3000
Alex Sherrah's career started with a bachelor of science in organic chemistry and pharmacology,
leading him to travel the world, to return home broke and in need of a job. Time spent as a
cellar rat at Tatachilla and a graduate diploma in oenology at Waite University were followed
by a job at Kendall Jackson's Napa Valley crown jewel, Cardinale, making ultra-premium

Bordeaux-blend wines. Stints at Knappstein and O'Leary Walker followed, punctuated by vintages in Burgundy and Austria. At the end of 2011 he moved to McLaren Vale and Coriole, where he became senior winemaker in '12, remaining there for 6 years, before moving on to head up winemaking at Haselgrove, his present-day job. I (James) cannot help but pass on some of his words of wisdom (and I'm not being sarcastic): 'Wine to me is not about tasting blackcurrant and cigar box but how the wine "feels" to drink. Flavour is obviously a big part of this, but how does the wine flow from the front to the back palate? It should transition effortlessly from first smell and sip to swallow, aftertaste and lingering influence of tannin and acid. I believe in balance, a great wine should have no sharp edges, it should have beautiful smooth curves from front to back.' Small wonder he makes such wonderful wines. Exports to the US, Luxembourg and China.

ŸŸŸŸŸ **Skin Party McLaren Vale Fiano 2020** Selectiv' machine–harvested, whole berries open-fermented in shallow vats, initially wild fermented, then overseeded with an aromatic cultured yeast, matured in used hogsheads for 4 months. A great success for a bold exercise, the wine complex but fresh, with no obvious tannins. The bright straw-green colour is another plus. Screw cap. 12% alc. **Rating** 94 To 2025 $30 JH **◐**

ŸŸŸŸŸ **Red et Al McLaren Vale Grenache Shiraz Nero d'Avola 2019** **Rating** 91 To 2024 $30 NG
McLaren Vale Nero d'Avola 2019 **Rating** 90 To 2023 $30 NG

Shingleback   ★★★★☆

3 Stump Hill Road, McLaren Vale, SA 5171 **Region** McLaren Vale
T (08) 8323 7388 www.shingleback.com.au **Open** 7 days 10–5
Winemaker John Davey, Dan Hills **Est.** 1995 **Dozens** 150 000 **Vyds** 120ha
Brothers Kym and John Davey planted and nurture their family-owned and sustainably managed vineyard on land purchased by their grandfather in the 1950s. Shingleback has been a success story since its establishment. Its 120ha of estate vineyards are one of the keys to that success, which includes winning the Jimmy Watson Trophy in 2006 for the '05 D Block Cabernet Sauvignon. The well-made wines are rich and full-flavoured, but not overripe (and hence, not excessively alcoholic). Exports to NZ, Canada, the US, the UK, China, Singapore, Cambodia and Vietnam.

ŸŸŸŸŸ **The Gate McLaren Vale Shiraz 2018** Estate-grown fruit. Deep crimson/purple colour; an unusual but extremely attractive wine, with characters normally encountered in cool climates. The intensity of the red/black cherry fruit comes with fine, tailored tannins. The result is a wine of great length, offering pleasure from the first to last sips. Screw cap. 14.5% alc. **Rating** 97 To 2035 $40 JH **◐**

ŸŸŸŸŸ **The Bio Project McLaren Vale Fiano 2020** Fiano is a variety that will surely achieve ever greater significance in Australia's varietal landscape. It holds its acidity and its lingering aftertaste wherever it is grown. Its almond and kaffir-lime flavours delicately coat the mouth, the next glass never far away. Screw cap. 12.5% alc. **Rating** 94 To 2026 $25 JH **◐**
D Block Reserve McLaren Vale Shiraz 2018 This is to type, for those drinkers expecting a fully loaded shiraz, brimming with scents of violet, blue-fruit allusions, licorice, baking and assorted spices. And yet it is not a caricature. Conversely, the texture is creamy and salubrious, without any obtuse angles or jarring acidity. The finish billows long across the palate, staining every pore. Big and robust, but plenty fresh. Screw cap. 14.5% alc. **Rating** 94 To 2030 $55 NG

ŸŸŸŸŸ **D Block Reserve McLaren Vale Cabernet Sauvignon 2018** **Rating** 93 To 2030 $55 NG
Unedited Single Vineyard McLaren Vale Shiraz 2019 **Rating** 92 To 2028 $70 NG
The Gate McLaren Vale Cabernet Shiraz 2019 **Rating** 92 To 2027 $40 NG
The Bio Project Dry McLaren Vale Monastrell Rosé 2020 **Rating** 91 To 2022 $25 NG

Local Heroes McLaren Vale Shiraz Grenache 2020 Rating 91 To 2028
$25 NG
Davey Estate Reserve McLaren Vale Cabernet Sauvignon 2019
Rating 91 To 2030 $25 NG
The Bio Project McLaren Vale Tempranillo Blend 2019 Rating 91 To 2023
$25 NG

Shining Rock Vineyard ★★★★☆

165 Jeffrey Street, Nairne, SA 5252 **Region** Adelaide Hills
T 0448 186 707 **www**.shiningrock.com.au **Open** By appt
Winemaker Con Moshos, Darren Arney **Est.** 2000 **Dozens** 1200 **Vyds** 14.4ha
Agronomist Darren Arney and psychologist wife Natalie Worth had the opportunity to
purchase the Shining Rock Vineyard from Lion Nathan in 2012. It had been established
by Petaluma in '00 and until '15 the grapes were sold to various premium wineries in the
Adelaide Hills. Darren graduated from Roseworthy Agricultural College in the late 1980s and
saw the vineyard as the opportunity of a lifetime to produce top-quality grapes from a very
special vineyard. They hit the ground running with the inaugural vintage of '15 made by Peter
Leske (Revenir), but since '16 the wines have been made by Con Moshos in conjunction with
Darren. It hardly need be said that the wines reflect the expertise of those involved, with the
eminence grise of Brian Croser in the background.

Shirvington ★★★★☆

107 Strout Road, McLaren Vale, SA 5171 **Region** McLaren Vale
T (08) 8323 7649 **www**.shirvington.com **Open** Thurs–Mon 11–4
Winemaker Kim Jackson **Est.** 1996 **Dozens** 950 **Vyds** 23.8ha
The Shirvington family began the development of their McLaren Vale vineyards in 1996
under the direction of viticulturist Peter Bolte and now have almost 24ha under vine, the
majority to shiraz and cabernet sauvignon, with small additional plantings of grenache
and mataro. A substantial part of the production is sold as grapes, the best reserved for the
Shirvington wines. Exports to the US.

 Row X Row McLaren Vale Rosé 2020 Straight-laced grenache. A light coral
hue belies the intensity of rosewater, lemon verbena, raspberry and dried thyme
flavours. Juicy, but not overtly fruity. A dry and thirst-slaking wine melding
European restraint with an effusive Australian joy. Screw cap. 12.8% alc. **Rating** 92
To 2021 $25 NG ❂
Row X Row McLaren Vale Fiano 2020 Hand picked from a single plot in the
Vale, a region so suited to this great Campanian variety. Lemon rind, grapefruit,
fennel and a briny spray of sea salt, lacing a vibrant finish. Mid weighted, saline
and crunchy. I like this variety riper and more textural, but a solid expression all
the same. Screw cap. 12.5% alc. **Rating** 91 To 2023 $25 NG
The Redwind McLaren Vale Shiraz 2018 A textbook interpretation of
full-bodied Vale shiraz. Blueberry, mulberry, anise, bitter chocolate to mocha
oak accents and a clove and pepper-laced finish. A riff of reductive tension is
deftly applied to promote a floral lift and a welcome belt of restraint across the
mid palate, keeping the fray focused and relatively savoury. Screw cap. 14% alc.
Rating 91 To 2032 $45 NG
McLaren Vale Shiraz 2018 Honest. Rich. Regional. Pulpy and fresh. Bergamot,
blackberry, violet, baking spice, Dutch licorice and pepper-grind notes flow with
a bit less effort than the regional shiraz norm. Solid drinking. Screw cap. 14% alc.
Rating 91 To 2026 $32 NG
McLaren Vale Cabernet Sauvignon 2018 The sort of full-bodied, maritime/
saline yet strongly varietal expression that is inimitably Vale. Aromas of spearmint,
blackcurrant, licorice, tapenade and bouquet garni, expanding across a pillar of oak.
Effusive intensity, persistence and impressive sage-doused length. Good drinking
for the medium term. Screw cap. 14% alc. **Rating** 91 To 2028 $32 NG

Row X Row Clare Valley Riesling 2020 Textbook Clare Valley riesling: kaffir lime, tonic and lemon rind. Gently mid weighted, with a skein of talcy acidity that is neither excessively sherbety, nor acerbic. A long, juicy flow. Solid kit for the local South East Asian–inspired takeout. Screw cap. 25% alc. **Rating** 90 **To** 2026 $25 NG

The Redwind McLaren Vale Cabernet Sauvignon 2018 A full-bodied, saline and highly maritime warm–climate cabernet. Piercing aromas of blackcurrant, sweet and indelible. Mint, bouquet garni, sage and crushed verdant herb douse a firm carriage of tannin, derived of both grape and mocha oak. No surprises here. Rich, sweet and a bit tangy. To type. Screw cap. 14% alc. **Rating** 90 **To** 2030 $45 NG

Sholto Wines   ★★★★

79 Noyes Lane, Gundaroo, NSW 2620 **Region** Canberra District
T 0413 746 883 **www.**sholtowines.com.au
Winemaker Jacob Carter **Est.** 2013 **Dozens** 500
Jake Carter began his career as a winemaker when he turned 18, working for Rob Howell of Jeir Creek Wine and Greg Gallagher of Gallagher Wines. That was 9 years ago, and he has now launched his own label to concentrate on alternative varieties (read natural) wines. He says he doesn't like the idea of sticking to any sort of recipe, so 'I change or tweak the ferment a bit for every wine coming through in the new vintage'. Fortune favours the bold it seems, and he's now embarking on planting a vineyard on a property purchased by his family just north of Canberra, outside the village of Gundaroo. There he will plant 2ha of 'alternative' varieties, and set up a rustic-style cellar door converted from an old horse barn.

♀♀♀♀♀ **Rouge Clair Canberra District 2019** A vibrant and refreshing red that's working off a savoury riff. Sure there's a medley of cassis, currants and florals with some licorice root too, but it's earthy with round tannins, some grip to the finish. Nice one. Diam. 12.5% alc. **Rating** 93 **To** 2026 $30 JF

Canberra District Syrah 2018 There's a lot of enjoyment across the Sholto range – it's all about refreshment and delicious drinking today. Excellent purple/black with loads of pepper cracked over the plum/cherry flavours with some licorice straps in the mix. Lighter framed, juicy yet very savoury with light and lightly drying tannins. Screw cap. 13% alc. **Rating** 92 **To** 2026 $35 JF

Canberra District Riesling 2019 Texture has been built into this via oak and a touch of skin contact – 3 days for one parcel, a day for the other, with 35% fermented in used French barriques. Good energy via acidity with a talc-like sensation across the palate. In the mix, lemon drops, peach fuzz and a tonic juiciness. Screw cap. 11.5% alc. **Rating** 90 **To** 2027 $30 JF

Shottesbrooke

101 Bagshaws Road, McLaren Flat, SA 5171 **Region** McLaren Vale
T (08) 8383 0002 **www.**shottesbrooke.com.au **Open** Thurs–Tues 11–5
Winemaker Hamish Maguire **Est.** 1984 **Dozens** 150 000 **Vyds** 30.64ha
Shottesbrooke is a proudly family-owned and -managed business with 2nd-generation Hamish Maguire as chief winemaker and general manager. Before taking the reins at Shottesbrooke, Hamish completed 2 vintages in France and 1 in Spain, giving him a personal knowledge of the world of wine. The investment of time and money over the past 33 years have taken Shottesbrooke to the position where it can embark on the next major step and undertake major improvements in the size and operation of its winery. The central theme is the investment in state-of-the-art equipment allowing more gentle fermentation, pressing, movement and maturation of the wines. Thus there has been a 25% increase in the temperature-controlled main barrel storage areas, sufficient to hold an additional 600 barrels. Once bottled and packaged, the wines are held in a purpose-built air-conditioned storage facility until shipped to customers in refrigerated containers to ensure quality and consistency throughout the entire process. Exports to all major markets, most importantly, China.

♟♟♟♟♟ Punch McLaren Vale Cabernet Sauvignon 2019 This is a very strong regional cab. The tannins are tightly composed, saline and doused with nori and wakame. Highly regional. The oak, nestled. The finish, long, immaculate and saturated with fruit, without coming across as sweet or overt. Cassis, graphite, verdant herb and sage. Ball-bearing precision about this. Screw cap. 14.5% alc. **Rating** 94 **To** 2033 $60 NG

♟♟♟♟♟ The Proprietor Reserve Series McLaren Vale 2019 Rating 93 **To** 2030 $60 NG
Big Dreams McLaren Vale Grenache 2019 Rating 92 **To** 2026 $95 NG
Single Vineyard Adelaide Hills Chardonnay 2019 Rating 91 **To** 2025 $33 TL
The Butchered Line McLaren Vale Shiraz 2019 Rating 91 **To** 2031 $95 NG
Measure Twice, Cut Once McLaren Vale Mataro 2019 Rating 91 **To** 2030 $95 NG
Engine Room McLaren Vale Cabernet Sangiovese 2019 Rating 90 **To** 2028 $19 NG ⊙

Shut the Gate Wines
8453 Main North Road, Clare, SA 5453 and 39 Jindabyne Road, Berridale, NSW 2628
Region Clare Valley
T 0488 243 200 **www**.shutthegate.withwine.com **Open** 7 days 10–4.30
Winemaker Contract **Est.** 2013 **Dozens** 6000
Shut the Gate is the venture of Richard Woods and Rasa Fabian, which took shape after 5 years' involvement in the rebranding of Crabtree Watervale Wines, followed by 18 months of juggling consultancy roles. During this time Richard and Rasa set the foundations for Shut the Gate; the striking and imaginative labels (and parables) catching the eye. The engine room of the business is the Clare Valley, where the wines are contract-made and the grapes for many of the wines are sourced. They have chosen their grape sources and contract winemakers with considerable care.

♟♟♟♟♟ For Hunger Single Site Clare Valley Shiraz 2018 The colour is an excellent dark garnet. A rich, voluptuous style that adds layers of flavour across its full-bodied palate. Dark plums, warm earth, bitumen, woodsy spices and steadfast tannins. It has a polish and it impresses now. Screw cap. 14.8% alc. **Rating** 93 **To** 2033 $48 JF
For Love Watervale Riesling 2020 The heady aromatics, all floral and citrus, are in sync with the palate. It's a lovely combo, with citrussy tang to the acidity, a wonderful slippery texture and all the flavours that Watervale can produce. Lemons and limes, stony with a touch of spice and pleasing to the last drop. Screw cap. 12% alc. **Rating** 92 **To** 2030 $28 JF
Rosie's Patch Watervale Riesling 2020 Shimmering with a pale olive shot through the straw hue and doesn't disappoint with its flavours. The talc-like texture of the acidity is the key to this refreshing drink, around which you can expect stone fruit, lemon/lime drops with some grapefruit pith. It finishes nice and dry. Drink now. Screw cap. 12% alc. **Rating** 90 **To** 2026 $22 JF

Shy Susan Wines
Billy Button Wines, 11 Camp Street, Bright, Vic 3741 **Region** Tasmania
T 0434 635 510 **www**.shysusanwines.com.au **Open** 7 days 11–6
Winemaker Glenn James **Est.** 2015 **Dozens** 300
'Shy Susan (*Tetratheca gunnii*) is a critically endangered wildflower endemic to a tiny part of Tasmania. Her survival depends completely on a little native bee, who alone is capable of pollination. Their fate is forever entwined.' After working with Tasmanian fruit for nearly 2 decades Glenn James and his wife, Jo Marsh, have released a range of unique wines from some of Tasmania's most exciting vineyards. Their initial release included Riesling, a Sylvaner Riesling blend, Gewürztraminer, Chardonnay, Pinot Noir and an Amphora Shiraz. Select

small parcels of fruit are crafted to reflect variety, vineyard and the stylistic approach forged from Glenn's skill and experience. Jo Marsh is owner and winemaker of Billy Button Wines (see separate entry).

Sidewood Estate

6 River Road, Hahndorf, SA 5245 **Region** Adelaide Hills
T (08) 8388 1673 **www.**sidewood.com.au **Open** Wed–Mon 11–5, Fri–Sat 11–8.30
Winemaker Darryl Catlin **Est.** 2004 **Vyds** 90ha

Sidewood Estate was established in 2004. It is owned by Owen and Cassandra Inglis who operate it as a winery and cidery. Situated in the Onkaparinga Valley, the vines weather the cool climate of the Adelaide Hills. Significant expenditure on regeneration of the vineyards was already well underway when Sidewood invested over $12 million in the expansion of the winery, increasing capacity from 500t to 2000t each vintage and implementing sustainable improvements including 100kW solar panels, water treatment works and insulation for the winery. The expansion includes new bottling and canning facilities capable of handling 6 million bottles of wine and cider annually. A multimillion-dollar restaurant, cellar door and cidery was opened in 2020. Wines are released under the Sidewood Estate, Stablemate and Mappinga labels. Exports to the UK, the US, Canada, the Netherlands, Malaysia, Thailand, Vanuatu, Singapore, Japan and China.

ŸŸŸŸŸ **Oberlin Adelaide Hills Pinot Noir 2019** One of 3 single-clone pinots in this range. 100% whole bunches and wild ferment. Alluring crimson colours in the glass, sophisticated cherry aromas that want to be swallowed up by the stems. Starts out a little reserved but builds on the palate with real power and depth. Dark cherry and raspberry notes in abundance, with layers and layers unfolding in the bottle for hours. Totally engaging. Screw cap. 13.5% alc. **Rating** 97 **To** 2028 $40 TL ✪

ŸŸŸŸŸ **Mappinga Shiraz 2018** Finely sculpted, with sophisticated balance of flavour and structure, delicious concentration of blacker fruits and berries, with fresh acidity, lip-smacking tannins, and white-pepper-led spices. Ticks all the boxes. Screw cap. 14.5% alc. **Rating** 96 **To** 2030 $60 TL ✪

Adelaide Hills Sauvignon Blanc 2020 A fragrant blossom-filled bouquet, with tropical notes feeding through to a lively, juicy palate that presents a dual stream of citrus and passionfruit flavours. Has the effortless charm that many sauvignon blancs lack. Ready now. Screw cap. 12% alc. **Rating** 95 **To** 2022 $22 JH ✪

Adelaide Hills Chardonnay 2020 Styled to be most respectful to the best that Hills fruit can offer, sourced across the best estate and grower blocks. Multi-clonal and cleverly steered through a range of barrel sizes (25% new). It's all about crisp, ripe stone fruit and subtle citrus-focused chardonnay with delightfully balanced oak sitting in support, developing a creamy palate while holding excellent length. Great value. Screw cap. 13% alc. **Rating** 95 **To** 2025 $24 TL ✪

777 Adelaide Hills Pinot Noir 2019 This 777 has an enticing aromatic that reflects its 30% whole-bunch inclusion. A delicate leafiness and mineral earthiness add savoury and terroir notes; spiced black cherry flavours following. Deliciously balanced, the palate is lively from fruit lift, and the acidity finishes with restraint. Screw cap. 13.5% alc. **Rating** 95 **To** 2028 $40 TL

Adelaide Hills Shiraz 2019 Quintessential Adelaide Hills shiraz. Dark berries and aromatic garden herbs, swirling fruit with a classy Amaro bitters edge and fine tannins providing a gently chewiness. A terrific expression of region and variety. Screw cap. 14% alc. **Rating** 95 **To** 2028 $26 TL ✪

Adelaide Hills Pinot Blanc 2020 Steered towards the fresh and crisp side of the variety's capacities with gentle treatment in hand picking, wild fermentation to start, then straight to barrel. It all contributes to a clear, citrus sense, specifically yellow grapefruit in its aromatics and flavours. A tiny sprinkle of sugariness for balance, some pithiness and bright acidity for textural feels. Mouth-watering. A top aperitif. Screw cap. 12.7% alc. **Rating** 94 **To** 2023 $24 TL ✪

Adelaide Hills Pinot Noir 2019 Fragrant with crushed red berries and flowering blackcurrant, slipping into black cherry. There's a delicate sourness and tangy acidity, lifting energy levels on the palate with light tannins holding everything together. Screw cap. 12.5% alc. **Rating** 94 **To** 2026 $32 TL

🍷🍷🍷🍷 **Adelaide Hills Pinot Gris 2020 Rating** 93 **To** 2023 $22 TL ✪
Mappinga Fumé Blanc 2019 Rating 92 **To** 2025 $35 TL
Adelaide Hills Rosé 2020 Rating 90 **To** 2023 $24 TL

Signature Wines   ★★★★
31 King Street, Norwood, SA 5067 **Region** Adelaide Hills
T (08) 8362 2020 **www.**signaturewines.com.au **Open** Wed–Sat 12–10
Winemaker Warwick Billings (Contract) **Est.** 2011 **Dozens** 15 000 **Vyds** 16ha
Signature Wines, owned by Daniel Khouzam and family, has formed a special relationship with core growers in the Adelaide Hills and the greater Barossa, complementing their own vineyards in the same regions and McLaren Vale. Daniel has been in the industry for over 20 years, and during that time has slowly developed its export markets. Previously operating out of the one-time Penfolds winery in the Eden Valley, Signature Wines moved to the leafy Adelaide suburb of Norwood in 2015, where it claims to have Adelaide's largest urban cellar door. Exports to Singapore, Japan and China.

🍷🍷🍷🍷 **Co-ordinates Range Adelaide Hills Tempinot 2019** Not something you see every day: a 60/40% tempranillo/pinot noir blend, the pinot matured for 8 months in barrels. The pinot rules the nose and softens the tempranillo on the palate, the flavour senses in the black cherry and cola territory. A bet each way. Palate acidity is lively, tannins supportive. Quirky yet worth the adventure. Screw cap. 13% alc. **Rating** 92 **To** 2026 $35 TL
Co-ordinates Range Adelaide Hills Sauvignon Blanc 2019 A remarkably textured sauvignon, given it has had no skin or oak impact. Perhaps lees contact in tank has done the work here: lovely fruit salad, grapefruit and faint fennel-like notes. Screw cap. 12% alc. **Rating** 91 **To** 2024 $27 TL

Silkman Wines   ★★★★★
c/- The Small Winemakers Centre, McDonalds Road, Pokolbin, NSW 2320
Region Hunter Valley
T 0414 800 256 **www.**silkmanwines.com.au **Open** 7 days 10–5
Winemaker Shaun Silkman, Liz Silkman **Est.** 2013 **Dozens** 4000
Winemaking couple Shaun and Liz Silkman (one-time dux of the Len Evans Tutorial) were both born and raised in the Hunter Valley. They both worked many vintages (both in Australia and abroad) before joining forces at First Creek Wines, where Liz is senior winemaker. This gives them the opportunity to make small quantities of the 3 classic varieties of the Hunter Valley: semillon, chardonnay and shiraz. Unsurprisingly, the wines so far released have been of outstanding quality. Exports to the the UK, the US and China.

🍷🍷🍷🍷🍷 **Reserve Hunter Valley Semillon 2014** Softer than the single-vineyard expression, yet no less a wine because of it. Lemon drop, yellow gummy bear, tonic, quince and toast. A lovely flow from fore to a very long aft. The acidity, buried amid the fruit essences as they are unpeeled with time and the wine's effusive freshness. Delicious drinking. Screw cap. 10.5% alc. **Rating** 95 **To** 2026 $50 NG
Reserve Hunter Valley Shiraz 2019 Medium bodied. Savoury. Floral. Firmly of the Hunter River 'Burgundy' idiom. Leather, suede, sweet cherry and fecund loamy earth scents. The tannins are wiry, lithe and expansive as they corral the fruit without impinging on its exuberance and the drinker's enjoyment. This is delicious. Again, a deft touch shines through this address' shiraz. If you are after something heavy, go elsewhere. Screw cap. 13.5% alc. **Rating** 95 **To** 2028 $50 NG

🍷🍷🍷🍷 **Single Vineyard Chardonnay 2019 Rating** 93 **To** 2028 $60 NG
Hunter Valley Shiraz 2019 Rating 92 **To** 2026 $30 NG

Silkwood Estate

2280 Channybearup Road, Pemberton, WA 6260 **Region** Pemberton
T (08) 9776 1584 **www.**silkwoodestate.com.au **Open** Fri–Mon & public hols 10–4
Winemaker Michael Ng **Est.** 1998 **Dozens** 20 000 **Vyds** 25ha

Silkwood Wines has been owned by the Bowman family since 2004. The vineyard is patrolled by a large flock of guinea fowl, eliminating most insect pests and reducing the use of chemicals. In '05 the adjoining vineyard was purchased, lifting the estate plantings to 23.5ha, which include shiraz, cabernet sauvignon, merlot, sauvignon blanc, chardonnay, pinot noir, riesling and zinfandel. The cellar door, restaurant and 4 luxury chalets overlook the large lake on the property. Exports to Malaysia, Singapore and China.

ŸŸŸŸŸ **The Bowman Pemberton Chardonnay 2020** A blend of 3 clones, wild ferment in barrel (50% new). Curry leaf, white peach, brine and apple. On the palate it follows suit. This is elegant and fine with a distinct saline curve through the finish. Screw cap. 13.5% alc. **Rating** 95 **To** 2031 $55 EL
The Walcott Pemberton Chardonnay 2020 Crushed cashew, white peach and layers of brine, rockmelon, pear and nectarine. More complex and layered than the Bowers chardonnay of the same vintage. This is very classy. Screw cap. 13% alc. **Rating** 94 **To** 2028 $30 EL ⊕
The Walcott Pemberton Shiraz 2019 Supple and chewy, this bursts with ripe red berries and lush spice that speaks of juniper berries, Bengal pepper and star anise. Very pretty, lithe, syrah-styled shiraz. A lot going on, a lot to like. Screw cap. 13.5% alc. **Rating** 94 **To** 2028 $30 EL ⊕

ŸŸŸŸŸ **The Bowers Pemberton Chardonnay 2020 Rating** 92 **To** 2027 $21 EL ⊕
The Walcott Pemberton Cabernet Sauvignon 2019 Rating 92 **To** 2028 $30 EL
The Bowman Pemberton Cabernet Sauvignon 2019 Rating 92 **To** 2031 $55 EL
The Walcott Pemberton Riesling 2020 Rating 91 **To** 2036 $28 EL
The Bowers Pemberton Pinot Noir Rosé 2020 Rating 91 **To** 2027 $21 EL ⊕
The Walcott Pemberton Pinot Noir 2020 Rating 90 **To** 2028 $30 EL

Silver Lining

60 Gleneagles Road, Mount Osmond, SA 5064 **Region** Adelaide Hills
T 0438 736 052 **www.**silverliningwine.com.au
Winemaker Leigh Ratzmer, Marty Edwards **Est.** 2020 **Dozens** 1200

The name alone says a lot about the positive and life-affirming attitude of this new venture by Marty Edwards, whose love of the Adelaide Hills was nurtured by his family's pioneering involvement with The Lane Vineyard in Hahndorf. They have all left that business now but after being diagnosed with Parkinson's Disease in 2012, Marty (previously an elite navy clearance diver) decided he still had a lot more to give. He focused on his health and young family, but couldn't give up his passion for Hills vineyards and wines. Silver Lining Wines was the result, with proceeds going to Parkinson's Disease research with the aim of helping others on the same challenging journey as this inspiring vigneron. Exports to the UK. (TL)

ŸŸŸŸŸ **Adelaide Hills Chardonnay 2020** From the Macclesfield district. This chardonnay is cast in a tight and linear style, clear and crisp with delicate opening lines that rise to burst with typical Hills white stone fruit and lemon-like acidity. After a short time in new and seasoned French barrels there's a faint background of lemon-zested cream biscuit. It's delicious. Deceptively so. Screw cap. 13% alc. **Rating** 94 **To** 2028 $30 TL ⊕
Adelaide Hills Shiraz 2020 The blueberry and blue floral notes to begin are vibrant and seductive, white pepper dusting the air. Fruit is sweet and smashable, with a line of sarsaparilla on the palate. There's a lot to be joyful about in this wine. Screw cap. 14% alc. **Rating** 94 **To** 2026 $35 TL

ŸŸŸŸŸ **Adelaide Hills Sauvignon Blanc 2020 Rating** 93 **To** 2025 $25 TL ⊕

Silver Spoon Estate

503 Heathcote-Rochester Road, Heathcote, Mount Camel, Vic 3523 **Region** Heathcote
T 0412 868 236 **www**.silverspoonestate.com.au **Open** W'ends 11–5 or by appt
Winemaker Peter Young **Est.** 2008 **Dozens** 1500 **Vyds** 22ha
When Peter and Tracie Young purchased an existing shiraz vineyard on the top of the
Mt Camel Range in 2008, they did not waste any time. They immediately planted a second
vineyard, constructed a small winery and in '13 acquired a neighbouring vineyard. The estate
name comes from the Silver Spoon fault line that delineates the Cambrian volcanic rock from
the old silver mines on the property. Peter became familiar with vineyards when working
in the 1970s as a geologist in the Hunter Valley and he more recently completed the master
of wine technology and viticulture degree at The University of Melbourne. Exports to China.

ŸŸŸŸŸ **The Ensemble Heathcote Shiraz Viognier 2018** From a dry ripening season,
The Ensemble generally tends towards riper, higher alcohols as evidenced here,
but there is also firm structure in 2018, and the intrinsic aromatic lift that viognier
brings. Plenty of upfront regional appeal with violet, black fruits, blackstrap
licorice and Middle Eastern spice. Finishes smooth and long. Screw cap. 15% alc.
Rating 90 **To** 2028 $35 JP

ŸŸŸŸ **Star Seeker Heathcote Shiraz Grenache 2017 Rating** 89 **To** 2025 $24 JP
The Fandango Heathcote Dry Red 2018 Rating 88 **To** 2024 $25 JP

Silverstream Wines

241 Scotsdale Road, Denmark, WA 6333 **Region** Denmark
T (08) 9848 2767 **www**.silverstreamwines.com **Open** Summer Tues–Sun 11–5, winter
by appt
Winemaker Michael Garland **Est.** 1997 **Dozens** 2500 **Vyds** 9ha
Tony and Felicity Ruse have 9ha of chardonnay, merlot, cabernet franc, pinot noir, riesling and
viognier in their vineyard 23km from Denmark. The wines are contract-made and, after some
hesitation, the Ruses decided their very pretty garden and orchard more than justified opening
a cellar door, a decision supported by the quality of the wines on offer at very reasonable
prices. Exports to the UK, Singapore and Japan.

ŸŸŸŸŸ **Limited Release Denmark Riesling 2018** In the hands of winemaker Andrew
Hoadley, who crafted the Limited Release range in 2018, this unexpected riesling
makes perfect sense; zippy, texturally complex, layered and long. Hoadley has a
way with wines that defies one's ability/desire to write down tech specifics …
you learn to just put down the pen, pick up a glass and listen. It's an undefinable
energy that he injects into his wines. This has a plush cheesecloth character on
the palate that begs another sip. And another. And, it's gone. Screw cap. 12.4% alc.
Rating 97 **To** 2041 $32 EL ✪

ŸŸŸŸŸ **Single Vineyard Denmark Cabernet Franc 2018** Pretty and fine, both
aromatically and flavour-wise. The tannins are the standout feature of this wine;
they are fine, chalky and cleverly woven through the fruit. Present at every stage of
the mouthful – they never overstay their welcome. A very elegant wine. Screw cap.
14.5% alc. **Rating** 95 **To** 2027 $30 EL ✪

ŸŸŸŸŸ **Denmark Blanc de Blancs 2014 Rating** 93 $38 EL
Cuvée Pinot Chardonnay 2011 Rating 93 $35 EL
Single Vineyard Denmark Pinot Noir 2018 Rating 92 **To** 2027 $35 EL

Simão & Co

PO Box 231, Rutherglen, Vic 3685 **Region** North East Victoria
T 0439 459 183 **www**.simaoandco.com.au
Winemaker Simon Killeen **Est.** 2014 **Dozens** 800
Simão is Portuguese for Simon, an inspiration far from Rutherglen where Simon Killeen
was born and bred. He grew up with vines all around him, and knew from an early age he

was going to become a winemaker. After working in wineries across Australia, France and Portugal he returned home to establish Simão & Co in 2014. It leaves time for him, by one means or another, to watch every minute of every game played by the Geelong Cats and hunt down the ruins of ghost wineries around Rutherglen.

 Simon Tolley Wines ★★★★

278 Bird In Hand Road, Woodside, SA 5244 **Region** Adelaide Hills
T 0400 710 677 **www**.simontolley.com.au **Open** 11–5 Thurs–Fri
Winemaker Simon Tolley, Leigh Ratzmer **Est.** 2015 **Dozens** 2000 **Vyds** 40ha
Simon Tolley is a 5th-generation grape grower who has managed vineyards across SA from Padthaway and Naracoorte to Clare and McLaren Vale as well as Margaret River in WA. Based in the Adelaide Hills, where he first worked in a technical role, then as a contract services manager and a regional manager, he also creates his own range of regionally suited sauvignon blanc, chardonnay, pinot noir and syrah, concentrating on growing specific clones in his family estate vineyard at Woodside. (TL)

🍷🍷🍷🍷🍷 **Perfectus Adelaide Hills Pinot Noir 2020** A small parcel only, from a block in the Verdun village. There's an earthy, gravelly note here to begin, with a pretty decent peppery, rocket-like spice hit on the palate that adds some gravitas to the cherry fruit notes. Quite captivating and well crafted. Screw cap. 13.5% alc. **Rating** 94 **To** 2027 $50 TL

🍷🍷🍷🍷🍷 **Perfectus Adelaide Hills Syrah 2017** **Rating** 92 **To** 2028 $50 TL
Adelaide Hills Pinot Noir 2020 **Rating** 91 **To** 2025 $30 TL
Perfectus Adelaide Hills Pinot Noir 2019 **Rating** 91 **To** 2025 $50 TL

Simonsens ★★★

30 Pax Parade, Curlewis, Vic 3222 **Region** Geelong
T (03) 5250 3861 **www**.barrgowanvineyard.com.au **Open** By appt
Winemaker Dick Simonsen **Est.** 1998 **Dozens** 150 **Vyds** 0.2ha
Dick and Dib (Elizabeth) Simonsen began planting their shiraz (with 5 clones) in 1994, intending to make wine for their own consumption. With all clones in full production, the Simonsens make a maximum of 200 dozen and accordingly release small quantities of Shiraz, which sell out quickly. The vines are hand pruned, the grapes hand picked, the must basket-pressed, and all wine movements are by gravity.

🍷🍷🍷🍷 **Barrgowan Vineyard Bellarine Peninsula Shiraz 2019** An elegant, cool-climate style featuring lively plum, dark cherry, earthy rhubarb and spicy lift. The fruit, quite rightly, is the star here, with nicely honed tannins lending support. Diam. 13.4% alc. **Rating** 89 **To** 2025 $35 JP

Sinapius ★★★★☆

4232 Bridport Road, Pipers Brook, Tas 7254 **Region** Northern Tasmania
T 0418 998 665 **www**.sinapius.com.au **Open** Mon–Fri 11–5, w'ends 12–5
Winemaker Vaughn Dell, Linda Morice **Est.** 2005 **Dozens** 200 **Vyds** 4.3ha
Vaughn Dell and Linda Morice purchased the former Golders Vineyard in 2005 (planted in 1994). More recent vineyard plantings include 14 clones of pinot noir and 11 clones of chardonnay, as well as small amounts of grüner veltliner, pinot gris, pinot blanc, gewürztraminer, riesling and gamay. The vineyard is close-planted, the density up to a backbreaking 11110 vines/ha, with the fruiting wire 40cm above the ground. The wines are made with a minimalist approach: natural ferments, basket pressing, extended lees ageing and minimal fining and filtration. Tragically, Vaughn died suddenly, days after celebrating his 39th birthday, in May 2020. Australia has lost a winemaker of ultimate skill and vision shared by a small handful of others.

🍷🍷🍷🍷🍷 **Single Vineyard Close Planted Chardonnay 2019** It's impossible not to be sentimental about a wine like this, but that's not why I like it. Such purity and precision are why Pipers River is not just all about pinot noir. This cool site sings in soprano high notes of textbook white fruits, eloquently harmonised with classy French oak, carrying a finish of delightful acid line and enduring persistence. Vale Vaughn. Screw cap. 13% alc. **Rating** 94 **To** 2034 $55 TS

Sinclair of Scotsburn ★★★☆

256 Wiggins Road, Scotsburn, Vic 3352 **Region** Ballarat
T 0419 885 717 **www.**sinclairofscotsburn.com.au **Open** W'ends by appt
Winemaker Scott Ireland **Est.** 1997 **Dozens** 150 **Vyds** 2ha
The late David and Barbara Sinclair purchased their property in 2001, an acquisition that 'wasn't even on the horizon of plan B'. At that time 1.2ha of chardonnay and 0.8ha of pinot noir had been planted but had struggled, the pinot noir yielding less than 0.25t in '02. So began a steep viticultural learning curve for David and Barbara. Winemaker Scott Ireland (Provenance Wines) was the winemaker from the beginning, making wine under the Sinclair of Scotsburn label and his own Provenance wines. With the passing of David Sinclair in December 2020, the future of the Sinclair of Scotsburn vineyard and brand remains unclear.

ŶŶŶŶŶ **Wallijak Chardonnay 2018** Juicy and complex with layers of flavours and interest from white peach, grapefruit and quince to lemon curd and almond meal. Nicely measured vanillan oak caresses. Elegance and freshness live here. Screw cap. 13.3% alc. **Rating** 95 **To** 2028 $25 JP ✪

ŶŶŶŶŶ **Manor House Pinot Noir 2018 Rating** 90 **To** 2023 $25 JP

Singlefile Wines ★★★★★

90 Walter Road, Denmark, WA 6333 **Region** Great Southern
T 1300 885 807 **www.**singlefilewines.com **Open** 7 days 11–5
Winemaker Mike Garland, Coby Ladwig, Patrick Corbett **Est.** 2007 **Dozens** 10000
Vyds 3.75ha
In 1986 geologist Phil Snowden and wife Viv moved from South Africa to Perth, where they developed their successful multinational mining and resource services company, Snowden Resources. Following the sale of the company in 2004, they turned their attention to their long-held desire to make and enjoy fine wine. In '07 they bought an established vineyard (planted in '89) in the beautiful Denmark subregion. They pulled out the old shiraz and merlot vines, kept and planted more chardonnay and retained Larry Cherubino to set up partnerships with established vineyards in Frankland River, Porongurup, Denmark, Pemberton and Margaret River. The cellar door, tasting room and restaurant are strongly recommended. The consistency of the quality of the Singlefile wines is outstanding, as is their value for money. Exports to the US, Singapore, Japan, Hong Kong and China.

ŶŶŶŶŶ **The Vivienne Denmark Chardonnay 2018** This is a wine of great provenance, with singular intensity. The fruit flavours hinge on grapefruit zest and juice alike, tightly framed acidity is also centrally involved. French oak is present, but in no way threatens the fruit. This will outlive the patience of many of those who purchase it. Screw cap. 13% alc. **Rating** 97 **To** 2035 $100 JH ✪

ŶŶŶŶŶ **Single Vineyard Mount Barker Riesling 2020** All class, as befits its Blue Lake Vineyard birthplace. The blossom and talc bouquet is shadowed by the intense, crisp palate where Granny Smith apple, crisp lemon-and-lime infusion, and detailed acidity carry the wine to a vibrantly fresh finish. Screw cap. 11.9% alc. **Rating** 96 **To** 2035 $35 JH ✪
Family Reserve Single Vineyard Denmark Chardonnay 2019 Chilled overnight and whole-bunch pressed direct to French barriques (40% new) for fermentation and 10% mlf, stirred weekly for 6 months. Opens with touches of smoky oak/grilled cashew on the bouquet. White peach, citrus and nashi pear follow on the long palate, which has layers of texture. Screw cap. 13.2% alc. **Rating** 96 **To** 2033 $60 JH ✪

Great Southern Chardonnay 2019 Chilled, whole-bunch pressed into French barriques (28% new). Lees stirred for 5 months, total time in oak 10 months. The oak is obvious on the bouquet, but fruit takes command on the rich and intense palate – grapefruit wrapped around white peach. Screw cap. 13.3% alc. **Rating** 96 To 2033 $30 JH ✪

Single Vineyard Frankland River Shiraz 2019 Frankland River is arguably the epicentre of Great Southern shiraz, the Riversdale Vineyard always in the frame. There is a combination of blackberry, pepper, spice and red licorice, classy tannins underwriting the longevity of a very good wine. Screw cap. 14.5% alc. **Rating** 96 To 2044 $39 JH ✪

The Philip Adrian Frankland River Cabernet Sauvignon 2018 Hand picked, 2 weeks cold soak, 6 weeks post-ferment maceration, pressed to French oak (50% new) for 14 months maturation. A sophisticated wine built for the long haul, not early consumption. It demands and deserves respect. Screw cap. 14.2% alc. **Rating** 96 To 2043 $100 JH

Run Free by Singlefile Riesling 2020 Great Southern fruit. The bright, crisp, mineral edge to the fruit is derived from the high acidity (8.7g/L) and nigh-on zero RS. Bursting with tingling lime sherbet flavours and aftertaste. Screw cap. 11.1% alc. **Rating** 94 To 2032 $25 JH ✪

Single Vineyard Pemberton Fumé Blanc 2020 There's plenty happening here, with mouth-pleasing tropical notes in a filigree of oak that has as much to do with structure as flavour. Ready now, although the citrussy acidity will underwrite its medium-term future. Screw cap. 12.5% alc. **Rating** 94 To 2023 $35 JH

Run Free by Singlefile Chardonnay 2019 Pressed direct to French barriques for a slow ferment and 8 months maturation, no mlf. White peach/nectarine/grapefruit sing together, oak spice a whisper. Overall intensity and length are impressive. Bargain. Screw cap. 13.4% alc. **Rating** 94 To 2029 $25 JH ✪

ŸŸŸŸŸ **Great Southern Malbec 2019 Rating** 93 To 2025 $25 JH ✪
Clement V 2019 Rating 92 To 2030 $35 JH
Great Southern Tempranillo 2019 Rating 92 To 2029 $25 JH ✪
Run Free by Singlefile Sauvignon Blanc 2020 Rating 91 To 2022 $25 JH
Run Free by Singlefile Shiraz 2019 Rating 91 To 2029 $25 JH

Sirromet Wines ★★★★

850 Mount Cotton Road, Mount Cotton, Qld 4165 **Region** Granite Belt
T (07) 3206 2999 **www.**sirromet.com **Open** 7 days 10–5
Winemaker Mike Hayes **Est.** 1999 **Dozens** 55 000 **Vyds** 30ha
An ambitious venture that succeeded in its aim of creating Qld's premier winery. The founding Morris family commissioned a leading architect to design the striking state-of-the-art winery; the state's foremost viticultural consultant to plant 3 major vineyards (in the Granite Belt); and the most skilled winemaker practising in Qld, Adam Chapman, to make the wine. It has a 200-seat restaurant and a wine club, and is firmly aimed at the tourist market, hosting 'a day on the green' concerts, taking full advantage of its location between Brisbane and the Gold Coast. Twenty years on, winemaker Mike Hayes (ASVO Winemaker of the Year 2017) is now at the helm. Mike is championing a shift in focus to emerging varieties, such as vermentino, fiano, pecorino, montepulciano, lagrein and aglianico, to withstand the warmer temperatures and lower rainfall of climate change. Exports to China, Japan and the US.

ŸŸŸŸŸ **Granite Belt Cabernet Sauvignon Shiraz 2019** Vibrant, crunchy, energetic and enduring, expressing the cool energy of the heights of the Granite Belt. Vibrant, medium purple hue. Brimming with tangy blackcurrant/berry fruit and screaming out for cellaring, thanks more to pronounced tangy acidity than bony, medium-grained tannins. Leading out strong and lively, it concludes a little short, but may build in time. Screw cap. 13.8% alc. **Rating** 91 To 2036 $50 TS

Sister's Run

PO Box 148, McLaren Vale, SA 5171 **Region** Barossa Valley/McLaren Vale/Coonawarra
T (08) 8323 8979 **www**.sistersrun.com.au
Winemaker Elena Brooks **Est.** 2001
Sister's Run is now part of the Brooks family empire, the highly experienced Elena Brooks making the wines. The Stiletto and Boot on the label are those of Elena, and the motto 'The truth is in the vineyard, but the proof is in the glass' is, I (James) would guess, the work of marketer extraordinaire husband Zar Brooks. Exports to all major markets.

ΨΨΨΨΨ **Bethlehem Block Gomersal Barossa Cabernet Sauvignon 2018** Give this
a little air and it will open up before your eyes. It has lovely ripe cabernet fruit in the blackberry spectrum with a delicate waft of mint-choc in the rear. Simple, well-toned fruit and even structures across the palate offer a good-value, easygoing cabernet that is ready to go now and might surprise with a few more years in its quiver. Screw cap. 14% alc. **Rating** 93 **To** 2028 $23 TL ✪
Calvary Hill Lyndoch Barossa Shiraz 2018 Rich, chocolatey plum, sweeter Asian and baking spices all weave together in this delicious, straight-up-and-down Barossa shiraz. Whatever oak has been employed offers a backdrop only. Simple pleasures. Screw cap. 14.5% alc. **Rating** 92 **To** 2026 $23 TL ✪

Sittella Wines

100 Barrett Street, Herne Hill, WA 6056 **Region** Swan Valley
T (08) 9296 2600 **www**.sittella.com.au **Open** Tues–Sun & public hols 11–5
Winemaker Colby Quirk, Yuri Berns **Est.** 1998 **Dozens** 15000 **Vyds** 25ha
Simon and Maaike Berns acquired a 7ha block (with 5ha of vines) at Herne Hill, making the first wine in 1998 and opening a most attractive cellar door facility. They also own the Wildberry Estate Vineyard in Margaret River. Plantings in Margaret River have increased with new clones of cabernet sauvignon, cabernet franc, P95 chardonnay and malbec. New clones of tempranillo and touriga nacional have also been added to the Swan Valley plantings. Consistent and significant wine show success has brought well deserved recognition for the wines. Exports to Japan and China.

ΨΨΨΨΨ **A-G Rare Series Golden Mile Swan Valley Grenache 2020** Boiled
raspberry lolly on the nose; both muscular and fine on the palate, with layers of salted blackberry, rosewater, strawberry pastille and red licorice. The Swan Valley GI gives a real tannic grunt to the finish, saving it from 'pretty' and elevating it to serious. Screw cap. 13.5% alc. **Rating** 96 **To** 2036 $50 EL ✪
Pedro Ximénez NV Rich and dense this is mini (tiny bottle) yet mighty. Luscious quince and dried fig are slathered upon nutmeg, date, toffee and crushed coffee grounds. The rancio characters that provide bitter foil to the sweetness on the palate serve only to engage and draw you back in for more. An astoundingly delicious wine of poise and stature. Length, too. 350ml. Screw cap. 18.5% alc.
Rating 96 $50 EL ✪
Cuvée Rosé Brut NV Disgorged 21 Mar '20. Rose petals, strawberry, red apple skins and pink peppercorn are overlaid by very fine market spice and curls of saffron. The fine acidity weaves the chalky phenolics and the fruit together. All in all, extremely classy, and clearly one of, if not the, greatest sparkling rosé in Western Australia released to date. Cork. 12.5% alc. **Rating** 95 $34 EL ✪ ♥
Show Reserve Liqueur Muscat NV This is viscous and dense. The older material from the solera is evident both visually and on the palate. Dense, rich and full of flavour, which carries on long after the wine has left the mouth. Not as complex as the Pedro Ximénez, but succulent, luxurious and very satisfying nonetheless. 375ml. Cork. 18.5% alc. **Rating** 95 $44 EL
Reserve Wilyabrup Margaret River Chardonnay 2020 From the Buckshot Ridge vineyard in Wilyabrup. High-impact toasty oak overlays intense yellow peach and red apple fruit on the palate. The fruit has very good concentration, almost piercing. Don't touch it for a year or so, or at the very least decant it – it

needs either the oxygen or your patience. Impressive wine. Screw cap. 13% alc.
Rating 94 **To** 2032 $37 EL

Avant-Garde Series Blanc de Blancs NV Méthode traditionnelle. Savoury, salty and layered with crushed nuts, preserved citrus and cheesecloth. Zero dosage, as the fruit has more than enough plush ripeness, making the need for extra sugar redundant. This is long and complex, with a real ripple to the flavour extension across the palate. Another classy sparkling release from Sittella. Cork. 12.5% alc. **Rating** 94 $50 EL

 **Reserve Swan Valley Shiraz 2020** Rating 93 To 2031 $29 EL
Cuvée Blanc NV Rating 93 $32 EL
Reserve Single Vineyard Margaret River Cabernet Malbec 2019
Rating 92 To 2036 $30 EL
Avant-Garde Series Swan Valley Tempranillo Touriga 2020 Rating 92
To 2031 $40 EL
Marie Christien Lugten Grand Vintage 2015 Rating 92 $45 EL
Vintage Fortified Shiraz Touriga 2019 Rating 92 $60 EL
El Vivero Blanco Swan Valley 2020 Rating 91 To 2024 EL
Swan Valley Chenin Blanc 2020 Rating 90 To 2027 $20 EL ✪

🍂 Sixty Eight Roses   ★★★☆

68 Chilton Road, Berri, SA 5343 **Region** Riverland
T 0416 983 720 **www.**sixtyeightroses.com.au
Winemaker Eric Semmler **Est.** 2020 **Dozens** 250 **Vyds** 8ha
Named for the roses dotting the property Theodora and George Koutsoukis have farmed since the 1970s. Originally from Greece, they met in Australia, raised a family of 4 and the Berri farm, rich with rows of orchards of apricots, pears and plums, and grapevines. Their son John is behind the Sixty Eight Roses wine label, which began in earnest in 2020 with the inaugural release of a 2019 syrah off vines planted by his parents 48 years ago. He's dreaming big. Plantings of alternative varieties are underway and certified organics is part of the story. (JF)

 Riverland Syrah 2019 Smells of Black Forest cake and cherry compote infused with licorice, an enticing start. A fair amount of smoky/charry flavours but pleasingly, it's not a big or overly rich wine. The tannins are ripe, supple and there's a softness throughout with a hint of raspberry acidity, with sweet fruit accents rendering this slurpy and refreshing. This is the first commercial release from Sixty Eight Roses. Bravo. Screw cap. 14.1% alc. **Rating** 91 **To** 2026 $25 JF

Small Island Wines   ★★★★

Drink Co, Shop 10, 33 Salamanca Place, Hobart, Tas 7004 **Region** Southern Tasmania
T 0414 896 930 **www.**smallislandwines.com **Open** Mon–Sat 10–8
Winemaker James Broinowski **Est.** 2015 **Dozens** 750 **Vyds** 4ha
Tasmanian-born James Broinowski completed his bachelor of viticulture and oenology at the University of Adelaide in 2013. He was faced with the same problem as many other young graduates wanting to strike out on their own: cash. While others in his predicament may have found the same solution, his was the first wine venture to successfully seek crowdfunding. The first year ('15) allowed him to purchase pinot noir from Glengarry in the north of the island, making 2100 bottles of pinot noir that won a gold medal at the Royal International Hobart Wine Show '16; and 200 bottles of rosé that sold out in 4 days at the Taste of Tasmania Festival '15. In '16 he was able to buy pinot from the highly rated Gala Estate on the east coast and back up the '15 purchase from the Glengarry Vineyard with a '16 purchase. It looks very much like a potential acorn-to-oak story, for the quality of the wines is seriously good.

Glengarry Single Vineyard Pinot Gris 2020 Skin contact builds a gris of full straw colour, richness, texture and structure. Ripe, spicy pear and grapefruit of generous, oily flesh are cut with cool Tasmanian acidity. Firm skin phenolics make for a finish of bite and grip, with almost (but not quite) the fruit length and presence to hold it. Screw cap. 13.5% alc. **Rating** 89 **To** 2022 $35 TS

Patsie's Blush Rosé 2020 Pretty, pale salmon/copper hue. A complex, savoury and serious rosé of ginger and spice, cut with pink grapefruit and tense lemon. Pronounced acidity holds a long finish, promising medium-term endurance in the cellar. Screw cap. 13.5% alc. **Rating** 89 **To** 2025 $35 TS

Smallfry Wines

13 Murray Street, Angaston, SA 5353 **Region** Barossa Valley/Eden Valley
T 0412 153 243 **www**.smallfrywines.com.au **Open** By appt
Winemaker Wayne Ahrens **Est.** 2005 **Dozens** 5000 **Vyds** 27ha
The engagingly named Smallfry Wines is the venture of Wayne Ahrens and partner Suzi Hilder. Wayne is from a 5th-generation Barossa family; Suzi is the daughter of well-known Upper Hunter viticulturist Richard Hilder and wife Del, former partners in Pyramid Hill Wines. Both have degrees from CSU, and both have extensive experience – Suzi was a consultant viticulturist, and Wayne's track record includes 7 vintages as a cellar hand at Orlando Wyndham and other smaller Barossa wineries. Their vineyards in the Eden Valley (led by cabernet sauvignon and riesling) and the Vine Vale area of the Barossa Valley (shiraz, grenache, semillon, mourvèdre, cabernet sauvignon and riesling) are certified biodynamic/organic. Exports to the US, Canada, Denmark, South Korea, Malaysia, Singapore, Hong Kong, Japan and China.

Smallwater Estate

52 Tramline Rd, Newlands WA 6251 **Region** Geographe
T (08) 9731 6036 **www**.smallwaterestate.com **Open** Sat–Sun 10–4
Winemaker Bruce Dukes, Remi Guise **Est.** 1993 **Dozens** 2500 **Vyds** 7.2ha
Smallwater Estate was planted in 1993 by John Small and his late wife Robyn, with the intention of developing a marron farm and a vineyard to grow contract grapes. After selling grapes to other wineries for over a decade, in 2005 John decided to make wine under the Smallwater Estate label. The 2006 release was small (zinfandel, 250 dozens), however since then, production has grown tenfold. Smallwater Estate focuses on shiraz, zinfandel, cabernet sauvignon, sauvignon blanc and chardonnay. (EL)

🍷🍷🍷🍷🍷 **Geographe Shiraz 2019** Pomegranate, blackberry, mulberry and raspberry are the first to jostle out of the glass, followed closely by red licorice, vanilla pod and anise. The palate is inky, layered and spicy, weaving its way across the tongue in a most hypnotic fashion. Good length of flavour finishes this off. Shiraz is another of Geographe's weapons, for this reason. One gold and 3 trophies Geographe Wine Show '20. Screw cap. 15.2% alc. **Rating** 95 **To** 2031 $35 EL ⊘

🍷🍷🍷🍷🍷 **Unwooded Geographe Chardonnay 2020 Rating** 90 **To** 2023 $22 EL

Smeaton Estate ★★★★☆

Level 1, 206 Greenhill Road, Eastwood, SA 5063 (postal) **Region** Adelaide Hills
T 0429 109 537 **www**.smeaton.estate
Winemaker Con Moshos **Est.** 1996 **Dozens** 450 **Vyds** 25ha
Janice and John Smeaton have planted their Martin Hill Vineyard to shiraz (6.5ha), sauvignon blanc (5.2ha), semillon (4.5ha), chardonnay (4ha), merlot (2.9ha), riesling (1.3ha) and pinot gris (0.6ha). The intention was to sell the grapes to Adelaide Hills wineries and this has been implemented. But in 2017 they teamed up with Con Moshos, an Adelaide Hills veteran with longstanding close ties to Brian Croser, to make 450 dozen of riesling. The wine is sold to retailers/wholesalers and if other wines are made in the future, they would be marketed the same way.

Smidge Wines ★★★★★

150 Tatachilla Road, McLaren Vale, SA 5171 **Region** McLaren Vale
T 0419 839 964 **www**.smidgewines.com **Open** By appt
Winemaker Matt Wenk **Est.** 2004 **Dozens** 5000 **Vyds** 4.1ha

Smidge Wines is owned by Matt Wenk and wife Trish Callaghan. It was for many years an out-of-hours occupation for Matt; his day job was as winemaker for Two Hands Wines (and Sandow's End). In 2013 he retired from Two Hands and plans to increase production of Smidge to 8000 dozen over the next few years. His retirement meant the Smidge wines could no longer be made at Two Hands and the winemaking operations have been moved to McLaren Vale, where Smidge is currently leasing a small winery. Smidge owns the vineyard in Willunga that provides the grapes for all the cabernet sauvignon releases and some of the McLaren Vale shiraz. The vision is to build a modern customised facility on the Willunga property in the not-too-distant future. The Magic Dirt shiraz wines are made in the same way, the purpose to show the impact of terroir on each wine: 14–16 days in an open fermenter, then after 10 months in barrel a selection of the best barrel is transferred to a single 2yo French barrique and a further 14 months of maturation follows. Exports to the UK, the US, South Korea and China.

🍷🍷🍷🍷🍷 **Pedra Branca VP 2018** A port for the big-dry-red drinker due to its contextual restraint. Far from cloying, it reels off thrilling aromas of cherry pith, blackberry, Chinese medicine, lilac, clove, pepper and suede. The tannins are impeccably hewn, chamois of feel. Real thrust of structure and parry of fruit. Immaculate and impressively long. Kudos! Screw cap. 17% alc. **Rating** 96 $45 NG ✪

Akeringa McLaren Vale Cabernet Sauvignon 2018 Matured for 2 years in (100% new) extra-tight-grained Cadus hogsheads. Fermented in open-top vessels on skins left dry. The skins serve as a conduit for pithy, nourishing, fine-grained tannins. Cassis, vanilla, bouquet garni, black cherry, kirsch and pencil lead. Savoury, saline and energetic. A beautifully made wine that is textural, impeccably detailed and undeniably salubrious. Plenty in the tank. Screw cap. 14.5% alc. **Rating** 95 To 2035 $85 NG

Uno Momento McLaren Vale Montepulciano 2018 A great colour: explosive in terms of its pulpy, inky opacity and purple edges. It almost glows! Possibly the finest iteration of this wonderful variety in Australia to date. Everything about it makes me smile. Black-fruit allusions, smoked meats, iodine, ample florals and best of all, a broad dissection of the rich palate by ferruginous tannins: burly, gritty and shaped to draw saliva to ready one for the meal ahead. Screw cap. 14% alc. **Rating** 95 To 2025 $38 NG

La Grenouille McLaren Vale Cabernet Sauvignon 2018 A stellar year in which old vines and sumptuous fruit make for a winning combination. The oak hangs off this a bit more than on its '17 predecessor. Yet here the fruit is denser, more vinous and surely, with patience, will deliver the more compelling wine. Blackcurrant, olive, dried sage, graphite, a herbal potpourri and spearmint. Tense, burly and a bit closed. The length is the signature. Screw cap. 14.5% alc. **Rating** 94 To 2031 $38 NG

🍷🍷🍷🍷🍷 **La Grenouille McLaren Vale Cabernet Sauvignon 2017** **Rating** 93 To 2026 $38 NG
Houdini Adelaide Hills Sauvignon Blanc 2020 **Rating** 91 To 2023 $25 TL
Il Piano McLaren Vale Fiano 2020 **Rating** 93 To 2023 $38 NG

Smithbrook ★★★★

Smithbrook Road, Pemberton, WA 6260 **Region** Pemberton
T (08) 9750 2150 **www**.smithbrook.wine **Open** By appt
Winemaker Ben Rector **Est.** 1988 **Dozens** 10 000 **Vyds** 57ha

The picturesque Smithbrook property is owned by Perth businessman Peter Fogarty and family, who also own Lake's Folly in the Hunter Valley, Deep Woods Estate in Margaret River and Millbrook in the Perth Hills. Originally planted in the 1980s and one of the first in the

Pemberton region, the Smithbrook Vineyard covers over 57ha of the 110ha property and focuses on sauvignon blanc, chardonnay and merlot.

ŦŦŦŦŦ Single Vineyard Pemberton Pinot Noir 2020 The Pemberton character comes through on the finish, in the form of cherry bramble, strawberry, black-olive tapenade and white spice. Working backwards, the palate is fine, spicy and laden with cherries and strawberries. This is pretty, delicate and quite delicious. Screw cap. 13.5% alc. **Rating** 92 **To** 2025 $25 EL ✪

Single Vineyard Pemberton Merlot 2019 Quite frankly, this is delicious. It has jubilant fruit and bright acid that is countersunk into the flavours. It doesn't have the tannin structure required for ageing, but the length of flavour is good and there is an appealing purity about it. Screw cap. 14.5% alc. **Rating** 92 **To** 2028 $25 EL ✪

Estate Pemberton Red Blend 2019 The varietal mix changes each year: 2019 sees a predominance of cabernet sauvignon, complemented by merlot, cabernet franc and petit verdot. This is astoundingly good value for money. Eyewatering. It is straightforward/simple – but who cares about that at this price? It is delicious, bouncy, elegant, supple, fresh and straight-out yum. Screw cap. 14% alc. **Rating** 92 **To** 2026 $15 EL ✪

Single Vineyard Pemberton Chardonnay 2019 $25 doesn't usually get you the whole 'hand picked, wild ferment, barrel maturation' gambit, but here it does. Fruit feels on the slim side initially, but this has texture and flavour and interest. The faint metallic vibe on the mid palate is the only quibble. Screw cap. 12.5% alc. **Rating** 91 **To** 2025 $25 EL

Snake + Herring ★★★★☆

3763 Caves Road, Wilyabrup, WA 6284 **Region** South West Australia
T 0427 881 871 **www**.snakeandherring.com.au **Open** 7 days 11–5 summer, 11–4 winter
Winemaker Tony Davis **Est.** 2010 **Dozens** 12 000
Tony (Snake) Davis and Redmond (Herring) Sweeny both started university degrees before finding that they were utterly unsuited to their respective courses. Having stumbled across Margaret River, Tony's life changed forever; he enrolled at the University of Adelaide, thereafter doing vintages in the Eden Valley, Oregon, Beaujolais and Tasmania, before 3 years at Plantagenet, next Brown Brothers, then a senior winemaking role at Yalumba, a 6-year stint designing Millbrook Winery in the Perth Hills and 4 years with Howard Park in Margaret River. Redmond's circuitous course included a chartered accountancy degree and employment with an international accounting firm in Busselton, and the subsequent establishment of Forester Estate in 2001, in partnership with Kevin McKay. Back on home turf he is the marketing and financial controller of Snake + Herring. Exports to the US.

ŦŦŦŦŦ Corduroy Karridale Chardonnay 2019 Cap gun and curry leaf on the nose, the palate is creamy and plush. Cool-climate acidity is like a spike through the fruit, holding it all together, salivating to the finish. This has breadth and depth, with a salted/preserved lemon character tying it all to the jetty. Smart. Screw cap. 12.5% alc. **Rating** 95 **To** 2028 $45 EL

Perfect Day Margaret River Sauvignon Blanc Semillon 2020 There's a distinct cassis note on the nose here, accompanied by green apple, lemon pith, brine and a really succulent delicious 'something' on the back of the palate. The effect is totally moreish and refreshing. The texture is standout – fine chalky phenolics elevate it from 'uncomplicated' to great. Screw cap. 12% alc. **Rating** 94 **To** 2027 $25 EL ✪

Hallelujah Porongurup Chardonnay 2019 So much going on at once here: the fruit shows its peachy stuff, with a brilliantly mouth-watering concentration; the acidity (even more mouth-watering) carves a searing line through the fruit, elevating the wine. Nutty/creamy oak cushions it all. Screw cap. 13% alc. **Rating** 94 **To** 2028 $45 EL

Redemption Great Southern Syrah 2019 This is juicy and redolent with red snakes and a stemmy crunch woven through the very heart of it. Spices like star

anise and aniseed embroider the edges of the jubilant fruit. Quite delicious, more delicate than the ripper 2018. Screw cap. 13.5% alc. **Rating** 94 **To** 2031 $25 EL ✪
At First Sight Great Southern Grenache 2020 Definitely stemmy and definitely crunchy, possessed of brilliant flavour and colour intensity. A slight little wine, defined in part by very fine, chalky tannins. The fruit has a way of permeating the palate from front to back and hooking in another sip. Yes. Screw cap. 13.5% alc. **Rating** 94 **To** 2027 $25 EL ✪

🍷🍷🍷🍷🍷 **Sabotage Great Southern Riesling 2020** Rating 93 **To** 2031 $25 EL ✪
Outshined Wilyabrup Cabernet Sauvignon 2019 Rating 93 **To** 2030 $33 EL
Tainted Love Margaret River Syrah Rosé 2020 Rating 91 **To** 2022 $25 EL

Snobs Creek Wines ★★★

132 Tranter Road, Toolleen, Vic 3551 **Region** Heathcote
T (03) 9596 3043 **www.**snobscreekvineyard.com.au **Open** W'ends 10–5
Winemaker Marcus Gillon **Est.** 1996 **Dozens** 5000 **Vyds** 28.3ha
In the 1860s, well-respected West Indian shoemaker 'Black' Brookes occupied a cottage at the bridge over Cataract Creek. After he passed away in the late 1880s the creek was renamed Snobs Creek, 'snob' being an old English term for cobbler (shoe repairer). The original vineyard, founded by Alex Gillon, was situated where Snobs Creek joins the Goulburn River, 5km below the Lake Eildon wall. In 2019 Alex's son Marcus Gillon moved operations to Heathcote, with an all-new cellar door and winery. The vineyards, on the slopes of Mount Carmel, were to be planted in '20 but Covid intervened: new plantings of shiraz, nebbiolo, cabernet sauvignon and malbec are planned.

🍷🍷🍷🍷 **Cordwainer Adelaide Hills Chardonnay 2018** An expression of ripe Adelaide Hills chardonnay, high in textural appeal with ripe fruits aplenty. Melon, white peach, nectarine, baked quince with almond meal. Opens wide, expansive and long. Lees contact and French oak are both evident but remain in balance, contributing to the general deliciousness. Screw cap. 13.7% alc. **Rating** 89 **To** 2027 $25 JP
VSP Heathcote Shiraz 2018 A wine of intensity, equal to this noticeable dose of both French and American oak. Mocha/chocolate/vanilla oak makes its presence known on the bouquet, but it's better assimilated on the palate. The fruit isn't complaining. It's up to the task with a solid core of blackberry, pepper and spice. A strong statement of its Heathcote origin with complexity and length. Screw cap. 14.2% alc. **Rating** 89 **To** 2027 $25 JP
Corviser Eden Valley Pinot Noir 2018 An Eden Valley pinot noir is an uncommon occurrence, particularly for a Victorian producer. Gently guides the drinker in with light florals, violet, strawberry and cherry aromas. Complexity and richness are not the main driver here, rather a flurry of sweet berry fruits persisting in league with spiced compote, a background of dried herbs and balanced oak. That, and a fleshy textural mouthfeel. Drink now. Screw cap. 12.7% alc. **Rating** 88 **To** 2025 $25 JP

Sons of Eden

Penrice Road, Angaston, SA 5353 **Region** Barossa Valley
T (08) 8564 2363 **www.**sonsofeden.com **Open** 7 days 11–6
Winemaker Corey Ryan, Simon Cowham **Est.** 2000 **Dozens** 9000 **Vyds** 60ha
Corey Ryan and Simon Cowham both learnt and refined their skills in the vineyards and cellars of Eden Valley. Corey is a trained oenologist with over 20 vintages under his belt, having cut his teeth as a winemaker at Henschke. Thereafter he worked for Rouge Homme and Penfolds in Coonawarra, backed up by winemaking stints in the Rhône Valley and in 2002 he took the opportunity to work in NZ for Villa Maria Estates. In '07 he won the Institute of Masters of Wine scholarship. Simon has had a similarly international career covering such diverse organisations as Oddbins, UK and the Winemakers' Federation of Australia. Switching from

the business side to grapegrowing when he qualified as a viticulturist, he worked for Yalumba as technical manager of the Heggies and Pewsey Vale vineyards. With these backgrounds, it comes as no surprise to find that the estate-grown wines are of outstanding quality. Exports to the UK, the US, Germany, Switzerland, Hong Kong, the Philippines, Taiwan and China.

ŦŦŦŦŦ **Notus Barossa Valley Grenache 2020** Luminous purple hue. A thrilling young grenache of gorgeous fruit and beautifully eloquent structure. These old vines deliver wonderful life and energy, popping with mulberries, black cherries, satsuma plums and rhubarb, lifted with pristine rose petals. Powder-fine tannins complete a finish of very good – if not outstanding – persistence. Screw cap. 14.5% alc. **Rating** 95 **To** 2028 $54 TS
Cirrus Single Vineyard High Eden Valley Riesling 2020 True to the 2020 season, this is a rich and powerful yet high-tensile riesling, launching out ripe and full with baked apple and kaffir lime fruit, morphing through the palate into a honed and tense finish of pure lemon and lime juice. Crystalline acidity unites seamlessly with powder-fine phenolic grip to lay out tension, structure and endurance. Screw cap. 12.5% alc. **Rating** 94 **To** 2030 $54 TS
Eurus Eden Valley Cabernet Sauvignon 2018 Density and definition. Impressive concentration of blackcurrant and blackberry fruit, even fresh licorice and touches of menthol, all backed with high-cocoa dark chocolate French oak. Firm, fine, confident tannins direct a long finish. Full and impacting. Screw cap. 14.5% alc. **Rating** 94 **To** 2033 $65 TS

ŦŦŦŦŦ **Romulus Old Vine Barossa Valley Shiraz 2018** Rating 93 To 2028 $80 TS
Remus Old Vine Eden Valley Shiraz 2018 Rating 91 To 2030 $80 TS
Kennedy Barossa Valley Grenache Shiraz Mourvèdre 2019 Rating 91 To 2024 $29 TS
Pumpa Eden Valley Cabernet Sauvignon 2019 Rating 90 To 2024 $30 TS

Soul Growers   ★★★★★

218 Murray Street, Tanunda, SA 5352 **Region** Barossa Valley
T (08) 8523 2691 **www.**soulgrowers.com **Open** By appt
Winemaker Paul Heinicke, Stuart Bourne **Est.** 1998 **Dozens** 10 000 **Vyds** 4.85ha
Friends and partners Paul Heinicke, Stuart Bourne (winemaker, ex Chateau Tanunda) Tom Fotheringham (sales and marketing, ex Penfolds) first met while all working at Barossa Valley Estate. Soul Growers source from multi-generational family growers (13 in total) in Moppa, Ebenezer, Kalimna, Vine Vale, Eden Valley and Nuriootpa with pocket-handkerchief vineyard blocks of mataro at Nuriootpa and grenache at Krondorf. Exports to the UK, Singapore, Malaysia and China.

ŦŦŦŦŦ **Hampel Single Vineyard Barossa Valley Shiraz 2019** The signature satsuma plum and blackberry core of Kalimna is inimitable, framed immaculately here in long straps of fresh licorice, high-cocoa dark chocolate and mixed spice. Its sweet fruit core carries long and strong, flanked confidently by firm, fine tannins. Cork. 14.5% alc. **Rating** 95 **To** 2039 $160 TS
Resurgence Barossa Valley Shiraz Cabernet Sauvignon 2019 The glossy, polished, spicy blackberry and black cherry fruit of Barossa shiraz is magnificently contrasted with the crunchy redcurrants, leaf and tangy acidity of cabernet. Considerable potential is amplified by finely textured dark chocolate oak, reinforcing a confident, fine tannin web. Its black fruit core holds bright, long and strong on a grand finish. Cork. 14% alc. **Rating** 95 **To** 2037 $60 TS
Serendipitous Adelaide Hills Pinot Noir 2019 Infused with black fruits and spice of all kinds, this is an extroverted pinot noir of impressive fruit depth. Vibrant purple in hue, it's laced with potpourri, anise and violets, over a core of blackberries, satsuma plums and black cherries. Classy, polished, fine tannins frame a long and harmonious finish. Screw cap. 14% alc. **Rating** 94 **To** 2029 $35 TS

ŦŦŦŦŦ **Equilibrium Barossa Valley GSM 2019** Rating 93 To 2025 $35 TS
Soul Sister Barossa Valley Rosé 2020 Rating 92 To 2021 $25 TS ✪

Hoffmann Single Vineyard Barossa Valley Shiraz 2019 Rating 92 To 2032 $160 TS
Defiant Barossa Valley Mataro 2019 Rating 91 To 2026 $60 TS
Eden Valley Riesling 2020 Rating 90 To 2022 $25 TS

SOUMAH   ★★★★☆

18 Hexham Road, Gruyere, Vic 3770 **Region** Yarra Valley
T (03) 5962 4716 **www.**soumah.com.au **Open** 7 days 10–5
Winemaker Scott McCarthy **Est.** 1997 **Dozens** 12 000 **Vyds** 19.47ha
Unravelling the story behind the exotically named SOUMAH and its strikingly labelled
Savarro (reminiscent of 19th-century baroque design) was a voyage of discovery. SOUMAH
is in fact an abbreviation of South of Maroondah (Highway); Savarro is an alternative name
for savagnin. This is the venture of Brett Butcher, who has international experience in the
hospitality industry as CEO of the Langham Group and a long involvement in retailing wines
to restaurants in many countries. The many varieties planted have been clonally selected and
grafted onto rootstock with the long-term future in mind, although some of the sauvignon
blanc has been grafted over to bracchetto. Exports to the UK, the US, Canada, Denmark,
Norway, South Korea, Singapore, Hong Kong, Japan and China.

�♟ **The Butcher Thomas Hendy Cut Syrah Cabernet Sauvignon Nebbiolo
2020** A more restrained, tighter style, although certainly full of vibrant fruit. It
has come together well. Cherry and red plums, peppery and powered ginger in
the mix, citrus peel and licorice root. Savoury through and through. Fuller bodied,
with lots of detail across the palate, led by finely chiselled tannins. Screw cap.
14% alc. **Rating** 95 To 2035 $50 JF
Equilibrio Single Vineyard Syrah 2019 An excellent, dark purple/garnet hue
befitting the density of the wine. It's no wallflower, built to last some distance and
packed with cedary, sweet oak, ripe fruit and a kitchen cupboard full of spices.
Despite its volume and richness, it has come together well, with the full-bodied
palate flush with velvety plush tannins and lovely texture. Screw cap. 14.5% alc.
Rating 94 To 2030 $80 JF

♟♟♟♟♀ **Hexham Single Vineyard Syrah 2020** Rating 93 To 2030 $40 JF
Ai Fiori Single Vineyard Rosato 2020 Rating 92 To 2022 $28 JH
Hexham Single Vineyard Syrah 2019 Rating 92 To 2039 $40 JH
Hexham Single Vineyard Pinot Noir 2020 Rating 91 To 2028 $40 JF
The Butcher Frank Wynyard Cut Syrah Cabernet Nebbiolo 2019
Rating 91 To 2033 $50 JF
Botrytis Viognier 2020 Rating 91 To 2024 $32 JF
Hexham Vineyard Chardonnay 2020 Rating 90 To 2025 $40 JF

South by South West   ★★★★★

9A Coronation Street, Margaret River, WA 6285 (postal) **Region** Margaret River
T 0438 001 181 **www.**southbysouthwest.com.au
Winemaker Livia Maiorana **Est.** 2016 **Dozens** 4000 **Vyds** 2ha
Livia (Liv) Maiorana and Mijan (Mij) Patterson, engineer and graphic designer, share a love of
travel. They embarked on a 'wine odyssey' to study the cycle of winemaking in different wine
regions around the world. 'We learned from masters of the craft at some of the biggest and
smallest players in California, Italy, France and British Columbia. We learned about terroirs
and varietals, viticultural practices, cultural winemaking tricks and techniques. We drank a lot
of wine.' They make the South by South West wines in small batches, the grapes sourced from
multiple districts within the Margaret River (Carbunup, Wilyabrup, Wallcliffe and Karridale).
Exports to Singapore.

♟♟♟♟♟ **Margaret River Chardonnay 2020** The 2020 vintage was warm and low
yielding, which has led to a tranche of wines that are powerful, concentrated
and scarce. This is no exception. Fresh pineapple, yellow peach, red apples and
a smattering of curry leaf gives us this salty, rich and racy little number.

Classy to the very end of its long finish. Screw cap. 13.5% alc. **Rating** 95 To 2031 $40 EL

Southern Forests Pinot Noir 2020 Very lifted, nouveau and crunchy. This is delicious. It is not traditional pinot in the elegant, silky sense, but it jumps into the booji gamay camp with red licorice, star anise, raspberry pip and lolly, and pomegranate. Epic. Screw cap. 13.5% alc. **Rating** 95 To 2027 $45 EL

Fieldie Margaret River Semillon Sauvignon Blanc 2020 It is difficult to draw the line between varieties once this aromatic and layered skin-contact wine is in the mouth, but it ceases to matter when the fruits cascade over one another creating a tidal wave of flavour. Kept in check by chalky phenolics and salty acid, this seems like a pretty perfect summer seafood wine. Screw cap. 12.7% alc. **Rating** 94 To 2031 $30 EL ✪

Super Margs 2020 Sangiovese/cabernet. Wild ferment, matured for 9 months in French/Hungarian oak. Sweet and juicy fruit upfront in a typically Australian way: glossy, juicy, bouncy and right behind the teeth. The prodigious (yet fine) tannins follow up right behind it, drawing out the fruit into a long finish. Diam. 13.5% alc. **Rating** 94 To 2031 $45 EL

 Margaret River Sauvignon Blanc 2020 Rating 93 To 2022 $25 EL ✪
Margaret River Nebbiolo 2020 Rating 93 To 2028 $50 EL
Margaret River Chenin Blanc 2020 Rating 92 To 2031 $35 EL
Arancia Margaret River Chenin Blanc 2020 Rating 92 To 2031 $35 EL
Margaret River Sangiovese 2020 Rating 92 To 2027 $35 EL
Miscela NV Rating 90 $30 EL

 # Southern Vales   ★★★★

PO Box 521, McLaren Vale SA 5171 **Region** McLaren Vale
T 0427 032 520
Winemaker Mike Farmilo **Est.** 2012 **Dozens** 17 000 **Vyds** 4.5ha
The Southern Vales winery in McLaren Vale was originally a regional cooperative, or shared production facility for grape growers to make wine from their own fruit, much in the way of the European model. Built in 1896, the large facility produced wines for domestic sales and export, until its sale in the mid 1990s. Subsequently, the brand went into hibernation. In 2012 it was purchased by 2 local families with winemaker Mike Farmilo at the helm. The fruit is proprietary sourced as well as purchased. The wines are corpulent, rich and heady. Shiraz is the mainstay. (NG)

 Princess Grace McLaren Vale Shiraz 2016 An unabashedly rich style, almost shameless in the way it hauls saturated dark-fruit references, pushing the envelope of maximum ripeness across a carriage of high-quality oak. And yet the effect is seamless. Classy, even. The fruit is far from desiccated and fresh enough. The oak, an adept harness for the excess, splaying mocha, vanilla and coffee bean scents. The finish, long and gently charred. Effortless and free-flowing, with no jagged edges. Crafted with a canny hand and a twinkle in the eye. Diam. 15% alc. Rating 95 To 2035 $70 NG

Encounter McLaren Vale Shiraz 2016 Rating 92 To 2026 $35 NG

Spence   ★★★★★

760 Burnside Road, Murgheboluc, Vic 3221 **Region** Geelong
T (03) 5265 1181 **www.**spencewines.com.au **Open** 1st Sun each month
Winemaker Peter Spence, Scott Ireland **Est.** 1997 **Dozens** 1300 **Vyds** 3.2ha
Peter and Anne Spence were sufficiently inspired by an extended European holiday – which included living on a family vineyard in Provence – to purchase a small property and establish a vineyard and winery. They have planted 3.2ha on a north-facing slope in a valley 7km south of Bannockburn, the lion's share to 3 clones of shiraz (1.83ha), the remainder to chardonnay, pinot noir and fast-diminishing cabernet sauvignon (it is being grafted over to viognier for use in the Shiraz). The vineyard attained full organic status in 2008, since then using only biodynamic practices.

🍷🍷🍷🍷 **Geelong Shiraz 2019** A strong follow-up to the 2018 shiraz, walking a similar path of cool-climate spiciness and medium-bodied elegance. Enticing right off the bat, with an arresting fragrance of black cherry, blueberry, stewed plum, dried herbs and black pepper. Flavours and texture glide on the palate, swept along with grainy, ripe tannins. A treat is in store for the drinker here. Screw cap. 13.8% alc. **Rating** 95 **To** 2034 $30 JP ✪

🍷🍷🍷🍷 **Geelong Pinot Noir 2019** Rating 92 To 2026 $35 JP
Geelong Chardonnay 2019 Rating 90 To 2027 $30 JP

Spinifex ★★★★★

PO Box 511, Nuriootpa, SA 5355 **Region** Barossa Valley
T (08) 8564 2059 **www**.spinifexwines.com.au **Open** At Vino Lokal, Tanunda
Winemaker Peter Schell **Est.** 2001 **Dozens** 6000 **Vyds** 12ha
Peter Schell and Magali Gely are a husband-and-wife team from NZ who came to Australia in the early 1990s to study oenology and marketing at Roseworthy College. They have spent 4 vintages making wine in France, mainly in the south where Magali's family were vignerons for generations near Montpellier. The focus at Spinifex is the red varieties that dominate in the south of France: mataro (more correctly mourvèdre), grenache, shiraz and cinsault. The wines are made in open fermenters, basket pressed, with partial wild (indigenous) fermentation and relatively long post-ferment maceration. This is a very old approach, but nowadays à la mode. Exports to the UK, Canada, Belgium, Singapore, Hong Kong, China and NZ.

🍷🍷🍷🍷 **Rostein Vineyard Flaxman Valley Eden Valley Shiraz 2018** A grand newcomer for Spinifex, this is the first time this vineyard has stepped up since it was purchased in 2014. Signature Eden Valley shiraz of full purple hue, reverberating with deep-set spice, powerful blackberry and satsuma plum fruit, fresh licorice and a full serve of dark chocolate oak. Impressive concentration is consummately backed with a fine yet taut frame of intricately suspended tannins that carry the finish very long indeed. Vino-Lok. 14.2% alc. **Rating** 96 **To** 2032 $125 TS

🍷🍷🍷🍷 **Dominion Barossa Valley Grenache 2019** Rating 92 To 2029 $45 TS
Esprit Barossa Valley 2019 Rating 91 To 2024 $35 TS
Barossa Valley Rosé 2020 Rating 90 To 2021 $28 TS

Spring Spur ★★★★

52 Fredas Lane, Tawonga, Vic 3697 **Region** Alpine Valleys
T (03) 5754 4849 **www**.springspurwine.com.au **Open** Thurs–Mon 8–6
Winemaker Alex Phillips **Est.** 2017 **Dozens** 80
Alex Phillips was born and raised in South Africa; one of the most vibrant and diverse wine-producing countries in the world. She graduated cum laude from the University of Stellenbosch in 2013, where she was awarded the prestigious Prof PA van der Bijl medal and crowned Best Academic Student: Viticulture and Oenology. After mentoring under celebrated winemaker Adam Mason at Mulderbosch Vineyards, she launched into vintages across the world before finding her feet as assistant winemaker at Billy Button Wines in the Alpine Valleys of North East Victoria. It is here she found love; not only in the picturesque winemaking region itself but in her fiancé, Lin. The pair live on Spring Spur – a beautiful working horse property in the Kiewa Valley, where Alex is free to spread her wings and do what she does best – bringing Spring Spur wines to life.

Spring Vale Vineyards ★★★★

130 Spring Vale Road, Cranbrook, Tas 7190 **Region** East Coast Tasmania
T (03) 6257 8208 **www**.springvalewines.com **Open** 7 days 11–4
Winemaker Barry Kooji **Est.** 1986 **Dozens** 15 000 **Vyds** 32.5ha
Lyn and Rodney Lyne have progressively established pinot noir (19ha), chardonnay (4ha), pinots gris and meunier (3ha each), syrah (2ha), sauvignon blanc (1ha) and gewürztraminer (0.5ha)

since 1986. The nearby Melrose Vineyard was purchased in 2007. Son Tim, armed with a degree in viticulture and a MBA, is now general manager and viticulturalist. Exports to Russia and Hong Kong.

🍷🍷🍷🍷🍷 **Sauvignon Blanc 2020** Precocious and flamboyant sauvignon filled with all the usual suspects of passionfruit, gooseberries and frangipani. Oak fermentation has been deployed to bring texture without imparting flavour, leaving a long finish to juicy, sweet fruit impact. Screw cap. 12.5% alc. **Rating** 90 **To** 2022 $28 TS

Springs Road Wines   ★★★★

761 Playford Highway, Cygnet River, SA 5223 **Region** Kangaroo Island
T 0499 918 418 **www.**springsroad.com.au **Open** 7 days 12–5 Oct–Apr, Wed–Mon 12–4 May–Sept
Winemaker Joch Bosworth **Est.** 1994 **Dozens** 4000 **Vyds** 11ha
Springs Road runs east–west across the northern part of Kangaroo Island. The Springs Road vineyards were established in 1994 on a small sheep property about 7km west of Kingscote and are now owned and operated by Joch Bosworth and Louise Hemsley-Smith from Battle of Bosworth in McLaren Vale (see separate entry). Small quantities of Chardonnay, Shiraz, Cabernet Sauvignon and a Cabernet Sauvignon Shiraz blend are made from the very low-yielding 20yo vines. The vineyards have been managed organically since Louise and Joch took over in 2016, and are awaiting certification. The wine label is adapted from Louis de Freycinet's 1808 map of the South Australian coastline, 'Terre Napoléon'. Exports to Hong Kong.

🍷🍷🍷🍷🍷 **Kangaroo Island Cabernet Sauvignon Shiraz 2018** You can see each of these varieties solo from the same vineyard, then this blending into a harmonious duet adds extra appeal; still full bodied, yet a more gentle, rounded style results. The 75% cabernet and mint note invite you in. The palate is complete, with the aromatics and plummy, spicy shiraz fruit, and while there's a decent tannin feel, there's a medium-bodied carry to the finish that encourages the next glass. Screw cap. 13.5% alc. **Rating** 94 **To** 2030 $35 TL

🍷🍷🍷🍷🍷 **Kangaroo Island Chardonnay 2019 Rating** 93 **To** 2025 $35 TL
Kangaroo Island Cabernet Sauvignon 2018 Rating 90 **To** 2028 $35 TL

Squitchy Lane Vineyard   ★★★★

Medhurst Road, Coldstream, Vic 3770 **Region** Yarra Valley
T (03) 5964 9114 **www.**squitchylane.com.au **Open** W'ends 11–5
Winemaker Medhurst Wines **Est.** 1982 **Dozens** 1500 **Vyds** 5.75ha
Mike Fitzpatrick acquired a taste for fine wine while a Rhodes scholar at Oxford University in the 1970s. Returning to Australia he guided Carlton Football Club to 2 premierships as captain, then established Melbourne-based finance company Squitchy Lane Holdings. The wines of Mount Mary inspired him to look for his own vineyard and in '96 he found a vineyard of sauvignon blanc, chardonnay, pinot noir, merlot, cabernet franc and cabernet sauvignon, planted in '82, just around the corner from Coldstream Hills and Yarra Yering.

🍷🍷🍷🍷🍷 **Yarra Valley Cabernet Franc 2019** A wine with charm and delicacy. There's a core of excellent fruit, lightly spiced and framed, with textural tannins, a youthful freshness yet there's depth too. Screw cap. 13.5% alc. **Rating** 93 **To** 2027 $40 JF
Light Dry Red Yarra Valley Cabernet Franc Merlot 2020 Yarra Valley seems to be cornering the 'light dry red' category. No complaints as here's another good one. It's bright, fresh and juicy with a savoury sway to the fruit. Light bodied with soft tannins and should come with a warning: irresistible drinking. Screw cap. 12% alc. **Rating** 92 **To** 2023 $28 JF
Yarra Valley Chardonnay 2018 This is one of those chardonnays that offers plenty of drinking pleasure without having to overthink what's in the glass. If you must know, there are some stone fruit and citrussy flavours, with a light touch of vanillan oak and spice. Refreshing and light on its feet. Screw cap. 13% alc. **Rating** 90 **To** 2026 $28 JF

Stage Door Wine Co

22 Whibley Street, Henley Beach, SA 5022 **Region** Eden Valley
T 0400 991 968 **www.**stagedoorwineco.com.au **Open** At Taste Eden Valley
Winemaker Graeme Thredgold, Phil Lehmann **Est.** 2013 **Dozens** 4000 **Vyds** 32.3ha
It took a long time for Graeme Thredgold to establish Stage Door Wine Co. Having been
a successful professional musician for 15 years during the 1980s and '90s, he developed vocal
nodules in the early '90s, putting an end to his musical career. Having spent so much time
working in hotels and night clubs, a new occupation stared him in the face: the liquor industry.
In '92 he began working for Lion Nathan as a sales representative, then spent 5 years with SA
Brewing and in '98 ventured into the world of wine as national sales manager for Andrew
Garrett. Around 2000 he moved on to the more fertile pasture of Tucker Seabrook as state
sales manager for SA. Further roles with Barossa Valley Estate and as general manager of Chain
of Ponds Wines added to an impressive career in sales and marketing, before he made his final
move – to general manager of Eden Hall Wines, which just happens to be owned by his
sister and brother-in-law, Mardi and David Hall. Grapes are sourced mainly from the family
vineyard, plus contract-grown fruit. Exports to Canada.

🍷🍷🍷🍷🍷 **Three Piece Barossa Grenache Shiraz Mataro 2020** Impressively vibrant,
full purple hue. Loaded with crunchy, spicy dark berry fruits, sarsaparilla root and
red licorice. Fine tannins bring up a long, bright and spicy finish. Quintessential
Barossa GSM and a barbecue quaffing special! Screw cap. 14.5% alc. **Rating** 90
To 2024 $25 TS

🍷🍷🍷🍷 **The Green Room Eden Valley Riesling 2020** Rating 89 To 2022 $25 TS
Eden Valley Cabernet Sauvignon 2019 Rating 89 To 2034 $50 TS

Staniford Wine Co

20 Jackson Street, Mount Barker, WA 6324 **Region** Great Southern
T 0405 157 687 **www.**stanifordwineco.com.au **Open** By appt
Winemaker Michael Staniford **Est.** 2010 **Dozens** 500
Michael Staniford has been making wine in Great Southern since 1995, principally as senior
winemaker for Alkoomi at Frankland River, with additional experience as a contract maker
for other wineries. The business is built around single-vineyard wines; a Chardonnay from
a 25+yo vineyard in Albany and a Cabernet Sauvignon from a 20+yo vineyard in Mount
Barker. The quality of these 2 wines is every bit as one would expect. Michael plans to
introduce a Riesling and a Shiraz with a similar individual vineyard origin, quality being the
first requirement.

Stanton & Killeen Wines

440 Jacks Road, Murray Valley Highway, Rutherglen, Vic 3685 **Region** Rutherglen
T (02) 6032 9457 **www.**stantonandkilleen.com.au **Open** Mon–Sat 9–5, Sun & public
hols 10–5
Winemaker Faustine Ropars **Est.** 1875 **Dozens** 10000 **Vyds** 34ha
In 2020 Stanton & Killeen celebrated its 145th anniversary. The business is owned and run
by 7th-generation vigneron Natasha Killeen and her mother and CEO, Wendy Killeen.
Fortifieds are a strong focus for the winery with around half of its production dedicated to
this style. Their vineyards comprise 14 varieties, including 7 Portuguese cultivars used for both
fortified and table wine production – 2 additional Portuguese varieties are planned for future
planting. A vineyard rejuvenation program has been implemented since 2014, focusing on
sustainable and environmentally friendly practices. Exports to the UK, Switzerland, Taiwan,
Hong Kong and China.

Stargazer Wine ★★★★★

37 Rosewood Lane, Tea Tree, Tas 7017 **Region** Tasmania
T 0408 173 335 **www.**stargazerwine.com.au **Open** By appt
Winemaker Samantha Connew **Est.** 2012 **Dozens** 1800 **Vyds** 3ha

Samantha (Sam) Connew has racked up a series of exceptional achievements, commencing with bachelor of law and bachelor of arts degrees, majoring in political science and English literature, from the University of Canterbury, Christchurch, NZ, then deciding her future direction by obtaining a postgraduate diploma of oenology and viticulture from Lincoln University, Canterbury, NZ. Sam moved to Australia, undertaking the Advanced Wine Assessment course at the Australian Wine Research Institute in 2000, being chosen as a scholar at the '02 Len Evans Tutorial, winning the George Mackey Award for the best wine exported from Australia in '04 and was awarded International Red Winemaker of the Year at the International Wine Challenge, London in '07. After a highly successful and lengthy position as chief winemaker at Wirra Wirra, Sam moved to Tasmania (via the Hunter Valley) to make the first wines for her own business, something she said she would never do. The emotive name (and label) is in part a tribute to Abel Tasman, the first European to sight Tasmania before proceeding to the South Island of NZ, navigating by the stars. Exports to the UK, the US, Singapore, Japan and Hong Kong.

Palisander Vineyard Coal River Valley Pinot Noir 2019 The seductive bouquet exudes dried rose petals, spices and some darker foresty notes underneath. The intense palate is all class, blending purity, precision and power. There's a freshness to the mouthfeel that carries through to the long finish and lingering aftertaste. Screw cap. 13% alc. **Rating** 98 **To** 2032 $55 JH ✪ ♥

Single Vineyard Derwent Valley Chardonnay 2018 A distinguished Tasmanian chardonnay, at once pure, yet complex, long, intense, and open for business. The interplay between fruit and barrel-ferment oak derivatives is masterful. Tasmanian chardonnay is not by any means a foregone conclusion. Screw cap. 13.5% alc. **Rating** 96 **To** 2030 $55 JH ✪

Tasmania Chardonnay 2019 Rating 92 **To** 2026 $55 TS
Coal River Valley Pinot Noir 2019 Rating 92 **To** 2031 $55 TS
Tupelo Tasmania 2020 Rating 91 **To** 2021 $32 TS

Steels Gate ★★★★
1974 Melba Highway, Dixons Creek, Vic 3775 **Region** Yarra Valley
T (03) 5965 2155 **www**.steelsgate.com.au **Open** Thurs–Mon 10.30–5.30
Winemaker Brad Atkins, Matthew Davis **Est.** 2010 **Dozens** 1400 **Vyds** 7ha
Brad Atkins and Matthew Davis acquired a 2ha vineyard of 25–30yo dry-grown chardonnay and pinot noir in 2009. For reasons unexplained, the owners have a particular love of gates, and as the property is at the end of Steels Creek, the choice of Steels Gate was obvious. The next step was to engage French designer Cecile Darcy to create what is known today as the Steels Gate logo.

Nagambie Vineyard Graciano 2019 Graciano is pretty in name and in the glass, a Spanish red wine that is showing a strong suitability to the Nagambie soils with a medium-bodied, fragrant and charming wine. Resplendent in forest fruits, plums, dried herbs and cedar aromas, it moves up a notch in intensity on the palate, abundant in deep fruit and sweet oak flavours. Framed in fine tannins, it should develop well. Diam. 13.4% alc. **Rating** 93 **To** 2029 $40 JP
Nagambie Vineyard Cabernet Sauvignon 2018 Everything is in its place here from the fine and leafy aromas to the elegant palate laid out before the drinker, velvety textured and understated in black fruits, spice and well-managed vanillan oak. Still, just not ready to shine. Would benefit from more time alone to blossom. Diam. 13.5% alc. **Rating** 92 **To** 2028 $50 JP
Shantell Vineyard Yarra Valley Chardonnay 2018 Quite a racy number, with the acidity whooshing through fresh grapefruit, lemon zest and creamed honey flavours and oak spices. Refreshing, tangy and uncomplicated. Diam. 12.5% alc. **Rating** 90 **To** 2027 $30 JF
Nagambie Vineyard Bastardo 2019 The Yarra Valley–based winery looked to fruit from Nagambie in 2019 and, in particular, this little-known grape more usually associated with Portuguese fortified-wine production. Strikes a sinewy,

medium-bodied and savoury pose which is immediately different from the usual red grape crowd. Briar, acacia, red cherry, earth, prune and wood smoke aromas. Despite some high-ish acidity, the wine is rich in ripe fruit and fills the mouth before finishing with a flourish of dry, savoury tannins. An interesting flavour sensation any way you look at it. Diam. 14.5% alc. **Rating** 90 **To** 2026 $40 JP

🍷🍷🍷🍷 **Estate Blend Yarra Valley Pinot Noir 2019** Rating 88 To 2027 $35 JF

Stefani Estate   ★★★★☆

735 Old Healesville Road, Healesville, Vic 3777 **Region** Yarra Valley
T 0492 993 446 **www**.stefaniwines.com.au **Open** Thurs–Fri by appt, Sat–Sun 11–5
Winemaker Peter Mackey **Est.** 1998 **Dozens** 5730 **Vyds** 18ha
Stefano Stefani came to Australia in 1985. Business success has allowed him and wife Rina to follow in the footsteps of his grandfather, who had a vineyard and was an avid wine collector. The first property they acquired was at Long Gully Road in the Yarra Valley, planted to pinot grigio, cabernet sauvignon, chardonnay and pinot noir. The next was in Heathcote, where they acquired a property adjoining that of Mario Marson (ex Mount Mary), built a winery and established 14.4ha of shiraz, cabernet sauvignon, merlot, cabernet franc, malbec and petit verdot. In 2003 a second Yarra Valley property, named The View, reflecting its high altitude, was acquired and Dijon clones of chardonnay and pinot noir were planted; that vineyard is currently undergoing organic conversion. In addition, 1.6ha of sangiovese have been established, using scion material from the original Stefani Vineyard in Tuscany. Exports to China.

🍷🍷🍷🍷🍷 **The View Yarra Valley Pinot Blanc 2019** What a delightful drink that flutters with compelling flavours of pear drops and essence, citrus, basil and other cool herbs. It's a touch estery, but there's a gentleness across the palate, an interesting texture, a quinine/lemon/saline thing going on, aside from mouth-watering lemon sorbet acidity. Screw cap. 13% alc. **Rating** 95 **To** 2023 $30 JF ❂
Barrel Selection Heathcote Shiraz 2019 The colour of Heathcote shiraz is amazing: black/purple shot with red. Awash with dark fruit, Middle Eastern spices, licorice root and a warm earth fragrance. The palate is full bodied yet flush with incredibly smooth tannins. There's a gloss to this, a refreshment throughout, and everything is in sync. Screw cap. 14.5% alc. **Rating** 95 **To** 2034 $65 JF

🍷🍷🍷🍷🍷 **The View Yarra Valley Chardonnay 2018** Rating 93 To 2028 $65 JF
Boccallupo Yarra Valley Sangiovese 2020 Rating 92 To 2026 $35 JF

Stefano Lubiana   ★★★★★

60 Rowbottoms Road, Granton, Tas 7030 **Region** Southern Tasmania
T (03) 6263 7457 **www**.slw.com.au **Open** Wed–Sun 11–4
Winemaker Steve Lubiana **Est.** 1990 **Vyds** 25ha
Monique and Steve Lubiana moved from the hot inland of a brown Australia to the beautiful banks of the Derwent River in 1990 to pursue Steve's dream of making high-quality sparkling wine. The sloping site allowed them to build a gravity-fed winery and his whole winemaking approach since that time has been based on attention to detail within a biodynamic environment. The first sparkling wines were made in 1993 from the initial plantings of chardonnay and pinot noir. Over the years they have added riesling, sauvignon blanc, pinot gris and merlot. The Italian-inspired Osteria restaurant is based on their own biodynamically produced vegetables and herbs, the meats (all free-range) are from local farmers and the seafood is wild-caught. In 2016 the Lubianas purchased the Panorama Vineyard, first planted in 1974, in the Huon Valley. Exports to the UK, Sweden, Singapore, Indonesia, South Korea, Japan, Taiwan, Hong Kong and China.

🍷🍷🍷🍷🍷 **Tasmania Chardonnay 2019** The refinement that Steve Lubiana has brought to his chardonnay over recent vintages is something to behold. He's achieved the holy grail of elegance without sacrificing definition, concentration, persistence or endurance. Pristine white fruits are ever-so-gently propelled by high-class French oak. Crystalline acidity illuminates a finish of pinpoint accuracy, undeterred line and magnificent persistence. Screw cap. 13% alc. **Rating** 96 **To** 2034 $58 TS ✪

Tasmania Pinot Noir 2019 Benchmark pinot from this celebrated, biodynamic estate vineyard in the Derwent Valley. A gorgeous core of exact black cherries and blackberries. Confident support from French oak brings impressive scaffolding of firm, fine, mineral tannins. The finish holds good (if not excellent) length, but may build with age. It certainly has the stamina to endure long. Screw cap. 13% alc. **Rating** 95 **To** 2034 $62 TS

Prestige Pinot Noir Chardonnay 1999 Tasted at a grand 21 years of age (13 on cork, 8 on lees), this is a magnificent testimony to Lubiana's longstanding mastery of sparkling. Primary, secondary and tertiary realms meet in a glorious fanfare, culminating in a triumphant crescendo of pipe smoke, green olive and toast. At once creamy and beautifully focused, it rides a long, clean line of pristine Tasmanian acidity. Cork. 12.5% alc. **Rating** 95 $210 TS

Tasmania Chardonnay 2018 There is a beautifully effortless, calm purity to this release from Steve Lubiana, eloquently articulating his certified biodynamic vineyard on the banks of the Derwent. A celebration of place and fruit before method or artefact, it presents perfectly ripe white stone fruits framed subtly in understated French oak, concluding magnificently with a long finish of scintillating Tasmanian acidity. Screw cap. 13% alc. **Rating** 94 **To** 2023 $50 TS

🍷🍷🍷🍷🍷 **Tasmania Riesling 2019 Rating** 93 **To** 2031 $33 TS
Primavera Chardonnay 2019 Rating 93 **To** 2024 $33 TS
Grande Vintage 2010 Rating 93 $85 TS
Primavera Pinot Noir 2019 Rating 92 **To** 2026 $38 TS
Tasmania Syrah 2019 Rating 92 **To** 2034 $62 TS
Chicane 2016 Rating 92 **To** 2031 $45 TS
Blanc de Blanc 2014 Rating 92 $58 TS
Primavera Chardonnay 2020 Rating 91 **To** 2025 $38 TS

Stella Bella Wines   ★★★★★

205 Rosabrook Road, Margaret River, WA 6285 **Region** Margaret River
T (08) 9758 8611 **www**.stellabella.com.au **Open** 7 days 10–5
Winemaker Luke Jolliffe, Jarrad Olsen **Est.** 1997 **Dozens** 40 000 **Vyds** 55.7ha
This enormously successful winemaking business produces wines of true regional expression with fruit sourced from the central and southern parts of Margaret River. The company owns and operates 6 vineyards, and also purchases fruit from small contract growers. Substantial quantities of wine covering all styles and price points make this an important producer for Margaret River. Exports of Stella Bella, Suckfizzle and Skuttlebutt labels to all major markets.

🍷🍷🍷🍷🍷 **Luminosa Margaret River Chardonnay 2019** Pink grapefruit, salted yellow peach, curry leaf and crushed nuts. It's worked, but it's got it all, including a core of pure fruit on the palate. Like a Tardis, this wine contains more flavour than it lets on. Ripples of flavour slowly radiate out from its centre, keeping the drinker engaged for quite some time. Gorgeous, salivating stuff. Screw cap. 13.3% alc. **Rating** 97 **To** 2036 $70 EL ✪

Luminosa Margaret River Cabernet Sauvignon 2018 Luminous is right … what a beautiful wine this is. Succulent raspberry, pomegranate, redcurrant and satsuma plum are sprinkled with pink peppercorn and sea salt and harnessed by supple, almost chewy tannins. The flavour undulates in waves. This is an incredible wine – do your future self a favour and seek this out. It's just pure pleasure. Screw cap. 14.1% alc. **Rating** 97 **To** 2041 $90 EL ✪

🍷🍷🍷🍷🍷 **Suckfizzle Margaret River Chardonnay 2019** More restrained and less obviously worked than the Luminosa, the power here comes from the undertow of fruit. It carries on far past the expected limit of endurance. If the key to quality is length of flavour, then this must be very good indeed. A spectacular wine. Screw cap. 13.6% alc. **Rating** 96 **To** 2036 $70 EL ✪

Suckfizzle Margaret River Sauvignon Blanc Semillon 2019 Ten months in oak (25% new). The 2019 vintage was cool, but by all accounts, great. Already the oak is seamlessly integrated aromatically, the palate exhibiting a melange of snow pea, jasmine, cassis and red apple skin, all laced up in briny acid. Texturally slippery and fine. Outstanding. Screw cap. 13.3% alc. **Rating** 95 **To** 2035 $45 EL

Skuttlebutt Margaret River Sauvignon Blanc Semillon 2020 Margaret River does this style so well it would be hard to deny at any price, let alone this. It's made in the vineyard, vinification without any embellishment – except perhaps a hint of sweetness. No matter; the blend of kaffir lime, white peach and passionfruit is balanced and freshened by crisp acidity. Screw cap. 12.9% alc. **Rating** 94 **To** 2025 $19 JH ❂

Suckfizzle Margaret River Cabernet Sauvignon 2018 Fragrant red berries, pink peppercorn and salted pomegranate lead the aromatic charge; the flavours in the mouth follow suit. On the palate the tannins take over, asserting a dominance that teeters on overthrowing the succulence of the fruit. Here, it is savoury and almost stalky. It all comes together again through the finish, leaving a trail of chewy tannins and sultry dark fruit in its wake. Screw cap. 14.4% alc. **Rating** 94 **To** 2036 $65 EL

♟♟♟♟♙ **Margaret River Sauvignon Blanc 2020 Rating** 93 **To** 2025 $25 EL ❂
Margaret River Semillon Sauvignon Blanc 2020 Rating 93 **To** 2026 $25 EL ❂
Margaret River Shiraz 2019 Rating 91 **To** 2027 $35 EL
Skuttlebutt Margaret River Cabernet Sauvignon Shiraz 2018 Rating 91 **To** 2026 $19 EL ❂
Skuttlebutt Margaret River Rosé 2020 Rating 90 **To** 2022 $19 EL ❂
Margaret River Cabernet Sauvignon 2018 Rating 90 **To** 2031 $38 EL

Steve Wiblin's Erin Eyes   ★★★★

58 Old Road, Leasingham, SA 5452 **Region** Clare Valley
T (08) 8843 0023 **www.erineyes.com.au**
Winemaker Steve Wiblin **Est.** 2009 **Dozens** 2500
Steve Wiblin became a winemaker accidentally when he was encouraged by his mentor at Tooheys Brewery who had a love of fine art and fine wine. This was 40 years ago and because Tooheys owned Wynns and Seaview, the change in career from beer to wine was easy. He watched the acquisition of Wynns and Seaview by Penfolds and then Seppelt, before moving to Orlando. He moved from the world of big wineries to small when he co-founded Neagles Rock in 1997. In 2009 he left Neagles Rock and established Erin Eyes, explaining, 'In 1842 my English convict forebear John Wiblin gazed into a pair of Erin eyes. That gaze changed our family make-up and history forever. In the Irish-influenced Clare Valley, what else would I call my wines but Erin Eyes?'

♟♟♟♟♙ **Stone of Destiny Clare Valley Shiraz Malbec 2018** A 64/36% blend, shiraz replacing the more usual cabernet in Clare Valley's approach. It's a very attractive wine, its bright colour, aromatic red and purple berry fruits taken through in a coat of dark chocolate on the light- to medium-bodied palate. Freshness is a major feature, suggesting early(ish) enjoyment. Screw cap. 14.5% alc. **Rating** 92 **To** 2030 $30 JH

Sticks   ★★★★

3/436 Johnston St, Abbotsford, Vic 3067 **Region** Yarra Valley
T (03) 9224 1911 **www.sticks.com.au**
Winemaker Anthony Fikkers **Est.** 2000 **Dozens** 15 000
One of many labels under the Joval Wine Group, headed by John Valmorbida, with a strong link to the Australian food and wine scene thanks to his Italian family heritage. The Valmorbida family is behind a host of successful enterprises including wine distribution, importing Italian comestibles, retail and of course their own wine labels. The Sticks brand is

all about offering entry-level yet fresh and simple everyday wines sourced from Yarra Valley floor sites at Coldstream, Dixon's Creek and Yarra Glen. The core comprises pinot grigio, chardonnay, pinot noir and cabernet sauvignon. In 2019, Anthony Fikkers took over as chief winemaker. Exports to Hong Kong, the UK and the US. (JF)

🍷🍷🍷🍷🍷 **Yarra Valley Cabernet Sauvignon 2018** It's bright. It's juicy. It's playful. It's Yarra Valley cabernet at a fair price. Don't expect complexity per se, but do expect mulberries and blackberries, almost-furry tannins and plenty of leafy eucalypt/mint woven into the body of the wine. Screw cap. 13.5% alc. **Rating** 91 **To** 2026 $24 JF

Yarra Valley Chardonnay 2019 An easygoing, drink-me-now wine with dabs of lemon and curd, herbs and spices. While it's short on the finish, it has savouriness and a hint of creamy lees texture. It meets the brief well. Screw cap. 12.5% alc. **Rating** 90 **To** 2025 $24 JF

Stockman's Ridge Wines

21 Boree Lane, Lidster, NSW 2800 **Region** Orange
T (02) 6365 6512 **www**.stockmansridge.com.au **Open** Thurs–Mon 11–5
Winemaker Jonathan Hambrook **Est.** 2002 **Dozens** 2000 **Vyds** 3ha
Stockman's Ridge Wines, founded and owned by Jonathan Hambrook, started its wine life in Bathurst, before relocating to its present vineyard on the northwest slopes of Mt Canobolas, at an elevation of 800m. Jonathan has planted pinot noir and grüner veltliner. His next-door neighbour is the Booree Lane Vineyard, owned by Bob Clark, who has shiraz, merlot, cabernet franc, chardonnay and gewürztraminer – a significant part of the grapes go to Stockman's Ridge. Exports to the US and China.

🍷🍷🍷🍷🍷 **Outlaw Orange Zinfandel 2017** This is good and has paid dividends with the bottle age given to it. Aromas of glühwein, spiced orange, clove and mulled cherry. Brambly, peppery and marked by wood smoke and sandalwood across the finish. The sweet/sour energy, typical of the variety's uneven ripening patterns, is a plus rather than a bane, mitigating the high-octane ripeness. Screw cap. 14.9% alc. **Rating** 92 **To** 2025 $40 NG

Stomp Wine ★★★★☆

504 Wilderness Road, Lovedale, NSW 2330 **Region** Hunter Valley
T 0409 774 280 **www**.stompwines.com.au **Open** Thurs–Mon 10–5
Winemaker Michael McManus **Est.** 2004 **Dozens** 1000
After a seeming lifetime in the food and beverage industry, Michael and Meredith McManus moved to full-time winemaking. They have set up Stomp Winemaking, a contract winemaker designed to keep small and larger parcels of grapes separate through the fermentation and maturation process, thus meeting the needs of boutique wine producers in the Hunter Valley. The addition of their own Stomp label is a small but important part of their business.

🍷🍷🍷🍷🍷 **Hunter Valley Shiraz 2019** These tannins have been extracted with aplomb: chewy, ripe and savoury; medium bodied as a result. The fruit, Hunter-style earthy but with a pulpy plum, mulberry and black-cherry joyousness. Lively, with a real thrust of extract and parry of structure, coating the palate. Wonderful vinosity, joy and length. Lovely wine. Screw cap. 14% alc. **Rating** 95 **To** 2030 $35 NG ✪

Stone Bridge Wines

20 Gillentown Road, Clare, SA 5453 **Region** Clare Valley
T (08) 8843 4143 **www**.stonebridgewines.com.au **Open** Thurs–Mon 11–4
Winemaker Craig Thomson, Angela Meaney **Est.** 2005 **Dozens** 3500 **Vyds** 85ha
'From little things, big things grow' is certainly true for Craig and Lisa Thomson, who planted 0.6ha of shiraz in 1997 and now own 85ha in 3 locations across the Clare Valley. They crush around 150t, more than 10 times their first batch in '05 when they launched the Stone Bridge Wines label and cellar door. They make grenache, riesling, shiraz, malbec, pinot gris and

sangiovese, along with sparkling wines made in the traditional method. Their winery is also a contract processing plant for local and interstate wine labels. Visitors to the rammed-earth cellar door can enjoy pizza from the wood-fired oven made by Craig, a baker by trade. Exports to Canada, Denmark, Singapore and China.

🍷🍷🍷🍷♀ **The Gardener Clare Valley Rosé 2020** A lovely rosé starting with its pastel pink hue and pretty aromas of rose petals. The palate fleshes out with strawberry and red licorice flavours. There's some texture, with bright acidity and a strong desire to pour another glass. Screw cap. 12.5% alc. **Rating** 91 **To** 2022 $25 JF

Stonefish   ★★★★★
3739 Caves Road, Wilyabrup, WA 6280 **Region** Various
T (08) 9755 6774 **www**.stonefish.wine **Open** 7 days 11–5
Winemaker Contract, Peter Papanikitas **Est.** 2000 **Dozens** 20000 **Vyds** 58ha
Peter Papanikitas has been involved in various facets of the wine industry for the past 30+ years. Initially his contact was with companies that included Penfolds, Lindemans and Leo Buring, then he spent 5 years working for Cinzano, gaining experience in worldwide sales and marketing. In 2000 he established Stonefish, a virtual winery operation, in partnership with various grapegrowers and winemakers, principally in the Barossa Valley and Margaret River, who provide the wines. The value for money has never been in doubt but Stonefish has moved to another level with its Icon and Reserve Barossa wines. Exports to Thailand, Vietnam, Indonesia, the Philippines, the Maldives, Singapore, Fiji, Hong Kong and China.

Stoney Rise   ★★★★☆
96 Hendersons Lane, Gravelly Beach, Tas 7276 **Region** Northern Tasmania
T (03) 6394 3678 **www**.stoneyrise.com **Open** Thurs–Mon 11–5
Winemaker Joe Holyman **Est.** 2000 **Dozens** 2000 **Vyds** 7.2ha
The Holyman family had been involved in vineyards in Tasmania for 20 years, but Joe Holyman's career in the wine industry – first as a sales rep, then as a wine buyer and more recently working in wineries in NZ, Portugal, France, Mount Benson and Coonawarra – gave him an exceptionally broad-based understanding of wine. In 2004 Joe and wife Lou purchased the former Rotherhythe Vineyard, which had been established in 1986, and set about restoring it to its former glory. There are 2 ranges: the Stoney Rise wines, focusing on fruit and early drinkability; and the Holyman wines – with more structure, more new oak and the best grapes, here the focus is on length and potential longevity. Exports to the UK, the Netherlands, Singapore and Japan.

🍷🍷🍷🍷🍷 **Tasmania Grüner Veltliner 2020** Grüner veltliner is a late-ripening variety that flourishes in a cool climate, the cooler the better. Its varietal signature of white pepper on the bouquet is present, but even more is the tightly wound spring of acidity. Its length is prodigious, and it is a wine built for the (very) long haul. Screw cap. 11.5% alc. **Rating** 97 **To** 2040 $32 JH

🍷🍷🍷🍷🍷 **Holyman Pinot Noir 2018** It's daring to throw in a large inclusion of whole bunches (60%) in Tasmania. Winemaker Joe Holyman executed it perfectly in '18, building fantastic aromatics and firmly textured structure without sacrificing fruit definition or tannin ripeness. The result is exotic and lifted, built on a core of rosehip, poached strawberries and morello cherries, with a tannin structure that promises longevity. It finishes a little short, but might build in time. Screw cap. 12% alc. **Rating** 94 **To** 2033 $50 TS

🍷🍷🍷🍷♀ **Holyman Chardonnay 2019 Rating** 93 **To** 2028 $50 TS
Chardonnay 2020 Rating 92 **To** 2027 $32 TS
Pinot Noir 2019 Rating 90 **To** 2024 $29 TS

Stonier Wines ★★★★★

Cnr Thompson's Lane/Frankston-Flinders Road, Merricks, Vic 3916
Region Mornington Peninsula
T (03) 5989 8300 **www.**stonier.com.au **Open** 7 days 11–5
Winemaker Michael Symons, Will Byron **Est.** 1978 **Dozens** 35 000 **Vyds** 17ha
This may be one of the most senior wineries on the Mornington Peninsula but that does not stop it moving with the times. It has embarked on a serious sustainability program that touches on all aspects of its operations. It is one of the few wineries in Australia to measure its carbon footprint in detail, using the officially recognised system of the Winemaker's Federation of Australia. It is steadily reducing its consumption of electricity; it uses rainwater, collected from the winery roof, for rinsing and washing in the winery, as well as for supplying the winery in general; it has created a balanced ecosystem in the vineyard by strategic planting of cover crops and reduction of sprays; and it has reduced its need to irrigate. All the Stonier wines are estate-grown and made with a mix of wild yeast (from initiation of fermentation) and cultured yeast (added towards the end of fermentation to ensure that no RS remains), and almost all are destemmed to open fermenters. All have a 2-stage maturation – always French oak and variable use of barriques and puncheons for the first stage. Exports to all major markets.

ᵀ ᵀ ᵀ ᵀ ᵀ **Reserve Mornington Peninsula Chardonnay 2020** This has the right amount of complexity and depth to warrant a Reserve stamp of approval. Ripe stone fruit, a thread of citrus, oak stitched in neatly and with creamy, lees inputs, all the flavours linger. Excellent acidity keeps things buoyant and bright. Screw cap. 13.5% alc. **Rating** 95 **To** 2028 $50 JF
KBS Vineyard Mornington Peninsula Chardonnay 2020 Nicely composed, with an immediately appealing, youthful and fragrant chardonnay nose of florals, stone fruit, melon and a dash of citrus. Flavours of classy vanilla-pod oak and lees, yet the palate is silky, luscious and neatly reined in with the acidity. Screw cap. 13% alc. **Rating** 95 **To** 2028 $50 JF

ᵀ ᵀ ᵀ ᵀ ᵀ **Mornington Peninsula Pinot Noir 2020 Rating** 93 **To** 2025 $30 JF
Gainsborough Park Vineyard Mornington Peninsula Chardonnay 2020 Rating 92 **To** 2025 $40 JF
Mornington Peninsula Chardonnay 2019 Rating 92 **To** 2025 $26 JF
Merron's Vineyard Mornington Peninsula Pinot Noir 2020 Rating 92 **To** 2030 $55 JF
Mornington Peninsula Pinot Noir 2019 Rating 91 **To** 2025 $30 JF

Stormflower Vineyard ★★★★☆

3503 Caves Road, Wilyabrup, WA 6280 **Region** Margaret River
T 0421 867 488 **www.**stormflower.com.au **Open** 7 days 11–5
Winemaker Stuart Pym, Joel Page **Est.** 2007 **Dozens** 2800 **Vyds** 10ha
Stormflower Vineyard was founded by David Martin, Howard Cearns and Nic Trimboli, 3 friends better known as co-founders of Little Creatures Brewery in Fremantle. They thought the location of the vineyard (planted in the mid '90s) was ideal for producing high-quality wines. Whether they knew that storms hit the property on a regular basis, with hail and wind impacting the crop in most seasons, isn't known. What is known is the investment they have made in the vineyard by pulling out one-third of the vines planted in the wrong way, in the wrong place, leaving almost 10ha of cabernet sauvignon, shiraz, chardonnay, sauvignon blanc, semillon and chenin blanc in place. Now the sole owner, David Martin is the driving force in the vineyard, with a family background in agriculture. The vineyard, certified organic by NASAA in 2016, is managed using natural soil biology and organic compost. A new winery was completed just in time for the 2020 vintage, with all wines now made onsite.

ᵀ ᵀ ᵀ ᵀ ᵀ **Wilyabrup Margaret River Cabernet Sauvignon 2018** Very aromatic, leafy cassis, juniper berry and pomegranate on the nose. It is attractively earthy, like freshly turned soil; the oak has a resin/licorice character. The palate is everything we expect, all of the flavours spooling out across the palate and through into the long finish. Screw cap. 14.7% alc. **Rating** 95 **To** 2041 $60 EL

🍷🍷🍷🍷🍷 **Wilyabrup Margaret River Chardonnay 2019** Rating 93 To 2031 $35 EL
Wilyabrup Margaret River Cabernet Shiraz 2019 Rating 93 To 2028
$27 EL **◑**
Margaret River Sauvignon Blanc 2020 Rating 92 To 2026 $25 EL **◑**
Wilyabrup Margaret River Shiraz 2018 Rating 91 To 2031 $38 EL
Silver Lining Wilyabrup Margaret River Sparkling 2019 Rating 90 $35 EL

SubRosa   ★★★★☆

PO Box 181, Ararat, Vic 3377 **Region** Grampians/Pyrenees
T 0478 072 259 **www**.subrosawine.com
Winemaker Adam Louder **Est.** 2013 **Dozens** 400
SubRosa, one of the best new wineries in the *Wine Companion 2019*, was created by 2 high-
performing partners in life and in this exceptional new winery. Adam Louder had completed
31 vintages in the Grampians, Pyrenees, Margaret River, Bordeaux and the Napa Valley, most
with famous names. He met Gold Coast–born partner Nancy Panter in the Napa Valley in '11
while she was working for Visa on projects that included the Olympic Games, FIFA World
Cup and NFL. After the '12 London Olympics, she and Adam moved between the US and
Australia, returning permanently to Australia in '15, having laid the groundwork for SubRosa
in '13. This is a business that will win gold medals galore should it enter wine shows. Exports
to Japan.

🍷🍷🍷🍷🍷 **Pyrenees Nebbiolo 2018** Attractive rose petal, Turkish delight, black cherry,
leafy aromas. Brambly spice, chewy fruit on the palate, but time in oak is also
apparent, delivering a varnish character which together with savoury tannins
completes a pretty complex nebbiolo picture. Give it time in the cellar. Screw
cap. 13.5% alc. **Rating** 93 **To** 2032 $45 JP
Grampians Shiraz 2018 Appealing aromatics with floral, raspberry, dry leaves
and a green edginess. Firm across the palate and fine in fruit density boasting
red cherry, baking spices, a hint of pepper, and mocha oak. A taut, well-tannined
shiraz. Screw cap. 14% alc. **Rating** 90 **To** 2026 $30 JP

Summerfield   ★★★★★

5967 Stawell-Avoca Road, Moonambel, Vic 3478 **Region** Pyrenees
T (03) 5467 2264 **www**.summerfieldwines.com **Open** Mon–Sat 10–5, Sun 10–3
Winemaker Mark Summerfield **Est.** 1979 **Dozens** 7000 **Vyds** 18.2ha
Founder Ian Summerfield handed over the winemaker reins to son Mark several years ago.
Mark has significantly refined the style of the wines with the introduction of French oak and
by reducing the alcohol without compromising the intensity and concentration of the wines.
If anything, the longevity of the wines produced by Mark will be even greater than that of
the American-oaked wines of bygone years. Exports to Japan and China.

Sunshine Creek   ★★★★

350 Yarraview Road, Yarra Glen, Vic 3775 **Region** Yarra Valley
T (03) 9882 1800 **www**.sunshinecreek.com.au
Winemaker Chris Lawrence **Est.** 2009 **Dozens** 7000 **Vyds** 20ha
Packaging magnate James Zhou has a wine business in China and, over the years, has
worked with an A–Z of distinguished Australian winemakers, including Grant Burge, Philip
Shaw, Phillip Jones, Pat Carmody and Geoff Hardy, to bring their wines to China. It was
a logical extension to produce Australian wine of similar quality and James commissioned
Mario Marson to find an appropriate existing vineyard. They discovered Martha's Vineyard,
which was planted in the 1980s by Olga Szymiczek. The site was a particularly good
one, which compensated for the need to change the existing spur-pruned vineyard (for
mechanisation) to vertical shoot position (VSP) for increased quality and hand picking. At the
same time, an extensive program of grafting was undertaken and new clones were planted. In
2011 Andrew Smith (formerly of Lusatia Park Vineyard) was appointed vineyard manager to
change the focus of management to sustainability and minimal interference. In '14 winemaker

Chris Lawrence joined the team and an onsite winery (capable of handling 275t) was completed prior to the '16 vintage. In '17 there was a changing of the guard in the winery as Mario decided to concentrate solely on his Vinea Marson brand and Chris took on the role of chief winemaker. Exports to Hong Kong, Japan and China.

🍷🍷🍷🍷🍷 **Ulysses Yarra Valley Cabernets 2018** This has come together well, with cassis and currant coated in savoury flavours of pepper, char and wild herbs. It's full bodied but not unwieldy, as the tannins are fine, long and ripe. Incredibly fresh. It's worth noting the top cabernets from the Yarra are not in monstrously heavy bottles like this one. Diam. 14% alc. **Rating** 95 **To** 2033 $120 JF

🍷🍷🍷🍷🍷 **Yarra Valley Chardonnay 2018 Rating** 93 **To** 2026 $45 JF
Yarra Valley Cabernets 2018 Rating 92 **To** 2028 $45 JF
Yarra Valley Pinot Noir 2018 Rating 91 **To** 2026 $45 JF
Yarra Valley Shiraz 2018 Rating 90 **To** 2030 $45 JF

 # Susuro

134/5 Hall St, Port Melbourne, Vic 3207 **Region** Various
T (03) 9646 1862 **www**.susuro.com.au
Winemaker Nikki Palun **Est.** 2019 **Dozens** 2500
Nikki Palun grew up in a family of backyard winemakers which left her with a deep-seated love of the grape. However, before becoming a winemaker she was a musician first, exploring different types and styles of music across the world. Her launch into wine was first at De Bortoli, where she was export manager for Asia Pacific, the Middle East and Africa, but soon took her to studying winemaking at Charles Sturt University. In 2014, she started the Octtava and Susuro wine labels. Nikki is a graduate of the Australian wine industry's Future Leaders Program, has served as a Wine Victoria board member, and has been involved in the Victorian Government wine ministerial advisory committee. She makes wine under both the Susuro (which specialises in Italian grape varieties) and Octtava wine labels. Exports to Taiwan and South Korea. (JP)

🍷🍷🍷🍷🍷 **Mornington Peninsula Friulano 2019** Heady aromas of wild flowers and fennel, with honeyed quince and spiced apple. Building on the palate, with neat phenolics adding to the glossy feel. It has the palate weight of, say, viognier but without its apricot flavour. This has a richness and a lusciousness, but not too much, and there's a lot of savouriness and bitter herbs throughout. Terrific drink. Screw cap. 12% alc. **Rating** 95 **To** 2025 $39 JF

🍷🍷🍷🍷🍷 **Octtava Pyrenees Shiraz 2019 Rating** 92 **To** 2032 $60 JP
Alpine Valleys Vermentino 2019 Rating 91 **To** 2024 $39 JP
South Australia Vermentino 2020 Rating 90 **To** 2022 $28 JF

Sutherland Estate

2010 Melba Highway, Dixons Creek, Vic 3775 **Region** Yarra Valley
T 0402 052 287 **www**.sutherlandestate.com.au **Open** W'ends & public hols 10–5
Winemaker Cathy Phelan, Angus Ridley **Est.** 2000 **Dozens** 1500 **Vyds** 4ha
The Phelan family established Sutherland Estate in 2000 when they purchased a mature 2ha vineyard at Dixons Creek. Further plantings followed: the vineyard now consists of 1ha each of chardonnay and pinot noir, and 0.5ha each of gewürztraminer, cabernet sauvignon, tempranillo and shiraz. Ron Phelan designed and built the cellar door, which enjoys stunning views over the Yarra Valley. Daughter Cathy, an inaugural member of Yarra Valley Wine Women, studied Wine Science at CSU and is now winemaker alongside her partner Angus Ridley, who spent over a decade at Coldstream Hills.

🍷🍷🍷🍷🍷 **Yarra Valley Blanc de Noirs 2016** Spends 4.5 years on lees. A mid gold hue with the lightest blush. Strong creamy leesy aromas including ripe camembert with lemon shortcake. It's refreshing, lively and the perky acidity leaves an imprint. Crown seal. 11.6% alc. **Rating** 90 **To** 2024 $36 JF

Sutton Grange Winery

★★★★★

Carnochans Road, Sutton Grange, Vic 3448 **Region** Bendigo
T (03) 8672 1478 **www**.suttongrange.com.au **Open** Sun 11–5
Winemaker Melanie Chester **Est.** 1998 **Dozens** 6000 **Vyds** 12ha
The 400ha Sutton Grange property is a horse training facility acquired in 1996 by Peter Sidwell, a Melbourne businessman with horseracing and breeding interests. A lunch visit to the property by long-term friends Alec Epis and Stuart Anderson led to the decision to plant shiraz, merlot, cabernet sauvignon, viognier and sangiovese. The winery is built from WA limestone. Exports to the UK, the US, Canada, Switzerland and China.

♟♟♟♟♟ **Estate Syrah 2019** Super-dense and packed with flavour but with real verve and brightness. Sutton Grange's location in the granite foothills of Mount Alexander is evident here. Granite provides mineral lift and natural balance, which makes an ideal background for a medium-bodied, black/blue-fruited young syrah. A dash of spice, a hint of cedary oak backed by fine chocolatey tannins rounds this charmer out very well. Screw cap. 14% alc. **Rating** 95 **To** 2030 $65 JP
Fairbank Syrah 2019 Fairbank shows the other side of the syrah coin, the plummy, juicy, sweet-fruited side that offers excellent drinking early, with the promise of some medium-term ageing. Brilliant purple hues, bright, jubey, cassis, plum and concentrated spice. Balance, texture and good length on display, together with some signature bush mint. It's all here. Screw cap. 14% alc. **Rating** 95 **To** 2033 $35 JP ✪

♟♟♟♟♟ **Estate Aglianico 2018** **Rating** 91 **To** 2027 $60 JP
Fairbank Sangiovese 2020 **Rating** 90 **To** 2026 $35 JP

Swan Valley Wines

★★★★

261 Haddrill Road, Baskerville, WA 6065 **Region** Swan Valley
T (08) 9296 1501 **www**.swanvalleywines.com.au **Open** Thurs–Sun & public hols 10–5
Winemaker Paul Hoffman **Est.** 1999 **Dozens** 1500 **Vyds** 6ha
Peter and Paula Hoffman, with sons Paul and Thomas, acquired their property in 1989. It had a long history of grapegrowing, the prior owner having registered the name Swan Valley Wines in '83. Courageously, the Hoffmans decided they would try to emulate the producers of chenin blanc in the Loire Valley, who use a classification system of Sec, Demisec, Moelleux (continuing with Doux and Liquoreux) in ascending order of sweetness. From Moelleux and above, the wines cruise through 30 years, the rare Liquoreux 100 years. Swan Valley Wines only attempted the first 3, but seem to have abandoned it.

♟♟♟♟♟ **Forest Blanc Semillon Sauvignon Blanc 2020** Wild ferment, zero additions, unfined, unfiltered. Creamy, nutty, savoury and saline with layered bitter orange, juniper berry, salted lychee, fresh baked bread and something else … Just like a walk in the bush after rain. Super-smart and concentrated with layers of interest and flavour. Screw cap. 13.1% alc. **Rating** 93 **To** 2028 $35 EL
Weip Country Chenin Blanc 2020 Chenin is so distinctive. You either love it or hate it. This is flinty apricot, Geraldton wax, wet river rocks (in the shade), and all kinds of great sheepy things (lanolin, for a start). On the palate, the beeswax phenolics integrate with the fruit and tart pop-rock acidity to create an intricately layered, highly engaging wine. Lots here for chenin lovers. Screw cap. 13.3% alc. **Rating** 93 **To** 2031 $40 EL
Warrine Chenin Blanc 2020 Beeswax, lanolin, apricot blossom and nectarine on the nose and palate. The acidity runs a bed of fine needles across the tongue. The lingering flavours and textures speak of cheesecloth, crushed limestone, white pepper and fennel flower. Screw cap. 12.2% alc. **Rating** 93 **To** 2031 $35 EL

Sweetwater Wines ★★★★

117 Sweetwater Road, Belford, NSW 2335 **Region** Hunter Valley
T (02) 4998 7666 **www**.sweetwaterwines.com.au
Winemaker Bryan Currie **Est.** 1998 **Vyds** 16ha
Sweetwater Wines is in the same ownership as Hungerford Hill and wouldn't normally have a separate winery entry in the *Wine Companion*. But it's a single-vineyard winery making only 2 wines, shiraz and cabernet sauvignon, the wines made by Andrew Thomas from 2003 to '16 and all stored in a temperature-controlled underground wine cellar that is part of the very large ornate house and separate guest accommodation built on the property. The reason for the seemingly unusual focus on cabernet sauvignon (true, second to shiraz) is the famed red volcanic soil over limestone. Exports to Hong Kong and China.

🍷🍷🍷🍷🍷 **Hunter Valley Shiraz 2019** As certain regional producers shift into a lighter and more digestible gear, reminiscent of the great Hunter reds of the past, this is a weighty shiraz of the more reductive, modern idiom. Polished. Oodles of vanillan oak. Floral aromas with undertones of iodine, clove, pepper and a rush of blue fruits. Aspirational. Well made. Will have plenty of fans. Screw cap. 14% alc. **Rating** 93 **To** 2028 $65 NG

🍷🍷🍷🍷 **Hunter Valley Cabernet Sauvignon 2018** **Rating** 88 **To** 2030 $65 NG

Swinging Bridge ★★★★★

701 The Escort Way, Orange, NSW 2800 **Region** Orange
T 0409 246 609 **www**.swingingbridge.com.au **Open** Tues–Wed by appt
Winemaker Tom Ward **Est.** 1995 **Vyds** 6ha
Swinging Bridge Estate was established in 1995 by the Ward and Payten families. In 2008, having been involved from the start, Tom and Georgie Ward took the helm and have since evolved Swinging Bridge into a premium supplier of cool-climate wines from Orange. The label had its founding in Canowindra with initial plantings of chardonnay and shiraz, named after the historic wooden pedestrian bridge that traverses the Belubula River at the foot of the vineyard. Today, Swinging Bridge has a variety of ranges on offer, including a number of Reserve wines, the Experimental Series, Winemaker Series and Estate Series. Tom and Georgie searched for a number of years for the perfect place to call home in Orange, both for their family and Swinging Bridge. Tom's pursuit of premium grapes resulted in a number of wines made from grapes grown on Peter and Lee Hedberg's Hill Park Vineyard (planted in 1998). Hill Park Vineyard is now the permanent home of Swinging Bridge; Tom and Georgie were able to realise their move when this outstanding property became available. Tom was a Len Evans scholar in 2012 and has been president of NSW Wine since '13.

🍷🍷🍷🍷🍷 **Tom Ward Block A Orange Chardonnay 2018** Tasting this after Block D 2015 confirms that chardonnay here has evolved. For the better: deft, detailed and precise. But with no sacrifice of flavour. Cool-climate jittery across the palate. More about texture than obvious fruit references. Nougatine, truffle and almond. Stone-fruit inflections, too. Long and juicy. The acidity is palpably natural and all the better because of it. I would drink without age on its side. Screw cap. 12.9% alc. **Rating** 95 **To** 2026 $60 NG

🍷🍷🍷🍷🍷 **Orange Shiraz 2019** **Rating** 92 **To** 2025 $22 NG ✪
Tom Ward William J. Orange Shiraz 2019 **Rating** 91 **To** 2025 $35 NG
Tom Ward #006 Orange Tempinot 2019 **Rating** 90 **To** 2023 $35 NG
Tom Ward #008 Orange Cabernet Franc Shiraz 2019 **Rating** 90 **To** 2024 $35 NG

Swings & Roundabouts ★★★★

2807 Caves Road, Yallingup, WA 6232 **Region** Margaret River
T (08) 9756 6640 **www**.swings.com.au **Open** 7 days 10–5
Winemaker Brian Fletcher **Est.** 2004 **Dozens** 10 000 **Vyds** 5ha

The Swings & Roundabouts name comes from the expression used to encapsulate the eternal balancing act between the various aspects of grape and wine production. Swings aims to balance the serious side with a touch of fun. The wines are released under the Swings & Roundabouts and Backyard Stories labels. The arrival of Brian Fletcher as winemaker has underwritten the quality of the wines. He has never been far from the wine headlines, with over 35 years of experience making wine all over the world. Exports to the US, Canada, Japan and China.

♀♀♀♀♀ Backyard Stories Margaret River Chardonnay 2019 Such buttery richness on the nose and palate that one assumes partial or full mlf. Extremely satisfying and quite delicious, with salted yellow peach, hints of curry leaf, some creamed French butter and a curling, lingering finish. The saline acid is a standout feature of the wine, weaving in and out of the rich fruit, freshening things up as it goes. Screw cap. 13% alc. **Rating** 94 **To** 2028 $50 EL
Backyard Stories Margaret River Cabernet Sauvignon 2018 Fleshy, ripe and creamy cabernet from a brilliant year. Red and black fruits course over the palate in concert, pulling through into the long finish. Plenty of stuffing and substance. Screw cap. 14.5% alc. **Rating** 94 **To** 2035 $55 EL

♀♀♀♀♀ Margaret River Sauvignon Blanc Semillon 2020 Rating 92 **To** 2022 $24 EL ✪
Novus Margaret River Malbec 2020 Rating 92 **To** 2025 $24 EL ✪
Margaret River Chardonnay 2019 Rating 91 **To** 2026 $24 EL
Backyard Stories Margaret River Sangiovese Rosé 2020 Rating 90 **To** 2024 $34 EL
Backyard Stories Pinot Noir Chardonnay NV Rating 90 $45 EL

Swinney   ★★★★☆

325 Frankland-Kojonup Road, Frankland River, WA 6396 **Region** Frankland River
T (08) 9200 4483 **www.**swinney.com.au
Winemaker Robert Mann **Est.** 1998 **Dozens** 2500 **Vyds** 160ha
The Swinney family (currently parents Graham and Kaye, and son and daughter Matt and Janelle) has been resident on their 2500ha property since it was settled by George Swinney in 1922. In the '90s they decided to diversify and now have 160ha of vines across 4 vineyards, including the Powderbark Ridge Vineyard in Frankland River (planted in '98, purchased in partnership with former Hardys winemaker Peter Dawson). The lion's share goes to shiraz (67ha) and cabernet sauvignon (48ha), followed by riesling, semillon, pinot gris, gewürztraminer, viognier, vermentino and malbec. They also pushed the envelope by establishing grenache, tempranillo and mourvèdre as bush vines, a rarity in this part of the world. Exports to the UK, Singapore and Hong Kong.

♀♀♀♀♀ Farvie Frankland River Syrah 2019 Bacon fat, maple, salted pomegranate, raspberry, graphite, red dirt, mulberry and pink peppercorn. Like the Hokusai wave, this crashes and courses with flavours and textures, ebbing and flowing on the palate. This is balanced, restrained, long, powerful and most importantly, shaped and structured by supple, chewy tannins. They hold the fruit in the cups of their hands and usher it through a very long finish. A weightlessly poetic wine. Screw cap. 14% alc. **Rating** 98 **To** 2031 $150 EL ✪ ❤
Farvie Frankland River Grenache 2019 What sets hearts on fire the world over for Châteauneuf-du-Pape is the muscular, ferrous, salty raspberry humbug and minerally hutzpah. It sets the high-tide mark for grenache. We grenache drinkers yearn for it. And here it is. The strength of Frankland River is its ability to marry sweet (glossy) red fruit to savoury, gravelly earth. The 2018 was a staggering showpiece, this is more restrained, cooler and finer, yet equally long. Choose your weapon. Screw cap. 14% alc. **Rating** 98 **To** 2041 $150 EL ✪ ❤

♀♀♀♀♀ Frankland River Grenache 2019 In a nutshell, this wine is supple, slinky, crunchy and very long; packed to the rafters with raspberry, exotic spice, and defined by fine, silty tannins. What a wine. Screw cap. 14% alc. **Rating** 96 **To** 2035 $42 EL ✪

Frankland River Riesling 2020 This has all the austere acidity that makes Frankland River riesling what it is, but it comes with a plump fruit profile that gives it a richness and almost an opulence. Lychee, lime, green apple and talc. The acidity has a zing and a pop and finishes with a crunch of sea salt. Screw cap. 12.5% alc. **Rating** 95 **To** 2031 $33 EL ✪

Frankland River Mourvèdre Syrah Grenache 2019 Layered, textural, elegant and robust all at once. Each variety calls 'present' on the roll call; syrah brings spice and structure, grenache succulent red berry fruits, while mourvèdre is the earthy bed upon which they all lay. Apart from the salty, ripe flavour, it's the cohesive and chewy texture that's really got me. Seriously great. Screw cap. 14% alc. **Rating** 95 **To** 2030 $42 EL

Frankland River Syrah 2019 Quite reductive initially, but it blows off. This is consistently an elegant and supple wine, with very fine structure and saturating density of flavour. The length of flavour endures long past the final sip, showing the pedigree of fruit and the care and attention in both the vineyard and winery. Screw cap. 14% alc. **Rating** 94 **To** 2031 $42 EL

Symphony Hill Wines ★★★★

2017 Eukey Road, Ballandean, Qld 4382 **Region** Granite Belt
T (07) 4684 1388 **www.**symphonyhill.com.au **Open** 7 days 10–4
Winemaker Abraham de Klerk **Est.** 1999 **Dozens** 6000 **Vyds** 3.5ha
Ewen Macpherson purchased an old table-grape and orchard property in 1996. A partnership with his parents, Bob and Jill Macpherson, led to development of the vineyard while Ewen completed his bachelor of applied science in viticulture (2003). The vineyard (now much expanded) was established using state-of-the-art technology. Exports to China.

♥♥♥♥♡ **Reserve Granite Belt Cabernet Sauvignon 2018** Juxtaposing full ripeness with the bright acid tension of this lofty site, this is an intense and age-worthy cabernet of cassis and blackcurrant fruit framed confidently in high-cocoa dark chocolate French oak. It holds its alcohol confidently on a persistent finish, sustained by lively natural acidity and firm, fine tannins. Screw cap. 15% alc. **Rating** 92 **To** 2033 $95 TS

Reserve Granite Belt Shiraz 2018 Savoury, spicy shiraz of medium purple/red hue. Dark berry fruits meet earthy, herbal complexity, confidently supported by firm, fine French oak tannins and the vibrant acid line of this high site. It lacks the lift, vibrancy and drive anticipated at this young age, yet holds the persistence and balance to improve over the coming decade. Screw cap. 13.5% alc. **Rating** 90 **To** 2033 $95 TS

♥♥♥♥ **Adelaide Hills Pinot Gris 2020** Rating 89 **To** 2022 $40 TS
Reserve McLaren Vale Sangiovese 2019 Rating 89 **To** 2024 $65 TS

Syrahmi ★★★★★

2370 Lancefield-Tooborac Road, Tooborac, Vic 3523 **Region** Heathcote
T 0407 057 471 **www.**syrahmi.com.au **Open** By appt
Winemaker Adam Foster **Est.** 2004 **Dozens** 2400 **Vyds** 0.8ha
Adam Foster worked as a chef in Victoria and London before moving to the front of house and becoming increasingly interested in wine. He then worked as a cellar hand with a who's who in Australia and France, including Torbreck, Chapoutier, Mitchelton, Domaine Ogier, Heathcote Winery, Jasper Hill and Domaine Pierre Gaillard. He became convinced that the Cambrian soils of Heathcote could produce the best possible shiraz, and since 2004 has purchased grapes from the region, using the full bag of winemaking techniques. In 2017 0.8ha of shiraz (3 clones) were planted at 8888 vines/ha at Tooborac, with a winery completed in time for the '19 vintage. Exports to the US, Japan and Hong Kong.

ΨΨΨΨΨ Garden of Earthly Delights Pinot Noir 2017 Open the bottle and the bouquet greets you, lifted and fragrant with just-squeezed red cherry, musky florals, a hint of forest floor and smoky, sweet spice. Runs true to those flavoursome characters, and long on the palate, with a spray of fine tannins. Super-elegant. Screw cap. 12.8% alc. **Rating** 95 **To** 2025 $55 JP
Garden of Earthly Delights Bruno Sangiovese 2012 Sourced from the Greenstone Vineyard, you sense the maker is making a statement here about the quality of, and his belief in, aged sangiovese out of Heathcote. He's staking a lot here and, boy, does he succeed! It takes you back to Tuscany, to the earth, tar and smoked meats savouriness of many an Italian style, with red, dusty, cherry pip flavours and all rolled up in a tight, medium-bodied wine. Stunning! Screw cap. 13.8% alc. **Rating** 95 **To** 2032 $70 JP

ΨΨΨΨΨ XV Heathcote Shiraz 2018 **Rating** 93 **To** 2032 $60 JP
Hugo Heathcote Shiraz 2017 Rating 93 **To** 2032 $55 JP
La Bise Heathcote Marsanne Roussanne 2019 Rating 92 **To** 2030 $47 JP
Heathcote Mourvèdre 2018 Rating 92 **To** 2028 $45 JP
Garden of Earthly Delights Sangiovese 2017 Rating 91 **To** 2027 $40 JP
Garden of Earthly Delights Riesling 2019 Rating 90 **To** 2024 $34 JP
Egg Heathcote Shiraz 2016 Rating 90 **To** 2026 $45 JP
Garden of Earthly Delights Nebbiolo 2017 Rating 90 **To** 2032 $40 JP

T'Gallant ★★★★

1385 Mornington-Flinders Road, Main Ridge, Vic 3928 **Region** Mornington Peninsula
T (03) 5931 1300 **www**.tgallant.com.au **Open** 7 days 9–5
Winemaker Tom Shanahan **Est.** 1990 **Vyds** 8ha
Husband and wife winemakers Kevin McCarthy and Kathleen Quealy carved out such an important niche market for the T'Gallant label that in 2003, after protracted negotiations, it was acquired by Beringer Blass (now part of TWE). The acquisition of a 15ha property and the planting of 8ha of pinot gris gave the business a firm geographic base, as well as providing increased resources for its signature wine.

ΨΨΨΨΨ Tribute Pinot Gris 2020 This is quite shy and only just makes a gris impression, as in more texture and richness on the palate. Lightly spiced pears, honeysuckle and some grated apple with a drizzle of lemon juice. Softish acidity and easy to enjoy. Screw cap. 13% alc. **Rating** 90 **To** 2023 $25 JF

Tahbilk ★★★★★

254 O'Neils Road, Tabilk, Vic 3608 **Region** Nagambie Lakes
T (03) 5794 2555 **www**.tahbilk.com.au **Open** Mon–Sat 9–5, Sun 11–5
Winemaker Alister Purbrick, Neil Larson, Alan George **Est.** 1860 **Dozens** 120 000
Vyds 221.5ha
A winery steeped in tradition (with National Trust classification) and which should be visited at least once by every wine-conscious Australian. It makes wines – particularly red wines – utterly in keeping with that tradition. The essence of that heritage comes in the form of their tiny quantities of shiraz made from vines planted in 1860. A founding member of Australia's First Families of Wine. *Wine Companion 2016* Winery of the Year. Exports to all major markets.

ΨΨΨΨΨ Museum Release Marsanne 2015 Just look at that straw-yellow colour! So youthful and just 6 years old! This is marsanne at its best, on the long road to a glorious future. It just gets better and better with each year, all without a skerrick of oak. Honeysuckle, buttered toast, jasmine and pear skin scents envelope the senses. The acidity tastes young and bright, belying the wine's age. What value lies here. Silver medal Alternative Varieties Wine Show '20. Screw cap. 12.5% alc. **Rating** 96 **To** 2030 $26 JP ✪ ♥
1860 Vines Shiraz 2017 A timeless beauty with time on its hands. Allow it a moment to spread its vinous wings. This is definitely a wine to contemplate.

Earth-baked and dusty – concentrated black fruits, Damson plum, woodsy spice, but then there's a sudden, beautiful moment of violets. Oak? Well, it's there in the background. It retains a modesty, a charming, understated grace, that is hugely appealing in a world of the super-shiraz. Screw cap. 14% alc. **Rating** 96 **To** 2043 $325 JP

Cane Cut Marsanne 2018 Marsanne gets to showcase its versatility at Tahbilk. Here, it knocks the dessert-style sweetie out of the park with its complexity and adroit winemaking. Striking gold/green hue. Orange peel, nougat, stone fruit and candied-fruit aromas transform into utter lusciousness on the palate. Smooth as glass. Can take chilling. 500ml. Screw cap. 11% alc. **Rating** 95 **To** 2026 $26 JP ✪

Grenache Mourvèdre Rosé 2020 Cast with a Rhône eye but delivered in a very Australian style with pristine, juicy, crunchy fruit to the fore. Bright confectionery pink. Red cherry, raspberry, strawberry, boiled lolly with pomegranate tartness that puckers just so. The degree of acidity/tannin meets the fruit and then just a little bit more. Got the balance just right. Screw cap. 12% alc. **Rating** 95 **To** 2025 $22 JP ✪ ♥

Eric Stevens Purbrick Shiraz 2017 Your classic Central Victorian shiraz in a nutshell, with a down-to-earth (literally) appeal of baked earth, Aussie bush scents mingling with ripe blackberries and woody oak spice. The palate is full and generous, with a lingering, smoky savouriness. Traditional, yes, in keeping with its namesake, who knew a thing or two and established the Tahbilk red wine style. Tasted months before release and still coming together, but with an assured confidence. Bronze medal at Perth Royal Wine Show '20. Screw cap. 14.5% alc. **Rating** 95 **To** 2034 $72 JP

Eric Stevens Purbrick Cabernet Sauvignon 2017 This is definitely about a taste of tradition, of measured oak, of ripe fruit allowed to fully express, and a sense of place in the earthy, dusty savouriness. This is no power cabernet. Aromas of the Aussie bush, sage, baked earth, light herbals and violets. A warm, inviting palate of dark chocolate and spice, finishing with firm tannins. Elegant and enticing now, but save some for later. Screw cap. 14% alc. **Rating** 95 **To** 2034 $72 JP

Old Vines Cabernet Shiraz 2018 A classic in many ways, not the least of which is the commitment to a distinctive Tahbilk style that is beyond trends. Baked earth, wood smoke, Aussie bush mint and dark plums. It combines a generous body of sustained flavour with toasty oak and ripe tannins, making for a harmonious whole. Screw cap. 14.5% alc. **Rating** 95 **To** 2034 $47 JP

ŶŶŶŶŶ **Marsanne 2020 Rating** 93 **To** 2028 $20 JH ✪
Shiraz 2019 Rating 93 **To** 2027 $26 JP ✪
Pinot Gris 2020 Rating 91 **To** 2025 $22 JP ✪
Cabernet Sauvignon 2018 Rating 91 **To** 2026 $26 JP
Grenache Shiraz Mourvèdre 2019 Rating 90 **To** 2024 $26 JP

Talisman Wines   ★★★★☆

Wheelman Road, Wellington Mill, WA 6236 **Region** Geographe
T 0401 559 266 **www.**talismanwines.com.au **Open** By appt
Winemaker Peter Stanlake **Est.** 2009 **Dozens** 3000 **Vyds** 9ha
Kim Robinson (and wife Jenny) began the development of their vineyard in 2000 and now have cabernet, shiraz, malbec, zinfandel, chardonnay, riesling and sauvignon blanc. Kim says that 'after 8 frustrating years of selling grapes to Evans & Tate and Wolf Blass, we decided to optimise the vineyard and attempt to make quality wines'. The measure of their success has been consistent gold-medal performance (and some trophies) at the Geographe Wine Show. They say this could not have been achieved without the assistance of vineyard manager Victor Bertola and winemaker Peter Stanlake.

ŶŶŶŶŶ **Gabrielle Ferguson Valley Chardonnay 2019** This label leaves a trail of gold medals and trophies in its wake, and the cooler vintage 2019 is no exception. Gunflint, curry leaf, brine, white peach and red apple skins define the aromatics, and more than clearly replicate themselves on the palate. The texture is fine and slippery. A lot to love and discover if you haven't tried it before. Screw cap. 13.6% alc. **Rating** 96 **To** 2031 $40 EL ✪

Ferguson Valley Malbec 2019 This is aromatically on the midnight end of the spectrum: blackberry, raspberry bramble, black pepper, star anise and szechuan peppercorns. Awesome. The palate delivers just what the nose promised, layering it with fine and grippy tannins. The acid energises this to unfurl both in the glass and the mouth. Savoury and plush at once. What a wine! Screw cap. 15% alc. **Rating** 95 **To** 2030 $35 EL ✪

Ferguson Valley Zinfandel 2019 A hallmark of this elevated vineyard in the Ferguson Valley, this wine is supple and bouncy, the high alcohol almost completely obscured, save for a brief suggestion through the finish. Dark-berry fruits, with a decidedly earthy edge (in a mulberry/raspberry-bramble spectrum), make it almost opulent, the major highlight being the medium body and grace with which it purports itself. Screw cap. 15.6% alc. **Rating** 95 **To** 2030 $45 EL

Ferguson Valley Cabernet Malbec 2019 The Talisman vineyard is one of the highest points in the Ferguson Valley, elevation giving the wines a poise and freshness. The fruit on the palate here is dense and yet restrained; it holds back, conserving its power, which it meters out over the long finish. This has all the hallmarks of good cellaring (fruit, acid, tannin, length), but it is also delicious now. And the price! Screw cap. 14.4% alc. **Rating** 94 **To** 2036 $30 EL ✪

Ferguson Valley Zinfandel 2018 Geographe does zinfandel very well. It's a combination of the warm days and cooler nights that really help it to excel here. This is no exception; pure, juicy, balanced and long, with all the raspberry and mulberry that we expect from the variety, bolstered by fine, salty acidity. The oak is imperceptible, save for the soft, plush tannins on the palate. Good length of flavour rounds it out into a complete package. Screw cap. 14.1% alc. **Rating** 94 **To** 2031 $45 EL

ΨΨΨΨ **Ferguson Valley Riesling 2020** Rating 93 **To** 2031 $25 EL ✪
Arida Ferguson Valley 2020 Rating 91 **To** 2026 $25 EL
Ferguson Valley Merlot 2019 Rating 90 **To** 2028 $40 EL

Talits Estate   ★★★★

722 Milbrodale Road, Broke, NSW 2321 **Region** Hunter Valley
T 0404 841 700 **www**.talitsestate.com.au **Open** Fri–Sun 9–5
Winemaker Daniel Binet **Est.** 2000 **Dozens** 400 **Vyds** 4ha

Gayle Meredith is the owner of this 4ha vineyard in the Broke Fordwich subregion of the Hunter Valley, resplendent with stellar accommodation and a forward-thinking mindset driven by winemaker, Daniel Binet. This manifests as a suite of wines stamped with a welcome savouriness. The hark back to a past, defined as much by the quintessential Hunter twang of sweet earth as by the uncanny regional blend of pinot noir and shiraz, is captivating. The quest for savoury, versatile expressions is also iterated across innovative work with sangiovese, admirably homegrown rather than outsourced to cooler zones. (NG)

ΨΨΨΨ **Summer Rosé of Merlot 2019** A bright light coral. We seldom see merlot rosé in Australia, but it works well. Verdant hedgerow scents give a savoury lift to sapid cherry and orange-rind notes. A plush core is bridled by a rail of phenolics and juicy acidity. Nothing pushed too far or hard. Dry, medium bodied and good drinking. Screw cap. 13.5% alc. **Rating** 90 **To** 2021 $25 NG

ΨΨΨ **The Rogue Rooster Sangiovese Merlot 2019** Rating 88 **To** 2023 $35 NG

Tallarook   ★★★☆

140 Ennis Road, Tallarook, 3569 **Region** Central Victoria
T 0423 205 370 **www**.tallarookwines.com.au
Winemaker Martin Williams MW **Est.** 1980 **Dozens** 7000 **Vyds** 12ha

Martin Williams collects degrees like those who collect postage stamps, his master of wine almost incidental to his wine career. He began with a degree in chemistry and biochemistry at The University of Sydney, followed by a master's at the University of California, working in Burgundy along the way. Years in the wine industry followed till Martin went on to obtain a doctorate in medicinal chemistry from Monash University in '12. He returned to the wine world in '15 and is now chief winemaker for Tallarook, a winery that has had a chequered existence after the vineyard was planted in 1980. It was intended to be a feature of a Porsche racing event centre, the track on the 475ha property on which the vineyard is planted. In '17 it was acquired by the Yang family. Only a token amount of wine is sold in Australia. Exports to China.

♥♥♥♥ **Shiraz 2019** Acacia, briar, Aussie bush scents mingle with black pepper and black fruits – very Central Victorian – and lively spice. Concentrated with choc-mocha, vanilla and sweet spice, plump, with dusty tannins. Screw cap. 13.5% alc. **Rating** 89 **To** 2031 $25 JP

Taltarni   ★★★★★

339 Taltarni Road, Moonambel, Vic 3478 **Region** Pyrenees
T (03) 5459 7900 **www**.taltarni.com.au **Open** 7 days 11–5
Winemaker Robert Heywood, Peter Warr, Ben Howell **Est.** 1969 **Dozens** 80 000
Vyds 78.5ha
The American owner and founder of Clos du Val (Napa Valley), Taltarni and Clover Hill (see separate entry) has brought the management of these 3 businesses and Domaine de Nizas (Languedoc) under the one roof, the group known as Goelet Wine Estates. Taltarni is the largest of the Australian ventures, its estate vineyards of great value and underpinning the substantial annual production. Insectariums are established in permanent vegetation corridors, each containing around 2000 native plants that provide a pollen and nectar source for the beneficial insects, reducing the need for chemicals and other controls of the vineyards. In recent years Taltarni has updated its winemaking techniques and in '17 celebrated 40 years of winemaking. Exports to all major markets.

♥♥♥♥♥ **Old Vine Estate Pyrenees Cabernet Sauvignon 2018** Harks back to some of the glorious cabernets of the 80s, with strong regional and varietal clarity, complexity and structure. Shows just how exciting the grape can be in a region dominated by shiraz. Densely coloured, with a roaming bouquet of dark plums, cassis, black cherries and subtle, spicy oak. Intense and concentrated, fine and long in tannic energy. Wow! Screw cap. 14% alc. **Rating** 96 **To** 2032 $45 JP ✪ ♥
Old Vine Estate Pyrenees Shiraz 2019 Winemaker Robert Heywood has been working on structural definition for his reds. His efforts would make Taltarni's early winemaker, Dominique Portet, very happy. The 2018 is very much about structure. It's firm and precise, with an equally well-deliberated, still-emerging, solid, blackberried fruit profile. Its future is beautifully laid out before it. Be patient. Screw cap. 14.5% alc. **Rating** 95 **To** 2034 $50 JP
Reserve Pyrenees Shiraz Cabernet 2019 In the Taltarni scheme of things, this Reserve Shiraz Cabernet can look forward to a long life ahead, yet even in its youth it shows its class. This is not a showy wine, but an elegant look at the classic Aussie red, albeit with a mass of beaut, concentrated flavour. Shiraz takes the lead here, all sweet blackberries, anise and plum, with a raft of woodsy spice. The palate lays out charming florals, dark chocolate and a long thread of dried herbs, all swept along by fine-cut, silky tannins. Cork. 14.5% alc. **Rating** 95 **To** 2032 $75 JP

♥♥♥♥♡ **Tasmanian Pinot Noir 2020 Rating** 92 **To** 2025 $32 JP
The Patron Pyrenees Cabernet Shiraz 2016 Rating 92 **To** 2036 $120 JP
Brut 2015 Rating 92 $26 JP
Taché Sparkling Rosé 2014 Rating 92 $26 JP
Cuvée Rosé 2014 Rating 92 $26 JP
Heathcote Shiraz 2018 Rating 91 **To** 2028 $35 JP
Sparkling Shiraz 2018 Rating 90 $26 JP

Tamar Ridge | Pirie ★★★★☆

1a Waldhorn Drive, Rosevears, Tas 7277 **Region** Northern Tasmania
T (03) 6330 0300 **www**.tamarridge.com.au **Open** 7 days 10–5
Winemaker Tom Wallace, Anthony De Amicis **Est.** 1994 **Dozens** 14000 **Vyds** 130ha
Tamar Ridge has been owned by Brown Brothers since 2010, its vineyards of inestimable value on an island unable to meet more than a small part of demand from the Australian mainland. It is focusing its attention on pinot noir for table wine and – along with chardonnay – sparkling wine. It goes without saying that the 14000 dozen production only accounts for a small part of the annual crop from 130ha. An outstanding suite of sparkling cuvées are branded 'Pirie' in honour of founder Dr Andrew Pirie. Exports to all major markets.

🍷🍷🍷🍷🍷 **Tamar Ridge Reserve Pinot Noir 2019** The distinguished side of Tamar pinot: sensitive, elegant and sophisticated. A captivating air of rose petal and potpourri. Unashamedly red-fruited, celebrating a vibrant core of morello cherry, spicy raspberry and strawberry hull, nuanced with a hint of white pepper. Whole bunches and barrels played gently and eloquently. Fine-grained tannins grace an outstanding finish. Tom Wallace's delicate side is something to behold, and has yielded my top Tasmanian pinot of the year! Screw cap. 13.1% alc. **Rating** 96 To 2034 $65 TS

🍷🍷🍷🍷🍷 **Tamar Ridge Pinot Gris 2019 Rating** 91 To 2021 $28 TS

Tambo Estate ★★★★

96 Pages Road, Tambo Upper, Vic 3885 **Region** Gippsland
T 0418 100 953 **www**.tambowine.com.au **Open** Thurs–Sun 11–5, 7 days January
Winemaker Alastair Butt **Est.** 1994 **Dozens** 1940 **Vyds** 5.11ha
Bill and Pam Williams returned to Australia in the early 1990s after 7 years overseas, and began the search for a property which met the specific requirements for high-quality table wines established by Dr John Gladstones in his masterwork *Viticulture and Environment*. They chose a property in the foothills of the Victorian Alps on the inland side of the Gippsland Lakes, with predominantly sheltered, north-facing slopes. They planted a little over 5ha: 3.4ha to chardonnay, as well as a little cabernet sauvignon, pinot noir and sauvignon blanc. They are mightily pleased to have secured the services of Alastair Butt (one-time winemaker at Seville Estate).

🍷🍷🍷🍷🍷 **Gippsland Lakes Sauvignon Blanc 2018** This wears its savouriness well although there's a smack of white peach and citrus. The palate fleshes out with lemon curd and nutty, leesy characters yet it has the acid line to keep it buoyant. The phenolic grip on the finish is tucked in neatly enough. Screw cap. 12.5% alc. **Rating** 92 To 2022 $28 JF
Gippsland Lakes Cabernet Sauvignon 2018 A heady wine, with fresh and dried currants, tomato-bush leaves, blackcurrant pastilles, pencil shavings and Kool Mints. Soft and plush, tannins have some give with leafy freshness throughout. It's old-school in a way and has a charm. Screw cap. 13.8% alc. **Rating** 92 To 2027 $28 JF
Gippsland Lakes Pinot Noir 2018 An intriguing and compelling wine, rich, slippery and ripe, yet with modest alcohol. It's full of licorice root, spiced rhubarb and Angostura bitters that follow through on the full-bodied palate. Tannins have a slight taste of green walnuts, although there is a plushness throughout. Screw cap. 12.9% alc. **Rating** 90 To 2026 $35 JF

🍷🍷🍷🍷 **Gippsland Lakes Chardonnay 2018 Rating** 88 To 2023 $28 JF

Taminick Cellars ★★★★

339 Booth Road, Taminick via Glenrowan, Vic 3675 **Region** Glenrowan
T (03) 5766 2282 **www**.taminickcellars.com.au **Open** Mon–Sat 9–5, Sun 10–5
Winemaker James Booth **Est.** 1904 **Dozens** 2000 **Vyds** 19.7ha

Peter Booth is a 3rd-generation member of the Booth family, who have owned this winery since Esca Booth purchased the property in 1904. James Booth, 4th generation and current winemaker, completed his wine science degree at CSU in 2008. The red wines are massively flavoured and very long-lived, notably those from the 9ha of shiraz planted in 1919. Trebbiano and alicante bouschet were also planted in 1919; the much newer arrivals include nero d'Avola.

🍷🍷🍷🍷🍷 **Durif 2017** A journey into the durif darkness, a place inhabited by the grape's propensity (when set free) for blackberries, bramble berry, tar and red earth. But, it's not for long. What is both apparent on the nose and upfront on the palate melds into an attractive, well-appointed durif with lifted aromatics of violet and spice. Quite a rich and varied little adventure. Screw cap. 13.8% alc. **Rating** 94 To 2031 $22 JP ✪

🍷🍷🍷🍷🍷 **Premium Shiraz 2015 Rating** 93 To 2030 $22 JP ✪
Liqueur Muscat NV Rating 93 $18 JP ✪
Cabernet Sauvignon 2015 Rating 91 To 2025 $18 JP ✪

Tapanappa   ★★★★★

15 Spring Gully Road, Piccadilly, SA 5151 **Region** Adelaide Hills
T (08) 7324 5301 **www**.tapanappa.com.au **Open** 7 days 11–4
Winemaker Brian Croser **Est.** 2002 **Dozens** 2500 **Vyds** 16.7ha

Tapanappa was founded by Brian Croser in 2002. The word Tapanappa is probably derived from the local Aboriginal language and likely translates to 'stick to the path'. Through Tapanappa, Brian is continuing a career-long mission of matching the climate, soil and geology of distinguished sites to the right varieties, and then developing and managing the vineyards to optimise quality. Tapanappa is dedicated to producing unique 'wines of terroir' from its 3 distinguished sites in SA with its winery located in the heart of the Piccadilly Valley. The brand's components are the Whalebone Vineyard at Wrattonbully (planted to cabernet sauvignon, shiraz and merlot in 1974), the Tiers Vineyard at Piccadilly in the Adelaide Hills (chardonnay) and the Foggy Hill Vineyard on the southern tip of the Fleurieu Peninsula (pinot noir). Exports to Canada, Europe, Sweden, the UK, Hong Kong, Japan and the UAE.

🍷🍷🍷🍷🍷 **Foggy Hill Vineyard Pinot Noir 2019** A darker note of berry here – blueberry and black cherry. It's fully fragrant, with the stems adding their woody spice and seasoning. What happens on the palate is unique, the structure of the wine taking your senses deeper into the flavour well, where a gastronomic heart of subtle amaro-like bitters dwells. Learned palates will want to sit on this and watch it unfold for hours, if not years. Cork. 13% alc. **Rating** 96 To 2030 $55 TL ✪ ♥
Whalebone Vineyard Cabernet Shiraz 2017 A cooler season works its magic, lifting the violet perfume of cabernet, the black pepper of shiraz, the bright tang of acidity and the fine-ground energy of enduring, chalk-bound tannins. Regional menthol assumes its rightful place. Medium-bodied effortlessness is refreshing. A keeper. Cork. 13.5% alc. **Rating** 95 To 2037 $55 TS
Whalebone Vineyard Merlot Cabernet Franc 2017 Signature Wrattonbully, from menthol-tinted aromatics and cassis-defined palate to fine-grained, powdery, chalk-dusted tannins. A cool season heightens tang, freshness, endurance and beauty. Everything works together confidently for a future as long as the cork holds out. Cork. 14.5% alc. **Rating** 94 To 2042 $90 TS
Definitus Foggy Hill Pinot Noir 2019 Characterful and energetic, this is probably the most distinctive pinot that Brian Croser has drawn from his Foggy Hill Vineyard yet. The best clones in the best part of the site unite in a savoury style, filled with beetroot, Moroccan souk and bay leaf. Juicy strawberries and red cherries of a warm season offer flesh and body, well countered by fine tannin bite. Sap and potpourri of whole bunches is well contained, delivering crunch and drive to a long finish. Cork. 12.5% alc. **Rating** 94 To 2034 $90 TS

🍷🍷🍷🍷🍷 **Tiers Vineyard Chardonnay 2019 Rating** 93 To 2025 $90 TS
Tiers Vineyard 1.5m Chardonnay 2019 Rating 92 To 2024 $55 TS

Tar & Roses
★★★★★

61 Vickers Lane, Nagambie, Vic 3608 **Region** Central Victoria
T (03) 5794 1811 **www**.tarandroses.com.au **Open** 1st w'end each month 10–4
Winemaker Narelle King **Est.** 2006 **Dozens** 40 000
Tar & Roses produces wines inspired by the classic Mediterranean varietals and was named
after the signature characteristics of nebbiolo. The name also ties back to the winemaking
team behind the venture, the legendary Don Lewis and his winemaking partner Narelle King.
Narelle is carrying on the Tar & Roses tradition after Don's passing in 2017. Exports to the
UK, the US, Canada, Singapore, Japan, China and NZ.

ΨΨΨΨΨ The Rose Heathcote Shiraz 2019 Contains a powerful fruit component from
ancient Cambrian soil, which helps explain the generosity, energy and textural
intrigue in this wine. Packed with blackberry, dark chocolate and dried herbs.
Rolls out across the palate with an earthy warmth and fine tannic edge. One to
age. Screw cap. 14.9% alc. **Rating** 95 **To** 2027 $60 JP
Heathcote Nebbiolo 2018 This has tapped into the beguiling, fragrant
aromatics and florals of the nebbiolo grape. Quite captivating, with rose petal,
violet, musk and sweet, wild herbs. The grape's notorious tannins are tamed
and fine, allowing the beauty of its red fruits, red licorice and bitter-chocolate
complexity to shine. Quite a star performance. Screw cap. 14% alc. **Rating** 95
To 2028 $50 JP

ΨΨΨΨΨ Central Victoria Sangiovese 2020 **Rating** 93 **To** 2028 $26 JP ✪
Heathcote Tempranillo 2020 **Rating** 93 **To** 2026 $26 JP ✪
Pinot Grigio 2020 **Rating** 91 **To** 2025 $22 JP ✪
Heathcote Nebbiolo Rosé 2020 **Rating** 91 **To** 2024 $29 JP
Heathcote Shiraz 2019 **Rating** 91 **To** 2026 $24 JP
Heathcote Sangiovese 2019 **Rating** 90 **To** 2025 $26 JP
King Valley Prosecco NV **Rating** 90 **To** 2022 $27 JP

Tarrahill.
★★★★

340 Old Healesville Road, Yarra Glen, Vic 3775 **Region** Yarra Valley
T (03) 9730 1152 **www**.tarrahill.com **Open** By appt
Winemaker Jonathan Hamer, Geof Fethers **Est.** 1992 **Dozens** 700 **Vyds** 6.5ha
Owned by former Mallesons Lawyers partner Jonathan Hamer and wife Andrea, a former
doctor and daughter of Ian Hanson, who made wine for many years under the Hanson-
Tarrahill label. Ian had a 0.8ha vineyard at Lower Plenty but needed 2ha to obtain a vigneron's
licence. In 1990 the Hamers purchased a property in the Yarra Valley and planted the requisite
vines (pinot noir – ultimately destroyed by the 2009 bushfires). Jonathan and company director
friend Geof Fethers worked weekends in the vineyard and in '04 decided that they would
undertake a wine science degree (at CSU); they graduated in '11. In '12 Jonathan retired
from law and planted more vines (cabernet sauvignon, cabernet franc, merlot, malbec and
petit verdot) and Ian (aged 86) retired from winemaking. Andrea has also contributed with a
second degree (horticulture); she is a biodynamics advocate.

ΨΨΨΨΨ Le Savant Cabernets 2019 Of the 4 reds from the 2019 vintage submitted, this
is the most youthful and the freshest. Cassis and blackcurrants, black licorice and
juniper in chocolate with lots of bay and tomato leaves. It feels cool and refreshing,
the tannins still adjusting and the finish pleasing. Better in a few years but not
for the long haul. Screw cap. 12.7% alc. **Rating** 91 **To** 2029 $42 JF

TarraWarra Estate
★★★★★

311 Healesville-Yarra Glen Road, Yarra Glen, Vic 3775 **Region** Yarra Valley
T (03) 5957 3510 **www**.tarrawarra.com.au **Open** Tues–Sun 11–5
Winemaker Clare Halloran, Adam McCallum **Est.** 1983 **Dozens** 9000 **Vyds** 28ha
TarraWarra is, and always has been, one of the top-tier wineries in the Yarra Valley. Founded
by Marc Besen AC and wife Eva Besen AO, it has operated on the basis that quality is

paramount, cost a secondary concern. The creation of the TarraWarra Museum of Art (twma.com.au) in a purpose-built building provides another reason to visit; indeed, many visitors come specifically to look at the ever-changing displays in the Museum. Changes in the vineyard include the planting of shiraz and merlot, and in the winery, the creation of a 4-tier range: a deluxe MDB label made in tiny quantities and only when the vintage permits; the single-vineyard range; a Reserve range; and the 100% estate-grown varietal range. Exports to France, Vietnam and China.

🍷🍷🍷🍷🍷 **South Block Yarra Valley Chardonnay 2019** This is so sparky, it could light up a room. Seriously mouth-watering acidity that crunches like lemon sorbet, leaving the palate enlivened and wanting more. There is more. There's the lime and tangerine, the dab of malty oak, the creamy, leesy nougatine and a fineness all the way. Screw cap. 13% alc. **Rating** 95 **To** 2029 $40 JF

Reserve Yarra Valley Chardonnay 2019 It's flavoursome, layered and complex, yet it's not too much of a good thing. Fine acidity seems to hold everything in place – the white nectarine, lemon zest and creamy leesy richness across the palate, and the oak just so, adding to its savoury tones. The flavours linger and it's moreish. Screw cap. 12.5% alc. **Rating** 95 **To** 2029 $50 JF

Reserve Yarra Valley Pinot Noir 2019 A more concentrated style of flavour, but it still retains the beautiful shape that stamps this Reserve. Perfumed with florals, spice and autumnal charm. Expect sweet red cherries, dabbed with basil and cooling menthol. While toasty bourbon oak flavouring is in the mix, it's mere seasoning. Tannins are plush, velvety and there's a gloss and a suppleness to the full-bodied palate. Screw cap. 13.8% alc. **Rating** 95 **To** 2030 $60 JF

Yarra Valley Barbera 2019 I love the way some varieties can inveigle their way into the landscape, such as barbera in the Yarra, and rise to the occasion. Among all those French grapes, this is the little wine that could. It's fragrant, different, really spicy with juniper and bitter herbs dousing the dark cherries within. Medium bodied with neat acidity, just so, light tannins and savoury stamp. Juicy and delicious. Saluté. Screw cap. 14% alc. **Rating** 95 **To** 2026 $30 JF ❂

Yarra Valley Chardonnay 2019 This estate chardonnay seems to be finer, a tad more complex and almost tighter than previous incarnations. It certainly has an amalgam of flavours, but is more citrus-toned and spiced with ginger. There's really fine, tangy acidity throughout and nothing is out of place. Screw cap. 13.2% alc. **Rating** 94 **To** 2028 $30 JF ❂

I Block Yarra Valley Pinot Noir 2019 While it comes across as sassy, with loads of ripe flavours from sweet black cherries to poached rhubarb, the palate backs off. It remains fuller bodied but not big. More complex flavours emerge from warm earth, charcuterie and juniper, all encased in toasty oak. Everything in its place and it's quite the charmer. Screw cap. 14% alc. **Rating** 94 **To** 2028 $45 JF

🍷🍷🍷🍷🍷 **Yarra Valley Roussanne Marsanne Viognier 2020 Rating** 93 **To** 2024 $35 JF
J Block Yarra Valley Shiraz 2018 Rating 93 **To** 2028 $40 JF
Yarra Valley Pinot Noir 2019 Rating 91 **To** 2025 $30 JF

 Tarrawatta   ★★★★

102 Stott Highway, Angaston, SA 5353 **Region** Eden Valley
T 0447 117 762 **www**.tarrawattawine.com.au
Winemaker Craig Isbel **Est.** 2017 **Dozens** 1700 **Vyds** 9.3ha
Tarrawatta's inaugural Shiraz and Grenache immediately secure its place among the who's who of the Barossa, making this one of the most exciting newcomers this year. Devoted exclusively to red wines, fruit is currently sourced entirely from the estate Ambervale vineyard in the northern Eden Valley. First planted in the mid 1800s, today the site boasts mostly dry-grown shiraz, cabernet sauvignon and a little grenache, with vines dating from 1968. A second site is earmarked for planting. Nick Radford oversees the vineyards and management of the estate, with Izway's Craig Isbel taking care of winemaking. The estate is owned by the Goldin Group, alongside Sloan Estate in the Napa and 3 Bordeaux châteaus including Château Le Bon Pasteur in Pomerol. Exports to Hong Kong. (TS)

♀♀♀♀♀ **Ambervale Eden Valley Shiraz 2018** Impressive hue of deep, vibrant purple, heralding an all-new Barossa shiraz of presence and distinction. Ticking all the boxes of impact of black fruits, licorice, coffee bean and dark chocolate oak. It holds integrity and poise, harmonised by an even acid line and most of all, by a fine, taut frame of impeccable tannins. Line and length promise great things in time. Cork. 14.9% alc. **Rating** 95 **To** 2033 $50 TS

Ambervale Eden Valley Grenache 2018 Tarrawatta has hit the ground running with its inaugural releases. The exotic spice of dry-grown old vines (planted 1968 in Moculta) and the black raspberry/blackberry fruit of grenache are eloquently framed in dark chocolate and coffee bean French oak. Warm alcohol reflects cherry liqueur. Firm, fine tannins and a long finish set it off for the cellar. Cork. 14.9% alc. **Rating** 94 **To** 2028 $50 TS

♀♀♀♀ **Ambervale Eden Valley Cabernet Sauvignon 2018 Rating** 89 **To** 2038 $50 TS

Tasmanian Vintners   ★★★★★

63 Kennedy Drive, Cambridge, Tas 7170 **Region** Southern Tasmania
T 0429 215 680 **www**.tasvintners.wine
Winemaker Liam McElhinney **Est.** 2019 **Vyds** 200ha
Tasmanian Vintners (TV) is a joint company owned 50/50% by Tasmanian businessman Rod Roberts and the Fogarty Wine Group, which acquired the assets of Winemaking Tasmania from the administrator of that business. TV will continue to process grapes and wine for a broad range of smaller Tasmanian producers, and also buy their excess fruit and assist them to market their wines. TV is well set up for small-batch production with Liam McElhinney as winemaker and responsible for business operation. Fogarty Wine Group (in its own right) has a number of other rapidly developing major projects in Tasmania.

Taylors   ★★★★☆

89A Winery Road, Auburn, SA 5451 **Region** Clare Valley
T (08) 8849 1111 **www**.taylorswines.com.au **Open** Mon–Fri 9–5, w'ends 10–4
Winemaker Mitchell Taylor, Adam Eggins, Phillip Reschke, Chad Bowman, Thomas Darmody **Est.** 1969 **Dozens** 250 000 **Vyds** 400ha
The family-founded and owned Taylors continues to flourish and expand – its vineyards are now by far the largest holding in the Clare Valley. Over the years there have been changes in terms of the winemaking team and the wine style and quality, particularly through the outstanding St Andrews range and more recently, The Visionary Cabernet Sauvignon and The Pioneer Shiraz. With each passing vintage, Taylors is managing to do for the Clare Valley what Peter Lehmann did for the Barossa Valley. Recent entries in international wine shows have resulted in a rich haul of trophies and gold medals for wines at all price points. A founding member of Australia's First Families of Wine, the family celebrated 50 years in 2019. Exports (under the Wakefield brand due to trademark reasons) to all major markets.

♀♀♀♀♀ **The Pioneer Exceptional Parcel Release Clare Valley Shiraz 2016** The Taylors crew love American oak with shiraz. Here it is unabashedly on display. And yet, it is latched onto this full-bodied wine, giving it support and the lead flavouring. Overall, it's smooth, opulent, rich, savoury and leathery, with a flutter of red fruits. All in all, amplified flavours, crafted to a style recipe. For its fan base, it works. Screw cap. 14.5% alc. **Rating** 95 **To** 2033 $200 JF

Masterstroke Coonawarra Cabernet Sauvignon 2019 This is quintessential Coonawarra: ripe cassis and currants, eucalyptus and earthy tones. Fuller bodied but not overwrought. Very youthful, a little puckering from the acidity, yet refreshing and bright, with smooth, fine tannins. Screw cap. 14.5% alc. **Rating** 95 **To** 2034 $50 JF

The Visionary Exceptional Parcel Release Clare Valley Cabernet Sauvignon 2016 Plenty of new wood flavour here. Cedary, tobacco, dusty, offsetting fruit compote flecked with spearmint and baking spices. Good flavours, with a savoury overlay alongside fine tannins and refreshing acidity. It comes together well for now and years more. Screw cap. 14.5% alc. **Rating** 95 **To** 2034 $200 JF

ŸŸŸŸŸ **Masterstroke McLaren Vale Shiraz 2019** Rating 93 To 2033 $50 JF
St Andrews Clare Valley Shiraz 2018 Rating 93 To 2032 $67 JF
Jaraman Coonawarra Clare Valley Cabernet Sauvignon 2018 Rating 93 To 2030 $32 JF
St Andrews Clare Valley Cabernet Sauvignon 2018 Rating 93 To 2034 $67 JF
Reserve Parcel Clare Valley Riesling 2019 Rating 92 To 2028 $25 JF
Jaraman Clare Valley McLaren Vale Shiraz 2019 Rating 91 To 2028 $32 JF
St Andrews Clare Valley Riesling 2020 Rating 90 To 2028 $37 JF
Margaret River Adelaide Hills Sauvignon Blanc 2020 Rating 90 To 2022 $20 JF ✪
St Andrews Clare Valley Chardonnay 2019 Rating 90 To 2026 $37 JF
Jaraman McLaren Vale Grenache 2020 Rating 90 To 2025 $32 JF

Tellurian   ★★★★☆

408 Tranter Road, Toolleen, Vic 3551 **Region** Heathcote
T 0431 004 766 **www.tellurianwines.com.au Open** W'ends 11–4.30 or by appt
Winemaker Tobias Ansted **Est.** 2002 **Dozens** 7000 **Vyds** 32ha
The vineyard is situated on the western side of Mt Camel at Toolleen, on the red Cambrian soil that has made Heathcote one of the foremost regions in Australia for the production of shiraz (Tellurian means 'of the earth'). Viticultural consultant Tim Brown not only supervises the certified organic Tellurian estate plantings, but also works closely with the growers of grapes purchased under contract for Tellurian. Further plantings on the Tellurian property in 2011 introduced small parcels of grenache, mourvèdre, carignan, nero d'Avola, marsanne, viognier, fiano, riesling and grenache gris to the 20ha of shiraz. Exports to the US, Singapore and China.

ŸŸŸŸŸ **Sommet Heathcote Shiraz 2017** Sourced from the highest point of the Tellurian vineyard, this is a flagship shiraz of some stature. Looks and feels the Heathcote part, with astounding deep colour, natural balance, the blackest of berries and tilled red earth resonating throughout. Fragrant and flavoursome, with savoury, fine tannins and a hint of bay leaf to finish. A top wine from a top year. Screw cap. 14.5% alc. **Rating** 96 **To** 2030 $75 JP ✪ ♥
Tranter Heathcote Shiraz 2018 There is a vitality present – real energy and effortless balance on display. Deep purple in hue, blackberry, violet, licorice and clove merge into graphite and baked earth. A framework of fine oak tannins brings the wine home. Screw cap. 14.6% alc. **Rating** 95 **To** 2030 $42 JP
Heathcote Marsanne 2019 This is definitely a richer, more expressive style of marsanne but doesn't it carry it well! Bright golden hues. A world of spice aromas with jasmine, wild honey, nougat, marzipan. Complex, but there is also a lightness. The fleshy palate is buoyed and brightened by a flinty edge and juicy acidity. Quite a quality statement for the variety. Screw cap. 13.9% alc. **Rating** 94 **To** 2025 $29 JP ✪

ŸŸŸŸŸ **GSM Heathcote Grenache Shiraz Mourvèdre 2019** Rating 92 To 2028 $29 JP
Heathcote Riesling 2020 Rating 90 To 2026 $29 JP
Heathcote Fiano 2020 Rating 90 To 2025 $29 JP

Temple Bruer   ★★★★

689 Milang Road, Angas Plains, SA 5255 **Region** Langhorne Creek
T (08) 8537 0203 **www.templebruer.com.au Open** Mon–Fri 9.30–4.30
Winemaker Kate Wall, Verity Cowley **Est.** 1980 **Dozens** 35 000 **Vyds** 123ha

Temple Bruer was in the vanguard of the organic movement in Australia and was the focal point for the formation of Organic Vignerons Australia. Part of the production from its estate vineyards is used for its own label, part sold. Owner David Bruer also has a vine propagation nursery, likewise run on an organic basis. Temple Bruer has 40ha of vineyards in Langhorne Creek, 59ha in Eden Valley, and 24ha in the Riverland (Loxton and Moorook). Exports to the UK, the US, Canada, Sweden, Japan and China.

𝗣𝗣𝗣𝗣𝗣 **The Agonist Riverland White Frontignac 2020** Sun-dried linen notes, field grasses, vanilla and Turkish delight on the palate. Distinctive dryish muscat styling. Has appeal for its unique expression. Screw cap. 13.5% alc. **Rating** 90 **To** 2023 $26 TL

𝗣𝗣𝗣𝗣 **Eden Valley Riesling 2020 Rating** 89 **To** 2023 $22 TL

Ten Minutes by Tractor ★★★★★

1333 Mornington-Flinders Road, Main Ridge, Vic 3928 **Region** Mornington Peninsula
T (03) 5989 6455 **www.**tenminutesbytractor.com.au **Open** 7 days 11–5
Winemaker Imogen Dillon, Martin Spedding **Est.** 1999 **Dozens** 12000 **Vyds** 38.3ha
Ten Minutes by Tractor is owned by Martin and Karen Spedding. It was established in 1997 with 3 Main Ridge vineyards – McCutcheon, Judd and Wallis – all located within a 10-min tractor ride from each other. Three vineyards have been added since: a recently replanted high-density vineyard at the cellar door and restaurant site (organically certified in 2004), the Coolart Road Vineyard in the north of the Peninsula, and the Main Ridge Spedding Vineyard, a high-density (12120 vines/ha) pinot noir vineyard planted in '16. The wines are released in 3 ranges: 10X, made from a number of estate-managed vineyards on the Mornington Peninsula; Estate, a reserve-level blend; and Single Vineyard, from the best-performing vineyard sites, usually a single block. In February 2018, a fire destroyed the main storage facility at the cellar door and restaurant site, with over 16000 bottles of wine lost (including a treasured collection acquired across 20 years for the restaurant cellar). The site was rebuilt, including a new private dining room and underground cellar for the restaurant, as well as a private cellar door tasting room and wine gallery. The wine gallery will formally open in late 2021 and includes many items from the Speddings' wine history collection, telling the story of the development of the wine industry in the Mornington Peninsula and the rest of Victoria. Exports to the UK, the US, Canada, Sweden, Switzerland, Hong Kong and China.

𝗣𝗣𝗣𝗣𝗣 **Coolart Road Mornington Peninsula Pinot Noir 2019** Of all the 2019 single-site pinots, this, on a warmer site, in a warmer vintage, is the pick. Go figure. It has more depth, more drive and energy. A neat composition of dark fruits, earthy, warm spices and woodsy flavours; a touch autumnal with hazelnut skins. The ripe, fuller-bodied palate extends out with pliable tannins and freshness ensuing. It has the right amount of complexity, yet is drinking well now. Screw cap. 14% alc. **Rating** 95 **To** 2028 $78 JF

𝗣𝗣𝗣𝗣𝗣 **Harmonia Mornington Peninsula Chardonnay 2020 Rating** 93 **To** 2029 $78 JF
Up The Hill Estate Mornington Peninsula Pinot Noir 2019 Rating 93 **To** 2028 $48 JF
Estate Mornington Peninsula Chardonnay 2019 Rating 92 **To** 2028 $44 JF
10X Mornington Peninsula Chardonnay 2019 Rating 91 **To** 2026 $30 JF
Down The Hill Estate Mornington Peninsula Pinot Noir 2019 Rating 91 **To** 2026 $48 JF
Wallis Mornington Peninsula Chardonnay 2019 Rating 90 **To** 2028 $86 JF
10X Mornington Peninsula Pinot Noir 2019 Rating 90 **To** 2024 $34 JF

Tenafeate Creek Wines ★★★★

1071 Gawler-One Tree Hill Road, One Tree Hill, SA 5114 **Region** Adelaide
T (08) 8280 7715 **www.**tcw.com.au **Open** Fri–Sun & public hols 11–5
Winemaker Larry Costa, Michael Costa **Est.** 2002 **Dozens** 3000 **Vyds** 1ha

Larry Costa, a former hairdresser, embarked on winemaking as a hobby in 2002. The property, with its 1ha of shiraz, cabernet sauvignon and merlot, is situated on the rolling countryside of One Tree Hill in the Mount Lofty Ranges. The business grew rapidly, with grenache, nebbiolo, sangiovese, petit verdot, chardonnay, semillon and sauvignon blanc purchased to supplement the estate-grown grapes. Michael Costa, Larry's son, with 18 vintages under his belt, mainly in the Barossa Valley, with Flying Winemaker stints in southern Italy and Provence, has joined his father as co-owner of the business. The red wines have won many medals over the years.

ŸŸŸŸŸ **One Tree Hill Basket Press Montepulciano 2017** In the house style, a big
red wine with an incredibly expressive nose: dark fruit, crushed and mulled with
plenty of sweet spice, prunes, blackberries and dark mint chocolate. The aromas all
follow through on the palate, structurally balanced to match the fuller-bodied feel,
with acidity and tannins all in play. A demonstrative wine suited to the campfire
and rustic cooking. Screw cap. 14.5% alc. **Rating** 94 **To** 2028 $30 TL ✪

ŸŸŸŸŸ **One Tree Hill Basket Press Sangiovese 2018 Rating** 93 **To** 2027 $30 TL
Museum Release Basket Press Shiraz 2010 Rating 92 **To** 2024 $70 TL
One Tree Hill Basket Press GSM 2019 Rating 92 **To** 2028 $30 TL
One Tree Hill Basket Press Tempranillo 2019 Rating 92 **To** 2028 $30 TL

Terindah Estate   ★★★★

90 McAdams Lane, Bellarine, Vic 3223 **Region** Geelong
T (03) 5251 5536 **www.**terindahestate.com **Open** 7 days 10–4
Winemaker Tim Byrne **Est.** 2003 **Dozens** 3000 **Vyds** 5.6ha
Retired quantity surveyor Peter Slattery bought the 48ha property in 2001, intending to plant the vineyard, make wine and develop a restaurant. He has achieved all of this (with help from others, of course), planting shiraz, pinot noir, pinot gris, picolit, chardonnay and zinfandel. Picolit is most interesting: it is a highly regarded grape in northern Italy, where it makes small quantities of high-quality sweet wine. It has proven very temperamental here, as in Italy, with very unreliable fruit set. In the meantime, he makes classic wines of very high quality from classic grape varieties – not wines for sommeliers to drool over because they're hip. Exports to Canada.

ŸŸŸŸŸ **Single Vineyard Bellarine Peninsula Shiraz 2019** Released as a youngster
with spunk, but will undoubtedly go the distance. A smooth, assured shiraz with
cool-climate varietal poise and spiciness. Red and blue berries layered through
with plums and spice. Flows beautifully onto the palate, bringing a warmth
of dusty oak and fine-edged tannins. Satiny texture seals the deal. Screw cap.
13.5% alc. **Rating** 92 **To** 2029 $44 JP
Single Vineyard Bellarine Peninsula Pinot Noir 2019 Unfiltered and lightly
cloudy by the looks of things. A good sign. Wild briar, bramble and herb with red
cherry and cranberry fill the senses. A fruit tingle/raspberry bon-bon brightness to
the pinot noir – very fruit-forward, very Bellarine Peninsula – with a streamlined
palate. Boasts a delicacy but the running herbal/acid line also gives the wine real
spine and tension. Screw cap. 12.5% alc. **Rating** 91 **To** 2026 $42 JP

Terra Riche   ★★★★☆

153 Jones Road, Mount Barker, WA 6234 **Region** Mount Barker
T 0432 312 918 **www.**terrarichewines.com.au
Winemaker Coby Ladwig, Luke Eckersley **Est.** 2017 **Dozens** 5000 **Vyds** 15ha
Luke Eckersley and Coby Ladwig are 2 of the most experienced winemakers in the Great Southern. In various ways, and for various businesses, they have demonstrated their winemaking skills again and again. Terra Riche brings a 3rd partner into the structure of this new business – Hong Chenggen (known as Ken) owns a Shanghai-based wine importing business, supplying to all cities throughout mainland China. Hitherto, his business has been focused on WA wines. Becoming a partner in Terra Riche puts the business in an enviable position. The quality of the wines made for the first releases is excellent, typical of Coby and

Luke's skills. The wines come in 4 ranges: Birds of Paint, Endgame, War of the Roses and Southern Navigator. Exports to Vietnam, Taiwan and China.

ŤŤŤŤŤ **Endgame the Rook Great Southern Riesling 2020** Brilliant acidity is cushioned by muscular, ripe fruit. Great Southern rieslings can go in a number of different directions; one is laser-sharp, austere, long and taut; another is muscular, rich, nutty, dense and long. Here we have both. There is a mineral/graphite edge through the finish that lingers long after the fruit has gone, making for an engaging drink. Screw cap. 11.8% alc. **Rating** 92 **To** 2031 $35 EL

Endgame the Rook Great Southern Shiraz 2019 Salted plums, mulberry and blackberry are bolstered by exotically spiced, resinous oak. The texture is very dense and powered by oak at this stage, but the fruit has oomph which suggests it will soften gracefully in the medium term. Screw cap. 14.5% alc. **Rating** 92 **To** 2031 $40 EL

Endgame the Rook Great Southern Cabernet Sauvignon 2019 The oak is well entrenched into the fruit at this early stage, which is fortunate given the delicacy of the red fruit flavours on the palate. Succulent redcurrant, pomegranate, red gravel and iodine make up the main, while saline acid and soft tannins frame it. Medium length of flavour at best hints at short-term drinking (and just beyond). Screw cap. 14.3% alc. **Rating** 92 **To** 2027 $40 EL

Endgame the Rook Pemberton Chardonnay 2020 Hand-picked Gingin clone, whole bunches, wild fermented in barrel then 8 months in French oak (30% new) with lees stirring weekly for 4 months. Creamy, intense and with tangy acid to get the mouth and the cheeks working. A surprising amount of chutzpah. Well put together. Glassy texture on the palate is the lingering impression. Screw cap. 13.1% alc. **Rating** 91 **To** 2028 $40 EL

Endgame Victory Frankland River Cabernet Sauvignon 2019 The regional stamp of Frankland River is evident in the gravelly, salted red berry fruit, but almost obscured by the tannins, which devour it. Tannins are the enduring memory of the wine. May come together in time. Screw cap. 14.4% alc. **Rating** 91 **To** 2038 $60 EL

Terre à Terre   ★★★★★

15 Spring Gunny Rd, Piccadilly, SA 5151 **Region** Wrattonbully/Adelaide Hills **T** 0400 700 447 **www.**terreaterre.com.au **Open** At Tapanappa **Winemaker** Xavier Bizot **Est.** 2008 **Dozens** 4000 **Vyds** 20ha
It would be hard to imagine 2 better-credentialled owners than Xavier Bizot (son of the late Christian Bizot of Bollinger fame) and wife Lucy Croser (daughter of Brian and Ann Croser). 'Terre à terre' is a French expression meaning down to earth. The close-planted vineyard is on a limestone ridge, adjacent to Tapanappa's Whalebone Vineyard. The vineyard area has increased, leading to increased production (the plantings include cabernet sauvignon, sauvignon blanc, cabernet franc and shiraz). In 2015, Terre à Terre secured the fruit from one of the oldest vineyards in the Adelaide Hills, the Summertown Vineyard, which will see greater quantities of Daosa and a Piccadilly Valley pinot noir. Wines are released under the Terre à Terre, Down to Earth, Sacrebleu and Daosa labels. Exports to the UK, the US, China, Canada, Japan and Hong Kong.

ŤŤŤŤŤ **Crayeres Vineyard Wrattonbully Sauvignon Blanc 2019** Cold-settled for 2 months, a technique developed by Brian Croser, but rarely duplicated. Fermentation in used 600L demi-muids, then matured on full lees for 8 months. The result is very complex, but the fruit is undaunted, with layers of lemon curd, citrus and a whisper of honey. Screw cap. 13.1% alc. **Rating** 96 **To** 2025 $50 JH ✪ ♥

Daosa Piccadilly Valley Blanc de Blancs 2016 From vigneron Xavier Bizot's own family vineyard in the Piccadilly Valley. The base wine spent 10 months in old oak, 42 months on lees in the bottle before disgorgement in September 2020. Chardonnay with a sense of native bush florals and leaf, ripe citrus flavours and a suggestion of mandarin – with a sophisticated palate texture and finish. Diam. 12.9% alc. **Rating** 94 $90 TL

Crayeres Vineyard Wrattonbully Cabernet Sauvignon Shiraz 2018
Ripe blackcurrant without the Ribena effect. Nine months in 21% new oak for
each of the varieties, then a further 9 months in old foudre casks, has brought a
sophistication to the overall glorious black-fruit profile; the shiraz adding a little
mid-palate plumpness without sweetening or dominating the flavour expression.
Classic cab/shiraz tannins are neatly balanced, even, and add a fulfilling conclusion.
Screw cap. 14.5% alc. **Rating** 94 **To** 2033 $50 TL

ᵧᵧᵧᵧᵧ **Crayeres Vineyard Wrattonbully Sauvignon Blanc 2020 Rating** 93
To 2026 $50 TL
Crayeres Vineyard Wrattonbully Cabernet Franc Shiraz 2018 Rating 93
To 2030 $32 TL
Daosa Piccadilly Valley Natural Reserve NV Rating 93 $50 TL

Tertini Wines

Kells Creek Road, Mittagong, NSW 2575 **Region** Southern Highlands
T (02) 4878 5213 **www.tertiniwines.com.au Open** 7 days 10–5
Winemaker Jonathan Holgate **Est.** 2000 **Dozens** 5500 **Vyds** 7.9ha
When Julian Tertini began the development of Tertini Wines in 2000, he followed in the
footsteps of Joseph Vogt 145 years earlier. History does not relate the degree of success that
Joseph had, but the site he chose then was, as it is now, a good one. Tertini has pinot noir and
riesling (1.8ha each), cabernet sauvignon and chardonnay (1ha each), arneis (0.9ha), pinot gris
(0.8ha), merlot (0.4ha) and lagrein (0.2ha). Winemaker Jonathan Holgate, who is responsible
for the outstanding results achieved at Tertini, presides over High Range Vintners, a contract
winemaking business also owned by Julian Tertini. Exports to Asia.

ᵧᵧᵧᵧᵧ **Southern Highlands Pinot Blanc 2019** A very solid wine, strongly European
in its chewy phenolics, gentle flow of acidity and intensity of fruit. Asian pear,
cinnamon, quince, fennel and tarte tatin. Long and forceful. Yet nothing is
overwrought, be it overripe or structurally pushed. Complex enough to feign
oak influence, yet none there. A delicious wine. Screw cap. 13% alc. **Rating** 93
To 2023 $30 NG
Tasmania Chardonnay 2019 This slightly warm season on the Coal River
has lent subtle exotic notes of mango and ripe fig to a lemon and white-peach
core of chardonnay. Malic acid has been tactically upheld to retain tension, and
will appreciate bottle age to integrate. It concludes long and energetic. Screw cap.
13% alc. **Rating** 92 **To** 2029 $60 TS
Southern Highlands Rosé 2019 A bright coral/cherry lipstick hue. Red
cherry, musk stick, bergamot and orange verbena notes. Dry and thirst-slaking,
with the sapid fruit flavours, astringency and body of a lighter-weight red. Versatile
at the table and plenty to like. Feels almost Italianate with its oomph and structural
detail. Screw cap. 13.5% alc. **Rating** 92 **To** 2021 $32 NG
Southern Highlands Pinot Gris 2019 A convincing gris. Baked apple, nashi
pear, cinnamon spice and a plume of acidity carrying it across the cheeks to a
long, vibrant finish. And here lies the rub – gris does not naturally boast this much
acidity. Still, loads of promise in terms of palate weight and aromatics. Screw cap.
12.5% alc. **Rating** 91 **To** 2023 $30 NG
Southern Highlands Riesling 2019 Courage displayed here. The usual whole-
bunch pressing, but on this occasion, the wine was racked to old puncheons for
a wild ferment, then inoculated to completion. Cheesecloth and a lees-derived
creaminess soaks the mid palate, buffering finger lime, pink grapefruit and
lemon-balm riffs. Long, dry and a bit tangy. Bodes well for the future. Screw cap.
12.3% alc. **Rating** 90 **To** 2024 $35 NG
Private Cellar Collection Southern Highlands Pinot Noir 2018 A lighter
shade of mid ruby. Quintessential cool-climate Australian scents of sarsaparilla,
fecund cherry, campfire and mulch. Admirable tannin structure. The fruit is a bit
sweet. This should age well across the early/medium term, facilitating greater
savouriness. Screw cap. 13.3% alc. **Rating** 90 **To** 2025 $51 NG

¶¶¶¶ Tasmania Pinot Noir 2019 Rating 89 To 2029 $60 TS
Private Cellar Collection Southern Highlands Riesling 2018 Rating 88
To 2023 $45 NG

Teusner   ★★★★★

95 Samuel Road, Nuriootpa, SA 5355 **Region** Barossa Valley
T (08) 8562 4147 **www.**teusner.com.au **Open** By appt
Winemaker Kym Teusner **Est.** 2001 **Dozens** 30 000 **Vyds** 120ha
Teusner is a partnership between former Torbreck winemaker Kym Teusner and Javier Moll,
and is typical of the new wave of winemakers determined to protect very old, low-yielding,
dry-grown Barossa vines. The winery approach is based on lees ageing, little racking, no fining
or filtration and no new American oak. As each year passes, the consistency, quality (and range)
of the wines increases; there must be an end point, but it's not easy to guess when, or even if,
it will be reached. Exports to the UK, the US, Canada, the Netherlands, Malaysia, Singapore,
Japan, Hong Kong and China.

¶¶¶¶¶ Avatar Barossa Valley 2019 A longstanding mainstay of the ever-diversifying
Teusner stable, Avatar has always been one of my Barossa GMS go-tos. Teusner's
mastery in championing fruit and integrity before oak and artefact make for
exquisite definition and detail, multi-dextrous food-matching versatility and
downright deliciousness. Oh, and nothing is lost in longevity, either. Its true greatness
is confirmed by superfine tannins, effortless fruit persistence and impeccable,
understated oak support. Screw cap. 14.5% alc. **Rating** 96 To 2029 $40 TS ✪
Righteous Barossa Valley Mataro 2018 Kym Teusner's juicy, polished,
delicious suave is arguably harder to translate in old-vine mataro than anywhere
else. That he is able to achieve this consistently is impressive; that he can uphold
varietal markers is what sets this apart as one of the Barossa's greatest single-
vineyard mataros. Glossy, ripe berry fruits maintain tang and freshness, set to a
backdrop of firm, fine tannins, and just the right amount of bitter high-cocoa dark
chocolate French oak. Great length and endurance. Cork. 15% alc. **Rating** 96
To 2033 $95 TS ♥
Big Jim Barossa Valley Shiraz 2019 This is Kym Teusner in fine form. Glossy,
supple, polished black fruits, nicely toned by a sprinkling of mixed spice, with a
backdrop of classic Barossa dark chocolate and licorice. Just the right volume of
fine tannins steady a long, generous finish. The Full Monty of Barossa shiraz, yet
not a bit too much. Screw cap. 14.5% alc. **Rating** 94 To 2024 $65 TS
Bilmore Barossa Valley Shiraz 2019 I've long marvelled at Kym Teusner's
superpower of delivering glossy density with vitality and accuracy. Few in the
Barossa do this with such consistency across every varietal and price point.
Particularly noble at the value end of the pool. The depth and just-picked
freshness of sweet black fruits that he has conjured here is not often seen without
spending double the dollars. Long, fine-grained, jubilant and irresistible. Yes, please.
Screw cap. 14.5% alc. **Rating** 94 To 2025 $27 TS ✪
Righteous FG Barossa Valley Shiraz 2017 An unashamed full-throttle Barossa
shiraz; loaded with the supple, spicy, ripe black fruits of old vines, supported by
the dark chocolate and fine-grained tannins of French oak (50% new). The finish
holds undeviating line and outstanding persistence, heightened by the acid drive
of this cool season, yet lacking nothing in generosity and integrity. Cork. 15% alc.
Rating 94 To 2027 $160 TS

¶¶¶¶¶ The Gentleman Barossa Valley Cabernet Sauvignon 2019 Rating 93
To 2027 $27 TS ✪
Teusner & Page Barossa Cabernet Sauvignon 2018 Rating 93 To 2028
$65 TS
The Dog Strangler Barossa Valley 2019 Rating 93 To 2024 $35 TS
Righteous FG Barossa Valley Shiraz 2018 Rating 92 To 2028 $165 TS
The Wark Family Shiraz 2019 Rating 91 To 2022 $30 TS
The Dog Strangler Barossa Valley 2018 Rating 90 To 2023 $35 TS

The Alchemists

PO Box 74, Cowaramup, WA 6284 **Region** Margaret River
T (08) 9755 5007 **www.**alchemistswines.com.au
Winemaker Mark Messenger, Luc Fitzgerald, Dave Johnson **Est.** 2008 **Dozens** 3000
Vyds 13.5ha

Brad and Sarah Mitchell were metallurgists for 15 and 20 years respectively, working on gold and hydro-metallurgical plants, having studied metallurgy and chemistry at university. Now they see themselves as alchemists, changing grapes into wine. When they purchased the vineyard in 2007 it was already 11 years old, the prior owners having sold the grapes to various well-known Margaret River wineries. Since taking control of the vineyard, they have removed vines on unsuitable soil and grafted others, moves that have paid dividends, resourcing the winemaking team to make a series of wines that have been consistent medal winners at significant wine shows.

Reserve Elixir Single Vineyard Margaret River Shiraz 2018 The spectrum of midnight fruit is more than enough to handle the oak that has been thrown at it. The only quibble is the spike of heat through the finish. Otherwise a full, dense, concentrated shiraz from one of the greatest vintages in the region, ever. Screw cap. 15% alc. **Rating** 92 **To** 2031 $40 EL

Elixir Margaret River Sauvignon Blanc 2018 Matured in 30% new French oak for 6 months. Chalky – almost grippy – phenolics frame the tart sugar snap and lychee fruit. Plenty of texture and interest here. Screw cap. 12.5% alc. **Rating** 91 **To** 2023 $28 EL

Elixir Margaret River Malbec 2018 Needs a vigorous swirl to get the energy going in this glass – once it's up and running, it's away. Sweet, juicy and plump, with tannins that lean towards the fierce but leave a slurpy impression instead. Brilliant mid-week wine. Screw cap. 14.3% alc. **Rating** 91 **To** 2027 $38 EL

Reserve Elixir Margaret River Chardonnay 2018 Rich, toasty and verging on tropical, the fruit carries over the tongue and descends into an oak-clad cavern of flavour and texture. There's a lot to like about the concentrated fruit in the process of drinking it, however the aftertaste and impression of oak is distracting. Screw cap. 13% alc. **Rating** 90 **To** 2027 $40 EL

The Cutting

439 Stonewell Road, Tanunda, SA, 5352 **Region** Barossa Valley
T 0467 596 340 **www.**the-cutting.com.au **Open** By appt
Winemaker Belinda van Eyssen **Est.** 2017 **Dozens** 90 **Vyds** 5ha

Viticulturist Daniel McDonald and partner winemaker Belinda van Eyssen launched The Cutting in 2018 on their Stonewell vineyard, bought by Daniel's parents in his birth year of 1980 and planted in 1998. An initial resolve to remain grapegrowers was thwarted by the temptation to make their own wines, inspired by other winemakers (to whom they were selling) producing single-vineyard wines from the site. Belinda gained winemaking experience in her home town of Cape Town, as well as in Portugal, France, California and NZ. Vinification and maturation in French oak barrels are carried out in a micro-winery in a shed onsite, 54m from the vineyard ('10 seconds by tractor!'). (TS)

Barossa Valley Shiraz 2018 A dry and savoury take on Barossa shiraz, contrasting firm, dusty, spicy oak with dark berry fruits. Fruit falls away rapidly, leaving oak tannins to dominate the finish. Screw cap. 14% alc. **Rating** 89 **To** 2028 $60 TS

The Hairy Arm

18 Plant Street, Northcote, Vic 3070 **Region** Sunbury/Heathcote
T 0409 110 462 **www.**hairyarm.com **Open** By appt
Winemaker Steven Worley **Est.** 2004 **Dozens** 1000 **Vyds** 3ha

Steven Worley graduated as an exploration geologist, then added a master of geology degree, followed by a postgraduate diploma in oenology and viticulture. Until December 2009 he was general manager of Galli Estate Winery. The Hairy Arm started as a university project in '04, and has grown from a labour of love to a commercial undertaking. Steven has an informal lease of 2ha of shiraz at Galli's Sunbury vineyard, which he manages, and procures 1ha of nebbiolo from the Galli vineyard in Heathcote. Exports to the UK, Canada and Hong Kong.

ŸŸŸŸŸ **Merrifolk Cote Nord Sunbury Syrah 2019** Merrifolk is a new label aimed at an earlier-drinking style, although this is an impressive wine in anyone's book. Excellent dark purple; awash with intensely flavoured black plums, laced with licorice root, coffee cream and meaty nuances. Full bodied, with luscious and expansive tannins, the palate glossy. It's a richer, riper style, more shiraz than syrah. Screw cap. 14.5% alc. **Rating** 95 **To** 2029 $26 JF ✪
Sunbury Shiraz 2019 The intensity of fruit flavour is astonishing. Deep, earthy and savoury. Full bodied with firm tannins, yet sweet and ripe. While it's imposing, quite big for sure, there's also an ease to this with lovely texture. It is complete. Screw cap. 14.8% alc. **Rating** 94 **To** 2033 $35 JF
Merrifolk Valhalla Shiraz Nebbiolo 2019 65% Sunbury shiraz, 35% Heathcote nebbiolo. A good combo that's knitted well. Dark fruit, licorice and bitumen, with intense woodsy spices, especially cardamom and clove. Full bodied and plush. The tannins have some grip, yet roll through quite effortlessly. A bargain at this price. Screw cap. 14% alc. **Rating** 94 **To** 2029 $26 JF ✪

ŸŸŸŸ♀ **Merri. Sunbury Shiraz 2019** **Rating** 91 **To** 2030 $50 JF

The Happy Winemaker ★★★★

16 Maddern Street, Black Hill, Vic 3350 **Region** Ballarat/Heathcote/Bendigo
T 0431 252 015 **www.**thehappywinemaker.com.au
Winemaker Jean-Paul Trijsburg **Est.** 2015 **Dozens** 700 **Vyds** 1ha
Jean-Paul Trijsburg graduated with an agronomy degree from the Wageningen University in the Netherlands and followed this with a joint master of science in viticulture and oenology in Montpellier, France, and Geisenheim, Germany. In between degrees he headed to Burgundy in 2007 and says, 'I started out picking grapes in Nuits-Saint-Georges, but somehow I ended up in the winery within a week'. The experience left him with a love of all things French, but he went on to work in wineries in Pomerol, the Rheingau, Rioja, Chile and South Africa. Since '12, he has called Australia home, having worked for Hanging Rock Winery in the Macedon Ranges and Lethbridge Wines in Geelong. He and wife Jessica live in Ballarat and, following the arrival of their second son, Jean-Paul runs a nearby 1ha vineyard of pinot noir and is an at-home dad for their children, Jessica working at a local health service. Jean-Paul moved from his garage-cum-winery to Hanging Rock for the '19 vintage (and ongoing thereafter). Additional grapes come from Heathcote, Bendigo and Ballarat.

ŸŸŸŸ♀ **Museum Release Heathcote Carménère by Jean-Paul 2015** A concentrated, dense wine which looks to have fully enjoyed the extra maturation in bottle. A warm, savoury, medium-bodied red wine with nicely restrained ripe black cherry, blueberry fruit and a world of sweet spice. Smooth on the palate and enjoying its time in the sun. Hugely enjoyable. Screw cap. 13.6% alc. **Rating** 92 **To** 2028 $40 JP
Heathcote Carménère by Jean-Paul 2019 This is the 4th vintage of carménère by the maker and it's looking pretty smart with a lush winescape of black cherries, wild berries, dried herbs and tilled earth. Smooth as silk on the palate with a touch of Mediterranean garrigue savouriness. Screw cap. 13.3% alc. **Rating** 92 **To** 2026 $33 JP
Strathbogie Ranges Nebbiolo by Jean-Paul 2019 Red/garnet in colour with good concentration of of typical nebbiolo floral aromatics, black cherry and dried herbs. Black pepper makes its mark on the palate in tandem with lifted spice, star anise and chalky, dusty tannins. A wine of some charm that speaks strongly of place. Screw cap. 13% alc. **Rating** 91 **To** 2034 $33 JP

ŸŸŸŸ **Mount Alexander Riesling by Jean-Paul 2020** **Rating** 89 **To** 2026 $25 JP
Mount Alexander Chardonnay by Jean-Paul 2019 **Rating** 89 **To** 2025 $25 JP

Mount Alexander Pinot Gris by Jean-Paul 2020 **Rating** 89 **To** 2025 $25 JP
Strathbogies Nebbiolo Rosé by Jean-Paul 2020 **Rating** 89 **To** 2023 $25 JP

The Islander Estate Vineyards ★★★★☆

78 Gum Creek Road, Cygnet River, SA 5223 **Region** Kangaroo Island
T (08) 8553 9008 www.iev.com.au **Open** Thurs–Tues 12–5
Winemaker Jacques Lurton, Yale Norris **Est.** 2000 **Dozens** 8000 **Vyds** 10ha
Established by one of the most famous Flying Winemakers in the world, Bordeaux-born and
trained and part-time Australian resident Jacques Lurton. He has established a close-planted
vineyard. The principal varieties are cabernet franc, shiraz and sangiovese, with lesser amounts
of grenache, malbec, semillon and viognier. The wines are made and bottled at the onsite
winery in true estate style. The property was ravaged by the terrible bushfire that devastated
many (not all) parts of the island in January 2020. The fire consumed the entire vineyard and
its infrastructure, the house, the laboratory and the office, which became the sacrificial lamb
slowing the fire sufficiently to allow the protection of the winery and its stock of bottled wine,
and the wines still in barrel and tank. Long-time friend and business partner Yale Norris cut
back every vine down to 20cm, hoping that shoots would appear – many have done so, but
far from all. If the regeneration ceases, the entire vineyard will be pulled out and replanted.
Exports to the UK, Ireland, the US, Canada, France, Switzerland, Germany, Abu Dhabi, Hong
Kong, Taiwan and China.

ŸŸŸŸŸ **The Wally White Kangaroo Island Semillon 2019** Going the extra step in
the semillon department, fermented in barrel and bringing something extra to its
already on-point ripe fruit. Creamy and complex, rather than austere and bracing
like many semillons. With a couple of years of initial development, the structural
foundations of acidity and a light pithiness carry this wine with the future in mind.
Screw cap. 14% alc. **Rating** 94 **To** 2027 $45 TL
Boxing Bay Kangaroo Island Shiraz Cabernet Sauvignon 2018 This blend
can come in so many stylistic variations, but rarely is it as bright-eyed, lifted and
crunchy as this. Fragrant with bush florals, dusted with sumac-like spice, tinted
with background eucalypt, while the varieties find a delicious harmony of flavours
and mouth-teasing structures. Screw cap. 14% alc. **Rating** 94 **To** 2028 $50 TL
Kangaroo Island Cabernet Sauvignon 2019 Here's a story in a bottle. After
several years/viticultural challenges, this cabernet came to fruition for the first time
in '19. A delicately teased cabernet, with all the varietal character on the nose,
beautiful clarity of flavour, medium-weighted concentration and a coat of classical
tannins. But after finally doing its thing in '19, the KI bushfires of '20 destroyed
the block and it sadly won't see the light of day again. Get into it while you can –
once in a lifetime. Screw cap. 13.5% alc. **Rating** 94 **To** 2028 $30 TL ✪

ŸŸŸŸŸ **Kangaroo Island Semillon Sauvignon Blanc 2019 Rating** 92 **To** 2025 $30 TL
Kangaroo Island Cabernet Franc 2019 Rating 92 **To** 2027 $30 TL
McLaren Vale Rosé 2020 Rating 91 **To** 2023 $30 TL

The Lake House Denmark ★★★★

106 Turner Road, Denmark, WA 6333 **Region** Denmark
T (08) 9848 2444 www.lakehousedenmark.com.au **Open** 7 days 10–5
Winemaker Harewood Estate (James Kellie) **Est.** 1995 **Dozens** 8000 **Vyds** 5.2ha
Garry Capelli and Leanne Rogers purchased the property in 2005 and have restructured
the vineyard to grow varieties suited to the climate – chardonnay, pinot noir, semillon and
sauvignon blanc – incorporating biodynamic principles. They also manage a couple of small
family-owned vineyards in Frankland River and Mount Barker with a similar ethos. Wines
are released in 3 tiers: the flagship Premium Reserve range, the Premium Block range and the
quirky He Said, She Said easy-drinking wines. The combined cellar door, restaurant and
gourmet food emporium is a popular destination. Exports to Singapore and China.

ŸŸŸŸŸ **Premium Reserve Single Vineyard Porongurup Riesling 2020** The
irrepressible purity and drive of Porongurup fruit is on display here. Lemon zest,

graphite, green apple and citrus blossom both on the nose and palate, backed by a coiled spring of salivating acid that crouches right behind the fruit mid palate. A lovely, long-lived wine with a distinct slate/gravel character on the nose. Screw cap. 12.5% alc. **Rating** 94 **To** 2036 $40 EL

Premium Reserve Frankland River Shiraz 2018 The 2018 was a brilliant vintage, producing wines of power and density. This is plush and opulent, illustrating the warmth and ripeness of the year. On the palate the tannins have that signature Frankland River ferrous/rust character (a positive). If anything, the fruit has a little too much oomph, but it is clear that Great Southern is capable of exceptional quality and consistency. Screw cap. 14.5% alc. **Rating** 94 **To** 2031 $45 EL

🍷🍷🍷🍷🍷 **Premium Reserve Premium Selection Cabernet Sauvignon 2018** Rating 93 To 2031 $55 EL
Premium Reserve Single Vineyard Chardonnay 2019 Rating 92 To 2032 $40 EL
Premium Reserve Single Vineyard Frankland River Shiraz 2019 Rating 92 To 2031 $45 EL
Single Vineyard Selection Semillon Sauvignon Blanc 2020 Rating 91 To 2025 $25 EL
Premium Block Selection Cabernet Sauvignon 2018 Rating 91 To 2028 $28 EL
Premium Block Selection Riesling 2020 Rating 90 To 2026 $25 EL
Premium Block Selection Shiraz 2019 Rating 90 To 2028 $25 EL

The Lane Vineyard ★★★★★

5 Ravenswood Lane, Balhannah, SA 5244 **Region** Adelaide Hills
T (08) 8388 1250 **www.**thelane.com.au **Open** 7 days 10–5
Winemaker Turon White **Est.** 1993 **Dozens** 25 000 **Vyds** 75ha
The Lane Vineyard is one of the Adelaide Hills' elite wine tourism attractions, with a cellar door and restaurant that offers focused tastings by region and style, with endless views. Established by the Edwards family in 1993, it was aquired by the UK's Vestey Group in 2012, following their establishment of Coombe Farm in the Yarra Valley. Four distinct tiers of single-vineyard wines are produced at The Lane; the entry-level Lane series from the Adelaide Hills, the Provenance range from in and around the Adelaide Hills and the top-tier Estate and Heritage ranges from their Hahndorf estate vines. Exports to the UK, Canada, South East Asia, Sweden and Norway.

🍷🍷🍷🍷🍷 **Provenance Adelaide Hills Syrah 2019** Estate vineyard, a mix of winemaking techniques, new and seasoned oak maturation. A delicious, uncomplicated syrah with expected and satisfying peppery spice lift. There's palate interest from a lovely mix of kitchen herbs in the flavour swirl. Simple, direct and elegant. Screw cap. 13.5% alc. **Rating** 95 **To** 2028 $40 TL

19th Meeting Single Vineyard Adelaide Hills Cabernet Sauvignon 2018 Estate grown in Hahndorf, half receiving a 72-day extended maceration on skins, all matured for 18 months in 40% new French barriques. Tick off the cabernet characters here: cassis and blackberry, leafy notes, choc-mint, with superfine chalky tannins that support the brighter fruit elements on the palate. Concentrated yet still lithe and busy on the finish. Screw cap. 13.5% alc. **Rating** 95 **To** 2030 $65 TL

Gathering Single Vineyard Adelaide Hills Sauvignon Blanc Semillon 2019 Oak influence here has softened any overt sauvignon expectations and helped to provide deeper, richer foundations. There's a little barrel-ferment flint in the background, lovely stone-fruit expression on the palate, and a satisfying spice and textural line on the finish. Will cover just about any white wine needs at the table. Screw cap. 13% alc. **Rating** 94 **To** 2026 $40 TL

Heritage RG Adelaide Hills Chardonnay 2019 An elite offering of the Hahndorf estate's chardonnay. Whole-bunch pressed, only free-run juice, fermented with both wild and inoculated yeasts, then 9 months in 66% new barrels. The fruit is the hero here, to have soaked in that oak. Gently teased, nectarine and ginger, a delicate grip to finish. Screw cap. 13% alc. **Rating** 94 **To** 2028 $100 TL

Reunion Single Vineyard Adelaide Hills Shiraz 2018 Estate sourced in Hahndorf, half receiving extended maceration on skins for 72 days. Matured for 18 months in 40% new French barrels. A darker-berried expression compared to its syrah siblings, with more concentration and depth, without resorting to overweight handling, finishing with a medium to full-bodied feel. Screw cap. 13.5% alc. **Rating** 94 **To** 2028 $65 TL

Adelaide Hills Cuvée Blanc de Blancs 2015 Traditional method. Chardonnay's citrus notes and lees-contact breadiness are the key layers here, a faint tonic bitterness in the background aiding the salivating nature of the style. A fine chalky finish leaves just enough dryness to encourage another quick splash. Diam. 12.5% alc. **Rating** 94 $65 TL

Heritage Late Disgorged Adelaide Hills 2010 Definite aged characters to start, polish and classical aldehydes in the mix, with fruit notes beginning to subside. A faint honeyed element treats the palate well, as does a slight salivating tonic bitterness. Heading into curio territory at this stage, yet a rare moment to see a high-end sparkling in such a mature setting. Diam. 12.5% alc. **Rating** 94 $100 TL

𝅘𝅥𝅮𝅘𝅥𝅮𝅘𝅥𝅮𝅘𝅥𝅮𝅘𝅥𝅮 **Provenance Adelaide Hills Riesling 2020** Rating 92 To 2025 $30 TL
Beginning Single Vineyard Adelaide Hills Chardonnay 2019 Rating 92 To 2026 $50 TL
Provenance Adelaide Hills Arneis 2019 Rating 91 To 2024 $30 TL

The Other Wine Co ★★★★

136 Jones Road, Balhannah, SA 5242 **Region** South Australia
T (08) 8398 0500 **www.theotherwineco.com Open** At Shaw + Smith
Winemaker Martin Shaw, Adam Wadewitz **Est.** 2015 **Dozens** 1000
This is the venture of Michael Hill Smith and Martin Shaw, established in the shadow of Shaw + Smith but with an entirely different focus and separate marketing. The name reflects the wines, which are intended for casual consumption; the whole focus being freshness combined with seductive mouthfeel. The concept of matching variety and place is one without any particular limits and there may well be other wines made by The Other Wine Co in years to come. Exports to the UK, Canada and Germany.

𝅘𝅥𝅮𝅘𝅥𝅮𝅘𝅥𝅮𝅘𝅥𝅮𝅘𝅥𝅮 **Tasmania Pinot Noir 2019** Interesting wine. In a savoury spectrum from the word go, there's the Tasmanian pinot birthmark, yet it's still to unfurl its sails. I'm sure it will start singing in 2–3 years' time. Screw cap. 13.5% alc. **Rating** 94 **To** 2030 $35 JH

Adelaide Hills Shiraz 2020 From an Adelaide Hills vineyard outside Shaw + Smith's usual remit, this time from the Echunga district, vinified in neutral concrete vats using a mix of whole berries and 15% whole bunches. A lighter-bodied style, redolent with bright plum fruit, offset with a subtle background of wood and stems, underpinned by a gentle spice and earthiness. Quite delicious and immensely drinkable. Screw cap. 13% alc. **Rating** 94 **To** 2024 $26 TL ✪

McLaren Vale Grenache 2020 Initial earthy, almost ironwork-like notes and bush herbals lead into a juicy style, a little ripper. It's fresh and vibrant, but then gathers an encouraging mouthfeel with powdery, earthy tannins. Very likeable. Screw cap. 13.5% alc. **Rating** 94 **To** 2025 $27 TL ✪

𝅘𝅥𝅮𝅘𝅥𝅮𝅘𝅥𝅮𝅘𝅥𝅮𝅘𝅥𝅮 **Adelaide Hills Pinot Gris 2020** Rating 93 To 2023 $26 TL ✪

The Pawn Wine Co. ★★★★

10 Banksia Road, Macclesfield, SA 5153 **Region** Adelaide Hills/Langhorne Creek
T 0438 373 247 **www.thepawn.com.au**
Winemaker Tom Keelan **Est.** 2004 **Dozens** 10000 **Vyds** 35ha

The Pawn Wine Co. began as a partnership between Tom Keelan and Rebecca Willson (Bremerton Wines) and David and Vanessa Blows. Tom was for some time manager of Longview Vineyards at Macclesfield in the Adelaide Hills, and consulted to the neighbouring vineyard, owned by David and Vanessa. In 2002 Tom and David decided to make some small batches of Petit Verdot and Tempranillo at Bremerton, where Tom is now vineyard manager. In 2017 Tom and Rebecca purchased David and Vanessa's share. David still supplies grapes to the Pawn Wine Co., and Tom works very closely with David and his 3 sons to produce food-friendly wines that reflect their origins. Exports to the UK and NZ.

🍷🍷🍷🍷🍷 **The Austrian Attack Adelaide Hills Grüner Veltliner 2019** This exhibits considerably more personality than most grüners on these shores. Aromas of sugar snap peas, green apple, apricot pith, citrus, asparagus and white pepper shimmy across a tensile grippy palate. I like the oxidative riff and the cuff of lees and oak. They serve to impart levity to the wine's tension while imparting a degree of nutty complexity. Pucker and freshness all at once. Fine length. Very good wine. Screw cap. 13.5% alc. **Rating** 93 **To** 2024 $26 NG

The Sicilian Defence Langhorne Creek Fiano 2019 Barrel-fermented and reductively handled. A fine nose: saline, pungently spicy and nutty, with stone fruits, orange blossom and wild fennel reverberating across a dense, well-packed palate. Dried mango, too. Assertive. Medium bodied. Real intensity of flavour playing off a chewy pumice-like texture, a skein of juicy acidity and a lick of oak, servicing poise and drive. Of which there is plenty! A superlative Campanian variety planted in what appears to be a region of real promise for it on these shores. Screw cap. 12.5% alc. **Rating** 92 **To** 2023 $26 NG

Jeu de Fin Clonal #76 Adelaide Hills Chardonnay 2019 Neatly toned 2019 Hills chardonnay in a vintage where many are quite broad. A lovely marriage of crunchy stone and citrus fruit, with subtle gingery spice adding an extra interest. Screw cap. 13.5% alc. **Rating** 91 **To** 2025 $36 TL

Jeu de Fin Adelaide Hills Shiraz 2018 This hits all the right notes: lilac florals on the nose segue to blueberry, blackberry, iodine, tapenade, anise, salami and a scrub of herb. Bitter chocolate, sure. A thread of peppery freshness and whole-bunch riffs on Indian spice, too. The oak regime is nicely appointed. Some reductive tension curtails the sweetness of fruit to an extent. Could be more savoury. This drinks like a medium-bodied luncheon quaff. Screw cap. 14.5% alc. **Rating** 91 **To** 2023 $40 NG

Pawn Star Maturana Tinta 2018 Maturana Tinta is a rare, near-extinct grape from Rioja. Grown on ironstone soils in Macclesfield, wild fermented in open-top vessels and matured in older French and Hungarian oak for 9 months. Pulpy. Juicy. Savoury. Whole-berry pastille, sarsaparilla and rosewater, too. Yet this wine's totem is the swathe of herb-soused tannins: gentle, peppery and amaro-like. This is a wine to drink in its youth. A paean to everything good about Europe's more savoury expressions, while celebrating the diversity here. A good drink. Cork. 14.5% alc. **Rating** 91 **To** 2022 $60 NG

The Gambit Adelaide Hills Sangiovese 2018 A multi-clonal blend from the southern sector of the Hills, with a small portion of whole-berry ferment accentuating a nose of blue violets and sour cherry sauce. There's a lovely fleshiness on the palate, yet more savoury, leafy and leathery elements drive the core, backed by a spicy tannin line as well. As always, wines like this simply need to be served with food to leverage their true worth. Screw cap. 14.5% alc. **Rating** 91 **To** 2026 $26 TL

Jeu de Fin Clonal #76 Adelaide Hills Chardonnay 2019 Macclesfield and Lenswood vineyards. Contemporary winemaking from wild fermentation, larger oak vessels and lees stirring. Neatly toned 2019 Hills chardonnay in a vintage where many are quite broad. A lovely marriage of crunchy stone fruit and citrus fruit, with subtle gingery spice adding an extra interest. Screw cap. 13.5% alc. **Rating** 91 **To** 2025 $36 NG

The Gambit Adelaide Hills Sangiovese 2019 A blend of 2 clones, one providing this wine's freshness in an almost sour-cherry sense, the other bringing more savoury, earthy, tea-leaf character, with accompanying tannins kept in balance. Italian meat dishes clearly fit perfectly with such a wine. Screw cap. 14.5% alc. **Rating** 90 **To** 2026 $36 TL

TTTT El Desperado Adelaide Hills Pinot Grigio 2020 **Rating** 89 **To** 2022 $20 TL
En Passant Adelaide Hills Tempranillo Montepulciano 2018 **Rating** 89
To 2026 $26 TL
El Desperado Adelaide Hills Pinot Noir 2019 **Rating** 88 **To** 2022 $21 NG

The Remarkable State ★★★★☆

GPO Box 1001, Adelaide, SA 5001 **Region** South Australia
T 0437 267 881 **www**.remarkablestate.com.au
Winemaker Various **Est.** 2018 **Dozens** 10 000
Owner Rob Turnbull moved to Australia from the UK in 1997, at that stage without any experience in the wine industry other than drinking it – and landed a vintage start with Peter Lehmann. One thing led to another in every part of the business, including study at the University of Adelaide. Fifteen years later he took the plunge and started his own business, calling on many of his friends as he built a portfolio of wines made by various winemakers using grapes grown in SA. His brief to those winemakers was simple: to make wines they'd want to take to dinner themselves. No capital cost, just working capital – then he went and spoilt it by purchasing tanks and equipment for the '19 vintage. But he does have an admirable marketing plan: make alternative varieties for Dan Murphy and mainstream varieties for export. The wine quality and value for money is good, the labels cleverly designed. Exports to the UK, Canada, NZ and China.

TTTTT One Remarkable Barrel No. 2 Barossa Valley Shiraz 2018 The 2nd
iteration from 2018 of the One Remarkable Barrel series, here from 120yo shiraz
in the Vine Vale district. It has spent 2 years in a 2nd-fill American oak puncheon,
which of course shows, though the fruit has the power-to-weight capacity here to
be able to lift on the palate and celebrate the much-loved generosity and opulence
of Barossa shiraz. It's old-school and grandfatherly and kind of loveable because of
it. Screw cap. 14.5% alc. **Rating** 95 **To** 2030 $65 TL

The Ridge North Lilydale ★★★★☆

106 Browns Road, North Lilydale, Tas, 7268 **Region** Northern Tasmania
T 0408 192 000 **www**.theridgenorthlilydale.com **Open** Sun 10.30–5 Oct–May
Winemaker Harry Rigney, Susan Denny **Est.** 2013 **Dozens** 1000 **Vyds** 2ha
This venture marks the return to Tasmania of husband and wife Harry Rigney and Susan Denny after more than 30 years on the east coast of the mainland. In his mid-20s Harry was the sole recipient of the prized Menzies Scholarship to undertake his master's degree at Harvard, becoming a highly acclaimed specialist in taxation law (while continuing to this day to play his electric guitar in a rock band). Susan completed a fine arts degree in the '70s (dux of her year) then moving into Applied Arts inter alia mastering oxy and electric welding. She also saw her father Tim's scientific, engineering and agricultural innovations trailblaze the world's lavender industry. So, they were equipped to purchase a 20ha property with north-facing slopes at an altitude of 350m and planted a 2ha close-planted 6000 vine vineyard in 2013/14. It earned them the title of Best Small Vineyard Tasmania '17.

The Stoke Wines ★★★★

98 Sneyd Road, Mount Jagged, SA 5211 **Region** Kangaroo Island/Adelaide Hills
T 0407 389 130 **www**.thestokewines.com **Open** Summer weekends
Winemaker Nick Dugmore, Rebecca Dugmore **Est.** 2016 **Dozens** 600
The Stoke Wines was born of a 6-month conversation that spanned Australia, Bali, Scotland, France and India. Wishing to escape their jobs in commercial winemaking, Nick and Rebecca Dugmore set off for a seachange in Bordeaux. Arriving in France, they realised that their half-baked attempt to learn French on the road was seriously insufficient. While left out of the conversation at their own party, the idea of The Stoke Wines was born. Nick's love affair with

Kangaroo Island had begun on a surf trip around Australia in a banana-yellow Ford Falcon in 2008. Kangaroo Island was the first stop, the rest of the itinerary is still awaiting completion. Making wine from Kangaroo Island is all about a connection to a place where Nick and Rebecca love to be and this is reflected in their winemaking. The '20 bushfires came as a terrible blow for those with vineyards, none more so than Jacques Lurton's The Islander Estate, which provided The Stoke Wines with some of its best grapes. But the island is much larger than most people realise and large parts were left untouched (and the vineyards in those parts). Nick and Rebecca produce the wines in a collective space in Mount Jagged where they have started a collective called Southern Artisans (SA) with another small producer, SKEW Wines. Their goal is to promote the Southern Fleurieu and Kangaroo Island. Nick is a winemaker at Wirra Wirra but with their support has gone part-time in '20 to be able to focus on the island. Rebecca is the part-time brand manager at Terre à Terre in the Adelaide Hills.

♀♀♀♀♀ Kangaroo Island Sauvignon Blanc 2020 Although the western side of Kangaroo Island was severely burned by bushfire, destroying key vineyards at that end of the island, the eastern side remained safe. This is a smashing summer drink, green/gold tones in the glass, a fruit salad of aromas, even some creaminess, with apple and lemon flavours and tangy acidity without greenness. Lighter bodied and moreish. Screw cap. 12.3% alc. **Rating** 93 **To** 2023 $30 TL

Kangaroo Island Syrah 2020 A bit of fun on the front label: rather than Syrah it says 'French for Shiraz'. Made from fruit that ripens slowly in KI's ocean-cooled terroir and crafted in what has become an Australian syrah style. There's a sense of stems to begin, a woodiness perhaps, with crunchy red-plum flavours on the palate, surrounded by pithy tannins with finishing flourishes of spice and tangy fruit. A summery drink-now shiraz. Screw cap. 13.3% alc. **Rating** 92 **To** 2024 $35 TL

Kangaroo Island Tempranillo Rosé 2020 Mid pink with a touch of-copper. Classic strawberry with earthy rhubarb aromas, neatly balanced sweet-and-spicy fruits with tangy mouthfeel and mild grip to finish. A rosé with a bit of substance to it. Screw cap. 13.5% alc. **Rating** 91 **To** 2023 $30 TL

The Story Wines   ★★★★★

170 Riverend Road, Bangholme, Vic 3175 **Region** Grampians
T 0411 697 912 **www.**thestory.com.au
Winemaker Rory Lane **Est.** 2004 **Dozens** 2500
Over the years I have come across winemakers with degrees in atomic science, doctors with specialties spanning every human condition, town planners, sculptors and painters; Rory Lane adds yet another to the list: a degree in ancient Greek literature. He says that after completing his degree and 'desperately wanting to delay an entry into the real world, I stumbled across and enrolled in a postgraduate wine technology and marketing course at Monash University, where I soon became hooked on … the wondrous connection between land, human and liquid'. Vintages in Australia and Oregon germinated the seed and he zeroed in on the Grampians, where he purchases small parcels of high-quality grapes. He makes the wines in a small factory where he has assembled a basket press, a few open fermenters, a mono pump and some decent French oak. Exports to the UK.

♀♀♀♀♀ R. Lane Vintners Westgate Vineyard Grampians Syrah 2019 The winemaker says this wine represents 'the best that I can do.' In 2019 the season was warm and yields were lower than usual. There are many layers of sometimes-intricate winemaking involved here and it shows. This is a most complex tale of syrah. Enjoy the unravelling that is ahead of you; dark and brooding fruit, tastes of the earth, fields of wildflowers, with savoury touches and rich in Grampians super-spice. It's all here. Screw cap. 13.5% alc. **Rating** 96 **To** 2034 $75 JP ❂

Grampians Marsanne Roussanne Viognier 2018 This is a beauty. Pretty, aromatic marsanne leads the way (a nice change from viognier) and sets the tone of spring blossom, jasmine, white musk, peach and pear. The palate is concentrated and textural, yet dances in bright acidity. Sensitive winemaking on display right here. Screw cap. 12.5% alc. **Rating** 95 **To** 2026 $30 JP ❂

Hyrdra Grampians Syrah 2019 This is another strong Grampians example of the breed (shiraz) with the addition of 10% grenache. Bursts out of the blocks, so fresh and arresting in tantalising spice and bright red/black berries. Keeps the pulse racing on the palate with a vibrancy and density of fruit, with restrained oak. Can imagine it settling down for a long time in bottle. Screw cap. 13.5% alc. **Rating** 95 To 2029 $30 JP ✪

Grampians Grenache 2019 As winemaker Rory Lane comments, late-ripening grenache is a recent arrival in the Grampians, warmer vintages opening the door. This has a perfumed bouquet of rose petals, violets and powder puff, the palate rapier-like with its savoury clothing of wild strawberry fruits. Screw cap. 13.5% alc. **Rating** 95 **To** 2029 $30 JH ✪

Super G Grampians Grenache Syrah Mourvèdre 2020 45/40/15% grenache/syrah/mourvèdre. A nod to the future stars of the Grampians, in addition to syrah. Complex, with the 3 varieties complementing each other beautifully here. In keeping with the vibrancy of fruit and lifted, aromatic style of the maker. Plush red cherry, dark plum cake and violets combine forces with an earthy, dried herb and spicy intensity. It's a powerful mix, but understated. This wine is still in building mode. Screw cap. 13.5% alc. **Rating** 95 **To** 2030 $30 JP ✪ ♥

Whitlands Close Planted Riesling 2019 Some (bright) colour pickup suggests good fruit flavours, and so it has. Acidity, the result of the vineyard's 800m elevation, is balanced by RS. It's an easy wine to enjoy. Screw cap. 12.5% alc. **Rating** 94 **To** 2027 $30 JH ✪

🍷🍷🍷🍷 **Grampians Grenache 2020 Rating** 89 **To** 2024 $30 JP

The Vintner's Daughter   ★★★★

5 Crisps Lane, Murrumbateman, NSW 2582 **Region** Canberra District
T (02) 6227 5592 **www.**thevintnersdaughter.com.au **Open** W'ends 10–4
Winemaker Stephanie Helm **Est.** 2014 **Dozens** 1000 **Vyds** 3ha
The Vintner's Daughter is Stephanie Helm, daughter of Ken Helm, who made her first wine when she was 9 and won her first trophy when she was 14. On finishing school she enrolled in an arts/law degree at the Australian National University, thereafter pursuing a career outside the wine industry until 2011, when she began the wine science degree at CSU. Along the way, while she was at ANU, she met a young bloke from Lightning Ridge at a pub and introduced him to the world of wine. It wasn't too long before he (Benjamin Osborne) was vineyard manager (with his background as a qualified horticulturist and landscaper) for Ken Helm. In late '14 all the wheels came full circle when a vineyard, originally planted in 1978 with traminer, crouchen and riesling, extended to 3ha in '99, came on the market. It was in an immaculate position between Clonakilla and Eden Road, and they purchased it in a flash and set about some urgently needed rejuvenation. Stephanie (and Ben) waltzed into the trophy arena at the Canberra International Riesling Challenge '15, winning the trophy for Best Canberra District Riesling and, for good measure, winning the trophy for Best Riesling at the Winewise Small Vignerons Awards '15. Gewürztraminer, pinot noir and shiraz are also part of the estate-based portfolio

🍷🍷🍷🍷🍷 **Canberra District Riesling 2020** As long as there's no extended skin contact, white wines do not normally suffer from smoke taint, and there is none here. Hand-picked fruit, free-run juice, cool fermentation in stainless steel, barely perceptible 5g/L RS. Still developing, and will jump out of its skin in 5 years. Screw cap. 12.5% alc. **Rating** 94 **To** 2033 $40 JH

🍷🍷🍷🍷🍷 **Canberra District Gewürztraminer 2020 Rating** 92 **To** 2022 $35 JH
Canberra District Pinot Noir 2019 Rating 90 **To** 2025 $35 JF
Canberra District Sparkling Chardonnay 2019 Rating 90 $45 JF

The Wanderer ★★★★★

2850 Launching Place Road, Gembrook, Vic 3783 **Region** Yarra Valley
T 0415 529 639 **www**.wandererwines.com **Open** By appt
Winemaker Andrew Marks **Est.** 2005 **Dozens** 500
The Wanderer wines are a series of single-vineyard wines made by Andrew Marks, winemaker and viticulturalist at Gembrook Hill Vineyard. Andrew spent 6 years as a winemaker with Penfolds before returning to Gembrook Hill in 2005. He has worked numerous vintages in France and Spain including Etienne Sauzet in Puligny Montrachet in '06 and more recently over 10 vintages in the Costa Brava, Spain. Andrew seeks to achieve the best expression of his vineyards through minimal handling in the winery. In '12 he founded The Melbourne Gin Company.

ΨΨΨΨΨ Upper Yarra Valley Chardonnay 2019 Only a puncheon and hogshead (800L) made. This is a classy wine. It has pristine fruit, a touch of lemon and white nectarine, a light dusting of spice, a lemon verbena and curd flavour adding some richness, yet this is very fine and long. The palate just flows beautifully and it's effortless to drink. I mean taste. Nah, drink. Diam. 12% alc. **Rating** 96 **To** 2030 $35 JF ✪
Upper Yarra Valley Pinot Noir 2019 There are 20% whole bunches in the mix here and they really pack a punch, enhanced by the 30% new French oak. Twigs, wood char, violets, cherries and pips, aniseed and more besides. Fuller-bodied sinewy tannins yet lots of sweet fruit. Needs more time to find itself. Diam. 13% alc. **Rating** 94 **To** 2033 $55 JF

ΨΨΨΨΨ Yarra Valley Pinot Noir 2019 **Rating** 93 **To** 2031 $38 JF

The Willows Vineyard ★★★★☆

310 Light Pass Road, Light Pass, SA 5355 **Region** Barossa Valley
T (08) 8562 1080 **www**.thewillowsvineyard.com.au **Open** Wed–Mon 10.30–4.30
Winemaker Peter Scholz **Est.** 1989 **Dozens** 6000 **Vyds** 42.74ha
The Scholz family have been grapegrowers for generations and they have over 40ha of vineyards, selling part of the crop. Current-generation winemaker Peter Scholz makes rich, ripe, velvety wines, some marketed with some bottle age. Exports to the UK, Canada, Switzerland, China and NZ.

ΨΨΨΨΨ G Seven Barossa Valley Shiraz 2019 A magnificent, full vibrant purple hue heralds all the dynamism and depth of youthful Barossa shiraz poised for a long life. With such lively vibrancy, this tastes like it's just out of the fermenter. Fantastic display of all the blue fruits of the Barossa, set to a grand display of fine tannins that shore up a very long finish. Oak is completely engulfed by confident fruit. All class. Screw cap. 14.6% alc. **Rating** 95 **To** 2034 $40 TS
Barossa Valley Riesling 2020 A tense and refined Barossa floor riesling, thanks partly to cool gully breezes of nearby Eden Valley, partly to early picking and not least to the fanatical expertise of Peter Scholz. The 2020 represents a benchmark at any price and a bargain at $20. Purity of exact lime, lemon and Granny Smith apple, magnificently honed acid line, persistence and phenolic management rarely seen in this drought season. Kudos. Screw cap. 11.3% alc. **Rating** 94 **To** 2030 $20 TS✪

ΨΨΨΨΨ G Seven Barossa Valley Mataro 2020 **Rating** 93 **To** 2025 $32 TS
Barossa Valley Old Vine Semillon 2020 **Rating** 92 **To** 2030 $20 TS✪
Bonesetter Barossa Valley Shiraz 2018 **Rating** 92 **To** 2031 $60 TS
The Doctor Sparkling Red NV **Rating** 92 $40 TS

Thick as Thieves Wines ★★★★★

355 Healesville-Kooweerup Road, Badger Creek, Vic 3777 **Region** Yarra Valley
T 0417 184 690 **www**.tatwines.com.au **Open** By appt
Winemaker Syd Bradford **Est.** 2009 **Dozens** 2000 **Vyds** 1.5ha

Syd Bradford is living proof that small can be beautiful and, equally, that an old dog can learn new tricks. A growing interest in good food and wine might have come to nothing had it not been for Pfeiffer Wines giving him a vintage job in 2003. In that year he enrolled in the wine science course at CSU; he then moved to the Yarra Valley in '05, gaining experience at a number of wineries including Coldstream Hills. Syd was desperate to have a go at crafting his own 'babies'. In '09 he came across a small parcel of arneis from the Hoddles Creek area, and Thick as Thieves was born. These days Syd farms 1.5ha of his own pinot noir (MV6 and Abel clones) and purchases other varieties from both the Yarra and King Valleys. The techniques used to make his babies could only come from someone who has spent a long time observing and thinking about what he might do if he were calling the shots. Exports to Japan.

🍷🍷🍷🍷🍷 **Plump Yarra Valley Pinot Noir 2020** What a delicious and thoroughly enjoyable drink. It's teeming with good things, including a heady fragrance, thanks in part to mostly whole bunches adopted in the ferment, so the fruit is poppy and crunchy and bright. But it's not a one-trick pony; it has depth, beautifully shaped silky tannins, fine acidity and an evenness across its medium-bodied palate. Screw cap. 13% alc. **Rating** 95 **To** 2030 $37 JF
Limited Release Yarra Valley Syrah 2020 I found this irresistible. It's crunchy, juicy, peppery and tangy. It has detail, yet it's a light- to medium-bodied wine filled with red fruits, fine sandpaper tannins and neat acidity. It just sings with vitality, freshness and style. Screw cap. 12.9% alc. **Rating** 95 **To** 2032 $45 JF
Limited Release Yarra Valley Pinot Syrah 2020 A new addition to the TAT range and a welcome one at that. Is it in the Light Dry Red category, the darling of the Yarra wine scene at the moment? Either way, this is fabulous. Juicy, tangy fruit, spiced up with black pepper, basil, pomegranate and wintergreen. The palate is lighter framed, with satiny, faint tannins. It hovers on the precipice of needing a touch more ripeness but the perky raspberry acidity pulls it back in and saves the day. Screw cap. 12.6% alc. **Rating** 94 **To** 2026 $45 JF

🍷🍷🍷🍷🍷 **Another Bloody Yarra Valley Chardonnay 2020** **Rating** 92 **To** 2028 $37 JF
The Aloof Alpaca Yarra Valley Arneis 2020 **Rating** 90 **To** 2023 $25 JF

Thistle Hill   ★★★★
74 McDonalds Road, Mudgee, NSW 2850 **Region** Mudgee
T (02) 6373 3546 **www.**thistlehill.com.au **Open** Thurs–Fri 10–4.30, Sun & public hols 10–4
Winemaker Tim White **Est.** 1976 **Dozens** 12 000 **Vyds** 33ha
Founders David and Lesley Robertson employed organic practices from Thistle Hill's inception in 1975, making it Australia's longest continuously running organic winery. New ownership saw the acquisition of neighbouring vineyard Erudgere in the early 2000s, with both properties now certified organic (no weedicides, insecticides or synthetic fertilisers). All wines are bottled under the Thistle Hill label. Exports to Mongolia and China.

Thistledown Wines   ★★★★★
c/- Revenir, Peacock Road North, Lenswood, SA 5240 **Region** South Australia
T 0405 038 757 **www.**thistledownwines.com
Winemaker Giles Cooke MW **Est.** 2010 **Dozens** 10 000
Founders Giles Cooke and Fergal Tynan are UK-based MWs with a collective 40+ years' experience in buying and selling Australian wines. They have been friends since 1998, when they met over a pint of beer on the evening before their first master of wine course. In 2006 they established Alliance Wine Australia, which purchases Australian wines for distribution in the UK; they took the process one step further when Alliance began the Thistledown Wines venture. This focuses on Barossa Valley shiraz, McLaren Vale grenache, and smaller amounts of Adelaide Hills chardonnay. Winemaker Giles, who splits his time between the UK and Adelaide, says he has particular affection for grenache and is precisely right (in my view) when he says, 'McLaren Vale grenache is world class, and it best expresses itself when made in the mould of pinot noir'. Exports to the UK, the US, Canada, Ireland, the Netherlands, Denmark, Czech Republic, Poland, Malta, South Korea, Singapore, China and NZ.

ΨΨΨΨΨ **Sands of Time Old Vine Single Vineyard Blewitt Springs McLaren Vale Grenache 2019** The beauty of this wine belies the label. Among the finest reds in Australia. A turbid mid ruby. Damson plum, strawberry, clove, rosemary, anise and turmeric flavours. A sandy weld of impeccable tannins, drawn taut and long by a beam of saline freshness. Ethereal and transparent. A blessed Australian site and an uncanny semblance to Rayas. Diam. 14.5% alc. **Rating** 97 **To** 2027 $80 NG ❂ ♥

ΨΨΨΨΨ **Cunning Plan McLaren Vale Shiraz 2019** A full-bodied shiraz that reflects cunning winemaking. Whole-berry fermentation has put a rich gloss on the palate without overloading the tannin structure. The predominantly black berry fruit is shot through with licorice, spice and an airbrush of dark chocolate. Screw cap. 14.5% alc. **Rating** 96 **To** 2039 $30 JH ❂

This Charming Man Single Vineyard Clarendon McLaren Vale Grenache 2019 More muscular than its svelte Blewitt brethren. The fruit, warmer: kirsch, orange peel, tangerine and black cherry. Floral. More overt and impactful. Mineral force, over sandy and ethereal detail. But it makes me no less giddy! Diam. 14.5% alc. **Rating** 96 **To** 2027 $80 NG

She's Electric Old Vine Single Vineyard McLaren Vale Grenache 2020 A limpid mid ruby. A nose suggestive of the sort of thirst-slaking succulence marking all wines here: rosehip, bracken, clove, kirsch, cranberry, bergamot, Turkish delight and iodine. Sweet of flavour, yet not an iota of jamminess. Measured. Savoury, spicy and honed by an attenuated limb of bony tannins. The extraction on a level that sets the bar. High. Screw cap. 13.5% alc. **Rating** 95 **To** 2026 $65 NG

The Distant Light Grenache Shiraz 2018 This is seamless. Again, the tannins maketh the wine: pithy, taut and juicy. Gorgeous aromas of mottled red plum, five-spice, white pepper, clove, cardamom and kirsch, expanding across the finish. Grenache the clear leader of the pack. For the better. Thrilling length. I'd drink this with youth on its side. Diam. 14.5% alc. **Rating** 95 **To** 2026 $125 NG

ΨΨΨΨΨ **Cunning Plan McLaren Vale Shiraz 2019 Rating** 93 **To** 2025 $30 NG
Suilven Adelaide Hills Chardonnay 2019 Rating 92 **To** 2026 $80 TL
Gorgeous Grenache White 2020 Rating 92 **To** 2025 $25 TL ❂
Gorgeous Grenache Rosé 2020 Rating 92 **To** 2023 $25 TL ❂
Thorny Devil Old Vine McLaren Vale Grenache 2019 Rating 92 **To** 2026 $32 NG
Gorgeous Grenache 2020 Rating 91 **To** 2028 $25 TL
Cloud Cuckoo Land Fiano Greco Zibibbo 2020 Rating 90 **To** 2023 $24 NG

Thomas St Vincent ★★★★★

PO Box 633, McLaren Vale, SA 5171 **Region** McLaren Vale
T 0438 605 694 **www**.thomasstvincent.com **Open** Not
Winemaker Gary Thomas **Est.** 2016 **Dozens** 240
Owner-winemaker Gary Thomas is the only vigneron I (James) know of who is a ruthless critic of his own wines. He explains he has come from a writing background in the (unspecified) media and has had a passion for Rhône wines since the mid-1980s. He made his way 'to the cool heart of McLaren Vale's Blewitt Springs, and its old vines, dry-grown on sand for flavour and purity. Wines in small batches, extended ferments, subtle blends, reflecting the terroir and the season. Bottled without fining or filtration. As wines used to be made.' He makes his wines at McLaren Vale winery La Curio.

Thomas Wines ★★★★★

28 Mistletoe Lane, Pokolbin, NSW 2320 **Region** Hunter Valley
T (02) 4998 7134 **www**.thomaswines.com.au **Open** 7 days 10–5
Winemaker Andrew Thomas **Est.** 1997 **Dozens** 10 000 **Vyds** 6ha

Andrew Thomas moved to the Hunter Valley from McLaren Vale to join the winemaking team at Tyrrell's Wines. After 13 years, he left to undertake contract work and to continue the development of his own label. He makes single-vineyard wines, underlining the subtle differences between the various subregions of the Hunter. The major part of the production comes from long-term arrangements with growers of old-vine semillon and shiraz. The acquisition of Braemore Vineyard in December 2017 was significant, giving Thomas Wines a long-term supply of grapes from one of the Hunter Valley's most distinguished semillon sites. The quality of the wines and the reputation of Andrew Thomas have never been higher. Exports to Japan and China.

The Cote Individual Vineyard Hunter Valley Shiraz 2019 Very fine. A majestic composition of tannins of noble detail and grit; blue/blackberry fruits, licorice straps and a smear of black olive and bincho charcoal. Feels ethereal, by virtue of the structural bones. All by virtue of a dry-grown vineyard, planted in '71. The finest tannin profile of the bunch. Screw cap. 14% alc. **Rating** 96 To 2035 $35 NG ✪

Kiss Limited Release Hunter Valley Shiraz 2019 From the sensory overhaul of Thomas' quality single-vineyard expressions, this one may win out. Not necessarily because it articulates the vineyard better than any other, but because the oak and grape tannins are handled with skill seldom seen in this country. Violet, blue/black-fruit aspersions, anise and clove. Then a resinous emergence of forensically detailed grape tannin and classy French oak. Screw cap. 13.8% alc. **Rating** 96 To 2035 $85 NG

Synergy Vineyard Selection Hunter Valley Semillon 2020 Multi-vineyard sources as usual, but there's nothing usual about the depth of varietal fruit expression on the palate. Lemongrass/lemon curd flavours run throughout, Hunter acidity the staff of the long life ahead. Great success in a difficult vintage. Screw cap. 11.5% alc. **Rating** 95 To 2035 $22 JH ✪ ♥

Sweetwater Individual Vineyard Hunter Valley Shiraz 2019 This vineyard always imparts verve and a thirst-quenching crunch to its wines: this is firmly marked. A boysenberry creaminess to the aroma. Less floral and iodine-lifted. Black olive and some salami smokiness. Yet the tannins run across the palate with detailed precision, not binding the wine too tightly. Long and compelling. Screw cap. 14% alc. **Rating** 95 To 2030 $35 NG ✪

Synergy Vineyard Selection Hunter Valley Shiraz 2018 Multiple vineyard sources separately vinified. The high-quality vintage shines through the expressive, dark berry-filled bouquet and into a sculpted, medium-bodied palate. Its freshness and savoury fruit/oak/tannin balance guarantee it will develop superbly over decades. Value+. Screw cap. 14.2% alc. **Rating** 95 To 2038 $25 JH ✪

Braemore Cellar Reserve Hunter Valley Semillon 2015 Compelling Hunter semillion aromas of lemon drop, barley water and buttered toast. Featherweight and balletic, with a strident reach across the palate of pumice-lime texture, juicy acidity and a skein of pungent mineral. Mouthfilling. Billows across the cheeks. The acidity feels natural. But it hasn't the length or intensity of flavour of better years. Screw cap. 10.5% alc. **Rating** 94 To 2028 $65 NG

The Dam Block Individual Vineyard Hunter Valley Shiraz 2019 Across the dam from the lauded Kiss vineyard. Of a similar blue-fruited disposition, the tannins assert more bitter chocolate but are less refined. Fullish bodied, but in the savoury regional style. Chewy finish. This pulls the saliva from the back of the mouth with an elastic timbre, whetting the palate for the next glass. The edgy tannins and teeming fruit serve up an intriguing tussle. Screw cap. 13.7% alc. **Rating** 94 To 2035 $45 NG

Belford Individual Vineyard Hunter Valley Shiraz 2019 On some levels, this is the most typically Hunter red of the Thomas wines: dark, dusty, savoury and appealing. The tannins are firm and nicely wrought. Medium-bodied feel, despite the alcohol. Sour cherry, damson plum and five-spice. Less reduction. Expansive and terracotta-scented, all across good length. I like this. Screw cap. 14.5% alc. **Rating** 94 To 2032 $45 NG

ΨΨΨΨ♀ **Braemore Individual Vineyard Hunter Valley Semillon 2020** Rating 93
To 2027 $35 NG
Elenay Barrel Selection Hunter Valley Shiraz 2019 Rating 93 To 2032
$55 NG
Two of a Kind Shiraz 2019 Rating 92 To 2032 $25 NG ✪
Déjà Vu Individual Vineyard Hunter Valley Shiraz 2019 Rating 92 To 2026
$35 NG
Joe's Block Barossa Valley Semillon 2020 Rating 91 To 2028 $30 NG
Synergy Vineyard Selection Hunter Valley Shiraz 2019 Rating 91 To 2026
$25 NG
Six Degrees Vineyard Selection Hunter Valley Semillon 2020 Rating 90
To 2024 $25 NG

Thompson Estate   ★★★★★

Tom Cullity Drive, Wilyabrup, WA 6284 **Region** Margaret River
T (08) 9755 6406 **www.**thompsonestate.com **Open** 7 days 10.30–4.30
Winemaker Paul Dixon **Est.** 1994 **Dozens** 10 000 **Vyds** 38ha
Cardiologist Peter Thompson planted the first vines at Thompson Estate in 1997, inspired by
his and his family's shareholdings in the Pierro and Fire Gully vineyards and by visits to many
of the world's premium wine regions. Two more vineyards (both planted in '97) have been
purchased, varieties include cabernet sauvignon, cabernet franc, merlot, chardonnay, sauvignon
blanc, semillon, pinot noir and malbec. Thompson Estate wines are made onsite at its state-
of-the-art winery. Exports to the UK, Canada, Belgium, the Netherlands, Denmark, Finland,
Singapore, Hong Kong and China.

ΨΨΨΨΨ **Margaret River Cabernet Sauvignon 2018** If you are tiring of reading about
the near-perfect 2018 vintage in Margaret River, look away now. It produced
wines of succulence, ripeness, density, power and balance, characters which are all
present here in this wine. The concentration of fruit and structuring tannins/oak
in this cabernet assure it a long and graceful life in the cellar for decades to come.
Screw cap. 14.5% alc. **Rating** 95 **To** 2041 $50 EL
The Specialist Margaret River Cabernet Sauvignon 2017 Aromas of ripe
cassis, black cherry and anise, set against a backdrop of glazed ham, pomegranate
and toasted, spicy oak. The palate is densely flavoured, with fruits on the red
spectrum rather than purple. An absolute mouthful of concentrated flavour. For
a cool vintage like '17, there is impressive weight and density here. Screw cap.
14.3% alc. **Rating** 95 **To** 2041 $90 EL
The Specialist Margaret River Chardonnay 2019 Pineapple, green apple
and white peach dominate the aromas that waft out of the glass, while the palate
trots obediently behind. The tart acid the only quibble, taut and trim. Texturally
this is quite creamy. The finish unfurls layers of citrus flavour. Screw cap. 13.3% alc.
Rating 94 **To** 2031 $80 EL

ΨΨΨΨ♀ **SSB Margaret River Semillon Sauvignon Blanc 2020** Rating 93 To 2027
$35 EL
Four Chambers Margaret River Cabernet Sauvignon 2019 Rating 93
To 2031 $25 EL ✪
Four Chambers Margaret River Chardonnay 2020 Rating 92 To 2027
$25 EL ✪
Four Chambers Margaret River Sauvignon Blanc 2020 Rating 90 To 2023
$25 EL

Thorn-Clarke Wines   ★★★★☆

266 Gawler Park Road, Angaston, SA 5353 **Region** Barossa Valley
T (08) 8564 3036 **www.**thornclarkewines.com.au **Open** Thurs–Mon 10–4, Tues–Wed
by appt
Winemaker Peter Kelly **Est.** 1987 **Dozens** 90 000 **Vyds** 222ha

Established by David and Cheryl Clarke (née Thorn), and son Sam, Thorn-Clarke is one of the largest family-owned estate-based businesses in the Barossa. Their winery is close to the border between the Barossa and Eden valleys and 3 of their 4 vineyards are in the Eden Valley: the Mt Crawford Vineyard is at the southern end of the Eden Valley, while the Milton Park and Sandpiper vineyards are further north in the Eden Valley. The 4th vineyard is at St Kitts, at the northern end of the Barossa Ranges. In all 4 vineyards careful soil mapping has resulted in matching of variety and site, with all the major varieties represented. The quality of grapes retained for the Thorn-Clarke label has resulted in a succession of trophy and gold medal–winning wines at very competitive prices. Exports to all major markets.

ŸŸŸŸŸ **Sandpiper Eden Valley Riesling 2020** Testimony to Pete Kelly's dexterity with riesling, this is a carefully tuned release, boasting a detail and elegance rarely seen in this vintage. Fresh, pure, signature lemon, lime and Granny Smith apple are graced with subtle nuances of star fruit. Graceful, crystalline acidity glides through a long finish. Enticing from the outset, and poised for a confident future. Screw cap. 11.5% alc. **Rating** 93 **To** 2030 $22 TS ✿

Shotfire Barossa Quartage 2018 A characterful and age-worthy blend in which malbec and cabernet franc play more than a support role, defining not only fragrant lift and savoury complexity but deepening a fine, dry tannin profile. The crunchy redcurrants of cabernet uphold a bright, tangy core of freshness and integrity, holding long through an even and enduring finish. One for the cellar. Screw cap. 14.5% alc. **Rating** 93 **To** 2033 $30 TS

Single Vineyard Selection Barossa Shiraz 2018 The Barossa's most northerly vineyard has produced a tangy, vibrant and medium-bodied style. Yet it's deep in colour and strong in its firm, fine, bony tannin shell. Acid and tannin unite to mark out a long future, confirmed by a long finish. Screw cap. 14% alc. **Rating** 92 **To** 2036 $40 TS

Sandpiper Barossa Rosé 2020 It takes a steady hand to craft such elegance and refinement from Barossa mataro. Fresh, vibrant strawberry and raspberry fruit is eloquently presented with vibrant acid drive that elongates a refreshing finish, sensitively backed with fine-ground tannins. Medium salmon crimson. Pretty and enticing in equal measure. Screw cap. 11.5% alc. **Rating** 91 **To** 2021 $22 TS ✿

Vintage Barossa Fortified Shiraz 2015 Young, lively, bright and spirity. Fresh, crunchy redcurrant and cassis fruit and red cherry liqueur underscored by dark chocolate oak and firm, fine tannins, concluding long and sweet. An extended spell in the cellar is called for, to soften and bring its disparate elements together. Great promise in a decade or three. 375ml. Cork. 19% alc. **Rating** 91 $28 TS

ŸŸŸŸ Eden Valley Brut Pinot Noir Chardonnay NV **Rating** 89 $26 TS

Thousand Candles ★★★★★

159 Killara Road, Gruyere, Vic 3770 **Region** Yarra Valley
T 0413 655 389 **www**.thousandcandles.com.au **Open** By appt
Winemaker Stuart Proud **Est.** 2010 **Dozens** 3000 **Vyds** 25.5ha

What is now called the Thousand Candles vineyard was originally known as Killara Estate, which was planted in 1997. The Thousand Candles name comes from a 19th-century account harking back to its Indigenous occupiers. A ceremony granting free passage to the lands around the property was witnessed by a European who, referring to the tribesmen dramatically holding aloft their firesticks, remarked, 'It's as if the twilight of the evening had been interrupted by a thousand candles.' And indeed the property is a dramatic one, plunging from a height of several hundred metres above the Yarra River down to its flood plains. After a rather odd launch of wines that had no variety/s specified on the labels (original winemaker Bill Downie said that he wished to be free to use whatever single or varietal blend best reflected the site and vintage), the vineyard is now producing superb Pinot Noirs and more than useful Shiraz, an ex post facto salute to the vision of Bill Downie. Exports the the UK, the US, Taiwan and China.

Three Dark Horses

307 Schuller Road, Blewitt Springs, SA 5171 **Region** McLaren Vale
T 0405 294 500 **www.3dh.com.au**
Winemaker Matt Broomhead **Est.** 2009 **Dozens** 5000 **Vyds** 8.9ha
Three Dark Horses is the project of former Coriole winemaker Matt Broomhead. After
vintages in southern Italy (2007) and the Rhône Valley, he returned to McLaren Vale in late
2009 and, with his father Alan, buys quality grapes, thanks to the many years of experience
they both have in the region. The 3rd dark horse is Matt's grandfather, a vintage regular.
They are expanding the plantings with grenache blanc, clairette and touriga nacional, and
reworking some of the shiraz vines planted in 1964. Part of the vineyard is sand soil–based
interspersed with ironstone, a highly desirable mix for shiraz and cabernet sauvignon. Exports
to NZ and China.

ŶŶŶŶŶ **Frank Ernest McLaren Vale Shiraz 2018** The most ambitious wine of the
suite, at least in terms of the oak. Opaque. Ovaltine-malty. Damson plum, Asian
five-spice, hoisin and Chinese duck lacquer. Avuncular. Varnished leather. A hark
to the past aromatically, melded with finer precision and oak/tannin management
of the present. Very attractive. Screw cap. 14.5% alc. **Rating** 94 **To** 2030 $50 NG
McLaren Vale Grenache 2019 Grenache is the raison d'être of the Vale.
And it will get even better! Here is the testing ground: thick and vinous. But
paradoxically, lithe and sprightly. Kirsch, black cherry, cardamom, licorice, dried
thyme and lavender. A complex potpourri of intrigue and great potential. Screw
cap. 14.5% alc. **Rating** 94 **To** 2026 $25 NG ✪

ŶŶŶŶŶ **McLaren Vale Shiraz Grenache Touriga 2019 Rating** 93 **To** 2023
$25 NG ✪
McLaren Vale Grenache Touriga 2019 Rating 93 **To** 2023 $25 NG ✪
The Bandy McLaren Vale Cabernet Sauvignon 2018 Rating 93 **To** 2025
$22 NG ✪
McLaren Vale Mataro 2019 Rating 93 **To** 2028 $25 NG ✪
McLaren Vale Shiraz 2019 Rating 90 **To** 2026 $25 NG

3 Drops

★★★★☆

PO Box 1828, Applecross, WA 6953 **Region** Mount Barker
T (08) 9315 4721 **www.3drops.com**
Winemaker Robert Diletti (Contract) **Est.** 1998 **Dozens** 3500 **Vyds** 21.5ha
3 Drops is the name given to the Bradbury family vineyard at Mount Barker. The name
reflects 3 elements: wine, olive oil and water – all of which come from the substantial property.
The vineyard is planted to riesling, sauvignon blanc, semillon, chardonnay, cabernet sauvignon,
merlot, shiraz and cabernet franc, and irrigated by a large wetland on the property. 3 Drops also
owns the 14.7ha Patterson's Vineyard, planted in 1982 to pinot noir, chardonnay and shiraz.
Exports to South Korea, Hong Kong and China.

ŶŶŶŶŶ **Great Southern Chardonnay 2019** A deliberately understated wine directing
all traffic to its varietal fruit, white stone fruit/grapefruit/apple flavours driving
the immensely long palate. Purity in a sip. Screw cap. 13% alc. **Rating** 96 **To** 2034
$28 JH ✪
Great Southern Pinot Noir 2019 Rob Diletti's touch is evident from start to
finish. Good colour and clarity. The red berry fruits of the bouquet flow directly
onto the palate, there joined by notes of spice and the impression of whole berry
and/or whole bunch. Superfine tannins give support to both the texture and
length of a classy pinot. Screw cap. 13.5% alc. **Rating** 95 **To** 2034 $32 JH ✪

ŶŶŶŶŶ **Great Southern Riesling 2020 Rating** 90 **To** 2031 $26 EL
Great Southern Nebbiolo Rosé 2020 Rating 90 **To** 2023 $25 EL

Three Elms

82 Riversdale Road, Frankland River, WA 6396 **Region** Frankland River
T 0458 877 734 **www**.threeelms.com.au
Winemaker Laura Hallett **Est.** 2017 **Dozens** 8000 **Vyds** 44ha
This venture is succession planning at its best. Merv and Judy Lange had a 1200ha wool and grain farm when, in 1971, they decided to plant a few vines as a possible diversification. They were the first to take this step in the Frankland River region and Alkoomi was born. My (James') first visit in '81 was illuminating. They had all the viticultural equipment required, and needed no outside help in creating and progressively expanding the size of the vineyard or building an initially small winery. Roll forward to 2014 and Alkoomi is one of the Top 100 Australian Wineries in my book published that year, with 104ha of estate vineyards and annual production of 60 000 dozen. Four years earlier (in '10) they had handed ownership to daughter Sandy and husband Rod Hallett, who had been an integral part of the business for many years as they raised their 3 daughters Emily, Laura and Molly. In '17 Three Elms was established, its name taking the first letter of the name of each daughter. Laura obtained a bachelor of agribusiness, majoring in viticulture, from Curtin University in '15. Her sisters both have admin/marketing roles in the business and are both part of the management group of Three Elms. Exports to the US, Denmark, Singapore, Taiwan and China.

🍷🍷🍷🍷🍷 **Timbertops Great Southern Riesling 2020** Pure citrus fruit driven by ripe and juicy acid. This is both pretty and gently austere, making for engaging drinking now and in a decade. Impressive. Screw cap. 11.6% alc. **Rating** 92 To 2031 $30 EL
Timbertops Chardonnay 2020 Crushed nuts and ripe stone fruit on the nose and palate. Creamy and textural, with a seam of fine acid that courses over the palate, this is a surprisingly soft, delicate and plump chardonnay that oozes balance. Agglomerate. 12.8% alc. **Rating** 92 **To** 2026 $35 EL

Three Kangaroos

268 Glen Osmond Road, Fullarton, SA 2583 **Region** Barossa Valley
T (08) 8212 0459 **www**.threekangaroos.com.au
Winemaker Contract **Est.** 2014 **Vyds** 30.4ha
What a surprise, and what a pleasure. Three Kangaroos began as a virtual wine business that owned neither vineyard nor winery, its primary business exporting wines to Vietnam, Japan and China. There is nothing unusual in this business strategy but it's rare for such wines to be of high quality. Owners Easan Liu and Tally Gao had previous successful business ventures in real estate and telecommunications and in 2012 they began an international wine distribution business, expanding this by establishing Three Kangaroos; they now own just over 30ha of vines in Stockwell. Exports to Vietnam, Japan and China.

3 Oceans Wine Company

Cnr Boundary Road/Bussell Highway, Cowaramup, WA 6284 **Region** Margaret River
T (08) 9756 5656 **www**.3oceanswine.com.au **Open** Thurs–Mon 10–5
Winemaker Jonathan Mettam **Est.** 1999 **Dozens** 145 000
After a period of spectacular growth and marketing activity, Palandri Wine went into voluntary administration in February 2008. In June of that year the Ma family, through their 3 Oceans Wine Company Pty Ltd, acquired the Palandri winery, its Margaret River vineyard and 347ha of the Frankland River vineyards. In October '08, 3 Oceans also acquired the Palandri and Baldivis Estate brands. There is a strong focus on the emerging markets of the Asia Pacific region, but no neglecting of the domestic market. Given the size of production, the quality of the wines is impressive. Exports to the UK, Singapore, Japan and China.

🍷🍷🍷🍷🍷 **The Explorers Frankland River Shiraz 2018** Provenance is everything and the vineyard speaks volumes here. The length of flavour leaves a lingering quibble, but there is no doubt of the quality of the fruit. Cork. 14.5% alc. **Rating** 94 **To** 2031 $35 EL

Vita Novus Frankland River Shiraz 2018 Intensely concentrated shiraz fruit forms the core of this wine. Layers of blackberry, mulberry and blueberry are the main notes, wrapped in grippy tannins and exotic spice. The oak is well integrated (present, but almost imperceptible in flavour), such is the intensity of the fruit. Screw cap. 14.5% alc. **Rating** 94 **To** 2031 $40 EL

ΨΨΨΨΨ **Fremantle Frankland River Shiraz 2018 Rating** 92 **To** 2031 $75 EL
The Explorers Margaret River Cabernet Sauvignon 2018 Rating 91
To 2028 $35 EL
The Explorers Margaret River Chardonnay 2019 Rating 90 **To** 2029 $45 EL

Tillie J   ★★★★

305 68B Gadd Street, Northcote, Vic 3070 (postal) **Region** Yarra Valley
T 0428 554 311 **www.**tilliejwines.com.au
Winemaker Natillie Johnston **Est.** 2019 **Dozens** 200
Mark my (James') words. Tillie Johnston is going to become a great winemaker. She began her career in 2012, one of the vintage crew at Coldstream Hills, and says her love for pinot noir began there. She then spent 4 of the next 8 years drifting between the Northern and Southern hemispheres unerringly picking the eyes out of an all-star cast of wineries: Leeuwin Estate, Brokenwood, Cristom (Oregon), Keller (Rheinhessen), Framingham (Marlborough) and Yarra Yering. Since then, she's been assistant winemaker at Giant Steps to Steve Flamsteed and Jess Clark. In '19 she was offered the opportunity to buy 2t of grapes from Helen's Hill of whatever variety she chose which was, of course, pinot noir. It came in 2 parcels: one Pommard and 943, hand-picked, whole bunches and destemmed; the second 777, Selectiv' harvested, 100% whole berries. Seven barriques: 1 new, 6 used.

ΨΨΨΨΨ **Yarra Valley Pinot Noir 2020** Bright, clear crimson/purple. The perfumed bouquet straddles red berry and plum; the relatively light-bodied palate brings substance to the purity promised by the bouquet. It does so with panache, surprising with the length and savoury finish/aftertaste. A dab of French oak also adds to the equation. Screw cap. 13% alc. **Rating** 95 **To** 2030 $35 JH ✪

Tim Adams   ★★★★☆

156 Warenda Road, Clare, SA 5453 **Region** Clare Valley
T (08) 8842 2429 **www.**timadamswines.com.au **Open** 7 days 10–4.30
Winemaker Tim Adams, Brett Schutz **Est.** 1986 **Dozens** 60 000 **Vyds** 195ha
Tim Adams and partner Pam Goldsack preside over a highly successful business. Having expanded the range of estate plantings with tempranillo, pinot gris and viognier, in 2009 the business took a giant step forward with the acquisition of the 80ha Leasingham Rogers Vineyard from CWA, followed in '11 by the purchase of the Leasingham winery and winemaking equipment (for less than replacement cost). The winery is now a major contract winemaking facility for the region. Exports to the UK, Sweden, Denmark, the Netherlands, South Korea, Taiwan, China, Hong Kong, Singapore and NZ.

ΨΨΨΨΨ **Clare Valley Shiraz 2018** Gee these wines are great value. This is a rich and ripe rendition, yet there's a lovely evenness across the full-bodied palate abetted by supple tannins. No harsh edges, just ripe, plump fruit and its spice friends having a party. The finish is warm and almost cuddly. It's definitely a winter drink. Screw cap. 14.8% alc. **Rating** 93 **To** 2028 $26 JF ✪
Schaefer Clare Valley Shiraz 2014 Gosh this has held on to to some youthful appeal, especially with the fruit profile very much in focus. It's topped up with a savouriness, mint-choc, new leather and toasty oak but it's all well controlled and balanced. Full bodied, ripe tannins and ready now but will easily notch up a few more years. Screw cap. 14.5% alc. **Rating** 93 **To** 2029 $40 JF
Clare Valley Riesling 2020 This starts out shy with more lemon barley water and saline flavours. Soft across the palate although neat acidity in the mix. It's refreshing, thoroughly enjoyable and dangerously easy to drink. Screw cap. 12% alc. **Rating** 92 **To** 2028 $24 JF ✪

Clare Valley Cabernet Malbec 2017 Stamped with regional spearmint and here it adds a refreshing lift to the cassis and plum flavours. Full bodied, with stern tannins holding fort. The malbec kicks in, adding savouriness and a little plumpness. The drying finish means food is essential and it will age well. Screw cap. 14.5% alc. **Rating** 90 **To** 2032 $26 JF

♀♀♀♀ **Clare Valley Shiraz 2017 Rating** 89 **To** 2029 $26 JF

Tim Gramp ★★★★

1033 Mintaro Road, Watervale, SA 5452 **Region** Clare Valley
T (08) 8843 0199 **www**.timgrampwines.com.au **Open** W'ends 12–4
Winemaker Tim Gramp **Est.** 1990 **Dozens** 6000 **Vyds** 16ha
Tim Gramp has quietly built up a very successful business, and by keeping overheads to a minimum, provides good wines at modest prices. Over the years, estate vineyards (shiraz, riesling, cabernet sauvignon, grenache and tempranillo) have been expanded significantly. Exports to Malaysia, Taiwan and China.

♀♀♀♀♀ **Watervale Riesling 2020** Reserved at first but it soon speeds up to reveal all the vitality, lemon flavouring, spice and lifting acidity that stamps this as a Watervale riesling. Refreshing now but will go some distance. Screw cap. 12% alc. **Rating** 90 **To** 2029 $21 JF❂
Watervale Riesling 2019 Mid straw hue and already offering aged flavours from baked ricotta to buttered toast with lime marmalade. Lots of lime juice across the palate, crisp acidity and it is refreshing. Drink this in the short term. Screw cap. 12.5% alc. **Rating** 90 **To** 2025 $21 JF❂

Tim McNeil Wines ★★★★

71 Springvale Road, Watervale, SA 5452 **Region** Clare Valley
T (08) 8843 0040 **www**.timmcneilwines.com.au **Open** Fri–Sun & public hols 11–5
Winemaker Tim McNeil **Est.** 2004 **Dozens** 1500 **Vyds** 2ha
When Tim and Cass McNeil established Tim McNeil Wines, Tim had long since given up his teaching career, graduating with a degree in oenology from the University of Adelaide in 1999. He then spent 11 years honing his craft at important wineries in the Barossa and Clare valleys. In Aug 2010 Tim McNeil Wines became his full-time job. The McNeils' 16ha property at Watervale includes mature dry-grown riesling. The cellar door overlooks the riesling vineyard, with panoramic views of Watervale and beyond. Exports to Canada.

♀♀♀♀♀ **Clare Valley Shiraz 2016** A bolshie, take-no-prisoners kind of shiraz yet it does come together. Black plums and currants, Dutch licorice, soy sauce and varnishy oak. Full bodied with firm tannins and somewhat drying on the finish. Screw cap. 14.5% alc. **Rating** 90 **To** 2028 $38 JF

Tim Smith Wines ★★★★☆

996 Light Pass Road, Vine Vale, SA 5352 **Region** Barossa Valley
T 0416 396 730 **www**.timsmithwines.com.au **Open** By appt
Winemaker Tim Smith **Est.** 2001 **Dozens** 6000 **Vyds** 1ha
With a talent for sourcing exceptional old-vine fruit from the Barossa floor, Tim Smith has created a small but credible portfolio of wines, currently including mataro, grenache, shiraz, viognier and, more recently, Eden Valley riesling and viognier. Tim left his full-time winemaking role with a large Barossa company in 2011, allowing him to concentrate 100% of his energy on his own brand. In '12 Tim joined forces with the team from First Drop (see separate entry) and moved winemaking operations to a winery fondly named 'Home of the Brave', in Nuriootpa. Exports to Hong Kong, China, the US, the UK and Denmark.

♀♀♀♀♀ **Barossa Shiraz 2018** Impressive full purple/red hue heralds deep, compact, dark berry/cherry/plum fruit of great concentration. Dark chocolate oak rises confidently to the challenging, uniting with firm, fine tannins on a long and full

finish. Glossy, polished and delicious. Screw cap. 14.5% alc. **Rating** 94 **To** 2028
$42 TS

ՊՊՊՊ Eden Valley Viognier 2020 Rating 91 To 2024 $30 TS

Tinklers Vineyard ★★★★★

Pokolbin Mountains Road, Pokolbin, NSW 2320 **Region** Hunter Valley
T (02) 4998 7435 **www.**tinklers.com.au **Open** 7 days 10–5
Winemaker Usher Tinkler **Est.** 1946 **Dozens** 7000 **Vyds** 41ha
Three generations of the Tinkler family have been involved with the property since 1942.
Originally a beef and dairy farm, vines have been both pulled out and replanted at various
stages and part of the adjoining 80+yo Ben Ean Vineyard has been acquired. Plantings include
semillon (14ha), shiraz (11.5ha), chardonnay (6.5ha) and smaller areas of merlot, muscat and
viognier. The majority of the grape production is sold to McWilliam's and Tyrrell's. Usher
has resigned his roles as chief winemaker at Poole's Rock and Cockfighter's Ghost to take
on full-time responsibility at Tinklers, and production has been increased to meet demand.
Exports to Sweden, Singapore and China.

ՊՊՊՊ Reserve Hunter Valley Semillon 2017 Youthful semillon, just shuffling from
adolescence into puberty, alluding to what we can expect with the iron will and
patience required by this classic variety. Bath salts, buttered toast and lemon-drop
scents. The palate, balletic and light, is still tense and elemental. Wait! Screw cap.
11.7% alc. **Rating** 95 **To** 2032 $35 NG ✪
Old Vines Hunter Valley Shiraz 2018 An inimitable expression of vinous
shiraz from the country's most historical wine region. Scents of camphor, black/
red cherry, anise, bitter chocolate; and that je ne sais quoi feel of terracotta and
loam that flows across a ripple of savoury tannins and defines the medium-bodied
luncheon wine that few other regions can make. This will age very well. Screw
cap. 14% alc. **Rating** 95 **To** 2035 $40 NG
School Block Hunter Valley Semillon 2019 This is very good, in the typically
understated way of a youthful classic. Aromas of lemongrass, verdant herb and
citrus balm skitter along a juicy rail of vibrant acidity and a pungent mineral
undercarriage. Subtle, but long and finely tuned. Nothing out of place. This will
go to very good places for those with patience. Screw cap. 11.5% alc. **Rating** 94
To 2032 $25 NG ✪

ՊՊՊՊ PMR Hunter Valley Merlot 2019 Rating 92 To 2024 $25 NG ✪
Hill Block Hunter Valley Chardonnay 2019 Rating 91 To 2024 $30 NG

Tobin Wines ★★★

34 Ricca Road, Ballandean, Qld 4382 **Region** Granite Belt
T (07) 4684 1235 **www.**tobinwines.com.au **Open** 7 days 10–5
Winemaker Adrian Tobin **Est.** 1964 **Dozens** 1400 **Vyds** 10ha
In the early 1960s the Rica family planted table grapes, followed by shiraz and semillon in
'64–66: these are said to be the oldest vinifera vines in the Granite Belt region. The Tobin
family (headed by Adrian) purchased the vineyard in 2000 and has increased the plantings,
which now consist of shiraz, cabernet sauvignon, merlot, tempranillo, semillon, verdelho,
chardonnay, muscat and sauvignon blanc.

ՊՊՊ Isabella Aged Semillon 2014 If the Hunter can make age-worthy dry
semillon, why not the Granite Belt? This is a strong case in point. Medium, bright
straw-yellow hue. Strong varietal pointers of cut grass, lemon and lanolin, with a
note of lemon drops and all the roast almond complexity of 7 years of maturity. It
leads out strong but fades on the finish. Screw cap. 12.2% alc. **Rating** 89 **To** 2024
$59 TS

Tokar Estate ★★★★★

6 Maddens Lane, Coldstream, Vic 3770 **Region** Yarra Valley
T (03) 5964 9585 **www**.tokarestate.com.au **Open** 7 days 10.30–5
Winemaker Martin Siebert **Est.** 1996 **Dozens** 5000 **Vyds** 12ha

Leon Tokar, a very successful businessman, and wife Rita dreamed of a weekender and hobby farm and it was largely by chance that in 1995 they found a scruffy paddock fronting onto Maddens Lane. By the end of the day they had signed a contract to buy the property, following in the footsteps of myself (James), and wife Suzanne, 10 years earlier when we also signed a contract to purchase what became Coldstream Hills on the day we first set foot on it (albeit several years after we first saw it). The Tokars wasted no time and by '99 had planted their 12ha vineyard and built a Mediterranean-inspired cellar door and restaurant. Martin Siebert has been winemaker for many years, making consistently good wines and, with son Daniel Tokar as general manager, has full responsibility for the day-to-day management of the business. Exports to the UK, Canada, Malaysia and China.

🍷🍷🍷🍷🍷 **Amphora Special Release Yarra Valley Tempranillo 2019** Succulent cherries, delicately spiced, savoury and a little meaty; but what makes this wine wonderful is the palate. Supple and flowing with polished tannins and, yes, with a texture of fine, fine sand. Bravo. Screw cap. 14% alc. **Rating** 95 **To** 2027 $60 JF
Coldstream Vineyard Yarra Valley Tempranillo 2019 Excellent dark colour, with deep and captivating flavours. Black cherries, juniper, woodsy earthy spices and wafts of jamon. It's medium bodied, the tannins sweet and textural. It falls short on the finish but what comes before it makes this a very good wine. Screw cap. 14% alc. **Rating** 94 **To** 2027 $50 JF

🍷🍷🍷🍷🍷 **Yarra Valley Shiraz 2019 Rating** 93 **To** 2028 $30 JF
Yarra Valley Chardonnay 2019 Rating 92 **To** 2025 $30 JF
Coldstream Vineyard Yarra Valley Pinot Noir 2019 Rating 92 **To** 2026 $50 JF
Carafe & Tumbler Yarra Valley Pinot Shiraz 2019 Rating 91 **To** 2024 $30 JF
Coldstream Vineyard Yarra Valley Chardonnay 2019 Rating 90 **To** 2026 $50 JF
Yarra Valley Pinot Noir 2019 Rating 90 **To** 2025 $30 JF
Yarra Valley Tempranillo 2019 Rating 90 **To** 2025 $39 JF

Tolpuddle Vineyard ★★★★★

37 Back Tea Tree Road, Richmond, Tas, 7025 **Region** Southern Tasmania
T (08) 8155 6003 **www**.tolpuddlevineyard.com **Open** At Shaw + Smith
Winemaker Martin Shaw, Adam Wadewitz **Est.** 1988 **Dozens** 1800 **Vyds** 20ha

If ever a winery was born with blue blood in its veins, Tolpuddle would have to be it. The vineyard was established in 1988 on a continuous downhill slope facing northeast; in '06 it won the inaugural Tasmanian Vineyard of the Year Award. Michael Hill Smith MW and Martin Shaw are joint managing directors. David LeMire looks after sales and marketing; Adam Wadewitz, one of Australia's brightest winemaking talents, is senior winemaker. Vineyard manager Carlos Souris loses nothing in comparison, with over 30 years of grapegrowing in Tasmania under his belt and an absolutely fearless approach to making a great vineyard even greater. Exports to the US, the UK, Canada, Denmark, China, Japan and Singapore.

🍷🍷🍷🍷🍷 **Chardonnay 2019** A strikingly beautiful chardonnay with its flowery bouquet bearing witness to the sheer purity of the incredibly long palate, the full palette of chardonnay flavours on display. Nectarine, white peach and grapefruit zest are sewn together by an invisible silver thread of acidity. Screw cap. 13% alc. **Rating** 98 **To** 2033 $84 JH ❂

Tomboy Hill

204 Sim Street, Ballarat, Vic 3350 (postal) **Region** Ballarat
T (03) 5331 3785
Winemaker Scott Ireland, Sam Vogel (Contract) **Est.** 1984 **Dozens** 500 **Vyds** 3.6ha
Former schoolteacher Ian Watson seems to be following the same path as Lindsay McCall of
Paringa Estate (also a former schoolteacher) in extracting greater quality and style than any
other winery in their respective regions. Since 1984 Ian has patiently built up a patchwork
quilt of small plantings of chardonnay and pinot noir. In the better years, single-vineyard
Chardonnay and/or Pinot Noir are released; Rebellion Chardonnay and Pinot Noir are
multi-vineyard blends, but all 100% Ballarat. After difficult vintages in 2011 and '12, Tomboy
Hill has been in top form since '15.

The Tomboy Ballarat Chardonnay 2019 Vibrant light straw. A taut, fine-
tuned, cool-climate chardonnay that reflects the winemaker's constant refining of
style in recent years, pulling back on oak (to just 20% new French barriques) and
promoting fruit over leesy flavours. Citrus blossom, white peach, Meyer lemon and
dusty lime. Hints of nashi pear, lemon drop and oyster shell/brine crunch lift the
palate. Touch of quince-like tartness makes for a clean exit. Screw cap. 13.2% alc.
Rating 95 **To** 2029 $55 JP
The Tomboy Ballarat Pinot Noir 2019 With poor winter and spring rains
followed by frost, little wonder the 2019 vintage was small. Quality remains high.
A fine delicacy on display enhanced by filigree-fine tannins. Each time you take
a sniff the landscape changes, at once violet and rose, then glacé cherry, blueberry,
then a mix of dried herbs. Quite the chameleon. Screw cap. 13.2% alc. **Rating** 95
To 2029 $80 JP

Rebellion Ballarat Pinot Noir 2019 Rating 91 **To** 2027 $35 JP

Tomich Wines

87 King William Road, Unley, SA 5061 **Region** Adelaide Hills
T (08) 8299 7500 **www.**tomich.com.au **Open** By appt
Winemaker Randal Tomich **Est.** 2002 **Dozens** 40 000 **Vyds** 85ha
Patriarch John Tomich was born on a vineyard near Mildura, where he learnt firsthand the
skills and knowledge required for premium grapegrowing. He went on to become a well-
known Adelaide ear, nose and throat specialist. Taking the wheel full circle, he completed
postgraduate studies in winemaking at the University of Adelaide in 2002 and embarked on
the master of wine revision course from the Institute of Masters of Wine. His son Randal is
a cutting from the old vine (metaphorically speaking), having invented new equipment and
techniques for tending the family's vineyard in the Adelaide Hills, resulting in a 60% saving in
time and fuel costs. Exports to China, Cambodia, the UK, Canada, India and the US.

Woodside Vineyard Q96 Adelaide Hills Chardonnay 2019 The Q is a
block designation on the estate vineyard, while 96 refers to the Bernard 96 clone
employed here. Straw gold colour. The nose is proud with the influence of barrel
use from start to finish. The fruit is classic Hills white nectarine with creamy
feels and good length. Drinking really well. Diam. 12.7% alc. **Rating** 95 **To** 2026
$60 TL
Woodside Vineyard Adelaide Hills Pinot Noir 2019 At this price, this is
a very smart wine. It brings cherry and plum to the flavour wheel, deliciously
balanced spice suggesting a note of fennel and thyme, even a light touch of mint,
sliding easily through its subtly sticky, grippy tannin curtains to finish. All-round
pinot goodness, at a very attractive price. Screw cap. 13% alc. **Rating** 95 **To** 2026
$30 TL ✪

Woodside Park Adelaide Hills Pinot Noir 2019 Rating 92 **To** 2024
$20 TL✪
H888 Adelaide Hills Shiraz 2019 Rating 92 **To** 2030 $60 TL

Duck & Weave Adelaide Hills Pinot Noir 2019 **Rating** 91 **To** 2024
$18 TL ✪
Tomich Hill Adelaide Hills Sauvignon Blanc 2020 **Rating** 90 **To** 2023
$20 TL ✪

Toolangi ★★★★★

At il Vigneto Pizzeria **Region** Yarra Valley
T (03) 5947 3388 **www**.toolangi.com **Open** Sat 11.30–8.30, Sun 11.30–5.30
Winemaker Kaspar Hermann, Kelly Healey **Est.** 1995 **Dozens** 7500 **Vyds** 14ha
Helmut Konecsny, owner of Rochford Wines, purchased Toolangi in 2018 and immediately
started ringing in the changes. Apart from new-look packaging, Konecsny and his winemaking
and vineyard team also set about rejuvenating and upgrading the vineyard and introducing
new winemaking practices. Exports to Fiji, Hawaii and China.

🍷🍷🍷🍷🍷 **F Block Yarra Valley Chardonnay 2020** This impresses immediately. It has a
certain stature and is well composed. Stone fruit, citrus, layered spices and a flutter
of oak are all in this together. The palate has an interesting texture of talc-like
acidity and a smidge of lemon pith phenolics, concluding long and convincing.
Screw cap. 13.5% alc. **Rating** 96 **To** 2032 $100 JF
Pauls Lane Yarra Valley Chardonnay 2020 Paring back on the winemaking
influences (no new oak) has left a brightness to this otherwise forceful wine. Fruit
in the riper spectrum, more white peach than citrus. The palate is lovely, with the
acidity just so. Screw cap. 13.4% alc. **Rating** 95 **To** 2028 $44 JF
Pauls Lane Yarra Valley Shiraz 2019 In a way, this sits halfway between the
D Block and the first-tier shiraz in terms of shape. It's complete. Dark plums
and juniper with baking spices, pepper and pine needles. There's more volume
here, but it's certainly not a big wine, just shy of full bodied. Tannins are ripe yet
quite fine, the finish long and there's a lot of appeal. No need to wait. Screw cap.
13.4% alc. **Rating** 95 **To** 2029 $44 JF
Block D Yarra Valley Shiraz 2019 So finely tuned and rather beautiful. While
there are flashes of fruit, this is savoury. Juniper, aniseed balls, ironstone, a woodland
of herbs and nori in the mix. It has definition and power but works off a medium-
bodied palate finishing with sandy tannins and great persistence. Bravo. Screw cap.
13.5% alc. **Rating** 95 **To** 2032 $100 JF
Yarra Valley Shiraz 2019 This is still in a youthful, primary phase, but that won't
stop anyone drinking it today. Super-bright fruit, laced with spices, well-handled
smoky/meaty reduction, more of the prosciutto variety. A grind of pepper, juniper
and mint add to the savoury flavours. The palate is taut, tannins giving, and bright
acidity to match. Well played. Screw cap. 13% alc. **Rating** 94 **To** 2030 $27 JF ✪

🍷🍷🍷🍷🍷 **E Block Yarra Valley Pinot Noir 2020 Rating** 92 **To** 2030 $100 JF
Pauls Lane Yarra Valley Pinot Noir 2020 Rating 91 **To** 2028 $44 JF
Yarra Valley Chardonnay 2020 Rating 90 **To** 2024 $30 JF

Top Note ★★★★

546 Peters Creek Road, Kuitpo, SA 5172 **Region** Adelaide Hills
T 0406 291 136 **www**.topnote.com.au **Open** W'ends & public hols 11–4 (closed Jun–Jul)
Winemaker Nick Foskett **Est.** 2011 **Dozens** 800 **Vyds** 17ha
Computer chip designer Nick and opera singer Cate Foskett were looking for a lifestyle
property in the Adelaide Hills after full-on careers in their very different occupations. By
chance they came across a 24ha property planted to 5 varieties, all mainstream except for
0.5ha of a rare mutation of semillon that turns the skin red. They say, 'Despite the small hurdles
of our not knowing much about anything and none of the grapes being under contract,
we sold our city house, enrolled in postgraduate viticulture and winemaking at the Waite
Campus, University of Adelaide, and became grapegrowers'. Two years on, Cate became
possibly the only qualified operatic viticulturist in the world, managing the vineyard and sales,
and still works as a singer between harvests.

ŦŦŦŦ♀ **Reserve Adelaide Hills Chardonnay 2016** The Reserve tag here reflects a level of complexity in layered stone fruits and, more importantly, textural cream and chalkiness. There's a balance beam of acidity underlying it all. A subtle wine that encourages contemplation. Screw cap. 12.5% alc. **Rating** 93 **To** 2026 **$35** TL
Adelaide Hills Chardonnay 2017 Ripe stone fruits, with a fair amount of oak – its vanillas and spices woven through – a touch of anise and lime in the background. Decent value. Screw cap. 12.5% alc. **Rating** 91 **To** 2026 **$25** TL

Torbreck Vintners ★★★★★

348 Roennfeldt Road, Marananga, SA 5352 **Region** Barossa Valley
T (08) 8562 4155 **www**.torbreck.com **Open** 7 days 10–5
Winemaker Ian Hongell, Scott McDonald **Est.** 1994 **Dozens** 70 000 **Vyds** 112ha
Torbreck Vintners was already one of Australia's best-known producers of high-quality red wine when, in Sept 2013, wealthy Californian entrepreneur and vintner Peter Kight (of Quivira Vineyards) acquired 100% ownership of the business. The brand structure remains as before: the top quartet led by The Laird (single-vineyard shiraz), RunRig (shiraz/viognier), The Factor (shiraz) and Descendant (shiraz/viognier). Exports to all major markets.

ŦŦŦŦŦ **The Laird 2016** Barossa shiraz on another scale, every detail exploded into larger-than-life proportions. Impenetrable black. Deeper presence of black plum, licorice and prune, more exotic old-vine spice, more smoky dark chocolate, more mineral tannin, more spirity alcohol, more coal dust, engine oil and unbridled horsepower. To achieve all this with profound persistence and consummate integrity is where The Laird leaves all other overpowered pretenders in its dust. The most spectacular monument to the sheer might of Barossa shiraz. Cork. 15.5% alc. **Rating** 98 **To** 2036 **$800** TS

ŦŦŦŦŦ **Les Amis Barossa Valley Grenache 2018** Monumental grenache of towering stature and enduring longevity. Deep wells of warm, spicy black fruits hover until kingdom come. Intricate, strong, slatey tannins mirror ancient geology. It completely laps up 50% new French oak, reinforcing spicy black density, shoring its scaffolding and heightening longevity. Cork. 15% alc. **Rating** 96 **To** 2033 **$200** TS
Eden Valley Viognier 2020 Detailed and intricately crafted are not words often associated with viognier. Plucked at a refreshing moment in its ripeness curve, it's themed with apple, pear and crunchy apricot. Wild fermentation and 8 months maturation in 60% new French oak barriques brings out enticing biscuit/toasted almond complexity. It remains astonishingly pale, considering. Soft acidity, well-toned phenolic texture and creamy mouthfeel unite in harmony. It holds with impressive determination and persistence, promising great things in the years to come. Screw cap. 13% alc. **Rating** 95 **To** 2028 **$49** TS ❤
The Growers' Cut Shiraz 2018 This label represents the standout parcel of a Torbreck grower for the year. Engineered for the long haul, it's a Marananga shiraz endowed with grand concentration of both fruit and structure. Black fruits of all kinds are tightly wrapped in a thick blanket of tannins, strong yet superfinely polished. Lingering persistence declares both distinction and endurance. Cork. 14.5% alc. **Rating** 95 **To** 2038 **$75** TS
The Factor 2018 The compact density and reverberating power that define The Factor are on grand display in 2018. Deep, penetrating layers of concentrated black fruits of all kinds meld with licorice and rich dark chocolate oak. For all its proportions, it upholds impeccable vitality and brightness. Tannins rise to the challenge in a surge of fine-grained, crafted presence. An exemplar of greatness at the big end of the Barossa. Cork. 15% alc. **Rating** 95 **To** 2033 **$125** TS
RunRig 2018 The full might of the 2018 harvest is rolled up in RunRig. A full purple hue heralds dense layers of spicy dark berry fruits, subtly accented by the orange/apricot aromas of a judicious touch of viognier. French oak rises to the occasion with dark chocolate presence and great depth of firm, fine tannins. It concludes long and generous with sweet, warm alcohol. For lovers of bold Barossa. Cork. 15% alc. **Rating** 95 **To** 2033 **$300** TS

Hillside Vineyard Barossa Valley Grenache 2018 Signature Barossa grenache, carefully executed in a strong season. Elegant red berries and spice are accurate and captivating, but it's the supple mouthfeel and intricate texture that really stand out here. Perfectly ripe, polished red cherry liqueur is impeccably set off by the creaminess of large oak foudres. Tannins sit so comfortably that you'd forget they were here at all, yet they hold a very long finish. Cork. 14.5% alc. **Rating** 95 To 2026 $75 TS

Hillside Vineyard Barossa Valley Shiraz Roussanne 2019 Inspired by co-fermenting shiraz and viognier, demonstrating that roussanne is equally adept at the counterintuitive art of deepening the colour of shiraz to a profound black purple. Violets and spice elevate a dense core of satsuma plum, compact blackberries and fresh, warm licorice straps. Grand density, magnificently structured with a burst of fine tannins. Depth for dollar is off the scale, with integrity that many Barossa shiraz wines (with another digit in the price tag) could only dream of. Screw cap. 14.5% alc. **Rating** 95 To 2027 $32 TS ✪

Descendant 2018 Torbreck's baby RunRig shows the full presence of viognier in 2018, lending subtle tropical and apricot nuances and a fragrant lift to the power and depth of shiraz. The density and concentration of the warm, dry 2018 season are well captured in impressive, compact black fruits and licorice. Dark chocolate and coffee-bean oak holds a long finish on rails of firm, enduring tannins. Cork. 15% alc. **Rating** 94 To 2038 $125 TS

The Steading 2019 Beautifully crafted, polished, seamless Barossa GSM. Bright and deep in colour and personality. Blessed with the expansive, effortless character that comes from maturation in large oak foudre. All 3 varieties and oak unite in seamless coherence, guided by superfine tannins through a long finish. Impossible to corner as fruity, savoury, herbal, peppery, spicy, fleshy or dry, it's consummately all of the above. Cork. 15% alc. **Rating** 94 To 2024 $40 TS

The Pict 2018 Rust, paprika, tomato and sweet leather encapsulate the savoury personality of mataro, with a faintly exotic twist of Greenock. Spicy ripe berry fruits are laid out neatly in a fine mesh of signature savoury, dry tannins and luscious, high-cocoa dark chocolate oak. A long finish accurately upholds every detail of grape and site. Grand mataro. Cork. 15% alc. **Rating** 94 To 2028 $75 TS

♀♀♀♀♀ **The Struie 2019** Rating 93 To 2034 $50 TS
The Gask 2019 Rating 93 To 2039 $75 TS
Harris Barossa Valley Grenache 2018 Rating 93 To 2025 $38 TS
Kyloe 2018 Rating 93 To 2026 $32 TS
Woodcutter's Barossa Valley Rosé 2020 Rating 92 To 2021 $25 TS✪
Woodcutter's Barossa Valley Shiraz 2019 Rating 92 To 2024 $29 TS
Cuvée Juveniles 2019 Rating 90 To 2021 $26 TS

 # Torrent

Great Northern Highway, Herne Hill, WA 6056 **Region** Swan Valley
T (08) 9250 7811 **www**.torrentwines.com.au
Winemaker Rino D'Angelo **Est.** 1963 **Dozens** 1000 **Vyds** 7ha
Grower-turned-producer Torrent Wines is owned by the 3rd-generation d'Angelo family in the Swan Valley. Mark d'Angelo (son of Guerino, who originally bought land in the Swan Valley in the '50s) runs the day-to-day operations, while son Rino is the winemaker (previously at Sittella under Colby Quirk and Yuri Berns). Established in 1963, Torrent has been bottling wines under its own label since 1978. The Swan Valley vineyard is planted to vermentino, chenin blanc, shiraz, grenache and cabernet sauvignon. Pinot noir is sourced from Manjimup. The wines are currently sold exclusively in WA. (EL)

♀♀♀♀♀ **Reserve Swan Valley Chenin Blanc 2018** Herbal nose. This is all about coriander, ripe green capsicum, white tea and apricot. The impact of the oak on the palate is evident in the texture and in the toasted spices through the finish. Fruit weight is minimal and slightly tart on the palate, but the length of flavour is very good. Screw cap. 13.6% alc. **Rating** 90 To 2028 $27 EL

Torzi Matthews Vintners ★★★★☆

Cnr Eden Valley Road/Sugarloaf Hill Road, Mt McKenzie, SA 5353 **Region** Eden Valley
T 0412 323 486 **www**.torzimatthews.com.au **Open** By appt
Winemaker Domenic Torzi **Est.** 1996 **Dozens** 3000 **Vyds** 10ha
Domenic Torzi and Tracy Matthews, former Adelaide Plains residents, searched for a number
of years before finding a block at Mt McKenzie in the Eden Valley. The block they chose is
in a hollow; the soil is meagre but they were in no way deterred by the knowledge that it
would be frost-prone. The result is predictably low yields, concentrated further by drying the
grapes on racks, thus reducing the weight by around 30% (the Appassimento method is used
in Italy to produce Amarone-style wines). Newer plantings of sangiovese and negroamaro, and
an extension of the original plantings of shiraz and riesling, have seen the wine range increase.
Exports to the UK and Denmark.

♀♀♀♀♀ **1920 Single Vineyard Barossa Shiraz 2019** All the deep spice, succulent
black fruits and supple tannins of old vines are transposed onto a backdrop of firm,
fine French oak. The result is generous, fleshy and meaty; an unabashed take on
Barossa shiraz that permeates every crevice of the mouth and the being. For all
its vast breadth, it carries impressive persistence. With soft tannins and understated
acidity, this is a vintage to enjoy in its youth. Cork. 14.5% alc. **Rating** 92 **To** 2025
$75 TS

♀♀♀♀ **Schist Rock Single Vineyard Barossa Shiraz 2020 Rating** 89 **To** 2025
$25 TS

Totino Estate ★★★☆

982 Port Road, Albert Park, SA 5014 (postal) **Region** Adelaide Hills
T (08) 8349 1200 **www**.totinowines.com.au
Winemaker Don Totino, Damien Harris **Est.** 1992 **Dozens** 15000 **Vyds** 29ha
Don Totino migrated from Italy in 1968, and at the age of 18 became the youngest barber in
Australia. He soon moved on, into general food and importing and distribution. Festival City,
as the business is known, has been highly successful, recognised by a recent significant award
from the Italian government. In 1998 he purchased a rundown vineyard at Paracombe in the
Adelaide Hills, since extending the plantings to 29ha of chardonnay, pinot grigio, sauvignon
blanc, sangiovese and shiraz. Various family members, including daughter Linda, are involved
in the business. Exports to Italy and China.

♀♀♀♀♀ **Adelaide Hills Cabernet Sauvignon 2017** No mistaking the cabernet here.
In a cooler year from the northern Paracombe district of the region, it has ripened
slowly, delivering concentrated cassis with spice and the cedar of oak maturation.
Drinking well now in this traditional style and will repay well with cellaring for
5–10 years. Screw cap. 14% alc. **Rating** 93 **To** 2030 $25 TL **☉**

Towerhill Estate ★★★★★

32288 Albany Highway, Mount Barker, WA 6324 **Region** Mount Barker
T 0427 323 073 **www**.towerhillwine.com.au
Winemaker Mike Garland, Andrew Hoadley **Est.** 1993 **Dozens** 350 **Vyds** 5ha
Towerhill Estate was established in 1993 by the Williams family, who began the planting of
the (now) 5ha vineyard of cabernet sauvignon, merlot, riesling and chardonnay. The venture
was acquired from former sheep farmer Julian Hanna in 2007; he runs the estate vineyard in
partnership with Leith Schmidt. The first vintage was in '08, its Riesling from that year
winning the Best Riesling trophy at the Perth Wine Show '12; yet another testament to the
skills of Robert Diletti at Castle Rock Estate. Since then winemaking has shifted to the nearer
Mount Shadforth contract winemaking facility run by Mike Garland and Andrew Hoadley.
Their wines are held back for release when mature. Exports to Singapore.

Tranquil Vale ★★★★

325 Pywells Road, Luskintyre, NSW 2321 **Region** Hunter Valley
T (02) 4930 6100 **www.**tranquilvalewines.com.au **Open** Fri–Sun 10–5
Winemaker Phil Griffiths, Connie Griffiths **Est.** 1996 **Dozens** 1000 **Vyds** 4ha
Phil and Lucy Griffiths purchased the property sight unseen from a description in an old copy of the Weekend Australian found in the Australian High Commission Office in London. The vineyard they established is on the banks of the Hunter River, opposite Wyndham Estate, on relatively fertile, sandy clay loam. Competent winemaking has resulted in good wines, some of which have already had show success. Exports to the UK.

🍷🍷🍷🍷🍷 **Hunter Valley Shiraz 2017** This is a delicious medium-bodied and utterly unpretentious wine, with the Hunter postcode stamped all over it. Scents of terracotta, Bing cherry, Asian five-spice and a smattering of herb. The extraction level perfect, promoting an ease of drinkability and savoury digestibility. Older French and American oak, a mere echo. Long and sappy. Screw cap. 14% alc. **Rating** 92 **To** 2027 $60 NG
Hunter Valley Chardonnay 2019 This is a mid-weighted chardonnay of admirable poise and ample flavour. Aromas of honeydew melon, white fig and peach. A curl of vanillan oak rallies the finish across a creamy mid palate defined by curd and mealy cashew scents. The finish, easygoing. Screw cap. 13% alc. **Rating** 90 **To** 2025 $35 NG

Traviarti ★★★★★

39 Elgin Road, Beechworth, Vic 3747 **Region** Beechworth
T 0439 994 075 **www.**traviarti.com **Open** By appt
Winemaker Simon Grant **Est.** 2011 **Dozens** 650 **Vyds** 0.43ha
After 15 years in the wine trade, first as a buyer in retail, then in sales and marketing roles for producers, Simon Grant and partner Helen Murray spent several years looking for the right place to grow nebbiolo, the wine which had the greatest appeal to them. They found a site at around 600m elevation on red decomposed shale and mudstone soils just above the town of Beechworth. Multiple clones of nebbiolo and tempranillo were planted on their own roots and rootstocks in 2011. The vineyard is now 100% nebbiolo.

Trentham Estate ★★★★

6531 Sturt Highway, Trentham Cliffs, NSW 2738 **Region** Murray Darling
T (03) 5024 8888 **www.**trenthamestate.com.au **Open** 7 days 10–5
Winemaker Anthony Murphy, Shane Kerr, Kerry Morrison **Est.** 1988 **Dozens** 60 000
Vyds 38.66ha
Remarkably consistent tasting notes across all wine styles from all vintages attest to the expertise of ex-Mildara winemaker Tony Murphy, a well-known and highly regarded producer. The estate vineyards are on the Murray Darling. With an eye to the future, but also to broadening the range of the wines on offer, Trentham Estate is selectively buying grapes from other regions with a track record for the chosen varieties. The value for money is unfailingly excellent. In 2018 Trentham Estate celebrated its 30th anniversary. Exports to the UK, Belgium, Sweden, Japan and China.

🍷🍷🍷🍷🍷 **The Family Vermentino 2020** Nothing welcomes summer more than a beach view and a glass of vermentino. Crack this open to enjoy a mix of citrus, a sprinkling of herbs with a kiss of lemon salt. Crisp, dry and refreshing. Screw cap. 12.5% alc. **Rating** 90 **To** 2022 $18 JF ✪
Cellar Reserve Great Western Shiraz 2019 Spicy, dark fruits abound, yet the essence is savoury with cigar box, twigs and a touch of menthol. It sits well. Just shy of full bodied. The tannins are ripe. It's refreshing in a way, but finishes raspy dry and short. Screw cap. 14% alc. **Rating** 90 **To** 2028 $28 JF
Reserve Heathcote Shiraz 2017 Quite a pared-back style given the usual intensity of Heathcote fruit. There is still a lot happening here with loads of

flavour, oak in check, tannins ripe and giving, a plushness across the palate without being a heavyweight. Good drinking now. Screw cap. 14.5% alc. **Rating** 90 To 2026 $28 JF

The Family Frizzante Maestri 2020 An outrageous dark purple hue, slightly fizzy and full of gorgeous sweet fruit flavour. Disco in a glass! Lots of fresh black cherries and sweet cherry essence, balanced with refreshing acidity. Nothing too serious, just a cheery drink. Chill this right down to boogie on. Screw cap. 9.5% alc. **Rating** 90 To 2021 $18 JF ✪

The Family Moscato 2020 Full of spring white flowers and lemon blossom, juicy and grapey with spicy moscato flavours. Some dried mango and pears too. Sweet and vibrant. Nice fizz. Hits the spot. Screw cap. 6% alc. **Rating** 90 To 2021 $18 JF ✪

ŸŸŸŸ   **Estate Shiraz 2019 Rating** 89 To 2023 $18 JF ✪
Reserve Tasmania Pinot Noir 2019 Rating 88 To 2024 $28 JF

Trevelen Farm   ★★★★

506 Weir Road, Cranbrook, WA 6321 **Region** Great Southern
T 0418 361 052 **www.**trevelenfarm.com.au **Open** By appt
Winemaker Harewood Estate (James Kellie) **Est.** 1993 **Dozens** 3000 **Vyds** 6.5ha
In 2008 John and Katie Sprigg decided to pass ownership of their 1300ha wool, meat and grain producing farm to son Ben and wife Louise. However, they have kept control of the 6.5ha of sauvignon blanc, riesling, chardonnay, cabernet sauvignon and merlot planted in 1993. When demand requires, they increase production by purchasing grapes from growers in Frankland River. Riesling remains the centrepiece of the range. Exports to the US and China.

ŸŸŸŸŸ   **Estate Riesling 2020** Picked at slightly higher baume than the Katie's Kiss, and fermented to dryness, this crunchy riesling runs a dermaroller of needling acid over the tongue. Taut and prickly, it has structural integrity and length of flavour, without final complexity and harmony. Screw cap. 12.5% alc. **Rating** 90 To 2028 $25 EL

Frankland Reserve Shiraz 2017 The nose and palate are imbued with an intense white-pepper character. Great flavour intensity is a feature, but there is an edge of hardness that means this either needs a decant or another year in bottle. Or perhaps that's just the way it is … Certainly the tannins create firm structure and cradle the fruit through the finish. Screw cap. 14.5% alc. **Rating** 90 To 2030 $25 EL

ŸŸŸŸ   **Katie's Kiss Riesling 2020 Rating** 89 To 2028 $18 EL ✪

Trifon Estate Wines   ★★★★

PO Box 258, Murchison, Vic 3610 **Region** Central Victoria
T (03) 9432 9811 **www.**trifonestatewines.com.au
Winemaker Jurie Germishuys **Est.** 1998 **Dozens** 180 000 **Vyds** 232ha
Trifon Estate has flown under the radar since it was established by Commodity Traders Australia in 1998. Since that time 232ha of vines have been planted to 15 varieties, the lion's share to shiraz (54ha), chardonnay (39ha), cabernet sauvignon (34ha) and merlot (28ha). Exports to China.

ŸŸŸŸŸ   **Lagoon View Winemakers Selection Cabernet Sauvignon 2016** As a 5yo cabernet sauvignon, this wine comes fully formed having been in bottle gathering itself together for some time before release. This is drinking beautifully now with a medium-bodied Goulburn Valley earthy richness. Very appealing with its leafy, Aussie bush notes, ripe plum, black cherry, woodsy spice. Completes the picture with a long line of ripe, fine tannins. Screw cap. 14.5% alc. **Rating** 92 To 2024 $30 JP

Lagoon View Riesling Traminer 2018 A blast from the past. The popularity of off-dry riesling traminer, so popular in the '70s and '80s, has waned. Good to see one producer keeping true and producing such a super-food-friendly style. The arresting scent of spring wildflowers, musky florals, potpourri, lime and spice. Exuberantly aromatic and light as a feather on the palate with lifted apple, citrus and kitchen spice. The sweetness level is well and truly balanced by brisk acidity. Nice job. Screw cap. 12% alc. **Rating** 90 **To** 2025 $22 JP

Lagoon View Winemakers Reserve Cabernet Sauvignon 2014 Now in its 7th year and moving into an easy, mature complexity that captures the regional stamp. Medium bodied, with the scent of the Australian bush, dark herbs, earth and blackberries. Time spent in French and American oak is now paying off handsomely. Looking pretty good for drinking right now. Cork. 14.5% alc. **Rating** 90 **To** 2024 $45 JP

♥♥♥♥ **Lagoon View Winemakers Selection Riesling 2019 Rating** 89 **To** 2026 $30 JP
Lagoon View Winemakers Selection Chardonnay 2018 Rating 88 **To** 2024 $30 JP
River View Goulburn Valley Rosé 2019 Rating 88 **To** 2023 $25 JP
River View Goulburn Valley Shiraz 2018 Rating 88 **To** 2026 $25 JP
Lagoon View Winemakers Selection Shiraz 2016 Rating 88 **To** 2023 $30 JP
Lagoon View Sparkling Chardonnay 2019 Rating 88 $30 JP

Trinchini Estate Wines ★★★★

6 Noble Street, Anglesea, Vic 3230 (postal) **Region** Geelong
T 0411 205 044 **www.**trinchini.com.au
Winemaker Marcus Trinchini **Est.** 2014 **Dozens** 1500
Marcus Trinchini was born in December 1975, after his father came from Italy to Australia when he was 21 years old. He had always made wine, like his father and his grandfather before him. From a childhood interest in everything about wine, in 2006 Marcus started working with wines and wineries. He moved to Victoria with his wife and in '12 started working with a small winery on the surf coast. This allowed him to begin the search for the perfect location for his first vineyard, which he found in Heathcote. He also found the old Pettavel winery in Geelong. He was underway making his own wine by '14, sourcing fruit from Heathcote, Geelong and the Yarra Valley. No machinery is used at any stage and while this is no doubt true of the crushing and pressing of the grapes, one assumes pumps are used to move the wine around the winery. Marcus certainly learnt his craft well. The wines submitted so far have all been of good quality. Marcus says, 'I continue to enjoy my craft, strive to master it, making a better piece of art each time so that one day I craft a Mona Lisa of wine'. Exports to China.

♥♥♥♥♥ **Limited Edition White S Heathcote Shiraz 2017** Only a small price difference between the Black and White S shiraz; white S is possibly the more polished of the two. Heathcote richness in fruit and depth of concentration is evident, but so too a flow of fine tannins, the oak so balanced you don't notice the joints and good length. Screw cap. 14% alc. **Rating** 94 **To** 2030 $50 JP

♥♥♥♥♀ **Limited Edition Black S Heathcote Shiraz 2017 Rating** 90 **To** 2026 $42 JP

tripe.Iscariot

20 McDowell Road, Witchcliffe, WA 6286 **Region** Margaret River
T 0414 817 808 **www.**tripeiscariot.com
Winemaker Remi Guise **Est.** 2013 **Dozens** 800
This has to be the most way-out winery name of the century. It prompted me (James) to email South African–born and trained winemaker/owner Remi Guise asking to explain its derivation and/or meaning. He courteously responded with a reference to Judas as 'the greatest black sheep of all time', and a non-specific explanation of 'tripe' as 'challenging in style'. He added, 'I hope this sheds some light, or dark, on the brand'. The wines provide a better answer, managing to successfully harness highly unusual techniques at various points of their elevage. His day job as winemaker at Naturaliste Vintners, the large Margaret River

contract winemaking venture of Bruce Dukes, provides the technical grounding, allowing him to throw the 'how to' manual out of the window when the urge arises. His final words on his Marrow Syrah Malbec are: 'So, suck the marrow from the bone, fry the fat, and savour the warm, wobbly bits'.

🍷🍷🍷🍷🍷 **Brawn Margaret River Chardonnay 2019** Wild ferment in barrel (40% new), matured for 10 months. Blocking mlf here has created a staunch line of acidity that spears through the very heart of the ripe orchard fruit. Concentrated, saline and very classy. This is for the acid freaks and the lovers of mineral Chablis; there is finesse, complexity, length and line here in spades. Screw cap. 12.8% alc. **Rating** 96 To 2036 $42 EL ✪

Absolution Karridale Margaret River Chenin Blanc 2019 Cheesecloth, green apple, saline and that sheepy little suggestion of unripe pear/lanolin. Karridale is cooler than Wilyabrup, which gives this wine a tension and poise. Classic chenin has that edgy phenolic drift on the palate – it is here, too. Screw cap. 12.5% alc. **Rating** 95 To 2036 $32 EL ✪

Absolution Wilyabrup Margaret River Chenin Blanc 2019 Being further north, Wilyabrup is slightly warmer than Karridale, lending this wine a plushness through the back palate. This is the fleshy, pristine and spicy one (the Karridale the lean, staunch and edgy one). Awesome to see. Very classy, totally delicious. Screw cap. 12.5% alc. **Rating** 95 To 2036 $32 EL ✪

Cock's Foot Madrigal 2019 An unbelievably pretty nose! Lychee and exotic spice, white spring florals and a host of delicate fruit. The balancing acidity is tight and tingly, giving the palate a real saline edge. This is lovely, almost chewy. It dances through the finish with an on-point, lyrical rhythm. The lighter, finer alternative to gewürz when pairing with spicy Thai cuisine. Screw cap. 12.4% alc. **Rating** 95 To 2020 $32 EL ✪

🍷🍷🍷🍷🍷 **Absolution Danse Macabre Blanc Sec 2020** **Rating** 92 To 2025 $25 EL ✪

Trofeo Estate   ★★★★☆

85 Harrisons Road, Dromana, Vic 3936 **Region** Mornington Peninsula
T (03) 5981 8688 **www.**trofeoestate.com **Open** Thurs–Sun 10–5
Winemaker Richard Darby **Est.** 2012 **Dozens** 7500 **Vyds** 18.5ha
This property has had a chequered history. In the 1930s Passiflora Plantations Company was set up to become Australia's leading exporter of passionfruit and associated products. By '37, 120ha was covered with 70000 passionfruit vines and a processing factory was in operation. The following year a disease devastated the passionfruit and the company went into receivership, never to be seen again. In '48 a member of the Seppelt family planted a vineyard on the exact site of Trofeo Estate and it was thereafter acquired by leading Melbourne wine retailer and wine judge, the late Doug Seabrook, who maintained the vineyard and made the wine until the vines were destroyed in a bushfire in '67. In '98 it was replanted but passed through several hands and fell into and out of neglect until the latest owner, Jim Manolios, developed the property as a cafe restaurant, vineyard and winery with pinot noir (8.2ha), chardonnay (5ha), shiraz (2.5ha), pinot gris (1.6ha) and cabernet sauvignon (1.2ha). Trofeo Estate is the exclusive Australian distributor of terracotta amphorae made in Italy, hence the involvement of amphorae in the making of a number of the wines. Exports to China.

🍷🍷🍷🍷🍷 **The Chosen Few Shiraz 2018** A compelling, savoury yet brightly-fruited wine. A whorl of dark fruit is doused in exotic spices, earthy, herbal and mouth-watering. There's a generosity on the palate, without it going overboard; the tannins are plump and velvety and the finish long. Cork. 14.7% alc. **Rating** 95 To 2030 $46 JF

The Chosen Few Pinot Noir 2019 There's a vibrancy throughout, red cherry accents, iodine, dried herbs and a dusting of spice. Squeezes in at medium bodied, the tannins light, textural and laced with lots of acidity. Refreshing and compelling. Screw cap. 14.3% alc. **Rating** 94 To 2029 $56 JF

ρρρρ² **The Chosen Few Mornington Peninsula Chardonnay 2019** Rating 92
To 2027 $49 JF
Aged in Terracotta Single Block Pinot Noir 2019 Rating 92 To 2028
$46 JF
Aged in Terracotta Rosé 2020 Rating 91 To 2022 $28 JF
Aged in Terracotta Mornington Peninsula Chardonnay 2019 Rating 90
To 2025 $34 JF
Blanc de Noir 2016 Rating 90 To 2021 $45 JF

Trove Estate

19 Villers Street, Cowaramup, WA 6284 **Region** Margaret River
T 0412 412 192 **www.**troveestate.com.au
Winemaker Laura Bowler **Est.** 2017 **Dozens** 8500 **Vyds** 16.03ha
The slick website could do with a spell and fact check here and there, and elsewhere
agreement on the establishment date ('16 or '17) and ownership (2 or 4 people). But that's
arguably beside the point, for its range of wines at 3 price points is well made and priced to sell.
The key players are business partners Paul Byron and Ralph Dunning, with decades of sales
and marketing in and around the wine industry. While Margaret River is (understandably)
the focus, the entry-point Secret Squirrel range of wines come from the Great Southern.
Next up the ladder is the Forest Grand group of Margaret River wines, and at the top is The
Laurels trio of Chardonnay, Shiraz and Cabernet. Part of the production comes from the estate
vineyards of 9.5ha cabernet sauvignon, 2.12ha shiraz and 4.41ha sauvignon blanc.

ρρρρρ **The Laurels Margaret River Cabernet Sauvignon 2019** Aniseed, cassis,
mulberry and licorice on the nose. On the palate, this is fine, layered and very
juicy, with sprinklings of exotic spice over the finish. Margaret River was cool
and wet in 2019, and for those who prepared for the conditions, the vintage was
of high aromas, delicacy and poise. Very smart. Screw cap. 14% alc. **Rating** 94
To 2036 $60 EL

ρρρρ **The Laurels Margaret River Shiraz 2019** Rating 89 To 2028 $60 EL

Tucks

37 Shoreham Road, Red Hill South, Vic 3937 **Region** Mornington Peninsula
T (03) 5989 8660 **www.**tuckswine.com.au **Open** Wed–Sun 11–5
Winemaker Simon Black **Est.** 1985 **Dozens** 2000 **Vyds** 3.4ha
Tucks has changed focus significantly since selling its large Red Hill vineyard, but it has
retained the Buckle Vineyard with chardonnay and pinot noir that consistently provide
outstanding grapes (and wine). In late 2017 Tuck's Ridge (as it was then called) was purchased
by John and Wendy Mitchell of neighbouring Montalto. They have revamped the cellar door
and restaurant, keeping the business as a separate operation.

ρρρρ² **Mornington Peninsula Chardonnay 2019** This is moreish and funky. Pleasing
too. The slip of sulphides lead the show, followed by fresh grapefruit, pith and
lemon zest, with judicious oak adding some toasty, slight vanillan flavour. It's
tight and linear. Refreshing and a few glasses will disappear quickly. Screw cap.
13.4% alc. **Rating** 93 To 2027 $45 JF
Mornington Peninsula Pinot Noir 2019 A plush, ripe and generous wine,
fittingly for the vintage. There's plenty of juicy fruit, woodsy spices with dabs of
sarsaparilla and licorice root. While it sits comfortably in its full-bodied frame
with plump tannins, it has plenty of refreshment and raspberry acidity to keep the
flavours at bay. Nice one. Screw cap. 14.2% alc. **Rating** 92 To 2025 $50 JF

Tulloch

Glen Elgin, 638 De Beyers Road, Pokolbin, NSW 2321 **Region** Hunter Valley
T (02) 4998 7580 **www.**tullochwines.com **Open** 7 days 10–5
Winemaker Jay Tulloch, First Creek **Est.** 1895 **Dozens** 40 000 **Vyds** 80ha

The Tulloch brand continues to build success on success. Its primary grape source is estate vines owned by part-shareholder Inglewood Vineyard in the Upper Hunter Valley. It also owns the JYT Vineyard, which was established by Jay Tulloch in the mid-1980s at the foot of the Brokenback Range, right in the heart of Pokolbin. Contract-grown fruit is also sourced from other growers in the Hunter Valley and futher afield. With Christina Tulloch a livewire marketer, skilled winemaking by First Creek Winemaking Services has put the icing on the winemaking cake. Exports to Belgium, the Philippines, Singapore, Hong Kong, Malaysia, Thailand, Japan and China.

Tumblong Hills ★★★★☆

1149 Old Hume Highway, Gundagai, NSW 2722 **Region** Gundagai
T 0408 684 577 **www**.tumblonghills.com
Winemaker Simon Robertson **Est.** 2009 **Dozens** 10 000 **Vyds** 200ha
This large vineyard was established by Southcorp Wines in the 1990s, as part of 'Project Max', an initiative to honour Max Schubert of Penfolds Grange fame. In 2009 it was acquired by business partners Danny Gilbert, Peter Leonard and Peter Waters. They were able to secure the services of viticulturist and general manager Simon Robertson, who knew the vineyard like the back of his hand, his experience stretching across the wine regions of Southern New South Wales. In '11, investors Wang Junfeng and Handel Lee came onboard to strengthen Tumblong Hills' presence in Australia and China. While shiraz and cabernet sauvignon remain the 2 most significant varieties, nebbiolo, barbera, sangiovese and fiano are increasingly important. Exports to China.

Turkey Flat ★★★★★

Bethany Road, Tanunda, SA 5352 **Region** Barossa Valley
T (08) 8563 2851 **www**.turkeyflat.com.au **Open** 7 days 11–5
Winemaker Mark Bulman **Est.** 1990 **Dozens** 20 000 **Vyds** 47.83ha
The establishment date of Turkey Flat is given as 1990 but it might equally have been 1870 (or thereabouts), when the Schulz family purchased the Turkey Flat Vineyard; or 1847, when the vineyard was first planted – to the very old shiraz that still grows there today and the 8ha of equally old grenache. Plantings have since expanded significantly, now comprising shiraz (24ha), grenache (10.5ha), cabernet sauvignon (5.9ha), mourvèdre (3.7ha) and smaller plantings of marsanne, viognier and dolcetto. The business is run by sole proprietor Christie Schulz. Exports to the UK, the US, China and other major markets.

🍷🍷🍷🍷🍷 **Barossa Valley Grenache 2019** Primarily produced from 100+yo estate vines, it is a model of consistent style, quality and supreme value. Its balance is marvellous, appropriate for a wine that makes its statement of juicy red berries, Turkish delight and rose petals without fuss or fanfare. Screw cap. 14.5% alc. Rating 97 To 2029 $45 JH ✪ ♥

🍷🍷🍷🍷🍷 **Barossa Valley White 2019** Marsanne/roussanne of breathtakingly sophisticated and intellectual heights. Uber-reductive, a veritable keg of gunpowder with lit fuse! Tension, energy and cut like the Barossa floor has never seen. It unites this maelstrom with astonishing coherence, grace and persistence that holds undeviating for a full 30 seconds. And it will live for decades. If you love grand cru Burgundy, you'll adore this. Outclasses its price point by a country mile! Screw cap. 13.1% alc. Rating 96 To 2034 $25 TS ✪
Butchers Block Barossa Valley Red Blend 2019 Grenache, shiraz and mataro from original vines on the estate Bethany vineyard. Marrying the exuberant, fragrant, exotic and herbal lift of whole-bunch fermentation while upholding varietal definition, integrity and graceful palate flow is an art form. Mark Bulman has again shown his talent in this bargain blend. Flamboyant and multi-faceted in its complexity, drawing into a tail of fine-grained texture and polished persistence. Benchmark bargain. Screw cap. 14.5% alc. Rating 95 To 2024 $22 TS ✪
Barossa Valley Sparkling Shiraz NV An enticingly medium-bodied Barossa sparkling shiraz, graced with white pepper and beetroot over a core of satsuma

plum skin, blackberries and morello cherries. A fine acid line marries with a stream of fine-grained tannins through a long, elegant finish. Such intricate engineering will confidently see it out for the next decade, but it's a delight from the outset. Crown seal. 13.9% alc. **Rating** 94 $45 TS

🍷🍷🍷🍷🍷 **Barossa Valley Rosé 2020** Rating 92 To 2021 $24 TS ⊙
Barossa Valley Shiraz 2019 Rating 91 To 2029 $55 TS

Turner's Crossing Vineyard ★★★☆

747 Old Bridgewater-Serpentine Road, Serpentine, Vic 3517 **Region** Bendigo
T 0427 843 528 **www**.turnerscrossing.com.au
Winemaker Various **Est.** 1999 **Dozens** 4000 **Vyds** 42ha
This outstanding, mature vineyard was named to remember the original landholder, Thomas Turner. During the 1800s, farmers and gold rush prospectors crossed the Loddon River beside the property, at what became known as Turners Crossing. During the Gold Rush period European settlers in the area started to plant vineyards, trusting that Bendigo's terroir would reveal itself as a suitable site on which to grow grapes. And they were right to be so confident. Its alluvial composition of rich limestone soils and Mediterranean climate make it a happy home for viticulture in particular. Turners Crossing Vineyard now spans 42ha of mature vines. The vineyard is virtually pesticide and chemical free; warm days and cool nights allow the grapes to ripen during the day and the vines to recover overnight. The vineyard bears shiraz, cabernet sauvignon, viognier and picolit (a rare white Italian variety). Exports to the UK, Canada, Vietnam and China.

🍷🍷🍷🍷🍷 **The Crossing Bendigo Shiraz 2018** Built large, this big, ripe shiraz delivers
something for everyone. Bursting in ripened plums, licorice, earth, sweet spiced
oak, and there's even a waft of eucalypt, too. It's warm and rich to taste, the
toasty oak and spice rolling in across a palate of supple tannins. Will definitely
build further. Diam. 14.9% alc. **Rating** 94 **To** 2034 $60 JP

🍷🍷🍷🍷 **Bendigo Shiraz 2017** Rating 89 To 2027 $25 JP

Turon Wines ★★★★☆

1760 Lobethal Road, Lobethal, SA 5241 **Region** Adelaide Hills
T 0423 956 480 **www**.turonwines.com.au **Open** By appt
Winemaker Turon White **Est.** 2013 **Dozens** 800 **Vyds** 2ha
This is the thoroughly impressive venture of newlyweds Turon and Alex White. Working for several small wineries while studying at university, Turon realised the potential of the ever-varying site climates within the Adelaide Hills. His overseas winemaking experience while completing his degree was appropriately lateral, with vintage winemaking at Argyle in Oregon and at Kovács Nimród in Eger, Hungary. Out of this has come a minimal-intervention approach to winemaking, being confident enough to stand back and let the wine develop and be itself, but equally being prepared to intervene if needs must. Selecting the right site, soil and meso climate within the region is, Turon believes, crucial in allowing the wines to reach their full potential. That said, experimentation of method is also of prime importance in understanding the potential of terroir and variety. One could go on with the philosophical side, but there is also a practical element. They have built a winery at their property in Lenswood and turned it into a cooperative winery from the outset, where young winemakers can work together, sharing equipment, resources and knowledge. They called the venture the Hills Handcrafted Collective, with wines to be released from the Collective a bit further down the track. Given the quality of the wines released under the Turon Wines label, one is tempted to say the sky's the limit. As it is, it was one of the top new wineries in the *Wine Companion 2019*.

🍷🍷🍷🍷🍷 **Artist Series Adelaide Hills Field Blend 2020** Here we have sauvignon blanc,
grüner veltliner and chardonnay, the 3 most lauded whites of the Hills region.
Do they get on together? They absolutely do. Attractive white orchard florals
and exciting palate zing, lemony and saline and tonic water in the flavour zone.

Technically whizz bang and simply yum. Screw cap. 12.9% alc. **Rating** 93 **To** 2024 $25 TL ⚪

Artist Series Balhannah Adelaide Hills Syrah 2019 Lifted dark-berry aromas and vibrant satsuma plum flavours, all with plenty of spice and laid-back oak notes supporting that delicious fruit. There's a delicate whiff of mint and eucalyptus on the finish. A generous and tasty syrah. Screw cap. 14.1% alc. **Rating** 93 **To** 2028 $32 TL

Artist Series Lenswood Adelaide Hills Chardonnay 2020 Classical white nectarine flavours through and through. The oak spice is subtly intermingled and there's a light tang on the back palate to define this fresh yet detailed style. Screw cap. 13% alc. **Rating** 92 **To** 2025 $32 TL

Project 5255 Langhorne Creek Grenache 2020 Grenache from the Watkins vineyard and a huge change to Turon White's usual style. An immediate blood lip/saline/wild bush sense of rusticity, yet it flows on the palate with a medium- to fuller-bodied viscosity. Flavours are cherry and licorice, with flinty tannins softly supportive. Recently bottled so give it a good decant at the moment. This feels like it will continue to build momentum. Screw cap. 16% alc. **Rating** 92 **To** 2028 $28 TL

Artist Series Adelaide Hills Rosé 2020 Pinot meunier. A fashionable pale pink. Ripe and aromatic. Crimson and darker berries at the fore, with a dash of bay rum in the background. This is not a shy rosé by any means, it has plenty of forthright personality. Screw cap. 13.1% alc. **Rating** 90 **To** 2023 $25 TL

Limited Series Adelaide Hills Syrah 2019 Lower alcohol, yet with plenty of energy on the palate. Showing some oak influence after 15 months in a French puncheon. A fuller-bodied style, quite powerful and intense, with a good show of cooler-climate black-pepper spice characters, and tangy tannins to finish. Will be worth checking back in 5–10 years. Screw cap. 13.2% alc. **Rating** 90 **To** 2030 $45 TL

🍷🍷🍷🍷 **Limited Series Adelaide Hills Pinot Noir 2019** **Rating** 89 **To** 2030 $45 TL

Twinwoods Estate   ★★★★☆

Brockman Road, Cowaramup, WA 6284 **Region** Margaret River
T 0419 833 122 **www.**twinwoodsestate.com
Winemaker Deep Woods Estate (Julian Langworthy), Aldo Bratovic **Est.** 2005
Dozens 2500 **Vyds** 8.5ha
This is a winery that was bound to succeed. It is owned by the Jebsen family, for many years a major player in the importation and distribution of fine wine in Hong Kong, more recently expanded into China. Jebsen invested in a NZ winery, following that with the acquisition of this vineyard in Margaret River in 2005. It brings together senior Jebsen managing director Gavin Jones, and peripatetic winemaker Aldo Bratovic, who began his career decades ago under the tutelage of Brian Croser. Its widespread distribution is interesting, not all the eggs being put in the Hong Kong/China markets. The quality of the wines I (James) have tasted fully lives up to what one would expect. (I tasted the wines without any knowledge of the background of Twinwoods.) It commenced selling wine in Australia in '14, with Terroir Selections its Australian partner, another intersection with Brian Croser. Exports to Denmark, Germany, Singapore, Taiwan, Hong Kong, China and NZ.

🍷🍷🍷🍷🍷 **Margaret River Chardonnay 2018** Flinty, funky and concentrated, this has a salivating seam of sea salt and curry powder on a bed of crushed nuts. What a cracking wine for the price! It has it all: fruit power, complex texture and good length of flavour. Yes. Screw cap. 13% alc. **Rating** 94 **To** 2028 $25 EL ⚪

🍷🍷🍷🍷♀ **Optivus Reserve Margaret River Cabernet Sauvignon 2016** **Rating** 90 **To** 2030 $45 EL
Margaret River Cabernet Sauvignon 2017 **Rating** 92 **To** 2027 $29 EL

Two Hands Wines   ★★★★★

273 Neldner Road, Marananga, SA 5355 **Region** Barossa Valley
T (08) 8562 4566 **www.**twohandswines.com **Open** 7 days 11–5
Winemaker Richard Langford **Est.** 1999 **Dozens** 55 000 **Vyds** 40ha
The 'hands' in question are those of SA businessmen Michael Twelftree and Richard Mintz, Michael in particular having extensive experience in marketing Australian wine in the US (for other producers). On the principle that if big is good, bigger is better, the style of the wines has been aimed squarely at the palate of Robert Parker Jr and *Wine Spectator*'s Harvey Steiman. Grapes are sourced from the Barossa Valley (where the business has 15ha of shiraz), McLaren Vale, Clare Valley, Langhorne Creek and Padthaway. The emphasis is on sweet fruit and soft tannin structure, all signifying the precise marketing strategy of what is a very successful business. At the end of 2015 Two Hands embarked on an extensive planting programme using vines propagated from a number of vineyards (including Prouse Eden Valley, Wendouree 1893, Kaelser Alte Reben, Penfolds Modbury, Kays Block 6, Kalimna 3C), as well as a high-density 1.4ha clos (a walled vineyard) with the vines trained in the goblet style of the Northern Rhône Valley. Exports to all major markets.

♀♀♀♀♀ **Holy Grail Single Vineyard Seppeltsfield Road Barossa Valley Shiraz 2019** The standout of Two Hands' Single Vineyard series, this is a grand statement of the power and bright definition of Seppeltsfield. Impressive depth of full, vibrant purple hue heralds a display of inky berry/cherry/plum fruit, layered with licorice and sensitively backed with dark chocolate oak. There's a brightness and confidence to this release, with acidity and fine-grained tannins coaxing out a finish of impressive line and lingering persistence. Diam. 14.5% alc. **Rating** 95 To 2034 $110 TS
Charlie's Garden Eden Valley Shiraz 2019 Two Hands' Garden Series snapshots the mood of 6 shiraz regions, adapting winemaking to highlight the character of each. This is one of the best, quintessential Eden Valley wines in all of its spicy, dark-berried glory, thanks to 10–81yo vines on Mengler's HIll at 460–490m elevation. Wonderful violet fragrance permeates a long palate in a sea of fine-boned tannins, dark chocolate oak and bright acidity. Diam. 14.7% alc. **Rating** 94 To 2034 $60 TS
Samantha's Garden Clare Valley Shiraz 2019 A pretty and endearing take on Clare Valley shiraz. Boasting a vibrant, full purple hue, a core of succulent black cherry and blackberry fruit is lifted by violet fragrance. Crunchy acidity and fine-boned tannins complete a seamless and enticing package. I'd like to see more persistence, but it may build in time. Diam. 14% alc. **Rating** 94 To 2029 $60 TS
Twelftree Brooks Road Clarendon McLaren Vale Grenache 2018 Identical on paper to Twelftree's Blewitt Springs, this is a wonderful contrast of terroirs. Clarendon infuses its spicy black fruits and black pepper; its tannin structure firmer yet every bit as fine, charged with a burst of acidity that splashes long and strong through the finish. An exemplar for the magnificence of grenache in Clarendon. Screw cap. 14.5% alc. **Rating** 94 To 2028 $45 TS

♀♀♀♀♀ **Max's Garden Heathcote Shiraz 2019 Rating** 93 To 2024 $60 TS
Bella's Garden Barossa Valley Shiraz 2019 Rating 92 To 2027 $60 TS
Dave's Block Single Vineyard Blythmans Road Blewitt Springs Shiraz 2019 Rating 92 To 2039 $110 TS
Brave Faces Barossa Valley Grenache Mourvèdre Shiraz 2019 Rating 92 To 2025 $30 TS
Fields of Joy Clare Valley Shiraz 2019 Rating 91 To 2031 $30 TS
Gnarly Dudes Barossa Valley Shiraz 2019 Rating 91 To 2025 $30 TS
Harriet's Garden Adelaide Hills Shiraz 2019 Rating 91 To 2029 $60 TS
Yacca Block Single Vineyard Menglers Hill Eden Valley Shiraz 2019 Rating 91 To 2029 $110 TS
Twelftree Schuller Blewitt Springs McLaren Vale Grenache 2018 Rating 91 To 2028 $45 TS
Sexy Beast McLaren Vale Cabernet Sauvignon 2019 Rating 91 To 2027 $30 TS

Aphrodite McLaren Vale Cabernet Sauvignon 2017 Rating 91 To 2037
$180 TS
The Boy Eden Valley Riesling 2020 Rating 90 To 2023 $30 TS

2 Mates ★★★★

160 Main Road, McLaren Vale, SA 5171 **Region** McLaren Vale
T 0411 111 198 **www.2mates.com.au**
Winemaker Mark Venable, David Minear, Matt Rechner, **Est.** 2003 **Dozens** 300
Vyds 20ha
The 2 mates are Mark Venable and David Minear, who say, 'Over a big drink in a small bar
in Italy a few years back, we talked about making "our perfect Australian Shiraz". When we
got back, we decided to have a go.' The wine ('05) was duly made and won a silver medal
at the Decanter World Wine Awards in London, in some exalted company. Eleven years on,
they hit the rarefied heights of 97 points for their $35 The Perfect Ten McLaren Vale Shiraz.

Two Rivers ★★★★

2 Yarrawa Road, Denman, NSW 2328 **Region** Hunter Valley
T (02) 6547 2556 **www.tworivers.com.au Open** 7 days 11–4
Winemaker Liz Silkman **Est.** 1988 **Dozens** 10 000 **Vyds** 67.5ha
A significant part of the viticultural scene in the Upper Hunter Valley with 67.5ha of
vineyards, involving an investment of several million dollars. Part of the fruit is sold under
long-term contracts and part is kept for Two Rivers. The emphasis is on chardonnay and
semillon. Two Rivers is also a partner in the Tulloch business, together with the Tulloch
and Angove families, and supplies grapes for the Tulloch label. A contemporary cellar door
adds significantly to the appeal of the Upper Hunter Valley as a wine-tourist destination. The
appointment of immensely talented winemaker Liz Silkman had an immediate impact.

 Museum Release Stone's Throw Hunter Valley Semillon 2015 A cool,
peripatetic vintage, albeit with many rewarding expressions, particularly with age.
This is such. Featherweight, with riveting aromas of lemon curd, tonic, dried hay
and barley sugar. Dry and balletic, with the flavours skittering to a long, chewy
finish across talcy acidity, all nicely measured. Screw cap. 10.5% alc. **Rating** 95
To 2027 $50 NG
Museum Release Thunderbolt Hunter Valley Shiraz 2014 A bright mid-
ruby hue with slight bricking at the edges. Aromas of suede, medicinal cola,
varnish, dark-cherry pith and the regional stamp of sweet fecund earth. Traditional,
medium bodied and very savoury, with fibrous tannins, expansive momentarily
and then drying across the finish. Yet this is more a sign of my precocity than the
wine's inability to age longer. Much longer, if the saliva drawn from the back of
my mouth, making me reach for the second glass, is any indication. Plenty in store.
Be patient. Screw cap. 13.7% alc. **Rating** 94 To 2028 $70 NG

 Yarrawa Road Hunter Valley Chardonnay 2019 Rating 93 To 2026
$50 NG
Vigneron's Reserve Hunter Valley Chardonnay 2019 Rating 91 To 2024
$40 NG
Vigneron's Reserve Hunter Valley Shiraz 2014 Rating 91 To 2024 $80 NG

Tyrrell's Wines ★★★★★

1838 Broke Road, Pokolbin, NSW 2321 **Region** Hunter Valley
T (02) 4993 7000 **www.tyrrells.com.au Open** Mon–Sun 9–4
Winemaker Andrew Spinaze, Mark Richardson, Chris Tyrrell **Est.** 1858
Dozens 220 000 **Vyds** 364ha
One of the most successful family wineries, a humble operation for the first 110 years of its
life that has grown out of all recognition over the past 40 years. Vat 1 Semillon is one of
the most dominant wines in the Australian show system and Vat 47 Chardonnay is one of the

pacesetters for this variety. Tyrrell's has an awesome portfolio of single-vineyard semillons released when 5–6 years old. Its estate plantings include over 100ha in the Hunter Valley and 26ha in Heathcote. In December '17 Tyrrell's purchased the 13.5ha Stevens Old Hillside Vineyard on Marrowbone Road; 6.11ha are planted to shiraz, including a 1.1ha block planted in 1867, the balance planted in 1963, notably to shiraz and semillon. There are 11 blocks of vines older than 100 years in the Hunter Valley and the Tyrrell family owns 7 of those blocks. A founding member of Australia's First Families of Wine. Exports to all major markets.

♟♟♟♟♟ **4 Acres Hunter Valley Shiraz 2019** This oscillates with the 8 Acres as my favourite of these single-vineyard expressions. An apotheosis of Hunter savouriness and a lightness of touch of yore. Truly ethereal. Fragrant, with mottled blue-fruit allusions, lilac, nori and chinotto. Clove, pepper grind and cardamom lace the finish. Yet frankly, words are a waste. The texture, the totem. Detailed tannins of immaculate precision. An airy grace. Elegance personified. Screw cap. 13% alc. **Rating** 97 **To** 2034 $135 NG ✪ ♥

♟♟♟♟♟ **Old Patch Hunter Valley Shiraz 2019** Medium of feel. Sappy and crunchy. Sour cherry, rosehip, bramble and root spice. An ethereal feel. Less reductive than the Johnno's cuvée at this stage. Beautiful, with a layer of sandalwood and orange rind across a spindly tannic frame, directing the effortless flow of fruit. One direction. Long. Screw cap. 13% alc. **Rating** 96 **To** 2035 $135 NG
8 Acres Hunter Valley Shiraz 2019 The most tannic and (for lack of a better word) powerful of these wines. A reductive whiff of violet, tapenade and nori. Ample blue fruits. Tense. But the unravelling of tannic precision is impressive. Almost ball-bearing precision; emery of texture. Long and staccato-like as fruit and tannins interchange roles. Screw cap. 13.5% alc. **Rating** 96 **To** 2035 $135 NG
Single Vineyard Belford Hunter Valley Semillon 2016 Belford boasts the most fruit intensity of Tyrrell's 3 single-vineyard semillons. The strongest immediate impact of the triumvirate. Talc, barley sugar and chalky riffs lead, with pink grapefruit and lemon balm. A linger of tonic, lemon myrtle and orange verbena. Extremely long and slaking already, with the confluence of fruit and structural components still elemental. Pulls the saliva from the back of the mouth. A little more time needed to really gel. Superb wine in the making. Screw cap. 11.5% alc. **Rating** 95 **To** 2030 $40 NG
Vat 1 Hunter Semillon 2016 Barley water, honeysuckle, lemon drop, dried straw and a skein of evergreen freshness that quenches, drives and balances myriad accents and textures. This is a long sheath of nervous energy, readying itself for calm into the later stages of development. Screw cap. 11% alc. **Rating** 95 **To** 2031 $98 NG
Vat 1 Hunter Semillon 2009 Delicious! An exceptional '09. Lemon drops, barley water, apricot pith, quince and buttered toast, the defining aroma of aged semillon. Feigns oak, but there is none. The dichotomy of lightness juxtaposed against riveting flavour intensity, riveting. This has life left, while offering imminent pleasure. Screw cap. 11.5% alc. **Rating** 95 **To** 2024 $150 NG
Old Hillside Vineyard Hunter Valley Shiraz 2019 Ethereal and nudging mid weight at best. Sappy and beautifully textured, without a skerrick of overt fruit sweetness emerging from polished tannic rails, chamois of texture. The oak, adding further restraint, is impeccably appointed. A wine of a pinot-like grace and lightness of being. Floral. Cherry. Rosewater. Sweet earth. A classic Hunter luncheon Burgundy, as this style was once called. Rightly so. Gorgeous wine. Screw cap. 13% alc. **Rating** 95 **To** 2032 $60 NG
Vat 9 Winemaker's Selection Hunter Valley Shiraz 2019 A reversion to delicacy. An homage to a noble past of sappy, savoury Hunter Burgundy, as it was once known. With this, there has been an adoption of larger-format oak, less agitation, and with that, superior tannin management. The result, sappy, floral, detailed and dangerously drinkable. Violet, dark cherry, clove, licorice straps and a sachet of spice. Yet the texture is the totem. And it is sumptuous. Screw cap. 13% alc. **Rating** 95 **To** 2034 $120 NG

Johnno's Hunter Valley Shiraz 2019 A mid-weight luncheon wine, with the strong possibility that it will be a very long lunch! Violet, dark cherry, nori and sappy sassafras tannins, lithe and attenuated, drawing an arc of effortless tension from the nose to the long finish. A little reductive, but nothing an aggressive decant or patience can't sort. I adore this delicate and spicy style. Screw cap. 13.5% alc. **Rating** 94 **To** 2035 $135 NG

Special Release Hunter Valley Shiraz Pinot Noir 2019 The Special Release label is reserved for one-off wines of merit, here a 60/40% blend. It's a fragrant wine that is deceptively elegant, its spiced red and black infusion of berry fruits suggesting it is ready now. However that may be, 10 years in bottle will result in a special wine. Screw cap. 13% alc. **Rating** 94 **To** 2034 $35 JH

🍷🍷🍷🍷 **Single Vineyard HVD Hunter Semillon 2016** Rating 93 To 2030 $40 NG
Vat 47 Hunter Chardonnay 2019 Rating 93 To 2026 $90 NG
Vat 9 Winemaker's Selection Hunter Valley Shiraz 2014 Rating 93 To 2026 $150 NG
Vat 8 Hunter Valley Shiraz Cabernet Sauvignon 2019 Rating 93 To 2032 $90 NG
Single Vineyard Stevens Hunter Semillon 2016 Rating 92 To 2026 $40 NG
Vat 63 Chardonnay Semillon 2019 Rating 92 To 2027 $55 NG
Single Vineyard Stevens Hunter Shiraz 2019 Rating 92 To 2030 $50 NG
Estate Grown Chardonnay 2019 Rating 91 To 2025 $35 NG
Lunatiq Heathcote Shiraz 2019 Rating 91 To 2029 $40 NG
Hunter Valley Shiraz 2019 Rating 90 To 2025 $25 NG
Rufus Stone Heathcote Shiraz 2019 Rating 90 To 2029 $25 NG

Ubertas Wines   ★★★

790 Research Road, Light Pass, SA 5355 **Region** Barossa Valley
T (08) 8565 7820 **www**.ubertaswines.com.au **Open** Wed–Sun 12–5
Winemaker Wine Wise, Philip Liu **Est.** 2013 **Dozens** 3800 **Vyds** 13.8ha
Brothers Phil and Kevin Liu followed their father from Taiwan to mainland China, working for their father's car component factory. In 2006 they made a life-changing decision to migrate to Australia and saw an opportunity to start a wine export business to China. They named their business Rytor. It succeeded and over the following years they both obtained master's degrees – Phil in oenology from the University of Adelaide, Kevin in marketing from the University of South Australia. By '14 they had taken another major step: building and managing their own winery at Light Pass in the Barossa Valley. Exports to Malaysia, Japan, Taiwan, Hong Kong and China.

🍷🍷🍷🍷 **Single Vineyard Barossa Valley Shiraz 2018** Honest Barossa shiraz of medium purple/red. A core of dark berry and plum fruit is evenly backed by dark chocolate oak and finely structured tannins. Good length and balance. More definition, vibrancy and fruit definition would take it to the next level. Diam. 14.5% alc. **Rating** 90 **To** 2025 $28 TS

Ulithorne

85 Kays Road, Blewitt Springs, SA 5171 **Region** McLaren Vale
T 0406 336 282 **www**.ulithorne.com.au **Open** By appt
Winemaker Matthew Copping **Est.** 1971 **Dozens** 2500 **Vyds** 7.2ha
Ulithorne produces small quantities of red wines from selected parcels of grapes from its estate vineyard in McLaren Vale, planted in 1950 by Bob Whiting. The small-batch, high-quality wines are influenced by Ulithorne's associate Laurence Feraud, owner of Domaine du Pegau of Châteauneuf-du-Pape. Exports to the UK, Canada, Sweden, Malaysia, Hong Kong and China.

Ulupna Winery

159 Crawfords Road, Strathmerton, Vic 3641 **Region** Goulburn Valley
T (03) 9533 8831 **www**.ulupnawinery.com.au **Open** By appt
Winemaker Vio Buga, Viviana Ferrari **Est.** 1999 **Dozens** 35 000 **Vyds** 22ha
Ulupna started out as a retirement activity for Nick and Kathy Bogdan. The vineyard on the banks of the Murray River is planted to shiraz (50%), cabernet sauvignon (30%) and chardonnay (20%); the plantings allowing for expansion in the years ahead. The wines are made under the direction of Vio Buga, who also designed and planted the vineyard. Exports are primarily directed to China, followed by Hong Kong, South Korea and Singapore.

Royal Phoenix Single Vineyard Shiraz 2019 A fine follow-up to the 2018 making a strong, muscular impression. Dark plum, licorice, chocolate and baked earth aromas bring a sense of the land and the place from where it hails. Slips nicely into a rich, seamless palate, finishing long. Cork. 15% alc. **Rating** 93 **To** 2031 $55 JP

Umamu Estate

★★★★

PO Box 1269, Margaret River, WA 6285 **Region** Margaret River
T (08) 9757 5058 **www**.umamuestate.com
Winemaker Bruce Dukes (Contract) **Est.** 2005 **Dozens** 1000 **Vyds** 16.8ha
Chief executive Charmaine Saw explains, 'My life has been a journey towards Umamu. An upbringing in both eastern and western cultures, graduating in natural science, training as a chef combined with a passion for the arts and experience as a management consultant have all contributed to my building the business creatively yet professionally.' The palindrome 'Umamu', says Charmaine, is inspired by balance and contentment. In practical terms this means an organic approach to viticulture and a deep respect for the terroir. The plantings, dating back to 1978, include cabernet sauvignon, chardonnay, shiraz, semillon, sauvignon blanc, merlot and cabernet franc. Exports to Canada, Malaysia, Indonesia, the Philippines, Singapore and Hong Kong.

Margaret River Chardonnay 2019 Unfettered purity of chardonnay fruit is at the very core of this wine. Silky, slippery, elegant, this is not made in the usual, fashionable way of modern Margaret River chardonnays. It is creamy and very soft, the length of flavour the ultimate key to its quality. This style of chardonnay often gets shunted into the shade in favour of more worked and obviously oaked styles. Screw cap. 13% alc. **Rating** 95 **To** 2036 $60 EL

Underground Winemakers

1282 Nepean Highway, Mt Eliza, Vic 3931 **Region** Mornington Peninsula
T (03) 9775 4185 **www**.ugwine.com.au **Open** 7 days 10–5
Winemaker Peter Stebbing **Est.** 2004 **Dozens** 10 000 **Vyds** 12ha
Owned by Adrian Hennessy, Jonathon Stevens and Peter Stebbing. Each has made wine in Alsace, Burgundy, Northern Italy and Swan Hill and each has extensive experience in the vineyards and wineries of the Mornington Peninsula. Their first step, in 2004, was to lease a small winery at Mt Eliza that had closed years earlier, but still had a vineyard with some of the oldest plantings of pinot noir, pinot gris and chardonnay on the peninsula. Their portfolio is nothing if not eclectic: Pinot Gris, Pinot Noir and Chardonnay from the Mornington Peninsula, and Durif, Moscato, Cabernet Merlot and Shiraz from Northern and Central Victoria. The San Pietro wines are made according to the philosophy of traditional Italian winegrower San Pietro, who has vineyards in the hills south of Benalla and the Mornington Peninsula (more information at www.sanpietrowine.com).

UG Mornington Peninsula Pinot Noir 2017 The forward colour confirms there is no need to hang onto this savoury wine – it's ready now to offer a balance of ripe cherries, poached rhubarb and licorice with some fragrant forest-floor aromas. The tannins have some give, the acidity is still fresh and it slips down rather easily. Screw cap. 13% alc. **Rating** 92 **To** 2024 $40 JF

San Pietro Pinot Noir 2019 A perky little number. Prickly acidity, raspberry and cranberry accents and blood orange too, with flecks of woodsy spices. It's not big, it's not overly complex, but it hits the spot. Screw cap. 13% alc. **Rating** 91 To 2027 $30 JF

Uplands ★★★★

174 Richmond Road, Cambridge, Tas 7170 **Region** Southern Tasmania
T (03) 6248 5460 **Open** By appt
Winemaker Tasmanian Vintners **Est.** 1998 **Dozens** 80 **Vyds** 0.5ha
Michael and Debbie Ryan bought the historic Uplands House (1823) in 1998 and decided to plant the front paddock with chardonnay, joining the grapegrowing trend in the Coal River Valley of Southern Tasmania. The vineyard is planted with the 2 most suitable clones for the area, 8127 for sparkling and the Penfold clone for their lightly wooded Chardonnay. They have developed a partnership with another small vineyard in the valley to produce a Pinot Noir Chardonnay that will spend at least 4 years on lees prior to disgorgement.

♡♡♡♡♡ **Coal River Valley Tasmania Chardonnay 2019** Exciting and delicious Tasmanian chardonnay. A bright, vibrant and energetic style of purity and fruit integrity. The lemon citrus crunch and acid line of the cool Coal River Valley expand magnificently into crunchy white peach and fig through a palate of integrity, line and persistence. Screw cap. 12.8% alc. **Rating** 94 To 2029 $35 TS

♡♡♡♡♡ **Coal River Valley Tasmania Chardonnay 2018** Rating 91 To 2028 $40 TS
Tasmanian Pinot Noir Chardonnay 2011 Rating 90 $55 TS

Upper Reach ★★★★☆

77 Memorial Avenue, Baskerville, WA 6056 **Region** Swan Valley
T (08) 9296 0078 **www**.upperreach.com.au **Open** 7 days 11–5
Winemaker Derek Pearse **Est.** 1996 **Dozens** 4000 **Vyds** 8.45ha
This 10ha property on the banks of the upper reaches of the Swan River was purchased by Laura Rowe and Derek Pearse in 1996. The original 4ha vineyard was expanded and plantings now include chardonnay, shiraz, cabernet sauvignon, verdelho, semillon, merlot, petit verdot and muscat. 90% of grapes are estate-grown; all wine is vinified onsite. The RiverBrook Restaurant serves share plates and the cellar door received a string of *Gourmet Traveller WINE* awards between 2013 and 2018.

♡♡♡♡♡ **Swan Valley Verdelho 2020** Concentrated and intense, this has loads of flavour packed in around the significant acidity that is coiled on the mid palate. The phenolics create a spicy and textural framework, from which the flavours of nashi pear, Granny Smith apples and white pepper can hang. Impressive. Some verdelhos from the Valley are showing well in their older age and this has those hallmarks. Screw cap. 13% alc. **Rating** 94 To 2031 $26 EL

♡♡♡♡♡ **Reserve Swan Valley Shiraz 2018** Rating 93 To 2030 $50 EL

Uraidla ★★★★☆

30 Swamp Road, Uraidla, SA 5142 **Region** Adelaide Hills
www.uraidlawines.com.au
Winemaker Frank Virgara **Est.** 2016
The Virgara family has been growing wine grapes in the Piccadilly Valley and Balhannah districts of the Adelaide Hills for more than 30 and 20 years respectively. Third-generation Uraidla boy Frank Virgara continues the tradition, following in the footsteps of his father Girolamo and grandfather, local market gardeners, fruit and vegetable retailers and well-known owners and operators of the fruit mart in the nearby Stirling township. Hills-based winemaker Turon White has sourced fruit from the Virgara vineyards and has been engaged as winemaker for the new releases of Momo wines under the Uraidla banner. (TL)

ΨΨΨΨΨ **Momo Adelaide Hills Chardonnay 2020** Textbook modern Australian chardonnay. The oak offers gingery spice and faint charriness and lees character as toasted nuttiness. The rich stone fruits sit comfortably just at the surface, lingering all the way through the palate. Well done. Screw cap. 13.5% alc. **Rating** 95 To 2026 $35 TL ✪

ΨΨΨΨ♀ **Momo Adelaide Hills Pinot Meunier Rosé 2020 Rating** 93 To 2024 $27 TL ✪
Momo Blanc Adelaide Hills Sauvignon Blanc 2020 Rating 91 To 2024 $27 TL

Utopos   ★★★★★

PO Box 764, Tanunda, SA 5352 **Region** Barossa Valley
T 0409 351 166 **www**.utopos.com.au
Winemaker Kym Teusner **Est.** 2015 **Dozens** 1500 **Vyds** 20ha
The fates were kind when Neil Panuja, a friend of Kym Teusner's from 'the big smoke', said he had the wish (and the cash) to get into fine-wine production and asked that Kym keep an eye out for something special. Shortly thereafter a vineyard that Kym had coveted from his beginnings in the Barossa Valley came onto the market. The 20ha vineyard was duly acquired, Kym investing in a small share that he couldn't really afford but had to have. The vineyard is perched on Roenfeldt Road at one of the highest points of the boundary between Greenock and Marananga. The depleted stony soils consistently produce low yields of high-quality grapes that loudly proclaim their Barossan origin. The X-factor is the site-driven savoury balance that Kym says he always longs for. The name they have given the business is the root word of Utopia. Everything is just so right: great vineyard, great winemaker, great story, great packaging. Exports to China.

ΨΨΨΨΨ **Shiraz 2018** Uniting the personalities of Marananga and Greenock, this is a shiraz at once delightfully plush and polished and magnificently structured for the cellar. Waves of deep black fruits, black pastilles and licorice wash with high-cocoa dark chocolate oak. Lively acidity and fantastically defined tannins sweep through a very long finish. One bottle was cork scalped. Screw caps please. Cork. 14.5% alc. **Rating** 96 To 2036 $65 TS ✪
Cabernet Sauvignon 2018 Kym Teusner has a talent for achieving the difficult juxtaposition of brooding power and impact with brightness, definition and varietal integrity. Exemplified here in deep wells of blackcurrant and satsuma plum, fresh licorice straps and high-cocoa dark chocolate. The 10% cabernet is cleverly and discreetly deployed. Top floral notes of the bouquet are subdued in its youth but swoop in in full force on the palate. It concludes, bright, long and magnificently framed in chalk-fine tannins. A showstopper. Cork. 14.5% alc. **Rating** 95 To 2038 $65 TS
Mataro Shiraz Grenache 2019 MSG is of course GSM turned on its head. The black fruits and firm, mineral, savoury tannins of mataro are the game here, which could threaten to topple the balance in the hands of mere mortals, but here perfectly in place in the succulent and glossy style of Kym Teusner. A benchmark of this blend, perfectly set off by high-cocoa dark chocolate French oak and impressive acid line. Patience. Cork. 14.5% alc. **Rating** 94 To 2039 $65 TS

🍇 Utter Wines   ★★★★

2427 Maroondah Highway, Buxton, Vic 3711 **Region** Upper Goulburn
T 0411 550 519 **www**.riverhousewineandtruffles.com.au **Open** By appt
Winemaker Adrian Utter, Robert Utter **Est.** 2012 **Dozens** 500 **Vyds** 2ha
Agronomist and viticulturist Adrian Utter and his father, Robert, farm a family property at Buxton in the Acheron River Valley, in the Murrindindi area of the Goulburn Valley. Initial plantings of grape vines have expanded slowly to just under 2ha of high-density vines, with further gradual expansion planned. The Utters believe the high continentality of the

mountain valley, with cool nights and warm days, allows longer ripening, preserving the vibrancy of the fruit. Sustainability guides vineyard practices, promoting biodiversity and maintaining plant health. The complete process from planting to bottling is performed by Adrian and Robert. The farm also supports a productive truffiere (Buxton Black Truffles) and beef cattle production. (JP)

ŸŸŸŸŸ Upper Goulburn Syrah 2019 Deep purple hue. Anise, black cherry, blueberry, pepperberry, sage. Packs plenty of fruit on the palate. There's a touch of musky floral with smoky oak, too. Looking good early on, which is a great sign for the future. The Utters labelled this vintage as syrah, a nod to the apparent and intrinsic high spice, not to mention all-round elegance. Diam. 13.6% alc. **Rating** 94 **To** 2025 $37 JP

ŸŸŸŸŸ Upper Goulburn Pinot Noir 2018 Rating 92 **To** 2025 $37 JP
Upper Goulburn Riesling 2019 Rating 91 **To** 2029 $27 JP
Upper Goulburn Shiraz 2018 Rating 90 **To** 2030 $37 JP

 # Valentine

31 Phillip Road, Woori Yallock, Vic 3184 **Region** Yarra Valley
T 0487 755 745 **www.**valentinewines.com.au
Winemaker Dominic Valentine **Est.** 2010 **Dozens** 2200
Dominic Valentine completed a science degree at the University of Western Australia in 1997, but the chance to work at leading Margaret River wineries such as Leeuwin Estate and Xanadu set him on a vinous journey. He completed a master in oenology from Roseworthy College in 2004 and has since worked in South Africa, Bordeaux and Alsace. Vintages in Germany ignited his love of riesling, and cool-climate varieties generally from a decade of work in the Yarra Valley. He sources fruit for his label from many sites across Victoria. Exports to China and Japan. (JF)

ŸŸŸŸŸ Heathcote Grenache 2019 There's a lot to like about this richly flavoured but not OTT grenache. Really perfumed, one of the appeals of the variety, with raspberries, dark cherries, red licorice, herbs and warm earth. Thankfully there are no confectionary flavours in this rendition. It's savoury, fuller bodied, with neatly packed sandy tannins. Very drinkable now. Screw cap. 13.5% alc. **Rating** 93 **To** 2027 $35 JF
Yarra Valley Chardonnay 2019 Juicy and tangy, led by citrus flavours and lots of acidity. A linear style and a touch austere at the moment but will plump out in time. Screw cap. 12.5% alc. **Rating** 92 **To** 2029 $40 JF
Lone Star Creek Vineyard Upper Yarra Pinot Noir 2019 The 2 Yarra Valley pinot noirs are made identically, this from a cooler site. It feels cool, too, with red cherries, tangy and tart. Sweeter fruit on the medium-bodied palate, woodsy spices, slightly raspy tannins but a refreshing outcome and led by decent acidity. Screw cap. 13% alc. **Rating** 91 **To** 2028 $40 JF
Yarra Valley Riesling 2019 Light aromatics on the palate. Tight acid line, although there is texture. Florals, citrus and ginger to the fore. Tangy and bright; looks good now and for the short term. Screw cap. 12.5% alc. **Rating** 90 **To** 2026 $35 JF

Valhalla Wines

163 All Saints Road, Wahgunyah, Vic 3687 **Region** Rutherglen
T (02) 6033 1438 **www.**valhallawines.com.au **Open** 7 days 10–4
Winemaker Anton Therkildsen **Est.** 2001 **Dozens** 1400 **Vyds** 2.5ha
Anton Therkildsen and wife Antoinette Del Popolo planted their vineyard in 2002 (shiraz and durif), and purchase viognier, marsanne, grenache and mourvèdre from local growers, reflecting their interest in the wines of the Rhône Valley. Anton uses traditional winemaking methods, making and cellaring the wines in their straw-bale winery. Sustainable viticulture practices are used, with minimal use of sprays and annual planting of cover crops between the rows. Rainwater harvesting, recycled packaging, a worm farm and the composting of grape skins and stalks complete the picture.

ITITT Rutherglen Riesling 2017 Mouth-wateringly good! Boasts one of the prettiest floral bouquets going around – white flowers, orange blossom – and fine-edged citrus notes of grapefruit, lime leaf. Plenty of verve and drive powering this youngster. Lime pith and lemon juice with developing spice makes it one to watch as it develops. Screw cap. 12.2% alc. **Rating** 95 **To** 2028 $25 JP ✪
Rutherglen Marsanne 2018 This white Rhône variety arrived in Rutherglen some time ago and seems to enjoy the warm climate, contributing a ripe, clean, well-focused citrussy edge to this wine. Jasmine, beeswax, lemon-curd bouquet. The grape's gentle acidity guides the palate with an almost Chablis-like nougat/apple/lemon drive. Bravo. Screw cap. 13.2% alc. **Rating** 95 **To** 2027 $28 JP ✪

ITITQ The Ranga 2018 Rating 92 **To** 2026 $25 JP ✪

Vanguardist Wines ★★★★☆

203 Main North Road, Clare, SA 5453 **Region** South Australia
T 0487 193 053 **www**.vanguardistwines.com
Winemaker Michael John Corbett **Est.** 2014 **Dozens** 1500 **Vyds** 7.5ha
Winemaker Michael John Corbett draws on established sources across SA to craft a delicious swag of Mediterranean-inspired wines of textural intrigue. A card of neutral wood, ambient ferments and plenty of whole bunch is dealt with a deft hand. The results, often compelling. Corbett's opus is grenache, specifically Blewitt Springs grenache, hewn of the region's low-yielding elevated old vineyards. His ripeness barometer challenges notions of what is optimal, flirting with marginal levels of alcohol on the lower side. Quantities are small, selling out fast. (NG)

ITITT V Rende Silver Sands Blewitt Springs McLaren Vale Grenache 2018 Skeletally defined as much by pinprick tannins – spindle, wiry brush and bone – as much as the fruit. A glimpse of Blewitt Springs' violet and kirsch, but more about sandalwood, bergamot, clove, cardamom and anise. A peacock-tail spread across the palate, with moreish tannins and juicy acidity a detailed exclamation of true quality. Cork. 13.6% alc. **Rating** 95 **To** 2027 $160 NG

ITITQ La Petite Vanguard McLaren Vale Grenache 2020 Rating 92 **To** 2024 $30 NG
La Petite Vanguard McLaren Vale Grenache Mourvèdre 2020 Rating 92 **To** 2024 $30 NG

Varney Wines ★★★★★

62 Victor Harbor Road, Old Noarlunga, SA 5168 **Region** McLaren Vale
T 0450 414 570 **www**.varneywines.com.au **Open** Thurs–Mon 11–5
Winemaker Alan Varney **Est.** 2017 **Dozens** 1050
Alan Varney's Australian career (based on an oenology degree from The University of Melbourne) grew out of a vintage stint with d'Arenberg into an 11-year employment, much of it as senior winemaker. He says that this period meant he came to be friends with many of the best local growers in McLaren Vale, the Adelaide Hills and Langhorne Creek. The d'Arenberg vintage typically included making 9 varieties, some mainstream, some alternative. He is a brilliant winemaker, saying, 'I am not afraid to step out of the box and go with my intuition … I only use old seasoned oak with no fining or filtration.' His ability to draw the varietal heart of each wine he makes with alcohol levels between 12% and 14% is extraordinary. He has built an environmentally sensitive winery alongside wife Kathrin's restaurant, Victor's Place, overlooking the rolling hills of the Onkaparinga Gorge. The unspoken question is whether he will increase the small amounts of each wine he makes; my (James') guess is not by much. Varney Wines were the *Wine Companion 2021* Best New Winery.

ITITT McLaren Vale GSM 2018 An exceptional Rhône blend. For the record, I loathe the GSM moniker, seeking wines that sublimate branding and the personality of each component with a juicy mouthful of spicy, Mediterranean herb-doused blue/black-fruit aspersions. This is THAT wine! The tannins, noble, savoury and thirst-slaking. Possibly the finest domestic 'GSM' yet tasted. A mini Gigondas. Screw cap. 14.6% alc. **Rating** 96 **To** 2024 $32 NG ✪

Adelaide Hills Chardonnay 2019 A very fine wine, relying as much on phenolic texture as reductive tension and bright acidity. A more complete, textural package as a result. Toasted hazelnut, oatmeal, white peach and tatami. Long, sprightly and effortless. Screw cap. 12.8% alc. **Rating** 95 **To** 2026 $32 NG **⬦**

Entrada McLaren Vale Grenache Mourvèdre Touriga 2019 A 60/30/10% blend, the grenache ex 60yo Blewitt Springs bush vines, all components picked early for vibrancy. Partial whole-bunch fermentation, briefly matured in used oak. Holding its hue well, and delivering a very complex yet juicy palate, jumping with spice and fine, savoury tannins. Screw cap. 13.1% alc. **Rating** 95 **To** 2029 $25 JH **⬦**

Adelaide Hills Cabernet Sauvignon 2018 An impressive, fully flared cabernet. All the bells and whistles. The result, a capacious wine of cassis, hedgerow, graphite, vanilla-pod oak and a firm seam of well-hewn tannin, verdant but just right. This will age very well. The oak as ambitious as the finish is long. It will settle into a nice groove. Screw cap. 14.4% alc. **Rating** 95 **To** 2024 $58 NG

McLaren Vale Grenache 2020 A fine grenache. Rich and sumptuous, but not short of freshness, deftness of touch, nor lightness of foot. Molten raspberry, cranberry and rosehip. Vibrant natural acidity, palpable. Old vines: vinous and pushing impressive length. Blewitt Springs sandiness melded to whole-bunch spice mix and some bitter-chocolate barrique accents. Of the zeitgeist, pushing richer flavour as much as pinosity. Impressive! Screw cap. 14.2% alc. **Rating** 94 **To** 2025 $35 NG

🍷🍷🍷🍷🍷 **McLaren Vale Adelaide Hills Shiraz 2018** **Rating** 90 **To** 2026 $42 NG

Vasse Felix   ★★★★★

Cnr Tom Cullity Drive/Caves Road, Cowaramup, WA 6284 **Region** Margaret River
T (08) 9756 5000 **www**.vassefelix.com.au **Open** 7 days 10–5
Winemaker Virginia Willcock **Est.** 1967 **Dozens** 150 000 **Vyds** 330ha
Vasse Felix is Margaret River's founding wine estate, established in 1967 by regional pioneer Dr Tom Cullity. Owned and operated by the Holmes à Court family since 1987, Paul Holmes à Court has brought the focus to Margaret River's key varieties of cabernet sauvignon and chardonnay. Chief Winemaker Virginia Willcock has energised the winemaking and viticultural team with her no-nonsense approach and fierce commitment to quality. Vasse Felix has 4 scrupulously managed vineyards throughout Margaret River that contribute all but a small part of the annual production. Wines include icons Tom Cullity (cabernet blend) and Heytesbury Chardonnay as well as Cabernet Sauvignon, Chardonnay, Sauvignon Blanc Semillon and Shiraz; Filius Chardonnay and Filius Cabernet Sauvignon; Classic Dry White and Classic Dry Red, plus limited quantities of Cane Cut Semillon and Blanc de Blancs. Exports to all major markets.

🍷🍷🍷🍷🍷 **Heytesbury Margaret River Chardonnay 2019** Everyone has their favourites. The Heytesbury chardonnay style is typically the wine that my heart reaches for. I love it. The 2019 iteration is minerally; laden with graphite and crushed rocks, brine, white currant, white peach and curry leaf. Heavily worked and wild, with an attractive rawness to it. Where 2018 was about fruit power, 2019 is about complex winemaking input. This still has my heart, but for different reasons to its predecessor. Screw cap. 13% alc. **Rating** 97 **To** 2036 $92 EL **⬦**

Tom Cullity Margaret River Cabernet Sauvignon Malbec 2017 This wine is undoubtedly one reason why Margaret River has such a powerful reputation for cabernet: concentration without weight, savoury statuesque tannins and layers upon layers of exotic spice, laid on a bed of ripe fruit. Coursing through the very heart of it is a steady beat of cool-vintage saline acid, pulling it over the coals of the tongue, through to the very long finish. Remarkable. Screw cap. 14.2% alc. **Rating** 97 **To** 2051 $180 EL ❤

🍷🍷🍷🍷🍷 **Margaret River Cabernet Sauvignon 2018** Powerfully ripe and dense, with epic length of flavour. This is a structural and concentrated cabernet capable of decades of graceful evolution in the cellar. Wild raspberry, salted licorice, aniseed, pomegranate, ferrous and kelp. Saline acid. It comes in at under $50, and long may that continue, for it is one of the great-value premium wines of the region. Agglomerate. 14.5% alc. **Rating** 96 **To** 2041 $47 EL ❂

Blanc X 2020 100% sauvignon blanc, 8 months in puncheon. Skin-contact white, a cloudy lemon/mandarin colour in the glass. This is enticingly structured – but make no mistake – it is tannic. And it's great. Chewy, shapely and supple – there's a fascinating, lean muscularity about it. A tangy citrus-rind vibe coupled with anise, five-spice and white pepper all jostle for space here. Saline and distinctly Mediterranean; its polished rusticity is at home on a deckchair on the bow of a wooden yacht, the coastal wind rustling its hair. Screw cap. 12.5% alc. **Rating** 95 **To** 2030 $39 EL

Margaret River Sauvignon Blanc 2019 Creamy, rounded and supremely textural, this moves away from the spiny sauvignon blanc we are accustomed to and moves into a New World European space. Heady Margaret River florals and leafy greens (coriander, broad beans and sugar snap peas) linger in the background, making this a brilliant excuse for lunch. From the land and into the glass – what a beauty. Screw cap. 13% alc. **Rating** 95 **To** 2030 $28 EL ❂

Margaret River Chardonnay 2019 Each year this wine presents an amalgam of creamy, chewy phenolics, ripe yet nervy fruit and exotic spice. The balance of these things depends on the year. In 2019, it's creamy and saline with white peach and fennel flower. Gorgeous stuff. Screw cap. 13% alc. **Rating** 95 **To** 2030 $40 EL

Margaret River Shiraz 2019 This is all about sunshine and shade; yin and yang. The fruit is both bright and red (vibrant and juicy), but it has shades of midnight depth and broodiness, too. It is fragrant, floral, spicy, satisfying and modern. The oak has been sensitively managed and as a result, is already integrated. Super-smart stuff. Agglomerate. 14% alc. **Rating** 94 **To** 2031 $37 EL

Filius Margaret River Cabernet Sauvignon 2018 This is the youngest brother in the family of cabernets at Vasse and has built a loyal following for its supple deliciousness and accessibility (both in price and quality). So: wild raspberry, red licorice, pomegranate, kelp, iodine, crushed pepper, spicy oak and the all important saline acid. The vintage has contributed a fruit power that gives the wine great length of flavour. Screw cap. 14.5% alc. **Rating** 94 **To** 2031 $29 EL ❂

🍷🍷🍷🍷   **Margaret River Classic Dry White 2020** Rating 93 To 2022 $19 EL ❂
Margaret River Classic Dry Red 2019 Rating 93 To 2027 $19 EL ❂
Filius Margaret River Chardonnay 2019 Rating 92 To 2027 $29 EL
Margaret River Classic Dry Rosé 2020 Rating 91 To 2022 $19 EL ❂

Vella Wines   ★★★★

PO Box 39, Balhannah, SA 5242 **Region** Adelaide Hills
T 0499 998 484 **www.**vellawines.com.au
Winemaker Mark Vella **Est.** 2013 **Dozens** 750
Mark Vella was blooded at Bloodwood Estate in 1995 (an appalling but inevitable pun). Over the following 22 years Mark has plied his trade as viticulturist in Orange, the Hunter Valley and now (and permanently) the Adelaide Hills. He manages to avoid conflicts of interest in running his vineyard management company, Vitiworks, and pinpointing outstanding parcels of fruit for the Vella brand. A broader conflict (which is in fact no conflict at all) comes from his 12 years of vineyard management, supplying contract-grown fruit for more than 40 of the leading wine producers in SA. He uses Andre Bondar to make his Chardonnay, Franco D'Anna his Pinot Noir, and Daryl Catlin his Pinot Blanc blend.

🍷🍷🍷🍷   **Gambler Adelaide Hills Gamay 2019** One of the earliest plantings of Gamay in the region. It looks like the variety will show distinct vintage variations. Here there's a little reductive funk to start, not off-putting but worth noting, as it adds interest to an otherwise red-cherry/berry focused style, a little stem character in play (though only 10% whole bunch employed). Spice on the palate adds a finishing lift. Definitely one to keep an eye on over the coming years. Screw cap. 13% alc. **Rating** 92 **To** 2025 $40 TL

Harvest Widow Chardonnay 2019 The 2019 vintage has influenced this iteration with a tad more fruit ripeness than cooler-vintage sibling. The wine is a touch fuller on the palate with nectarine/peach flavours more redolent, and palate tension a little softer. Screw cap. 13% alc. **Rating** 90 **To** 2024 $32 TL

 Gambler Adelaide Hills Gamay 2020 Rating 89 **To** 2024 $40 TL

Velo Wines ★★★★

755 West Tamar Highway, Legana, Tas 7277 **Region** Northern Tasmania
T (03) 6330 3677 **www.velowines.com.au Open** 7 days 10–5
Winemaker Michael Wilson, Winemaking Tasmania **Est.** 1966 **Dozens** 3000 **Vyds** 1.4ha
The 0.9ha of cabernet sauvignon (apparently Tasmania's oldest) and 0.5ha of pinot noir of Tamar Valley's Legana Vineyard were planted in 1966 by Graham Wiltshire, one of the 3 great pioneers of the Tasmanian wine industry. Viticulturalist (and Olympic cyclist) Michael Wilson and his wife Mary Wilson purchased the Legana Vineyard in 2011, painstakingly rehabilitating the almost 50yo vines. Shiraz, sauvignon blanc, riesling, pinot gris and chardonnay have since been planted. The estate changed hands again in 2017 and It's now under the ownership of trio Ken Hudson, Peter Bond and David Vaution. (TS)

 Legana Estate Tasmania Cabernet Sauvignon 2019 Crunchy and characterful, energised by the electric acidity of Tasmania and sustained by a firm, medium-grained tannin profile, this is a wine to bury deep in the cellar and forget about. Boasting a vibrant, medium purple hue and crunchy, exact red/blackcurrant fruit, it holds a very long and enduring finish. Screw cap. 13.5% alc. **Rating** 93 **To** 2049 $32 TS

Legana Estate Tasmania Rosé 2020 Just the thing to serve when rosé is too light and pinot noir is too heavy. A characterful pinot noir rosé of medium crimson hue. Flamboyant strawberry and red cherry flesh is filled with layers of spice, pink pepper and rosehip lift, toned by a spine of Tassie acidity. It holds the flesh, drive, confidence and persistence to support a fine tannin frame. Screw cap. 12.5% alc. **Rating** 91 **To** 2021 $30 TS

Legana Estate Old Vine Tasmania Pinot Noir 2018 The biscuity, cashew nut complexity and confident tannin structure of French oak builds an enduring framework and savoury mood around old-vine Tamar River pinot noir. Spicy, dark berry/cherry fruits and black pepper unite with lively acid drive on a long finish. Give it plenty of time for oak to soften and integrate. Screw cap. 13.5% alc. **Rating** 91 **To** 2033 $40 TS

Legana Estate Tasmania Pinot Noir 2019 Pale purple/crimson in hue, this is a refreshingly light-bodied pinot with versatile food pairing dexterity. Crucially, it lacks nothing in definition, persistence or integrity. Confidently carrying blackberry, black cherry and black pepper through a long finish, it rides on equal rails of crunchy, fine tannins and bright acidity. Screw cap. 13.5% alc. **Rating** 90 **To** 2024 $32 TS

Vickery Wines ★★★★☆

7 Belvidere Road, Nuriootpa, SA 5355 **Region** Clare Valley
T (08) 8362 8622 **www.vickerywines.com.au**
Winemaker John Vickery, Keeda Zilm **Est.** 2014 **Dozens** 10 000 **Vyds** 18ha
It must have been a strange feeling for John Vickery to begin at the beginning again, 60 years after his first vintage in 1951. His interest in, love of and exceptional skills with riesling began with Leo Buring in '55 at Chateau Leonay. Over the intervening years he became the uncrowned but absolute monarch of riesling makers in Australia until, in his semi-retirement, he passed the mantle on to Jeffrey Grosset. Along the way he had (unsurprisingly) won the Wolf Blass Riesling Award at the Canberra International Riesling Challenge 2007 and had been judged by his peers as Australia's Greatest Living Winemaker in a survey conducted

by *The Age*'s Epicure in '03. His new venture has been undertaken in conjunction with Phil Lehmann, with 12ha of Clare and Eden valley riesling involved and wine marketer Jonathon Hesketh moving largely invisibly in the background. The Da Vinci–code letters and numerals are easy when it comes to EVR (Eden Valley Riesling) and WVR (Watervale Riesling), but thereafter the code strikes. The numerics are the dates of harvest, thus '103' is 10 March, '172' is 17 February. The initials that follow are even more delphic, standing for the name of the vineyard or those of the multiple owners. Exports to the UK, EU and Asia.

ŸŸŸŸŸ **The Reserve Zander Kosi Block Eden Valley Riesling 2018** It's really, really hard to put this wine down. Expect to be wooed by the fragrance as much as the palate. A perfect blend of freshness and pulsing acidity, with some complexity of age starting to unfurl: preserved lemons with ginger spice, candied lime jellies, buttered toast and lime marmalade. But not too much. It has some way to go. Screw cap. 12% alc. **Rating** 96 **To** 2033 $32 JF ❂
Eden Valley Riesling 2020 Immediately enticing, with a bouquet of lavender, lime blossom and wafts of ginger cream and white pepper. It feels almost luscious and juicy as it fills the palate, then the fine line of acidity brings everything together neatly, finishing long. Screw cap. 12% alc. **Rating** 95 **To** 2030 $23 JF ❂
The Reserve Castine Hay Shed Block Watervale Riesling 2018 Already revealing toasty characters of baked ricotta and lime marmalade, as if kissed by the sun. They're adding an extra depth to the wine now, but perhaps without the acid drive to shift it into long-term drinking. That's OK. Make the most of it now. Screw cap. 12.5% alc. **Rating** 95 **To** 2028 $32 JF ❂

ŸŸŸŸŸ **Watervale Riesling 2020 Rating** 93 **To** 2026 $23 JF ❂

Victory Point Wines ★★★★★

92 Holben Road, Cowaramup, WA 6284 **Region** Margaret River
T 0417 954 655 **www**.victorypointwines.com **Open** Wed–Sun 11–4
Winemaker Mark Messenger (Contract) **Est.** 1997 **Dozens** 2500 **Vyds** 13.7ha
Judith and Gary Berson have set their sights high. They established their vineyard without irrigation, emulating those of the Margaret River pioneers (including Moss Wood). The fully mature plantings comprise 4.2ha of chardonnay and 0.4ha of pinot noir; the remainder Bordeaux varieties with cabernet sauvignon (6.2ha), cabernet franc (0.5ha), malbec (1.7ha) and petit verdot (0.7ha). The cellar door overlooks the 20+yo vineyard.

ŸŸŸŸŸ **Margaret River Pinot Noir 2019** This is beautiful. Layered and spicy, with folds of delicate red berry flavours, marbled with exotic spice like pink peppercorn, cardamom and succulent, ripe acidity. There is a lot of pleasure here, all of which can be experienced at any time over the long, lingering finish. The cool year has helped craft a wine of finesse and balance, making this one of the smartest pinots in the state. Screw cap. 13.5% alc. **Rating** 96 **To** 2036 $55 EL ❂
Margaret River Cabernet Sauvignon 2018 Rich, ripe and with a meaty undertow, this cabernet makes a serious statement on both the nose and palate. Powerful fruit and dense weight shows a wine capable of immense pleasure in the short term, but with all the generous stuffing that will ensure it a long and graceful future in the cellar, too. This has grunt and Euro structuring, aniseed and clove through the long finish. Screw cap. 14% alc. **Rating** 96 **To** 2041 $45 EL ❂
The Mallee Root Margaret River Cabernet Sauvignon Malbec Petit Verdot 2018 Some wines demand that you smell them over and over … this is one. Elegant, savoury and aromatic, it's all about salted cassis, pomegranate, whiffs of pink peppercorn and loads of exotic spice. The palate is shaped by curvy tannins. Demanding though it may be, you get more than you pay for. Impressive. Screw cap. 14% alc. **Rating** 95 **To** 2035 $29 EL ❂

ŸŸŸŸŸ **Margaret River Cabernet Franc 2019 Rating** 92 **To** 2031 $35 EL

View Road Wines

Peacocks Road, Lenswood, SA 5240 **Region** Adelaide Hills
T 0402 180 383 **www.**viewroadwines.com.au
Winemaker Josh Tuckfield **Est.** 2011 **Dozens** 3000
View Road Wines sources prosecco, arneis, chardonnay, sangiovese, merlot, sagrantino and
syrah from Adelaide Hills vineyards; shiraz, aglianico and sagrantino from McLaren Vale
vineyards; and nero d'Avola and fiano from the Riverland. All of the wines are wild-yeast
fermented and matured in used oak.

Vigena Wines

★★★★☆

210 Main Road, Willunga, SA 5172 **Region** McLaren Vale
T 0433 966 011 **www.**vigenawine.com **Open** By appt
Winemaker Ben Heide **Est.** 2010 **Dozens** 20000 **Vyds** 15.8ha
The principal business of Vigena Wines is exporting to Singapore, Hong Kong and China.
In recent years the vineyard has been revitalised, with one significant change: chardonnay has
been grafted to shiraz, giving the business a 100% red wine focus. Exports to Singapore, Hong
Kong and China.

🍷🍷🍷🍷🍷 **McLaren Vale Cabernet Sauvignon 2019** A wine built to impress.
Full bodied and laden with the bells and whistles of assiduous, fully invested
winemaking. Blackcurrant and oak-derived cedar scents dominate the nose. Classy
oak, this. A work-out in the glass reveals tapenade, sage, thyme and a sachet of
herb. The oak sits atop the fruit, still unresolved. Yet the wine's sheer extract, purity
of fruit, tenacious length and finely tuned, graphite tannins leave no doubt that all
parts will synchronise in time. Cork. 14.5% alc. **Rating** 94 **To** 2034 $65 NG

🍷🍷🍷🍷🍷 **McLaren Vale Shiraz 2019 Rating** 93 **To** 2028 $79 NG
McLaren Vale Cabernet Sauvignon Shiraz 2019 Rating 92 **To** 2034 $55 NG

Vigna Bottin

★★★★

192 Main Road, Willunga SA 5172 **Region** McLaren Vale
T 0414 562 956 **www.**vignabottin.com.au **Open** Fri 11–4, Sat–Sun 11–5
Winemaker Paolo Bottin **Est.** 2006 **Dozens** 1500 **Vyds** 15.22ha
The Bottin family migrated to Australia in 1954 from Treviso in northern Italy, where they
were grapegrowers. The family began growing grapes in McLaren Vale in '70, focusing on
mainstream varieties for sale to wineries in the region. When son Paolo and wife Maria made
a trip back to Italy in '98, they were inspired to do more, and, says Paolo, 'My love for barbera
and sangiovese was sealed during a vintage in Pavia. I came straight home to plant both
varieties in our family plot. My father was finally happy!' They now trade under the catchy
phrase 'Italian Vines, Australian Wines'.

🍷🍷🍷🍷🍷 **Mclaren Vale Fiano 2019** Great promise. There may be better fiano out there,
but this is top tier. A superior wine. Winning because of the optimal ripeness and
additional textural intrigue, binding a sea-spray freshness with a savoury chewiness.
Aromas of apricot pith, fennel, samphire, pistachio and marzipan. A long driver
and an intense player. Delicious wine! Screw cap. 12.9% alc. **Rating** 94 **To** 2024
$27 NG❂
McLaren Vale Barbera 2019 Some used French oak and bunches (15%) guide
this down a savoury path. Impeccably done. Bing cherry, tar and violet. The finish
is calm – soothing, even. Little heat. Impeccable balance. Screw cap. 14.7% alc.
Rating 93 **To** 2022 $47 NG
McLaren Vale Nero d'Avola 2019 A delicious wine, full bodied, yet with
pulpy fruity energy and dusty tannic swagger. Nothing excessive. Poised and ready
to give pleasure. Aromas of sweet black cherry, root spice, pepper and orange
zest reverberate across a juicy palate. A core of molten sweetness, quintessentially
McLaren Vale, finishes with some heat. Easily negotiated with a chill. Screw cap.
14.4% alc. **Rating** 93 **To** 2023 $40 NG

McLaren Vale Vermentino 2020 The wines at Vigna Bottin are on an inexorable quality ride upwards. This is arguably the finest expression of vermentino in the country. I can only wish for more. Salty and mineral. Pumice-like texture. It could be riper, even more layered and intense, in my view. But a very solid wine, all the same. Lemon pith, pink grapefruit and quince teem long. Screw cap. 12.7% alc. **Rating** 92 **To** 2022 $27 NG

Compare's McLaren Vale Shiraz 2017 Wild fermented, aged in older French oak for 9 months and blended with a dollop (10%) of nero d'Avola. The result is full bodied, umami savoury and rewarding. Espresso oak, boysenberry, anise and clove. The mid palate, porcini, salumi and beef bouillon. The finish, far from gushing and sweet. Instead, moreish and easygoing. Screw cap. 14.5% alc. **Rating** 91 **To** 2024 $27 NG

McLaren Vale Sangiovese 2018 This sort of heat does not suit sangiovese as it may more firmly Mediterranean varieties. The tannins are splendid all the same: all coffee grind and bitter chocolate; expansive, spindly, frisky and firm. They assuage the phalanx of dark-fruit flavours and heat. Almost enough, but perhaps not quite. Loads of promise. Drink with meat. Screw cap. 14.7% alc. **Rating** 91 **To** 2024 $32 NG

♟♟♟♟ **McLaren Vale Sangiovese Rosato 2020 Rating** 88 **To** 2021 $27 NG

Vignerons Schmölzer & Brown ★★★★☆

39 Thorley Road, Stanley, Vic 3747 **Region** Beechworth
T 0411 053 487 **www.**vsandb.com.au
Winemaker Tessa Brown, Jeremy Scholzer **Est.** 2014 **Dozens** 1800 **Vyds** 2ha
Winemaker/viticulturist Tessa Brown graduated from CSU with a degree in viticulture in the late 1990s and undertook postgraduate winemaking studies at the University of Adelaide in the mid-2000s. Her self-description of being 'reasonably peripatetic' covers her winemaking in Orange in '99 and also in Canberra, SA, Strathbogie Ranges, Rioja and Central Otago before joining Kooyong and Port Phillip Estate in '08. In '09 Mark Walpole showed Tessa and architect partner Jeremy Schmölzer a property that he described as 'the jewel in the crown of Beechworth'. When it came onto the market unexpectedly in '12, they were in a position to jump. The property (named Thorley) was 20ha and cleared; they have planted chardonnay, shiraz, riesling and nebbiolo. By sheer chance, just across the road from Thorley was a tiny vineyard, a bit over 0.4ha, with dry-grown pinot and chardonnay around 20 years old. When they realised it was not being managed for production, they struck up a working relationship with the owners, getting the vineyard into shape and making their first (very good) Brunnen wines in '14. The Obstgarten wines come from a small, high-altitude riesling vineyard in the King Valley. Exports to the UK and Hong Kong.

♟♟♟♟♟ **Obstgarten K King Valley Riesling 2019** A wine of clarity and purity that also comes with 31g/L RS, something that sits so well among the lime peel, lemon sherbet, green apple and layered spice as to go all but unnoticed. Juicy acidity works the mouth, providing line and length. Helps put King Valley's underrated riesling grape on the map. Screw cap. 10.5% alc. **Rating** 95 **To** 2026 $39 JP

Thorley Beechworth Chardonnay 2019 Just biding its time. It knows how good it is. A super-confident chardonnay from a region that shines with the grape variety. Still unfolding. The bouquet is working on a big reveal with white flowers, nectarine, ruby grapefruit, citrus zest and wild herbs in train. Love the rapier-like acidity, the conductor of this fine orchestra of fruit. Already has it together. The road will be long with this one. Screw cap. 12.5% alc. **Rating** 95 **To** 2028 $42 JP

Brunnen Beechworth Chardonnay 2019 A striking Beechworth chardonnay already in balance, with fruit concentration playing a starring role. Not bad for a youngster. A picture of cool restraint, opening with grapefruit, lime, lemon rind and pear. Tight, almost lean on the palate, but a depth of fruit is developing. White peach, apple, honeysuckle and chalky, nutty oak. No questioning the role of the vineyard's quartz-laden site in the lingering sherbet, mineral-tang acidity. Screw cap. 12.5% alc. **Rating** 95 **To** 2029 $46 JP ♥

Thorley Beechworth Shiraz 2019 A beauty in repose that was tasted before release but had all the hallmarks of an assured, elegant future. Dark-plum fruit, anise, pepper, dusty oak spice. Palate is lithe with fine tannins and a composed core of berry, peppery flavour. A wine that will reward patience. Screw cap. 13% alc. **Rating** 94 **To** 2032 $42 JP

🍷🍷🍷🍷🍷 Selection King Valley Riesling 2019 **Rating** 93 **To** 2026 $45 JP
Brunnen Beechworth Pinot Noir 2019 **Rating** 90 **To** 2028 $46 JP
Beechworth Nebbiolo 2019 **Rating** 90 **To** 2026 $42 JP

Vinaceous Wines

49 Bennett Street, East Perth, WA 6004 (postal) **Region** Various
T (08) 9221 4666 **www.**vinaceous.com.au
Winemaker Gavin Berry, Michael Kerrigan **Est.** 2007 **Dozens** 8000
This somewhat quirky venture was the baby of wine marketer Nick Stacy, Michael Kerrigan (winemaker/partner Hay Shed Hill) and Gavin Berry (winemaker/partner West Cape Howe). Nick Stacy separated from the business in August 2020 (John Waldron, managing partner of Risky Business Wines, has since stepped in), taking the Reverend V and Clandestine Vineyards brands with him. Fruit is now all sourced from Margaret River and Great Southern. The wines are of seriously good quality and equally good value. Exports to the UK, the US, Canada, South America, Denmark, Finland, Indonesia, the Philippines, Thailand, Singapore and Hong Kong.

Vindana Wines

PO Box 705, Lyndoch, SA 5351 **Region** Barossa Valley
T 0437 175 437 **www.**vindanawines.com.au
Winemaker Scott Higginson **Est.** 1968 **Dozens** 350 **Vyds** 1ha
Scott Higginson is a 7th-generation vigneron, whose family history starts in 1846 on the banks of Jacobs Creek and continues there for 111 years until an ill-fated decision to sell and move to the Riverland where a series of Peter Lehmann–like moves to protect growers from collapses in the wine-grape market turned sour. Scott has returned to the Barossa Valley, completing the wine marketing degree at Roseworthy Agricultural College and adding extensive work with medium to large (Foster's group) wineries. In 2013 he purchased a housing block at Lyndoch with enough room for 1ha of vines. He also purchases small parcels of premium fruit, making wine on a minimum-intervention basis. With a couple of 8th-generation feet on the ground, some very good wines have materialised overnight. Exports to China.

Vinden Wines ★★★★★

138 Gillards Road, Pokolbin, NSW 2320 **Region** Hunter Valley
T 0488 777 493 **www.**vindenwines.com.au **Open** 7 days 10–5
Winemaker Angus Vinden **Est.** 1998 **Dozens** 6000 **Vyds** 22ha
Angus Vinden may be young in the context of regional winemakers, but he lacks neither moxie nor experience. A 2nd-generation farmer with 22ha under vine, Angus' deft touch is due as much to his regional nous as to the mentorship of Glen Howard and the influence of his backyard sites. A traditional suite of semillon and shiraz galvanises the crowd at the Vinden cellar door, but for those seeking intrigue there are exciting tremors beyond. With the use of amphorae, long macerations and whole-bunch fermentations across varieties that augur well for the future, the atmosphere at Vinden is one of febrile excitement, strung across a bow of great possibility and high expectations. The tempranillos are possibly the finest in the country. Full and plump, but savoury and marked by a detailed tannic mettle and Hunter earthiness. The chenin, electrifying. Stay tuned! Exports to the UK, the US and Singapore. (NG)

🍷🍷🍷🍷🍷 Single Vineyard Reserve Hunter Valley Semillon 2015 This is lightweight, tightly furled and as tensile as much as it is sandy and saline across the whiplash of a finish. Despite what the back label says, I'd hedge my bets on close to another decade of age-worthiness. Scents of Meyer lemon, citrus balm, lemongrass and tonic. Dry. Subdued for its age. A noble austerity about it, boding well. Screw cap. 11% alc. **Rating** 95 **To** 2029 $60 NG

Basket Press Hunter Valley Shiraz 2018 An elegant, high-quality shiraz, with balance and length its cornerstones. Hunter Valley soil flows in its veins, with a savoury/earthy undercarriage to the blackberry fruits. Screw cap. 13.9% alc. **Rating** 95 **To** 2033 $40 JH

Somerset Vineyard Fountainhead Hunter Valley Shiraz 2019 A fine shiraz, stamped firmly with the regional decal of sweet earth and polished leather, as much as a subdued tannic refinement. An aura of coolness to this. Clearly a fine site. Sweet cherry pie, mace, violet, pastille and anise, underlain by a ripple of mineral brightness and impeccably nestled French oak (25% new). The finish, long and refined. A delicious drink. Screw cap. 13.9% alc. **Rating** 94 **To** 2031 $60 NG

The Vinden Headcase Somerset Vineyard Single Barrel #1 Northern Slope Hunter Valley Shiraz 2019 Delicious. The tannins, beautifully placed. Refined, delicate and flimsy. A quilt with a thread coarse enough to service interest and savouriness to the sweet cherry, briar and anise notes; fine enough to allow the fruit to float in an ethereal gauze. Diam. 14% alc. **Rating** 94 **To** 2032 $60 NG

The Vinden Headcase Somerset Vineyard Single Barrel #2 Western Slope Hunter Valley Shiraz 2019 Beautiful. Hunter, to be sure, with its sweaty earth scents, fecund with promise. Red and blue fruit incantations. Pepper, clove, anise, Seville Orange and lilac. Yet the veil of tannic detail promotes the inherent freshness of the wine while guiding its flow long. Very fine. Diam. 14% alc. **Rating** 94 **To** 2023 $60 NG

ΨΨΨΨῩ **Lignée Hunter Valley Orange Semillon Sauvignon Blanc NV** The Lignée label is a collaboration between Angus Vinden and Will Gilbert in Orange. Equal parts '20 Hunter semillon and '19 Orange skin-contact sauvignon. Delicious. The phenolic element successfully knocks out sauvignon's overt pungency, while buffering semillon's austerity. Nicely done! Drinks like the army of incandescent wine served in a Parisian boîte: a bit turbid, dried-hay leesy, orange-and-tamarind-chutney skinsy, with tangy sauvignon greengage and durian scents. Judiciously chewy, long and saline. Cork. 11.6% alc. **Rating** 93 **To** 2024 $60 NG

Lignée Hunter Valley Orange Shiraz Pinot Noir 2018 A hark to a past of mid-weight, digestible 'Hunter River Burgundy', or luncheon styles as I call them, Orange serving up high-country pinot lift. An even split of varieties. Mid turgid ruby. Fecund strawberry, rosewater, white pepper, lilac, Seville Orange and clove. Lithe, gently pliant and very easy to drink. Magnum only. Cork. 13% alc. **Rating** 92 **To** 2024 $90 NG

Basket Press Hunter Valley Shiraz 2019 Rating 93 **To** 2032 $40 NG

The Vinden Headcase Somerset Vineyard Single Barrel 73 Block Hunter Valley Tempranillo 2019 Rating 93 **To** 2029 $40 NG

Somerset Vineyard Hunter Valley Chardonnay 2020 Rating 90 **To** 2025 $30 NG

The Vinden Headcase Single Barrel Hunter Valley Shiraz 2016 Rating 90 **To** 2026 $60 NG

Vinea Marson

★★★★☆

411 Heathcote-Rochester Road, Heathcote, Vic 3523 **Region** Heathcote
T 0430 312 165 **www.**vineamarson.com **Open** W'ends
Winemaker Mario Marson **Est.** 2000 **Dozens** 2500 **Vyds** 7.12ha

Owner-winemaker Mario Marson spent many years as the winemaker/viticulturist with the late Dr John Middleton at the celebrated Mount Mary. Mario has over 35 years of experience in Australia and overseas, having undertaken vintages at Isole e Olena in Tuscany and Piedmont and at Domaine de la Pousse d'Or in Burgundy, where he was inspired to emulate the multi-clonal wines favoured by these producers, pioneered in Australia by John Middleton. In 1999 he and his wife, Helen, purchased the Vinea Marson property on the eastern slopes of the Mt Camel Range. They have planted shiraz and viognier, plus Italian varieties of sangiovese, nebbiolo, barbera and refosco dal peduncolo. Marson also sources northeastern Italian varietals from Porepunkah in the Alpine Valleys. Exports to China.

ŦŦŦŦŦ **Sangiovese 2017** Early days for this wine, which hails from a strong vintage and includes 12 clones. A most complex and reserved wine. A savoury exposé of the grape in earth, truffle, leather and anise, gathering around blackberry/cherry-spiced fruits. Each time you go to the glass, there is something new to explore. Gotta love that. And so taut in cherry-pip tannins. Be patient with this one. Diam. 14% alc. **Rating** 95 **To** 2034 $42 JP

Prosecco 2019 An exceptional vintage in 2019 delivers not only a delicious drink but a complex one. Complexity and prosecco are not mutually exclusive. Honeysuckle, apple blossom, grapefruit and mandarin skin. Flows seamlessly with a quiet savouriness. There's lemon curd, crab apple and poached pear, with a gentle sweetness. Another top prosecco from this maker. Crown seal. 11% alc. **Rating** 95 **To** 2023 $32 JP **○**

Viognier 2018 A memorable drinking experience. Brilliant, glistening yellow/green hues. Complex, aromatic fragrance of acacia, grapefruit, lime zest, quince and orange peel. Boasts considerable concentration of fruit, liveliness and an energy that lifts it beyond the run of the mill. Screw cap. 13.5% alc. **Rating** 94 **To** 2030 $34 JP

ŦŦŦŦŶ **Shiraz Viognier 2017 Rating** 93 **To** 2034 $42 JP
Grazia 2018 Rating 92 **To** 2028 $34 JP
Nebbiolo 2016 Rating 91 **To** 2034 $46 JP

Vineyard Road   ★★★★

697 Langhorne Creek Road, Belvidere, SA 5255 **Region** Langhorne Creek
T (08) 85368 334 **www**.vineyardroad.com.au **Open** Wed–Mon 10–5
Winemaker Project Wine (Peter Pollard) **Est.** 2016 **Dozens** 10 000 **Vyds** 1500ha
This business is owned by Fabal Wines Pty Ltd. Fabal has been growing grapes and managing vineyards Australia-wide for over 30 years and decided to venture into wine production in 2016. It currently has 13 wines on offer at the cellar door, half the Vineyard Road business is dedicated to Vasse Virgin Natural Olive Oil skin products. The majority of the estate vineyards are situated in Langhorne Creek, with 565ha of the major varieties. There are also outlying vineyards in the Clare Valley (riesling) and Heathcote (tempranillo). Exports to the US, Singapore and China.

ŦŦŦŦŶ **Reserve Eden Valley Riesling 2018** Springton. The marriage of early- and late-harvest fruit unites a succulent, amiable personality of white stone fruits with a focused line of Springton acidity. Impressively backward and primary at 2.5 years of age, it has built gentle nuances of mixed spice and honeysuckle, retaining a core of grapefruit, lemon and pear. Screw cap. 12.2% alc. **Rating** 90 **To** 2025 $30 TS

Vinifera Wines   ★★★★☆

194 Henry Lawson Drive, Mudgee, NSW 2850 **Region** Mudgee
T (02) 6372 2461 **www**.viniferawines.com.au **Open** Mon–Fri 11–4, Sat–Sun 10–5
Winemaker Lisa Bray, Jacob Stein **Est.** 1994 **Dozens** 1200 **Vyds** 11ha
Having lived in Mudgee for 15 years, Tony McKendry (a regional medical superintendent) and wife Debbie succumbed to the lure of winemaking; they planted their small (then 1.5ha) vineyard in 1995. In Debbie's words, 'Tony, in his spare two minutes per day, also decided to start Wine Science at CSU in 1992'. She continues, 'He's trying to live 27 hours per day (plus we have four kids!). He fell to pieces when he was involved in a severe car smash in 1997. Two months in hospital stopped his full-time medical work, and the winery dreams became inevitable'. Financial compensation finally came through and the small winery was built. The now-expanded vineyard includes 3.25ha each of chardonnay and cabernet sauvignon, 1.5ha of tempranillo and 1ha each of semillon, grenache and graciano.

ΥΥΥΥΩ Organic Mudgee Cabernet Sauvignon 2018 One of the finest reds of the Vinifera swag by virtue of the detailed tannins and quality oak, no matter how aspirational and ever-so-slightly clumsy. The former, due to a long extraction regime; the latter, finding an impressive equilibrium with the quality of grape tannins as a result. Less time in oak could be a savvier choice. Bitter chocolate, oaky cedar, blackcurrant, olive, bouquet garni. The oak tannins, a Zildjan gong across the finish. Will find its place with a bit more patience. Screw cap. 14% alc. **Rating** 93 **To** 2030 $45 NG

Reserve Mudgee Cabernet Sauvignon 2016 Bottle age has made this approachable; the sheer density of fruit and ambitious French oak cladding suggests that it would've been impenetrable before now. Sweet cocoa on the nose. Coffee bean, wet earth, breakfast tea leaves, mulch, sage and blackcurrant, all. The oak, still very palpable but no longer domineering. The tannins, detailed, thickly textured and nicely pliant, guiding a long finish. Will age further. Well. Screw cap. 14% alc. **Rating** 93 **To** 2032 $60 NG

Organic Mudgee Graciano 2018 For me, one of the finest reds of this Vinifera suite and one of the more exciting of Mudgee. The confluence of dark fruits, pepper grind, clove, Seville orange and coffee grind, complex and somewhat confident. The acidity, a bit too shrill. Still, great promise. Screw cap. 14.5% alc. **Rating** 92 **To** 2023 $45 NG

Organic Mudgee Shiraz 2019 Among the more loosely knit and free-flowing reds of the Vinifera suite, marked by vanilla/bourbon scents of older American oak where it sat for 9 months. Oak handling can be aggressive at this address, but this works well. Red/blue-fruit allusions, some orange peel, mocha, sweet earth and clove scents drawn to a gentle tension by a bow of acidity, peppery and juicy enough in the context. Screw cap. 14% alc. **Rating** 91 **To** 2028 $50 NG

Gran Tinto 2018 Shiraz, garnacha and tempranillo. Plum, baking spice, kirsch and bitter cherry. Pithy and firm, with a curb of vanillan bourbon/mocha/cedar oak, conferring a savoury edge of restraint and a brûlée sweetness, all at once. This is a solid interpretation, auguring well for a promising future as this canny blend evolves at the source. Screw cap. 14.5% alc. **Rating** 91 **To** 2026 $38 NG

Organic Mudgee Grenache 2019 Subdued, requiring a real suck of air to reveal scents of kirsch, briar, pepper and bergamot. I like this. The level of ripeness far less than South Australian iterations but by the same token, savoury, almost joyous and just ripe enough to impart an edgy freshness best enjoyed in its youth. The tannins, curt. Needing work. This is good. The potential, excellent. Screw cap. 14% alc. **Rating** 90 **To** 2022 $32 NG

ΥΥΥΥ Organic Madeleine Mudgee Sparkling Chardonnay 2019 Rating 88 $40 NG

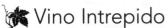
Vino Intrepido

22 Compton Street, Reservoir, Vic, 3078 (postal) **Region** Victoria
T 0488 479 999 **www**.intrepido.com
Winemaker James Scarcebrook **Est.** 2016 **Dozens** 850
Before the grape crush took hold, James Scarcebrook started out in wine retail, working his way from cellar door assistant to marketing coordinator at Domaine Chandon in the Yarra Valley and most recently in sales with leading importers. A love of Italian varieties had been cemented earlier when he took off overseas for 16 months in 2011 after finishing a master of wine business at Adelaide University. Then in 2016, a small parcel of Heathcote sangiovese morphed into the inaugural Vino Intrepido. Dedicated solely to Italian varieties with fruit sourced mostly from Victorian growers, the range has expanded to include vermentino, friulano, fiano, nero d'Avola and nebbiolo. (JF)

ΥΥΥΥΩ Blood Of My Blood Heathcote Sangiovese 2020 The name just rolls off the tongue doesn't it? So, too, the wine. Winemaker James Scarcebrook loves this grape and it shows. Even in its youth, it comes fully formed with emerging complexity. Everything is in its place for a wonderful future. Black cherry, caper, leather, spice and earth lay the foundation. Savoury tight tannins and an already-developing texture do the rest. Screw cap. 14.5% alc. **Rating** 92 **To** 2028 $37 JP

🍷🍷🍷🍷 **Sacred & Profane Heathcote Sagrantino 2020 Rating** 89 **To** 2032 $33 JP
Nero's Fiddle Midura Nero d'Avola 2020 Rating 88 **To** 2024 $28 JF

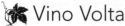 Vino Volta

184 Anzac Road, Mount Hawthorn, WA 6016 **Region** Swan Valley
T (08) 9374 8050 **www**.vinovolta.com.au/ **Open** By appt
Winemaker Garth Cliff **Est.** 2018 **Dozens** 1800
Garth Cliff was winemaker at Houghtons in the Swan Valley for 10 years prior to starting Vino Volta with his partner Kristen McGann in January 2019. Vino Volta largely (although not exclusively) focuses on chenin blanc (they make 4, pushing the grape in 4 different directions) and grenache from the Valley. Chenin blanc is in a revival phase currently, much of it thanks to Cliff, culminating in the inaugural nationwide Chenin Blanc Challenge in 2020, held in the Swan Valley. Together they have also started their own wine import portfolio called Wine Terroirists, calling on McGann's long experience in the trade. Cliff is an active (in every sense) member of the Swan Valley Winemakers Association and a tireless proponent for the region. Exports to Singapore. (EL)

🍷🍷🍷🍷🍷 **Funky And Fearless Swan Valley Chenin Blanc 2019** This has that stern, textural edge that chenin can have, plumped out by crushed cashew, native bush blossoms and oyster shell. It's still sheepy, it's layered, and the acidity that weaves in and out of the fruit is salty and very fine. A lot going on here, and a beautiful expression of one of the many directions in which chenin will be amiably pushed. Screw cap. 13.5% alc. **Rating** 95 **To** 2031 $35 EL ❂
La Chingadera Tempranillo Grenache Touriga 2019 Dense, layered and delicious – this packs pure red fruits in with exotic market spice. The salty and refreshing acidity laces it all together. The tannins are pervasive, but that's OK given the mix of varieties. Long, modern and exciting – another win for Vino Volta. Screw cap. 14% alc. **Rating** 95 **To** 2031 $35 EL ❂
Nothing Wrong With Old Skool Swan District Chenin Blanc 2020 Super-pretty; Geraldton wax, shaved macadamia, Pink Lady apple, cheesecloth, lanolin, fennel flower and beeswax. The palate follows in exactly this manner, leaving a trail of nashi pear on the tongue. Gorgeous. Screw cap. 12.5% alc. **Rating** 94 **To** 2036 $30 EL❂
Funky And Fearless Swan Valley Chenin Blanc 2020 Green apricots, salted preserved lemons, nashi pear, white pepper and briny acid. The oak is integrated, but alters the inherent chenin texture on the palate – that edgy line of phenolic grip that so distinguishes the variety is wrapped up in a softly textured, almost creamy, structure. Quite delicious, very long, and finely structured. Super-smart wine. Screw cap. 13.5% alc. **Rating** 94 **To** 2036 $35 EL
Post Modern Seriousism Swan Valley Grenache 2020 This is crunchy and juicy with fine, furry, pervasive tannins that shape the raspberry fruit. The mid palate has an edgy bramble laced through it, and to top it all off, the Peters Raspberry Freeza finish (best ice cream of all time) is laced with salty, earthy minerality that elevates it from delicious to serious. Ripping example of modern Swan Valley grenache. Screw cap. 13.5% alc. **Rating** 94 **To** 2031 $30 EL❂

🍷🍷🍷🍷🍷 **Nothing Wrong With Old Skool Swan District Chenin Blanc 2019**
Rating 93 **To** 2028 $30 EL
So Well Then Swan District Fiano 2020 Rating 93 **To** 2028 $30 EL
Different Skins Gewürztraminer Frontignac 2020 Rating 93 **To** 2027 $35 EL
Méthode Ancestrale Swan Valley Grenache 2020 Rating 92 **To** 2023 $35 EL

Vintage Longbottom

15 Spring Gully Road, Piccadilly, SA 5151 **Region** McLaren Vale/Adelaide Hills
T (08) 8132 1048 **www.**vintagelongbottom.com
Winemaker Matt Wenk **Est.** 1998 **Dozens** 48000 **Vyds** 94.9ha
Kim Longbottom has moved her wine business from Padthaway to the Adelaide Hills, where
Tapanappa has taken on the responsibility of making 3 tiers of wines. At the top is Magnus
Shiraz from Clarendon and Blewitt Springs; the middle is the H Range from the McLaren
Vale floor districts; and there is a sparkling range from the Adelaide Hills. Her daughter Margo
brings experience in fashion, digital marketing and business administration. Exports to the
UK, the US, Canada, Denmark, Singapore, Hong Kong, China and NZ.

????? **Henry's Drive H Adelaide Hills Sauvignon Blanc 2019** A serious take on
Hills sauvignon blanc, away from the familiar wild aromatic style, with 5 months
in French oak puncheons, albeit without using the word fumé anywhere on the
bottle. The wine expresses initial vanilla and baking spice from the barrel time,
while the citrus and herbal elements harmonise on the palate, creating a unique
tang, intriguingly rich yet refreshing at the same time. I'm convinced. Screw cap.
12.7% alc. **Rating** 94 **To** 2025 $28 TL ❂
Henry's Drive H Adelaide Hills Chardonnay 2019 This has sat for 8 months
in French oak puncheons. In doing so it has picked up all those good elements of
contemporary chardonnay, a touch of oak and barrel character to begin, nothing
overblown, then pure fruit expression – trademark Hills white nectarine – on
the palate, a nice little tang of citrus and spice on the finish, keeping it fresh and
vibrant. A lovely, balanced approach. Screw cap. 13.5% alc. **Rating** 94 **To** 2026
$28 TL ❂

????? **Henry's Drive H Adelaide Hills Sangiovese Rosé 2020** Rating 91 **To** 2023
$28 TL
Henry's Drive McLaren Vale Shiraz 2019 Rating 91 **To** 2030 $40 NG

Vintners Ridge Estate ★★★★

Lot 18 Veraison Place, Yallingup, Margaret River, WA 6285 **Region** Margaret River
T 0417 956 943 **www.**vintnersridge.com.au **Open** By appt
Winemaker Flying Fish Cove (Simon Ding) **Est.** 2001 **Dozens** 250 **Vyds** 2.1ha
When Maree and Robin Adair purchased the Vintners Ridge Vineyard in 2006 (cabernet
sauvignon), it had already produced 3 crops, having been planted in November '01. The
vineyard overlooks the picturesque Geographe Bay.

????? **Margaret River Cabernet Sauvignon 2019** Energetic cabernet laden
with cassis and spice. The tannins serve to bolster the fruit, and while firm and
structuring, are perfectly in balance. Good length of flavour rounds it all out. Screw
cap. 14.4% alc. **Rating** 92 **To** 2031 $25 EL ❂

Virago ★★★★

5a Ford Street, Beechworth, Vic 3747 **Region** Beechworth
T 0411 718 369 **www.**viragobeechworth.com.au **Open** By appt
Winemaker Karen Coats, Rick Kinzbrunner **Est.** 2007 **Dozens** 175 **Vyds** 1ha
Karen Coats was a tax accountant but has now completed the bachelor of wine science at
CSU. It was her love of nebbiolo and the Beechworth region that made Virago Vineyard
her new office of choice. Prue Keith is an orthopaedic surgeon but devotes her free time
(whatever is not occupied by mountain biking, skiing and trekking to the peaks of mountains)
to Virago Vineyard. The vines had been removed from the property long before Karen and
Prue purchased it, but the existing terracing, old posts and broken wires laid down a challenge
that was easily accepted, although the planting of nebbiolo was not so easy. The one and only
Rick Kinzbrunner has a more than passing interest in nebbiolo, so it was inevitable that he
would be the consultant winemaker.

ΨΨΨΨ **Nebbiolo 2017** An excellent year on full display, giving rise to a dark and brooding nebbiolo of wild rosemary, thyme, saltbush, incense, black cherry and mandarin skin. A most complex and accomplished wine of intrigue and discovery – such is nebbiolo's power – finishing firm, with a savoury tannin presence. Diam. 14% alc. **Rating** 96 **To** 2035 $50 JP ✪

ΨΨΨΨ **La Mistura Nebbiolo 2018** **Rating** 93 **To** 2025 $30 JP

Virgara Wines ★★★☆

143 Heaslip Road, Angle Vale, SA 5117 **Region** Adelaide Plains
T (08) 8284 7688 **www**.virgarawines.com.au **Open** Mon–Fri 10–5, w'ends 11–5
Winemaker Tony Carapetis **Est.** 2001 **Dozens** 50 000 **Vyds** 118ha
In 1962 the Virgara family – father Michael, mother Maria and 10 children – migrated to Australia from southern Italy. Through the hard work so typical of many such families, in due course they purchased land (1967) and became market gardeners, acquiring an existing vineyard in Angle Vale in the early '90s. The plantings have since been expanded to almost 120ha of shiraz, cabernet sauvignon, grenache, malbec, merlot, riesling, sangiovese, sauvignon blanc, pinot grigio and alicante bouschet. In 2001 the family purchased the former Barossa Valley Estates winery and today the 2nd generation of the Virgara family run the estate, employing ex-Palandri (and before that, Tahbilk) winemaker Tony Carapetis. Exports to the US, Canada, China, Thailand, Malaysia and Japan.

ΨΨΨΨ **Legacy Adelaide Sauvignon Blanc 2020** Although grown on the Adelaide Plains north of Adelaide (not a district renowned for crisp white wines) this vineyard is shaded from afternoon sun by a huge gum tree, the fruit picked at night at its coolest. Ripe fruit-salad notes with plenty of tangy acidity for a mouth-watering expression. Screw cap. 13.7% alc. **Rating** 91 **To** 2022 $15 TL ✪
Five Brothers Adelaide Cabernet Sauvignon 2016 Sourced from 50yo vines, this is warm-climate cabernet wearing a decent coat of oak yet providing enough varietal fruit power to carry it – if this style floats your boat. Everything is massive: bottle, style and price. Cork. 14.5% alc. **Rating** 90 **To** 2030 $100 TL

ΨΨΨ **Five Brothers Adelaide Shiraz 2016** **Rating** 89 **To** 2030 $100 TL

Voyager Estate ★★★★★

Lot 1 Stevens Road, Margaret River, WA 6285 **Region** Margaret River
T (08) 9757 6354 **www**.voyagerestate.com.au **Open** 7 days 10–5
Winemaker Steve James, Travis Lemm **Est.** 1978 **Dozens** 40 000 **Vyds** 112ha
The late mining magnate Michael Wright pursued several avenues of business and agriculture before setting his sights on owning a vineyard and winery. It was thus an easy decision when he was able to buy what was then called Freycinet Estate from founder and leading viticulturist Peter Gherardi in 1991. Peter had established the vineyard in '78 and it was significantly expanded by Michael over the ensuing years. Apart from the Cape Dutch–style tasting room and vast rose garden, the signpost for the estate is the massive Australian flagpole – after Parliament House in Canberra, it's the largest flagpole in Australia. Michael's daughter, Alexandra Burt, has been at the helm of Voyager Estate for many years, supported by general manager Chris Furtado and a long-serving and committed staff. Michael is remembered as a larger-than-life character, more at home in his favourite work pants and boots than a suit, and never happier than when trundling around the estate on a four-wheeler or fixing a piece of machinery. Exports to all major markets.

ΨΨΨΨ **MJW Margaret River Chardonnay 2018** The pinnacle. A culmination of different clones, parcels and processes. The Gingin clone brings explosive power and density, Clone 95 provides linearity, line, focus and acidity. Partial mlf (50%) softens the 95 on the palate, and 10 months maturation knits the whole piece together. Sophisticated winemaking and top-notch fruit selection come together in this perfect vintage. Screw cap. 13% alc. **Rating** 98 **To** 2041 $110 EL ✪

MJW Margaret River Cabernet Sauvignon 2016 Small components of petit verdot and merlot in the blend. Matured for 20 months in French oak (50% new). Elegant, supple, finely textured and very long. This is seriously classy cabernet from a vintage that produced wines of singular density, muscularity and tannins. Screw cap. 14% alc. **Rating** 97 **To** 2051 $180 EL

🍷🍷🍷🍷🍷 **Margaret River Cabernet Sauvignon 2017** Having stood in all 3 source vineyards, each component is clear in this wine: density from the Old Block, suppleness from the Block 12 and red fruits and brine from the Weightmans Block. Savoury, long, fine-knit and of supreme elegance. It's not intense cabernet, but it is persistent and very long. Screw cap. 14% alc. **Rating** 96 **To** 2041 $85 EL
Margaret River Chardonnay 2019 Always a very classy wine, this vintage is no exception. A blend of clones and partial mlf really set this off to a silky start. The explosive power of the Gingin clone is kept in check by the tension and citrus line of the Dijon clones, the mlf serving as the glue that binds it all together. Acidity freshens the day, and the spicy fruit hooks you in for a 2nd glass. Lovely stuff. Screw cap. 13% alc. **Rating** 95 **To** 2036 $50 EL
Broadvale Block 6 Margaret River Chardonnay 2019 An exposé of clone 95, this is taut and linear, with winemaking texture built in around the fruit to plump and soften the track that it makes across the tongue. Malolactic fermentation softens the high acid from Clone 95, dropping in crushed cashew and red apple skins along the way. As usual, very classy from Voyager. Screw cap. 12.5% alc. **Rating** 95 **To** 2036 $65 EL
Margaret River Chenin Blanc 2020 White pear, summer apricot, jasmine tea and white spice. The palate has a waxy Vouvray vibe going on, which really builds on itself through the evolution over the palate. Desperately pleasurable, jolly good drinking. Screw cap. 13.5% alc. **Rating** 95 **To** 2030 $20 EL ✪
The Modern Margaret River Cabernet Sauvignon 2018 No explanation forthcoming on what it is that makes this modern as opposed to previous vintages of Voyager's cabernets. The fragrant, medium-bodied, juicy cassis fruit-filled palate may of itself provide the answer. It's a pretty wine. Screw cap. 14.5% alc. **Rating** 95 **To** 2030 $50 JH
The Modern Margaret River Cabernet Sauvignon 2019 Fourteen months in French oak (39% new). Salted raspberry, licorice and Mariposa plum, the '19 vintage has birthed a wine of restraint and class. Far more layered, fine and spicy than the previous vintage. It needs time to unfurl and flower, which it should have done by the time it is released. Gorgeous, New World cabernet: power without weight. Screw cap. 14% alc. **Rating** 94 **To** 2036 $45 EL

🍷🍷🍷🍷🍷 **Girt by Sea Margaret River Chardonnay 2019 Rating** 93 **To** 2027 $28 EL
Girt by Sea Margaret River Chardonnay 2020 Rating 92 **To** 2028 $28 EL
Project Margaret River Sparkling Chenin Blanc 2020 Rating 92 $32 EL
Margaret River Sauvignon Blanc Semillon 2020 Rating 90 **To** 2025 $24 EL
Project Margaret River Sparkling Rosé 2020 Rating 90 $35 EL

Walsh & Sons   ★★★★★

4/5962 Caves Road, Margaret River, WA 6285 **Region** Margaret River
T (08) 9758 8023 **www**.walshandsons.com.au
Winemaker Ryan Walsh, Freya Hohnen **Est.** 2014 **Dozens** 1500 **Vyds** 20ha
The name Walsh & Sons has a Burgundian twist, the only difference is that Walsh & Sons would be Walsh et Fils. The analogy continues: the sons Roi and Hamish (Ryan Walsh and Freya Hohnen their parents) are in turn from McHenry Hohnen, of Margaret River blue-blood wine aristocracy. Ryan and Freya have had a Burgundian family association, having made wine for McHenry Hohnen from 2004 to '12, and over that time visiting/working for wineries in France, Spain, Switzerland and the US. At present, part of the crop from their 11ha Burnside Vineyard (where they base themselves) and the Walsh 7ha Osmington Vineyard is sold to McHenry Hohnen, Yalumba and Domain & Vineyards. The Burnside Vineyard is in biodynamic conversion. Exports to the US.

ŶŶŶŶŶ Felix Margaret River Syrah 2019 A gorgeous midnight ruby colour. The nose has crunchy black fruits, licorice and exotic spice, but most of all, it is interesting. Engaging, with brilliant density and intensity. A core of berry fruits huddle in the centre of the palate, the surrounding characters dominated by pepper, anise and toasty oak. Good length of flavour. A lot to love here. Modern rusticity and charm. Cork. 13.5% alc. **Rating** 95 **To** 2030 $30 EL ✪

Roi Margaret River Cabernet Sauvignon 2019 The nose is completely different from every other cabernet on the bench – stemmy, crunchy and yet ripe, giving a Rhône-esque bacon fat vibe. OK, I'm listening. It is a brooding rendition of Margaret River cabernet on the palate. Savoury tannins encase sweet purple fruit, all in all it tends to tip-toe across the tongue, rather than plod. If you're looking for the right side of 'different', look no further. Cork. 13.5% alc. **Rating** 95 **To** 2041 $45 EL

Burnside Margaret River Chardonnay 2020 All of the Walsh & Sons whites have a similar phenolic profile, somewhere between mineral/ash/graphite/pencil shavings. Once you get a feel for it, it's both distinctive and delicious. This is layered and briny, with a spicy pull across the palate. White peach, nectarine and curry leaf. Screw cap. 13% alc. **Rating** 94 **To** 2031 $50 EL

Little Poppet White 2019 Semillon/chardonnay blend. Mineral and spiced, this is saline with fresh garden herbs and bags of warm citrus (think along the lines of pink grapefruit, salted/preserved lemon and tangerine). The palate is zingy, textural and exciting – both lean and fleshy at once. Engaging phenolic grip through the mid palate and finish. Esoteric style owing to the distinctive fine ash character on the nose. Screw cap. 12.2% alc. **Rating** 94 **To** 2025 $26 EL ✪

ŶŶŶŶ♀ Lola Red Margaret River 2019 Rating 90 **To** 2027 $26 EL

Wangolina ★★★★☆

8 Limestone Coast Road, Mount Benson, SA 5275 **Region** Mount Benson
T (08) 8768 6187 **www**.wangolina.com.au **Open** 7 days 10–4
Winemaker Anita Goode **Est.** 2001 **Dozens** 4000 **Vyds** 11ha
Four generations of the Goode family have been graziers at Wangolina Station, but Anita Goode has broken with tradition by becoming a vigneron. She has planted sauvignon blanc, shiraz, cabernet sauvignon, semillon and pinot gris.

ŶŶŶŶ♀ A Series Limestone Coast Tempranillo 2019 Give this time to open up, revealing a flood of flavour from morello cherries, dark plums to sarsaparilla, thick hoisin sauce and boot polish. A dense, full-bodied palate with chewy tannins. It's a little rough and raw, in need of more time or hearty fare, but it's a solid offering. Screw cap. 14% alc. **Rating** 93 **To** 2028 $25 JF ✪

Lagrein 2019 Ah, the colour of lagrein. It's so pleasing. Lots to enjoy here with layers of flavour from dark cherries, woodsy spices, cooling acidity and grainy tannins. While there's a fair whack of eucalyptus/mint in the mix, it would be tamed by food. Screw cap. 13.5% alc. **Rating** 90 **To** 2024 $28 JF

Wanted Man ★★★★☆

School House Lane, Heathcote, Vic 3523 **Region** Heathcote
T (03) 9639 6100 **www**.wantedman.com.au
Winemaker Shadowfax, Adrian Rodda, Mark Walpole **Est.** 1996 **Dozens** 2000
Vyds 8.19ha
The Wanted Man vineyard was planted in 1996 and was managed by Andrew Clarke, producing Jinks Creek's Heathcote Shiraz. That wine was sufficiently impressive to lead Andrew and partner Peter Bartholomew (a Melbourne restaurateur) to purchase the vineyard in 2006 and give it its own identity. The vineyard, now managed by Callan Randall, is planted to shiraz (4ha), marsanne, viognier, grenache, roussanne and mourvèdre. The quirky Ned Kelly label is the work of Mark Knight, cartoonist for the *Herald Sun*. Exports to the UK.

�♀♀♀ **Black Label Heathcote Marsanne Roussanne 2019** A Rhône Valley white
blend with character and poise. Wanted Man is rewarded for its faith in these
2 grapes with a real stunner, boasting a lifted scent of white flowers, honeysuckle,
apple and citrus. Lovely. Fleshy and juicy, it is the combination of soft acidity
and creamy texture that brings this wine home, together with a lemon balm and
almond nut complexity. Screw cap. 14% alc. **Rating** 95 **To** 2027 $60 JP
Black Label Heathcote Marsanne Roussanne 2018 Adrian Rodda, the
talented contract winemaker, always manages to build a degree of complexity into
his white wines. Signature marsanne introduction here, like a burst of spring, with
apple and citrus blossom, jasmine, wild herbs, Golden Delicious apple and spice.
Rich layers of flavour flow across the palate, a creamy mouthfeel finishes with fresh
lemony acidity. Gives serious insight into what these varieties are capable of. Screw
cap. 13.5% alc. **Rating** 94 **To** 2027 $60 JP
White Label Heathcote Marsanne Rousanne 2017 A bright, fresh, zippy
Rhône blend that combines the prettiness of marsanne with the palate weight
and strength of roussanne. Delicious aromas of honeysuckle, citrus, tarte tatin and
buttered toast. Gaining bottle complexity as it ages with stone fruits, almond meal,
nougat and wet stone. Brisk acidity ties it together beautifully. Gently savoury, too.
Screw cap. 13% alc. **Rating** 94 **To** 2026 $27 JP ✪

♀♀♀♀♀ **Single Vineyard Heathcote Shiraz 2017** **Rating** 93 **To** 2027 $80 JP

Wantirna Estate ★★★★★

10 Bushy Park Lane, Wantirna South, Vic 3152 **Region** Yarra Valley
T (03) 9801 2367 **www.**wantirnaestate.com.au
Winemaker Maryann Egan, Reg Egan **Est.** 1963 **Dozens** 700 **Vyds** 4.2ha
Reg and Tina Egan were among the early movers in the rebirth of the Yarra Valley. The
vineyard surrounds the house they live in, which also incorporates the winery. These days
Reg describes himself as the interfering winemaker but in the early years he did everything,
dashing from his legal practice to the winery to check on the ferments. Today much of the
winemaking responsibility has been transferred to daughter Maryann, who has a degree
in wine science from CSU. Both have honed their practical skills among the small domaines
and châteaus of Burgundy and Bordeaux, inspired by single-vineyard, terroir-driven wines.
Maryann was also winemaker for many years in Domaine Chandon's infancy. Exports to
Thailand, Hong Kong and China.

♀♀♀♀♀ **Amelia Yarra Valley Cabernet Sauvignon Merlot 2018** Predominantly
cabernet sauvignon and merlot, with smaller amounts of cabernet franc and petit
verdot. Classic aromas you want to see from this blend, with subtle blackcurrant,
redcurrant, tobacco, mulberry, mint and just a touch of green herb and leaf.
Perfectly medium bodied, the wine flows evenly along the palate, escorted by
superfine tannin. The flavours really linger on the finish. Screw cap. 13% alc.
Rating 95 **To** 2038 $77 SC
Lily Yarra Valley Pinot Noir 2019 Staggered picking times to capture different
flavour profiles; some parcels saw longer post-ferment skin contact to increase
tannin extract. You have to get through the spicy oak on the bouquet to find the
cherry and cranberry fruit character, but it's there. It blossoms on the palate with
a beautifully silky texture, and that tannin is perfectly balanced and integrated.
Should develop very well. Screw cap. 14.5% alc. **Rating** 94 **To** 2029 $77 SC

♀♀♀♀♀ **Isabella Yarra Valley Chardonnay 2019** **Rating** 93 **To** 2029 $77 SC

Warner Vineyard ★★★★☆

PO Box 344, Beechworth, Vic 3747 **Region** Beechworth
T 0438 331 768 **www.**warnervineyard.com.au
Winemaker Gary Mills **Est.** 1996 **Dozens** 350 **Vyds** 4.48ha
The Warner family – Graeme, Gwen, Stuart and Katie – planted their vineyard in 1996,
astutely choosing shiraz (2.3ha) and chardonnay (1.4ha) as their main game, with 0.8ha of

roussanne and marsanne as a side bet. As the vines began to move to maturity, it became clear that their choice of the decomposed granitic soils was 100% correct, and the grapes were much in demand, Giaconda taking the shiraz and Jamsheed the chardonnay. In the lead-up to the '12 vintage, the family decided to keep enough grapes to have Gary Mills (Jamsheed) make around 200 dozen of each wine.

ŸŸŸŸŸ The Rest Beechworth Shiraz 2017 A contrasting style to the '16, one more elegant and lifted. Maintains a tighter structure, too. Red fruits to the fore, including redcurrant, violet and licorice. Firms on the palate. A cool-climate shiraz with the kind of energy and layers of bright fruit and spice that we come to expect from Beechworth. Screw cap. 13.8% alc. **Rating** 95 **To** 2027 $40 JP

ŸŸŸŸŸ The Rest Beechworth Chardonnay 2018 Rating 93 **To** 2028 $44 JP
The Rest Beechworth Roussanne 2015 Rating 93 **To** 2023 $36 JP
The Rest Beechworth Shiraz 2016 Rating 93 **To** 2026 $40 JP
The Rest Beechworth Chardonnay 2019 Rating 92 **To** 2027 $42 JP
Beechworth Roussanne Marsanne 2016 Rating 90 **To** 2024 $36 JP

Warramate   ★★★★☆
27 Maddens Lane, Gruyere, Vic 3770 **Region** Yarra Valley
T (03) 5964 9267 **www**.warramatewines.com.au
Winemaker Sarah Crowe **Est.** 1970 **Dozens** 3000 **Vyds** 6.6ha
A long-established and perfectly situated winery reaping the full benefits of its 50yo vines; recent plantings have increased production. All the wines are well made, the Shiraz providing further proof (if such be needed) of the suitability of the variety to the region. In 2011 Warramate was purchased by the partnership that owns the adjoining Yarra Yering; the Warramate brand is kept as a separate operation, using the existing vineyards. Exports to the UK, the US, Singapore, Hong Kong and China.

ŸŸŸŸŸ RS76 Yarra Valley Riesling 2020 When botrytis turns up in a riesling vineyard it's best to craft a sweeter style, hence the RS of 76g/L here. Thanks to lively acidity, this doesn't feel overly sweet – more generous and luscious. It's a delightful outcome with glacé lemon, white nectarine and cinnamon spice, refreshing throughout. Now the bad news: this is a one-off, as the riesling has since been replanted to malbec. 500ml bottle. Screw cap. 10.5% alc. **Rating** 92 **To** 2025 $35 JF
Yarra Valley Pinot Noir 2020 Sit back and relax with this uncomplicated, juicy wine. It's floral and fragrant with a neat combo of lightly spiced cherries, fresh herbs and a some charcuterie flavours. Tannins are compact, the acidity is brisk and it's very refreshing. Screw cap. 13% alc. **Rating** 91 **To** 2026 $35 JF

Warramunda Estate   ★★★★☆
860 Maroondah Highway, Coldstream, Vic 3770 **Region** Yarra Valley
T 0412 694 394 **www**.warramundaestate.com.au **Open** Thurs–Sun 10–5
Winemaker Robert Zak-Magdziarz **Est.** 1998 **Dozens** 6000 **Vyds** 25.2ha
The Magdziarz family acquired Warramunda from the Vogt family in 2007, producing their first vintage in '13. The Magdziarz family have built on the existing solid foundations with a deep respect for the surrounding landscape and a vision for terroir-driven wines. Viticulture follows biodynamic principles, vines are unirrigated and wines are all naturally fermented with wild yeast. Second label Liv Zak (named for daughter Olivia, studying viticulture, winemaking and business at Charles Sturt university) was launched in 2015. Exports to the UK, the US, Canada, Japan and China.

ŸŸŸŸŸ Coldstream Yarra Valley Pinot Noir 2019 This manages to offer considerable depth and power, yet appear light and pure. A neat confluence of cherries, exotic spice and savouriness. The oak adds a touch of seasoning and a carapace to holding everything together. Fine tannins and juicy acidity seal the deal. Diam. 12% alc. **Rating** 95 **To** 2033 $55 JF

Coldstream Yarra Valley Syrah 2019 Layers of flavour and definitely appealing, starting with its heady aroma. Floral, spicy, earthy and welcoming. The fuller-bodied palate fills out with sweet, dark fruits, pepper and cardamom, and a touch of cedary oak that is otherwise neatly in place. Textural tannins and vibrant acidity complete the picture. Diam. 13.5% alc. **Rating** 95 **To** 2030 $55 JF
Coldstream Yarra Valley Cabernets 2019 A blend of 80/15/5% cabernet sauvignon/cabernet franc/petit verdot that has come together very nicely, thank you very much. It's medium bodied at best, savoury and spicy, with lovely tannins, lightly drying on the finish. Diam. 14% alc. **Rating** 95 **To** 2035 $65 JF

♥♥♥♥♡ **Liv Zak Yarra Valley Syrah 2019** Rating 93 To 2027 $38 JF
Coldstream Yarra Valley Viognier 2019 Rating 91 To 2027 $45 JF
Block 1 Coldstream Yarra Valley 2019 Rating 91 To 2025 $45 JF
Liv Zak Yarra Valley Rosé 2019 Rating 90 To 2021 $28 JF
Coldstream Yarra Valley Malbec 2019 Rating 90 To 2027 $45 JF

Water Wheel

Bridgewater-Raywood Road, Bridgewater-on-Loddon, Vic 3516 **Region** Bendigo
T (03) 5437 3060 **www**.waterwheelwine.com **Open** Mon–Fri 9–5, w'ends 12–4
Winemaker Bill Trevaskis, Amy Cumming **Est.** 1972 **Dozens** 35 000 **Vyds** 136ha
Peter Cumming, with more than 2 decades of winemaking under his belt, has quietly built on the reputation of Water Wheel year by year. The winery is owned by the Cumming family, which has farmed in the Bendigo region for more than 50 years, with horticulture and viticulture special areas of interest. Over half the vineyard area is planted to shiraz (75ha), followed by chardonnay and sauvignon blanc (15ha each), cabernet sauvignon and malbec (10ha each) and smaller plantings of petit verdot, semillon, roussanne and grenache. Water Wheel continues to make wines that over-deliver at their modest prices. Exports to the UK, the US, Canada and China.

♥♥♥♥♥ **Bendigo Viognier 2019** A complex, barrel-fermented viognier that reveals a
dab winemaking hand. Everything is nicely in place (not easy with this grape,
which can tend towards the oily) from the spring blossom, orange peel and
ripe stone fruits through to the spicy, citrussy and restrained palate. It's a winner.
Smooth and totally hedonistic. Screw cap. 14.6% alc. **Rating** 94 **To** 2026 $24 JP ❂

♥♥♥♥♡ **Bendigo Chardonnay 2019** Rating 91 To 2025 $18 JP ❂
Royal Selection Bin 998 Old Vine Shiraz 2017 Rating 90 To 2030 $50 JP
Bendigo Grenache 2019 Rating 90 To 2025 $24 JP

Watershed Premium Wines

Cnr Bussell Highway/Darch Road, Margaret River, WA 6285 **Region** Margaret River
T (08) 9758 8633 **www**.watershedwines.com.au **Open** 7 days 10–5
Winemaker Severine Logan, Conrad Tritt **Est.** 2002 **Dozens** 100 000 **Vyds** 137ha
Watershed Wines has been set up by a syndicate of investors, with no expense spared in establishing the substantial vineyard and striking cellar door, with a 200-seat cafe and restaurant. Situated towards the southern end of the Margaret River region, its neighbours include Voyager Estate and Leeuwin Estate. The vineyard development occurred in 3 stages (2001, '04 and '06), the last in Jindong, well to the north of stages one and two. The first stage of the winery was completed prior to the '03 vintage, with a capacity of 400t, increased the following year to 900t, then another expansion in '05 to 1200t. March '08 saw the crush capacity reach 1600t; wine storage facilities have increased in lockstep with the crush capacity, lifted by a further 170 000kl. Exports to Germany, Indonesia, Fiji, Thailand, Papua New Guinea, Singapore, Hong Kong and China.

Waterton Hall Wines

61 Waterton Hall Road, Rowella, Tas 7270 **Region** Northern Tasmania
T 0417 834 781 **www**.watertonhall.com.au **Open** By appt
Winemaker Tasmanian Vintners **Est.** 2006 **Dozens** 1200 **Vyds** 2.52ha
The homestead that today is the home of Waterton Hall Wines was built in the 1850s.
Originally a private residence, it was modified extensively in 1901 by well-known neo-
Gothic architect Alexander North and ultimately passed into the ownership of the Catholic
church from '49–96. Together with various outbuildings it was variously used as a school, a
boys' home and a retreat. In 2002 it was purchased by Jennifer Baird and Peter Cameron and
in '15 passed into the family ownership of 'one architect, one farmer, one interior designer,
one finance director and one labradoodle'. Their real names are David and Susan Shannon
and John Carter and Belinda Evans. (Dog's name is unknown.) Susan and John are sister and
brother. Planting is underway and will see the current 2.5ha progressively extended to 10ha.

99999 **Tamar Valley Viognier 2019** The holy grail of viognier is varietal integrity
with elegance and tension. This wine epitomises all 3, contrasting pristine, crunchy
apricot and lemon fruit with apricot kernel and bright Tasmanian acidity. Wild
fermentation in old oak barrels brings creamy texture that holds its phenolic grip
comfortably through a long finish. Well executed. Screw cap. 12.5% alc. **Rating** 94
To 2026 $38 TS

99999 **Tamar Valley Riesling 2019 Rating** 93 To 2032 $27 TS ●
20-Year-Old Vines Tamar Valley Shiraz 2019 Rating 93 To 2029 $40 TS
Tamar Valley Shiraz 2019 Rating 90 To 2023 $35 TS

 Watkins

59 Grants Gully Road, Chandlers Hill, SA, 5159 **Region** Langhorne Creek
T 0422 418 845 **www**.watkins.wine **Open** Fri 1–7 Sat–Sun 11–5
Winemaker Sam Watkins **Est.** 2019 **Dozens** 2500 **Vyds** 120ha
Sibling trio Ben, Sam and Jo Watkins, under the guidance of parents David and Ros Watkins,
have established Watkins as a new label based at their Chandlers Hill winery and cellar door.
They are tapping into their well-established estate vineyards there and in Langhorne Creek:
both regions' vines are maritime influenced, with afternoon sea breezes tempering summer
ripening temperatures. The top-of-the-ridge cellar door overlooks rolling hillside vines on
one side and St Vincent Gulf on the other. Winemaker Sam Watkins has worked in Napa
Valley, USA, and Porto, Portugal, as well as Orange, NSW, and Coonawarra, Barossa and
McLaren Vale, SA. Brother Ben is commercial director, and sister Jo is brand director and cellar
door manager. (TL)

99999 **Langhorne Creek Shiraz 2019** Estate grown, 10 parcels in the winery,
maturing in a range of mostly larger, old oak vessels with some newer barrels
also in the mix. Rich, ripe shiraz as well as that faint background of mint and
chocolate, more milk than dark. Chewy palate textures while the fruit lingers.
A good-value shiraz with genuine regional expression. Screw cap. 14.2% alc.
Rating 91 To 2025 $20 TL ●
Langhorne Creek Cabernet Sauvignon 2019 Estate cabernet, with 10%
merlot. Matured in American and French barrels. Ripe cabernet fruit characters,
some earthiness which expresses itself in a faint mint/eucalyptus forest feel. Not
holding back in the tannin department, thick yet soft. Screw cap. 14.2% alc.
Rating 91 To 2026 $20 TL ●

9999 **Langhorne Creek Rosé 2020 Rating** 89 To 2023 $20 TL

 Watson Family Wines

3948 Caves Road, Wilyabrup, WA 6280 **Region** Margaret River
T (08) 9755 6226 **www**.watsonfamilywines.com.au **Open** 7 days 10–5
Winemaker Stuart Watson **Est.** 1973 **Dozens** 1000 **Vyds** 2ha

Watson Family Wines is owned and operated by the Watson Family of Woodlands Wines (est. 1973) in Margaret River. The Watson Family Wines are an affordable (sub $30) set of Margaret River varietals, focusing on shiraz, cabernet merlot, chardonnay and semillon sauvignon blanc; they also make a nebbiolo. Exports to Denmark, Belgium, Japan, South Korea, China, Singapore, Sweden, Taiwan, the Czech Republic and Poland. (EL)

ŶŶŶŶ **Margaret River Nebbiolo 2016** Savoury and layered, there is a core of cherry fruit wrapped in chalky nebbiolo tannins. Creamy texture drags this over the palate, through to the moderately long finish. Interesting, but more tannin and freshness here would justify the more savoury aspects of this wine. Screw cap. 13% alc. **Rating** 89 **To** 2024 $32 EL

WayWood Wines

Vale Cru Wine Experience at 190 Main Rd, McLaren Vale, SA 5171 **Region** McLaren Vale **T** (08) 8323 8468 **www**.waywoodwines.com **Open** At Vale Cru, McLaren Vale **Winemaker** Andrew Wood **Est.** 2005 **Dozens** 1500 **Vyds** 3ha
This is the culmination of Andrew Wood and Lisa Robertson's wayward odyssey. Andrew left his career as a sommelier in London and retrained as a winemaker, working in Portugal, the UK, Italy and the Granite Belt (an eclectic selection), settling in McLaren Vale in early 2004. Working with Kangarilla Road winery for the next 6 years, while making small quantities of shiraz, cabernets and tempranillo from purchased grapes, led them to nebbiolo, montepulciano and shiraz. The wines are available from Vale Cru at the McLaren Vale Visitors Centre, Main Road, McLaren Vale; private tastings by appointment at WayWood. Exports to Canada and China.

Weathercraft Wine

1242 Beechworth-Wangaratta Road, Everton Upper, Vic 3678 **Region** Beechworth **T** (03) 5727 0518 **www**.weathercraft.com.au **Open** Fri–Sat 11–4 (except during winter) or by appt
Winemaker Raquel Jones, Mark O'Callaghan **Est.** 1998 **Dozens** 1800 **Vyds** 4ha
After 2 years of searching, Hugh and Raquel Jones discovered a vineyard 10 min out of Beechworth. It had an immaculate 20yo vineyard, set up by Roland Wahlquist, the ex-CEO of Brown Brothers. For years the fruit had only ever been sold to Yalumba for a single-vineyard shiraz and it had the best possible address with nearby neighbours Giaconda, Sorrenberg, Golden Ball, Savaterre, Castagna and Fighting Gully Road. So it was that Hugh and Raquel followed their own advice and surrounded themselves with the best advisors possible. They retained Mark Walpole for the vineyard and Mark O'Callaghan for winemaking advice to Raquel, helping her on her winemaking journey. Dr Mary Cole, an academic from Melbourne and Monash universities and a renowned scientist, has advised on their move to organic certification. The Weathercraft winery was built in 2019, and while Raquel runs the winery and vineyard production, Hugh continues to run their property advisory practice Garcia & Jones.

ŶŶŶŶŶ **Beechworth Shiraz 2019** This cooler-climate shiraz asks for a 2nd look and a 3rd, just to make sure that you haven't missed anything. It's easy to overlook the fine detail. Blue and red berries, a handful of dried herbs, a pinch of spice, a bunch of violets and smattering of coffee grounds. Still young and vigorous and fruit forward, with nicely managed oak and earthy tannins. Screw cap. 13.9% alc. **Rating** 93 **To** 2025 $40 JP
Beechworth Tempranillo 2019 Winemaker Raquel Jones has Spanish heritage and has chosen an early-drinking joven style for her tempranillo. Plenty of life and energy here. Bursts free with juicy dark cherries, red plums, dried herbs and a hint of tomato leaf. A dry, lightly savoury expression with grainy tannins. The result is a youngster that almost demands the company of food. Screw cap. 13.5% alc. **Rating** 90 **To** 2023 $34 JP

Welland Wines   ★★★☆

Lot 1 Welland Road, Nuriootpa, SA 5355 **Region** Barossa Valley
T 0438 335 510 **www.**wellandwines.com
Winemaker Soul Growers **Est.** 2017 **Dozens** 5000 **Vyds** 1.7ha
Surrounded by the sprawling northern expanse of the township of Nuriootpa and destined
to be sold for development, the 1923-planted Welland shiraz vineyard was rescued in 2017 by
a group of friends led by Ben and Madeleine Chapman. The neglected vineyard of 30 rows
was resurrected in 2019 with new trellising, irrigation and replanting of dead vines. Fruit
from the site is supplemented by shiraz and cabernet sauvignon from other vineyards around
the Barossa and Eden valleys. Contract winemaking is handled by the talented team at Soul
Growers. Exports to Singapore and China. (TS)

ΨΨΨΨΨ **Old Hands Barossa Cabernet Sauvignon 2018** Full purple red. Powerful
and ripe Barossa cabernet, brimming with cassis and blackcurrant fruit and high-
cocoa dark chocolate French oak. It has the fruit density and firm, fine tannins to
handle warming alcohol on a finish of even persistence. Well assembled for a bold
style. Cork. 15% alc. **Rating** 91 **To** 2033 $70 TS

ΨΨΨΨ **Old Hands Barossa Shiraz 2018 Rating** 89 **To** 2028 $70 TS
Valley & Valley Barossa Cabernet Sauvignon 2019 Rating 89 **To** 2034
$30 TS

 ## Wellington & Wolfe   ★★★★

3 Balfour Place, Launceston, Tas 7250 **Region** Tasmania
T 0474 425 527 **www.**wellingtonwolfe.com
Winemaker Hugh McCullough **Est.** 2017 **Dozens** 250
There are many routes to winemaking, and a master's degree in modern history from Scotland
is among the more unusual. Hugh McCullough came to love wine through hospitality work
to fund his studies, ultimately culminating in a master's in viticulture and oenology, focusing
on sparkling and aromatic wine production. Vintages in Oregon, Washington, the Barossa
and Tasmania followed, finally settling in Launceston with his partner winemaker Natalie
Fryar (Bellebonne), establishing Wellington & Wolfe in 2017. The aromatic expression, depth
of flavour and racy acidity of Tasmanian riesling are his first love: second label Wolfe at the
Door was introduced in 2020 to showcase the 'supporting' varietals. Production is tiny and
fruit is sourced from growers in Pipers River and the Tamar Valley. A talented newcomer to
watch. (TS)

ΨΨΨΨΨ **Eylandt Off Dry Tasmania Riesling 2020** Pale, vibrant straw green. Fines
herbes, white pepper, kaffir lime. Even a suggestion of classic Pipers River oyster
shell. A tactical lick of RS brings harmony and grace without sweetness. It feels
Germanic, in the best way. Eylandt is engineered for the cellar, and 2020 especially
so. Screw cap. 8.5% alc. **Rating** 93 **To** 2035 $48 TS
Tasmania Riesling 2020 The contrast of texture and tension is a tricky
balancing act in Tasmanian riesling and Hugh McCullough has nailed it here with
careful and judicious exploitation of every clever trick in the book: wild yeast, old-
oak fermentation, soaking, and maturation on solids with stirring. He's masterfully
achieved the holy grail of luscious texture with just a lick of residual sweetness
(5g/L). Pure lime, lime jube and Granny Smith apple build a palate that unites
juicy concentration with zesty freshness. It's eminently food-versatile and delicious.
Screw cap. 12% alc. **Rating** 92 **To** 2025 $38 TS
Wolfe at the Door Pinot Noir 2020 The world needs more light, fruity and
affordable reds and this is an unashamedly light-bodied take on cool-climate pinot.
Think Beaujolais meets Tassie. Poached strawberry, raspberry and pink pepper are
structured by understated acidity and super-subtle tannins that promise immediate
joy. Screw cap. 12.5% alc. **Rating** 90 **To** 2021 $29 TS

ΨΨΨΨ **Wolfe at the Door RGG White Blend 2020 Rating** 89 **To** 2021 $25 TS

Wendouree

★★★★★

Wendouree Road, Clare, SA 5453 **Region** Clare Valley
T (08) 8842 2896
Winemaker Tony Brady **Est.** 1895 **Dozens** 2000 **Vyds** 12ha

An iron fist in a velvet glove best describes these extraordinary wines. They are fashioned with commitment from the very old vineyard (shiraz, cabernet sauvignon, malbec, mataro and muscat of Alexandria), with its unique terroir, by Tony and Lita Brady, who rightly see themselves as custodians of a priceless treasure. The 100+yo stone winery is virtually unchanged from the day it was built; this is in every sense a treasure beyond price. Wendouree has never made any comment about its wines, but the subtle shift from the lighter end of full-bodied to the fuller end of medium-bodied seems to be a permanent one (always subject to the dictates of the vintage). The best news of all is that I (James) will get to drink some of the Wendourees I have bought over the past 10 years before I die and not have to rely on my few remaining bottles from the 1970s (and rather more from the '80s and '90s).

🍷🍷🍷🍷🍷 **Clare Valley Shiraz 2019** This has a density, richness and ripeness, yet a beauty, too. Wafts of spice and Aussie bush aromas, with baking spices slipping through plums and blackberries. There's a buoyancy throughout, and bright fruit across the palate; the oak steadfast as a support and seasoning. The palate is perfectly shaped, fuller bodied, with expansive, textural tannins and acidity working in unison. Screw cap. 13.6% alc. **Rating** 96 **To** 2039 $65 JF ✪
Clare Valley Shiraz Mataro 2019 A 55/45% shiraz/mataro combo means the mataro is buffering or softening out the tannins so they feel ripe and velvety. A neat confluence of bright, dark fruit, savoury inputs via oak and more besides. Dark chocolate and mint, hazelnut-skin tannins, charcuterie and cedary oak. Its youthful vibrancy, while enticing, will be tamed in time. Screw cap. 13.6% alc. **Rating** 96 **To** 2042 $50 JF ✪
Clare Valley Cabernet Malbec 2019 With no straight cabernet this vintage, this ends up as 70/30% cabernet/malbec. While shiraz and malbec are good friends, cabernet and malbec are lovers. This is the wine that smells of Wendouree: the bush, the winery and the vineyards resplendent with gnarly centenarian and 'younger' vines. Plush, ripe fruit, all currant and blackberry accented, perfumed with aniseed, wild herbs and dark chocolate studded with mint. Lovely tannins and time on its side. If you can wait. If you can get some. Screw cap. 13.9% alc. **Rating** 96 **To** 2039 $60 JF ✪
Clare Valley Shiraz Malbec 2019 An even blend between these varieties that do like each other's company. The flavours, texture and tannins of each morph into a complete wine. This is particularly savoury, full of wild herbs and juniper, meaty and yet juicy fruit and tangy acidity in the mix. Screw cap. 13.5% alc. **Rating** 95 **To** 2039 $50 JF
Clare Valley Malbec 2019 A vibrant dark purple colour and the most approachable in the range this vintage, yet as always, this is something else. Such a unique offering to the world of wine. A core of bright fruit, laced with spice, a squeeze of blood orange and wafts of ironstone and warm earth. The flavours play off a medium-bodied palate with furry, grainy tannins, and great persistence. A star of the vintage, but each to their own – it's hard to pick a favourite. Screw cap. 13.8% alc. **Rating** 95 **To** 2035 JF

West Cape Howe Wines

★★★★★

Lot 14923 Muir Highway, Mount Barker, WA 6324 **Region** Mount Barker
T (08) 9892 1444 **www.**westcapehowewines.com.au **Open** 7 days (various hours)
Winemaker Gavin Berry, Caitlin Gazey **Est.** 1997 **Dozens** 60 000 **Vyds** 310ha

West Cape Howe is owned by a partnership of 4 WA families, including winemaker/managing partner Gavin Berry and viticulturist/partner Rob Quenby. Grapes are sourced from estate vineyards in Mount Barker and Frankland River. The Langton Vineyard (Mount Barker) has 100ha planted to cabernet sauvignon, shiraz, riesling, sauvignon blanc, chardonnay and semillon; the Russell Road Vineyard (Frankland River) has 210ha. West Cape Howe also sources select parcels of fruit from valued contract growers. Best Value Winery in the *Wine Companion 2016*. Exports to the UK, the US, Denmark, Switzerland, South Korea, Singapore, Japan, Hong Kong and China.

ŸŸŸŸŸ **Mount Barker Riesling 2020** Pure and beautiful. This has it all – lean austerity, ripe citrus fruit, taut acid and long length of flavour. It's a little ripper, and the price is well below the pleasure it delivers. Don't miss it. Screw cap. 11.5% alc. Rating 95 To 2036 $22 EL ✪

Two Steps Mount Barker Shiraz 2018 Intense and full bodied, with a red-fruited core that nestles into the mid palate – raspberry, mulberry, and pink peppercorn. The oak is quite robust (but tight) at the front of the palate, and thanks to that succulent reserve of fruit, this is balanced and serious. Good length of flavour means this is a very good wine indeed. Screw cap. 14.5% alc. Rating 95 To 2035 $30 EL ✪

Porongurup Riesling 2020 The irrepressible purity of Porongurup permeates every corner of this wine. The palate is plush and plump, with characters of mandarin blossom, lemon pith and green apple; the acid a mineral-laden river coursing below it all. 5g/L of RS plumps out the texture, giving it a slip and slide that is most attractive. Not quite sweet, but not quite dry either. A thoroughly quenching and lovely riesling. Screw cap. 12.5% alc. Rating 94 To 2031 $30 EL ✪

Styx Gully Mount Barker Chardonnay 2019 Toasted nuts and grilled yellow peach on both nose and palate. Plenty to touch and feel here, the texture courtesy of oak fermentation. A creamy wine with electrifying acidity that props up the orchard fruit. Lovely stuff. Screw cap. 13% alc. Rating 94 To 2028 $30 EL ✪

Book Ends Mount Barker Cabernet Sauvignon 2018 Brilliant intensity of flavour and tannins, and brilliant value for money. Good length of flavour indicates some potential joy in the cellar going forward. It's got that attractive Mount Barker muscle about it … Screw cap. 14.5% alc. Rating 94 To 2031 $30 EL ✪

Frankland River Tempranillo 2019 Violets, raspberries and fresh mulberries off the bush, with black pepper, licorice and anise sprinkled around the edges. The fruit on the palate has a sweet core – this is juicy and pleasurable and great. A modern, glossy rendition of temp – it basically begs for a barbecue. Screw cap. 14.5% alc. Rating 94 To 2027 $22 EL ✪

ŸŸŸŸŸ **Rosé 2020** Rating 93 To 2022 $17 EL ✪
Mount Barker Sauvignon Blanc 2020 Rating 90 To 2022 $22 EL

Whicher Ridge   ★★★★

200 Chapman Hill East Road, Busselton, WA 6280 **Region** Geographe
T 0448 531 399 **www.**whicherridge.com.au **Open** Thurs–Mon 11–5
Winemaker Cathy Howard **Est.** 2004 **Dozens** 2500 **Vyds** 9ha
It is hard to imagine a founding husband-and-wife team with such an ideal blend of viticultural and winemaking experience accumulated over a combined 40+ years. Cathy Howard (née Spratt) was a winemaker for 16 years at Orlando and St Hallett in the Barossa Valley, and at Watershed Wines in Margaret River. She now has her own winemaking consulting business as well as making the Whicher Ridge wines. Neil Howard's career as a viticulturist began in the Pyrenees region with Taltarni and Blue Pyrenees Estate, then he moved to Mount Avoca as vineyard manager for 12 years. When he relocated to the west, he managed and developed a number of vineyards throughout the region. Whicher Ridge's Odyssey Creek Vineyard at Chapman Hill in Geographe supplies sauvignon blanc and cabernet sauvignon, as well as a little viognier, malbec, mataro and petit verdot. Shiraz and cabernet are also sourced from a leased vineyard in Margaret River. Exports to Singapore.

ŸŸŸŸŸ **Elevage Geographe Sauvignon Blanc 2020** 100% sauvignon blanc, 30% fermented in seasoned oak, the balance in tank. There is a savoury crushed-ant character on the nose, that sits alongside the grapefruit, gooseberry and guava. On the palate it is mineral and flinty, with lovely line and length through the finish. Screw cap. 12.5% alc. Rating 94 To 2025 $32 EL

Elevation Geographe Cabernet Sauvignon 2018 Brambly cassis, satsuma plum, mulberry and blackberry. The tannins are fine and gravelly in texture; oak plays a dominant role through the finish at this stage. All things in place. Screw cap. 14.3% alc. **Rating** 94 **To** 2036 $50 EL

🍷🍷🍷🍷 **Mademoiselle V Margaret River Viognier 2019** Rating 93 To 2026 $38 EL
Tapalinga Margaret River Shiraz 2019 Rating 93 To 2031 $38 EL
Henry Road Margaret River Chardonnay 2019 Rating 91 To 2031 $38 EL
Odyssey Garden Geographe Sauvignon Blanc 2020 Rating 90 To 2025 $25 EL

Whimwood Estate Wines   ★★★★

2581 Nannup-Balingup Road, Nannup, WA 6275 **Region** Blackwood Valley
T 0417 003 235 **www**.whimwoodestatewines.com.au **Open** W'ends & public hols 11–4
Winemaker Bernie Stanlake **Est.** 2011 **Dozens** 550 **Vyds** 1.2ha
Maree Tinker and Steve Johnstone say they fell in love with the property at first sight in 2011, without even knowing that it had a vineyard. The name draws on the region's past timber-milling history, where horse-drawn whims were used for hauling logs. The vineyard had been planted in 2004 to chardonnay, with an agreement in place for the purchase of the grapes by a local winemaker. The grape shortage of '04 had turned into a grape surplus by '11, and it was left to Maree and Steve to remove 6000 of the 8000 chardonnay vines, and increase the handful of shiraz vines originally planted by grafting onto chardonnay rootstock. They now have 0.7ha of chardonnay and 0.5ha of shiraz.

🍷🍷🍷🍷 **Blackwood Valley Chardonnay 2018** Rich and toasty, this is complex, worked and loaded with spiced yellow peach, curry leaf, cashew and apple. The oak contributes a fresh marzipan character to the wine, the acidity swooshes in and cleanses it all. A lovely, complete, and very big wine. Very satisfying, very smart. Screw cap. 12.6% alc. **Rating** 93 **To** 2031 $32 EL

🍷🍷🍷🍷 **Blackwood Valley Shiraz 2018** Rating 89 To 2027 $28 EL

Whispering Brook   ★★★★★

Rodd Street, Broke, NSW 2330 **Region** Hunter Valley
T (02) 9818 4126 **www**.whispering-brook.com **Open** Fri–Sun 10.30–5
Winemaker Susan Frazier, Adam Bell **Est.** 2000 **Dozens** 1100 **Vyds** 3ha
It took some time for partners Susan Frazier and Adam Bell to find the property on which they established their vineyard over 20 years ago. It has a combination of terra rossa loam soils on which the reds are planted, and sandy flats for the white grapes. The partners have also established an olive grove and accommodation for 10–18 guests in the large house set in the vineyard, offering vineyard and winery tours. Exports to Canada and Japan.

Whistler Wines   ★★★★☆

241 Seppeltsfield Road, Stone Well, SA 5352 **Region** Barossa Valley
T (08) 8562 4942 **www**.whistlerwines.com **Open** 7 days 10.30–5
Winemaker Michael J. Corbett, Josh Pfeiffer, Adam Hay **Est.** 1997 **Dozens** 6000
Vyds 14.2ha
Whistler was established in 1999 by brothers Martin and Chris Pfeiffer but is now in the hands of the next generation, brothers Josh and Sam Pfeiffer. Josh took over the winemaking and viticulture in 2013 and has incorporated the sustainable approach of organic and biodynamic techniques. Sam has stepped into the general manager role, largely focused on sales and marketing. Whistler maintains the traditional Estate range of wines as well as the fun, easy drinking 'next gen' range, which has more adventurous labelling and names. Exports to Norway, Hong Kong, Canada, the US, Denmark, Mauritius and South Korea.

🍷🍷🍷🍷 **Get in my Belly Barossa Valley Grenache 2020** A refreshingly medium-bodied grenache of fragrance, spice and appeal. Bright red berry fruits intermesh

seamlessly with the rose petal and potpourri aromatics and exotic spice of well-measured whole-bunch inclusion. Powder-fine tannins guide a graceful and inviting finish. Screw cap. 13% alc. **Rating** 93 **To** 2024 $40 TS
Estate Barossa Valley Shiraz 2019 Density of crunchy mulberry and blackberry fruit pops with fresh raspberry and red cherry vibrancy. This is a dignified take on this drought vintage, framed eloquently in fine-grained tannins and just the right amount of crunchy acidity. Screw cap. 14% alc. **Rating** 92 **To** 2029 $60 TS
Estate Barossa Shiraz Cabernet 2019 Shiraz and cabernet interlock to compelling effect here, subsuming any evidence of where one ends and the other commences. Blackberry and black cherry fruit pops with crunchy acidity, fine-grained tannins and nicely restrained oak. A strong vintage for Whistler, promising medium-term potential. Screw cap. 13.5% alc. **Rating** 92 **To** 2029 $40 TS

Whistling Eagle Vineyard ★★★★★

2769 Heathcote-Rochester Road, Colbinabbin, Vic 3559 **Region** Heathcote
T (03) 5432 9319 **www**.whistlingeagle.com **Open** By appt
Winemaker Ian Rathjen **Est.** 1995 **Dozens** 950 **Vyds** 20ha
This is a remarkable story. Owners Ian and Lynn Rathjen are 4th-generation farmers living and working on the now famous Cambrian red soil of Heathcote. Henning Rathjen was lured from his birthplace in Schleswig Holstein by the gold rush, but soon decided farming provided a more secure future. In 1858 he made his way to the Colbinabbin Range, and exclaimed, 'We have struck paradise.' Among other things, he planted a vineyard in the 1860s, expanding it in the wake of demand for the wine. He died in 1912, and the vineyards disappeared before being replanted in '95, with 20ha of immaculately tended vines. The core wine is Shiraz, with intermittent releases of Sangiovese, Viognier, Cabernet Sauvignon and Semillon.

🍷🍷🍷🍷🍷 **Eagles Blood Heathcote Shiraz 2017** This captures the rust-coloured iron-oxide-rich soils and the brightness and mineral edge they can bring to shiraz. Built around a core of Heathcote black fruits and spice and supported by nicely restrained French and American oak, this is bold and generous. Ultra-ripe fruits mingle with savoury elements and sturdy tannins. This one is a keeper. Screw cap. 14.8% alc. **Rating** 95 **To** 2034 $60 JP
Heathcote Cabernet Sauvignon 2018 Shows impressive poise from the outset with a tight-knit grouping of ripe, bright cassis and black cherry, plum fruit and hazelnut oak. And there's a wealth of layers to traverse on the palate. Approachable yet intense, with fine tannins. Cork. 14% alc. **Rating** 95 **To** 2028 $40 JP ♥

🍷🍷🍷🍷 **Heathcote Arinto 2019** **Rating** 92 **To** 2025 $35 JP
Heathcote Grenache 2018 **Rating** 91 **To** 2026 $35 JP
Heathcote Sangiovese 2018 **Rating** 91 **To** 2026 $30 JP

Whistling Kite Wines ★★★★

73 Freundt Road, New Residence via Loxton, SA 5333 **Region** Riverland
T (08) 8584 9014 **www**.whistlingkitewines.com.au **Open** By appt
Winemaker 919 Wines (Eric and Jenny Semmler) **Est.** 2010 **Dozens** 360 **Vyds** 16ha
Owners Pam and Tony Barich have established their vineyard and house on the banks of the Murray River, which is a haven for wildlife. They believe custodians of the land have a duty to maintain its health and vitality – their vineyard has had organic certification for over 2 decades, and biodynamic certification since 2008.

🍷🍷🍷🍷 **Riverland Chardonnay 2020** Biodynamic. No oak. Considering the hot vintage, this has remained tight and bright. A touch of tropical fruit but also lemon juice and zest. Soft and plush across the palate and while it doesn't have length, it has drinkability plus. Screw cap. 13% alc. **Rating** 90 **To** 2024 $25 JF

Wicks Estate Wines

21 Franklin Street, Adelaide, SA 5000 (postal) **Region** Adelaide Hills
T (08) 8212 0004 **www**.wicksestate.com.au
Winemaker Adam Carnaby **Est.** 2000 **Dozens** 25 000 **Vyds** 53.96ha
Tim and Simon Wicks had a long-term involvement with orchard and nursery operations at
Highbury in the Adelaide Hills prior to purchasing their property at Woodside in 1999. They
planted fractionally less than 54ha of sauvignon blanc, shiraz, chardonnay, pinot noir, cabernet
sauvignon, tempranillo and riesling. Wicks Estate has won more than its fair share of wine
show medals over the years, the wines priced well below their full worth. Exports to the US,
Singapore, Hong Kong and China.

ŸŸŸŸŸ Adelaide Hills Cabernet Sauvignon 2012 Museum Release. Well reviewed
when first released with just 2 years under its belt. This Tim Knappstein-steered
Hills cabernet is peaking now at 8 years, releasing astonishingly intense cabernet
aromatics in full crushed-blackberry/currant mode. Unmistakably varietal. The
concentration of those sweet fruits and peppery spice on the palate just adds more
thrills, with the tannins smoothing off, round and supportive. Extraordinary value.
Screw cap. 14.5% alc. **Rating** 95 **To** 2025 $25 TL **✪**

ŸŸŸŸŸ C.J. Wicks Adelaide Hills Pinot Noir 2019 Rating 91 **To** 2028 $45 TL
Eminence Adelaide Hills Shiraz 2018 Rating 91 **To** 2030 $100 TL
Adelaide Hills Pinot Gris 2020 Rating 90 **To** 2022 $20 TL **✪**
Pamela Adelaide Hills Chardonnay Pinot Noir 2015 Rating 90 $30 TL

Wignalls Wines

448 Chester Pass Road (Highway 1), Albany, WA 6330 **Region** Albany
T (08) 9841 2848 **www**.wignallswines.com.au **Open** Thurs–Mon 11–4
Winemaker Rob Wignall, Michael Perkins **Est.** 1982 **Dozens** 7000 **Vyds** 18.5ha
While the estate vineyards have a diverse range of sauvignon blanc, semillon, chardonnay, pinot
noir, merlot, shiraz, cabernet franc and cabernet sauvignon, founder Bill Wignall was one of
the early movers with pinot noir, producing wines that, by the standards of their time, were
well in front of anything else coming out of WA (and up with the then limited amounts being
made in Victoria and Tasmania). The establishment of an onsite winery and the assumption of
the winemaking role by son Rob, with significant input from Michael Perkins, saw the quality
and range of wines increase. Exports to Denmark, Japan, Singapore and China.

ŸŸŸŸŸ Single Vineyard Albany Pinot Noir 2019 Strawberry, raspberry, green olive
and black pepper on the nose. On the palate the flavours follow suit, cushioned by
soft tannins, all of which flow through to the moderately long finish. Redcurrant,
pomegranate, a hint of crushed ant and saline acid form the closing act. Screw cap.
14.9% alc. **Rating** 92 **To** 2028 $34 EL

ŸŸŸŸ Single Vineyard Albany Sauvignon Blanc 2020 Rating 89 **To** 2022
$19 EL **✪**

Willoughby Park

678 South Coast Highway, Denmark, WA 6333 **Region** Great Southern
T (08) 9848 1555 **www**.willoughbypark.com.au **Open** 7 days 10–5
Winemaker Elysia Harrison **Est.** 2010 **Dozens** 13 000 **Vyds** 19ha
Bob Fowler, who comes from a rural background and had always hankered for a farming
life, stumbled across the opportunity to achieve this in early 2010. Together with wife
Marilyn, he purchased the former West Cape Howe winery and surrounding vineyard that
became available when West Cape Howe moved into the far larger Goundrey winery. In '11
Willoughby Park purchased the Kalgan River Vineyard and business name, and winemaking
operations have been transferred to Willoughby Park. There are now 3 labels: Kalgan
River single-vineyard range (Kalgan River Ironrock from single sites within the Kalgan River
Vineyard); Willoughby Park, the Great Southern brand for estate and purchased grapes; and
Jamie & Charli, a sub-$20 Great Southern range of wines. Exports to China.

ΨΨΨΨΨ **Kalgan River Albany Riesling 2020** Cheesecloth, lanolin, salted preserved
lemon, citrus pith and white pepper. There's a lot going on here, built within
the confines of lacy phenolics and saline acidity. Screw cap. 13% alc. **Rating** 93
To 2031 $32 EL

Ironrock Kalgan River Albany Riesling 2020 Green apple, lemon sherbet and
lime blossom. Very pretty and savoury; taut acidity and saline threads through the
fruit. Screw cap. 12.8% alc. **Rating** 91 **To** 2031 $35 EL

Kalgan River Albany Shiraz 2018 Showing surprising development on the
nose, this has soft fruit characters on the palate: bruised plum, blackberry and
mulberry. The tannins are very soft also, creating the overall impression of plump,
plush wine. If one were to be picky, one might suggest this is further along the
development path than perhaps it should be at this point, however, its soft comfort
will bring pleasure to many. Screw cap. 14.5% alc. **Rating** 91 **To** 2028 $32 EL

Ironrock Albany Shiraz 2018 Crushed coffee grounds and hints of formic on
the nose, the palate is driven by tannins which ensconce the fruit. The ovoid-
shaped palate has a streaming tail, constructed by oak, that at no point allows the
fruit to either shine or escape. Screw cap. 14.5% alc. **Rating** 90 **To** 2031 $55 EL

Kalgan River Albany Great Southern Cabernet Sauvignon 2018
Concentrated cassis and raspberry form the fruit core on the palate, frilled
with herbs such as sage and parsley. It is saturated and full of flavour, the length
moderate at best. Licorice, aniseed and blackcurrant are the enduring memory.
Screw cap. 14.5% alc. **Rating** 90 **To** 2028 $32 EL

ΨΨΨΨ   **Kalgan River Great Southern Pinot Noir 2019 Rating** 89 **To** 2026 $32 EL

Willow Bridge Estate   ★★★★★

178 Gardin Court Drive, Dardanup, WA 6236 **Region** Geographe
T (08) 9728 0055 **www.**willowbridge.com.au **Open** 7 days 11–5
Winemaker Kim Horton **Est.** 1997 **Dozens** 25 000 **Vyds** 59ha
Jeff and Vicky Dewar have followed a fast track in developing Willow Bridge Estate since
acquiring the spectacular 180ha hillside property in the Ferguson Valley. Chardonnay, semillon,
sauvignon blanc, shiraz and cabernet sauvignon were planted, with merlot, tempranillo, chenin
blanc and viognier following. Many of its wines offer exceptional value for money. Kim
Horton, with 25 years of winemaking in WA, believes that wines are made in the vineyard;
the better the understanding of the vineyard and its unique characteristics, the better the wines
reflect the soil and the climate. Exports to the UK, China and other major markets.

ΨΨΨΨΨ **Bookends Fumé Geographe Sauvignon Blanc Semillon 2020** An
outstanding example of the style, at a reasonable price. The fruit is ripe, almost
tropical (guava, green pineapple, with hints of green mango, Granny Smith apples
and sugar snap peas). Oak is seamlessly integrated into the fruit (in fact, it is almost
invisible, save for the complexiity and softening effect it has had on the texture).
Classy to the end. Screw cap. 13.7% alc. **Rating** 95 **To** 2027 $25 EL ✪

Rosa de Solana Geographe 2020 87/13% tempranillo/grenache. A Turkish
delight vibe on the nose. The fruit on the mid palate plumes generously, showing
pomegranate, redcurrant, raspberry pip and rosewater. There's a suggestion of
pistachio, joined by cumin and a whiff of cinnamon. The acid that binds the fruit
together is tense and nervy, bringing this home as a balanced, structured, pure and
layered rosé, worthy of any stage of a meal. Yes. Screw cap. 13% alc. **Rating** 95
To 2022 $25 EL ✪

Gravel Pit Geographe Shiraz 2019 An unbelievably vibrant colour –
somewhere between magenta, fuschia and midnight. The Geographe region excels
in shiraz and winemaker Kim Horton is a master at protecting fruit purity in his
wines. This is layered, with rippling intensity of flavour, imperceptible oak, and
exotic spices that net szechuan, star anise, aniseed and much more. A gorgeous
wine and a flag-bearer for the region. Screw cap. 14.2% alc. **Rating** 95 **To** 2035
$30 EL ✪

Black Dog Geographe Shiraz 2017 Full bodied and dense, with chewy tannins, an opulent black-fruit profile and spice that colours the edges of perception on the palate. The fruit retains a purity at the very centre, but the oak influence and density of the style mean this is not anything other than a big, concentrated shiraz. Definitely a style, and executed well here. The length is the key. Screw cap. 14% alc. **Rating** 95 **To** 2035 $65 EL

Geographe GSM 2020 A bouncy, pure, and delicious wine. Raspberry lolly, salami, blackberry, licorice and satsuma plum mingle on the palate, within the confines of fine, chalky tannins. With length of flavour that punches well above its price, this is a very compelling little wine. Screw cap. 14.5% alc. **Rating** 95 **To** 2028 $25 EL ✪

Solana Geographe Tempranillo 2019 100% barrel matured in new and old oak puncheons and hogsheads. The new oak component is evident on the nose, but once this wine is in your mouth the fruit intensity is on high: it can wear the oak gracefully. Purity and texture are the calling cards here. Crunchy acidity keeps this refreshing and taut; the length of flavour is very good. Screw cap. 14% alc. **Rating** 95 **To** 2035 $30 EL ✪

G1-10 Geographe Chardonnay 2020 Glassy texture and bright, briny acidity pave the way for an avalanche of ripe stone fruits to tumble across the palate. Once the dust settles (so to speak), the pockets of flavour unfurl through the finish. Impressive and affordable. Screw cap. 13.8% alc. **Rating** 94 **To** 2027 $30 EL ✪

♟♟♟♟♟ **Dragonfly Geographe Sauvignon Blanc Semillon 2020 Rating** 92 **To** 2024 $22 EL ✪

Willow Creek Vineyard ★★★★★

166 Balnarring Road, Merricks North, Vic 3926 **Region** Mornington Peninsula
T (03) 5931 2502 **www.rarehare.com.au Open** 7 days 11–5
Winemaker Geraldine McFaul **Est.** 1989 **Dozens** 6000 **Vyds** 11ha
Significant changes have transformed Willow Creek. In 2008, winemaker Geraldine McFaul, with many years of winemaking in the Mornington Peninsula under her belt, was appointed and worked with viticulturist Robbie O'Leary to focus on minimal intervention in the winery; in other words, to produce grapes in perfect condition. In '13 the Li family arrived from China and expanded its portfolio of hotel and resort properties in Australia by purchasing Willow Creek, developing the luxury 46-room Jackalope Hotel, the Rare Hare and Doot Doot Doot restaurants, a cocktail bar and tasting room.

♟♟♟♟♟ **Mornington Peninsula Chardonnay 2019** Pitch perfect with its combo of white nectarine, grapefruit and ginger spice, all spruced up with lemony tangy acidity. Oak is seamlessly integrated and adds depth to the palate and a flutter of woodsy spices. And yet with all this, it has a lightness of touch belying the layers of flavour within. Screw cap. 13.5% alc. **Rating** 95 **To** 2029 $45 JF

Mornington Peninsula Pinot Noir 2019 A classy wine that has a whole lot of detail, yet is almost understated because it's not showy. While there's a core of very good fruit woven throughout, its groove is distinctly savoury. There's a hint of smoky reduction and oak spices, raw silk tannins and texture across the medium-bodied palate. The finish lingers. Screw cap. 13.5% alc. **Rating** 95 **To** 2034 $45 JF

♟♟♟♟♟ **Mornington Peninsula Pinot Gris 2020 Rating** 93 **To** 2024 $35 JF
Mornington Peninsula Brut 2016 Rating 92 $45 JF
Rare Hare Sparkling 2017 Rating 90 $35 JF

Wills Domain ★★★★★

Cnr Abbeys Farm Road/Brash Road, Yallingup, WA 6281 **Region** Margaret River
T (08) 9755 2327 **www.willsdomain.com.au Open** 7 days 10–5
Winemaker Richard Rowe **Est.** 1985 **Dozens** 20 000 **Vyds** 20ha
When the Haunold family purchased the original Wills Domain Vineyard in 2000, they were adding another chapter to a family history of winemaking stretching back to 1383 in what

is now Austria. Their Yallingup vineyard is planted to shiraz, semillon, cabernet sauvignon, sauvignon blanc, chardonnay, merlot, petit verdot, malbec, cabernet franc and viognier. The onsite restaurant has won numerous accolades. Exports to the US.

🍷🍷🍷🍷🍷 **Paladin Hill Margaret River Matrix 2019** Brambly cassis pastille, pomegranate and ripe summer raspberry. This is supple, bouncy, beautiful and long, with elegance and harmony to spare. Glorious expression of cabernet from a cool and aromatic year. Screw cap. 14% alc. **Rating** 97 **To** 2046 $110 EL ✪

🍷🍷🍷🍷🍷 **Paladin Hill Margaret River Chardonnay 2020** Very young and very toasty, with brilliant concentration. The phenolics have the structure and rigidity that we expect from the low-yielding but excellent 2020 vintage. The length of flavour pulls out through the finish and shows the pedigree of the fruit. Very smart wine, but give it another year – it is very early in its life right now. Drink from late 2021 onwards. Screw cap. 13.5% alc. **Rating** 96 **To** 2035 $80 EL
Paladin Hill Margaret River Shiraz 2019 This was a cool year in Margaret River, and it has produced a swathe of wines that are highly aromatic, detailed and nuanced. This is no exception. Sweet and juicy blackberry fruit on the core of the palate, surrounded by exotic spice tannins and fine French oak. The wine is supple, balanced and delicious. Screw cap. 14% alc. **Rating** 95 **To** 2036 $85 EL
Eightfold Margaret River Shiraz 2019 Salted red fruits and exotic spice are the entree, main and dessert of this wine. The supple way that it twists and contorts on the tongue is made infinitely better by the finely woven acid (crunchy sweet red apples) that is through all aspects of the fruit and tannins. The whole package is quite delicious and has good length of flavour. Screw cap. 13.5% alc. **Rating** 94 **To** 2031 $39 EL

🍷🍷🍷🍷♀ **Eightfold Margaret River Chardonnay 2020 Rating** 93 **To** 2031 $39 EL
Eightfold Margaret River Cabernet Sauvignon 2019 Rating 93 **To** 2031 $39 EL
Mystic Spring Margaret River Cabernet Sauvignon 2019 Rating 91 **To** 2027 $25 EL

Willunga 100 Wines   ★★★★

PO Box 2239, McLaren Vale, SA 5171 **Region** McLaren Vale
T 0417 401 856 **www.**willunga100.com
Winemaker Tim James, Mike Farmilo, Skye Salter **Est.** 2005 **Dozens** 9500 **Vyds** 19ha
Willunga 100 is owned by Liberty Wines (UK), sourcing its grapes from McLaren Vale (it owns a 19ha vineyard in Blewitt Springs). The winemaking team is decidedly high powered with the hugely experienced Tim James and Mike Farmilo the conductors of the band. The focus is on the diverse districts within McLaren Vale and dry-grown bushvine grenache. Exports to the UK, Canada, Singapore, Hong Kong and NZ.

🍷🍷🍷🍷♀ **The Tithing Grenache 2020** Blood plum, Asian spice, orange peel, cherry amaro and white pepper. I initially thought it callow, but aeration brings life. Long, sandy and fine boned. Screw cap. 14% alc. **Rating** 93 **To** 2027 $55 NG
The Hundred Single Vineyard Clarendon McLaren Vale Grenache 2020 A round, rich and juicy wine, with a chord of reduction imparting tension to the mid palate. Riffs on violet, dark cherry, raspberry bon-bon, Seville orange and iodine. Smoky and saline across the finish, like biting into a sheet of nori. Good pushy length. Screw cap. 14.5% alc. **Rating** 92 **To** 2027 $45 NG
McLaren Vale Grenache 2020 This is best drunk as if a lighter frisky red, despite the weight. Again, a bit hollow. Kirsch, bergamot, tamarind and darker cherry scents. A spindle of fibrous tannins, sandy and gritty, promote verve and an ease of drinkability. Screw cap. 14.5% alc. **Rating** 90 **To** 2025 $25 NG
McLaren Vale Tempranillo 2020 A drink defined by a carapace of detailed sandy tannins, as much by violet, anise and jubilant accents of blue fruits. To be churlish, the mid palate is a bit hollow. But a satisfying and savoury wine, all the same. Screw cap. 14% alc. **Rating** 90 **To** 2026 $25 NG

Wilson Vineyard

Polish Hill River, Sevenhill via Clare, SA 5453 **Region** Clare Valley
T (08) 8822 4050 **www**.wilsonvineyard.com.au **Open** W'ends 10–4
Winemaker Daniel Wilson **Est.** 1974 **Dozens** 3000 **Vyds** 11.9ha
In 2009 the winery and general operations were passed on to son Daniel Wilson, the
2nd generation. Daniel, a graduate of CSU, spent 3 years in the Barossa with some of
Australia's largest winemakers before returning to Clare in '03. Parents John and Pat Wilson
still contribute in a limited way, content to watch developments in the business they created.
Daniel continues to follow John's beliefs about keeping quality high, often at the expense of
volume, and rather than talk about it, believes the proof is in the bottle.

🍷🍷🍷🍷🍷 **Polish Hill River Riesling 2020** While the warm, dry vintage has offered
some richer flavours, overall, this has taken it all in its stride. Lovely pristine citrus
flavours with freshly grated Granny Smith apples, spicy with ginger and some
daikon. It has a fine texture and the refreshing acidity adds to its considerable
length. Nice one. Screw cap. 12.5% alc. **Rating** 92 **To** 2025 $29 JF
DJW Polish Hill River Riesling 2020 For a young riesling, this is quite open
and approachable, with stone fruit and lemon curd plus a sprinkling of dried
herbs. It has a softness and juiciness with just enough refreshing acidity. Screw cap.
12% alc. **Rating** 90 **To** 2024 $24 JF

Windance Wines

2764 Caves Road, Yallingup, WA 6282 **Region** Margaret River
T (08) 9755 2293 **www**.windance.com.au **Open** 7 days 10–5
Winemaker Tyke Wheatley **Est.** 1998 **Dozens** 4500 **Vyds** 8.65ha
Drew and Rosemary Brent-White founded this family business, situated 5km south of
Yallingup. Cabernet sauvignon, shiraz, sauvignon blanc, chardonnay, merlot, grenache, semillon
and grenache have been established. The estate wines are all certified organic. Daughter
Billie and husband Tyke Wheatley now own the business: Billie, a qualified accountant, was
raised at Windance and manages the business and the cellar door; and Tyke (with winemaking
experience at Picardy, Happs and Burgundy) has taken over the winemaking and manages
the vineyard.

🍷🍷🍷🍷🍷 **Margaret River Shiraz 2019** An elegant, medium-bodied wine with red and
black cherry fruit on the smooth and supple palate. Exemplary handling of extract
and the use of oak puts this in the class of its '18 predecessor, even if the show
record of that wine was momentous. Great balance and mouthfeel. Screw cap.
14% alc. **Rating** 96 **To** 2034 $28 JH ✪
Wild Things Amphora Margaret River Shiraz 2020 Inky, skinsy, intense
shiraz with squid-ink concentration that stains both the glass and the teeth.
There is a lot going on here; jasmine tea, salted licorice, bitter orange, mulberry,
blackberry, aniseed and brine. It all comes wrapped in a vibrant package of fruit
that feels totally alive. Not for everyone, but for those who chase this style, pleasure
awaits. Cork. 13.5% alc. **Rating** 94 **To** 2028 $42 EL
Glen Valley Margaret River Shiraz 2018 A full-on, full-bodied Margaret
River shiraz. Layered plum and blackberry fruits have the depth to underwrite
long-term development. From a near-top-rated vintage, and will flourish with
time. Screw cap. 14% alc. **Rating** 94 **To** 2038 $42 JH
Margaret River Cabernet Merlot 2019 Organic. 71/15/14% cabernet
sauvignon/merlot/malbec. Vibrant, soft, layered and leafy with oodles of
cassis, raspberry, and spice. This is a masterstroke in easy-drinking and clever
construction. Gold at Perth Royal Show 2020. Screw cap. 14% alc. **Rating** 94
To 2028 $26 EL ✪
Wild Things Amphora Margaret River Cabernet Sauvignon 2020 Wild
ferment, pressed directly to new French oak, then transferred to clay egg amphora
for 5 months. Maturation in egg amphora softens the tannins and maintains a
minerality and finesse. Very good length of flavour; the succulence of red berries

on the palate carries through the finish, making this very moreish. Cork. 13.5% alc.
Rating 94 **To** 2036 $55 EL
Margaret River Cabernet Sauvignon 2019 Supple and succulent, the fruit
here is loaded with raspberry, cassis, pomegranate, pink peppercorn and redcurrant.
The tannins are finely textured, and the refreshing, briny acid is woven through
it all, holding it together. Cracking little wine, especially for the price. Screw cap.
14% alc. **Rating** 94 **To** 2036 $34 EL

🍷🍷🍷🍷♀ **Margaret River Chenin Blanc 2020 Rating** 93 **To** 2025 $20 EL ✪
Glen Valley Margaret River Blanc de Blancs 2018 Rating 92 $35 EL
Margaret River Sauvignon Blanc Semillon 2020 Rating 90 **To** 2024
$21 EL ✪

Windfall Wine Estate   ★★★★

7 Dardanup West Road, North Boyanup, WA 6237 **Region** Geographe
T 0408 930 332 **www.**windfallwine.com.au
Winemaker Luke Eckersley **Est.** 1996 **Dozens** 3000 **Vyds** 3ha
Julie and Phil Hutton put their money where their hearts are, electing to plant a merlot-only
vineyard in 1996. Presumably knowing the unpredictable habits of merlot when planted on
its own roots, they began by planting 3500 Schwartzman rootstock vines and then 12 months
later field-grafted the merlot scion material. Small wonder their backs are still aching. I (James)
don't doubt for a millisecond the sincerity of their enthusiasm for the variety when they say,
'Fruity, plummy, smooth and velvety. Hints of chocolate too. If you're new to wine and all
things merlot, this is a wonderful variety to explore.' The previous name, Bonking Frog, was
fun but became wildly unsuited to what has become a serious player in the Geographe region.
Exports to China and Mauritius.

🍷🍷🍷🍷♀ **Ivor Reserve Geographe Merlot 2018** With layers of red fruit and plush
tannins, this is densely packed with flavour. The oak makes an obvious impact at
this stage, but thanks to the concentrated fruit, this will no doubt be absorbed in a
short time. Screw cap. 14.8% alc. **Rating** 92 **To** 2031 $40 EL
Single-Handed Great Southern Chardonnay 2019 Flavours of green
pineapple, papaya, guava and honeydew melon. The phenolics have an attractively
bitter edge to them that offsets the fruit, all of it pinioned up by austere acidity.
Screw cap. 13.5% alc. **Rating** 90 **To** 2027 $30 EL

Windows Estate   ★★★★★

4 Quininup Road, Yallingup, WA 6282 **Region** Margaret River
T (08) 9756 6655 **www.**windowsestate.com **Open** 7 days 10–5
Winemaker Chris Davies **Est.** 1999 **Dozens** 2000 **Vyds** 7ha
Chris Davies planted the Windows Estate vineyard (cabernet sauvignon, shiraz, chenin blanc,
chardonnay, semillon, sauvignon blanc and merlot) in 1996, at the tender age of 19. He has
has tended the vines ever since, gaining organic certifcation in 2019. Initially selling the grapes,
Chris moved into winemaking in 2006 and has had considerable show success for the
consistently outstanding wines. Exports to the UK, the US and Italy.

🍷🍷🍷🍷🍷 **La Fenetre Margaret River Chardonnay 2017** PSA: There is a new kid
on the block (in case you didn't already know). Chris Davies performs sensitive
and detailed winemaking, which sees every clone and parcel treated differently
in bâtonnage, oak and skin contact. Scintillating acidity lays the track for the taut
citric fruit to glide along. In every respect this oozes elegance, restraint and pure
beauty. If it isn't obvious already, I love it. Heartily. Screw cap. **Rating** 97 **To** 2036
$85 EL ✪

🍷🍷🍷🍷🍷 **Petit Lot Chardonnay 2019** A scintillating wine. The acidity is like a jolt right
through the centre of the tongue, getting the saliva coursing through the mouth.
Citrus pith, white peach, red apple skins, brine, fennel flower and crushed cashews
are at the heart of this very pure chardonnay. Quite simply outstanding. Trophy

Best Single Vineyard White, Margaret River Wine Show '20. Screw cap. 13% alc.
Rating 96 To 2036 $48 EL ✪

Petit Lot Chenin Blanc 2019 There's a lot to love about this family-owned
and -operated estate. Nectarine, green apple, nashi pear and apricot. The palate is
where the beauty lies: intense fruit concentration, briny acid, built on very fine,
waxy phenolics. The length of flavour is brilliant – it courses with no sign of
slowing down. Manages restraint, as well. Screw cap. 11.5% alc. **Rating** 96 To 2030
$37 EL ✪ ♥

Petit Lot Fumé Blanc 2019 Typical of Windows Estate is the intense
concentration of fruit flavour on the palate – this is no exception. Textural, svelte
and layered. Another cracker from Chris and Jo Davies. Keep an eye on this little
producer if you like to stay ahead of the curve ... Screw cap. 12% alc. **Rating** 95
To 2030 $37 EL

Petit Lot Violette 2018 This has all of the 2018 vintage hallmarks of intense
vibrancy, ripeness and concentration. The fruit is layered with blackberry, raspberry,
aniseed and pomegranate, the acidity a bright spark on the tongue. At this stage,
the oak is asserting itself, but the fruit shows it will claim dominance in the end.
Certified organic. Screw cap. 14% alc. **Rating** 95 To 2042 $39 EL

Petit Lot Violette 2017 Cabernet franc/merlot/petit verdot/malbec. Matured
in French oak for 18 months (35% new). Spicy, layered, juicy and long. There
is a lot to like here. The wine has a bounce and a chewiness that makes it jolly
good drinking. The length of flavour is the ultimate key to its quality. This is a
crowd pleaser for sure, but it has enough layers of interest to engage the nerds (us).
Brilliant. Screw cap. 14% alc. **Rating** 95 To 2030 $39 EL

Petit Lot Semillon Sauvignon Blanc 2019 68/27/5% semillon/sauvignon
blanc/chardonnay. Hand-picked fruit. Each variety was wild-yeast fermented
separately in barrel. Nine months in oak (500L barriques, 25% new). Incredibly
exciting and energetic. The oak contributes a sweaty, corporeal funk to the
crystalline fruit, the combination of which creates a salty party in the mouth.
This is happening. Screw cap. 12% alc. **Rating** 94 To 2030 $30 EL ✪

Petit Lot Malbec 2017 Finer and softer than many malbecs, this leads with
succulent berry fruit and plush tannins. The oak has been absorbed by the fruit,
and the tannins are well matched to the fresh acid – all of which give grace and
balance to the overall experience. Lovely wine. Screw cap. 14% alc. **Rating** 94
To 2035 $49 EL

Wine Architect   ★★★★

38a Murray Street, Tanunda, SA 5352 **Region** Adelaide Hills
T 0439 823 251 **www.**winearchitect.com.au **Open** Wed–Thurs 2–6, Fri 2–late, or by appt
Winemaker Natasha Mooney **Est.** 2006 **Dozens** 3000
This is a reasonably significant busman's holiday for Natasha Mooney, a well-known and
highly talented winemaker whose 'day job' (her term) is to provide winemaking consultancy
services for some of SA's larger wineries. This allows her to find small, unique parcels of grapes
that might otherwise be blended into large-volume brands. She manages the arrangements so
that there is no conflict of interest, making wines that are about fruit and vineyard expression.
She aims for mouthfeel and drinkability without high alcohol, and for that she should be
loudly applauded. Wines are released under La Bise (named for the southerly wind that blows
across Burgundy) and The Thief? labels.

♟♟♟♟♟ **La Bise Whole Bunch Pressed Adelaide Hills Pinot Gris 2020** From the
renowned Amadio Vineyard at Kersbrook, whole-bunch pressed juice kept on
full solids for a week before fermentation. Full flavoured pear – heading in the
Buerre Bosc direction – with a delicate musk note there too. Delicious, mouth-
watering texture and spice on the palate. All round goodness. Screw cap. 12.9% alc.
Rating 94 To 2024 $22 TL ✪

♟♟♟♟♟ **La Bise Adelaide Hills Nero d'Avola 2020** Rating 93 To 2025 $29 TL
La Bise Adelaide Hills Sangiovese 2019 Rating 92 To 2028 $25 TL ✪

Wine Unplugged

2020 Upton Road, Upton Hill, Vic 3664 (postal) **Region** Victoria
T 0432 021 668 **www**.wineunplugged.com.au
Winemaker Callie Jemmeson, Nina Stocker **Est.** 2010 **Dozens** 5000
Nina Stocker and Callie Jemmeson believe that winemaking doesn't have to have barriers:
what it does need is quality, focus and a destination. With a strong emphasis on vineyard
selection and a gentle approach to their small-batch winemaking, the wines are a true
reflection of site. The wines are released under the pacha mama, La Vie en Rose, Cloak &
Dagger, Motley Cru and Harvest Moon labels. Exports to China.

ŸŸŸŸŸ pacha mama Yarra Valley Chardonnay 2018 Smoky sulphides at play here, so
it smells of chicken soup at first, all savoury and umami-like. There is the requisite
white stone fruit and citrus elements, too, but very much behind the scenes. Also
tucked in neatly, the acidity and perfectly integrated oak. Screw cap. 13% alc.
Rating 95 **To** 2028 $30 JF ❂
pacha mama Pinot Gris 2019 Opens with the telltale varietal inputs of ginger-
spiced poached pears/apples, fresh pears too, and a fleck of aniseed. There is a
juiciness and tang with lemon/tangerine notes, then it glides into richer territory,
with creamy lees adding texture and flavour. Screw cap. 13% alc. **Rating** 95
To 2024 $28 JF ❂
pacha mama Heathcote Shiraz 2019 Outrageous colour – vibrant black/
purple and what's so appealing with this wine is its beautifully tamed tannins.
They have shape but are not at all brutish, giving definition to the fuller-bodied
wine. In the mix, dark, sweet fruit, Chinese five-spice, charry wood flavours and a
guarantee of an excellent drink. Screw cap. 14% alc. **Rating** 95 **To** 2028 $30 JF ❂

ŸŸŸŸ♀ pacha mama Yarra Valley Chardonnay 2019 **Rating** 93 **To** 2027 $30 JF
pacha mama Yarra Valley Pinot Noir 2019 **Rating** 92 **To** 2025 $34 JF
Cloak & Dagger The Cloak Sangiovese 2019 **Rating** 90 **To** 2023 $28 JF

Wine x Sam   ★★★★☆

69-71 Anzac Avenue, Seymour, Vic 3660 **Region** Central Victoria
T 03 57 990 437 **www**.winebysam.com.au **Open** Fri–Sun 9–4
Winemaker Sam Plunkett, Mark Hickin, Sophie Fromont **Est.** 2012 **Dozens** 70 000
Vyds 10.2ha
Since 1991 Sam Plunkett and partner Bron Dunwoodie have changed shells as often as a lively
hermit crab: 1991, first estate vineyard established and mudbrick winery built; 2001, created
a new winery at Avenel; 2004, purchased the large Dominion Wines in partnership with the
Fowles family; 2011, Fowles purchased the Plunkett family's shareholding, except 7ha of shiraz
and 3.2ha of chardonnay. Winemaking moved to the Taresch family's Elgo Estate winery.
Within 2 years the Plunkett interests had leased the entire Elgo winery, now making the Elgo
wines as well as their own brands. A large contract make for Naked Wines saw production
increase, and a few blinks of the eye later, production is now 70 000 dozen. Exports to the
UK, the US and China.

ŸŸŸŸŸ The Victorian Strathbogie Ranges Riesling 2019 Riesling is always a
strength with this maker. Maybe a little more forward in comparison to last
year. Zesty, sherbet fresh with apple blossom, talc and musk, fine citrus and spice.
Shimmies over the tongue with an added note of lemon butter texture. Finishes
with lingering, mouth-watering acidity. Screw cap. 11.8% alc. **Rating** 94 **To** 2025
$24 JP ❂

ŸŸŸŸ♀ The Victorian Strathbogie Ranges Primitivo 2020 **Rating** 92 **To** 2027
$24 JP ❂
Stardust & Muscle Strathbogie Ranges Chardonnay 2020 **Rating** 90
To 2025 $32 JP
The Victorian Strathbogie Ranges Rosé 2019 **Rating** 90 **To** 2024 $24 JP
The Victorian Heathcote Shiraz 2019 **Rating** 90 **To** 2026 $24 JP

Wines by KT

20 Main North Road, Watervale, SA 5452 **Region** Clare Valley
T 0419 855 500 **www**.winesbykt.com **Open** Fri–Sun 11–4
Winemaker Kerri Thompson **Est.** 2006 **Dozens** 4500 **Vyds** 9ha
KT is winemaker Kerri Thompson. Kerri graduated with a degree in oenology from Roseworthy Agricultural College in 1993, and thereafter made wine in McLaren Vale, Tuscany, Beaujolais and the Clare Valley, becoming well known as the Leasingham winemaker in the Clare Valley. She resigned from Leasingham in 2006 after 7 years at the helm, and after a short break became winemaker at Crabtree. Here she is also able to make Wines by KT, sourcing the grapes from 2 local vineyards, one biodynamic, the other farmed with sulphur and copper sprays only.

ŸŸŸŸŸ **Peglidis Vineyard Watervale Aged Release Riesling 2013** Mid gold hue, galloping to the tertiary line. It's complex and heady, with toasty, baked ricotta, drizzled with lemon, honey, beeswax and lime marmalade, sans sweetness, just the tang. Super-dry, with plenty of laser-sharp acidity keeping it buoyant on the palate. Pitch-perfect now. Screw cap. 12% alc. **Rating** 95 **To** 2025 $50 JF

ŸŸŸŸŸ **Peglidis Vineyard Watervale Riesling 2020 Rating** 93 **To** 2026 $38 JF
Churinga Vineyard Watervale Riesling 2020 Rating 93 **To** 2028 $34 JF
5452 Watervale Shiraz 2019 Rating 93 **To** 2029 $29 JF
Melva Wild Fermented Riesling 2020 Rating 92 **To** 2027 $33 JF
Churinga Vineyard Watervale Cabernet Sauvignon 2016 Rating 92 **To** 2028 $40 JF
Tinta by KT Clare Valley Tempranillo Monastrell 2019 Rating 92 **To** 2026 $29 JF
5452 Watervale Riesling 2020 Rating 91 **To** 2026 $29 JF
Churinga Vineyard Watervale Riesling 2019 Rating 91 **To** 2029 $34 JF
Rosa by KT Garnacha Tempranillo Rosada 2019 Rating 91 **To** 2022 $29 JF

Wines of Merritt

PO Box 1122, Margaret River, WA 6285 **Region** Margaret River
T 0438 284 561 **www**.winesofmerritt.com.au
Winemaker Nick James-Martin **Est.** 2017 **Dozens** 600
Nick James-Martin grew up in a tiny Riverland town, spending his early working life in some of Adelaide's better restaurants, helping his family establish a vineyard in McLaren Vale. Two years working for WINE Magazine in London offered him the opportunity of travelling through France, Spain, Portugal and Italy, immersing himself in wine in those countries. He then studied wine marketing and oenology at the University of Adelaide, sitting for a master's degree. He worked at Rosemount, Vasse Felix and Stella Bella, plus overseas vintages in Hawke's Bay, NZ and Languedoc, France. Sarah James-Martin is a hospitality professional and prior to moving to Margaret River she ran the acclaimed Salopian Inn in McLaren Vale and worked for other wineries in the region. She's currently mastering the art of cheesemaking at Yallingup Cheese Company.

ŸŸŸŸŸ **Single Vineyard Small Batch Margaret River Syrah 2020** A luminscent fuschia colour in the glass. Salted heirloom tomato, pomegranate, raspberry, red licorice and pink peppercorn notes. This is skinsy and textural and totally delicious. The oak is almost imperceptible: rustic, svelte, saturated and verging on nouveau … a lot to love. An exciting wine. Screw cap. 13.5% alc. **Rating** 95 **To** 2027 $40 EL
Single Vineyard Small Batch Margaret River Chenin Blanc 2020 Slightly cloudy in the glass; cheesecloth, apple cider, lanolin, saffron, white pepper and brine. While this has very soft phenolic texture, it is combined with almost formidable acid, which gives the impression of duality on the tongue. There's a lot going on, but it retains elegance. Very smart. Screw cap. 12.5% alc. **Rating** 94 **To** 2036 $40 EL

Wirra Wirra ★★★★★

463 McMurtrie Road, McLaren Vale, SA 5171 **Region** McLaren Vale
T (08) 8323 8414 **www**.wirrawirra.com **Open** Mon–Sat 10–5, Sun & public hols 11–5
Winemaker Paul Smith, Tom Ravech, Kelly Wellington **Est.** 1894 **Dozens** 140 000
Vyds 21.5ha

Wirra Wirra has established a formidable reputation. The wines are of exemplary character, quality and style; The Angelus Cabernet Sauvignon and RWS Shiraz battling each other for supremacy, with The Absconder Grenache one to watch. Long may the battle continue under managing director Andrew Kay and the winemaking team of Paul Smith, Tom Ravech and Kelly Wellington, who forge along the path of excellence first trod by the late (and much loved) Greg Trott, the pioneering founder of modern-day Wirra Wirra. Its acquisition of Ashton Hills in 2015 added a major string to its top-quality bow. Exports to all major markets.

🍷🍷🍷🍷🍷 **Woodhenge Basket-Pressed McLaren Vale Shiraz 2018** Black fruits of many types glide across the palate on a magic carpet of savoury but fine tannins. Its overall balance is perfect. Just lovely. Screw cap. 14.5% alc. **Rating** 96 **To** 2033 $35 JH ✪

The Angelus McLaren Vale Cabernet Sauvignon 2018 Fresher, fleet of foot and more detailed than not too long ago. Kudos! A herbal and mineral confluence of sage, graphite and bay leaf laces the tannins, lithe, attenuated and refined. Tapenade and currant, too. The oak is impeccably integrated. Long and seamless. A refined classic, sacrificing neither richness nor the inimitable nori salinity that stamps its regional pedigree. Cellarworthy. Screw cap. 14% alc. **Rating** 96 **To** 2035 $70 NG ✪

Church Block McLaren Vale Cabernet Sauvignon Shiraz Merlot 2018 It is lightning fast out of the blocks, the colour bright, the bouquet flowery, the medium-bodied palate with a silky smooth mouthfeel. The fruit flavours are predominantly red cherry/berry-accented, the tannins sewn skilfully into the fabric of the wine. Screw cap. 14.5% alc. **Rating** 95 **To** 2029 $25 JH ✪

🍷🍷🍷🍷🍷 **Chook Block Shiraz 2018 Rating** 93 **To** 2033 $150 NG
The Absconder McLaren Vale Grenache 2019 Rating 93 **To** 2025 $70 NG
The Lost Watch Adelaide Hills Riesling 2020 Rating 92 **To** 2026 $25 TL✪
Hiding Champion Select Vineyards Adelaide Hills Sauvignon Blanc 2020 Rating 92 **To** 2023 $25 TL✪
Catapult Elevated Vineyards McLaren Vale Shiraz 2019 Rating 92 **To** 2027 $26 NG
RSW McLaren Vale Shiraz 2018 Rating 92 **To** 2032 $70 NG
Farmer's Heart McLaren Vale Grenache 2019 Rating 92 **To** 2025 $28 NG
The 12th Man Adelaide Hills Chardonnay 2020 Rating 91 **To** 2026 $35 NG

Wise Wine ★★★★★

237 Eagle Bay Road, Eagle Bay, WA 6281 **Region** Margaret River
T (08) 9750 3100 **www**.wisewine.com.au **Open** 7 days 11–5
Winemaker Andrew Siddell, Matt Buchan, Larry Cherubino (Consultant) **Est.** 1986
Dozens 10 000 **Vyds** 2.5ha

Wise Wine, headed by Perth entrepreneur Ron Wise, has been a remarkably consistent producer of high-quality wine. The vineyard adjacent to the winery (2ha of cabernet sauvignon and shiraz, and 0.5ha of zinfandel) in the Margaret River is supplemented by contract-grown grapes from Pemberton, Manjimup and Frankland River. The value for money of many of the wines is extraordinarily good. Exports to Switzerland, the Philippines and Singapore.

🍷🍷🍷🍷🍷 **Dr. RW Frankland River Cabernet Sauvignon 2018** Impenetrable midnight ink in the glass. The nose reveals a fortress of aromas; salted licorice, graphite, blood plum and raspberry. Mulberry, blackberry, exotic Asian spice and star anise all colour the edges. A laughably dense wine, built like a Barossa shiraz of old – muscular and ripped. Brawny and extracted, not delicate. This will live for decades with ease. A tour de force. Screw cap. 14.5% alc. **Rating** 96 **To** 2051 $125 EL

Eagle Bay Margaret River Cabernet Sauvignon 2018 This is unreal. Concentrated cassis, pomegranate and raspberry fruits are bolstered by licorice tannins and toasty exotic spices. Drink it tonight or decades from now – your call. We live in hallowed times as Margaret River '18s like this are finally released onto the market. Collect them voraciously. Screw cap. 14% alc. **Rating** 96 **To** 2056 $85 EL

Eagle Bay Margaret River Chardonnay 2019 Creamed macadamia is met with salty Pink Lady acidity and grilled white peach. This is all about purity and drive, wrapped in subtle, spicy toast. Concentrated, elegant and brilliant. Screw cap. 13.2% alc. **Rating** 95 **To** 2036 $75 EL

Margaret River Cabernet Sauvignon 2019 Earthy, brambly cassis and spicy oak rise up out of the glass. A layered, powerful and almost opulent palate, such is the cascade of flavours. Fine tannins hold it all in place. This is beautiful now, and will be in a decade or 2 as well. The cool '19 lives in the shadow of the ripe '18 vintage, but its inherent restraint and spiciness has produced wines of grace and elegance. Screw cap. 14.2% alc. **Rating** 95 **To** 2036 $45 EL

Leaf Series Margaret River Cabernet Sauvignon 2018 Excellent colour; a full-bodied cabernet with exemplary varietal expression from start to finish. Cassis, dried herbs, tapenade and savoury, ripe tannins rule the roost. Screw cap. 14.2% alc. **Rating** 95 **To** 2038 $45 JH

Leaf Series Porongurup Riesling 2020 Eminently pure, fermented in stainless steel and bottled early. This speaks wholeheartedly of the Porongurups; that is to say, jasmine florals, citrus pith, chalky phenolics and subtle, yet coiled acidity. Glorious. Screw cap. 12% alc. **Rating** 94 **To** 2036 $30 EL ✪

🍷🍷🍷🍷🍷 **Leaf Series Margaret River Fumé Blanc 2020 Rating** 90 **To** 2025 $35 EL
Frankland River Fiano 2020 Rating 90 **To** 2025 $35 EL

Witches Falls Winery ★★★★

79 Main Western Road, Tamborine Mountain, Qld 4272 **Region** Queensland
T (07) 5545 2609 **www**.witchesfalls.com.au **Open** Mon–Thurs 10–4, Fri–Sun 10–5
Winemaker Jon Heslop, Allan Windsor, Ren Dalgarno **Est.** 2004 **Dozens** 12000
Vyds 10.5ha
Witches Falls is the venture of Jon and Kim Heslop. Jon has a deep interest in experimenting with progressive vinification methods in order to achieve exceptional and interesting results. He has a degree in applied science (oenology) from CSU and experience working in the Barossa and Hunter valleys, as well as at Domaine Chantal Lescure in Burgundy and with a Napa-based winegrower. Witches Falls' grapes are sourced from the Granite Belt (in addition to its 0.4ha of estate pecorino and some fruit from SA). Exports to Singapore, Taiwan and China.

🍷🍷🍷🍷 **Prophecy Granite Belt Cabernet Sauvignon 2019** A solid and age-worthy Granite Belt cabernet. Accurate varietal hallmarks of blackcurrant, capsicum and cassis trace an accurate palate line. Barrel work is clunky and domineering, imposing charry personality and grainy tannins. Give it time to find its way through the forest. Screw cap. 14.2% alc. **Rating** 89 **To** 2034 $64 TS

Wolf Blass ★★★★★

97 Sturt Highway, Nuriootpa, SA 5355 **Region** Barossa Valley
T (08) 8568 7311 **www**.wolfblass.com **Open** 7 days 10–4.30
Winemaker Chris Hatcher, Steve Frost **Est.** 1966
The Wolf Blass wines are made at all price points, ranging through Red, Yellow, Gold, Brown, Grey, Black, White and Platinum labels covering every one of the main varietals. In 2016 a new range of wines labelled BLASS was introduced. The style and range of the wines continue to subtly evolve under the leadership of chief winemaker Chris Hatcher. Exports to all major markets.

ΨΨΨΨΨ **Platinum Label Medlands Vineyard Barossa Valley Shiraz 2016** This is the complete package, with a 10-gun salute to a more serious side of the Blass style. There's a wealth of black and blue fruits cradled in firm, fine-grained tannins and the usual healthy oak. Screw cap. 14.5% alc. **Rating** 96 **To** 2031 $200 JH
The Master Single Vineyard Greenock Barossa Valley Cabernet Shiraz 2018 Refreshingly, this leans more heavily on cabernet than traditional Blass blends, with a long post-ferment maceration building silkiness in its tannin profile. Supple, graceful and consummately polished, with an effortlessness that sets the pace for the modern Blass style. Confidently crafted tannins and grand persistence bode well for the future. Cork. 14% alc. **Rating** 96 **To** 2038 $350 TS

ΨΨΨΨΨ **Makers' Project Reserve McLaren Vale Grampians Shiraz 2019** **Rating** 92 **To** 2022 $26 NG
Maker's Project Malbec 2019 Rating 91 **To** 2027 $20 TS
Grey Label McLaren Vale Shiraz 2018 Rating 90 **To** 2030 $45 NG

Wood Park   ★★★★☆

263 Kneebones Gap Road, Markwood, Vic 3678 **Region** King Valley
T (03) 5727 3778 **www**.woodparkwines.com.au **Open** At Milawa Cheese Factory 7 days 10–5
Winemaker John Stokes **Est.** 1989 **Dozens** 7000 **Vyds** 16ha
John Stokes planted the first vines at Wood Park in 1989 as part of a diversification program for his property at Bobinawarrah, in the hills of the Lower King Valley, east of Milawa. The vineyard is managed with minimal chemical use and a mix of modern and traditional winemaking techniques are used (wild-yeast open fermentation and hand plunging). The reach of Wood Park has been expanded with Beechworth Pinot Noir and Chardonnay, the mix of mainstream and alternative varieties all well made.

ΨΨΨΨΨ **Reserve King Valley Cabernet Sauvignon 2018** A top vintage with small yields has the making of a wine of concentration and class. Already in harmony, deep in colour, with the inviting aroma of spice, dark chocolate, blackberries and sweet oak. Refined palate with smooth spice, savoury notes and firm, cabernet tannins. Wow! Screw cap. 13.8% alc. **Rating** 95 **To** 2030 $45 JP
Reserve King Valley Zinfandel 2018 Rich, lustrous red/garnet hues. A wine of substance but not heavy, maintaining a level-headed winemaking approach which is so often not the case with this variety. Also shows a more primitivo/wild-herbal savouriness than the smart-edged zin we sometimes see. Bramble berry, briar, wild berry, wood-smoke aromas entice. So smooth across the tongue, with truffle, earth and spice gaining traction. Impressive. Screw cap. 14.9% alc. **Rating** 95 **To** 2028 $45 JP

ΨΨΨΨΨ **Whitlands King Valley Pinot Noir 2018 Rating** 92 **To** 2025 $30 JP
Reserve King Valley Shiraz 2018 Rating 92 **To** 2028 $45 JP
Home Block Yarra Valley Roussanne 2019 Rating 90 **To** 2026 $28 JP
Whitlands King Valley Pinot Gris 2019 Rating 90 **To** 2026 $26 JP
King Valley Pinot Noir Rosé 2020 Rating 90 **To** 2024 $26 JP
Premium Reserve King Valley Shiraz Saperavi 2018 Rating 90 **To** 2030 $80 JP
The Tuscan King Valley 2018 Rating 90 **To** 2026 $29 JP
Forgotten Patch King Valley Sangiovese 2019 Rating 90 **To** 2026 $26 JP

Woodhaven Vineyard   ★★★☆

87 Main Creek Road, Red Hill, Vic 3937 **Region** Mornington Peninsula
T 0421 612 178 **www**.woodhavenvineyard.com.au **Open** By appt
Winemaker Lee Ward, Neil Ward **Est.** 2003 **Dozens** 250 **Vyds** 1.6ha
Woodhaven is the venture of Lee and Neil Ward, both qualified accountants for 30 years in Melbourne, albeit working in different industries. They spent 2 years looking for a suitable site on the Mornington Peninsula, ultimately finding one high on Red Hill. Bringing the

venture to the point of production has been a slow and, at times, frustrating business. They decided from the outset to be personally responsible for all aspects of growing the grapes and making the wines, relying on the advice readily given to them by George and Ruth Mihaly of Paradigm, David and (the late) Wendy Lloyd of Eldridge, John and Julie Trueman of Myrtaceae and Nat and Rose White, formerly of Main Ridge. They also decided to grow the vines organically and biodynamically; it took 8 years to produce their first 2 barrels of wine in 2010. In '13 the 0.8ha each of pinot noir and chardonnay finally produced more than one barrel of each wine.

♀♀♀♀ **Chardonnay 2019** Matured for 15 months in 66% new French oak barriques, with mlf. There's ripe stone fruit, beeswax and cinnamon flavours striding across the creamy and luscious palate, but the winemaking dominates. Screw cap. 13.5% alc. **Rating** 89 **To** 2022 $40 JF

Desailly Chardonnay 2018 Lee and Neil Ward like their chardonnays infused with lots of oak and flavour via mlf and lees stirring. If that's your style, knock yourself out. This is very rich and layered with vanillan oak and stone fruit with a hint of caramel. It does have good acidity cutting through the winemaking artefact and keeping everything in line. The fruit here is very good, and with less winemaking inputs, the wine would shine so much brighter. Screw cap. 13.5% alc. **Rating** 88 **To** 2025 $60 JF

Woodlands   ★★★★★

3948 Caves Road, Wilyabrup, WA 6284 **Region** Margaret River
T (08) 9755 6226 **www**.woodlandswines.com **Open** 7 days 10–5
Winemaker Stuart Watson **Est.** 1973 **Dozens** 16 000 **Vyds** 26.58ha
Founders David Watson and wife Heather had spectacular success with the cabernets he made in 1979 and the early '80s. Commuting from Perth on weekends and holidays, as well as raising a family, became all too much and for some years the grapes from Woodlands were sold to other Margaret River producers. With the advent of sons Stuart and Andrew (Stuart primarily responsible for winemaking), the estate has bounced back to pre-eminence. The wines come in 4 price bands, the bulk of the production under the Chardonnay and Cabernet Merlot varietals, then a series of Reserve and Special Reserves, then Reserve de la Cave and finally Cabernet Sauvignon. The top end wines primarily come from the original Woodlands Vineyard, where the vines are almost 50 years old. Exports to the UK, the US, Sweden, Denmark, Finland, South Korea, Mauritius, Indonesia, Malaysia, the Philippines, Singapore, Japan and China.

♀♀♀♀♀ **Chloe Anne Margaret River Cabernet Sauvignon 2017** As with all Woodlands cabernets, once you get past the oak, the fruit is of the highest pedigree; rippling with layers of complexity and nuance. Their potential for grace in the cellar is proven. Raspberry, pomegranate, bitter cocoa, aniseed, salted tomato, Dutch licorice, sage and exotic spice hide within the savoury folds of flavour that forms the backbone of this wine. The oak envelopes it all now, but will emboss into the fruit over time. Screw cap. 13.5% alc. **Rating** 96 **To** 2051 $189 EL

Emily Margaret River 2019 A cabernet franc-led Bordeaux blend, with merlot, malbec, cabernet sauvignon and petit verdot in support. A supple and chewy style that oozes restraint, pedigree and charm. Redcurrant, pink peppercorn, clove, star anise, fennel, red licorice, pomegranate and raspberry all mingle within the constraints of judiciously handled oak, laced up by saline acidity. The length is awesome, telling us we can either drink it now or cellar it with confidence. Screw cap. 13.5% alc. **Rating** 96 **To** 2041 $45 EL **✪**

Woodlands Brook Vineyard Margaret River Chardonnay 2020 Grilled yellow peach, red apple skins, hints of curry leaf, salt bush and crushed cashews. The palate is precisely as expected: concentrated and creamy, with layers of rich fruit flavours and secondary characters from the fermentation and oak. Complex and full bodied, a worthy sibling to the Chloe. Screw cap. 12.5% alc. **Rating** 95 **To** 2036 $45 EL

Wilyabrup Valley Margaret River Chardonnay 2020 This wine is routinely one of the great-value chardonnays from Margaret River. It exemplifies intensity of stone-fruit flavour, creamy crushed nuts on the palate and taut salty acidity. Through the lens of the warmer, lower-yielding but brilliant 2020 vintage, this is concentrated, punchy and, above all, very classy. Screw cap. 13% alc. **Rating** 94 To 2028 $28 EL **○**

ŸŸŸŸŸ **Margaret River Cabernet Franc Merlot 2018** Rating 92 To 2027 $28 EL

Woods Crampton   ★★★★★
P O Box 417, Hamilton, NSW 2303 **Region** Various
T 0417 670 655 **www.**woods-crampton.com.au
Winemaker Nicholas Crampton, Aaron Woods **Est.** 2010 **Dozens** 11 000
This is one of the most impressive ventures of Nicholas Crampton (his association with McWilliam's is on a consultancy basis) and winemaking friend Aaron Woods. The two make the wines at the Sons of Eden winery with advice from Igor Kucic. The quality of the wines and the enticing prices have seen production soar from 1500 to 11 000 dozen, with every expectation of continued success. Exports to the UK, Canada, Denmark, Switzerland, Russia, Singapore, Hong Kong, China and NZ. (NG)

ŸŸŸŸŸ **Michael John Centenarian Vines Single Vineyard Barossa Valley Shiraz 2018** A self-professed 'herculean' wine in an overweight bottle. Medium purple hue. A compact and focused core of satsuma plum, blackberry/cherry fruit is accented with licorice and spice. French oak masterfully elevates structure and persistence without interrupting impressive fruit flow. Grand potential. One bottle was cork scalped. Reliable closures please. Cork. 14.5% alc. **Rating** 95 To 2038 $125 TS
Frances & Nicole Old Vine Single Vineyard Eden Valley Shiraz 2018 Full purple red. Impressively coiled and crafted. Quintessential Eden Valley old-vine shiraz, brimming with deep black/blueberry fruit and lifted fragrant spice, amplified by whole-bunch fermentation. Fine tannins have been well polished, uniting with natural acidity to draw out a long finish. Give it time. Screw cap. 14.5% alc. **Rating** 94 To 2033 $60 TS
Phillip Patrick Old Vines Single Vineyard Eden Valley Shiraz 2018 Medium purple hue. Glossy blackberry/cherry and blueberry proclaim classy, signature Eden Valley character. Grand fruit integrity takes a confident lead before the spicy lift of whole-bunch fermentation and the fine scaffolding of new French oak. Compact and coiled, this is a vintage for the cellar. One bottle was cork scalped. Cork. 14.5% alc. **Rating** 94 To 2038 $125 TS

Woodstock   ★★★★☆
215 Douglas Gully Road, McLaren Flat, SA 5171 **Region** McLaren Vale
T (08) 8383 0156 **www.**woodstockwine.com.au **Open** 7 days 10–5
Winemaker Ben Glaetzer **Est.** 1905 **Dozens** 22 000 **Vyds** 18.44ha
The Collett family is among the best known in McLaren Vale, the late Doug Collett AM was known for his World War II exploits flying Spitfires and Hurricanes with the RAF and RAAF, returning to study oenology at Roseworthy Agricultural College and rapidly promoted to take charge of SA's largest winery, Berri Co-operative. In 1973 he purchased the Woodstock estate, built a winery and in '74 he crushed its first vintage. Son Scott Collett, once noted for his fearless exploits in cars and on motorcycles, became winemaker in '82 and has won numerous accolades; equally importantly, he purchased an adjoining shiraz vineyard planted circa 1900 (now the source of The Stocks Shiraz) and a bushvine grenache vineyard planted in '30. In '99 he joined forces with Ben Glaetzer, passing responsibility for winemaking to Ben, but retaining responsibility for the estate vineyards. Exports to most major markets.

ŸŸŸŸŸ **Scott Collett McLaren Vale Shiraz Cabernet Sauvignon 2016** A massive wine that could come from almost anywhere. Dark-fruit allusions, crushed rock, garden herb, kirsch and smattered spice, curbed by a phalanx of Ovaltine malty oak. All impeccably integrated to the point where the wine could be called 'smooth'. The alcohol, sublimated by the morass until the second glass. Then, comes the heat. A very well-made wine firmly stamped by maker. Cork. 15.5% alc. **Rating** 94 **To** 2030 $180 NG

🍷🍷🍷🍷♀ The Stocks Single Vineyard McLaren Vale Shiraz 2018 **Rating** 92 **To** 2033 $95 NG
Naughty Monte Montepulciano 2017 **Rating** 92 **To** 2023 $30 NG
McLaren Vale Shiraz 2016 **Rating** 91 **To** 2024 $26 NG
McLaren Vale Very Old Fortified NV **Rating** 90 $48 NG

Woodvale   ★★★★☆

PO Box 54, Watervale, SA 5453 **Region** Clare Valley
T 0417 829 204 **www.**woodvalevintners.com.au
Winemaker Kevin Mitchell **Est.** 2014 **Dozens** 3000 **Vyds** 7ha
This is the personal venture of Kevin Mitchell and wife Kathleen Bourne, not an offshoot of Kilikanoon (see separate entry). The main targets are what Kevin describes as 'modest, sustainable growth, working with the varieties that Clare does so well: riesling, shiraz, cabernet sauvignon, mataro, semillon, pinot gris, and of course, grenache'. Given he is a 3rd-generation Clare Valley grapegrower, procuring grapes from mates to supplement the estate shiraz, pinot gris and riesling should not be a problem.

🍷🍷🍷🍷🍷 Watervale Riesling 2020 This falls into place very quickly, offering pure Watervale charm. The lemons and limes, the light dusting of spice and herbs and the neat line of acidity take it to a long finish. Screw cap. 12% alc. **Rating** 95 **To** 2028 $25 JF ✪

🍷🍷🍷🍷♀ Skilly Clare Valley Riesling 2020 **Rating** 93 **To** 2027 $25 JF ✪
Spring Gardens Clare Valley Shiraz 2018 **Rating** 92 **To** 2030 JF

Woody Nook   ★★★★

506 Metricup Road, Wilyabrup, WA 6280 **Region** Margaret River
T (08) 9755 7547 **www.**woodynook.com.au **Open** 7 days 10–4.30
Winemaker Digby Leddin, Courtney Dunkerton **Est.** 1982 **Dozens** 8000 **Vyds** 14.23ha
Woody Nook, with a backdrop of 18ha of majestic marri and jarrah forest, doesn't have the high profile of the biggest names in Margaret River but it has had major success in wine shows over the years. It was founded by Jeff and Wynn Gallagher in 1978 and purchased by Peter and Jane Bailey in 2000, with Jeff and Wynn's son Neil involved in the vineyards and winery until very recently. Major renovations by the Bailey family transformed Woody Nook with a new winery, a gallery tasting room for larger groups and an alfresco dining area by the pond. Exports to the UK, China, Singapore and Malaysia.

🍷🍷🍷🍷🍷 Gallagher's Choice Margaret River Cabernet Sauvignon 2017 This is rich (almost opulent?) and chocolatey rather than purely driven by cassis. The oak has been largely absorbed by the fruit; what remains through the finish will no doubt be mopped up in time as well. Bitter cocoa, star anise, mulberry, resinous oak, exotic spice and very little hint of the cool year that birthed it. Powerfully structured and with unfurling length. A wine for the cellar. Screw cap. 14.5% alc. **Rating** 94 **To** 2036 $65 EL

🍷🍷🍷🍷♀ Limited Release Margaret River Fumé Blanc 2020 **Rating** 91 **To** 2028 $28 EL

Word of Mouth Wines   ★★★★☆

42 Wallace Lane, Orange, NSW 2800 **Region** Orange
T 0429 533 316 **www.**wordofmouthwines.com.au **Open** Fri–Sun 10.30–5 and by appt
Winemaker David Lowe, Paul Martung, Will Rikard-Bell **Est.** 1998 **Dozens** 1500 **Vyds** 3ha

Peter Gibson, formerly a teacher of fine art, has been the one constant figure in Word of Mouth, his involvement dating back to 1999 when he established Pinnacle Wines with an early planting of pinot gris. Word of Mouth was formed when Pinnacle amalgamated with neighbouring Donnington Vineyard. In 2013 the Donnington parcel was sold and has since become Colmar Estate. Peter retained his original block and continues under the Word of Mouth label, with pinot gris, petit manseng, grüner veltliner, mencia, albariño, riesling, chardonnay and pinot noir planted. The cellar door is attached to a working pottery studio.

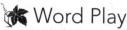 # Word Play ★★★★

41 Jenke Road, Marananga, SA 5355 **Region** Barossa Valley
T 0499 618 260 **www**.wordplaywines.com.au **Open** By appt
Winemaker Fiona Donald, Matthew Pick **Est.** 2015 **Dozens** 350 **Vyds** 6ha
Wordplay Wines is the side project of Seppeltsfield winemakers Matthew Pick and Fiona Donald. Their compact range consists of just 1500 bottles each of Shiraz and Cabernet Sauvignon from their 4ha Jenke Road Block vineyard planted in 1999 in Marananga, and 1100 bottles of Yarra Valley Pinot Noir. This little operation is quite a contrast to their day jobs, where they have enjoyed long and varied careers making wines for larger brands including Hardys, Barossa Valley Estate, Penfolds, Chateau Reynella, Leasingham, Leo Buring and Yalumba. First released in 2018, their reds are generous, characterful and age-worthy. (TS)

🍷🍷🍷🍷🍷 **An Anagram Barossa Valley Shiraz 2017** When played right, the cool 2017 season proved to be a blessing, particular in the Barossa's most generous districts. Crunchy blackberry, blueberry, black plum and licorice fruit receives good backing from French oak's dark chocolate and coffee notes, building a fine splay of confident tannins and drawing out a long finish. One for the cellar. Screw cap. 14.8% alc. **Rating** 93 **To** 2037 $90 TS
41 Across Barossa Valley Cabernet Sauvignon 2017 A generous and characterful take on Barossa cabernet. The cool 2017 season coaxes out a panoply of varietal distinction in crunchy redcurrants, roast capsicum, bay leaf and cedar. It culminates in the ripeness and density of cassis. Furry tannins are a little lacking in polish, but will come together in sufficient time. It holds the line, length and integrity to go the distance. Screw cap. 14.6% alc. **Rating** 93 **To** 2037 $75 TS

 # Worlds Apart ★★★☆

Hellbound, 201 Rundle Street, Adelaide, SA 5000 **Region** Adelaide Hills
T 0422 454 665 **www**.worldsapartwines.com **Open** Wed–Sun 4–12
Winemaker Louis Schofield **Est.** 2017 **Dozens** 1600
Worlds Apart is Louis Schofield, former sommelier, wine rep, fine-wine retailer, current assistant winemaker at Ochota Barrels and part-owner of Adelaide wine bar Hellbound; along with partner Hannah Jeffery, a chef with experience in several Adelaide restaurants. They call the Adelaide Hills home, but take fruit from exceptional vineyards in Eden Valley and McLaren Vale as well. Drawing equal influence from their peers in natural wine and the fine wines of the world, the style is fresh, low-alcohol wines with an underlying seriousness. Their venture was established in 2017 and by 2020 they were producing 400 dozen. There is no cellar door, but wines can be tasted at Hellbound, address and opening hours above. Exports to Malaysia, Singapore and the UK. (TL)

🍷🍷🍷🍷🍷 **In the Flowers Eden Valley Riesling 2020** Barrel-fermented riesling, floral and grapey, lovely fresh-cut green-apple bite with the faintest of spiced sugars on the finish. Tasty and moreish. Screw cap. 12.4% alc. **Rating** 92 **To** 2023 $33 TL

Wren Estate ★★★★★

389 Heathcote-Rochester Road, Mt Camel, Vic 3523 **Region** Heathcote
T (03) 9972 9638 **www**.wrenestate.com.au **Open** W'ends & public hols 10–5
Winemaker Michael Wren **Est.** 2017 **Dozens** 10000 **Vyds** 14.5ha

Michael Wren, winemaker and owner of Wren Estate, has been making wine for over 15 years across multiple continents. For 10 years he was a Flying Winemaker for one of Portugal's top wineries, Esporao, and was particularly struck by the use of lagares for top-quality wines. Lagares are low, wide, open red-wine fermenters that allow foot treading (or stomping) with the level of must little more than knee deep. The consequence is the very soft, yet high, extraction of colour, flavour and soft tannins. The red wine fermenters in the Wren winery are replicas of the traditional lagares. The vineyard (of 14.5ha) sits in a 52ha property and was planted in 2002, the shiraz with 16 different clone and rootstock combinations, giving Michael priceless information on the vagaries of the site. Each block is picked, fermented and aged separately, the best in a limited release single block series. All the premium wines are individually barrel selected. Exports to the US and China.

ꭚꭚꭚꭚꭚ **MXW Heathcote Shiraz 2018** This asks a lot of the drinker, like 'try not opening the bottle for another 10 years at least'. Built to last, MXW presents a dense, rich Heathcote shiraz with a nod to the Old World – fermentation in a bees wax-lined lagar – and an eye on presenting an age-worthy shiraz with a modern New World oak sheen. Oozes class with savoury tannins running firm from edge to edge. Cork. 14.9% alc. **Rating** 95 **To** 2036 $225 JP
Heathcote Marsanne 2019 The alcohol gives you a clue to style here, early picked and delicate. It displays the variety's pretty honeysuckle and jasmine florals, in tandem with its citrus, acacia and lemon balm herbals. The palate is fresh and alive, with emerging texture and a wealth of citrus/pear/honeysuckle/spice flavour. A wine to watch. Screw cap. 12.9% alc. **Rating** 94 **To** 2029 $25 JP ✪

ꭚꭚꭚꭚꭚ **Block 5 Heathcote Shiraz 2018 Rating** 93 **To** 2036 $159 JP

Wynns Coonawarra Estate ★★★★★

Memorial Drive, Coonawarra, SA 5263 **Region** Coonawarra
T (08) 8736 2225 **www**.wynns.com.au **Open** 7 days 10–5
Winemaker Sue Hodder, Sarah Pidgeon **Est.** 1897
Large-scale production has not prevented Wynns (an important part of TWE) from producing excellent wines covering the full price spectrum from the bargain-basement Riesling and Shiraz through to the deluxe John Riddoch Cabernet Sauvignon and Michael Shiraz. Even with steady price increases, Wynns offers extraordinary value for money. Investments in rejuvenating and replanting key blocks, under the direction of Allen Jenkins and skilled winemaking by Sue Hodder, have resulted in wines of far greater finesse and elegance than many of their predecessors. Exports to the UK, the US, Canada and Asia.

ꭚꭚꭚꭚꭚ **Johnsons Single Vineyard Cabernet Sauvignon 2019** There's an opulence to the 2018 vintage reds and yet Wynns always manages to coat the wines with a layer of elegance. It helps to have access to the oldest cabernet vines in Coonawarra, Johnson's Block planted in 1954. This is only the 2nd release as a single-vineyard wine. It's all about precision, from a core of ripe fruit, its length to beautifully shaped silk-coated tannins. Screw cap. 13.3% alc. **Rating** 97 **To** 2032 $90 JF ✪
Black Label Cabernet Sauvignon 2019 The 64th vintage. A wine of provenance. A wine of excellence. It ages superbly, yet is flattering when young. Perfect fruit at its core, with gentle flavours of cassis, blackberries and blueberries. It has depth, length and line, thanks to the fine, detailed tannins. Classy cabernet. This is up there as one of the finest to date. Bravo. Cork. 13.8% alc. **Rating** 97 **To** 2043 $45 JF ✪
Harold Single Vineyard Cabernet Sauvignon 2018 In a way, this captures the very essence of Coonawarra cabernet. It has all the heady aromas and flavours from blackberries/currants, black olives to dried herbs, pulled together by a sheath of tannins. And yet, it is distinctly Wynns – or rather, Harold. It has elegance. The oak is completely absorbed into the wine and those tannins are so finely plied. A bit like a Stradivarius violin – this is finely tuned and polished. It is the pick of the 2018 cabernets. Screw cap. 13.4% alc. **Rating** 97 **To** 2038 $80 JF ✪

John Riddoch Limited Release Cabernet Sauvignon 2018 Tasting young John Riddoch simply throws a spotlight on its quality as the cornerstone, because this wine evolves into something special with age. It's a majestic wine. Full bodied and deep, with an abundance of tannins, but all in place, with a brightness to the acidity. There's nothing harsh here. Earthy flavours, cedary oak and excellent fruit make it a bit of a tease: it is rather easy to open a bottle to enjoy now, yet its best years are ahead of it. Screw cap. 14% alc. **Rating** 97 **To** 2045 $150 JF ✪ ♥

🍷🍷🍷🍷🍷 **Michael Limited Release Shiraz 2018** The star of the shiraz line-up at Wynns. An impressive wine built for longevity as much as sheer enjoyment. There's a certain refinement to this vintage, echoed in this wine. Florals, cherries dusted with pepper, cinnamon and crushed herbs. Full bodied yet buffered by finely chiselled tannins and pulsing acidity. Exceptional balance. Screw cap. 14% alc. **Rating** 96 **To** 2038 $150 JF

V&A Lane Shiraz 2019 V&A Lane shiraz seems to be on cruise control these days. It doesn't need to overtake or slow down, even if the handbrake has been hit on the very modest alcohol. This a wine of finesse. Certainly flavoursome, with its puff of perfume and spicy red and black plums infused with Pontefrac licorice. It's lighter framed in a Coonawarra context, but it has shape. A very good V&A Lane Shiraz. Screw cap. 12.3% alc. **Rating** 95 **To** 2033 $60 JF

Old Vines Shiraz 2019 This has slipped comfortably into a seamless wine. Supple, ripe fruit, lightly spiced with cedar, licorice root and cinnamon. The palate is fuller bodied but so restrained. The tannins are absurdly fine, with length like no tomorrow. Screw cap. 13.4% alc. **Rating** 95 **To** 2034 $45 JF

V&A Lane Cabernet Shiraz 2019 Taking inspiration from the lighter clarets made in the 1950s and '60s, this modern version's beat is all savoury, with juniper, licorice root and fennel. It's medium bodied (just) and the tannins are gossamer-fine, yet spun together to a gentle hold. Compelling wine. Screw cap. 12.4% alc. **Rating** 95 **To** 2035 $60 JF

Black Label Shiraz 2018 Good colour; a very expressive bouquet, with interlocking red and black fruit and cedary oak, the palate bringing ripe tannins into play. All the components are here, but are yet to join each other. Screw cap. 13.8% alc. **Rating** 94 **To** 2038 $45 JH

🍷🍷🍷🍷🍷 **Cabernet Rosé 2020 Rating** 93 **To** 2023 $25 JF ✪
Shiraz 2018 Rating 93 **To** 2026 $25 JF ✪
Riesling 2020 Rating 92 **To** 2026 $25 JF ✪
Cabernet Shiraz Merlot 2018 Rating 91 **To** 2027 $25 JF

Xabregas
★★★★☆

Spencer Road, Mount Barker, WA 6324 **Region** Mount Barker
T (08) 9200 2267 **www.**xabregas.com.au
Winemaker Luke Eckersley **Est.** 1996 **Dozens** 16 000 **Vyds** 80ha
The Hogan family have 5 generations of WA history and family interests in sheep grazing and forestry in the Great Southern, dating back to the 1860s. Terry Hogan AM (1939–2018), founding Xabregas chairman, felt the Mount Barker region was 'far too good a dirt to waste on blue gums', and vines were planted in 1996. The Hogan family concentrates on the region's strengths – shiraz and riesling. Exports to China.

Xanadu Wines
★★★★★

316 Boodjidup Road, Margaret River, WA 6285 **Region** Margaret River
T (08) 9758 9500 **www.**xanaduwines.com **Open** 7 days 10–5
Winemaker Glenn Goodall, Brendan Carr, Steve Kyme, Darren Rathbone **Est.** 1977
Dozens 45 000 **Vyds** 82.8ha
Xanadu Wines was established in 1977 by Dr John Lagan. In 2005 it was purchased by the Rathbone family and together with Glenn Goodall's winemaking team they have significantly improved the quality of the wines. The vineyard has been revamped via soil profiling, improved drainage, precision viticulture and reduced yields. The quality of the

wines made since the acquisition of the Stevens Road Vineyard in '08 has been consistently outstanding. Exports to most major markets.

🍷🍷🍷🍷🍷 **Reserve Margaret River Cabernet Sauvignon 2018** It should be said from the outset – this is quite likely the best wine, white or red, ever made at Xanadu. The intersection between a perfect vintage, pedigree fruit and sensitive winemaking look just like this: cassis, blackberry pastille, marri blossom, raspberry, pomegranate, black pepper and star anise. Hints of fennel flower and salty licorice are the lingering impressions. What a wine. Screw cap. 14% alc. **Rating** 98 **To** 2051 $110 EL ✪

Reserve Margaret River Chardonnay 2019 As ever, sophisticated, lithe, glassy and svelte. Through the lens of the cool 2019 vintage, this wine has a scintillating energy, the acid jolts a burst onto the tongue, stinging it into life. The length of flavour goes on and on. Xanadu chardonnays have a proven track record of graceful ageing in the cellar, often not truly coming into their own until 3+ years after release. Pedigree, in a word. Screw cap. 13% alc. **Rating** 97 **To** 2041 $110 EL ✪

Stevens Road Margaret River Chardonnay 2019 This 2019 Stevens Road provided a moment of unadulterated joy when I drank it on Christmas Day. The salty acid and taut citrus fruit cut through the conversation and the heat of the day, injecting pleasure and calm. This is svelte, with salty limes. Briny and delicious. Buy both the 2019 Reserve and Stevens Road chardonnays: cellar the Reserve, drink this. Screw cap. 13% alc. **Rating** 97 **To** 2036 $80 EL ✪

Stevens Road Margaret River Cabernet Sauvignon 2018 Dutch licorice on the nose and shining on the palate. The tannins really steal the attention from the pristine fruit. Such finely knit tannins, cleverly inlaid into the fruit without being hidden, are one of the standouts of this beautiful wine. They shape and structure the pure cassis fruit, ushering it through to a long and lingering finish. Screw cap. 14% alc. **Rating** 97 **To** 2051 $80 EL ✪

🍷🍷🍷🍷🍷 **Margaret River Cabernet Sauvignon 2019** Scintillatingly pure and taut, this is elegant, supple cabernet at its finest. Garden mint and purple fruit dominates; the length of flavour an enduring ripple on a still lake. Brilliant stuff, even more so given the price and its ability to age gracefully. Screw cap. 14% alc. **Rating** 96 **To** 2035 $40 EL ✪

DJL Margaret River Sauvignon Blanc Semillon 2020 A very classy wine, especially at this price: clean and layered, with crystalline purity and good length of flavour. Some barrel influence enhances the beauty of the fruit, lending elegance to the passionfruit, snow pea and Geraldton wax. The texture is a highlight – slippery and fine. Screw cap. 12.5% alc. **Rating** 94 **To** 2027 $26 EL ✪

Margaret River Chardonnay 2019 Nashi pear, white peach and briny acid form the core of this wine, but they are joined by crushed salted cashews and red apple skins. Demands decanting to soften the edges, if drinking in its youth – this label really kicks into gear about 2 years after release (if you have any left). Screw cap. 13% alc. **Rating** 94 **To** 2030 $40 EL

DJL Margaret River Shiraz 2019 This is pristine; crunchy, juicy and pure, with layers of cassis, blueberry, mulberry, red licorice and raspberry. There's a supple bounce on the palate that might lend it to a slight chill in warmer weather. A delight for the price. Screw cap. 14% alc. **Rating** 94 **To** 2026 $26 EL ✪

Exmoor Margaret River Shiraz 2018 With 0.5% viognier. All cool-area fruit (Wallcliffe and Karridale), matured 14 months in French oak (25% new). Pure, slippery, juicy, bouncy, delicious shiraz. What more could you possibly want for $20? This has structure, length, line and succulent fruit. The oak is countersunk into the salty, juicy fruit. Cracking little wine. Screw cap. 14.5% alc. **Rating** 94 **To** 2027 $20 EL ✪

DJL Margaret River Cabernet Sauvignon 2019 Super-pretty raspberry, raspberry lolly and red licorice aromas give an indication of what to expect … the palate does not disappoint. Supple, verging on slinky; fine tannins provide seamless structure and shape. Modern, lithe and darn delicious. Screw cap. 14% alc. **Rating** 94 **To** 2028 $26 EL ✪

ᵐᵐᵐᵐᵐ Exmoor Margaret River Chardonnay 2020 Rating 93 To 2027 $20 EL ○
DJL Margaret River Chardonnay 2020 Rating 93 To 2028 $26 EL ○
DJL Margaret River Shiraz Graciano Rosé 2020 Rating 93 To 2022
$26 EL ○
DJL Margaret River Malbec 2019 Rating 93 To 2031 $26 EL ○
Exmoor Margaret River Sauvignon Blanc Semillon 2020 Rating 92
To 2023 $20 EL ○
Exmoor Margaret River Cabernet Sauvignon 2019 Rating 91 To 2028
$20 EL ○
Exmoor Margaret River Rosé 2020 Rating 90 To 2022 $20 EL ○

XO Wine Co   ★★★★☆

13 Wicks Road, Kuitpo, SA 5172 **Region** Adelaide Hills
T 0402 120 680 **www.**xowineco.com.au
Winemaker Greg Clack, Kate Horstmann **Est.** 2015 **Dozens** 1800
Greg Clack spent 11 years in McLaren Vale with Haselgrove Wines. In 2014 he took himself
to the Adelaide Hills as chief winemaker at Chain of Ponds – this remains his day job, nights
and days here and there devoted to XO. Its raison d'être revolves around small-batch, single-
vineyard wines chiefly made from grenache, barbera, chardonnay and gamay. The winemaking
minimises wine movements, protecting freshness.

ᵐᵐᵐᵐᵐ Single Vineyard Small Batch Adelaide Hills Barbera 2020 From the
Kuitpo district, 10% whole bunch, wild ferment, matured on lees and stirred in
older French barrels. Total purity in the nose – cherry with thyme, sweetly lifted
on the palate, while kept tight underneath with neatly integrated and sympathetic
tannins. Delicious all the way. Screw cap. 14% alc. Rating 95 To 2026 $32 TL ○
Single Vineyard Small Batch Adelaide Hills Pinot Noir 2020 Plenty of
small-batch winemaking, including a good portion of carbonic maceration, which
shows in the aromatic feel: juicy, plump, with an orange skin/aperol note. A small
amount of new oak adds some woody herb and forest sensibilities to the palate.
Peppery spice adds some tension. Has plenty to admire. Screw cap. 13.5% alc.
Rating 94 To 2026 $32 TL
Single Vineyard Games Night McLaren Vale Grenache Shiraz 2019
Sourced from a vineyard just southwest of the Willunga township, a small
percentage of whole bunch in both varieties, the shiraz seeing one new oak
barrel during maturation. And it's that cedary oak note that really lifts this wine
to start, crimson cherry juices as well. Everything works nicely together here, the
palate with lovely easy grip and deliciously upbeat. Lovely. Screw cap. 14.5% alc.
Rating 94 To 2025 $27 TL ○

ᵐᵐᵐᵐᵐ Single Vineyard Small Batch Adelaide Hills Chardonnay 2019 Rating 92
To 2025 $32 TL
Games Night Adelaide Grenache Barbera Rosé 2020 Rating 92 To 2023
$24 TL ○

Yabby Lake Vineyard   ★★★★★

86–112 Tuerong Road, Tuerong, Vic 3937 **Region** Mornington Peninsula
T (03) 5974 3729 **www.**yabbylake.com **Open** 7 days 10–5
Winemaker Tom Carson, Chris Forge, Luke Lomax **Est.** 1998 **Dozens** 3350 **Vyds** 50ha
This high-profile wine business was established in 1998 by Robert and Mem Kirby (of
Village Roadshow), who had been landowners in the Mornington Peninsula for decades. The
vineyard enjoys a north-facing slope, capturing maximum sunshine while also receiving sea
breezes. In the midst of conversion to organic viticulture, the main focus is on 25ha of pinot
noir, 14ha of chardonnay and 8ha of pinot gris; 3ha of shiraz, merlot and sauvignon blanc take
a back seat. The arrival of the hugely talented Tom Carson as group winemaker in 2008 added
lustre to the winery and its wines, making the first Jimmy Watson Trophy–winning pinot noir
in 2014 and continuing to blitz the Australian wine show circuit with single-block pinot noirs.
Exports to the UK, Canada, Sweden, Hong Kong and China.

🍷🍷🍷🍷🍷 Single Vineyard Mornington Peninsula Syrah 2019 Aside from the striking deep garnet hue that immediately beckons, this starts out a bit shy. Let it be. Let it breathe. It will then unfurl to reveal a savoury, refined wine. Dark fruit, a dusting of pepper and licorice, mocha, warm earth and Aussie bush aromas. It works off a medium-bodied palate with the most exquisite tannins. Top of the class. Screw cap. 14% alc. **Rating** 96 **To** 2032 $36 JF ✪

Red Claw Mornington Peninsula Pinot Noir 2019 Hand picked and sorted, open-fermented with 25% whole bunches, matured in used French puncheons. Bright crimson-purple; the fragrant bouquet weaves a tapestry of red berry blossom, with a darker note picked up on the complex palate and its long finish. Screw cap. 14% alc. **Rating** 95 **To** 2029 $30 JH ✪

Single Vineyard Mornington Peninsula Pinot Noir 2019 There's a richness and ripeness of flavour perfectly reflecting the warmer vintage, without going over the top. Fragrant and floral, dark cherries spiced to the max, dabs of licorice, herbs and a smidge of wood char, with the oak neatly tucked in. Tannins have some emery board grip and the acidity is bright enough that you can enjoy it now or hold for a while. Screw cap. 13.5% alc. **Rating** 95 **To** 2030 $64 JF

🍷🍷🍷🍷🍸 Late Disgorged Single Vineyard Mornington Peninsula Cuvée Nina 2010 **Rating** 93 $100 JF

Single Vineyard Mornington Peninsula Chardonnay 2019 **Rating** 92 **To** 2029 $45 JF

Red Claw Mornington Peninsula Chardonnay 2019 **Rating** 90 **To** 2025 $28 JF

Yal Yal Estate   ★★★★

15 Wynnstay Road, Prahran, Vic 3181 (postal) **Region** Mornington Peninsula
T 0416 112 703 **www**.yalyal.com.au
Winemaker Rollo Crittenden **Est.** 1997 **Dozens** 2500 **Vyds** 7ha
In 2008 Liz and Simon Gillies acquired a vineyard in Merricks, planted in 1997 to 1.6ha of chardonnay and a little over 1ha of pinot noir. It has since been expanded to 7ha, half devoted to chardonnay, half to pinot noir.

🍷🍷🍷🍷🍸 Yal Yal Rd Mornington Peninsula Pinot Noir 2019 Vibrant and vivacious. It's a good combo. But there's more: red cherries and tangy, barely ripe raspberries, yet savoury through and through. Medium bodied, blessed with raw silk tannins and crunchy acidity. All in all, refreshment in a glass. Screw cap. 13.5% alc. **Rating** 93 **To** 2028 $32 JF

Winifred Mornington Peninsula Pinot Noir 2019 Gee these wines are well pitched and placed. They are made respectfully, with no overt winemaking inputs. Everything is in its place. Cherries, blood orange and zest, woodsy spices and light sandpaper tannins sashaying across the full-bodied palate. Screw cap. 13.5% alc. **Rating** 93 **To** 2029 $45 JF

Edith Mornington Peninsula Chardonnay 2019 While this isn't overly complex, it is thoroughly appealing and balanced. Everything is just so, from the stone fruit and citrus nuances to its texture. Oak is integrated, adding palate plushness as much as flavour, with a hint of vanilla and woodsy spices. Screw cap. 13.5% alc. **Rating** 92 **To** 2027 $45 JF

Yal Yal Rd Mornington Peninsula Rosé 2019 Entices from the moment this is poured, starting with its pastel pink/copper hue. Lightly aromatic. The palate offering both texture (thanks to barrel fermentation and ageing in used French oak) and pleasure, as it complements the spiced red fruits and ginger cream flavours. Screw cap. 13.5% alc. **Rating** 91 **To** 2022 $23 JF ✪

🍷🍷🍷🍷 Yal Yal Rd Mornington Peninsula Chardonnay 2019 **Rating** 88 **To** 2026 $30 JF

Yalumba ★★★★★

40 Eden Valley Road, Angaston, SA 5353 **Region** Eden Valley
T (08) 8561 3200 **www.**yalumba.com **Open** 7 days 10–5
Winemaker Louisa Rose (chief), Kevin Glastonbury, Natalie Cleghorn, Sam Wigan,
Heather Fraser, Will John, Teresa Heuzenroeder **Est.** 1849 **Dozens** 930 000 **Vyds** 180ha
Owned and run by the Hill-Smith family, Yalumba has a long commitment to quality and
great vision in its selection of vineyard sites, new varieties and brands. It has always been a
serious player at the top end of full-bodied Australian reds and was a pioneer in the use of
screw caps. It has a proud history of lateral thinking and rapid decision-making by a small
group led by Robert Hill-Smith. The synergy of the range of brands, varieties and prices is
obvious, but it received added lustre with the creation of The Caley. A founding member of
Australia's First Families of Wine. Exports to all major markets.

ΤΤΤΤΤ **The Caley Coonawarra Barossa Cabernet Shiraz 2016** Yalumba began
blending Coonawarra cabernet with Barossa shiraz more than a half century ago.
This is one of the greatest expressions of this great Australian blend of recent
decades. Perfect, compact, fragrant blackcurrant and blackberry fruit depth pauses
time as it hovers motionless for minutes, propelled by the most intricate, chalk
mineral framework of perfectly interlocked fruit and French oak tannins. A vintage
to hark back to for another half century yet. Cork. 14% alc. **Rating** 99 **To** 2066
$365 TS ♥

Carriage Block Dry Grown Barossa Valley Grenache 2017 The ruby
colour is just gaining a little dark brick red around the rims, and the red fruits that
cover the rainbow of cherry to raspberry notes are just showing the introduction
of delicate and delicious sourness. Adults-only palate complexity. There's a clarity
and directness to the palate, pure grenache juiciness and a tender touch of tannin
to finish. The whole picture of this wine is bright and beautiful. Cork. 13.5% alc.
Rating 97 **To** 2027 $50 TL ✪

ΤΤΤΤΤ **Vine Vale Barossa Valley Grenache 2019** The medium-bodied, red-fruited
persona of Barossa grenache is compelling, all the more so when lifted by the
fragrance and exotic spice of whole-bunch fermentation. With the full, glorious
detail accurately preserved under screw cap, this is a joyous celebration of dark
raspberries, wild strawberries, rosehip and incense. Super-fine tannins are perfectly
matched to its fragrant mood. Benchmark. Screw cap. 14% alc. **Rating** 96 **To** 2029
$40 TS ✪

The Signature Barossa Cabernet Sauvignon Shiraz 2017 Embracing
Yalumba's deep reach in to the great sites of the Barossa, this cool vintage was
sourced entirely from the Valley floor. Compact, concentrated and exact, cabernet's
varietal integrity takes a bright, fragrant, compelling lead. Impressive black-fruit
depth is backed by a splay of superfine, enduring tannins. Testimony to the
blending wizardry of Yalumba, this is one of the wines of the vintage and one of
the greats of the hallowed Signature lineage. Cork. 14.5% alc. **Rating** 96 **To** 2052
$65 TS ✪

The Cigar Coonawarra Cabernet Sauvignon 2018 A terrific vintage for
the great Menzies vineyard. Textbook, crunchy blackcurrants and blackberries are
wrapped in cedary, fine-boned French oak, nuanced with roast coffee bean and
high-cocoa dark chocolate. Firm, fine-grained tannins unite with vibrant acidity
on a finish of fantastic energy and endurance. Now under screw cap, every detail is
upheld. Screw cap. 14% alc. **Rating** 94 **To** 2043 $35 TS

FSW Wrattonbully Botrytis Viognier 2020 Viognier's unctuous glacé apricot
finds an enticing place between the honey and exotic spice of botrytis. Carefully
handled fermentation makes for a pristine style of impressive line and length. 2020
furnished the acidity to uphold freshness and poise. One of the greatest under this
label yet. Screw cap. 10.5% alc. **Rating** 94 **To** 2030 $30 TS ✪

ΤΤΤΤΤ **Ringbolt Margaret River Cabernet Sauvignon 2019 Rating** 90 **To** 2027
$28 EL

Yangarra Estate Vineyard ★★★★★

809 McLaren Flat Road, Kangarilla SA 5171 **Region** McLaren Vale
T (08) 8383 7459 **www**.yangarra.com.au **Open** Mon–Sat 11–5
Winemaker Peter Fraser **Est.** 2000 **Dozens** 15000 **Vyds** 100ha
This is the Australian operation of Jackson Family Wines, one of the leading premium wine producers in California, which in 2000 acquired the 172ha Eringa Park Vineyard from Normans Wines (the oldest vines dated back to 1923). The renamed Yangarra Estate Vineyard is the estate base for the operation and has moved to certified biodynamic status with its vineyards. Peter Fraser has taken Yangarra Estate to another level altogether with his innovative winemaking and desire to explore all the possibilities of the Rhône Valley red and white styles. Thus you will find grenache, shiraz, mourvèdre, cinsault, carignan, tempranillo and graciano planted, and picpoul noir, terret noir, muscardin and vaccarese around the corner. The white varieties are roussanne and viognier, with grenache blanc, bourboulenc and picpoul blanc planned. Then you see ceramic eggs being used in parallel with conventional fermenters. In 2015 Peter was named Winemaker of the Year at the launch of the *Wine Companion 2016*. Exports to the UK, the US, China and other major markets.

🍷🍷🍷🍷🍷 **Old Vine McLaren Vale Grenache 2019** From vines planted in '45 on a deep sandy dune dubbed 'The Beach' by Yangarra. Whole bunches are open-fermented. The bouquet exudes fresh-picked raspberries which form the nucleus of the powerful and intense palate, with grainy tannins that underline the complexity of the wine. Screw cap. 14% alc. **Rating** 96 **To** 2034 $35 JH ✪

Hickinbotham Clarendon Grenache 2019 This cuvée is akin to the finest pinot; svelte, detailed and uplifting. Aromas of sour cherry, raspberry, rosewater, mace and orange zest. The superior wine of 2019 here, or at least what I've tasted to date. Stunning. The tannins, growing with air and the next sip. The finish, jitterbug energetic, chiselled and chamois of texture. Long and succulent. Another addition to the Australian stable of finessed world-class grenache. Screw cap. 14.5% alc. **Rating** 96 **To** 2027 $60 NG ✪

High Sands McLaren Vale Grenache 2018 This is an imperious grenache if that adjective can be ascribed to a grape variety this joyous; this giddy of fruit and yet, underlying it all, a defining totem of immaculately extracted tannins. Kirsch, bramble, anise, clove, sandalwood and wood smoke drive long against a tannic parry: sandy, granular and emery-like. Screw cap. 14.5% alc. **Rating** 96 **To** 2026 $200 NG

McLaren Vale Roussanne 2020 Warm vintages service this doyen of white Rhône varieties so well, almost forcing the phenolic amplitude and textural quilt that would otherwise be lacking, at least in this country. This has it in spades. Scintillating aromas of bitter almond, apricot pith, rooibos, pistachio and freshly lain tatami mat. À point! Pucker and freshness; textural detail personified. The French oak (25% new) and lees work, apposite. The finish, long and rippling across the textural crevices. I'd love to drink this in 5 years. Screw cap. 14.5% alc. **Rating** 95 **To** 2027 $35 NG ✪

King's Wood McLaren Vale Shiraz 2019 I like this. A bit looser knit than the Ironheart. Floral and lifted. Sappy and crunchy. A powerful wine, to be sure, but light on its feet. An energetic cadence, weaving a thread of peppery acidity into a quilt of blue-fruit allusions, violet, nori, smoked meat and Asian spice. Firm across the finish, the tannins pulling the saliva forth in readiness for the next glass. Screw cap. 14.5% alc. **Rating** 95 **To** 2026 $60 NG

Ironheart McLaren Vale Shiraz 2018 The 25% whole bunches bring a briary complexity, while building a tannic bridge between the attack and mid palate. The tannins, grape and oak, serve as a long arc across blue/boysenberry, anise, clove and violet. Peppery and vibrant as much as it is plush and firm. Screw cap. 14.5% alc. **Rating** 94 **To** 2032 $120 NG

🍷🍷🍷🍷 **Roux Beauté McLaren Vale Roussanne 2019 Rating** 93 **To** 2026 $60 NG
Ovitelli McLaren Vale Grenache 2019 Rating 93 **To** 2024 $60 NG
Old Vine McLaren Vale Grenache 2020 Rating 92 **To** 2027 $42 NG

PF McLaren Vale Shiraz 2020 Rating 91 To 2023 $27 NG
McLaren Vale Shiraz 2019 Rating 91 To 2025 $35 NG
PF McLaren Vale Grenache 2020 Rating 91 To 2022 $27 NG
McLaren Vale Noir 2020 Rating 91 To 2024 $28 NG
McLaren Vale Rosé 2020 Rating 90 To 2021 $27 NG

Yarra Edge   ★★★★☆

455 Edward Road, Chirnside Park, Vic 3116 **Region** Yarra Valley
T 0428 301 517 **www**.yarraedge.com.au
Winemaker Dylan McMahon **Est.** 1983 **Dozens** 3500 **Vyds** 12.73ha
Yarra Edge was established by the Bingeman family in 1983, who were advised and guided by
John Middleton (of Mount Mary). The advice was, of course, good and Yarra Edge has always
been able to produce high-quality fruit if the vineyard was properly managed. Up to '98 the
wines were made onsite under the Yarra Edge label, but in that year the vineyard was leased
by Yering Station, which used the grapes for their own wines. Subsequently the vineyard
received minimal care until it was purchased by a Chinese-owned company, which set about
restoring it to its full glory. This has been achieved with Lucas Hoorn (formerly of Hoddles
Creek Estate and Levantine Hill) as full-time vineyard manager and Dylan McMahon as
contract winemaker, the wines made at Seville Estate. The quality of the wines speaks for
itself. Exports to China.

🍷🍷🍷🍷🍷 **Edward Single Vineyard Cabernet Sauvignon Cabernet Franc Merlot
2019** A thread of cooler flavours run through this, all ripe fruit yet there's restraint.
Lifted aromatics, currants and cassis, pine needles and wintergreen with woodsy
spices settling into the medium-bodied palate. Tannins are slightly coarse but will
soften in time. A lovely claret style. Screw cap. 13.2% alc. **Rating** 93 To 2034
$49 JF
**Ally Single Vineyard Cabernet Sauvignon Merlot Cabernet Franc
Malbec 2019** This shares a similar lightness and coolness as its sibling Edward,
but more oak influence, not much but it is noticeable. The tannins are drier and
stern. More time should resolve that. Screw cap. 13.2% alc. **Rating** 91 To 2034
$59 JF
Premium Single Vineyard Chardonnay 2019 There's enough stone fruit,
citrus, nougatine and spice here to keep a chardonnay drinker happy. It's fine and
long with the tight palate led by acidity. The toasty oak needs to subside to make
this more delicious. Screw cap. 13% alc. **Rating** 90 To 2026 $59 JF
Single Vineyard Pinot Noir 2019 A soft, gentle and easy-to-like wine. The
aromatics set the scene: cherry and plums strewn with baking spices, a waft of
autumn with warm earth. While the tannins are plush, the wine is medium bodied
with light acidity. Screw cap. 13.2% alc. **Rating** 90 To 2025 $49 JF

🍷🍷🍷🍷 **Yarra Valley Chardonnay 2019** Rating 89 To 2026 $45 JF

Yarra Yering   ★★★★★

Briarty Road, Coldstream, Vic 3770 **Region** Yarra Valley
T (03) 5964 9267 **www**.yarrayering.com **Open** 7 days 10–5
Winemaker Sarah Crowe **Est.** 1969 **Dozens** 5000 **Vyds** 112ha
In September 2008, founder Bailey Carrodus died and in April '09 Yarra Yering was on the
market. It was Bailey Carrodus' clear wish and expectation that any purchaser would continue
to manage the vineyard and winery, and hence the wine style, in much the same way as he
had done for the previous 40 years. Its acquisition in June '09 by a small group of investment
bankers has fulfilled that wish. The low-yielding, unirrigated vineyards have always produced
wines of extraordinary depth and intensity. Dry Red No. 1 is a cabernet blend; Dry Red
No. 2 is a shiraz blend; Dry Red No. 3 is a blend of touriga nacional, tinta cão, tinta roriz, tinta
amarela, alvarelhão and sousão; Pinot Noir and Chardonnay are not hidden behind delphic
numbers; Underhill Shiraz (planted in 1973) is from an adjacent vineyard purchased by Yarra
Yering in '87. Sarah Crowe was appointed winemaker after the 2013 vintage. She has made

red wines of the highest imaginable quality right from her first vintage in '14 and, to the delight of many, myself (James) included, has offered all the wines with screw caps. For good measure, she introduced the '14 Light Dry Red Pinot Shiraz as a foretaste of that vintage and an affirmation of the exceptional talent recognised by her being named Winemaker of the Year in the *Wine Companion 2017*. Exports to the UK, the US, Singapore, Hong Kong, China and NZ.

ＹＹＹＹＹ **Carrodus Shiraz 2019** From the small block of shiraz planted in 1969 comes a wine of distinction, thanks to the constant fine tuning orchestrated by winemaker Sarah Crowe. Wafts of pepper, woodsy spices, iodine and florals end up mingling with the pure fruit flavours within. Ribbons of fine tannin grace the palate, as does gossamer-like acidity, holding everything perfectly in place and just allowing the finish to linger and impress even more. Screw cap. 14% alc. **Rating** 98 **To** 2039 $275 JF

Dry Red No. 2 2019 Shiraz, mataro, viognier. It's easy to be bowled over by this wine's beauty, from its bright colour to its heady fragrance of violets, Middle Eastern spices, fresh currants and blue fruits. Then magic happens. It is superfine, graced with perfectly formed silky tannins. The oak is seamlessly integrated, then flavour builds across the barely medium-bodied palate. While there's a lightness of touch, it's layered and complex. A complete wine full of style, elegance and substance. Screw cap. 13.5% alc. **Rating** 98 **To** 2034 $120 JF ✪ ♥

Carrodus Cabernet Sauvignon 2019 There is such clarity to this wine, from the exuberant colour to the masterful combination of flavours within, centred exclusively on this majestic variety. Blackberries and currants, bay leaves and lead pencil plus deep-etched cedary oak. It has a juiciness thanks to the acidity, and while it is fuller bodied, as with all YY reds, a defining feature is beautiful tannins: here they are, insistent yet super fine. Screw cap. 13.5% alc. **Rating** 98 **To** 2044 $275 JF ♥

Dry Red No. 1 2019 This is mesmerising. Do take time to bask in its fragrance – all floral and spicy with some aniseed and fresh herbs. Enjoy the poised fruit flavours of blackberries, mulberries and a hint of blueberries coated in spicy oak and tethered to the body of the wine. Pulsing acidity and beautiful tannin structure shape this and offer a promise of more to come in time. Wow – what a wine. Screw cap. 13.5% alc. **Rating** 98 **To** 2039 $120 JF ✪ ♥

Carrodus Pinot Noir 2019 This is all about refinement, and in a way, it has a deceptive gentleness, as the flavours are subtle, the oak has meshed into the body of the wine and the silky tannins weave across the palate. Arguably the finest Carrodus pinot to date. Screw cap. 14% alc. **Rating** 97 **To** 2034 $275 JF

ＹＹＹＹＹ **Chardonnay 2019** While YY makes its mark as a red wine producer of excellence, of late its chardonnay is really standing out. It's changing. It's finer. It's pristine, with layers of citrus and tangy acidity lengthening out a palate that's seamless and textural. It has the right amount of moreish sulphides to the fruit weight. Try putting this down. Screw cap. 13% alc. **Rating** 96 **To** 2029 $105 JF

Pinot Noir 2019 A beautifully balanced and complete wine to either drink now or cellar so it garners more complexity. The former option is hard to beat, revealing plump plums and black cherries, layers of spice and integrated oak. Precision across the palate, raw silk tannins and a freshness to the acidity ensure there's a lingering quality. Screw cap. 13.5% alc. **Rating** 96 **To** 2031 $105 JF

Underhill 2019 There's so much restraint and purity of fruit across the YY range this vintage, Underhill is no different. Perfumed, savoury, delicate yet complex, pure and long. Lacy tannins and fine acidity work across a lithe palate. Screw cap. 13.5% alc. **Rating** 96 **To** 2033 $120 JF

Agincourt Cabernet Malbec 2019 Could this be any more aromatic, with its perfect mix of florals, fruit and spice? The savouriness of (30%) malbec comes through as a mere accompaniment to the heady cabernet. Oak remains in the background, tannins are perfectly judged and acidity is bright. It promises to delight now and for some years hence. Screw cap. 13% alc. **Rating** 96 **To** 2029 $105 JF

Carrodus Viognier 2019 Just 2 barrels. A labour of love. It is not easy to maintain varietal purity for viognier without it turning broad and oily. None of that here. It's almost delicate, with just a smidge of apricot and kernels. Infused with lemon, orange and woodsy spices, it's textural, but light as a feather across the palate. Bravo. Screw cap. 14% alc. **Rating** 95 **To** 2029 $160 JF

New Territories Shiraz Touriga 2019 This has an approachability similar to the Light Dry Red, so there's no crime cracking it open now. But there's some depth and stuffing here, allowing it to unfurl over the next few years. It starts off with lavender, pepper and new leather, plus a core of fruit, tinted with Middle Eastern spices and lightly drying, fine tannins. It's definitely savoury, medium bodied and stamped with drinkability. Screw cap. 13% alc. **Rating** 95 **To** 2029 $55 JF

Dry Red No. 3 2019 This blend of Portuguese varieties has come together seamlessly and offers immediate drinking appeal. Heady with violets and lavender, blackcurrants and szechuan pepper, blackstrap licorice and Mediterranean herbs, all adding to its youthful beauty. Fine tannins, raspberry-like acidity and complexity raise it way above ordinary. Screw cap. 12.5% alc. **Rating** 95 **To** 2028 $105 JF

ŢŢŢŢŢ **Merlot 2019 Rating** 93 **To** 2030 $105 JF
Light Dry Red Pinot Shiraz 2020 Rating 93 **To** 2026 $95 JF
Dry White No. 1 2019 Rating 92 **To** 2030 $55 JF
Sparkling Blanc de Noir 2016 Rating 90 $60 JF

Yarradindi Wines   ★★★★☆

1018 Murrindindi Road, Murrindindi, Vic 3717 **Region** Upper Goulburn
T 0438 305 314 **www**.mrhughwine.com
Winemaker Hugh Cuthbertson **Est.** 1979 **Dozens** 90 000 **Vyds** 70ha
Murrindindi Vineyards was established by Alan and Jan Cutherbertson as a minor diversification from their cattle property. Son Hugh Cutherbertson (with a long and high-profile wine career) took over the venture and in 2015 folded the business into his largest customers to create Yarradindi Wines. The main focus now is export to China with distribution organisations in Hangzhou, shipping 1 million bottles annually. Exports to the UK and China.

ŢŢŢŢŢ **Mr Hugh Sipping Bliss Aperitif NV** A rich, nutty apera style using very old base wines once owned by Melbourne's famous W.J. Seabrook & Son. The winemaker, Hugh Cuthbertson (ex Seabrook) bought the apera and fortified soleras and had them freshened by master fortifier David Morris. This piece of history is stunning in flavour intensity, complexity and price. A drink of the ages, golden amber in colour with the scent of dried citrus, vanilla and hazelnut, running long and rich, warming the soul. 375ml. Cork. 18% alc. **Rating** 95 $45 JP

Mr Hugh Sipping Bliss Digestif NV In another time this would have been called a tawny port and was made in the dry, nutty Portuguese style. No ordinary digestif, the name doesn't go anywhere near revealing the seriousness of this fortified or its richness and utter complexity. Reveals its age in the walnut brown colour and deep scent of molasses, dried fruit, caramel, coffee. Flows seamlessly and long across the palate. An absolute beauty in the glass. 375ml. Screw cap. 18% alc. **Rating** 95 $35 JP ✪

ŢŢŢŢŢ **Mr Hugh Penbro Vineyard White Pony Cabernet Franc Cabernet Sauvignon 2019 Rating** 91 **To** 2029 $45 JP

Yarran Wines   ★★★★☆

178 Myall Park Road, Yenda, NSW 2681 **Region** Riverina
T (02) 6968 1125 **www**.yarranwines.com.au **Open** Mon–Sat 10–5
Winemaker Sam Brewer **Est.** 2000 **Dozens** 20 000 **Vyds** 30ha
Lorraine Brewer (and late husband John) were grapegrowers for over 30 years and when son Sam completed a degree in wine science at CSU, they celebrated his graduation by crushing 1t of shiraz, fermenting the grapes in a milk vat. The majority of the grapes from the estate

plantings are sold but each year a little more has been made under the Yarran banner; along the way a winery with a crush capacity of 150t has been built. Sam worked for Southcorp and De Bortoli in Australia, and overseas (in the US and China), but in 2009 decided to take the plunge and concentrate on the family winery with his parents. The majority of the grapes come from the family vineyard but some parcels are sourced from growers, including Lake Cooper Estate in the Heathcote region. Over the past 3 years Sam has focused on improving the quality of the estate-grown grapes, moving to organic conversion. Yarran was the *Wine Companion 2021* Dark Horse of the Year. Exports to Canada, Singapore and China.

🍷🍷🍷🍷🍷 **A Few Words ... Whole Bunch Heathcote Shiraz 2019** Ethereal and sassy. Violet, yeasty bouillon notes and ample red cherry amaro riffs. The palate, pliant but gently so. Some powdery real oak tannin, defining the seams. The flavours running a line of decent intensity, juxtaposed against the overall light framework. A good drink. Screw cap. 14.2% alc. **Rating** 92 **To** 2023 $32 NG

Bendigo Heathcote Hilltops Shiraz 2019 Violet, boysenberry and clove. Plump yet sinewy and savoury enough to evince a modicum of sophistication. This drinks akin to a wine twice its price. My overall impression is one of intuition and an admirably deft touch. Screw cap. 14.2% alc. **Rating** 91 **To** 2023 $15 NG ✪

B Series Heathcote Shiraz 2019 Dark fruit of tone, rich and laden with bourbon/mocha American oak accents. The calling card is far from the uncanny lightness of touch that defines other wines under this banner. Still, if you are after oomph there is plenty here. Screw cap. 14.2% alc. **Rating** 91 **To** 2025 $32 NG

Botrytis Semillon 2018 This hits all the right notes from tangerine, canned pineapple and peach, to grape spice, citrus verbena and dried mango. Lightweight, yet a luscious oscillation of decadent sweetness is juxtaposed with an undercarriage of bright acid crunch for refreshment and tone. Screw cap. 11.5% alc. **Rating** 91 **To** 2028 $28 NG

Limited Release Block Series Riverina Durif 2019 A burly wine. The oak at the fore, corseting violet, boysenberry, molten cherry and dried herb flavours. The finish, maple and cedar. This is a wine of rustic charm and considerable power over any pretence of finesse. Screw cap. 14% alc. **Rating** 90 **To** 2025 $28 NG

🍷🍷🍷🍷 **A Few Words ... Pale Dry Rosé 2020 Rating** 88 **To** 2021 $20 NG

Yarrh Wines   ★★★★

440 Greenwood Road, Murrumbateman, NSW 2582 **Region** Canberra District
T (02) 6227 1474 **www.**yarrhwines.com.au **Open** Fri–Sun 11–5
Winemaker Fiona Wholohan **Est.** 1997 **Dozens** 2000 **Vyds** 6ha

Fiona Wholohan and Neil McGregor are IT refugees; both now work full-time running the Yarrh Wines Vineyard and making the wines. Fiona undertook the oenology and viticulture course at CSU and has also spent time as an associate judge at wine shows. They spent 5 years moving to a hybrid organic vineyard with composting, mulching, biological controls and careful vineyard floor management. The vineyard includes cabernet sauvignon, shiraz, sauvignon blanc, riesling, pinot noir and sangiovese. They have recently tripled their sangiovese plantings with 2 new clones. Yarrh was the original Aboriginal name for the Yass district.

🍷🍷🍷🍷🍷 **The Brunette Canberra District Sangiovese 2018** Dark, spicy cherries, Mediterranean herbs and radicchio bitterness too. Woodsy spices via oak, which is in check. The palate is pure sangiovese – textural tannins, sinewy and tangy, with refreshing acidity in the driver's seat and leading the way to the finish line. Screw cap. 13.5% alc. **Rating** 95 **To** 2028 $35 JF ✪

🍷🍷🍷🍷 **Canberra District Sangiovese 2019 Rating** 91 **To** 2024 $32 JF

Yelland & Papps ★★★★

279 Nuraip Road, Nuriootpa, SA 5355 **Region** Barossa Valley
T 0408 628 494 **www.**yellandandpapps.com **Open** By appt
Winemaker Michael Papps, Susan Papps **Est.** 2005 **Dozens** 4000 **Vyds** 2ha
Michael and Susan Papps (née Yelland) set up this venture after their marriage in 2005. It is easy for them to regard the Barossa Valley as their home because Michael has lived and worked in the wine industry in the Barossa Valley for more than 20 years. He has a rare touch, producing consistently excellent wines, but also pushing the envelope; as well as using a sustainable approach to winemaking with minimal inputs, he has not hesitated to challenge orthodox approaches to a number of aspects of conventional fermentation methods. Exports to Norway and China.

ℙℙℙℙ **Second Take Barossa Valley Shiraz 2019** The exotic spice, Campari and sappy tannins of whole-bunch fermentation lead out, over a core of tangy, dark berry fruits and cherry liqueur. A bright purple hue, fine tannin frame and lingering persistence confirm its youthful potential. For those who enjoy a bunchy style. Screw cap. 13.4% alc. **Rating** 89 **To** 2029 $45 TS

Yering Station ★★★★★

38 Melba Highway, Yarra Glen, Vic 3775 **Region** Yarra Valley
T (03) 9730 0100 **www.**yering.com **Open** 7 days 10–5
Winemaker Brendan Hawker, James Oliver, Darren Rathbone **Est.** 1988 **Dozens** 60 000 **Vyds** 112ha
The historic Yering Station (or at least the portion of the property on which the cellar door and vineyard are established) was purchased by the Rathbone family in 1996; it is also the site of Yarrabank. A spectacular and very large winery was built, handling the Yarrabank sparkling and the Yering Station table wines, immediately becoming one of the focal points of the Yarra Valley – particularly as the historic Chateau Yering, where luxury accommodation and fine dining are available, is next door. Exports to all major markets.

ℙℙℙℙℙ **Reserve Yarra Valley Shiraz Viognier 2019** Everything is just so with this tip-top reserve. It's full bodied and very rich with lovely spiced plums, mocha and licorice root flavours. The tannins are velvety and plush and this feels quite sumptuous, even decadent. Hard to resist now, but will reward more in time. Screw cap. 14% alc. **Rating** 96 **To** 2035 $130 JF
Reserve Yarra Valley Pinot Noir 2019 There's a density, a plushness and a level of complexity that puts this in reserve territory. Nicely layered with sweet fruit, spice, cedary oak and ripe, textural tannins. It has a certain savouriness, almost ferrous and of all things, this feels cool across the full-bodied palate. Screw cap. 13.5% alc. **Rating** 95 **To** 2033 $130 JF
Yarra Valley Shiraz Viognier 2019 This is firmly in the riper spectrum, yet composed. It's silky and textured, full of dark plums, wood char, licorice and dried herbs. The full-bodied palate is fleshy and satisfying, with expansive tannins. Drinking well right now. Screw cap. 14.5% alc. **Rating** 95 **To** 2027 $40 JF
Reserve Yarra Valley Cabernet Sauvignon 2019 A fragrant and very fine reserve. It kicks off with violets and cassis, menthol and blackberries, licorice and mocha then freshly rolled tobacco. The oak is well integrated, the tannins precise and persuasive and really, nothing is out of place. But given its youth, it is tightly wound and needs more time. Screw cap. 13.5% alc. **Rating** 95 **To** 2034 $130 JF
Reserve Yarra Valley Chardonnay 2019 Flavoursome yet somewhat reticent. Yes, there's a lovely fragrance and the palate is full of citrus and some stone fruit, all spiced up with a layer of creamy lees; not much, just enough. There's an evenness across the palate, it just doesn't have the drive of previous vintages. This is good but not great as a Reserve must be. Screw cap. 13.5% alc. **Rating** 94 **To** 2028 $130 JF

ℙℙℙℙℙ **Laura Barnes Pinot Noir 2019 Rating** 92 **To** 2028 $70 JF
Yarra Valley Chardonnay 2019 Rating 90 **To** 2026 $40 JF

Yarra Valley Pinot Noir 2019 **Rating** 90 **To** 2027 $40 JF
Yarra Valley Cabernet Sauvignon 2018 **Rating** 90 **To** 2028 $40 JF

Yeringberg ★★★★★

Maroondah Highway, Coldstream, Vic 3770 **Region** Yarra Valley
T (03) 9739 0240 **www.**yeringberg.com.au **Open** By appt
Winemaker Sandra de Pury **Est.** 1863 **Dozens** 1500 **Vyds** 3.66ha
Guill de Pury and daughter Sandra, with Guill's wife Katherine in the background, make
wines for the new millennium from the low-yielding vines re-established in the heart of
what was one of the most famous (and infinitely larger) vineyards of the 19th century. In the
riper years, the red wines have a velvety generosity of flavour rarely encountered, while never
losing varietal character; the long-lived Marsanne Roussanne takes students of history back to
Yeringberg's fame in the 19th century. Exports to the UK, the US, Switzerland, Hong Kong
and China.

ɁɁɁɁɁ **Yarra Valley Cabernet Sauvignon 2019** While this has the exuberance
of youth, it is also a composed and classy cabernet. A harmonious blend of
mulberries and plums, cedary oak, cigar box and a touch of iodine. The palate is
detailed from the ultrafine tannins, the brightness of the acidity to its impressive
length. Elegance in a glass. Screw cap. 13.5% alc. **Rating** 97 **To** 2042 $95 JF ✪
Yeringberg 2019 This was tasted less than a month after it was bottled and
while it's a very fine Yeringberg with its beauty on show, it's reserved and needs
time to adjust and settle. Everything is in sync. Lovely aromas of violets, autumn
leaves, mulberries and more. The medium-bodied palate is layered with fine,
textural tannins, dazzled with fresh acidity and exceptional length. Screw cap.
13% alc. **Rating** 97 **To** 2044 $95 JF ✪

ɁɁɁɁɁ **Yarra Valley Cabernet Sauvignon 2017** This is the first 100% cabernet
made by Yeringberg, and celebrates the 650th anniversary of the de Pury family
in Switzerland. No more than medium bodied, it reflects the cool, high-quality
Yarra Valley vintage, striking for its purity of blackcurrant varietal fruit and
bay leaf/black olive adornments drawing out the finish. Screw cap. 13.5% alc.
Rating 96 **To** 2032 $98 JH
Yeringberg 2018 A gentle Yeringberg, with its heady fragrance of mulberries,
florals, cedary oak and the kitchen cupboard full of spices and herbs. So enticing.
The palate is medium-bodied, with astonishingly fine, powdery tannins, finishing
long and pure. As usual, an elegant wine that delights now and will do more so in
a few years' time. Screw cap. 13.5% alc. **Rating** 96 **To** 2038 $95 JF
Yarra Valley Chardonnay 2019 Where to start? There's a lot of flavour and
depth here. It's not too big, although full of stone fruits and citrus, candied and
fresh, with some spicy grilled nuts and a creamy lusciousness. Savouriness, too,
with oak neatly in place. The overall impression is a stylish wine. Screw cap.
13% alc. **Rating** 95 **To** 2030 $65 JF
Yarra Valley Viognier 2019 Few producers can match Yeringberg's viognier.
Harmony is the aspiration, achieved by picking fruit over 8 days, so there's
acidity, freshness and ripeness. There's also wild fermentation in barrel, no mlf
and maturation in large-format, used oak. Ripe stone fruit, apricot and kernel,
with ginger cream drizzled in honey. All tempered by lemon zest acidity and
lime marmalade tang. There's richness here, without heaviness. A lovely viognier.
Screw cap. 13.5% alc. **Rating** 95 **To** 2027 $35 JF ✪
Yarra Valley Pinot Noir 2018 Gosh, if the aromatics don't seduce you, the
palate will. Starts off with an autumnal, forest-floor fragrance, moving towards
cherries and pips, with a smattering of herbs. Amaro and pomegranate add tang,
with tannins the texture of a fine emery board. Elegant and suave. Screw cap.
13% alc. **Rating** 95 **To** 2033 $95 JF
Yarra Valley Shiraz 2019 A lot of complexity and savouriness come out to
play this vintage, alongside a wonderful coolness across the palate. Expect dark
plums, licorice and menthol, juniper, a dash of pepper and roasted root vegetables.

It's fuller-bodied, with a covering of textural tannins and bright acidity. Screw cap. 13.5% alc. **Rating** 95 **To** 2033 $85 JF

ΨΨΨΨ♀ Yarra Valley Pinot Noir 2019 **Rating** 93 **To** 2038 $95 JF
Yarra Valley Marsanne Roussanne 2019 **Rating** 92 **To** 2032 $65 JF
Yarra Valley Shiraz 2018 **Rating** 92 **To** 2027 $85 JF

Yes said the seal   ★★★★

1251-1269 Bellarine Highway, Wallington, Vic 3221 **Region** Geelong
T (03) 5250 6577 **www**.yessaidtheseal.com.au **Open** 7 days 10–5
Winemaker Darren Burke **Est.** 2014 **Dozens** 1200 **Vyds** 8ha
This is the newest venture of David and Lyndsay Sharp, long-term vintners on Geelong's Bellarine Peninsula. It is situated onsite at the Flying Brick Cider Co's Cider House in Wallington. The estate vineyard includes 3ha of pinot noir, 2ha each of chardonnay and shiraz and 1ha of sauvignon blanc.

ΨΨΨΨΨ The Bellarine Rosé 2020 A most serious-looking rosé in copper/orange hues. The expectation is for a fuller-flavoured rosé style and you won't be disappointed. Shiraz is the basis here, displaying red-fruit aromas in abundance with wild herbs. Lays out a crisp, even and juicy palate with tangy, summer raspberry, cherry and musk, macaroon. A serious rosé, indeed. Screw cap. 12.5% alc. **Rating** 94 **To** 2023 $35 JP

ΨΨΨΨ♀ The Bellarine Shiraz 2018 **Rating** 93 **To** 2026 $45 JP
Reserve Blanc de Blanc 2016 **Rating** 92 $45 JP
The Bellarine Chardonnay 2019 **Rating** 91 **To** 2025 $38 JP
The Bellarine Pinot Noir 2019 **Rating** 91 **To** 2025 $45 JP

Z Wine   ★★★★★

Shop 3, 109-111 Murray Street, Tanunda, SA 5352 **Region** Barossa Valley
T (08) 8563 3637 **www**.zwine.com.au **Open** Mon–Wed 10–5, Thurs–Sun 10–late
Winemaker Janelle Zerk **Est.** 1999 **Dozens** 10000
Z Wine is the partnership of sisters Janelle and Kristen Zerk, whose heritage dates back 5 generations at the Zerk Vineyard in Lyndoch. Vineyard resources include growers that supply old-vine shiraz, old-bushvine grenache and High Eden riesling. Both women have completed degrees at the University of Adelaide (Janelle winemaking and Kristen wine marketing). Janelle also has vintage experience in Puligny Montrachet, Tuscany and Sonoma Valley. Wines are released under the Z Wine, Rustica and Section 3146 labels. Z Wine's cellar door is in the main street of Tanunda. Exports to the US, Singapore, NZ, Taiwan, Hong Kong and China.

ΨΨΨΨΨ Julius Barossa Valley Shiraz 2019 Impressive full, vibrant, luminous purple hue. These old vines encapsulate the compelling mood of Lyndoch, contrasting great depth of black fruits with lift and drive. A deep core of blackberry, black cherry, satsuma plum and licorice is confidently backed with high-cocoa dark chocolate oak. Impressively scaffolded tannins rise to the occasion. Screw cap. 14.5% alc. **Rating** 95 **To** 2039 $70 TS
Hein Ancestor Vine Barossa Valley Shiraz 2019 Medium, vibrant purple. A complex interplay of red/black fruits of all kinds, with the exotic spice of old vines (believed to be more than 140yo) indistinguishable from the fragrant overlay of a touch of whole-bunch influence. Coffee-bean oak is kept in the background, supporting fine tannin profile through a finish of good length. More about interest than impact, and all the better for it. Diam. 14.5% alc. **Rating** 94 **To** 2039 $300 TS

ΨΨΨΨ♀ Saul Night Havest Eden Valley Riesling 2020 **Rating** 93 **To** 2030 $35 TS
Roman Old Vine Barossa Valley GSM 2020 **Rating** 93 **To** 2023 $40 TS
Rohrlach Survivor Vine Barossa Valley Grenache 2019 **Rating** 92 **To** 2024 $120 TS

Audrey Barossa Valley Cabernet Sauvignon 2018 Rating 92 To 2028 $40 TS
Plowman Dry Grown Barossa Valley Shiraz 2018 Rating 91 To 2023 $120 TS
Julius Barossa Valley Shiraz 2012 Rating 91 To 2021 $150 TS
Section 3146 Barossa Valley Cabernet Sauvignon 2018 Rating 91 To 2033 $35 TS
Rustica Reserve Barossa Valley Shiraz 2018 Rating 90 To 2028 $34 TS
Laverin Old Vine Barossa Valley Bonvedro 2019 Rating 90 To 2022 $30 TS

Zarephath Wines

424 Moorialup Road, East Porongurup, WA 6324 **Region** Porongurup
T (08) 9853 1152 **www**.zarephathwines.com.au **Open** Mon–Sat 10–5, Sun 10–4
Winemaker Robert Diletti **Est.** 1994 **Dozens** 1500 **Vyds** 8.9ha
The Zarephath vineyard was owned and operated by Brothers and Sisters of The Christ Circle, a Benedictine community. In 2014 they sold the property to Rosie Singer and her partner Ian Barrett-Lennard, who live on the spot full-time and undertake all the vineyard work, supplemented by the local Afghani community during vintage and pruning. They have diverse backgrounds, Ian's roots in the Swan Valley, while Rosie has worked in various aspects of fine arts, first in administration and thereafter as a practising visual artist with galleries in north Queensland and regional WA.

Porongurup Syrah 2018 Graphite and mineral. Blackberry and mulberry. This is luscious – and that's the vintage. The 2018 season yields wines like this: power with inky ripeness. The cool-climate acid is the key to giving an extra dimension of pedigree. Concentrated and intense – a beautiful wine. Screw cap. 13.5% alc. Rating 95 To 2035 $30 EL **❂**
Porongurup Pinot Noir 2018 There are a number of things converging in this glass: a near-perfect vintage, the tiny, carefully tended vineyard (by owners Rosie and Ian) at the far end of the Porongurup range and the skill of winemaker Rob Diletti. Elegant, layered, spicy, with lacy tannins and good length of flavour. Pomegranate, raspberry, pink peppercorn and something soft, like freshly grated nutmeg. Very pretty. Screw cap. 14% alc. **Rating** 94 To 2031 $35 EL

Single Vineyard Porongurup Riesling 2019 Rating 92 To 2036 $30 EL
Porongurup Petit Chardonnay 2017 Rating 90 To 2027 $25 EL

Zema Estate

14944 Riddoch Highway, Coonawarra, SA 5263 **Region** Coonawarra
T (08) 8736 3219 **www**.zema.com.au **Open** Mon–Fri 9–5, w'ends & public hols 10–4
Winemaker Joe Cory **Est.** 1982 **Dozens** 15 000 **Vyds** 61ha
The Zema family have always hand pruned this vineyard set in the heart of Coonawarra's terra rossa soil. Winemaking practices are straightforward; if ever there was an example of great wines being made in the vineyard, this is it. Exports to Hong Kong, Singapore, China and NZ.

Coonawarra Cabernet Sauvignon 2018 As with so many cabernets, lots of air and time to open up makes such a big difference. This appeared raw and closed at first, with raspy tannins. It then revealed cassis, leafy freshness, dark chocolate, herbs and menthol. A core of sweet fruit works in unison with the cedary oak and while more bottle age is need to smooth out the tannins, they are knitted into the body of the wine. Screw cap. 14.5% alc. **Rating** 93 To 2033 $30 JF
Saluti Coonawarra Cabernet Shiraz 2016 Sweet, cedary oak is still upfront but as this is built for ageing, it should become merely a stitch in the overall tapestry, given time. Black fruit, savoury mostly, with roasted hazelnuts and dark chocolate. Full bodied, dense across the palate, a richness too, before the grip of the tannins take hold. Screw cap. 14.5% alc. **Rating** 93 To 2034 $130 JF

Sparkling Coonawarra Merlot 2018 Excellent dark purple hue. The bubbles anchor in, lasting seemingly longer than many sparkling reds. It's vibrant, teeming with plums, brambly fruit and cassis with loads of spices and cedar. The tannins have some give, a dab of sweetness throughout yet it finishes nice and dry. Cork. 14% alc. **Rating** 92 $35 JF

Coonawarra Shiraz 2018 Released with 4 years under its belt yet fresh as can be. The oak has fallen into place, adding extra oomph on the palate. Full bodied with ample tannins. It's in a good place: fruit is still in the mix yet savouriness abounds. Screw cap. 14.5% alc. **Rating** 90 **To** 2028 $29 JF

Zerella Wines

182 Olivers Rd, McLaren Vale, SA 5171 **Region** McLaren Vale
T (08) 8323 8288/0417 766 699 **www**.zerellawines.com.au **Open** Mon–Sat 11–4
Winemaker Jim Zerella **Est.** 2006 **Dozens** 2500 **Vyds** 58ha

In 1950 Ercole Zerella left his native Campania in southern Italy to seek a better life in SA. With a lifetime of farming and grapegrowing, the transition was seamless. Ercole's son Vic followed in his father's footsteps, becoming an icon of the SA farming and wine industries. He founded Tatachilla, where his son Jim began as a cellar hand, eventually controlling all grape purchases. While working there, Jim purchased land in McLaren Vale and, with help from family and friends, established what is now the flagship vineyard of Zerella Wines. He also established a vineyard management business catering to the needs of absentee owners. When Tatachilla was purchased by Lion Nathan in 2000 he declined the opportunity of continuing his role there and by '06 had purchased 2 more vineyards, and become a shareholder in a 3rd. These all now come under the umbrella of Zerella Wines, with its 58ha of vines. The winemaking techniques used are thoroughly à la mode and definitely not traditional Italian. Exports to the UK and Canada.

Home Block Single Vineyard McLaren Vale Shiraz 2017 A forceful wine with the envelope pushed in terms of palate-saturating ripeness, staining extract and a salty, powerful finish. The fruit, however, is true to region and variety: a warm-climate expression of shiraz's blueberry, fruitcake, charcuterie, black olive, baking spice, iodine and floral notes. Thickly textured, with a bitter chocolate and barbecue-doused splay of tannins across the long, thick finish. Screw cap. 14.5% alc. **Rating** 93 **To** 2032 $60 NG

La Gita Etrurian McLaren Vale Sangiovese 2016 This highly savoury mid-weighted wine was not racked other than its single transport to French oak (40% new) for 15 months. Sensitive oak handling has galvanised the flavours into a sheath of sour cherry, sandalwood and dried herb. Sangiovese's frisky tannins stain the gums while placating any excess. The acidity is unnecessarily bright. Nevertheless, a delicious wine. Screw cap. 14% alc. **Rating** 93 **To** 2026 $60 NG

La Gita McLaren Vale Nero d'Avola 2019 Fine aromas suggest a keen understanding of the variety: faithful black cherry, fruitcake, and orange rind, spooled along a thick thread of broad dusty tannins by some maritime salinity and dutiful freshness. Screw cap. 14.5% alc. **Rating** 92 **To** 2024 $35 NG

La Gita McLaren Vale Arneis 2018 This dry, lively and texturally intriguing wine spent a further 5 months on lees to build layers and tension. Very successfully! Aromas of lemon drop, nashi pear and bitter almond reverberate on a mid-weighted to fullish palate. The finish, comparatively relaxed and long. Screw cap. 13.5% alc. **Rating** 91 **To** 2023 $30 NG

4056 McLaren Vale Cabernet Sauvignon 2019 Superlative value. A rich, pulpy and energetic cabernet, sacrificing nothing in terms of the expected chocolatey richness, ample mouthfeel and regional saltiness. Yet the wine is handled in such a way – wild-yeast ferment and no racking other than a shift to neutral wood for 12 months – that it is a joy to drink already. Blackcurrant, sage, tapenade and hedgerow. All in just the right amounts. Screw cap. 14.5% alc. **Rating** 91 **To** 2025 $30 NG

La Gita McLaren Vale Barbera 2019 Pulpy texture, grapey and lilac/floral aroma. Presumably plenty of whole berries in the mix. Loads of mulberry, boysenberry and blueberry flavours billow across a rich but gentle palate. The tannins, just palpable enough to guide the cavalcade of fruit. The acidity, bright. This is a variety best drunk in its youth. Screw cap. 14.5% alc. **Rating** 91 **To** 2023 $35 NG

ŸŸŸŸ **Workhorse McLaren Vale Shiraz 2019 Rating** 88 **To** 2024 $30 NG

Zig Zag Rd ★★★★

201 Zig Zag Road, Drummond, Vic 3446 **Region** Macedon Ranges
T (03) 5423 9390 **www**.zigzagwines.com.au **Open** Thurs–Mon 10–5
Winemaker Henry Churchill, Harriet Churchill, Gilles Lapalus **Est.** 1972 **Dozens** 1500
Vyds 4.5ha
Henry and Harriet Churchill, Brits with a background in sustainable agriculture, took over the Zig Zag vineyard from Eric and Anne Bellchambers in 2018. With a new baby in tow, Henry and Harriet were then 'new to winemaking, viticulture and parenting'. The focus is on regenerative farming, and they have launched a 2nd label, 'Kind Folk', for experimental wines, including an amber wine, a barrel-fermented rosé and a pet nat. (TS)

ŸŸŸŸŸ **Macedon Ranges Riesling 2019** New owners. New labels. New energy. Opaque straw hue with wafts of lemon blossom and just-cut herbs of an Alpine persuasion. Flavours of lemon drops, white pepper and radish. The palate has texture and depth, citrus comes into play, with lemon and mandarin. It tastes slightly off-dry, although there's no shortage of acidity, so it feels racy and refreshing to the last drop. Screw cap. 12% alc. **Rating** 94 **To** 2028 $25 JF ✪
Macedon Ranges Shiraz 2019 This is certainly showing off its cool-climate credentials with a heady fragrance, florals, a flash of pepper, aniseed and mint. Some tart and tangy Angelina plums and cherries in the mix. Medium bodied, nicely savoury, with a fine emery board of tannins and crunchy, raspberry acidity. A fresh style, yet some substance too. Screw cap. 13% alc. **Rating** 94 **To** 2026 $27 JF ✪

ŸŸŸŸŸ **Heritage '72 Vines Macedon Ranges Pinot Noir 2019 Rating** 92 **To** 2026 $55 JF

Zilzie Wines ★★★★

544 Kulkyne Way, Karadoc, Vic 3496 **Region** Murray Darling
T (03) 5025 8100 **www**.zilziewines.com **Open** By appt
Winemaker Jonathan Creek **Est.** 1999 **Vyds** 700ha
The Forbes family has been farming since the early 1900s. Zilzie is currently run by Roslyn Forbes and sons Steven and Andrew, the diverse range of farming activities now solely focused on grapegrowing from substantial vineyards. Having established a dominant position as a supplier of grapes to Southcorp, Zilzie formed a wine company in '99 and built a winery in 2000, expanding it to its current capacity of 60 000t. The wines consistently far exceed expectations, given their enticing prices, that consistency driving the substantial production volume in an extremely competitive market. The business includes contract processing, winemaking and storage; the winery is certified organic. Exports to the US, China, Singapore, South Korea, Indonesia and Malaysia.

ŸŸŸŸŸ **Platinum Edition Arinto 2020** This is a terrific rendition. Pressings fermented in older barrels, free-run juice into stainless steel, then partial transfer to barrel and left on lees to build texture. Spicy, juicy pears, lemon juice, and grated Granny Smith apples. Excellent length, with fine, chalky acidity and grapefruit pith phenolics. It's crisp, very dry and deliciously good. Screw cap. 14% alc. **Rating** 95 **To** 2025 $35 JF ✪

ŸŸŸŸ **Ferghana Shiraz 2019 Rating** 91 **To** 2029 $50 JF
Limited Edition McLaren Vale Shiraz 2019 Rating 91 **To** 2033 $70 JF

Regional Collection Clare Valley Rosé 2020 Rating 90 To 2022 $22 JF
Regional Collection Barossa GSM 2018 Rating 90 To 2024 $22 JF
Regional Collection Langhorne Creek Malbec 2019 Rating 90 To 2024
$22 JF

Zitta Wines   ★★★★

3 Union Street, Dulwich, SA 5065 (postal) **Region** Barossa Valley
T 0419 819 414 **www**.zitta.com.au
Winemaker Angelo De Fazio **Est.** 1864 **Dozens** 3200 **Vyds** 28ha
Owner Angelo De Fazio says that all he knows about viticulture and winemaking came from
his father (and generations before him). It is partly this influence that has shaped the label and
brand name: Zitta is Italian for 'quiet', and the seeming reflection of the letters of the name
Zitta on the label is in fact nothing of the kind: turn the bottle upside down, and you will
see it is the word 'Quiet'. The Zitta vineyard dates back to 1864, with a few vines remaining
from that time, and a block planted with cuttings taken from those vines. Shiraz dominates
the plantings (24ha), the balance made up of grenache and a few mataro and nero d'Avola
vines. The property has 2 branches of Greenock Creek running through it and the soils reflect
the ancient geological history of the site, in part with a subsoil of river pebbles, reflecting the
course of a long-gone river. Exports to Denmark, Sweden, Norway and China.

�♥♥♥♀ **Single Vineyard Greenock Barossa Valley Nero d'Avola 2018** A
compellingly light and refreshing take, more rosso and viola than it is nero. Two
years in puncheons has done nothing to diminish its hue or its primary take
on black cherry and blueberry fruit. Bright acidity and finely textured tannins
energise a long and harmonious finish. Enticingly vibrant nero, all the more
impressive for a dry, warm season in Greenock. Bravo! Screw cap. 13.7% alc.
Rating 93 **To** 2033 $45 TS
Single Vineyard Bernardo Greenock Barossa Valley Shiraz 2018
Zitta's flagship unites the full impact and depth of Greenock with layers of dark
chocolate oak. Full, vibrant purple. Impressive density of satsuma plum, blackberry,
black cherry and licorice carries long and strong. A little extractive bitterness and
alcohol warmth lend a firm edge to the finish. Screw cap. 14.8% alc. **Rating** 91
To 2033 $55 TS

♥♥♥♥ **Single Vineyard Union Street Greenock Barossa Valley Shiraz 2018**
Rating 89 **To** 2028 $35 TS

Zonte's Footstep   ★★★★☆

The General Wine Bar, 55a Main Road, McLaren Flat, SA 5171 **Region** McLaren Vale
T (08) 7286 3088 **www**.zontesfootstep.com.au **Open** Mon–Sat by appt
Winemaker Brad Rey **Est.** 2003 **Dozens** 20000 **Vyds** 214.72ha
Zonte's Footstep has been very successful since a group of long-standing friends, collectively
with deep knowledge of every aspect of the wine business, decided it was time to do
something together. Along the way there has been some shuffling of the deck chairs but all
achieved without any ill feeling from those who moved sideways or backwards. The major
change has been a broadening of the regions (Langhorne Creek, McLaren Vale, the Barossa
and Clare valleys and elsewhere) from which the grapes are sourced. Even here, however, most
of the vineyards supplying grapes are owned by members of the Zonte's Footstep partnership.
Exports to the US, Canada, Ireland, Belgium, Finland, Sweden, Denmark, Thailand, Singapore,
South Korea, Hong Kong and China.

♥♥♥♥♥ **Blackberry Patch Fleurieu Cabernet 2019** Fruit from Langhorne Creek
and a block in Blewitt Springs, McLaren Vale. Cabernet with 5% tempranillo,
finding a delicious companionship with aromas of warm sun-kissed blackberries.
There's delicious, pure fruit and a delicate touch of licorice on the palate, leaving
you with a sense of honesty and immense satisfaction – a vinous hug, if you will.
Screw cap. 14% alc. **Rating** 94 **To** 2028 $30 TL

Canto Fleurieu Sangiovese Lagrein 2019 An 87/13% blend with sangio in the lead. Plenty to love here, and no need to dissect each variety's contribution, as the wine works in its own right. Part earthy and savoury, part dark plum and chocolate; with juicy, crunchy tart satsuma plum flavours and lip-smacking tannins that carry the flavours for quite some time. Screw cap. 14% alc. **Rating** 94 To 2028 $30 TL ○

ŸŸŸŸŸ **Madrugador Fleurieu Tempranillo 2020** Rating 93 To 2028 $35 TL
Chocolate Factory McLaren Vale Shiraz 2019 Rating 92 To 2027 $30 NG
Violet Beauregard Langhorne Creek Malbec 2019 Rating 92 To 2026 $30 TL
Lady of the Lake Single Site Langhorne Creek Viognier 2020 Rating 91 To 2025 $30 TL
Scarlet Ladybird Fleurieu Rosé 2020 Rating 91 To 2024 $25 TL
Globe Skimmer Fleurieu Rosé 2020 Rating 91 To 2025 $30 TL
Age of Enlightenment McLaren Vale Shiraz 2018 Rating 91 To 2030 $75 NG
Love Symbol McLaren Vale Grenache 2019 Rating 91 To 2024 $30 NG

Zonzo Estate

957 Healesville-Yarra Glen Road, Yarra Glen, Vic 3775 **Region** Yarra Valley
T (03) 9730 2500 **www**.zonzo.com.au **Open** Wed–Sun 12–4
Winemaker Caroline Mooney **Est.** 1998 **Vyds** 18.21ha
This is an iteration of Train Trak, best known by Yarra Valley locals for the quality of its wood-fired oven pizzas. The vineyard was planted in 1995, the first wines made from the 1998 vintage. The business was acquired by Rod Micallef in 2016. The restaurant is open Wed–Sun for lunch and Fri–Sun for dinner. Exports to China.

ŸŸŸŸŸ **Yarra Valley Pinot Noir 2020** This is good, actually very good, given the price. It delivers big time. A complete package of dark cherries, chinotto and blood-orange zest with smoky, meaty, savoury inputs and the oak neatly in place. It's fuller bodied but not big. The palate is actually very smooth with light and fine tannins and a juiciness throughout. It's a terrific drink right now. Screw cap. 13.5% alc. **Rating** 93 To 2026 $27 JF ○

ŸŸŸŸ **Yarra Valley Chardonnay 2020** Rating 89 To 2023 $27 JF

Index

Wineries are arranged alphabetically under geographical indications (see page 8), to help you find a wine or winery if you're looking locally or on the road. If you are hoping to visit, the following key symbols will be of assistance.

Ⓨ   **Cellar door sales**

🍴   **Food:** lunch platters to à la carte restaurants

⊨   **Accommodation:** B&B cottages to luxury vineyard apartments

♪   **Music events:** monthly jazz in the vineyard to spectacular yearly concerts

Adelaide Plains (SA)

Albany (WA)

Alpine Valleys (Vic)

Beechworth (Vic)

Coonawarra (SA)

Cowra (NSW)

Currency Creek (SA)

Great Southern (WA)

Byron & Harold 141
Castelli Estate 152 ♀ ⅋ ⊨ ⌕
Forest Hill Vineyard 253 ♀ ⅋ ⌕
Kings Landing 361
Lowboi 398
Marchand & Burch 413
Oranje Tractor 481 ♀
Paul Nelson Wines 492 ♀
Plan B Wines 517
Rockcliffe 547 ♀ ⅋ ⌕
Rosenthal Wines 551
Singlefile Wines 593 ♀
Staniford Wine Co 606 ♀
Trevelen Farm 662 ♀
Willoughby Park 703 ♀ ⅋ ⌕

Great Western (Vic)

Best's Wines 110 ♀ ⅋ ⌕
Black & Ginger 117

Greater Perth (WA)

Paul Conti Wines 491 ♀ ⅋

Gundagai (NSW)

Nick Spencer Wines 468
Tumblong Hills 666

Hastings River (NSW)

Cassegrain Wines 152 ♀ ⅋ ⌕

Heathcote (Vic)

Anderson Fort 75
Armstead Estate 83 ♀

Bull Lane Wine Company 137
Burke & Wills Winery 139 ♀ ⌕
Cavalry Wines 155
Chalmers 159
Condie Estate 178 ♀
Devil's Cave Vineyard 212 ♀
Domaine Asmara 220 ♀ ⊨
Ellis Wines 236 ♀
Heathcote Estate 305 ♀ ⅋
Humis Vineyard 328 ♀
Idavue Estate 331 ♀ ⅋ ⌕
Jasper Hill 340 ♀
Kennedy 356
Lake Cooper Estate 372 ♀ ⅋
Merindoc Vintners 426 ⅋ ⊨
Mia Valley Estate 429 ♀ ⅋
Munari Wines 459 ♀ ⅋ ⌕
Paul Osicka 492 ♀
Rogues Lane Vineyard 548
Sanguine Estate 565 ♀ ⌕
Silver Spoon Estate 591 ♀
Snobs Creek Wines 600 ♀ ⌕
Syrahmi 619 ♀
Tellurian 629 ♀ ⅋
Vinea Marson 685 ♀
Wanted Man 692
Whistling Eagle Vineyard 702 ♀
Wren Estate 718 ♀ ⅋

Henty (Vic)

Basalt Wines 99 ♀ ⅋
Bochara Wines 121 ♀
Crawford River Wines 188 ♀
Henty Estate 313
Hentyfarm Wines 313 ♀
Jackson Brooke 336

Mornington Peninsula (Vic)

Mornington Peninsula (Vic) continued

Paradigm Hill 486 ♀

Paringa Estate 487 ♀ ⫪

Phaedrus Estate 507 ♀

Pt. Leo Estate 519 ♀ ⫪

Port Phillip Estate 522 ♀ ⫪ ⊨

Portsea Estate 522 ♀

Principia 524 ♀

Quealy Winemakers 530 ♀ ⫪

Scorpo Wines 571 ♀

Sedgley & Sons 573

Stonier Wines 613 ♀ ⫪

T'Gallant 620 ♀ ⫪ ⚲

Ten Minutes by Tractor 630 ♀ ⫪

Trofeo Estate 664 ♀ ⫪ ⊨

Tucks 665 ♀ ⫪ ⚲

Underground Winemakers 673 ♀

Willow Creek Vineyard 705 ♀ ⫪ ⊨ ⚲

Woodhaven Vineyard 714 ♀

Yabby Lake Vineyard 722 ♀ ⫪

Yal Yal Estate 723

Mount Barker (WA)

Galafrey 265 ♀

Gilberts 276 ♀ ⫪ ⚲

Plantagenet 517 ♀ ⫪ ⚲

Poacher's Ridge Vineyard 518 ♀ ⊨

Terra Riche 631

3 Drops 650

Towerhill Estate 660

West Cape Howe Wines 699 ♀ ⫪

Xabregas 720

Mount Benson (SA)

Cape Jaffa Wines 146 ♀ ⫪ ⚲

Mount Benson Estate 450 ♀ ⫪ ⊨ ⚲

Norfolk Rise Vineyard 472

Wangolina 692 ♀ ⚲

Mount Gambier (SA)

Coola Road 179

Herbert Vineyard 314 ♀

Mount Lofty Ranges (SA)

Macaw Creek Wines 401 ♀

Michael Hall Wines 430 ♀

Mudgee (NSW)

Bunnamagoo Estate 138 ♀ ⫪ ⚲

Craigmoor | Montrose 188 ♀ ⫪ ⚲

Ernest Schuetz Estate Wines
239 ♀ ⫪ ⊨

Huntington Estate 329 ♀ ⚲

Logan Wines 393 ♀ ⫪

Lowe Wines 398 ♀ ⫪ ⚲

Mansfield Wines 412 ♀

Robert Stein Vineyard 545 ♀ ⫪

Rosby 550 ♀ ⊨

Thistle Hill 645 ♀ ⊨

Vinifera Wines 686 ♀ ⫪

Murray Darling (Vic and NSW)

Trentham Estate 661 ♀ ⫪ ⚲

Zilzie Wines 735 ♀

Nagambie Lakes (Vic)

Box Grove Vineyard 124 ♀ ⫪

Dalfarras 198 ♀ ⫪

Acknowledgements

It goes without saying that it takes a cast of thousands to create a project of this magnitude, but never more than this year, with James' herculean workload disseminated across an ever-growing and immensely talented team.

This book is the shared labour and passion of the tasting team like never before, and if I had my way each of their names would appear on the cover. The mandate of delivering the most up-to-date reviews calls for a punishing tasting and writing schedule. Turning a mountain of thousands of tasting samples into articulate reviews in a clunky and complicated database is hardly the idyllic life that a wine writer is imagined to lead! Each and every one of these pages is a testimony to the devotion and talent of these seven incredible individuals. As one commented after the dust settled: 'It brings new appreciation for the job that James has done singlehandedly over the previous decades.'

The unique and distinctive voice of each taster coming to life on these pages loud, clear and captivating is an inspiration to me, second only to seeing the finest wines and wineries of the year rise to the top. Erin, you bring wine to life like nobody else. Ned, your vocabulary ever captivates and challenges me. Jane, I love that you can simultaneously make wine no-nonsense and fun. Tony, every word carries the dignified confidence that you personify. Jeni, you make wine real and keep us all honest. And James, you are the master of capturing a wine authoritatively, concisely and eloquently.

The true credit for pulling this edition together is due to Emily Lightfoot, our talented and tireless Tasting Manager, who achieved the impossible of assembling countless pieces of this vast puzzle, reinventing the process at the same time. She became the superstar of the tasters for her brilliance and patience, her appointment this year 'serendipitous alignment' and her work behind the scenes 'made the daunting doable; the highs, a bit higher and the lows, surmountable!' Her name deserves front-cover status, too.

At Hardie Grant headquarters, huge thanks to Sandy Grant for his unwavering support and to the HGX team, who are responsible for the day-to-day operations of the *Companion* online, its print magazines and its annual awards. It is a real team effort, led by Jacinta (and, during maternity leave, Nick) Hardie-Grant. Special thanks to marketeers Erin Ivanka and Meg Nunan; to the technical one-man band that is Sanjay Robson; to the editorial team of Amelia Ball, Eliza Campbell and Casey Warrener, and the commercial team under Claire Teisseyre, in particular J'aime Cardillo and Natalie Sakarintr (special thanks to Eliza, J'aime and Natalie for their all-hands-on-deck support in the final moments of this book); to the finance team of Christine Dixon and Sammi Gui; and, of course, Emily Lightfoot. My thanks also to the Hardie Grant Books team who help bring this book together; to Roxy Ryan, managing director; Jane Willson, publishing director; Joanna Wong, project editor; Rosanna Dutson, editor and fact-checker extraordinaire; Megan Ellis, typesetter; Marg Bowman, proofreader; and Kasi Collins and the rest of the Hardie Grant Books marketing team.

Personal thanks from me to Jody Rolfe for surmounting my mountain of samples and data entry, and to Rachael, Linden, Huon and Vaughn Stelzer for your patience and support. Ned's thanks go to Matilda, Jack, Don and Dianne Goodwin, and to Gregory and Gaye Ross, for receiving so many deliveries on his behalf. Erin thanks her friend Wendy, for unpacking, cataloguing and filing every wine and tech sheet and faithfully tasting almost all, and Jesse, without whom, nothing is possible. Tony to Marina for putting up with all the interruptions to normal family life; to the dedication of several courier drivers; and to Graham Lough and Blackwood Rotary Club for fundraising efforts sourced from wine remainders. Jeni, to GT, always. Emily, to Alice, Jack and Tom Percival for their support. And James to Paula on her 30th year with the *Companion* and to Beth on more than 20.

Finally, to the 1300 wineries who sent wines and answered our calls for wine and vintage background, this edition owes its existence to you all.

Paula Grey

16 May 1960 – 12 June 2021

My world and the world lost a truly wonderful person when Paula Grey suddenly passed away on the night of 12 June, aged 61. Her husband Doug's description of her as a gentle and kind person is absolutely right, and he should know better than anyone, given that they married in England on 25 November 1978, she 18, he 20. They had five children who share Doug's desolation at the loss of someone who died long before her due time.

Paula came into my life on 11 January 1991 as my PA, and became my eyes, ears, fingers, hands, and above all else, my brains – and, on occasion, the Pinocchio on my shoulder (that was as close as we came to ever exchanging cross words). Her output via her computer was phenomenal, and there was no way that the *Wine Companion* could have grown as it did without her acute intelligence in database building and management, extending to shortcuts to the point where it was akin to artificial intelligence. On occasion, it would fail and very odd words would appear in the printed document, when her self-deprecating sense of humour would break out, never far from the surface.

She never stopped learning and asking questions about technical wine issues, and, where and when needed, softly polish my tasting notes where she was sure of her ground. Her skill in handling incoming phone calls was one of her greatest strengths. No matter how ill she felt, she would respond to the 'How are you?' question saying 'I'm lovely!' and find out what the caller needed to speak to me about. More often than not, she would be able to answer the question or provide the information so deftly that the caller would completely forget the need to speak to me.

Time may fill the hole in my heart but will never heal it.

James Halliday